I0759755

PRAISE FOR *ESSENTIALS OF REFORMED SYSTEMATIC THEOLOGY*

"Every Christian should own a handbook of Christian doctrine. But not everyone is likely to begin with the four massive volumes of Joel Beeke and Paul Smalley's *Reformed Systematic Theology*—despite all their value. Thankfully, we now have 'Beeke and Smalley Junior' in one volume at a simpler level. Still comprehensive and substantial, it is never 'dumbed down.' Wonderfully accessible and readable, it provides an ideal go-to volume for Christians of all ages and stages who want to 'grow in the grace and knowledge of our Lord and Savior Jesus Christ' (2 Pet. 3:18)."

Sinclair B. Ferguson, Chancellor's Professor of Systematic Theology, Reformed Theological Seminary; Teaching Fellow, Ligonier Ministries

"I praise God that the same great biblical truths that are set forth in the exhaustive *Reformed Systematic Theology* are now made available to all in a more concise and accessible edition. It will be an incalculable blessing and benefit to the laity, our youth, and the global church. This is a remarkable achievement."

Paul Washer, Director, HeartCry Missionary Society

"The mighty four volumes of Beeke and Smalley's *Reformed Systematic Theology*, in their 5,200 pages, are an achievement that may never again be approached in the thoroughness, length, piety, doxology, accessibility, pithiness, sobriety, and trustworthiness of the creation. It is a deeply spiritual work—heavenly, profitable, and full of practical application. It is also a precious companion for every preacher, suitable for the man in his first pastorate and fresh for the retired preacher who still hungers and thirsts for wisdom and righteousness. Now the essentials have appeared—a synopsis, a compression of four volumes into a single book of 1,088 pages with summaries at the beginning of individual chapters, a focus on their highlights, and references to the enlargements of the themes in the more comprehensive four volumes for more needed study. This brilliant summary is where many will begin. It seems almost indispensable to have this single volume as a launching pad or as the handmaiden to the genius of the four giants of truth and godliness."

Geoffrey Thomas, Former Pastor, Alfred Place Baptist Church, Aberystwyth, Wales

"This condensed version of Beeke and Smalley's more compendious volumes is to be greatly welcomed. It is to be hoped that a new readership will be reached and stimulated to search further into the riches of Reformed theology."

Robert Letham, Senior Research Fellow, Union School of Theology

PRAISE FOR THE *REFORMED SYSTEMATIC THEOLOGY* FOUR-VOLUME SET

"This resource will instruct the mind and inflame the heart."

John MacArthur, Pastor, Grace Community Church, Sun Valley, California; Chancellor, The Master's University and Seminary

"Theology for the church of God and not just for the academy."

Ian Hamilton, President, Westminster Presbyterian Theological Seminary, United Kingdom

"Here is truth presented to make you think, pray, and sing."

Jeremy Walker, Pastor, Maidenbower Baptist Church, Crawley, UK; author, *Life in Christ*; *Anchored in Grace*; and *A Face Like a Flint*

"Chapter after chapter of *Reformed Systematic Theology* not only takes readers into the depths of our triune God but also shows what these great truths have to do with the Christian life."

Matthew Barrett, Professor of Christian Theology, Midwestern Baptist Theological Seminary; author, *Simply Trinity* and *None Greater*

ESSENTIALS OF REFORMED SYSTEMATIC THEOLOGY

ESSENTIALS OF
REFORMED SYSTEMATIC THEOLOGY

Joel R. Beeke and Paul M. Smalley

WHEATON, ILLINOIS

Essentials of Reformed Systematic Theology

Published by Crossway
1300 Crescent Street
Wheaton, Illinois 60187

Cover design: Jordan Singer

First printing 2025

Printed in China

All emphases in Scripture quotations have been added by the authors.

Hardcover ISBN: 978-1-4335-9091-7
ePub ISBN: 978-1-4335-9093-1
PDF ISBN: 978-1-4335-9092-4

Library of Congress Cataloging-in-Publication Data

Names: Beeke, Joel R., 1952- author | Smalley, Paul M. author
Title: Essentials of Reformed systematic theology / Joel R. Beeke and Paul M. Smalley.
Description: Wheaton, Illinois: Crossway, [2025] | Includes bibliographical references and index.
Identifiers: LCCN 2024038815 | ISBN 9781433590917 hardcover | ISBN 9781433590924 pdf | ISBN 9781433590931 epub
Subjects: LCSH: Reformed Church—Doctrines
Classification: LCC BX9422.3 .B43 2025 | DDC 230/.42—dc23/eng/20250529
LC record available at https://lccn.loc.gov/2024038815

Crossway is a publishing ministry of Good News Publishers.

RRD 35 34 33 32 31 30 29 28 27 26
13 12 11 10 9 8 7 6 5 4 3 2

For

David and Vicky McWilliams,

faithful and encouraging friends (Phil. 1:3)

—Joel R. Beeke

For

Levi, Elizabeth, and Michael,

the sons and daughter of many prayers

—Paul M. Smalley

Contents

Section 3B: Man as Sinner before God

PART 4: THE DOCTRINE OF CHRIST

Section 4A: The Covenant of Grace

Section 4B: The Person and Work of Christ

PART 5: THE DOCTRINES OF THE HOLY SPIRIT AND SALVATION

Section 5A: The Spirit and the History of Salvation

Section 5B: The Spirit and the Application of Salvation

Section 5C: The Spirit and the Experience of Salvation

PART 6: THE DOCTRINE OF THE CHURCH

Section 6A: The Church's Identity

Section 6B: The Church's Authority and Work

Section 6C: The Church's Means of Grace

PART 7: THE DOCTRINE OF THE LAST THINGS

Section 7A: Introduction and Special Issues in the Last Things

Section 7B: The Glorious Hope of Christ

Abbreviations

ANF — *The Ante-Nicene Fathers.* Edited by Alexander Roberts and James Donaldson. Revised by A. Cleveland Coxe. 9 vols. New York: Charles Scribner's Sons, 1918.

BDAG — Walter Bauer. *A Greek-English Lexicon of the New Testament and Other Early Christian Literature.* Revised and edited by Frederick W. Danker. 3rd ed. Chicago: University of Chicago Press, 2000.

Comm. — John Calvin. *Commentaries.* 22 vols. Grand Rapids, MI: Baker, 2003.

CRS — Wilhelmus à Brakel. *The Christian's Reasonable Service.* Edited by Joel R. Beeke. Translated by Bartel Elshout. 4 vols. Grand Rapids, MI: Reformation Heritage Books, 1992–1995.

Denzinger — Heinrich Denzinger. *Enchiridion Symbolorum Definitionum et Declarationum de Rebus Fidei et Morum; Compendium of Creeds, Definitions, and Declarations on Matters of Faith and Morals.* Edited by Peter Hünermann, Helmut Hoping, Robert Fastiggi, and Anne Englund Nash. 43rd ed. San Francisco: Ignatius, 2012.

Institutes — John Calvin. *Institutes of the Christian Religion.* Edited by John T. McNeill. Translated by Ford Lewis Battles. Library of Christian Classics 20–21. Philadelphia: Westminster, 1960.

LSJ — Henry George Liddell and Robert Scott, compilers. *A Greek-English Lexicon.* Revised by Henry Stuart Jones and Roderick McKenzie. 9th ed. Oxford: Oxford University Press, 1996.

LW — Martin Luther. *Luther's Works.* Edited by Jaroslav Pelikan et al. 79 vols. St. Louis: Concordia, 1958–2016.

NIDNTTE *The New International Dictionary of New Testament Theology and Exegesis*. Edited by Moisés Silva. 5 vols. Grand Rapids, MI: Zondervan, 2014.

NIDOTTE *The New International Dictionary of Old Testament Theology and Exegesis*. Edited by Willem A. VanGemeren. 5 vols. Grand Rapids, MI: Zondervan, 1997.

NPNF[1] *A Select Library of Nicene and Post-Nicene Fathers of the Christian Church, First Series*. Edited by Philip Schaff. 14 vols. New York: Christian Literature Co., 1888.

NPNF[2] *A Select Library of Nicene and Post-Nicene Fathers of the Christian Church, Second Series*. Edited by Philip Schaff and Henry Wace. 14 vols. New York: Christian Literature Co., 1894.

Psalter *The Psalter, with Doctrinal Standards, Liturgy, Church Order, and Added Chorale Section*. Preface by Joel R. Beeke and Ray B. Lanning. 1965. Reprint, Grand Rapids, MI: Eerdmans for Reformation Heritage Books, 2003.

RC *Reformed Confessions of the 16th and 17th Centuries in English Translation: 1523–1693*. Compiled by James T. Dennison Jr. 4 vols. Grand Rapids, MI: Reformation Heritage Books, 2008–2014.

RD Herman Bavinck. *Reformed Dogmatics*. Edited by John Bolt. Translated by John Vriend. 4 vols. Grand Rapids, MI: Baker Academic, 2003–2008.

RST Joel R. Beeke and Paul M. Smalley. *Reformed Systematic Theology*. 4 vols. Wheaton, IL: Crossway, 2019–2024.

SPT Johannes Polyander, Antonius Walaeus, Antonius Thysius, and Andreas Rivetus. *Synopsis Purioris Theologiae, Synopsis of a Purer Theology: Latin Text and English Translation*. Translated by Riemer A. Faber. Edited by Dolf te Velde, Rein Ferwerda, Willem J. van Asselt, William den Boer, Riemer A. Faber, Henk van den Belt, and Harm Goris. 3 vols. Studies in Medieval and Reformation Traditions: Texts and Sources. Leiden: Brill, 2014, 2016, 2020.

TDNT *Theological Dictionary of the New Testament*. Edited by Gerhard Kittel, Geoffrey W. Bromiley, and Gerhard Friedrich. 10 vols. Grand Rapids, MI: Eerdmans, 1964.

TFU	*The Three Forms of Unity*. Birmingham, AL: Solid Ground, 2010.
THBap	*Trinity Hymnal—Baptist Edition*. Edited by David Merck. Suwanee, GA: Great Commission Publications, 1995.
WJE	*The Works of Jonathan Edwards*. 26 vols. New Haven, CT: Yale University Press, 1957–2008.
WJF	*The Works of John Flavel*. 6 vols. Edinburgh: Banner of Truth, 1968.
WJO	*The Works of John Owen*. Edited by William H. Goold. 16 vols. Edinburgh: Banner of Truth, 1965–1968.
WJO-H	John Owen. *An Exposition of the Epistle to the Hebrews*. 7 vols. 1854. Reprint, Edinburgh: Banner of Truth, 1991. Originally part of *The Works of John Owen*.
WRS	*The Works of Richard Sibbes*. Edited by Alexander Grosart. 7 vols. Edinburgh: Banner of Truth, 1973.
WSChar	*The Works of Stephen Charnock*. 5 vols. 1864–1865. Reprint, Edinburgh: Banner of Truth, 1986.
WTB	*The Complete Works of the Late Rev. Thomas Boston, Ettrick*. Edited by Samuel M'Millan. 1853. Reprint, Stoke-on-Trent, England: Tentmaker, 2002.
WTG	*The Works of Thomas Goodwin*. 12 vols. 1861–1866. Reprint, Grand Rapids, MI: Reformation Heritage Books, 2006.
WWP	*The Works of William Perkins*. Edited by Joel R. Beeke and Derek W. H. Thomas. 10 vols. Grand Rapids, MI: Reformation Heritage Books, 2014–2020.

Preface

WILLIAM TYNDALE DEVOTED himself to translating the Bible into the language of the people. A theologian once said to him that it was not a good idea to let people read God's Word for themselves. We are told that Tyndale replied, "If God spares my life . . . I will cause a boy that drives the plow to know more of the Scripture than you do."[1] Tyndale ultimately died as a martyr so that ordinary people could know, believe, and obey the truth of God.

Christians have long labored to bring the Word to everyone and explain what it means. For example, the first edition of John Calvin's systematic theology was much smaller than the book you are reading. Calvin wanted the book to be a summary of the Christian life presented in basic truths for everyone who desired to pursue godliness.[2]

Though we are neither Tyndale nor Calvin, we also desire to bring the truth of God's Word to as many people as are willing to learn it. To that end, we have abridged the four large volumes of *Reformed Systematic Theology* into a single shorter volume. The material was cut back to about one-sixth of its original length. Many sentences were simplified. But our aim was still to present a systematic theology that would be biblical, doctrinal, experiential, and practical.[3]

1 John Fox[e], *Book of Martyrs*, ed. Charles A. Goodrich (Hartford, CT: Edwin Hunt, 1845), 259, language modernized.

2 John Calvin, *Institutes of the Christian Religion: 1536 Edition*, trans. and annot. Ford Lewis Battles, rev. ed. (Grand Rapids, MI: The H. H. Meeter Center for Calvin Studies; Eerdmans, 1986), 1. The subtitle reads, "Embracing almost the whole sum of piety and whatever is necessary to know of the doctrine of salvation." Calvin commended it to be "read by all persons zealous for piety."

3 Portions of *Reformed Systematic Theology* were adapted from other published materials by Joel Beeke and thus have passed into this book in abridged and simplified form. Please see *RST* for the appropriate acknowledgments.

To help the reader, a summary is presented at the beginning of each chapter, highlighting key words. These theological terms and many others appear with definitions in a glossary at the end of the book. We also include a list of theologians from the past whom we quote or mention in the book, providing their dates and brief comments on their lives. You will also find at the end of the book a guide to the parts of *Reformed Systematic Theology* that explain the topics covered here in much more depth.

As you read this book, please pray for God to teach you. Apart from Christ working by the Holy Spirit, we cannot understand the Word in a way that benefits and changes us. And remember that all Christian truth aims at obedience. Take time to respond to what you read. Look to Christ for grace. Repent of sin. Worship God. Resolve to keep his commandments. And tell someone else the truths that you learn.

With the completion of this volume, we wish to wholeheartedly thank our blessed triune God for his grace from beginning to end. We also thank our wives (Mary and Dawn) and families, and the Crossway team (especially our able editor, Greg Bailey). They have persevered with us over the last decade as we have persevered in writing *Reformed Systematic Theology* and *Essentials of Reformed Systematic Theology*. We thank Wouter Pieters for proofreading the book and making many helpful suggestions. We also thank Fraser Jones for reviewing the material and particularly for writing the short biographical notes in the list of theologians at the end of the book.

Please pray with us that God will use this book to grow his people, save the lost, glorify his name, and provide an on-ramp for many young people and adults to know and experience biblical Reformed theology more richly than before. *Soli Deo gloria!* ("Glory to God alone!")

PART 1

THE DOCTRINE OF THE KNOWLEDGE OF GOD

Section 1A

Questions about Theology

1

The What, Who, Where, and When of Theology

Chapter Summary and Key Terms

In Christian *theology*, the church explains and applies the Bible's *doctrine*, or teaching, about God. Theology is human reflection on the knowledge and wisdom revealed in God's Word. The goal of theology is that we may know God and live unto him through Jesus Christ. *Systematic theology* is a presentation of all the doctrines of Christianity organized by topic. Systematic theology answers the question, What does the whole Bible teach about each of its major topics and its relation to other topics? People do theology as God's creatures made in his image. If we are Christians, we are being renewed in that image. Christians study and talk about theology as members of Christ's church in a world that is against God. We are learning theology during our journey as pilgrims on our way to glory. We live in the last days between Christ's first and second coming.

AT THE COMMAND OF the angel of the Lord, Philip the evangelist traveled south to a desert road. There he encountered an Ethiopian court official who was returning home from Jerusalem, where he had worshiped the God of Israel. The man sat in his chariot reading the words of Isaiah about one who quietly submitted to death like a meek lamb. Philip asked him if he understood what he was reading. The Ethiopian replied, "How can I, except some man should guide me?" (Acts 8:26–33). Anyone who has spent more than a little time reading the Bible has experienced this need, wondering, "How can I understand unless someone guides me?" This guidance is the work of theology.

What Is Theology?

Theology frightens some people and fascinates others. It introduces us to an unseen world, one far greater and more lasting than the world we see and touch. Doing theology is the most important task that any human being can take on. In fact, as R. C. Sproul said, "Everyone's a theologian."[1] Even the atheist's rejection of God is an act of theology.

The word *doctrine* means "teaching." Christian doctrine is the church's teaching based on the Bible, God's Word (2 Tim. 3:16). The term *theology* literally means "words or speech about God," and thus it is the study of God and questions about the doctrines he has revealed. More specifically, Christian theology is a human description of the authoritative knowledge and wisdom that God has revealed in his Word so that we may know him and live unto him through Jesus Christ.

Systematic theology answers the question, What does the whole Bible teach about each of its major topics and its relation to other topics? Louis Berkhof said that systematic theology "seeks to give a systematic presentation of all the doctrinal truths of the Christian religion."[2] It builds in our minds a way of thinking in which each doctrine is clearly understood and rightly connected to other doctrines. It proves how every part of doctrine is deeply rooted in the Holy Scriptures. It neither ignores the theologies of the past nor accepts any one of them blindly. Rather, systematic theology compares all things to the Word of God in order to defend true Christianity while deepening our understanding of God's revelation. Systematic theology is not just a description of what people have believed in the past but an attempt to declare God's Word to the present generation.

The aim of theology should be a right relationship with God through Christ (2 Tim. 3:15). Paul says, "I count all things but loss for the excellency of the knowledge of Christ Jesus my Lord: for whom I have suffered the loss of all things, and do count them but dung, that I may win Christ" (Phil. 3:8).

William Ames wrote, "Theology is the doctrine of living to God."[3] Petrus van Mastricht slightly expanded Ames's definition to "the doctrine of living

1 From the title of R. C. Sproul, *Everyone's a Theologian: An Introduction to Systematic Theology* (Lake Mary, FL: Reformation Trust, 2014).

2 Louis Berkhof, *Introduction to Systematic Theology* (Grand Rapids, MI: Baker, 1979), 58–59.

3 William Ames, *The Marrow of Theology*, trans. John D. Eusden (Grand Rapids, MI: Baker, 1968), 1.1.1 (77).

to God by Christ."[4] This definition shows that theology is a careful study of "doctrine," which is the teaching of God's Word. Theology is about God. The goal of theology is "living to God"—that is, seeking his pleasure and glory. We can do this only through the Mediator ("by Christ").

Theology is both knowledge and wisdom. Knowledge is important because we must know the truth about God and his ways to have a relationship with him. Wisdom refers to skill or competency. Sometimes wisdom is skill in a trade or art. But more generally it is skill in one's whole approach to life. Wisdom includes knowledge. But wisdom is broader than knowledge, including the ability to live skillfully and joyfully for the glory of God.

Theology involves both theory and practice. We do not need to choose between having full heads with cold hearts and empty heads with warm hearts. We must know God in a manner that engages our heads, hearts, and hands. Jeremiah 9:24 says, "Let him that glorieth glory in this, that he understandeth and knoweth me, that I am the LORD which exercise lovingkindness, judgment, and righteousness, in the earth: for in these things I delight, saith the LORD."

Knowing God involves knowing his attributes and actions that set him apart from the false gods of man (Jer. 10:1–16). However, theology demands action, for knowing God moves us to glorify him: "Who would not fear thee, O King of nations? For to thee doth it appertain" (v. 7). Also, knowing God means imitating him: "He judged the cause of the poor and needy; then it was well with him: was not this to know me? saith the LORD" (22:16).

Who Does Theology?

In the art of photography, one crucial factor is the point of view. For example, you can take a picture of a volcano looking up from the ground or down from a helicopter. Similarly, in doing theology, we must be conscious of our point of view. Theology is "the knowledge or wisdom of the divine matters that God has revealed to people in this world . . . and that he has adapted to their capability."[5]

First, we do theology as creatures of God (Gen. 1:1). We are not God. Therefore, we must acknowledge that he is beyond our ability to fully

4 Petrus van Mastricht, *Theoretical-Practical Theology*, vol. 1, trans. Todd M. Rester, ed. Joel R. Beeke (Grand Rapids, MI: Reformation Heritage Books, 2018), 1.1.26 (98).

5 Polyander, Walaeus, Thysius, and Rivetus, *SPT*, 1.9 (1:35).

understand (Rom. 11:33). One danger of theology is that "knowledge puffeth up" (1 Cor. 8:1). John Owen rightly said, "Our thoughts, our meditations, our expressions of him are low, many of them unworthy of his glory, none of them reaching his perfections."[6] The true theologian does theology with an attitude of dependence, submission, and godly fear toward the Lord.

Second, we also do theology as God's image bearers (Gen. 1:26–27). Part of being created in God's image is the ability to know and acknowledge God (Col. 3:10; cf. Rom. 1:21). However, our theology is not God's theology but "image theology," or only the faint echo and dim reflection of the original. Franciscus Junius said that our theology is "a certain copy and, rather, shadowy image . . . [of the] unbounded wisdom which God possesses."[7]

Third, we do theology as sinners against God. No one on earth does theology from a standpoint of neutrality. Our first response to true theology is resistance: "This is the condemnation, that light is come into the world, and men loved darkness rather than light, because their deeds were evil" (John 3:19). Mankind generates its own false theology by which it can never find God (1 Cor. 1:19–21). John Calvin said, "They do not therefore apprehend God as he offers himself, but imagine him as they have fashioned him in their own presumption."[8] Therefore, we must repent of our resistance to God's Word. We must depend every day on Christ to open our minds to understand the Scriptures (Luke 24:25, 45).

Fourth, we do theology as born-again children of God, if by grace we have repented of our sins and trusted in Christ alone for salvation. God is our inner teacher (John 6:45). This does not take away the need for studying God's Word. It does not mean we do not need to learn from the human teachers that the Holy Spirit gives to the body of Christ. But it opens a whole new world of possibilities. We were blind, but now by grace we can see (2 Cor. 3:17–18; 4:4–6).

Fifth, we may also do theology as pastors and teachers in the church, if God calls us to serve him in those ways. Pastors and teachers have a special calling to study theology, for they are sent by Christ to build up the church in "the unity of the faith, and of the knowledge of the Son of God" (Eph.

6 Owen, *The Mortification of Sin in Believers*, in *WJO*, 6:64.

7 Franciscus Junius, *A Treatise on True Theology, with the Life of Franciscus Junius*, trans. David C. Noe (Grand Rapids, MI: Reformation Heritage Books, 2014), 104.

8 Calvin, *Institutes*, 1.4.1.

4:11–13). God requires them to be "apt to teach" (1 Tim. 3:2) and "able by sound doctrine both to exhort and to convince the gainsayers" (Titus 1:9). Pastors and teachers should never rest in what they already know. Paul exhorted Timothy, "Meditate upon these things; give thyself wholly to them; that thy profiting may appear to all" (1 Tim. 4:15).

Where Do We Do Theology?

Where, in this case, does not refer to our location but to our situation among men.

We study theology among mankind in rebellion against God. True theology always takes a stand against the world. The calling of a theologian is to suffer persecution (Matt. 23:33–35). He is a servant of the gospel that the world rejects. The theologian can say with Paul, "I endure all things for the elect's sakes, that they may also obtain the salvation which is in Christ Jesus with eternal glory" (2 Tim. 2:10).

We learn theology in the church. The apostle Paul does not sharply distinguish what is taught to ministerial students from what is taught in the church. He says, "The things that thou hast heard of me among many witnesses, the same commit thou to faithful men" (2 Tim. 2:2). We need the church. Perseverance in sound doctrine and holy living requires godly relationships (Heb. 3:13; 10:23–25). Paul says that our theology is enriched as we worship with the church: "Let the word of Christ dwell in you richly in all wisdom; teaching and admonishing one another in psalms and hymns and spiritual songs, singing with grace in your hearts to the Lord" (Col. 3:16).

Life is not about merely exchanging ideas through reading and writing but face-to-face fellowship with real people. John said, "Having many things to write unto you, I would not write with paper and ink: but I trust to come unto you, and speak face to face, that our joy may be full" (2 John 12). Communion with God and godly people is the goal of theology: "That which we have seen and heard declare we unto you, that ye also may have fellowship with us: and truly our fellowship is with the Father, and with his Son Jesus Christ" (1 John 1:3).

When Do We Do Theology?

In asking, When do we do theology? *when* does not refer to seasons in our lives or times in our schedules but to the time of history in which we stand.

Christians are theologians during their pilgrimage to glory. We have not yet arrived (Phil. 3:12). We are travelers and wayfarers. Wise theologians, like the saints of old, have "confessed that they [are] strangers and pilgrims on the earth" (Heb. 11:13). Only foolish and immature Christians think that they already reign and have become wise (1 Cor. 4:8, 10). So our theology is not yet the theology of vision, for we do not yet see Christ (1 John 3:2). "We know in part," but one day we will see "face to face" (1 Cor. 13:9–12). Junius said, "The more we are called along in the whole course of this our miserable life, the more we feel our own ignorance and weakness." Thus, "true humility . . . occupies the first and most important place in theology."[9]

Christians are also theologians during the last days. The "last days" are not just the few years before Christ's return. Rather, they are the entire period between Christ's first and second comings (Heb. 1:1–2). Theologians today have the privilege of reading the full revelation that God's Son gave us after his incarnation. Doing theology in the last days also implies, however, that our task is full of danger. The last days are times of error in the professing church (1 Tim. 4:1; 1 John 2:18). We therefore must not shrink from the call to defend the faith and to discipline professing Christians when false teachings infiltrate the church.

Conclusion

We may compare theology to the telling of a story. It is the grand story of God, creation, the fall of man, redemption accomplished, redemption applied, a new people formed, and the restoration of all things. It is not just a story that we read but *our story*. Therefore, we cannot pretend to be neutral or detached observers. Instead, we must do theology aware of our place in the story.

Pause at this point to examine yourself. Are you a worshiper and loving servant of the Creator? Do you believe yourself to be one created in God's image, a person who can have true knowledge of God but never reach his infinite depths?

Do you acknowledge the moral corruption of your soul? Do you depend upon Christ to bring light to your inner darkness and conquer your heart's rebellion?

9 Junius, *A Treatise on True Theology*, 232.

If you are a pastor, teacher, or student of theology, do you approach it with a sense of divine calling to "labour in the word and doctrine" (1 Tim. 5:17)?

Do you regard theology as a call to suffer persecution or as an opportunity to exalt or promote yourself in this world? Are you doing theology in relationship with true Christian friends with whom you regularly worship in the church?

Do you study theology as a pilgrim who is still far from glory? How does the conviction of living in the last days put a sense of privilege, urgency, and anticipation of judgment day into your study of theology?

Suggested Songs to Sing to the Lord

- Psalm 119:33–40, "Teach me, O Lord, Thy way of truth," in *Psalter*, No. 325; *THBap*, No. 451
- "Break thou the bread of life, dear Lord, to me," in *THBap*, No. 256

Questions for Meditation or Discussion

1. What is doctrine?
2. What is theology?
3. What is systematic theology?
4. What definition of theology was given by Ames and enhanced by van Mastricht?
5. How does this definition encourage us that true theology is practical?
6. Is theology best considered knowledge, wisdom, or both? Why?
7. How does our creation in God's image enable us to do theology?
8. How does it affect you personally to know that a faithful witness to true theology will suffer persecution? How have you experienced this?
9. What difference does it make to study theology as pilgrims on their way to glory as opposed to those who have already arrived in glory?
10. How might living in friendships in the church help us to be better theologians?

2

The Which, Why, and How of Theology

Chapter Summary and Key Terms

Theology that is faithful to God's Word is Christian, catholic, evangelical, and Reformed. *Christian* means "having to do with the disciples of Christ." The term *catholic* means "universal." It refers not to *Roman Catholicism* but to the common teachings of Christ's churches throughout the world, as in the ancient creeds. *Evangelical* means "characterized by the gospel." Evangelical theology centers on the preaching of the gospel according to the Reformation teachings of *sola Scriptura* ("Scripture alone"), *sola gratia* ("grace alone"), *solus Christus* ("Christ alone"), *sola fide* ("faith alone"), and *soli Deo gloria* ("glory to God alone"). *Reformed theology* is teaching that is in agreement with the confessions and catechisms of the Reformed churches. It centers on the glory and sovereignty of God. We must do theology because God has spoken, and we have his Word in the Scriptures. Theology is both a spiritual work of pursuing godliness and a mental work of study and learning.

JOHN DUNCAN was a Scottish Presbyterian scholar and missionary. He was known as "Rabbi" Duncan both for his knowledge of Hebrew and his love for the Jewish people. He once said, "I'm first a Christian, next a Catholic, then a Calvinist, fourth a Paedobaptist, and fifth a Presbyterian. I cannot reverse this order." These categories, Duncan said, were not so much like concentric circles as like levels of a tower: "The first is the broadest, and is the foundation laid by Christ; but we are to build on that foundation."[1]

Which Theology Do We Do?

In a world of many religions and diverse and conflicting beliefs, which theology should we seek to do? Systematic theology faithful to God's Word is Christian, catholic, evangelical, and Reformed.

First, our theology, at its foundation, must be *Christian*—that is, we do theology as disciples of Jesus Christ (Acts 11:26). God the Father testifies of Jesus, "This is my beloved Son, in whom I am well pleased; hear ye him" (Matt. 17:5). Christ's teachings are the rock on which we must build our lives (7:24). Submission to Christ requires submission to the words of the prophets and apostles by whom God spoke, the words that make up the Old and New Testaments of the Bible.[2] Christian theology is done with faith in Christ and in submission to his Word.

Second, our theology must be *catholic*. The word *catholic* does not refer to the Roman Catholic Church but means "general" or "universal." The "catholic church" is the church in all places and times as opposed to a single congregation. Catholic theology acknowledges the ancient creeds that are recognized all over the world, especially the *Apostles' Creed*, the *Nicene Creed*, the Definition of the *Council of Chalcedon*, and the *Athanasian Creed*. A related term is *orthodoxy*, which refers to holding to the fundamental doctrines of Christianity as expressed in creeds, confessions, and catechisms. The opposite of orthodoxy is *heresy*. Not all error is heresy, only that which radically opposes saving faith by denying fundamental truths.

Third, our theology must be *evangelical*, a term meaning "of the gospel" or "good news."[3] Paul gives us a summary of the gospel in 1 Corinthians 15:1–5:

> Moreover, brethren, I declare unto you the gospel which I preached unto you, which also ye have received, and wherein ye stand; by which also

1 Cited in William Knight, *Colloquia Peripatetica: Deep-Sea Soundings, Being Notes of Conversations by the Late John Duncan*, 3rd ed. (Edinburgh: Edmonstron and Douglas, 1871), 8. *Paedobaptist* means one who believes in the baptism of infant children of confessing church members (see chap. 83). *Presbyterian* here refers to a form of church government by councils of elders who rule over individual churches and federations of churches (see chap. 76).

2 Luke 24:25–27, 44–48; John 5:39; 16:13–14; 1 Pet. 1:11; 2 Pet. 3:2.

3 See Joel R. Beeke, *What Is Evangelicalism?* (Darlington, England: Evangelical Press, 2012).

> ye are saved, if ye keep in memory what I preached unto you, unless ye have believed in vain. For I delivered unto you first of all that which I also received, how that Christ died for our sins according to the scriptures; and that he was buried, and that he rose again the third day according to the scriptures: and that he was seen of Cephas, then of the twelve.

Historically, "evangelical theology" is Reformation theology—that is, theology taught by the Protestant Reformers such as Martin Luther and John Calvin in the sixteenth century. We can summarize it in five phrases that begin with some form of the Latin word *sola* ("alone").

- *Sola Scriptura* ("Scripture alone") means that the Holy Scriptures are our supreme and divine rule of faith and life. The Scriptures are the Word of God (1 Thess. 2:13).
- *Sola gratia* means that God's "grace alone," not human goodness and effort, saves sinners (Rom. 3:24; Eph. 2:4–10). All people by nature are deeply corrupted by sin and unable to save themselves (Rom. 3:10–12; 8:7–8; Eph. 2:1–3).
- *Solus Christus* means that "Christ alone," not the saints, the angels, or the priests of the church, acts as our Mediator, Redeemer, and Savior (1 Tim. 2:5).
- *Sola fide* teaches us that "faith alone," not a person's works, is the instrument by which he is forgiven and counted righteous by God (Rom. 4:4–5; Gal. 2:16).
- *Soli Deo gloria* means "glory to God alone." All the praise for any good in us must be given to God through Jesus Christ (1 Cor. 4:7; Gal. 6:14).

Fourth, our theology must be *Reformed*. Reformed doctrines are taught by the Reformed confessions of the sixteenth and seventeenth centuries, such as the Belgic Confession of Faith (1561), the Heidelberg Catechism (1563), the Second Helvetic Confession (1566), the Canons of Dort (1618–1619), and the Westminster Confession of Faith (1646), Shorter Catechism (1647), and Larger Catechism (1647). The Westminster Confession was adapted for use by congregational churches as the Savoy Declaration (1658). That congregationalist declaration was then modified by Particular Baptist theologians to be the Second London Baptist Confession of Faith (written in 1677 and reaffirmed in 1689).

The heart of Reformed theology is the knowledge of the triune God and his sovereignty. For this reason, Reformed theology is called "God-centered" theology. To be Reformed is to fear the Lord and to live to glorify and enjoy him forever. The Reformed doctrine of salvation can be summarized in the five points of eternal election, definite redemption, total depravity, effectual calling, and the perseverance of the saints. Reformed theology is also experiential. That means it not only addresses the mind but also engages the heart. The Puritans said, "The knowledge we especially commend, is not a brain-knowledge, a mere speculation . . . but an inward, a savoury, an heart knowledge."[4] God-centered theology aims to form God-centered souls.

Why Do We Do Theology?

Objections to Theology

The question of why we do theology presses hard against us in our day. People raise a number of objections to theology.

Objection 1: Only science is real. Theology is just opinions about religion.

We answer that this objection is logically inconsistent. The statement that we can know only what is proven by science cannot itself be proven by science. What experiment would we do to prove it? Also, theology has real foundations. Though we cannot see the invisible or measure the infinite God, through his Son he has spoken with us (John 1:18; Col. 1:15).

Objection 2: The only thing that matters is what works to grow the church. Theology is a waste of time.

We reply that sound theology is essential to evangelism and building the church. Our theology shapes both our message and methods. The church must guard against a false, accursed gospel (Gal. 1:8–9). Christ gives pastors and teachers to the church to build up the body "till we all come in the unity of the faith, and of the knowledge of the Son of God" (Eph. 4:13).

Objection 3: Doctrine divides, damaging the unity of the body of Christ. Therefore, many doctrines of the Bible are best left alone.

4 "Epistle to the Reader," in *Westminster Confession of Faith* (Glasgow: Free Presbyterian Publications, 2003), 6.

We answer that *sound* doctrine unites (Eph. 4:13) but *false* doctrine divides. Paul warned the Ephesian elders, "Also of your own selves shall men arise, speaking perverse things, to draw away disciples after them" (Acts 20:30). A church without good theology is more vulnerable to division, not less.

Objection 4: We should just read and teach the Bible. Theology is too academic. Theologians and seminaries are often unfaithful to the Bible.

We respond by asking, What does the Bible teach? It is impossible to teach biblical truth without reflecting on the Bible in a systematic fashion. The discipline of theology is not unfaithfulness but obedience to the call to "meditate upon these things" (1 Tim. 4:15).

Objection 5: Godliness is a feeling in the heart. Friedrich Schleiermacher said, "Christian doctrines are accounts of the Christian religious affections set forth in speech."[5] Therefore, theology is not the study of truth so much as the study of experience.

We reply by quoting our Lord's words: "If ye continue in my word, then are ye my disciples indeed; and ye shall know the truth, and the truth shall make you free" (John 8:31–32). True theology in the heart is living and vital knowledge; it is "life eternal" (17:3).

Objection 6: God is too great for us to know. Any attempt to build a system of truths dishonors his infinity. Therefore, it is arrogant to do theology.

We answer that it is not arrogant to believe God's Word with all our hearts. Rather, faith in what God says is the greatest expression of humility (Isa. 66:2). The Bible is not a cloud of darkness but a light that brings clarity (Ps. 119:105).

Objection 7: Theology is too dogmatic. We are on a never-ending journey into truth. We never arrive at any definite conclusions.

We respond by noting our duty to "hold fast the form of sound words, which thou hast heard of me, in faith and love which is in Christ Jesus" (2 Tim. 1:13). We must "earnestly contend for the faith which was once delivered unto the saints" (Jude 3).

Objection 8: We can believe only what is reasonable to our minds. Many Christian doctrines, such as the Trinity, the incarnation, and the

5 Friedrich Schleiermacher, *The Christian Faith*, ed. H. R. Mackintosh and J. S. Stewart (New York: Harper and Row, 1963), sec. 15 (1:76).

substitutionary atonement, are irrational or illogical. Therefore, Christian theology is not true.

We answer that the most rational action we can take is to believe all that God has said, even if we cannot fully understand it. God cannot lie. John 3:31–33 says, "He that cometh from above is above all. . . . He that hath received his testimony hath set to his seal that God is true."

Objection 9: There is no absolute truth. Everything is relative. Therefore, we have no right to force our opinion on others. That means theology is an attempt to oppress others. It is an act of hatred or abuse.

We reply that this objection contradicts itself. It asserts as absolute truth that there is no absolute truth.[6] Are relativists absolutely sure that there is no absolute truth? We, however, acknowledge that there is absolute truth. But that is not hate. The Lord is truth (John 14:6) and love (1 John 4:8). It is therefore no contradiction to speak the truth in love (Eph. 4:15).

While we reject these arguments against doing theology, we can also learn from them. We must not do theology in a way that is abstract, impractical, divisive, cold, arrogant, illogical, oppressive, or hateful. Instead, our theology should be practical, loving, humble, and wise.

The Reason for Theology: God Has Spoken

We read in Hebrews 1:1–2, "God, who at sundry times and in divers manners spake in time past unto the fathers by the prophets, hath in these last days spoken unto us by his Son, whom he hath appointed heir of all things, by whom also he made the worlds." This is the great reason why we can and must do theology: God has spoken, and we have his Word.

God has spoken, so we must hear him. In the book of Deuteronomy, the prophet Moses says repeatedly, "Hear, O Israel" (Deut. 4:1; 5:1; 6:3–4; 9:1). Luther said, "To hear God is bliss. . . . Therefore we must pay attention with trembling."[7]

God has spoken, so we must obey him. Deuteronomy 5:1 says, "Hear, O Israel, the statutes and judgments which I speak in your ears this day, that ye may learn them, and keep, and do them." Hearing God's Word receives the whole counsel of God to guide the whole life.

6 John Frame, *The Doctrine of the Knowledge of God*, A Theology of Lordship (Phillipsburg, NJ: P&R, 1987), 120.

7 Luther, *Lectures on Deuteronomy*, in *LW*, 9:48.

God has spoken, so we must teach others about him. The Lord commanded Moses to teach the people so that they would teach their children and grandchildren (Deut. 4:9–10). God also entrusted the teaching office to the priests in the old covenant (17:9–12). In the new covenant, the teaching office belongs to ministers and elders (1 Tim. 3:2; 2 Tim. 2:24; Titus 1:9).

God has spoken, so we must glorify him. Deuteronomy 6:4–5 says, "Hear, O Israel: The Lord our God is one Lord: and thou shalt love the Lord thy God with all thine heart, and with all thy soul, and with all thy might." All our study, obedience, and teaching aim to give to the Lord the all-encompassing love that he deserves of us. Calvin said, "If we will know whether we have profited in God's law or no, we must always sift and search ourselves whether we have such desire and zeal that God should be honored and glorified by us."[8] Thus, the theologian should not be motivated by merely accumulating knowledge. Rather, he or she should study and teach, as Richard of St. Victor said, by "the fervor of my burning soul."[9]

How Do We Do Theology?

The Spiritual Work of Theology

J. I. Packer said, "All theology is also spirituality." He explained, "If our theology does not quicken the conscience and soften the heart, it actually hardens both; if it does not encourage the commitment of faith, it reinforces the detachment of unbelief; if it fails to promote humility, it inevitably feeds pride."[10] What does the discipline of theology require of you spiritually?

First, *be a disciple of Christ.* A disciple is a student. The goal of discipleship is to take on the mind and character of one's master. Discipleship requires submission to Christ's instruction and imitation of his conduct. Jesus says, "The disciple is not above his master: but every one that is perfect shall be as his master" (Luke 6:40). Are you a faithful follower of Christ?

Second, *depend on Christ, the Prophet, Priest, and King.* The labor of a theologian is an exercise of faith in Christ. Jesus Christ is the great Prophet,

8 John Calvin, *Sermons on Deuteronomy* (1583; facsimile repr., Edinburgh: Banner of Truth, 1987), 266.

9 Richard of St. Victor, *On the Trinity: English Translation and Commentary*, trans. and ed. Ruben Angelici (Eugene, OR: Cascade, 2011), 3.1 (116).

10 J. I. Packer, *A Quest for Godliness: The Puritan Vision of the Christian Life* (Wheaton, IL: Crossway, 1990), 15.

the living Word who makes God known (John 1:1, 14, 18). Theologians are guilty sinners. They must receive the grace to serve God by faith in the great High Priest, who offered himself for sinners and now intercedes for them (Heb. 10:12). Theology is a work of spiritual warfare. Theologians must draw strength from their King to powerfully proclaim his Word (2 Cor. 10:3–4; Eph. 6:10–13).

Third, *pray for the Holy Spirit's illumination.* Paul prayed "that the God of our Lord Jesus Christ, the Father of glory, may give unto you the spirit of wisdom and revelation in the knowledge of him: the eyes of your understanding being enlightened" (Eph. 1:17–18). Every believer has blind spots that hinder his grasp of God's truth. We must pray, "Open thou mine eyes, that I may behold wondrous things out of thy law" (Ps. 119:18).

Fourth, *study the Word of God with trembling.* We must never treat it "as the word of men, but as it is in truth, the word of God, which effectually worketh also in you that believe" (1 Thess. 2:13). The Lord of heaven and earth, who created all things, says, "To this man will I look, even to him that is poor and of a contrite spirit, and trembleth at my word" (Isa. 66:2). Humility is the only proper posture of the theologian. John Owen said, "I personally do not claim . . . to be able to do more than stammer pitifully when I come to discuss such high matters."[11]

Fifth, *submit your mind to God's Word.* An elder must be a man who is "holding fast the faithful word as he hath been taught" (Titus 1:9). The people should be able to say of the theologian, "The law of truth was in his mouth. . . . For he is the messenger of the LORD of hosts" (Mal. 2:6–7). We must study, write, and teach out of a solid conviction that God's Word is truly perfect and perfectly true. We dare not do theology by subjecting God to our finite and fallen minds. Rather, we must subject ourselves to God's Word.

Sixth, *endure suffering for the sake of God's Word.* The teacher must "endure hardness, as a good soldier of Jesus Christ" (2 Tim. 2:3). The theologian is an ambassador of the risen King (v. 8). He must, like Paul, "suffer trouble . . . even unto bonds . . . [and] endure all things for the elect's sakes, that they may also obtain the salvation which is in Christ Jesus with eternal

11 John Owen, *Biblical Theology: The History of Theology from Adam to Christ*, trans. Stephen P. Westcott (Orlando, FL: Soli Deo Gloria, 1994), 6.1 (591).

glory" (vv. 9–10). You may face the slander of the elites and the loss of friends. Psalm 119:23 says, "Princes also did sit and speak against me: but thy servant did meditate in thy statutes."

Seventh, *cultivate a spiritual appetite for God's Word*. Love the Word. Embrace the attitude of Psalm 119:131: "I opened my mouth, and panted: for I longed for thy commandments." Crave the Word of God like babies crave milk (1 Pet. 2:2). Delight in the Word as your mouth delights in sweet honey (Pss. 19:10; 119:103). Treasure the Word more than thousands of gold coins (Ps. 119:72, 127). Search it as if you were seeking for buried treasure (Prov. 2:4). Herman Witsius said, "Let the theologian be ravished with these heavenly oracles—let him be occupied with them day and night, let him meditate in them, let him live in them."[12]

Eighth, *live what you learn*. No theology can be pleasing to God if it does not breathe a spirit of holiness and love. Paul warns, "Knowledge puffeth up, but charity edifieth" (1 Cor. 8:1). The Lord Jesus Christ threatened to take away the spiritual lamp of a church when it lost its first love, even though it was an active church that rejected false teachers (Rev. 2:1–5). As those who spend much time in reading and thinking, theologians must guard themselves from being hearers but not doers of the Word (James 1:22–25). Theology without application is like a horse without legs. Jonathan Edwards said, "Practice according to what knowledge you have. This will be the way to know more."[13]

Ninth, *be a faithful member of a faithful church*. The Christian theologian must seek not to walk alone. Just as Paul writes to every member of Christ's body, so we say to its teachers, "The eye cannot say unto the hand, I have no need of thee: nor again the head to the feet, I have no need of you" (1 Cor. 12:21). Faithfulness to God's Word is a community project (Prov. 13:20).

Tenth, *use theology as fuel for praise*. Psalm 119:171 says, "My lips shall utter praise, when thou hast taught me thy statutes." Our studies should regularly move us to praise the Lord. Our highest aim in teaching should be to lead others to worship the one true God. Witsius said, "By a theologian I mean one who, imbued with a substantial knowledge of divine things

12 Herman Witsius, *On the Character of a True Theologian*, ed. J. Ligon Duncan III (Greenville, SC: Reformed Academic Press, 1994), 31.

13 Edwards, "The Importance and Advantage of a Thorough Knowledge of Divine Truth," in *WJE*, 22:102.

derived from the teaching of God Himself, declares and extols, not in words only, but by the whole course of his life, the wonderful excellencies of God and thus lives entirely for his glory."[14]

The Mental Work of Theology

It is a grave mistake to set the knowledge of the heart against that of the head. We should not despise the careful and rigorous study of theology. We would offer the following guidelines for those desiring to start learning theology.

1. Read the Bible completely and repeatedly.
2. Study particular books of the Bible.
3. Interpret Scripture with Scripture.
4. Ask questions about the text's meaning and application.
5. Become familiar with good confessions of faith and catechisms.
6. Read good books, especially older ones, about theology.
7. Take notes on what you learn.
8. Discuss doctrine with thoughtful Christians.
9. Receive correction and criticism humbly, always going back to God's Word.

As you look at this list, think about where you can start becoming a theologian today. Consider what practical steps you could take even this week to grow in your understanding of God's Word. But do not just think about them—do them.

Suggested Songs to Sing to the Lord

- Psalm 25, "Lord, I lift my soul to Thee," in *Psalter*, No. 64; *THBap*, No. 583
- "God, my King, thy might confessing," in *THBap*, No. 2

Questions for Meditation or Discussion

1. What four words describe which theology we do? What does each mean?
2. How would you respond to the statement "Doctrine divides"?

14 Witsius, *On the Character of a True Theologian*, 27.

3. What is the fundamental reason why we do theology?
4. Of the objections to theology listed in this chapter, which pose the greatest danger to your church or denomination? How can you resist them?
5. What does it mean to be a disciple of Christ? Why is discipleship crucial for theology?
6. Why is it important for the theologian to rely upon Christ as

    - Prophet to reveal the truth of God?
    - Priest to reconcile guilty sinners to God?
    - King to lead us in spiritual warfare against God's enemies?

7. What can you do to build habits of prayer into your study of theology? Why must you not neglect to seek God's illumination for yourself and those whom you teach?
8. What does this statement imply for theologians: "To this man will I look, even to him that is poor and of a contrite spirit, and trembleth at my word" (Isa. 66:2)?
9. What would you say to a theologian who was not an active member of a church, neglecting to worship, serve, and fellowship in a local congregation?
10. How do you respond to criticism? What does that say about your spiritual condition? What kind of attitude toward criticism should we desire? How can we develop it?

Section 1B

God's Revelation to Man

3

Introduction to God's Revelation

Chapter Summary and Key Terms

God's *revelation* is his communication of truths that people otherwise would not know, or at least not know with certainty. God has revealed himself and his will on a level that human beings can understand and communicate to one another so that we may know his glory. People have the ability to know God and receive his revelation because he made man in his image. He communicates with people through *general revelation*, which he gives naturally through the created world, and *special revelation*, his Word, which he gave supernaturally to select people. God applies special revelation to his people so that they respond with faith, love, obedience, and prayer.

WHEN WE RAISED THE QUESTION Why do we do theology? our basic answer was, God has spoken. But what do we mean by that? How has the invisible God disclosed himself? The answer shakes the foundations of our modern and postmodern secular culture. Carl Henry said, "Nowhere does the crisis of modern theology find a more critical center than in the controversy over the reality and nature of divine disclosure."[1]

The Bible's Words for God's Revelation

Throughout the Bible, we read of how God has communicated with people. Since we cannot see God, we must hear him if we are to know him. Though God sent prophets and apostles to declare his Word, the Bible portrays

1 Carl F. H. Henry, *God, Revelation and Authority*, 6 vols. (Waco, TX: Word, 1976), 2:7.

God himself as the great communicator. In the Bible, God appears, speaks, and reveals. When we speak of God's revelation, we mean that God makes known truths that we cannot otherwise know, or at least that we would not know with absolute certainty.

Old Testament Words for God's Revelation

Divine revelation sometimes took place when the Lord "appeared" to someone (Gen. 12:7). A "prophet" could also be called a "seer," one who had seen a supernatural appearance of the Lord (1 Sam. 9:9). Prophecy was sometimes called a "vision" (3:1).

The Hebrew Bible often tells us that God "says" things or "speaks" to people with "words." The phrase "Thus saith the LORD" is used more than four hundred times in the Old Testament. It tells us that God sent messages to man with solemn authority. Expressions such as "the word(s) of the LORD" or "of God" appear more than three hundred times in the Bible.

God could "shew" or "make known" (ESV) his ways and covenant (Ps. 25:4, 14) and his salvation (98:2). He could "teach" people, "lead" them, and "guide" or "instruct" (ESV) them in his truths (25:4–5, 8–9). From the verb rendered as "instruct" comes the term we translate as "law" or "instruction" (torah), which appears more than two hundred times in the Hebrew Bible. There are many other terms associated with "law," such as "statute," "judgment," "testimony," "precept," and "commandment."

Another Hebrew term is the verb translated as "to reveal," which means "to uncover or disclose." Amos 3:7 says, "Surely the Lord GOD will do nothing, but he revealeth his secret unto his servants the prophets." Daniel 2:22 uses a similar word in the Aramaic language when Daniel says, "He revealeth the deep and secret things: he knoweth what is in the darkness, and the light dwelleth with him" (cf. Job 12:22).

New Testament Words for God's Revelation

Like the Old Testament, the Greek New Testament uses terms for human speech to describe God's communication with men. The word translated as "speak" is "characteristic of the way in which Jesus himself refers to his own revelation" in the Gospel of John.[2] For example, Jesus says, "These things

2 *NIDNTTE*, 3:78.

have I spoken unto you."[3] This term appears in a key text of divine revelation, Hebrews 1:1–2: "God, who . . . spake in time past unto the fathers by the prophets, hath in these last days spoken unto us by his Son."

Also very common are the verb translated as "to say" and the related noun translated as "word" (*logos*). Revelation 21:5 says, "And he that sat upon the throne said, Behold, I make all things new. And he said unto me, Write: for these words are true and faithful." Christ himself is the "Word" (*Logos*) who is from God and is God (John 1:1; Rev. 19:13). Christ uniquely "declared," or explained, the invisible God (John 1:18).

The New Testament also uses other terminology, such as another term for "word" (*rhema*, Rom. 10:17; Eph. 6:17). God is also said in the New Testament to "teach" (John 8:28; cf. 6:45) and give "knowledge" (1 Cor. 1:5; Col. 1:9–10). The Holy Spirit "signifies," or makes clear, certain truths in the Scriptures that he inspired (Heb. 9:8; 1 Pet. 1:11). God "shows," or exhibits, unknown realities so that they can be known (John 5:20; Rev. 1:1).

The verb translated as "to reveal" and the noun "revelation" are important words for God's communication (Matt. 10:26). In a parallel text in another Gospel, instead of "revealed" we read "manifested," which means "made visible" or "made known" (Mark 4:22; cf. John 2:11; 17:6). The opposite of "made manifest" is "kept secret" (Rom. 16:25–26). Another term, sometimes translated as "revealed," which was used in Greek literature for public or official actions, in the New Testament "expresses the fact that God instructs someone by revelations," such as through dreams or by angels.[4]

The terminology of God's communication in the Old and New Testaments revolves around three major ideas. First, God communicated a message in words in a form that human beings can receive, understand, and repeat. Second, there is a gracious revelation of hidden truth from God that man cannot discover on his own. Third, God's eternal glory breaks into our ordinary lives through his revelation.

Basic Truths about God's Revelation

Herman Bavinck wrote, "A true concept of revelation can be derived only from revelation itself."[5] We learn about revelation in the way that children

3 John 14:25; 15:11; 16:1, 25, 33.

4 *TDNT*, 9:481. See Matt. 2:12, 22; Luke 2:26; 10:22; Heb. 8:5; 11:7; 12:25.

5 Bavinck, *RD*, 1:299.

learn language—by listening to our Father speak and responding with trust and obedient imitation.

God's Revelation to His Image Bearers

Bavinck said, "The creation is the first revelation of God, the beginning and foundation of all subsequent revelation. The biblical concept of revelation is rooted in that of creation."[6] The Bible does not open with an argument to prove God's existence. It simply declares, "In the beginning God created the heaven and the earth" (Gen. 1:1). The simple phrase "God said" appears ten times in Genesis 1, telling us that the Creator of the world is the God who speaks. This God reveals himself as the Lord who reigns without limitation or competitor and as the overflowing fountain of all blessing and goodness. Genesis 1 sets the tone for the entire Bible as the self-disclosure of the living God.

God designed creation so that mankind would know him. God's creative work reached its high point in the creation of man in God's image (Gen. 1:26–27). As soon as God created man, he began speaking to him (v. 28; 2:16–17). God continued to reveal himself in words after man's rebellion and fall (Genesis 3). His revelation now serves his purpose to redeem and renew his corrupted and condemned image bearers on earth.

God reveals himself to his image bearers in three kinds of works involving creation, communication in words, and the re-creation of fallen man in God's image. We see this pattern in Psalm 19.

First, there is God's creation (Ps. 19:1–6). God gives *general revelation* by his works known by all people.

Second, there is the Word of God (Ps. 19:7–9). God gives *special revelation* by his words, but it is given not to all but first to Israel and then, through the preaching of God's Word, to many nations.

Third, there is the response to the Word from a renewed heart (vv. 10–14). God works *applied revelation*. This does not consist of new content in addition to general and special revelation. Instead, it accompanies the preaching of the Word to illuminate the heart. It makes people willing and eager to receive God's truth.

6 Bavinck, *RD*, 1:307.

The Revelation of God by His Creation (General Revelation)

David says, "The heavens declare the glory of God; and the firmament sheweth his handywork" (Ps. 19:1). Though the skies, sun, moon, and stars have no mouths, David writes of their "speech" (v. 2) and "voice" (v. 3).

This revelation is happening all the time, going on "day unto day" and "night unto night" (Ps. 19:2). It is everywhere, "through all the earth" (v. 4). God designed creation to reveal his nature to us all. In the blazing colors of the sun we see the happiness of God like a "bridegroom," the power of God like "a strong man," and the presence of God, for "there is nothing hid from the heat" of the sun (vv. 5–6). As we look around us, we see that God has made his creation a theater for his glory; as John Calvin said, it is "this magnificent theater of heaven and earth, crammed with innumerable miracles."[7]

The revelation of God through his works in creation is often called *natural revelation*. It occurs through God's ordinary works. It is received by our ordinary senses and reasoning. B. B. Warfield wrote, "There is the revelation which God continuously makes to all men: by it his power and divinity are made known." It is "adapted to man as man" and "is communicated through the media of natural phenomena, occurring in the course of nature or of history."[8]

The Revelation of God by His Word (Special Revelation)

David, after celebrating the revelation of God in his works in Psalm 19, turns his attention to God's Word. He writes, "The law of the LORD is perfect, converting the soul: the testimony of the LORD is sure, making wise the simple. The statutes of the LORD are right, rejoicing the heart: the commandment of the LORD is pure, enlightening the eyes. The fear of the LORD is clean, enduring for ever: the judgments of the LORD are true and righteous altogether" (vv. 7–9).

The qualities that belong to the Holy Scriptures mark it as the Word of God: perfect, sure, right, pure, clean, true, and righteous. General revelation communicates the reality and majesty of the Creator ("glory," Ps. 19:1), but special revelation brings to light his moral perfections of faithfulness and righteousness and reveals his holy will for our lives.

7 Calvin, *Institutes*, 2.6.1; cf. 1.5.8; 1.6.2; 1.14.20.

8 Benjamin B. Warfield, *The Inspiration and Authority of the Bible* (Phillipsburg, NJ: Presbyterian and Reformed, 1948), 73–74.

David says that God uses his Word to apply his revelation to the heart and life ("converting . . . making wise . . . rejoicing," etc.). David's description of general revelation says nothing about it changing people. We need God's Word to enjoy spiritual blessings.

Just as general revelation may be called natural revelation, so special revelation is *supernatural*. Douglas Kelly writes, "Special (or supernatural) revelation . . . was necessary from man's beginning, because man's finite nature could not of itself grasp the full understanding necessary to please God in all things, and it became even more necessary because of the negative effects the fall of Adam has had on the minds of all his descendants."[9]

God creates a covenant relationship between himself and man through his Word. Psalm 19 speaks of "God" (*El*) in its first section on God's creation. But then, six times in six lines of poetry about God's Word, we read the name "the Lord" (*YHWH*). That is the personal name that God used for himself when he redeemed the children of Israel and made his covenant with them as his people (Ex. 6:2–8; 20:1–2). This reminds us that God's Word is all about his glory as the Redeemer and King of his people. Thus, special revelation after the fall has focused on Jesus Christ, the Mediator of the covenant of grace.

The Response of God's Servants to His Word (Applied Revelation)

God's Word calls forth a response from his people as his Spirit works within them. The last part of Psalm 19 focuses particularly on this response. The believer loves the Word, treasuring it more "than gold, yea, than much fine gold," and delighting in it as "sweeter also than honey" (v. 10). The believer listens to the Word as God's "servant," cherishing it as a valuable source of warning and following it as a trustworthy guide that leads to "great reward" (v. 11).

The believer also prays to God in response to his Word. He confesses the depth of his sins: "Who can understand his errors?" (Ps. 19:12a). He seeks grace for justification and release from his guilt: "Cleanse thou me from secret faults" (v. 12b). He also seeks grace for sanctification: "Keep back thy servant also from presumptuous sins; let them not have dominion over me:

9 Douglas F. Kelly, *Systematic Theology: Grounded in Holy Scripture and Understood in the Light of the Church*, 3 vols. (Fearn, Ross-shire, Scotland: Christian Focus, 2008–2021), 1:155.

then shall I be upright, and I shall be innocent from the great transgression" (v. 13). The believer prays because he longs to please God: "Let the words of my mouth, and the meditation of my heart, be acceptable in thy sight" (v. 14).

The last words of Psalm 19 reveal the center of a right response to the Word. David says, "O Lord, my strength [literally "my rock"], and my redeemer" (v. 14). These are words of trust (18:2). The essential response of man to special revelation is faith. Here we find the seventh use of God's name (Lord) in this psalm, showing that the revelation of God calls us to rest our hearts upon the faithful covenant Savior and Lord. In his Word, God calls us to faith in Christ.

This response is crucial for salvation. Therefore, examine yourself. Ask, How have I responded to God's revelation? Do I love his Word? Do I listen to it as the voice of God? Do I echo it back to him in my prayers for justifying and sanctifying grace? Do I long to please God? Do I have faith in Christ?

Suggested Songs to Sing to the Lord

- Psalm 119:169–76, "O let my supplicating cry," in *Psalter*, No. 342
- "How firm a foundation, ye saints of the Lord," in *THBap*, No. 80

Questions for Meditation or Discussion

1. What are some words that the Bible uses for God's revelation?
2. What are the three central truths the authors draw out of the Old and New Testament words for divine revelation?
3. Bavinck said, "A true concept of revelation can be derived only from revelation itself." Is this true or false? Why?
4. What does the biblical doctrine of creation (Genesis 1) imply about divine revelation?
5. How would you explain the three kinds of works that God does to reveal himself: (1) general revelation, (2) special revelation, and (3) applied revelation?
6. How does each kind of revelation appear in Psalm 19?
7. Why is general revelation sometimes called "natural revelation"?
8. Why is special revelation sometimes called "supernatural revelation"?
9. What effects of applied revelation are found in Psalm 19?
10. How has God applied his revelation to you? How has his Word affected you?

4

General Revelation

Chapter Summary and Key Terms

In *general revelation*, God reveals himself through the created world we see around us. God also reveals himself through his image in human beings. We see evidence of his image in our skill and conscience, though the human race is corrupted by sin. The *conscience* is God's witness within human nature to his judgment against sin and his blessing on righteousness. Conscience testifies on the basis of *natural law*, the knowledge of moral principles that God embedded in human nature. General revelation gives all people a basic knowledge of God, but it does not save anyone from foolishness and sin. The church can appeal to general revelation to convince people that they have sinned against God and need salvation. General revelation also shows the church God's beauty and glory, leading us to worship him.

ALEKSANDR SOLZHENITSYN was a Russian historian and author. He was imprisoned for his criticism of the Soviet Union and later expelled from his homeland. In 1983 he said,

> More than half a century ago, while I was still a child, I recall hearing a number of older people offer the following explanation for the great disasters that had befallen Russia: "Men have forgotten God; that's why all this has happened." Since then I have spent well-nigh fifty years working on the history of our Revolution. . . . But if I were asked today to formulate as concisely as possible the main cause of the ruinous Revolution that

> swallowed up some sixty million of our people, I could not put it more accurately than to repeat: "Men have forgotten God; that's why all this has happened."[1]

Solzhenitsyn did not say this to single out Russia but as part of his critique of other nations as well. He said that "the principal trait of the entire twentieth century" is that "men have forgotten God."[2] Sadly, we see the same pattern continuing today.

Revelation around Man in Creation

The apostle Paul summarizes the history of all nations: "When they knew God, they glorified him not as God, neither were thankful; but became vain in their imaginations, and their foolish heart was darkened" (Rom. 1:21). To believe that mankind has turned away from God, we must first recognize that "they knew God." This is possible because God has revealed himself to all nations by his general revelation.

General Revelation of God's Nature

Paul says, "That which may be known of God is manifest in them; for God hath shewed it unto them. For the invisible things of him from the creation of the world are clearly seen, being understood by the things that are made, even his eternal power and Godhead; so that they are without excuse" (Rom. 1:19–20). God's general revelation reveals him to a limited degree. It shows "that which may be known of God." Yet it reveals him in an open and plain manner. Certain truths about God are "manifest." God has showed himself, the invisible God, so that "the invisible things of him . . . are clearly seen."

General revelation reveals God's divine nature. Creation shows "his eternal power" (Rom. 1:20), "the glory of the uncorruptible God" (v. 23), and "the Creator, who is blessed for ever" (v. 25). This revelation has happened throughout history: "from the creation of the world" (v. 20). The verbs "are clearly seen" and "being understood" are in the present tense, which shows

1 Aleksandr Solzhenitsyn, "Men Have Forgotten God," in *In the World: Reading and Writing as a Christian*, ed. John H. Timmerman and Donald R. Hettinga, 2nd ed. (Grand Rapids, MI: Baker, 2004), 145.

2 Solzhenitsyn, "Men Have Forgotten God," in *In the World*, 145.

that this revelation continues to make God known. It reveals God through his created world: "the things that are made" (v. 20).

General Revelation of God's Wrath

Paul also says, "For the wrath of God is revealed from heaven against all ungodliness and unrighteousness of men, who hold the truth in unrighteousness" (Rom. 1:18). God reveals his saving righteousness in the gospel (vv. 16–17). But there is also a revelation "from heaven" of God's wrath against all sinners (v. 18).

The verb translated as "is revealed" is in the present tense. God is making known his wrath even now by his acts in history. For example, he is giving sinners over to corrupting desires and a worthless mindset as a judgment for rejecting him (Rom. 1:22–32). The doctrine of providence teaches us that physical calamities should also be received as general warnings of God's wrath and loving calls to repentance (Luke 13:4–5).

Revelation within Man

God also reveals himself through his creation in mankind. General revelation includes our creation in God's image and inner sense of obligation to him.

General Revelation according to God's Image

Created in God's image (Gen. 1:26–27), human nature is imprinted with a representation of God. In his original state of being "very good" (v. 31), man was a living revelation of God's knowledge, righteousness, and holiness, and this image is being renewed in those who are united to Christ (Eph. 2:10; 4:24; Col. 3:10).

Traces of God's image remained in man after his fall into sin against God (Gen. 9:3–6). We see something about God in man's intelligence and skill in farming, architecture, music, technology, and poetry (4:2, 17, 20–24). John Calvin said that man "is a rare example of God's power, goodness, and wisdom, and contains within himself enough miracles to occupy our minds."[3] Therefore, we encounter God's general revelation not only in forests and oceans but also in cities, gardens, factories, libraries, kitchens, and offices.

3 Calvin, *Institutes*, 1.5.3.

General Revelation through the Human Conscience

Fallen humanity is aware that God exists and is a righteous Judge. The worst sinners know "the judgment of God, that they which commit such things are worthy of death" (Rom. 1:32).

All nations have this awareness of God and his judgment. Paul says, "For when the Gentiles, which have not the law, do by nature the things contained in the law, these, having not the law, are a law unto themselves: which shew the work of the law written in their hearts, their conscience also bearing witness, and their thoughts the mean while accusing or else excusing one another" (Rom. 2:14–15). Paul does not say that Gentiles "do the law," but literally do "the things of the law." They partially conform their actions to some of its teachings, such as "a man should not steal" (v. 21).

Moral behavior in people who do not have God's Word comes from the inner "work of the law" to reveal God's will and condemn sin (Rom. 2:15; cf. 3:20). This is *natural law*, which is God's general revelation embedded in the hearts of all people, even those who are ignorant of special revelation. The "work of the law written in their hearts" (v. 15) does not refer to the saving work of the Holy Spirit (2:29), but to what all human beings have "by nature" as God's creatures.

Paul calls the inner testimony of natural law the "conscience" (Rom. 2:15). The conscience is the sense that one has offended or pleased God (John 8:9; Acts 23:1; 24:16). Paul compares the conscience to a witness in a court (Rom. 2:15; 9:1; 2 Cor. 1:12). The conscience uses the mind's knowledge of God's law to testify whether we have done right or wrong in his sight, with the anticipated verdict from the Judge (Rom. 2:15–16). Thus, the conscience speaks as a representative of God.

Sadly, man's conscience is defiled by human impurity (Titus 1:15). It can lose its sensitivity as if "seared with a hot iron" (1 Tim. 4:2). It can falsely accuse (1 Cor. 8:7). Yet man cannot escape his conscience without ceasing to be man.

The Effectiveness of General Revelation

We must ask what effect general revelation has upon humanity. The Bible tells us that all mankind has fallen away from God (Gen. 6:5; Ps. 14:2–3). Even many of the people in ancient Israel did not know God, despite having his Word (Judg. 2:10; Jer. 9:3). It is possible to have knowledge of God in the mind and yet not know him with faith and love in the heart. One can be exposed to God's light and yet remain in darkness (John 3:19–20; 8:19; 16:3).

The Knowledge Granted to All

The effects of general revelation are that all men know the following truths. First, God exists and created all things (Rom. 1:20–21). Also, atheism is foolish (Ps. 14:1). This is not an insult to an atheist's intelligence. It is simply a recognition that the atheist refuses to acknowledge what he knows (Prov. 1:7, 22) because of his pride and wickedness (Ps. 10:4). Furthermore, general revelation causes all people to know that God has a unique nature as God. The Creator is glorious (Pss. 8:1; 19:1), supremely wise (104:24), good to all (Acts 14:15–17), sovereign over our lives (Acts 17:24–25, 27), and eternal and all-powerful (Rom. 1:20–21).

General revelation does not reveal the Trinity or God's work of salvation for sinners. But people know enough to understand that idolatry is wicked (Acts 14:15; 17:24, 29). They also know that God holds man accountable to his moral law (Rom. 2:14–15). Sinners are under God's wrath and without excuse (1:18, 20).

The Response of Man to This Knowledge

The Bible never represents general revelation as the pathway by which sinners return to the true God. General revelation leaves men unchanged in their foolishness and sin (Rom. 1:21–32). Men have the truth about the Creator, but they "hold the truth in unrighteousness" (v. 18). That means they restrain or hold back the truth from making any progress in their lives. Rather than glorifying God, people plunge into the worship of idols (vv. 23, 25).

The Bible depicts mankind as wallowing in idolatry: "All the wise men of the nations . . . are altogether brutish and foolish" (Jer. 10:7–8). Worshiping rocks and wood is plainly ridiculous, even in the light of human reason. But man still "feedeth on ashes: a deceived heart hath turned him aside, that he cannot deliver his soul, nor say, Is there not a lie in my right hand?" (Isa. 44:9–20).

Mankind responds to the inner witness of conscience with "the vanity of their mind, having the understanding darkened, being alienated from the life of God through the ignorance that is in them, because of the blindness of their heart: who being past feeling have given themselves over unto lasciviousness, to work all uncleanness with greediness" (Eph. 4:17–19). Despite general revelation, the nations do not know God (Jer. 10:25; Gal. 4:8).

The Proper Christian Use of General Revelation

General revelation is very useful for the church in its work in at least two ways.

First, *general revelation is useful for the church's witness.* Christians can use general revelation to show people their need for the gospel and to call them to repent of their idolatry. Paul introduces general revelation in Romans 1 not as another way to be saved, but as a means of showing people their guilt and need for the righteousness of Christ (Rom. 1:16–21). When Paul's missionary team "preached the gospel," they called their hearers away from worshiping idols and men. The missionaries urged them to "turn from these vanities unto the living God" who created all things, appealing to the "witness" of God's good gifts in creation (Acts 14:7, 15, 17). Paul's sermon at Mars Hill attacked idolatry with facts about God and his world that even pagan poets and philosophers acknowledged (17:24–29). Paul used these remnants of truth as the basis upon which to build a call for his hearers to turn toward the risen Lord Jesus Christ as he is revealed in the gospel (vv. 30–31). All sinners have an inward witness that confirms the law of God. That helps them to make sense of the good news of salvation. By itself, general revelation saves no one. But with the gospel and the work of the Holy Spirit, general revelation can be a means of awakening sinners.

Second, *general revelation is useful for the church's worship.* When our eyes are opened by the special revelation of the Word and by the applied revelation of the Spirit, we see God's creation in a new way. The world that appeared drab and frightening now bursts with majesty, beauty, wisdom, and delight as the handiwork of our God. We join the angels in singing, "Thou art worthy, O Lord, to receive glory and honour and power: for thou hast created all things" (Rev. 4:11). The Psalms celebrate God's glory in creation (Psalms 8, 19, 29, 104, 145, 147). They say, "In his hand are the deep places of the earth: the strength of the hills is his also. The sea is his, and he made it: and his hands formed the dry land. O come, let us worship and bow down: let us kneel before the LORD our maker" (Ps. 95:4–6).

General Revelation and Science

All knowledge and skill come from the Lord. Just as surely as God gave us ears and eyes, so he "teacheth man knowledge" (Ps. 94:9–10). Only the proud and foolish refuse to acknowledge that it is "God my maker . . . who teacheth us more than the beasts of the earth, and maketh us wiser than the fowls of heaven" (Job 35:10–11). This applies to all forms of knowledge, including such matters as politics, zoology, and botany.[4]

Calvin said, "If we regard the Spirit of God as the sole fountain of truth, we shall neither reject the truth itself, nor despise it wherever it shall appear, unless we wish to dishonor the Spirit of God."[5] Christians recognize in the arts and sciences many good gifts from God. But believers must be careful in their use of human culture, for sin has corrupted all human endeavors.

A Christian approach to science must begin with recognizing that it is not just a report of the results of experiments. Rather, science is a form of human philosophy that seeks to explain the physical world and to form a view of reality to guide and improve our lives. But science is not necessary to know and glorify God. It does teach some valid and useful truths—we see that in medicine and technology. But non-Christian scientists propose systems of thought that contradict God's Word. Even non-Christians, though, recognize legitimate methods of reasoning, such as logical deduction. Christians may use these methods to serve God in various scientific fields.

A biblical approach to science does not strangle scientific progress. Rather, it empowers scientists to do their work under God's direction and blessing. Scientists operate with delegated authority from God. Science is rooted in his command to "subdue" the earth and "have dominion" over all its animals and plants (Gen. 1:28–29). When human beings engage in scientific work, they act as God's servant-kings upon the earth (Prov. 25:2; cf. 1 Kings 4:33). Scientists can investigate nature with confidence that God created the human mind to know the truth. Christianity promotes a culture within which science makes sense and is valued. Christian doctrine teaches that the universe is an orderly system that shows the regular patterns created by the God of wisdom, law, and covenantal faithfulness. As created by God, the world is good, useful, and understandable to people created

4 1 Kings 3:9, 12; 4:29–34; Job 12:13; Prov. 8:15–16; Dan. 1:3–4, 17; 2:20–21.

5 Calvin, *Institutes*, 2.2.15.

in his image.[6] Atheists have no rational basis on which to believe that the universe operates according to logical or mathematical principles, or even to believe that we can know reality.

Scientists must do their work with humility. As God reminded Job, we were not present when he created the earth, have not visited the full extent of his world, and do not fully understand the creatures all around us (Job 38:4, 16; 39:1). Scientists must realize that their theories possess only limited human certainty. On the other hand, the Word of God has divine certainty (Prov. 30:5–6).

Science and Christianity, when done rightly, support each other. The scientist Galileo Galilei said, "The Holy Bible can never speak untruth—whenever its true meaning is understood." However, the expressions of the Bible are not written in technical, scientific language. Instead, as Galileo said, the Bible communicates truths in a manner designed "to accommodate them to the capacities of the common people."[7] Scientists should pursue knowledge with prayer for God's help, for the Lord is still their Teacher (Isa. 28:26, 29).

Scientific study of the world is also not able to make us wise. Science has provided us with nuclear power and computer technology. But the atrocities of the modern world prove that science cannot solve mankind's most pressing problems, for "the fear of the Lord, that is wisdom; and to depart from evil is understanding" (Job 28:28). Scientists must work with God-fearing integrity. Just as a Christian must not check his mind at the door of the church, so a scientist must not check his faith and conscience at the door of the laboratory. This requires that scientific studies be made part of a larger, God-centered worldview (Prov. 1:7).

Scientists should use their findings for the glory of God. David says, "When I consider thy heavens, the work of thy fingers, the moon and the stars, which thou hast ordained; what is man, that thou art mindful of him? And the son of man, that thou visitest him? . . . O Lord our Lord, how excellent is thy name in all the earth!" (Ps. 8:3–4, 9). The astronomer

6 Nancy R. Pearcey and Charles B. Thaxton, *The Soul of Science: Christian Faith and Natural Philosophy* (Wheaton, IL: Crossway, 1994), 22–36. On the regular patterns or laws of nature as rooted in God's covenant faithfulness, see Gen. 8:22; 9:1, 9–11; Jer. 31:35–36; 33:20–21, 25–26.

7 Cited in Olaf Pederson, "Galileo and the Council of Trent: The Galileo Affair Revisited," *Journal for the History of Astronomy* 14 (February 1983): 17.

and mathematician Johannes Kepler wrote, "Even in astronomy my work worships God."[8]

Whether or not you are a scientist, be a worshiper of the Creator. Take time to look up at the skies, look around at the mountains and oceans, and look down at the flowers and insects. Remind yourself constantly that God made them. And give him the praise and glory.

Suggested Songs to Sing to the Lord

- Psalm 19, "The spacious heav'ns declare the glory of our God," in *Psalter*, No. 37
- Psalm 104, "O Lord, how manifold the works," in *Psalter*, No. 288; *THBap*, No. 10

Questions for Meditation or Discussion

1. What truths about general revelation do the authors draw out of Romans 1:19–20?
2. How does the conscience reveal God? How is it distorted by sin?
3. What knowledge does God's general revelation give to all mankind?
4. How does mankind respond to God's general revelation?
5. How can Christians use general revelation in evangelism? In worship?
6. What principles should guide Christians in how they view science?
7. Is science sufficient to make us wise? Why or why not?
8. What counsel would you give on how to be a good scientist and a good Christian at the same time?
9. What attitude should scientists have toward the certainty of their conclusions?
10. Is it appropriate for a scientist to pray to God for understanding? Why or why not?

8 Cited in Rhonda Martens, *Kepler's Philosophy and the New Astronomy* (Princeton, NJ: Princeton University Press, 2000), 14.

5

Special Revelation

Chapter Summary and Key Terms

In *special revelation*, all three persons of the Trinity work together to reveal God's Word to people. God reveals himself on a human level so that we can understand him. He gave special revelation through words, appearances (*theophanies*), events, and Jesus Christ's coming in the flesh. It is wrong to say that the church's traditions are God's Word, as in *Roman Catholicism*. It is also an error to be skeptical of the Bible and base religion on our reasoning and felt experience of God (*theological liberalism* or *modernism*). Another error is *religious pluralism*, the belief that God draws people to himself through many religions, not just Christianity. Nor it is correct to say, with *neoorthodoxy* (also called *dialectical theology*), that God revealed himself through Christ, but his revelation is not words in the Bible but a personal encounter with God. The Holy Scriptures are the Word of God.

HAVING EXAMINED the doctrine of general revelation, we now consider God's special revelation. It is called "special" because it is not granted generally to all mankind through natural means. God gave special revelation through supernatural means to his chosen messengers. They must then tell it to others.

In special revelation, God spoke with human beings in language that they could understand and repeat. God revealed himself in this way because he chose to do so out of his love. He made known hidden truths that men cannot discover on their own. When God spoke, his eternal glory shone into our ordinary, mundane existence.

Special Revelation by the Trinity through the Mediator

All works of God outside of himself engage all three persons of the Trinity. The three share one divine essence and one power. John 3:34–35 says, "For he whom God hath sent speaketh the words of God: for God giveth not the Spirit by measure unto him. The Father loveth the Son, and hath given all things into his hand." The Father sent the Son in his love and gave the Spirit to equip the Son for his work. The Son spoke the words of the Father and worked by the power of the Spirit. The Spirit accompanied the Son with infinite fullness to accomplish the Father's will. The three acted as one God to reveal the Word to men.

Therefore, the whole Trinity gives us special revelation through the Mediator. John Owen said, "This revelation of God's will, gifted to Christ by the Father, communicated by Christ through the Holy Spirit to the apostles and others for the benefit of the entire church, taken at its greatest extent, is the divine teaching or theology of the gospel."[1]

The Son is the only Mediator of God's revelation. Christ says, "All things are delivered to me of my Father: and no man knoweth who the Son is, but the Father; and who the Father is, but the Son, and he to whom the Son will reveal him" (Luke 10:22). Christ is "the Word" (John 1:1). No one has ever known God unless "the only begotten Son, which is in the bosom of the Father, . . . hath declared him" (v. 18).

The Father is the author of revelation in the Son. Christ explains, "My doctrine is not mine, but his that sent me" (John 7:16). He says, "I have not spoken of myself; but the Father which sent me, he gave me a commandment, what I should say, and what I should speak" (12:49). He who has seen Christ has seen the Father (14:9). Christ is in the Father, and the Father in him; thus, the Son says, "The words that I speak unto you I speak not of myself: but the Father that dwelleth in me, he doeth the works" (v. 10).

The Spirit is the agent of revelation through the Son. Christ said, "The Spirit of the Lord is upon me, because he hath anointed me to preach the gospel to the poor" (Luke 4:18). The Spirit of Christ worked upon the prophets in ancient times as they wrote of Christ (1 Pet. 1:10–12; 2 Pet. 1:21). The Lord Jesus promised that after he ascended to the Father, he would obtain

1 John Owen, *Biblical Theology: The History of Theology from Adam to Christ*, trans. Stephen P. Westcott (Orlando, FL: Soli Deo Gloria, 1994), 6.2 (602).

the gift of "the Spirit of truth," by whom gospel witness would expand into the world (John 14:16–17; 15:26–27).

Franciscus Junius said that the "cause of our theology is God the Father in the Son through His own Spirit breathing life into it, as He is the sole author and highest and most perfect creator of this wisdom in His own servants."[2]

The Human Character of Special Revelation

God's special revelation is his intentional communication to human beings, who are created in his image and likeness (Gen. 1:26–27). Therefore, it must come to us in the form of a limited, created likeness of his own infinite knowledge. God does reveal himself and his will to human beings, but he does so not at his level but at ours. An analogy would be how Albert Einstein might talk to a little child about physics.

One aspect of our turning back to God (Isa. 55:6–7) is acknowledging that he is far above our thinking: "For my thoughts are not your thoughts, neither are your ways my ways, saith the Lord. For as the heavens are higher than the earth, so are my ways higher than your ways, and my thoughts than your thoughts" (vv. 8–9).

God's Word bridges the gap. He adapts it to our capacities so that it nourishes us as rain and snow nourish the plants (Isa. 55:10–11). The call to repentance is a call to faith in God's Word. The Lord says, "Incline your ear, and come unto me: hear, and your soul shall live" (v. 3).

The point of contact between God's infinite mind and our finite and fallen minds is the incarnation of Jesus Christ. God's special revelation to sinners could reach its intended fullness only through the incarnation of our Lord. He is "the brightness of [God's] glory, and the express image of his person" (Heb. 1:3). God the Son lowered himself to take our form—human nature (Phil. 2:7). He bears God's perfect truth in our limited human patterns of thought (John 1:14).

The Ways God Gave Special Revelation

God spoke to men "in divers manners" (Heb. 1:1) or "in many ways" (ESV). He gave special revelation in words, appearances, events, and the incarnate

2 Franciscus Junius, *A Treatise on True Theology, with the Life of Franciscus Junius*, trans. David C. Noe (Grand Rapids, MI: Reformation Heritage Books, 2014), thesis 29 (196).

person of Jesus Christ. Each of these ways was supernatural in how it communicated God's truth.

Supernatural Revelation in Words

The most fundamental way by which God gave special revelation was through words. Ninety-two times the prophetic message begins, "The word of the LORD came" (Gen. 15:4; 2 Sam. 7:4; etc.). Sometimes, such as at Mount Sinai, God spoke with an audible voice. At other times, he sent angels to speak to men. It is possible that in other cases he caused the words to arise supernaturally within the prophets' minds (1 Cor. 14:29–30). Sometimes God directed and controlled a person's study of history so that he could write it with perfect "certainty" (Luke 1:1–4). Sometimes God stimulated and guided a person's careful crafting of poetry so that he wrote the Word of the Holy Spirit (2 Sam. 23:1–3). Whatever the method, the result was God's words in human language (Acts 1:16; 28:25).

Supernatural Revelation in Appearances

Other means of revelation were theophanies, dreams, and visions (Num. 12:6, 8). A *theophany* is a visible appearance of the invisible Lord. Herman Bavinck noted that these appearances did not mean that God has a body but were "perceptible signs by which his presence is made known."[3] Revelation by dreams and visions was a picture of supernatural realities that God impressed directly upon the minds of the recipients. Dreams and visions were often interpreted through words from God. Visions, in contrast to dreams, generally took place with "eyes open" and the person awake (Num. 24:4, 16).

Supernatural Revelation in Events

God also gave revelation by his sovereign acts in history. He worked miracles, he said, so that people would "know that I am the LORD" (Ex. 7:5). Revelation also took place through ordinary, natural processes. Like the supernatural inspiration of writers of biblical history, these means of revelation were supernatural but not by a display of miraculous power. Rather, God controlled ordinary events or natural means to communicate supernatural information. For example, God revealed his will to the priest through objects called the

3 Bavinck, *RD*, 1:328.

Urim and Thummim (Ex. 28:30; Lev. 8:8; Num. 27:21) and sometimes by the casting of lots (Lev. 16:8–9; Num. 26:55–56; 33:54).

Supernatural Revelation in the Incarnate Person of Jesus Christ

All of Christ's life "in the flesh" (incarnate) is revelation from God, for he is the Son of God and the living truth. Jesus says, "I am the way, the truth, and the life: no man cometh unto the Father, but by me. If ye had known me, ye should have known my Father also: and from henceforth ye know him, and have seen him. . . . He that hath seen me hath seen the Father" (John 14:6–9). In the incarnate Lord, all other ways of divine revelation reach their richest fulfillment. Christ's every word is the Word of God. He reveals God with every ordinary act of love and every extraordinary miracle. Christ is the most perfect appearance of God ever known.

God's Personal Revelation in True Words

God reveals *himself*. He speaks and acts so that "ye shall know that I am the Lord your God" (Ex. 6:7). Christ says, "This is life eternal, that they might know thee the only true God, and Jesus Christ, whom thou hast sent" (John 17:3). J. I. Packer says, "As God's act, revelation is the personal self-disclosure whereby He brings us actively and experimentally [experientially] to know Him as our own God and Saviour."[4] Therefore, special revelation is relational, for in it we meet God.

However, it is misleading to set the personal, relational quality of special revelation against revelation coming in true words. That would make the knowledge of God into no knowledge at all but only a feeling. A personal encounter that leads to a relationship is much more than true beliefs. But it cannot be less or we have no basis to say that we know the other person. Revelation communicates knowledge. For example, God reveals man's secrets and his plan for the future (Dan. 2:20–23), who Jesus is as God's Son (Matt. 16:16–17), and "the things that are freely given to us of God" so that we can know and speak about them (1 Cor. 2:9–13).

That is not to say that God's revelation is like science. The Bible is not a list of truths about God. It contains a wide variety of divinely inspired

4 J. I. Packer, "God Speaks to Man: Revelation and the Bible," in *Christian Foundations* (Philadelphia: Westminster, 1965), 2:55.

literature, such as historical narrative, doctrinal instruction, prophetic rebuke, songs of praise, and lamentation. It aims to shape not only our beliefs but our entire existence as individuals and churches. However, the Bible is full of truth claims. Apart from the truth, God's Word would have no power to form relationships or change lives.

The gospel itself consists of the "good news" that "Christ died for our sins according to the scriptures; and that he was buried, and that he rose again the third day according to the scriptures: and that he was seen of Cephas, then of the twelve," and many others (1 Cor. 15:3–5). These are not just feelings. They are facts of history.

Errors regarding Special Revelation

The ancient church faced theological attacks mainly with regard to the doctrines of the person of Christ and the Trinity. The church from the Reformation to the modern era has found itself forced to defend the doctrine of special revelation from many errors.

Special Revelation Extended to Include Man's Tradition

The Roman Catholic Church teaches that divine revelation has been passed down in two forms: "Sacred Tradition and Sacred Scripture."[5] The church, it says, "does not derive her certainty about all revealed truths from the holy Scriptures alone. Both Scripture and Tradition must be accepted and honored with equal sentiments of devotion and reverence." The Roman Catholic Church's pope and bishops assert the supreme authority to interpret the Word of God. When they define doctrine, they claim that everyone must accept it by faith as completely true.[6]

The pope, "as supreme pastor and teacher of all the faithful," supposedly speaks with "infallibility" when "he proclaims by a definitive act a doctrine pertaining to faith or morals." Even when he is not making a definitive pronouncement, his teachings must be received by the faithful "with religious assent."[7]

In response, we note that there is no indication in the Holy Scriptures of a second, equally authoritative source of divine revelation. The Roman

5 *Catechism of the Catholic Church* (New York: Doubleday, 1994), secs. 76, 80.

6 *Catechism of the Catholic Church*, secs. 82, 85, 88.

7 *Catechism of the Catholic Church*, secs. 891–92; cf. 2035.

Church attempts to find biblical support for its position by quoting Christ's promise that the Holy Spirit will teach his church (John 16:12–13).[8] But Christ did not say anything here about the infallibility of the bishop of Rome or any church organization. He promised the Holy Spirit's teaching, first to the apostles, who were with him at the time, and generally to all believers, whom the Spirit illuminates to know the truth of God's Word.

Roman Catholics also appeal to references to tradition in the New Testament (2 Thess. 2:15; 3:6). They claim these prove that God also speaks through the church's tradition.[9]

We reply that if tradition is faithful to God's Word, it should be obeyed (1 Cor. 11:2). Those who heard the preaching of the apostles were to pass it along to others (2 Tim. 2:2). However, there is no promise in the Bible that the traditions of the church will always preserve the Word of God in its purity and entirety. Tradition must always be tested by the written Word of Christ, not blindly followed (Col. 2:6–8, 22).

Special Revelation Set below Man's Reason

Instead of lifting human tradition to the level of God's authority, Enlightenment philosophers lifted man to a position of independence from God in his quest for truth. Rather than believing that the Bible was inspired by God, people who accepted this perspective tended to view the Bible as simply a collection of ancient human writings containing legends, superstitions, historical mistakes, doctrinal and moral errors, and unscientific views of the world. The study of the Bible based on such assumptions developed into an academic field known as *higher criticism*. Beginning in the late eighteenth century and especially in the nineteenth century, some people attempted to wed this unbelieving approach to the Bible with a major revision of Christianity—actually a different religion from Christianity—called *theological liberalism* or *modernism*.

A central teaching of liberal modernism is the denial of supernatural miracles. Theological liberals critically sift the teachings of the Bible to supposedly find the true message of Jesus. This message is said to be the

8 John Eck, *Enchiridion of Commonplaces against Luther and Other Enemies of the Church*, trans. Ford Lewis Battles (Grand Rapids, MI: Baker, 1979), 4.1 (46).

9 Eck, *Enchiridion*, 4.1 (46); and Dave Armstrong, *A Biblical Defense of Catholicism* (Manchester, NH: Sophia Institute Press, 2003), 8–13.

fatherhood of God for all people, the brotherhood of all people, and the importance of loving one another. The message, they say, is not that Christ is the only begotten Son of God and the Savior.[10] The Bible is not viewed as accurate history but as a collection of legends that modern people must reject because miracles cannot be true.[11]

In response to liberal modernism, we observe that people who teach it claim to be Christians but teach unbelief toward the Word of God. Modernists may speak warmly of Christ, yet they refer not to the Christ of the Bible but to a Christ they invented. These theologians and preachers continue to use traditional Christian language but try to convince people of a belief system not found in the Bible. Furthermore, the modernist objection against the supernatural has no basis in reason or science. Miracles are entirely reasonable if God exists. He is the almighty Creator and Sustainer of all things (Jer. 32:17).

Liberal modernism brings no living union with the living Christ. Jesus says, "If ye continue in my word, then are ye my disciples indeed; and ye shall know the truth, and the truth shall make you free" (John 8:31–32). Liberalism's confidence in human reasoning and feeling runs directly against the truth that fallen man has a "whorish heart" that quickly departs from God to pursue idols (Ezek. 6:9). Our only hope lies in the light that shines in Scripture alone (Isa. 8:20). This is the light of Christ, our supernatural Teacher (9:2, 6).

Special Revelation Spread to All Religions

Theological liberalism replaces the truths of Christianity with experiences of God's love. *Religious pluralism* is the belief that God works through the experiences of all religions so that they are pathways to God.[12] It is illustrated by a parable in which blind men approach an elephant. One man touches its side and declares the elephant to be like a wall. A second, feeling its trunk, compares the animal to a snake. A third, touching its leg, thinks the beast

10 Adolf Harnack, *What Is Christianity? Lectures Delivered in the University of Berlin During the Winter-Term 1899–1900*, trans. Thomas Bailey Saunders, rev. 2nd ed. (New York: G. P. Putnam's Sons, 1902), 73, 154–57.

11 Harnack, *What Is Christianity?*, 21–22, 30; and Rudolf Bultmann, *New Testament Mythology and Other Basic Writings*, trans. Schubert M. Ogden (Minneapolis: Fortress, 1984), 4.

12 Friedrich Schleiermacher, *On Religion: Speeches to Its Cultured Despisers*, trans. and ed. Richard Crouter, Texts in German Philosophy (Cambridge: Cambridge University Press, 1988), 194; and John Hick, *The Metaphor of God Incarnate: Christology in a Pluralistic Age* (Louisville: Westminster/John Knox, 1993), 141.

to be much like a tree. The blind men argue among themselves, each sure that he alone is right.[13]

Pluralism appeals to our appreciation for humility, compassion for all people, and the mystery of a God we cannot completely understand. However, religious pluralism arrogantly claims to see the truth about God even while it contradicts itself by saying that religions only grope after him like blind men and no one can really know him.[14] Religious pluralism does not really accept different religions. Rather, it insults and denies them because it declares them all to be wrong. The skepticism of religious pluralism starts with the assumption that God does not communicate in words. To put it in terms of the parable, what if the elephant speaks? We know the true God because he has spoken.

Special Revelation Replaced with Meeting God

Karl Barth and Emil Brunner began a theological movement in the twentieth century that came to be known as *neoorthodoxy* or *dialectical theology*. Unlike liberal theologians, they taught that revelation is the sovereign, gracious act of God toward man, not something arising from inside of man. However, neoorthodox theologians said that the Word of God is not a book but Jesus Christ.

The Bible, they said, is not God's Word and revelation. It is only the record of the prophetic and apostolic witness to divine revelation. The Bible supposedly contains doctrinal and historical errors. Yet neoorthodox theologians regard it to be the means through which God reveals himself to us so that it *becomes* God's Word to us. When God reveals himself to a person through the Bible, revelation is reconciliation and life. In revelation we encounter God, and he engages us in faith and obedience. To simply identify the Bible as the Word of God is "bibliolatry."[15]

13 John Godfrey Saxe, "The Blind Men and the Elephant: A Hindoo Fable," in *The Poems of John Godfrey Saxe* (Boston: James R. Osgood and Company, 1873), 260.

14 Lesslie Newbigin, *The Gospel in a Pluralist Society* (Grand Rapids, MI: Eerdmans; Geneva: WCC, 1989), 10.

15 Karl Barth, "The Christian Understanding of Revelation," in *Against the Stream: Shorter Post-War Writings, 1946–52*, ed. Ronald Gregor Smith (New York: Philosophical Library, 1954), 207–25; and Emil Brunner, *Revelation and Reason: The Christian Doctrine of Faith and Knowledge*, trans. Olive Wyon (Philadelphia: Westminster, 1946), 2.1, 4; 3.1; 4.2–6; 9.1 (23–24, 28–29, 32, 43–47, 120).

In response to Barth's and Brunner's view of special revelation, we must say that we are grateful for their emphasis on the gracious, sovereign character of divine revelation and the centrality of Christ in God's act of making himself known. But by separating revelation from the Bible, they have not been faithful to the witness of Scripture. Revelation is not merely a personal encounter. It is truth we can know and believe (Eph. 3:4–6). Revelation does not always mean that people receive the truth and are reconciled to God (John 3:19). Christ, the personal Word of God, bears witness that the Bible is the written Word of God (Mark 7:9–13; John 10:35).

If the Bible were not God's revelation but only a fallible human witness to divine revelation, then there would be no basis for us to teach God's truth with authority. Consequently, the neoorthodox view of revelation, for all its talk of encounter, leaves man stranded on an island of ignorance. People must grope after Christ through the uncertain means of feelings. Millard Erickson asks, "Can the advocates of this view be sure that what they encounter is really the God of Abraham, Isaac, and Jacob?"[16]

The good news is that God has spoken and revealed himself in his Word. The Bible repeatedly claims to be words from God that reveal him and his will. The Holy Scriptures are not merely man's interpretation of God's revelation. The Bible *is* God's revelation of himself. It is the Word of God, which was produced by the Holy Spirit and cannot be broken (John 10:35; 2 Pet. 1:20–21). Therefore, beware of these false views of special revelation. Instead, receive the Bible for what it is: the Word of God. Resolve even now to accept all that it teaches as truth and to build your life on it.

Suggested Songs to Sing to the Lord

- Psalm 19, "Most perfect is the law of God," in *Psalter*, No. 42; *THBap*, No. 450
- "O Word of God Incarnate," in *THBap*, No. 267

Questions for Meditation or Discussion

1. Show from Scripture that special revelation is a work of the Trinity. What function does the Father perform in special revelation? The Son? The Spirit?

16 Millard J. Erickson, *Christian Theology*, 3rd ed. (Grand Rapids, MI: Baker, 2013), 159.

2. What do the authors mean by "the human character of special revelation"?
3. What four modes of special revelation are found in the Bible?
4. What does Roman Catholicism teach concerning Scripture and tradition?
5. What is liberal modernism, and why is it so called?
6. What arguments do the authors bring against liberal modernism?
7. What is religious pluralism?
8. What is the parable of the elephant? What does it mean? How does the parable show the inconsistency and arrogance of pluralistic claims?
9. What was Barth and Brunner's view of divine revelation? Of the Bible?
10. Someone says, "My problem with your religion is that you turn the Bible into an idol. The Word of God is not an ancient book but the person of Jesus Christ." How do you respond?

6

The Inspiration, Authority, and Clarity of the Bible

Chapter Summary and Key Terms

The word of the prophets and apostles is the *Word of God*, God's speech or message to man. God's messengers spoke his word and wrote it down in books that formed the Holy Scriptures. The Holy Spirit produced the Scriptures by his work of *inspiration*. As a result, all the words of the Bible are both human words and God's words, exactly what God wanted these writings to say (*plenary, verbal inspiration*). Therefore, the Bible has divine *authority*. We should believe all that it teaches and obey all that it commands us. By the Spirit's work of illumination, people recognize the Bible's inherent authority as God's Word, its property of *self-authentication*. Thus, the church recognized the *canon* (the sixty-six books belonging to the Holy Scriptures). The Spirit also gave the Bible such *perspicuity* (or clarity) that anyone can understand its basic message. The plenary inspiration and clarity of the Scriptures allow us to interpret more difficult passages by the *analogy of Scripture*, comparing one passage with others that address the same topic.

GOD HAS SPOKEN. This special revelation is the basis of our eternal hope (Titus 1:1–3). Trusting in his Word, we find a solid resting place for our confidence and a way of taking refuge in God's salvation. Proverbs 30:5 says, "Every word of God is pure: he is a shield unto them that put their trust in him."

When we call the Bible the Word of God, we do not mean that it is merely a message from men about God. The Bible is not just the writers' reports of God's message insofar as they understood it rightly. Rather, the written words of the Bible are God's Word to us.

The Word of the Prophets and Apostles Is the Word of God

Even before the Bible was written, God spoke to men like Noah and Abraham. His word came with authority and power to call forth their faith in what they could not see (Heb. 11:7–8). Later, he spoke through other prophets and the apostles. The Bible represents their words as nothing less than the words of God. We should receive these words as if we heard them from God's own mouth.

The Word of God Preached through the Prophets and Apostles

The message God's prophets preached is the word of the Lord (2 Kings 20:16; Ezra 1:1). Elisha says, "Hear ye the word of the LORD; thus saith the LORD" (2 Kings 7:1). Micaiah says, "Therefore hear the word of the LORD" (2 Chron. 18:18). The apostle Paul says, "For this cause also thank we God without ceasing, because, when ye received the word of God which ye heard of us, ye received it not as the word of men, but as it is in truth, the word of God, which effectually worketh also in you that believe" (1 Thess. 2:13).

When the Bible says that the prophets and apostles spoke God's word, it means that God was speaking through them (2 Sam. 23:2). What the prophets said, the Lord said. It is "the word of the LORD, which he spake by his servants the prophets" (2 Kings 24:2). This was not something that happened once in a while—it was true of all God's prophets: God "spake by the mouth of his holy prophets, which have been since the world began" (Luke 1:70). Likewise, the authority of the apostles arose from the supernatural work of the Spirit to give them their words (Matt. 10:20; 1 Cor. 2:13).

The Written Word of God: The Old Testament

At God's command, Moses wrote God's words in a book (Ex. 17:14; 24:4; 34:27). The Lord himself wrote the Ten Commandments on tablets of stone (24:12; 31:18; 34:1, 28). Not all prophets wrote down the words God gave them. But at God's command some prophets and wise men did write them down to preserve them for future generations (1 Sam. 10:25; Isa. 30:8; Jer. 30:2). The result was a growing collection of materials that were the written word of God. The "words of the book" were "the word of the Lord" (2 Chron. 34:21; cf. Jer. 36:2, 10–11).

The apostles and other New Testament authors believed that the Old Testament was the Word of God. Together with other pious Jews, the early Christians viewed the various sacred writings of Israel—the Law and the Prophets—as God's inspired books (Acts 24:14). The New Testament refers to the Old Testament as the "Scriptures" (John 5:39; Rom. 1:2). That word, which means "writings," is consistently used in the New Testament for the Bible, not for other writings. Peter quotes a psalm, saying, "This scripture must needs have been fulfilled, which the Holy Ghost by the mouth of David spake" (Acts 1:16; cf. Heb. 3:7; 10:15–17).

Christ has a very high view of the Old Testament. The Lord Jesus explains,

> Think not that I am come to destroy the law, or the prophets: I am not come to destroy, but to fulfil. For verily I say unto you, till heaven and earth pass, one jot or one tittle shall in no wise pass from the law, till all be fulfilled. Whosoever therefore shall break one of these least commandments, and shall teach men so, he shall be called the least in the kingdom of heaven: but whosoever shall do and teach them, the same shall be called great in the kingdom of heaven. (Matt. 5:17–19)

The Old Testament Scriptures have God's eternal authority in their smallest details, down to the jot and tittle, the smallest parts of Hebrew letters (Luke 16:17).

The Lord Jesus believed that Moses wrote the law. He called it "the word of God." He also severely criticized those who set the law aside for the sake of human traditions (Mark 7:10–13). He said that "the scripture cannot be broken" (John 10:35).

The Written Word of God: The New Testament

The New Testament also claims to be the word of God, just like the Old Testament. Christ places his words on the same level as the words of the Holy Scriptures: "Heaven and earth shall pass away, but my words shall not pass away" (Matt. 24:35; Luke 21:33). He says we should believe both what is written in the Old Testament and "the words which I spake unto you" (Luke 24:44). Believing Christ's words goes hand in hand with believing the writings of Moses (John 5:47). To be ashamed of Christ's words and not to believe them will bring dire consequences on judgment day (Luke 9:26; John 12:47–48).

One New Testament writer could call the writings of another New Testament author "Scripture" on the same level as the Old Testament. In 1 Timothy 5:18, Paul writes, "For the scripture saith, thou shalt not muzzle the ox that treadeth out the corn. And, The labourer is worthy of his reward." The first quotation is from the Old Testament (Deut. 25:4), but the second is found in the Gospels (Matt. 10:10; Luke 10:7). Paul considered the Gospels to be Scripture. Peter compares the way that some people abused Paul's letters to the way they abused "the other scriptures" (2 Pet. 3:16). Peter believed that Paul's letters were part of the Holy Scriptures.

The apostles believed that their teachings had God's authority. For church members to ignore instructions from an apostle was enough of a reason for the church to rebuke them (2 Thess. 3:14–15). If a teacher contradicted the gospel of an apostle's letters, he doomed himself to damnation (Gal. 1:8–9). It was not merely the apostle who was writing but "Christ speaking in me" (2 Cor. 13:3). Paul, though giving detailed instructions not found in previous teachings by God or Christ, says, "The things that I write unto you are the commandments of the Lord" (1 Cor. 14:37). The book of Revelation opens with the claim to be divine revelation through Jesus Christ (Rev. 1:1). The book says that the Lord promises, "These words are true and faithful" (21:5). Revelation concludes with a fearsome warning against anyone who adds or takes away from the prophecy (22:18–19). The New Testament teaches that it is God's Word.

The Spirit's Inspiration of the Written Word of God

The Bible consists of human words that are also God's words. How did such a thing take place? The answer is the *inspiration* of the Holy Spirit. The Bible identifies the Holy Spirit particularly as the One who spoke through the prophets and apostles (Neh. 9:30; Eph. 3:5). David writes, "The Spirit of the Lord spake by me, and his word was in my tongue" (2 Sam. 23:2). His reference to the tongue shows the direct influence that the Spirit had on the prophets. As a result, what they thought in their minds and spoke with their mouths was the word of God.

The Lord Jesus Christ promised his apostles that he would grant them a special influence of the Spirit of truth. By that influence, they could accurately remember the words that he spoke on earth and deeper revelations that he would grant them later (John 14:25–26; 16:12–14).

God's Inspiration of Words

Nowhere does the Bible suggest that God merely gave insight to the prophets, who then spoke the message in their own words. The Lord assured a fearful Moses, "I will be with thy mouth, and teach thee what thou shalt say" (Ex. 4:12). God gave Jeremiah the same promise: "I have put my words in thy mouth" (Jer. 1:9). The plural term "words" implies that God inspired not just general ideas but gave the specific words by which the speakers or writers communicated the ideas. God led the prophets to exactly what they should say, and they said exactly that (Num. 22:38; 23:5, 12, 16). The prophet became the mouth of the Lord (Ex. 4:16). This does not mean that God took over the prophet's body. Each human writer expressed himself in his own style. But God sovereignly controlled the prophets' process of thinking and writing so that the result is the Word of God.

The result of this process of *verbal inspiration* was that the words written in the Bible are the words of God. Christ's confidence in the text of the Holy Scriptures is so strong that he bases an argument on a single word in Psalm 110:1 (Matt. 22:41–45). The apostle Paul bases an argument on the fact that a word in the Old Testament is singular instead of plural (Gal. 3:16).

God Breathed Out the Words of the Whole Bible

Paul writes, "All scripture is given by inspiration of God, and is profitable for doctrine, for reproof, for correction, for instruction in righteousness" (2 Tim. 3:16). Peter says,

> We have also a more sure word of prophecy; whereunto ye do well that ye take heed, as unto a light that shineth in a dark place, until the day dawn, and the day star arise in your hearts: knowing this first, that no prophecy of the scripture is of any private interpretation. For the prophecy came not in old time by the will of man: but holy men of God spake as they were moved by the Holy Ghost. (2 Pet. 1:19–21)

The apostles are teaching us how far God's inspiration reaches. Paul writes about "all scripture." The entire Bible is inspired. Similarly, Peter says that "no prophecy of the scripture" arises merely from man's interpretation or will, but all is from the Holy Spirit.

Therefore, we may speak of *plenary, verbal inspiration*, the divine inspiration of the whole Bible in every word of the original manuscripts. All writings of the prophets and apostles are the Word of God. The Westminster Confession of Faith lists the sixty-six books of the Bible and says, "All . . . are given by inspiration of God to be the rule of faith and life."[1]

The apostles are also teaching us the meaning of inspiration. Paul's expression "given by inspiration" literally means "God-breathed" or "breathed out by God" (ESV). God breathed out the Scriptures themselves, just as our words are produced by our breath. The Greek word translated as "breathe" is closely related to "Spirit," implying the special work of the Holy Spirit. Inspiration is the work of the Holy Spirit to produce the Bible through human authors so that the Bible is God's Word just as surely as the breath of our mouths produces our own words.

Peter says that the prophets "spake as they were moved by the Holy Ghost." The word translated as "moved" means "carried from one place to another." The Holy Spirit carried the prophets to write exactly what God wanted them to communicate. We should remember, too, that God sovereignly shaped their personalities and experiences by his providence to prepare them to write what he wanted them to write.

The inspiration of the Bible means that the Bible is God's Word. It has divine properties, including divine authority, clarity, inerrancy, and sufficiency. We will explore these properties in the remainder of this chapter and also in the next.

The Authority of the Bible

The people who heard Christ teach "were astonished at his doctrine: for he taught them as one having authority" (Matt. 7:28–29). By the inspiration of the Spirit of Christ, authority shines in every part of Holy Scripture.

The Bible's authority as the Word of God means that everyone who hears or reads it should submit to what it teaches us to believe and do. Paul considers it a mark of conversion "that you who were once slaves of sin

1 The Westminster Confession of Faith (1.2), in *RC*, 4:235. Cf. the Second London Baptist Confession (1.2), in *RC*, 4:533.

have become obedient from the heart to the standard of teaching to which you were committed" (Rom. 6:17 ESV). Human authorities may make rules for many parts of our outward lives. But the Word of God alone has the authority to bind our consciences with respect to doctrine, worship, morality, and conduct.

The Bible has this authority because it comes from God and is his Word. The testimony of God has infinitely more authority than the testimony of man (1 John 5:9; cf. 1 Thess. 2:13). The Westminster Confession of Faith says, "The authority of the Holy Scripture, for which it ought to be believed, and obeyed, dependeth not upon the testimony of any man, or Church; but wholly upon God (who is truth itself) the author thereof: and therefore it is to be received, because it is the Word of God."[2]

The Bible says more than four hundred times, "Thus saith the Lord." This is the way a king's proclamations are presented.[3] God speaks as the supreme Lord and King. All who hear must submit to his word. We cannot make any leader or council of leaders into our final authority. History has shown that leaders and councils have made mistakes and contradicted each other.[4]

Faith in the Holy Scriptures does not depend on the authority of mere men but arises from the inward illumination of the Holy Spirit. By this illumination, God gives sinners the ability to see that the Bible is the Word of God. Paul explains, "My speech and my preaching was not with enticing words of man's wisdom, but in demonstration of the Spirit and of power: that your faith should not stand in the wisdom of men, but in the power of God" (1 Cor. 2:4–5). The Spirit works in the heart to show and confirm the truth of the gospel.

The Holy Spirit accompanies the gospel with power to produce "assurance" (1 Thess. 1:5). That refers to the confidence of saving faith that God's Word is true (Heb. 6:11; 10:22). Reformed theologians, therefore, teach that the Bible has the property of *self-authentication*.[5] This means that God's

2 The Westminster Confession of Faith (1.4), in *RC*, 4:235. Cf. the Second London Baptist Confession (1.4), in *RC*, 4:533.

3 Ex. 5:10–11; 1 Kings 2:30; 20:1–3; 22:27; 2 Kings 9:18–19; 18:29, 31; 2 Chron. 18:26; Isa. 36:14, 16.

4 The Westminster Confession of Faith (1.10); and the Second London Baptist Confession (1.10), in *RC*, 4:236, 535.

5 Calvin, *Institutes*, 1.7.3, 5; cf. Westminster Confession of Faith (1.5), in *RC*, 4:235.

Word contains marks that it comes from God. As a result, when the Holy Spirit opens the eyes of the heart, people recognize the Bible's authority as God's Word.

By the Spirit's illumination, God's people recognized long ago which books were inspired by God and belonged to the list of authentic writings of the Holy Scriptures (this list is called the *canon*). Ancient Israel recognized the thirty-nine books of the Hebrew Old Testament. The early church recognized the twenty-seven books of the Greek New Testament. Several other ancient books by Jews and Christians, though they might be of some value for history and wisdom, were not inspired by God. Such books belong not to God's Word but to what is called the *Apocrypha*.

Our response to God's Word is our response to God. Isaiah writes,

> Thus saith the Lord, The heaven is my throne, and the earth is my footstool: where is the house that ye build unto me? And where is the place of my rest? For all those things hath mine hand made, and all those things have been, saith the Lord: but to this man will I look, even to him that is poor and of a contrite spirit, and trembleth at my word. (Isa. 66:1–2)

The Clarity of the Bible

The Holy Scriptures contain "some things in them that are hard to understand" (2 Pet. 3:16 ESV). Therefore, God's Word calls for teachers gifted by the Spirit (1 Cor. 12:28–29). God especially works through those ordained as ministers of the Word and elders (Titus 1:7). However, the Bible does not belong just to a special group of teachers. It is the treasure of the whole family of God. God commands believers to meditate on his words and to "teach them diligently unto thy children" (Deut. 6:6–7; cf. 4:9). The Bible has been compared to a river deep enough for an elephant to swim and shallow enough at its shores for a lamb to safely wade.[6]

The Westminster Confession of Faith says,

> All things in Scripture are not alike plain in themselves, nor alike clear unto all: yet those things which are necessary to be known, believed, and

6 Gregory the Great, *Morals on the Book of Job*, 3 vols. (Oxford: John Henry Parker, 1844), epistle to Leander, sec. 4 (1:9).

> observed for salvation, are so clearly propounded, and opened in some place of Scripture or other, that not only the learned, but the unlearned, in a due use of the ordinary means, may attain unto a sufficient understanding of them.[7]

The Reformers called this doctrine the *perspicuity* (clarity) of Scripture.[8] Much to the dismay of the pope and his followers, the Reformers brought the whole Bible to the whole church. They translated it into the language of the people, preached its message to everyone, and made the reading and preaching of it the central activity of the church's worship.

The Bible often shows us its clarity by comparing God's Word to a light to guide us. Psalm 119:105 says, "Thy word is a lamp unto my feet, and a light unto my path." Proverbs 6:23 says, "The commandment is a lamp; and the law is light." Peter also compares "the word of prophecy" to "a light that shineth in a dark place" (2 Pet. 1:19). Therefore, the Bible is not a dark and cloudy book to which men must add light and clarity. The Bible is God's light that shines into the darkness of men's ignorance of God.

The great obstacle to our understanding of the truths of God is not the Bible. Our problem is the sin and satanic unbelief that control the wicked (John 8:43–45; 2 Cor. 4:4) and remain to some extent in the godly (Luke 24:25, 45). However, those who have the Spirit of God dwelling in them "have the mind of Christ" (1 Cor. 2:16) As believers, they are able to understand the Scriptures, especially as they press on to maturity (3:1–3). The veil has been lifted from their hearts, and by the Spirit they behold the glory of Christ and are transformed into his likeness (2 Cor. 3:14–18). All of the Bible is profitable for our instruction and spiritual development (Rom. 15:4; 2 Tim. 3:16).

One practical implication of the clarity of Scripture is that we should search the Bible with great anticipation. If we are believers and pray for God to illuminate us so that we can see the wonders in his Word (Ps. 119:18), then we have every reason to expect to see those wonders set forth and their mystery unveiled in the pages of Scripture. This expectation should motivate us to read the Bible, teach it to our children, and come to hear it

7 The Westminster Confession of Faith (1.7), in *RC*, 4:236. Cf. the Second London Baptist Confession (1.7), in *RC*, 4:534.

8 Polyander, Walaeus, Thysius, and Rivetus, *SPT*, 5.1 (1:129).

preached with eagerness and appetite. Furthermore, since the Bible is clear enough for people to understand its doctrines, the church has an obligation to translate the original Hebrew, Aramaic, and Greek texts into the languages of the world.[9]

Another practical implication of the clarity of the Bible is the principle of interpretation known as *the analogy of Scripture*. If the great doctrines of the Bible are clearly taught in some texts, then it follows that less clear passages can be interpreted by the clearer texts.[10] This principle of interpretation is a great aid to studying the Bible. It helps to keep the teacher under the authority of the Holy Spirit, who inspired the whole Bible, rather than inventing new and heretical interpretations.

Thank God for the divine authority and clarity of his Word! Far from imprisoning us, these glorious properties set us free. They deliver us from being controlled by false leaders in the church. They put the Word of God in the hands of all God's people. They liberate us to surrender our lives to God's truth with confidence in our Christian faith. They establish the lordship of Jesus Christ over his church. The least child of God may learn from the Lord and know that his or her salvation rests not upon the wisdom of men but on the Word of God.

Suggested Song to Sing to the Lord

- Psalm 119:1–2, 9–10, 105–106, in "How blessed are the perfect in the way," *Psalter*, No. 428

Questions for Meditation or Discussion

1. Why should we regard the word preached by the prophets and apostles to be the word of God?
2. How did Christ and the New Testament writers regard the Old Testament documents?
3. How did Christ and his apostles teach us to view the words of the New Testament?
4. What is the doctrine of inspiration? How is it taught in 2 Timothy 3:16 and 2 Peter 1:19–21?

9 The Westminster Confession of Faith (1.8), in *RC*, 4:236.

10 The Westminster Confession of Faith (1.9), in *RC*, 4:236.

5. How would it affect the faith of God's people if they concluded that they cannot trust that all the Bible's words were inspired by God, but only some words or perhaps the main ideas?
6. What do we mean by the authority of the Bible? What is the basis of the Bible's authority?
7. How does God convince us that the Bible is his authentic Word?
8. What response does the authority of God's Word call for in us?
9. What is the perspicuity of Scripture? How is it taught in the Bible?
10. How should the doctrine of perspicuity help you to approach your own reading of the Bible with greater anticipation?

7

The Inerrancy and Sufficiency of the Bible

Chapter Summary and Key Terms

Since the Bible is God's Word, it is true in all that it teaches. We call this property of the Bible its *inerrancy*—that is, the quality of having no error. This perfect truthfulness includes anything that Scripture teaches in relation to every field of knowledge. Therefore, we should give it our complete trust. We should also accept the Bible as the source of all knowledge necessary for salvation and all moral principles for a life pleasing to God. This property of Scripture is called its *sufficiency*. We should not add to the Bible or take away from it. Rather, for any questions we might have about spiritual life or how the church should function, we should seek the answers in the Bible.

THE BIBLE IS TRUE. John Calvin said, "This is a principle that distinguishes our religion from all others, that we know that God hath spoken to us, and are fully convinced that the prophets did not speak at their own suggestion, but that, being organs [instruments] of the Holy Spirit, they only uttered what they had been commissioned from heaven to declare."[1] The Heidelberg Catechism says that true faith includes "a certain knowledge, whereby I hold for truth all that God has revealed to us in His Word."[2] The Bible is God's perfect instruction for his people.

1 Calvin, *Comm.* on 2 Tim. 3:16.

2 The Heidelberg Catechism (LD 7, Q. 21), in *TFU*, 73. The Heidelberg Catechism adds in this answer that true faith also includes "an assured confidence" in the gospel of Christ produced by the Spirit's work in the heart.

The Inerrancy of the Bible

The word *inerrant* means "without error." Therefore, when we refer to the Bible's inerrancy, we mean that it does not declare anything contrary to what is true and real. All that it does declare is faithful and accurate.[3] The Belgic Confession states that we receive the Holy Scriptures "for the regulation, foundation, and confirmation of our faith; believing without any doubt all things contained in them . . . because the Holy Ghost witnesseth in our hearts that they are from God."[4] The Westminster Confession of Faith refers to "the infallible truth" of the Bible.[5]

The Bible's Teaching on Scripture's Inerrancy

The Bible is God's Word. Every word of it is inspired by God's Spirit (2 Tim. 3:16; 2 Pet. 1:20–21). Therefore, the trustworthiness of the Bible is the trustworthiness of God. He is not a liar (Num. 23:19; 1 Sam. 15:29) and cannot make mistakes. He knows all things in all places and times (Pss. 33:14; 139:1–4; 147:5). Therefore, the Bible is truth without error.

God has revealed the inerrant truthfulness of his Word. Christ says to his Father, "Thy word is truth" (John 17:17). The message of the Scriptures is "the word of truth" (Ps. 119:43; 2 Tim. 2:15). We may say of the Bible what the widow of Zarephath said to Elijah: "The word of the LORD in thy mouth is truth" (1 Kings 17:24).

The psalmist rejoices, "Thy word is true from the beginning: and every one of thy righteous judgments endureth for ever" (Ps. 119:160; cf. vv. 142, 151). God's servants say, "Thy words be true" (2 Sam. 7:28). One of the last statements in the Bible is "These sayings are faithful and true" (Rev. 22:6; cf. 21:5). God's Word never fails (Josh. 21:45; 23:14; 1 Sam. 3:19; 9:6; 1 Kings 8:20, 56).

The Lord also teaches that his Word is utterly pure. Psalm 12:6 says, "The words of the LORD are pure words, like silver refined in a furnace on the ground, purified seven times" (ESV). Notice the plural term "words," which draws attention to the details of Scripture. The image in Psalm 12 is of a refiner refining silver again and again until it is absolutely pure.

3 See *The Chicago Statement on Biblical Inerrancy*, Alliance of Confessing Evangelicals, http://www.alliancenet.org/the-chicago-statement-on-biblical-inerrancy.

4 The Belgic Confession (Art. 5), in *TFU*, 20.

5 The Westminster Confession of Faith (1.5), in *RC*, 4:235. Cf. the Second London Baptist Confession (1.5), in *RC*, 4:533.

Proverbs 30:5–6 says, "Every word of God is pure: he is a shield unto them that put their trust in him. Add thou not unto his words, lest he reprove thee, and thou be found a liar." The purity of the Bible extends to "every word." It is completely worthy of our trust.

Our faith in the inerrant written Word is ultimately faith in the Son of God, who cannot make a mistake. Jesus Christ is the Word of God (John 1:1) and the living truth (14:6). Matthew Barrett says, "This [truth] raises a dilemma for those who oppose the inerrancy of Christ's words. If they find error in what Christ has spoken, what are they to make of Christ's person?"[6]

Objections to Inerrancy

People raise a number of objections to the doctrine of inerrancy.

Objection 1: People make mistakes. Though God inspired the Bible, it was written by imperfect human beings. Therefore, the Bible must contain mistakes.

In reply, we say that the whole Bible is both human and divine. We cannot separate its teaching into parts that are God's truth and parts that are human errors. Furthermore, as John Frame notes, "Human beings do not necessarily err. Even unregenerate people sometimes speak the truth. So we should not think it impossible that God could reveal himself through human agents, keeping them from error, without violating their humanity."[7]

Objection 2: History is not essential to religion. The Bible's historical accounts are often flawed. However, it does not matter if the Bible fails to teach true history because it does not fail in its teaching about Christ and salvation.

In reply, we say that the gospel centers on historical events (1 Cor. 15:3–8). Apart from those events, its doctrines cannot stand (vv. 14, 17). Jesus Christ affirms the complete reliability of the historical accounts of the Bible, including Genesis (Matt. 12:39–42; 19:4–6; 23:35).

Objection 3: The Bible contradicts modern history and science. The Bible does in fact contain errors, some modern historians and scientists tell us.

In reply, we note that we should be willing to check our theology when it is questioned. Perhaps we are not rightly understanding what God is saying

6 Matthew Barrett, *God's Word Alone—The Authority of Scripture: What the Reformers Taught . . . and Why It Still Matters*, The 5 Solas Series (Grand Rapids, MI: Zondervan, 2016), 283.

7 John Frame, *The Doctrine of the Word of God*, A Theology of Lordship (Phillipsburg, NJ: P&R, 2010), 73–74.

in his Word. But we can also question what historians and scientists say. Many factors make human studies of history and science less than certain. The bottom line is this: Who has higher authority, man or God? Is not God the best historian and scientist?

Objection 4: Parts of the Bible contradict other parts. Therefore, the Holy Scriptures cannot be entirely true.

In reply, we say that when faced with what looks like a contradiction in the Scriptures, we should approach it believing God's witness that the Bible is his Word. It is possible that an error was added to the original inspired text by those who copied the ancient manuscripts. Scholars can compare manuscripts to determine the original reading. Or perhaps we are not properly translating or interpreting either or both texts. It also might be that the two texts do fit together. They might address the same situation from somewhat different but equally true perspectives. And there are cases where we are not able to resolve problems in a manner that fully satisfies our minds. This calls for humility and patience.

But difficult questions about the Bible do not give us reason to reject its inerrancy. Augustine said, "If we are perplexed by an apparent contradiction in Scripture, it is not allowable to say, The author of this book is mistaken; but either the manuscript is faulty, or the translation is wrong, or you have not understood."[8]

Practical Applications of the Bible's Truthfulness

Since the Word of God is pure truth, we should place our complete trust in what God has said. To trust in the Bible for truth is to trust in the God who cannot lie. We glorify God when we trust in his Word, especially when everything around us fights against that trust (Rom. 4:20). Furthermore, when we trust in God's Word, we discover that he is a "shield" to us (Prov. 30:5; cf. Gen. 15:1). Without faith in the Word, it will not profit us (Heb. 4:2), but by faith in God's Word, we please him (11:5–6). Inerrancy is the foundation of all comfort and solid hope. We know that God will never break his promises to us in Christ.

We must never try to correct the Bible with our own reasoning. Paul is our model here, "believing all things which are written in the law and in the

8 Augustine, *Reply to Faustus the Manichaean*, 11.5, in *NPNF*[1], 4:180.

prophets" (Acts 24:14). Not just some things in the Bible but "whatsoever things were written aforetime were written for our learning, that we through patience and comfort of the scriptures may have hope" (Rom. 15:4). Our Lord Jesus Christ teaches us that the Bible is "the word of God" and "cannot be broken" (John 10:35). That is not fanaticism but simply the fullness of faith.

The Sufficiency of the Bible

The sufficiency of the Holy Scriptures is often expressed with the Latin phrase *sola Scriptura*, "Scripture alone." The Geneva Confession declares, "For the rule of our faith and religion, we wish to follow the Scripture alone."[9]

The Bible's Sufficiency Defined

The sufficiency of the Holy Scriptures means that everything necessary for saving faith and spiritual life is taught in the Bible. The Westminster Confession of Faith says, "The whole counsel of God concerning all things necessary for His own glory, man's salvation, faith and life, is either expressly set down in Scripture, or by good and necessary consequence may be deduced from Scripture: unto which nothing at any time is to be added, whether by new revelations of the Spirit or traditions of men."[10]

The Bible does not claim to be a comprehensive guide to astronomy, business, history, or medicine. But it does claim to be "able to make thee wise unto salvation through faith which is in Christ Jesus" and "profitable for doctrine, for reproof, for correction, for instruction in righteousness" (2 Tim. 3:15–16).

The Bible's Sufficiency Clarified

The Bible's sufficiency does not mean that we do not need teachers and scholars or creeds and confessions. These are not to be rejected but welcomed as means that the Holy Spirit uses in the body of Christ (1 Cor. 12:28; Eph. 4:11–13). Rather, the *sola* of *sola Scriptura* means that the Bible alone is the source of all teaching with God's authority. Any teaching that is not derived from the Holy Scriptures has only human authority.

Though the sufficiency of Scripture informs all of life, it especially applies to the holy activities of the church and its officers. In the actions of

9 The Geneva Confession (Art. 1), in *RC*, 1:395.

10 The Westminster Confession of Faith (1.6), in *RC*, 4:235. Cf. the Second London Baptist Confession (1.6), in *RC*, 4:533–34.

the church as the church, the sufficiency of Scripture implies the *regulative principle of worship*. This is the teaching that we must worship as God has commanded, not according to human ideas of worship (Deut. 12:30–32). We will explore that principle under the doctrine of the church's work (chap. 80).

The Bible's Teaching on Scripture's Sufficiency

Negatively, we find the sufficiency of Scripture taught when the Bible commands us not to add to God's Word. Moses said, "You shall not add to the word that I command you, nor take from it, that you may keep the commandments of the LORD your God that I command you" (Deut. 4:2 ESV; cf. Prov. 30:5–6; Rev. 22:18–19). Isaiah, the Lord Jesus, and the apostle Paul all warn against teaching based on man's doctrines (Isa. 29:13; Mark 7:6–7; Col. 2:22).

Positively, the Bible tells us that its revelation is complete for moral instruction and direction on how to go to heaven: "He hath shewed thee, O man, what is good; and what doth the LORD require of thee" (Mic. 6:8).

Jesus speaks about a rich man who goes to hell. He calls out to Abraham in heaven to send someone to his living brothers to warn them. Abraham says, "They have Moses and the prophets; let them hear them." The rich man argues that they need more, and suggests that if someone returns from the dead, his brothers will repent. Abraham replies, "If they hear not Moses and the prophets, neither will they be persuaded, though one rose from the dead" (Luke 16:27–31). In other words, the Old Testament is sufficient to lead sinners to eternal life. If they reject God's Word, not even a miracle will be enough for them to believe.

Paul teaches the Bible's sufficiency when he says that all Scripture is breathed out by God (2 Tim. 3:15–16). Even when taught to children, the Scriptures "are able" to lead them to wisdom and salvation. They are sufficient to guide Christian parents to give moral and spiritual instruction to their sons and daughters. This should give great encouragement to all parents to teach the Word to their children and bring it into every aspect of their family life (Deut. 6:6–7; Eph. 6:4).

The Bible is also sufficient to direct the church and its ministries. God's minister is fully equipped by the Word for "all good works," the whole ministry required of him by God, because the Bible is "profitable" for all those works (2 Tim. 3:16–17). Paul says, "I charge thee therefore before God, and the Lord Jesus Christ, who shall judge the quick and the dead at his appearing and his kingdom; *preach the word*; be instant in season, out of season; reprove, rebuke, exhort with all long suffering and doctrine" (4:1–2).

Practical Applications of the Bible's Sufficiency

We must stand on the Bible as the fully sufficient revelation of God for our salvation and spiritual growth. The church does not need to add its own traditions to the Bible in order to have the full Word of God. Neither should we follow modern prophets and apostles who claim continuing special revelation.

The sufficiency of the Bible implies that no matter what spiritual question or trial we may face as individual Christians, we must go to the Word of God for answers. When we lack wisdom, we must pray for God to grant it (James 1:5) and seek it eagerly from his mouth (Prov. 2:3–6). Augustine said, "In all these books those who fear God and are of a meek and pious disposition seek the will of God. . . . For among the things that are plainly laid down in Scripture are to be found all matters that concern faith and the manner of life, to wit, hope and love."[11]

Church leaders must also be careful to build their churches on the Bible alone. Extrabiblical advice from pastors should be presented as human opinion. Such advice might be helpful, but it also might be mistaken because it is not directly from God. Paul exhorts pastors to build the church on no other foundation than Jesus Christ. They must build God's temple with the gold and silver of his wisdom, not the wood and straw of man's wisdom (1 Cor. 3:10–13).

Suggested Songs to Sing to the Lord

- Psalm 12, "O Lord, be Thou my helper true," in *Psalter*, No. 21; *THBap*, No. 45
- "Thy Word is like a garden, Lord," in *THBap*, No. 257

Questions for Meditation or Discussion

1. What is the doctrine of inerrancy?
2. How can we argue for inerrancy based on God's inspiration of the Holy Scriptures?

11 Augustine, *On Christian Doctrine*, 2.9, in *NPNF*[1], 2:539.

3. What Scripture passages declare the absolute purity of God's Word?
4. What practical implications does inerrancy have for our lives?
5. Someone asks, "Why can't I continue to trust in Jesus as my Lord and Savior, and at the same time think that the Bible is wrong about some points of history?" How do you respond?
6. What is the sufficiency of the Holy Scriptures?
7. What Scripture passages warn against adding to God's Word?
8. How does the Bible testify to its sufficiency as God's law and gospel for mankind?
9. How does 2 Timothy 3:15–4:2 give us confidence that the Bible is sufficient?
10. What practical implications does the doctrine of the Bible's sufficiency have for us?

8

Applied Revelation for Practical Fruit

Chapter Summary and Key Terms

Revelation benefits us only when, by God's grace, it is applied to our lives. On a personal level, God calls each of us to trust and study his Word so that we know him in our hearts. In the family, we should teach the Word to our children. The church must receive the Word so that it transforms us from the inside out and makes us into witnesses and worshipers. As we are changed by the Word, we become means by which God changes others in society around us. The result is that God is glorified among all nations as the church fulfills its mission.

GOD PRODUCES the people of the Word by applying special revelation to individual people to form the body of Christ. Applied revelation creates the church's practical response to the Holy Scriptures. By God's grace, his elect become people who turn away from the corrupting lies of this world to meditate with delight on the Word (Ps. 1:1–2).

Whatever your reason for reading this book, we present these truths not merely to inform your mind. We desire that the Lord will transform your heart and life by his Word.

The Fruit of Applied Revelation in Each Person

Personal Faith in the Scriptures

Nothing is more essential to the profitable study of Holy Scripture than personal faith in it as the Word of God. It is this Word that shows us God and offers us Christ. Saving faith is clinging to God with confident trust (Deut. 10:20–21; 30:20)—that is, receiving Christ (John 1:12). Ralph Robinson said, "Faith is a uniting grace: it knits the soul to Christ, and Christ to the soul."[1] We must "hold fast the form of sound words . . . in faith and love which is in Christ Jesus" (2 Tim. 1:13). Do you have personal faith in the Word of God, shown by the works of genuine love?

God's saving grace rests upon those who tremble at his Word (Isa. 66:2). By grace, the believer receives the gospel "not as the word of men, but as it is in truth, the word of God, which effectually worketh also in you that believe" (1 Thess. 2:13). Trust in God's Word. Count all Scripture to be the absolute truth of God. Stake your life on it. Build upon it with personal obedience as the rock-solid foundation of your life.

Personal Study of the Scriptures

Those who have eyes to see count the Bible to be their greatest earthly treasure. They say with the psalmist, "I have rejoiced in the way of thy testimonies, as much as in all riches. I will meditate in thy precepts, and have respect unto thy ways. I will delight myself in thy statutes: I will not forget thy word" (Ps. 119:14–16).

Are you an active student of the Bible? Do you read it daily? Do you compare Scripture with Scripture to increase your understanding? Do you sit under pastors who preach God's Word from their hearts to your heart every Lord's Day? Do you make good use of the many Bible study helps available to you, including edifying books and the recorded sermons of faithful ministers of the Word?

Paul exhorted Timothy, "Consider what I say; and the Lord give thee understanding in all things" (2 Tim. 2:7). Those who listen to preaching must "take heed" how they hear (Luke 8:18). Nourish your soul in a continual feast on the Holy Scriptures (Jer. 15:16). You can be in the school of Christ every day, sitting like Mary at the feet of Jesus (Luke 10:39).

Personal Experience through the Scriptures

Paul was not content to teach the truth. He also prayed "that the God of our Lord Jesus Christ, the Father of glory, may give unto you the spirit of

1 Ralph Robinson, *Christ All, and in All* (London: Richard D. Dickinson, 1868), 174.

wisdom and revelation in the knowledge of him" (Eph. 1:17). By the Spirit's illumination, the saints have a heart knowledge of all that God is for them in Christ (vv. 18–20). The Father works mightily on the inner man through the Spirit. Then the heart experiences the indwelling Christ and all his benefits. The Christian begins to better know the love of God in Christ that goes beyond our understanding (3:16–19).

Through the Word, the Spirit of the Lord shows us the glory of Christ. The Spirit sets us free from our corrupt love for sin and self. He transforms us to share Christ's glory (2 Cor. 3:16–18; 4:4–6).

Do you enjoy God in the Word? Do you long after him as a deer pants for water? Does your soul seek him earnestly because his lovingkindness is better than life?

The Fruit of Applied Revelation in the Family

God's revelation aims to impact not just one man or woman at a time but their children and grandchildren as well. The Bible should sit at the center of family life. Wilhelmus à Brakel said, "A home without a Bible is a ship without a rudder."[2] God revealed his testimonies and laws to the people of Israel "that they should make them known to their children" (Ps. 78:5).

Moses said to fathers and mothers in Israel, "These words, which I command thee this day, shall be in thine heart: and thou shalt teach them diligently unto thy children, and shalt talk of them when thou sittest in thine house, and when thou walkest by the way, and when thou liest down, and when thou risest up" (Deut. 6:6–7). Matthew Henry wrote, "Those that love the Lord God themselves should do what they can to engage the affections of their children to him."[3] When we teach the Holy Scriptures to children, the Word is able to make them "wise unto salvation through faith which is in Christ Jesus" (2 Tim. 3:15).

The Fruit of Applied Revelation in the Church

The Spirit applies the Word to the body of Christ. He brings light to our darkness. God promises his church, "Arise, shine; for thy light is come, and the glory of the Lord is risen upon thee. For, behold, the darkness shall

2 Brakel, *CRS*, 1:76.

3 Matthew Henry, *Matthew Henry's Commentary*, 6 vols. (Peabody, MA: Hendrickson, 1991), 1:586.

cover the earth, and gross darkness the people: but the Lord shall arise upon thee, and his glory shall be seen upon thee" (Isa. 60:1–2).

Transformation in the Life of the Church

The Lord promises his covenant people that he will put his law "in their inward parts, and write it in their hearts; and will be their God, and they shall be [his] people" (Jer. 31:33). Christ is the Mediator of the new covenant between God and his people. His blessings are for his church (Heb. 8:6–13; 10:14–17).

Edmund Clowney said, "The church, according to Scripture, is not a religious club, a voluntary association of like-minded Christians who cultivate friendship and engage in joint projects. It is rather the institution of Christ and of the Spirit, formed by his power and governed by his Word."[4]

Are you a member of a local church that is faithful to Christ? The people who receive God's Word by the Spirit do not stand alone. They stand as one church in Christ. Are you and your church people of the Word?

Balance in Pastoral Ministry

The God who promises to transform his people (Jer. 3:17) also promises to give them competent shepherds. He says, "I will give you pastors according to mine heart, which shall feed you with knowledge and understanding" (v. 15). These shepherds serve the church with a beautiful combination of faithfulness in their lives and their teaching.

Ministers and elders, you must nurture the church in both experiential godliness and doctrinal truth. As John Murray liked to say, we aim for "intelligent piety."[5] Your ministry should exhibit the loving heart of God. You must faithfully expound his unchanging truth. And you must lead people to the throne of grace in prayer.

Zeal in Evangelism

Since God gives his Word to his church, the people of the Word must engage in evangelism and missions. Paul says, "How then shall they call on him in whom they have not believed? And how shall they believe in him of whom

4 Edmund P. Clowney, *The Church*, Contours of Christian Theology (Downers Grove, IL: InterVarsity Press, 1995), 58.

5 Cited in the introduction to *Collected Writings of John Murray*, 4 vols. (Edinburgh: Banner of Truth, 1982), 4:vii.

they have not heard? And how shall they hear without a preacher? And how shall they preach, except they be sent?" (Rom. 10:14–15).

Though not all Christians are preachers, all Christians should invest in God's cause. It begins with devoting ourselves to prayer (Col. 4:2). We must pray particularly for those who preach the Word, that God would open doors for them to speak and give them boldness (vv. 3–4). We must give money to support the ministry of the gospel and the schools in which ministers are trained for their work. When we talk with those outside the church who are perishing without Christ, we must learn to season our speech with the salt of grace. We should sprinkle winsome words about our Lord into daily conversation (vv. 5–6).

Dependency in Leadership

The ministers and elders of Christ's church should learn from the doctrine of revelation that wisdom does not begin in them but comes from the mouth of the Lord (Prov. 2:6). Being wise in their own eyes is not fitting for those who teach others to submit to God's Word. What do we have that we did not receive? When did we become infallible? "Trust in the Lord with all thine heart; and lean not unto thine own understanding" (3:5).

In the Scriptures, God has given the man of God a holy manual that, if humbly studied and followed, will equip him completely for all the good works of ministry (2 Tim. 3:16–17). Every leader should have the attitude of Solomon, who said, "I am but a little child," and therefore plead for God to give him "an understanding heart" (1 Kings 3:7–9). It was said of John Cotton, "He had learned to study, because he had learned to pray."[6]

Priority in Education

The church has ministries that address social or physical needs. But it must remember that its core calling is the ministry of the Word. Like the apostles, pastors and teachers today must not "leave the word of God, and serve tables," but resolve to give themselves "continually to prayer, and to the ministry of the word" (Acts 6:2, 4).

6 John Norton, *Abel Being Dead, Yet Speaketh; or, the Life and Death of That Deservedly Famous Man of God, Mr John Cotton* (London: by Tho. Newcomb for Lodowick Lloyd, 1658), 27.

Paul says,

> If thou put the brethren in remembrance of these things, thou shalt be a good minister of Jesus Christ, nourished up in the words of faith and of good doctrine, whereunto thou hast attained. . . . Meditate upon these things; give thyself wholly to them; that thy profiting may appear to all. Take heed unto thyself, and unto the doctrine; continue in them: for in doing this thou shalt both save thyself, and them that hear thee. (1 Tim. 4:6, 15–16)

Whether we teach the catechism to children or systematic theology to graduate students, we must encourage people to bring together truth and godliness. Do not present yourself as a master of the Word, but as one who longs to be mastered by the Word.

Saturation in Worship

Preaching is a major means of grace, but the Bible is for more than preaching. Paul says, "Let the word of Christ dwell in you richly in all wisdom; teaching and admonishing one another in psalms and hymns and spiritual songs, singing with grace in your hearts to the Lord" (Col. 3:16). Few things bring the Word of God into the heart more effectively than singing it.

This command to fill worship with the Bible extends to the whole worship service. Mark Dever and Paul Alexander say, "Church leaders who have been committed to seeing the church reformed according to God's Word down through the ages have had a common method: read the Word, preach the Word, pray the Word, sing the Word, see the Word (in the ordinances)."[7] We should use all such God-appointed means to fill our worship services with the Word of God. Why water down the soup when God has made it so rich and flavorful for his children with the nutrients of his Word?

The Fruit of Applied Revelation in Society

Christ's church is called to be the light of the world and a city set on a hill (Matt. 5:14). Through the church's life and witness, Christ continues to perform his mission to be "a light of the Gentiles; to open blind eyes, to bring out the prisoners from the prison, and them that sit in darkness out of the prison house" (Isa. 42:6–7).

7 Mark Dever and Paul Alexander, *How to Build a Healthy Church: A Practical Guide for Deliberate Leadership* (Wheaton, IL: Crossway, 2021), 101.

God confirms the truth of his Word by the fruits it produces in our lives. Christ says, "Let your light so shine before men, that they may see your good works, and glorify your Father which is in heaven" (Matt. 5:16). Similarly, Paul says, "Be blameless and harmless, the sons of God, without rebuke, in the midst of a crooked and perverse nation, among whom ye shine as lights in the world" (Phil. 2:15).

By transforming his people through applied revelation, God makes them into agents of change in society. They become living images of his mercy and justice. This is God's plan to influence society—the witness of Christians made beautiful by their good works. Too often churches rely on programs and events to attract visitors. The best attraction the church has is radiant, obedient servants of God.

The Fruit of Applied Revelation in All Nations

When we consider the implications of God's Word in the lives of his people, we must remember that his purpose is worldwide. The Lord says, "Look unto me, and be ye saved, all the ends of the earth: for I am God, and there is none else" (Isa. 45:22). We must lift our eyes and see the nations as the inheritance of Christ (Ps. 2:8).

John Calvin said,

> We must daily desire that God gather churches unto himself from all parts of the earth; that he spread and increase them in number; that he adorn them with gifts; that he establish a lawful order among them; on the other hand, that he cast down all enemies of pure teaching and religion; that he scatter their counsels and crush their efforts.[8]

Such faith breathes forth mighty prayers that call down the kingdom of God among all nations.

The Fruit of Applied Revelation for the Glory of God

The Word of God reveals the glory of God for the worship of God: "Declare his glory among the heathen, his wonders among all people. For the LORD is great, and greatly to be praised: he is to be feared above all gods"

8 Calvin, *Institutes*, 3.20.42.

(Ps. 96:3–4). John Owen wrote, "The ultimate end of true theology is the celebration of the praise of God, and His glory and grace in the eternal salvation of sinners."[9]

We begin praising him now, even as we wait for the full display of glory, because the victory of Christ is sure. Calvin said, "Indeed, we are quite aware of what . . . lowly little men we are. . . . But our doctrine must tower unvanquished above all the glory and above all the might of the world, for it is not of us, but of the living God and his Christ whom the Father has appointed to 'rule from sea to sea, and from the rivers even to the ends of the earth' [Ps. 72:8]."[10]

Oh, what a gift God has given to us in his Word! We have the very words of God, the truth of God, the light of God, the glory of God, and the name of God. Through the Word, the Lord becomes our strength and our song. He is our salvation. With the Word bearing fruit in our lives, we are set free to fulfill the purpose for which God created us: to glorify God alone and enjoy him forever. *Soli Deo gloria!*

Suggested Songs to Sing to the Lord

- Psalm 119:129–36, "Thy wondrous testimonies, Lord," in *Psalter*, No. 337
- "The Spirit breathes upon the Word," in *THBap*, No. 258

Questions for Meditation or Discussion

1. How does God's Word describe the personal faith created by applied revelation?
2. Why are those to whom God applies his revelation faithful to study the Scriptures? What is the goal of such study?
3. What is the spiritual experience of those who have received God's Word?
4. When you examine yourself regarding your faith, study, and experience of the Word, what do you see? How do you desire to change?
5. Why should the Bible be at the center of family life? How are you practicing this principle?

9 John Owen, *Biblical Theology: The History of Theology from Adam to Christ*, trans. Stephen P. Westcott (Orlando, FL: Soli Deo Gloria, 1994), 6.4 (619).

10 Calvin, *Institutes*, "Prefatory Address to King Francis I of France," sec. 2.

6. After reading the section titled "The Fruit of Applied Revelation in the Church," what are some specific requests you could start praying for your church? Make a list and use it in your prayers.
7. How does the application of revelation cause the church to influence the world?
8. Why must we not rest satisfied until God's Word impacts every nation and people on earth?
9. How does applied revelation lead us to live to the glory of God alone (*soli Deo gloria*)?
10. Given your gifts, relationships, and situation, what does it mean for you to be an evangelistic and missionary-minded Christian?

PART 2

THE DOCTRINE OF GOD

Section 2A

Who God Is

9

Introduction to the Doctrine of God

Chapter Summary and Key Terms

Knowing God gives strength to his people. It is possible to know God because he has chosen to make himself known to us. Since the whole world is a revelation of God, atheism is foolish. Seeking to know God should be our highest priority, for it is our greatest privilege. However, knowing God is not just about knowledge in the head; it involves humility and love in the heart, and obedience and righteousness in a person's life. God reveals his *divine nature*—who he is in his being or essence that makes him different from all other beings. The *attributes of God* are the characteristics that belong to him by his divine nature, such as his infinite power. Something is an attribute of God if we can use it to complete the sentence "By nature, God is," such as, "By nature, God is love." All our knowledge of God is by way of analogy (*analogical language*) because he is infinite, and we are his image bearers.

KNOWING GOD CHANGES A PERSON. We see this in the life of Daniel, who suffered horribly in his youth. The Babylonians conquered the kingdom of Judah and carried Daniel away as a captive to a foreign land. He could easily have grown bitter or conformed to Babylon's brutal, pagan ways to advance his career. Instead, he served the one true God. The secret of Daniel's godly conduct is that he knew his God and gave him all the glory (Dan. 2:20–21). Wilhelmus à Brakel said, "The foundation of religion is the character of God."[1]

1 Brakel, *CRS*, 1:3.

The True Knowledge of God

The Power of Knowing the True God

Our purpose in studying the doctrine of God is to live to God through Christ. Knowing God gives us the strength to do that. Daniel foresaw a time of great trials and temptations for God's people, but he said, "The people that do know their God shall be strong, and do exploits" (Dan. 11:32).

The knowledge of God has strengthened his people through the ages. It can strengthen us today if, by grace, we receive it into our hearts. It is possible to have much knowledge of theology in our heads with no godliness at all in our hearts (James 2:19). However, when someone knows God truly, this knowledge unites him to God through Jesus Christ by faith. David said, "They that know thy name will put their trust in thee: for thou, LORD, hast not forsaken them that seek thee" (Ps. 9:10).

The Possibility of Knowing the True God

True worship must be a thoughtful response to something real. Skeptics argue that we cannot know God. If theology were man's quest to discover God, we could never know anything about God for certain. But Christian theology arises from God's pursuit of man.

It is possible for us to know God because he chooses to be known: "Ye are my witnesses, saith the LORD, and my servant whom I have chosen: that ye may know and believe me, and understand that I am he: before me there was no God formed, neither shall there be after me" (Isa. 43:10).

The Perversity of Rejecting the True God

God has shown by the world all around us that he exists (Rom. 1:20; 2:14–15). Greg Nichols writes, "No man needs to have God's existence proved to him. He already knows it. Anyone who denies this is a liar."[2]

God's revelation of himself exposes the foolishness of atheism: "The fool hath said in his heart, There is no God. They are corrupt, they have done abominable works, there is none that doeth good" (Ps. 14:1). The fear of God in the heart is the fountain of righteousness. The denial of God in the heart is the fountain of sin. Stephen Charnock said, "All sin is founded in

2 Greg Nichols, *Lectures in Systematic Theology*, ed. Rob Ventura, 4 vols. to date (Seattle: CreateSpace Independent Publishing Platform, 2017–2024), 1:97.

a secret atheism." Every sin says, "I would be a lord to myself, and would not have a God superior to me."[3]

The Priority of Knowing the True God

The denial of God brings forth all kinds of poisonous fruit, but knowing God and making him known is the heartbeat of real human life. Augustine said, "Thou hast formed us for Thyself, and our hearts are restless till they find rest in Thee."[4]

Knowing God is

- the highest human privilege: "Let him that glorieth glory in this, that he understandeth and knoweth me, that I am the Lord" (Jer. 9:24).
- the heart of the covenant: "They shall all know me, from the least of them unto the greatest of them" (Jer. 31:34).
- the essence of eternal life: "This is life eternal, that they might know thee the only true God, and Jesus Christ, whom thou hast sent" (John 17:3).
- the engine of holiness: God "hath given unto us all things that pertain unto life and godliness, through the knowledge of him" (2 Pet. 1:3).

Nothing is more central to human life than the knowledge of God through Christ. Do you regard knowing God as your greatest privilege? Do you eagerly desire to know him better? That desire is a mark of saving grace.

The Piety of Seeking to Know the True God

How can we "press on to know the Lord" (Hos. 6:3 ESV)? We seek to know him by having humble hearts, open ears to his Word, and repentance for our sins against him. To know him rightly is to fear him (Prov. 9:10), and the fear of God moves us to turn away from sin (Job 28:28). To fear him rightly we must also love him (Deut. 10:12). This is true *piety*.

John Calvin said, "Indeed, we shall not say that, properly speaking, God is known where there is no religion or piety. . . . I call 'piety' that reverence

3 Charnock, *The Existence and Attributes of God*, in *WSChar*, 1:186.

4 Augustine, *Confessions*, 1.1.1, in *NPNF*[1], 1:45.

joined with love of God which the knowledge of his benefits induces."[5] Such piety requires faith in Christ. We are far from God until we are reconciled to him by the blood of Christ (Eph. 2:13).

Growing in the knowledge of God requires righteous action. Christ said, "He that hath my commandments, and keepeth them, he it is that loveth me: and he that loveth me shall be loved of my Father, and I will love him, and will manifest myself to him" (John 14:21).

We learn to know God better in the school of suffering. The psalmist confessed, "Before I was afflicted I went astray: but now have I kept thy word. Thou art good, and doest good; teach me thy statutes" (Ps. 119:67–68).

Knowing God in His Nature and Attributes

From the earliest days of the church, the saints have confessed their faith in God according to the attributes of his divine nature. The people of Israel said that God is "righteous," "ready to pardon, gracious and merciful, slow to anger, and of great kindness," "great," and "mighty" (Neh. 9:8, 17, 32). God's *attributes* are qualities or characteristics that permanently belong to him. They are his virtues and perfections. God's attributes make him God.

The Bible's Testimony to God's Unique Nature

God's nature puts him above all creation. It also casts down the proud claims of idols. Paul writes, "When ye knew not God, ye did service unto them which *by nature* are no gods" (Gal. 4:8). Therefore, "we ought not to think that the Godhead ["divine being," ESV] is like unto gold, or silver, or stone, graven by art and man's device" (Acts 17:29). Paul also describes the "divine nature" as God's "eternal power" and "the glory of the immortal God" (Rom. 1:20, 23 ESV). The divine nature is known through the Lord Jesus, in whom dwells the fullness of the "Godhead" (KJV) or "deity" (Col. 2:9 ESV).

To be godly people, we must know the divine nature. John Owen said, "Our whole duty in general respects the nature of God. It is our giving glory to him because he is God, and as he is God, glorifying him as God (Ex. 20:2; Isa. 42:8; Deut. 28:58; Rom. 1:21)."[6]

5 Calvin, *Institutes*, 1.2.1.

6 Owen, *WJO-H*, 4:365.

Some Important Scripture Texts on God's Attributes

The Lord taught his people to know him through his attributes. Though all Scripture reveals God, some passages of Scripture especially present his attributes.

God says of himself, "The Lord, the Lord God, merciful and gracious, longsuffering, and abundant in goodness and truth, keeping mercy for thousands, forgiving iniquity and transgression and sin, and that will by no means clear the guilty; visiting the iniquity of the fathers upon the children, and upon the children's children, unto the third and to the fourth generation" (Ex. 34:6–7). We find these words repeated in various forms throughout the Scriptures.[7] This passage presents a two-sided description of God. He declares himself first "the Lord" (twice) and "God," which are names of his lordship. Second, he lists aspects of his love and justice, which we call his moral perfections.

Psalm 145 reveals God's majesty and his mercy. Consider the attributes praised:

- God's greatness, might, and majesty (vv. 3–6)
- God's goodness, righteousness, grace, compassion, and mercy (vv. 7–9)
- God's glory, power, majesty, and eternity (vv. 11–13)
- God's kindness, righteousness, mercy, and holiness (vv. 14–21)

In Jeremiah 9:24, God commends the supreme value of knowing "that I am the Lord which exercise lovingkindness, judgment, and righteousness, in the earth: for in these things I delight." Here again we find, first, a declaration that God is the Lord. Second, there is a list of moral perfections, and also God's affection ("delight"). The next chapter of this prophecy lifts up God's lordship. He is the great, mighty, true, living, everlasting, wrathful, and wise Creator, and cannot be compared to man's idols (10:6, 10, 12).

In the New Testament, Paul writes of Christ's saving "mercy," "grace," and "longsuffering" (1 Tim. 1:12–16). He then glorifies God's supremacy: "Now

7 Num. 14:18; 2 Chron. 30:9, Neh. 9:17, 31; Pss. 86:15; 103:8; 111:4; 116:5; 145:8; Joel 2:13; Jonah 4:2; Nah. 1:3.

unto the King eternal, immortal, invisible, the only wise God, be honour and glory for ever and ever. Amen" (v. 17). Later, Paul praises "the blessed and only Potentate, the King of kings, and Lord of lords; who only hath immortality, dwelling in the light which no man can approach unto; whom no man hath seen, nor can see: to whom be honour and power everlasting. Amen" (6:15–16).

Therefore, we find that biblical religion is a faith grounded in the attributes of God. These attributes sharply distinguish God from his creatures. They rule out idolatry and condemn the false worship of this world. The knowledge of his attributes gives content to our worship so that we adore the true God. The better we know his attributes, the more they give color and clarity to our praises. The attributes sparkle brilliantly in God's saving work in Christ. The study of God's attributes is the joy of evangelical theology. It leads to the greatest of gifts: the knowledge of the Lord.

A Biblical Approach to Studying God's Attributes

If we want to think clearly about God's attributes, we need to go beyond what we can see about him in his creation and study what he reveals about himself in his Word.

God reveals his attributes through biblical words and doctrines. God has given us specific words to describe him, such as *power*, *wisdom*, and *goodness*. We may also describe him with terms implied by biblical teaching, such as *eternity* and *simplicity*. God requires us to ponder what he says about himself and recognize its logical implications (Matt. 22:29–32).

Though God has many attributes, there is only one divine nature. Moses wrote, "Hear, O Israel: the Lord our God is one Lord" (Deut. 6:4). Like the sparkling facets of one diamond and the spectrum of colors emitted by the one sun, the attributes are beams of God's radiant perfection. They are not additions to his being, and they cannot be subtracted from him. The attributes are God, and God is his attributes.

The attributes of God belong to each person of the Trinity. The Father, the Son, and the Holy Spirit share one "name," or one glorious nature (Matt. 28:19). They are all present everywhere (Ps. 139:7; Matt. 28:20) and are all without beginning (Gen. 1:2; John 8:58). Our proof of the Trinity begins with our study of God's attributes. We will see that each person of the Godhead fully shares in the one divine nature with all its attributes.

God also reveals his attributes in his acts. From the exodus of Israel to the crucifixion and resurrection of Christ, God's great works of redemption display his attributes. He is the Lord who keeps his covenant with his people.

God teaches us his attributes for our faith, adoration, and imitation. Abraham trusted in God's promise because he was "fully persuaded that, what he had promised, he was able also to perform" (Rom. 4:21). Sarah conceived Isaac "through faith," for "she judged him faithful who had promised" (Heb. 11:11). Knowing God's attributes moves his children to exclaim, "Who is a God like unto thee, that pardoneth iniquity, and passeth by the transgression of the remnant of his heritage? He retaineth not his anger for ever, because he delighteth in mercy" (Mic. 7:18). One of the greatest honors true believers give to God is that they live as "imitators" of him (Eph. 5:1 ESV).

Analogy in Our Knowledge of God

We can never fully comprehend God. He is infinite and incomprehensible (chap. 12). But this does not mean that we cannot know him truly, for God's Word is true. Herman Bavinck said, "As God reveals himself, so he is."[8]

We must remember that when we describe God using human words (the only words we have), we speak of him by way of analogy, as Thomas Aquinas explained.[9] Some analogies about God in the Bible are fairly obvious, as when we read about God's "hand." This is figurative language describing God as if he had a human body with its limitations and passions.[10] But even when we read something more literal, such as "Be merciful, even as your Father is merciful" (Luke 6:36 ESV), there is an analogy. God's mercy is infinite, eternal, unchangeable, and incomprehensible. But his mercy is similar to ours in his loving choice to show kindness to the hurting and vulnerable, so we can know his mercy and imitate it (Eph. 4:32). This is possible because we were created in God's image and likeness (Gen. 1:26).

8 Bavinck, *RD*, 2:111.

9 Thomas Aquinas, *Summa Theologica*, trans. Fathers of the English Dominican Province (London: R. & T. Washbourne, 1914), Part 1, Q. 13, Art. 5. We cannot talk about God in *univocal language* (as if "love" means the same for him as it does when applied to human love). But we are not trapped in *equivocal language* ("love" means something totally different for God, so we know nothing about his love). Instead, we speak of him in *analogical language* (his "love" is similar in some ways to human love but must be understood in a way fitting for God).

10 Speaking about God as if he had a human form is called *anthropomorphism*. Speaking about him as if he had a human soul with human passions is called *anthropopathism*.

Our knowledge of God can be compared to a little girl's first visit to the ocean. As the waves splash over her feet, she says, "Wet!" She dips her hand in the water, puts it to her mouth, and says, "Salty!" Then she lifts her eyes to take in the vast sea, and she whispers, "Big!" This child has only the smallest understanding of the ocean's properties. But her knowledge is true: the ocean is wet, salty, and big. Such is our knowledge of God's attributes—it is a true yet childlike knowledge. Brakel said, "We can only perceive the uttermost fringes of His Being by reflecting upon the divine attributes."[11] This should fill us with awe and humility.

Let us therefore take up the study of God's attributes with this prayer: "May I know thee more clearly, love thee more dearly, and follow thee more nearly, day by day."[12]

Suggested Songs to Sing to the Lord

- Psalm 103, "O come, my soul," in *Psalter*, No. 283; *THBap*, No. 10
- Psalm 115, "Not unto us, O Lord of heav'n," in *Psalter*, No. 308; *THBap*, No. 20

Questions for Meditation or Discussion

1. What is the power of knowing God?
2. Why is it possible to know God?
3. Why is atheism foolish, even if it is held by very intelligent people?
4. Why should we make knowing God our highest priority?
5. How is piety—or godly fear and love—important for knowing God?
6. What is an attribute of God? What are some examples of his attributes?
7. How does the Bible tell us that God has a unique nature?
8. What are some passages of Scripture that list God's attributes?
9. Why can we talk about God only by way of analogy? Why should that humble us?
10. What is something about studying God's attributes that you are looking forward to? Pray that God would make this study helpful to your spiritual life.

11 Brakel, *CRS*, 1:88.

12 Ascribed to Richard of Chichester, in *The Westminster Collection of Christian Prayers*, comp. Dorothy M. Stewart (Louisville: Westminster John Knox, 2002), 41 (21.15).

10

The Holy "I Am," the Only God

Chapter Summary and Key Terms

One way that God has revealed himself is by his name, *YHWH*, often pronounced as Yahweh or Jehovah, and translated as "the Lord." This name means "I Am." It shows us God's independence from everything outside of himself ("I Am That I Am") and his faithfulness ("I am with you"). The Bible also reveals the *holiness of God*. Holiness is the incomparable glory of the divine nature in his majesty, moral excellence, and mercy to the humble. The Holy Scriptures teach *monotheism*, the belief that there is only one true God—he alone is holy. False beliefs about God include *atheism* (there is no God), *polytheism* (there are many gods), *pantheism* (all is God, and all is one), *panentheism* (God is the spirit or life force of all things), and *finite theism* (there is a God, but he is limited in power and knowledge). We must turn away from these false beliefs about God and fear the holy Lord with all our hearts.

WHO IS GOD? We can start by considering his name. Although the Bible uses many names and titles for God, he says that *YHWH* is "my name" (Ex. 6:3; Isa. 42:8). This is sometimes pronounced Yahweh or Jehovah. It is often translated as "the Lord" (note the capital letters). This is God's special name, which he shares with no other (Ps. 83:18).

We also can consider God's attributes, which we discussed briefly in the previous chapter. However, only one attribute of God is declared three times in one verse: "Holy, holy, holy" (Isa. 6:3). Surely holiness is something very important for us to understand about God.

In this chapter, we will begin our study of the doctrine of God by looking at the meaning of his special name and his attribute of holiness. Then we will use what we learn to show how many so-called gods that people worship are not the true God at all.

The Name of "the Lord"

God appeared to Moses in a burning bush and sent him to bring Israel out of Egypt. Moses asked, "Behold, when I come unto the children of Israel, and shall say unto them, The God of your fathers hath sent me unto you; and they shall say to me, What is his name? What shall I say unto them?" (Ex. 3:13). God replied, "I Am That I Am: and he said, Thus shalt thou say unto the children of Israel, I Am hath sent me unto you" (v. 14). The word translated as "I Am" is a form of God's name "the Lord" (*YHWH*). "I Am" explains what his name means.

God's Name of Sovereign Independence

The name "I Am" reveals that God *is* simply because he is God. When a human being says, "I am," he adds other words, such as "the son of John Smith." However, when God says, "I Am," he is asserting that, although he has relationships, he is not defined by any relationship outside of his own being. God exists of himself.[1] Stephen Charnock explained that God is saying, "I am, that is, I receive from no other what I am in myself. He depends upon no other in his essence, knowledge, purposes, and therefore [another] hath no changing power over him."[2]

The longer form, "I Am That I Am" or "I am who I am" (ESV), also tells us that God is sovereign and independent. The expression could also be translated as "I will be who I will be." In Hebrew, it is quite similar to the Lord's words "I will . . . be gracious to whom I will be gracious, and will shew mercy on whom I will shew mercy" (Ex. 33:19). That is a statement of God's absolute sovereignty to give grace and mercy to whomever he pleases (Rom. 9:15–18). Therefore, "I Am That I Am" indicates that God is sovereign and free from all limitations outside of himself. When God said this to Moses, he was showing his servant his sovereignty. God

1 This is called his *aseity*, an attribute we will explore in chapter 12.

2 Charnock, *The Existence and Attributes of God*, in *WSChar*, 1:392.

has the power to work miracles (Ex. 3:20; 4:1–9) and rules over all human ability or disability (4:11).

God's Name of Covenant Faithfulness

God's name "I Am" also tells us that he is near to his people to keep the promises of his covenant. The same verb in the same form is translated in the phrases "I will be with thee" (Ex. 3:12) and "I will be with thy mouth" (4:12, 15). These promises to Moses echo God's promises to be with Abraham's offspring to give them salvation and an inheritance (Gen. 26:3; 31:3). In the same passage where God says, "I Am," he also says that he is "the Lord God of your fathers, the God of Abraham, the God of Isaac, and the God of Jacob" (Ex. 3:14–15). We can depend on God to be present with his people throughout history. He will do what he says he will do.

God is telling Moses that he has compassion for his suffering people and will save them (Ex. 2:24–25; 3:7–10, 16–17). God's eternal, sovereign independence does not hold him back from personal relationships, for "thus saith the Lord, Israel is my son, even my firstborn" (4:22). Therefore, "the Lord" is a name of redeeming love and covenant faithfulness.

God's Name and Jesus Christ

Christ says that he is the Lord who appeared to Moses. Jesus says, "Before Abraham was, *I am*" (John 8:58). He does not say, "I was," but "I am." Christ claims to be the joy of Abraham (v. 56), the eternal Lord who existed long before his human birth in Bethlehem (cf. Mic. 5:2). Bruce Milne comments, "He is the eternal Christ sharing the everlasting life of the Father, the changeless Lord who towers over history, Master of time, Ruler of the ages, undiminished by the passing of the centuries."[3]

Christ uses these same words to tell us that he is everything we need. The Lord Jesus declares, "*I am* the bread of life" (John 6:35), "*I am* the light of the world" (8:12), "*I am* the door" (10:7, 9), "*I am* the good shepherd" (10:11, 14), "*I am* the resurrection, and the life" (11:25), "*I am* the way, the truth, and the life: no man cometh unto the Father, but by me"

3 Bruce Milne, *The Message of John: Here Is Your King!*, The Bible Speaks Today (Downers Grove, IL: InterVarsity Press, 1993), 136.

(14:6), and, "*I am* the vine, ye are the branches . . . without me ye can do nothing" (15:5).

Christ is God with us. He is the sovereign and eternal God come in human flesh to be our spiritual food, wisdom, strength, and fruitfulness. And the Holy Spirit whom Christ sends is also "I AM." Words spoken by "the LORD" in the Old Testament (Jer. 31:33–34) are said in the New Testament to be spoken by the Holy Spirit (Heb. 10:15–17).

Therefore, let us turn away from all other gods and trust only in the Trinity, who is "I AM. He is the sovereign, independent, faithful, loving God, who is with his people to keep his covenant.

The Holiness of God

When Moses approached the burning bush, the Lord commanded him to come no closer, "for the place whereon thou standest is holy ground" (Ex. 3:5). The great "I AM" is holy. John Howe said that holiness "is an attribute of attributes," so that we many think of God's "holy power, holy truth, [and] holy love," for it is the "glory of his other perfections."[4] To be "holy" is to be sacred, set apart from all that is unclean, and set above all that is ordinary (Lev. 10:10; 11:44).

God's Majestic Holiness

God's holiness is first his glory and majesty as God. Moses says, "Who is like unto thee, O LORD, among the gods? Who is like thee, glorious in holiness, fearful in praises, doing wonders?" (Ex. 15:11). Hannah says, "There is none holy as the LORD: for there is none beside thee: neither is there any rock like our God" (1 Sam. 2:2). God's holiness "is used as a synonym for his deity," R.C. Sproul writes. "The word *holy* calls attention to all that God is."[5]

Isaiah had a vision of "the Lord sitting upon a throne, high and lifted up, and his train filled the temple" (Isa. 6:1). Heavenly spirits fly above the divine throne, calling out, "Holy, holy, holy, is the LORD of hosts: the whole earth is full of his glory" (v. 3). The declaration of this attribute three times shows that God is holy in a supreme and absolute sense. He is "the Lord"

4 John Howe, *The Blessedness of the Righteous*, in *The Works of the Rev. John Howe* (London: William Tegg and Co., 1848), 2:59.

5 R. C. Sproul, *The Holiness of God* (Wheaton, IL: Tyndale House, 1985), 57.

and "the King" over all heaven and earth (vv. 1–5). God's holiness "signifies everything about God that sets Him apart from us and makes Him an object of awe, adoration, and dread to us."[6]

God's Moral Holiness

The Lord's holiness is also his moral excellence and purity. He is the "Holy One," who is "of purer eyes than to behold evil." He cannot "look on iniquity" with indifference, much less approval (Hab. 1:12–13). Isaiah 5:15–16 says, "The eyes of the lofty shall be humbled: but the Lord of hosts shall be exalted in judgment, and God that is holy shall be sanctified in righteousness." The Lord is "holy and true," and so will certainly "judge and avenge" every sin committed against him and his people (Rev. 6:10). The moral excellence of God's holiness blazes forth in his law, which is "holy, and just, and good" (Rom. 7:12).

Since God is holy, we must be holy (1 Pet. 1:16). J. C. Ryle describes "true practical holiness" as follows: "Holiness is the habit of being of one mind with God . . . hating what He hates—loving what He loves—and measuring everything in this world by the standard of His Word." A holy person will "endeavour to shun every known sin, and to keep every known commandment." He will "strive to be like our Lord Jesus Christ."[7]

God's Merciful Holiness

God's holiness also includes his grace: "For thus saith the high and lofty One that inhabiteth eternity, whose name is Holy; I dwell in the high and holy place, with him also that is of a contrite and humble spirit, to revive the spirit of the humble, and to revive the heart of the contrite ones" (Isa. 57:15). This is the wonder of holiness—it puts God above all creation but also brings him near to tenderly care for those broken over their sins.

Again, this attribute not only sets God against sin but also draws him near to dwell with sinners in "the holy place" of the tabernacle (Ex. 25:8; 26:33–34). This was possible by the sacrifices of the priests. The high priest wore a golden plate on his forehead that bore the words "Holiness To The Lord" (28:36). Once a year, the high priest brought the blood of sacrifices

6 *The Reformation Study Bible*, ed. R. C. Sproul (Orlando, FL: Ligonier Ministries, 2005), 168.

7 J. C. Ryle, *Holiness: Its Nature, Hindrances, Difficulties, and Roots* (Cambridge: James Clarke and Co., 1956), 34–38.

into the Most Holy Place (Lev. 16:16). The ancient priestly work of sacrifice typified the person and work of our great High Priest, Jesus Christ. He offered himself once for all as a sacrifice for sins.

The holiness of God is also seen in the work of the Holy Spirit to make sinners holy. Thus, the gospel is a message about the holiness of the Trinity. God is holy in judging sinners, holy in redeeming sinners, and holy in sanctifying sinners. How sweet, then, is the holiness of God when we meet it through faith in Christ! Christians can have "boldness to enter into the holiest by the blood of Jesus" (Heb. 10:19).

False Gods That Are Not the Holy Lord

The Bible teaches *monotheism*, the doctrine that there is only one true God:[8] "The Lord he is God; there is none else beside him" (Deut. 4:35). Knowing that God is the Lord and that he is holy teaches us enough to tell the difference between the true God and most false gods. We can see this difference in several false systems of belief.

Atheism is the belief that there is no god, no Lord, no Holy One. However, man is inevitably a worshiper. Atheists, like all others, give their adoration to something as god. Secular humanism tries to elevate man to the place of a god. Marxism views the socialist government as a godlike entity that promises to bring mankind into a world of justice and peace.

Polytheism is the belief that there are many gods. According to polytheism, there is not one Lord who is different from all others. The gods of polytheism are not holy, especially in their moral lives. In animism, the world is full of spirits. There are the spirits of trees, mountains, animals, dead ancestors, and so on. These spirits must be appeased through rituals and sacrifices. They may be controlled by sorcery and divination. *Hinduism*, Shinto, and some kinds of *Buddhism* are also examples of polytheism.

Pantheism is the belief that everything is God. Therefore, pantheists believe that there is no Creator. Although Hinduism has many gods, its deeper teaching is pantheism. Hinduism teaches that there is one supreme and impersonal reality. It is beyond good and evil in its infinite, universal, absolute oneness. Another form of pantheism appears in Daoism (or Taoism), a religion teaching that all things are a combination of *yin* ("dark")

8 We will return to the doctrine of monotheism under the doctrine of the Trinity (chaps. 19–20).

and *yang* ("light"). The New Age movement is a mixture of these kinds of beliefs, with the main idea that "you are God." Ecospirituality, or "green religion," is the belief that nature is sacred and spiritual.

Panentheism is the belief that God is in everything. He is regarded as the soul of the universe—its spirit or life force. Again, this assumes there is no Creator who is holy. Some kinds of Buddhism call people to practice the worship of many gods but teach panentheism. The Buddha is said to live in everything. A popular example of panentheism is belief in "the force" in the *Star Wars* movies.[9]

Finite theism is the belief in a god limited by the world he created and other factors outside of his control. He is not the sovereign "I Am." It is popular today for people to believe in a god who is always there for us in emotional support. But such a god rarely if ever acts directly in the world. This view is sometimes called "moralistic therapeutic deism." According to open theism, God is limited by his love—he is not the absolute King and cannot know the future for certain. God is said to take risks that may not succeed and sometimes regrets decisions he makes.

Each of these false views of God rejects the Lord who is absolutely sovereign over the world that he created and that is distinct from him. These gods are not holy. They are impersonal, immoral, or part of the world. Against all such false gods, the true God declares, "Thus says the Lord, who created the heavens . . . who formed the earth and made it . . . 'I am the Lord, and there is no other. . . . Turn to me and be saved, all the ends of the earth! For I am God, and there is no other' " (Isa. 45:18, 22 ESV).

Do not think that you are above taking a false god into your heart. Every time we sin, we commit "practical atheism." If our hearts are divided in loyalty, we are guilty of polytheism. Whenever we give our adoration to created things, we live like pantheists. Trusting in our own thoughts as if they were God's word is no better than panentheism. Failing to trust in God's plan and providence is finite theism.

Be watchful against idols. And consider this: your actions show more about what you believe about God than your words. Examine yourself for false views of God. Cling always to the God of the Bible.

9 A more philosophical form of panentheism is *process theology*, which teaches that God is the collective spirit of all living things, and each of us is like a cell in God's brain.

Suggested Songs to Sing to the Lord

- Psalm 135, "Exalt the Lord, His praise proclaim," in *Psalter*, No. 375; *THBap*, No. 12
- "Holy, Holy, Holy, Lord God Almighty!" in *THBap*, No. 87

Questions for Meditation or Discussion

1. What is the name of God that he revealed to Moses in Exodus 3?
2. How does God's name reveal his sovereign independence?
3. How does God's name reveal his covenant faithfulness?
4. How does the Bible show us that Christ is the God of Exodus 3?
5. What does it mean for God to be holy?
6. How does Isaiah 6 show the majesty of God's holiness?
7. What Scripture passages teach us about the moral excellence and mercy of God's holiness?
8. What is the definition of each of the following: (1) atheism, (2) polytheism, (3) pantheism, (4) panentheism, and (5) finite theism?
9. Of these false views of God, which has had the greatest influence on you? How?
10. Someone says, "The only god that I worship is Mother Nature." How do you respond?

11

God's Spirituality and Simplicity

Chapter Summary and Key Terms

The Bible says, "God is spirit." This teaches the *spirituality of God*. He is a spirit, somewhat like angels and human spirits, but infinite and eternal. He has no body and is therefore invisible, but is a living, intelligent, personal being. Since God is spirit, we must worship him in spirit and truth, not just with outward actions. The Scriptures also say, "God is love." These biblical statements teach the *simplicity of God*. The divine attribute of simplicity means that God is not composed of parts but is one in nature. It also means that his attributes are his very essence—he is love, righteousness, wisdom, power, life, and so on. God's simplicity shows us that we must serve him with the simplicity of a sincere and wholehearted devotion to keeping his commandments.

CHRIST SAYS, "God is a Spirit: and they that worship him must worship him in spirit and in truth" (John 4:24). Jesus's words may also be translated as "God is spirit" (ESV).

God is not the only one who may be described as "spirit." Angels are spirits (Heb. 1:7, 14). Human beings consist of "flesh and spirit" (2 Cor. 7:1). However, when we say that God is "a Spirit," we should not think that he is the same as angels or men, though he is somewhat like them in certain ways. God is, in the words of the Westminster Confession of Faith, "a most pure spirit" or a supremely spiritual spirit.[1]

1 The Westminster Confession of Faith (2.1), in *RC*, 4:236. Cf. the Second London Baptist Confession (2.1), in *RC*, 4:535.

In this chapter, we will consider what it means that God is spirit. We will also consider a closely related doctrine, God's simplicity.

The Spirituality of God

God Has No Body

Christ's statement "God is a Spirit" teaches us that God has no physical body. Christ says, "A spirit hath not flesh and bones" (Luke 24:39). Isaiah 31:3 reads, "Now the Egyptians are men, and not God; and their horses flesh, and not spirit." As Jesus explains, since God is spirit, his worship does not require us to be in a special physical place, such as a temple (John 4:20–24).

Physical bodies exist in particular places and times. God created all places and physical matter, and started time itself (Gen. 1:1). Moreover, he is present everywhere: "Do not I fill heaven and earth? saith the LORD" (Jer. 23:24). Bodies have height, length, and width. God's being is infinite, for "the heaven and heaven of heavens cannot contain him" (2 Chron. 2:6).

Some people object that God must have a body because he appeared to people as a man (Gen. 18:1–2) or a glorified man (Ex. 24:10). But God's visible appearances do not teach that he has a body, just as the visible appearances of angels do not prove that they have physical bodies. Like God, they are spirits (Ps. 104:4; Heb. 1:7). God appeared in a variety of forms in the Old Testament, including a cloud and a consuming fire (Deut. 4:11–19), to show he has no body.

Others may object that the Bible often speaks of God's body parts—his hand, arm, eye, foot, and so on. But these are metaphors for his power, knowledge, and other attributes or actions.[2] Shall we think that God has wings and feathers because the Bible uses that metaphor for his care (Ps. 91:4)? Isaiah compared God to both a warrior in battle and a woman in labor pains (Isa. 42:13–14; 59:16–18). None of this language contradicts the fact that God is spirit; his divine nature has no physical material or shape.

God Is Invisible

Christ's words "God is a Spirit" (John 4:24) also teach that we cannot see God with our eyes. The worship of God is not about things we see. Worship is our response to truths we read in the Scriptures and receive by faith. As

2 A metaphor describing God as if he has a human body is called an *anthropomorphism*.

Jesus says, people "worship the Father in spirit and in truth" (John 4:23). When God the Son became "flesh" that people could see, that was because he became a man (1:14). However, "no man hath seen God at any time" (v. 18).

God's invisibility means that he has no size, shape, or color that our eyes can behold. His attributes are made known through the things that he has made, but his "eternal power and Godhead" are themselves "invisible" (Rom. 1:20). We perceive God in this age in the same way most saints have through history. It is "by faith" that we see "him who is invisible" (Heb. 11:27).

God's invisibility shows how different he is from us and our world. It is one reason why we worship him. Paul says, "Now unto the King eternal, immortal, invisible, the only wise God, be honour and glory for ever and ever. Amen" (1 Tim. 1:17). God's invisibility also wraps his ways in mystery. Job says, "Lo, he goeth by me, and I see him not: he passeth on also, but I perceive him not" (Job 9:11).

God Is Intelligent and Personal

When Christ says, "God is a Spirit," he also shows that God is a personal, conscious being. The word translated as "spirit" commonly refers to a person's inner life, what he thinks, loves, and chooses (Luke 1:46–47). Charles Hodge said, "If God be a spirit, it follows of necessity that He is a person—a self-conscious, intelligent, voluntary agent."[3]

God's very name means "I Am" (Ex. 3:14), not "It Is." For anyone to say "I am" is to show that he is a person who is aware of his existence. God says, "Look unto me, and be ye saved, all the ends of the earth: for I am God, and there is none else" (Isa. 45:22).

God is a personal, intelligent, and affectionate spirit. Therefore, we worship him rightly only when we do so in a personal, thinking, and feeling manner through Christ (John 4:24).

God Is Alive

To say that God is spirit is to say that he is life—mighty, immortal life. The word translated as "spirit" sometimes means "wind," which suggests energy

3 Charles Hodge, *Systematic Theology*, 3 vols. (1871–1873; repr., Peabody, MA: Hendrickson, 1999), 1:379.

and motion (John 3:8). It can also mean "breath," indicating life (6:63). When Christ says, "God is a Spirit," he has just spoken to the woman at the well about "living water" that satisfies every thirst and becomes in a person "a well of water springing up into everlasting life" (4:10, 14). Therefore, Christ's words teach us that God is a living, powerful being who gives life to others.

The Lord is "the living God" who created the world (Jer. 10:10–12; Acts 14:11–17). He is very different from the dead idols of men, which cannot speak or do anything. There is no "breath [or spirit] in their mouths" (Ps. 135:15–18).

From the truth that God is spirit we may learn that he is totally active—he is pure act. A "spirit" is, by definition, living and dynamic. There is no such thing as motionless wind or breath.

Each person in the Trinity is life. Jesus says, "The Father hath life in himself" (John 5:26). Christ is "the life" (John 14:6). And Paul says, "The Spirit is life" (Rom. 8:10).

Practical Applications of God's Spirituality

The doctrine of God's spirituality has several rich applications.

First, *God's spirituality prohibits idol worship.* Any teaching that God has physical matter or form is a lie. The holy "I Am" is infinitely more glorious than earth or flesh.

Second, *God's spirituality demands simplicity in his worship.* God made the old covenant ceremonies obsolete by the finished work of Christ (Heb. 8:13; 9:1–14). He replaced them with worship in spirit and truth, the new covenant form of worship that is remarkably simple (see chap. 80). We no longer need holy places such as temples or sacred mountains (John 4:20–24). We have Christ.

Third, *God's spirituality calls for worship marked by sincerity and understanding.* Since "God is a Spirit," true worshipers "must worship him in spirit and in truth" (John 4:24). God's spirituality implies that he is thinking and personal. He cannot be pleased with mindless or hypocritical worship.

Fourth, *God's spirituality implies that true worshipers bear holy fruit.* Since God is spirit, he is life itself. To know the living God is to have a fountain of eternal life springing up in one's soul (John 4:14; 7:37; 17:3). Eternal life must produce practical results in our behavior. Spiritual life begins in the mindset and affections of our spirits, for God is spirit.

The Simplicity of God

The Bible's Doctrine of Simplicity

God's simplicity means that he has no parts. His attributes are not what God has so much as who he is. Christ does not say that God *has* a spirit but that "God *is* a Spirit" (John 4:24). John says, "God *is* light" (1 John 1:5). Light refers to God's knowledge and moral purity as opposed to the darkness of lies and sin (vv. 6–10). John also says, "God *is* love" (4:8, 16).

The Scriptures do not say that God is partly spirit, partly light, and partly love. Rather, the whole of God is spirit. All of God is light. Everything in God is love. Each of his attributes describes the other attributes, so that his power is "eternal power" (Rom. 1:20), and in his love he "loveth righteousness" (Ps. 33:5).

However, simplicity does not mean that God's attributes are all identical. The word "power" does not mean the same as "wisdom" or "love." Each attribute of God is a distinct way in which he reveals himself on a human level. Yet all God's attributes are one in his one simple essence. We find an analogy to God's simplicity in how the light of one sun makes all the colors of the rainbow. For us to understand and appreciate God's glory, we must view the full spectrum of colors through the prism of his Word. In God himself, the attributes shine as a single, infinitely brilliant light.

God's attributes describe his very being. Augustine said, "In God to be is the same as to be strong, or to be just, or to be wise, or whatever is said of the simple multiplicity, or multifold simplicity, whereby we signify his substance."[4]

The Whole Doctrine of God and Simplicity

God's simplicity fits with other truths about him. This simple God is the Trinity. God the Father is pure light without change or shadow (James 1:17). God the Son, incarnate in Jesus Christ, not only *brings* the light but also *is* the light (John 8:12). Similarly, "the Spirit is truth" (1 John 5:6). The doctrine of the Trinity does not divide God into three parts. Rather, the three persons share one simple and undivided divine essence. The Father, the Son, and the Spirit have one goodness, one power, one eternity, and one wisdom.

4 Augustine, *On the Trinity*, 6.4.6, in *NPNF*[1], 3:100.

God is simple because he is one (1 Cor. 8:4; 1 Tim. 2:5). Deuteronomy 6:4 says, "Hear, O Israel: The Lord our God is one Lord." God is not divided or in conflict with himself. Therefore, our love should not be divided among various objects but focused fully on the one God with our whole hearts (v. 5).

The simplicity of God also fits with his independence as "I Am" (Ex. 3:14). Beings made of parts get them from a source outside of themselves. Another person or power must assemble those parts to make a complex being. The independent God has no parts. He simply *is*.

The doctrine of divine simplicity is part of the legacy of truth that the church has passed down through the centuries. Irenaeus said, "He is a simple, uncompounded Being."[5] Augustine said that God "is what He has. . . . Thus, He is in Himself living, for He has life, and is Himself the Life which He has." He said that God's nature cannot lose its attributes "because it is not one thing and its contents another, as a cup and the liquor, or a body and its color, or the air and the light or heat of it, or a mind and its wisdom."[6] As several Reformed confessions say, he is "without body, parts, or passions."[7]

Practical Applications of Divine Simplicity

This attribute also has numerous applications:

First, *God's simplicity shows us that wherever God is present, he is fully present with all his attributes.* We constantly dwell in the presence of the infinite, eternal, and unchangeable God of wisdom, power, justice, and love. Therefore, we must fear him. At the same time, however, this truth is comforting. All of God is with his children for their good.

Second, *God's simplicity means that we should never dwell just on one attribute to the neglect of others.* We should not focus on God's sovereignty to the neglect of his mercy. We must not make much of his love while making little of his justice. It is a mistake to talk only about his presence with us and lose sight of his glory beyond all our understanding. If we fall into errors such as these, we will end up worshiping a false god instead of the Lord.

5 Irenaeus, *Against Heresies*, 2.13.3, in *ANF*, 1:374.

6 Augustine, *The City of God*, 11.10, in *NPNF*[1], 2:211.

7 The Thirty-Nine Articles (Art. 1); the Irish Articles (Art. 8); the Westminster Confession of Faith (2.1); the Savoy Declaration (2.1); and the Second London Baptist Confession (2.1), in *RC*, 2:754; 4:92, 236–37, 461, 535.

Third, *God's simplicity shines most brightly at the cross of Christ.* There, Christ glorified all the attributes of God. William Bates wrote, "It is here that wisdom, goodness, justice, holiness, and power, are united in their highest degree and exaltation."[8]

Fourth, *God's simplicity promotes sincere holiness and love.* The Lord put statements such as "God is light" and "God is love" in parts of the Bible that call people to turn from hypocrisy and sincerely follow Christ (1 John 1:5–7; 4:7–8). God is completely one with his righteousness and love. It is impossible to know him savingly without walking in light and love.

Fifth, *God's simplicity means that no fruit of the Spirit can be separated from any other fruit.* There is profound unity in holiness, for it faintly reflects the simplicity of God. Love is patient, kind, joyful, righteous, and true (1 Cor. 13:4–6). Self-control and slowness to anger are real power, greater than the strength of a conquering warrior (Prov. 16:32; 25:28). We cannot abound in love without also growing in knowledge and discernment (Phil. 1:9). Let us therefore pursue holiness with our whole lives, for holiness is the essence of bearing the image of God.

Suggested Songs to Sing to the Lord

- Psalm 18, "I love the Lord, His strength is mine," in *Psalter*, No. 34
- "Immortal, invisible, God only wise," in *THBap*, No. 35

Questions for Meditation or Discussion

1. What is the biblical evidence that God has no body?
2. How would you explain the references to God's body and physical appearance in the Bible?
3. Prove from Scripture that God's being is invisible.
4. Imagine that someone tells you that God is the impersonal force in the world. How would you prove from Scripture that this is not what "God is a Spirit" means?
5. Show from the Holy Scriptures that the word "spirit" includes the idea of life.
6. What is God's simplicity?

8 William Bates, *The Harmony of the Divine Attributes in the Contrivance and Accomplishment of Man's Redemption* (1853; repr., Homewood, AL: Solid Ground, 2010), 73.

7. What is the biblical basis for the doctrine of God's simplicity?
8. How do other doctrines about God fit well with the doctrine of simplicity?
9. What are some practical applications of the doctrine of divine simplicity?
10. Take one of those practical applications and turn it into a prayer: "I praise Thee, O Lord, because Thou art . . ."

12

God's Infinity, Incomprehensibility, Aseity, Immensity, and Eternity

Chapter Summary and Key Terms

The *infinity of God* is his attribute of being matchlessly perfect in every way without any limitation. God's infinity with respect to the minds of created beings is his *incomprehensibility*: he is far beyond our full understanding. The *aseity of God* is his independence from all other things. He exists, lives, and acts from himself as the "I Am." He is not caused and does not receive any good from any being outside of himself. The other side of God's aseity is his *sufficiency*, the attribute of being the infinite fullness of all goodness and glory. God dwells in his *special presence*, where he makes his glory known to us. But his *essential presence*, or presence of his being, is not confined to places where he especially reveals his glory. He cannot be limited by space (*immensity*), and he is fully present in every location (*omnipresence*). God's attribute of *eternity* teaches us that he possesses the fullness of his infinite life as one complete whole, not spread out over a span of time. He has no beginning, end, or succession of moments. Rather, he is fully present at all times. He will be his people's everlasting joy.

When we encounter something great and magnificent, we find it both humbling and fascinating. Towering mountains, thundering waterfalls, deep canyons, and vast oceans remind us of how small we are. There is "no one greater" than God (Heb. 6:13 ESV). He is the Supreme Being. Compared to God, the angels are mere servants, and the heavens are like a garment that wears out and is changed (1:10–14).

In this chapter, we will consider God's infinity, or unlimited glory. His infinity has several aspects, including his incomprehensibility, aseity and sufficiency, immensity and omnipresence, and eternity. We will explain each of these terms in turn.

God's Infinity

When the Bible speaks of God's *infinity*, it means that he is perfect in every way without limitation. God is matchless in his glory: "To whom then will ye liken God? Or what likeness will ye compare unto him?" (Isa. 40:18). All the nations of mankind are to him but a drop in a bucket or dust on the scales, "less than nothing" in his sight (vv. 15–17). God never gets tired. His knowledge is limitless. He will never fail to uphold the cause of his people (vv. 27–28). Psalm 145:3 says, "Great is the Lord, and greatly to be praised; and his greatness is unsearchable."

The infinity of God is essential to the gospel. The guilt of our sins is enormous. Christ compared it to a debt of "ten thousand talents" (Matt. 18:24). That is an amount of money that would require many lifetimes to repay. Who could repay such a debt for us? Only our "great God and Savior Jesus Christ" (Titus 2:13 ESV). Christ died on the cross in his human nature, for his divine nature could not die. But the person who died on the cross was the infinitely valuable Son of God. Therefore, we may rest assured that his blood redeemed more people than we can count from all nations (Rev. 7:9, 14). His blood can save the worst sinners (1 Tim. 1:15).

God's Incomprehensibility

The *incomprehensibility* of God is the doctrine that he is beyond anyone's full understanding except his own. The statement that "his greatness is unsearchable" (Ps. 145:3) means that it is impossible for us to completely measure or grasp how great he is. God's power goes far beyond anything that we can imagine (Eph. 3:20–21). Even our worship falls short of his worthiness. His "glorious name . . . is exalted above all blessing and praise" (Neh. 9:5).

Zophar says, "Canst thou by searching find out God? Canst thou find out the Almighty unto perfection? It is as high as heaven; what canst thou do? Deeper than hell; what canst thou know? The measure thereof is longer than the earth, and broader than the sea" (Job 11:7–9). Christ's riches are "unsearchable" and his love "passeth knowledge" (Eph. 3:8, 18–19). We can no more hold the infinite God in our minds than a boy can scoop up the ocean in a seashell. Therefore, we should submit our minds entirely to God's Word, that we might know the truth revealed by his Spirit (1 Cor. 2:9–10).

God is incomprehensible in his works. Eliphaz says that God "doeth great things and unsearchable; marvellous things without number" (Job 5:9). Likewise, Job says that God "doeth great things past finding out; yea, and wonders without number" (9:10). God's works are "wondrous," "great," and "very deep" (Pss. 72:18; 92:5).

When the godly see that God is beyond their ability to understand (Job 38:1–4), they repent of their complaints when his ways are hard (42:1–6). They learn to meekly endure his discipline (40:1–5). God alone knows the way of true wisdom (28:20–23)—it begins with the fear of the Lord (v. 28).

Let us learn, then, to glorify the incomprehensible God. The stars he created and the storms he ordains "are but the outskirts of his ways, and how small a whisper do we hear of him! But the thunder of his power who can understand?" (Job 26:14 ESV). May God teach us to say with Paul, "O the depth of the riches both of the wisdom and knowledge of God! How unsearchable are his judgments, and his ways past finding out!" (Rom. 11:33).

God's Aseity and Sufficiency

God's *aseity* teaches us that he is independent from all things. He is self-existent—he lives and acts without help from anyone or anything else. As we saw earlier in this book, his name "the Lord" (*YHWH*) means "I Am" (Ex. 3:14). It declares his eternal, independent existence. God has "life in *himself*" (John 5:26). Aseity implies that he has no cause, needs none, and is the first cause of all (Isa. 44:6; Rev. 1:8).

No creature can add any good to his Creator, for everything good comes from him (Pss. 24:1–2; 50:7–13). The Holy Scriptures say, "Can a man be profitable unto God, as he that is wise may be profitable unto himself? Is it any pleasure to the Almighty, that thou art righteous? Or is it gain to him, that thou makest thy ways perfect?" (Job 22:2–3). Our obedience does not add to the glory of who he is, nor does our sin cause him loss (35:6–7). Paul says, "Who hath first given to him, and it shall be recompensed unto him again?" (Rom. 11:35; citing Job 41:11).

The doctrine of God's *sufficiency* teaches that he is the infinite fullness of all goodness and glory. God is "the overflowing fountain of all good," as the Belgic Confession says.[1] He is the "fountain of living waters" (Jer. 2:13; 17:13). David says,

> Thine, O Lord, is the greatness, and the power, and the glory, and the victory, and the majesty: for all that is in the heaven and in the earth is thine; thine is the kingdom, O Lord, and thou art exalted as head above all. Both riches and honour come of thee, and thou reignest over all; and in thine hand is power and might; and in thine hand it is to make great, and to give strength unto all. (1 Chron. 29:11–12)

The Creator is always the giver in all his relationships with his creatures (Acts 17:24–25; James 1:17). Paul exults, "For of him, and through him, and to him, are all things: to whom be glory for ever. Amen" (Rom. 11:36). God always works from a position of wealth, not need. Yet he freely chooses to live in covenant relationship with finite, sinful people. All God's love for his creatures is freely given.

The Westminster Confession of Faith says,

> God hath all life, glory, goodness, blessedness, in and of Himself; and is alone in and unto Himself all-sufficient, not standing in need of any creatures which He hath made, nor deriving any glory from them, but only manifesting His own glory in, by, unto, and upon them. He is the alone fountain of all being, of whom, through whom, and to whom are all things.[2]

We must learn to trust in God's aseity and sufficiency. The knowledge of these attributes can give us the power to worship him with joy and to trust him when our circumstances are discouraging. He is the all-sufficient portion of his people (Ps. 73:25–26).

The Lord is also our sufficiency in ministry. Christ supernaturally turned five loaves and two fish into enough food to feed thousands (Mark 6:33–44). He says to his servants as they feel their weakness, "My grace is sufficient for thee" (2 Cor. 12:9).

1 The Belgic Confession (Art. 1), in *TFU*, 17.

2 The Westminster Confession of Faith (2.2), in *RC*, 4:237. Cf. the Second London Baptist Confession (2.2), in *RC*, 4:535.

God's sufficiency can fill believers in Christ with hope. They can anticipate their future inheritance in "the riches of his glory" (Rom. 9:23). They have God! He is enough.

God's Immensity and Omnipresence

The God who declared "I Am" also promised, "I will be with thee" (Ex. 3:12, 14). Moses clung to this word, for he did not want to go anywhere "if thy presence go not with me" (33:15). God's presence includes his special presence and his essential presence.

God's *special presence* is his dwelling with us (Ex. 29:45). It refers to displays of his glory when he acts to keep his covenant through judgment and salvation. Heaven is the place where God dwells with the angels and the spirits of dead believers (Heb. 12:22–23) to display his holiness and beauty (Isa. 63:15). On earth, God dwells in his temple (Jonah 2:7). In the new covenant, that is not a building but the assembly of his people (Eph. 2:20–22). When Christ returns, the Lamb that was slain will be our temple, for God's glory will shine from Christ to fill the new creation (Rev. 21:1–3, 22–23). Then we will say, "The Lord is there" (Ezek. 48:35). However, God's *essential presence*, or the presence of his being, is not confined to the places of his special presence—as his attributes of immensity and omnipresence reveal.

God's *immensity* is the truth that he cannot be limited to any location or by any boundary: "The whole earth is full of his glory" (Isa. 6:3). Solomon says, "Behold, the heaven and heaven of heavens cannot contain thee" (1 Kings 8:27; cf. 2 Chron. 2:6). Stephen Charnock said, "Innumerable worlds cannot be a sufficient place to contain God; he can only be a sufficient place to himself."[3]

God's *omnipresence* teaches us that he is fully present in every place. David says, "If I ascend up into heaven, thou art there: if I make my bed in hell, behold, thou art there" (Ps. 139:8). In Jeremiah 23:23–24 we read, "Am I a God at hand, saith the Lord, and not a God afar off? Can any hide himself in secret places that I shall not see him? saith the Lord. Do not I fill heaven and earth? saith the Lord."

Every person of the Trinity is omnipresent. God the Father dwells with all his children behind the closed doors of their homes. He "seeth in secret"

3 Charnock, *The Existence and Attributes of God*, in *WSChar*, 1:432.

their faithful acts of devotion and will reward them (Matt. 6:1, 4, 6, 9, 18). Christ promised his church, "For where two or three are gathered together in my name, there am I in the midst of them" (18:20). He said, "Lo, I am with you always, even unto the end of the world" (28:20). The Holy Spirit also is the omnipresent God (Ps. 139:7, 9–10); he dwells in every Christian in the world (Rom. 8:9).

God's omnipresence is a warning to us not to commit sin. Proverbs 15:3 says, "The eyes of the LORD are in every place, beholding the evil and the good." The omnipresence of the Lord should fill us with the fear of God. We daily dwell in the presence of the Lord of heaven and earth.

This doctrine encourages believers to rely on God wholeheartedly: "The eyes of the LORD run to and fro throughout the whole earth, to shew himself strong in the behalf of them whose heart is perfect [fully devoted] toward him" (2 Chron. 16:9). He calls us to "walk before" him in righteous integrity (Gen. 17:1).

The omnipresence of God can make Christians fearless. Wherever trials may meet you, hear his promise: "Fear thou not; for I am with thee: be not dismayed; for I am thy God: I will strengthen thee; yea, I will help thee; yea, I will uphold thee with the right hand of my righteousness" (Isa. 41:10).

God's Eternity

The *eternity* of God is the truth that he is not limited in any way by time. God possesses the infinite fullness of his life as one complete whole. Job 36:26 says, "Behold, God is great, and we know him not, neither can the number of his years be searched out." Time is part of God's creation (Gen. 1:14).

We read in Genesis 21:33, "Abraham planted a grove in Beersheba, and called there on the name of the LORD, the everlasting God"—literally "God of eternity." Abraham confessed his faith that no amount of time, not even centuries, can stop God from being and doing all that he promised in his covenant. Two thousand years later, Paul glorified "the everlasting God" for keeping his promises through Abraham's great offspring, Jesus Christ (Rom. 16:25–27).

Human beings come and go, but the Lord is "our dwelling place in all generations" (Ps. 90:1). The eternal God has no beginning or end. Moses says, "Before the mountains were brought forth, or ever thou hadst formed the earth and the world, even from everlasting to everlasting, thou art God" (v. 2).

The eternal God has no succession of moments in time. Moses writes, "For a thousand years in thy sight are but as yesterday when it is past, and as a watch in the night" (Ps. 90:4). A thousand years is more than a million times longer than a few hours in the night ("a watch"). But to God a millennium is like minutes. Peter also says, "One day is with the Lord as a thousand years, and a thousand years as one day" (2 Pet. 3:8). For us a day may pass quickly and then fade into the past. God has access to every second as if it were stretched over the span of days. How could it be true of God that one day is like a thousand years and a thousand years like one day? He is independent of the motion of time. He is the Lord of time.

Eternity fills all God's attributes (Pss. 93:2; 103:17; 104:31; 119:142, 144). The eternity of God with respect to time is like his immensity with respect to space. Just as God's "place" is himself, so his "time" is his own eternity: the Lord "inhabiteth eternity" (Isa. 57:15). God's eternity reminds us that he is incomprehensible. How can we fully understand a being without beginning, without end, and not subject to the flow of time?

We can trust the eternal God: "Trust ye in the LORD for ever: for in the LORD JEHOVAH is everlasting strength" (Isa. 26:4). Literally he is "the Rock of ages" (KJV mg.). Fallen humanity is as weak and unreliable as the grass of the field (Isa. 40:6–7), quickly passing away. However, the word of God is powerful, unchangeable, and eternal, for God is eternal (v. 8).

God's eternity calls us to turn our attention from this short life to the ages to come: "The world passeth away, and the lust thereof: but he that doeth the will of God abideth for ever" (1 John 2:17). For believers, our present trouble is a "light" matter compared to the "eternal weight of glory" (2 Cor. 4:17). God's eternity should awaken the wicked to the everlasting terrors of hell. God calls sinners "to flee from the wrath to come," which "will burn with fire unquenchable" (Luke 3:7, 17). However, the eternity of God helps us to trust in Christ for eternal salvation. The Scriptures say, "Jesus Christ the same yesterday, and to day, and for ever" (Heb. 13:8). He is "able also to save them to the uttermost that come unto God by him, seeing he ever liveth to make intercession for them" (7:25). Therefore, this doctrine offers solid comfort to God's people. Moses says, "The eternal God is thy refuge, and underneath are the everlasting arms" (Deut. 33:27).

God's eternity teaches his people to anticipate everlasting joy. Our Savior will spend the coming ages showering the riches of his kindness on us in Christ Jesus (Eph. 2:4, 7). Charnock said, "The enjoyment of God will be as fresh and glorious after many ages, as it was at first," for "God is always vigorous and flourishing; a pure act of life, sparkling new and fresh rays of life and light," and life with him will never get boring or come to an end as we enjoy the infinite and eternal God.[4]

Suggested Songs to Sing to the Lord

- Psalm 90, "O God, our help in ages past," in *Psalter*, No. 247; *THBap*, No. 26
- Psalm 139, "Lord, Thou hast searched me," in *Psalter*, No. 382; *THBap*, No. 33

Questions for Meditation or Discussion

1. Define God's infinity and demonstrate it from Scripture.
2. What does the word *aseity* mean? What is the basis for this doctrine in the Bible?
3. What is one Scripture passage that clearly teaches God's sufficiency?
4. What is God's special presence? His immensity? His omnipresence?
5. How should we respond to the doctrine of God's omnipresence?
6. What can we learn about God's eternity from Psalm 90:2, 4?
7. What does 2 Peter 3:8 teach us about God and time?
8. What are the practical applications of God's eternity to our lives?
9. Psalm 90:12 says, "So teach us to number our days, that we may apply our hearts unto wisdom." Pray this prayer and consider this: How can you live more wisely before the eternal God?
10. If God were living one day at a time as we do, what would that tell us about God, his plan, and his relationship with the world? How would it lessen his glory?

4 Charnock, *The Existence and Attributes of God*, in *WSChar*, 1:364–65.

13

God's Immutability

Chapter Summary and Key Terms

The *immutability of God* is his attribute of being without change. God's attributes do not change, for they are infinite and eternal. His eternal will or decree is also unchangeable; his plan never fails. God's relationships with his creatures change as they change, but that does not mean there is any change in God himself. Though the Bible speaks of God repenting, relenting, or changing his mind, it is not teaching us that God feels regret over his decisions or changes his plan. The Bible simply uses human language for the infinite, eternal, and immutable God. However, he makes no mistakes. Therefore, we can rest our hope fully in him.

CHANGE FILLS OUR LIVES. The Greek philosopher Heraclitus famously said that you cannot step into the same river twice.[1] The Roman poet Ovid said, "Time is the devourer of things."[2] We grow up and grow old in years that, in hindsight, seem to have passed as swiftly as a flying bird.

Some theologians say that God changes. However, the Bible teaches that he never changes. This is the doctrine of God's *immutability*. For us, the prospect of never changing would be horrible, for it would trap us in our

1 Cited in Plato, *Cratylus*, 402a, in *Plato*, vol. 4, *Cratylus, Parmenides, Greater Hippias, Lesser Hippias*, trans. Harold North Fowler, Loeb Classical Library (Cambridge, MA: Harvard University Press, 1926), 67.

2 Ovid, *Metamorphoses*, 15.234, in *Ovid*, vol. 4, *Metamorphoses*, trans. Frank Justus Miller, Loeb Classical Library (Cambridge, MA: Harvard University Press, 1916), 380.

limited, imperfect lives. But as Johannes Wollebius said, "The immutable life of God is absolutely perfect and absolutely blessed."[3]

God's Unchangeable Being

"In the beginning," God already existed in all the power, wisdom, and goodness by which he created the universe (Gen. 1:1). There is no history of how God was born and grew up. In Psalm 90:2, Moses says, "From everlasting to everlasting, thou art God." What God was, he is now and always will be, for he is eternal.

Men's lives are disappearing "like smoke," passing "like a shadow," and withering "like grass" (Ps. 102:3, 11). But the believer can say to God, "Of old hast thou laid the foundation of the earth: and the heavens are the work of thy hands. They shall perish, but thou shalt endure: yea, all of them shall wax old like a garment; as a vesture shalt thou change them, and they shall be changed: but thou art the same, and thy years shall have no end" (vv. 25–27). "We ought therefore," John Calvin said, "to seek stability nowhere else but in God."[4]

Immutability, then, marks a basic difference between the Creator and his creation, including humanity. God says, "I am the Lord, I change not" (Mal. 3:6). This verse links God's immutability to his name "the Lord" (*YHWH*), or "I Am" (Ex. 3:14). God is the One who is. His self-existence and faithfulness guarantee that he will not change but will keep his ancient promises.

God's attributes do not change. His love and faithfulness cannot change (Psalm 136). God never loses any of the infinite power he used to create all things (Isa. 40:28). God's wisdom is immutable, for no one has ever "instructed him . . . [or] taught him knowledge" (Isa. 40:14). Nothing can increase his insight, for that would imply that his knowledge was limited, but "there is no searching of his understanding" (v. 28).

God is immutable because of his infinite perfection and sufficiency. He already has an unlimited fullness of goodness and glory. He can neither decrease nor increase. All change comes from a cause, but God's aseity teaches us that he receives nothing from causes outside of himself (Acts

3 Johannes Wollebius, *Compendium Theologiae Christianae*, 1.1.(3).3.iii.3, in *Reformed Dogmatics*, ed. and trans. John W. Beardslee III, A Library of Protestant Thought (New York: Oxford University Press, 1965), 39.

4 Calvin, *Comm.* on Ps. 102:25–27.

17:24–25). However, though God is unchanging, he is the living, personal, and active God, "the fountain of living waters" (Jer. 2:13).

The Bible uses various pictures for God's immutability. He is called the "Rock," a massive cliff or mountain (Deut. 32:4). This image shows his strength and stability. Another picture of God's immutability is light. James writes, "Every good gift and every perfect gift is from above, and cometh down from the Father of lights, with whom is no variableness, neither shadow of turning" (1:17). The sun, moon, and stars are always moving in the sky and changing in appearance. God, the Creator of these lights, is the eternal light that never changes.

God's Unchangeable Will

God is immutable not just in the perfections of his nature but also in the purposes of his heart. God's immutable purpose of grace flows out of his immutable nature. He says, "I am the LORD, I change not; therefore ye sons of Jacob are not consumed" (Mal. 3:6). The immutability of God's will is reflected in the stability of his Word (Ps. 119:89). Heaven and earth will pass away before his words pass away (Matt. 5:18; 24:35).

Even wicked Balaam had to say, "God is not a man, that he should lie; neither the son of man, that he should repent: hath he said, and shall he not do it? Or hath he spoken, and shall he not make it good?" (Num. 23:19). Men are changing and unreliable. Sometimes they lie, promising one thing but doing another. Sometimes they commit to do something, but afterward change their minds. However, God is not human. He does not lie or change his mind or purposes. Thus, his blessing on his chosen people will not fail (v. 20). Greg Nichols writes, "The church will never perish. Persecution will never destroy it. Temptation will never overwhelm it. Its enemies strive in vain. God has decreed its preservation and victory."[5]

God has absolute freedom to decide what he pleases. His decree is "the counsel of his own will" (Eph. 1:11). He freely decided his good pleasure in eternity (v. 4) and now performs that unchanging plan in time (Dan. 4:24, 35). Man's plans are often frustrated and have to be changed. God's plan is never frustrated and will stand forever (Ps. 33:10–11).

5 Greg Nichols, *Lectures in Systematic Theology*, ed. Rob Ventura, 4 vols. to date (Seattle: CreateSpace Independent Publishing Platform, 2017–2024), 1:256.

Therefore, Christians have a hope that is "an anchor of the soul, both sure and stedfast" (Heb. 6:19). God has revealed "the immutability of his counsel" (v. 17). His promises will never expire, for his plan will never change. We can trust his Word. Over the whole Bible flies this banner: "These words are true and faithful" (Rev. 21:5).

Questions about God's Immutability

The doctrine of God's immutability has rich implications for our faith and obedience. But like God's eternity, it can puzzle our minds. Two major theological questions confront us when we consider God's immutability. We may summarize them in the words *relationships* and *repentance*.

God's Relationships and Immutability

As we have seen, the Holy Scriptures teach us that God does not change in his being or plan. But the Scriptures plainly say that God's relationships change. Unbelievers live under God's wrath, but when they repent of their sins and believe the gospel, they come under God's forgiveness (John 3:16–18, 36). Thus, the gospel of Christ demands that we recognize that God's relationships change.

Some evangelical theologians argue that though God does not change in his attributes or plan, he changes in his experiences and emotions as his relationships with us change.[6] This would mean that one part of God is unchanging (his attributes and plan) and the other part is changing (his experiences and emotions). However, there can be no change in God, for he says, "I am the Lord, I change not" (Mal. 3:6). The Bible also says nothing about God having two parts. Rather, God is one (Deut. 6:4). He is simple. His very essence is love (1 John 4:8). Therefore, if his love changed, his very being would change. God's affections are not changing emotions (chap. 18).

God's relationships with creatures in time, though very real, are not part of his essence. Relationships are outward actions of God. Changes in them involve no change in God himself. His relationships change, but he never changes.

6 Bruce A. Ware, "An Evangelical Reformulation of the Doctrine of the Immutability of God," *Journal of the Evangelical Theological Society* 29, no. 4 (December 1986): 440–41; and *God's Greater Glory: The Exalted God of Scripture and the Christian Faith* (Wheaton, IL: Crossway, 2004), 148, 150.

God's Repentance and Immutability

In light of the Bible's teaching that God is unchanging in the perfection of his nature and purpose, it sometimes confuses people to read that God does "repent" or, as it also can be translated, "regret" or "relent" (ESV). For example, Genesis 6:6–7 says, "And it repented the LORD that he had made man on the earth, and it grieved him at his heart. And the LORD said, I will destroy man whom I have created from the face of the earth; both man, and beast, and the creeping thing, and the fowls of the air; for it repenteth me that I have made them."

Teachers of open theism point to Scripture passages such as Genesis 6 as evidence that God does not have an unchanging plan.[7] Rather, he is said to change his plan to respond sensitively to those whom he loves. This means that when evil spread on the earth in the time of Noah, God felt regret over his decision to make man. Under this view, God had not known that man would sin. But if this is true, God makes decisions with horrible outcomes.

On the contrary, God is eternal and perfect in wisdom. He is not limited by time and cannot make mistakes. When this passage says that God "repented," it tells us that he was very displeased with human sin, as the word "grieved" shows (Gen. 6:6). The Creator of the perfect world thus became the destroyer of the sinful world. However, that does not mean God changed his plan because of events he did not foresee. That would contradict the message of Genesis that God knows events many years before they happen (15:13–16; 25:23; 37:5–8).

Sin does not cause God's plan to fail but mysteriously fulfills it. Joseph could tell his brothers, "Ye thought evil against me; but God meant it unto good" because of results that came years later (Gen. 50:20). Therefore, we should interpret God's repentance in Genesis 6:6–7 to refer not to a change of his plan but to a change in his dealings with man. God planned the flood from the beginning for his glory in judgment and salvation. Augustine said, "Thou . . . changest Thy ways, leaving unchanged Thy plans."[8]

Trusting the Unchangeable Lord

God's immutability entered our changeable world when the Word became flesh and dwelt among us (John 1:14). In his human nature, Christ has

7 Open theism is a form of finite theism or belief in a limited god. See chaps. 10 and 14.

8 Augustine, *Confessions*, 1.4, in *NPNF*[1], 1:46.

changed and developed (Luke 2:40). In his eternal divine nature, he never changes. The Son remains the immutable Creator (Heb. 1:10–12). Once he became man, he is forever the God-man. Hebrews 13:8 celebrates "Jesus Christ the same yesterday, and to day, and for ever."

Therefore, if we trust in Christ alone for salvation, we can know that God has loved us with an everlasting love (Ps. 103:17; Isa. 54:7–10). John Preston said, "When thou knowest that God is knit to thee by an unchangeable bond, that he is a friend whom thou mayest build upon forever, whom thou mayest trust; this makes thy heart to cleave to him."[9]

We should imitate God's immutability by keeping our word. We should be reliable people by God's grace (2 Cor. 1:17–20). We must change through the lifelong process of repentance. However, our repentance pursues greater steadiness and stability in the image of God.

Though we strive to imitate God's faithfulness and admire the saints for their perseverance, we must view mere men realistically. People are full of changes: "As for man, his days are as grass: as a flower of the field, so he flourisheth" (Ps. 103:15). Therefore, we cannot hope in any mere man.

Only God's immutability can be the basis of our hope. We must say with the psalmist, "My soul, wait thou only upon God; for my expectation is from him. He only is my rock and my salvation: he is my defence; I shall not be moved" (Ps. 62:5–6).

Samuel Willard said, "Live upon this attribute; it is enough to keep up your spirits, and strengthen you with patience to run that weary and difficult race that you are called unto. It is true, you meet with many changes among creatures . . . yet faint not, nor be weary, for in all these you have an unchangeable God to stand by you."[10]

Suggested Songs to Sing to the Lord

- Psalm 33, "Let all the earth Jehovah fear," in *Psalter*, No. 86; *THBap*, No. 40
- "Great is thy faithfulness, O God my Father," in *THBap*, No. 27

9 John Preston, *Life Eternall, or, A Treatise of the Divine Essence and Attributes*, 2nd ed. (London: by R. B., 1631), 2:88.

10 Samuel Willard, *A Compleat Body of Divinity in Two Hundred and Fifty Expository Lectures on the Assembly's Shorter Catechism* (Boston: by B. Green and S. Kneeland for B. Eliot and D. Henchman, 1726), 64–65.

Questions for Meditation or Discussion

1. What does *immutability* mean?
2. How does Psalm 102 reveal the immutability of God?
3. How does Malachi 3:6 teach us about God's immutability?
4. How do God's other attributes confirm his immutability?
5. How does knowing that God is the unchangeable Rock give you confidence and hope?
6. How should we view God's immutability and relationships?
7. What argument do open theists make from Genesis 6:6–7?
8. How should we understand Genesis 6:6–7 when it says God "repented," taking the context of Genesis into account?
9. If God were changing, how would it affect the Christian's life?
10. Why is God's immutability a source of great strength and comfort?

14

God's Knowledge

Chapter Summary and Key Terms

God is infinite in knowledge. He has *omniscience*, the attribute of knowing all things. That means he has perfect knowledge of himself, of all possible things and events, and of all actual things and events that will ever be. God also has perfect *wisdom*, his infinite skill to create the world and rule it well. In his wisdom, he has chosen excellent goals and excellent means to accomplish them—though those means are sometimes mysterious and surprising to us. Another aspect of God's infinite knowledge is his *foreknowledge* or complete knowledge of all future events. But God's foreknowledge is denied by *open theism*, a form of finite theism. Open theism teaches that God's power and knowledge of the future are severely limited by our choices, so he changes his plan as he seeks relationships with people. On the contrary, the foreknowledge of God is well established by many prophecies in Scripture that foretell the future. God is the Lord of the future, so we can trust his promises.

HAGAR HAD FLED FROM HER MISTRESS, Sarai, turning her face toward her homeland of Egypt. In her womb grew Abram's son Ishmael. As a foreigner, a woman, and a slave in the ancient Near East, she hardly seemed like a candidate for a visit from God. Yet the angel of the Lord came to her in the wilderness. God told her to go home and gave her great promises about her son and his posterity. In response, Hagar named the place "Beer-lahai-roi," which means, "Well of the Living One who sees me" (Gen. 16:14 ESV).

We cannot see God, but he always sees us. Whoever or wherever we are, God knows us and the whole panorama of our lives—past, present, and future. The doctrine of his unlimited knowledge of all things helps us to trust and love him.

God's Infinite Knowledge

God is "perfect in knowledge" (Job 36:4; 37:16). The psalmist says, "He telleth the number of the stars; he calleth them all by their names. Great is our Lord, and of great power: his understanding is infinite" (Ps. 147:4–5). God's understanding cannot be measured, and his thoughts are far above ours (Isa. 40:28; 55:8–9).

Paul compares God's knowledge and wisdom to a bottomless vault of treasure. He says, "O the depth of the riches both of the wisdom and knowledge of God! How unsearchable are his judgments, and his ways past finding out!" (Rom. 11:33). Therefore, we have nothing to add to what he already knows (v. 34; cf. Job 21:22; Isa. 40:13–14).

God knows truth by an act of his infinite glory, quite different from how we know truth. Human beings know by a process that involves observation and experience, listening to other people, and thinking about particular matters in our minds. Our knowledge increases and decreases over time. But God's way of knowing is not like ours (Job 21:22; Isa. 40:13–14). Louis Berkhof said, "The knowledge of God may be defined as that perfection of God whereby He, in an entirely unique manner, knows Himself and all things possible and actual in one eternal and most simple act."[1]

God is light (1 John 1:5). In the Bible, light is often used to represent knowledge. Light reveals things. God does not receive light from any outside source—his nature is his own light. All knowledge is in him. All knowledge in his creatures radiates from him (Ps. 36:9), either from his essential glory as the triune God or from his will concerning his creation. All our knowledge comes from him. Our greatest knowledge is to know him.

1 Louis Berkhof, *Systematic Theology* (Edinburgh: Banner of Truth, 1958), 66.

The doctrine of divine knowledge should humble us. We are tempted to be proud of what we know, thinking that we have deep insights into God. But our minds, compared to God's mind, are like a spark to the sun and a drop to the ocean. John Owen said, "All our notions of God are but childish in respect of his infinite perfections."[2] However, we should not retreat into thinking we cannot know anything about God. Rather, we should seek to learn more from his Word, the Holy Scriptures. Whatever the topic may be, God knows it completely.

God's Omniscience

The Scriptures say that God "knoweth all things" (1 John 3:20). Theologians call this all-encompassing divine knowledge God's *omniscience.*

God knows himself, saying, "I am God" (Isa. 45:22). The Father, the Son, and the Holy Spirit know one another in a way that no one else can fathom, even to the depths of the divine being (Matt. 11:27; 1 Cor. 2:10). Compared to God's knowledge of his own infinite glory, his knowledge of the whole universe is "a very little thing" (Isa. 40:15).

God knows the world that he created and everything in it. He is the great watcher, listener, and evaluator of creation (Job 28:24; Heb. 4:13). Psalm 33:13–15 says, "The Lord looketh from heaven; he beholdeth all the sons of men. From the place of his habitation he looketh upon all the inhabitants of the earth. He fashioneth their hearts alike; he considereth all their works." God knows all things in his creation because he is present in all places (Prov. 15:3).

God gives perfect attention to each individual man, woman, and child (Matt. 10:30). He knows us better than we know ourselves. David says, "O Lord, thou hast searched me, and known me" (Ps. 139:1). The Lord knows when you sit and when you stand. He knows your travel and your rest, your thoughts and your words (vv. 2–4). There is no place you can go to escape his knowledge (vv. 7, 12).

God's knowledge is a powerful motive to repent of sin and seek forgiveness through Christ's blood. The God who knows everything is not an indifferent observer. He is the Lord and Judge of all the earth. Hannah warns, "Talk no more so exceeding proudly; let not arrogancy come out of

2 Owen, *The Mortification of Sin in Believers,* in *WJO,* 6:65.

your mouth: for the Lord is a God of knowledge, and by him actions are weighed" (1 Sam. 2:3). God knows the secret thoughts and motives of a man (1 Sam. 16:7; 1 Kings 8:39). He says to sinners, "I know the things that come into your mind" (Ezek. 11:5). God alone searches the hearts of men (2 Chron. 6:30; Jer. 17:9–10).

God's omniscience is a marvelous comfort to his people. God hears our groaning and sees our afflictions (Ex. 2:23–25; 3:7). He understands our weaknesses and responds with tender pity (Ps. 103:14). The Father knows what his children need before they ask him (Matt. 6:8).

God's Wisdom

The Lord is "the only wise God" (Rom. 16:27 ESV). Job says, "He is wise in heart, and mighty in strength: who hath hardened himself against him, and hath prospered?" (Job 9:4). He adds, "With him is wisdom and strength, he hath counsel and understanding" (12:13).

God's wisdom means that he is infinitely skilled to create the world and rule it well. The psalmist says, "O Lord, how manifold are thy works! In wisdom hast thou made them all: the earth is full of thy riches" (Ps. 104:24). Daniel prays, "Blessed be the name of God for ever and ever: for wisdom and might are his: and he changeth the times and the seasons: he removeth kings, and setteth up kings: he giveth wisdom unto the wise, and knowledge to them that know understanding" (2:20–21). By his wisdom, God makes "everything beautiful in its time" (Eccles. 3:11 ESV). Our wisdom is to fear the Lord (Ps. 111:10; Prov. 1:7).

Jesus Christ is God's wisdom in human flesh. Christ is the Wonderful Counselor (Isa. 9:6). He is the King who knows things only God could know and makes amazingly excellent plans. He is anointed by the Spirit of wisdom and understanding (11:1–5). In Christ "are hid all the treasures of wisdom and knowledge" (Col. 2:3).

God both concealed and revealed his wisdom in "Christ crucified . . . Christ the power of God, and the wisdom of God" (1 Cor. 1:23–24). For those united to Christ by God's effectual calling, Christ "is made unto us wisdom" (v. 30). In Jesus Christ, God has manifested to heaven and earth the unsearchable riches of his wisdom by saving the church (Eph. 3:10). God's wisdom has ordered all things in Christ so that "he that glorieth, let him glory in the Lord" (1 Cor. 1:31).

Practical Applications of God's Knowledge and Wisdom

We should seek to grow in knowledge. If the God of glory is wise, it is our glory to receive more wisdom from him.

Rely on God's wisdom when you are suffering trials and do not know what to do. Be often in prayer for more wisdom (James 1:5).

Admire God's knowledge and wisdom displayed in all his works (Jer. 51:15). Contemplate his mighty deeds. Consider especially his wisdom in the cross of Jesus Christ.

Live in sincere piety because God's eye is always on you. Trust his wisdom when you cannot understand his ways (Prov. 3:5). Remember that God can draw a straight line with a crooked stick.

When you are falsely accused of wrongdoing, quiet yourself with the knowledge that the Judge of all the earth knows and will make it right (1 Pet. 2:23).

Do not give in to the temptation to believe that God has forgotten you. Rather, say to yourself that he is "the everlasting God, the Lord, the Creator of the ends of the earth . . . there is no searching of his understanding." Wait on the Lord, and he will renew your strength (Isa. 40:27–31).

God's Foreknowledge

God's omnipresence implies that his knowledge reaches to all places. His eternity implies that his knowledge reaches to all times: past, present, and future. God's omniscience of the future is called his *foreknowledge*. Throughout the Bible, God reveals future events before they take place, and his Word proves true.

Objections to God's Foreknowledge

The Bible tells us about God's foreknowledge so often that it has been taught by all branches of true Christianity. However, there are false teachers, such as open theists, who deny that God foreknows the future free choices of angels and men. They make the following objections.

Objection 1: God regrets some of his decisions in light of how people later act (Gen. 6:6–7).

In reply, we note—as we argued in the previous chapter—that biblical statements about God's repentance reveal changes in his relationships and actions. Neither God nor his plan changes (Ps. 33:10–11; Mal. 3:6).

Objection 2: God tests people to see how they will act. For example, he said to Abraham, "Now I know that thou fearest God" (Gen. 22:12). Thus, God did not know what Abraham would choose.

In response, we assert that this argument would prove that God was ignorant not only of the future but also of Abraham's heart. On the contrary, "now I know" expresses God's pleasure and blessing on Abraham's course of life (compare "know" in Pss. 1:6; 37:18).

Objection 3: God says that people do some things that never entered his mind, such as child sacrifice (Jer. 7:31; 19:5; 32:35). Thus, God did not know they would do those things.

In reply, we must say that this is a ridiculous argument. God knew about child sacrifice and prohibited it in the law of Moses centuries earlier (Lev. 18:21; 20:2). God's statement means that he never would have commanded Israel to commit such evil acts.

Objection 4: God's prophecies about the future are either about what he will do (Isa. 46:10) or are conditional on what we will do (Jer. 18:7–11), which God does not know for certain.

In response, we note that though some of God's promises are conditional, not all are. Isaiah 46:10–11 is not just about God's actions. He foretold the actions of Cyrus, by whom God would restore Israel two centuries later (44:28; 45:1).

Objection 5: God cannot know what has not yet been determined, such as our future choices. If they were determined, we would have no freedom to choose.

In reply, we say that this argument bases doctrine on human reasoning. If God's foreknowledge and human choices are both taught in the Word of God, then we must believe in both. Furthermore, foreknowledge and human freedom do not logically contradict each other.

Examples of God's Foreknowledge in the Scriptures

The testimony to God's perfect knowledge of the future spans the Bible from Genesis through Revelation. Tertullian quipped that God's foreknowledge "has for its witnesses as many prophets as it inspired."[3] Consider some examples.

God told Abraham that his offspring would go to a foreign land and be slaves for four centuries (Gen. 15:13). God revealed to Joseph the future

3 Tertullian, *Against Marcion*, 2.5, in *ANF*, 3:301.

of individuals and nations years ahead of the actual events (Genesis 37, 40, 41). The Lord made it a test of a true prophet that his prophecies must certainly come true (Deut. 18:22).

God foretold through a prophet that a descendant of David named Josiah would destroy a particular altar (1 Kings 13:2). That prophecy came true centuries later (2 Kings 23:15–17). The prophet Micaiah announced that Ahab would die in battle and said, "If thou return at all in peace, the LORD hath not spoken by me" (1 Kings 22:28).

The greatest event of history that fulfilled predictive prophecy was the coming and work of God's Son—the grand theme of the Old Testament (Luke 24:44–47). The prophets foretold that Christ would come from the tribe of Judah (Gen. 49:10) and from the family of David (Isa. 9:6–7). He would be born of a virgin (7:14) in the town of Bethlehem (Mic. 5:2). He would bring the light of God to Galilee (Isa. 9:1–2). He would be a prophet like Moses, declaring God's word and working miracles (Deut. 18:15–19; 34:10–12). Another preacher would go ahead of him, calling Israel to prepare itself for the coming of the Lord (Isa. 40:3; Mal. 3:1).

Christ would be rejected by the leaders of the nation, but God would make him the foundation of his new temple (Ps. 118:22–26). The humble King would ride into Jerusalem on a donkey (Zech. 9:9). His sorrows would overwhelm him as his enemies pierced his hands and feet, mocking him as he died and as God himself abandoned him to judgment (Ps. 22:1, 7, 13, 16). He would meekly bear the sins of his people and suffer the punishment they deserved, yet he would be buried in the place of the rich (Isa. 53:5–9).

God would raise Christ from the dead (Ps. 16:10–11) and exalt him to sit at his right hand in supreme glory (110:1). Then he would send out the good news so that people from all nations would become worshipers of God (22:22, 27). At the heart of the gospel is the proclamation that Christ's death and resurrection took place "according to the scriptures" (1 Cor. 15:3–4)—that is, in fulfillment of God's plan revealed in the Bible (Rom. 1:1–2).

Applications of God's Foreknowledge for Life

God's perfect knowledge of all future events has rich applications to the Christian life. We should acknowledge that he is Lord of the future and we are not. Rather, we must make our plans meekly, for we "do not know what tomorrow will bring." We ought to say, "If the Lord wills, we will live and do this or that" (James 4:14–15 ESV).

We should trust God's promises for the future. Not one of his words can fall to the ground (1 Sam. 3:19; 2 Kings 10:10). We should especially trust the great promise that the Lord Jesus Christ will return in divine glory to judge the earth and bring everlasting joy to his people. Nothing can stop God's plan to glorify himself in Christ. He says to us, "These words are true and faithful" (Rev. 21:5). Let us stake our lives on them and lift up our heads in hope.

Suggested Songs to Sing to the Lord

- Psalm 33, "Jehovah from His throne on high," in *Psalter*, No. 87
- Psalm 139, "All that I am I owe to Thee," in *Psalter*, No. 383; *THBap*, No. 34

Questions for Meditation or Discussion

1. How do the Holy Scriptures show us that God's knowledge is infinite?
2. Where does the Bible teach us God's omniscience of (1) all creation, (2) each individual person, and (3) the thoughts and motives of our hearts?
3. What is God's wisdom?
4. How has God shown his wisdom in the world he made and rules?
5. What did Tertullian mean when he said that God's knowledge of the future "has for its witnesses as many prophets as it inspired"?
6. What are some Scripture passages that show that God foreknows man's future free decisions?
7. What are some prophetic predictions that have been fulfilled in Jesus Christ?
8. Meditate on the doctrine that God knew your whole life before you were born. How does this truth affect you? How can you use it to cultivate amazement, worship, humility, and hope?

15

God's Sovereignty

Chapter Summary and Key Terms

The *sovereignty of God* is his effectual rule as supreme Lord over all things. His very names identify him as "I Am," "God," "Most High," "God Almighty," "Lord," and "the Lord of hosts." God is sovereign in his will. His *preceptive will* is his choice of what men and angels should do as their duty to him. His *decretive will* is his decree of all that will take place. God also has sovereign *authority*. That is his right to do and command what he pleases with his creatures. God's absolute authority arises from his nature as the only God and his relationship to the world as its Creator. Another aspect of God's sovereignty is his *omnipotence*, or infinite power, to do all his decretive will. God is able to do anything consistent with his holiness. He gives creatures all the power they have and exercises sovereign control over all things. Since God is sovereign, we should repent of rebelling against him, seek his sovereign grace, and submit to his commandments.

THE SOVEREIGNTY OF GOD is one of the great doctrines of the Bible, filling its pages. It is the root of the believer's godliness and comfort. It is also the strong foundation of his hope.

The doctrine of God's sovereignty teaches that he reigns effectually as Lord over all that he has made. This doctrine has many parts. God's decree, election and reprobation, and providence will each receive our attention in later chapters. In this chapter, we will offer an introduction to God's sovereignty as one of the perfections of his lordship.

God's Names of Sovereignty

God reveals his sovereignty in the names that he gives to himself in his Word.

We have already talked about the meaning of *YHWH*. That is the name by which God reveals his self-existence as "the Lord." He is the independent "I Am" on whom all else depends (Ex. 3:14).

However, the first of the Lord's names to appear in Scripture is "God" (*Elohim*). This name is used thirty-five times in the first thirty-four verses of the Bible (Gen. 1:1–2:3). God's creation of the heaven and the earth presents him as the powerful King. He made all things and controls them with his mere word. This name denotes him as the God of all power.

The Holy Scriptures also name God the "Most High" (*Elyon*). This is a title of supremacy over the world (Pss. 83:18; 97:9).

He is also "Almighty God" (*El Shaddai*, Gen. 17:1). Job 37:22–23 shows us that this is a name of majestic power: "With God is terrible majesty. Touching the Almighty [*Shaddai*], we cannot find him out: he is excellent in power, and in judgment, and in plenty of justice."

Abraham and his offspring also spoke to God as "Lord" (*Adonai*, Gen. 15:2). This term, which means "Master," is a different word from the one that is translated as "the Lord." When Isaiah reported his vision of the exalted, holy King of angels and "the whole earth," he said, "I saw the Lord [*Adonai*]" (Isa. 6:1–3).

We find many references in the Bible to "the Lord of hosts" (*YHWH Tsebaot*, 1 Sam. 1:3, 11). This title describes God as a military commander of vast forces. A host is an army (Deut. 20:9; 2 Sam. 10:7).

In summary, the names of God display his sovereignty. This is the God who inspires both dread in his enemies and hope in his servants. It is no surprise to read in Scripture that God is "King for ever and ever" (Ps. 10:16), "the King of glory" (24:7–10), "a great King over all the earth" (47:2), and "the blessed and only Potentate, the King of kings, and Lord of lords" (1 Tim. 6:15).

God's Sovereign Will

God is a personal being who makes choices (Deut. 4:37; 12:14; 18:5). His choices are called his "will." The will of God is sovereign. It is supreme over all, for it is the will of the great King. The Scriptures speak of God's will toward his creatures in two ways: his preceptive will and decretive will.

God's *preceptive will* is what *should* happen. It has to do with obedience to God's commands and rules—his precepts. For example, Paul writes, "For this is the will of God, even your sanctification, that ye should abstain from fornication" (1 Thess. 4:3). David prays, "Teach me to do thy will" (Ps. 143:10).

God's *decretive will* is what he determines *will* happen—his decrees. It has to do with his power and reign. Daniel 4:17 says, "The most High ruleth in the kingdom of men, and giveth it to whomsoever he will." God "worketh all things after the counsel of his own will" (Eph. 1:11).

The distinction between God's decretive will and preceptive will guards two great doctrines: God's sovereignty and man's responsibility. We see both in the crucifixion of Jesus Christ. Peter preached to sinners in Jerusalem that Christ, "being delivered by the determinate counsel and foreknowledge of God, ye have taken, and by wicked hands have crucified and slain" (Acts 2:23). On the one hand, the crucifixion of our Lord Jesus was clearly against God's preceptive will. It was the murder of God's righteous servant. On the other hand, the death of Christ fulfilled God's decretive will. All these things took place according to God's plan.

This distinction also has enormous practical value for the Christian life. We must learn to distinguish between what God will do with our lives and what our duty is toward God. When we pray for God to teach us his will, we must seek to know our responsibility. We must also learn to be content to leave his plans for our future hidden in the secrecy of his wise decree.

God's Sovereign Authority

God's authority is his right to do with all creatures as he pleases. He has this right because he is the Creator of all things: "The earth is the Lord's, and the fulness thereof; the world, and they that dwell therein" (Ps. 24:1). Therefore, God may freely and justly impose his will on his creatures, both in what he decrees and what he commands. No one has a greater right to reign than the Lord.

Nebuchadnezzar confessed, "All the inhabitants of the earth are reputed as nothing: and he doeth according to his will in the army of heaven, and among the inhabitants of the earth: and none can stay his hand, or say unto him, What doest thou?" (Dan. 4:35). God is not accountable to anyone. No one may question his right to do what he does, much less accuse him of wrongdoing (Job 9:12).

God's ownership of the world also confirms his supreme right to demand from angels and men complete obedience to his commands. He gives us enough reason to keep all his statutes by simply saying, "I am the LORD" (Lev. 18:4–5; 19:37). When it comes to moral law that binds the conscience, "there is one lawgiver"—God alone (James 4:12).

God's Sovereign Power

The Lord has infinite power to accomplish all his decretive will and enforce the full rights of his authority. He demonstrated that power in the work of creation. His mere word of command brought the world into existence (Ps. 33:6). William Ames wrote that faith says to God, "Lord, if you will, you can," and the Lord replies, "I will; therefore, it is done" (cf. Matt. 8:2–3).[1] The majestic heavens express only a "little" of his strength, and "the thunder of his power who can understand?" (Job 26:14).

Since all things come from God the almighty Creator, all power is first in God before it belongs to anyone else (Job 12:16; Ps. 62:11; Dan. 2:20). God does not merely give strength to his people—he is their strength. In fact, "my Strength" or "our Strength" is another name for God (Ex. 15:2; Pss. 28:7–8; 46:1).

There is no limit to the amount of power that God can exercise. Though tested by his troubles, Job learned to say, "I know that thou canst do every thing, and that no thought of thine can be hindered" (Job 42:2 KJV mg.).

Neither can God's power ever be diminished or exhausted: "The LORD, the Creator of the ends of the earth, fainteth not, neither is weary" (Isa. 40:28). When the armies of Babylon prepared to destroy Jerusalem, Jeremiah prayed, "Ah Lord GOD! Behold, thou hast made the heaven and the earth by thy great power and stretched out arm, and there is nothing too hard for thee" (Jer. 32:17).

In Christ, the Almighty came to us hidden in human flesh. The angel assured Mary that Christ would be born of her though she was a virgin: "With God nothing shall be impossible" (Luke 1:37). The Lord Jesus controlled

1 William Ames, *The Marrow of Theology*, trans. John D. Eusden (Grand Rapids, MI: Baker, 1968), 1.6.8 (92).

the storms of nature with his mere word. That prompted his disciples to exclaim, "What manner of man is this, that even the winds and the sea obey him!" (Matt. 8:27). It was no mere man but God (Ps. 107:29).

We call God's infinite power his *omnipotence* ("all power"). James Ussher explained God's omnipotence as follows. God is able to perform whatever he wills or is not contrary to his nature. He can do all things very easily. He can do them either with means, without means, or contrary to means, as pleases him. No power can resist him. All power is in God alone. No creature can do anything unless he or she continually receives power from God to do it.[2]

We should not make omnipotence into nonsense. Someone might foolishly ask if God has the power to destroy himself or the power to create something greater than himself. Philosophers debate whether God can make a stone too heavy for him to lift. But that would be a sign of weakness, not power. Augustine said, "He cannot do some things for the very reason that he is omnipotent."[3]

Practical Applications of God's Sovereignty

The great doctrine of God's sovereignty has numerous practical applications.

First, *God's sovereignty calls us to repent of rebelling against him.* Job 9:4 says, "He is wise in heart, and mighty in strength: who hath hardened himself against him, and hath prospered?" The most foolish thing in the world is to fight against the omnipotent God. The psalmist marvels, "Why do the heathen rage, and the people imagine a vain thing?" (Ps. 2:1).

Second, *God's sovereignty calls us to trust in his promises.* It seemed impossible that God could give a son to old Abraham and barren Sarah. But God said, "Is any thing too hard for the Lord?" (Gen. 18:14). Whatever dangers you may face, believe that God is able to sustain you in them or rescue you from them.

Third, *God's sovereignty calls us to fear him.* We should meditate on the power of the King. We should say, "Great and marvellous are thy works, Lord God Almighty. . . . Who shall not fear thee, O Lord, and glorify thy name?" (Rev. 15:3–4). Yet the infinite resources of his power are for the good

2 Adapted from James Ussher, *A Body of Divinity: Being the Sum and Substance of the Christian Religion*, intro. Crawford Gribben (Birmingham, AL: Solid Ground, 2007), 2nd head (39).

3 Augustine, *The City of God*, 5.10, in *NPNF*[1], 2:92.

of those who fear him, not against them. We may fear him with childlike confidence in our heavenly Father.

Fourth, *God's sovereignty calls us to humbly praise him*. We should "sing unto the LORD" and "make a joyful noise," for he is "a great God, and a great King above all gods," who holds the earth and the sea in his hands (Ps. 95:1–6).

Fifth, *God's sovereignty calls us to faithfully serve him*. Even if you are a "master" on earth, remember that you have a "Master" in heaven (Eph. 6:9). Wilhelmus à Brakel said, "All that God wills, the servant of God also wills, because the will of God is the object of his desire and delight."[4]

Sixth, *God's sovereignty calls us to submit to him in sorrows*. When bad news strikes our families, God's grace enables us to say, "It is the LORD. Let him do what seems good to him" (1 Sam. 3:18 ESV). God's omnipotence grates harshly on the sufferer's ear when he is in rebellion against his Maker. But this truth enables the saint to repent of his complaints, put his hand over his mouth, and bow before the incomprehensible majesty of God (Job 40:1–5; 42:1–6).

Seventh, *God's sovereignty calls us to have hope for the salvation of others*. When we consider the hardness of men's hearts and their slavery to sin, we may despair of their conversion. We might cry out, "Who then can be saved?" Christ answers, "With men it is impossible, but not with God: for with God all things are possible" (Mark 10:27).

Eighth, *God's sovereignty calls us to pray for great things*. Paul's prayers for the spiritual growth of the saints are staggering in the great things he seeks for them. But Paul reminds us that the Father "is able to do exceeding abundantly above all that we ask or think" (Eph. 3:20).

Suggested Song to Sing to the Lord

- "The Lord is King! Lift up thy voice," *THBap*, No. 58

Questions for Meditation or Discussion

1. What do each of the following biblical names communicate about God: (1) *Elohim*, (2) *Elyon*, (3) *El Shaddai*, (4) *Adonai*, (5) *Lord of hosts*?

4 Brakel, *CRS*, 1:4.

2. What is the difference between God's preceptive will and his decretive will?
3. What two truths are protected by the difference between God's preceptive and decretive will?
4. Why does God have absolute authority over the entire world?
5. How can we define omnipotence?
6. Of the several applications given for God's sovereignty, which do you find most comforting?
7. Of these applications, which do you find most convicting? Why?
8. How does it affect the gospel if we deny that God rules over all events? Why?

16

God's Goodness and Love

Chapter Summary and Key Terms

The *goodness of God* is the moral excellence of all he is and does. Goodness includes mercy, grace, patience, love, truth, and righteousness. God's *mercy* is his kindness that moves him to show compassion to the suffering. His *grace* is his generosity to give favor and help to those who do not deserve it. His *patience* is his slowness to anger ("longsuffering"), waiting before punishing sinners and gladly forgiving those who repent. The *love of God* is his attribute of giving himself to others. The three persons of the Trinity love one another infinitely. God has a general love for all mankind and a special love for his people. God's *love of benevolence* is his kindness to his creatures, especially shown in sending his Son. His *love of complacency* is his delight in those whom he loves and has brought into saving union with Christ. (God's truth and righteousness are discussed in the next chapter.)

SOME PEOPLE WRONGLY THINK of the sovereign God as a harsh, distant, and coldhearted dictator. But the Bible celebrates his magnificent goodness. By his judgment on Egypt, God showed Israel that "I am the LORD" (Ex. 6:2–8; 10:2). The Israelites quickly turned aside from the Lord to worship an idol, but rather then destroying them, the Lord revealed his goodness (Ex. 33:19).

Stephen Charnock said, "Goodness is the brightness and loveliness of our majestic Creator. To imagine a God without it, is to imagine a miserable, [stingy], narrow-hearted, savage God, and so an unlovely [ugly] and horrible being; for he is not God that is not good."[1]

1 Charnock, *The Existence and Attributes of God*, in *WSChar*, 2:281.

The Bible's Words for God's Goodness

God tells of his "goodness" (Ex. 33:19) in a list of attributes: "The LORD, The LORD God, merciful and gracious, longsuffering, and abundant in goodness and truth" (34:6).

The Lord is "good," which means kind and forgiving (Pss. 25:8; 34:8; 136:1). God showed his goodness in the work of creation (Gen. 1:31). He showers it on his people so that they marvel at his great "goodness" (Pss. 31:19; 145:7). God's generosity to his creatures comes from his perfect goodness (Matt. 19:17). He is the supreme good, the infinite good, the source of all good, and the all-satisfying good (Pss. 4:6–7; 36:7–9; 73:25–28; Hab. 3:17–19). Herman Witsius said that God is a limitless fountain of all the good that a believer desires. In fact, he is far greater than what man desires or can even imagine.[2]

The word "merciful" is related to the term for a mother's womb. It means compassion, like that of a mother (or father) for a child (Ps. 103:13–14).[3] God's mercy is described as his "bowels" to communicate strong inner affection (Isa. 63:15; Jer. 31:20). In the New Testament, God is named "the Father of mercies" (2 Cor. 1:3). Richard Sibbes commented, "Everything that comes from God to his children, it is a mercy. It is as it were dipped in mercy before it comes to us."[4] The Lord's "mercy" is his compassion that moves him to act to help those in misery (Matt. 9:27; 20:30–31) or those vulnerable to misery (Matt. 18:33 ESV; 2 Tim. 1:18).

"Gracious" means showing unmerited favor and kindness, often to the poor or needy (Ex. 22:26–27; cf. Prov. 3:34). Mercy emphasizes the kindness shown to someone in misery; grace stresses free generosity to someone to whom the giver owes nothing. For the apostle Paul, grace is not merely God's good attitude to people. It is his loving purpose and power to save sinners through Christ (Rom. 3:24; 5:21; 6:14; 11:5–6). In addition to saving grace, there is serving grace, the free gift of power to serve (Eph. 3:7–8).

God is patient. The Lord describes himself in Exodus 34:6 as "longsuffering" or "slow to anger" (ESV). Such patience is the wisdom and moral

2 Herman Witsius, *Sacred Dissertations on the Apostles' Creed*, trans. Donald Fraser (1823; repr., Grand Rapids, MI: Reformation Heritage Books, 2010), 1:111.

3 *NIDOTTE*, 3:1093–95.

4 Sibbes, *A Learned Commentary or Exposition upon the First Chapter of the Second Epistle of S. Paul to the Corinthians*, in *WRS*, 3:30.

power to control oneself when one is offended (Prov. 14:29; 16:32). God desires to forgive rather than pay back wrong quickly (Num. 14:18; Neh. 9:17). If he intends to punish sin, he waits until the right time to execute justice (Nah. 1:2–3). John Calvin said that God "patiently waits for those who have sinned and invites them to repentance by his long-suffering. For this reason he is called 'slow to anger,' because he would not be severe unless man's wickedness required him to execute punishment on his sins."[5]

God loves people. When the Lord says he is "abundant in goodness" (Ex. 34:6), the word rendered as "goodness" (*khesed*) is more often translated as "kindness," "lovingkindness," or "steadfast love." It means faithful love and affectionate loyalty. It is God's unbreakable husbandly love for his bride (Isa. 54:5–10). This word appears in a common refrain of worship: "his mercy endureth for ever"; literally, "his love is forever."[6]

The Old Testament employs another term for God's love that also can be used for human affection. But his love is not a fickle passion like much human love. The Lord loves righteousness and justice (Ps. 33:5). He loves according to his sovereign choice of whom he will love and how he will show kindness to them (Deut. 4:37; 7:8; 10:15).

The New Testament mainly uses the word *agapē* to describe God's "love" in Christ. God demonstrated his love by sending his Son to die for lawless, wicked men (Rom. 5:6–10).

A Study of God's Love

"God is love" (1 John 4:8, 16). However, this does not mean that love is God. Nor does it mean that God is only love (and not other attributes such as power and justice). What it means is that love is his nature. Love fills God's attributes. His holiness is a loving holiness, and his love is a holy love. God is pure love—there is no evil in him. God's love is his very life—the infinite act of which his very essence consists. Therefore, no one has a saving relationship with God unless he or she, too, loves other people (vv. 7–8).

God's love means that even before creation there were relationships of self-giving within the Trinity: "The Father loveth the Son" (John 3:35). This love is the foundation of the partnership of the three persons of the

5 Calvin, *Comm.* on Ex. 34:5–7, language modernized.

6 Pss. 100:5; 106:1; 107:1; 118:1–4, 29; 136:1–26, etc.

Godhead in all of God's works (5:20). Christ is God's *beloved* Son (Matt. 3:17; 17:5; Col. 1:13). The Father's love for the Son in the Spirit is the infinite and eternal act of the whole life of God. Robert Traill said, "Where God the Father is the lover, and God the Son is the beloved, who can tell what that love is! . . . Here faith must believe and adore, and cry out, O the depths!"[7]

God loves people in both kindness and delight. His *love of benevolence* is his gracious and merciful kindness for people apart from what they deserve. Its highest display was Christ's death on the cross: "not that we loved God, but that he loved us" (1 John 4:10). God loved those whom he saved with "great love" when they were the objects of "wrath" (Eph. 2:3–4). Paul explains that God saved us because he is "rich in mercy, because of the great love with which he loved us" (v. 4 ESV). His love springs from the riches of his compassion for those in misery. Augustine noted, "In a wonderful and divine manner, even when he hated us, he loved us."[8]

God's *love of complacency* is his delight in those whom he loves. God rejoices in all his works (Ps. 104:31). This love especially appears in God's rejoicing in his Son and those united to him. The Father said to Christ, "Thou art my beloved Son; in thee I am well pleased" (Luke 3:22). Though God's grace to sinners is at its root the love of benevolence, in its fruits it includes God's pleasure in his people: "The Lord taketh pleasure in them that fear him, in those that hope in his mercy" (Ps. 147:11). Christ Jesus says, "He that hath my commandments, and keepeth them, he it is that loveth me: and he that loveth me shall be loved of my Father, and I will love him, and will manifest myself to him" (John 14:21). The saints please God with their good works (Col. 1:10; 3:20; 1 John 3:22). This is the pleasure of a kind Father who has counted his children righteous for Christ's sake and sent his Spirit into their hearts to produce sincere though imperfect obedience to his will.

We need to keep in mind both sides of God's love. The doctrine of God's love of benevolence guards the truth of salvation by grace alone. The doctrine of God's love of complacency encourages the saved to be holy to please God.

Since "God is love" (1 John 4:8), he is loving to all: "Every good gift . . . cometh down from the Father of lights" (James 1:17). However, God exercises sovereign freedom in how he loves each of his creatures. The Lord says,

7 Robert Traill, *Sixteen Sermons on the Lord's Prayer, in John XVII.24*, in *The Works of the Late Reverend Robert Traill* (Edinburgh: J. Ogle et al., 1810), 2:280.

8 Augustine, *On the Gospel of St. John*, 110.5, in *NPNF*[1], 7:411.

"I will have mercy on whom I will have mercy, and I will have compassion on whom I will have compassion" (Rom. 9:15; cf. Ex. 33:19).

God shows *universal goodness* to all his creatures: "The LORD is gracious, and full of compassion; slow to anger, and of great mercy. The LORD is good to all: and his tender mercies are over all his works" (Ps. 145:8–9).

God has a *general love* toward all humanity. He provides sunshine and rain for both the good and the wicked (Matt. 5:44–45; Luke 6:35–36). However, if sinners despise and abuse the goodness of God's general love by refusing to repent, the result will be God's pure wrath on them (Rom. 2:4–5).

In addition to God's general love for all men, the Bible reveals God's *special love* toward his chosen people (Rom. 1:7; 9:10–13; Col. 3:12). God the Father chose them in love (Eph. 1:3–5). God the Son loved his church in particular (5:25). He gave himself for each person in it individually (Gal. 2:20). In his special love for foolish, hateful sinners, God the Holy Spirit regenerates and renews them (Titus 3:3–6). This special love saves sinners to the end.

Practical Applications of God's Goodness and Love

The truths of God's goodness and love have very practical applications for believers.

First, *have absolute confidence that God is good.* Believe that those who trust in such a good God are blessed by him (Ps. 34:8). Trust in Christ as the supreme example of God's love and the only Mediator by whom you will be saved by his love (1 John 4:9–10).

Second, *turn from your sins and come to God in repentance.* He is good. He will welcome you and teach you his ways (Ps. 25:8). Then, by faith in his goodness, keep his commandments. Trust that his laws are for your good (Deut. 6:24; 10:13).

Third, *hope in God's love in the darkest times.* David said, "How long wilt thou forget me, O LORD? For ever? . . . But I have trusted in thy mercy" (Ps. 13:1, 5). Look to the cross for proof that God loves us. When God's providence hurts you deeply, see in Christ's hands and his side the marks of his love. Patiently bear your sorrows with confidence that he will give you all good things and work all things for your good (Rom. 8:28, 31–32).

Fourth, *love God for his goodness* (Luke 7:47; 1 John 4:19). Desire God as your supreme good (Ps. 73:25, 28). Meditate on the love of God and praise him until his love ignites your love.

Fifth, *imitate God's goodness to all.* Show kindness to the animals and even the plants that God created (Deut. 25:4; Prov. 12:10). Love all men, even your enemies (Matt. 5:44–45). Love others fervently and sacrificially in the church of Christ (Eph. 4:32; 1 Pet. 1:22).

Sixth, *worship God for his goodness and love.* This was the response of Moses when the Lord proclaimed his goodness and the greatness of his love: "Moses made haste, and bowed his head toward the earth, and worshipped" (Ex. 34:8). Sing to him, "For the Lord is good; his mercy is everlasting; and his truth endureth to all generations" (Ps. 100:5).

Suggested Song to Sing to the Lord

- Psalm 146, "Hallelujah, praise Jehovah," in *Psalter*, No. 400; *THBap*, No. 53

Questions for Meditation or Discussion

1. What passage of Scripture lists the attributes of God's goodness? What are they?
2. What is the difference between God's mercy and his grace? Give an example of each.
3. What does the Bible mean when it says that God is "longsuffering"?
4. What does the Hebrew word *khesed* mean?
5. When John says, "God is love" (1 John 4:8), what does he not mean? What does he mean?
6. What has God revealed about the Father's love for his Son in the Trinity?
7. What is God's love of benevolence and his love of complacency?
8. What basis is there in the Bible for saying that God has a general goodness toward all creatures?
9. What basis is there in the Bible for speaking of God's special love for his chosen people?
10. Select one of the applications of God's goodness and love listed at the end of this chapter. What are some key Scripture passages that support it? Read them and ask God for grace to make that application in your life and your church.

17

God's Truth and Righteousness

Chapter Summary and Key Terms

The goodness of God, his infinite moral excellence, includes his truth and righteousness. The *truth of God* means that he is real and reliable. He is the true God, not a fiction. He is true to reality in all that he thinks and says, without error or falsehood. He is faithful to act consistently with what he says. We can rest our souls in his perfect trustworthiness, for not one word of God can fail. The *righteousness of God*, also called his *justice*, means that he is the standard of moral perfection. God commands righteousness in his laws, rules in righteousness, brings righteous order among his people, and punishes acts contrary to righteousness. He honors righteousness in salvation, and trains and rewards his children in righteousness. God directs all things toward the most righteous end—namely, the display of his glory. Thus, we must walk in his righteous ways.

AS WE STUDIED IN THE LAST CHAPTER, God's goodness includes his mercy, grace, slowness to anger, and love (Ex. 33:19; 34:6). However, Moses's encounter with God's glory also shows us that he is "abundant in goodness and truth" and "will by no means clear the guilty" (34:6–7). Therefore, God's goodness includes his "truth" and faithfulness, and his righteousness and justice.

In this chapter, we will focus first on God's truth and faithfulness, and then on his righteousness and justice. A key Scripture text for these attributes is Deuteronomy 32:4: "He is the Rock, his work is perfect: for all his ways are judgment: a God of truth and without iniquity, just and right is he."

God's Truth

God is truth in three ways. First, he is truth because he is real, as opposed to all false gods, which are illusions. Moses says, "He is the Rock… a God of truth" (Deut. 32:4). But of the people who worship other gods, he says, "Their rock is not as our Rock. . . . Where are their gods, their rock in whom they trusted?" (vv. 31, 37).

Second, God is true in the sense of fidelity to the facts. Truth can mean the facts, such as truth proven in a court of law (Deut. 13:14; 17:4). God knows all things as they are. His words are without error, for truth is the opposite of lies and deceit (Prov. 12:19). God cannot lie.[1] God's word is truth in its fidelity to what is real and right (2 Sam. 7:28; 1 Kings 17:24). William Perkins said that Christ's word is "authentic, sufficient of itself, and needs no other confirmation." Christ "speaks the truth, according as everything is in itself, without error, deceit, or falsehood."[2]

Third, God lives, speaks, and acts with unfailing faithfulness, consistency, and integrity. Truth can mean being loving, faithful, and righteous. "True" frequently appears alongside "righteous" and "just" in the Bible (Ps. 19:9; Rev. 15:3). Lamentations 3:22–23 says, "It is of the Lord's mercies that we are not consumed, because his compassions fail not. They are new every morning: great is thy faithfulness."

The gospel of salvation is closely connected to God's truthfulness. The gospel is the "good news" that, in the fullness of time, God faithfully kept his word. He sent his Son into the world for our salvation. Christ came to the offspring of Abraham "for the truth of God, to confirm the promises made unto the fathers" (Rom. 15:8). The Lord Jesus says, "He that sent me is true" (John 7:28; 8:26). Whoever receives Christ's testimony affirms that "God is true" (3:33).

Caspar Olevianus said,

> So great and constant is the truth of God that one word of divine truth surpasses that of all the angels and people. . . . When, therefore, we are anxious or in doubt about something, why not see whether there is some word of Jehovah about that matter that has us perplexed? Once such a

1 Num. 23:19; 1 Sam. 15:29; Titus 1:2; Heb. 6:18.

2 Perkins, *A Godly and Learned Exposition or Commentary upon the Three First Chapters of the Revelation*, in *WWP*, 4:334, 595.

word has been found, we can give rest to our souls, knowing for certain that the slightest point of divine truth is more firm than the entire fabric of heaven and earth.[3]

The Bible's Words for God's Righteousness

"God is light" (1 John 1:5). In part, that means "he is faithful and just" (v. 9). He is pure of sin: "In him is no darkness at all" (v. 5). To find a description of God's moral perfection, we return to the key Scripture text we quoted earlier: "He is the Rock, his work is perfect: for all his ways are judgment: a God of truth and without iniquity, just and right is he" (Deut. 32:4). Let's consider the different words used here for righteousness.

The word translated as "perfect" means "whole" and "complete." It was used of a sacrificial animal "without blemish" (Ex. 12:5; Lev. 1:3). David says, "As for God, his way is perfect; the word of the LORD is tried: he is a buckler to all them that trust in him. For who is God, save the LORD? And who is a rock, save our God?" (2 Sam. 22:31–32; Ps. 18:30–31). God's perfection means that his acts display the fullness of moral excellency in flawless beauty. God is "without iniquity," or utterly sinless (Deut. 32:4).

God's "judgment" is his justice. The Hebrew term refers to the character, decisions, and acts of a good judge. Abraham said that it would be far from God "to slay the righteous with the wicked: and that the righteous should be as the wicked. . . . Shall not the Judge of all the earth do right?" (Gen. 18:25).

God loves justice (Pss. 33:5; 37:28; 99:4). All justice is from him and belongs to him (Deut. 1:17). His justice is infinitely great (Ps. 36:6). Justice is the foundation of his throne (89:14; 97:2). John Calvin said, "It [is] impossible for God, who is the Judge of the world, . . . [to] in the least degree swerve from righteousness."[4]

As noted above, God is also said to be "just" (Deut. 32:4), a word meaning "righteous." All of God's character, words, and actions are righteous: "The righteous LORD loveth righteousness" (Ps. 11:7). "All the words of my mouth are righteous; there is nothing twisted or crooked in them" (Prov. 8:8 ESV). "The LORD is righteous in all his ways" (Ps. 145:17). God never does wrong (Job 8:3; 34:10, 12).

3 Caspar Olevianus, *An Exposition of the Apostles' Creed*, trans. Lyle D. Bierma (Grand Rapids, MI: Reformation Heritage Books, 2009), 24.

4 Calvin, *Comm.* on Gen. 18:25.

The word translated as "right" or "upright" (Deut. 32:4; Pss. 25:8; 92:15) literally means straight as opposed to crooked. God's Word is the straight-edge, the plumb line, and the laser level of right and wrong. It is the standard to which all should be compared (Pss. 19:8; 33:4; 111:8; 119:137).

A Study of God's Righteousness

God's righteousness or justice comes to us like a diamond with many sparkling facets.

First, *God reveals his righteousness in his laws.* Righteousness fulfills a moral standard, particularly God's law (Deut. 6:25). The law is his revelation of righteousness for mankind (4:8; Ps. 19:9). Human righteousness consists of keeping God's commandments (Ezek. 18:5–9; Matt. 5:17–20).

God's law is not a higher power over him. It is a display of his own righteousness: "Righteous art thou, O Lord, and upright are thy judgments. Thy testimonies that thou hast commanded are righteous and very faithful" (Ps. 119:137–138). George Swinnock said, "The law or rule of God's justice is within him, yea, it is himself; he is his own law."[5]

Therefore, let us resist every temptation to despise God's law. Let us never accuse his law of being harsh or unrealistic. Rather, let us humble ourselves to receive its correction.

Second, *God works righteously according to his covenant.* God's faithful dealings with Israel revealed his righteousness: "Thou art the Lord the God, who didst choose Abram . . . and madest a covenant with him . . . and hast performed thy words; for thou art righteous" (Neh. 9:7–8). God punished the people of Israel, and they had to confess, "Thou art just in all that is brought upon us; for thou hast done right, but we have done wickedly" (v. 33).

God's righteousness appears in his faithful keeping of his promises of grace (Ps. 103:17–18) and threats of punishment (Dan. 9:14). We may not understand why God is doing what he is doing. But we can know for sure that he always keeps his Word, for he is righteous.

Third, *God orders the community of his people with righteousness.* In his righteousness, he defines proper behavior and right relationships among

5 George Swinnock, *The Incomparableness of God*, in *The Works of George Swinnock*, 5 vols. (1868; repr., Edinburgh: Banner of Truth, 1992), 4:412.

people. Justice requires fairness in business. The Lord says, "Just balances, just weights, a just ephah, and a just hin, shall ye have" (Lev. 19:36). Justice also requires treating all people without prejudice. In doing so, it guards against the abuse of power and the oppression of the vulnerable (Deut. 10:17–18). God's justice is the foundation of human rights (Job 29:13–17).

Fourth, *God will punish the wicked with his righteous judgments*. His righteous punishment of the wicked arises from his justice: "Upon the wicked he shall rain snares, fire and brimstone, and an horrible tempest: this shall be the portion of their cup. For the righteous Lord loveth righteousness" (Ps. 11:6–7).

God hates sin and those who commit it (Lev. 26:30; Deut. 12:31; Ps. 5:4–5). His justice pays back the wicked for their hatred of God and rebellion against his law (cf. Rom. 8:7). Paul says, "For the *wages* of sin is death" (6:23), and, "They which commit such things are *worthy* of death" (1:32).

Fifth, *God glorifies his righteousness in salvation*. God saves people in a way that glorifies his moral perfection, so his salvation can be called "righteousness" (Isa. 51:5–8).

In justification, God satisfies his justice by Christ's death for the sins of his people (Isa. 53:6). They are redeemed, and God's wrath is appeased (Rom. 3:21–26). They are counted righteous for Christ's obedience (5:19).

In sanctification, Christ establishes his kingdom of justice by working in believers by the power of the Holy Spirit (Isa. 9:6–7; 11:1–5). Believers have died with Christ to sin and live for righteousness (Rom. 6:2–6; 1 Pet. 2:24).

We must never be content unless we know that we have this double grace. Are you looking to Christ alone for your justification by a Spirit-worked faith? Are you sincerely, though imperfectly, obeying Christ by Spirit-worked holiness? Only in justification and sanctification do we fully honor God's righteousness.

Sixth, *the righteous Father disciplines and rewards his children*. Christ, when praying for his people, addressed God as the "righteous Father" (John 17:24–25). The Father disciplines every son or daughter whom he loves (Heb. 12:5). He trains them for maturity to be "partakers of his holiness" (v. 10).

The Father also rewards his children for their love and obedience with treasure in his heavenly kingdom (Matt. 6:4, 6, 18–20). "For God is not unrighteous to forget your work and labour of love, which ye have shewed toward his name, in that ye have ministered to the saints, and do minister" (Heb. 6:10). God's fatherly gifts are not based on any merit in his children—they are the reward of grace. He rewards them because he is their Father and he loves them (Luke 12:32; 17:10). Therefore, to strive after the Father's reward is not legalistic or selfish. It is the heart of a child to long to please his or her father and to hear him say, "Well done."

Seventh, *God's righteousness aims at the display of his glory.* Justice demands that our highest goal be the greatest good—and no good can be greater than the glory of God. The Lord has sworn an oath "in righteousness" that to him every knee will bow and every tongue will confess allegiance (Isa. 45:22–23). He called his Servant "in righteousness" to give sight to the blind and freedom to the prisoners, and declared, "I am the LORD: that is my name: and my glory will I not give to another, neither my praise to graven images" (42:6–8).

Let us begin to sing the praises of God's righteousness now. Such worship is a foretaste of the new heaven and the new earth, where righteousness dwells (2 Pet. 3:13):

> O sing unto the LORD a new song; for he hath done marvellous things: his right hand, and his holy arm, hath gotten him the victory. The LORD hath made known his salvation: his righteousness hath he openly shewed in the sight of the heathen. . . . For he cometh to judge the earth: with righteousness shall he judge the world, and the people with equity. (Ps. 98:1–2, 9)

Practical Applications of God's Truth and Righteousness

We close this chapter with some thoughts on how to apply God's beautiful, magnificent attributes of truth and righteousness to our lives.

First, *rest your hope on the rock, the God who is real.* David exulted, "The LORD is my rock, and my fortress, and my deliverer; my God, my strength, in whom I will trust; my buckler, and the horn of my salvation, and my high tower" (Ps. 18:2).

Second, *believe all that God says in his Word, both promises and threats.* Build your life on them. Jesus Christ says, "Therefore whosoever heareth these sayings of mine, and doeth them, I will liken him unto a wise man, which built his house upon a rock" (Matt. 7:24).

Third, *imitate God's faithfulness by keeping your word.* Paul says, "But as God is true, our word toward you was not yea and nay" (2 Cor. 1:18). Say what you mean and do what you say.

Fourth, *receive the righteousness of God in Jesus Christ as your salvation.* Paul summarizes his confidence in the gospel: "For I am not ashamed of the gospel of Christ: for it is the power of God unto salvation to every one that believeth. . . . For therein is the righteousness of God revealed from faith to faith: as it is written, The just shall live by faith" (Rom. 1:16–17).

Fifth, *walk in the righteousness of keeping God's commandments.* "Praise ye the Lord. Blessed is the man that feareth the Lord, that delighteth greatly in his commandments. His seed shall be mighty upon earth: the generation of the upright shall be blessed. Wealth and riches shall be in his house: and his righteousness endureth for ever" (Ps. 112:1–3).

Suggested Song to Sing to the Lord

- Psalm 119, "Forever settled in the heav'ns," in *Psalter*, No. 332; *THBap*, No. 54

Questions for Meditation or Discussion

1. In what three ways is God the truth? How is each shown in the Bible?
2. How did God show his faithfulness by the incarnation and work of Jesus Christ?
3. How does your faith in the Lord reflect his faithfulness? How does it not?
4. What is the meaning of each word used of God's righteousness in Deuteronomy 32:4?
5. How is God's righteousness related to his law?
6. How does God execute righteousness according to his covenant?
7. How did Christ's cross demonstrate God's justice?
8. How does God the Father show justice in his discipline of his children?
9. Do you have a hearty anticipation that the Father will reward you? Why or why not?
10. How does God's justice relate to his glory?

18

God's Affections and Impassibility

Chapter Summary and Key Terms

The *affections of God* toward us are his attitudes and actions expressing his attributes in a way similar to human emotions. God's *jealousy* expresses his ardent love for his glory and his people. That does not imply that God has the evil jealousy often seen in human beings. God has no *passions* and does not pass through changing emotional states, as is taught in the doctrine of his *impassibility*. By passions, we mean emotions not regulated by wisdom, righteousness, and peace. By impassibility, we mean the immutability of God's affections. The *beatitude of God* is his possession of infinite joy because of the fullness of his perfection and his sovereignty over the world to manifest his glory in it. The *wrath of God* is the affection of God's justice against sin and his will to punish sinners. God's *compassion* is the affection of his mercy to the suffering. He delights to show kindness to those in misery. But God's compassion implies no physical feelings or suffering in him. He remains the eternal and unchangeable Lord.

GOD IS FULL OF AMAZING goodness and beauty. We saw that in the previous two chapters as we explored the divine attributes listed in Exodus 34:6–7 and Deuteronomy 32:4. These attributes lead us to consider God's affections. Just as human love involves human affections, so God's infinite love involves his infinite affections.

God is spirit (John 4:24). John Gill observed that our spirits are like God in that they have "understanding, will, and affections." He noted, "God not only loves his creatures, but is love itself (1 John 4:16). His mercy is from everlasting to everlasting, on them that fear him; and he pities them as a father pities his children (Ps. 103:13, 17)." These attributes are different from our affections because they never disturb God. But, as Gill said, they "may be called affections" because they are "similar to affections in intelligent beings."[1]

God's affections toward his creatures are not his attributes themselves, but his attitudes and actions according to his attributes. Thus, God's affection of wrath is his attitude and action toward sinners according to his attribute of righteousness. His affection of compassion is his attitude and action toward sufferers according to his attribute of love. His affection of joy is his attitude and action toward all in creation that reflects his perfections, according to his beatitude, or his complete happiness in himself.

God's Jealousy: The Intensity of His Affections

The Lord tells us that he is "a jealous God" (Ex. 20:5; 34:14). The Bible warns that human jealousy can be evil and lead to destructive anger (Pss. 37:1; 73:3; James 3:14, 16; 4:2). On the other hand, righteous jealousy burns for the glory of God's Word and worship (Pss. 69:9; 119:139). Jesus Christ displayed this affection when he took a whip and cleared the temple (John 2:17). "Jealous" can mean "zealous" in a positive sense. God's jealousy is like a husband's love for his wife (Ezek. 16:38) or a warrior's energy to fight for what is right (Isa. 42:13).

God's jealousy stirs up his wrath to punish sinners (Ex. 20:5; Nah. 1:2) and his mercy to save his people (Isa. 59:17). It is the fiery energy of his holiness (Josh. 24:19). He says he "will be jealous for [his] holy name" so that he will be "sanctified" in the sight of men and they will "know that I am the LORD" (Ezek. 39:25, 27–28). We can define God's jealousy as his limitless, fervent zeal to glorify himself. God is not half-hearted in anything that he wills. His very essence is an eternal act of infinite love (1 John 4:8).

Therefore, we should cultivate godly affections as much as possible in order to love God with great zeal. Jonathan Edwards said, "True religion, in great part, consists in holy affections."[2] God's jealousy should move us to love him exclusively as our only Bridegroom (2 Cor. 11:2). We should

1 John Gill, *A Complete Body of Doctrinal and Practical Divinity* (1839; repr. Paris, AR: The Baptist Standard Bearer, 1995), 33, 78.

2 Edwards, *Religious Affections*, in *WJE*, 2:95.

fear committing spiritual adultery by giving our hearts to this world (James 4:1–5). Biblical zeal will not make us wild, but wise, meek, and diligent (Rom. 12:11–12). God's grace trains us to live "soberly, righteously, and godly, in this present world," and to be "zealous of good works" as we wait in hope of the glory of God (Titus 2:12, 14).

God's Impassibility: The Immutability of His Affections

Human affections and emotions are often passions. By *passions*, we mean disturbing feelings that lead us to act foolishly or sinfully. God, however, is "without body, parts, or passions."[3] There is never any sin, suffering, or change in God. Instead, his affections express his perfections in relation to particular people and situations. Our emotions are only faint and changing shadows of his perfect affections. God's *impassibility*, or lack of passions, means that his affections are sovereign and immutable.

Antonius Thysius wrote of "God's good affections (which in human beings are the passions)," saying that they are "nothing other than God's ardent will towards us, and its power and effect in creatures."[4] The word *ardent* means "burning, fiery, or hot." God's love, for instance, is strong, zealous, and energetic.

But God's love is eternal. It never changes. "God is love"—not just what he does but who he is—in the simplicity of his being (1 John 4:8). His faithful love is "from everlasting to everlasting" (Ps. 103:17). As we saw when we studied God's immutability, he says, "I am the Lord, I change not" (Mal. 3:6).

In light of God's simplicity, infinity, eternity, and immutability, we cannot say that his affections toward us mean that he changes as we change. However, God does have distinct affections with respect to events at different points in time. His eternity does not stop him from knowing what takes place in time or having real relationships with people in time. God has a distinct attitude toward each person at each point in time as appropriate to his holy nature.

Consider a woman who lives in unbelief for some years. She then turns to Christ in true conversion. For the rest of her life, she follows him through

3 The Thirty-Nine Articles (Art. 1), the Westminster Confession of Faith (2.1), and the Second London Baptist Confession (2.1), in *RC*, 2:754; 4:236–37, 535.

4 Polyander, Walaeus, Thysius, and Rivetus, *SPT*, 6.39 (1:177).

many trials. God's affections toward her are many. He has wrath toward her before her conversion. His mercy leads her to salvation. He delights in her repentance. As his child, she is the object of his compassion in her suffering. He is displeased with her remaining sins. He rejoices at her sincere but imperfect obedience.

But God is not passing through time day by day as we are. He is entirely present with each person at every point of space and time, yet he is not limited by space and time. We are changing but he is not.

Sound theology requires biblical balance. There are different views of God's impassibility. It is best to believe both that God has affections and that he never changes. R. C. Sproul said, "We must not let a speculative form of impassibility strip God of his personal attributes, especially his attribute of love. . . . If he has no capacity for affection, he has no capacity for love."[5] Herman Bavinck said, "Without losing himself, God can give himself, and, while absolutely maintaining his immutability, he can enter into an infinite number of relations with his creatures."[6]

God's impassibility reminds us that it is good, even Godlike, to have affections, as long as those affections are righteous and pure. We should cultivate holy affections as fruit of the Holy Spirit. On the other hand, God's impassibility also reminds us that we should not be ruled by disorderly passions. Our affections should be steady and consistent, as is appropriate for each situation. We are not immutable like God. But we can reflect his immutability by being faithful and stable in our characters and attitudes.

God's Beatitude: The Joy of His Affections

God reveals himself in the Holy Scriptures to be limitless in his pleasure and joy. The boundless happiness of God is called his *beatitude*. He is infinitely "blessed" (1 Tim. 1:11; 6:15). God's love, faithfulness, righteousness, and justice are great beyond all measure. As a result, he has "abundant" satisfaction, a "river" of pleasure, and "the fountain of life" (Ps. 36:5–9). In his presence are "honour and majesty," "strength and beauty" (96:6). He needs nothing outside of himself to be happy, for he is sufficient in himself, being a bottomless fountain of good (1 Chron. 29:10–12; Jer. 2:13). As Augustine

5 R. C. Sproul, *Loved by God* (Nashville: Word, 2001), 133.

6 Bavinck, *RD*, 2:159.

said, God is the fullness and unfailing abundance of unfading joy.[7] Since he is the eternally blessed King, there is no unhappiness in him. God loves but is never upset. He is jealous but free from worry. He changes his ways but is never sorry. He is angry yet always peaceful.[8]

God has pleasure in those who fear him and hope in him (Ps. 147:11). But that does not mean they give him some benefit or increase his happiness. Job 22:3 says, "Is it any pleasure to the Almighty, that thou art righteous? Or is it gain to him, that thou makest thy ways perfect?" God's joy is in giving us all good. He has pleasure in saving his people by grace (Jer. 32:40–41): "He delighteth in mercy" (Mic. 7:18).

God's joy encourages us to seek to please him. We should strive to keep his commandments so that we may be near him (John 14:21, 23). His delight in his own perfections should attract us to rejoice in him "with joy unspeakable and full of glory" (1 Pet. 1:8).

Knowing God's unchanging happiness should give us invincible hope. If we belong to Jesus Christ, then our destiny is to dwell in the glory of the eternally happy God (Rom. 5:2). We will spend unending ages discovering the infinitely beautiful affections of God as we fellowship with him through his Son. Set your heart on this hope, and your soul will feast daily.

God's Wrath: The Justice of His Affections

God's wrath is his holy hatred of or ardent will to punish all who transgress his law. It is his burning justice against sin. God says, "If your soul abhor my judgments, so that ye will not do all my commandments," then "my soul shall abhor you" (Lev. 26:15, 28, 30). The just God loves righteousness and hates sin (Ps. 11:5–7).

The anger of God is his attitude to all sin and only to sin: "The wrath of God is revealed from heaven against all ungodliness and unrighteousness of men" (Rom. 1:18). However, his anger does not burst out in foolish, wicked rage: "The day of wrath" is the day of the "revelation of the righteous judgment of God; who will render to every man according to his deeds" (2:5–6).

The severity of God's wrath goes hand in hand with the sweetness of his goodness (Nah. 1:6–7; Rom. 11:22). We should not accuse God of

7 Augustine, *Confessions*, 2.6.13, in *NPNF*[1], 1:58.
8 Augustine, *Confessions*, 1.4.4, in *NPNF*[1], 1:46.

cruelty—it is only the evil of our sins that makes his wrath so strong. God's wrath is "his strange work" (Isa. 28:21). The Bible says, "God is love" (1 John 4:8); it never says, "God is wrath." Strictly speaking, wrath is not an attribute of God's nature. It is the attitude and exercise of his justice against sin.

In some Scripture passages, God's displeasure with sin is expressed in terms of his grief (Gen. 6:6; Ps. 78:40; Isa. 63:10). However, this is a human metaphor for God's wrath. These Scripture passages do not speak of harm done to God by sinners, as if he were in pain. But God's displeasure does harm to sinners. Edward Leigh said that God "cannot be hurt, for that were a weakness; but he may be wronged, for that is no weakness, but a fruit of excellency."[9]

God has holy joy even in his wrath. He does not enjoy hurting his creatures (Lam. 3:33; Ezek. 33:11). But he rejoices in his justice when he executes the law's curse on sinners (Deut. 28:15, 63). His wrath is not a passion that upsets him, for it arises from invincible sovereignty and wisdom (Ps. 2:4–6; Jer. 10:10–12).

Few people think about God's anger against sin. Most people, acting in unrighteousness, obstruct the truth of God and do not fear him (Rom. 1:18; 3:18). We foolishly fear men who can do no more than kill the body, but not the God who is able to destroy both soul and body in hell (Matt. 10:28). Our first response to God's wrath should be to cast off all hypocrisy and run to Christ in true repentance and faith (Luke 3:7–8). Christ alone can rescue us from the wrath that is to come; all other so-called saviors are mere idols (1 Thess. 1:9–10).

The doctrine of God's wrath does not make us vengeful. It releases us from bitterness. Paul says, "Dearly beloved, avenge not yourselves, but rather give place unto wrath: for it is written, Vengeance is mine; I will repay, saith the Lord" (Rom 12:19).

We honor the wrath of God by appealing to civil authorities to punish criminals. These authorities are God's servants "to execute wrath upon him that doeth evil" (Rom. 13:1, 4).

Since God's wrath is his ardent justice, loving God will make us more concerned for justice (Ps. 119:53, 136). We can love justice even as we

9 Edward Leigh, *A Treatise of Divinity* (London: by E. Griffin for William Lee, 1646), 2:75.

grow in meekness, becoming more like Christ (1 Pet. 2:23). The knowledge of God's wrath against oppression should make us advocates for the oppressed, insofar as we have the power to help them (Job 29:12–17; Prov. 31:8–9).

God's Compassion: The Mercy of His Affections

God is unchangeable in his perfect happiness. But he loves and comforts the hurting. As Justin Martyr said, God is "impassible," yet he cares deeply about the repentance and salvation of men, for he is not "like a stone."[10] This is his *compassion*. This affection does not cause him any suffering. It is his special kindness for the suffering (Ex. 22:27; Deut. 10:18; Ps. 10:17–18), especially his suffering people (Deut. 32:10; Acts 9:4).

God knows his people's suffering with a compassionate will to support and deliver them. When the people of Israel were enslaved in Egypt, the Lord heard their cries, saw their situation, knew their sorrow, and came down to save them (Ex. 2:23–25; 3:7–8, 16). Isaiah looked back to the exodus and wrote, "In all their affliction he was afflicted, and the angel of his presence saved them: in his love and in his pity he redeemed them; and he bare them, and carried them all the days of old" (Isa. 63:9). It is as though God counted his people's oppression in Egypt as his own. But God did not save Israel to relieve himself of pain that he was suffering. Rather, his choice to be "afflicted" with his suffering people means that his "love" and "pity" for them moved him to rescue them.

Some theologians have said that Christ's cross reveals the suffering of God. But this is not true. Rather, the cross reveals God's grace in the incarnate Mediator. Christ crucified is one person with two natures, fully divine and fully human. As God, the Son is immutable and immortal (Heb. 1:12)—he cannot suffer. He had to become a partaker of human flesh and blood so that in his human nature he could suffer and die as the atoning sacrifice for his brothers (2:14, 17). Now we have a Savior who is able to sympathize with us, for he knows what it is to suffer as a man in this world (4:15).

The kind affection of the Lord should draw us like a magnet to seek him in all our sorrows. Psalm 34:17–18 says, "The righteous cry, and the LORD heareth, and delivereth them out of all their troubles. The LORD is nigh

10 Justin Martyr, *First Apology*, chaps. 25, 28, in *ANF*, 1:171–72.

unto [near to] them that are of a broken heart; and saveth such as be of a contrite spirit."

If God the Son was willing to become human in order to suffer with his brothers, how much more should we be willing to enter the sufferings of our fellow men and women insofar as is necessary to love them! Let us therefore "rejoice with them that do rejoice, and weep with them that weep" (Rom. 12:15). The more we do so, the more we will become finite human images of the glorious living God. And one day, Jesus will wipe every tear from our eyes and welcome us into his glory.

Suggested Songs to Sing to the Lord

- Psalm 102, "The Lord has heard and answered prayer," in *Psalter*, No. 273, stanzas 5–7; *THBap*, No. 25
- "Lord, with glowing heart I'd praise thee," in *THBap*, No. 69

Questions for Meditation or Discussion

1. In what sense is God jealous, according to the Bible?
2. What does *impassibility* mean?
3. What is God's beatitude? Demonstrate this doctrine from the Holy Scriptures.
4. Why is it important for the Christian faith that we believe that God is infinitely happy?
5. How do God's affections encourage us to glorify him and enjoy him forever?
6. How do the Holy Scriptures show that God's wrath is personal and righteous?
7. How can God be angry against sin and yet not change or be disturbed?
8. Which of the following statements describes you? (More than one may apply.)

    - I don't believe in God's wrath against sin.
    - I believe in God's wrath, but he has never been angry against me.
    - I deserve God's wrath, even to the point of deserving hell.
    - I am afraid that I will be punished forever by God's wrath.

- I have been rescued by Christ from God's wrath and will never have to face it.
- I am not bitter, for I trust in God's wrath to deal justly with those who wrong me.
- I approve of God's wrath and share in his love for justice and hatred of sin.

9. How would you summarize what the Bible says about God's compassion?
10. How are you showing compassion of both heart and action toward people in need?

19

The Trinity, Part 1: The Son and the Holy Spirit

Chapter Summary and Key Terms

The *doctrine of the Trinity* is the teaching that the one true God eternally exists as three persons. The Father, the Son, and the Holy Spirit are distinct persons, yet they share one divine nature, so each is fully God. Both the Son and the Holy Spirit are God, as the Bible makes clear by their divine names, attributes, actions, relationships, and other factors. *Arianism* claimed that God the Father created the Son. This teaching was condemned as heresy by the Council of Nicaea, which declared that the Son is the "same in essence" (*homoousion*) with the Father. The Father did not create the Son at a point in time but "begets" him by *eternal generation*. The Holy Spirit is also a distinct person. The Father and the Son "breathe" the Spirit in his *eternal procession* from them. Thus, he shares the same divine life and essence as they do.

WHEN JESUS CHRIST WAS BAPTIZED in the River Jordan, we read that "straightway coming up out of the water, he saw the heavens opened, and the Spirit like a dove descending upon him: and there came a voice from heaven, saying, Thou art my beloved Son, in whom I am well pleased" (Mark 1:10–11). Here, at "the beginning of the gospel of Jesus Christ" (v. 1), we encounter the Father, the Son, and the Holy Spirit. These three persons act as one God in Christ's mission.

The gospel cannot be separated from the doctrine of the Trinity (Titus 3:4–6). Paul says, "When the fulness of the time was come, God sent forth his Son, made of a woman, made under the law, to redeem them that were under the law, that we might receive the adoption of sons. And because ye are sons, God hath sent forth the Spirit of his Son into your hearts, crying, Abba, Father" (Gal. 4:4–6). Every person of the Trinity works for our salvation.

The word *trinity* does not appear in the Bible. But the doctrine of the Trinity may be summarized by truths taught in the Bible. There is one God, who is the Father, the Son, and the Holy Spirit. The Father is God. The Son is God. The Holy Spirit is God. The Father, the Son, and the Holy Spirit are three persons. The Son is the only begotten Son of the Father. The Spirit proceeds from the Father and the Son.

In this chapter, we begin our consideration of the doctrine of the Trinity by looking at who the Son and the Holy Spirit are.

The Son of God Is God

Clearly, the Father is God (John 17:11; 1 Cor. 8:6; James 1:17). However, we must prove from the Holy Scriptures that the Son is God.

In the fourth century, the church needed to respond to *Arianism*. According to that heresy, Christ had a beginning. If that were true, Christ would be one of God's creations, and therefore different from God. The false doctrine of Arianism continues today in religious groups such as the Jehovah's Witnesses.

The Council of Nicaea (AD 325) declared the church's faith in "one Lord Jesus Christ, the Son of God, the only-begotten of the Father, that is of the substance [*ousia*] of the Father; God of God and Light of light; true God of true God; begotten, not made, consubstantial [*homoousion*] with the Father."[1] The Greek word *homoousion* means "the same in essence." Athanasius of Alexandria was a great defender of this truth, for he understood that salvation hinged on the Son's being God, for only God could redeem sinners and glorify them.[2]

Arguments for the Deity of Christ

We present seven arguments to show that Christ, the Son of God, is fully God himself.

1 Cited in Socrates Scholasticus, *Ecclesiastical History*, 1.8, in *NPNF*², 2:10.

2 Athanasius, *On the Incarnation of the Word*, secs. 7–9, in *NPNF*², 4:39–41.

First, *the preexistence of Christ proves that he is God.* Christ was living and active before he came into this world as a human being (Mic. 5:2). Jesus says, "I came down from heaven, not to do mine own will, but the will of him that sent me" (John 6:38). He even says, "Before Abraham was, I am" (8:58). The Son was with the Father before the foundation of the world (17:5, 24). John says, "In the beginning was the Word" (1:1). Christ is the "Alpha and Omega, the beginning and the end, the first and the last" (Rev. 22:13).

Second, *the prophecies about Christ prove that he is God.* The prophets foretold that God himself would come to his people (Isa. 40:3, 5, 9–10; Mal. 3:1–6). These prophecies were fulfilled when Jesus came (Mark 1:1–9). The prophets also taught that the Christ to come would be the Lord and God. David said, "The LORD said unto my Lord, Sit thou at my right hand, until I make thine enemies thy footstool" (Ps. 110:1). Isaiah foretold that the child to be born would be the "mighty God" (Isa. 9:6).

Third, *the names of Christ prove that he is God.* He is the "Son" of the Father (Mark 1:1, 11; 9:7). He is not just an adopted son, but someone with a unique relationship to God the Father. Jesus says, "No man knoweth the Son, but the Father; neither knoweth any man the Father, save the Son, and he to whomsoever the Son will reveal him" (Matt. 11:27). The Bible also names Christ "God":[3] "The Word was God" (John 1:1).[4] The New Testament often calls Christ the "Lord," such as the "Lord of glory" (1 Cor. 2:8), the "Lord of lords" (1 Tim. 6:15; Rev. 17:14; 19:16), and the "Lord of all" (Acts 10:36). When the New Testament quotes Old Testament statements about "the LORD" (Jehovah) and applies them to Jesus as "Lord," God's Word is calling Jesus "Jehovah."[5]

Fourth, *the attributes of Christ prove that he is God.* He has the attributes of holiness (Acts 3:14), eternity (John 8:58), sovereign power (Matt. 8:26),

3 Isa. 9:6; John 20:28; Rom. 9:5; Titus 2:13; Heb. 1:8; 2 Pet. 1:1.

4 The Jehovah's Witnesses mistranslate the last clause of John 1:1 as "the Word was a god," noting that the Greek definite article is not present before the word translated as "God" by the King James Version and most other translations. *The Kingdom Interlinear Translation of the Greek Scriptures* (Brooklyn, NY: Watchtower Bible and Tract Society of New York, 1985), 401, 1139. But if we translated the Bible in this way, we would have to read "a god" in John 1:6, 12, 13, 18, too. The Greek language often omits the definite article, especially in a predicate nominative that precedes the verb, as in John 1:1.

5 Rom. 10:9, 13; 14:9–12; Phil. 2:10–11; 1 Thess. 1:8–9; Heb. 1:10–12.

infinite knowledge (John 16:30), omnipresence (Matt. 28:20), self-existence (John 5:26), and immutability (Heb. 1:10–12). When we examine these divine attributes of Christ, we are led to confess with Paul, "In him dwelleth all the fulness of the Godhead bodily" (Col. 2:9).

Fifth, *the relationships of Christ prove that he is God.* He is the only begotten Son of the Father (John 3:16). Also, the Spirit of God is the Spirit of the Son (Gal. 4:6). We will discuss these relationships more later.

Sixth, *the actions of Christ prove that he is God.* The Son is the sovereign author of election (Matt. 24:31; John 15:19). The work of creation is the work of God alone (Isa. 44:24), but it was done not by the Father alone but also by the Son. John writes, "All things were made by him; and without him was not any thing made that was made" (John 1:3; cf. 1 Cor. 8:6; Col. 1:16; Heb. 1:2, 10). Christ also engages in God's work of providence: "By him all things consist" (Col. 1:17). He is "upholding all things by the word of his power" (Heb. 1:3). The Lord Jesus demonstrates his deity by working miracles by a mere word (Matt. 8:8–9, 16, 26–27, 31–32). Christ gives forgiveness of sins (Mark 2:5, 7, 10), which only God can do (Isa. 43:25; Mic. 7:18). Christ raises sinners from spiritual death to life (John 5:24–25). He pours out the promised Spirit on the church, a work that is said to be God's (Joel 2:28–29; Acts 2:16–18, 33). Christ guards those whom he saves so that "they shall never perish" (John 10:28). He will raise the dead on the last day when he judges all men (5:27–29). Stephen Wellum says, "In the Bible's presentation of Christ, he is in an entirely different category than any created thing. Jesus alone is identified with the Creator-Covenant Lord in all his actions, character, and work."[6]

Seventh, *the honors of Christ prove that he is God.* People rightly pray to Christ.[7] Men and angels rightly worship Christ.[8] We should give our worship not to any creature, not even to an apostle or angel, but to God alone.[9]

Christ is fully God. Do you worship him? It is one thing to acknowledge his deity as a doctrine, but another thing to see his glory with the eyes of your heart. Meditate on Christ and pray for the Spirit to show you his glory.

6 Stephen Wellum, *Christ Alone: The Uniqueness of Jesus as Savior: What the Reformers Taught . . . and Why It Still Matters,* The Five Solas Series (Grand Rapids, MI: Zondervan, 2017), 56.

7 John 14:13–14; Acts 7:59; Rom. 10:9, 13; 1 Cor. 1:2.

8 Matt. 2:1–12; 14:33; John 5:23; Heb. 1:6; Rev. 5:9, 12–13.

9 Matt. 4:9–10; Acts 10:25–26; Rev. 19:10; 22:8–9.

The Eternal Generation of the Son

We distinguish the Son from the Father and the Spirit by his eternal generation. That is, the Father begets the Son without a beginning in time. The Westminster Confession of Faith says, "In the unity of the Godhead there [are] three persons, of one substance, power, and eternity: God the Father, God the Son, and God the Holy Ghost: the Father is of none, neither begotten, nor proceeding; the Son is eternally begotten of the Father; the Holy Ghost eternally proceeding from the Father and the Son."[10] The verb *to beget* refers to a father's act of producing a child. The Father's generation of the Son is not a work of creation, for both are eternal. However, the Father is always the Father of the Son.

Several passages in the writings of John speak of God's Son as the "only begotten" of the Father.[11] Several English translations since the mid-twentieth century have rendered the word translated as "only begotten" simply as "only." But the term is often used for an only child born to a parent.[12] In every context where John uses the term, it refers to God's Son and contrasts him as God's natural Son to people "born" or "begotten" of God by his saving grace.[13] Therefore, in its literal sense, the meaning of the word is "only begotten."[14]

Christ is God's Son in a unique (Matt. 11:27; Rom. 8:32) and eternal (John 17:24) manner. In a natural father-son relationship, the son is from the father. The Gospel of John teaches that Christ is "of" or "from" the Father.[15] Christ says, "For as the Father hath life in himself; so hath he given to the Son to have life in himself" (5:26). The Son is the Father's "Word" (1:1) and "image" (Col. 1:15–16), "the brightness of his glory and the express image" of him (Heb. 1:3). As the Nicene Creed says, Christ is "God of God."[16]

10 The Westminster Confession of Faith (2.3), in *RC*, 4:237. See also the Nicene Creed, in *TFU*, 7; and the Belgic Confession (Art. 10), in *TFU*, 25. The Second London Baptist Confession (2.3) similarly says, "In this divine and infinite Being there are three subsistences, the Father, the Word (or Son) and Holy Spirit, of one substance, power, and eternity, each having the whole divine essence, yet the essence undivided: the Father is of none, neither begotten nor proceeding; the Son is eternally begotten of the Father; the Holy Spirit proceeding from the Father and the Son." Cited in *RC*, 4:536.

11 John 1:14, 18; 3:16, 18; 1 John 4:9.

12 Luke 7:12; 8:42; 9:38; Heb. 11:17.

13 John 1:13–14, 18; 3:3–8, 16, 18; 1 John 4:7, 9.

14 *TDNT*, 4:739.

15 John 1:14; 6:46; 7:29; 8:42; 13:3; 16:27–28.

16 The Nicene Creed, in *TFU*, 7.

The eternal generation of the Son is a mystery. Irenaeus of Lyon said, "If any one, therefore, says to us, 'How then was the Son produced by the Father?' we reply to him, that no man understands that production, or generation . . . which is in fact altogether indescribable." No man or angel comprehends it, "but the Father only who begat, and the Son who was begotten."[17]

We can say on the basis of God's Word that the person of the Son is begotten of the Father. Therefore, he is always the Son from the Father. This helps us to see how the Father and the Son are one God (John 10:30). It reveals that the person of the Son is from the Father, and so the Father is in the Son (14:10). It also explains the order in their relationship and acts. The Father sends the Son (1 John 4:9–10). But the Son never sends the Father.

The Holy Spirit Is God

The Holy Spirit is not the Father or the Son. But the Spirit shares the same divine nature with them and is rightly called God the Spirit.

Arguments for the Deity of the Holy Spirit

We present the following seven arguments for the deity of the Holy Spirit.

First, *the Holy Spirit has the names of God.* Words spoken by "the Lord" in the Old Testament are characterized as words spoken by the Spirit (Heb. 10:15–16). The Spirit is "the Lord," Jehovah. To lie to the Holy Spirit is to lie to "God" (Acts 5:3–4).

Second, *the Holy Spirit has the attributes of God.* The Bible reveals the Spirit's omniscience (Isa. 40:13; 1 Cor. 2:9–11), omnipotence (Luke 1:34–37), omnipresence (Ps. 139:7; 1 Cor. 6:19), eternity (Gen. 1:2), foreknowledge (Acts 1:16; 1 Pet. 1:11–12), goodness (Neh. 9:20; Ps. 143:10–11), love (Rom. 15:30), truth (John 14:17), holiness (Isa. 63:10–11; Rom. 1:4), infinity (John 3:34), life (2 Cor. 3:3, 6), and simplicity (Rom. 8:10; 1 John 5:6).

Third, *the Holy Spirit has the relationships of God.* The Spirit is the Spirit of the Father (Matt. 10:20). He proceeds from the Father (John 15:26). And he is called the Spirit of the Son (Gal. 4:6) and the Spirit of Christ (Rom. 8:9). The Father, the Son, and the Spirit appear together repeatedly in the New Testament.[18]

17 Irenaeus, *Against Heresies*, 2.28.6, in *ANF*, 1:401.

18 Mark 1:9–11; 1 Cor. 12:4–6; Gal. 4:4–6; Eph. 1:17–20; 3:14–17; Titus 3:4–6.

Fourth, *the Holy Spirit performs the actions of God.* The Spirit created all things and people (Gen. 1:2; Job 33:4). He gives life to the creatures (Ps. 104:30). He inspired God's Word (2 Sam. 23:2; Acts 1:16; 2 Pet. 1:21). He worked miracles through Christ and the apostles (Luke 4:14; Rom. 15:19; Heb. 2:4). He regenerates and gives spiritual life to sinners (John 3:3–6; 2 Cor. 3:6). He raises the dead (Rom. 1:4; 8:11; 1 Cor. 15:42–45).

Fifth, *the Holy Spirit manifests the presence of God.* The Spirit is the divine person living in the temple of God (1 Cor. 3:16–17; Eph. 2:21–22). If the Holy Spirit is not God, then how can our bodies be "the temple of the Holy Ghost" (1 Cor. 6:19)? Since God's temple is a people scattered across the world among the nations, the Holy Spirit must be God to dwell in them all at the same time.

Sixth, *the Holy Spirit has the authority of God.* The Spirit exercises sovereignty over the church "as he wills" (1 Cor. 12:11 ESV; cf. Acts 13:2). The Spirit led Israel through the wilderness (Isa. 63:14). He leads God's children in the ways of righteousness (Ps. 143:10; Rom. 8:14). The Spirit even led the incarnate Mediator (Matt. 4:1).

Seventh, *the Holy Spirit receives the honors of God.* The Spirit is equally honored with the Father and the Son in baptism (Matt. 28:19). Paul invokes the Spirit with the Father and the Son when blessing believers (2 Cor. 13:14). Thus, the church confesses in the Nicene Creed that the Holy Spirit "with the Father and the Son together is worshiped and glorified."[19]

The deity of the Holy Spirit is central to Christian doctrine and worship. Do you love the Holy Spirit? Do you desire the Spirit to fill you? Do you seek the Spirit just to get power? Or do you want to know more of his glory and help others to do the same?

The Personality of the Holy Spirit

Some false teachers have claimed that the Holy Spirit is merely God's energy or an impersonal force. But the Lord Jesus teaches that the Spirit is a person. Christ describes the Spirit not with the impersonal word "comfort" but with the personal term "Comforter" and with masculine pronouns ("he," "him").[20] The Spirit teaches, guides, testifies, reproves, and intercedes.[21]

19 The Nicene Creed, in *TFU*, 7.

20 John 14:16, 26; 15:26; 16:7, 13–14.

21 John 14:26; 15:26; 16:8, 13; Rom. 8:26.

Someone might object that being poured out like water (Acts 2:17) and quenched like fire (1 Thess. 5:19) prove that the Spirit is impersonal.

In reply, we note that the Bible compares God himself to a "fountain of living waters" (Jer. 2:13) and "a consuming fire" (Deut. 4:24). Thus, pouring and quenching are figures of speech, images for ways that the Spirit works, not literal descriptions of him as a mere thing.

We can lie to the Holy Spirit (Acts 5:3). Who can lie to mere energy? Christ said that one can sin "against the Holy Ghost" (Mark 3:28–29). No one can sin against an impersonal force.

The Spirit commands men and refers to himself as "I" (Acts 10:19–20; 13:2). He knows the things of God and reveals them (1 Cor. 2:10–12). Sin displeases him (Isa. 63:10; Eph. 4:30). He makes moral judgments about what is good (Acts 15:28). The Spirit has a will, even the sovereign will that determines the distribution of gifts in Christ's body (1 Cor. 12:11). The Holy Spirit is the personal Lord of all.

You must not treat the Holy Spirit as a mere power to be used or an experience to be pursued. Do you treat the Holy Spirit as a mere force or as the personal Lord? He dwells in each believer as a divine person within a human person. Dear believers, how aware are you of the fact that you are hosting God as a royal guest in your heart? "There is nothing in the world so great and sweet a friend that will do us so much good as the Spirit, if we give him entertainment," Richard Sibbes wrote.[22] Marvel over his love, undeserved grace, and patience to live within you.

The Eternal Procession of the Holy Spirit

Christ says that the Holy Spirit "proceedeth from the Father" (John 15:26). This might be interpreted as simply a repetition of what Christ said earlier in the same verse: "I will send" the Comforter. But that would seem redundant. Plus, "I will send" is in the future tense, but "proceedeth" is in the present tense. Therefore, this procession is the Spirit's relation to the Father at all times.

The Holy Spirit proceeds from the Father *and* the Son. He is the Spirit of the Father (Matt. 10:20). The Father says of Christ, "I will put my Spirit upon him" (12:18 ESV). Yet the Spirit of God is called "the Spirit of Christ" (Rom. 8:9; 1 Pet. 1:11) and "the Spirit of Jesus Christ" (Phil. 1:19).

22 Sibbes, *A Fountain Sealed*, in *WRS*, 5:431.

The Spirit is sent by the Father and the Son (John 14:26; 15:26; 16:7). Paul says that "God sent forth his Son" and "God hath sent forth the Spirit of his Son" (Gal. 4:4, 6). The word "Spirit" can also mean breath. Christ seemed to compare the Holy Spirit to his living breath when he "breathed on them, and saith unto them, Receive ye the Holy Ghost" (John 20:22).

The Nicene Creed, as formulated by the Council of Constantinople (AD 381), simply said that the Spirit proceeds "from the Father." But in Western, Latin-speaking Christianity, people became convinced that the Spirit also proceeds from the Son. The Spirit is sent by the Son to save sinners, and he is the Spirit of the Son, as Augustine said.[23] Therefore, churches in the West changed the Nicene Creed to say that the Holy Spirit "proceedeth from the Father and the Son."[24] The Eastern, Greek-speaking churches rejected the addition of "and the Son." This disagreement was one reason why the churches in the West and the East split in AD 1054.

Knowing that the Holy Spirit is always the Spirit of Christ reminds us that we should never separate true spiritual experiences from faith in Christ and the knowledge of God's Word. The Holy Spirit always glorifies Christ (John 16:14).

The Trinity as the Heart of Christianity

There is more for us to discuss about the Trinity in the next chapter. But it should already be clear that this doctrine is central to Christian theology and life. The Heidelberg Catechism says,

> Q. What is thy only comfort in life and death?
> A. That I with body and soul, both in life and death, am not my own, but belong unto my *faithful Savior Jesus Christ*; who, with His precious blood, hath fully satisfied for all my sins, and delivered me from all the power of the devil; and so preserves me that without the will of my *heavenly Father*, not a hair can fall from my head; yea, that all things must be subservient to my salvation, and therefore, by His *Holy Spirit*, He also assures me of eternal life, and makes me sincerely willing and ready, henceforth, to live unto Him.[25]

23 Augustine, *On the Trinity*, 15.26.45, in *NPNF*[1], 3:224.

24 The Nicene Creed, in *TFU*, 7. The Latin phrase *filioque* ("and from the Son") became the center of controversy.

25 The Heidelberg Catechism (LD 1, Q. 1), in *TFU*, 68, emphasis added.

Without all three of the divine persons, we would have no salvation, no hope, and no everlasting joy. Therefore, Christian, give your wholehearted worship to the whole Trinity. Worship the Father for choosing to bless you forever. Worship the Son for dying for you and preserving you from the Devil. And worship the Holy Spirit for giving you the love, joy, and peace to live for him.

Suggested Song to Sing to the Lord

- "Come, thou Almighty King," *THBap*, No. 89

Questions for Meditation or Discussion

1. What is Arianism? Who teaches this heresy today?
2. What does *homoousion* mean and how did the Council of Nicaea use it to explain Christ's relationship to God?
3. Prove from the Holy Scriptures that the Son is God by his (1) preexistence, (2) prophecies, (3) names and titles, (4) attributes, (5) relationships, (6) actions, and (7) honors.
4. What is the eternal generation of the Son? How is it different from human generation of a son?
5. Prove from the Holy Scriptures that the Holy Spirit is God by his (1) names and titles, (2) attributes, (3) relationships, (4) actions, (5) presence, (6) authority, and (7) honors.
6. Someone says, "The Holy Spirit is not a person, just the power of God." What do you say?
7. What is the eternal procession of the Spirit? From whom does he proceed? Prove your answers from the Bible.
8. Why is the doctrine of the Trinity essential to the Christian life?
9. How would it affect you if Christ were not God? If the Holy Spirit were not God?

20

The Trinity, Part 2: Three Persons and One God

Chapter Summary and Key Terms

There is only one God—this is the doctrine of *monotheism*. The false teaching of *modalism* says that the Father, the Son, and the Holy Spirit are one person who appears under three names. But the Holy Scriptures reveal that God exists in three persons. By the term *person*, we mean someone unique, rational (thinking), and volitional (choosing) by nature, and in relationships with other persons. The three persons of the Trinity dwell in one another and share one divine nature. The Father begets the Son. The Father and the Son breathe the Spirit. The Trinity is not a logical contradiction, for God is three in persons but one in nature, but it is a mystery beyond comprehension. Yet by grace believers can have intimate fellowship with the triune God—the Father, the Son, and the Holy Spirit.

THE TRINITY IS A MYSTERY of one God who exists in three persons. The Belgic Confession says, "We believe in one only God, who is one single essence, in which are three persons, really, truly, and eternally distinct, according to their incommunicable [unique] properties; namely, the Father, and the Son, and the Holy Ghost."[1]

In this chapter, we will study God's oneness and threeness. We will also consider practical applications of the doctrine of the Trinity.

1 The Belgic Confession (Art. 8), in *TFU*, 22.

The One and Only God

Many religions teach that there are multiple gods (polytheism). Some even claim to be Christianity. For example, Mormonism teaches that the Father, the Son, and the Holy Spirit are three distinct gods (*tritheism*). But God's Word teaches *monotheism*, the doctrine that there is only one true God.

Moses says, "The LORD he is God; there is none else beside him. . . . The LORD he is God in heaven above, and upon the earth beneath: there is none else" (Deut. 4:35, 39). God declares, "See now that I, even I, am he, and there is no god with me: I kill, and I make alive; I wound, and I heal: neither is there any that can deliver out of my hand" (32:39).

The great confession of the Old Testament is "The LORD our God is one LORD" (Deut. 6:4). It can also be translated, "The LORD our God, the LORD is one" (ESV). Christ agreed with a Jewish scribe who said this means that "there is one God; and there is none other but he" (Mark 12:32). The apostles of the church likewise said that God is one (Gal. 3:20; 1 Tim. 2:5; James 2:19).

Therefore, "thou shalt love the Lord thy God with all thine heart, and with all thy soul, and with all thy might" (Deut. 6:5). We must not divide our love among different beings but give God everything. The more we see that there is only one God, the more we desire "one thing"—namely, to dwell with God as his worshipers and see his beauty (Ps. 27:4).

The Three Persons of the Trinity

The Father, the Son, and the Holy Spirit are not three ways that one person shows himself to us. They are three persons sharing one divine nature. The Son is not the Father. God the Father sent Christ into the world (John 3:17). The Father loves the Son and speaks to him not as "me" but as "thee" (Luke 3:22). Christ prayed to the Father (Mark 14:36). The Spirit is not the Father or the Son. Rather, the Father anoints the Son with the Spirit (Acts 10:38). The Spirit leads the Son (Luke 4:1). Christ calls the Spirit "another Comforter" besides himself (John 14:16). The Father and the Son send the Spirit to God's people (v. 26; 15:26).

We use the term *person* to distinguish the Father, Son, and Holy Spirit. Tertullian said that they are not the same "person" but that Christianity "distributes the Unity into a Trinity, placing in their order the three Persons—the Father, the Son, and the Holy Ghost . . . yet of one substance, and of one condition, and of one power, inasmuch as He is one God."[2] Tertullian opposed the error of *modalism*, which is the idea that the Trinity is one Lord who takes on different names, manifestations, and functions. Modalism teaches that God is like one man who is a husband, father, and employee. That is not the biblical Trinity.

Although each of the three persons is equally God, their relations reflect an order among them. Such an order is implied in the very names "Father" and "Son." That is not a relationship in which the roles can be reversed. The Father sent the Son (1 John 4:9). The Son never sends the Father. The Son's work glorifies the Father (John 17:4). The Father and the Son send the Spirit (14:26; 15:26). The Spirit does not send them. The Holy Spirit glorifies the Son (16:14). God's Word gives us a basis for calling the Father the first person, the Son the second person, and the Holy Spirit the third person of the Trinity. However, this is not an order of time, as if one person existed before another. It is also not an order of greatness, as if one person has more glory than another. It is an order of relationship.

What do we mean by the word *person* when we use it in the doctrine of the Trinity? A person is someone unique, rational (thinking), and volitional (choosing) by nature, and in relationships with other persons. A person is someone, not something. Each person is unique. God speaks of Christ as his "only begotten Son" (John 3:16)—not just *a son* but *the Son* (v. 35). The Holy Spirit is never called the Father or the Son. The persons are rational and volitional, for they know and love one another (5:20; 16:13–15). And the three persons are in relationships with one another and with other, created persons. The Father says to Christ, "Thou art my beloved Son; in thee I am well pleased" (Luke 3:22). The Holy Spirit says to the church, "Set apart for me Barnabas and Saul for the work to which I have called them" (Acts 13:2 ESV).

God is eternally personal and relational. This is the sweetness and beauty of the mysterious doctrine of the Trinity. We may rejoice that "God is love" and know that we must "love one another" (1 John 4:7–8). Insofar as we refuse to love God and one another, we diminish our own personhood and fail to bear God's image as a personal and relational being.

2 Tertullian, *Against Praxeas*, chap. 2, in *ANF*, 3:598.

The Three Persons as One God

The divine persons are distinct from one another. But they are not separated. The Father, the Son, and the Holy Spirit dwell in one another. John writes that "the only begotten Son . . . is in the bosom of the Father" (John 1:18), the place of intimate friendship. Christ says, "I am in the Father, and the Father in me" (14:10–11; cf. 10:38; 17:21). Each person of the Trinity completely embraces the others in mutual sharing of all divine glory.

As John of Damascus taught, the mutual indwelling of the persons of the Trinity does not mean that they merge into one person. They remain three persons even as they cling to one another with no separation. They live in one another as the Father, the Son, and the Spirit.[3] The Bible says, "God is love" (1 John 4:8), and love seeks union with the beloved. There is no more glorious union than that shared in God among the Father, the Son, and the Holy Spirit. They love one another infinitely.

The first and second persons of the Trinity are the Father and the Son. But we must not think of the Trinity merely as a family. We do not believe in three Gods. The Son is begotten of the Father (John 3:16). The Spirit proceeds from the Father and the Son (Gal. 4:6). Therefore, God is one in his essence and work.

The three persons of the Trinity share one activity, one knowledge, and one power. Jesus Christ says, "My Father is working until now, and I am working. . . . The Son can do nothing of his own accord, but only what he sees the Father doing. For whatever the Father does, that the Son does likewise. For the Father loves the Son and shows him all that he himself is doing" (John 5:17, 19–20 ESV). The Holy Spirit also shares in the same activity, knowledge, and power of the Father and the Son (Gen. 1:2; Isa. 11:2).

The three persons of the Trinity share one divine life and one divine will. Christ says, "For as the Father raises the dead and gives them life, so also the Son gives life to whom he will. . . . For as the Father has life in himself, so he has granted the Son also to have life in himself" (John 5:21, 26 ESV). Likewise, the Spirit comes to believers through Christ as "rivers of living water" (7:37–39). The Holy Spirit exercises the same divine will with the Father and the Son. The Spirit distributes various spiritual gifts to each mem-

3 John of Damascus, *Orthodox Faith*, 1.14, in *Saint John of Damascus: Writings*, trans. Frederic H. Chase Jr., The Fathers of the Church 37 (Washington, DC: The Catholic University of America Press, 1958), 202.

ber of the church "as he wills" (1 Cor. 12:11 ESV). And yet, "God arranged the members in the body, each one of them, as he chose" (v. 18 ESV). The Father, the Son, and the Holy Spirit are the one living and choosing God.

In the Athanasian Creed, the church confesses,

> We worship one God in Trinity, and Trinity in Unity; neither confounding the Persons nor dividing the substance. For there is one Person of the Father, another of the Son, and another of the Holy Spirit. But the Godhead of the Father, of the Son, and of the Holy Spirit is all one, the glory equal, the majesty coeternal. . . . So the Father is God, the Son is God, and the Holy Spirit is God; and yet they are not three Gods, but one God.[4]

The Trinity and Logic

It is sometimes argued that the Trinity is a logical contradiction and thus cannot be true.

In reply, we say that the doctrine of the Trinity would be a contradiction only if it asserted that God is one and three in the same respect. That would be the case if Christians said there is one God and three Gods, or that God is one person and three persons. But the Trinity is one God in three persons. There is no formal contradiction here.

Someone might object that the doctrine still does not make sense, asking, How can we believe in a God whom we cannot understand?

In response, we say that our lack of comprehension is no argument against the doctrine. We should expect that our knowledge of God will always fall short of who he is (Ps. 145:3; Rom. 11:33). He is the infinite Lord. We are finite creatures. Recognizing that the Trinity is a mystery produces the practical fruit of humility. The only way to know God is to humble ourselves and let his Word teach us what is true.

Practical Applications: Friendship with the Triune God

The triune God is the life and joy of his people. As some Reformed theologians have said, the "doctrine of the Trinity is the foundation of all our communion with God, and comfortable dependence on him."[5] In this

4 The Athanasian Creed, in *TFU*, 8–9.

5 The Savoy Declaration (2.3) and the Second London Baptist Confession (2.3), in *RC*, 4:461, 536.

instance, “communion” means fellowship and companionship as with a friend.

Paul says, “For through him [Christ] we both have access in one Spirit to the Father” (Eph. 2:18 ESV). That means the following:

- Fellowship with God is “through” God the Son. He is “the way” through whom alone we can come to the Father (John 14:6). Christians trust in what Christ has done, not what they have done.
- Fellowship with God is “in” God the Holy Spirit. The Spirit is God dwelling in us as his temple (Eph. 2:22). He strengthens us in the inner man. As a result, we know Christ dwelling in our hearts with his unspeakable love and experience the riches of the Father’s glory (3:16–19).
- Fellowship with God is “to” God the Father. Through the Son and in the Holy Spirit, Christians increasingly know by faith that they are the Father’s chosen, adopted, and beloved children, and they respond by blessing the Father forever and living “to the praise of the glory of his grace” (Eph. 1:3–6).

Believers in the gospel find nothing more delightful, awe-inspiring, and unifying than drawing near to the Father through the Son in the Spirit.

The saints have a distinct relationship with each person in the Godhead. Paul says, “The grace of the Lord Jesus Christ and the love of God and the fellowship of the Holy Spirit be with you all” (2 Cor. 13:14 ESV). That means the following:

- Our communion with God the Father is especially in his “love,” for by his love he sent his Son to the cross (John 3:16; Rom. 5:8; 1 John 4:9–10). We fellowship with him as the Father who loves us (1 John 3:1).
- Our communion with God the Son is especially in his “grace,” for he is “full of grace” (John 1:14). We fellowship with him as the Son in whom are all spiritual blessings from the Father (Eph. 1:2–3).
- Our communion with God the Holy Spirit is especially in his “fellowship,” for he brings people together to be God’s temple in Christ (1 Cor. 3:16; 6:17). We fellowship with him as the Spirit who binds

us to one another and to the Father and the Son in a living, eternal relationship.

While trusting and loving each person of the Trinity, we must not forget that the three are one God. As Basil the Great said, the persons of the Trinity are like links in a chain, and you cannot grasp one without drawing the others near.[6]

Gregory of Nazianzus said, "No sooner do I conceive of the One than I am illumined by the splendor of the Three; no sooner do I distinguish them than I am carried back to the One. . . . When I contemplate the Three together, I see but one flame, and cannot divide or measure out the undivided light."[7]

Though we cannot fully understand the Trinity, we must love the triune God. Do you love him? We hope that after reading these chapters on this doctrine that you have a clearer and more biblical understanding of the Trinity. Yet this is not the ultimate goal. Do you live to glorify and enjoy the one God who is the Father, the Son, and the Holy Spirit? Does your heart burn for this God? Does your life shine for his honor? There is no higher or nobler aim.

Suggested Songs to Sing to the Lord

- "Praise God, from whom all blessings flow," *Psalter*, page 415, #1; *THBap*, page xvi
- "O God, we praise thee; and confess," *THBap*, No. 90

Questions for Meditation or Discussion

1. Is the doctrine of the Trinity a logical contradiction? Why or why not?
2. What is monotheism? Prove it from the Holy Scriptures.
3. How would you show that the Father, the Son, and the Holy Spirit are three persons?
4. What is modalism? Why is this heresy?
5. What do we mean by a *person* in the Trinity?

6 Basil the Great, *Epistles*, 38.4, in *NPNF*^{2}, 8:139.

7 Gregory of Nazianzus, *Oration on Holy Baptism*, 40.41, in *NPNF*^{2}, 7:375, spelling modernized. "Flame" was "torch" in the cited translation.

6. How does the Bible show that the divine persons dwell in one another?
7. Show from the Bible that the persons of the Trinity are one in essence and life.
8. What does it mean to have communion with the Father through the Son in the Spirit?
9. How does 2 Corinthians 13:14 show that we have communion with each person in the Trinity?
10. How has reading this chapter helped you to want to love the triune God more?

Section 2B

What God Does

21

God's Eternal Decree

Chapter Summary and Key Terms

God's actions in time are rooted in his *decree*. That is his eternal and sovereign will, according to his wisdom and goodness. He has decided everything that will take place outside of himself, for his glory. God's decree includes the evil acts of demons and sinful men. But God is not evil, for he decreed to sovereignly permit evil for his good purposes. Furthermore, the free choice of our will is real, but God's choice rules over all things. Nor is the doctrine of God's decree *fatalism*. That is the belief that everything moves to predetermined results, regardless of what we choose or do. Fatalism destroys human responsibility. The doctrine of God's decree establishes responsibility, for God decreed both causes and effects, means and ends. Trusting in God's decreed leads us to take wise and righteous action with confidence that God planned all things for good.

NEBUCHADNEZZAR WAS A "king of kings" (Dan. 2:37), but he was forced to face the "God of gods" (v. 47). Daniel brought bad news to the Babylonian emperor and said, "This is the decree of the most High" (4:24). And it happened just as God said.

Centuries later, the great Caesar Augustus issued a "decree" that had the direct result of Jesus Christ being born in Bethlehem (Luke 2:1–7). This happened exactly as God had revealed to the prophet Micah (Mic. 5:2). Just as kings issue decrees and presidents issue executive orders, so God has made a decree.

In this chapter, we will consider God's eternal decree, another part of the doctrine of his sovereignty (see chap. 15). From mighty kings to infant children, the Lord God reigns over all according to his decree. The Westminster Shorter Catechism says, "The decrees of God are his eternal purpose, according to the counsel of his will, whereby, for his own glory, he hath foreordained whatsoever comes to pass."[1]

The Characteristics of God's Decree

A *decree* is an order issued by an authority. God's plan is the wise decree of the supreme King. It is neither an idle foreknowledge nor an arbitrary will. Rather, it is an act of both God's supreme intelligence and sovereign decision. His decree is his wise "counsel" (Ps. 33:11; Prov. 19:21) that he "purposed" (Isa. 14:24, 26–27). It is his "pleasure" (46:10) that he "commandeth" (Lam. 3:37). In a word, it is God's "will" that he decided would take place (Eph. 1:11).

God's Word reveals several qualities of the divine decree.

First, *God's decree is eternal.* He made it before creating the world, before time began (1 Cor. 2:7; Eph. 1:4; 3:9–11). God's "purpose and grace . . . was given us in Christ Jesus before the world began" (2 Tim. 1:9–10).

Second, *God's decree is sovereign.* Daniel said to Nebuchadnezzar, "This is the decree of the most High, which is come upon my lord the king . . . till thou know that the most High ruleth in the kingdom of men, and giveth it to whomsoever he will" (Dan. 4:24–25).

Third, *God's decree is infallible.* It cannot fail. Proverbs 19:21 says, "Many are the plans in the mind of a man, but it is the purpose of the LORD that will stand" (ESV). No one can resist his will (Rom. 9:19). The Lord says, "I am God, and there is none like me, declaring the end from the beginning, and from ancient times the things that are not yet done, saying, My counsel shall stand, and I will do all my pleasure" (Isa. 46:9–10).

Fourth, *God's decree is immutable.* It cannot change. Men's plans are often frustrated and must be altered. But "the counsel of the LORD standeth for ever, the thoughts of his heart to all generations" (Ps. 33:10–11).

Fifth, *God's decree is unconditional.* A conditional decree would imply, "God will do this or that if it is our will." But the Bible teaches us to say, "We

1 The Westminster Shorter Catechism (Q. 7), in *RC*, 4:354. Cf. the Baptist Catechism (Q. 10), in *RC*, 4:574.

will do this or that if it is God's will" (cf. James 4:15). This follows from the sovereignty, infallibility, and immutability of the decree.

Sixth, *God's decree is specific.* God decreed the characteristics of each kind of seed (1 Cor. 15:38). He decreed which woman Isaac would marry (Gen. 24:44). He decreed the flight of ravens to bring food to Elijah (1 Kings 17:4). He decreed the motions of clouds, tornadoes, rain, and lightning (Job 28:26; 37:12–13). And he decreed the military victories of the king of Assyria (Isa. 10:6). God's decree encompasses the details of history.

Seventh, *God's decree is comprehensive.* The Lord does all his pleasure in all places of his created universe (Pss. 115:3; 135:6). His saints are "predestinated according to the purpose of him who worketh all things after the counsel of his own will" (Eph. 1:11).

Eighth, *God's decree is mysterious.* Our limited knowledge of the decree depends on divine revelation (Dan. 2:20–22; 1 Cor. 2:7–10). God's decree expresses his infinite wisdom for all things in creation throughout history. Thus, it defies our full comprehension (Ps. 40:5).

Ninth, *God's decree is good.* All of God's activities are righteous, faithful, just, and good, for that is what he loves (Ps. 33:4–5). Isaiah says, "Thy counsels of old are faithfulness and truth" (Isa. 25:1).

Tenth, *God's decree is wise.* The Lord gives to all men their skill and wisdom (Isa. 28:23–29). He himself is "wonderful in counsel," extraordinarily wise in forming his plans (v. 29). Paul says, "We speak the wisdom of God in a mystery, even the hidden wisdom, which God ordained before the world unto our glory" (1 Cor. 2:6–7).

Eleventh, *God's decree is Christ-centered.* Paul says, "All things were created by [the Son], and for him" (Col. 1:16). God has so ordered the plan of salvation "that in all things [the Son] might have the preeminence" (v. 18).

Twelfth, *God's decree is God-glorifying.* Paul exults, "For of him, and through him, and to him, are all things: to whom be glory for ever. Amen" (Rom. 11:36). God is the originating source, the sustaining agent, and the ultimate goal of all things.

In summary, God's decree is his eternal and sovereign plan, based on his will alone, according to his incomprehensible wisdom and goodness, in which he has decided all persons, things, events, and relationships ever to take place outside of himself, directing all things for the display of his glory in Jesus Christ.

Objections to God's Decree

The doctrine of God's decree certainly has enemies. They say that it misrepresents God as malicious and his providence as determinism. They also say that it leads to fatalism and despair. On the contrary, the doctrine of the decree encourages faith, love, diligence, and hope.

Is God Evil?

One accusation leveled against the doctrine of God's decree is that it portrays him as evil and malicious because he decreed the disasters and atrocities of our fallen world. But the Bible says God is love (1 John 4:8) and cannot tempt others to sin (James 1:13). Thus, we are told that we should reject the doctrine of the divine decree.

In reply, we say that *God is not evil, but he decrees evil for good purposes.* Lamentations 3:37–38 says, "Who is he that saith, and it cometh to pass, when the Lord commandeth it not? Out of the mouth of the most High proceedeth not evil and good?" No sorrow can touch us unless the Lord ordains it. But God does not delight in suffering: "For he doth not afflict willingly [literally "from his heart"] nor grieve the children of men" (v. 33).

For those who hope in him, the Lord remains the God of unfailing love and faithfulness (Lam. 3:21–23). He is the portion of his people (v. 24). In the mystery of their sufferings, they find that God is still good (v. 25). He knew that it was good for them to bear this yoke for a time (vv. 26–27).

God decrees sin and then permits people to commit it, not because he loves it but because it serves his good purposes. Joseph, the son of Jacob, was betrayed by his brothers. They sold him into slavery. He was then falsely accused of sexual assault and imprisoned for years (Genesis 37–41). Yet he later said to his brothers, "Ye thought evil against me; but God meant it unto good, to bring to pass, as it is this day, to save much people alive" (50:20).

We should respond to this doctrine by fearing God. The Lord is light, but he does not shrink from decreeing darkness on sinners. He is love, but he is willing to command that burning sorrows fall on his enemies and that flaming trials refine his children.

The children of God must expect his painful discipline. But they must believe that it springs from love, not malice (Heb. 12:5–11). Christ despised the accursed cross for "the joy that was set before him" (v. 2). We must "run with patience the race that is set before us, looking unto Jesus" (vv. 1–2).

Is Free Choice an Illusion?

Another objection raised against the divine decree is that it means that nothing is the result of genuine choice. All comes to pass as a matter of necessity. But we know that we make choices. Therefore, the doctrine of God's sovereign and unconditional decree, it is said, cannot be true.

In reply, we affirm that *free choice is real, but God's choice rules over all.* He decreed the details of Christ's suffering and death. Yet the people involved acted freely and were accountable for their choices. Christ said, "Truly the Son of man goeth, as it was determined: but woe unto that man by whom he is betrayed!" (Luke 22:22). Peter told his fellow Jews that Christ was handed over to crucifixion "by the determinate counsel and foreknowledge of God" (Acts 2:23). But Peter also said that "ye have crucified" Christ, for which he urged them, "Repent," and, "Save yourselves" (vv. 36, 38, 40).

We are not claiming that man's acts are caused by what is in and around him before he makes a choice. Man is not a machine. Each person's choices come spontaneously from his heart. He perceives his situation and makes a rational judgment about what is good for him. The Westminster Confession of Faith says,

> God from all eternity, did, by the most wise and holy counsel of His own will, freely, and unchangeably ordain whatsoever comes to pass: yet so, as thereby neither is God the author of sin, nor is violence offered to the will of the creatures; nor is the liberty or contingency of second causes taken away, but rather established.[2]

One great application of this doctrine is that we must personally deal with the Lord of lords. Fallen mankind foolishly pretends to live independently from the will of God. The decree confronts us with God's absolute lordship. How will we respond to this Lord?

2 The Westminster Confession of Faith (3.1), in *RC*, 4:238. Cf. the Second London Baptist Confession (3.1), in *RC*, 4:536.

Wilhelmus à Brakel asked, "Do you wish God to be your servant in order that you might receive your foolish desires? Or is it your joy that He is Lord, that He acts freely, and that as supreme Sovereign He rules everything according to His will?"[3]

Is This Fatalism?

Yet another objection brought against the doctrine of the decree is that it subjects our lives to an iron fate that destroys human responsibility. If God decreed all that happens, it is said, then it does not matter what we choose or how much effort we exert—the end will be the same.

In reply, we say that this doctrine does not lead to *fatalism*, for God's decree establishes human responsibility. It is God who connects wise diligence and reward, or foolish disobedience and sorrow. God decreed both the event and the means by which the event comes to pass.

Knowing that God is ultimately in control gives us the strength to do what we can when our situation is grim. In one battle, Joab saw that Israel's armies were far outnumbered. But he said to his brother, "Be of good courage, and let us play the men for our people, and for the cities of our God: and the LORD do that which seemeth him good" (2 Sam. 10:12).

Paul's ship was driven about by a violent storm during his voyage to Rome. But an angel told the apostle, "Fear not, Paul; thou must be brought before Caesar: and, lo, God hath given thee all them that sail with thee" (Acts 27:24). The revelation of God's decree did not encourage those on the ship to neglect the means of safety. On the contrary, Paul encouraged them to take nourishment (vv. 34–35). When the sailors tried to abandon the ship, Paul told his guards, "Except these abide in the ship, ye cannot be saved" (v. 31). Paul's faith in God's decree led him to act with prudence and diligence.

The fatalist might object, "Why should I pray? God has already decreed what will happen. He will not alter it in response to my prayers." However, God decreed our prayers too. And he included his answers to our prayers as part of his eternal, wise plan. If someone then says, "Why should I pray? God does not need my help," the Scriptures answer that God does not call us to pray because he needs our advice. We pray that we may know, honor, and enjoy God as our Father (Matt. 6:6–9; 7:11).

3 Brakel, *CRS*, 1:208.

God has revealed little of his decree to us. We should focus on his promises and our duties, not the specifics of the future (Deut. 29:29). Rather than obsessing about what lies ahead, wondering what God has planned, we can entrust it to him. We may not know his decree, but if we are believers, we do know the decreeing God. He is ever faithful.

Suggested Song to Sing to the Lord

- "Lord, my weak thought in vain would climb," *THBap*, No. 93

Questions for Meditation or Discussion

1. How would you show from the Scriptures that God has decreed all that takes place?
2. How do we know that God's decree is (1) eternal, (2) sovereign, (3) infallible, (4) immutable, and (5) unconditional?
3. Why is it crucial for us to believe that God's decree is good and wise?
4. A friend says, "I think that God has a plan for his major goals, but not a plan for everything that happens. Many events are random or meaningless." How do you respond?
5. What Scripture passages teach us that God's decree orders all things for his glory in Christ?
6. How would you answer the following objections to this doctrine? (1) If God decreed evil, then he must be evil. (2) If God decreed everything, then our choices are mere illusions. (3) If God decreed the end results, then there is no point in our hard work.
7. How should the doctrine of God's decree humble us? How should it comfort us?
8. Meditate on Lamentations 3:22–42. What does this text show us about a proper response to God's sovereign decree in times of great distress?

22

Election and Reprobation

Chapter Summary and Key Terms

Predestination is the aspect of God's decree, for his glory, of all things that concern salvation and damnation. It consists of *election* and *reprobation*. God's act of election was his selection of those whom he would save by grace in Christ and the means by which he would save them. Election was part of the decree of God. It was an eternal act of love in the Trinity. In election, God freely and unconditionally chose certain individuals for salvation to the praise of his grace, not because of any merit or faith he saw in them via his foreknowledge. Those whom God elected, he calls, justifies, sanctifies, and glorifies in union with Christ. God's act of reprobation was also part of his decree. In reprobation, he eternally chose to abandon certain individuals to hardness of heart so that they would be damned, to the praise of his justice. Believing these doctrines, we must call all people to trust in Christ alone for salvation and to pursue holiness by the grace of Christ, for faith and holiness are the fruit and evidence of election.

THE CROWN JEWEL of the doctrine of God's sovereignty is his election of those whom he would save by grace. According to the doctrine of election, God selected certain people for salvation by grace unto eternal glory, as well as the means by which he would bring them to saving faith. According to the doctrine of reprobation, God decided that other people would be justly damned forever for their sins.

Election and reprobation are the two sides of God's decree of predestination and together serve to display God's sovereign glory in his grace and justice. Like a diamond reflecting the sunlight, these doctrines sparkle with God's glory shining from Jesus Christ. At the same time, they are a theological battlefield. Fierce debates rage about them. However, avoiding them does not help the church, for the Bible is full of these doctrines.[1] The doctrines of election and reprobation highlight a truth that all Christians know: salvation is entirely of God's grace.

Election to Gracious Salvation

Paul says,

> Blessed be the God and Father of our Lord Jesus Christ, who hath blessed us with all spiritual blessings in heavenly places in Christ: according as he hath chosen us in him before the foundation of the world, that we should be holy and without blame before him in love: having predestinated us unto the adoption of children by Jesus Christ to himself, according to the good pleasure of his will, to the praise of the glory of his grace, wherein he hath made us accepted in the beloved. (Eph. 1:3–6)

This passage teaches us several important truths about election.

First, election was *an act of God's love.* The Lord of election is the God who so richly "hath blessed" his people that he is gladly "blessed" by them in return (Eph. 1:3). He chose them "in love" (v. 4). The God of predestination is not stingy or cruel. He is the "Father" who aims at "the adoption of children" into his family (vv. 3, 5). In a word, election was "grace" (v. 6). It was the source of "all spiritual blessings" that Paul lists in this epistle (v. 3).

Second, election involved *a covenant between the Father and the Son.* The person who elected his people is called "the God and Father of our Lord Jesus Christ" (Eph. 1:3). Paul also names him "the God of our Lord Jesus Christ" (v. 17). This title, similar to "the God of Abraham" (Gen. 26:24; 28:13), and the word "bless" (cf. 12:2, 3) echo God's covenant with Abraham. God's election of the nation of Israel was linked to his covenant with Abraham. So too, God's election of people to salvation was linked to

1 For references to "elect" or "election," see Matt. 20:16; 22:14; 24:22, 24, 31; Mark 13:20, 22, 27; Luke 18:7; John 15:16, 19; Rom. 8:33; 9:11; 11:5, 7, 28; 16:13; 1 Cor. 1:27–28; Eph. 1:4; Col. 3:12; 1 Thess. 1:4; 2 Tim. 2:10; Titus 1:1; James 2:5; 1 Pet. 1:2; 2:9; 2 Pet. 1:10; 2 John 1, 13; Rev. 17:14.

an eternal covenant between God the Father and God the Son regarding the Son's mission of salvation. Christ is the Lamb of God, "foreordained before the foundation of the world" (1 Pet. 1:20).

Third, election resulted in *union with Christ*. Paul repeatedly says that election and the grace that flows from it are "in" or "by" Christ (Eph. 1:3, 4, 5, 6). We can know that we were chosen by God by believing the gospel of Christ and following him (1 Thess. 1:4–6). John Calvin said, "How do we know that God has elected us before the creation of the world? By believing in Jesus Christ."[2]

Fourth, election consisted of *God's sovereign selection of whom he would save*. God "hath blessed us . . . according as he hath chosen us" (Eph. 1:3–4). Paul does not write that God chose a course of action, such as to save the people who trusted in him. Rather, God chose particular people ("us"). He selected the individuals he would bless. Believers can rejoice that their "names are written in heaven" (Luke 10:20), even "from the foundation of the world" (Rev. 17:8).

Fifth, election was *an aspect of God's eternal decree of all things* (see chap. 21). God chose his saints "before the foundation of the world" (Eph. 1:4). He "predestinated us . . . to himself" (v. 5). The word translated as "predestine" means to decide or decree something beforehand. God's saints were "predestinated according to the purpose of him who worketh all things after the counsel of his own will" (v. 11). Hence, election unto salvation was part of the larger decree by which God decided everything that would ever take place. God chose not only whom he would save but also the means by which he would save them. It is comforting to believers to know that God included everything necessary in his plan to accomplish his good purposes.

Sixth, election is *the root of the Christian's holiness*. God chose us "that we should be holy and without blame before him" (Eph. 1:4). Paul writes, "For whom he did foreknow, he also did predestinate to be conformed to the image of his Son, that he might be the firstborn among many brethren" (Rom. 8:29). The legalist would claim that God chose us because we were worthier than others. But in reality, all our holiness results from God's election of grace (2 Thess. 2:13), which he did with no regard to the worthiness

2 John Calvin, *Sermons on the Epistle to the Ephesians* (Edinburgh: Banner of Truth, 1973), 47.

of our works (Rom. 11:5–6). On the other hand, an antinomian would say that if God chose us, we will be saved regardless of how we live. But the Scriptures teach that God's election brings a holy calling that creates a faithful person who overcomes the world through Christ (Rev. 17:14). Only by exercising a faith that bears fruit in true godliness and love does a person make his "calling and election sure" (2 Pet. 1:4–10). Calvin said, "Our election must be as a root that yields good fruits."[3]

Seventh, election aimed at *the praise of God's glory*. God chose and predestined his people "to the praise of the glory of his grace" (Eph. 1:6). Paul repeats the same idea in verses 12 and 14. God directed all of salvation "to the praise of his glory" (v. 14). He predestined people to eternal life "that he might make known the riches of his glory" (Rom. 9:23). Christ is our model and leader in how to respond to election. He joyfully praised God for his sovereign gift of grace to whomever he pleased (Luke 10:21).

In summary, election is that aspect of God's eternal decree of all things in which he sovereignly and lovingly selected those whom he would call, justify, sanctify, and glorify by union with Jesus Christ to the praise of his glory alone. He made this selection according to the incomprehensible counsel of his will alone and nothing good that he foresaw in us. The Father entered an eternal covenant with the Son that he would be the Mediator of grace applied by the Spirit.

Reprobation to Just Damnation

When we studied God's decree, we saw that God planned human sin, which he hates, for his own good purposes (Gen. 50:20). Reprobation glorifies God not because he delights in human suffering but because he delights in justice. In this section, we will trace three themes of the Bible related to reprobation.

Sinners Forsaken to Hardness of Heart

God chose to abandon some sinners to impenitence and unbelief. The high priest Eli pleaded with his sons to repent of their scandalous sins against God's holiness. But "they would not listen to the voice of their father, for it was the will of the Lord to put them to death" (1 Sam. 2:25 ESV). These wicked priests

3 Calvin, *Sermons on the Epistle to the Ephesians*, 35.

acted of their own will. Yet the ultimate reason why they did not repent was that God had chosen to glorify his justice by destroying them for their sins.

God hardened the heart of Pharaoh (Ex. 10:1). As a result, he proudly and stubbornly resisted the Lord (v. 3). Pharaoh hardened his own heart (8:15, 32; 9:34), so he was responsible for his sins (9:17, 34). But ten times Moses wrote that the Lord hardened Pharaoh's heart.[4] Furthermore, the hardness of Pharaoh's heart ultimately failed to serve his sinful purposes. Rather, it served God's holy purpose to glorify himself (7:3–4; 9:16; 10:1).

God also hardened the hearts of people in Israel. The Lord said, "Make the heart of this people fat, and make their ears heavy, and shut their eyes; lest they see with their eyes, and hear with their ears, and understand with their heart, and convert, and be healed" (Isa. 6:10).

God's hardening of sinners does not mean that he motivates them to sin. God gives only good gifts (James 1:17). He cannot entice anyone to evil (v. 13). God hardens sinners by withdrawing those gifts that would restrain them from certain sins (cf. Gen. 20:6). He hardens not by adding evil but by subtracting good. He leaves sinners to their sin (Ps. 81:11–12).

People Destined for Righteous Damnation

God destined some unbelieving sinners for his just punishment. Solomon teaches us, "The Lord hath made all things for himself: yea, even the wicked for the day of evil" (Prov. 16:4). God created all things good (Gen. 1:31), so he is not the author of sin. Man chose to sin, and God reserves certain sinners for his just wrath (Job 21:30).

Jude 4 speaks of false teachers "who were before of old ordained to this condemnation." The word translated as "ordained" here literally means "written beforehand." Jude is probably speaking of God's decree as if it were a book (Pss. 40:8; 139:16). A very similar text is 2 Peter 2:3: "Their condemnation from long ago is not idle" (ESV).

Peter says that those who "stumble at the word, being disobedient, . . . [were] appointed" to this doom (1 Pet. 2:8). The word translated as "appointed" is the same verb that Peter uses earlier of God's appointing of Christ to be the cornerstone of God's living temple (v. 6). God predestined

4 Ex. 4:21; 7:3; 9:12; 10:1, 20, 27; 11:10; 14:4, 8, 17. Exodus also says six times that Pharoah's heart was hard with no cause named (7:13, 14, 22; 8:19; 9:7, 35).

Christ's death and exaltation. He also predestined some people to unbelief and opposition to Christ (cf. Acts 4:27–28). Peter goes on to contrast these people with God's elect: "But ye are a chosen generation" (1 Pet. 2:9).

Someone might object that Peter also says, "The Lord is not slack concerning his promise, as some men count slackness; but is longsuffering to us-ward, not willing that any should perish, but that all should come to repentance" (2 Pet. 3:9). This, it is said, clearly teaches that God wills the repentance and salvation of all people.

In response, we note that the words "any" and "all" may be defined in context as "us," which refers to God's "beloved" people (2 Pet. 3:1, 8, 14, 17). Or if we take "all" in its broadest sense, then the verb "willing" can refer not so much to a decision as to a delight. We know that God delights in repentance (Luke 15:7). However, we also know that the Lord rejoices to punish the wicked (Deut. 28:63), for he is the God of justice (32:4). Thus, he calls all men to repentance, but he has chosen to punish some for their sins.

Those whom God has not elected are reserved for his righteous hatred against sinners: "Was not Esau Jacob's brother? saith the Lord: yet I loved Jacob, and I hated Esau" (Mal. 1:2–3). God laid the land of Edom waste and called the nation "the people against whom the Lord hath indignation forever" (vv. 3–4). Paul quotes these words as evidence that the Lord has mercy not according to works but on those whom he chooses (Rom. 9:11–15). The rest are objects of his just wrath (v. 22).

Enemies Ordained for God's Glory

God ordains the destruction of some sinners for his glory in Christ. The betrayal of Christ by Judas was a great sin, but it all happened "as it was determined" (Luke 22:22). Peter says that "the Scripture had to be fulfilled, which the Holy Spirit spoke beforehand by the mouth of David concerning Judas" (Acts 1:16 ESV). God ordained Judas's sin unto his damnation so that Christ would die for the salvation of many people.

The Lord declared to Pharaoh, "For this cause have I raised thee up, for to shew in thee my power; and that my name may be declared throughout all the earth" (Ex. 9:16). Why did the armies of Egypt chase the people of Israel into the Red Sea? The Lord said, "And I will harden Pharaoh's heart, that he shall follow after them; and I will be honoured upon [glorified over] Pharaoh, and upon all his host; that the Egyptians may know that I am the

Lord" (14:4). As a result of Pharaoh's hardening and destruction, Israel glorified the Lord for his great work of salvation (15:1–21).

God's dealings with Pharaoh are an example of how he has mercy on whom he wills and hardens whom he wills, for his glory (Rom. 9:17–18). God is like a potter forming clay pots for different purposes. God willed to make known his wrath and power through "vessels of wrath prepared for destruction" in contrast to "vessels of mercy, which he has prepared beforehand for glory" (vv. 21–23 ESV).

In summary, reprobation is that aspect of God's eternal decree of all things in which he sovereignly selected those whom he would abandon to their sins and damn forever, to the praise of his glory. He made this selection according to the incomprehensible counsel of his will. He does not abandon the reprobate by motivating them to sin but by withholding his unmerited grace. Their damnation is an act of justice, fully deserved because of their sins.

Practical Applications of the Doctrines of Election and Reprobation

These doctrines are rich in applications for believers.

First, *trust in Christ, in whom is all election and no reprobation.* As we saw, God's election revolved around Christ and union with him by faith (Eph. 1:3–6). No one who is in Christ is reprobate. Therefore, our first response to election and reprobation should be to flee to Christ. By his grace, we must hide ourselves in him as our only righteousness and salvation. Then we need not fear. "In him we have redemption through his blood, the forgiveness of our trespasses, according to the riches of his grace" (v. 7 ESV).

Second, *pursue holiness and love as God's chosen people.* Election produces holiness (Eph. 1:4). Therefore, the only pathway by which the elect attain glory is the road of holiness. Knowing that God elected us should move us to love one another. Paul says, "Put on therefore, as the elect of God, holy and beloved, bowels of mercies, kindness, humbleness of mind, meekness, longsuffering" (Col. 3:12).

Third, *seek and enjoy assurance of election and glory.* No one can know in this life that he is a reprobate. God has not revealed in his Word whom he has reprobated. However, it is possible to be assured of one's election. Do you have faith in Jesus Christ? It is because of your election: "As many as were ordained to eternal life believed" (Acts 13:48). Do you love God's holy ways and walk in sincere, though imperfect, obedience to his holy laws? It is because "he hath chosen us in him before the foundation of the world, that we should be holy" (Eph. 1:4). Are you striving to increase in knowledge, purity, and love? This is how to "make your calling and election sure" (2 Pet. 1:10).

Fourth, *evangelize the lost with confidence in the God of sovereign grace.* Paul says, "I suffer trouble, as an evil doer, even unto bonds; but the word of God is not bound. Therefore I endure all things for the elect's sakes, that they may also obtain the salvation which is in Christ Jesus with eternal glory" (2 Tim. 2:9–10). Christ has his sheep, including those not yet in his fold (John 10:16). The Father gave them to him (v. 29). He died for them (v. 11). They will hear his voice and follow him to the end (vv. 27–28). Be faithful, speak the gospel, and trust God.

Fifth, *have great optimism for the future of Christ's church.* The church will face many troubles. False teachers will arise and draw disciples after themselves (Acts 20:30). In fact, "if it were possible, they shall deceive the very elect" (Matt. 24:24). But it is *not* possible. False teachers may make some progress. Some professing Christians will fall away. "Nevertheless the foundation of God standeth sure, having this seal, The Lord knoweth them that are his" (2 Tim. 2:19).

Sixth, *receive with hope the afflictions that God ordains for his elect.* Those "whom he did foreknow, he also did predestinate to be conformed to the image of his Son" (Rom. 8:29). The elect are "joint-heirs with Christ; if so be that we suffer with him, that we may be also glorified together" (v. 17). Paul says, "No man should be moved by these afflictions: for yourselves know that we are appointed thereunto" (1 Thess. 3:3). Persevere, Christian, for God has chosen you to pass through sufferings on the way to eternal glory.

Suggested Song to Sing to the Lord

- "How vast the benefits divine," *THBap*, No. 95

Questions for Meditation or Discussion

1. What is the doctrine of election?
2. What motivated God to elect sinners for salvation?
3. Why is the God of election called "the God and Father of our Lord Jesus Christ" (Eph. 1:3–4)?

4. What does it mean to be "chosen in Christ" (see Eph. 1:4)?
5. How would you show from Scripture that election involved God's selection of the particular individuals whom he would save?
6. How does God's election relate to all events that take place in history (cf. Eph. 1:11)?
7. What is the doctrine of reprobation?
8. How would you prove that reprobation is a biblical teaching?
9. What is the ultimate purpose of divine election and reprobation?
10. How does your heart react to election and reprobation? Why? Has reading this chapter made any difference in how you view this subject? How?

23

Questions about Predestination

Chapter Summary and Key Terms

Adherents of *Pelagianism* and *Arminianism* oppose the biblical doctrine of predestination because they believe that it contradicts human free will. Instead, Pelagians and Arminians teach a different view of predestination, such as the doctrine that God chose individuals because he knew that they would believe in Christ and follow him to the end (*conditional election*). Or they may teach that God chose to save a category of people: "whoever will believe" (*corporate election*). On the contrary, the Scriptures teach that God chose individuals for salvation, and his election is eternal and unconditional. Predestination does not violate God's goodness or justice, for God is free to show mercy as he pleases, and all sinners deserve damnation. The doctrine of predestination should move us to humble ourselves, find comfort and hope in God's sovereign grace to save us to the end, and give all praise to him for grace and eternal life.

THE DOCTRINE OF PREDESTINATION, including both election and reprobation, has long been controversial. The Bible clearly teaches that God is sovereign over all things. He saves sinners by his grace alone. As we saw in the last chapter, God elects his people and rejects others. Yet the Bible also teaches that people bear personal responsibility for their actions.

In this chapter, we will provide a short survey of the history of the debate over this doctrine. We will then offer answers to some questions related to it. Our goal is not to solve every problem. As mere human beings, we cannot fully comprehend God. We strive to receive all of God's Word with as much understanding as possible. John Calvin said, "Let this then be our sacred rule, to seek to know nothing concerning [predestination], except what Scripture teaches us: when the Lord closes his holy mouth, let us also stop the way, that we may go no farther."[1]

The History of the Controversy over Predestination

Predestination first received serious attention from theologians in the controversy over *Pelagianism* (we will discuss this view in more detail in chap. 34). In the fifth century, Pelagius taught that people have the power to choose to be good, and God predestined to salvation those whom he foreknew would repent and believe. According to Augustine, however, Adam's sin enslaved people to sin. But God elected some people to salvation. God saves his chosen ones by grace so that they choose him and follow him to the end, Augustine said.

The Christian church rejected Pelagius's teaching. But only some people followed Augustine's doctrine. Others taught that we need God's grace, but his grace does not have the power to save us unless we choose to cooperate with it. This view is called *synergism* (see chap. 58). Like Pelagius, these synergists also taught that God chooses whom he will save based on his knowledge of who will choose him.

Predestination remained a controversial subject in the Middle Ages. In the ninth century, church leaders condemned Gottschalk of Orbais for teaching election and reprobation. Some theologians of the twelfth and thirteenth centuries, such as Bernard of Clairvaux and Thomas Aquinas, taught that God chose whom he would save as a free act of his love. However, in the fourteenth and fifteenth centuries, other theologians took large steps away from Augustine's teaching. They said that God gives saving grace to whoever does the best he can to love God. This doctrine was opposed by Thomas Bradwardine, John Wycliffe, and Jan Hus, who agreed with what Augustine had taught.

In the sixteenth century, the Protestants taught the doctrines of salvation by grace alone and God's election of whom he would save. Martin Luther said that God predestined some people to salvation. He taught that God's

1 Calvin, *Comm.* on Rom. 9:14.

election was not based on anything good that people would do. But he insisted that his teaching should not be taken as fatalism but should be seen as a doctrine of comfort for God's people.

After Luther died, bitter disputes erupted among Lutherans about sin, grace, and predestination. Most Lutheran churches found unity in the Formula of Concord (1577). They said that God elected some people to salvation. But they denied that God reprobated anyone. Instead, they said that God's will to save all people is frustrated by those who resist his grace.[2]

Early Reformed theologians, such as Ulrich Zwingli, Heinrich Bullinger, Martin Bucer, Peter Martyr Vermigli, and John Calvin, said that God unconditionally chose those whom he would save. Saving faith is the gift of God's grace alone. This means, they said, that God chose to damn some sinners as their sins deserve. The doctrine of predestination was clearly stated in the early Reformed confessions, such as the Belgic Confession.[3] It was also taught by Reformed orthodox theologians such as William Perkins.

However, a controversy about God's grace arose within the Reformed Church of the Netherlands. Jacob Arminius and his followers insisted that election simply means that God chose to save those who would believe and obey him to the end. Salvation was said to depend at every point on man's choosing to do what he can.

At the Synod of Dort (1618–1619), the doctrine of *Arminianism* was rejected. God's election and reprobation were affirmed by the Canons of Dort to be the teaching of the Bible.[4] A few decades later, the Reformed doctrine of predestination reached one of its most mature expressions in the Westminster Confession of Faith.[5] Though debates about predestination continue to the present day, the Belgic Confession, the Canons of Dort, and the Westminster Confession remain the definitive confessional statements of Reformed theology on predestination.

2 The Formula of Concord (Epitome, 11.12, 19; Solid Declaration, 11.5, 9, 40), in *The Book of Concord: The Confessions of the Evangelical Lutheran Church*, ed. Robert Kolb and Timothy J. Wengert, trans. Charles Arand et al. (Minneapolis: Fortress, 2000), 518–19, 641–42, 647.

3 The Belgic Confession (Art. 16), in *TFU*, 33.

4 The Canons of Dort (Head 1), in *TFU*, 120–33.

5 The Westminster Confession of Faith (3.3–8), in *RC*, 4:238–39. Cf. the Second London Baptist Confession (3.3–7), in *RC*, 4:536–37.

Questions about Predestination

People have many questions about predestination. Here are some of the most common ones.[6]

First, *does God will the salvation of all people?* Paul says that God "will have all men to be saved, and to come unto the knowledge of the truth" (1 Tim. 2:4). However, this Scripture cannot mean that God chooses to save every human being. God accomplishes all his will (Ps. 135:6), but he does not save all mankind (Matt. 7:13–14).

It is better to understand "all men" to refer to people from every kind and category. God saves kings and subjects, rich and poor, educated and uneducated, women and men, young and old. Paul calls for prayer for "all men; for kings, and for all that are in authority" (1 Tim. 2:1–2). Therefore, we should tell the gospel to all kinds of people. We do not know whom God chose until, by his grace, they are saved by faith in Christ to the praise of his glory (Eph. 1:3–4, 11–14).

Second, *how could a good and loving God choose to damn some people?* It is certainly true that God is love (1 John 4:8). He is good to all people (Luke 6:35). But God is free to exercise his love as he chooses (Ex. 33:19). He did not choose to give eternal life to all sinners. Rather, he chose to save some sinners but to give others the punishment that their sins deserve.

God is the source of all good (James 1:17). Likewise, suffering comes as God's punishment of sin (Rom. 5:12; 6:23). Thus, God damns sinners not because of any malice in him, but because of his justice against sin. Even in his wrath, God remains good.[7] It is sinners who are evil. The Lord says, "O Israel, thou hast destroyed thyself; but in me is thine help" (Hos. 13:9).

Third, *why should we teach predestination instead of just preaching the gospel?* We should preach the gospel. But we should also teach predestination. It gives solid hope to those who believe the gospel. Paul says,

> We know that all things work together for good to them that love God, to them who are the called according to his purpose. For whom he did foreknow, he also did predestinate to be conformed to the image of his Son,

6 Some questions related to predestination will be addressed under other topics. For example, we will show that a biblical view of the free choice of the will (chap. 35) and the free offer of the gospel (chap. 56) are both taught by Reformed theology.

7 On the wrath of God in connection to his justice and goodness, see chap. 18.

> that he might be the firstborn among many brethren. Moreover whom he did predestinate, them he also called: and whom he called, them he also justified: and whom he justified, them he also glorified. (Rom. 8:28–30)

Since God chose whom he would save, he will bring his chosen ones to glory.

Paul then asks a series of questions (Rom. 8:31–39). If God is for us, who can be against us? If God gave up his Son for us, how will he not also grace us with all things? Who will bring any charge against God's elect? Who will condemn us? What can separate us from God's love in Christ? Every one of these questions drives us to the same happy conclusion: those in Christ may rest assured that God's love will never fail them. God will bring them safely through every sorrow to be "more than conquerors" (v. 37). Therefore, election is a message of enduring hope.

Fourth, *did God choose those whom he foreknew would trust and obey him to the end?* The golden chain of salvation begins with those "whom he did foreknow" (Rom. 8:29; cf. 1 Pet. 1:2). This might be taken to mean that he chose them because he knew they would believe—a doctrine called *conditional election*. But Paul rejects the idea that God's predestination was based on man's future actions. He says of Jacob and Esau, "For the children being not yet born, neither having done any good or evil, that the purpose of God according to election might stand, not of works, but of him that calleth" (Rom. 9:11).

What, then, does it mean that God "foreknew" those whom he predestined (Rom. 8:29)? In the Holy Scriptures, "to know" often means to love or to choose with approval and blessing (Gen. 18:19; Ps. 1:6; Jer. 1:5). Therefore, Paul means that God predetermined those whom he loved and chose beforehand to become like Christ. Augustine said, "He chose us, not because we believed, but that we might believe, lest we should be said first to have chosen Him, and so His word be false (which be it far from us to think possible), 'Ye have not chosen me, but I have chosen you [John 15:16].' "[8]

Fifth, *if God's election cannot fail, then why did his chosen people reject Christ?* Paul was very sad that many of his fellow Jews did not believe in Christ (Rom. 9:1–3). He said, "My heart's desire and prayer to God for Israel

8 Augustine, *On the Predestination of the Saints*, 19.38, in *NPNF*[1], 5:517.

is, that they might be saved" (10:1). We, too, must grieve over the lost and pray for their salvation.

But the sad condition of many Jews does not mean that God's plan failed. Paul says, "They are not all Israel, which are of Israel" (Rom. 9:6). There are two Israels, the physical descendants of Abraham and his spiritual descendants (v. 8). The latter are Abraham's descendants by God's election. God chose Isaac but not Ishmael, though they had the same father (vv. 7–9). God chose Jacob but not Esau, though they had the same father and mother (vv. 10–12). Therefore, God's election did not fail. He has always chosen some but not others.

Sixth, *did God choose people for salvation as a group or as individuals?* Some people argue that Romans 9 is not about individuals but about groups. They say that God does not choose individual people for salvation but only the whole group of those who believe in Christ—whoever they might be. This idea is called *corporate election*.

But Romans 9 is about the salvation of individuals whom God chose. The main idea of Romans is salvation. In chapters 9 and 10 of Romans, Paul focuses on the salvation of Jewish individuals (Rom. 9:1–3; 10:1). He talks about being "children of God" (9:8). God's saving "call" is "not of works" (v. 11; cf. 2 Tim. 1:9). Paul speaks in terms of individuals, what each one does, and whether God has mercy on each one.

God predestined individuals, just as he calls individuals, justifies individuals, and will glorify individuals (Rom. 8:30). He did not choose an idea ("believers" or "the church"). He chose people (Eph. 1:4; 2 Thess. 2:13). Paul can even say to an individual Christian that he is "chosen in the Lord" (Rom. 16:13).

Seventh, *is God unjust in choosing to save some but not all?* Paul expects someone to ask, "Is there unrighteousness with God?" He answers firmly, "God forbid" (Rom. 9:14). Paul explains that God has total freedom to show mercy on whom he pleases. He quotes the Lord's statement, "I will have mercy on whom I will have mercy, and I will have compassion on whom I will have compassion" (v. 15). God's grace is a free gift apart from any human choice or effort: "So then it is not of him that willeth, nor of him that runneth, but of God that sheweth mercy" (v. 16).

Paul also quotes what the Lord said to wicked Pharaoh: "For this same purpose have I raised thee up, that I might shew my power in thee, and that my name might be declared throughout all the earth" (Rom. 9:17).

God ordained Pharaoh's defiance and disobedience to glorify himself. Paul concludes, "Therefore hath he mercy on whom he will have mercy, and whom he will he hardeneth" (v. 18). This is not about God being just or fair, but about the absolute sovereignty and freedom of his mercy to sinners.

Eighth, *if God chose whom he saves, how can he blame man for his sin?* Paul again expects an objection: "Why doth he yet find fault? For who hath resisted his will?" (Rom. 9:19). Paul's answer is breathtaking, for he makes no attempt to explain God's ways. Instead, the apostle says, "Who are you, O man, to answer back to God?" (v. 20 ESV). The greatness of God demands that we be silent in such matters.

Paul compares God to a potter who has the right to make different vessels out of the same clay (Rom. 9:21). Some people are "vessels of wrath fitted to destruction" for God "to shew his wrath, and to make his power known" (v. 22). Others are "vessels of mercy, which he had afore prepared unto glory" so he could "make known the riches of his glory" (v. 23). God has the right to choose because he is God. He also has the right to judge because he is God. Ultimately, it boils down to this: *God is God.* Predestination brings us to face the absolute and incomprehensible glory of God, and we must worship him (11:33–36).

Practical Applications of the Doctrine of Predestination

What applications can we make from the doctrine of predestination?

First, *we should meditate on the nature of God revealed in predestination.* Consider his wisdom in crafting a marvelous plan of salvation and damnation that included every person who would ever live. Think about his authority to save whom he wills. Ponder his mercy in selecting for salvation those who would otherwise be utterly lost and worthy of damnation. Contemplate his justice in saving the elect by the blood of his Son and in damning the reprobate for their sins. Adore his eternity in deciding all this before time began. Stand in awe at his majesty that predestined men in a fashion that we can never fully understand.

Second, *we should put no faith in works, but trust Christ for justification by faith alone.* Election is the ultimate cause of our justification (Rom. 8:30), and election is by grace, not by works (11:6). Therefore, believers are justified apart from their works (3:28). Election teaches us to put no trust in our own righteousness, but in Christ alone.

Third, *we should reject pride and walk in godly fear toward the Lord.* People tend to twist God's election into a cover for hypocrisy. They may think that the so-called "elect people" can do what they please and still boast proudly in God's promises. Against this, Paul warns that God broke off the unbelieving branches from the tree of his church, adding, "Thou standest by faith. Be not highminded, but fear" (Rom. 11:20). Are we any better than the vessels of wrath? Only God's sovereign grace lifts us up out of damnation. We must humbly trust in him.

Fourth, *we should give our grateful praises to the God of election.* Paul exults, "Blessed be the God and Father of our Lord Jesus Christ, who hath blessed us with all spiritual blessings in heavenly places in Christ: according as he hath chosen us in him before the foundation of the world" (Eph. 1:3–4). Without God's election of us, we would never have been saved. In and of ourselves, we are only sinners. But praise be to God, election is the friend of sinners! Furthermore, we should continually thank God for his election and calling of our brothers and sisters in the Lord (2 Thess. 2:13). How marvelous is his grace!

Suggested Songs to Sing to the Lord

- Psalm 65, "Praise waits in Zion, Lord, for Thee," *Psalter*, No. 166
- "How sweet and awful is the place," *THBap*, No. 271

Questions for Meditation or Discussion

1. What did Augustine teach about salvation, grace, and predestination?
2. What does Lutheranism teach about salvation, grace, and predestination?
3. What does Reformed theology teach about predestination?
4. What did Paul mean when he wrote that God "will have all men to be saved" (1 Tim. 2:4)?
5. How is the doctrine of election a source of assurance for believers?
6. Does Romans 8:29 teach that God elected those whom he foreknew would trust and follow Christ to the end? Why or why not?
7. How does Paul answer the objection that the God of predestination is unjust?
8. How is the doctrine of predestination a cause of great humility?
9. How is the doctrine of predestination a cause of great hope?

24

God's Creation of the World

Chapter Summary and Key Terms

In God's work of *creation*, he made the universe and all that is in it, and all very good. Creation was the first step in the execution of God's decree for his glory. It began time and history. It showed that God, the Creator, is infinitely greater than his creatures. The work of creation distinguishes the biblical view of God from polytheism, pantheism, panentheism, and atheism. The doctrine of *creation ex nihilo* ("out of nothing") teaches that God did not form the world out of material that already existed. Genesis 1 says that God made the whole world, including mankind, in six days. The *gap theory* says that long ages passed between the first two verses of Genesis. The *day-age view* says that each "day" in Genesis 1 was really an age. The *framework view* reads Genesis 1 as if it were a parable or poem. But it is best to interpret Genesis 1 as teaching the creation of all things in six literal days at the beginning of the history of the universe (*calendar day view*).

THE DOCTRINE OF CREATION anchors our faith in God, directs our lives to his glory, and protects us against idolatry (Acts 14:15; Rev. 4:11). His act of creation began the execution of his decree and launched history. The Genesis account of it is the starting point for the Bible and the beginning of God's revelation of himself. It also lays the foundation for ethics and worship, and it grounds the gospel of Jesus Christ in the nature of God, the nature of man, and their relationship as Creator and creature. Second only to redemption by the incarnate Lord, the act of creation was the greatest display of the glory of God.

False Beliefs about the Origin of the Universe

False views of creation spring from belief in false gods. Some believe that there were two or more first causes to the world (polytheism). According to ancient pagan religions, the origin of the world (and many of its gods) arose from gods mating or warring with one another. Other religions say that both spirit and matter have always existed, and neither made the other.

If all things are one (pantheism), there is no real difference between God and creation. God could say, "I indeed am this creation," as Hindus claim.[1] Other people believe that God is the soul of the universe, and the world is like his body (panentheism). God, then, did not create the world and does not rule it. Rather, he is one with the world, so he suffers with it, develops with it, and seeks to persuade it to develop toward good. These views of God are very different from faith in the "God that made the world and all things therein," for "he is Lord of heaven and earth" (Acts 17:24).

Some people think that the physical matter and energy of the universe have always existed, and this is all that has ever existed (atheism). Physical and chemical reactions drive everything that happens in the universe.

People often hold to a mixture of these views. For example, they might believe the universe is all that exists but also believe there is a kind of spirit or life-force in the universe. As a result, they give their devotion to things in the universe as if those things were gods. As Paul explains, those who refuse to glorify God exchange his glory for the visible things of creation (Rom. 1:21–23).

God's Work of Creation

The doctrine of creation is taught in many places in the Bible, but it is good for us to begin "in the beginning," with the foundation of the whole Bible, Genesis 1:1–2:3. There we learn that God created the world in six days:

- *Day One*: In the beginning, God created the heavens and the earth. He made light, resulting in the beginning of day and night.

1 Brihadaranyaka Upanishad, 1.4.1–5, cited in *The Upanishads*, trans. F. Max Müller (Oxford: Oxford University Press, 1884), 2:85–86.

- *Day Two*: God divided the waters above, most likely the clouds, from the waters below, which are the rivers, lakes, oceans, and subterranean aquifers.
- *Day Three*: God gathered the waters so that the dry land appeared. He named the former "seas" and the latter "earth." God also made the plants.
- *Day Four*: God created lights in the heaven to distinguish seasons and years.
- *Day Five*: God created sea creatures and flying creatures. He blessed them to be fruitful and multiply.
- *Day Six*: God created land animals. He then created man in his image. God blessed man to be fruitful, multiply, and rule over the other living creatures.
- *Day Seven*: God ceased from his work of creation. He blessed and sanctified that day.

We learn two important lessons from Genesis 1 about God's work of creation.

First, *God's work of creation was unique.* It marked the beginning of the universe (Gen. 1:1; Mark 10:6), the first day of history (Gen. 1:5). Prior to that day, there was no time. There was only God "before the ages began" (2 Tim. 1:9; Titus 1:2 ESV).

Second, *God's work of creation was universal.* God made all parts and places of the whole universe. He is "the living God, which made heaven, and earth, and the sea, and all things that are therein" (Acts 14:15).

Creation and the Glory of God

God revealed his work of creation to his people to show his glory. The Westminster Confession of Faith says, "It pleased God the Father, Son, and Holy Ghost, for the manifestation of the glory of His eternal power, wisdom, and goodness, in the beginning, to create, or make of nothing, the world, and all things therein whether visible or invisible, in the space of six days; and all very good."[2]

2 The Westminster Confession of Faith (4.1), in *RC*, 4:239. Cf. the Second London Baptist Confession (4.1), in *RC*, 4:538.

By the work of creation, God showed that he is *unique*, the only true God. Hezekiah says, "O Lord of hosts, God of Israel . . . thou art the God, even thou alone, of all the kingdoms of the earth: thou hast made heaven and earth" (Isa. 37:16). We must give our worship and supreme allegiance to no being other than the Creator of heaven and earth.

This unique Creator is *the Trinity*, one God in three persons. When the text says, "God created the heaven and the earth" (Gen. 1:1), the verb "created" is in the singular form, for it is the action of one God. However, we read next, "And the Spirit of God moved upon the face of the waters" (v. 2). "Spirit of God" is the same expression used elsewhere for the Holy Spirit (Ex. 31:3; 1 Cor. 12:3). The Spirit of God acted on creation like a mother bird tenderly nurturing its chicks (cf. Deut. 32:10–12). Then God said, "Let *us* make man in *our* image" (Gen. 1:26). God was in conversation with God as more than one person.

Later, in the New Testament, John writes, "In the beginning was the Word, and the Word was with God, and the Word was God. The same was in the beginning with God. All things were made by him; and without him was not any thing made that was made. . . . And the Word was made flesh, and dwelt among us" (John 1:1–3, 14). Therefore, Christ is the Creator of the world along with the Father and the Holy Spirit (Heb. 1:10).

The work of creation also shows us God's immense *power*. The universe he made is too large for us to imagine. Yet he made it with ease, merely by speaking (Ps. 33:6, 9). Our sun is over three hundred thousand times more massive than the earth. God created innumerable stars with a mere word. The power of the Creator should fill us with awe and astonishment. When a construction worker does his job, he needs tools and raw materials such as lumber or bricks. God needed only his will and his power to make the universe. Jeremiah exclaims, "Ah Lord God! Behold, thou hast made the heaven and the earth by thy great power and stretched out arm, and there is nothing too hard for thee" (Jer. 32:17).

Through creation, we understand God's *authority* over everything and everyone. God made all things. Therefore, he owns them. David says in Psalm 24:1–2, "The earth is the Lord's, and the fulness thereof; the world, and they that dwell therein. For he hath founded it upon the seas, and established it upon the floods." This truth should make us want to understand and obey God's laws, for we belong to him. Psalm 119:73 says, "Thy hands have made me and fashioned me: give me understanding, that I may learn thy commandments."

God's work of creation shines with his *wisdom*. Proverbs 3:19 says, "The LORD by wisdom hath founded the earth; by understanding hath he established the heavens." God chose to make the world at first "without form, and void" (Gen. 1:2). Then, over six days, he gave it structure, order, and form until it was prepared to be a good home for mankind. God also created the many kinds of living creatures (vv. 11–12, 21, 24–25), bringing them together to form a harmonious system of life. Only a being of great intelligence and skill could make such a complex and beautiful world. We can trust this wise God.

When we consider the beauty and bounty of God's world, especially as it was before sin and the curse marred it, we should be overwhelmed at the *goodness* of God. Over and over again we read in Genesis 1 that God made something and saw that "it was good." The creation account ends with the statement that "God saw every thing that he had made, and, behold, it was very good" (v. 31). Paul says, "Every creature of God is good, and nothing to be refused, if it be received with thanksgiving: for it is sanctified by the word of God and prayer" (1 Tim. 4:4–5). God "giveth us richly all things to enjoy" (6:17).

We conclude that God created the universe to declare his glory (Ps. 19:1): "The whole earth is full of his glory" (Isa. 6:3). Therefore, we should use all things for God's glory. John Calvin asked in his catechism, "What is the chief end of human life?" and answered, "To know God." He went on, "Why do you say that?" and replied, "Because He created us and placed us in this world to be glorified in us. And it is indeed right that our life, of which He himself is the beginning, should be devoted to His glory."[3]

Creation out of Nothing

God created everything that exists. He did not just shape material that already existed. Rather, he made the very substances of which all things consist. Thus, we say that he created the world "out of nothing" (Latin *ex nihilo*). Christians believe this for several reasons.

First, when the creation account says, "In the beginning God created the heaven and the earth" (Gen. 1:1), it is declaring that God created all that

3 Calvin's Catechism of 1545 (Q. 1–2), in *RC*, 4:469.

exists. The rest of the chapter tells us that he made every kind of thing there is. It is utterly silent about any matter that existed beforehand. The work of creation was the "beginning" of everything.

Second, many Scripture passages state that God created "all things."[4] Psalm 146:6, which Paul quotes in Acts 14:15, shows that the phrase "all things" refers to everything in every realm of the universe: "heaven and earth, the sea, and all that is in them" (ESV).

Third, Hebrews 11:3 denies that God made the universe out of anything we can see: "By faith we understand that the universe was created by the word of God, so that what is seen was not made out of things that are visible" (ESV). F. F. Bruce paraphrased, "The visible universe, he says, was not made out of equally visible raw material; it was called into being by divine power." He goes on to say, "The writer to the Hebrews . . . affirms the doctrine of *creatio ex nihilo*."[5]

Fourth, Colossians 1:16 states that by Christ "were all things created, that are in heaven, and that are in earth, visible and invisible." There is no person, material, or substance, not even something undetectable by our senses, that Christ did not create.

Fifth, Romans 4:17 affirms that God "calls into existence the things that do not exist" (ESV). At the very least, this says that God has the power to create *ex nihilo*.

Sixth, the doctrine of creation out of nothing is essential to a biblical view of God. If the universe consists of material not created by God, the universe is independent of God. Thus, the Bible's view of God as the sovereign Lord over all things collapses.

God's creation of the universe out of nothing greatly magnifies his power and asserts his absolute sovereignty over the world. Stephen Charnock said, "Greater power cannot be imagined than that which brings something out of nothing."[6] This doctrine should humble us. Thomas Watson said, "How little cause have they to boast who came from nothing."[7]

4 Neh. 9:6; John 1:3; Acts 14:15; 17:24; 1 Cor. 8:6; Eph. 3:9; Col. 1:16; Rev. 4:11.

5 F. F. Bruce, *Hebrews*, New International Commentary on the New Testament (Grand Rapids, MI: Eerdmans, 1964), 280–81.

6 Charnock, *The Existence and Attributes of God*, in *WSChar*, 2:128.

7 Thomas Watson, *A Body of Divinity* (Edinburgh: Banner of Truth, 1965), 114.

Creation in Six Days

The Bible says that God made the world in the span of six days (Gen. 1:31; Ex. 20:11). Christians have interpreted these texts in different ways.

The *gap theory* proposes that there were many ages between Genesis 1:1 and verse 2. This is sometimes called the ruin-reconstruction view because the condition of the earth as "without form, and void" is said to be the result of a disaster. The gap allows for long geological ages. The disaster explains the deaths of creatures represented in the fossil record.

But there is no evidence in Genesis 1 for a gap of billions of years. Verse 2 does not say the earth "*became* without form," but that it "*was* without form." The Bible nowhere teaches that there was a worldwide disaster after the first creation. Genesis 1 reveals a world without conflict, sin, or judgment—a "very good" world (v. 31). The entire work of creation took place "in six days" (Ex. 20:11). Christ explicitly says that Adam and his son Abel lived at the beginning of the world (Mark 10:6; Luke 11:50–51). These factors leave no room for a gap in the Bible's history.

The *day-age view* interprets the "six days" as six long ages. It is argued that the Bible says a "day" is like "a thousand years" (Ps. 90:4; 2 Pet. 3:8).

But those Scripture passages are not teaching us about the time of creation. They are about God's eternity and patience. We have no basis in Scripture to import this figurative use of "day" into the Genesis account. Genesis 1 reads as history. We cannot allow the theories of modern science to control how we read the Bible. If we do, we will end up surrendering the authority of the Bible as God's Word.

The *framework view* says that the "six days" are not history but theology presented in a form like a parable. This is clear, we are told, because in the first three days God formed parts of his world (light, sky/sea, land) and in the next three days he filled them (lights in the sky, fish/birds, animals/people). So it was all one creative work, not a work on separate days.

But the well-organized structure of Genesis 1 does not mean that it is not history. There is structure in the account of the ten plagues on Egypt (Exodus 7–12). The perfect harmony and order of Genesis 1 remind us that God is the sovereign and wise Creator. It makes much more sense to read Genesis 1 not as a theological poem but as a chronological sequence of days in which each act of creation prepares for what follows it.

The *calendar day view* understands Genesis 1 to present six literal days at the beginning of history. The repetition of the phrase "the evening and the morning" on each of the six days suggests an ordinary cycle of night and day. The appeal to the six days and the seventh in the Sabbath commandment only makes sense if creation took place in a literal week (Ex. 20:11; 31:17). The omnipotent God would have had no difficulty making the world in six days.

People may raise objections to the calendar day view, which we answer as follows:

1. God is said to have created light on the first day but the sun on the fourth. But God can make light without the sun.
2. Too many events take place on the sixth day (Gen. 1:24–31) to fit into a twenty-four-hour day. There was the creation of animals, the creation of man, man's naming of the animals, the creation of woman, and man's speech about her (cf. chap. 2). But we do not know how long these events took. This argument is speculative.
3. The seventh day has no reference to evening and morning. Therefore, it is an age that continues to the present time (Gen. 2:1–3). But this is an argument from silence. Besides, the Sabbath law would make no sense if the seventh day lasts forever, for the Sabbath originally fell on the seventh day of each week (Ex. 20:11).
4. Genesis 2:4 says God created all things in a day: "In the day that the Lord God made the earth and the heavens." Therefore, the days are not literal. But "in the day" is a Hebrew way of saying "when" (v. 17; 5:1). It is not the same as a list of numbered days that tells about historical events (cf. Num. 7:12–83).

In the end, we find the plain and simple reading of Genesis 1 as the history of six calendar days to be the most compelling. Calvin said, "Moses wanted to indicate that one entire day was made up of two parts: from evening till morning, and from morning till the following evening"—that is, "the day and the night," or "twenty-four hours."[8]

8 John Calvin, *Sermons on Genesis, Chapters 1–11*, trans. Rob Roy McGregor (Edinburgh: Banner of Truth, 2009), 29, 60.

Suggested Songs to Sing to the Lord

- Psalm 96, "Sing to the Lord, sing His praise, all ye peoples," *Psalter*, No. 259; *THBap*, No. 65
- "Each little flow'r that opens," *THBap*, No. 636

Questions for Meditation or Discussion

1. Explain these false views of the origin of the universe: (1) polytheism, (2) pantheism, (3) panentheism, and (4) atheism.
2. What did God create on each of the days of the first week?
3. How does God's work of creation show his uniqueness?
4. What hints of the Trinity do we find in Genesis 1?
5. How did God display his power, authority, wisdom, and goodness in the work of creation?
6. What does creation *ex nihilo* mean? How do we know it is true?
7. Explain each of the following views of the six days of Genesis 1 and the problems with it: (1) the gap theory, (2) the day-age view, (3) the framework view.
8. What is the "calendar day" interpretation of Genesis 1? What is its greatest strength?
9. What objections do people raise against the calendar day view? How can these be answered?
10. How has studying God's work of creation encouraged you to trust him more?

25

Questions about Creation

Chapter Summary and Key Terms

Though the Bible is not a science textbook, we still should believe what it says about when and how God created the world. Despite assertions to the contrary, Genesis 1 is not a myth or legend. Rather, it is God's Word concerning the origin of all things. Furthermore, it is written in the form of history, not poetry. The Bible indicates that the world is only several thousand years old. Scientists cannot prove that the universe is billions of years old, for they can observe only current events. People must speculate about what happened in the distant past. The Bible is not compatible with *evolution*, the theory that all life on earth developed from a common ancestor by a natural process over billions of years. Genesis 1–2 says that God supernaturally created each kind of plant and animal, and lastly made man of the earth, all in the span of six days. Genesis also presents the flood of Noah as a global cataclysm that destroyed all human beings and animals on the earth except those in the ark.

IN THE LAST TWO CENTURIES, the Christian doctrine of creation has been challenged by modern theories about the origin of the universe and life in it. This raises questions. In this chapter, we will discuss some of those questions to show that it is reasonable to believe the Bible's teaching about how God created the world.

Is Genesis 1 a Myth?

Some theologians say that Genesis 1 is a "myth"—that is, a traditional story or religious legend. But to call Genesis 1 a myth is to treat it like other ancient ideas that few people believe today. It is to make it like Greek or Norse mythology. This is wrong because Genesis is part of the Holy Scriptures, the Word of God, which is always true in its teaching and profitable in its application (Prov. 30:5; 2 Tim. 3:16).

Some people argue that the Bible teaches an ancient view of the universe contrary to modern science. For example, some claim that the writers of the Bible believed that the sky is a solid dome holding up a heavenly sea (Gen. 1:6–8; cf. Ps. 148:4).

In reply, we note that people who say this are reading ancient beliefs about astronomy into the Bible. The Holy Scriptures never teach such a thing. The Bible does not teach us much about the structure of the universe. For example, it speaks of "the circle of the earth" (Isa. 40:22), but it also speaks of "the four corners of the earth" (11:12; Acts 10:11; Rev. 7:1). The point is not whether the world is a circle or a square. These are figures of speech.

The "waters which were above the firmament" (Gen. 1:7) are probably best understood as the clouds. Ancient peoples understood that rain comes from clouds (Judg. 5:4; Job 26:8).

The Bible is not a book of ancient mythology. Edward Young said, "Genesis one is a document *sui generis* [in a category of its own]; its like or equal is not to be found anywhere in the literature of antiquity. And the reason for this is obvious. Genesis one is a divine revelation to man concerning the creation of heaven and earth."[1]

Is Genesis 1 Real History?

Some people have said that Genesis 1 is a kind of poetry. It is intended to teach us that God created the world, but not, we are told, to present a history of how he did so.

In reply, we say that the early chapters of Genesis present themselves as history. They read like history as found in other parts of the Bible, not like poetry.

Hebrew poetry is written in parallel lines. One line makes a point, and the next either repeats the same thought in somewhat different words or states its opposite. For example,

1 Edward J. Young, *Studies in Genesis One* (Phillipsburg, NJ: Presbyterian and Reformed Publishing, 1964), 82.

Then the earth shook and trembled;
The foundations also of the hills moved. (Ps. 18:7)

Or,

For the LORD knoweth the way of the righteous:
  but the way of the ungodly shall perish. (Ps. 1:6)

We do not find poetry like that in Genesis 1. Instead, the text is a string of sentences written in the grammar used in Hebrew for a series of real events. It says, "And God said," "And God saw," "And God called," and, "And God made." This is the style of history, not poetry.

As we continue to read through Genesis, we find that the early chapters are part of a larger narrative. Genesis links creation to real people and events through genealogies that trace Adam's family to Noah (Genesis 5), Abraham (11:10–27), Isaac (25:19), Jacob (37:2), and his children and grandchildren (46:8–27). The first book of Chronicles picks up the family tree and carries it through the descendants of David after the exile (1 Chronicles 1–3). The New Testament traces the genealogy of Jesus Christ back to Adam (Luke 3:23–38).

Jesus Christ, our supreme authority, treated Genesis as true history. He says, "But from the beginning of creation, 'God made them male and female.' 'Therefore a man shall leave his father and mother and hold fast to his wife, and the two shall become one flesh.' So they are no longer two but one flesh" (Mark 10:6–8 ESV). Here Christ refers to Genesis 1:27 and 2:24. He says that the events described in those passages took place at "the beginning of creation." Jesus also speaks of Abel, Adam's son, as an example of how things were "from the foundation of the world" (Luke 11:50–51). If God's Son, our Lord, believed the history reported in the early chapters of Genesis, so should we.

Does Science Prove That the World Is Billions of Years Old?

Since ancient times, some philosophers and scientists have believed that the earth had no beginning. Since the mid-twentieth century, the most popular theory has been that the universe erupted as a "big bang" about fourteen billion years ago. But a plain reading of the Bible's history leads the Christian to conclude that the earth is only several thousand years old.

We must remember that science is not just gathering facts that people can measure but also making theories that explain those facts. Theories are open to debate. There are even non-Christian scientists who question the big bang theory.

God created the world, at least in some respects, with the appearance of age. God made human beings as adults ready to marry. Trees were already grown and bearing fruit when he created them. Science cannot trace the age of a supernatural act, such as creation, by comparing it to natural processes. Imagine that a scientist analyzed the wine that Christ miraculously made from water (John 2:1–11). He probably would conclude that it came from the juice of grapes fermented over some weeks or months. But Christ made it in an instant.

Someone may object that radioactive dating shows that some rocks are billions of years old.

In reply, we point out that scientists must make assumptions to estimate the age of a rock. Radioactive dating involves theories about how much of a chemical element was in rocks ages ago and how much was added or taken away by physical processes over time. One must know how much radiation came from outside the material. One must also have a theory as to how the rate of radioactive decay changes or does not change over time.

Others may object, based on the size of the universe, that it must have taken starlight billions of years to get from distant stars to our planet so that we can see them.

In reply, we note that some scientists (and not just creationists) argue that the speed of light was much faster in past times than it is today. Furthermore, some current astrophysicists say that the visible universe has a radius of forty-six billion light years. But they claim that the universe is only fourteen billion years old. They explain this discrepancy by saying that space itself is expanding. If that is so, the size of the universe may not tell us much about the age of the universe.

Though scientists are very intelligent, there is still much they do not understand. When scientific theories contradict the Bible, we should have the humility to remember that the Lord said to Job, "Where wast thou when I laid the foundations of the earth?" (Job 38:4).

Is the Bible Compatible with the Evolution of the Species?

For thousands of years, people such as the Epicurean philosophers of ancient Greece have tried to explain the universe and life within it by means of entirely natural processes. This atheistic, naturalistic idea was given a modern scientific form in the theory of *evolution*. This is the belief that all life developed by natural processes from the elements of the earth. Life is said to have begun three billion to four billion years ago. For many eons, life supposedly consisted of very simple, single-celled organisms. These led to more complex plant life and then animals by the process of natural selection. Human beings developed from apes.

However, there are serious scientific problems with evolution. The fossil record does not show a smooth development of one kind of living being to another. We observe adaptation, and mankind has bred animals to produce different kinds of pets and livestock. But we have not observed one kind of animal become another kind. Breeding dogs still produces dogs. The most fundamental units of life, cells, have been discovered to be amazingly complex. Cells are not things that could happen by accident. Each cell's genetic code (DNA) contains enough information to fill a library. Mere chemical reactions do not create new information. Information is produced by intelligence.

Evolution also raises moral problems. If human beings are animals, why not kill them if we find it useful? People who believe in evolution may believe that we should treat one another with justice and kindness, but they have little reason for that belief. Only when we see that we have a Creator, that people are made in his image, and that he gives us laws to obey do we have reason to do what is right and loving.

The most serious problem with evolution is that it contradicts the Word of God. Genesis 1 teaches that God created the universe, plants, animals, and man in the space of six days. It did not take the billions of years necessary for evolution. The Bible also teaches us that plants, animals, and mankind came into existence by supernatural acts of God, not slow, natural development (Gen. 1:11, 20–28).

God made each plant or animal "according to its kind" (Gen. 1:11–12, 21, 25 ESV). The order of the creation days does not match the order of evolutionary theory. Birds appear in the creation account before land animals.

Evolution's principle of natural selection—survival of the fittest—assumes that animals have suffered and died for millions of years in order to produce the species we observe today. But God made the animals at first to eat plants (Gen. 1:29–30). His world was "very good" (v. 31), not full of killing and death. God made the first man "of the dust of the ground" (2:7). He did not make him out of another animal, such as an ape. The Lord made the first woman out of part of Adam's body (vv. 21–23). She became "the mother of all living" (3:20). It is impossible to believe in evolution without doing violence to the text of Scripture.

Was the Flood Global or Local?

The Bible also teaches that God destroyed the world and nearly all who lived in it by a great flood. Only those in the ark survived (Genesis 6–9). Some people regard the flood as a legend. Maybe, they say, there was a significant local flood. But they insist there was never a worldwide flood.

But the account of the flood in the Bible is presented as real history. It is recorded with specific dates and periods of time, as if drawn from a diary. Genesis teaches that God destroyed all living creatures outside the ark on the surface of the earth in the flood (Gen. 6:7; 7:4, 19–23). Why would Noah need to save all kinds of animals from a regional flood? Why bring birds into the ark when they could fly away? Why would Noah need to build such a large boat? Why would he not simply move to a safe location, such as a mountain? Furthermore, this flood was an unusual disaster involving a geological disturbance, not just a large flood produced by rain (7:11).

If we treat the flood as a legend, we overthrow the authority of God's Word to speak to any historical event. What else is a legend? For example, did Christ even rise from the dead?

Regarding the flood as legendary also calls into question the trustworthiness of God's promises. God said he would never send such a flood again (Gen. 9:11). But there have been many floods since then. For God's promise to be true, the biblical flood had to be unique—a worldwide flood that destroyed all life outside of the ark, just as God's judgment will one day fall on everyone who is not saved by faith in Christ.

Suggested Songs to Sing to the Lord

- "Praise the Lord in heav'nly places," Psalm 148, *Psalter*, No. 405
- "I sing th' almighty pow'r of God," *THBap*, No. 106

Questions for Meditation or Discussion

1. Why should we not call Genesis 1–3 a "myth"?
2. Why should we view Genesis 1–3 as history, not just poetry?
3. Why should we be cautious about using science to determine the age of the universe?
4. What are some scientific problems with the theory of evolution?
5. Why does the idea that human life evolved from animals by chemical reactions make it difficult to find reasons to act with justice and kindness?
6. How does the theory of evolution contradict the Bible?
7. How does Genesis show that Noah's flood was worldwide?
8. If the flood of Genesis was not worldwide, what does that imply about God's promises?
9. Someone says, "I don't see why I have to take Genesis literally to be a Christian. Why can't I accept evolution and still believe in Christ for my salvation?" How do you respond?

26

God's Providence

Chapter Summary and Key Terms

God's *providence* is his work of executing his decree in history after creating the world. God sustains and rules all his creatures for his glory and the good of his people. In the *concurrence* of his providence, God gives his creatures power to act according to their natural properties, but he also directs them to fulfill his purposes, whether they act necessarily, freely, or contingently. Christians experience God's providence under the loving sovereignty of the Father; in union with the submissive, incarnate Son; and by the inward power of the Holy Spirit. God's providence cannot be limited by natural laws, excluded from the details of life, or hindered by human choices. Nor should we deny providence because of the *problem of evil.* That is the claim that an all-good and all-powerful God would not permit evil to exist. However, God has good reasons to permit evil, though we do not understand them all. Practically speaking, believing in God's providence gives us patience in adversity, thankfulness in prosperity, and confidence about the future.

IN PROVIDENCE, the God who decreed all things for his glory in Christ executes his decree in history. Having created the world, he now directs his creation to fulfill his purpose.

The Heidelberg Catechism says the "providence of God" is "the almighty and everywhere present power of God; whereby, as it were by His hand, He upholds and governs heaven, earth, and all creatures; so that herbs and grass, rain and drought, fruitful and barren years, meat and drink, health and sickness, riches and poverty, yea, and all things come, not by chance, but by His fatherly hand."[1] This doctrine calls us to trust God in everything.

Providence Described

The Westminster Shorter Catechism tells us of three parts of God's providence: "God's works of providence are, his most holy, wise, and powerful preserving and governing all his creatures, and all their actions."[2] Let us look at these three parts more closely.

God's Preservation of All His Creation

The Creator of heaven, earth, and all that is in them did not abandon his creation after he made it. Paul says, "[The] God that made the world and all things therein, seeing that he is Lord of heaven and earth, dwelleth not in temples made with hands; neither is worshipped with men's hands, as though he needed any thing, seeing he giveth to all life, and breath, and all things" (Acts 17:24–25).

Creation constantly receives God's care. Whenever a wild donkey drinks water, a bird perches on a tree branch, cattle graze on grass, or men eat bread, God is present and active as the giver of these good things (Ps. 104:10–15). Lions must hunt for their food, but they "seek their meat from God" (v. 21). God feeds the birds. He clothes the fields with flowers. And he cares for his children so that they can seek his kingdom without the burden of earthly anxiety (Matt. 6:25–33). James writes, "Every good gift and every perfect gift is from above, and cometh down from the Father of lights" (James 1:17).

God's Control of All His Creation

God rules over everything and directs it all according to his good and wise decree. The plagues on Egypt proved that the Lord controls rivers, frogs, insects, livestock, storms, light, darkness, human health, and life itself (Exodus 7–11). His control is absolute and unstoppable: "Whatsoever the LORD pleased, that did he in heaven, and in earth, in the seas, and all deep places" (Ps. 135:6). Nebuchadnezzar acknowledged, "All the inhabitants of the earth are reputed as nothing: and he doeth according to his will in the

1 The Heidelberg Catechism (LD 10, Q. 27), in *TFU*, 76.

2 The Westminster Shorter Catechism (Q. 11), in *RC*, 4:354. Cf. the Baptist Catechism (Q. 14), in *RC*, 4:575.

army of heaven, and among the inhabitants of the earth: and none can stay his hand, or say unto him, What doest thou?" (Dan. 4:35).

In his Word, God reveals that he controls these things:

- the weather (Lev. 26:4–5; 19–20; Pss. 107:25, 29; 147:15–18)
- the plants and animals (Gen. 41:25–32; Lev. 26:22; Jonah 1:17; 2:10; 4:6–7)
- the nations of mankind (Deut. 2:3–5, 9, 19; Dan. 4:17; Acts 17:26)
- the life of every human being (Ex. 4:11; 1 Sam. 2:6–7; Ps. 139:13–15; James 4:15)
- the decisions of every human being (2 Sam. 17:14; 1 Kings 12:15; Prov. 21:1)
- the demons and Satan (Job 1:10, 12; 2:3–6; Luke 8:30–33)
- the sins of men (Gen. 50:20; Ps. 105:25; Acts 4:27–28; Rom. 11:32)

God does not cause sin, "for God cannot be tempted with evil, neither tempteth he any man" (James 1:13). He is the pure source of good (v. 17; cf. 1 John 1:5). However, the Lord's providence over man includes his control of human sin for his good purpose.

In summary, God "worketh all things after the counsel of his own will" (Eph. 1:11).

God's Working with the Acts of All His Creation

God works in and through everything he made so that it also works according to his plan. This is called his *concurrence*. The Westminster Confession of Faith says, "Although, in relation to the foreknowledge and decree of God, the first Cause, all things come to pass immutably, and infallibly; yet, by the same providence, He ordereth them to fall out, according to the nature of second causes, either necessarily, freely, or contingently."[3]

God works with *natural, necessary causes* in the created order. For example, we read in Psalm 104:13–14, "He watereth the hills from his chambers. . . . He causeth the grass to grow for the cattle." The fall of rain from the clouds (Eccles. 11:3) and the growth of plants from seeds in the earth (Mark

3 The Westminster Confession of Faith (5.2), in *RC*, 4:240. Cf. the Second London Baptist Confession (5.2), in *RC*, 4:538–39.

4:27–28) are natural processes—scientists can analyze them according to mathematical laws. But they are also providential acts of God (Ps. 147:8).

God works with *the free choices of angels and people*. The Lord declared the king of Assyria to be "the rod of mine anger" (Isa. 10:5), no more able to do anything than a "saw" or a "staff" can lift itself up without a man to move it (v. 15). However, the Assyrian king was a morally responsible person. He did not act out of obedience to God. He had plans of his own to glorify himself (v. 7). Therefore, the Lord used him to punish Israel and then punished him when God's purpose for Israel was fulfilled (vv. 12–13).

God also works in *contingent, apparently random events*. When God foretold Ahab's death, the king disguised himself in battle. But an arrow still pierced him at the joint of his armor so that he died (1 Kings 22:17, 20, 34–37). If a man cuts wood and the ax-head slips from the handle and kills another man, humanly speaking it is an accident. But it is still an act of God (Ex. 21:13; Deut. 19:5). Events as random as the casting of lots (somewhat like flipping coins or throwing dice today) are determined by God (Prov. 16:33).

In his providence, God generally works through means. But God is the primary and sovereign cause. He can work without means (John 2:1–11). He can work against means (Ex. 1:17; Acts 8:1). And he can use means to do things far above the ordinary power of those means (Josh. 6:20; Judg. 7:22). We must, therefore, live by faith and not by sight (2 Cor. 5:7).

Providence Experienced

God is the Trinity. The Father, the Son, and the Holy Spirit live and act as one God. This shapes the Christian's experience of providence.

God's providence is fatherly. It is the good pleasure of God the Father to bless his children and give them the kingdom (Luke 12:22–32). The Heidelberg Catechism teaches the Christian to confess that since God is our Father through Jesus Christ, "He will provide me with all things necessary for soul and body; and further, that He will make whatever evils He sends upon me, in this valley of tears, turn out to my advantage; for He is able to do it, being Almighty God, and willing, being a faithful Father."[4]

Christians also experience God's providence in union with God the Son. God's providence toward his Son was wrapped in dark mystery,

4 The Heidelberg Catechism (LD 9, Q. 26), in *TFU*, 76.

as Christ suffered to redeem us from our sins (Matt. 27:40). Likewise, God's ways toward his adopted sons and daughters are often hidden by clouds of suffering. We follow Christ along the path of sorrow to glory (Rom. 8:17, 28–29). God's providences toward his children drive them ever more deeply into a Christlike life of praying, "Abba, Father" (v. 15; cf. Mark 14:36).

Believers experience providence as children of God through the work of God the Holy Spirit. The Spirit assures us, despite our sins and sorrows, that we are the children of God (Rom. 8:16). By the Spirit, we come to see God's sending of Jesus Christ to the cross as a marvelous display of divine love for us, a love that "is shed abroad in our hearts" (5:5–8). The Holy Spirit, given to us as the "firstfruits" of our adoption, stirs us to "groan within ourselves" after the glory to which God is leading his creation (8:23).

The God of providence is the Father who loves us, the Son who died and rose again in union with us, and the Spirit who indwells us and leads us home. His providence is personal.

Providence Defended

The doctrine of providence is attacked from a number of directions. Let us consider four of them and how the Holy Scriptures equip us to respond.

Providence Falsely Limited by the Laws of Nature

Secular Western culture presses us to believe that the world is a vast machine operating according to the unbreakable principles of science. Therefore, it may seem impossible for God to reign over what happens lest he "break" the laws of nature.

In response, we assert that God is the sovereign Creator and Lord of all things (Acts 17:24). The laws of nature are not powers independent of God. Rather, they are patterns that he created, sustains, and directs by his sovereign word. They exist because Christ is "upholding all things by the word of his power" (Heb. 1:3).

God works through natural processes. He also works miracles, as the Bible repeatedly tells us. It is not unreasonable to believe in miracles unless we assume that the God of the Bible does not exist. Why would it be difficult for the God who created all things by supernatural power to act on his creation with the same supernatural power today?

Providence Falsely Excluded from Details

Some theologians teach that God does not have "specific sovereignty," but only a "general sovereignty" over the "general structures" of the world. As a result, his plans sometimes fail.[5]

In response, we note that we have already shown from the Bible that God is constantly preserving and sovereignly ruling over everything, including human life.

Christ taught that God's providence extends to the smallest details when he said, "Are not two sparrows sold for a farthing? And one of them shall not fall on the ground without your Father. But the very hairs of your head are all numbered" (Matt. 10:29–30). The word translated as "farthing" refers to money worth about an hour's wage. Though little birds were bought cheap, not one of them could perish apart from God's will. How much more can we be sure that God cares for us—even for the individual hairs on our heads? The providence of God extends to the smallest details of life.

Providence Falsely Subjected to Man's Free Will

Some theologians argue that God's providence, though still sovereign over life's general circumstances, is frustrated by poor human choices.

In reply, we say that we must not assume that God's sovereignty and human responsibility contradict each other. The Bible teaches both that God is sovereign and man is responsible even in the same events. For example, the Word of God says that the following events were determined by the Lord's will. Solomon took the throne instead of his rivals (1 Kings 2:15, 24). He removed Abiathar from the priesthood (v. 27). Israel enjoyed a season of rest from the attacks of neighboring nations (5:4, 12). Solomon built God's temple (8:15, 20). The northern tribes broke away from the kingdom (11:11–12). An enemy leader arose among the Edomites (v. 14). Solomon's son acted foolishly and harshly (12:15). The northern tribes followed Jeroboam (v. 24). Wicked Baasha exterminated Jeroboam's male descendants (14:10, 14; 15:25–34). These events involved many human choices, often bad choices. But the Bible says that they took place by God's providence.

5 John Sanders, *The God Who Risks: A Theology of Providence* (Downers Grove, IL: InterVarsity Press, 1998), 213, 230.

God's providence does not depend on man's choices. The opposite is true. Man is not king—God is. The message of God's Word from beginning to end is: *the Lord reigns.*[6] We cannot subject God's will to man's will.

Providence Falsely Denied Because of Evil

Atheists argue that if there were an all-good and all-powerful God, he would not allow evil to exist. This is known as the *problem of evil.*

In reply, we note that the argument assumes that there is no sufficient reason why God would permit evil, such as the accomplishment of a greater good. But Joseph said to his brothers after they sold him into slavery, "Ye thought evil . . . but God meant it unto good" (Gen. 50:20).

Though the problem of evil is not convincing on a logical level, it can be a challenge on a personal level. It can be very difficult to overcome the horror, distress, doubt, anger, and perplexity someone feels because of evil. Evil threatens faith in the goodness of God.

The teachings of God's Word equip us to face evil with a wise mind and a vibrant faith. Consider the basic doctrines of creation, fall, redemption, and completion.

The doctrine of creation vindicates God because he made all things "very good" (Gen. 1:31). God did not create evil. The Creator is also the Lord and owner of all things. He has the right to do with us as he pleases (Rom. 9:20).

The doctrine of the fall traces all our misery back to man's disobedience against God. The sin of Adam plunged us all into a state of sin and misery that we constantly make worse with our own sins (Rom. 3:10–12; 5:12). We are not to blame God for our sorrows. Death is God's righteous judgment against our sin (6:23). Rather, we should be amazed at "the problem of good." Why does God continue to show such goodness to sinners?

The doctrine of redemption highlights God's goodness even more gloriously than creation. We may not understand why we face certain problems, but we can know for sure that since God sacrificed his Son for sinners, God is love (1 John 4:8–10). He has shown extraordinary love for the undeserving (Rom. 5:7–8). God is wise enough to plan the apparently meaningless injustice of his Son's murder for the salvation of many. He knows how to

6 Ex. 15:18; 1 Chron. 16:31; Pss. 47:8; 93:1; 96:10; 97:1; 99:1; 146:10; Isa. 24:23; 52:7; Mic. 4:7; Rev. 19:6.

use any evil for good (1 Cor. 1:18–25). God the Son walked through the valley of the shadow of death. He is now seated at God's right hand, full of sympathy and grace for believers as they suffer temptation (Heb. 4:14–16).

Finally, the doctrine that God will bring his purposes to completion in the new heaven and new earth promises that all who repent and believe in Christ will be raised up to share his glory. They will enjoy a new world that no longer groans in bondage (Rom. 8:17–25). God's servants are often discouraged and sometimes despair of life itself (2 Cor. 1:8; 4:8). But these present sufferings are "not worthy to be compared with the glory which shall be revealed in us" (Rom. 8:18). "Our light affliction, which is but for a moment, worketh for us a far more exceeding and eternal weight of glory" (2 Cor. 4:17). All the evil we suffer now will not be worth comparing to the joy of being with God forever (Ps. 73:24–26).

Providence Applied

The Heidelberg Catechism highlights three benefits of knowing God's providence: "that we may be patient in adversity; thankful in prosperity; and that in all things, which may hereafter befall us, we place our firm trust in our faithful God and Father, that nothing shall separate us from His love; since all creatures are so in His hand, that without His will they cannot so much as move."[7] Let us consider these benefits more closely.

First, *the doctrine of providence teaches us patience in adversity.* When trouble comes, our natural response is to resent it, sink into self-pity, become bitter, and complain. However, in chaos the Christian can cultivate an inner quietness. Thomas Brooks said, "It is the great duty and concernment of gracious souls to be mute and silent under the greatest afflictions, the saddest providences, and sharpest trials that they meet with in this world."[8]

We may groan *to* God but may not grumble *against* God.[9] Faith in his providence produces active endurance, prayerful dependence, and open-eyed watchfulness. Such patience arises from an awareness that God afflicts his children so that we will share in his holiness and ultimately in his glory (Prov. 3:11–12; Rom. 5:1–5; Heb. 12:5–11). This means that when adversity

7 The Heidelberg Catechism (LD 10, Q. 28), in *TFU*, 76.

8 Thomas Brooks, *The Mute Christian under the Smarting Rod*, in *The Works of Thomas Brooks*, ed. Alexander Grosart, 6 vols. (1866; repr., Edinburgh: Banner of Truth, 1980), 1:295.

9 Brooks, *The Mute Christian under the Smarting Rod*, in *Works*, 1:306, 310.

comes, we can rejoice (James 1:2–4), depending on the Holy Spirit to fill us with hope (Rom. 15:13). Then we can confess with William Cowper, "Behind a frowning providence, he hides a smiling face."[10]

Second, *the doctrine of providence teaches us thankfulness in prosperity.* We should respond to "every good gift" by acknowledging that it "cometh down from the Father of lights" (James 1:17). We never lack good gifts for which to praise the God of providence (Eph. 5:20).

Though we naturally desire prosperity, it exposes us to great temptation to forget the Lord who gives us wealth and to lift up our hearts in pride (Deut. 8:11, 14, 17–18). Adversity is a bitter cup to drink, but prosperity is an intoxicating wine. We must stay sober by humble thanksgiving. Even an ice cube to cool one's mouth is cause for thanksgiving, for we all deserve the fire of hell with not a drop of water to reduce our pain (Luke 16:24). Just think of all the good things God freely gives!

Third, *the doctrine of providence teaches us confidence about the future.* If we are believers who love God, he directs everything in history for our good (Rom. 8:28). Therefore, we may conclude, "If God be for us, who can be against us? He that spared not his own Son, but delivered him up for us all, how shall he not with him also freely give us all things?" (vv. 31–32).

No matter what we face, "tribulation, or distress, or persecution, or famine, or nakedness, or peril, or sword" (Rom. 8:35), nothing will separate us from God's love (v. 39). And one day we will enjoy "the glorious liberty of the children of God" (v. 21). No one has a better reason for optimism than the Christian.

Suggested Songs to Sing to the Lord

- Psalm 104, "He waters the hills with rain from the skies," *Psalter*, No. 286
- Psalm 135, "O praise ye the Name of Jehovah," *Psalter*, No. 373

Questions for Meditation or Discussion

1. What is the doctrine of preservation? What are some key texts in the Bible that teach it?

10 William Cowper, "God Moves in a Mysterious Way," in *Olney Hymns* (London: J. Johnson, 1807), 255.

2. Demonstrate from the Holy Scriptures that God controls (1) weather, (2) plants and animals, (3) nations, (4) every human life, (5) human decisions, (6) demons, and (7) man's sin.
3. Prove from the Scriptures that God sovereignly works in concurrence with our free choices.
4. According to the Scriptures, how do the laws of nature relate to God and his will?
5. How would you show from the Bible that it is not enough to say that God has "general sovereignty"?
6. How can the following truths help us to face the problem of evil: (1) the doctrine of creation, (2) the doctrine of the fall, (3) the doctrine of redemption, (4) the doctrine that God will bring his purposes to completion in the new creation?
7. What are the three applications that the Heidelberg Catechism makes of the doctrine of providence? Which of the three is most relevant to you now? Why?
8. Why is the doctrine of God's providence important for the Christian faith?

27

Angels and Demons

Chapter Summary and Key Terms

Angels are created, intelligent, heavenly spirits. They are not the spirits of human beings but are a distinct order of beings who serve as God's worshipers, messengers, and warriors. The concept of a *guardian angel*, who is supposedly assigned to guard and guide a specific human being, has no clear biblical support. We must not worship angels but should imitate them in their worship and obedience to God. The Scriptures also speak of *demons*. Those are angels that rebelled against God and now rule over this sinful world. The leader of the demons is known as *Satan* or the *Devil*, who works largely through deception. Believers in the Lord Jesus must resist the Devil by relying on Christ and putting on their spiritual armor.

WE LIVE IN A WORLD full of unseen spirits. We learn this from the biblical account of the time when the king of Syria sent an army by night to capture the prophet Elisha. When Elisha's servant got up in the morning, he was terrified to see their city besieged by enemies. However, Elisha said, "Fear not: for they that be with us are more than they that be with them." Elisha prayed, "and the LORD opened the eyes of the young man; and he saw: and, behold, the mountain was full of horses and chariots of fire round about Elisha" (2 Kings 6:15–17). The capture of Elisha turned into the capture of the Syrian army by angelic powers.

In this chapter, we take up the study of good and evil spirits: angels and demons.

The Angels of God

The Bible's Terms for Angels

The words in Hebrew and Greek that are translated as "angel" mean "messenger" and are also used for human messengers (Gen. 32:3; James 2:25). Angels are called "cherubim," winged creatures that guarded paradise after the fall (Gen. 3:24). Cherubim appeared in the art of the tabernacle and temple (Ex. 25:20; 1 Kings 6:24–27). In one passage, they are called "seraphim" (Isa. 6:2, 6), a term that means "to burn." Angels are compared to flames of fire or perhaps bolts of lightning (Ps. 104:4). Another word used for an angel is "spirit" (Heb. 1:7, 14). The Bible also refers to angels as "sons of God" (Job 1:6; 2:1; 38:7) and the "host of heaven" (2 Chron. 18:18; Neh. 9:6)—that is, God's armies. Paul writes of them with words for mighty rulers, such as "principalities" and "powers" (Eph. 3:10; 6:12; Col. 1:16).

The Nature of Angels

Angels are *spirits* (Heb. 1:14). They are not the spirits of dead people (12:22–23) or the Holy Spirit (who is God) but a distinct kind of created spirit (Ps. 104:4; Heb. 1:7). They are heavenly beings (Matt. 24:36). Since angels are spirits, they are not made of physical matter like our "flesh and bones" (Luke 24:39). Angels are also invisible by nature, though they can make themselves visible (2 Kings 6:17; Col. 1:16). Unlike mankind and animals, angels are not sexual and do not mate with each other (Matt. 22:30). They do not die (Luke 20:36). The angel Gabriel visited Daniel and Mary hundreds of years apart (Dan. 8:16; Luke 1:26).

Angels are God's *servants* (Heb. 1:7, 14). They exist to do the will of God for his glory (Ps. 103:20). They are intelligent, personal beings (2 Sam. 14:17, 20; Luke 1:19). Angels have "joy" (Luke 15:10) and "desire" (1 Pet. 1:12). Apart from those spirits that rebelled against the Lord, the angels are holy (Matt. 25:31; Acts 10:22). God holds them morally responsible for their actions (1 Cor 6:3; 2 Pet. 2:4). The angels that continued in holiness are preserved by God's sovereignty, for he chose them (1 Tim. 5:21). But angels are not redeemed by Christ. Jesus came to save only human beings (Heb. 2:16).

Angels are God's *army*. They are the "host," or army, of the Lord (Ps. 148:2; Luke 2:13). They are the soldiers of heaven, fighting against Satan

(Rev. 12:7). There are many of them (Ps. 68:17; Dan. 7:10). They are organized according to the Lord's will, some having higher authority than others (Dan. 10:13; cf. Col. 1:16). Angels are very fast. The Bible compares them to wind or lightning (Ps. 18:10; Ezek. 1:14). They can come from heaven to earth before we finish a prayer (Dan. 9:21). Angels are also powerful (Ps. 103:20), and they are frightening and majestic (Dan. 10:4–9; Matt. 28:3–4). They are instruments of God's glory (Matt. 16:27; Luke 2:9).

Angels are God's *creatures* made by him (Ps. 148:2, 5; Col. 1:16). That means they are not gods and that they can be present in only one place at a time (Matt. 4:11; Luke 2:15). They are limited in their power (Dan. 10:13), authority (2 Pet. 2:4), and knowledge (Matt. 24:36); for instance, they do not have direct knowledge of our hearts (2 Chron. 6:30). Angels are not immutable but are capable of change (2 Pet. 2:4). All these creaturely limitations mean that angels are not worthy of worship (Rev. 19:10; 22:8–9).

The Work of Angels

God made angels for the works of worship and service. David said, "The Lord hath prepared his throne in the heavens; and his kingdom ruleth over all. Bless the Lord, ye his angels, that excel in strength, that do his commandments, hearkening unto the voice of his word" (Ps. 103:19–20). Let us consider these angelic works briefly.

First, angels *observe God's works*. They watched God make the earth (Job 38:4–7) and they watch Jesus save sinners (Luke 15:10; 1 Tim. 3:16; 1 Pet. 1:11–12).

Second, angels *praise God's glory*. In heaven, the angels "rest not day and night," but constantly "give glory and honor and thanks to him that [sits] on the throne" (Rev. 4:8–9).

Third, angels *guard God's holy places*. They were the guardians of paradise (Gen. 3:24) and God's temple (1 Kings 6:27; 8:6–7), and are depicted as guarding the heavenly Jerusalem (Rev. 21:12, 27).

Fourth, angels *proclaim God's message*. They sometimes communicated God's word, though not all the Holy Scriptures came through them (Acts 7:53; Rev. 1:1).

Fifth, angels *care for God's children*. "Are they not all ministering spirits, sent forth to minister for them who shall be heirs of salvation?" (Heb. 1:14).

Sixth, angels *protect God's ministers.* Angels released the apostles from prison (Acts 5:19–20; 12:5–11). An angel killed a king who persecuted the apostles (12:23–24).

Seventh, angels *execute God's judgments.* They will return with Christ to judge the world (Matt. 13:39; 2 Thess. 1:7–8).

Eighth, angels *serve God's Son.* They were "created by him, and for him" (Col. 1:16). Jesus Christ is "the head of all principality and power" (2:10).

Does Each Person Have a Guardian Angel?

Some Christians have taught that each believer has a guardian angel. They base this idea on two passages of the Holy Scriptures. Jesus says, "Take heed that ye despise not one of these little ones; for I say unto you, That in heaven their angels do always behold the face of my Father which is in heaven" (Matt. 18:10). When disciples gathered for prayer for Peter, whom they presumed was still in prison, and Rhoda reported that Peter was knocking at the door, they said, "It is his angel" (Acts 12:15).

However, neither of these passages says that God assigns one angel to guard (much less to guide) each person. "Their angels" could refer to the many angels caring for all of God's children—a sign of his great love for them—not specific angels assigned to individuals (Matt. 18:10). As to the disciples who said of Peter, "It is his angel" (Acts 12:15), they were not at that moment examples of strong faith or clear thinking. Furthermore, if these passages do refer to guardian angels, then those angels were derelict in their duties.The passages indicate that they were not with the people they were supposed to be guarding!

The doctrine of guardian angels encourages people to pray to angels and look to them for help. Instead, we should pray to God through Christ alone.

Implications of the Doctrine of Angels

The doctrine of angels implies that we must worship God alone. Angels are awesome beings, but they themselves worship God (Rev. 4:8–9; 5:11). The angel of Revelation twice insists that we give no worship to angels but "worship God" alone (19:10; 22:9).

Since God delivered his revelation through the ministry of angels, we must listen to God's Holy Word. Since the law of God given through angels was trustworthy and brought severe penalties on those who rejected it, "we must pay much closer attention" to the message of salvation declared by God's Son, or "how shall we escape" punishment (Heb. 2:1–3 ESV)?

The ministry of angels to believers calls us to trust God's gracious protection. God's people are safe in "the shadow of the Almighty" (Ps. 91:1), for God employs the mighty armies of heaven "to guard you in all your ways" (v. 11 ESV).

We must keep God's commands as the angels do. Angels are constantly "obeying the voice of his word" (Ps. 103:20 ESV). When we pray, "Thy will be done in earth, as it is in heaven" (Matt. 6:10), we are asking God that we would serve him "as willingly and faithfully as the angels do in heaven."[1]

We also should willingly serve God's lowly people as the angels do. They are servants to God's children (Heb. 1:14). If the very angels are willing to serve us, we should gladly serve one another.

The future coming of the angels with Christ teaches us to fear God's righteous judgment. Heaven will one day unleash a vast army of holy warriors led by the King of kings. They will come to wage war and shatter sinners as an iron rod shatters clay pots (Rev. 19:11–16).

Finally, we must live for God's only begotten Son in the manner of the angels. Just as they sing, "Worthy is the Lamb that was slain" (Rev. 5:12), so those whom he redeemed with his blood must "no longer live for themselves but for him who for their sake died and was raised" (2 Cor. 5:15 ESV).

Satan and the Demons

Angels are real, but not every angel is good. All believers in Jesus Christ are engaged in a spiritual war against Satan and his demons (Eph. 6:10–13).

The Bible's Terms for Demons

The Bible speaks of one evil spirit as the "Devil" (Matt. 4:1), which means "opponent," "slanderer," or "accuser" (1 Tim. 3:11). The Devil is the "Serpent" or "dragon" that tempted the first man and woman to sin (Gen. 3:1–4), deceives the world (Rev. 12:9), and assaults Christ and his church (vv. 4, 17). He is "Satan" (Job 1:6–9; Matt. 4:10), which means "the adversary."

1 The Heidelberg Catechism (LD 49, Q. 124), in *TFU*, 113.

Christ calls the Devil the "enemy" (Luke 10:19). He is "the accuser of our brethren" (Rev. 12:10). He is "the angel of the abyss," called "Abaddon," or "destruction," and "Apollyon," or "destroyer" (9:11). The Devil is also called "the Wicked One" or "the Evil One" (1 John 2:13–14; 3:12).

Scripture describes Satan's power by calling him "the prince of demons" (Matt. 9:34 ESV) and "the prince of the power of the air" (Eph. 2:2). He is the "king" over the swarming hordes of demons (Rev. 9:11). He is even called "the god of this world" (2 Cor. 4:4).

The Holy Scriptures also speak of many "evil spirits" (Luke 7:21) and "unclean spirits" (4:36). It calls them "demons" (Matt. 8:31; 1 Cor. 10:20–21 ESV), also translated as "devils" (KJV). Paul describes demons with words of power and authority (Eph. 6:11–12).

The Origin and Nature of Demons

The demons are angels (Matt. 25:41; Rev. 12:7, 9). Therefore, what is true about angels pertains to demons as well—they are intelligent, organized, and powerful but limited spirits created by God to serve him. There are many demons (Mark 5:9), perhaps even hundreds of millions (Rev. 9:16–21).

God made the angels, like all other created things, very good (Gen. 1:31). But some angels rebelled against his will. Peter says, "God spared not the angels that sinned, but cast them down to hell, and delivered them into chains of darkness, to be reserved unto judgment" (2 Pet. 2:4). Jude writes, "The angels which kept not their first estate, but left their own habitation, he hath reserved in everlasting chains under darkness unto the judgment of the great day" (Jude 6).

We do not know much about the fall of Satan and the demons. It may have begun with the sin of pride (cf. Ezek. 28:11–19). These angels turned from their mission to serve mankind (Heb. 1:14) to attempt to destroy the human race (Gen. 3:1–4).

The Kingdom of Darkness

The Holy Scriptures teach the horrifying truth that Satan now rules over mankind. Christ said to people who would not listen to his word, "Ye are of your father the devil, and the lusts of your father ye will do" (John 8:44). Satan is "the prince of this world" (12:31; 14:30; 16:11). John says, "He that committeth sin is of the devil; for the devil sinneth from the beginning. For this purpose the Son of God was manifested, that he might destroy the works of the devil" (1 John 3:8). He adds, "In this the children of God are manifest, and the children of the Devil: whosoever doeth not righteousness is not of God, neither he that loveth not his brother" (v. 10).

The apostle Paul says that Christians formerly "were dead in trespasses and sins; wherein in time past ye walked according to the course of this world, according to the prince of the power of the air, the spirit that now worketh in the children of disobedience" (Eph. 2:1–2). We were saved when God "delivered us from the power of darkness, and . . . translated us into the kingdom of his dear Son" (Col. 1:13). When God gives sinners repentance, they "escape from the snare of the devil, after being captured by him to do his will" (2 Tim. 2:26 ESV).

Although Satan rules over sinners, he does so as a limited being created by God and still subject to his decree and providence. Satan could do nothing against Job until "the Lord said unto Satan, Behold, all that he hath is in thy power; only upon himself put not forth thine hand" (Job 1:12).

Satan was behind Christ's betrayal, arrest, and murder (Luke 22:3, 53; John 13:2, 27; 14:30). But Satan's actions resulted in his own defeat and the release of many sinners from his captivity (John 12:31–32; 16:11). Therefore, we should fear God, not the Devil. Samuel Rutherford said that Christ holds the Devil on the "chain of omnipotence."[2]

The Activity of Satan and the Demons

How do Satan and his demons work in the world?

First, Satan works through *deception*. Christ says, "When he speaketh a lie, he speaketh of his own: for he is a liar, and the father of it" (John 8:44). Deception is the Devil's great strategy. He "deceiveth the whole world" (Rev. 12:9). He can appear as "an angel of light" (2 Cor. 11:14). Satan uses people to spread his lies—false teachers in the church teach the "doctrines of devils" (1 Tim. 4:1–3).

Second, Satan works through *demonization*. Sometimes a demon dwells in a person's body and gains a measure of control over him (Mark 1:23;

2 Samuel Rutherford, *The Trial and Triumph of Faith* (Edinburgh: Banner of Truth, 2001), 389.

3:11). Such a person is said to be "possessed" by the demon or literally to be "demonized" (1:32; 5:15–16, 18). Demonized people can have superhuman strength (5:4) and knowledge (1:24, 34; Acts 16:16–18).

Jesus and his servants in the New Testament cast out demons, but exorcism appears to have been a special gift given to the apostles and evangelists (Matt. 10:1; Luke 10:17; Acts 8:5–7). The ultimate solution to demonization is salvation and receiving the Holy Spirit. John says to believers, "Greater is he that is in you, than he that is in the world" (1 John 4:4).

Third, Satan works through *disease and death*. Demonization often brings physical problems. Demons can cause blindness, deafness, inability to speak, and violent convulsions (Matt. 12:22; Mark 9:17–27). (Of course, these problems can also arise without demons, for we live in a fallen world.) The Devil also kills when he can, for he "was a murderer from the beginning" (John 8:44). However, Satan is not the lord of death. God determines the day when each man dies (Job 14:5).

Fourth, Satan works toward the goal of *damnation*. In Eden, Satan did not attempt to strike down Adam and Eve. He led them into sin so that God would condemn the human race (Genesis 3). The Devil is "the accuser of our brothers . . . who accuses them day and night before our God" (Rev. 12:10 ESV).

But Satan is not the lord of hell. Rather, the "everlasting fire [is] prepared for the devil and his angels" (Matt. 25:41). Satan will be "cast into the lake of fire" to be "tormented day and night for ever and ever" (Rev. 20:10).

The Saints' Warfare against Satan and the Demons

The Christian life is a constant battle to overcome Satan by the grace of God. The saints live in the hope that "the God of peace shall bruise Satan under your feet shortly," not because of their strength but by "the grace of our Lord Jesus Christ" (Rom. 16:20). Let us consider how Christians are called to wage this warfare.

First, *Christians must rely on Christ's victory*. Paul says, "Be strong in the Lord, and in the power of his might" (Eph. 6:10). This battle requires God's power (2 Cor. 6:7; 10:4). Paul writes of "the working of his mighty power, which he wrought in Christ, when he raised him from the dead, and set him at his own right hand in the heavenly places, far above all principality, and power, and might, and dominion" (Eph. 1:19–21). The power to overcome the forces of Satan is not from themselves; they receive it by faith in the exalted Lord Jesus.

Christ overcame Satan particularly through his death and resurrection (Col. 2:13–15; Rev. 5:5–6). Therefore, we overcome the Devil "by the blood of the Lamb" (Rev. 12:11).

Second, *Christians must resist Satan's schemes*. Paul says, "Put on the whole armour of God, that ye may be able to stand against the wiles of the devil" (Eph. 6:11). The word translated as "wiles" refers to the schemes or strategies by which the Devil tries to deceive and overcome us. It is our duty, therefore, to know Satan's tactics, to keep watch against them, and to resist them with all our might.

For example, Satan promises that disobedience will make us happy, but obedience will ruin our lives (Gen. 3:4–5). He can use one sin as a beachhead in a believer's soul to launch further attacks, such as through bitterness (Eph. 4:26–27). The Devil intimidates us by persecution like "a roaring lion" (1 Pet. 5:8).

Satan is insidious and subtle. He may use bad advice from other Christians to discourage us from following God fully (Matt. 16:21–23). Satan may shock us with temptations we never thought would move us (Luke 22:31, 33). He makes strategic retreats so that he may attack again (4:13). He uses false reasoning to burden the believer's conscience with guilt (Rev. 12:10). We must watch for Satan's devices and resist them.

Third, *Christians must stand in God's armor*. The positive call to spiritual warfare is to "stand" against the Devil's forces while using "the whole armour of God" (Eph. 6:13). Paul lists six pieces of spiritual armor and concludes with a call to prayer (vv. 14–18). We must know the truth; embrace the righteousness of our justification and practice the righteousness of our sanctification; stand firm on the peace we have with God through Christ; trust in God's promises; have hope in our ultimate salvation and victory; speak the Word of God; and constantly pray for God's assistance. Bernard of Clairvaux said, "The enemy's temptation is a burden to us, but our prayer to God is far more burdensome to the enemy!"[3]

3 Bernard of Clairvaux, *For the Dedication of a Church*, 3.2, in *Sermons for the Autumn Season*, trans. Irene Edmonds, rev. Mark Scott, intro. Wim Verbaal, Cistercian Fathers Series 54 (Collegeville, MN: Liturgical Press, 2016), 189.

Suggested Songs to Sing to the Lord

- Psalm 103, "In the heav'ns the Lord Almighty," *Psalter*, No. 282
- "A mighty Fortress is our God," *THBap*, No. 81

Questions for Meditation or Discussion

1. What terms does the Bible use for angelic beings? What do they mean?
2. What does the Bible tell us about the nature of angels as (1) spirits, (2) God's servants, (3) God's warriors, and (4) creatures?
3. What is the work of angels?
4. What practical lessons can we learn from the doctrine of angels?
5. How do we know that Satan and the demons were originally angels?
6. How does the Devil work through (1) deception, (2) demonization, (3) disease and death, and (4) damnation?
7. What are Satan's common schemes to attack believers? Which of them do you believe he is using to attack you now?
8. Which piece of God's armor is most lacking in your life? What are you going to do about it?

PART 3

THE DOCTRINE OF MAN

Section 3A

Man as Servant of God

28

God's Creation of Man

Chapter Summary and Key Terms

The doctrine of man is a major theme of the Holy Scriptures. Human beings are at the center of God's purpose for his creation. The world attempts to define humanity in terms of our mind, biology, freedom, relationships, or emotions. But none of these can completely capture who we are because human identity cannot be separated from our relationship with God. Regarding that relationship, we may speak of the *fourfold state of man*. These four spiritual conditions are the states of innocence, sin, grace, and glory. God made man in the state of innocence with special honor in the creation, bearing the image of God. God also made man with special relationships under the covenant of God's loving lordship. From the beginning, God established the *creation ordinances* of work and Sabbath rest, and marriage and procreation. Man began with a single individual, Adam. If we deny the historical Adam, we undermine the entire Christian faith, including faith in Christ, the last Adam.

IT WAS PART OF CHRIST'S WISDOM that "he knew what was in man" (John 2:25). In other words, Christ understood people. As the light of the world, he revealed who he is and who we are (John 3:19; 15:22). Our Lord Jesus not only said many "I am" statements but also made some very pointed "Ye are" statements (John 8:23, 44).

When the writers of the Bible asked, "What is man?" they sought the answer from God (Job 7:17). David gazed up at the stars in wonder and exclaimed, "What is man, that thou art mindful of him? And the son of man, that thou visitest him?" (Ps. 8:4; cf. 144:3). According to the Bible, the question of who mankind is cannot be separated from God and our relationship with him.

Why Study the Doctrine of Man?

The Lord devotes much of the Bible to teaching us about who we are. Louis Berkhof wrote that "man occupies a place of central importance in Scripture," for "man is not only the crown of creation, but also the object of God's special care."[1] It is good to study the works of God (Pss. 92:4–5; 111:2). Certainly, then, we should consider the high point of God's work of creation (8:4, 6).

Studying the doctrine of man sheds light on the doctrine of God, for man was created in God's image (Gen. 1:26). Also, understanding humanity helps us to understand the person of our Lord Jesus Christ. God's Son became like his brothers in all things human except sin (Heb. 2:17; 4:15). What God made us to be in the beginning points ahead to what we will become in the future if we are united to Christ. The new creation will be like paradise—only better, because the Lamb of God will be there (Rev. 22:1–5).

The nations of Europe and North America are reaping the bitter fruit of rejecting their Christian heritage, including the biblical doctrine of man. We see human culture falling apart all around us. Consider the decline in morality, education, public safety, and the media and the arts. Many people feel anxiety and even despair. They are asking questions: Who am I? What are my roots? Do I belong to something bigger than myself? Why is my life so painful and confusing? What does it mean to be human? How are we different from animals? How can I know what is right and wrong? Is morality merely relative? Why are we in the mess that we are in? Why can't we solve problems such as social injustice and war? Why do people commit atrocities such as genocide, terrorism, human trafficking, and ethnic oppression? Where is our world going? Do I have any cause for hope?

The Bible gives us answers to such questions that are *realistic*—they help us to deal wisely with ourselves and other people. The Bible's answers are also *idealistic*—we need ideals to aim for high and worthy goals. The Bible is also *optimistic*—its promises give us hope that God is changing people and will win in the end.

1 Louis Berkhof, *Systematic Theology* (Edinburgh: Banner of Truth, 1958), 181.

How Does the World Approach the Doctrine of Man?

The world tries to define us in various ways. Some people think that the most real thing about human beings is their mind or spirit. The body is viewed at best as a shell around the person and at worst as an evil to escape. On the other hand, many people today think we are just brains and bodies, and our whole lives can be explained by biology and chemistry. Some people think that our lives are defined by our sexual desires. Still others believe that human life is all about possessions, wealth, and economics.

In some cultures, especially in the global West, human life is thought to be all about the freedom to do whatever one pleases as long as it does not harm others. Relativism and postmodernism say that each person has the right to construct his or her own reality. This means that teaching absolute truth and morality is a form of hatred. In other cultures and to some social scientists, man is defined by his relationships, such as family dynamics or power structures in the community. From another point of view, the most important thing about us is our emotional health and feeling good about ourselves.

It is common for people to define the meaning of their lives by a combination of these things. Or people may cynically believe that life is absurd and meaningless—they say we must create our own purpose by being authentic to ourselves.

All these views touch on things that are real about human life, but they fail to fully explain who we are and why we exist. Ultimate answers must come from God's Word.

How Does the Bible Approach the Doctrine of Man?

The Bible teaches us that our identity and meaning cannot be separated from the God who made us. The Westminster Shorter Catechism says, "What is the chief end of man? Man's chief end is to glorify God (1 Cor. 10:31; Rom. 11:36), and to enjoy him for ever (Ps. 73:25–28)."[2]

The Bible also teaches us to view man in the light of the history of redemption. Human beings are best understood according to where they stand in the *fourfold state of man*:[3]

2 The Westminster Shorter Catechism (Q. 1), in *RC*, 4:353.

3 Thomas Boston, *Human Nature in Its Fourfold State* (Edinburgh: Banner of Truth, 1964). We will speak more of these four states in chap. 35.

1. the state of innocence
2. the state of sin
3. the state of grace
4. the state of glory

The doctrine of man, which we are discussing in this part of our systematic theology, focuses on the first two states. The third is the subject of the doctrine of salvation, and the fourth the doctrine of the last things, both of which we will treat in later parts.

Man's Special Honor in God's Cosmos (Gen. 1:26–2:3)

The first chapter of Genesis shows that God created man with great dignity. He made man after he made heaven and earth, light and darkness, seas and dry land with living plants, sun and stars, fish and birds, and land animals. Man is the crown of creation. God prepared the world for his sake. Genesis 1:27 repeats the verb translated as "created" three times in reference to man's creation, whereas it appears only twice before (vv. 1, 21). Only after man and woman were on earth was God's creation done and declared "very good" (v. 31). God gave mankind all things richly so that we might enjoy them and be rich in thanksgiving and good works (1 Tim. 4:4; 6:17).

God also honored human beings by the announcement of his special plan for them. When God made other animate creatures, he said, "Let the waters bring forth," or, "Let the earth bring forth" (Gen. 1:20, 24). However, we read in Genesis 1:26, "And God said, Let us make man." This surprising "us" reveals God consulting with God. In the light of later revelation, we see this statement as part of a conversation within the Trinity. Martin Luther commented, "Man was created by the special plan and providence of God."[4] Thus, man stands at the center of the wise and eternal counsel of the Trinity. We learn from the New Testament that this counsel centered on one man, the God-man, our Lord Jesus Christ (Eph. 3:9, 11; 2 Tim. 1:9). When the Father, Son, and Holy Spirit made Adam, they had already planned that the Son would become the last Adam to redeem our fallen race. How marvelous is God's love!

4 Luther, *Lectures on Genesis*, in *LW*, 1:56 (Gen. 1:26).

God showed how special he intended mankind to be by announcing that he would make man "in our image" (Gen. 1:26), unlike the other living creatures, each of which he made simply according to its "kind" (vv. 11–12, 21, 24–25). Of all earthly things, only man is called the image of God. With this great honor came the right to have "dominion" over all the earth and its creatures (vv. 26, 28; cf. Ps. 8:3–8). God still does "whatsoever he hath pleased," and yet, "the earth hath he given to the children of men" (Ps. 115:3, 16). The making of man in this manner prepared the way for the coming of God's incarnate Son. He is the "image of the invisible God" (Col. 1:15), now lifted up to rule over all (Heb. 2:5–10).

Genesis says that God "sanctified" the seventh day (Gen. 2:3). Luther said, "To sanctify means to set aside for sacred purposes, or for the worship of God."[5] God set aside the seventh day as a day for man to stop his ordinary work and worship God. This shows that man, unlike plants and animals, has a special ability to worship his Creator. Though all the universe displays God's glory (Ps. 19:1), God created man in a special way to praise him (Isa. 43:7, 21).

Man's Special Relationships in God's Covenant (Gen. 2:4–25)

Genesis 1:1–2:3 gives us the big picture of the creation of the universe by "God," but the next part of Genesis describes in more detail the creation of man as male and female. Genesis 2:4–25 is a more personal account of the creation of man by "the LORD God" (*YHWH Elohim*). That name reminds us of God's covenant faithfulness to his people (Ex. 3:13–17). In Genesis 2, God reveals himself in relationship to man. What does this revelation teach us?

First, *God is the Lord of our life.* "The LORD God formed man of the dust of the ground, and breathed into his nostrils the breath of life; and man became a living soul" (Gen. 2:7). Man did not come into being by a process of evolution from animals. God formed his body directly from the "dust," which means "earth" or "soil" (3:14, 19; 26:15). It should humble us that we are of the dust (18:27). God also gave the "breath of life" to that body, which refers to physical, biological life (6:17; 7:15, 22). Our living bodies are like the bodies of the animals.[6] When Genesis says the Lord God "breathed"

5 Luther, *Lectures on Genesis*, in *LW*, 1:79 (Gen. 2:3).

6 It may surprise the reader to learn that the Hebrew words translated as a "living soul" are the same words used to call an animal a "living creature" (Gen. 1:20–21, 24, 30; 9:10, 12, 15–16). However, as we will discuss later, "soul" can also mean the human spirit (chap. 31).

into man "the breath of life," it tells us that human life started in face-to-face intimacy with God. Man is not a god or a part of God, but he is the special work of the Holy Spirit, who is the living breath of God (Job 32:8; 33:4). Our new creation must be worked by the same Spirit of Christ (John 20:22).

Second, *God is the Lord of our location.* He provided man with a rich, beautiful, and holy home, a garden full of beautiful plants and delicious food (Gen. 2:8–9). "Eden" is the Hebrew word for "delight" or "luxury." The area had abundant water, which in the ancient Near East meant wealth. Nearby lands had gold and gemstones (vv. 11–12). In the garden, the Lord God spoke with man and communed with him (vv. 15–25). The garden was guarded by angelic cherubim, God's heavenly warriors (3:24). Trees, fruit, cherubim, and water all would later appear in God's temple (1 Kings 6–7). The garden was like a holy temple where God lived with man (Ezek. 28:13–14; 31:8–9).

Third, *God is the Lord of our law.* The Lord God asserted his authority over the man by assigning him a place to live and work to do (Gen. 2:15). God also gave man a law to obey, with life and death hanging on his obedience (vv. 16–17). The covenant name of God ("the Lord") suggests that God related to man as his covenant Lord, directing human life by his covenant word. Man may have been king over creation, but he remained the servant of the Creator. Man always stands before God under a combination of holy privilege and holy obligation. So long as man is man, he cannot escape the law of God.

Fourth, *God is the Lord of our love.* God made man to be a creature in relationships. Adam needed a "help meet for him," or a helper who was suitable to him (Gen. 2:18, 20). God made the woman and presented her to the man, making the first marriage, and so "God hath joined together" husband and wife (Matt. 19:6). Man received the woman from God to love and cherish as his own body, calling her "bone of my bones, and flesh of my flesh" (Gen. 2:23). By making the woman out of the man, God also indicated his will that husband and wife should be "one flesh" (v. 24). Husbands and wives must be committed and bound together for a lifetime. The first man and woman lived together in the garden without fear or shame to separate them, enjoying total openness and intimacy.

God designed marriage to reflect his relationship with his covenant people (Isa. 54:5; Hos. 2:19–20). The man's words to the woman, "bone of my bones, and flesh of my flesh," are like what the Israelites said when they made a covenant with David to be their king (2 Sam. 5:1–3; cf. 19:13). The "deep sleep" of Adam is the same term used when the Lord made a covenant with Abram (Gen. 15:12). The marriage of the first man and woman foreshadowed the covenant relationship between Christ and his church (2 Cor. 11:2–3; Eph. 5:28–32).

Therefore, though God is the Lord of our love relationships with one another, more importantly he is the Lord of his gracious covenant of love. God created man for a special relationship with himself. God showered his image bearer with blessings and privileges. He desired that man would be close to him. This shows us how marvelous his kindness is, and how sad man's fall away from God is. But it also shows us how glorious God's grace is through the last Adam, Jesus Christ.

In summary, we learn from Genesis 1–2 that God established certain *creation ordinances* when he made the human race. These are the ordered structures in human life ordained by the Creator from the beginning until the age to come. There are four creation ordinances that come in two pairs: work to subdue the earth and rest on the weekly Sabbath, and marriage and procreation (bearing and raising children) to fill the earth with the image of God.

The Importance of the Historical Adam

Given the claims of the theory of evolution, some people have said that we should abandon the doctrine that there was a real, historical first man named Adam. Some suggest that "Adam" is just a symbol for "everyman," the common human experience of temptation and sin. However, the existence of Adam is the basis for many of our beliefs as Christians.

The Scriptures insist that man is not just a highly developed animal but a special creation of God, made in his image to rule over the animals (Gen. 1:26). Adam was originally and uniquely formed as the first man (2:7; cf. 1 Cor. 15:45). If we do not believe in Adam, we lose our greatest reason to think that man is different from the animals.

Also, if we deny that Adam really existed, we undermine the truth that the human race is one race. Acts 17:26 says that God "hath made of one blood all nations of men for to dwell on all the face of the earth, and hath determined the times before appointed, and the bounds of their habitation." Some translations even say "made from one man" (ESV). Black or white,

Chinese or Russian, Arab or Jew, we are all blood brothers—since we all came from Adam.

Our Lord Jesus Christ taught us to look to the creation of Adam and Eve as the basis for the Creator's order for gender and sex (Matt. 19:3–6). So did the apostle Paul (1 Cor. 11:8–9; 1 Tim. 2:13–14). Both Christ and Paul grounded their teaching in the Creator's original design for men and women. If we treat the Genesis account as a myth, it loses its authority to reveal God's will for all mankind.

How do we explain the sin and misery of the human race? Paul says, "By one man sin entered into the world, and death by sin" (Rom. 5:12). Later, in verse 17, he says, "By one man's offence death reigned by one." But if there was no Adam, there was no fall. This means that God created a world full of pain and death, not one that was very good.

Our doctrines of God, creation, and sin turn on the hinge of Adam's fall. If we break the hinge, the whole system of biblical doctrine collapses.

Indeed, without a real Adam, the gospel itself is compromised. Paul says that Adam was a "type," or foreshadowing, of Christ (Rom. 5:14 ESV). He writes, "Since by man came death, by man came also the resurrection of the dead. For as in Adam all die, even so in Christ shall all be made alive" (1 Cor. 15:21–22). In verse 45, Paul calls Christ "the last Adam." If there was no real Adam, then Paul's theology is wrong.

To deny the reality of Adam is to deny the authority of the Holy Scriptures as God's Word. If Adam never existed, why should we believe that Abraham, Moses, and David were real people? Once we reject the historical Adam, we trigger an earthquake that sends a tsunami of skepticism surging over the Bible, wiping out our faith in its reliability. If we deny Adam, what is to keep us from denying Christ's historical birth, life, death, and resurrection?

People who deny that Adam truly existed may say that the Bible is God's Word. But they think the Bible contains errors and false teachings derived from the cultures in which it was written. They believe that the Bible must give way to the ever-changing theories of science. They may try to separate the Bible's teachings about spiritual things from its statements about history, but in the end, they leave us with no certain basis for our faith. The Bible's message is not just ideas and commands, but good news about what God has done in history to save us. As Paul writes in 1 Corinthians 15:17, "If Christ be not raised, your faith is vain; ye are yet in your sins." Indeed, if we believe that the Holy Scriptures contain errors, we are opposing Jesus Christ, for he says that the words of the prophets and his own words are all eternal truth (Matt. 5:18; 24:35).

Suggested Songs to Sing to the Lord

- Psalm 25, "To Thee I lift my soul," *Psalter*, No. 60
- "Come, sound his praise abroad," *THBap*, No. 102

Questions for Meditation or Discussion

1. Why is it important and helpful to study the Bible's doctrine of man?
2. What are some ways the world tries to define who we are?
3. In what sense is the creation of man the high point of God's work of creation?
4. How does Genesis 1 give special honor to the human race among all God's creatures?
5. What does Genesis 2:7 teach about the origin of the first human being?
6. What does Genesis 2:15–17 imply about man's relationship to God?
7. What does it mean that God made the woman to be a "help meet for him" (Gen. 2:18)?
8. Why is the existence of Adam as a real person in history important for Christian doctrine?
9. What does the denial of Adam's historicity logically imply about the rest of the Bible's historical accounts?
10. Someone says, "I don't need to worry about whether Genesis is history or legend. I know Jesus Christ. He is enough for me." How do you respond?

29

The Image of God

Chapter Summary and Key Terms

Man was created in the *image of God.* God's image makes human beings unique among earthly creatures. People are visible expressions of God's attributes, relationships, and activities. The image of God appears in many aspects of human life. The image of God consists especially in man's knowledge, righteousness, and holiness. It is exercised in mankind's dominion over the earth. Man has brought ruin to the divine image by sin. But that image still abides in the human race. Christ is the supreme Image of God. By bringing people into union with Christ, the Holy Spirit renews the image of God within them until it is fully restored at Christ's return. Being created in God's image has massive implications for the sanctity and dignity of human life.

THE WORDS "God created man in his own image" (Gen. 1:27) tell us how excellent God made the human race to be. Nothing could honor man more than bearing the image of the Creator. Therefore, we must grasp what God has revealed about man's creation in God's image in order to understand who we are, what we were created to do, and how we should relate to God, our fellow men and women, and the other creatures.

The Bible's Teaching about God's Image

The Created Image of God

We have already noted that in Genesis 1:27 the word translated as "created" appears three times to emphasize that man is the crown of creation. In verses

26–27, we read of "image" three times and "likeness" once, highlighting how central the image of God is to man's identity and purpose.

When God said he would make man "in our image, after our likeness," he revealed that the human race would be created to display his attributes. The Lord designed human beings to be limited, visible, earthly creatures that resemble God for his glory. God's image in man is a finite reflection of the infinite power, authority, wisdom, and goodness of the Creator of the world. Thus, God's image implies personality. Man can think, choose, and communicate through words, somewhat as God does. Man was made to reveal God in his speech and conduct as God's prophet.

People also bear God's image for his worship. The word translated as "image" is sometimes used in the Bible for images of false gods (Num. 33:52; 2 Kings 11:18; 2 Chron. 23:17). God forbade people to use images to represent him or to aid in worship (Ex. 20:4–6). Ironically, the very people God designed to glorify him as his living images have glorified dead images—idols—that cannot represent the living God (Rom. 1:21–23). But it was not so in the beginning. Man was made to worship God alone. Just as sacred images dwell in temples, God made man to be his image in the garden of Eden. The garden was like a holy temple where man served God as his priest. As both image and priest, man exists for the worship of God.

God's creation of man in his image is also closely connected to man ruling the world as its king. We see this in Genesis 1:26: "And God said, Let us make man in our image, after our likeness: and let them have dominion over the fish of the sea, and over the fowl of the air, and over the cattle, and over all the earth, and over every creeping thing that creepeth upon the earth" (see also vv. 27–28). In the ancient world, kings often set up man-made images of themselves to represent their authority. But God set up living images to represent his authority on earth. The God of creation has supreme authority over his works. Man as his image bearer is granted a measure of authority as God's servant-king (Ps. 8:4–8).

Another aspect of being created in God's image is being part of a family. God, though one, revealed himself to be more than one person when he created man. He said, "Let *us* make man in *our* image" (Gen. 1:26). God made man to dimly reflect the Trinity through each man's relationships with other people. These relationships begin with the human family, for God created man in his image "male and female" to "be fruitful and multiply" (vv. 27–28). In this way, they would fill the earth with children who also would bear God's image.

Furthermore, man in God's image was made to be God's son. Genesis 5:1 says, "God created man, in the likeness of God made he him." Then, verse 3 says Adam "begat a son in his own likeness, after his image." On the one hand, the text contrasts God's *creating* and Adam's *begetting*. We should not think that the image of God implies that people are gods. They are creatures. On the other hand, Genesis 5 shows that Adam was created to be a son of God (see also Luke 3:38). It should not surprise us, then, that in the Bible God's image is closely related to his eternal Son, Jesus Christ.

The Continuing Image of God

The fall of man brought terrible harm to our race (Genesis 3). God saw "that the wickedness of man was great in the earth, and that every imagination of the thoughts of his heart was only evil continually" (6:5). However, man did not become an animal. We read that people got married, raised children, farmed, built cities, performed music, and worked with metal after the fall (4:2, 17, 20–22). Man still bears the image of the Creator in some sense.

When God gave the animals to man to kill and eat, he warned that he would call to account anyone who murdered a human being. The reason was that God had made man in his image (Gen. 9:5–6). James rebukes his readers for blessing God but cursing men, "who are made in the likeness of God" (James 3:9 ESV). Fallen people still bear God's image, at least in broken fragments.

The Incarnate Image of God

The supreme Image of God is Jesus Christ (Heb. 1:3). Paul writes of "the light of the glorious gospel of Christ, who is the image of God" (2 Cor. 4:4). Just as Adam was "the son of God," so God said to Christ, the descendant of Adam, "Thou art my beloved Son; in thee I am well pleased" (Luke 3:22, 38). But whereas Adam disobeyed God when tempted by the Devil, Christ obeyed when the Devil tempted him (4:1–13).

Paul says Christ is "the image of the invisible God, the firstborn of every creature: for by him were all things created, that are in heaven, and that are in earth, visible and invisible, whether they be thrones, or dominions, or principalities, or powers: all things were created by him, and for him: and he is before all things, and by him all things consist" (Col. 1:15–17). In this passage, Paul both compares and contrasts Christ to Adam. Like Adam, Christ in his human nature is God's Image and King on earth. He is "the last Adam" (1 Cor. 15:45), come to redeem the fallen image bearers of God and restore them for God's glory. However, Christ is the Creator and Lord of heaven and earth. In him dwells the very fullness of God (Col. 1:19; 2:9). Christ is the Image of God because he is God's eternal Son who shares the Father's divine nature.

The Renewed Image of God

God saves sinners by uniting them to Christ in his death and resurrection by a Spirit-worked faith. The light of Christ, the Image of God, shines in their hearts as an act of new creation through the preaching of the gospel (2 Cor. 4:4–6). United to him who is the Image of God, they are renewed in God's image. Paul writes, "But we all, with open face beholding as in a glass the glory of the Lord, are changed into the same image from glory to glory, even as by the Spirit of the Lord" (2 Cor. 3:18).

The truth that God is remaking Christians in his image is clear from Scripture. Paul says, "Lie not one to another, seeing that ye have put off the old man with his deeds; and have put on the new man, which is renewed in knowledge after the image of him that created him" (Col. 3:9–10). He also says that Christians should "put off . . . the old man . . . ; and be renewed in the spirit of your mind; and . . . put on the new man, which after God is created in righteousness and true holiness" (Eph. 4:22–24).

The Completed Image of God

In Romans 8:29, Paul says, "For whom he did foreknow, he also did predestinate to be conformed to the image of his Son, that he might be the firstborn among many brethren." John Murray commented, "The apostle has in view the conformity to Christ that will be realized when they will be glorified with Christ . . . the final and complete conformity of resurrection glory. . . . It is noteworthy that this should be described as conformity to the image of the Son; it enhances the marvel of the destination."[1]

1 John Murray, *The Epistle to the Romans*, The New International Commentary on the New Testament, 2 vols. (Grand Rapids, MI: Eerdmans, 1968), 1:319.

Christians will be "glorified together" with Christ and will share in "the glory which shall be revealed in us" (Rom. 8:17–18), the vivification and redemption of our mortal bodies (vv. 11, 23). We will dwell in a creation that has been set free from sorrow and corruption, brought "into the glorious liberty of the children of God" (v. 21). Having borne the image of the first Adam, we will bear the image of the last Adam in heavenly, resurrected glory (1 Cor. 15:45–49).

Therefore, the image of God spans history from creation to new creation. It sums up the destiny of man in Christ. It is a glorious image, an image of sonship, the image of Christ. The Bible's doctrine of God's image draws our hearts upward to Christ, who is seated at the right hand of the Father. It is not merely about our past and present but also about the future of believers in the Lord Jesus Christ. It is a doctrine of hope.

Different Ideas about the Meaning of God's Image

There is a mystery wrapped around the words "image of God." What exactly makes us God's image? Some theologians have said that the image of God has to do with who we are as human beings; others have said that it is about what we do. The Reformed tradition emphasizes both.

Views That God's Image Is Something We Are

Some people have thought that God has a body, so man bears his image by having a body like God. But that is a heresy, for God is an infinite spirit and has no physical likeness (Isa. 40:18–26; John 4:24). However, the human body is God's noble creation.

More commonly, Christians have thought that God's image is to be found in the abilities of the mind to think and choose. One can see this idea in the teachings of Gregory of Nyssa.[2] Early in church history, Christians started teaching that God's "image" is man's mental abilities, but God's "likeness" is man's moral virtues.[3] For a long time, this was the standard Roman Catholic teaching, but modern Roman Catholicism recognizes that it is not correct. The Bible uses "image" and "likeness" in the same way to describe mankind (Gen. 1:26–27; 5:1–3).

2 Gregory of Nyssa, *On the Making of Man*, 16.9, 11, 17, in *NPNF*[2], 5:405–6.

3 Irenaeus, *Against Heresies*, 5.6.1, 5.8.1, in *ANF*, 1:532–33.

The Reformers realized that righteousness is a very important part of bearing God's image (Eph. 4:24; Col. 3:10). Lutheran theologians went so far as to say that the fall of man into sin destroyed God's image entirely.[4] However, that view has serious problems with the Bible's teaching that God's image continues in all men (Gen. 9:6; James 3:9).

Views That God's Image Is Something We Do

Some Christians have said that God's image is to be found in man's work to rule the world. This view is also very old; it was taught as early as John Chrysostom.[5] There is an obvious connection between the image of God and human dominion in Genesis 1:26–28 (see also Ps. 8:5–8). However, Genesis 1:26–28 does not say the image is dominion, but that God gave man dominion after he made man in his image. Furthermore, if the image is entirely about ruling the earth, that might imply that disabled people lack the image of God.

Other Christians say that the image is about man's personal relationships, just as Genesis highlights God's use of the plural pronoun "us" and man's identity as "male and female" (Gen. 1:26–27). This view has become popular in modern times. There is a measure of truth to this. We saw earlier that bearing God's image is connected to being a family, even God's family. But if the image is entirely about relationships, what happens to the image when relationships are shattered by sin? Anthony Hoekema rightly said that "the image of God consists of more than mere functioning; it concerns not only what man does but also what he is." "Image" is not a verb but a noun, one that "refers to the uniqueness of man's existence, and . . . is inseparable from man's being man."[6]

The View That God's Image Is in the Whole Life

John Calvin taught that God's image is "the whole excellence by which man's nature towers over all the kinds of living creatures."[7] In his view, the core of the image is truth in the mind and righteousness in the heart (Eph.

4 Apology of the Augsburg Confession, 2.18–22; Formula of Concord, Solid Declaration, 1.10–11, in *The Book of Concord: The Confessions of the Evangelical Lutheran Church*, ed. Robert Kolb and Timothy J. Wengert, trans. Charles Arand et al. (Minneapolis: Fortress, 2000), 114–15, 533–34.

5 John Chrysostom, *Homilies on Genesis, 1–17*, trans. Robert C. Hill, The Fathers of the Church 74 (Washington, DC: The Catholic University of America Press, 1986), 9.6 (120).

6 Anthony A. Hoekema, *Created in God's Image* (Grand Rapids, MI: Eerdmans, 1986), 64–65.

7 Calvin, *Institutes*, 1.15.3.

4:24; Col. 3:10).[8] Calvin wrote, "Although the primary seat of the divine image was in the mind and heart, or in the soul and its powers, yet there was no part of man, not even the body itself, in which some sparks did not glow."[9] Therefore, though the lines of God's image in us are so "maimed, that they may truly be said to be destroyed," nevertheless we may still trace them faintly in fallen man.[10] "God's image was not totally annihilated and destroyed" in Adam's fall, he said. But what remains in man is deformed and corrupted. God begins its renewal in man's spiritual rebirth, and "it will attain its full splendor in heaven."[11]

How can God's image be in both who we are and what we do? The answer lies in seeing that we do what we do because we are who we are. An eagle's ability to fly depends on its having wings. Mankind's ability to fulfill its purpose depends on having certain abilities. God made us to be his servant-kings. For a king to rule well, he must have a thinking mind, a wise and righteous heart, and a strong and able body to take action.[12] The image of God in man must involve all that we are so that we can serve him with all our heart, soul, mind, and strength.

Think of human nature as a temple in which God's glory was intended to dwell. When the priest fell into idolatry, the temple was ruined and the glory departed. But the ruins of the temple remain and await their reconstruction, cleansing, consecration, and renewed filling with glory. Though the sanctuary is no longer functioning, it remains God's "holy temple" (Ps. 79:1). Similarly, all the parts of man's being and function were made to represent God's presence on earth. Even though the fall has ruined us, we remain the bearers of God's image.

Practical Applications of Man Being Created in God's Image

Bearing the image of God has many implications for human life.

1. *Sanctity*. Man is sacred, and to take away his life without just cause is to assault the glory of God (Gen. 9:6). People are not animals. We must cherish human life.

8 Calvin, *Institutes*, 1.15.4.

9 Calvin, *Institutes*, 1.15.3.

10 Calvin, *Comm.* on Gen. 1:26.

11 Calvin, *Institutes*, 1.15.4.

12 Polyander, Walaeus, Thysius, and Rivetus, *SPT*, 13.41 (1:331).

2. *Spirituality*. God is a spirit (John 4:24). Man, created in his image, reflects that spirituality as a being made to worship. We are all priests, whether to the Lord or to a false god.

3. *Rationality*. Man is a thinking, personal being, just like the God of Genesis 1. We must treat people as thinkers and help them to think more clearly and wisely.

4. *Dignity*. We may not treat people with contempt and curses (James 3:17). We should honor them all (1 Pet. 2:17). People are not things for us to buy, use, and sell.

5. *Equality*. Since our first father and mother were both created in God's image (Gen. 1:27), the dignity of the image belongs to both genders, every ethnic group, and all classes within society.

6. *Benevolence*. Do good to all people. As we love them, we are loving the God who made them in his image.

7. *Stewardship*. Man rules as God's servant-king. He is a steward of God's possessions. He must represent the Lord, whose "tender mercies are over all his works" (Ps. 145:9).

8. *Morality*. At the heart of the image of God stands knowledge, righteousness, and holiness (Eph. 4:24; Col. 3:10). Man cannot escape morality, and therefore, his only hope is for God to make him holy through the Spirit of Christ.

9. *Destiny*. Created in God's image, man exists for God's glory. Whether God glorifies himself by saving us from our sins or by damning us for our sins, mankind will glorify God in the end. It is our inescapable destiny.

10. *Mystery*. We cannot fully understand what it means to be created in God's image because we live at a time when that image is corrupted in everyone we see. But it will not always be so: "Beloved, now are we the sons of God, and *it doth not yet appear what we shall be*: but we know that, when he shall appear, *we shall be like him*; for we shall see him as he is" (1 John 3:2).

Suggested Songs to Sing to the Lord

- Psalm 8, "Lord, our Lord, Thy glorious Name," *Psalter*, No. 15; *THBap*, No. 107
- "My dear Redeemer and my Lord," *THBap*, No. 171

Questions for Meditation or Discussion

1. How does the image of God relate to the attributes of God, worship, kingship, and family?
2. How would you prove from Scripture that the image of God continued in man after the fall?
3. How is Christ the image of God?
4. What does Paul say about God's image or likeness when discussing our renewal by the Spirit?
5. How does the ultimate goal of our salvation relate to the image of God?
6. What mistaken ideas have some people taught concerning God's image and the human body?
7. How do some Christians define the image of God in terms of who we are?
8. How do some Christians define the image of God in terms of what we do?
9. How did Calvin explain that the image of God is found in the whole person?
10. What are the practical implications of man being created in God's image?

30

Human Gender and Sexuality

Chapter Summary and Key Terms

One aspect of God's creation of human beings is *gender*. There are only two genders among human beings—male and female. One's gender corresponds to one's biological sex at birth. A man is an adult male human being. A woman is an adult female human being. Both genders are very good. People of both genders bear the image of God with equal dignity. At creation, God also instituted *marriage*. Marriage is the union of one man and one woman in an exclusive, lifelong covenant. The purposes of marriage include mutual help, intimate companionship, and producing and raising children. God designed men to be leaders in the family, and women to be helpers to their husbands. Homosexual desires and actions are unnatural and contrary to the law of God. Sexual activity can be righteous and good only in marriage.

GOD HAS REVEALED how men and women should relate to each other. The first two chapters of Genesis lay the foundation for a Christian view of marriage, sex, and the family. God's law also makes known what pleases him in these relationships.

Major shifts in Western culture since the 1960s have challenged the church's teaching on gender and sexuality. Feminism insists that marriage and motherhood are oppressive for women. The LGBTQ-rights movement demands as a matter of justice that everyone affirm homosexuality, bisexuality, transgenderism, and other "queer" expressions of sexuality as good.[1]

1 LGBTQ is an acronym for "lesbian, gay, bisexual, transgender, and queer."

We cannot answer all the scientific, political, legal, and practical questions related to these matters. However, the Bible addresses the basic questions about human sexuality.

The Bible's Basic Teaching on Gender

God created mankind in two distinct genders. Genesis 1:27 says, "So God created man in his own image, in the image of God created he him; *male and female* created he them." Gender is not merely about how we feel about ourselves or how society expects us to behave. Gender is God's fixed order in creation. Since the words "male" and "female" are used of animals as well as humans (Gen. 6:19; 7:3, 9), gender clearly has a biological component. This implies that the gender of each person corresponds to his or her physical sex.[2]

God created people of both genders "in the image of God" (Gen. 1:27). This is the basis of the equal dignity of men and women. It is very good for a man to be a man, and very good for a woman to be a woman (v. 31). Men and women should live as equals with different genders, a difference visible in clothing and hairstyles (Deut. 22:5; 1 Cor. 11:14–16).

God reveals in Genesis 2–3 that he made man to be a leader and woman to be a helper. The man was given relative authority over his wife. God created the man first (Gen. 2:7), which Paul saw as evidence of a leadership role: "But I suffer not a woman to teach, nor to usurp authority over the man, but to be in silence. For Adam was first formed, then Eve" (1 Tim. 2:12–13). While the man was yet alone, the Lord God gave his commandment to him (Gen. 2:15–17). This implies that the man was called to teach God's word to the woman, not vice versa.

God then made the woman of the man to help him (2:22). This is a sign that "the head of the woman is the man. . . . For the man is not of the woman: but the woman of the man. Neither was the man created for the woman; but the woman for the man" (1 Cor. 11:3, 8–9). When the Lord God brought the woman to the man, he named her (Gen. 2:23; cf. 3:20). Giving a name is an act of authority (1:5, 8, 10; 2:19), just as a higher king can name a lesser king or official (Gen. 41:45; 2 Kings 23:34; 24:17).

2 In rare cases, people are born with a mixture of male and female anatomy or genetics. This "intersex" condition is not the same as transgenderism.

After Adam and Eve sinned, the Lord God "called unto Adam, and said unto him, Where art thou?" (Gen. 3:9). The first to receive the command was the first to be called to account for breaking it. God's punishment on the woman aimed at her status as a mother and wife, but it was Adam whose disobedience brought death to all (3:16–19; Rom. 5:12–19). The entire race is named after the first man, "Adam," or "man," showing his headship (Gen. 5:2). Thus, it is appropriate to refer to the human race generically as "man," "men," or "mankind."

Christian feminists object that Genesis 3:16 teaches us that a husband's authority over his wife comes from the fall: "Thy desire shall be to thy husband, and he shall rule over thee."

In response, we agree that Genesis 3:16 speaks of the authority of a husband over his wife, but it does not tell us that this rule is a consequence of the fall. We have already noted evidence that the first man had authority over his wife before the fall. What is new after the fall is the wife's "desire" toward her husband—the same word God uses to describe sin's "desire" to conquer Cain (4:7). The point is that sin will now drive women to try to conquer their husbands, though husbands will still exercise authority over their wives.

Though Genesis 2–3 teaches the authority of the husband, it also stresses the equality of the woman. God calls her the "help meet for him" (Gen. 2:18). "Help" does not mean a less capable assistant. In fact, the word is used for God himself, who gives strength to people in need (Pss. 70:5; 124:8). The woman has strengths that the man lacks. He needs her. The phrase "meet for him" means a fitting match for the man, something no animal could be (Gen. 2:20).

God made the woman from the man's rib. She was, by the man's glad confession, "bone of my bones, and flesh of my flesh" (Gen. 2:23). She shares the same human life. As Paul says, God intended for husbands to love and cherish their wives as a part of themselves. They should imitate Christ, who loved his bride and sacrificed himself for her (Eph. 5:25, 28–31).

Even the history of the fall portrays the woman as a responsible moral agent who thinks and chooses (Gen. 3:1–6, 13, 16). God included the woman in the first statement of the gospel, promising to turn her back to him and making her a means by which he would bring victory over Satan (v. 15).

In sum, Genesis 1–3 offers a balanced perspective that honors both men and women while recognizing that they are different. Andreas and Margaret Köstenberger write, "God's plan for humanity is one of partnership in which the man, as God-appointed leader, and his wife alongside him jointly represent the Creator by exercising dominion over the earth."[3]

The Bible's Basic Teaching on Sex and Marriage

Marriage is the union of one man and one woman in an exclusive, lifelong covenant for mutual help, intimate companionship, and bearing and raising children. According to God's Word, one purpose for marriage is an intimate sexual relationship between husband and wife. We read in Genesis 2:24, "Therefore shall a man leave his father and his mother, and shall cleave unto his wife: and they shall be one flesh." "Leave" implies starting a new household. "Cleave" means to cling to or hold tightly (Ruth 1:14), as if glued together (2 Sam. 23:10). Christ warns, "What therefore God hath joined together, let not man put asunder" (Matt. 19:6).

We should not think that sex in marriage is sinful or unspiritual. Everything God created is good (1 Tim. 4:1–5). It is a saying of the wise, "Let thy fountain be blessed: and rejoice with the wife of thy youth. Let her be as the loving hind and pleasant roe; let her breasts satisfy thee at all times; and be thou ravished always with her love" (Prov. 5:18–19).

Another purpose for marriage is human procreation in the nurture of a family. In Genesis 1:27–28, "Male and female created he them" leads to "Be fruitful and multiply." For those created in God's image, sexual relationships serve to fill the earth with more image bearers. Thus, children are a blessing from God (Ps. 127:3).

God also intended marriage for the purpose of protecting people from sexual immorality. It is written, "Marriage is honourable in all, and the bed undefiled: but whoremongers and adulterers God will judge" (Heb. 13:4). "The bed" is a figure of speech for sexual activity (Rom. 13:13). Thus, sex in marriage is not unclean in God's sight, but sex outside of marriage is forbidden.

The Westminster Confession of Faith says, "Marriage was ordained for the mutual help of husband and wife (Gen. 2:18), for the increase of mankind

3 Andreas J. Köstenberger and Margaret E. Köstenberger, *God's Design for Man and Woman: A Biblical-Theological Survey* (Wheaton, IL: Crossway, 2014), 35.

with a legitimate issue, and of the Church with an holy seed (Mal. 2:15); and for preventing of uncleanness (1 Cor. 7:2, 9)."[4]

The Bible's Teaching on Homosexuality

God's Word condemns homosexuality as a sin from which people must be saved by Christ. There is not a single positive statement in Scripture about homosexuality.

One reason that the Lord destroyed the city of Sodom was its sexual perversion. The men of Sodom wanted to "know" other men (Gen. 19:4–5), a figure of speech for sex (v. 8). Jude says that the men of Sodom suffered God's fiery destruction for "giving themselves over to fornication, and going after strange flesh" (Jude 7). Peter speaks of the "filthy" conduct of Sodom (2 Pet. 2:7).

The law of Moses prohibits sexual acts between men, calling such sexual relations an "abomination" (Lev. 18:22; 20:13).

Paul says in 1 Timothy 1:9–10 that God's law condemns "them that defile themselves with mankind"—literally "men who go to bed with males." Paul also says,

> For this cause God gave them up unto vile affections: for even their women did change the natural use into that which is against nature: and likewise also the men, leaving the natural use of the woman, burned in their lust one toward another; men with men working that which is unseemly, and receiving in themselves that recompence of their error which was meet. (Rom. 1:26–27)

Sexual activity between people of the same sex is "against nature." Homosexual desires and actions are "vile" and "unseemly," which means they bring dishonor and shame to those who exercise them.

Elsewhere, Paul writes, "Know ye not that the unrighteous shall not inherit the kingdom of God?" (1 Cor. 6:9). Among other forms of unrighteousness, Paul includes being "effeminate" and "abusers of themselves with mankind" (vv. 9–10). The word translated as "effeminate" literally

4 The Westminster Confession of Faith (24.2), in *RC*, 4:263. Cf. the Second London Baptist Confession (25.2), in *RC*, 4:561.

means "men who are soft." It refers to men who seek to attract and please homosexuals. The phrase translated as "abusers of themselves with mankind" means "men who go to bed with males." People who have willingly engaged in homosexual sex and do not repent of their sin will not "inherit the kingdom of God."

Paul told the Corinthians, "And such were some of you: but ye are washed, but ye are sanctified, but ye are justified in the name of the Lord Jesus, and by the Spirit of our God" (1 Cor. 6:9, 11). They were no longer unrighteous. God had changed who they were by saving them "in Christ Jesus" (1:2).

Believers in Christ have a new identity by union with him. There is no such thing as a gay or lesbian Christian any more than there is a Christian adulterer or a Christian drunkard. To be sure, believers must still fight sin that remains in their hearts (Rom. 7:14–25; Gal. 5:17). Sin in a believer's life remains sin, including homosexual desires and actions. God calls his children to cling to Christ by faith and to strive in holy fear to put off all sin and pursue holiness (2 Cor. 6:16–7:1). And he promises that he counts them as washed clean and justified in his sight by the grace of Christ.

Someone might object that the people who wrote the ancient Scriptures did not have our modern understanding of sexual orientation. Such an orientation is said to define a person's identity by emotions and sexual desires. However, we each must define our identity not by our feelings but by what our Creator reveals in his Word. Denny Burk writes, "In God's world, we are who God says we are. We are not merely the sum total of our fallen sexual desires."[5]

The most basic question about our identity is not How do I feel? but How am I related to God and representing him as his living image by obeying his Word? This question goes beyond sexuality. We must remember that sex and marriage are temporary gifts (Matt. 22:30). We were made for something far greater—spiritual union with the God of glory.

Suggested Song to Sing to the Lord

- Psalm 128, "Blest the man that fears Jehovah," *Psalter*, No. 360; *THBap*, No. 626

5 Denny Burk, "Is Homosexual Orientation Sinful?" *Journal of the Evangelical Theological Society* 58, no. 1 (2015): 113.

Questions for Meditation or Discussion

1. What are two modern movements in Western culture that affect our views of sexuality?
2. How have these movements affected you in your background and experience?
3. What is the basic teaching on gender in Genesis 1:27?
4. How does the Bible describe the roles of men and women in relation to each other?
5. What does Genesis 1 teach us about sex in terms of procreation?
6. What does Genesis 2 teach us about sex in terms of relationships?
7. What does the Old Testament teach about homosexuality? List specific texts.
8. What does the New Testament teach about homosexuality? List specific texts.
9. What is the modern idea of sexual orientation? What is the problem with it?
10. How should a church treat homosexual or transgender people who desire to attend its services? What if they want to become members of the church?

31

The Human Body and Soul

Chapter Summary and Key Terms

A whole human person consists of a body and a soul. Some theologians have taught that human beings have three parts: body, soul, and spirit (*trichotomy*). But the Scriptures often use the terms "soul" and "spirit" for the same thing. Thus, human beings have two parts, not three. The body is a good creation by God. It is important for spiritual life now and for the hope of eternal life after the resurrection of the dead. The *soul* is an invisible, immortal human spirit. It has the personal faculties of thought, emotion, and will. It is a distinct substance from the body and continues in conscious existence after the body dies. The soul also is central to pleasing God, who requires not just right behavior but right thought and motive. Salvation begins in the soul.

GOD CREATED A WORLD with physical plants and animals on the earth below and intelligent spirits in heaven above. However, there is one creature who shares in both a physical body and a rational spirit: *man*. Herman Bavinck said, "Creation culminates in humanity where the spiritual and material world are joined together."[1]

Body and Soul: Different but Joined Together

Both the body and the soul are important parts of our lives as human beings.[2] They function as one and affect each other deeply. God calls us

1 Bavinck, *RD*, 2:511.

2 In this chapter, we use "soul" and "spirit" to refer to the immaterial part of the human person, but we recognize that the words translated as "soul" and "spirit" in the Bible have a wide range of meanings, including biological life. See Beeke and Smalley, *RST*, 2:230–31.

to cleanse "flesh and spirit" for the sake of holiness (2 Cor. 7:1). Antonius Thysius said that a human being "is composed from both, that is from the rational soul and the body which a very tight and close bond binds together into one nature, united in one person."[3]

However, there is a difference between man's body and soul. Christ compares gaining the whole world with losing one's "soul" (Matt. 16:26), implying that the soul is different from the things of the body. Another word for the soul is the "spirit." When Christ raised a dead girl to life, "her spirit returned" (Luke 8:55 ESV). Therefore, her spirit "is seen as distinct from and surviving the death of the physical body."[4] The Lord Jesus said that people can "kill the body, but are not able to kill the soul" (Matt. 10:28). This clearly means that the body and the soul are different substances.

It is helpful to compare human beings to angels and to animals. Angels are spirits (Ps. 104:4). They cannot die (Luke 20:36). They are personal (1:19). God will judge them for their works (Matt. 25:41). Animals, on the other hand, have bodies. They die. The Bible does not speak of them as personally responsible before God for their actions. It mentions no judgment day for animals. Human beings are somewhat like angels and animals but different from both. Humans have spirits and, like angels, are persons who think and choose. God will judge them for their works (16:27). Humans also have bodies, like the animals, and can die. But only human beings were created in God's image, and as a result, they have dominion over the animals (Gen. 1:26–28). Jesus says that each human being is worth more than many animals (Matt. 6:26; 10:30; 12:12). People are unique creatures made of earthly bodies and everlasting, personal souls.

The Human Body

Someone might wonder why theology pays any attention to the body. Gregg Allison writes, "The normal state of human existence is an embodied existence."[5] Therefore, we must learn from God's Word how to properly view our bodies.

3 Polyander, Walaeus, Thysius, and Rivetus, *SPT*, 13.3 (1:315).

4 Robert H. Stein, *Luke*, The New American Commentary 24 (Nashville: Broadman & Holman, 1992), 263.

5 Grgg R. Allison, "Toward a Theology of Human Embodiment," *Southern Baptist Journal of Theology* 13, no. 2 (2009): 5.

The doctrine of creation teaches us *the goodness of the body*. It arose by the supernatural work of God on the elements of the earth (Gen. 2:7). The body is "very good" (1:31). Its natural functions, such as sex in marriage and the enjoyment of food, are gifts from the Creator (1 Tim. 4:1–5). David says, "I will praise thee; for I am fearfully and wonderfully made: marvellous are thy works; and that my soul knoweth right well" (Ps. 139:14). Our bodies are sacred works of art. John Calvin said, "The human body shows itself to be a composition so ingenious that its Artificer is rightly judged a wonder-worker."[6] Therefore, it pleases God for Christians to take care of their bodies and to use them to build things, plant and harvest crops for food, and work in the skilled trades, the sciences, and the arts.

The doctrine of sanctification teaches us *the spiritual importance of the body*. Paul says, "Let not sin therefore reign in your mortal body, that ye should obey it in the lusts thereof" (Rom. 6:12). Paul even says to Christians, "Your bodies are the members of Christ" (1 Cor. 6:15). Therefore, we must not live merely to please our bodies. Instead, we should use our bodies for the glory of God (v. 20).

The doctrine of last things teaches us *the ultimate restoration of the body*. Christ said, "Marvel not at this: for the hour is coming, in the which all that are in the graves shall hear his voice, and shall come forth; they that have done good, unto the resurrection of life; and they that have done evil, unto the resurrection of damnation" (John 5:28–29). The hope of believers is that when Christ returns in glory, he will "change our vile body, that it may be fashioned like unto his glorious body, according to the working whereby he is able even to subdue all things unto himself" (Phil. 3:21). Even our bodies will enjoy eternal life with God in glory.

The Human Soul

There is much mystery about the human soul. However, we know certain truths about it because God has revealed them in his Word.

First, *the human soul is immortal*. By the will of God, the soul cannot die or cease to exist. Christ says that men "kill the body, but are not able to kill the soul" (Matt. 10:28). Even when Jesus says, "Fear him which is able to destroy both soul and body in hell" (v. 28), he does not mean that the soul

6 Calvin, *Institutes*, 1.5.2.

ceases to exist. "Destroy" means "ruin" here.[7] God will punish the wicked with ruin in pain and torment, though they will continue to exist forever (25:46; Rev. 14:11). Other Scripture passages also teach that the human spirit departs the body but continues in conscious existence after death.[8]

Second, *the human soul is immaterial.* It is not made of matter that we can see or touch. When Jesus rose from the dead, he said, "Behold my hands and my feet, that it is I myself: handle me, and see; for a spirit hath not flesh and bones, as ye see me have" (Luke 24:39). But as we saw, the soul is a real substance that continues after the body dies and returns to earth.

Third, *the human soul is the same as the human spirit.* Some theologians teach *trichotomy*, the idea that human beings have three parts: body, soul, and spirit. They argue that Paul refers to the human "spirit and soul and body" (1 Thess. 5:23). Another text speaks of "the dividing asunder of soul and spirit" (Heb. 4:12). But if we take this approach, then Mark 12:30 would mean that human beings have *four* parts: "Thou shalt love the Lord thy God with all thy heart . . . soul . . . mind, and . . . strength." Scripture passages like these are not teaching us how many parts human beings have. In many Scripture passages, "soul" and "spirit" mean the same thing. Hannah said, "I am a woman of a sorrowful spirit . . . [and] have poured out my soul before the Lord" (1 Sam. 1:15). Isaiah prayed, "With my soul have I desired thee in the night; yea, with my spirit within me will I seek thee early" (Isa. 26:9). Mary worshiped God, saying, "My soul doth magnify the Lord, and my spirit hath rejoiced in God my Saviour" (Luke 1:46–47). Therefore, whether the Bible uses "soul" or "spirit" for the invisible part of our person, it refers to the same thing.

Fourth, *the human soul has personal faculties or abilities.* The soul has the faculty of thought, including knowledge (1 Cor. 2:11), understanding (Isa. 29:24), memory, and meditation (Ps. 77:6). It also has the faculty of emotion, such as desire (Isa. 26:9), anguish (Job 7:11), sorrow (Matt. 26:38; Mark 8:12), and joy (Luke 1:47). And the soul has the faculty of will, such as choices (Ex. 35:21; Ezra 1:1, 5) and inclinations (Matt. 26:41).

Fifth, *the human soul is central for pleasing God.* Mere outward acts of worship do not please God (Matt. 15:8). David cried out for God to renew

7 The Greek word translated as "destroy" in Matt. 10:28 is also used in Matt. 9:17, where it is translated as "perish": "Neither do men put new wine into old bottles: else the bottles break, and the wine runneth out, and the bottles *perish*."

8 Eccles. 12:7; Luke 16:22–23; 23:43, 46; Acts 7:59; Phil. 1:21, 23; Heb. 12:23, etc. See chap. 89.

his spirit (Ps. 51:10). He understood that the worship God desires arises from a spirit broken over sin (v. 17). The root of Israel's disobedience against God was that the people were "a generation whose heart was not steadfast, whose spirit was not faithful to God" (78:8 ESV). God does not merely judge outward conduct, but "the Lord weigheth the spirits" (Prov. 16:2). A major promise of salvation is that God will give people "a new heart . . . and a new spirit" (Ezek. 36:26).

Have you been born again? It is not enough to know the truth and improve your behavior. Jesus Christ said to a man who had devoted his life to studying the Bible and to practicing religion, "Ye must be born again" (John 3:7). Therefore, examine yourself. Do you have a new heart and a new spirit that loves God?

Where are your priorities? How are you using your time and the means of grace to cultivate your soul? Do not be deceived. Jesus says, "For what is a man profited, if he shall gain the whole world, and lose his own soul? Or what shall a man give in exchange for his soul?" (Matt. 16:26).

Suggested Songs to Sing to the Lord

- "Be still my soul: the Lord is on thy side," *THBap*, No. 579
- "O Lord of Hosts, how lovely the place where thou dost dwell!," *THBap*, No. 305

Questions for Meditation or Discussion

1. How do we know that the human soul or spirit is different from the body?
2. How do human beings compare to angels and animals?
3. What does God's creation of the human body imply about it?
4. Why are our bodies important for the pursuit of holiness?
5. What will eternal life mean for the Christian's body?
6. How would you prove from the Holy Scriptures that the soul is immortal?
7. How do the Scriptures reveal that the soul is immaterial?
8. What is the doctrine of trichotomy? How do the Scriptures show it is not correct?
9. What are the faculties of the soul?
10. Why is the soul central to pleasing God?

32

God's Covenant with Adam

Chapter Summary and Key Terms

God has chosen to relate to human beings through covenants. A *covenant* is a solemn promise that legally defines a relationship of loyalty. God's covenants define a Lord-servant relationship and often include laws to obey. A covenant may include a grant of authority to perform an office, representation of a group by an individual, and visible signs. God made a covenant with Adam in the garden of Eden. This is often called the *covenant of works*. God promised life or death to Adam and his offspring depending on whether he honored God as Lord by obeying his law about the tree of the knowledge of good and evil. This covenant is also called the covenant of creation, the covenant of friendship, and the covenant of life. The covenant of works reveals that God is our covenant Lord, man is his covenant servant, our sin is covenant breaking, and Christ came to be the covenant Lord and Servant for the redemption of his people.

ROBERT ROLLOCK SAID, "God speaks nothing to man without the covenant."[1] The history of the world is also the history of God's covenants. Herman Bavinck said, "Covenant is the essence of true religion."[2] From the beginning, God has coupled law with promise to show his abundant goodness and enduring faithfulness, and to woo people to glorify him and enjoy him forever.

1 Robert Rollock, *A Treatise of God's Effectual Calling*, in *Select Works of Robert Rollock*, 2 vols. (Grand Rapids, MI: Reformation Heritage Books, 2008), 1:33.

2 Bavinck, *RD*, 2:569.

When we consider the doctrine of Christ, we will discuss God's covenant of grace (chaps. 38–41). Here, in our study of the doctrine of man, we must address God's covenant with Adam. This is often called the *covenant of works*. The doctrine of the covenant of works lays an important foundation for understanding Christ's work of salvation.

Someone might object that the word *covenant* does not appear in Genesis 2, and neither God nor Adam swore an oath. Another objection might be that "covenant of works" is too legalistic a term for God's fatherly and gracious dealings with Adam.

But the fact that the word *covenant* is not in Genesis 2 does not mean the idea is not there. Marriage is revealed in Genesis 2, but it is not called a covenant until much later in the Bible. Neither a formal oath nor the word covenant appears in God's promise to David (2 Samuel 7), but other Scripture passages call that promise a covenant and an oath (Ps. 89:3, 34–35). The term "covenant of works" is not legalistic, for the Bible uses the word "works" for the loving obedience of God's children by his grace (Matt. 5:16; Eph. 2:10). The real question is whether God's arrangement with Adam fits the definition of a covenant.

The Definition and Description of Covenants

What is a covenant? Theologians sometimes define a covenant as a contract. But it is better to say that a covenant is *a solemn promise that legally defines a relationship of loyalty*.

At the heart of a covenant is a solemn promise. The term *covenant* first appears in the Bible in God's promise to save Noah and never to destroy the earth with a flood again (Gen. 6:18; 9:9–17). Other Scripture passages say that God's covenant is his promise or oath (Ps. 105:9; Luke 1:72–73; Gal. 3:15–18). A covenant legally defines the loyalty expected in a personal relationship. Moses said, "The Lord your God is God, the faithful God who keeps covenant and steadfast love with those who love him and keep his commandments" (Deut. 7:9 ESV).

There are other things that are true of many covenants, though not all. One person or group in a covenant may be declared to be under the lordship of the other party (Ex. 6:7; 20:1–17). A covenant may require obedience to laws, such as in God's covenant with Israel (19:5). These laws may come with warnings of punishments for disobedience (Lev. 26:15–17). Also, a covenant may authorize someone to perform an office (a special position and responsibility to serve). By covenant, God made David and his offspring into his servant-kings (2 Samuel 7). In a covenant, someone may represent a larger group. God's covenants with Noah, Abraham, and others were with them and their offspring (Gen. 9:9; 17:7). God sometimes chose a visible sign as a reminder of a covenant, such as the rainbow (9:12–13) or circumcision (17:11).

The Covenant in Genesis 2

God's words to Adam in Genesis 2:15–17, in their context, fit the definition of a covenant. The text says, "And the Lord God took the man, and put him into the garden of Eden to dress it and to keep it. And the Lord God commanded the man, saying, Of every tree of the garden thou mayest freely eat: but of the tree of the knowledge of good and evil, thou shalt not eat of it: for in the day that thou eatest thereof thou shalt surely die."

God spoke to Adam in solemn legal words. This is God's only direct speech to man in the entire chapter. The phrases "freely eat" and "surely die" are literally "eating you shall eat" and "dying you shall die." These are formal sayings as in a legal death sentence (Gen. 26:11) or a sworn oath (Num. 26:65; cf. Ps. 95:11).

Genesis 2 implies a promise of life. God gave Adam the right to eat of "the tree of life" (v. 9). It would enable him to "live for ever" (3:22). The threat of death for violating God's prohibition implies that man would not die if he kept the law. This fits with the principle of "do this and live" that appears throughout the Scriptures.[3] God's words define his relationship to Adam like the loyalty between a good king and his obedient servant or the love between a kind father and his faithful son. By refusing to eat fruit that looked good (2:9; 3:6), Adam would have said, "The Lord is my supreme good. I choose him and his will."

Therefore, the Lord made a covenant with Adam—a solemn promise that legally defined a relationship of loyalty with him and his family.

Other common elements of covenants appear in this passage. God is described with a name of lordship: "the Lord God." He authorized Adam to serve in the offices of prophet, priest, and king. In chapter 29, we saw that

3 Lev. 18:5; Ezek. 20:11; Matt. 19:17; Gal. 3:12.

creation in the image of God implies the abilities to reveal God (prophet), to worship God (priest), and to reign for God (king). Genesis 2 tells us that God called man to serve him in those ways. God spoke directly to Adam in the garden (vv. 16–17). Martin Luther argued that since Adam was alone when God spoke to him, he had the responsibility of speaking God's word to others, beginning with his wife (once God created her) and later with their children.[4] He was God's prophet to them. The garden was also like a temple, where Adam served in God's presence. Adam's work was literally "to serve" and "to guard" the garden (v. 15), the same words used for the service of the Levites and priests in the temple (Num. 3:7–8; 8:26; 18:7). Adam was king of the world (Gen. 1:26), the animals were his subjects, and the garden was his palace (2:19–20). Luther said that God "places man into that garden as into a castle and temple" to be his "dwelling place and royal headquarters."[5] Hence, the Lord God commissioned Adam to serve him as a prophet, a priest, and a king.

God treated Adam as the representative of his natural descendants. Though the Lord would soon create a wife for Adam with whom he would have children, God spoke to Adam with the singular "thou" (Gen. 2:16–17). Adam represented his family in this legal arrangement. God had threatened Adam with the penalty of death. Yet Genesis 5 reports not only the death of Adam but the death of his descendants. Finally, God's arrangement with Adam involved visible signs: the tree of the knowledge of good and evil and the tree of life. These are all common marks of a covenant.

Therefore, though the word *covenant* does not appear in Genesis 2, there is every reason to believe that God made a covenant with Adam.

We may offer this summary of the first covenant made in history: the Lord God freely made a covenant with Adam as the representative of all his natural descendants. In that covenant, God threatened death for disobedience but promised eternal life for perfect obedience. The visible signs of the covenant were the tree of the knowledge of good and evil and the tree of life.

We must not underestimate how serious a crime it was for Adam to violate God's covenant. By that one act of rebellion, our first parents broke, in principle, all of the Ten Commandments. (1) They abandoned their God

4 Luther, *Lectures on Genesis*, in *LW*, 1:105 (Gen. 2:16–17).

5 Luther, *Lectures on Genesis*, in *LW*, 1:101 (Gen. 2:15).

and made gods out of themselves and the Devil. (2) They did not keep the ordinance God had appointed for his glory, but made an idol out of creation. (3) They despised the name of God in his attributes of goodness, wisdom, trustworthiness, and so on. They profaned the sacramental sign, ignored his word, and misconstrued his providential works. (4) They made themselves unfit for holy worship on the Sabbath. (5) They overthrew their duties as husband and wife, abandoned their descendants, and did not honor their heavenly Father. (6) They murdered themselves and all mankind. (7) They gave themselves over to sensual desires. (8) They stole what was not their own. (9) They bore false witness against the Lord. (10) They became discontent and covetous. Truly this one sin contained a world of evils.

Other Scripture Passages That Reveal the Covenant of Works

We also find references to the covenant of works in other Scripture passages. In Hosea 6:6–7, the Lord rebuked Israel: "For I desired mercy, and not sacrifice; and the knowledge of God more than burnt offerings. But they like men have transgressed the covenant: there have they dealt treacherously against me." In the phrase "like men," the Hebrew word translated as "men" is the singular *adam*. The same phrase appears in Job 31:33: "If I covered my transgressions as Adam" (cf. Gen. 3:12). Therefore, Hosea 6:7 is best taken to refer to Adam breaking God's covenant. Even if *adam* means "man," it implies a covenant made with all humanity. When was such a covenant made except at creation? When was it broken except by Adam?

Another significant passage regarding the covenant of works is Isaiah 24:5–6: "The earth also is defiled under the inhabitants thereof; because they have transgressed the laws, changed the ordinance, broken the everlasting covenant. Therefore hath the curse devoured the earth, and they that dwell therein are desolate: therefore the inhabitants of the earth are burned, and few men left." God would send a "curse" on the whole world because its people had "broken the everlasting covenant." This chapter is not just about Israel. It refers to "the isles of the sea" ("the coastlands of the sea," ESV) and "the kings of the earth" (vv. 15, 21). Edward Young said, "The eternal covenant here spoken of designates the fact that God has given His Law and ordinances to Adam, and in Adam to all mankind."[6]

6 Edward Young, *The Book of Isaiah*, 3 vols. (Grand Rapids, MI: Eerdmans, 1969), 2:158.

The apostle Paul compared and contrasted Adam and Christ in Romans 5:12–19. Adam's sin brought "condemnation" on our race (vv. 16, 18). The punishment is "death" (vv. 12–17). That is precisely the judgment God threatened against Adam in the garden of Eden. Paul's argument in Romans 5 assumes that God set up a legal arrangement so that Adam's disobedience would bring mankind under guilt and punishment. Christ saves his people as their representative in the covenant of grace. Therefore, Adam brought destruction on his people as their representative in the first covenant.

The History of the Doctrine of the Covenant of Works

The idea of God's covenant of works with Adam is an ancient doctrine. Augustine said, "For the first covenant, which was made with the first man, is just this: 'In the day ye eat thereof, ye shall surely die.'" He said that Adam represented all mankind, so people "have all broken God's covenant in that one in whom all have sinned"—that is, our first father.[7]

Reformed theologians developed this doctrine over the course of the sixteenth century. John Calvin said that the tree of life given to Adam, like the rainbow given to Noah, was a sacrament and seal of God's covenant.[8] Zacharias Ursinus may have been the first Reformed theologian to write of a "covenant of creation" and a "natural covenant" between God and Adam.[9] Dudley Fenner may have been the first person to use the phrase "covenant of works."[10]

In the seventeenth century, the covenant of works became a standard teaching of Reformed theology. The Westminster Confession of Faith says, "The first covenant made with man was a covenant of works (Gal. 3:12), wherein life was promised to Adam; and in him to his posterity (Rom. 10:5; 5:12–20), upon condition of perfect and personal obedience (Gen. 2:17; Gal. 3:10)."[11]

Reformed theologians have given different names to the covenant with Adam. Some have called it a "covenant of friendship" because God and

7 Augustine, *The City of God*, 16.27, in *NPNF*[1], 2:326.

8 Calvin, *Institutes*, 4.14.18.

9 Zacharius Ursinus, *The Larger Catechism*, Q. 36, trans. Lyle D. Bierma, Fred Klooster, and John Medendorp, in *An Introduction to the Heidelberg Catechism*, Texts and Studies in Reformation and Post-Reformation Thought (Grand Rapids, MI: Baker Academic, 2005), 168–69.

10 Dudley Fenner, *Sacra Theologia*, 2nd ed. ([Geneva]: Eustathium Vignon, 1586), 4.1 (39).

11 The Westminster Confession of Faith (7.2), in *RC*, 4:242.

Adam were already at peace with each other and needed no reconciliation. Some have named it a "covenant of creation" or "covenant of nature" because it stood on the purity of human nature as God created it. Some have called it a "covenant of life" for its promise of life. Others have called it a "legal covenant" or "covenant of works" because its condition was obedience to God's command.

Reformed theologians have stressed that the covenant of works shows God's goodness: "He is a rewarder of them that diligently seek him" (Heb. 11:6). This may be illustrated by a parable adapted from the writings of Thomas Boston.[12] Let us imagine that a farmer desires to pass on the family business to his son. The father promises his son that he will receive the whole farm and all its equipment. The only condition is that the son must manage a small vineyard according to his father's instructions. To show that he really means this, the father draws up legal papers. However, this is no cold, commercial transaction. It is a fatherly act drenched with love. This is a weak analogy to the infinite goodness of God to his son, Adam, before the fall. In the garden, Samuel Rutherford said, we find that "law is honeyed with love."[13]

Practical Applications of the Covenant of Works

Although the covenant of works may seem to be a highly theological concept, it has numerous practical applications. Let us consider several.

The Covenant of Works Shows Us the Covenant Lord

In the covenant of works, the Creator pledged himself to Adam to be mankind's all-sufficient Lord and Father forever if Adam would obey him.

First, *the covenant of works reveals God to be the Lord of our life.* He gave man life and all good things in paradise. He warned that he would take life away if man sinned, but if man obeyed, he would enjoy it forever. We should be amazed at how generous God is. Yet the covenant also calls us to fear God's justice: "The wages of sin is death" (Rom. 6:23).

Second, *the covenant of works reveals God to be the Lord of our location*—our homes and callings in life. God made the covenant in the garden,

12 Boston, *A View of the Covenant of Works*, in *WTB*, 11:181.

13 Samuel Rutherford, *The Covenant of Life Opened: Or a Treatise of the Covenant of Grace* (Edinburgh: by Andre Anderson, for Robert Broun, 1655), 35.

where he put the man and assigned him his work (Gen. 2:15). The Lord has set each of us in a particular place. He has given us callings to fulfill in each season of our lives. We must submit to that providence. The covenant also shows us our calling to persevere under God's fatherly training. The garden was a beautiful paradise, but it was also a place where faith and obedience were tested.

Third, *the covenant of works reveals God to be the Lord of our law.* We must obey God's commands. We must obey even if we do not understand why. Some may ask what was wrong with eating a piece of fruit. It was a test of obedience. The covenant's promises and threats also impose on us the obligation to believe God's word: "Without faith it is impossible to please him" (Heb. 11:6).

Fourth, *the covenant of works reveals God to be the Lord of our love.* After God made his covenant with Adam, he created the woman and instituted the marriage covenant (Gen. 2:18–25). Human marriage foreshadows Christ's marriage to the church (Eph. 5:25–33). Therefore, we should rejoice in God's graciousness to lower himself to join with us in a covenant relationship. Though the first covenant was broken, we can have a relationship with God by the covenant of grace in Jesus Christ. By grace, Christ can be our Bridegroom!

The Covenant of Works Shows Us the Covenant Servant

The presence of the covenant Lord implies a covenant servant. Man is not a menial slave but a servant in the sense of an officer of the great King, who serves him with dignity and power.

First, *the covenant of works shows us that God commissioned man to serve him as a prophet.* God made man to hear and meditate on God's Word. The faithful servant is quick to say, "Speak, LORD; for thy servant heareth" (1 Sam. 3:9). Adam's work as a prophet in the covenant also teaches us to speak God's Word to one another.

Second, *the covenant of works shows us that God commissioned man to serve him as priest.* It is our duty to worship the holy Lord. It also implies our responsibility to keep God's worship holy. We must guard the sacred garden, so to speak, from anything that would pollute God's worship. We must worship him only according to his Word.

Third, *the covenant of works shows us that God commissioned man to serve him as a king.* As God's royal servant, you have freedom to enjoy

God's world. God "giveth us richly all things to enjoy" (1 Tim. 6:17). But as a servant-king, you must also own your responsibility to do God's will. Human beings are stewards. God is the owner of all.

The Covenant of Works Shows Us the Servant's Apostasy from the Lord

Genesis 2 was written not for Adam but for us, who live in a fallen world because of Adam's sin. It helps us to understand our apostasy (or falling away) from our Creator.

First, *the covenant of works teaches us that we did not fall away from God as individuals but as a whole race in Adam.* Our first father was righteous, but he fell. We must acknowledge that the best of men is a changeable creature, not the immutable Creator. Let us set aside our illusions about how strong and stable we are. The covenant also teaches us to recognize that we are not neutral. We have already fallen with Adam into the state of sin (Rom. 5:12, 16, 18).

Second, *the covenant of works teaches us that our apostasy is rebellion against God's law.* This helps us to understand man's attempt to be righteous by his works. To convince ourselves that we are righteous, we often replace God's law with man's traditions, which are easier to keep. The covenant of works also calls us to humble ourselves. When God says through his law, "You have sinned and are sinful, and deserve the wrath of God in hell forever," we should reply with sorrow, "Yes, Lord, it is true."

Third, *the covenant of works teaches us that man's fall was a great crime against God.* The covenant presses us to grieve over our ingratitude and treason. By breaking God's law, man treated his generous Lord as if he were a wicked tyrant. Man became a traitor, rebel, and enemy of the sovereign God. The covenant of works also calls us to renounce all false hopes of saving ourselves. If sinless Adam did not stand, how do we think that we sinners will stand?

The Covenant of Works Shows Us the Redeeming Lord and Servant

Adam was a type of Christ (Rom. 5:14). The covenant revealed God as the covenant Lord and engaged man as God's covenant servant. Thus, it also foreshadowed Christ both as Lord and Servant.

First, *the covenant of works foreshadows Christ as the Lord and Servant of our life.* It calls us to believe in Christ as the Lord and life giver. God breathed life into the first man (Gen. 2:7). Christ breathes on his people the life-giving Holy Spirit (John 20:22). We must also believe in Christ as the last and life-giving Adam. Death came by the first Adam's sin, but resurrection life by Christ's obedience (Rom. 5:17; 1 Cor. 15:21–22). Stop trying to be your own Adam. Rest all your hopes on the last Adam appointed by God.

Second, *the covenant of works foreshadows Christ as the Lord and Servant of our location.* Since Jesus is Lord, we must serve him where he has put us in the work he has given us (Col. 3:23–24). We must follow him and imitate him as the Servant of our Lord (Isa. 42:1), who endured many trials in this world to do the will of God (Heb. 12:1–2). By grace, Christ's perseverance becomes the perseverance of his redeemed people.

Third, *the covenant of works foreshadows Christ as the Lord and Servant of our law.* We must obey the Lord Christ as the Lawgiver. If we do not keep Christ's commands, then we do not love him (John 14:15). And we must rest in Christ as the Servant who perfectly obeyed God in our place. He satisfied the demands of God's justice for us (Heb. 7:22, 26–27). We plead with you, dear reader, to flee to Christ for your righteousness. Flee from the broken covenant of works to the covenant of grace.

Fourth, *the covenant of works foreshadows Christ as the Lord and Servant of our love.* God brought Adam and Eve together in the first marriage. By grace, God brings together Christ and his church. Christ loved the church as her husband and gave himself for her (Eph. 5:25–27). The covenant of grace is a covenant of faithful love. Those who are joined to Christ by a Spirit-worked faith may live in Christian freedom, not under the covenant of works. The covenant of works was a covenant of life for Adam in his righteousness. But let us in our sins never seek life through it or we will find nothing but bondage and death. The high privilege of the Christian is to live in the freedom of the sons of God, a freedom that will expand into glory when God's Son is revealed.

Suggested Songs to Sing to the Lord

- Psalm 1, "That man is blest who, fearing God," *Psalter*, No. 1; *THBap*, No. 446
- Psalm 111, "O give the Lord wholehearted praise," *Psalter*, No. 304; *THBap*, No. 767

Questions for Meditation or Discussion

1. How do the authors define a covenant?
2. What other things are often true of a covenant?
3. How do this definition and description fit with God's arrangement with Adam in Genesis 2?
4. How do Hosea 6:6–7, Isaiah 24:5–6, and Romans 5:12–19 show us the covenant with Adam?
5. What ancient church theologian spoke of God's dealings with Adam as a covenant?
6. How can we illustrate the covenant of works with a parable of a farmer and his son?
7. How does the covenant of works show us that God is the covenant Lord?
8. What can we learn from the covenant of works about man as a covenant servant?
9. How does the covenant of works shed light on man's apostasy from God?
10. What does the covenant of works foreshadow about Christ as the Lord and Servant?

Section 3B

Man as Sinner before God

33

Sin and the Fall of Man

Chapter Summary and Key Terms

God created man in his image and in a state of innocence. But the first man, Adam, brought ruin on himself and his natural descendants by committing sin, breaking God's commandment in the garden. The essence of *sin* is hatred against God, whether in attitude or action. All sin involves rebellion against God's law, unbelief toward his word, and worship of his creatures, especially ourselves, instead of him, the Creator. Adam's sin broke the covenant of works. This resulted in the *fall of man*, the human race's loss of the state of innocence and its imprisonment in the state of sin. The punishment that sin deserves is *death*. Death separates the soul from God to be ruled by sin (spiritual death). It separates the body from the soul to be ruled by decay (physical death). And it separates the body and soul from all happiness, to be ruled by God's wrath (eternal death).

GOD CREATED MAN in a state of pure goodness but put his obedience to the test. Man's response was tragic: "God hath made man upright; but they have sought out many inventions" (Eccles. 7:29), or "schemes" (ESV).

In this chapter, we will trace man's fall into sin, recorded in Genesis 3. First, however, we will step back to look at the big picture of what the Holy Scriptures say about sin in general. Sin is amazingly deceitful and blinding in its effects on the human heart (Jer. 17:9). Therefore, we must listen carefully to God's Word and pray earnestly that God's Spirit would cause us to see sin for what it is.

The Bible's Words for Sin

The Old Testament uses many words for sin, but three are most common (Ex. 34:7). To "sin" literally means to miss a mark (Judg. 20:16). But sin is not a mistake; it is shooting at the wrong target on purpose. To "transgress" or "rebel" (1 Kings 12:19) means to defy authority (2 Kings 1:1). "Iniquity" (Gen. 15:16) means moral evil, guilt, or punishment. These three ideas provide a good summary of sin. When someone sins, he turns away from his created purpose, rebels against the Lord's authority, and becomes guilty and liable to punishment.

Sin is also called "evil" (1 Kings 11:6), "wickedness" (Prov. 11:5), "guiltiness" (Gen. 26:10), and "uncleanness" (Ezek. 36:29). In committing sin, people have refused to "hear" God's Word (2 Kings 17:14), "rebelled against the commandment of the LORD" (Deut. 1:26), and "like sheep have gone astray" (Isa. 53:6).

The New Testament also uses three main words for this sad subject: "sin" (Rom. 3:23), "unrighteousness" (6:13), and "lawlessness" (1 John 3:4 ESV). It also speaks of "evil" (Matt. 9:4), "transgression" of the law (Rom. 4:15), "disobedience" (5:19), and the state of being "unclean" (2 Cor. 6:17).

The Deep Roots and Core Motives of Sin

What does all sin have in common? What is the central thrust of sin that makes it sinful? Let's consider various answers to these questions, each of which contains a measure of truth.

1. *Passions of the body.* The first sin involved grasping after physical gratification in the forbidden fruit (Gen. 3:6). Worldliness is allowing our lusts to reign over us to please our eyes and flesh, and to feed our pride (1 John 2:16).

But sin must be more than sensual passion, for it often involves the spirit, such as in the case of pride. The Devil has no body but is the worst sinner of all. The body is not evil or the source of evil, but is God's good creation.

It is true, though, that sin preoccupies us with this world—what we can experience now by our senses. Sin deadens us to the glory of God, whom we cannot see (Matt. 6:19–24). The message of God's kingdom is often choked out in people's hearts by "the care of this world, and the deceitfulness of riches" (13:22).

2. *Pride and selfishness.* The bait with which Satan lured Adam and Eve to their deaths was "Ye shall be as gods" (Gen. 3:5) or even "like God" (ESV).

The day of the Lord is against everything "proud and lofty" (Isa. 2:12). Sinners are "lovers of their own selves (2 Tim. 3:2), but true love does not seek its own (1 Cor. 13:5).

But if we define sin as pride or selfishness, we risk becoming man-centered rather than God-centered. The emphasis of Scripture falls on sin's rebellion and treason against God, not just how we view ourselves. Selfishness also does not explain why people expend, humiliate, or even destroy themselves to pursue their sins.

3. *Idolatry*. The great offense against which God's wrath burns is man's refusal to glorify his Creator and willingness to worship images of created things (Rom. 1:18–23). Pride and self-love are deeply connected to seeking glory in the things of this world.

But when God summarized the moral law in the Ten Commandments, he devoted only the second commandment to forbidding idols. The rest address other matters. We do not find that the Bible uses idolatry as a master category for all sin, but only as one category among others.

4. *Unbelief*. The temptation in the garden hinged on whether Adam and Eve would believe God's word (Gen. 3:4). The great failure of Israel in the wilderness was that "they believed not his word" (Ps. 106:24). The Bible says, "Whatsoever is not of faith is sin" (Rom. 14:23). Martin Luther said, "Unbelief is the root, sap, and chief power of all sin."[1]

But if we take unbelief as the core of all sin, we must understand it not in a merely negative way, as a lack of faith. Unbelief is active opposition to God. There is a perverse energy in sin that can be explained only by its hatred against God.

5. *Rebellion against God's law*. "Sin is the transgression of the law" (1 John 3:4) or "Sin is lawlessness" (ESV). It is a stubborn refusal to be "subject to the law of God" (Rom. 8:7). The Westminster Shorter Catechism says, "What is sin? Sin is any want [lack] of conformity unto, or transgression of, the law of God."[2]

But if we define the core of sin as a violation of God's law, we must make it clear that the law cannot be separated from God, the Lawgiver. Opposing God's law means acting as an enemy of God. When people break God's law,

1 Luther, *Preface to the Epistle of St. Paul to the Romans*, in *LW*, 35:369.

2 The Westminster Shorter Catechism (Q. 14), in *RC*, 4:355. Cf. the Baptist Catechism (Q. 17), in *RC*, 4:575.

they "walk contrary" to God (Lev. 26:21–28, 40–41). Thomas Watson said that sin strikes at God. It not only seeks to dethrone him but to make him no longer to be God.[3]

6. *Hatred against God*. This is perhaps the best approach to understanding sin. At the core of sin is hatred against God as our Creator and Lawgiver, and the futile attempt to proudly exalt ourselves over him (Rom. 1:20–25; 8:7). Sin corrupts each part of the threefold office of God's covenant servants, whether it is considered as "unbelief" (prophet), "idolatry" (priest), or "rebellion" (king). Sin's definitive act is rebellion against God's law. Its defiling desire is turning from God's glory to creatures. Its deepest mindset is unbelief toward God's revelation. All of these descriptions of sin reveal its damnable character as enmity against God.

Consider what it means that you are a sinner. John Owen reminded us that the least degree of sin is hostility against God, just as "every drop of poison is poison, and will infect, and every spark of fire is fire, and will burn."[4] The smallest motion of sin in your heart is a criminal act of hatred against God. Surely this truth calls us to humble ourselves. We should cry out in horror, "What am I, and what have I done?"

The Fall of Man into Sin and Misery

Sin is not a mere idea but a real evil that appeared in history at a specific time. The Bible records the entrance of sin into this world in Genesis 3.

The Transgression of Creatures against Their God

The first enemy of God was "the serpent" in the garden (Gen. 3:1). Though it acted in some ways like a snake (vv. 1, 14–15), its crafty skill in tricking the first woman shows that it was no animal but rather an evil intelligence. It was "that old serpent, called the Devil, and Satan, which deceiveth the whole world" (Rev. 12:9).

Satan deceived the woman regarding the trustworthiness of God's word. The Devil began by suggesting doubt about what God had said: "Yea, hath God said, Ye shall not eat of every tree of the garden?" (Gen. 3:1). In other words, "Did God actually say that? Is he that stingy?"

3 Thomas Watson, *A Body of Divinity* (Edinburgh: Banner of Truth, 1965), 133–34.

4 Owen, *Indwelling Sin in Believers*, in *WJO*, 6:177.

The Serpent next led the woman into a distortion of God's word. She replied, "We may eat of the fruit of the trees of the garden: but of the fruit of the tree which is in the midst of the garden, God hath said, Ye shall not eat of it, neither shall ye touch it, lest ye die" (Gen. 3:2–3). Her answer was mostly true, but she exaggerated God's restriction by adding "neither shall ye touch it," as if God were harsh. She also weakened God's warning, changing "thou shalt surely die" (2:17) into "lest ye die."

The Devil went on to make a bold denial of God's word. He said, "Ye shall not surely die" (Gen. 3:4). He contradicted God's warning that he would judge sinners. Satan added, "For God doth know that in the day ye eat thereof, then your eyes shall be opened, and ye shall be as gods, knowing good and evil" (v. 5). The tempter attacked God's justice, truthfulness, and love. Satan aimed to cultivate unbelief in God's word while proposing his own promise. In other words, the Devil sought to dethrone God in man's heart and take his place. Luther said, "The source of all sin truly is unbelief and doubt and abandonment of the Word. Because the world is full of these, it remains in idolatry, denies the truth of God, and invents a new god."[5]

The woman and the man responded to this temptation in defiance of God's word. Genesis 3:6 says, "And when the woman saw that the tree was good for food, and that it was pleasant to the eyes, and a tree to be desired to make one wise, she took of the fruit thereof, and did eat, and gave also unto her husband with her; and he did eat." Here we have an anatomy of sin. It begins with false perceptions based on unbelief ("the woman saw"). It grows into corrupt desires—the desire to satisfy the body, to possess beautiful things, and to be one's own source of wisdom (cf. 1 John 2:16). It produces disobedient action.

Someone might say that eating a piece of fruit was a small sin. But as William Perkins said, this one sin contained "unbelief . . . of the truth of God's word," "contempt of God," "pride and ambition," ingratitude for God's good gifts, a craving to be wiser than God, the blasphemies of charging God "with lying and envy," the murder of themselves and their descendants, and discontentment—in short, "the breach of the whole law of God."[6]

5 Luther, *Lectures on Genesis*, in *LW*, 1:149.

6 Perkins, *An Exposition of the Symbol*, in *WWP*, 5:87–88.

The Righteousness of God toward Sinners

As soon as the man and his wife sinned, God's secret judgment began to fall on them. They felt shame and tried to cover themselves (Gen. 3:7). Sin estranged them from God and from each other. They also felt guilt and fear in God's presence. When Adam and Eve heard God coming to them, they "hid themselves from the presence of the LORD God amongst the trees of the garden" (v. 8). They knew that they deserved punishment.

God patiently confronted the sinners. He came asking questions. He desires sinners to examine themselves and repent of their sins. He spoke to Adam first, inviting him to come and confess what he had done. But Adam first avoided the issue, then blamed his wife and God for giving her to him (Gen. 3:12). Once full of love for God and his bride, Adam was now controlled by selfishness and hatred. God then questioned the woman. She said, "The serpent beguiled [deceived] me, and I did eat" (v. 13).

The Lord God pronounced his judgment on each of the three sinners in the garden. God spoke his supreme curse on Satan (Gen. 3:14). Then God afflicted the woman in her household relationships (v. 16). Her joy in bearing children would be mingled with great pain, and her relationship with her husband would be disturbed by conflict as she tried to control him. Finally, God punished the man with hard labor and death (vv. 17–19). When God's steward-king over the earth fell, God's curse fell on man's earthly dominion (1:28). Now all creation groans with mankind in misery (Rom. 8:20–22).

God's Judgment of Threefold Death for Sin

The Lord God had said, "In the day that thou eatest thereof thou shalt surely die" (Gen. 2:17). The Holy Scriptures show us that this death is threefold.

First, *sin merits spiritual death*. Death, even before the demise of the body, separates the soul from God to be ruled by sin. Man's sin tore open a chasm of hatred against God. We saw that in man's guilt, fear, and unwillingness to accept personal responsibility (Gen. 3:7–13). This was a shocking fall from spiritual life to spiritual death (Eph. 2:1–3; 4:18). It destroyed the core of God's image: righteousness and holiness (Eph. 4:24).

Second, *sin merits physical death*. Man would now experience weariness, pain, and the death of his body (Gen. 3:16, 19). The human body, once so full of life and beauty, decays horribly into earth. God's image bearer on earth was subjected to futility.

Third, *sin merits eternal death*. The full doctrine of hell is not revealed in the account of the garden, but we find it foreshadowed there. God banished man from paradise and eternal life, and he armed his holy angels against man (Gen. 3:24). God's curse fell on the Devil (v. 14). It also falls on people who follow the Devil (4:11; 9:25; 12:3). Christ will say to the wicked, "Depart from me, ye cursed, into everlasting fire, prepared for the devil and his angels" (Matt. 25:41). This is the ultimate death (Rev. 20:14). The very thought of hell should make us tremble. This is the condemnation that Adam brought on the human race.

God's Seed Promise of the Victor

In the darkest chapter in the Bible, we find the light of God's goodness shining in the promise of Christ. God said to the Serpent, "I will put enmity between thee and the woman, and between thy seed and her seed; it shall bruise thy head, and thou shalt bruise his heel" (Gen. 3:15).

God promised *the application of salvation*. Satan had tempted the woman to turn away from God and toward himself. But God said that he would put "enmity," or hatred, between them to shatter their unholy alliance. By his sovereign grace, God would turn the woman and her seed back to himself in repentance and faith. He divided Satan's seed and the woman's seed—that is, people who follow the Devil in sin and people who are saved by sovereign grace.

God also promised *the accomplishment of salvation*. He foretold a decisive battle between the Serpent and the great Seed of the woman—Jesus Christ. God granted Satan the power to bruise the heel of the Seed. But God promised that the Seed would bruise the Serpent's head. To tread on an enemy with one's foot shows total victory (Ps. 91:13). Genesis 3:15 foreshadowed both the cross and the empty tomb of Christ.

Finally, God promised *the agent of salvation*. As the Seed of the woman, he must be a human being, born of a woman (Gal. 4:4). He must be capable of suffering, for Satan would "bruise his heel" (Gen. 3:15). However, he must also be almighty God to conquer the Devil. The promise hints at the coming of the incarnate Lord, God in the flesh, Jesus Christ.

If God could call people to faith with such a brief promise, how much more should we, equipped with the whole Bible, hope entirely in Jesus Christ? God promises those in union with Christ that he will "bruise Satan under your feet shortly" (Rom. 16:20). However, this promise belongs only to those who receive Christ by faith.

Consider the alternative. Adam's sin has plunged you into sin. Apart from Christ, you are already in a state of spiritual death. You are subject to the Devil's power. Physical death will one day kill you. After this will come eternal death. You will suffer torment forever for your sins. How will you escape?

Thanks be to God for Jesus Christ our Lord! In Christ, believers have victory over the Devil, sin, death, and hell itself. Take hold of Christ by faith, and you will discover that he has taken hold of you. By his grace, follow him to the end, and he will welcome you into paradise.

Suggested Songs to Sing to the Lord

- "Praise the Saviour now and ever," *THBap*, No. 174
- "Before thee, God, who knowest all," *THBap*, No. 409

Questions for Meditation or Discussion

1. What are some important words for sin in the Bible? What can we learn from them?
2. What are the strengths and weaknesses of saying that the core of sin is (1) passions of the body, (2) pride and selfishness, (3) idolatry, (4) unbelief, and (5) rebellion against God's law?
3. What do the authors say about sin's definitive act, defiling desire, deepest mindset, and damnable character?
4. What strategy did Satan use to tempt the sinless man and woman in the garden?
5. How did listening to Satan's lies change how the woman saw the forbidden fruit?
6. What judgments did the Lord pronounce on the man and woman?
7. What threefold death came on mankind for our fall in Adam?
8. How does Genesis 3:15 reveal the application, accomplishment, and agent of salvation?
9. How has reading this chapter affected how you think and feel about sin?

34

Original Sin and Total Depravity

Chapter Summary and Key Terms

Mankind has fallen in Adam into the state of sin. *Pelagianism* denies this and teaches that human beings by nature always have the power to choose to be good. Pelagius opposed Augustine's teaching that sinners are saved by grace alone (*sola gratia*). Augustine recognized the Bible's teaching that all human beings descended from Adam by natural generation are born in the guilt and corruption of *original sin*. That is the *imputation* (legal reckoning) of the guilt from Adam's breaking of the covenant of works, the lack of Adam's original righteousness, and the total depravity of man's nature, from which come all actual sins. By *total depravity*, we mean the corruption of man's whole nature by sin. Total depravity does not mean that everyone is as bad as he could be. It means that every part of who we are is stained by sin and unacceptable to God apart from the saving grace of Christ.

SIN POISONS OUR SOULS even in the cradle. It raises its ugly head in childish lies and playground cruelty. Sin distorts our relationships, dirties our business dealings, defiles our sexuality, and damages our world. It leads to broken marriages, murders, and wars. Sin clings to our last breath. There is no more horrifying end than to die in one's sins without the Savior.

Our study of sin must dig down to its deepest roots: original sin. The term *original sin* refers not to the first sin but to the guilt and sinfulness that affects all of Adam's natural descendants and is the origin of all other sins (Rom. 5:12). As the *New England Primer* said, "In Adam's fall, we sinned all."[1] A related doctrine is called *total depravity*. The word *depravity* means corruption or distortion. *Total* does not mean that everyone is as sinful as he possibly could be, but that sin corrupts our thoughts, emotions, choices, and actions—the whole human life.

The History of the Doctrine of Original Sin

The doctrine of sin did not receive much attention until Pelagianism arose at the end of the fourth century AD. Before then, theologians taught man's fall in paradise into a state of sin and death, as well as man's free choice of the will and moral responsibility. But they did not give careful thought to how these truths fit together in a balanced and biblical way.

Pelagius taught that man did not become a slave of sin after Adam's fall. Instead, man still has the power in himself to choose good. For Pelagius, salvation by grace meant three things. First, God created us with free will. Second, he teaches us in his Word what to believe and do. Third, he offers forgiveness by the blood of Christ. But man does not need a supernatural change of heart. Each person chooses whether to be good or bad, Pelagius said.

Augustine strongly opposed Pelagianism. He taught that Adam and Christ are "the two men by one of whom we are sold under sin, by the other redeemed from sins."[2] Augustine quoted Ambrose of Milan, who had said, "All of us human beings are born under the power of sin, and our very origin lies in guilt."[3]

The Pelagian view of sin and grace was condemned as heretical (outside the bounds of true Christianity) by a synod at Carthage (AD 418) and the Council of Ephesus (AD 431). However, other theologians, such as John Cassian, tried to find middle ground between Pelagius and Augustine. They said that we cannot be saved apart from the grace of God working in our hearts. But they also said his grace works in all people, and only those who choose to cooperate with God's grace are saved.

1 *The New England Primer: A Reprint of the Earliest Known Edition, and Many Facsimiles and Reproductions, and an Historical Introduction*, ed. Paul Leicester Ford (New York: Dodd, Mead, and Co., 1899), 64.

2 Augustine, *On Original Sin*, 2.28.24, in *NPNF*[1], 5:246.

3 Augustine, *Answer to Julian*, 2.3.5, in *The Works of Saint Augustine: A Translation for the Twenty-First Century* (Hyde Park, NY: New City Press, 2002), 1/24:307. See Ambrose, *Penance*, 1.3.13, in *NPNF*[2], 10:331.

Augustine's teachings strongly influenced Christian doctrine in the West for centuries. But in the late medieval period, William of Ockham and Gabriel Biel taught that unsaved sinners can still love God well enough to be worthy to receive saving grace. That was a big step toward Pelagianism and salvation by works.

The Reformers of the sixteenth century believed that Augustine's view of sin and grace was faithful to the Bible. They taught and defended the doctrines of original sin and salvation by grace alone apart from works. The Lutheran Church declared in the Augsburg Confession, "Since the fall of Adam all human beings who are propagated according to nature are born with sin, that is, without fear of God, without trust in God, and with concupiscence [sinful desire], . . . [which] damns and brings eternal death to those who are not born again."[4]

Likewise, the Reformed churches said in the Belgic Confession,

> We believe that through the disobedience of Adam original sin is extended to all mankind, which is a corruption of the whole nature and an hereditary disease, wherewith infants themselves are infected even in their mother's womb, and which produceth in man all sorts of sin, being in him as a root thereof; and therefore is so vile and abominable in the sight of God that it is sufficient to condemn all mankind.[5]

At the Synod of Dort, Reformed theologians declared that all men "have derived corruption from their original parent," which includes "blindness of mind, horrible darkness, vanity and perverseness of judgment," so that man has become "wicked, rebellious, and obdurate [hardened] in heart and will, and impure in his affections."[6] The "unregenerate man" is "utterly dead in sin" and "destitute of all powers unto spiritual good."[7] Original sin "by itself suffices to condemn the whole human race."[8]

4 The Augsburg Confession (Art. 2), in *The Book of Concord: The Confessions of the Evangelical Lutheran Church*, ed. Robert Kolb and Timothy J. Wengert, trans. Charles Arand et al. (Minneapolis: Fortress, 2000), 39.

5 The Belgic Confession (Art. 15), in *TFU*, 32.

6 The Canons of Dort (Heads 3/4, Arts. 1–2), in *TFU*, 140.

7 The Canons of Dort (Heads 3/4, Rej. 4), in *TFU*, 149.

8 The Canons of Dort (Heads 3/4, Rej. 1), in *TFU*, 148.

However, people with high confidence in human reasoning and feelings have often denied the doctrine of original sin. Instead, they teach the basic goodness of man. Pelagianism is alive today in theological liberalism. Furthermore, some Christian theologians continue to seek middle ground, such as in Arminianism, so that they can say both that sinners are saved by grace and that man has some ability either to cooperate with God's grace or to resist it.

The Bible's Teaching on the Universal State of Sin

The state of sin is the condition of every person until God gives saving grace. Paul says, "There is none righteous, no, not one: there is none that understandeth, there is none that seeketh after God. They are all gone out of the way, they are together become unprofitable; there is none that doeth good, no, not one" (Rom. 3:10–12). Sin corrupts everyone's words (vv. 13–14), actions (vv. 15–17), and minds (v. 18).

All people sin. Solomon said, "There is no man that sinneth not" (1 Kings 8:46). He added, "There is not a just man upon earth, that doeth good, and sinneth not" (Eccles. 7:20). Thomas Goodwin said that sin is a "universal flood that covers the face of the earth."[9]

Children, too, are sinful. Man's heart "is evil from his youth" (Gen. 8:21). From the moment of conception, a human being is "in iniquity" and "in sin" (Ps. 51:5). "The wicked are estranged from the womb: they go astray as soon as they be born, speaking lies" (58:3).

John warns, "If we say that we have no sin, we deceive ourselves, and the truth is not in us. . . . If we say that we have not sinned, we make him a liar, and his word is not in us" (1 John 1:8, 10). James says, "We all stumble in many ways" (James 3:2 ESV). Paul writes, "For all have sinned, and come short of the glory of God" (Rom. 3:23).

The Deadly Dimensions of Original Sin

The Westminster Shorter Catechism gives us an excellent summary of the extent of original sin: "The sinfulness of that estate whereinto man fell, consists in the guilt of Adam's first sin, the want of original righteousness, and the corruption of his whole nature, which is commonly called Original

9 Goodwin, *An Unregenerate Man's Guiltiness before God*, in *WTG*, 10:6.

Sin; together with all actual transgressions which proceed from it."[10] Let us look more closely at these aspects.

The Imputation of Adam's Sin

Adam did not sin merely as a private individual. His first sin broke the covenant in which he represented all mankind. Though God said to Adam in particular, "In the day that thou eatest thereof thou shalt surely die" (Gen. 2:17), death came to all Adam's descendants after the fall (Genesis 5). Death is the penalty for sin (Rom. 6:23). This implies that Adam's guilt rests on the entire human race. Paul says, "In Adam all die" (1 Cor. 15:22). Theologians refer to the legal reckoning of Adam's guilt to all his natural offspring as the *imputation* of Adam's sin.

Elsewhere, the apostle explains, "As by one man sin entered into the world, and death by sin; and so death passed upon all men, for that all have sinned" (Rom. 5:12). The last phrase can be translated as "because all sinned" (ESV). Paul is teaching the immediate imputation or direct counting of Adam's sin to his natural descendants. Paul does not say that "all became sinful" or "all were sinning," but that "all sinned." That is, they sinned in Adam's sin—even those who did not personally and knowingly break a commandment as Adam did (v. 14). Paul writes, "By one man's offense death reigned by one" (v. 17). The sin of one man is the basis for all mankind's "condemnation" (vv. 16, 18). Although our sinful acts increase our condemnation, our guilt begins not with personal sins but with Adam's sin.

Someone might object that it would not be fair for God to condemn Adam's offspring for a sin they did not personally commit. Each person is liable for his own sins, not the sins of his fathers (Deut. 24:16; Ezek. 18:20).

In reply, we admit that God does not count sin to a person just because one of his ancestors sinned. But Adam was not just our forefather. He was our representative in the covenant of works. If we think that God should not have made Adam our representative, we must remember that God is God, and we are mere creatures. If God does not have the right to count Adam's sin to those whom he represented, God also cannot count Christ's righteousness to those whom he represents (Rom. 5:15–19). In other words,

10 The Westminster Shorter Catechism (Q. 18), in *RC*, 4:355. Cf. the Baptist Catechism (Q. 21), in *RC*, 4:575.

if we reject the imputation of Adam's sin, we undermine the gospel. And everyone in Adam shares his corruption and commits actual sin as soon as he is able. No one is innocent.

We must feel the weight of our guilt in Adam. Edward Reynolds rightly said that Adam's sin contained "pride, ambition, rebellion, infidelity, ingratitude, idolatry, concupiscence, theft, apostasy, unnatural affection, violation of covenant, and an universal renunciation of God's mercy promised."[11] Woe unto mankind for the guilt of our fall!

The Lack of Original Righteousness

When Adam sinned, he destroyed his spiritual legacy to his children. The Lord created man in his image (Gen. 1:27). The heart of that image is to be alive to God in knowledge, righteousness, and holiness (Eph. 4:24; Col. 3:10). When God threatened death against man if he disobeyed (Gen. 2:17), part of that death was the loss of spiritual life in fellowship with God. Man's spiritual goodness was not merely lessened by the fall—it was extinguished. As a result, none of fallen man's thoughts are good (6:5).

Mankind is not merely weakened by sin but is "dead in trespasses and sins" (Eph. 2:1; cf. Rom. 8:6; Col. 2:13). Salvation is a change "from death unto life," from hatred to Christian love (1 John 3:13–14). Jesus said that the repentant prodigal son "was dead, and is alive again" (Luke 15:24, 32). The self-indulgent are dead even while they live (1 Tim. 5:6).

We must reject false optimism about human goodness. Friedrich Schleiermacher wrongly taught that godliness is "already present in human nature," though "feeble and suppressed," and waiting to be "stimulated" by Christ's influence.[12] Thus, theological liberalism tends to view mankind as improving through education and social justice. But apart from saving grace, human beings exist in the total absence of spiritual life. They may pray and fast, be kind to friends, and give gifts to their children. But they are morally evil and displeasing to God (Matt. 5:46–47; 6:5; 7:11). To those who think that they keep God's commandments, the Lord Jesus says, "There is none good but one, that is, God" (19:17).

11 Edward Reynolds, *The Sinfulness of Sin*, in *The Whole Works of the Right Rev. Edward Reynolds*, 6 vols. (1826; repr., Morgan, PA: Soli Deo Gloria, 1996), 1:118.

12 Friedrich Schleiermacher, *The Christian Faith*, ed. H. R. Mackintosh and J. S. Stewart (New York: Harper and Row, 1963), sec. 106 (2:476).

God made us wealthy in holiness, but Adam made beggars of us all. David Clarkson said, "Man's soul is left like a ruined castle; the bare ragged walls, the remaining faculties, may help you to guess what it has been; but all the ornaments and precious furniture is gone."[13]

So long as we think that we are spiritually rich, we will say that we "have need of nothing" from Christ. Only when we know that we are "wretched, and miserable, and poor, and blind, and naked" are we ready to receive his riches (Rev. 3:17–18). Do you see yourself as impoverished by nature, with nothing to offer to God? Or are you "rich" in self-righteousness? If so, ask God to show you your poverty.

The Total Depravity of Man's Whole Nature

Death goes beyond the absence of life to include the corruption of man by sin. The spiritually dead are under the influence of this world and the Devil, and they seek whatever their rebellious minds and bodies desire (Eph. 2:1–3). Man bears within himself the secret death of "enmity against God" (Rom. 8:7; cf. James 4:4).

As we noted above, the doctrine of total depravity does not mean that every person is as bad as he could be (2 Tim. 3:13). Sinners have consciences and are aware of their sin (Rom. 1:32; 2:14–15). They may appreciate moral and compassionate behavior (Acts 2:47). They may disapprove of certain kinds of sin (1 Cor. 5:1). They may even show great kindness (Acts 28:2).

Total depravity means that corruption infects the whole person and stains every act he performs. The reason, the will, and the affections of man are all corrupt. Paul says, "For we ourselves also were sometimes foolish, disobedient, deceived, serving divers lusts and pleasures, living in malice and envy, hateful, and hating one another" (Titus 3:3). Reynolds said that just as there is saltiness "in every drop of the sea . . . so is there sin in every faculty of man."[14] Even the prayers and worship of an unrepentant sinner are abominations to God (Prov. 15:8; 28:9).

The stronghold of reigning sin is the heart. Christ said, "From within, out of the heart of men, proceed evil thoughts, adulteries, fornications, murders, thefts, covetousness, wickedness, deceit, lasciviousness, an evil

13 David Clarkson, "Of Original Sin," in *The Works of David Clarkson*, 3 vols. (Edinburgh: Banner of Truth, 1988), 1:6.

14 Reynolds, *The Sinfulness of Sin*, in *Works*, 1:122.

eye, blasphemy, pride, foolishness: all these evil things come from within, and defile the man" (Mark 7:21–23).

The defilement of the soul contaminates the whole life of sinners. Sin corrupts men's speech, actions, relationships, purposes, and mindset (Ps. 36:1–4). Their desires have become evil lusts (James 4:1–4; 1 Pet. 2:11). Their thinking has become worthless in spiritual matters (Rom. 1:21; Eph. 4:17). Even their "conscience is defiled" (Titus 1:15). Mankind is "in the flesh," without God's Spirit (Rom. 7:5–6; 8:9). From this corruption arise all actual sins that we commit, for they are "the works of the flesh" (Gal. 5:19–21).

Depravity still stains the whole being of the believer, though God has given him spiritual life that produces good works (Gal. 5:17). Never in all his earthly days has he loved God with all his heart, soul, and might. But that is what God's law requires (Deut. 6:5). Even godly Isaiah had to cry out in the presence of the Holy One, "Woe is me! For I am undone; because I am a man of unclean lips, and I dwell in the midst of a people of unclean lips" (Isa. 6:5). Therefore, even the believer's praises and good works must be offered up through Christ the Mediator. By his perfect righteousness alone are they pleasing to God (Heb. 13:15–16).

Suggested Song to Sing to the Lord

- Psalm 14, "The God Who sits enthroned on high," *Psalter*, No. 23; *THBap*, No. 474 (first verse omitted)

Questions for Meditation or Discussion

1. What do the terms *original sin* and *total depravity* mean?
2. What did Pelagius teach about sin? How did Augustine oppose him?
3. What do the Lutheran and Reformed churches say about original sin in their confessions?
4. How do the Holy Scriptures show that all people on earth are sinners?
5. How does Romans 5 teach the immediate imputation of Adam's sin to mankind?
6. Why should we not complain that it is unfair for God to count us sinners for what Adam did?
7. What Scripture passages show us that all in Adam are spiritually dead?

8. What Scripture passages testify that the human heart is corrupted by sin?
9. How would you demonstrate from the Bible that sin has corrupted man's entire nature?
10. How does the knowledge of your sinfulness affect you personally? How should it?

35

Total Inability and Free Choice

Chapter Summary and Key Terms

Human beings by nature have *free choice of the will.* That is the liberty to choose what they believe is good without being compelled by outside forces or acting automatically like machines. How people use this liberty depends on where they stand in the fourfold state of man. In the *state of innocence*, as created by God, human nature was very good. People had the ability to freely choose God and his will but also could change by choosing sin. In the *state of sin*, since the fall of man, human nature is corrupt. People have *total inability* to choose God and his will, the complete lack of power and inclination to please God. Instead, they are the willing slaves of sin. In the *state of grace*, after salvation, human nature is renewed in its ability to freely choose God and his will. But people do so imperfectly due to remaining sin. In the *state of glory*, Christ's perfected people have glorious liberty so that they always freely choose God and cannot sin.

SIN RULES UNSAVED SINNERS (Rom. 3:9; 5:21). Christ says, "Whosoever committeth sin is the servant of sin" (John 8:34). The word rendered here as "servant" may also be translated as "slave" (ESV), the opposite of one who is "free" (v. 36). However, Christ does not speak of slavery against one's will but enslavement of the will. He said, "Ye are of your father the devil, and the lusts of your father ye will do"—literally "you choose to do" (v. 44).

When Adam first sinned, he turned from listening to God's word to listening to Satan's lies. Since then, man has been in bondage to the Devil

(Heb. 2:14–15). Satan is "the ruler of this world" (John 12:31; 14:30; 16:11 ESV). He is even called "the god of this world" (2 Cor. 4:4). Human beings are in "the snare of the devil," and only God can deliver them by the gift of repentance (2 Tim. 2:25–26).

Therefore, we must reject Pelagianism and its teaching of man's moral ability. Charles Finney wrongly claimed, "The human will is free, therefore men have power or ability to do all their duty."[1] Rather, we must accept the Bible's doctrine of man's *total inability* to do good apart from Christ.

Total Inability under the Dominion of Sin

The Holy Scriptures contain several statements that deny that a sinner is able to serve God. As long as they are in the state of sin, sinners are

- *unable to speak what God counts as good.* Matthew 12:34, 37 says, "O generation of vipers, how can ye, being evil, speak good things? For out of the abundance of the heart the mouth speaketh. . . . By thy words thou shalt be condemned."
- *unable to obey God's law and please him.* Romans 8:7–8 says, "The carnal mind is enmity against God: for it is not subject to the law of God, neither indeed can be. So then they that are in the flesh cannot please God."
- *unable to be saved.* Matthew 19:25–26 says, "When his disciples heard it, they were exceedingly amazed, saying, Who then can be saved? But Jesus beheld them, and said unto them, With men this is impossible; but with God all things are possible."
- *unable to spiritually perceive or enter God's kingdom.* John 3:3, 5 says, "Except a man be born again, he cannot see the kingdom of God. . . . Except a man be born of water and of the Spirit, he cannot enter into the kingdom of God."
- *unable to listen to God's Word with an open mind.* John 8:43 says, "Why do ye not understand my speech? Even because ye cannot hear my word" (cf. Jer. 6:10).

1 Charles G. Finney, *Lectures on Systematic Theology: Embracing Ability, (Natural, Moral, and Gracious,) . . . and Perseverance* (Oberlin, OH: James M. Fitch, 1847), 17.

- *unable to receive truth revealed by God's Spirit.* First Corinthians 2:14 says, "But the natural man receiveth not the things of the Spirit of God: for they are foolishness unto him: neither can he know them, because they are spiritually discerned."
- *unable to come to Christ in faith.* John 6:44, 65 says, "No man can come to me, except the Father which hath sent me draw him: and I will raise him up at the last day. . . . No man can come unto me, except it were given unto him of my Father."
- *unable to believe in Christ for salvation.* John 12:39–40 says, "Therefore they could not believe, because that Esaias said again, He hath blinded their eyes, and hardened their heart; that they should not see with their eyes, nor understand with their heart, and be converted, and I should heal them" (cf. Isa. 6:9–10).
- *unable to confess with saving faith that Jesus is Lord.* First Corinthians 12:3 says, "No man can say that Jesus is the Lord, but by the Holy Ghost."
- *unable to receive the Holy Spirit.* John 14:17 says, "Even the Spirit of truth; whom the world cannot receive, because it seeth him not, neither knoweth him: but ye know him; for he dwelleth with you, and shall be in you."
- *unable to bear good fruit that glorifies God.* John 15:5 says, "I am the vine, ye are the branches: he that abideth in me, and I in him, the same bringeth forth much fruit: for without me ye can do nothing."

Thus, the Canons of Dort say, "All men are conceived in sin, and by nature children of wrath, incapable of saving good, prone to evil, dead in sin, and in bondage thereto, and without the regenerating grace of the Holy Spirit, they are neither able nor willing to return to God, to reform the depravity of their nature, or to dispose themselves to reformation."[2]

The Free Choice of the Will

If people indeed are slaves of sin, unable to turn to God until he gives them saving grace, someone might ask how can they be responsible for their actions. Do they have freedom of choice?

2 The Canons of Dort (Heads 3/4, Art. 3), in *TFU*, 141.

People are responsible for their actions, and they do exercise the free choice of their wills. But we must be clear about what we mean by "free choice" and "freedom of the will."

The Bible often speaks of people choosing and willing, and God clearly holds people responsible for their choices. But phrases such as "free choice" or "freedom of the will" do not appear in the Scriptures. In the original language of the Bible, "freewill offerings" (Lev. 22:18) literally means "willingness" and does not mention freedom. God's Word refers to the control center of human thought and action not as the "will" but as the "heart" (Prov. 4:23; Mark 7:21). The heart is not neutral but is inclined to either good or evil (Ps. 73:1; 125:4; Matt. 12:35).

The idea of the free choice of the will does have an important place in the Christian tradition and can be useful, if rightly defined. Augustine recognized that there is "always within us a free will," but that does not mean the human will is good, for sin has made us evil.[3] John Calvin said, "If freedom is opposed to coercion, I both acknowledge and consistently maintain that choice is free, and I hold anyone who thinks otherwise to be a heretic."[4]

The Westminster Confession of Faith says, "God hath endued the will of man with that natural liberty, that it is neither forced, nor, by any absolute necessity of nature, determined to good, or evil."[5] Specific choices are not the result just of one's nature, experiences, and circumstances. We are not machines or robots. Our choices are not like the natural instincts of an animal. Instead, we have true liberty of will. We might define the liberty of the will as the capacity to choose what one judges to be good without external compulsion or internal necessity.

Freedom of Will in the Fourfold State of Man

Human freedom of choice means different things depending on the spiritual state of man. Theologians often speak of four states of human life (see chap. 28).

3 Augustine, *On Grace and Free Will*, 31.15, in *NPNF*[1], 5:456.

4 John Calvin, *The Bondage and Liberation of the Will*, ed. A. N. S. Lane, trans. G. I. Davies, Texts and Studies in Reformation and Post-Reformation Thought (Grand Rapids, MI: Baker, 1996), 68.

5 The Westminster Confession of Faith (9.1), in *RC*, 4:246. Cf. the Second London Baptist Confession (9.1), in *RC*, 4:544.

The State of Innocence: A Changeable Ability to Choose God

The Westminster Confession of Faith says, "Man, in his state of innocency, had freedom and power to will and to do that which was good and well pleasing to God; but yet, mutably, so that he might fall from it."[6] God's covenant with Adam implied human choice. Created very good in God's image (Gen. 1:27, 31), man was righteous and could do righteousness. But God's command implied that man could also change for the worse. Augustine said, "The first freedom of will which man received when he was created upright consisted in an ability not to sin, but also in an ability to sin."[7]

The State of Sin: An Inability to Choose God

The Westminster Confession of Faith says, "Man, by his fall into a state of sin, hath wholly lost all ability of will to any spiritual good accompanying salvation: so as, a natural man, being altogether averse from that good, and dead in sin, is not able, by his own strength, to convert himself, or to prepare himself thereunto."[8] Augustine said, "The free will taken captive does not avail, except for sin; but for righteousness, unless divinely set free and aided, it does not avail."[9]

However, man in the state of sin still has a will. It retains a shadow of its former liberty. Sinners may choose whom they will marry (Gen. 6:2) and who will be their king (1 Sam. 8:18). The wicked choose what God hates (Isa. 65:12; 66:3). They choose what false gods and idols they will worship (Judg. 10:14; Isa. 1:29; 41:24). Those with power over the righteous abuse them however they will (Matt. 17:12). Those who hear the gospel call of Christ are not willing to come to him (23:37; John 5:40). Sinners choose what seems good to their minds and pleases their hearts (Gen. 3:6; Josh. 7:21). The tragedy is that their minds are darkened and their wills depraved, so that they are slaves of sin and yet responsible for their choices.

The State of Grace: A Renewed but Imperfect Ability to Choose God

The Westminster Confession of Faith says, "When God converts a sinner, and translates him into the state of grace, He freeth him from his natural

6 The Westminster Confession of Faith (9.2), in *RC*, 4:246. Cf. the Second London Baptist Confession (9.2), in *RC*, 4:544.

7 Augustine, *The City of God*, 22.30, in *NPNF*[1], 2:510.

8 The Westminster Confession of Faith (9.3), in *RC*, 4:246. Cf. the Second London Baptist Confession (9.3), in *RC*, 4:544–45.

9 Augustine, *Against Two Letters of the Pelagians*, 3.24.8, in *NPNF*[1], 5:414.

bondage under sin; and, by His grace alone, enables him freely to will and to do that which is spiritually good; yet so, as that by reason of his remaining corruption, he doth not perfectly, nor only, will that which is good, but doth also will that which is evil."[10]

Conversion is the transition from slavery to freedom, yet freedom under a new Master. Paul says, "But God be thanked, that ye were the servants of sin, but ye have obeyed from the heart that form of doctrine which was delivered you. Being then made free from sin, ye became the servants of righteousness" (Rom. 6:17–18). Augustine said, "He will not be free to do right, until, being freed from sin, he shall begin to be the servant of righteousness. And this is true liberty, for he has pleasure in the righteous deed; and it is at the same time a holy bondage, for he is obedient to the will of God."[11] Paul says, "The law of the Spirit of life in Christ Jesus hath made me free from the law of sin and death" (Rom. 8:2).

Free will is then no longer an empty shadow but a living (though imperfect) reality. Christians have a new willingness that is worked in them by God: "For it is God which worketh in you both to will and to do of his good pleasure" (Phil. 2:13). Thomas Boston said, "Regenerating grace is powerful and efficacious, and gives the will a new turn. It does not indeed force it, but sweetly, yet powerfully draws it, so that His people are willing in the day of His power (Ps. 110:3)."[12]

However, these Spirit-worked desires and choices are met with bitter opposition from the indwelling sin that remains in believers. As a result, they feel frustration and heartache over their remaining sin and imperfect obedience (Rom. 7:15–24; Gal. 5:17).

The State of Glory: A Perfect and Unchangeable Ability to Choose God

The Westminster Confession of Faith says, "The will of man is made perfectly and immutably free to good alone in the state of glory only."[13] Only in heaven do we find "the spirits of the righteous made perfect" (Heb. 12:23 ESV). When Christ will return in the visible glory of God and raise

10 The Westminster Confession of Faith (9.4), in *RC*, 4:246. Cf. the Second London Baptist Confession (9.4), in *RC*, 4:545.

11 Augustine, *Enchiridion*, chap. 30, in *NPNF*[1], 3:247.

12 Thomas Boston, *Human Nature in Its Fourfold State* (Edinburgh: Banner of Truth, 1964), 213.

13 The Westminster Confession of Faith (9.5), in *RC*, 4:246. Cf. the Second London Baptist Confession (9.5), in *RC*, 4:545.

the dead to life, the image of God will be fully perfected in the children of God (1 John 3:2). They will return to the paradise of God, where there will be no Serpent or tree of the knowledge of good and evil to test them, but only the tree of life—"and they shall reign for ever and ever" (Rev. 22:1–5).

At that time, believers will attain the highest level of freedom that human beings can possess: "the glorious liberty of the children of God" (Rom. 8:21). Augustine explained,

> Neither are we to suppose that because sin shall have no power to delight them, free will must be withdrawn. It will, on the contrary, be all the more truly free, because set free from delight in sinning to take unfailing delight in not sinning. For the first freedom of will which man received when he was created upright consisted in an ability not to sin, but also in an ability to sin; whereas this last freedom of will shall be superior, inasmuch as it shall not be able to sin.[14]

Therefore, the freedom of the will is not the will's neutrality between good and evil, but the power to rationally choose what is truly good, especially the supreme good. Someone might object that we will not be truly free if we have an inability to choose sin. But Augustine said, "Are we to say that God Himself is not free because He cannot sin?"[15] True freedom consists in our likeness to God, for we were made to bear his image.

Practical Applications of the Will's Freedom and Bondage

Given that sinners are responsible for their choices and yet are enslaved to sin, how should we evangelize the lost? We can learn the following lessons from Isaiah 55.

We should offer Christ as the sufficient Savior for sinners (Isa. 55:1–2). Let us not worry about who God has chosen but simply call people to trust in him. At the same time, let us point them to the faithfulness of God in his covenant (v. 3). He is worthy of our trust. As we urge sinners to turn to the Savior, we should rely on God to gather them to Christ (vv. 4–5). Only he can bring them out of the dominion of sin and into the kingdom

14 Augustine, *The City of God*, 22.30, in *NPNF*[1], 2:510.

15 Augustine, *The City of God*, 22.30, in *NPNF*[1], 2:510.

of Christ. Yet we must call them, as responsible moral agents, to turn to God and righteousness (vv. 6–7). Even in the state of sin, people still have minds and wills, and they will be saved when, by God's grace, they use them to come to Christ.

You might object that you do not understand how these truths of God's sovereignty and human responsibility fit together. We cannot fully understand God's ways. But we can trust him. Therefore, we should submit to God's Word in those matters that we do not understand, such as his sovereign mercy (Isa. 55:8–9). And we should have confidence in God's Word as his instrument to give new life (vv. 10–11). Though sinners are spiritually dead, God gives life to his elect through the Word. So keep declaring the Word.

Finally, in our struggles with sin, we should trust that God will completely save our wills. We can hope in the ultimate freedom that Christ will give his people when he returns in glory (Isa. 55:12–13).

Suggested Songs to Sing to the Lord

- Psalm 51, "God be merciful to me," *Psalter*, No. 140; *THBap*, No. 415
- Psalm 119:25–32, "My grieving soul revive, O Lord," *Psalter*, No. 324

Questions for Meditation or Discussion

1. How do the Holy Scriptures reveal that fallen man is enslaved to the Devil?
2. What is the doctrine of total inability? Prove it from the Bible.
3. When you consider your own inability by nature, how does it move you to praise God for his grace?
4. How does the Bible speak of (1) the human will, (2) the human heart, and (3) freedom or liberty?
5. How do the authors define the free will of man?
6. Describe the condition of man and his will in (1) the state of innocence, (2) the state of sin, (3) the state of grace, and (4) the state of glory.
7. How does the doctrine of the freedom of the will encourage zealous, humble, and hopeful evangelism?
8. What is one way that reading this chapter has helped you better understand man's slavery and liberty?

36

Actual Sins and God's Punishment of Sin

Chapter Summary and Key Terms

The corruption of original sin produces *actual sins*—thoughts, words, or deeds that wrong God or people. Actual sins include *sins of omission* (failing to do what God commands) and *sins of commission* (doing what God forbids). Though all sins deserve death, some sins are worse than others, and there are *heinous sins* that are especially evil in God's sight. Factors that make a sin worse include who commits the sin, who is wronged by the sin, and what is done. Sin earns the just penalty of loss and the penalty of sense. The *penalty of loss* is the punishment of sin consisting in the loss of God's good gifts. The greatest loss that unsaved sinners can experience is God himself, for they were created to fellowship with him but will be separated from him forever. The *penalty of sense* is the punishment of sin consisting in the suffering of God's wrath in this life and forever in hell.

SINFUL HEARTS PRODUCE SINFUL ACTS, which lead to punishment from God. James writes, "When lust hath conceived, it bringeth forth sin: and sin, when it is finished, bringeth forth death" (James 1:15). Christ says, "A corrupt tree bringeth forth evil fruit" (Matt. 7:17). This fruit is *actual sins*. Man's rebellion against God works itself out in a variety of actual sins.

Actual Sins Committed by Sinners

The Dimensions of Actual Sins

The variety of actual sins can be considered in three dimensions.

First, *there are sins against God and sins against our neighbors.* Christ taught us that the whole law hangs on two commandments. We must love the Lord our God with all our hearts and love our neighbors as ourselves (Matt. 22:36–40). Yet all sins are against God, even sins such as murder or adultery, which directly strike at human beings (Gen. 39:7–9; Ps. 51:4). This is because God created man in his image (Gen. 9:6; James 3:9–12). To wrong people is to wrong God.

Second, *there are sins of omission and sins of commission.* Sins of commission take place when we do what God has forbidden. Sins of omission occur when we fail to do what God has required of us in his law: "Therefore to him that knoweth to do good, and doeth it not, to him it is sin" (James 4:17).

Third, *there are sins of thought, sins of word, and sins of deed.* External acts of praise and worship do not please God when the heart is far from him (Isa. 29:13). Sin in any part of our lives displeases God. Solomon shows us the varied nature of sins when he says, "These six things doth the Lord hate: yea, seven are an abomination unto him: a proud look, a lying tongue, and hands that shed innocent blood, an heart that deviseth wicked imaginations, feet that be swift in running to mischief, a false witness that speaketh lies, and he that soweth discord among brethren" (Prov. 6:16–19).

The Domains of Actual Sins

God has taught us much about sin in the Ten Commandments, where he summarized his moral law. We will study God's moral law later in this book (chaps. 68–70). Here we simply outline how the first four commandments show us kinds of sins against God and the last six commandments kinds of sins against our neighbors.

Sins can be committed against God's (1) unique glory, (2) prescribed worship, (3) awesome name, and (4) holy day (Ex. 20:3–11). Sins can also be violations of human beings' (5) proper authority, (6) sacred life, (7) faithful sexuality, (8) rightful property, (9) true testimony, and (10) submissive contentment (vv. 12–17).

The Ten Commandments show us that the scope of sin is as wide as human existence, and it corrupts every aspect of human life and culture.

The Different Circumstances of Actual Sins

Some sins are committed in public and some in secret. Some sins are open to be seen, as when Peter denied that he was a disciple of Christ (Matt. 26:69–75). Other sins are hidden for a time, as when Achan took forbidden treasure from Jericho (Josh. 7:1, 21) or when David committed adultery with Bathsheba (2 Sam. 12:12; cf. Prov. 9:17). We should fear God in all that we do, "for God shall bring every work into judgment, with every secret thing, whether it be good, or whether it be evil" (Eccles. 12:14).

Some sins are the acts of individuals and others are generally true of whole societies. The Bible teaches individual responsibility and accountability. Paul says, "For we must all appear before the judgment seat of Christ; that every one may receive the things done in his body, according to that he hath done, whether it be good or bad" (2 Cor. 5:10). But God also judges groups of people for their sins, whether nations (Isaiah 13–23; Amos 1–2), towns (Luke 10:12–15), or churches (Revelation 2–3). This does not mean that the Lord lumps people together in guilt by association. God treats differently those individuals who do not participate in the sins that are generally committed by people in groups that he judges (2:24; 3:4).

Some sins are done by oppressors and others by victims of oppression. The Lord takes the oppression of the poor and vulnerable very seriously (Ex. 22:21–24; Lev. 19:33–34). True religion that pleases God shows itself in caring for the needy (James 1:27) and serving our brothers in Christ who suffer need (Matt. 25:31–46). But God does not favor someone simply because he is poor or suffers unjust treatment. God will judge all men impartially (Col. 3:25). He will punish the poor and vulnerable for their sins, too, if they do not repent (Isa. 9:17). We all must repent lest we perish for our sins (Luke 13:1–5).

The Degrees of Actual Sins

The Roman Catholic Church defines some sins as mortal and other sins as venial.[1] The first are said to put a person out of a state of grace, so they are

1 *Catechism of the Catholic Church* (New York: Doubleday, 1994), secs. 1854–1863, 2268.

deadly to the soul while the others are not. But "the wages of sin is death" (Rom. 6:23), regardless of which sin is committed. John Calvin said, "All sin is mortal. For it is rebellion against the will of God, which of necessity provokes God's wrath, and it is a violation of the law, upon which God's judgment is pronounced without exception."[2]

However, it is also a mistake to think that all sins are of equal weight. The Lord showed Ezekiel some sins of the people but said that he would see "greater abominations" (Ezek. 8:6, 13, 15). The person who handed Christ over to Pilate committed a "greater sin" than Pilate did (John 19:11). The wicked can become "worse and worse" (2 Tim. 3:13).

What makes *heinous sins* more offensive to God than others? The various factors include the following:

- *the person of the sinner.* Sin may be aggravated by privileges enjoyed by the sinner, such as greater knowledge of God's Word (Matt. 11:21–24; Luke 12:47–48) or a position of influence over others (Gal. 2:11–14; James 3:1).
- *the person who is sinned against.* Sins are more heinous when committed in direct contempt for God himself (2 Kings 19:4, 16, 22) or against a person to whom God has given authority (Prov. 30:17). Sins of injustice against the weak and vulnerable are also great offenses in God's sight (Ex. 22:21–24; Amos 5:11–12).
- *the extent of sin's action.* Sin's motion in the heart is a serious matter, but it becomes worse when it erupts into physical acts of wickedness (James 1:14–15). We see this when Cain's anger broke out in the murder of his brother (Gen. 4:5–12).
- *the perversity of the sinner's reason.* Sin that aims to meet real needs in unlawful ways is not as great an offense as sin that needlessly destroys people and things. The theft of food by a hungry man is not as great a sin as adultery (Prov. 6:30–35).
- *the height of the sinner's defiance.* If people persist in sinning after witnessing God's judgment, they aggravate their guilt (Jer. 5:3; Dan. 5:18–23). Bold, shameless, and brazen sins provoke God to greater anger (Num. 15:30; Jer. 3:3; 6:15).

2 Calvin, *Institutes*, 2.8.59.

- *the depth of sin's abnormality.* Scripture speaks with special horror against sins committed "against nature" (Rom. 1:26). Similarly, the Word sharply rebukes sins that violate the common decency of man (1 Cor. 5:1; 1 Tim. 5:8).
- *the holiness of the sinner's situation.* Gross sins committed in sacred acts of worship are greatly aggravated. Examples are hypocrisy in giving to the church's ministry to the poor (Acts 5:1–11), disorder at the Lord's Supper (1 Cor. 11:17–34), and abuse of an office of leadership in the church (1 Sam. 2:12–17; Mal. 2:1–9).

After reading about actual sins, take time for prayerful self-examination. What are your sins? Do you hear God's declarations against sin with humility and brokenness? Do you seek God's grace in Jesus Christ for the forgiveness of sin and victory over its dominion? Are you striving against sin by faith in Christ's cross as the Spirit strives against sin within you?

God's Punishment of Sin

The Reasons for Punishment

God punishes sin because it is an offense against him. That punishment includes the *penalty of loss* (the loss of fellowship with God and enjoyment of his good gifts) and the *penalty of sense* (the infliction of pain under God's wrath).

Sin contradicts who God is and breaks fellowship with him. John says, "This then is the message which we have heard of him, and declare unto you, that God is light, and in him is no darkness at all" (1 John 1:5). If we claim to walk with God as his friends but conduct ourselves in habitual unrepentant sin, we are liars and hypocrites (v. 6; cf. Amos 3:3).

Sin also offends God's justice and provokes his wrath. Paul says, "For the wrath of God is revealed from heaven against all ungodliness and unrighteousness of men" (Rom. 1:18). God's wrath is not an uncontrolled passion or an impersonal process. Rather, it is his wise and righteous anger against moral wrong. The Heidelberg Catechism says, "Is not God then also merciful? God is indeed merciful, but also just; therefore His justice requires, that sin which is committed against the most high majesty of God, be also punished with extreme, that is, with everlasting punishment of body and soul."[3]

3 The Heidelberg Catechism (LD 4, Q. 11), in *TFU*, 71.

The Punishment Partly Begun in This Life

God's wrath is already active in this world to punish sin in part. He punishes sin by judgments on the soul. He gives sinners over to the power of their sin (Acts 7:42; Rom. 1:24, 26, 28) and hardens them in their unbelief (Rom. 9:17–18; 11:7–10). God also punishes sin by judgment on the body (Ps. 7:11–13). We cannot blame every loss on the personal sin of the sufferer, for God afflicts the righteous for his glory (Job 1–2; John 9:1–3). But God can strike the wicked for their sins. He can punish them in any area of life, even with death itself (Acts 12:23; Rev. 2:23).

God may use human means to punish sin. He judges sin inwardly by the conscience. Paul says that the nations ignorant of God's Word still have "the work of the law written in their hearts, their conscience also bearing witness, and their thoughts the mean while accusing or else excusing one another" (Rom. 2:14–15). Calvin said, "They have a sense of divine judgment, as a witness joined to them, which does not allow them to hide their sins from being accused before the Judge's tribunal."[4] God also uses civil government to judge sin outwardly. Civil justice tends to restrain crime in society (Deut. 19:20; Eccles. 8:11), but its primary purpose is to justly punish sin: to "execute wrath upon him that doeth evil" (Rom. 13:4).

However, the worst punishment a sinner experiences in this life is far from the full wrath of God. Samuel Willard said, "His hand of compassion holds back his hand of vengeance; and though they feel some of the scalding drops of his anger at present, yet they do not suffer all his fury."[5]

The Punishment Fully Inflicted Forever

God executes the full and eternal punishment of sin after death (see chap. 89), and will do so especially after judgment day (see chaps. 93–94). At death, the souls of the wicked suffer torment for their sins (Luke 16:22–25). When Christ returns, he will raise all people from the dead and summon them to judgment. He will sentence the wicked to eternal damnation (John 5:28–29). Then they will experience the penalty of loss and the penalty of sense in the greatest degree. Johannes Wollebius said, "This state consists of

4 Calvin, *Institutes*, 3.19.15.

5 Samuel Willard, *A Compleat Body of Divinity in Two Hundred and Fifty Expository Lectures on the Assembly's Shorter Catechism* (Boston: by B. Green and S. Kneeland for B. Eliot and D. Henchman, 1726), 221.

the loss of the highest good and the undergoing of the highest evil."[6] Christ will say, "Depart from me, ye cursed, into everlasting fire, prepared for the devil and his angels" (Matt. 25:41).

On that day, sinners will discover that God's wrath is irresistible in its force (Nah. 1:6), inconceivable in its power (Ps. 90:11), unbearable in its effects (Isa. 33:14), unavoidable in its punishment (Heb. 2:3), eternal in its duration (Rev. 14:11), and righteous in its judgment (Rom. 2:5). Thomas Boston said, "See here the great evil of sin. Many reckon it but a small matter to transgress God's holy and righteous law. . . . But if they would consider the dreadful effects of sin, they would be of another mind. Sin is the worst of evils."[7]

Have you fled from the coming wrath by taking refuge in Jesus Christ? Or are you storing up wrath for yourself in the day of judgment by your unrepentant heart? Make no mistake—you cannot avoid judgment day. Either you will be saved from your sins by Christ's grace and brought into his kingdom forever, or you will be damned for your sins and suffer forever.

Suggested Songs to Sing to the Lord

- Psalm 64, "Hear, Lord, the voice of my complaint," *Psalter*, No. 165; *THBap*, No. 753
- "Teach me, O Lord, thy holy way," *THBap*, No. 456

Questions for Meditation or Discussion

1. What are actual sins? How are they different from original sin?
2. What are sins of commission and sins of omission? What are examples of each?
3. Briefly describe the ten domains in which we can sin according to the Ten Commandments.
4. What are some of the different circumstances of actual sins?
5. What factors make one sin more offensive than others in God's sight?
6. What judgments might God send against a sinner's soul as punishment for sin?

6 Johannes Wollebius, *Compendium Theologiae Christianae*, 1.12.(1).viii, in *Reformed Dogmatics*, ed. and trans. John W. Beardslee III, A Library of Protestant Thought (New York: Oxford University Press, 1965), 74.

7 Boston, *An Illustration of the Doctrines of the Christian Religion*, in *WTB*, 1:300.

7. What judgments might God send against a sinner's body as punishment for sin?
8. How does God employ both the conscience and the civil government to judge sin?
9. When and how will God fully punish sinners?
10. Do you deserve to suffer God's wrath forever? How will you escape it?

37

Sin, Suffering, and the Believer

Chapter Summary and Key Terms

The believer's experience with sin deeply humbles him. He fights against his remaining sin and longs to be free of it. The believer also suffers in union with Christ while living in this fallen world, passing through deep trials while clinging to the promises of God. Therefore, the Christian life involves *paradox*. A paradox is something that seems to be a contradiction (though it may be true), causing tension and even inward conflict. Christians experience the paradoxes of loving righteousness while grieving over remaining sin and of knowing they are God's beloved children while enduring great suffering. These paradoxes, as painful as they are, serve God's loving purpose to make them like Christ.

NOTHING REVEALS MORE about a person than how he responds to his sins and sorrows. Many people feel remorse about sin. But only people with new hearts from God hate sin as an offense to him and turn from it to serve him. Yet their lives are still mixtures of sin and righteousness. So believers feel much inner conflict. Similarly, suffering produces emotional struggles in many people. But in believers, it is the battle to trust the Lord amid suffering that refines their faith and purifies their lives. Christians live in the midst of these paradoxes, and God uses these struggles to prepare them for glory.

In other chapters, we discuss God's providence over all things, including suffering (chap. 26), his work of effectual calling and regeneration (chaps. 58 and 59), and sanctification, the process by which the Holy Spirit makes believers more like Christ (chap. 63). Here our focus is on the Christian's experience as he or she responds to remaining sin and the painful trials of this life.

Sin and the Believer in Christ

The Believer's Humble Response to Sin

When God saves a sinner, he produces in that person's heart an inward brokenness and humility over sin (Matt. 5:3–4). The spiritual sight of God's holiness calls forth confession (1 John 1:8–9) and repentance of sin (Mark 1:15). True repentance always comes with faith in Christ alone. By faith we are justified with God (Gal. 2:16). By faith we live for God by Christ (vv. 19–20). John Owen said, "Set faith at work on Christ for the killing of thy sin. His blood is the great sovereign remedy for sin-sick souls. Live in this, and thou wilt die a conqueror."[1]

Faith breathes out prayer for God to make one holy (Ps. 19:13). As believers pray, they must also "watch and be sober" (1 Thess. 5:6), keeping themselves alert against spiritual danger. Wilhelmus à Brakel said, "Spiritual watchfulness consists in watching over our soul in a careful and circumspect manner in order that no evil may befall her."[2]

Believers are spiritual warriors in a battle against their own sins. They must "flee" from evil desires, "follow after righteousness," "fight the good fight of faith," and "lay hold on eternal life" (1 Tim. 6:11–12). Archibald Alexander wrote, "The Christian is a soldier and must expect to encounter enemies, and to engage in many a severe conflict."[3]

Though God's children pass through many conflicts with sin, they still have great cause to give thanks to the Father. He delivered them from Satan and brought them into "the kingdom of his dear Son: in whom [they] have redemption through his blood, even the forgiveness of sins" (Col. 1:12–14). Thanksgiving is not just a duty but is also a necessary part of overcoming sin and unbelief.

The Paradox of a Believer's Experience with Sin

Believers are one with Christ and indwelt by the Holy Spirit. But they are still contaminated by remaining sin. Thus, in this age, Christians live out a

1 Owen, *The Mortification of Sin in Believers*, in *WJO*, 6:79.

2 Brakel, *CRS*, 4:11.

3 Archibald Alexander, *Thoughts on Religious Experience* (1844; repr., Edinburgh: Banner of Truth, 1967), 130.

paradox, which is something that seems to be a contradiction. They know forgiveness of their guilt but feel shame for sins past and present (Ezek. 16:62–63; Rom. 6:21–23). As William Greenhill said, God's forgiveness teaches sinners to say, "Ah, what have we done! How have we sinned against a God of love, against mercy, against grace! We will do it no more."[4] Their shame is strangely mingled with the peace and confidence that God will never reject them.

Believers have deliverance from sin's ruling dominion but must endure the frustration of their remaining depravity. Sin is no longer their master (Rom. 6:14). They are now spiritually married to Christ to bear fruit for God (7:4, 6). But they still find that "evil is present" in them (v. 21). Brakel wrote, "Indwelling corruption greatly torments and grieves believers."[5]

Many believers enjoy, at least in some measure, assurance of salvation even as they walk in fear and trembling before the holy Lord. He has given them precious promises that he will dwell with them as their loving Father (2 Cor. 6:16–18). Yet these very promises motivate them to purify themselves and pursue holiness "in the fear of God" (7:1). Assurance and fear grow side by side in the hearts of God's children because of the holiness of their Father (1 Pet. 1:15–17) and the price of their redemption by Christ's blood (vv. 18–19).

The true Christian lives in this paradox. The higher he rises in love and hope, the lower he sinks in humility and hatred of his sins.

The Believer's Fervent Hope for Complete Purity from Sin

One day, Christ will present believers as "a glorious church, not having spot, or wrinkle, or any such thing; but . . . holy and without blemish" (Eph. 5:27). They will be his perfect bride.

William Cowper said it well,

Dear dying Lamb, thy precious blood
Shall never lose its power,
Till all the ransomed church of God
Be saved, to sin no more.[6]

4 William Greenhill, *An Exposition of the Prophet Ezekiel*, ed. James Sherman (Edinburgh: James Nichol, 1864), 411.

5 Brakel, *CRS*, 4:251.

6 William Cowper, "There is a fountain filled with blood" (1771), in *THBap*, No. 188.

The Christian hope of final holiness makes God's people sing his praises. The day of our full holiness will be our wedding day to Jesus Christ (Rev. 19:6–8). All our righteousness and freedom from sin will be for his pleasure. This hope motivates Christians to pursue holiness: "Every man that hath this hope in him purifieth himself, even as he is pure" (1 John 3:3).

Suffering and the Believer in Christ

Putting Suffering in Perspective

Christians will suffer as long as they remain in this world. The apostles taught new converts, "We must through much tribulation enter into the kingdom of God" (Acts 14:22).

To view their sorrows in the proper perspective, Christians must remember that they still live in a world that was cursed because of Adam's sin (Gen. 3:17). Much of their affliction comes from being part of a fallen race subject to death and misery (Rom. 5:12) in a world that is groaning for the lifting of the curse (8:20–22). Believers may also suffer because of God's judgments against their nations (Jer. 9:1; Luke 21:20–23). God will shake everything in creation, but the church need not fear. The Lord is with believers, and his kingdom will never be shaken (Hag. 2:5–7; Heb. 12:26–29).

Christians should learn to see their sorrows through the lens of the gospel. Ezekiel Hopkins said, "If I have an interest in the righteousness of Christ, justice is already satisfied, the curse removed, and all the sorrows and afflictions I suffer, are but the corrections of a gracious Father, not the revenge of an angry God."[7]

The Father's Purposes in Afflicting His Children

God may afflict his beloved people, but he always has good fatherly reasons in doing so.

First, *through affliction God humbles believers deeply.* He shows them their inadequacy and his absolute sufficiency and supremacy so that they repent of questioning the ways of the Almighty (Job 42:1–6).

Second, *through affliction God exposes believers' sins.* In trials, the Holy Spirit searches the soul for sins. He drags sins out of their hiding places in the heart and sets them in the light of God's holy and all-searching eye (Ps. 90:7–8).

7 Ezekiel Hopkins, *The Doctrine of the Two Covenants* (London: Richard Smith, 1712), 82–83.

Suffering has a way of uncovering sins that lie hidden in seasons of prosperity and of compelling us to face those sins.

Third, *through affliction God purges believers' corruption.* In the hand of God, the rod of affliction subdues our pride, bridles our inordinate affections, and chastens our disobedience. "Before I was afflicted I went astray," the psalmist confessed, "but now have I kept thy word" (Ps. 119:67).

Fourth, *through affliction God draws believers near to him.* They learn experiential lessons about prayer in the school of affliction that can be learned nowhere else. The Lord said of Israel, "In their affliction they will seek me early" (Hos. 5:15).

Fifth, *through affliction God conforms believers to Christ.* The Lord trains us through hardship "that we might be partakers of his holiness" (Heb. 12:10).

Sixth, *through affliction God expands believers' joy.* David says, "For his anger endureth but a moment; in his favour is life: weeping may endure for a night, but joy cometh in the morning" (Ps. 30:5). Where godly suffering abounds, consolation also abounds (2 Cor. 1:4–5).

Seventh, *through affliction God increases believers' faith.* Affliction works for good by helping us walk by faith and not by sight (2 Cor. 5:7).

Eighth, *through affliction God weans believers from this world.* They learn to say, "Although the fig tree shall not blossom, neither shall fruit be in the vines . . . yet I will rejoice in the LORD, I will joy in the God of my salvation" (Hab. 3:17–18).

Ninth, *through affliction God prepares believers for their heavenly inheritance.* Affliction elevates our souls heavenward so that we look for "a city which hath foundations, whose builder and maker is God" (Heb. 11:10).

Let us therefore trace all our sorrows back to the tender love of our heavenly Father. Paul says, "If God be for us, who can be against us? He that spared not his own Son, but delivered him up for us all, how shall he not with him also freely give us all things?" (Rom. 8:31–32).

The Saints' Communion with Christ in Affliction

Although Christians suffer with all creation, in a special sense they are "joint-heirs with Christ . . . [and] suffer with him, that [they] may be also glorified together" with him (Rom. 8:17). The most effective means for living as a Christian in affliction is to consider Christ (Heb. 3:1).

First, *consider the piety of Christ.* Christ's enduring obedience, even to death on the cross, is the model for our humility (Phil. 2:5–8), the merit for our righteousness before God (3:9), and the mighty power by which God works obedience in us now (2:11–13).

Second, *consider the perseverance of Christ.* Christ provides us the strength to persevere day by day, even in the severest of sorrows. He earned that provision for us by enduring his own sufferings to the end. Drop by drop of blood, for six long hours he poured out his life. Jesus "endured the cross" (Heb. 12:2).

Third, *consider the passion of Christ.* Ask yourself this: If Jesus suffered so much on behalf of his people, should I not be able to endure in his strength the daily afflictions I must bear? What are my afflictions compared to his?

Fourth, *consider the power of Christ.* Christ shepherds his people "in the strength of the Lord, in the majesty of the name of the Lord his God" (Mic. 5:4). If he chooses to load you with affliction—even staggering affliction—do not be alarmed but look to him for strength.

Fifth, *consider the prayers of Christ.* He continually prays in heaven for all his church (Heb. 7:25; 1 John 2:1). No condemnation can come on his people while he who died for their sins intercedes for them (Rom. 8:34). Trusting in his prayers, you, too, should pray (Heb. 4:15–16).

Sixth, *consider the presence of Christ.* He is at no time absent from you, even when your faith does not actively grasp him (Matt. 28:20; Heb. 13:5). He is with you as your Prophet, Priest, and King. John Flavel said, "Behold, then, a sanctified affliction is a cup, whereinto Jesus hath wrung and pressed the juice and virtue of all his mediatorial offices. Surely, that must be a cup of generous, royal wine, like that in the supper, a cup of blessing to the people of God."[8]

Seventh, *consider the plan of Christ.* The Lord Jesus persevered because of the joy set before him (Heb. 12:2). Having suffered, he entered his glory, just as God had foreordained and foretold (Luke 24:25–26). When he returns, "then shall the righteous shine forth as the sun in the kingdom of their Father" (Matt. 13:43). Remember the order of God's plan. As Frances Havergal wrote,

8 Flavel, *Navigation Spiritualized*, in *WJF*, 5:252.

Light after darkness,
Gain after loss,
Strength after weakness,
Crown after cross.[9]

Suggested Songs to Sing to the Lord

- "Stricken, smitten, and afflicted," *THBap*, No. 192
- "When peace, like a river," *THBap*, No. 580

Questions for Meditation or Discussion

1. Why is humility a believer's response to sin?
2. Why must a believer repeatedly exercise faith in Christ to triumph over sin?
3. What reason does every believer have to give thanks to God, even when facing his or her sins?
4. What is the Christian's ultimate hope regarding his or her sin? Quote specific promises of God.
5. Why do God's saints suffer simply by being part of this world and their nations?
6. How does God the Father use affliction to deal with the sins of his children?
7. In what ways do sorrows serve to deepen the relationship between Christians and God?
8. How do sorrows help believers to let go of this world and embrace God's kingdom?
9. What encouragements can Christians find in Christ's piety and perseverance?
10. Of the various ways to consider Christ, which are most helpful to you? Why?

9 Frances R. Havergal, *Under the Surface*, 3rd ed. (London: J. Nisbet and Co., 1876), 175.

PART 4

THE DOCTRINE OF CHRIST

Section 4A

The Covenant of Grace

38

Introduction to the Covenant of Grace

Chapter Summary and Key Terms

The Bible revolves around the covenants that God made with people. How do these covenants relate to one another? According to *Marcionism*, the Old Testament presents the evil god who made the physical world, while the New Testament is about the good Father of Christ. Christians rejected this view as heresy and offered various other explanations. For example, *dispensationalism* teaches an absolute distinction between Israel and the New Testament church, saying that the one God has two plans for his two peoples. By contrast, Reformed *covenant theology* says that God has revealed one moral law, one gospel, one covenant of grace, and one saved people throughout history. The *covenant of grace* consists of God's solemn promises concerning Christ and salvation that bind God to his people in all ages. God made various historical covenants with his saved people, each of which was an administration of the one covenant of grace.

THE WESTMINSTER SHORTER CATECHISM ASKS, "Did God leave all mankind to perish in the estate of sin and misery?" It then answers, "God having, out of his mere good pleasure, from all eternity, elected some to everlasting life, did enter into a covenant of grace, to deliver them out of the estate of sin and misery, and to bring them into an estate of salvation by a Redeemer."[1]

1 The Westminster Shorter Catechism (Q. 20), in *RC*, 4:355–56. Cf. the Baptist Catechism (Q. 23), in *RC*, 4:576.

We have already studied the doctrine of God and the doctrine of man (parts 2 and 3 of this volume). Now we will study the doctrine of Christ, beginning with the covenant of grace and later continuing to the person and work of Christ.

What is a covenant? As we said in our study of God's covenant with Adam (chap. 32), a covenant is *a solemn promise that legally defines a relationship of loyalty*. A covenant often has other features. It may place a person or group under another's lordship and require obedience to laws. It may give someone authority to perform an office. It may involve someone representing a larger group. And it may employ visible signs.

God made a variety of covenants, which we will consider in more detail in the next chapter. All the covenants throughout history that promise Christ and salvation are joined together as one covenant of grace.

Why Study the Covenant of Grace?

The covenant of grace is a valuable topic of study for several reasons.

First, *the covenant of grace stands in closest connection to Christ*. God gave Christ to be "a covenant of the people" (Isa. 42:6). Edward Young said, "All the blessings of the covenant are embodied in, have their root and origin in, and are dispensed by him."[2] The covenant is like a gold ring that clasps the diamond of our Lord Jesus. It presents Christ to us as silver dishes serve up a delicious feast.

Second, *the covenant of grace provides the basic structure of history*. The key figures of history in the Bible—Abraham, Moses, David, and ultimately Christ—stand at the center of the covenants that unfold God's eternal covenant of grace step by step.

Third, *the covenant of grace supports God-centered faith*. In the promises of his covenant, the Lord reveals himself so that people may trust in him. He is the "God, that keepeth covenant and mercy for them that love him and observe his commandments" (Neh. 1:5).

Fourth, *the covenant of grace shapes spiritual experience*. David says, "The secret of the LORD is with them that fear him; and he will shew them his covenant" (Ps. 25:14). If we desire to understand true Christian experience, then we must learn about the covenant of grace.

2 Edward Young, *The Book of Isaiah*, 3 vols. (Grand Rapids, MI: Eerdmans, 1969), 3:120–21.

Fifth, *the covenant of grace directs the church's practice.* God's covenant defines the identity, membership, privileges, and obligations of those he calls "my people" (Lev. 26:12; cf. Ex. 6:7). The Lord's Supper is an ordinance of the new covenant (Luke 22:20).

Sixth, *the covenant of grace glorifies God in his attributes.* In making and keeping the covenant, he has revealed his faithfulness (Deut. 7:9), merciful love (Ps. 89:1–2), righteousness (Neh. 9:8), eternity (Ps. 105:8), immutability (Isa. 54:10), and redeeming power (Ex. 6:2–6).

Different Views of God's Covenants

God's covenant ways are complex. The Holy Scriptures present us with several covenants. Some of God's requirements for his people have changed over time. But God's basic promises and moral principles have always remained the same, for he is the same God who never changes. How do we fit together the sameness and differences in the covenants?

One very bad solution was *Marcionism*, taught by Marcion of Pontus. He argued that the Creator of the earth, the God of Israel, was evil. Marcion rejected the Old Testament and much of the New Testament. Against Marcion, Irenaeus said that "the two covenants" are "of one and the same substance, that is, from one and the same God. . . . For there is one salvation and one God."[3]

Augustine said that as he read the Old Testament, "everywhere Christ meets me and refreshes me."[4] The stages of history, he added, can be called different covenants, and the "old" is cancelled by the "new." However, the covenant God made with Abraham did not pass away because it is the covenant "of justification and an eternal inheritance."[5]

Martin Luther taught a strong contrast between the old covenant and the new covenant. The old promised physical blessings based on obedience. The new promises "the forgiveness of sins, grace, righteousness, and eternal life freely, for Christ's sake."[6] But Luther also taught that God revealed the

3 Irenaeus, *Against Heresies*, 4.9.1, 3, in *ANF*, 1:472–73.

4 Augustine, *Against Faustus*, 12.27, cited in Michael Cameron, "The Christological Substructure of Augustine's Figurative Exegesis," in *Augustine and the Bible*, ed. and trans. Pamela Bright (Notre Dame, IN: University of Notre Dame Press, 1999), 94.

5 Augustine, *Expositions on the Book of Psalms*, trans. H. M. Wilkins, 6 vols. (Oxford: John Henry Parker, 1847–1857), 105.7 (5:152).

6 Luther, *Lectures on Galatians, 1535*, in *LW*, 26:301, 437–39.

promise of Christ as early as Genesis 3:15. He even called that promise "the spiritual covenant."[7] The Old Testament saints were justified by faith, not by works of the law. Their faith, like ours, was in Christ.[8] Luther saw two covenants in God's dealings with Abraham and his offspring: "the material one involving the land of Canaan and the spiritual one involving the eternal blessing."[9]

Ulrich Zwingli may have been the first teacher of *Reformed covenant theology*. He argued that "the Christian people also stand in the gracious covenant with God in which Abraham stood with him."[10] John Calvin said, "All men adopted by God into the company of his people since the beginning of the world were covenanted to him by the same law and by the bond of the same doctrine as obtains among us."[11]

Reformed covenant theology is summarized well in the Westminster Confession of Faith (chap. 7). It says God's covenants express his free choice to lower himself to meet his creatures on their level so that they can enjoy him. His first covenant with man was the covenant of works, in which he promised life to Adam and his offspring "upon condition of perfect and personal obedience." God made the covenant of grace to meet the needs of fallen man. In that covenant, he offers life in Christ, requires faith in Christ, and promises the Spirit of Christ to convert the elect. God has administered this covenant in different ways under the law and the gospel. These are not "two covenants of grace, different in substance, but one and the same, under various dispensations."[12]

Particular Baptist theology, known today as Reformed Baptist theology, agreed that God saves all his people throughout history by one covenant of grace revealed in the gospel of Christ from man's first fall (Gen. 3:15).[13] Some Particular Baptist theologians, such as Nehemiah Coxe and Benjamin Keach, taught that God's dealings with Abraham involved two covenants.

7 Luther, *Lectures on Genesis*, in *LW*, 2:71.

8 Luther, *Lectures on Galatians, 1535*, in *LW*, 26:85, 239.

9 Luther, *Lectures on Genesis*, in *LW*, 3:111.

10 Cited in Peter A. Lillback, *The Binding of God: Calvin's Role in the Development of Covenant Theology*, Texts and Studies in Reformation and Post-Reformation Thought (Grand Rapids, MI: Baker Academic, 2001), 95–96.

11 Calvin, *Institutes*, 2.10.1.

12 The Westminster Confession of Faith (chap. 7), in *RC*, 4:242–43.

13 The Second London Baptist Confession (7.3), in *RC*, 4:541.

They noted that Abraham had physical offspring (ethnic Israel) and spiritual offspring (believers in Christ, Gal. 3:7). The law of Israel was taken as a covenant of works. The covenant of grace was promised from the beginning but not fully implemented until the new covenant.[14] Other Particular or Reformed Baptists have believed that the various covenants are different administrations of the one covenant of grace.

According to *dispensationalism*, the Old Testament and the New Testament express two entirely different covenants. There is no covenant of grace for all of history. Charles Ryrie said, "A dispensationalist keeps Israel and the church distinct" because God is working out "two distinct purposes" through "two peoples."[15] Dispensationalist theologians believe that God's promises to Israel must be fulfilled to the Jewish people in a very literal manner. However, progressive dispensationalism allows for the application to the church of some promises made to Israel, especially the new covenant (Jer. 31:31–34).

Finally, theologians have made two recent proposals for understanding God's covenants. *New covenant theology* teaches that Israel and the church are one people. However, there is no covenant of grace that brings together both testaments, nor was there a covenant of works with Adam. Also, the commands of the Old Testament do not apply today unless repeated in the New Testament.[16] *Progressive covenantalism* affirms that God made a covenant with Adam and that God's promises to Israel are fulfilled in Christ and all in union with him. However, Israel and the new covenant church are essentially different, and the Ten Commandments apply to Christians only in the manner that they are fulfilled in Christ.[17]

Basic Principles of Covenant Theology

With so many different views of God's covenants, what should we believe? In this section, we will present some basic principles for understanding

14 See Pascal Denault, *The Distinctiveness of Baptist Covenant Theology: A Comparison between Seventeenth-Century Particular Baptist and Paedobaptist Federalism* (Birmingham, AL: Solid Ground, 2013).

15 Charles Ryrie, *Dispensationalism*, rev. ed. (Chicago: Moody, 1995), 38–39.

16 See Tom Wells and Fred Zaspel, *New Covenant Theology* (Frederick, MD: New Covenant Media, 2002).

17 See Stephen J. Wellum and Brent E. Parker, eds., *Progressive Covenantalism: Charting a Course between Dispensational and Covenant Theologies* (Nashville, TN: B&H Academic, 2016).

God's covenants. These principles are consistent with Reformed theology and some versions of Reformed Baptist theology.

First, *God's gospel of salvation has always been the same.* Paul rebuked the Galatians for beginning to turn aside from the gospel of faith in Christ alone. They were looking to their works to justify them (Gal. 3:1–5). Paul showed from the history of God's people that justification by faith alone was not something new. Rather, it was the ancient promise by which God had saved his people in all ages. Salvation comes to people not by works of the law but "by the hearing of faith" (vv. 2, 5), "even as Abraham believed God, and it was accounted to him for righteousness" (v. 6). Justification by faith is "the gospel" that God preached to Abraham, not just for him but for the blessing of "all nations" (vv. 8–9). Believers were justified the same way under the Old Testament as they are under the New. The gospel is not new, but was the same for Abraham as it is for us.

Second, *God made the covenant of works according to his law.* The gospel says, "The just shall live by faith" (Gal. 3:11). But the law says, "The man that doeth them shall live in them" (v. 12). The law pronounces God's "curse" against everyone who does not do everything commanded (v. 10). As a result, those who desire to be righteous before God by their works must keep the whole law (v. 10; cf. 5:3). These two principles of righteousness by law and righteousness by gospel are "two covenants" (4:24).

Third, *God rooted the covenant of grace in his promises to his Son and all in union with him.* The promise of "seed" in God's covenant with Abraham particularly refers to one person, Jesus Christ (Gal. 3:16). It also refers to his people. Those who have "faith in Christ Jesus" and "have put on Christ" are "Abraham's seed, and heirs according to the promise" (vv. 26–29).

Fourth, *God's covenant of grace has had different administrations at different times.* Centuries after God made his covenant with Abraham, the law was "added" by God "till the seed [Christ] should come to whom the promise was made" (Gal. 3:19). But the law did not nullify the promise (v. 17). It just changed how God administrated his covenant. Today, God no longer requires circumcision, which was demanded under the administration of his covenant to Abraham (5:2–6). God has administrated his covenant differently for Abraham, Israel, and those in the new covenant today.

Fifth, *God's covenant of grace is one in its essence.* Though it has had different administrations, its core has remained the same through the ages.

This follows from what we already have said. Abraham had the same gospel as Paul (Gal. 3:6). The law "was added" to the covenant, not to replace the promise as the basis for the inheritance, but to regulate the life of Israel until Christ came (vv. 17–19). Christ himself is the preeminent "seed" of Abraham (v. 16). Just as Abraham was counted righteous by faith, so justified believers in Christ "are the children of Abraham" who receive "the blessing of Abraham" (3:7, 14). Paul says, "And if ye be Christ's, then are ye Abraham's seed, and heirs according to the promise" (v. 29). In the Holy Scriptures, the people of Israel are the "seed" of Abraham (Ps. 105:6; Isa. 41:8). Abraham is Israel's "father" (Josh. 24:3; Isa. 51:2). In effect, Paul says that believers in Jesus Christ are the true Israel. John Gill wrote, "The covenant of grace is but one and the same in all ages, of which Christ is the substance. . . . For though the covenant is but one, there are different administrations of it; particularly two, one before the coming of Christ, and the other after it."[18]

Sixth, *there is an abiding duty to obey God's moral law.* Christ came "to redeem them that were under the law" (Gal. 4:5). One might conclude that believers are no longer bound to keep God's commandments. But Paul says that we must use our "liberty" in Christ to serve one another in love, "for all the law is fulfilled in one word, even in this; Thou shalt love thy neighbor as thyself" (5:13–14). Here Paul quotes the law of Moses (Lev. 19:18). Christians still have the duty to obey the moral precepts revealed in the covenant of law given through Moses (Rom. 13:8–10). Paul firmly opposes placing Christians under the obligation of circumcision and other ancient ceremonies (Gal. 2:3; 4:10–11; 5:2–3, 6). But the moral law still binds us. Paul says, "Circumcision is nothing, and uncircumcision is nothing, but the keeping of the commandments of God" (1 Cor. 7:19). As Calvin said, the law no longer condemns believers but guides them as "a kind adviser."[19]

Seventh, *the church is united to her covenant God through faith.* From first to last, God's covenant of grace calls for the answer of man's faith to embrace the promises and receive salvation (Gal. 3:6–14, 22–26). Such faith is not a bare mental belief but saving knowledge, assent, and trust in Christ alone for salvation. Saving faith unites people to Jesus Christ (vv. 26–27) and receives the Holy Spirit (vv. 2, 14), so that believers cry, "Abba, Father"

18 John Gill, *A Complete Body of Doctrinal and Practical Divinity* (1839; repr., Paris, AR: The Baptist Standard Bearer, 1995), 345.

19 Calvin, *Comm.* on Gal. 5:18.

(4:6). Faith also unites believers in Christ to one another (3:28). Therefore, by the covenant of grace God creates a living union and experiential communion between himself and his people.

Reformed covenant theology is experiential theology. It is not merely a way to interpret the Bible or an exercise of systematic thinking. True covenant theology involves knowing God and being known by him—a relationship forged through faith in Christ by the Holy Spirit. Covenant theology trains the soul to cry out to the Lord as "my rock, and my fortress, and my deliverer; my God, my strength, in whom I will trust" (Ps. 18:2).

We will develop each of these basic principles of covenant theology in greater detail in future chapters, except for the doctrine of the covenant of works, which we taught earlier in this volume (see chap. 32).

Before we proceed, however, ask yourself, Is the Lord my God, and am I one of his people? In other words, are you personally in covenant with God? Do you know him? Are you known by him? Have you trusted in Jesus Christ alone to save you from the guilt of your sins and make you a child of God? Has God given you the Holy Spirit's saving work so that you are becoming more like your Father?

Suggested Song to Sing to the Lord

- Psalm 103, "The tender love a father has, for all his children dear," *Psalter*, No. 278; *THBap*, No. 85

Questions for Meditation or Discussion

1. What is the authors' basic definition of a covenant? What common elements do they say can be found in many biblical covenants?
2. Someone says to you, "I have no interest in studying the covenant of grace. I simply want to know Christ." How do you respond?
3. What was the teaching of Marcion? How did Irenaeus respond?
4. What does the Westminster Confession of Faith state regarding the covenant of grace?
5. What did the Particular Baptists teach about the covenant of grace?
6. What is dispensationalism? How does it interpret God's promises to Israel?
7. How would you show that God has saved people by the same gospel through the ages?

8. What arguments do the authors make that the covenant of grace is one in its essence?
9. How do the authors argue that Christians still have an obligation to obey God's moral law?
10. Is the Lord your covenant God? How do you know?

39

God's Gospel and His Covenant with His Son

Chapter Summary and Key Terms

Salvation has always been through faith in Christ, the only Mediator. One reason for this is that salvation is based on the eternal plan made by the persons of the Trinity. That plan is called the *counsel of peace* or the *covenant of redemption*. Some Reformed theologians regard the counsel of peace to be the covenant of grace from eternity. Others see it as a separate covenant. In this eternal covenant, the Father promised the Son a people and a kingdom, the Son promised the Father that he would do the work of redemption, and the Holy Spirit promised his effectual working in it all. Therefore, we should trust in Christ alone for salvation, study the Scriptures to see Christ in the whole Bible, and learn to imitate God's faithfulness to his eternal promises.

GOD'S COVENANT OF GRACE IS ANCIENT. He announced the gospel through the earliest prophets. God's people, whether in the Old Testament or the New, have always shared the same salvation. Indeed, the covenant of grace is eternal. It began with the plan formed by the Trinity before the world began.

In this chapter, we will show that God has always saved sinners by the gospel of Jesus Christ. We will also show that God made a covenant not just with his people but with his Son in eternity. These principles of covenant theology help us to see that there is one covenant of grace. By that covenant, God works out the salvation of his elect from the beginning of time to the end of the world.

Salvation Always through the One Mediator

Christ alone is the Mediator of saving grace. Paul says, "For there is one God, and one mediator between God and men, the man Christ Jesus; who gave himself a ransom for all" (1 Tim. 2:5–6). William Perkins said, "Christ stands alone in the work of redemption, without colleague or partner."[1] No mere man can save himself or others. But Jesus Christ is no mere man. He is the God-man, God who became a man to save us (John 1:1, 14).

Christ is the only revealer of God. He says, "No man knoweth who the Son is, but the Father; and who the Father is, but the Son, and he to whom the Son will reveal him" (Luke 10:22). He also is the only way to God. As he put it, "I am the way, the truth, and the life: no man cometh unto the Father, but by me" (John 14:6). Peter explains, "Neither is there salvation in any other: for there is none other name under heaven given among men, whereby we must be saved" (Acts 4:12).

Therefore, we conclude that whomever God has saved since the fall of man, he saved through faith in Jesus Christ. Caspar Olevianus said, "All the elect are granted the same faith, by which from the beginning they were engrafted into the Son of God."[2]

Salvation by Faith in Christ through All Ages

How can God have saved people through Christ before Christ came? God revealed Christ from the beginning. The Heidelberg Catechism says that we know the Mediator, Jesus Christ, "from the holy gospel, which God Himself first revealed in Paradise; and afterwards published by the patriarchs and prophets, and represented by the sacrifices and other ceremonies of the law; and lastly, has fulfilled it by His only begotten Son."[3]

As soon as man fell into sin, God promised to send a "seed" who would conquer the Devil (Gen. 3:15).[4] Herman Bavinck said that this promise "contains the entire covenant in a nutshell."[5] Some of Adam and Eve's descendants lived by faith in God's promises, such as Abel, Enoch, and Noah

1 Perkins, *Commentary on Galatians*, on Gal. 4:8–11, in *WWP*, 2:272.

2 Caspar Olevianus, *An Exposition of the Apostles' Creed*, trans. Lyle D. Bierma (Grand Rapids, MI: Reformation Heritage Books, 2009), 132.

3 The Heidelberg Catechism (LD 6, Q. 19), in *TFU*, 73.

4 See the section on God's seed promise at the end of chap. 33.

5 Bavinck, *RD*, 3:221.

(Heb. 11:4–7). In addition to God's word, they also had types of Christ. Sacrifices for sin foreshadowed Christ (Gen. 4:4; 8:20–21). The worldwide flood was a type of judgment for mankind's sins and salvation by grace through the obedience of one man (Gen. 6–9; see Isa. 54:9; Matt. 24:37–38).

God revealed more of the plan of salvation in his call to Abraham (Gen. 12:1–3). In the first part of this call, God promised an inheritance in the land, many offspring, blessing, and honor (vv. 1–2a). These promises were partly fulfilled in the kingdom of Israel in the Promised Land. But the promises also looked ahead to an inheritance in God's heavenly city (Heb. 11:13–16). They belong to those who trust in the Lord as Abraham did (John 8:39–40; Rom. 4:16–17). God's purpose for the spiritual seed of Abraham is nothing less than the glory for which he first created man (Heb. 2:5–10, 16).

In the second part of the call of Abraham, God promised to make him a channel of blessing to many others, though not to all (Gen. 12:2b–3). The Lord called Abraham to "be a blessing" to others (v. 2b). God said, "I will bless them that bless thee, and curse him that curseth thee" (v. 3). Those who love God's people will be blessed forever (Matt. 25:34–40). Those who do not love God's people will be cursed forever (vv. 41–46). This principle of spiritual discrimination between the blessed and the cursed is central to the gospel. The blessing will, however, reach every clan on earth (Gen. 12:3). In this promise, God "preached the gospel beforehand to Abraham" (Gal. 3:8 ESV).

Abraham "believed in the LORD; and he counted it to him for righteousness" (Gen. 15:6). He may not have known as much as we do today, but he had faith in Christ. The Lord Jesus said, "Abraham rejoiced to see my day: and he saw it, and was glad" (John 8:56, 58).

Moses foretold that God would raise up "a Prophet . . . like unto me" (Deut. 18:15–19). Jesus is the Prophet (Acts 3:22–23). Israel's redemption from Egypt was a type of salvation in Christ (1 Cor. 5:7; Titus 2:14). God's law for Israel required sacrifices for sin as another type of Christ (Heb. 10:1–10). Even in the old covenant, believers enjoyed the forgiveness of sins (Ps. 32:1; 103:3, 12). They hoped in Christ for their justification (Isa. 53:11).

In conclusion, from the garden of Eden to the later Hebrew prophets, God has revealed the gospel of his Son (Rom. 1:1–3). The Spirit of Christ testified to the prophets of "the sufferings of Christ, and the glory that should follow" (1 Pet. 1:10–11). The Old Testament reveals Christ, his sufferings, and his resurrection (Luke 24:25–27, 44–47). The first principle of covenant theology is that God has always saved sinners by the same gospel.

Yet we also recognize that God's revelation of Christ grew over time. John Calvin said,

> At the beginning when the first promise of salvation was given to Adam it glowed like a feeble spark. Then, as it was added to, the light grew in fullness, breaking forth increasingly and shedding its radiance more widely. At last—when all the clouds were dispersed—Christ, the Sun of righteousness, fully illumined the whole earth.[6]

Practical Applications of Salvation by Christ Alone

The principle that Christ is the only Mediator of salvation has several important applications.

First, *we should trust in Christ alone for salvation*. From beginning to end, God has saved sinners only by faith in Christ. Do you think that you will be saved in a manner different from Abraham, David, or Peter?

Second, *we should read the whole Bible to know Christ*. Since God revealed the same gospel from Genesis to Revelation, we should read all of Scripture praying for the Holy Spirit to show us Christ.

Third, *we should preach Christ from all Scripture*. If God has called you to preach the Word, do so believing that all Scripture aims to make us wise unto salvation by faith in Christ.

Fourth, *we should trust in the faithfulness of the God and Father of Jesus Christ*. God has followed the same plan of salvation for thousands of years. What a demonstration of his faithfulness!

Fifth, *we should count all true believers in Christ from all times and places as our family*. Cherish your ancient heritage. Love God's people from all nations.

Sixth, *we should send the gospel of Christ to all nations*. The gospel has been God's means of salvation throughout history. It is the only means of salvation today. For the sake of Christ's name, do what you can to spread the good news to all people.

6 Calvin, *Institutes*, 2.10.20.

Seventh, *we should look forward to the joy of all nations in the eternal city of God.* Christ will save people of all kinds to glorify God and enjoy him forever.

The Father's Counsel of Peace with His Son

The covenant of grace goes even further back than the first revelation of the gospel to man. Salvation is an eternal promise between the Father and the Son. The Westminster Larger Catechism says, "The covenant of grace was made with Christ as the second Adam, and in him with all the elect as his seed."[7] Christ is an eternal person, God the Son. Therefore, the covenant of grace is an eternal agreement in the Trinity. This may be called "the counsel of peace" (Zech. 6:13), the covenant of redemption, or the covenant of grace from eternity. The Bible reveals the counsel of peace in several ways.

First, *God predestined Christ.* God has blessed his saints "in Christ" because "he hath chosen us in him before the foundation of the world" (Eph. 1:3–4). Christ himself is God's chosen one (Isa. 42:1; 1 Pet. 2:6). He was "foreordained before the foundation of the world" to redeem God's people (1 Pet. 1:18–20). In the purposes of God, he is "the Lamb slain from the foundation of the world" (Rev. 13:8). But Christ already existed "in the beginning" (John 1:1). He is not just someone elected by God; he is the God who elects (Matt. 24:31; John 15:16). Therefore, when the Father elected the Son, the Son agreed with the Father to save the chosen people.

Second, *God swore an oath to Christ.* David says, "The Lord hath sworn, and will not repent, Thou art a priest for ever after the order of Melchizedek" (Ps. 110:4). This promise reveals a covenant between God and Christ. It is like God's covenant oath with David (89:3). By this oath, Jesus was made the Priest and Surety of the new covenant (Heb. 7:21–22). This commitment was already settled in God's mind a thousand years before Christ came, when David wrote Psalm 110. Therefore, this passage also points to the eternal counsel of peace.

Third, *God made ancient promises to Christ.* God promised his Servant that God would "be glorified" in him (Isa. 49:3). He would suffer humiliation (v. 4), but the Lord would make him to be "salvation unto the end of the earth" (v. 6). As the conquering King, he would release "the prisoners" and those "in darkness," then bring them from all lands to a place of safety

7 The Westminster Larger Catechism (Q. 31), in *RC*, 4:305.

and satisfaction (vv. 9–12). The Lord said, "I will . . . give thee for a covenant of the people" (v. 8). God's covenant with his people, then, is rooted in his promises to Christ.

Fourth, *God promised a covenant seed to Christ.* God consistently made his covenants with individuals and their seed or offspring (Gen. 9:9; 17:7; 2 Sam. 7:12). Christ has no physical offspring. But Christ is the "everlasting Father" of his people (Isa. 9:6)—he has spiritual offspring, born of his death. God promised that he would "see his seed . . . [and] justify many; for he shall bear their iniquities" (53:10–11). This justified seed is the true Israel: "In the LORD shall all the seed of Israel be justified, and shall glory" (45:25). God promised to make with them "the covenant of my peace" (54:10). Therefore, God made a covenant with Christ and his seed, just as he did with Abraham and David, and their seed.

Fifth, *God made the counsel of peace with Christ.* God commanded the prophet Zechariah to crown the priest Joshua. God then declared, "The BRANCH . . . shall sit and rule upon his throne; and he shall be a priest upon his throne: and the counsel of peace shall be between them both" (Zech. 6:11–13). "The Branch" is a title of Christ (Jer. 23:5–6; 33:15; Zech. 3:8). The crowning of a priest symbolized that Christ would be both King and Priest. The "counsel of peace" is the plan formed by God and Christ from eternity to make peace with sinners by Christ's blood (cf. 3:8–9; 9:9–11).

Sixth, *God made a covenant to give the kingdom to Christ.* The Lord Jesus says, "I appoint unto you a kingdom, as my Father hath appointed unto me" (Luke 22:29). The verb translated as "appoint" commonly means to make a covenant (Acts 3:25; Heb. 8:10). Jesus had just spoken of the new covenant in his blood (Luke 22:20). So Christ says that the Father made a covenant with him for a kingdom. Christ's disciples are included as well by his shed blood.

Seventh, *God made Adam a foreshadowing of Christ.* Adam is a "figure," or type, of Christ (Rom. 5:14). Adam's disobedience resulted in mankind falling into a state in which they are counted as sinners under God's condemnation. Christ's obedience brought those in him into a state in which they are counted as righteous by God's justification (vv. 16, 19). As we saw (chap. 32), God made a covenant with Adam to represent all people united to him. In a similar way, God made a covenant with Christ to represent all people united to him.

Eighth, *God is the covenant God of Christ.* Christ speaks of his Father as "my God" (John 20:17). The Son is fully God (v. 28). But as the Mediator, he stands in covenant with the Father. God the Father is "the God of our Lord Jesus Christ" (Eph. 1:17). This is a covenant name, like "the God of Abraham" (Gen. 26:24) and "the God of David" (2 Kings 20:5). Thus, the Father made a covenant with the Son.

Ninth, *God promised before time began to give eternal life in Christ.* Paul writes of the "hope of eternal life, which God, that cannot lie, promised before the world began" (Titus 1:2)— literally "before times everlasting." To whom did God make this promise? No one existed then except the Trinity. In this epistle, Paul has just written of "God" and "Jesus Christ" (v. 1). Therefore, God the Father made a commitment to God the Son to grant eternal life to the elect through faith in him (v. 1).

In summary, the Holy Scriptures reveal that God the Father made a plan, a solemn promise, and a covenant with God the Son before time began to save the elect through Christ's work. William Ames said that God bound Christ to his office as the Mediator "through a special covenant," expressed in Isaiah 53:10. He added that "the agreement between God and Christ was a kind of advance application of our redemption."[8] In that covenant, God gave us to Christ and Christ to us in his eternal decree. He executes this plan in time by regenerating us and giving us saving faith in Christ. All this is accomplished by the power of God the Holy Spirit.

Theological Applications of the Counsel of Peace

The doctrine of the counsel of peace helps us to see clearly that the Trinity is three persons in the one true God. God has one will, but it is related to the perspective of each divine person. "God is love" in his undivided essence (1 John 4:8). But we also read that "the Father loveth the Son" (John 3:35) and "I [the Son] love the Father" (14:31). These words express distinct persons loving one another in God.

As a distinct, eternal, divine person, God the Son accepted his mission to lay down his life for sinners (John 10:17–18). The cross was a revelation of the Son's love for sinners no less than the Father's love (Gal. 2:20; Eph.

8 William Ames, *The Marrow of Theology*, trans. John D. Eusden (Grand Rapids, MI: Baker, 1968), 1.19.4–6; 1.24.3 (132, 149).

5:2, 25). Furthermore, the cross was not the Father's will imposed on the Son; that could be seen as unfair to Jesus. Christ's dying for sinners was a counsel, or plan, formed by the whole Trinity before time began.

The doctrine of the counsel of peace shows us that God's covenant of grace is rooted in eternity (2 Tim. 1:9). Of course, we speak of a covenant in the Trinity by way of analogy, according to our limited understanding of God. Reformed theologians disagree whether the covenant between the Father and the Son is a distinct covenant (called "the covenant of redemption") or essentially the same as the covenant of grace (so that the counsel of peace could also be called a "covenant of grace from eternity"). In either case, it is clear that God's love for his covenant people is "from everlasting to everlasting" (Ps. 103:17–18).

Practical Applications of the Counsel of Peace

The doctrine of the counsel of peace is deep theology, but it is also practical in several ways.

First, it teaches us that we should *trust in Christ*. Let us go to Christ with empty hands, poor in spirit, knowing that all our riches must come from him. We have said it before and cannot emphasize it too much: Christ is the only Mediator between God and man. He is the only Savior.

Second, we should *marvel at God's eternal love*. Wilhelmus à Brakel said, "This covenant reveals a love which is unparalleled, exceeding all comprehension. How blessed and what a wonder it is . . . to have been the object of the eternal, mutual delight of the Father and the Son to save you!"[9]

Third, we should *examine ourselves to see if we are in Christ*. All our hope is bound up in being united to Christ (Col. 1:27). Apart from him, we are without God and hopeless (Eph. 2:12).

Fourth, we should *contemplate the loyalty of true love*. By God's will, the strongest bonds of love express themselves in covenants. Love delights to bind itself in commitments.

Fifth, we should *honor our covenant commitments*. God thought that a covenant was the best way to glorify the love shared among the Father, the Son, and the Holy Spirit. Therefore, we should regard our covenants as excellent ways to live out the highest love.

9 Brakel, *CRS*, 1:263.

Sixth, we should *rest confidently in our hope*. If we are in Christ, then God will save us to the end. God has not only promised salvation to us but also has promised our salvation to Christ. The Father and the Son will keep their promises to each other and save the elect forever.

Seventh, we should *glorify God for his covenant in Christ*. The doctrine of the counsel of peace grounds all of salvation in the will of the eternal, triune God. Thus, it is all for his glory.

Suggested Songs to Sing to the Lord

- Psalm 32, "How blest is he whose trespass hath freely been forgiv'n," *Psalter*, Nos. 83–84; *THBap*, No. 462
- Psalm 110, "The Lord unto His Christ hath said," *Psalter*, No. 303

Questions for Meditation or Discussion

1. How does the Bible show us that salvation is always through Christ?
2. How did believers before Abraham know and trust in the gospel of Christ?
3. What did God reveal about salvation in his promises to Abraham (Gen. 12:1–3)?
4. How did Moses and the law point to Christ?
5. The authors urge us to read the whole Bible to know Christ and to preach Christ from all Scripture. What are some ways that we can find Christ in the Old Testament?
6. What is the counsel of peace or covenant of redemption?
7. How do the following Scripture passages show that God the Father made a counsel of peace with God the Son: (1) Ephesians 1:3–4; (2) Psalm 110:4; (3) Isaiah 49:1–12; (4) Isaiah 53:10–11; (5) Zechariah 6:11–13; (6) Luke 22:29–30; (7) Romans 5:14–19; (8) John 20:17; (9) Titus 1:2?
8. What does the doctrine of the counsel of peace show us about the Trinity and Christ's work of giving himself for our sins?
9. What does the doctrine of God's eternal covenant of grace show us about his love for us?
10. What does the doctrine of the counsel of peace teach us about how we should love one another?

40

The Different Administrations of the Covenant of Grace

Chapter Summary and Key Terms

God revealed and applied the covenant of grace through the *historical covenants* he made with Noah, Abraham, Israel, David, and believers under the new covenant in Christ. The covenant with Noah is an administration of common grace. The covenants with Abraham, Israel, and David were *old covenant* forms of the covenant of grace. Under these covenants of promise, God gave his grace through *temporary administrations* of the covenant of grace before Christ came to establish the new covenant. God also provided *types*, which were people, events, institutions, and religious rites that he designed to foreshadow Christ and his work. The *new covenant* is the last of the historical covenants. It was foretold by the prophets and instituted when Christ accomplished redemption. The saving grace of the new covenant was given through the covenant of grace in all ages, but it comes with greater glory since Christ's incarnation and exaltation.

THERE ARE DIFFERENCES and similarities among God's covenants with men. When Christians read the Old Testament, some things may seem strange to us, such as circumcision in the covenant with Abraham and animal sacrifices by priests in the covenant with Israel. But others things in the Old Testament make the hearts of Christians rejoice, such as David's trust in God and in his experience of God's grace. This is because there are several *historical covenants* that God made at different stages of history after the fall of man, but in a very importance sense these covenants are one.

In this chapter, we will survey those historical covenants. In the next chapter, we will present arguments that there is one covenant of grace that ties the historical covenants together.

Introduction to the Ancient Covenants

After Adam broke the covenant of works, the Lord began to reveal promises of the covenant of grace to fallen mankind. He then made the first historical covenant with Noah. As history progressed, God made a series of other historical covenants with his particular people. We may call them God's redemptive historical covenants—the covenants with Abraham, Israel, and David, and the new covenant.

Every redemptive historical covenant is, at its core, the covenant of grace. But every redemptive historical covenant before the new covenant dispensed God's grace through a temporary administration with types that revealed Christ. The Westminster Confession of Faith says that the covenant of grace "was differently administered in the time of the law, and in the time of the gospel." The first included "promises" and "types" of Christ. The second centers on the display of "Christ, the substance."[1]

The redemptive historical covenants before Jesus Christ were, in part, *temporary administrations* of Christ's grace. Paul called them "the covenants of promise" (Eph. 2:12), literally "covenants of *the* promise." The plural "covenants" shows that we can speak of them as distinct historical covenants. Yet they revealed the one covenant of grace: "the promise." We call these covenants "administrations" because through them God administered (or dispensed) his mercies to his people through specific promises, commands, offices, and forms of worship (cf. Rom. 9:4). But the external administrations of these covenants were temporary. That is why requirements such as circumcision and the ceremonial laws of Moses have passed away in Christ (Eph. 2:11, 15).

The covenants prior to Christ's coming offered *types* that revealed Christ. By *types* we mean people, events, institutions, and religious rites that God designed to foreshadow Christ and his kingdom. For example, the temple

1 The Westminster Confession of Faith (7.5–6), in *RC*, 4:243.

in Israel foreshadowed how Christ and his people are a "holy temple in the Lord" (Eph. 2:21). Thomas Boston called these covenants, "covenants typical of the covenant of grace."[2]

The Covenant of Preservation with Noah and His Seed

The first covenant explicitly mentioned in the Bible is the one God made with Noah. The Lord commanded Noah to build the ark to escape the worldwide flood. He said, "Every thing that is in the earth shall die. But with thee will I establish my covenant; and thou shalt come into the ark, thou, and thy sons, and thy wife, and thy sons' wives with thee" (Gen. 6:17–18).

When the flood was over, God said to Noah, "I establish my covenant with you, and with your seed after you; and with every living creature that is with you. . . . I will establish my covenant with you; neither shall all flesh be cut off any more by the waters of a flood; neither shall there any more be a flood to destroy the earth" (Gen. 9:9–11). God appointed the rainbow to be the sign of the covenant (vv. 12–17).

God's covenant with Noah was not a temporary administration of *saving* grace to God's particular people. Rather, it was an administration of God's *common* grace to all mankind. But this historical covenant was also closely connected to the covenant of grace. It restrains God's wrath against mankind's sin. It preserves God's creation until he fulfills his saving purposes.

The flood was a type of eternal judgment (Matt. 24:37–39; 2 Pet. 2:5–7). The salvation of eight people through water was a picture of the salvation of sinners by Christ's death, resurrection, ascension, and session at God's right hand (1 Pet. 3:18–22). God compares the covenant of preservation to his unbreakable "covenant of peace" (Isa. 54:9–10).

The Covenant of Promise with Abraham and His Seed

God unfolded his covenant with Abraham over time. It began when God called him to go up from Ur of the Chaldees to an unknown land (Gen. 12:1–7). The Lord promised to give him blessing, the land, and many offspring. Later God renewed his promise of offspring, stirring Abraham to the exercise of justifying faith (15:4–6). The Lord then formally "made a covenant" with Abraham to give the land to his seed (vv. 8, 13, 18). God called

2 Boston, *An Illustration of the Doctrines of the Christian Religion*, in *WTB*, 1:328.

Abraham to walk before him in righteous integrity and again promised to multiply his offspring and give them the land (17:1–2, 7–8). The Lord demanded that Abraham and his seed "keep my covenant" by circumcising every male born (or bought as a slave) in Abraham's household—the household God promised to expand into a nation (vv. 9–14).

We may picture the seed of Abraham as two overlapping circles. One circle is his physical offspring through Isaac and Jacob (Gen. 17:19; Acts 3:25). The other circle is Abraham's spiritual offspring, those who share in his faith in God's promise, whether they are Jews or Gentiles (Rom. 4:11–12). The area where the circles overlap is the Israelites who are saved by faith in Christ. At the center of that overlap is Christ, the great Seed (Gal. 3:16).

The historical covenant with Abraham was a temporary administration of the covenant of grace. God used it as a means to dispense saving grace to true believers, Abraham and his spiritual seed in Israel. Their justifying faith came by hearing the promises of God, just as ours does today (Gen. 15:5–6). God's word nurtured their hope in the coming of Christ, the Son of Abraham (Matt. 1:1). The blessing promised to Abraham was not merely physical but centered on salvation from sin (Mic. 7:18–20) and included justification and the work of the Spirit (Gal. 3:8, 14).

God's covenant with Abraham also included types that revealed Christ. The land of Canaan was the temporary home for the patriarchs as pilgrims on their way to the city of God (Heb. 11:13–16). Circumcision of the flesh was a type of circumcision of the heart in Christ (Deut. 30:6; Rom. 2:25–29). Christ accomplished spiritual circumcision by dying for our sins and rising again (Col. 2:11–13).

God no longer requires circumcision of the body (1 Cor. 7:18–19; Gal. 6:15). But God's promises to Abraham continue today in Christ (Luke 1:72–73). Both Jewish and Gentile believers in Christ are the spiritual seed of Abraham (Gal. 3:26, 29). They can say, "We are the circumcision, which worship God in the spirit, and rejoice in Christ Jesus, and have no confidence in the flesh" (Phil. 3:3).

The Covenant of Law with Israel through Moses

After Abraham, Isaac, and Jacob died, their offspring found themselves enslaved in Egypt. God saved them from slavery through Moses and brought them to Mount Sinai. There the Lord made the covenant of law. He said,

> Ye have seen what I did unto the Egyptians, and how I bare you on eagles' wings, and brought you unto myself. Now therefore, if ye will obey my voice indeed, and keep my covenant, then ye shall be a peculiar treasure unto me above all people: for all the earth is mine: and ye shall be unto me a kingdom of priests, and an holy nation. (Ex. 19:4–6)

Was the covenant of law a covenant of works? If people take the commandments themselves as a way to be justified, the law becomes a covenant of works. It promises eternal life for perfect obedience (Matt. 19:16–19; Rom. 10:5; Gal. 3:12) and threatens a curse against all lawbreakers (Gal. 3:10). But in the context of God's word to Israel, the covenant of law was another temporary administration of the covenant of grace. The law did not nullify the promise given to Abraham (Gal. 3:15–17), nor was it "against the promises of God" (v. 21). The law's blessings and curses mostly pertained to national prosperity, not eternal salvation (Leviticus 26; Deuteronomy 28). Under this national covenant, unbelievers received many temporal benefits of the covenant of grace, but they remained personally under the broken covenant of works in Adam.[3] Believers suffered temporal afflictions when the nation disobeyed God, but they remained saved through Christ under the covenant of grace.

In the covenant of law, God expanded the number of types that revealed Christ. The redemption and exodus of Israel, the Passover lamb, the Aaronic priesthood, the tabernacle, and the laws of cleanness and uncleanness were all types pointing to Christ. These "types and ordinances" served "to instruct and build up the elect in faith in the promised Messiah, by whom they had full remission of sins, and eternal salvation."[4]

The Covenant of Kingdom with David and His Seed

The Lord promised to establish the kingdom of David's "seed" forever (2 Sam. 7:12). This royal son would build the house of the Lord—his temple (v. 13). God also promised to be a father to the king and to take him as his son in a lasting relationship of faithful love (vv. 14–15).

The Lord gave his covenant with David as a temporary administration of the covenant of grace for his people. Through David and his seed, the Lord

3 For a distinction between external and internal participation in the covenant of grace, see the argument for infant baptism in chap. 83.

4 The Westminster Confession of Faith (7.5), in *RC*, 4:243.

gave Israel salvation from pagan enemies and a political system to protect justice in society (2 Sam. 8:1–15; 23:3–5). God's covenant with David gave Israel a more stable status under God's love (Ps. 89:28–34). Through David and Solomon came a greater revelation of true spirituality in the Psalms and the Proverbs. The Lord also secured his special presence with Israel in the temple, his house.

The covenant of kingdom contained types that revealed Christ, the true King. When believers went to the house of the Lord and observed the rituals, by faith they saw God's beauty, power, and glory (Pss. 27:4; 63:2; 84:1–2). They found spiritual satisfaction in his goodness and holiness (65:4). And they perceived the coming judgment (73:17–19). David himself was a type of Christ in humiliation and exaltation.

The New Covenant through Our Lord Jesus Christ

The later Hebrew prophets looked ahead to a "covenant of peace" (Isa. 54:10; Ezek. 34:25; 37:26) and an "everlasting covenant" (Isa. 61:8; Jer. 32:40; 50:5; Ezek. 16:60; 37:26). God promised "a new covenant . . . not according to the covenant" he made when he saved the people of Israel from Egypt, which they broke (Jer. 31:31–32).

The new covenant contains the following promises (Jer. 31:33–34):

- *Inward covenant faithfulness*: "I will put my law in their inward parts, and write it in their hearts." God promised to give his people new hearts (Ezek. 11:19; 36:26–27).
- *Covenantal union and communion*: "[I] will be their God, and they shall be my people. . . . They shall all know me, from the least of them unto the greatest of them, saith the Lord." God's people would know him experientially (Hos. 2:20).
- *Permanent atonement for sin's guilt*: "For I will forgive their iniquity, and I will remember their sin no more." To not "remember" sin is to not reject sinners or punish them (Jer. 14:10; Hos. 8:13). Guilt is gone and forgiveness is total (Jer. 33:8).

As a "testament," the new covenant was not formally ratified until "the death of the testator" (Heb. 9:16–17). Christ's death accomplished redemption "once for all" (10:10). Therefore, the new covenant is not a temporary administration of the covenant of grace, but an "everlasting covenant" (13:20). Its glory will not fade away like that of the old covenant (8:13).

There are several differences between the old covenant and the new covenant. These differences spring from Christ's coming in the flesh. The new covenant brings the following:

- a greater revelation of God's saving grace (John 1:14, 17)
- the substance of the shadows given in the old covenant (Col. 2:16–17; Heb. 10:1)
- a greater boldness to draw near to God through the Savior who always makes intercession for us (Heb. 4:14–15; 7:25; 10:19–22)
- a transformed people who enjoy real, spiritual communion with God, instead of a nation of covenant breakers (Heb. 8:9, 11)
- God's saving grace sent out to all nations (Isa. 49:6; Acts 13:47)

We should not consider the new covenant without hungering and praying for its promises to be fulfilled in our lives. Apart from the grace promised in this covenant, God's laws can do nothing but condemn us, for they are not written in our hearts and we are blind to Christ (2 Cor. 3:1–4:6). We must know the Lord, for there is no greater treasure, wisdom, or power (Jer. 9:24–25). Therefore, let us earnestly pray with John Calvin:

> Grant, Almighty God, that as thou hast favoured us with so singular a benefit as to make through thy Son a covenant which has been ratified for our salvation—O grant, that we may become partakers of it, and know that thou so speakest with us, that thou not only shewest us by thy Word what is right, but speakest also to us inwardly by thy Spirit, and thus renderest us teachable and obedient, that there may be an evidence of our adoption, and a proof that thou wilt govern and rule us, until we shall at length be really and fully united to thee through Christ our Lord. Amen.[5]

Suggested Song to Sing to the Lord

- Psalm 105, "Unto the Lord lift thankful voices," *Psalter*, No. 425; *THBap*, No. 763

5 Calvin, *Comm.* on Jer. 31:33.

Questions for Meditation or Discussion

1. What are the "covenants of promise" (Eph. 2:12)? What does the plural "covenants" imply? What does the singular term "promise" imply?
2. What does it mean that the covenants of promise were temporary administrations of the covenant of grace?
3. What does it mean that the covenants of promise contained types that revealed Christ?
4. How did God promise in the covenant with Noah to support our world with common grace?
5. What did God promise to Abraham concerning his seed? How did those promises apply to his physical seed and to his spiritual seed?
6. How was God's covenant of law with Israel in some ways a national covenant? How was it a gracious covenant?
7. What did God promise to David concerning his "seed"?
8. What specific promises did the Lord give in Jeremiah 31:31–34?
9. In what five ways does the new covenant excel the old covenant?
10. Can you claim the promises of the new covenant as your own? Why or why not?

41

The One Covenant of Grace

Chapter Summary and Key Terms

Though God made several redemptive historical covenants with his people through history, there are good reasons to see all of them as administrations of the one covenant of grace. God has been saving sinners since the fall of man by the same gospel of Christ. All God's promises of salvation are rooted in the covenant the Trinity made before time began. The ancient covenants implemented temporary administrations of God's saving grace and revealed Christ through types. Many Old Testament promises have been fulfilled in Christ and his church in the New Testament. One promise stands at the center of God's covenants: "You shall be my people, and I will be your God." Each covenant advanced the covenants before it, linking them together. And the Bible uses the singular word *covenant* to refer to groups of redemptive historical covenants. Therefore, there is one covenant of grace. This covenant is God's instrument to create the relationship of faith and love that God's people have with him.

BEHIND THE REDEMPTIVE historical covenants stands the one covenant of grace. In the last chapter, we saw that we can speak of God's covenants with Abraham, Israel, and David with the plural word "covenants" (Eph. 2:12). But all of these covenants were administrations of the covenant of grace in Jesus Christ. Their promises are fulfilled in its final administration, the new covenant.

John Calvin said, "The covenant made with all the patriarchs is so much like ours in substance and reality that the two are actually one and the same. Yet they differ in the mode of dispensation."[1] John Gill wrote, "The

1 Calvin, *Institutes*, 2.10.2.

covenant of grace is but one and the same in all ages, of which Christ is the substance," though "there are different administrations of it."[2]

The Arguments for One Covenant of Grace

In previous chapters, we laid out three arguments for the doctrine of the covenant of grace.

First, *God has been saving sinners by the same gospel since the fall of man.* Therefore, God has one people saved by one Mediator through one faith (chap. 39).

Second, *God promised salvation in a covenant with Christ before time began.* Every promise of salvation flows from this eternal counsel of peace (chap. 39).

Third, *the ancient redemptive historical covenants implemented temporary administrations of God's saving grace.* They also offered types that revealed Christ and pointed to the new covenant (chap. 40).

To these three arguments we may add a fourth: *many promises of the Old Testament are fulfilled in Christ and his church in the New Testament.* For instance, God promised that David's descendant would reign on his throne. Peter says this promise was fulfilled when Christ was lifted up to sit at God's right hand (Acts 2:30–36). Peter also applies to the church titles and promises given to Israel (1 Pet. 2:9). James says that the gathering of the Gentiles into the church fulfills the prophecy of Amos concerning David's kingdom (Acts 15:13–17). The new covenant promised to Israel is applied to the church (2 Cor. 3:3, 6; Heb. 8:6–13). Paul says, "If ye be Christ's, then are ye Abraham's seed, and heirs according to the promise" (Gal. 3:29). Therefore, God does not have two purposes for two peoples, as dispensationalism claims. Rather, one covenant of grace spans the Old and New Testaments.

We will now add three more arguments for the covenant of grace. They are the core promise of all the redemptive historical covenants, their organic unity, and the use of the singular term "covenant" in the Bible.

The Core Promise: Your God, My People

Fifth, one promise stands at the center of all of God's redemptive historical covenants. The Lord says again and again, "You shall be my people,

2 John Gill, *A Complete Body of Doctrinal and Practical Divinity* (1839; repr. Paris, AR: The Baptist Standard Bearer, 1995), 345.

and I will be your God." This is a promise of "union and communion with God."[3]

God promised Abraham, "I will establish my covenant between me and thee and thy seed after thee in their generations for an everlasting covenant, to be a God unto thee, and to thy seed after thee. . . . I will be their God" (Gen. 17:7–8). The Lord repeated this promise when he said that he would redeem Israel from Egypt (Ex. 6:7). He said it again after making a covenant with the Israelites at Mount Sinai (29:45–46; Lev. 26:12). God said of David's seed, "I will be his father, and he shall be my son" (2 Sam. 7:14). David responded, "Thou hast confirmed to thyself thy people Israel to be a people unto thee for ever: and thou, Lord, art become their God" (v. 24).

In the new covenant, the Lord says, "[I] will be their God, and they shall be my people" (Jer. 31:33). This promise belongs to the church of Christ (2 Cor. 6:16; Heb. 8:10). It is at the heart of our eternal hope: "They shall be his people, and God . . . [will] be their God. . . . He that overcometh shall inherit all things; and I will be his God, and he shall be my son" (Rev. 21:3, 7).

Running through all of God's redemptive historical covenants with his chosen people is one great promise that he will give himself to them as their God and take them as his people. Calvin called it "the very formula of the covenant" and noted that "life and the whole of blessedness are embraced in these words."[4] Therefore, God's ancient covenants with Abraham, Israel, and David, as well as his new covenant in Christ, are one covenant in substance.

The Organic Unity of the Covenants

Sixth, beginning with the covenant with Abraham, each subsequent redemptive historical covenant was rooted in the ones before it, sustained their basic commitments, and advanced their fulfillment. Though they all were distinct historical covenants, they grew organically from one to the next to form one covenant.

The covenant with Israel through Moses expanded and advanced the covenant with Abraham. The Lord saved Israel from Egypt because "God remembered his covenant with Abraham" (Ex. 2:24). He then revealed himself to Israel as "the Lord God of your fathers, the God of Abraham"

3 John Murray, *The Covenant of Grace* (1953; repr., Phillipsburg, NJ: Presbyterian and Reformed, 1988), 21.

4 Calvin, *Institutes*, 2.10.8. He also cited Lev. 26:11–12; Ps. 144:15; Hab. 1:12.

(3:15; cf. 4:5). He redeemed his people and led them to Canaan because of his oath to the patriarchs (6:2–8).

Moses called the Israelites to "enter into covenant with the LORD thy God, and into his oath, which the LORD thy God maketh with thee this day: that he may establish thee to day for a people unto himself, and that he may be unto thee a God, as he hath said unto thee, and as he hath sworn unto thy fathers, to Abraham, to Isaac, and to Jacob" (Deut. 29:12–13; cf. 30:20). Thus, God's covenant with Abraham was still in effect under the covenant of law.

The covenant with David expanded and advanced the covenants with Abraham and Israel. In the covenants of promise and law, God said that he would raise up kings for Israel (Gen. 17:6, 16) and gave directions for their selection and conduct (Deut. 17:14–20). When the Lord made the covenant of kingdom, David praised God for redeeming the Israelites from Egypt and for taking them as his people forever, saying, "The LORD of hosts is the God over Israel: and let the house of thy servant David be established before thee" (2 Sam. 7:22–26).

When Solomon built the temple, he said, "There hath not failed one word of all his good promise, which he promised by the hand of Moses his servant" (1 Kings 8:56). Nor did the covenant with David replace the law. Solomon asked God to incline the people's hearts "to keep his commandments . . . which he commanded our fathers" (v. 58). O. Palmer Robertson says, "Each successive covenant with Abraham's descendants advanced the original purposes of God to a higher level of realization."[5]

The new covenant continues and fulfills the ancient covenants. It began a new era with the coming of Christ in the flesh and his complete accomplishment of redemption. But God has not abandoned his ancient covenants. The first words in the New Testament are "The book of the generation of Jesus Christ, the son of David, the son of Abraham" (Matt. 1:1). Christ says, "Think not that I am come to destroy the law, or the prophets: I am not come to destroy, but to fulfil," and that with regard to the "commandments" (5:17, 19).

Jesus Christ was born to sit on "the throne of his father David" (Luke 1:32). Mary rejoiced that God "has helped his servant Israel, in remembrance of his mercy, as he spoke to our fathers, to Abraham and to his

5 O. Palmer Robertson, *The Christ of the Covenants* (Phillipsburg, NJ: Presbyterian and Reformed, 1980), 29.

offspring forever" (vv. 54–55 ESV). In Christ, God was raising up salvation "in the house of his servant David," for he remembered "his holy covenant; the oath which he sware to our father Abraham" (vv. 69, 72–73). The blessed seed of Abraham consists of those united to Christ by faith, whether Jew or Gentile (Gal. 3:28–29).

The unity of God's redemptive historical covenants in the eternal covenant of grace comes from the unity of God's promises in the one Lord Jesus Christ. Christ did not come to discard God's promises to the patriarchs but "to confirm the promises" to honor God's faithfulness (Rom. 15:8). In Christ, all of God's promises are fulfilled for God's glory (2 Cor. 1:19–20). Christ is the substance of the covenants. Therefore, in substance they are one.

The Singular Term "Covenant" in the Bible

Seventh, the Bible sometimes uses the singular term "covenant" for the redemptive historical covenants as a group. Therefore, we have a biblical basis to speak of one covenant of grace.

The Lord said of Israel, "I will not cast them away, neither will I abhor them, to destroy them utterly, and to break my covenant with them: for I am the Lord their God" (Lev. 26:44). To which covenant was the Lord referring? It was both the covenant of law that God made with Israel after the exodus (vv. 9, 15, 25, 45–46) and his covenant of promise with Abraham (v. 42).

When Moses called the Israelites to "enter into covenant with the Lord thy God," they did so to be his people and have him as their God, "as he hath sworn unto thy fathers, to Abraham, to Isaac, and to Jacob" (Deut. 29:12–13). Therefore, the singular term "covenant" in Deuteronomy refers to both the promises to Abraham and to Israel.

Psalm 111 speaks of God's "covenant" (Ps. 111:5, 9). But the psalm refers to the inheritance (v. 6) promised to Abraham and the commandments (v. 7) given through Moses.

Nehemiah 9 records a prayer that speaks of God's "covenant" with Abraham and Israel's history from the exodus through the exile. The prayer appeals to "our God . . . who keepest covenant" (v. 32). The singular word "covenant" refers to the covenant of promise with Abraham, the covenant of law through Moses, and the covenant of kingdom with David.

The emphasis of the Holy Scriptures regarding the new covenant falls on its superiority over the ancient covenants. Christ has come and accomplished redemption. But some passages use the singular term "covenant" for both the old and the new. Consider a prophecy that weaves together the fulfillment of all the redemptive historical covenants under the banner of one covenant (Ezek. 37:24–26). In that prophecy, we read of

- the covenant with David: "David my servant shall be king over them; and they all shall have one shepherd."
- the covenant through Moses: "they shall also walk in my judgments, and observe my statutes, and do them."
- the covenant with Abraham: "they shall dwell in the land that I have given unto Jacob my servant, wherein your fathers have dwelt."
- all of these through the new covenant: "I will make a covenant of peace with them; it shall be an everlasting covenant with them."

Therefore, the redemptive historical covenants are one covenant of grace. It is true that God revealed more truth to his people over time, that there are differences among the redemptive historical covenants, and that the new covenant is superior to the ancient covenants. But we may rightly speak of the singular covenant of grace that is revealed and implemented in them all.

The Relationship Created by the Covenant of Grace

God's covenant of grace defines his relationship of faithful love with his people in Christ. J. I. Packer said, "The goal of grace . . . is to create a love relationship between God and us who believe, . . . and the bond of fellowship by which God binds Himself to us is His covenant. . . . This covenant relationship is the basis of all biblical religion."[6] Therefore, as we conclude our study of the covenant of grace, we will consider two key experiential aspects of this covenant relationship: faith and love.

Faith in the Lord as Our Covenant God

God calls us to enter the spiritual relationship promised in the covenant of grace. William Strong said, "It's our duty to enter our covenant with

6 J. I. Packer, *Knowing God* (Downers Grove, IL: InterVarsity Press, 1993), 261–62.

the Lord; and this is the great end of the publishing of the gospel, to bring men into the bond of the covenant."[7] The living relationship offered in the covenant does not begin until we trust in Christ (Gal. 3:26, 29). Only then can we say, "O my God, I trust in thee" (Ps. 25:2). Like Ruth, we must take refuge under his wings (Ruth 2:12). We must say to God's children, "Thy people shall be my people, and thy God my God" (1:16).

Hear the voice of Christ calling. He promises, "I am the bread of life: he that cometh to me shall never hunger; and he that believeth on me shall never thirst" (John 6:35). He lovingly pleads, "If any man thirst, let him come unto me, and drink" (7:37).

If you have not yet come to Christ by faith, consider who calls you. He is the Son of God, the Mediator of the new covenant. He has all the promises of the covenant in his hand. He can write the law on your heart by the Spirit so that you delight to do God's will. Christ can give you the knowledge of God so that the Lord becomes your God and you become one of his people. Christ died for sinners. He can take away the guilt of your sins so that God will never give you what you deserve or remember your guilt against you. Christ needs nothing from you, but he offers you everything in the covenant of grace. Will you receive this Christ?

Consider, too, what will happen to those who neglect this great salvation. You are already a covenant breaker in Adam. If you refuse to trust in Christ after hearing the gospel, you also make yourself a covenant despiser. One day, God will summon you to his throne of judgment. His wrath will punish you forever. Sinner, flee from the wrath that is to come! Turn from sin, trust in Christ, and embrace the covenant of grace.

Repentant believer, marvel and rejoice that you are in the covenant of grace! John Brown of Haddington said, "Now, O my soul, think what astonishing displays of Jehovah's perfections appear in this covenant! Behold . . . infinite mercy, grace, and love . . . ! How infinite wisdom plans! Infinite persons engage! How all infinite perfections work for the redemption of sinful men—of sinful *me*!"[8]

7 William Strong, *A Discourse of the Two Covenants*, Westminster Assembly Project (1678; facsimile repr., Grand Rapids, MI: Reformation Heritage Books, 2011), 165.

8 John Brown of Haddington, *Systematic Theology: A Compendious View of Natural and Revealed Religion* (1817; repr., Grand Rapids, MI: Reformation Heritage Books, 2015), 255, emphasis original.

Love for the Lord as Our Covenant God

God's covenant of grace creates a relationship of love that Scripture compares to a marriage in which the husband loves his wife with his dearest affections and undying commitment. The Lord is the Bridegroom of his people. They are his bride.

The Lord said of Israel, when it was "the time of love," that "I sware unto thee, and entered into a covenant with thee, . . . and thou becamest mine" (Ezek. 16:8). "As the bridegroom rejoiceth over the bride, so shall thy God rejoice over thee" (Isa. 62:5).

God the Son is the Bridegroom for whom believers long (Mark 2:19–20). Jesus Christ has entered a particularly intimate relationship with his people. He shares their human nature and experiences in a fallen world (Heb. 2:14–18). He is united to them more closely than a husband is to his wife. They are "one spirit" with Christ (1 Cor. 6:17). He is their life (Col. 3:4).

John Owen said that this spiritual marriage results in a relationship between Christ and his people that is accompanied by affections suitable for such a marriage.[9] Christ and his bride willingly give themselves to each other in faithful love. Christ takes his bride to himself, saying, "I will be yours, and you will be mine, and for no one else" (cf. Hos. 3:3). Christ accepts us with delight. He treasures us with compassion and generosity. The church receives Christ with joy. We treasure him with single-minded devotion and submission.[10]

Therefore, cultivate love for Christ. Meditate on the covenant and its specific promises in Christ. Exercise your faith to trust him more. Pray for God to fulfill his promises increasingly in you. Stir up your affections of love to this loving and lovely Savior. Put your love into action with good works. Persevere in faithful love in imitation of the covenant-keeping God. This is the fruit that grows from the covenant of grace.

Suggested Songs to Sing to the Lord

- Psalm 89, "My song forever shall record," *Psalter*, No. 241; *THBap*, No. 101
- "A debtor to mercy alone," *THBap*, No. 99

9 Owen, *Communion with God*, in *WJO*, 2:54.

10 Owen, *Communion with God*, in *WJO*, 2:56, 118.

Questions for Meditation or Discussion

1. The authors write, "Behind the redemptive historical covenants stands the one covenant of grace." How would you explain this statement in your own words?
2. What three arguments for the one covenant of grace were given in previous chapters?
3. What argument can be made against dispensationalism from the fulfillment of Old Testament promises in the New Testament?
4. What core promise is found in all of the redemptive historical covenants?
5. What does that core promise imply about the covenant of grace?
6. How would you show from the Holy Scriptures that (1) the law of Moses expanded and advanced the covenant with Abraham, (2) the covenant with David expanded and advanced the previous covenants, and (3) the new covenant continues and fulfills the ancient covenants?
7. What are some Scripture passages that use the singular word "covenant" to refer to multiple covenants?
8. What does the use of the singular term "covenant" for multiple covenants imply?
9. How does the covenant of grace call people into a relationship of faith and love? Do you have this covenant relationship? If not, what must you do to gain it? If so, how can you grow in it?

Section 4B

The Person and Work of Christ

42

Introduction to the Person and Work of Christ

Chapter Summary and Key Terms

The doctrine of the person and work of Christ is well worth our study, for the knowledge of him is of surpassingly great value. God has revealed this doctrine in part through names such as *Jesus* (the human name of the Savior who delivers his people from sin); *Christ* (a title of office for the Spirit-anointed Prophet, Priest, and King); and *Son of God* (a title of deity for the only begotten Son of the Father). A biblical approach to this doctrine considers Christ's deity, humanity, states of humiliation and exaltation, and work as the Mediator. Studying the person and work of Christ is a spiritual work. It requires the power of the Holy Spirit to overcome our blindness and transform us into Christ's image as the glory of God shines in our hearts through the gospel.

THE CHRISTIAN LIFE is a long and difficult race. We must "run with patience the race that is set before us, looking unto Jesus" (Heb. 12:1–2). We cannot endure as Christians merely by keeping a list of rules, following a philosophy of life, or pursuing a series of experiences. The Christian must have Christ. Jesus Christ, the Son of God, is everything to the believer.

Jesus Christ prayed that his people might "be with me where I am; that they may behold my glory" (John 17:24). This should also be our fervent desire. John Owen said, "One of the greatest privileges . . . of believers, both in this world and unto eternity, consists in their beholding the glory of Christ."[1] Therefore, let us press on to know the Lord Jesus.

The Value of Studying the Doctrine of Christ

Here are a few reasons why the knowledge of Christ is so excellent that all else is worthless by comparison (Phil. 3:8).

First, *the doctrine of Christ is central.* At the core of Christianity is the gospel. At the core of the gospel is Jesus Christ (1 Cor. 15:1–4). The Father intends that "in all things [the Son] might have the preeminence" (Col. 1:18).

Second, *the doctrine of Christ is controversial.* Satan's servants work hard to draw people away from devotion to Christ by preaching "another Jesus" (2 Cor. 11:3–4, 13–15).

Third, *the doctrine of Christ is necessary.* "Whosoever denieth the Son, the same hath not the Father" (1 John 2:23). Anyone who denies that Christ came in the flesh "is not of God" (4:3).

Fourth, *the doctrine of Christ is awakening.* God uses the preaching of Christ to revive the church by the Holy Spirit. Christ says of the Spirit, "He shall glorify me" (John 16:14).

Fifth, *the doctrine of Christ is captivating.* The study of Christ enthralls the heart because no one is as beautiful as Christ (Ps. 45:2). He is "altogether lovely" (Song 5:16).

Sixth, *the doctrine of Christ is glorious.* In Christ, we find the "riches" of God's "glory" (Phil. 4:19; Col. 1:27). Paul writes of "the unsearchable riches of Christ" (Eph. 3:8).

The Names of Christ

Christ's names reveal who he is and what he has done.[2] The Apostles' Creed confesses faith in "Jesus Christ, [God's] only begotten Son, our Lord."[3] We will examine his human name ("Jesus"), his names of office (such as "Christ"), and his names of deity ("Son," "Lord," etc.).

Our Lord bears the human name Jesus. That is a form of "Joshua," the name of the servant of the Lord who led Israel into the Promised Land

1 Owen, *Meditations and Discourses on the Glory of Christ*, in *WJO*, 1:286.

2 In the Bible, the word "name" includes not just personal names but also titles such as "Lord" (Phil. 2:9–11) and "Son" (Heb. 1:4–5).

3 The Apostles' Creed, in *TFU*, 5.

(Josh. 1:1–2). But Jesus is the greater Joshua. He brings his people into their inheritance, the kingdom of God. Both names, Jesus and Joshua, mean "the Lord is salvation." The angel of the Lord, who announced the coming of Jesus to Joseph, said, "Thou shalt call his name Jesus: for he shall save his people from their sins" (Matt. 1:21). The Heidelberg Catechism says, "Why is the Son of God called Jesus, that is, a Savior? Because He saveth us, and delivereth us from our sins; and likewise, because we ought not to seek, neither can find salvation in any other."[4]

The Lord Jesus has the official name of the Christ. This title means "Anointed." An "anointed one" is someone ordained for an office as God's servant, such as a prophet (1 King 19:16; Ps. 105:15), a priest (Ex. 28:41; 29:9; Lev. 4:3, 5), or a king (1 Sam. 2:10; 10:1; 15:1). Christ is the Prophet (Acts 3:22), Priest (Heb. 2:17), and King (Matt. 25:34) on whom our salvation hangs.[5]

Christ bears many other names of office as well. He is the Mediator (1 Tim. 2:5; Heb. 9:15), God's Servant (Isa. 42:1; 53:11), and the Savior (Luke 2:11). He is the last Adam (1 Cor. 15:45), the Son of Abraham, and the Son of David (Matt. 1:1). He is the Word (John 1:1), the Truth (14:6), the Image of God (Col. 1:15), and the Faithful Witness (Rev. 1:5). He is the Light (John 8:12) and the Sun of Righteousness (Mal. 4:2). He is the Advocate (1 John 2:1), the Forerunner (Heb. 6:20), and the Surety of the covenant (7:22). He is the Lamb of God (John 1:29). He is the Temple (John 2:19–21) and the Cornerstone (Isa. 28:16). He is the Door (John 10:7–10) and the Way (14:6). He is the Son of Man (Dan. 7:13–14). He is the Head (Eph. 1:22; 4:15). He is the Prince of Life (Acts 3:15) and the Captain of Salvation (Heb. 2:10). He is the Life (John 14:6), the Bread of Life (6:35), and the Resurrection and the Life (11:25). He is the Bridegroom of his church (Matt. 9:15). He is the Judge of all mankind (Acts 10:42). He is the Vine (John 15:1–8). He is the Wonderful Counselor, the Mighty God, the Everlasting Father, and the Prince of Peace (Isa. 9:6–7). He is the Good Shepherd (John 10:11).

Christ also bears the names of deity.[6] He is the Son of God (Mark 1:1). He is not just one of God's adopted children. He is the only begotten Son

4 The Heidelberg Catechism (LD 11, Q. 29), in *TFU*, 77.

5 The Heidelberg Catechism (LD 12, Q. 31), in *TFU*, 78.

6 On the names of deity given to Christ, see the third argument that the Son of God is God in chap. 19.

(John 3:16). He is the Son with the power to control creation (Matt. 4:3; 14:33). He has a unique relationship to the Father (11:27).

Indeed, Christ is God (John 1:1; 20:28). He is Immanuel (Isa. 7:14), which means "God with us" (Matt. 1:23). He is the eternal "I AM" (John 8:58). Christ is the alpha and omega, the beginning and the end, the first and the last (Rev. 22:13).

Jesus is the Lord. He is the Lord of glory (1 Cor. 2:8), the Lord of lords (1 Tim. 6:15; Rev. 17:14; 19:16), and the Lord of all (Acts 10:36). "LORD" is the term used to translate the name Jehovah (*YHWH*) in the Old Testament. The New Testament quotes Old Testament statements about Jehovah and applies them to Jesus as "Lord." Jesus is Jehovah.[7]

After such an overwhelming list of names, it is not surprising to read that Christ is our all (Col. 3:11). He is the fullness of God's grace and glory given to fill all the needs of all God's people from all nations for all eternity (John 1:14; Col. 2:9–10).

A Basic Approach to the Doctrine of Christ

Given the riches of what the Bible says about Christ, how can we organize our approach to this doctrine? Paul gives us a model in Philippians 2:6–11.

First, Paul writes of *Christ's deity*. He, "being in the form of God, thought it not robbery to be equal with God" (Phil. 2:6). The Greek word translated as "form" refers to something's distinctive appearance, character, or nature. "The form of God" in this context means "true divine nature" in contrast to "human nature."[8] For Christ to exist in the form of God means that he possesses "the whole fullness of attributes which make God God," as B. B. Warfield said.[9] But Christ did not regard his equality with God as "robbery" (v. 6). That means that the Son regarded his nature as God not as something to selfishly exploit but as an opportunity to give. Similarly, we should view our goods and abilities not as something to exploit for selfish reasons but as resources with which to serve others.

7 Rom. 10:9, 13; 14:9–12; Phil. 2:10–11; 2 Thess. 1:8–9; Heb. 1:10–12.

8 Moisés Silva, *Philippians*, 2nd ed., Baker Exegetical Commentary on the New Testament (Grand Rapids, MI: Baker Academic, 2005), 101.

9 Benjamin B. Warfield, "The Person of Christ according to the New Testament," in *The Person and Work of Christ*, ed. Samuel G. Craig (Philadelphia: Presbyterian and Reformed, 1950), 39.

Second, Paul writes of *Christ's humanity.* Christ "made himself of no reputation, and took upon him the form of a servant, and was made in the likeness of men" (Phil. 2:7). The Greek verb translated as "made . . . of no reputation" does not imply that Christ stripped himself of the attributes of God. Rather, he "took" to himself a human nature that was weak and mortal. Christians call this the *incarnation*, which means that the Son of God became a man: "The Word became flesh" (John 1:14 ESV). Christ's incarnation did not subtract from his divine nature but added his human nature. If the Lord Christ was willing to become what we are, we should be willing to be what we already are—God's servants who exist to do his will.

Third, Paul writes of *Christ's states of humiliation and exaltation.* "And being found in fashion as a man, he humbled himself. . . . Wherefore God also hath highly exalted him" (Phil. 2:8–9). Christ chose to take a position lower than others that he might serve them, just as we should (vv. 3–4). This self-humbling led to his death on the cross. God then made Christ the Most High over all creation (cf. Ps. 97:9). By the Father's decree, all people will confess that Jesus is Lord. Paul applies to Christ what Isaiah wrote about Jehovah, the only God (Isa. 45:22–23). In Christ's state of exaltation, the person who has always been God is honored as God, though he is now also a man. Christians should set their minds on Christ seated at God's right hand in glory (Col. 3:1–2). Wilhelmus à Brakel said, "That is the beginning of heaven, where the beholding of Christ in His glory will be the eternal joy and occupation of the elect."[10]

Fourth, Paul writes of *Christ's work as the Mediator* in those two states. We saw that the titles "servant" and "Lord" reveal Christ's humanity and deity. But these words also highlight his work as the Mediator. Key leaders under God's covenants were called the Lord's servants (Gen. 26:24; Josh. 1:2; 24:29; 2 Sam. 7:5). Christ is God's great "servant" (Isa. 49:3–8). At the heart of Christ's work is his obedience, even to the point of suffering God's curse on the cross (Phil. 2:8). God the Father blessed his obedient Son by greatly honoring him (v. 9). This was also for our sake, that we might be lifted from humiliation to glory (3:21). As "Lord," Christ still serves as the Mediator to save God's people and punish his enemies (Psalm 110; Acts 2:32–36). Christ's work as Lord results in "the glory of God the Father" (Phil. 2:11).

10 Brakel, *CRS*, 1:653.

Paul lays out a beautiful model for the doctrine of Christ's person and work. It begins with Christ's deity. We have already studied that glorious topic under the doctrine of the Trinity (chap. 19). What remains for us is to study Christ's incarnation as a man, his two states of humiliation and exaltation, and his work as the Mediator. These will be the topics of the next several chapters.

The Spiritual Dynamics of the Doctrine of Christ

We rightly know the Lord Jesus Christ only when we trust, submit to, and adore him. Therefore, the study of Christ is a spiritual exercise. Paul makes that clear in 2 Corinthians 3–4.

We need the Holy Spirit. Without the Spirit, our hearts are hardened against the gospel (2 Cor. 3:14–16). But "where the Spirit of the Lord is, there is liberty" (v. 17), for "with the Spirit of the living God," Christ writes the word on the heart (v. 3).

By the Spirit, Christ's glory transforms us. Paul says, "We all, with unveiled face, beholding the glory of the Lord, are being transformed into the same image from one degree of glory to another. For this comes from the Lord who is the Spirit" (2 Cor. 3:18 ESV). What we see in the gospel is "glory"—not just truth but also true majesty and splendid beauty in Jesus Christ, the very "glory of God" (4:6). As a result, we experience a process of transformation into "glory," sanctification into the image of God by conformity to Christ (v. 4).

God performs this transforming work by the plain teaching of the truth. His revelation of his glory in the gospel strikes a deathblow to all lies and manipulations that people may use to promote themselves and their parties. Instead, "by manifestation of the truth" the faithful servants of God can declare, "[We are] commending ourselves to every man's conscience in the sight of God" (2 Cor. 4:2).

Satan resists the truth by blinding unbelievers. The gospel is "hid to them that are lost" because "the god of this world hath blinded the minds of them that believe not" (2 Cor. 4:3–4). Specifically, Satan blinds unbelievers to "the light of the gospel of the glory of Christ" (v. 4 ESV). The gospel does not evoke their trust, love, and worship.

Preachers and teachers of Christ's glory must deny their lust for glory. Paul says, "For we preach not ourselves, but Christ Jesus the Lord; and ourselves your servants for Jesus' sake" (2 Cor. 4:5). We must put to death our selfishness that screams for recognition.

God makes Christ's glory to shine in our hearts. That is why knowing Christ honors God, not the preacher or teacher. Paul says, "For God, who commanded the light to shine out of darkness, hath shined in our hearts, to give the light of the knowledge of the glory of God in the face of Jesus Christ" (2 Cor. 4:6). When God created the world, he said, "Let there be light: and there was light" (Gen. 1:3). In the same way, Owen wrote, "the act of God working faith in us is a creating act: 'We are his workmanship, created in Christ Jesus' (Eph. 2:10)."[11]

The servants of Christ are just "earthen vessels, that the excellency of the power may be of God, and not of us" (2 Cor. 4:7). God has chosen to keep Christ's glory not in treasure chests but in easily broken clay jars. People can see our weakness and distress. They then see that the gospel's glory comes from no mere man but from God (vv. 8–14). Take heart, dear believer, as you grieve over your sins and suffer in the world. Your tears will water the seed of this doctrine so that it bears much fruit.

Suggested Songs to Sing to the Lord

- Psalm 27, "Jehovah is my light," *Psalter*, No. 71
- "Join all the glorious names," *Trinity Psalter Hymnal* (Willow Grove, PA: OPC and URCNA, 2018), No. 377

Questions for Meditation or Discussion

1. What is the value of studying the doctrine of Christ?
2. What do the following names mean: (1) Jesus, (2) Christ, (3) Son of God, (4) the Lord?
3. Of the other names of Christ, what is one that is especially meaningful to you? Why?
4. What model for approaching the doctrine of Christ can we learn from Philippians 2:6–11?
5. What does the word *incarnation* mean?
6. Why do we need the work of the Holy Spirit to know Christ?
7. How is the knowledge of Christ a transforming sight?
8. How are the teachers of the doctrine of Christ like jars of clay? How does this glorify God?

11 Owen, *Discourse Concerning the Holy Spirit*, in *WJO*, 3:321.

43

Christ's Incarnation, Part 1: The Bible's Basic Teaching

Chapter Summary and Key Terms

The *incarnation* of the Son of God is his taking of a human nature, body and soul, to himself. The incarnation resulted in one person having two natures, the divine nature and a human nature. The *virgin birth* of Jesus took place after his miraculous conception in the womb of the virgin Mary without the involvement of a physical father. Christ's human nature was formed from Mary's body without sexual intercourse by the power of the Holy Spirit. This joining of the divine nature and a human nature in one person is called the *hypostatic union*. The two natures are united in a way that preserves their distinct attributes. Christ is fully God and truly man, not a hybrid or demigod. As a man, Christ has experienced suffering, fatigue, limitation, and change. Jesus is sinless before the Father, filled with the Holy Spirit, and the brother of his people.

FOR THOUSANDS OF YEARS, God's people hung their hope on the promise of a coming Savior. The prophets eagerly received God's promises about Christ and searched them diligently (1 Pet. 1:10–12). When Jesus was born of Mary, believers rejoiced with great joy. Their Savior and Lord had come.

We have already discussed the deity of Christ as God the Son (chap. 19). In this chapter, we will begin to discuss his incarnation. The Heidelberg Catechism says, "God's eternal Son, who is, and continueth true and eternal God, took upon Him the very nature of man, of the flesh and blood of the

Virgin Mary, by the operation of the Holy Ghost; that He might also be the true seed of David, like unto His brethren in all things, sin excepted."[1]

The Incarnation of God the Son

The Gospel of John begins, "In the beginning was the Word, and the Word was with God, and the Word was God. . . . And the Word was made flesh, and dwelt among us, (and we beheld his glory, the glory as of the only begotten of the Father,) full of grace and truth" (John 1:1, 14). With these words, John introduces a person who is both God and human.

The Word became "flesh" (John 1:14). This term can refer to the human body (6:54), but more generally it refers to humanity (17:2). "Flesh" communicates man's "frail and perishing nature."[2] John's statement that God became flesh is surprising, even shocking. Yet John insists in his epistles that we must believe that "Jesus Christ is come in the flesh" (1 John 4:2–3; 2 John 7).

John also says the Word "dwelt among us"—literally "made his tabernacle" or "pitched his tent" among us—in his "glory" (John 1:14). This tells us that Christ is the true tabernacle where God's glory dwells with his people (Ex. 40:34–35).

Christ is the God-man. Augustine said, "God's Son, assuming humanity without destroying His divinity, established and founded this faith, that there might be a way for man to man's God through a God-man."[3] If we want to receive Christ and become children of God (John 1:12), we must receive Christ for who he is—the Word become flesh (v. 14).

The Virgin Birth of Christ

The Lord said, "Behold, a virgin shall conceive, and bear a son, and shall call his name Immanuel" (Isa. 7:14). "Immanuel" means "God with us." The word translated as "virgin" refers to a young woman who is not married. In ancient Israel, such a woman presumably would not have been sexually active. The same word is used of Rebekah (Gen. 24:43) when she was a young woman of marriageable age but had never had sexual relations with a man (v. 16).

1 The Heidelberg Catechism (LD 14, Q. 35), in *TFU*, 79.

2 Calvin, *Comm.* on John 1:14.

3 Augustine, *The City of God*, 11.2, in *NPNF*[1], 2:206.

Centuries after Isaiah wrote his words, the angel Gabriel came to Mary, a "virgin" betrothed to Joseph but not yet married (Luke 1:26–27). The angel said, "Behold, thou shalt conceive in thy womb, and bring forth a son, and shalt call his name JESUS" (v. 31). Jesus is the promised Immanuel (Matt. 1:22–23), conceived "of the Holy Ghost" (vv. 18, 20). Mary was the physical mother of Jesus in his human nature (Luke 1:42–43). But Joseph had no biological relation to Jesus (Matt. 1:25).

The miracle of Christ's virgin birth shows that God saves sinners by his supernatural power. The angel concluded, "With God nothing shall be impossible" (Luke 1:37). J. Gresham Machen said, "The overwhelming majority of those who reject the Virgin Birth reject also the supernatural content of the New Testament. . . . And the question concerning all miracles is simply the question of the acceptance or rejection of the Saviour that the New Testament presents."[4]

Mary believed God's promise (Luke 1:45). But she sought a deeper understanding, asking, "How shall this be, seeing I know not a man?" (v. 34). The angel said, "The Holy Ghost shall come upon thee, and the power of the Highest shall overshadow thee: therefore also that holy thing which shall be born of thee shall be called the Son of God" (v. 35). These words weave together promises rooted in the Old Testament. The Holy Spirit came in Christ to renew creation (Isa. 32:15–17). God's power came down in Jesus like the cloud of glory that came on the tabernacle (Ex. 40:35). The child formed by the Holy Spirit was holy, preserved from original sin (Ps. 51:5). Jesus is "the Son of God," the Lord come as a human child (Luke 2:11).

The virgin birth calls us to submit our minds and hearts to God's Word regardless of how difficult the Word may be to accept. If we cannot believe God about the virgin birth, how can we trust him to save us from hell and raise us from the dead to reign with Christ?

The Two Natures of God the Son Incarnate

Christ is fully God and fully man. Since the beginning of the incarnation, he has been both at the same time: one person existing in two natures. The

4 J. Gresham Machen, *Christianity and Liberalism* (1923; repr., Grand Rapids, MI: Eerdmans, 1992), 108–9.

joining of the divine nature and a human nature in one person is called the *hypostatic union.*

The Holy Scriptures foretold that this unique person was to be both a child and the mighty God (Isa. 9:6). He would be both born in Bethlehem and yet eternal and omnipotent (Mic. 5:2, 4). When he came, he was baptized in a river (Matt. 3:13–15). He experienced hunger and temptation (4:1–2). But he also called men to leave everything to follow him, spoke with absolute authority, and hung men's eternal destinies on whether they obeyed his words (4:19–22; 5:22, 28; 7:24, 26, 29). He slept deeply from fatigue but calmed a storm with a mere word (8:23–27). He suffered and died but is the Son of God (16:16, 21). He rose from the dead with a body that people could touch (28:9). But he has all authority, shares one "name" with the Father and the Spirit, and is present with all his people in all nations at all times (vv. 18–20).

Gregory of Nazianzus said, "What He was He continued to be; what He was not He took to himself."[5] His natures are not mixed, but each retains its own attributes. John Calvin said, "We affirm his divinity so joined and united with his humanity that each retains its distinctive nature unimpaired, and yet these two natures constitute one Christ."[6]

The Need for the Incarnation

Christ's becoming a man must have been necessary for him "to seek and to save that which was lost" (Luke 19:10). Why else would his loving Father have sent him to suffer so much in our flesh?

It is written, "For it became him, for whom are all things, and by whom are all things, in bringing many sons unto glory, to make the captain of their salvation perfect through sufferings" (Heb. 2:10). The verb translated as "became" means to be suitable, proper, or fitting. The passage also says, "Therefore he had to be made like his brothers in every respect, so that he might become a merciful and faithful high priest" (v. 17 ESV). The verb translated as "he had to" ("behoved" KJV) means to owe a debt or be under obligation. The priestly work of sacrifice and intercession required that God's Son become a flesh-and-blood man.

5 Gregory of Nazianzus, *Third Theological Oration: On the Son*, sec. 19, in *NPNF*[2], 7:308.

6 Calvin, *Institutes*, 2.14.1.

Only the God-man can rescue sinners from God's wrath. Satisfaction of God's justice is necessary for salvation. Anselm of Canterbury said, "No one save God can make it, and no one save man ought to make it, [so] it is necessary for a God-Man to make it."[7]

Francis Turretin said that the Mediator must be "God-man . . . man to suffer, God to overcome; man to receive the punishment we deserved, God to endure and drink it to the dregs; man to acquire salvation for us by dying, God to apply it to us by overcoming; man to become ours by the assumption of flesh, God to make us like himself by the bestowal of the Spirit."[8]

God did not need to send his Son. Saving sinners was God's free choice. But to save sinners, God the Son had to become a man. God's own justice demanded it. This is one of our greatest causes to praise the Lord, for we need nothing as much as we need Jesus.

The True Humanity of God the Son Incarnate

While remaining fully God, the Son became truly "man" (Rom. 5:15; 1 Tim. 2:5). He is human in body and soul.

Christ's Human Body

Christ has a real human body. He has a head, hands, and feet (Matt. 8:3, 20; 15:30). He slept, spat, and wept (Mark 4:38; 7:33; Luke 19:41). Jesus is not a spirit that merely appears human. He has flesh and bones that can be grasped and felt (Luke 24:39).

His body is in one place at a time. We read of Jesus "walking by the sea of Galilee" and "walking in the temple" (Matt. 4:18; Mark 11:27). After he rose from the dead, the angel announced at his tomb, "He is not here" (Matt. 28:6).

The body of Jesus was susceptible to pain and death during his state of humiliation. He felt hunger (Matt. 4:2; 21:18) and thirst (John 19:28). He could be struck and injured (Matt. 27:26, 29–30). He died on the cross (Mark 15:37). Only after his resurrection is it said that "Christ being raised

7 Anselm, *Why God Became Man*, 2.6, in *A Scholastic Miscellany: Anselm to Ockham*, ed. Eugene R. Fairweather, Library of Christian Classics, Ichthus Edition (Philadelphia: Westminster, 1956), 151.

8 Francis Turretin, *Institutes of Elenctic Theology*, trans. George Musgrave Giger, ed. James T. Dennison Jr., 3 vols. (Phillipsburg, NJ: P&R, 1992–1997), 13.3.19 (2:302–3).

from the dead dieth no more; death hath no more dominion over him" (Rom. 6:9).

When we survey the Bible's teaching on Christ's human body, it is striking how ordinary Jesus was among men. His neighbors scoffed, "Is not this the carpenter, the son of Mary?" (Mark 6:3). It is only now, in his state of exaltation, that Christ's human body is "glorious" (Phil. 3:21).

Christ's Human Spirit

Christ's humanity includes a fully human "spirit" or "soul" (Mark 2:8; John 12:27). The incarnate Son has *a limited human mind.* As a child, he "increased in wisdom" over time (Luke 2:52). As a man, he did not know everything. He said, "Of that day and that hour [when he will return] knoweth no man, no, not the angels which are in heaven, neither the Son, but the Father" (Mark 13:32). Athanasius of Alexandria explained that Christ said this not about his knowledge as the Word but about his human knowledge.[9] As God, he knows all things. As man, his knowledge is limited.

Jesus has *changeable human emotions.* He was sometimes angry and grieved (Mark 3:5). He rejoiced (Luke 10:21). He marveled (Matt. 8:10; Mark 6:6). He had compassion on people (Mark 6:34). In the garden of Gethsemane, he said, "My soul is exceeding sorrowful, even unto death" (Matt. 26:38). On the cross, he felt the horror of being forsaken by God (27:46). In his exaltation, he exchanged his sorrows for the fullness of joy (Pss. 16:11; 45:7).

Christ has *a freely choosing human will.* Jesus exercised his power and mercy willingly (Matt. 8:3; 15:32). He chose his apostles (Mark 3:13). His human will is distinct from the divine will, yet fully submitted to it. He said, "I seek not mine own will, but the will of the Father which hath sent me" (John 5:30). He prayed, "Not my will, but thine, be done" (Luke 22:42).

The incarnate Son of God offers to God his *faithful human worship.* Jesus was often in prayer (Luke 5:16; 6:12). He addressed God not only as "my Father" but also as "my God" (Mark 15:34; John 20:17). He praises God and leads his people to do the same (Heb. 2:12).

As a man in the state of humiliation, Jesus had *vulnerable human relationships.* In his greatest trial, he asked his three closest friends to stay up with him and was disappointed when they fell asleep (Matt. 26:38, 40). It was

9 Athanasius, *Against the Arians*, 3.28.43, 45, in *NPNF*², 4:417–18.

foretold of his passion, "Reproach hath broken my heart; and I am full of heaviness: and I looked for some to take pity, but there was none; and for comforters, but I found none" (Ps. 69:20).

We conclude that "in all things" Christ became "like unto his brethren" (Heb. 2:17). The only exception is that he alone is "without sin" (4:15). He is the last Adam (1 Cor. 15:45). His assumption of the entire human nature was necessary for our entire salvation. Gregory of Nazianzus said, "For that which He has not assumed He has not healed."[10]

The love of Christ should amaze us. As God the Son, he has never experienced the least pain, shame, or grief, but dwells in infinite glory and joy. Every spark of sorrow that touched him was something he willingly embraced by becoming one of us. He did it all for our salvation.

The Relationships of God the Son Incarnate

The Son of God enjoys unique divine relations to the Father and the Holy Spirit in the eternal Trinity. In taking to himself a human nature, God the Son has also taken to himself a new set of relationships to the Father, the Holy Spirit, and God's people.

Christ is *sinless before God the Father*. Jesus is the man perfectly obedient to all of God's commandments. He has been "holy" from his conception (Luke 1:35; Acts 3:14). Christ is God's delightful Son and righteous Servant (Isa. 42:1; 53:11; Mark 1:11). Jesus could make the astounding claim, "I do always those things that please him" (John 8:29).

Though absolutely pure from the beginning, Christ's human holiness developed (Luke 2:52). His temptations were real and painful (Heb. 2:18), but though he was tempted, he is "without sin" (4:15). John Murray said, "He came into the closest relation to sinful humanity that it was possible for him to come without thereby becoming himself sinful."[11] An athlete, though already in good health, develops his strength and skill through strenuous exercise and practice. Thus, it is said of Jesus that "though he were a Son, yet learned he obedience by the things which he suffered" (5:8). Now exalted to heaven, he is "holy, harmless, undefiled, separate from sinners" (7:26).

10 Gregory of Nazianzus, *Epistles*, no. 101, in *NPNF*[2], 7:440.

11 John Murray, *Collected Writings of John Murray*, 4 vols. (Edinburgh: Banner of Truth, 1982), 2:133.

Christ is *filled with the Holy Spirit.* The Spirit of God formed Christ's humanity at his conception (Matt. 1:18, 20; Luke 1:35). The Spirit came upon him at his baptism (Luke 3:22). The Spirit filled him to face Satan's temptations and to preach the word (4:1, 14, 18). With his exaltation to God's right hand, Christ received an even greater filling so that he could pour out the Spirit on all his people (Acts 2:17–18, 33). The Holy Spirit fills Christians because he first filled Christ. We receive the Spirit "through Jesus Christ" (Titus 3:5–6).

Christ has a *brotherly relationship with God's people.* He calls his disciples "my brethren" (Matt. 28:10; John 20:17; Heb. 2:11–12). Christ truly has entered human experience (Heb. 4:15). He understands us. B. B. Warfield said, "It was not merely the mind of a man that was in him, but the heart of a man as well."[12] God the Son bound himself to his people forever by entering their world and taking their very nature to himself. A closer union of man to God is inconceivable.

Suggested Songs to Sing to the Lord

- Psalm 69 (messianic), "Save me, O God, because the floods," *Psalter*, No. 184
- "Hark the herald angels sing," *THBap*, No. 168

Questions for Meditation or Discussion

1. What does John 1:14 mean when it says that "the Word was made flesh"?
2. What does it mean to say that Jesus Christ is the God-man?
3. What does the Bible teach about Christ's virgin birth?
4. How does the Bible show that Christ is one person with two natures?
5. How does the Bible show that Christ has a real human body?
6. How do the Holy Scriptures indicate that Christ has a limited human mind?
7. What are some human emotions ascribed to Jesus Christ? List Scripture references.

12 Benjamin B. Warfield, *Selected Shorter Writings*, ed. John E. Meeter (Nutley, NJ: Presbyterian and Reformed, 1970), 1:161.

8. What did Christ show us about himself when he prayed, "Not my will, but thine be done" (Luke 22:42)?
9. What evidence do we have in the Scriptures that Christ is righteous and sinless?
10. How is it encouraging to know that Christ counts God's people as his brothers and sisters?

44

Christ's Incarnation, Part 2: History and Theology

Chapter Summary and Key Terms

The church has needed to defend the doctrine of Christ's person against many errors. First, there are errors about Christ's relation to the Father:

- The Father and Christ are two gods (a form of *polytheism*).
- The Father and Christ are the same person (*Sabellianism*).

Second, there are errors about Christ's deity and humanity:

- Jesus was a mere man (according to *Judaism*, *Islam*, and *theological liberalism*).
- Jesus was a god or spirit that only appeared human (*docetism*).
- Jesus was a mere man anointed with the Christ-Spirit (some forms of *Gnosticism*).
- Jesus was a mere man adopted and glorified by the Father (*adoptionism*).
- Christ is the Son created by the Father, not the eternal God (*Arianism*).
- Christ is two persons, one God and the other man (*Nestorianism*).
- Christ is one person with one divine-human nature (*Eutychianism* or *monophysitism*).

Third, there are errors about Christ's body and soul:

- Christ's body was from heaven (some forms of Gnosticism and *Anabaptism*).
- Christ's soul was the divine Word (*Apollinarianism*).
- Christ had only a divine will but no human will (*monothelitism*).

Against these errors, the early councils of the church confessed that the Son of God is "of one substance (*homoousion*) with the Father" and has two natures, divine and human, joined in one person without confusion, change, or separation. The incarnation also does not mean that Christ emptied himself of his divine attributes during his humiliation (*kenosis theory*). Even then, Christ was fully God, though his glory was largely hidden. Therefore, we should glorify God the Son because he was willing to become a man for our salvation. We should trust in his almighty power to save us, rejoice that he is our brother who understands us, and imitate his human holiness.

THE DOCTRINE OF THE INCARNATION developed through history with the doctrine of the Trinity. During the centuries after the apostles died, the church passed through a series of controversies that forced it to consider who Jesus Christ is. In this furnace of controversy, the Holy Spirit forged the orthodox confession of Christ's person based on God's Word.

The church fathers understood that our salvation rests on Christ. If we slip on the doctrine of the person of Christ, we slide away from the gospel. God the Father has designed all things for his Son. We glorify Christ when we believe in him as he truly is.

In this chapter, we will consider how the church's understanding of the doctrine of Christ developed in history, answer some theological questions, and make practical applications.

Errors about Christ Faced by the Church

Even in the first century, Paul needed to warn against preachers of "another Jesus" (2 Cor. 11:4). John said, "Whosoever denieth the Son, the same hath not the Father" (1 John 2:23). Not surprisingly, the early church confronted various false teachings about Christ. We list twelve errors here.

The first two errors have to do with Christ's person in relation to the Father.

Error 1. *Christ is another god than the Father.* This is polytheism (belief in many gods) or tritheism (the idea that the Trinity is three gods). This was an ancient heresy among the Gnostics and has reappeared in Mormonism. But there is only one God (Deut. 4:39). The Father and the Son are one in essence and power (John 10:28–30).

Error 2. *Christ is the same person as God the Father.* This is modalism or *Sabellianism* (chap. 20). But the Father and the Son speak to each other as distinct persons (Matt. 3:17; 14:23). The Father did not die on the cross, but the Son did out of obedience to the Father (Phil. 2:8).

The next several errors have to do with the deity and humanity of Christ's person.

Error 3. *Christ is one person, merely a man.* This is taught by Judaism and Islam, as well as in theological liberalism. But Christ is God (John 1:1). He is the Judge of the living and the dead (2 Tim. 4:1). He will be glorified by all angels and people as Lord over all (Phil. 2:9–11).

Error 4. *Christ is one divine person, but not human.* This is called *docetism*, the idea that Jesus only appeared to be human. But Christ is truly a man (1 Tim. 2:5). He was born of a woman, ate and drank, and suffered and died. He is the God-man.

Error 5. *The human Jesus and the divine Christ are two persons.* The Christ supposedly came upon the man Jesus and left him before he was crucified. This is a form of *Gnosticism*. But Christ "has come in the flesh" (1 John 4:2 ESV) and "died for our sins" (1 Cor. 15:3).

Error 6. *Christ is one person, a man adopted and glorified by God.* This is called *adoptionism*. But Christ already existed at the beginning of time (John 1:1). He is "the Word" who "was made flesh, and dwelt among us" (v. 14). He is the eternal "I am" (8:58).

Error 7. *Christ is one person, the supernatural Son created by the Father.* This is called Arianism and is taught by the Jehovah's Witnesses today. But God's names, attributes, and actions belong to Christ (Heb. 1:10–12). He is God (chap. 19.)

Error 8. *Jesus and the Son are two persons, one a man and the other God.* This is called *Nestorianism*. But Christ is one person addressed with the singular, personal "thou" (Mark 1:11). Thomas addressed the man with nail-scarred hands as "my Lord and my God" (John 20:25–28).

Error 9. *Christ is one person with one divine-human nature.* This is called *Eutychianism* or *monophysitism*. It dissolves Christ's humanity into his deity, so that even his human nature has become divine. But Christ has a distinct human nature (Luke 2:52). He obeyed God as a man in our place and conquered sin for our sake.

The last three errors concern Christ's human body and soul.

Error 10. *Christ's body was not earthly but from heaven.* This is another teaching of Gnosticism that reappeared in some forms of *Anabaptism*. But Jesus is a descendant of David through his mother (Luke 1:27, 31–32). Thus, his humanity is the fruit of the womb of Mary, who was truly his mother according to his human nature (vv. 42–43).

Error 11. *Christ has no human soul but is the divine Word in a body.* This is called *Apollinarianism*. But Christ has a human soul (John 12:27). He was tempted (Heb. 4:15). He had a truly human experience of life in his thoughts, emotions, and will (see chap. 43).

Error 12. *Christ is God and man in one person but has no human will.* This is *monothelitism*. But Christ has a human will that he submitted to the divine will (Luke 22:42). He did not seek his own human will, but the will of the Father who sent him (John 5:30).

The Great Councils on the Doctrine of Christ

Confronted by this swarm of errors, how did the early church respond? Church leaders dug deeply into the Holy Scriptures. They wrestled with how to express the Bible's teaching about Jesus Christ. They also gathered in councils to hammer out confessions of faith.

The Council of Nicaea (AD 325) confessed, "The Son of God, the only-begotten of his Father, of the substance of the Father, God of God, Light of Light, very God of very God, begotten, not made, being of one substance (*homoousion*) with the Father." The word *homoousion* means that the Father and the Son share the same divine nature. The council condemned the Arian teaching (error 7) that "there was a time when the Son of God was not."[1]

1 The Creed of Nicaea, in *NPNF*², 14:3.

The Council of Constantinople (AD 381) condemned as heresy both Sabellianism (error 2) and Apollinarianism (error 11).[2] The council affirmed that the Father and the Son are two distinct persons, and that the Son took to himself a human body and a human soul while remaining God in one substance with the Father.

The Council of Ephesus (AD 431) condemned Nestorianism (error 8). The council affirmed that Christ is one person, though both divine and human.

The Council of Chalcedon (AD 451) rejected Eutychianism (error 9). This council stated,

> Jesus Christ, the only-begotten Son must be confessed to be in two natures, unconfusedly, immutably, indivisibly, inseparably, and that without the distinction of natures being taken away by such union, but rather the peculiar property of each nature being preserved and being united in one person and subsistence, not separated or divided into two persons, but one and the same Son.[3]

Jesus Christ shares in the divine nature and has a human nature in a manner that does not change God into man or man into God, but allows him to work as the God-man for our salvation.

In a later Council of Constantinople (AD 680–681), church leaders rejected monothelitism (error 12), declaring that Christ has two wills just as he has two natures, though his human will always follows his divine will in wholehearted submission.

The statements of these councils about Christ have defined true Christianity, including Reformed Christianity. For example, the Westminster Confession of Faith states,

> The Son of God, the second person in the Trinity, being very and eternal God, of one substance and equal with the Father, did, when the fulness of time was come, take upon Him man's nature, with all the essential properties, and common infirmities thereof, yet without sin; being conceived

2 The Canons of the First Council of Constantinople, canon 1, in *NPNF*[2], 14:172.

3 The Acts of the Council of Chalcedon, in *NPNF*[2], 14:264–65.

> by the power of the Holy Ghost, in the womb of the virgin Mary, of her substance. So that two whole, perfect, and distinct natures, the Godhead and the manhood, were inseparably joined together in one person, without conversion, composition, or confusion. Which person is very God, and very man, yet one Christ, the only Mediator between God and man.[4]

John Owen said of Christ's incarnation, "This is the glory of the Christian religion—the basis and foundation that bears the whole superstructure—the root whereon it grows. This is its life and soul."[5] The great works of salvation could never have succeeded if they had not come through God the Son incarnate. Owen added, "The faith of this mystery ennobles the mind wherein it is—rendering it spiritual and heavenly, transforming it into the image of God."[6] Therefore, rest your faith in Immanuel, striving to know him ever better in the mystery of his incarnation.

Theological Questions about the Incarnation

The doctrine of the incarnation is a great mystery known only by faith in God's Word. Yet faith seeks a deeper understanding that it may offer higher praise to God. Thus, we will consider two common theological questions about the incarnation of Christ.

Is the Doctrine of the Incarnation Illogical?

Someone might object that one person with one life cannot have two natures or that one person cannot be both infinite and finite.

In response, we acknowledge that the incarnation is beyond our understanding. God and his ways are incomprehensible to us (Ps. 145:3). But there is no logical contradiction in the orthodox doctrine of the person of Christ. This doctrine does not teach that the one person of Christ has one life, but that he has a divine life and a human life. It would be a contradiction to say that Christ is both infinite and finite in the same respect. But the orthodox doctrine is that Christ is infinite in his divine nature and finite in his human nature.

4 The Westminster Confession of Faith (8.2), in *RC*, 4:244. Cf. the Second London Baptist Confession (8.2), in *RC*, 4:542.

5 Owen, *Christologia*, in *WJO*, 1:48.

6 Owen, *Christologia*, in *WJO*, 1:50.

The confessions of Nicaea and Chalcedon remain the best way to express this mystery. Herman Bavinck said,

> Whatever the objections that have been advanced in earlier and later times against the two-natures doctrine, it has the advantage that it does not neglect any of the scriptural data, maintains the name of Christ as the only mediator between God and humankind, and in addition still offers the plainest and clearest understanding of the mystery of the incarnation.[7]

Did Christ Set Aside His Divine Attributes?

According to the theory of "kenosis," Christ "emptied himself" of some of his divine attributes when he became a man (Phil. 2:7 ESV). He supposedly took up those attributes again when he rose again to glory. Christ's kenosis was his temporary limitation of himself.

But this theory is not based on what the Bible says about Christ or God. The verb translated as "emptied himself" is best understood by the next phrase, "taking the form of a servant" (Phil. 2:7 ESV). He emptied himself not by subtracting his divine nature but by adding a human nature. Christ was fully God during his state of humiliation. He had divine knowledge of the Father (Matt. 11:27) and sovereignty over his own life (John 10:17–18). If Christ has ever been God, he must always be God in all the divine attributes, for God cannot change (Ps. 102:25–27). The very words of that psalm are applied to Christ in Hebrews 1:10–12.

Rather than saying that God the Son emptied or limited himself in the incarnation, it is better to say that his glory was mostly hidden during his humiliation (Isa. 49:2; 53:1–3). The Word became flesh and was present with us (John 1:14). His glory was manifest to those who had the faith to see it. But most people, even in Israel, did not know or receive him (vv. 10–11).

The Glory of the Mystery of the Incarnation

When we consider these questions, we realize how precious it is to have a Mediator who is God and man. B. B. Warfield said,

7 Bavinck, *RD*, 3:304.

> The glory of the Incarnation is that it presents to our adoring gaze, not a humanized God or a deified man, but a true God-man—one who is all that God is and at the same time all that man is: on whose almighty arm we can rest, and to whose human sympathy we can appeal. We cannot afford to lose either the God in the man or the man in the God; our hearts cry out for the complete God-man whom the Scriptures offer us.[8]

Practical Applications of the Incarnation

The incarnation of Christ is an unrepeatable event, just as surely as the incarnate Lord is a unique person. But the incarnation has great practical applications for life. In light of it, we should do the following.

First, *seek after Christ through the gospel.* Thomas Watson said, "So look unto him, as to believe in him, that so Christ may not only be united to our nature, but to our persons."[9]

Second, *receive Christ as the only Mediator.* Thomas Goodwin urged, "Is Christ every way so fit a Saviour? Then choose him, and rest in him alone."[10]

Third, *magnify God's love for giving us his Son.* Goodwin said, "For him to be made a creature is more than for us to become nothing, or for an angel to become a worm."[11]

Fourth, *marvel at Christ as the supernatural Savior.* Christ is a living miracle, God's glory in human form. Owen said that Christ's incarnation "is above all miracles."[12]

Fifth, *look to Christ to reveal God's glory to you.* The Word became flesh (John 1:14). Thus, as James Ussher said, Christ is "God revealed in the flesh."[13]

Sixth, *know Christ as your elder brother.* Christ "is not ashamed to call them brethren" (Heb. 2:11). Wilhelmus à Brakel said, "This yields boldness and familiarity to bring all our needs before Him, who, being man Himself, understands man's frame of mind when he suffers pain."[14]

8 Benjamin B. Warfield, *Selected Shorter Writings*, ed. John E. Meeter (Nutley, NJ: Presbyterian and Reformed, 1970), 1:166.

9 Thomas Watson, *A Body of Divinity* (Edinburgh: Banner of Truth, 1965), 165.

10 Goodwin, *Of Christ the Mediator*, in *WTG*, 5:63.

11 Goodwin, *Of Christ the Mediator*, in *WTG*, 5:65.

12 Owen, *Christologia*, in *WJO*, 1:45–46.

13 James Ussher, *A Body of Divinity: Being the Sum and Substance of the Christian Religion*, intro. Crawford Gribben (Birmingham, AL: Solid Ground, 2007), 12th head (147).

14 Brakel, *CRS*, 1:516.

Seventh, *follow Christ in holiness*. Goodwin said, "As he took our nature, let us take his; [let us labor] to be changed into his image, being made partakers of the divine nature [2 Pet. 1:4]."[15]

Eighth, *imitate Christ in humility*. William Perkins said, "Christ's incarnation must be a pattern unto us of a most wonderful and strange humility. . . . He was content to lie in the manger, that we might rest in heaven."[16] We should also humble ourselves to serve others.

Ninth, *defend the doctrine of Christ against errors*. Caspar Olevianus said, "Satan has always tried . . . to deny or at least to weaken one of the natures in the Mediator of the covenant. When the root of a tree is damaged, the branches wither and there can be no hope for fruit."[17]

Tenth, *glorify the incarnate Son*. Herman Witsius said,

> Hosanna, blessed Jesus, thou true and eternal God, thou true and holy man! In the unity of thy person, we recognize both natures, each possessing its own distinct properties. Thee we acknowledge. Thee we worship. From thy hand alone we expect salvation. May the whole world of thine elect unite in knowing, acknowledging, and adoring thee, and thus be saved through thy blessed name! Amen.[18]

Suggested Songs to Sing to the Lord

- "O come, all ye faithful" (the song quotes the Nicene Creed), *THBap*, No. 151
- Psalm 40 (messianic psalm), "The off'ring on the altar burned," *Psalter*, No. 109

Questions for Meditation or Discussion

1. What are two errors about the Son's relationship to the Father?
2. What are the following errors: (1) docetism (error 4), (2) Arianism (error 7), (3) Nestorianism (error 8), (4) Eutychianism (error 9), and (5) Apollinarianism (error 11)?

15 Goodwin, *Of Christ the Mediator*, in *WTG*, 5:66–67.

16 Perkins, *An Exposition of the Symbol*, in *WWP*, 5:122, 132.

17 Caspar Olevianus, *An Exposition of the Apostles' Creed*, trans. Lyle D. Bierma, intro. R. Scott Clark (Grand Rapids, MI: Reformation Heritage Books, 2009), 68.

18 Herman Witsius, *Sacred Dissertations on the Apostles' Creed*, trans. Donald Fraser (1823; repr., Grand Rapids, MI: Reformation Heritage Books, 2010), 14.46 (2:35).

3. What did the Council of Nicaea (AD 325) say about Christ?
4. What did the Council of Chalcedon (AD 451) say about Christ's two natures?
5. Why is the doctrine that the one Christ has two natures not a logical contradiction?
6. What is the kenosis theory? Why is it incorrect?
7. According to B. B. Warfield, what is the glory of the incarnation?
8. Which of the practical applications in this chapter is most helpful to you? Why?

45

Christ's Threefold Office and Two States

Chapter Summary and Key Terms

Christ serves as the one *Mediator* in his *two states* according to the *threefold office* given him by the Father. He is the only Mediator between God and man, which is the *office* he bears in the covenant of grace. Christ's *state of humiliation* lasted from the beginning of his incarnation through his death and burial. His *state of exaltation* began with his *resurrection*, encompasses his *ascension* and *session* (sitting at God's right hand), and will last through his second coming and eternal reign in glory. The threefold office of Christ is his position as *Prophet*, to give his people the knowledge of God and his will; *Priest*, to make reconciliation between them and God; and *King*, to deliver them from their enemies and rule them as citizens of God's kingdom. Therefore, we should look to Christ to meet our every spiritual need, whether it is our ignorance and blindness, our guilt and condemnation, or our enslavement and deadness.

SAUL OF TARSUS traveled to Damascus to arrest Christians. Instead, Jesus Christ arrested Saul. Blinded by Christ's glory, Saul finally saw the truth that his heart had been unable to see. He wasted no time in taking up his new calling as Christ's minister. To everyone's astonishment, "he preached Christ in the synagogues, that he is the Son of God" (Acts 9:20). As Paul would later write, the person and work of Christ are the core of the Christian message (1 Cor. 2:2).

Therefore, having studied the doctrine of Christ's person, we now enter the study of his saving work as our Mediator.

The Office of the One Mediator

Christ's work is so rich that it is difficult to describe it in its fullness. Some people focus too much on just one thing Christ does, such as his teaching, sacrifice, or coming judgment. They become imbalanced and lose sight of the whole. How are we to bring together the various parts of Christ's work? Reformed theology offers a good one-two-three solution: the *one Mediator* performs his incarnate work in *two states* according to his *threefold office*. The Westminster Shorter Catechism says, "Christ, as our Redeemer, executeth the offices of a prophet, of a priest, and of a king, both in his estate of humiliation and exaltation."[1]

The term "office" refers to a special trust or commission laid on a person to perform tasks assigned him by an authority. A mediator is a middleman chosen to establish a good relationship between two parties. Christ bears the office of Mediator to execute the covenant of grace. This office is summed up in the title "the Christ," which means the One anointed by the Holy Spirit to be God's chosen servant. The Christ is the Prophet, Priest, and King of our salvation.

Christ is the only Mediator of saving grace to reunite God and people (1 Tim. 2:5). The Lord Jesus says, "I am the door: by me if any man enter in, he shall be saved" (John 10:9); "I am the way . . . no man cometh unto the Father, but by me" (14:6); and, "I am the vine, ye are the branches . . . without me ye can do nothing" (15:5). Christ is the only person who is both God and man. He alone is qualified to mediate salvation from God to man.

Since Christ is the only Mediator of salvation (1 Tim. 2:5), we should pray for evangelism and missions. Paul says, "I exhort therefore, that, first of all, supplications, prayers, intercessions, and giving of thanks, be made for all men. . . . For this is good and acceptable in the sight of God our Saviour; who will have all men to be saved, and to come unto the knowledge of the truth" (vv. 1, 3–4). We should pray regularly and fervently for the conversion of all kinds of people. We should pray for "kings, and for all that are in

1 The Westminster Shorter Catechism (Q. 23), in *RC*, 4:356. Cf. the Baptist Catechism (Q. 26), in *RC*, 4:576.

authority" (v. 2). And we should participate in the church's prayer meetings. Paul says, "I desire then that in every place the men should pray, lifting holy hands without anger or quarreling" (v. 8 ESV). Doing this shows that we believe that there is only one Mediator and that all people need him.

Christ's Threefold Office

The threefold office of Christ perfectly matches the spiritual needs of sinners. As Prophet, Christ takes away our foolishness and ignorance. As Priest, he takes away our guilt and condemnation. As King, he takes away our corruption and spiritual enslavement.

God revealed Christ's threefold office in the Old Testament. As we saw earlier (chap. 32), God made Adam to be a prophet, priest, and king in the garden of Eden (Gen. 2:15–17). Christ is the last Adam (1 Cor. 15:45).

Christ is the angel, or messenger, of the Lord, who himself is God. That angel is the Lord of the prophets (Ex. 3:1–6; 2 Kings 1:3, 15). He is the Warrior-King who fought for Israel (Ex. 23:20–22; 2 Kings 19:34–35). He is the Priest who intercedes for his people (Zech. 1:12; 3:1–5).

The title "Christ," or "Anointed," links his office to the prophets, priests, and kings of the Old Testament. They served as God's officers in the covenants God made through Moses and David. They were "anointed," whether with oil, the Holy Spirit, or both (Ex. 28:41; 1 Sam. 16:13; 1 Kings 19:16).

The prophets foretold that Christ would fulfill the threefold office. Moses said that God would raise up a "Prophet" like him (Deut. 18:15). God made known to David that his Lord was set apart by divine oath to serve as "priest" forever (Ps. 110:4). The Psalms celebrate God's Son, who would be enthroned as "king" and inherit the nations (2:6–8).

The New Testament says that Christ came in the flesh as his people's Prophet, Priest, and King. Jesus called himself a "prophet" (Luke 4:24; 13:33). The apostles preached that Christ is the great "prophet" foretold by Moses (Acts 3:22–24). Jesus identified Psalm 110 as a prophecy of the Christ (Matt. 22:41–45), which declares that he is "a priest for ever" (Ps. 110:4). At the Last Supper, Christ said that his blood would be "shed for many for the remission of sins" (Matt. 26:28). This is the same thing that the old covenant said about the sin offering presented by its priests (Lev. 4:25–26). The Lord Jesus taught his disciples that "the Son of man shall come in his glory" and sit on his throne, for he is "the King" (Matt. 25:31, 34).

The Heidelberg Catechism summarizes the teaching of the Holy Scriptures:

> Q. Why is He called Christ, that is, anointed?
> A. Because He is ordained of God the Father, and anointed with the Holy Ghost, to be our chief Prophet and Teacher, who has fully revealed to us the secret counsel and will of God concerning our redemption; and to be our only High Priest, who by the one sacrifice of His body, has redeemed us, and makes continual intercession with the Father for us; and also to be our eternal King, who governs us by His Word and Spirit, and who defends and preserves us in (the enjoyment of) that salvation He has purchased for us.[2]

Practical Applications of Christ's Offices

What are the practical applications of Christ's office as Mediator?

First, *since Christ is the one Mediator, you must have Christ to save you.* As John Flavel said, it is utter foolishness to reject Jesus Christ. Since he is the only Mediator between God and man, there is no one else to step in and shield you from the devouring fire and everlasting burning of God's anger. Those who are reconciled to God should give thanks to the Lord Jesus Christ for all the peace, grace, and comfort they have received from God.[3]

Second, *the knowledge of Christ's office brings great joy and peace to his people* (Luke 2:10–14). Jesus came not to do his own will but the will of God. He was chosen, anointed, and sent by God for the great work of redemption (John 5:30; 6:27, 38; 10:36). Christ comes to us as the One fully authorized by the Father to save sinners and bring them to God. Therefore, we have a solid basis to fully trust in him. We can boldly rejoice that salvation and glory belong to us if we belong to him.

Third, *the doctrine of Christ's threefold office encourages us to seek in Christ all we need to live unto God and enjoy him forever.* Richard Sibbes said that by nature we are "ignorant and blind," but "he is a prophet to teach us . . . not only the outward, but the inward man." We are powerless before "the rebellion and sinfulness" of our hearts, but "he is a king to subdue whatsoever is ill in us, and likewise to subdue all opposite power [outside] us."

2 The Heidelberg Catechism (LD 12, Q. 31), in *TFU*, 78.

3 Flavel, *The Fountain of Life*, in *WJF*, 1:114–16.

We are "cursed by reason of our sinful condition, so he is a priest to satisfy the wrath of God for us."[4] In him we find all the fullness of God, and in him we are complete (Col. 2:9–10).

Fourth, *the doctrine of Christ's threefold office greatly enriches preaching.* Preachers are often told that they must preach Christ. This might seem repetitive. They might feel as though they must force Christ on any passage of Scripture they are preaching. But this doctrine opens up a wealth of ways to preach the grace of Christ from various texts of the Bible. For instance, he is not just a sacrificing Priest on earth but also an interceding Priest in heaven. And he is also the Prophet and King.

Fifth, *given the price Christ paid to save us from sin and wrath, we should stand up for him when wicked men attack his holy name and kingdom.* Flavel said that it is better that the wicked would turn their weapons on us than attack the name of our Mediator with no one to vindicate him. Christ is the holy Servant of the Lord, the great office bearer of the covenant. We must be zealous for his honor.[5]

The Two States of the Incarnate Christ

The Mediator performs his threefold office in two states. The Holy Spirit showed the prophets both "the sufferings of Christ, and the glory that should follow" (1 Pet. 1:11). Paul says that Christ "humbled himself . . . [so] God also hath highly exalted him" (Phil. 2:8–9).

Christ is the God-man in both his humiliation and his exaltation. But during his humiliation, his divine glory was mostly hidden (John 12:38). In his state of exaltation, his divine glory shines visibly through his humanity (17:5).

Both states are required for salvation. The state of humiliation was necessary for the accomplishment of salvation. The state of exaltation is necessary for the full application of salvation.

Christ's saving works in his states of humiliation and exaltation were all performed in union with his people. Christ's life on earth, suffering, death, resurrection, and glorification were all done *for* his people, and they died and rose *with* him (Rom. 6:1–14; 1 Pet. 2:24).

4 Sibbes, *A Description of Christ*, in *WRS*, 1:16.

5 Flavel, *The Fountain of Life*, in *WJF*, 1:117–18.

Steps in Christ's State of Humiliation

Christ is God the Son. He could not have suffered any humiliation he did not choose (Matt. 4:3; 26:53; John 10:17–18). Paul says, "He humbled himself" (Phil. 2:8). We may consider Christ's humiliation at various points along his life history as a man.

We see Christ's humiliation in *his relationship to the law*. As God, he is not subject to the law (Matt. 17:24–27), but is rather the Lawgiver (James 4:12). For the sake of his mission, God the Son became man and was "made under the law" (Gal. 4:4). He took on the obligation to keep the whole law of Moses. He also took the obligation to suffer the curse that his lawbreaking people had earned (3:10, 12).

His humiliation is evident in the circumstances of *his birth*. His mother was from Nazareth (Luke 1:26), a town of bad reputation (John 1:46). He was born in Bethlehem, a "little" place (Mic. 5:2). At the time, "there was no room for them in the inn" (Luke 2:7). The infant was laid "in a manger"—a feeding trough for livestock (vv. 7, 12, 16).

His childhood and early adulthood were neither easy nor elegant. Jesus's family took refuge in a foreign land for a time to escape great danger (Matt. 2:13–15). Jesus grew up as the "carpenter's son" (13:55). He took up the same trade (Mark 6:3).

Christ started *his public ministry* when he was "about thirty years of age" (Luke 3:23). He suffered the Devil's temptations, from which he emerged proven as a fully obedient Son (4:1–13). Christ preached, taught, prayed, healed, worked miracles, and trained apostles and evangelists. Men viciously accused him of being a sinner (John 9:16) and deceiver (7:12). He was "a man of sorrows" (Isa. 53:3). He was weary (John 4:6). He wept (11:35). But despite his sufferings, he did his Father's will, which he cherished more than his daily food (4:34; 6:38).

The humiliation of Christ intensified greatly in *his passion and death*. Great anguish seized him in the garden of Gethsemane, but he submitted to his Father's will (Mark 14:32–36). One of the apostles betrayed him with a kiss (vv. 43–45). Another denied that he knew him (vv. 66–72).

False witnesses accused Jesus before the Jewish high council. The council members condemned him to death for claiming to be the Christ, spat on him, struck him, and mocked him (Mark 14:57–65). They took him to

Pilate, the Roman governor, whose soldiers scourged him, forced a crown of thorns on his head, mocked him, and struck him (John 19:1–5). Pilate found no fault in him, but still handed him over to be crucified (vv. 4, 6, 16).

The Roman soldiers hung Jesus like a criminal on a cross while people mocked him in his agony (Mark 15:25–32). To be killed on a "tree" or wooden pole was a public sign of dying as a lawbreaker under God's curse (Deut. 21:22–23). Darkness fell on the land. Christ cried out, "My God, my God, why hast thou forsaken me?" (Mark 15:33–34). Then the Son of God died.

The conclusion of Christ's humiliation was *his burial.* His lifeless body was laid in a tomb (Acts 13:29; 1 Cor. 15:4). In experiencing death in its fullness, "Christ fully bore the punishment of sin," Herman Bavinck said.[6]

Thus, we may summarize the lowest point of Christ's humiliation with words from the Apostles' Creed: "He descended into hell."[7] That is not to say that Christ literally went to hell, for his spirit went to heaven after he died (Luke 23:43, 46). Rather, Christ experienced the spiritual anguish of hell on the cross and the physical humiliation of dying and being buried in the ground.[8] We should marvel at the unspeakable love of Christ, that he was willing to endure hellish humiliation to deliver his people from the depths of hell.

Steps in Christ's State of Exaltation

Christ's state of exaltation began with *his resurrection* from the dead. His tomb was found to be empty (Matt. 28:1–7). He appeared to many of his disciples (1 Cor. 15:4–7). Jesus proved that he was not a ghost but a living man. He said, "Behold my hands and my feet, that it is I myself: handle me, and see; for a spirit hath not flesh and bones, as ye see me have" (Luke 24:39). From Christ's resurrection springs the resurrection of his people from spiritual death (Eph. 2:4–5) and their resurrection from physical death on the last day (Rom. 8:11).

Forty days after Christ's resurrection, his disciples watched *his ascension* into heaven (Luke 24:51). He rose into the sky (Acts 1:9) and "ascended up far above all heavens" (Eph. 4:10). He entered God's holy presence as our "forerunner" (Heb. 6:20).

6 Bavinck, *RD*, 3:410.

7 The Apostles' Creed, in *TFU*, 5.

8 On the interpretation of "he descended into hell," see Beeke and Smalley, *RST*, 2:912–25.

Christ's ascension led to *his session*, or *sitting at God's right hand*. David prophesied, "The LORD said unto my Lord, Sit thou at my right hand, until I make thine enemies thy footstool" (Ps. 110:1). Christ's sitting at the right hand of God began his ministry as the glorified Priest-King (vv. 2–4). He is enthroned with supreme authority (Eph. 1:20–21).

The first public act of the glorified Lord was *his outpouring of the Holy Spirit* on his people at Pentecost (Acts 2:4, 32–36). The Spirit came in Jesus's name to powerfully advance the progress of the word of Christ in the world (John 14:26; 15:26–27).

The final step of Christ's exaltation will be *his coming in glory*. Just as he ascended bodily into heaven, so he will descend bodily to earth again (Acts 1:9–11). He will judge the world in righteousness (Acts 17:31). And he will regenerate creation (Matt. 19:28) to be a "new heavens and a new earth" (2 Pet. 3:13).

Practical Applications of Christ's Two States

The doctrine of the two states of Christ has several beautiful applications.

First, the most important application is that *we should trust the gospel of Christ's humiliation and exaltation*. The center of the gospel is "Christ died for our sins . . . [and] rose again" (1 Cor. 15:3–4). We must believe that Christ suffered and entered his glory (Luke 24:25–26). Have you trusted in him to save you by his humiliation and exaltation?

Second, the doctrine of Christ's two states reminds us that Christianity requires that *we should follow Christ in the humble road to glory* (Luke 9:20–23; Heb. 12:1–2). Understanding this doctrine can bring great comfort to suffering Christians. Following Christ under the cross is a sign that we will share in his glory. Gregory of Nazianzus said, "Sweet are the nails . . . for to suffer with Christ and for Christ is better than a life of ease with others."[9]

Third, Christ's two states should also teach us that *we should evaluate people by their obedience, not their circumstances* (John 8:15; 2 Cor. 5:12, 16). When godly people suffer trouble, Christ's example of humiliation should encourage them. Some of those most despised by the world have been people "of whom the world was not worthy" (Heb. 11:38).

9 Gregory of Nazianzus, *Orations*, 45.23, in *NPNF*[2], 7:431.

Fourth, the doctrine of Christ's humiliation and exaltation means that *we should rejoice daily in Christ's victory*. Wilhelmus à Brakel said,

> He who for our sake became poor, was a man of sorrows, and endured the contempt of men, has conquered all and triumphantly ascended into heaven.... With what joy the heavenly legions must have accompanied Him upon His entry! With what joy the glorified saints must have beheld Him! With what delight the Father must have received Him![10]

Therefore, let us join the heavenly celebration of Jesus Christ, saying with joy, "Who is this King of glory? The Lord strong and mighty, the Lord mighty in battle" (Ps. 24:8).

Suggested Song to Sing to the Lord

- Psalm 24, "The earth, with all that dwell therein," *Psalter*, No. 59; *THBap*, No. 66

Questions for Meditation or Discussion

1. What is the one-two-three pattern that Reformed theology uses to summarize the work of Christ?
2. How is Christ's threefold office revealed in the Old Testament?
3. How is Christ's threefold office revealed in the New Testament?
4. Which of the practical applications of Christ's office is most relevant to you? Why?
5. What Scripture passages show us that Christ's saving work involved two states?
6. What does it mean that Christ was "made under the law"?
7. How is Christ's humiliation seen in his (1) birth, (2) childhood and early adulthood, (3) public ministry, (4) passion, (5) death, and (6) burial?
8. What are the steps of Christ's exaltation? Why is each one important?
9. How can Christ's humiliation and exaltation give patience and hope to Christians?

10 Brakel, *CRS*, 1:642.

46

Christ's Revelation as Prophet

Chapter Summary and Key Terms

Christ is the supreme Prophet of his people. Moses foretold the coming of a prophet like himself, who would enjoy close communion with God and work mighty miracles. Even before the Son came in the flesh, he worked to reveal the word of God through the ancient prophets. After Christ's incarnation, he preached and sent out apostles, prophets, and evangelists. Christ himself was the Image of God on earth in his life and death. When Christ rose from the dead and ascended into heaven, he poured out the Spirit of truth to inspire the writing of the New Testament. Today, whenever the Bible is read or heard, Christ is speaking in the Word. Furthermore, Christ ministers as Prophet to the human heart, granting the *illumination* of the Holy Spirit. By Christ's work as Prophet, blind sinners see the glory of divine truth in the Holy Scriptures, and God's saved people grow in their understanding and faith in the Word.

THE LORD JESUS CHRIST SAYS, "I am the way, the truth, and the life" (John 14:6). Christ is the Mediator of the truth. Indeed, he is the truth. Through him, we know God and his will for our salvation. Christ is the Prophet of his people.

Christ is the perfect person to serve as our Prophet. He is the Word of God. John says, "In the beginning was the Word, and the Word was with God, and the Word was God" (John 1:1). When "the Word was made flesh" (v. 14), the perfect self-expression of God became human. Christ is the Son of God. Jesus said, "No one knows the Son except the Father, and no one knows the Father except the Son and anyone to whom the Son chooses to reveal him" (Matt. 11:27 ESV). Christ "is the image of the invisible God" (Col. 1:15). He is not just a created image of God, like mankind. This Image is the Creator himself (v. 16). He is the brightness of the Father's glory (Heb. 1:3).

Christ came to deliver the truth of God to perishing men, women, and children. He said, God "hath anointed me to preach the gospel" (Luke 4:18). He added, "I must preach the good news of the kingdom of God to the other towns as well; for I was sent for this purpose" (v. 43 ESV).

Christ says, "I am the light of the world: he that followeth me shall not walk in darkness, but shall have the light of life" (John 8:12). Satan blinds this world to God's glory (2 Cor. 4:4). Without Christ, people *are* darkness (Eph. 5:8). Therefore, all sinners need Christ so that they may know the truth and respond rightly to it. Jesus would have died in vain if his people could not hear his gospel and have their eyes opened to turn to God and receive his forgiveness (Acts 26:18). Thanks be to God for the light of the world!

The Prophet Foretold by Moses

Moses, the great prophet of the Old Testament, said that God would raise up another prophet like him (Deut. 18:15–19). That Prophet is Jesus Christ (Acts 3:22–23; 7:37).

A prophet is a spokesman called by God to tell others the word that God gives him. The Lord said to Moses, "See, I have made thee a god to Pharaoh: and Aaron thy brother shall be thy prophet. Thou shalt speak all that I command thee: and Aaron thy brother shall speak unto Pharaoh, that he send the children of Israel out of his land" (Ex. 7:1–2). In other words, a prophet is God's "mouth" to speak to people (4:15–16). Prophets speak what God has revealed (1 Cor. 14:29–30).

Moses said that God would raise up the great Prophet from the Israelites' "brethren" (Deut. 18:15, 18). Christ regards his people as his brothers and sisters. He "is not ashamed to call them brethren, saying, I will declare thy name unto my brethren" (Heb. 2:11–12). Douglas Kelly writes, "He speaks with a human voice that can be understood by other humans. He shares our experiences. . . . His full humanity welcomes us to come."[1]

1 Douglas F. Kelly, *Systematic Theology: Grounded in Holy Scripture and Understood in the Light of the Church*, 3 vols. (Fearn, Ross-shire, Scotland: Christian Focus, 2008–2021), 2:189.

The promised Prophet would be "like" Moses (Deut. 18:15, 18). Deuteronomy later says,

> There arose not a prophet since in Israel like unto Moses, whom the Lord knew face to face, in all the signs and the wonders, which the Lord sent him to do in the land of Egypt to Pharaoh, and to all his servants, and to all his land, and in all that mighty hand, and in all the great terror which Moses shewed in the sight of all Israel. (34:10–12)

Thus, it was clear that the Prophet like Moses would enjoy remarkable intimacy with God and work great miracles. This is what we find in the Son of God.

The Prophet would be the Mediator of God's words. Moses said, "To him you shall listen" (Deut. 18:15 ESV), for he would have God's "words in his mouth" (vv. 18–19). Jesus says, "My doctrine is not mine, but his that sent me. . . . I do nothing of myself; but as my Father hath taught me, I speak these things" (John 7:16; 8:28). Therefore, if we do not listen to Christ the Prophet, God will judge and destroy us (Deut. 18:19; Acts 3:23). John Flavel said, "His commands are to be obeyed, not disputed."[2]

Christ's Revelation by the Word

We need Christ as our Prophet because we need the gospel. We are saved by faith (Eph. 2:8), and faith is grounded in knowledge (Ps. 9:10). Therefore, Christ's work as the Prophet centers on the Word. The Westminster Shorter Catechism says, "Christ executeth the office of a prophet, in revealing to us, by his word and Spirit, the will of God for our salvation."[3]

The Mediator of God's Truth before the Incarnation

John writes, "No man hath seen God at any time; the only begotten Son, which is in the bosom of the Father, he hath declared him" (John 1:18). Therefore, every special revelation of God through the ages has come through the Son. Flavel said, "Christ is the original and fountain of all that light which guides us to salvation."[4] He is the only revealer of God.

2 Flavel, *The Fountain of Life*, in *WJF*, 1:120.

3 The Westminster Shorter Catechism (Q. 24), in *RC*, 4:356. Cf. the Baptist Catechism (Q. 27), in *RC*, 4:576.

4 Flavel, *An Exposition of the Assembly's Catechism*, 24.2, in *WJF*, 6:182.

God the Son was the Lord of the ancient prophets. When the Lord appeared to Isaiah and called him to be a prophet (Isaiah 6), it was Christ whom Isaiah saw (John 12:37–41). The prophets spoke by "the Spirit of Christ" (1 Pet. 1:10–11).

Christ was the wisdom of the wise men of Israel. All God's saving wisdom is in Christ (Col. 2:3). Jesus taught that he is the wisdom of God (Luke 7:34–35; 11:49). He is the personal Wisdom who speaks in the book of Proverbs (Prov. 8:12–30).

The Incarnate Prophet in His State of Humiliation

The arrival of the incarnate Son brought God's final word to this world. Hebrews 1:1–2 says, "God, who at sundry times and in divers manners spake in time past unto the fathers by the prophets, hath in these last days spoken unto us by his Son." God the Son incarnate is the supreme revelation of God (John 1:14). He has received the truths of God in his human mind and heart. He is able to communicate God's truths to us in a human way.

Christ is the Teacher anointed by the Holy Spirit. The Father loves the Son and sent him to speak the words of God with the fullness of the Spirit (John 3:34–35). The Holy Spirit descended on Christ at his baptism (Luke 3:22). After rejecting the Devil's temptations, Jesus went out "in the power of the Spirit . . . [and] taught in their synagogues" (4:14–15). He declared that in him the ancient promise of the Spirit-anointed preacher had been fulfilled (vv. 18–21; cf. Isa. 61:1–2). Those who heard him "were astonished at his teaching, for his word possessed authority" (Luke 4:32 ESV). The Gospels contain his teachings, including many individual sayings and longer blocks of instruction (such as Matthew 5–7, 10, 13, 18, 23–25; and John 14–17). Faith in Christ means submitting to him as our Master and Teacher. Christ's call is "Come unto me. . . . Take my yoke upon you, and learn of me" (Matt. 11:28–29).

Christ sent apostles, prophets, and evangelists to Israel. He "ordained twelve, that they should be with him, and that he might send them forth to preach, and to have power to heal sicknesses, and to cast out devils" (Mark 3:14–15). He also sent out other messengers of his word (Matt. 23:34; Luke 10:1).

Every act of God the Son incarnate was a revelation of God and his will. He was God's living Image among men (2 Cor. 4:4). We must be imitators of the Lord (1 Thess. 1:6). Christ's example teaches us that we must deny ourselves for him (Matt. 16:24). We must humbly obey God, even unto death (Phil 2:5, 8). We must live for God's glory (1 Cor. 10:31; 11:1). We must serve one another in love (John 13:15; Eph. 5:2). We must bear with one another in meekness and forgiveness (Col. 3:12–13). We must endure unjust suffering patiently (1 Pet. 2:21–23). William Perkins said that Christian conduct consists of "such a course of life whereby we following Christ's example do by him perform new obedience to God."[5]

Christ's greatest work of revealing God in his state of humiliation was his suffering and death for our sins. Christ was our Prophet on the cross. In his passion, Jesus Christ revealed the priceless worth of God's will (Mark 14:36) and our total inability to justify ourselves (Gal. 2:21). He revealed God's justice and righteousness (Rom. 3:25–26), love for sinners (5:8), and wisdom and power (1 Cor. 1:23–24). In the paradox of the cross, God was revealed most gloriously when Christ's deity was most hidden in weakness and shame.

The Incarnate Prophet in His State of Exaltation

Christ's work of mediating God's Word continues with his exaltation. By rising from the dead, Jesus revealed God's faithfulness to his Word (1 Cor. 15:4). Christ demonstrated his reliability as a true prophet (Matt. 28:6), showed God's power (Eph. 1:18–20), and confirmed the gifts of eternal life (John 11:25; 14:19–20) and justification (Rom. 4:25). Also, he proved that God had vindicated him (1 Tim. 3:16) and appointed him to judge the world (Acts 17:31).

After Christ rose from the dead, he launched the church's mission to the whole world (Matt. 28:18–20). He also gave further teachings to his disciples to prepare them for their work (Luke 24:25–27, 44–47; Acts 1:1–3).

Christ then ascended into heaven, sat down at the right hand of God, and poured out the Holy Spirit on the church (Acts 1:9–11; 2:33). This is "the Spirit of truth," who, Jesus had promised, would "teach you all things" (John 14:16–17, 26). Christ gave this promise especially to the apostles (15:26–27). Robert Letham says, "Thus, the apostles' teaching was to be derived from the Holy Spirit and, in consequence, from Christ himself."[6]

5 Perkins, *A Golden Chain*, chap. 39, in *WWP*, 6:190.

6 Robert Letham, *The Work of Christ*, Contours of Christian Theology (Downers Grove, IL: InterVarsity Press, 1993), 97.

The lasting benefit of Christ's sending the Spirit of truth is the apostles' writing of the New Testament. Though the Lord Jesus did not write a book, the inspired writings of the apostles communicate the truths revealed to them by Christ (Gal. 1:12; Rev. 1:1).

The ascended Christ is the Lord of the church's present ministry of the Word. Paul writes, "He that descended is the same also that ascended up far above all heavens, that he might fill all things. And he gave some, apostles; and some, prophets; and some, evangelists; and some, pastors and teachers; for the perfecting of the saints, for the work of the ministry, for the edifying of the body of Christ" (Eph. 4:10–12).

We hear Christ's voice whenever we read or hear the Holy Scriptures. Paul says, "Christ [is] speaking in me" (2 Cor. 13:3), and, "The things that I write unto you are the commandments of the Lord" (1 Cor. 14:37). The Bible's authority, inerrancy, and sufficiency arise from the authority, inerrancy, and sufficiency of Christ. John Owen wrote, "All these are absolutely secured in the divine person of the great prophet of the church. His infinite wisdom, his infinite goodness, his essential veracity, his sovereign authority over all, give the highest assurance . . . that there is no possibility of error or mistake in what is declared unto us."[7]

Christ also continues to speak through the ministry of the Word today. Gospel preachers are "ambassadors for Christ," so that Paul says, "God [is] making his appeal through us" (2 Cor. 5:20 ESV). Those who reject the messengers of Christ reject Christ himself (Luke 10:16). Christ's "sheep hear his voice . . . and the sheep follow him: for they know his voice" (John 10:3–4).

The greatest act of revelation by Christ in his state of exaltation will take place at his second coming. On that day, "the Lord Jesus shall be revealed from heaven with his mighty angels" (2 Thess. 1:7–8). The saints look ahead with anticipation to "the revelation of Jesus Christ" (1 Pet. 1:7 ESV). For the unrepentant sinner, the day of Christ will be "the day of wrath and revelation of the righteous judgment of God" (Rom. 2:5). To the child of God, it is promised, "We shall be like him; for we shall see him as he is" (1 John 3:2).

Is it your great desire to be with Christ and to see his glory? David said, "One thing have I desired of the Lord, that will I seek after; that I may dwell

7 Owen, *Christologia*, in *WJO*, 1:94.

in the house of the Lord all the days of my life, to behold the beauty of the Lord" (Ps. 27:4). Make this your prayer, too.

Christ's Illumination of People by the Holy Spirit

Sinners are unable to receive the gospel (1 Cor. 2:14). The Mediator saves us from this blindness, too. Thomas Boston said, "Christ teaches his elect . . . by his Spirit, who joins inward illumination to external revelation."[8] Christ the Prophet reveals the truth and heals the eyes of the heart to see it.

The Lord promised to give Christ to be "a light of the Gentiles; to open the blind eyes" (Isa. 42:6–7). People are afflicted with blindness to the things of God (vv. 16–19; 43:8). By God's saving power, the light of God's glory shines in our hearts "in the face of Jesus Christ" (2 Cor. 4:6). Richard Sibbes said, "God can create a new spiritual eye to discern of spiritual things. . . . God, and only God, that created light out of darkness, can create light in the soul."[9]

Christ continues to teach the hearts of those whom he has saved (John 14:21). After he rose from the dead, he appeared to his disciples and "opened their minds to understand the Scriptures" (Luke 24:45 ESV). They were already believers, but foolishness and resistance to believing God's Word remained in their hearts (v. 25). Christ's saving illumination changes his people over time (2 Cor. 3:18). By the Spirit, believers "have the mind of Christ" (1 Cor. 2:12, 16). Therefore, we should pray, "Open thou mine eyes, that I may behold wondrous things out of thy law" (Ps. 119:18), and, "Lord, teach us" (Luke 11:1).

Christ's inward illumination does not reveal new truth. Rather, he applies truth already revealed in the Scriptures (Luke 24:45). Isaiah warns, "To the law and to the testimony: if they speak not according to this word, it is because there is no light in them" (Isa. 8:20). Flavel said that illumination was not intended "to take men off from reading, and studying, and searching the scriptures . . . but to make their studies and duties the more fruitful."[10] Gerard Wisse said, "This inner, prophetical ministry of Christ is under no circumstances to be divorced from the Word."[11]

8 Boston, *An Illustration of the Doctrines of the Christian Religion*, in *WTB*, 1:418.

9 Sibbes, *The Glorious Feast*, in *WRS*, 2:464.

10 Flavel, *The Fountain of Life*, in *WJF*, 1:132.

11 Gerard Wisse, *Christ's Ministry in the Christian: The Administration of His Offices in the Believer* (Grand Rapids, MI: Free Reformed Publications, 2013), 18.

Through the Word, Christ reveals God to the soul (Matt. 11:27; 1 John 5:20–21). We once were "so enamored of ourselves that we hated God," as Wisse said. But now we delight in God and hate our sin. Furthermore, by Christ's illumination, "we will discover that we do not only have an aversion for the law, but also for the gospel." Christ "lets us see that we have nothing, but also that we need not have anything in order to be objects of free grace. In Christ there is an all-sufficiency." Christ also shows us the loveliness of his law. We come to see that "to be obedient is to love." In short, Christ teaches us "that God is . . . God!"[12]

Suggested Song to Sing to the Lord

- Psalm 25, "Lord, to me Thy ways make known," *Psalter*, No. 67; *THBap*, No. 583

Questions for Meditation or Discussion

1. Why is Christ the perfect Prophet of God?
2. What can we learn about Christ from Deuteronomy 18:15–19?
3. What does John 1:18 imply about all of God's revelations of himself through history?
4. What evidence is there that God the Son gave God's word in the Old Testament?
5. How did Christ exercise his prophetic ministry in Israel during his state of humiliation?
6. Why can we say the New Testament is from Christ when he wrote nothing himself?
7. How will the Son of Man reveal God when he returns?
8. Why do people need Christ to illuminate their hearts by his Spirit?
9. How does Christ's illumination relate to the Holy Scriptures?
10. What are some things that Christ continues to show Christians by his illumination?

12 Wisse, *Christ's Ministry in the Christian*, 9–12, 21, 37.

47

Christ's Sacrifice as Priest, Part 1: Substitution and Satisfaction

Chapter Summary and Key Terms

Christ, as the Priest of his people, offered himself as a sacrifice to appease God's anger (*propitiation*). He paid the price to set them free (*redemption*) and give them peace with God (*reconciliation*). It is true that Christ died as the Prophet to exert *moral influence* by his revelation of love and righteousness. Christ also died as the King to win *victory* over sin and Satan. But most fundamentally, Christ died as the Priest to offer a sacrifice of *penal substitution*, for he suffered the penalty that his people deserved for their sins. Acting as their *surety* in the covenant of grace, he made *satisfaction* to God's law by paying the debt they owed. Their guilt is thus removed (*expiation*). Christ's sacrifice should cause us to marvel at the love of God, who paid such a price to save his enemies. We should also stand in awe at his justice. It could not be satisfied except by the death of his Son.

JESUS CHRIST, God the Son incarnate, is the great Priest. His work as Prophet and King is toward man. His work as Priest is toward God (Heb. 5:1). Hugh Martin said, "It propitiates God; it intercedes to God. It satisfies God's justice; it pacifies God's wrath; it secures God's favour; it seals God's covenant love; and gives effect to God's eternal purpose and grace."[1]

1 Hugh Martin, *The Atonement: In Its Relation to the Covenant, the Priesthood, the Intercession of Our Lord* (Edinburgh: James Gemmell and George Bridge, 1887), 59.

God taught Israel about Christ's priesthood through the types or shadows of the priesthood granted to the sons of Aaron. A priest is a person chosen by God to serve him in his holy presence (Ex. 28:1; 29:44). He must be without "blemish" (Lev. 21:16–24) and clothed with glory and holiness (Ex. 28:36–40). Mankind's sin and uncleanness greatly offend God's holiness (Lev. 15:31). To reconcile God and his people, a priest offers sacrifices for sins (Heb. 5:1; 8:3) and intercedes for sinners (Lev. 16:12–19). The Westminster Shorter Catechism says, "Christ executeth the office of a priest, in his once offering up of himself a sacrifice to satisfy divine justice (Heb. 9:14, 28), and reconcile us to God (Heb. 2:17); and in making continual intercession for us (Heb. 7:24–25)."[2]

The Sacrifice to Make Atonement

The primary purpose of a priest's sacrifice is to "make atonement" (Lev. 1:4; 4:20, 26, 31, 35). This refers to appeasing an offended party by a gift that makes right an injustice done. The result is the restoration of a relationship (Gen. 32:20). The Bible gives us three ways of understanding atonement.

First, atonement is *propitiation*. This word means the appeasing, or pacifying, of someone's anger. God's wrath is against sinners (Rom. 1:18). He sent Christ to be their "propitiation through . . . his blood" (3:25). The Son became "a merciful and faithful high priest . . . to make propitiation for the sins of the people (Heb. 2:17 ESV). Without his sacrifice, there is only "fiery indignation, which shall devour the adversaries" (10:27).

We should not think, though, that Christ persuaded an angry Father not to destroy us. The Father sent the Son to accomplish propitiation. John says, "Herein is love, not that we loved God, but that he loved us, and sent his Son to be the propitiation for our sins" (1 John 4:10). Leon Morris writes, "It is to God himself that we owe the removal of God's wrath."[3]

Christ made propitiation by sacrificing himself. Jesus is God's beloved Son, who always pleases his Father. But Christ bore the wrath of the righteous Judge against lawbreakers. As a result, God's wrath is removed

2 The Westminster Shorter Catechism (Q. 25), in *RC*, 4:356. Cf. the Baptist Catechism (Q. 28), in *RC*, 4:576.

3 Leon Morris, *The Apostolic Preaching of the Cross*, 3rd ed. (Grand Rapids, MI: Eerdmans, 1965), 207.

from them (Isa. 54:8–9). Instead, God rejoices in his redeemed as a bridegroom delights in his bride (62:4–5).

Second, atonement is *redemption*. This has to do with the rescue of someone from loss, slavery, or death by the payment of a price or ransom. Jesus laid down his life as a "ransom for many" (Matt. 20:28; Mark 10:45). This same term is used for the price paid to rescue a lawbreaker from punishment (Ex. 21:29–30). Christ paid this ransom price not to the Devil but to God (Heb. 9:14–15). "In [Christ] we have redemption through his blood, the forgiveness of sins, according to the riches of his grace" (Eph. 1:7).

God's law places all who break it "under the curse," but "Christ hath redeemed us from the curse of the law, being made a curse for us: for it is written, Cursed is every one that hangeth on a tree" (Gal. 3:10, 13). John Murray wrote, "He became so identified with the curse resting on his people that the whole of it in all its unrelieved intensity became his. That curse he bore and that curse he exhausted."[4] By redemption in Christ, God adopts believers as his sons and daughters (4:4–5).

Third, atonement is *reconciliation*. This word refers to a change of relationship from hostility and division to friendship and peace. The gospel invitation, "Be reconciled to God," means trusting in Christ so that God will not count your trespasses against you (2 Cor. 5:19–20). Paul says, "For if, when we were enemies, we were reconciled to God by the death of his Son, much more, being reconciled, we shall be saved by his life. And not only so, but we also joy in God through our Lord Jesus Christ, by whom we have now received the atonement," literally "the reconciliation" (Rom. 5:10–11).

The root of reconciliation is God's amazing love. Thomas Manton said, "When we had alienated our hearts from God, refused his service, and could expect nothing but the rigour of his law and vindictive justice, then he spared not his own Son to bring about this reconciliation for us."[5] The fruit of reconciliation is friendship with God. Irenaeus said, "In the last times the Lord has restored us into friendship through His incarnation, having become the Mediator between God and men; propitiating indeed for us the Father against whom we had sinned."[6]

4 John Murray, *Redemption Accomplished and Applied* (Grand Rapids, MI: Eerdmans, 1955), 44.

5 Thomas Manton, *Christ's Eternal Existence*, in *The Complete Works of Thomas Manton*, 22 vols. (London: James Nisbet & Co., 1873), 1:498.

6 Irenaeus, *Against Heresies*, 5.17.1, in *ANF*, 1:544.

The good news of Christ's sacrifice calls us to faith in him (Rom. 3:25). Faith throws away as trash and dung everything else men claim as their righteousness (Phil. 3:4–9). Do you sense God's anger against your sins? Rest in the propitiation of Christ that has won God's approval. Does your sin place you under a burden of guilt? Find hope in the Redeemer who paid the ransom price with his own blood. Do you know that you deserve rejection and eternal shame? Look to the blood of Christ to give you peace with God forever.

Christ's Sacrifice as Penal Substitution

Christ's sacrifice unto God was his offering of himself in the place of his people under God's law and judgment. This doctrine is called *penal substitution*. It is "substitution" because Christ lived and died as his people's representative before God, offering himself in their place. It is "penal" because he suffered the punishment of God's legal judgment that they deserved.

Some theologians argue that Christ died to save us by *moral influence*. According to this view of the atonement, his death reveals God's love and justice in a way that the Holy Spirit uses to move us to faith and repentance. Other theologians say that Christ died to win *victory* over evil powers, such as the Devil. We agree with both statements, as the reader can see in our discussions of Christ's work as the crucified Prophet (chap. 46) and crucified King (chap. 50). But the work of the Priest is to offer a sacrifice for sins (Heb. 5:1). Without penal substitution, neither influence nor victory is enough to save us.

God promised penal substitution in the Old Testament. The killing of animals as sacrifices for sin showed that sinners deserve death and need a substitute to die in their place. The Lord tested Abraham by commanding him to sacrifice Isaac, but then directed him to sacrifice "a ram . . . in the stead of his son" (Gen. 22:13). At the Passover, the punishment of death fell on all the firstborn in Egypt (Ex. 11:4–5). The only way for the firstborn to escape was by the family killing a sacrificial lamb instead and placing its blood on the doorposts (Ex. 12:3–7, 13, 27).

Atonement by substitution is prophesied in Isaiah 53. The prophet writes, "He was wounded for our transgressions, he was bruised for our iniquities. . . . The Lord hath laid on him the iniquity of us all" (vv. 5–6). God placed the punishment for sin on his righteous Servant: "It pleased the Lord to bruise him" as "an offering for sin" (v. 10).

God performed penal substitution in the New Testament. Christ says, "The Son of man came . . . to give his life as a ransom for many" (Matt. 20:28; Mark 10:45). Paul says, "For he hath made him to be sin for us, who knew no sin; that we might be made the righteousness of God in him" (2 Cor. 5:21). As David Clarkson explained, Christ's righteousness was counted to us, so that the Lord treats us as righteous people. But our sins were counted against Christ, so that the Lord punished him as a sinner. He was punished for our guilt, not his own.[7]

We have already seen penal substitution in the three ways the Bible explains atonement. Christ "redeemed" his people by taking their place "under the law" and suffering the curse of that law for them (Gal. 3:13; 4:4–5). Jesus is their "propitiation" by his "blood" (Rom. 3:25), having made the sacrifice by which he appeased God's wrath by receiving it upon himself. The Mediator is their "reconciliation" to God, for by the transfer of their guilt to him and his righteousness to them (2 Cor. 5:18–21), they have peace with God (Rom. 5:1, 9–10; Eph. 2:14–17).

This truth makes us exclaim, "O sweet exchange! . . . That the wickedness of many should be hid in a single righteous One, and that the righteousness of One should justify many transgressors!"[8]

Christ's Sacrifice for the Satisfaction of God's Justice

The Reformed confessions speak of Christ making "satisfaction" to God.[9] They use the term *satisfaction* in the old sense of paying a debt or fulfilling an obligation. Jesus taught us to call our sins "debts" (Matt. 6:12; Luke 7:41–43). He compared our guilt to a financial debt that would take us thousands of lifetimes to pay off ("ten thousand talents," Matt. 18:24). Christ must pay the debt to release his people. His sacrifice is the "ransom" (Mark 10:45; 1 Tim. 2:6) and the "price" (1 Cor. 6:20; 7:23). The effect of Christ's satisfaction is sometimes called *expiation*, which is the removal of legal guilt and

7 David Clarkson, *Christ's Dying for Sinners*, in *The Works of David Clarkson*, 3 vols. (Edinburgh: Banner of Truth, 1988), 3:68.

8 Anonymous, *Epistle to Diognetus*, chap. 9, in *ANF*, 1:28.

9 The Belgic Confession (Art. 20), in *TFU*, 37; the Westminster Confession of Faith (11.3), in *RC*, 4:247–48; and the Second London Baptist Confession (11.3), in *RC*, 4:547.

liability to punishment. By Christ's blood, transgression and uncleanness are removed from believers (Ps. 103:12; 1 John 1:7).

God provided this satisfaction because he loves us. Though we were neither "righteous" nor "good," God demonstrated his love for us in that "Christ died for us" (Rom. 5:6–8). Robert Letham says, "Rather than presenting a cruel and distorted picture of God, what penal substitution shows us is that God's love for us is such that he was prepared to pay the ultimate price that love can pay."[10] Let us be quick to run to this loving God when we sin so that he may forgive us. And let us learn to love one another as he loves us (John 13:34).

Christ's satisfaction was necessary because of God's justice. In its essence, sin is hatred against God and rebellion against his law (Rom. 8:7; 1 John 3:4). Therefore, God's righteousness demands the just punishment of all who break his law (Ex. 23:7; Ps. 11:6–7). John Owen said, "Sin is contrary to the nature of God." It would be "inconsistent" with his nature for him to pass by sin unpunished. This is not because God is bound by "any external rule or law." Rather, "his law . . . is the holiness and righteousness of his own nature."[11]

Paul says that God has "forgiven you all trespasses" by "blotting out the handwriting of ordinances that was against us, which was contrary to us, and took it out of the way, nailing it to his cross" (Col. 2:13–14). The Greek word translated as "handwriting" refers to a legal paper of financial obligation. At the cross of Christ, God cancelled the debt, nailing the paper to the cross, as it were.

Christ satisfied God's justice by acting as the "surety" of his people (Heb. 7:22). A *surety* is a person who takes on the legal obligations of another, either paying his debts or suffering his punishment. Christ committed himself to discharge his people's obligations to God's law so that the promises of grace would be fulfilled. The context in which Christ is called a surety is his priesthood (vv. 20–21). Christ acts as a surety by his sacrifice and unending intercession (vv. 23–27). He is the covenant representative of his people.

Someone might object that it is not necessary for God to punish Christ in the place of others. God is so kind, it is said, that he can forgive sin without price.

10 Robert Letham, *The Work of Christ*, Contours of Christian Theology (Downers Grove, IL: InterVarsity Press, 1993), 137.

11 Owen, *WJO-H*, 2:110–11.

In response, we agree that God is infinitely kind. But his kindness is shown in paying the debt of sinners by the death of his Son. God is both mercy and justice, love and light (1 John 1:5; 4:8). It would not be right for God to ignore injustice instead of punishing it. His judgments on sinners display his righteousness (Rev. 15:3–4; 16:5, 7; 19:2). Anselm of Canterbury said, "Nothing is less tolerable in the order of things, than for the creature to take away the honor due to the Creator and not repay what he takes away."[12]

Another might object that it would be unjust for God to punish someone for the sins of another. God forbids human judges to do such a thing (Deut. 24:16; 2 Kings 14:6; Ezek. 18:20).

In reply, we must point out that Christ was not forced to die but died willingly for his people (Eph. 5:25). God the Son is sovereign over his life and freely laid it down (John 10:17–18). We also note that Christ was the legal representative of his people in the covenant of grace. William Perkins said,

> In the passion, Christ must not be considered as a private person—for then it could not stand with equity that He should be plagued and punished for our offences—but as one in the eternal counsel of God set apart to be a public surety or pledge for us [Heb. 7:22] to suffer and perform those things which we in our own persons should have suffered and performed.[13]

Christ was able to make satisfaction for our sins by penal substitution because he is joined with us in the covenant. His death in our place was just because of "the covenant oneness of Christ and His members," as Martin said.[14] This is no legal fiction, but the consequence of the legal bond formed between the Son and the elect in the eternal counsel of peace.

The doctrine that Christ satisfied God's justice by penal substitution shows us God's faithfulness. He will never compromise his justice or break his promises. Let us, therefore, rest our whole confidence on him, even though the circumstances of our lives may scream at us that God is unjust and unworthy of our trust. Trust him for the forgiveness of your sins by the

12 Anselm, *Why God Became Man*, 1.13, in *A Scholastic Miscellany: Anselm to Ockham*, ed. Eugene R. Fairweather, Library of Christian Classics, Ichthus Edition (Philadelphia: Westminster, 1956), 122.

13 Perkins, *An Exposition of the Symbol*, in *WWP*, 5:140.

14 Martin, *The Atonement*, 14–15.

blood of Christ. Trust him to give you eternal life and glory on the basis of what Christ has accomplished. And trust him to care for you through all of life and to use the worst of evils for your good. The more you live by faith in Christ crucified, the more you will be able to confess with confidence, "The Lord is upright: he is my rock, and there is no unrighteousness in him" (Ps. 92:15).

Suggested Songs to Sing to the Lord

- Psalm 130, "From out the depths I cry to Thee," *Psalter*, No. 364
- "Man of Sorrows! What a name," *THBap*, No. 175

Questions for Meditation or Discussion

1. Is Christ's work as Priest mainly directed toward God or men? Why?
2. What can we learn from the sons of Aaron about Christ's priesthood?
3. What does it mean that Christ accomplished (1) propitiation, (2) redemption, and (3) reconciliation?
4. What does "penal substitution" mean?
5. How did God promise penal substitution in the Old Testament?
6. How did God perform penal substitution in the New Testament?
7. What does Christ's "satisfaction" mean?
8. How does Christ's work of satisfaction relate to God's (1) love and (2) justice?
9. How has this chapter helped you to see God's faithfulness more clearly?

48

Christ's Sacrifice as Priest, Part 2: Obedience and Perfection

Chapter Summary and Key Terms

How did Christ make satisfaction to God's justice for the sins of his people? In a word, he did it by his obedience. Christ flawlessly kept God's law (*active obedience*). He also fully suffered its penalty against sinners (*passive obedience*). As a result, his sacrifice was perfect. It has unlimited worth to save all who repent and trust in him (this is known as the *sufficiency of Christ's sacrifice*). He completed redemption, and no sacrifice for sins needs to be added (the *finality of Christ's sacrifice*). It effectively accomplished the salvation of all for whom he died, so that they will be saved through faith (the *efficacy of Christ's sacrifice*). As a work of *particular redemption*, Christ's sacrifice saved God's elect people from all nations. When we consider Christ's obedience and the perfection of his work, we should trust him alone to save us from God's wrath and imitate him by walking in obedience to God and submission to his providence.

THE CORE OF CHRIST'S WORK as Priest is his obedience to the Father's will. John Murray said, "The Scripture regards the work of Christ as one of obedience."[1] Christ's perfect obedience accomplished the redemption of God's elect.

A priest had to do exactly what "the LORD commanded" (Lev. 9:6–10). God did not want mere rituals of "sacrifice and offering," but a faith-

1 John Murray, *Redemption Accomplished and Applied* (Grand Rapids, MI: Eerdmans, 1955), 19.

ful servant who would say, "I delight to do thy will, O my God; yea, thy law is within my heart" (Ps. 40:6–8). That servant was Jesus Christ. His obedience to God's will led him to offer himself as a sacrifice for our sins (Heb. 10:4–12).

Christ satisfied the demands of the law for righteousness. Paul says, "For Christ is the end of the law for righteousness to every one that believeth" (Rom. 10:4). By "the end of the law," Paul most likely means its goal. Christ accomplished for believers the law's aim of "righteousness." Matthew Poole said, "Whatever the law required that we should do or suffer, he hath perfected it on our behalf."[2]

The Obedience of Christ Our Sacrifice

Christ's Active and Passive Obedience

The Second London Baptist Confession states that God counts believers righteous "by imputing Christ's active obedience unto the whole law and passive [obedience] in his death for their whole and sole righteousness."[3] Christ's *active obedience* was his perfect keeping of God's commandments. His *passive obedience* was his submission to God's purpose that he should suffer and die for our sins.

Johannes Wollebius said, "Just as the passion of Christ is necessary for the expiation of sin, so his active obedience and righteousness are necessary for the gaining of eternal life." This is because "the law binds us both to punishment and to obedience." Wollebius added, "To punishment, because it places a curse on anyone who does not perform all the words of the law. To obedience, because it promises life only to those who keep it completely."[4]

The Heidelberg Catechism says, "God, without any merit of mine, but only of mere grace, grants and imputes to me the perfect satisfaction, righteousness and holiness of Christ; as if I never had had, nor committed any sins; yea, as if I had fully accomplished all that obedience which Christ has accomplished for me."[5]

2 Matthew Poole, *Annotations upon the Holy Bible*, 3 vols. (New York: Robert Carter and Brothers, 1853), on Rom. 10:4 (3:513).

3 The Second London Baptist Confession (11.2), in *RC*, 4:546.

4 Johannes Wollebius, *Compendium Theologiae Christianae*, 1.18.(2).4.i, in *Reformed Dogmatics*, ed. and trans. John W. Beardslee III, A Library of Protestant Thought (New York: Oxford University Press, 1965), 106–7.

5 The Heidelberg Catechism (LD 23, Q. 60), *TFU*, 87.

Jesus obeyed God's commandments perfectly in an ordinary human life for his first thirty years or so. Then, at his baptism, the Father declared, "Thou art my beloved Son; in thee I am well pleased" (Luke 3:22–23). He is the last Adam. The first Adam was God's created son (v. 38), but he sinned when Satan tempted him. Christ is God's eternal Son, and he succeeded in obeying God and defeating Satan by the word of God (4:1–13). Paul says, "For as by one man's disobedience many were made sinners, so by the obedience of one shall many be made righteous" (Rom. 5:19). John Calvin wrote, "The obedience of Christ is reckoned to us as if it were our own."[6]

Christ's passive obedience began at the moment of his incarnation as a human being and continued in his sufferings throughout his state of humiliation (see chap. 45). He was a "man of sorrows" (Isa. 53:3). But he was no helpless pawn forced into tragedy. He was the sovereign Lord, fully in control of what happened to him. He laid down his life by his own authority (John 10:17–18). He "gave himself" (Titus 2:14).

Both Christ's active and passive obedience were needed to fulfill the demands of God's law. The law curses lawbreakers and promises life to the man who keeps its commands (Gal. 3:10, 12). Christ redeemed his people from the curse (v. 13) and granted them the blessing (v. 14). Therefore, he must have performed the obedience and suffered the curse in our place. He was "made under the law, to redeem them that were under the law," so that they would be heirs of God (4:4–5, 7). Christ took on himself the full obligations to satisfy the law so that believers would gain the inheritance that he earned.

To be "righteous" in God's sight is to be counted as one who has obeyed God's law (Deut. 6:25; 24:13). If Christ's righteousness is not imputed to us, then our righteousness must stand on something in ourselves, either our good works, love, or faith. But Paul writes of "not having mine own righteousness, which is of the law, but that which is through the faith of Christ, the righteousness which is of God by faith" (Phil. 3:9). The righteousness given to believers is the obedience of Christ. Paul says, "For he hath made him to be sin for us, who knew no sin; that we might be made the righteousness of God in him" (2 Cor. 5:21).

6 Calvin, *Institutes*, 3.11.23.

Christ's Supreme Obedience in His Passion

All of Christ's human life during his state of humiliation involved sinless obedience through suffering. But he exercised his human soul in increasing levels of submission to God's will over the course of his life. This was especially true in his passion, when he submitted to bear the full wrath of God against his people. He exercised new heights of obedience as he entered new depths of sorrow.

In the garden of Gethsemane, Jesus "began to be greatly distressed and troubled." He said, "My soul is very sorrowful, even to death" (Mark 14:33–34 ESV). He "fell on the ground" as under crushing weight. He prayed, "Abba, Father, all things are possible unto thee; take away this cup from me: nevertheless not what I will, but what thou wilt" (v. 36). This "cup" from God was "the cup of his fury" (Isa. 51:17). It contained the "fire and brimstone" that sinners deserved (Ps. 11:6; Rev. 14:10). When Jesus went out to meet those who came to arrest him, he said, "The cup which my Father hath given me, shall I not drink it?" (John 18:11). Behold the obedience of Christ! He willingly drank into himself the flaming wrath of almighty God against sin.

Christ was seized and falsely accused. He was brutally beaten and mocked—first by the Jewish high council and then by Roman soldiers (Mark 14:53–65; 15:15–20). Jesus endured these injustices meekly (Isa. 53:7). He "committed himself to him that judgeth justly" (1 Pet. 2:23). At any moment, he could have summoned an army of angels to destroy his foes (Matt. 26:53). Instead, he quietly submitted to God's will.

Then they crucified Jesus (Matt. 27:33–35). Crucifixion is a horribly shameful and painful way to die. Christ was rejected and mocked by men (vv. 39–44). He cried out, "My God, my God, why hast thou forsaken me?" (v. 46). God forsakes those who forsake him, break his covenant, and provoke his wrath (Deut. 31:16–17). Christ "was numbered with the transgressors; and he bare the sin of many" (Isa. 53:12). He accepted this willingly (Luke 22:37). He was "obedient unto death, even the death of the cross" (Phil. 2:8).

The Perfections of Christ's Sacrifice

Christ's obedience unto death perfectly accomplished the redemption of his chosen people, so that they all will be saved through faith in the gospel.

The Sufficient Sacrifice

The *sufficiency of Christ's sacrifice* is its more-than-adequate value to pay the ransom price for the sins of everyone who trusts in him. The Canons of Dort say, "The death of the Son of God is the only and most perfect sacrifice and satisfaction for sin, and is of infinite worth and value, abundantly sufficient to expiate the sins of the whole world."[7] Christ's sacrifice is more valuable than all the treasures of the earth. God's chosen people "were not redeemed with corruptible things, as silver and gold, . . . but with the precious blood of Christ, as of a lamb without blemish and without spot" (1 Pet. 1:18–19).

The person who offered himself is God. Paul exhorted the Ephesian elders to care for "the church of God, which he hath purchased with his own blood" (Acts 20:28). He is "our great God and Savior Jesus Christ, who gave himself for us to redeem us" (Titus 2:13–14 ESV). Stephen Charnock explained that though only Christ's human nature died, his sacrifice has infinite value "because it is offered by an infinite person."[8]

Therefore, let us never think that our good works (or the works of any mere man or woman) can atone for our sins. If such an infinitely precious ransom price was required for our forgiveness, shall we think our pitiful works will save us? We must trust in Christ alone.

The Final Sacrifice

The *finality of Christ's sacrifice* is its completeness, such that no one needs to add anything to the merit of what he has done to save his people from God's wrath. Just before Christ died, "knowing that all things were now accomplished," he declared, "It is finished" (John 19:28, 30). Christ finished the work of making a sacrifice for sins to deliver people from God's judgment. The redemption price had been paid in full (Mark 10:45). Christ offered himself once for all (Heb. 7:27; 9:12; 10:10, 12): "For by one offering he hath perfected for ever them that are sanctified" (10:14).

Any attempt by people to make satisfaction to God for their own sins directly contradicts the sufficiency and finality of Christ's sacrifice. We do not need an earthly priest to offer a sacrifice for us. We do not need to do penance prescribed by a priest. We only need Jesus Christ.

7 The Canons of Dort (Head 2, Art. 3), in *TFU*, 134.

8 Charnock, *A Discourse on the Acceptableness of Christ's Death*, in *WSChar*, 4:570.

Wilhelmus à Brakel said that Christians should meditate often on the finished work of Christ. Such meditation will "yield strong consolations." By grace, it will help us to "perceive the perfect satisfaction of divine justice and how perfect the sinner is before God in Christ" and "how certainly and truly salvation has been merited." This will bring "peace of conscience in God and free access to the Father."[9]

The Effectual Sacrifice

The *efficacy of Christ's sacrifice* is its effective accomplishment of the salvation of all those for whom he died. Two thousand years ago, God blotted out his people's legal debt, "nailing it to his cross" (Col. 2:14). Christ has "obtained eternal redemption" (Heb. 9:12), "hath redeemed us" (Gal. 3:13), and has "bought" us with a price (1 Cor. 6:20). The Lamb of God "redeemed" people from every nation, many of them before they even heard the gospel (Rev. 5:9).

Therefore, if Christ died for us, we will certainly be saved. Paul says, "What shall we then say to these things? If God be for us, who can be against us? He that spared not his own Son, but delivered him up for us all, how shall he not with him also freely give us all things?" (Rom. 8:31–32). "All things" includes calling, justification, becoming like Christ, and glorification with him (vv. 29–30). The "us all" for whom God gave his Son (v. 32) is not all without exception. In context, "us all" refers to all whom God predestined to glory, the elect (vv. 30, 33).

Greg Nichols says,

> This blessed truth gives every Christian solid ground for confidence and assurance. It calls every Christian to stand fast, with one mind and heart striving for the faith of the gospel. It calls every Christian to sing the praises of the Lamb, for he is worthy, for his blood accomplished and obtained redemption (Rev. 5:9–10).[10]

The Particular Sacrifice

According to the doctrine of *particular redemption* or definite redemption, Christ did not die to save everyone or to make it possible for everyone to

9 Brakel, *CRS*, 1:614.

10 Greg Nichols, *Lectures in Systematic Theology*, ed. Rob Ventura, 4 vols. to date (Seattle: CreateSpace Independent Publishing Platform, 2017–2024), 3:696–97.

be saved. He died to fully accomplish the redemption of his elect people.[11] The Canons of Dort say, "It was the will of God, that Christ by the blood of the cross . . . should effectually redeem out of every people, tribe, nation, and language, all those, and those only, who were from eternity chosen to salvation and given to Him by the Father."[12]

Christ died to save "many." They are the "many" whom he justifies (Isa. 53:11), to whom he gives forgiveness of sins (Matt. 26:28), and whom he brings to glory (Heb. 2:10). His name is Jesus because "he shall save his people from their sins" (Matt. 1:21). Christ said, "I came down from heaven . . . [to do] the will of him that sent me" (John 6:38). God's will was that Christ should save all whom the Father had given him (vv. 38–39). The Lord Jesus Christ said, "I am the good shepherd, and know my sheep, and am known of mine . . . and I lay down my life for the sheep" (10:14–15). The sheep of Christ are those whom the Father "gave" him (v. 29).

Isaiah says that Christ died "for the transgression of my people" (Isa. 53:8). Paul says that Christ "gave himself for us, that he might redeem us from all iniquity, and purify unto himself a peculiar people, zealous of good works" (Titus 2:14). He adds, "Husbands, love your wives, even as Christ also loved the church, and gave himself for it" (Eph. 5:25).

Christ intercedes for those for whom he died (Isa. 53:12; 1 John 2:1–2). He does not intercede for everyone, but only those whom the Father gave him (John 17:9, 20). Christ is the Mediator who applies redemption to their lives so that they are saved (Heb. 8:6–12).

Therefore, Christ accomplished particular redemption for his particular people.

Someone might object that the doctrine of particular redemption discourages evangelism because it will not allow us to tell unbelievers, "Christ died for you."

In response, we note that the assurance that Christ "loved me, and gave himself for me" belongs to those who have died with him and risen with him to a new life (Gal. 2:20). In the New Testament, evangelism is preaching

11 It is also called *limited atonement*, but this term does not appear in the Reformed confessions or the writings of sixteenth- or seventeenth-century Reformed theologians. For an explanation of this doctrine, see Joel R. Beeke, *Living for God's Glory: An Introduction to Calvinism* (Lake Mary, FL: Reformation Trust, 2008), 89–100.

12 The Canons of Dort (Head 2, Art. 8), in *TFU*, 136.

Christ and calling sinners to him—not telling unbelievers that "Christ died for you." There is no example in the New Testament where Christians say this to unbelievers.

Another might object that the Holy Scriptures speak of Christ's coming and dying to save "all" or "the world." So, it is said, Christ died for everyone without exception.

In response, we say that a closer look at these Scripture passages shows that this is not what they are saying. For example, Paul says that Christ "gave himself a ransom for all" (1 Tim. 2:6). The word translated as "all" here means "all kinds of" (v. 1; 6:10). "All" can also mean "many" (Luke 16:16; John 3:26). Similarly, "world" does not always mean everyone in the world (John 16:20). When John writes, "God so loved the world, that he gave his only begotten Son" (3:16), the word translated as "world" means people in rebellion against God (v. 19). "All the world" can mean "many nations" (Col. 1:5–6). Christ is said to be the propitiation for "the whole world" (1 John 2:2), but "the whole world" can refer to God's people among many nations (Rom. 1:8). Christ's sacrifice is universal because he redeemed many people from all nations (Rev. 5:9).

Remember what we saw in the last chapter about Christ's sacrifice. Christ made propitiation for his people to turn away God's wrath. He made satisfaction to God's justice for their sins. As we argued in the last section, Christ's death is an effectual sacrifice that will result in the salvation of all for whom he died. But only some people will be saved from God's wrath. Others will be punished by God for their sins. Therefore, Christ died as the substitute only for his chosen ones.

Practical Applications of Christ's Perfect Sacrifice

We may draw numerous practical applications from the sacrifice of Christ.

First, *we should recognize that God will glorify his righteousness and his law*. He will execute justice either in Christ's death or in the sinner's punishment. But justice will be served.

Second, *we should rely on Christ alone to deliver us from the punishment that we deserve*. He is the Lamb of God. Trust him to save you from hell. Receive him as your righteousness.

Third, *we should consider the high value of obedience in the sight of God*. Learn from Christ's sacrifice that nothing is more precious than doing the will of God—not even life itself.

Fourth, *we should run the race of obedience in imitation of Christ.* Focus your mind and engage your energies to the great aim of obeying the will of God.

Fifth, *we should remain patient and faithful through suffering, even unto death.* The One who saved you by his obedient sufferings waits for you at the end of your journey.

Sixth, *we should humble ourselves under the truth that Christ redeemed us only because of his sovereign grace.* As Brakel taught, say to yourself, "Why is Jesus my Surety? Why does Jesus love me with an everlasting love, considering that so many millions go to hell?"[13]

Seventh, *we should glorify the great Redeemer.* Brakel directed us to say to Jesus, "I truly rejoice that Thou hast taken my place, hast satisfied for my sins, and hast merited eternal life for me. To all eternity I desire to acknowledge this, and to love and thank Thee."[14]

Suggested Songs to Sing to the Lord

- "And can it be that I should gain," *THBap*, No. 731
- "To God be the glory, great things he hath done!," *THBap*, No. 667

Questions for Meditation or Discussion

1. How do the Holy Scriptures show us that obedience is the heart of Christ's work as the Priest?
2. What does Paul mean by saying, "Christ is the end of the law" (Rom. 10:4)?
3. What do theologians mean by Christ's active and passive obedience?
4. How did Christ obey God to the utmost in the garden of Gethsemane, his trial, and his crucifixion?
5. What gives the sacrifice of Christ its infinite value? Support your answer from Scripture.
6. What did Christ mean when he said, "It is finished" (John 19:30)?
7. How do the Scriptures teach that Christ redeemed his particular people?
8. How can we answer the objection that Christ died for "all" and the "world"?

13 Brakel, *CRS*, 1:617.

14 Brakel, *CRS*, 1:618–19.

9. What are some practical applications of the truth that Christ saved us by his perfect sacrifice?
10. How should the doctrine of particular redemption humble us and move us to glorify God?

49

Christ's Intercession as Priest

Chapter Summary and Key Terms

Christ's office as Priest requires him not only to offer a sacrifice for sins but also to make intercession for his people and to bless them. The *intercession of Christ* in his state of exaltation is his appearing before God as the representative of his elect people in the covenant of grace. He offers perpetual and authoritative prayer as their *Advocate* for their salvation to the end. His intercession displays the efficacy of his sacrifice and the sympathy of his human heart so that his people receive the mercy they need in their trials. As the interceding High Priest, Christ blesses his people with the blessings of the covenant in all saving grace. Believers can find comfort and boldness in this doctrine of Christ's intercession as they depend on him to give them grace and access to God.

CHRIST ROSE FROM THE DEAD as the triumphant Priest. He ministers before God for our sake even now in heaven. His *intercession* is his appearing before God as our representative and obtaining grace for us by his prayers. The sacrifice of Christ is the foundation of our salvation. The intercession of Christ is central to its application. Christ ever lives as the Mediator of the new covenant. All grace comes to us through him.

The doctrine of Christ's intercession is one of the most comforting doctrines of the Christian faith. John Owen wrote, "The actual intercession of Christ in heaven is . . . a principal foundation of the church's consolation."[1] Robert Murray M'Cheyne said, "If I could hear Christ praying for me in the

1 Owen, *WJO-H*, 5:538.

next room, I would not fear a million of enemies. Yet the distance makes no difference; He is praying for me."[2]

The Gospels tell us that Christ prayed often.[3] He foretold that Satan would tempt Peter and said, "But I have prayed for thee, that thy faith fail not" (Luke 22:32). An entire chapter in the Gospel of John records Christ's prayer to his Father for his people (John 17).

After Christ rose from the dead, ascended into heaven, and sat at God's right hand, he began his intercession as the exalted High Priest. John says that when Christians sin, they have "an advocate with the Father, Jesus Christ the righteous" (1 John 2:1). Paul says, "Who is he that condemneth? It is Christ that died, yea rather, that is risen again, who is even at the right hand of God, who also maketh intercession for us" (Rom. 8:34). We also read in the epistle to the Hebrews, "He is able also to save them to the uttermost that come unto God by him, seeing he ever liveth to make intercession for them" (Heb. 7:25).

The Perfections of Christ's Heavenly Intercession

The Holy Scriptures, especially the epistle to the Hebrews, reveal the following perfections of Christ's priestly intercession.

First, *Christ's intercession is holy.* The Mediator has "holiness to the Lord" engraved, as it were, on his very person (Ex. 28:36). He is "without sin" (Heb. 4:15) and is "holy, harmless, undefiled, separate from sinners" (7:26). As a result, the intercession of Christ glorifies God's holiness, for God wills to be honored by those who draw near to him (Lev. 10:3).

Second, *Christ's intercession is heavenly.* "We have a great high priest, that is passed into the heavens, Jesus the Son of God" (Heb. 4:14). He is "set on the right hand of the throne of the Majesty in the heavens" (8:1). William Gouge noted that this position reveals the High Priest's "divine dignity" as God the Son (1:2–3).[4]

Third, *Christ's intercession is perpetual.* He ministers by "the power of an endless life" (Heb. 7:16). God the Father promised, "Thou art a priest for

2 Robert Murray M'Cheyne, "Reformation," in *Memoir and Remains of Robert Murray M'Cheyne*, ed. Andrew Bonar (1892; Edinburgh: Banner of Truth, 1966), 154.

3 For example, Luke 3:21; 5:16; 6:12; 9:18, 28–29; 10:21; 11:1; 22:17, 19, 32, 41–45; 23:34, 46.

4 William Gouge, *Commentary on the Whole Epistle to the Hebrews*, 3 vols. (Edinburgh: James Nichol, 1866), 1:18.

ever" (v. 17). Christ "holds his priesthood permanently, because he continues forever. . . . He always lives to make intercession" (vv. 24–25 ESV).

Fourth, *Christ's intercession is authoritative.* We must not imagine the heavenly Priest pleading for mercy for his people. Our Lord Jesus intercedes as the Servant appointed by God to this very work and exalted to sit at God's right hand (Heb. 5:4–6; 7:21; 8:1). He mediates to sinners the graces that God promised to give them in his covenant (8:6–12). He intercedes as One who has already accomplished redemption by his blood (9:12).

Fifth, *Christ's intercession is legal.* His intercession turns away the condemnation of those charged with breaking the law and establishes their justification (Rom. 8:33–34). John writes, "If any man sin, we have an advocate with the Father, Jesus Christ the righteous" (1 John 2:1). The word translated as "advocate" refers to a person called in to help in a legal case, perhaps not a lawyer but certainly a witness or representative in court.

Sixth, *Christ's intercession is protective.* It defeats the saints' great "accuser," Satan, "who accuses them day and night before our God" (Rev. 12:10 ESV; cf. Zech. 3:1–5).

Seventh, *Christ's intercession is personal.* He intercedes by the very presence of his incarnate person before God the Father. He ascended to heaven as the priestly "forerunner" of his people (Heb. 6:20). "By his own blood he entered in once into the holy place, having obtained eternal redemption for us" (9:12). He went "into heaven itself, now to appear in the presence [literally "to the face"] of God for us" (v. 24).

Eighth, *Christ's intercession is effectual.* Jesus warned Peter that Satan aimed to "sift" him "like wheat," a violent trial. But Christ said, "I have prayed for you that your faith may not fail. And when you have turned again, strengthen your brothers" (Luke 22:31–32 ESV). Christ did not say "if" but "when" in regard to Peter's turning. No one can condemn "God's elect" when Christ "is interceding for us, [for] who shall separate us from the love of Christ?" (Rom. 8:33–35 ESV). The writer to the Hebrews says, "He is able also to save them to the uttermost that come unto God by him, seeing he ever liveth to make intercession for them" (Heb. 7:25). The phrase translated as "to the uttermost" could be translated as "to the all-completion."

Ninth, *Christ's intercession is particular.* His intercession secures the salvation of "God's elect" (Rom. 8:33–34). Jesus said to the Father, "I pray not for the world, but for them which thou hast given me; for they are thine" (John 17:9; cf. 6:39). Christ said to Peter, "I have prayed for thee [singular], that thy [singular] faith fail not" (Luke 22:32).

Tenth, *Christ's intercession is complete.* He intercedes for everything needed for salvation. Christ makes intercession for "transgressors" (Isa. 53:12), those presently unconverted (Ps. 51:13). As to his saved people, in John 17, Christ prayed for their spiritual preservation (vv. 11–16), sanctification (vv. 17–19), unity (vv. 20–23), and glorification (v. 24).

Eleventh, *Christ's intercession is compassionate.* He took "flesh and blood" like ours "that he might be a merciful and faithful high priest" (Heb. 2:14, 17). Since "he himself hath suffered being tempted," he is able to help his tempted, suffering people (v. 18): "For we have not an high priest which cannot be touched with the feeling of our infirmities; but was in all points tempted like as we are, yet without sin" (4:15). He relates to his people as a friend (John 15:14–15), a brother (Heb. 2:11–12), and a husband (2 Cor. 11:2).

Twelfth, *Christ's intercession is unique.* He is the way; no one can come to God except through him (John 14:6). Other people may pray for us, but Christ alone intercedes as the Mediator who gave himself as the ransom for our sins (1 Tim. 2:5–6). We should look to no other supposed intercessor in heaven—such as Mary or the saints—for our salvation.

In summary, Christ is the holy, heavenly, perpetual Intercessor. He has entered God's presence as the authoritative legal representative of his particular people. He intercedes on the basis of his finished work of making propitiation for their sins. He overcomes Satan's accusations against them. He effectually secures their complete salvation from beginning to end. He views them with the most tender compassion as they strive against temptation and sometimes fail. Christ is the perfect Advocate and Intercessor. He is the only Mediator we need to bring us to God.

Someone might ask, "Why is Christ's intercession necessary? God does not need to be reminded that Christ finished the work of redemption."

In response, we note that Christ's intercession brings about the application of his finished work in a way that best glorifies God and strengthens our faith. He sits at God's right hand as the Mediator who was sent by God's love and has perfectly honored his holiness. His work as intercessor encourages believers to constantly depend on him and to boldly draw near to God in

Jesus's name. Christ's very presence in heaven is a living testimony to the fact that God accepts believers, for Christ is their surety and representative in the covenant.

Christ's intercession shows that his work as Priest is central to his work as Prophet and King. Christ's sacrifice accomplished our entire redemption. So, too, his intercession obtains every grace needed to apply redemption to us. What Christ works in us as Prophet and King, he first receives from God as interceding Priest. William Bridge said that the blessings of Christ's kingly and prophetic offices are founded on his priestly office. The life and power of the other offices flow from his office as Priest.[5]

The Blessing of Our Great High Priest

One function of a priest is to pronounce God's blessing (or benediction) on his people (Gen. 14:18–20; Deut. 10:8; 21:5). In this blessing, the priest calls on God to give grace and peace (Num. 6:22–26). Theologians have different views of whether the priest's blessing is a distinct third work after sacrifice and intercession, or a part of intercession. But it is clear that Christ blesses his people as their Priest. "Aaron lifted up his hand toward the people, and blessed them" (Lev. 9:22). Likewise, just before Christ ascended into heaven, "he lifted up his hands, and blessed" his disciples (Luke 24:50–51).

Blessing is the opposite of curse. Sinners are under God's curse for breaking the commandments of his law (Gal. 3:10). In his redeeming sacrifice, Christ received the curse of the law. As a result, his believing people are delivered from the curse (v. 13). They receive the blessing "through Jesus Christ" by faith (v. 14). The main benefits of God's blessing are justification and the grace of the Holy Spirit (vv. 8, 14).

Christ mediates all saving blessings to us through his intercession. Through Christ, God sends the Spirit to regenerate us and indwell us richly (Titus 3:5–6). Christ's intercession obtains for us the Comforter (John 14:16). By his intercession, we receive the grace of sanctification and victory over Satan's temptations (17:15, 17; Heb. 2:17–18). Our Advocate preserves us in a state of justification despite our sins (Rom. 8:33–34; 1 John 1:7–2:2). His prayers ensure that our faith will not fail (Luke 22:31–32). By his intercession, we will

5 William Bridge, *The Great Gospel Mystery of the Saints' Comfort and Holiness Opened and Applied from Christ's Priestly Office*, in *The Works of the Rev. William Bridge*, 5 vols. (London: Thomas Tegg, 1845), 1:5.

be saved to the end (Heb. 7:25). He will confess our names before the Father when he judges the world and welcomes his saints into glory (Rev. 3:5).

The exaltation of our great High Priest is a sign that God is fulfilling the covenant of grace and has begun the last days (Heb. 1:2–3; 9:26). Therefore, Christ's intercession unlocks all promised grace and glory for his people. In union with Christ, they are blessed by the Father with "all spiritual blessings" (Eph. 1:3).

Practical Applications of Christ's Intercession

The intercession of our Lord Jesus is a boundless field full of flowers from which we may draw sweet nectar for our souls. Let us consider some of the riches of knowing our Intercessor.

First, *this doctrine can form in us constant reliance on the exalted Christ.* We must run the race set before us while "looking unto Jesus" (Heb. 12:2).

Second, *this doctrine can afford us strong consolation and hope.* Christ's entrance into heaven as our forerunner confirms God's unbreakable promise to bless his people (Heb. 6:17–20). We can exult in hope.

Third, *this doctrine can help us have confidence in our justification.* Christ was raised for our justification and intercedes to deliver us from condemnation (Rom. 4:25; 8:33–34). We should assure our consciences with this doctrine.

Fourth, *this doctrine can encourage promptness to confess sin to God.* We must not remain silent when God convicts us of sin (Ps. 32:3–5). Rather, let us confess our sins with faith in Christ's propitiation and intercession. We can trust that God "is faithful and just to forgive us our sins, and to cleanse us from all unrighteousness" (1 John 1:9; 2:1–2).

Fifth, *this doctrine can increase expectation and comfort in prayer.* What is more comforting in trials than to go to a friend who knows how we feel? "Let us therefore come boldly unto the throne of grace, that we may obtain mercy" (Heb. 4:15–16).

Sixth, *this doctrine can help us exercise trust in Christ for the grace of the Holy Spirit.* Let us never separate the Spirit from Jesus Christ. He is the Spirit of God's Son (Gal. 4:6). Believers overcome trials by "the supply of the Spirit of Jesus Christ" (Phil. 1:19). Owen said, "The great duty of tempted souls, is to cry out unto the Lord Christ for help and relief."[6]

6 Owen, *WJO-H*, 3:486.

Seventh, *this doctrine can cultivate dependence on Christ in worship.* Christ's blood alone can cleanse our consciences so that we may boldly draw near and worship God (Heb. 9:13–14; 10:19–25). "By him therefore let us offer the sacrifice of praise to God continually, that is, the fruit of our lips giving thanks to his name" (13:15). John Calvin wrote, "God cannot be really invoked by us and his name glorified, except through Christ the Mediator."[7]

Eighth, *this doctrine can help us increase in assurance of ultimate salvation and blessedness as we meditate on it.* We will be able to rejoice and exult, for he is able "to save . . . to the uttermost" (Heb. 7:25). As long as this Intercessor stretches out his hands of blessing, we may be sure that the true Israel will prevail over its enemies (Ex. 17:8–13).

Suggested Song to Sing to the Lord

- "O the deep, deep love of Jesus!," *THBap*, No. 453

Questions for Meditation or Discussion

1. What is Christ's heavenly intercession?
2. What Scripture passages tell us that Christ makes intercession or is the Advocate?
3. What are the perfections of Christ's intercession? How is each revealed in the Scriptures?
4. Why is Christ's intercession unique? What does that imply about trusting in other supposed intercessors in heaven, such as Mary or the saints?
5. Of the perfections of Christ's intercession, which is most comforting to you? Why?
6. What is Christ's blessing on his people? What does this blessing include?
7. What is the relationship between Christ blessing his people and the Holy Spirit?
8. Based on the practical applications of the doctrine of Christ's intercession, what are two reasons why understanding and believing this doctrine is especially important for you right now?

7 Calvin, *Comm.* on Heb. 13:15.

50

Christ's Reign as King

Chapter Summary and Key Terms

Christ is the victorious *King* appointed by God over his people. He obtained victory over sin by obeying the Father even unto death on the cross. In this way, the sacrificing Priest paid the price to redeem people from sin's enslavement. The Servant-King broke the power of sin by bringing his human nature into the deepest submission to God's will. Christ then triumphed over all the powers of evil by rising from the dead and ascending into heaven. Now seated at God's right hand, Christ reigns in his *threefold kingdom* with universal power, spiritual grace, and heavenly glory. He exercises his reign to fulfill his commission to rule over God's people, build his temple, and conquer his enemies. The *kingdom of God* and Christ is the treasure of his people and should be their highest aim in all their pursuits.

JESUS CHRIST MAY SEEM like an unlikely candidate for kingship. He himself acknowledged, "My kingdom is not of this world" (John 18:36). His title "King of the Jews" was displayed not on a throne or battle chariot but on the cross where he died (19:19–22). But Christ is "King of kings and Lord of lords" (Rev. 19:16).

The kingdom of God is a major theme of the Bible. In the Old Testament, God's kingdom sometimes has to do with his sovereignty over all creation (Pss. 103:19; 145:9–15; Dan. 4:34–35). At other times, God's kingdom refers to his people (Ex. 19:6; Ps. 114:2), especially as they were ruled by the sons of David (1 Chron. 28:5; 2 Chron. 13:8).

Jesus Christ came to fulfill the ancient prophecies of the great Son of David (Luke 1:31–33). Christ's gospel is the "gospel of the kingdom" (Matt. 4:23; 9:35; 24:14). Jesus often spoke of the "kingdom of heaven" and the "kingdom of God," which refer to the same thing (19:23–24). Christ is the divine King, God the Son incarnate (Isa. 9:6–7).

We may speak of the Son's kingdom in two ways. Since Christ is God the Son, the second person of the Trinity, he shares by nature in God's sovereignty over all creation (Heb. 1:2–3). We may also speak of Christ's kingdom as it relates to his role as the Mediator. Christ's mediatorial kingdom is God's reigning work through Christ by the Spirit to deliver people from Satan's dominion and bring them to grace so that they will enjoy his glory forever (Matt. 12:28; 13:41–53).

The Victory of the Crucified King

In each part of Christ's threefold office, we may speak of Christ's finished work and his continuing work—redemption accomplished and applied. The King fully accomplished victory at the cross and now reigns to apply it. This victory was by price and power.

The Price of Victory

Victory over sin and Satan was one of the great purposes for which Christ came: "He that committeth sin is of the devil; for the devil sinneth from the beginning. For this purpose the Son of God was manifested, that he might destroy the works of the devil" (1 John 3:8).

Christ suffered and died as the Priest to offer himself as a sacrifice for sins. At the same time, Christ was also conquering and winning victory as the King. How is it that "the Lion of the tribe of Judah, the Root of David, has conquered"? The answer appears in "a Lamb standing, as though it had been slain" (Rev. 5:5–6 ESV).

By picturing salvation as penal substitution, the Passover lamb was a type of Christ's sacrificial work as our only High Priest (see chap. 47). The same type also foreshadowed his victory as King. The Lord said, "For I will pass through the land of Egypt this night, and will smite all the firstborn in the land of Egypt, both man and beast; and against all the gods of Egypt I will execute judgment: I am the Lord" (Ex. 12:12). By the Passover plague, God broke the enslaving power of false gods over his people. By Christ, the Passover lamb, God broke the power of sin and Satan over his people.

Peter says, "You were ransomed from the futile ways inherited from your forefathers, not with perishable things such as silver or gold, but with the precious blood of Christ, like that of a lamb without blemish or spot" (1 Pet. 1:18–19 ESV). The blood of Christ was the price of victory (Rev. 5:5, 9; 12:11). Christians are no longer to live in sin because they were "bought with a price" (1 Cor. 6:20). Our deliverance "from the power of darkness" is inseparable from our "redemption through his blood, even the forgiveness of sins" (Col. 1:13–14; cf. Eph. 1:7).

Why was Christ's satisfaction to justice needed to rescue his elect from the Devil? Satan has no right to lead people in rebellion against God. But God justly gave sinners over to the power of sin when they rejected him (Rom. 1:24, 26, 28). The penalty of Adam's sin and our sins is death (5:12; 6:23). Spiritual death includes hostility against God, so that people are unwilling and unable to submit to his law (8:6–8).

Christ saved his people from the power of evil by paying their debt to God's justice. Paul says that God has "forgiven you all trespasses; blotting out the handwriting of ordinances that was against us, which was contrary to us, and took it out of the way, nailing it to his cross; and having spoiled principalities and powers, he made a shew of them openly, triumphing over them in it" (Col. 2:13–15). Thus, Christ's victory as King comes from his sacrifice as Priest.

The Power of Victory

John Eadie said, "Redemption is a work at once of price and power, of expiation and conquest. On the cross was the purchase made; on the cross was the victory gained. The blood that wipes out the sentence was there shed, and the death which was the death-blow of Satan's kingdom was there endured."[1]

Christ overcame the Devil by obedience to God. In the fires of suffering, Christ forged a new humanity that obeys the will of God. He pressed his human nature into the deepest submission to God. At Gethsemane, he prayed, "Abba, Father . . . not what I will, but what thou wilt" (Mark 14:36).

1 John Eadie, *A Commentary on the Greek Text of the Epistle of Paul to the Colossians*, ed. W. Young, 2nd ed. (Edinburgh: T&T Clark, 1884), 169.

Christ reigned as King on the cross (John 19:19–21). True kingship begins with ruling oneself (Prov. 16:32). Paul says, "For in that he died, he died unto sin once" (Rom. 6:10). John Murray said, "It is because Christ triumphed over the power of sin in his death that those united to him in his death die to the power of sin (vv. 2, 11)."[2] Christ now imparts by his Spirit the human holiness he perfected in his own human nature. By the Spirit, "we have the mind of Christ" (1 Cor. 2:16), the mindset of self-denial (Phil. 2:5, 8).

Christ won a perfect victory by his obedience. By his perseverance unto death on the cross, he became "the author and finisher of our faith" and attained glory at God's right hand (Heb. 12:2). In other words, Christ won the victory by perfecting his own human faith and obedience through trials.

The incarnate Son "learned obedience by the things which he suffered" (Heb. 5:8). He experienced obedience by patiently submitting himself to God's will, though it was extremely hard. By this experience, Christ was "made perfect" (v. 9) as the cause of eternal salvation to his people. That does not mean any sin needed to be removed from him (there was none). Rather, he was "made perfect" by the building of godly maturity and proven character.

God found it fitting, "in bringing many sons unto glory, to make the captain of their salvation perfect through sufferings" (Heb. 2:10). The Greek word translated as "captain" means founder or leader of a people. Christ leads a new family ("many sons") into the "glory" of "the world to come." He did so by suffering, dying, and being "crowned with glory and honour" to take up dominion over creation (vv. 5–10).

In Christ, we are truly free because he won the victory over all that would oppress us. This victory is the basis of Christian courage. We need not fear. No power of earth or hell can conquer us since Christ died for our sins. The Lamb has overcome!

The Triumph of the Risen King

In the ancient world, when a ruler won a great military victory, he would return home in a triumphal procession. He would receive honor, glorify his gods, and often consolidate his power. The exaltation of Jesus Christ is

2 John Murray, *The Epistle to the Romans*, The New International Commentary on the New Testament, 2 vols. (Grand Rapids, MI: Eerdmans, 1968), 1:225.

his heavenly triumph for the glory of God the Father and salvation of his people. Christ's triumph began with his resurrection. He is "the firstborn from the dead; that in all things he might have the preeminence" (Col. 1:18).

When Jesus rose from the dead, he entered his glory as the Lord of eternal life (Luke 24:26; Rom. 6:4, 9). Christ died for our sins (1 Cor. 15:3), then rose as the last Adam to rescue his people from the death they deserve and to give eternal life to them by God's Spirit (1 Cor. 15:21–22, 45).

The resurrection was the first step of Christ receiving supremacy over all. In him, the prophecy of Psalm 110:1 was fulfilled: "The LORD said unto my Lord, Sit thou at my right hand, until I make thine enemies thy footstool." Such supremacy is fitting only for the God-man, God the Son incarnate. As God, the Son always had this supremacy. But as the incarnated Mediator, he is now exalted as Lord to show his glory in a way not previously seen during his humiliation (Rom. 14:9; Phil. 2:11).

Christ's resurrection displays his conquest over the powers of evil. Paul says that God raised Christ and seated him "far above all principality, and power, and might, and dominion, and every name that is named" (Eph. 1:21).

When Christ rose, he took up the position of being God's human Servant-King over the world. Paul says that God "hath put all things under his feet" (Eph. 1:22). This was God's original purpose for man (Ps. 8:6). When God exalted Christ, he fulfilled his plan to give his people dominion over creation (Heb. 2:5–10).

Christ rose to enrich his church. God granted the risen Christ "to be the head over all things to the church, which is his body, the fulness of him that filleth all in all" (Eph. 1:22–23). He fills us until we reach the full measure of his glorified humanity in union with God by the Spirit (3:19; 4:15; 5:18). John Calvin wrote, "If we have and possess his only Son, Jesus Christ, we have the full perfection of all good, so that if we cast our eye upon him, we may see all that can be desired."[3]

Christ's triumph does not give us a reason to think that we or our church will triumph over all earthly problems and enjoy material success in this world. Rather, it teaches us to depend on Christ with great confidence. We do not yet reign as kings in glory. The greatest leaders of the church

3 John Calvin, *Sermons on the Epistle to the Ephesians* (Edinburgh: Banner of Truth, 1973), 111.

remain weak, poor, mortal, and despised men (1 Cor. 4:8–13). Our souls are battlegrounds in the conflict between sin and righteousness (Gal. 5:17; 1 Pet. 2:11). But Christ is King. He has won the victory. In union with him, Christians are overcoming the world (1 John 5:4–5). Indeed, we are "more than conquerors" (Rom. 8:37).

Christ's Threefold Kingdom

Reformed theologians speak of Christ's kingdom of power, kingdom of grace, and kingdom of glory. These are not three kingdoms but three ways that Christ reigns in his one kingdom.

First, *Christ reigns with universal power*. He has authority over all (Matt. 28:18). He is sovereign over the nations (Ps. 72:8; Dan. 7:13–14). The Father has "given him power over all flesh, that he should give eternal life to as many as thou hast given him" (John 17:2). He is Lord of all (Acts 10:36; Phil. 2:9–11). He is crowned with glory and honor, and reigns over all things, including all animals (Ps. 8:4–8; Heb. 2:5–9).

Christ's reign from God's right hand ensures the advance of the gospel and the spiritual triumph of the church. John Owen said, "Though our persons fall, our cause shall be as truly, certainly, and infallibly victorious, as that Christ sits at the right hand of God. . . . The cause in which we are engaged shall surely conquer as Christ is alive and shall prevail at last."[4]

Second, *Christ reigns with spiritual grace*. The Spirit of the Lord rests on this King (Isa. 11:1–2). People enter his kingdom through the new birth by the Holy Spirit (John 3:3, 5). Christ writes his laws "not with ink but with the Spirit of the living God, not on tablets of stone but on tablets of human hearts" (2 Cor. 3:3 ESV). Christ came as the last Adam to conquer sin and bring the reign of righteousness, that "as sin hath reigned unto death, even so might grace reign through righteousness unto eternal life by Jesus Christ our Lord" (Rom. 5:21). "The kingdom of God" is among his people in "righteousness, and peace, and joy in the Holy Ghost" (14:17).

Third, *Christ reigns with heavenly glory*. We tend to think of the kingdom of glory as in the future. But Christ has already entered his glory by his resurrection from the dead, ascension into heaven, and session at God's right hand (Luke 24:26; Acts 7:55; 1 Pet. 1:11). His resurrected body

4 Owen, "The Use of Faith, If Popery Should Return upon Us," in *WJO*, 9:507–8.

radiates glorious light (Acts 9:3, 17; 22:6, 11; 26:13). His human nature is now immortal (Rom. 6:9). His glory is presently hidden in heaven, but he will appear in glory (Col. 3:1, 3–4). Even now, he reigns as "the head of all principality and power" (2:10).

The Royal Acts of Christ's Present Reign

David's kingship involved three main responsibilities. First, "David executed judgment and justice unto all his people" through the officers of his kingdom (2 Sam. 8:15–18). Second, he accumulated treasures so that his son could construct and furnish the temple (1 Chron. 18:8; 29:1–5; 2 Chron. 5:1). Third, he subdued Israel's enemies (2 Sam. 8:1–6, 13–14). Christ serves God as the King for the same three purposes.

First, *Christ rules in righteousness over God's people.* Christ appoints ministers in the church (Eph. 4:10–12). He is present with the church to direct its worldwide mission (Matt. 28:18–20). He is the Lord of angels (1 Pet. 3:22), sending them to protect the church (Heb. 1:14). He liberates his disciples from sin by the Word (John 8:31–36) and renews the image of God in them (2 Cor. 3:3, 18; 4:4, 6). His presence in his people by the Holy Spirit is their sanctification and hope of glory (Rom. 8:9–10; Col. 1:27). As the bridegroom, Christ loves his bride (Mark 2:19–20) and cares for her as his body (Eph. 5:28–30). He reigns even now over his righteous people in heaven (Heb. 12:23–24).

Second, *Christ builds the temple of God's presence.* That temple is the people of the church, built together as living stones resting on Christ as the living cornerstone (1 Pet. 2:4–6). Christ constructs God's temple on earth (Matt. 16:18). He established the laws and ordinances of God's temple with his Word (28:20), equips the servants of God's temple with spiritual gifts (Eph. 4:7–8), and purifies God's temple with discipline (Mal. 3:1; Rev. 3:19). Christ reigns over God's temple in heaven (Rev. 21:22).

Third, *Christ conquers the enemies of God.* Christ restrains the powers of evil. He conquered the Devil by his death (Heb. 2:14–15) and now reigns "far above" all powers for the sake of his church (Eph. 1:21, 23). He also judges the nations (Ps. 2:10–12; Rev. 1:5). The Lord sent an angel to strike Herod dead for persecuting the church and boasting as if he were a god (Acts 12:1–2, 21–23). Christ converts the lost and rescues Satan's captives (Mark 3:27; Acts 5:31). He leads God's army and equips his servants for spiritual battle (Eph. 6:10–12; Rev. 17:14). Christ will execute final judgment (Matt. 25:31–46; Rev. 19:11–16) and will subdue all his enemies for the sake of his people, even the "last enemy," death itself (1 Cor. 15:26).

The Preciousness of Christ's Glorious Kingdom

We should view the kingdom of God and Christ as the greatest treasure. The world seeks after earthly goods and benefits. Christ says, "Seek ye first the kingdom of God, and his righteousness; and all these things shall be added unto you" (Matt. 6:33).

Jesus compares the kingdom to a treasure hidden in a field, which, when discovered, is worth selling all to gain (Matt. 13:44). This is because when we gain the kingdom, we gain the King. When God's kingdom purposes come to complete fulfillment, God will be "all in all" (1 Cor. 15:28). Therefore, pursue Christ's kingdom as your highest priority and ultimate goal. Seek Christ's grace as your riches on earth and his eternal glory as your inheritance forever.

Suggested Songs to Sing to the Lord

- Psalm 21, "Now the King in Thy strength shall be joyful, O Lord," *Psalter*, No. 45
- Psalm 72, "Christ shall have dominion over land and sea," *Psalter*, No. 200; *THBap*, No. 678

Questions for Meditation or Discussion

1. In what two senses may we speak of God's "kingdom"? Show both from the Holy Scriptures.
2. Why is Christ's satisfaction to God's justice necessary to set sinners free from Satan?
3. What do the authors mean when they write, "In the fires of suffering, Christ forged a new humanity that obeys the will of God"? Why was this work needed for our salvation?
4. What are some ways that Christ's resurrection is his triumph?
5. How does Christ have a threefold kingdom? Show from Scripture how Christ reigns over his kingdom in each of these three ways.
6. What are the three main responsibilities of the King? Give examples of each.

7. Someone says to you, "Christ's kingdom will begin only when he returns to earth." In light of what you have learned in this chapter, how do you reply?
8. Why should the truths of this chapter increase our fear and joy toward Christ?

51

The People of the Prophet, Priest, and King

Chapter Summary and Key Terms

By union with Christ, believers already share in some of the privileges of his threefold office. They are a prophetic people in Christ. God anoints them with the Holy Spirit to know the truth of God and to speak it as witnesses to unbelievers and for the building up of the church. Believers are also a priestly people in Christ. They have access to God to enjoy bold communion with him in prayer and worship. They are likewise a kingly people in Christ. They already reign in saving grace and are overcomers in their sufferings and spiritual warfare against evil because of the finished work of Christ. Therefore, they no longer live for themselves but for the Lord.

GREAT ARE THE BENEFITS of Christ's threefold office. Believers enjoy some privileges of their Prophet, Priest, and King by union with Christ. Christians "are a chosen generation, a royal priesthood, an holy nation, a peculiar people; that ye should shew forth the praises of him who hath called you out of darkness into his marvellous light" (1 Pet. 2:9). Like Christ, God's Anointed One, those in Christ are also "anointed" (2 Cor. 1:21).

The Heidelberg Catechism asks, "But why art thou called a Christian?" and answers, "Because I am a member of Christ by faith, and thus am partaker of His anointing; that so I may confess His name, and present myself a living sacrifice of thankfulness to Him; and also that with a free and good conscience I may fight against sin and Satan in this life, and afterwards reign with Him eternally, over all creatures."[1] We live unto Christ, then, as prophets, priests, and kings.

Christ's Prophetic People

The Lord revealed that all his people would become prophets by the Holy Spirit (Num. 11:29; Joel 2:28–29). This promise began to be fulfilled when Christ ascended into heaven and poured out the Holy Spirit (Acts 2:17–18). This does not mean that every Christian receives and declares new special revelation. The spiritual gift of prophecy has ceased in the church (see chap. 54). In the age to come, all Christians will be fully prophets who see God "face to face" (1 Cor. 13:12). But in these last days, believers are indwelt and baptized by the Holy Spirit to know and speak the truth. This gives them great privileges as Christ's prophetic people.

First, *Christians are anointed to know the truth of Christ.* John says, "Ye have an unction from the Holy One" (1 John 2:20). This "unction" (or "anointing") preserves them in the knowledge of true doctrine and protects them from receiving heresy (vv. 21–22). Christians must respond to this great privilege by clinging to the truth of Christ. They should study the truth and let it rule their thoughts and feelings. John says, "Let that therefore abide in you, which ye have heard from the beginning" (v. 24).

Second, *Christians are empowered to witness for Christ.* Jesus says, "Ye shall receive power, after that the Holy Ghost is come upon you: and ye shall be witnesses unto me both in Jerusalem, and in all Judaea, and in Samaria, and unto the uttermost part of the earth" (Acts 1:8). Not all Christians are called to be preachers, but all are called to speak God's Word to unbelievers around them as they have opportunity. Paul writes, "Walk in wisdom toward outsiders, making the best use of the time. Let your speech always be gracious, seasoned with salt, so that you may know how you ought to answer each person" (Col. 4:5–6 ESV).

Third, *Christians are equipped to edify Christ's body.* Paul says, "Speaking the truth in love, we are to grow up . . . into Christ, from whom the whole body . . . when each part is working properly, makes the body grow" (Eph. 4:15–16 ESV). By Christ's grace, believers are "full of goodness, filled with all knowledge, able also to admonish one another" (Rom. 15:14). The Lord

1 The Heidelberg Catechism (LD 12, Q. 32), in *TFU*, 78.

requires Christians to "consider one another to provoke unto love and to good works . . . exhorting one another" (Heb. 10:24–25). They should exhort one another daily to beware of sin (3:13), give and receive painful rebuke in faithful love when needed (Ps. 141:5), and encourage one another, saying, "Let us go" to meetings for worship and prayer (Isa. 2:3; Zech. 8:21).

Christ's Priestly People

The Holy Scriptures reveal the marvelous privileges of the priesthood of believers in Christ. Isaiah says that believers "shall be named the Priests of the Lord" because he has clothed them "with the robe of righteousness" (Isa. 61:6, 10). Peter says, "Ye also, as lively stones, are built up a spiritual house, an holy priesthood, to offer up spiritual sacrifices, acceptable to God by Jesus Christ" (1 Pet. 2:5). This is possible because Christ saved us from our sins by his blood, redeeming a people from all nations to be "priests unto God" (Rev. 1:5–6; 5:9–10). They enjoy the following priestly privileges.

First, *the priesthood of believers grants them access to God's holy presence.* Hebrews 10:19–22 says, "Having therefore, brethren, boldness to enter into the holiest by the blood of Jesus, by a new and living way, which he hath consecrated for us, through the veil, that is to say, his flesh; and having an high priest over the house of God; let us draw near." God's priestly people have access to God's heavenly presence through Jesus Christ. His blood cleanses us from guilt. His living intercession as our High Priest secures our welcome.

Second, *the priesthood of believers grants them the satisfaction of communion with God.* People often seek satisfaction through the sensory experiences of external religion, but "it is good for the heart to be strengthened by grace, not by foods, which have not benefited those devoted to them. We have an altar from which those who serve the tent have no right to eat" (Heb. 13:9–10 ESV). Christ is "the bread of life" on whom we feed by faith to the satisfaction of our deepest needs and desires (John 6:35). The glorified Christ pours on his people the living waters of the Holy Spirit to satisfy them forever (4:14; 7:37–39). What joys believers may partake of in their communion with God each Lord's Day and, indeed, every day!

Third, *the priesthood of believers grants them the joy of pleasing God.* Though the Lord knows our sins (Revelation 2–3), there is a great difference between those in a state of sin who "cannot please God" and those in

Christ who have his Spirit (Rom. 8:8–9). People who live by faith please God (Heb. 11:5–6) by their good works (1 Thess. 4:1; 1 John 3:22). If you are a believer, God is "working in you that which is wellpleasing in his sight, through Jesus Christ; to whom be glory for ever and ever" (Heb. 13:21).

Fourth, *the priesthood of believers grants them the freedom of Christian prayer.* "We have a great high priest, that is passed into the heavens, Jesus the Son of God. . . . Let us therefore come boldly unto the throne of grace, that we may obtain mercy, and find grace to help in time of need" (Heb. 4:14–16). God's "throne" symbolizes his supreme power, authority, righteousness, and justice by which he reigns over all things (Pss. 93:1–2; 97:1–2; 103:19), but for those in union with the Son of God, it is "the throne of grace." Believers can come to God with the liberty and boldness won by Christ's blood.

Fifth, *the priesthood of believers grants them the right and responsibility to offer spiritual sacrifices to God.* Believers are a "holy priesthood, to offer up spiritual sacrifices, acceptable to God by Jesus Christ" (1 Pet. 2:5). Christians may offer:

- the sacrifice of repentance (Ps. 51:17)
- the sacrifice of self (Rom. 12:1–2)
- the sacrifice of praise (Heb. 13:15)
- the sacrifice of care and companionship for others (Heb. 13:16)
- the sacrifice of missions (Rom. 15:16)
- the sacrifice of financial gifts (Phil. 4:18)
- the sacrifice of martyrdom (2 Tim. 4:6)

Christ's Kingly People

Christ's kingly office creates a kingly people. The redeemed are restored to bear the image of God as his servant-kings in the new creation. They are not just priests but "a royal priesthood" (1 Pet. 2:9). Christ has made them "kings and priests unto God and his Father" by his blood (Rev. 1:5–6). They enjoy several privileges as a result of Christ's office as King.

First, *God's children reign in grace, though not yet in glory.* Sin and death reign over mankind because of the disobedience of Adam (Rom. 5:12). But Christ has delivered his people from sin's dominion (6:14). Paul says, "For if by one man's offence death reigned by one; much more they which receive abundance of grace and of the gift of righteousness shall reign in life by one, Jesus Christ" (5:17). The full glory of this reign is in the future kingdom. But God's grace is reigning even now through Christ (v. 21).

Second, *God's children reign over all things*. They are "more than conquerors," for "all things work together for good to them that love God" (Rom. 8:28, 37). Paul writes, "Therefore let no man glory in men. For all things are yours; whether Paul, or Apollos, or Cephas, or the world, or life, or death, or things present, or things to come; all are yours; and ye are Christ's; and Christ is God's" (1 Cor. 3:21–23).

That does not mean that Christians are already enthroned in glory. Paul says sarcastically to the proud Corinthians, "Now ye are full, now ye are rich, ye have reigned as kings without us: and I would to God ye did reign, that we also might reign with you" (1 Cor. 4:8). Rather, we conquer by suffering and overcome through death. Martin Luther wrote,

> The power of which we speak is spiritual. It rules in the midst of enemies and is powerful in the midst of oppression. This means nothing else than that "power is made perfect in weakness" [2 Cor. 12:9] and that in all things I can find profit toward salvation, so that the cross and death itself are compelled to serve me and to work together with me for my salvation.[2]

Third, *God's children have a noble and courageous faith*. Christ gives his people true liberty (Gal. 5:1). They will inherit the fullness of liberty in the glory to come (Rom. 8:21), but the Holy Spirit already brings a measure of this liberty to them (2 Cor. 3:17). "The wicked flee when no man pursueth: but the righteous are bold as a lion" (Prov. 28:1). God's adopted children need not cringe and cower before their Father (Rom. 8:15), and if not before God, not before anyone.

Wilhelmus à Brakel said that God's children have "a royal heart" to be courageous and to persevere with the eternal kingdom of Christ in view.[3] Therefore, Johannes VanderKemp wrote,

> Conduct yourself with a holy, but humble greatness of mind, as kings, "who will not be brought under the power of any[thing]," as that great man

2 Luther, *The Freedom of a Christian*, in *LW*, 31:355.

3 Brakel, *CRS*, 1:572.

> [Paul] said (1 Cor. 6:12). Ye are too noble, and of too high a condition to suffer yourself to be enslaved to any sin, or to any creature, without and contrary to the will of God.[4]

Fourth, *God's children have certain victory in spiritual warfare*. Christians are overcomers. John says that they "have overcome the wicked one" (1 John 2:13–14). He adds, "For whatsoever is born of God overcometh the world: and this is the victory that overcometh the world, even our faith. Who is he that overcometh the world, but he that believeth that Jesus is the Son of God?" (5:4–5).

Zacharius Ursinus said, "The kingly office of Christians is to oppose and overcome, through faith, the devil, the world, and all enemies." We fight by faith. Ursinus added, "Christ conquers his enemies by his own power, but we overcome our foes in and through him—by his grace and assistance." Yet we must imitate our Warrior-King to follow in his footsteps to glory. Ursinus said, "Since we are kings it becomes us to fight manfully against sin, the world, and the devil, that we may reign with Christ."[5] Paul says, "Be watchful, stand firm in the faith, act like men, be strong. Let all that you do be done in love" (1 Cor. 16:13 ESV).

Fifth, *God's children have a stewardship as God's royal servants*. God created man in his image so that people would rule as his servant-kings on earth (Gen. 1:26–28). God's stewards manage, enjoy, and care for his creation. The Christian view of work and possessions is profoundly shaped by knowing that Christ is the Lord and heir of all things (Matt. 28:18; Heb. 1:2). Perhaps we labor in the home, a trade, the arts, or some other professional vocation. Every object and person is under Christ's sovereignty and exists for his glory (Col. 1:16–17). Paul says, "Whatsoever ye do, do it heartily, as to the Lord, and not unto men; knowing that of the Lord ye shall receive the reward of the inheritance: for ye serve the Lord Christ" (3:23–24). Christians serve Christ in this world but do not seek this world; instead, they seek "treasures in heaven" in "the kingdom of God" (Matt. 6:19–20, 33).

4 Johannes VanderKemp, *The Christian Entirely the Property of Christ, in Life and Death, Exhibited in Fifty-Three Sermons on the Heidelberg Catechism*, trans. John M. Harlingen, 2 vols. (repr., Grand Rapids, MI: Reformation Heritage Books, 1997), 1:271.

5 Zacharias Ursinus, *The Commentary of Dr. Zacharias Ursinus on the Heidelberg Catechism*, trans. G. W. Williard (repr., Phillipsburg, NJ: Presbyterian and Reformed, 1985), 179–80.

In Christ, believers already enjoy a foretaste of their future as prophets, priest, and kings. Richard Sibbes said, "The life of heaven is begun on earth. We are kings now; we are priests now; we are conquerors now; we are new creatures now. We must praise God, and begin the employment of heaven now; for what they do perfectly, that we begin to do."[6]

The People Who Live for Christ

God's people live for Christ. Paul writes, "For whether we live, we live unto the Lord; and whether we die, we die unto the Lord: whether we live therefore, or die, we are the Lord's. For to this end Christ both died, and rose, and revived, that he might be Lord both of the dead and living" (Rom. 14:8–9).

Similarly, Paul says, "For the love of Christ controls us, because we have concluded this: that one has died for all, therefore all have died; and he died for all, that those who live might no longer live for themselves but for him who for their sake died and was raised" (2 Cor. 5:14–15 ESV). Thus, the believer can say, "To live is Christ, and to die is gain" (Phil. 1:21).

What does it mean to live unto the Lord Jesus? It means that our concerns are no longer confined to that narrow circle of *self*. Instead, we live as those who are not our own. We know we were bought at a price (1 Cor. 6:19–20), so we deny ourselves to serve the Lord (Luke 9:23). Our whole lives are aimed at Christ, for our whole lives belong to him. We live *to* Christ because we live *by* Christ—by faith in him. By his grace, we surrender our wills to do his will in obedience to the Holy Scriptures. We live and, indeed, we die with the aim that Christ will be magnified (Phil. 1:20). We do this with the confidence that God's glory is our ultimate happiness. To live for him is to seek the best for ourselves, not in this world but in the age to come. We understand that man does not exist for himself, but for God. Therefore, the best life is one that is lived for God through Christ, who is the God-man.[7]

Suggested Songs to Sing to the Lord

- Psalm 18, "As Thou, O Lord, hast made me strong," *Psalter*, No. 36
- Psalm 62, "My soul in silence waits for God," *Psalter*, No. 161; *THBap*, No. 571

6 Sibbes, *The Hidden Life*, in *WRS*, 5:216.

7 This paragraph summarizes Sibbes, *The Christian's End*, in *WRS*, 5:292–300.

Questions for Meditation or Discussion

1. Why is it possible for Christians to enjoy spiritual privileges as prophets, priests, and kings?
2. What are three privileges that Christians have as prophets in Christ?
3. In which of these prophetic privileges do you especially desire to grow? What is a practical step you can take toward growing in that area?
4. What are five applications of the priesthood of believers in Christ?
5. What kinds of spiritual sacrifices can believers offer to God through Christ? How are you already offering sacrifices such as these?
6. What are five benefits believers enjoy as kings in Christ?
7. In what ways do Christians already reign in Christ? In what ways do they not yet reign?
8. How does the Bible show us that Christ's people live for him and not for themselves?
9. What is something precious that you learned about the Lord Jesus in your study of the doctrine of Christ in this part of systematic theology? How has that truth affected your life?

PART 5

THE DOCTRINES OF THE HOLY SPIRIT AND SALVATION

Section 5A

The Spirit and the History of Salvation

52

The Spirit in Creation, Common Grace, and Israel

Chapter Summary and Key Terms

Since the Holy Spirit is God and the person of the Trinity who applies salvation to people, to know him is extremely valuable. God the Holy Spirit has been working from the beginning of creation. All things depend on him for life, and all human knowledge and skill come from him. God's works of kindness to human beings in general are called *common grace*. This is distinct from *saving grace*, which he gives only to the elect by union with Christ. Common grace is the cause of much good in society and restrains much evil, but it cannot save anyone. The Holy Spirit worked much common grace in Old Testament Israel, including giving prophecies and power to his servants. The Spirit also manifested God's special presence in Israel and worked salvation and holiness in Old Testament believers. If the saints under the Old Testament needed the Spirit's work, we certainly need it today as we seek to perform the new covenant ministry of the church.

IF WE TREASURE CHRIST, we treasure the work of the Holy Spirit whom he sent. Jonathan Edwards said, "The Holy Spirit, in his indwelling, his influences and fruits, is the sum of all grace, holiness, comfort and joy, or in one word, of all the spiritual good Christ purchased for men in this world: and is also the sum of all perfection, glory and eternal joy, that he purchased for them in another world."[1]

1 Edwards, *An Humble Attempt to Promote Explicit Agreement and Visible Union of God's People in Extraordinary Prayer*, in *WJE*, 5:341.

Someone might say that we should not study the Spirit but must simply be filled with the Spirit. We agree that we should not rest in mere knowledge about the Spirit. We must seek the Spirit's power to serve God with all our hearts. But we must also learn the difference between the work of God's Spirit and the many "spirits" in the world (1 John 4:1–2).

We should not avoid the Holy Spirit out of a concern about unbiblical spirituality. Martyn Lloyd-Jones said, "The doctrine of the Holy Spirit is neglected because people are so afraid of the spurious, the false, and the exaggerated that they avoid it altogether." But since "the Holy Spirit is the one who applied salvation, it is of the utmost practical importance that we should know the truth concerning Him."[2]

The Importance of Studying the Holy Spirit

We should study all that God's Word reveals, including its abundant teaching about the Holy Spirit. There are several reasons why this area of study is crucial.

First, *to know the Spirit is to know our God*. The Holy Spirit is God. Therefore, to study the person and work of the Holy Spirit is a great way to know God better. The Holy Spirit is the third person of the Trinity, so knowing him also brings us into communion with the Father and the Son (2 Cor. 13:14; Gal. 4:4–6).

Second, *to know the Spirit is to know our salvation*. God brings sinners into the kingdom by causing them to be born again by the Spirit (John 3:3–5). No one can confess Jesus as Lord without the Holy Spirit (1 Cor. 12:3). The Spirit is "the Lord and Giver of life."[3]

Third, *to know the Spirit is to understand sanctification*, the process of spiritual growth in holiness. Sanctification is "of the Spirit" (2 Thess. 2:13; 1 Pet. 1:2). John Owen noted, "All this increase of holiness is immediately the work of the Holy Ghost."[4] If we listed every part of the Christian life, beside each item we could add "by the Spirit."

Fourth, *to know the Spirit is to balance the Christian life*. We must maintain a proper balance between our knowledge of doctrine (from the Word)

2 Martyn Lloyd-Jones, *Great Doctrines of the Bible*, vol. 2, *God the Holy Spirit* (Wheaton, IL: Crossway, 1997), 5–6.

3 The Nicene Creed, in *TFU*, 7.

4 Owen, *Pneumatologia*, in *WJO*, 3:393. The "Holy Ghost," of course, is the same as the "Holy Spirit."

and our experience of spiritual life (from the Spirit). J. van Genderen and W. H. Velema wrote, "The Word does not exist apart from the Spirit. It is the Word of the Spirit. The Spirit does not come without the Word. He is the Spirit of the Word."[5]

Fifth, *to know the Spirit is to worship God rightly.* Our worship should be Trinitarian. We are baptized "in the name of the Father, and of the Son, and of the Holy Ghost" (Matt. 28:19). The church worships through Christ, with access to the Father, and in one Spirit (Eph. 2:18).

Sixth, *to know the Spirit is to appreciate historic Christian doctrine.* In the Apostles' Creed, the Christian confesses, "I believe in the Holy Ghost."[6] B. B. Warfield called John Calvin "the Theologian of the Holy Spirit."[7]

Seventh, *to know the Spirit is to be equipped to speak to our culture.* People desire to experience something transcendent and glorious. The doctrine of the Holy Spirit equips us to show people that Christianity offers true knowledge and genuine spiritual experience.

Eighth, *to know the Spirit is to be prepared for spiritual warfare.* When Christ fought against the Devil's temptations, he did so as a man "full of the Holy Ghost" (Luke 4:1). His great weapon, and ours, is "the sword of the Spirit, which is the word of God" (Eph. 6:17).

Ninth, *to know the Spirit is to feel our dependence.* The doctrine of the Holy Spirit is full of man's inability and God's sovereignty. The Lord's word to Zerubbabel remains true: "Not by might, nor by power, but by my spirit,[8] saith the Lord of hosts" (Zech. 4:6).

Tenth, *to know the Spirit is to know Christ.* The great work of the Spirit is union with Christ (1 Cor. 6:17). Calvin wrote, "The Holy Spirit is the bond by which Christ effectually unites us to himself."[9]

5 J. van Genderen and W. H. Velema, *Concise Reformed Dogmatics*, trans. Gerrit Bilkes and Ed M. van der Maas (Phillipsburg, NJ: P&R, 2008), 767.

6 The Apostles' Creed, in *TFU*, 5.

7 Benjamin B. Warfield, *Calvin and Calvinism*, in *The Works of Benjamin B. Warfield*, 10 vols. (Bellingham, WA: Logos Research Systems, 2008), 5:21.

8 The lowercased word "spirit" in English Bible translations does not necessarily mean that the reference is not to the personal Holy Spirit. The languages in which the Bible was originally written do not use capital letters to designate proper nouns. Even in English texts written in the sixteenth through eighteenth centuries, capitalization did not follow modern conventions. In many places in the King James Version, the reader can understand "spirit" to mean "Spirit."

9 Calvin, *Institutes*, 3.1.1.

Do you know the Holy Spirit? Have you experienced his power to convict, convert, and increasingly consecrate people to the Lord? If so, you will love the Holy Spirit. You will want to have a right understanding of how he works in people's lives.

The Holy Spirit's Work in Creation and Providence

At the very beginning of the creation account, we meet the Holy Spirit. Genesis 1:1–2 says, "In the beginning God created the heaven and the earth. And the earth was without form, and void; and darkness was upon the face of the deep. And the Spirit of God moved upon the face of the waters." The verb translated as "moved" is used elsewhere of the hovering of a mother bird over its young (Deut. 32:11). The Spirit of God cared for creation and brought it to life and completion. Gregory of Nyssa said, "Every operation which extends from God to the creation . . . has its origin from the Father, and proceeds through the Son, and is perfected in the Holy Spirit."[10]

All living things depend on the Spirit. The psalmist says, "Thou hidest thy face, they are troubled: thou takest away their breath, they die, and return to their dust. Thou sendest forth thy spirit, they are created: and thou renewest the face of the earth" (Ps. 104:29–30). Ambrose of Milan said, "The Holy Spirit gives life to all things; since both He, as the Father and the Son, is the Creator of all things."[11] To declare that the Holy Spirit is the personal life giver is very different from saying that the Spirit is the life force of all things. The Spirit is the Creator, not part of this created world.

The Holy Spirit makes each human being. Thus, we can confess, "The spirit of God hath made me, and the breath of the Almighty hath given me life" (Job 33:4). The Spirit of the Lord gives each man his intelligence and knowledge: "It is the spirit in man, the breath of the Almighty, that makes him understand" (Job 32:8 ESV). The Spirit gives leadership ability, as we see in Joshua (Deut. 34:9) and Saul (1 Sam. 10:6, 10; 11:6). God filled people in Israel with the Spirit of wisdom so that they would have skill to work with wood, metal, and cloth, and the ability to teach others to do the same (Ex. 28:3; 31:1–11; 35:31–35).

10 Gregory of Nyssa, *On "Not Three Gods,"* in *NPNF*², 5:334.

11 Ambrose, *Of the Holy Spirit*, 2.5.32, in *NPNF*², 10:118.

Therefore, we must depend on the Holy Spirit daily for all skill and ability. We must also value all human knowledge. Calvin said, "If we regard the Spirit of God as the sole fountain of truth, we shall neither reject the truth itself, nor despise it wherever it shall appear, unless we wish to dishonor the Spirit of God." Calvin included law and civics, science, public speaking, medicine, and mathematics among the truths given us by God.[12] Of course, that does not place ordinary human thinking on the same level as the inspired Word of God (2 Tim. 3:15–17). But if all abilities come from the Spirit, then we must use them for God's glory. Paul says, "Whatsoever ye do, do it heartily, as to the Lord, and not unto men" (Col. 3:23).

God's Common Grace to Mankind

The Doctrine of Common Grace

We have seen that the Holy Spirit showers many gifts on mankind. The Lord's goodness extends to the whole world (Ps. 145:8–9). The Lord Jesus teaches God's children to love their enemies, "for he maketh his sun to rise on the evil and on the good, and sendeth rain on the just and on the unjust" (Matt. 5:44–45). God "is kind to the ungrateful and the evil" (Luke 6:35 ESV). The Lord preserves the world today just as he promised in his covenant with Noah (Gen. 9:1–17).

God restrains much sin that could break out in this evil world (Gen. 20:6; 35:5; Ex. 34:24). Most people, though evil sinners, still give good things to their children (Matt. 7:11; 1 Tim. 5:8). They avoid behaviors regarded as shameful in their cultures (1 Cor. 5:1). They love those who love them (Matt. 5:46–47). Calvin said, "God by his providence bridles perversity of nature, that it may not break forth into action; but he does not purge it within."[13]

Many Reformed theologians use the term *common grace* for God's kindness to human beings in general, which does not produce salvation. Common grace includes the free offer of the gospel, God's restraint of human sin in the unconverted, and his promotion of good behaviors that benefit society. Common grace is different from *saving grace*, which God gives only to his elect by union with Christ.[14] Without the saving graces of the fear of

12 Calvin, *Institutes*, 2.2.15.

13 Calvin, *Institutes*, 2.3.3.

14 See Abraham Kuyper, *Common Grace*, trans. Nelson D. Kloosterman and Ed M. van der Maas, ed. Jordan Ballor and Stephen Grabill, 3 vols., Abraham Kuyper Collected Works in Public

the Lord and hope in his mercy, no human work pleases God (Ps. 147:10–11). A sinner's religious acts are abominations in God's sight (Prov. 15:8; 28:9).

Common grace is a doctrine taught in the Old Testament. The Hebrew word translated as "grace" in the Old Testament does not mean friendship but freely given favor. God's "grace" included rescuing Lot out of Sodom before its destruction (Gen. 19:19) and providing men to help Moses to lead Israel (Num. 11:11, 15). Isaiah 26:10 says, "Let favour be shewed [literally "grace be given"] to the wicked, yet will he not learn righteousness."

In the New Testament, "grace" most often refers to God's saving grace (Eph. 2:8). But not all of God's gifts of grace result in salvation. All gifts for service in the church are grace (Rom. 12:6; Eph. 4:7; 1 Pet. 4:10). But these graces may be possessed by hypocrites who will ultimately be damned (Matt. 7:22–23; John 6:70). God's kindness and goodness to the wicked will result in greater condemnation to those who refuse to repent (Rom. 2:4–5).

Therefore, we may speak of God's common grace to sinners, but we must make it clear that common grace cannot save or make someone worthy of saving grace.[15] G. H. Kersten said,

> Common grace has a threefold purpose: (1) It serves to glorify God's goodness shown to Adam's posterity. (2) It serves to perform God's good pleasure in the salvation of the elect [by sustaining the world into which they will be born]. (3) It serves to exalt the righteousness of God even more in the judgment of the wicked. "So that they are without excuse" (Rom. 1:20).[16]

Practical Applications of the Doctrine of Common Grace

Since God shows common grace to mankind, we should seek his blessing on the societies in which we live (1 Tim. 2:1–5). The Lord told the exiles that they must "seek the peace of the city whither I have caused you to be carried away captives, and pray unto the Lord for it: for in the peace thereof shall ye have peace" (Jer. 29:7). Likewise, Christians are pilgrims and exiles in

---

Theology (Bellingham, WA: Lexham; Grand Rapids, MI: Acton Institute, 2015, 2019, 2020). On the controversy among Reformed theologians over common grace, see Beeke and Smalley, *RST*, 3:83–90.

15 The Canons of Dort (Heads 3/4, Rej. 5), in *TFU*, 150.

16 G. H. Kersten, *Reformed Dogmatics: A Systematic Treatment of Reformed Doctrine Explained for the Congregations*, trans. Joel R. Beeke and J. C. Westrate, 2 vols. (Grand Rapids, MI: Netherlands Reformed Book and Publishing Committee, 1980), 1:78.

this world (1 Pet. 2:11). Many an unbeliever, if honest, would have to admit to some Christian, "The LORD hath blessed me for thy sake" (Gen. 30:27).

By loving, doing good to, and praying for the wicked, God's children display the image of their kind and loving Father in heaven (Matt. 5:44–45). Godly Christians are the salt of the earth and the light of the world (vv. 13–16) as they bear the fruit of saving grace.

But we must not put too much emphasis on common grace or erase the difference between the church and the world. God's word to the church is still "Come out from among them" (2 Cor. 6:17). "The friendship of the world is enmity with God" (James 4:4).

We must also take care that we do not rest in common grace for our own souls. Merely outward morality is not evidence of salvation. The Spirit leads God's children to fight against their inner lusts and to love with sincerity (Gal. 5:16–24). We must be born again of the Spirit or we will never enter God's kingdom (John 3:3, 5).

The Spirit of God with Old Covenant Israel

Since Christ poured out the Holy Spirit on the day of Pentecost, someone might assume that the Spirit was absent before then. It is certainly true that the Holy Spirit does not appear as often in the Old Testament as in the New. He empowered relatively few people for ministry, not the whole people of God (Num. 11:29). However, the Spirit was not absent from Israel.

First, *the Spirit worked in the Old Testament as the Spirit of prophecy*. Peter says, "For the prophecy came not in old time by the will of man: but holy men of God spake as they were moved by the Holy Ghost" (2 Pet. 1:21). David said, "The Spirit of the LORD spake by me, and his word was in my tongue" (2 Sam 23:2). Whenever we read the words of the Old Testament, we should receive them as the words that "the Holy Ghost saith" (Heb. 3:7).

Second, *the Spirit worked in the Old Testament as the Spirit of power*. The Holy Spirit gave his servants effectual power to rule people for God's glory. Joshua was "a man in whom is the Spirit" (Num. 27:18 ESV). It is written of Othniel, "The Spirit of the LORD came upon him, and he judged Israel, and went out to war" (Judg. 3:10). When David was anointed with oil, "the Spirit of the LORD came upon [him] from that day forward" (1 Sam. 16:13).

Third, *the Spirit worked in the Old Testament as the Spirit of presence*. God was present with Israel at the exodus through the "Holy Spirit"

(Isa. 63:10–11 ESV). The Lord said to Israel, "I am with you . . . according to the word that I covenanted with you when ye came out of Egypt, so my spirit remaineth among you: fear ye not" (Hag. 2:4–5). Each Old Testament saint could rejoice that God's Spirit was with him wherever he went (Ps. 139:7–8).

Fourth, *the Spirit worked in the Old Testament as the Spirit of piety*. The Holy Spirit who saves people and works to make them holy today performed the same ministry before Christ came. After he sinned, David prayed, "Cast me not away from thy presence; and take not thy holy spirit from me" (Ps. 51:11). In the context, he was praying for spiritual cleansing, joy, forgiveness, and inward renewal (vv. 7–10). We read in another prayer, "Teach me to do thy will; for thou art my God: thy spirit is good; lead me into the land of uprightness" (143:10). This could be translated, "Let your good Spirit lead me" (ESV). God's Wisdom says, "Turn you at my reproof: behold, I will pour out my spirit unto you" (Prov. 1:23).

Our Lord Jesus Christ said, "Verily, verily, I say unto thee, Except a man be born again, he cannot see the kingdom of God. . . . Except a man be born of water and of the Spirit, he cannot enter into the kingdom of God" (John 3:3, 5). Christ also said that Abraham, Isaac, and Jacob—and the prophets who followed them—will be in the kingdom (Luke 13:28). Therefore, these saints were born of the Spirit. The new birth produces a life of righteousness, a radical break from sin, authentic Christian love, faith in Christ, and ability to overcome the world (1 John 2:29; 3:9; 4:7; 5:1, 4, 18). Unless we think that Abraham, Moses, David, and Isaiah had no repentance, faith, love, and obedience, we must conclude that they were born of the Spirit.

The indwelling of the Holy Spirit is necessary for a life of obedience. The Lord says, "I will put my Spirit within you, and cause you to walk in my statutes and be careful to obey my rules" (Ezek. 36:25–27 ESV). Similarly, Paul contrasts life in the Spirit with death in the flesh, saying that "they that are in the flesh cannot please God. But ye are not in the flesh, but in the Spirit, if so be that the Spirit of God dwell in you" (Rom. 8:8–9). Therefore, wherever we encounter spiritual life toward God, we meet a person indwelt by the Spirit. The saints of the Old Testament did walk in obedience to God's laws (Gen. 26:5; Ps. 119:60, 63, 67). Though the Holy Spirit was not poured out to the extent he is under the New Testament, he was dwelling in believers to make them holy.

The Old Testament saints craved and enjoyed fellowship with God. They found satisfaction in his presence (Ps. 36:8–9). They thirsted for God, their "exceeding joy" (42:1–4; 43:4). They declared that God was present like a river that makes people glad (46:4–5). They longed to see his power, glory, and love (63:1–8). They received spiritual illumination about the end of the wicked and the inheritance of the righteous, which is God himself (73:17–28). They longed to meet God and counted one day in his house as better than a thousand spent with the wicked (84:1–12). Are we to imagine that they desired and experienced communion with the living God apart from the grace of the Holy Spirit?

Practical Applications of the Spirit's Old Covenant Work

Although God's people are no longer under the old covenant (Heb. 8:13), the books of the Old Testament were written for our instruction and hope (Rom. 15:4). We can learn from the Spirit's work in ancient Israel that we must submit to the Spirit's words through the prophets. Whenever we read the Old Testament Scriptures, we are hearing the Holy Spirit speaking to us.

We must also rely on the Spirit's power. Throughout history, no one has been able to serve the Lord without the assistance of the Holy Spirit. Indeed, we need the Spirit's power to trust in the Lord and walk in obedience. Therefore, we must pray for the Spirit to work in us and in our churches. Since it is the Spirit's special work to bring God's presence to his people, we need the Holy Spirit if we are to commune with God in worship.

As much as we admire the Holy Spirit's work in the old covenant, we should be grateful for our privileges in the new covenant. We enjoy brighter revelation of Christ and his ways. The Spirit gives broader empowerment for ministry to members of Christ's body. There are multiplied opportunities to enter God's special presence wherever churches gather in Jesus's name. The Spirit grants greater liberty and assurance to God's children by the finished work of Christ. Do not take these privileges for granted. Instead, thank God for them.

The greatest lesson to learn is that Christ is always the Mediator. The same Spirit saved people in ancient times because there is only one Mediator of salvation. Athanasius said, "Surely as, before His becoming man, He, the Word, dispensed to the saints the Spirit as His own, so also when made man, He sanctifies all by the Spirit and says to His disciples, 'Receive ye the

Holy Ghost.' . . . Therefore 'Jesus Christ is the same yesterday, to-day, and for ever.' "[17] Therefore, may our study of the Spirit in the Old Testament lead us to Christ, to trust in him.

Suggested Songs to Sing to the Lord

- Psalm 104, "Thy Spirit, O Lord, makes life to abound," *Psalter*, No. 287; *THBap*, No. 110
- "Spirit, strength of all the weak," *THBap*, No. 244

Questions for Meditation or Discussion

1. Why is it important to know the Holy Spirit and his work?
2. What evidence is there in the Bible that the Holy Spirit is the Creator?
3. How is the Holy Spirit active in sustaining and ruling creation today?
4. What is common grace? How do the Holy Scriptures reveal God's common grace?
5. How do we need to be careful to think rightly about common grace?
6. How was the Holy Spirit at work in the Old Testament as the Spirit of (1) prophecy, (2) power, and (3) presence?
7. What evidence do we find in the Psalms and Proverbs that the Holy Spirit was working holiness in the Old Testament saints?
8. What do the words of Jesus in John 3:3 imply about the Old Testament saints? Why?
9. How would you explain the following statement by the authors: "Wherever we encounter spiritual life toward God, we meet a person indwelt by the Spirit"?
10. What practical applications can we draw from the Spirit's old covenant work?

17 Athanasius, *Discourses against the Arians*, 1.12.48, in *NPNF*[2], 4:334.

53

The Spirit of Christ and of Pentecost

Chapter Summary and Key Terms

The Holy Spirit is central to the work of Christ. The Spirit formed Christ's human nature in the womb of the virgin Mary. The Spirit came on Jesus at his baptism to empower him for ministry. Christ willingly offered himself as a sacrifice to God by the Spirit, and God raised Christ from the dead by the power of the Spirit. After Jesus ascended into heaven, he poured out the Holy Spirit on his church, baptizing his disciples with a greater fullness of the Spirit's power. *Pentecostalism* claims that *baptism with the Spirit* is a special empowerment given to some believers, shown by speaking in tongues. But the Scriptures teach that all believers have been baptized with the Spirit. This baptism fulfills what Jesus promised about the *Comforter* or *Advocate* sent by the Father and the Son to bear witness to Christ. We should always seek the power of the Spirit with the aim of glorifying Christ, for that is the Spirit's mission.

CHRIST STARTED HIS MINISTRY in Nazareth by reading the prophecy of Isaiah 61:1–2, which begins, "The Spirit of the Lord is upon me, because he hath anointed me." He then announced, "This day is this scripture fulfilled in your ears" (Luke 4:16–21). Though all the saints share in his anointing (2 Cor. 1:21), Christ is supremely the Anointed.

When we consider Christ's anointing with the Holy Spirit, we must remember the doctrines of the Trinity (chaps. 19–20) and the incarnation (chaps. 43–44). The Son and the Spirit are distinct persons, both fully God. They are one God with the Father. The incarnate Son is both God and man in one person. As the human Servant of the Lord, Christ received the graces of the Spirit to live in godliness and fulfill his earthly mission. As God the Son, the Mediator was anointed by the Father to give the Holy Spirit to sinful men.

God the Son had been working to save sinners by his Spirit long before he came as an incarnate man. His coming in the flesh with the fullness of the Spirit inaugurated the kingdom of God. After Christ died for our sins, rose from the dead, and ascended into heaven, he poured out the Holy Spirit on his church on the day of Pentecost. That event marked the beginning of a new era in which the Spirit's work increased in both power and extent.

The Holy Spirit and Christ's Earthly Life and Ministry

The Holy Spirit was with Jesus from his human beginning. Jesus was conceived in Mary "of the Holy Ghost" (Matt. 1:18, 20). The angel Gabriel told Mary, "The Holy Ghost shall come upon thee, and the power of the Highest shall overshadow thee: therefore also that holy thing which shall be born of thee shall be called the Son of God" (Luke 1:35). Christ would not be the God-man apart from the Spirit forming his humanity from Mary's flesh.

The Spirit filled Christ's ministry with power. God had promised, "Behold my servant, whom I uphold; mine elect, in whom my soul delighteth; I have put my spirit upon him: he shall bring forth judgment to the Gentiles" (Isa. 42:1). The Father fulfilled this promise at Christ's baptism: "The Holy Ghost descended in a bodily shape like a dove upon him, and a voice came from heaven, which said, Thou art my beloved Son; in thee I am well pleased" (Luke 3:22). Afterward, "Jesus being full of the Holy Ghost returned from Jordan, and was led by the Spirit into the wilderness" (4:1). So, too, believers are led by the Spirit, who bears witness to them that they are children of God (Rom. 8:14–16). Richard Sibbes said, "Whatsoever the Holy Ghost doth in us, he doth the same in Christ first, and he doth it in us because in Christ."[1]

The Holy Spirit gave Christ power to preach the gospel with grace and authority (Luke 4:14–19, 22, 32). John says, "He whom God hath sent speaketh the words of God: for God giveth not the Spirit by measure unto him" (John 3:34). Christ's words are "spirit" and "life," for through them the Holy Spirit gives eternal life (6:63).

1 Sibbes, *A Description of Christ*, in *WRS*, 1:18.

The Spirit equipped Christ to wage spiritual warfare against Satan, then "led" Jesus "into the wilderness to be tempted of the devil" (Matt. 4:1). Having overcome the Devil, Christ cast demons out of many people "by the Spirit of God" (12:28). Peter says, "God anointed Jesus of Nazareth with the Holy Ghost and with power: who went about doing good, and healing all that were oppressed of the devil; for God was with him" (Acts 10:38).

The Holy Spirit and Christ's Death, Resurrection, and Ascension

Since the Spirit led Christ in the path of obedience during his life, it is no surprise that the Spirit led Christ in his obedience unto death on the cross.

The Gospels do not mention the Spirit when Christ cried, "Abba, Father," in Gethsemane (Mark 14:36). But Paul says the Spirit moves God's adopted children to pray to their "Abba, Father" (Rom. 8:15; Gal. 4:6). The connection suggests that Jesus, too, was praying in the Spirit.

Christ "through the eternal Spirit offered himself without spot to God" (Heb. 9:14). Some theologians have taken the term "eternal Spirit" to mean Christ's deity. But "Spirit" often refers to the Holy Spirit in Hebrews, not to the divine nature. Therefore, "through the eternal Spirit" most likely means that the Holy Spirit gave Christ the strength to offer himself on the cross. The Spirit filled his human soul with love for the Father and compassion toward sinners so that he willingly gave his life for them, as John Owen said.[2]

God raised Christ from the dead by the power of the Holy Spirit (Rom. 1:4). Paul says, "If the Spirit of him that raised up Jesus from the dead dwell in you, he that raised up Christ from the dead shall also quicken your mortal bodies by his Spirit that dwelleth in you" (8:11). Christ was put to death in the flesh but made alive in the Spirit (1 Pet. 3:18).

Though the Spirit filled Christ throughout his life, Christ received a greater fullness to pour out on his people when he ascended into heaven (Acts 2:32–33). John Flavel said, "Whatever spiritual grace or excellency is in Christ, it is not appropriated to himself, but they do share with him: for indeed he was filled with the fulness of the Spirit, for their sakes and use: as the sun is filled with light, not to shine to itself, but to others; so is Christ with grace."[3]

2 Owen, *Pneumatologia*, in *WJO*, 3:177.

3 Flavel, *The Method of Grace*, in *WJF*, 2:142.

Christ now reigns as King through the sevenfold fullness of the Spirit (Isa. 11:2; Rev. 3:1; 5:6). The Holy Spirit is the agent of Christ's grace throughout the world. The Spirit joins Christ to his redeemed people (1 Cor. 6:17, 19). Paul says that the saints are "the epistle of Christ ministered by us, written not with ink, but with the Spirit of the living God; not in tables of stone, but in fleshy tables of the heart" (2 Cor. 3:3). Christ does not merely give his commands to his people. He gives them life by the Holy Spirit (v. 6).

Practical Applications of the Spirit of Christ for the Christian Life

The main application of this doctrine is that we should exercise faith in Jesus Christ. Whenever we perceive any spiritual need in ourselves or others, we must go to Christ, in whom the fullness of the Spirit dwells, to ask him to meet that need. Sibbes said, "We have a full treasury to go to. All treasure is hid in Christ for us."[4]

This doctrine rebukes Christians for their spiritual weakness. Sibbes said, "Men live as if Christ were nothing, or did nothing concerning them . . . as if he had received the Spirit only for himself and not for them, whereas all that is in Christ is for us."[5] Let us, therefore, stir ourselves up to take hold of Christ by faith. In grasping Christ, we will receive the Spirit of God for our every need. Then we will be able to say, "I can do all things through Christ which strengtheneth me" (Phil. 4:13).

If we truly know the Spirit of Christ, we will walk in increasing holiness in the image of Christ. The Heidelberg Catechism says, "Christ, having redeemed and delivered us by His blood, also renews us by His Holy Spirit after His own image."[6] Follow Christ in faith, prayer, suffering, and obedience by the power of the Spirit.

Christ's Baptism of His People with the Spirit at Pentecost

During the celebration of Pentecost after Christ's ascension, God poured out the Holy Spirit with great power. The biblical term for this outpouring of grace is *baptism with the Spirit*. John the Baptist said, "I baptize you with water, but he who is mightier than I is coming, the strap of whose sandals I am not worthy to untie. He will baptize you with the Holy Spirit and fire"

4 Sibbes, *A Description of Christ*, in *WRS*, 1:20–21.

5 Sibbes, *A Description of Christ*, in *WRS*, 1:21.

6 The Heidelberg Catechism (LD 32, Q. 86), in *TFU*, 98.

(Luke 3:16 ESV). Baptism with the Spirit is a figure of speech for being flooded with God's grace.

John echoed ancient prophecy. The Lord had said, "Fear not, O Jacob, my servant; and thou, Jesurun, whom I have chosen. I will pour water upon him that is thirsty, and floods upon the dry ground: I will pour my spirit upon thy seed, and my blessing upon thine offspring: and they shall spring up as among the grass, as willows by the water courses" (Isa. 44:2–4). The Lord further said, "I will pour out my spirit upon all flesh" (Joel 2:28).

After Jesus Christ died and rose from the dead, he told his disciples that they would be his "witnesses" to "all nations, beginning at Jerusalem," and commanded them to wait in Jerusalem until "I send the promise of my Father upon you . . . until ye be endued with power from on high" (Luke 24:47–49). Christ explained, "For John truly baptized with water; but ye shall be baptized with the Holy Ghost not many days hence. . . . But ye shall receive power, after that the Holy Ghost is come upon you: and ye shall be witnesses unto me both in Jerusalem, and in all Judaea, and in Samaria, and unto the uttermost part of the earth" (Acts 1:5, 8).

After Christ ascended into heaven, the disciples gathered in Jerusalem, seeking God in prayer and waiting for baptism with the Spirit as the Lord had commanded. On the day of Pentecost, there was "a sound from heaven as of a rushing mighty wind, and . . . tongues like as of fire . . . sat upon each of them. And they were all filled with the Holy Ghost, and began to speak with other tongues, as the Spirit gave them utterance" (Acts 2:2–4). Filled by the power of the Spirit, Peter preached Christ in the very city where he had been crucified. Three thousand were saved (v. 41).

Pentecost was an annual feast in the Jewish calendar on the fiftieth day after the Passover. Also called "the feast of weeks," it was when Israel brought the firstfruits of the wheat harvest to the Lord (Ex. 23:16; 34:22; Lev. 23:15–22). The salvation of Jews from many places during this feast suggests that Christ gathered the firstfruits of a great harvest from the nations (cf. Rom. 16:5; 1 Cor. 16:15) by the power of the Spirit (Luke 24:47–49; Acts 1:8).

Since Pentecost, Christ grants baptism with the Holy Spirit to the whole church and every true member of it, Jew or Gentile (Acts 11:16–17). Peter said at Pentecost, "Repent, and be baptized every one of you in the name of Jesus Christ for the remission of sins, and ye shall receive the gift of the Holy Ghost" (Acts 2:38).

Paul explains, "For as the body is one, and hath many members, and all the members of that one body, being many, are one body: so also is Christ. For by one Spirit are we all baptized into one body, whether we be Jews or Gentiles, whether we be bond or free; and have been all made to drink into one Spirit" (1 Cor. 12:12–13). Baptism with the Spirit unites all those who belong to Christ. Though the Corinthian church was very immature (3:1–3), Paul did not command its members to be baptized with the Spirit. He taught them that they already shared in this baptism as members of Christ's body. Just as believers are "one spirit" with Christ (6:17), so they are united by "one Spirit" with one another in Christ (12:13; Eph. 2:18; 4:4).

Christ baptized his people with the Holy Spirit beginning at Pentecost and continues to bring each new convert into the same grace. By baptizing his people with the Spirit, Christ floods them with grace, gives them all power to serve him for the building of his church, and unites them as one people. Therefore, baptism with the Spirit is not the same as being born again by the Spirit. It is a newly increased work of Christ that he gives to all God's children, though all do not experience this gift to the same degree.

The doctrine of baptism with the Spirit displays the great spiritual advance that God accomplished for his people through his Son. Formerly the Spirit of Christ empowered only a limited number of people to serve God's kingdom. Now the Spirit empowers every saint to build up the body. In previous times, the Spirit focused his activity on the nation of Israel. Now he powerfully evangelizes and unites individuals from all nations and social classes to form one body in Christ. Pentecost launched Christ's worldwide assault on Satan's kingdom. How zealous are we for the advance of the gospel among all nations?

The Claims of Pentecostalism

Contrary to Reformed teaching about baptism with the Spirit, a key doctrine of *Pentecostalism* is that baptism with the Spirit is a special empowerment for life and service, often received after salvation and shown by speaking in tongues. Pentecostal theologians argue that many Christians have received authentic spiritual experiences of a baptism with power after their conversion.

In reply, we say that experiences must always be tested and interpreted according to the Holy Scriptures. Some spiritual experiences are demonic (2 Cor. 11:13–15; 1 John 4:1–6). Some are merely human. Some are human responses to God that are not caused by God's saving grace (Mark 4:16–17; John 18:6). It is also possible for a Christian who has already been baptized with the Spirit to have a fresh experience of the Spirit's filling (Acts 4:31).

Pentecostal theologians also argue that the book of Acts shows that believers often received baptism with the Spirit after conversion (Acts 2:1–4; 8:12–17; 9:17–18).

In reply, we note that in the book of Acts, Luke tells us about many unique events after Christ ascended. Some of those baptized with the Spirit were Jewish disciples who already had been saved before Christ began his reign in glory (2:1–4). Some were Gentiles long estranged from the Jews, such as the Samaritans, who were included for the first time in Christ's kingdom by faith (8:12–17). We should not treat such unique events as patterns to follow. Luke does not present a consistent pattern in Acts about the baptism or gift of the Spirit. Cornelius and his household were baptized with the Spirit as soon as they were converted (Acts 10:44–48; 11:15–18). Peter promises the gift of the Spirit to *all* who repent (2:38).

As we observed earlier, Paul says, "By one Spirit are we all baptized into one body" (1 Cor. 12:13). Paul uses the same Greek words and grammar to describe Spirit baptism as other references to it in the Gospels and the book of Acts.[7] The words "we all" show that every true member of Christ's body—all the saved—are now baptized with the Spirit.

Christ's Promise of the Advocate

If baptism with the Holy Spirit is a new gift to the whole church, something begun after Christ ascended into heaven, what is new about it? The Holy Spirit regenerated and indwelt people under the old covenant (see chap. 52). But the Lord Jesus said that the Holy Spirit was going to come as "another Comforter" (John 14:16). As another *Comforter*, the Spirit's work extends the mission of the Son in a new way on earth.

In ancient Greek literature, the word translated as "Comforter" meant an advocate, a person called to speak for another in court.[8] The same word is used of Christ as the "advocate" who intercedes for his people with the Father on the basis of his sacrifice (1 John 2:1–2).

7 Compare Matt. 3:11; Mark 1:8; Luke 3:16; John 1:33; and Acts 1:5.

8 *TDNT*, 5:800–803; and Leon Morris, *The Gospel according to John*, The New International Commentary on the New Testament (Grand Rapids, MI: Eerdmans, 1995), 665–66.

Therefore, Christ promised to send the Spirit as the Advocate to testify to men. The context of this teaching was Christ's arrest, trial, and sentencing to death by the wicked world (John 18–19). Christ explained that the world unjustly hates him and his disciples because he exposes sin (15:18–25). God and the world are like two contenders in court. Christ said that the Advocate would "testify of me" when the apostles bore witness (vv. 26–27). The Spirit would come to "reprove the world of sin" (16:8).

The world hates and persecutes Christ's disciples (John 15:18–20; 16:1–3). But God and Christ send the Advocate to vindicate them. By the Spirit's presence in them (14:16–17), the Father and the Son come to them and dwell in them (vv. 20–21, 23), so that they are not "orphans" after Christ's ascension (v. 18, KJV mg., ESV). By sending the Advocate, Christ leaves peace with his disciples that fortifies them against fear (v. 27; 16:33).

The Advocate always works as "the Spirit of truth" (John 14:17; 15:26; 16:13). The Father sent the Advocate in Christ's name to teach his disciples and keep in their minds the truths revealed by Christ (14:26). He said the Spirit of truth would teach them truths that Christ had not revealed in his earthly ministry because his disciples could not receive them yet (16:12–13). But the Spirit would not teach truth apart from Christ. Jesus said, "He shall glorify me" (v. 14).

Christ said that he would send the Advocate after his ascension to heaven (John 16:5, 7). His promise was fulfilled on the day of Pentecost, as we can see by what God did through Peter's preaching. Sinners were convicted, Christ was glorified, and believers had much joy in the Lord (Acts 2:31–37, 46). Peter later said, "We are his witnesses of these things [Christ's exaltation]; and so is also the Holy Ghost, whom God hath given to them that obey him" (5:32). The Spirit continues this same work today through the ministry of the Word.

Do you know the ministry of the Advocate in your life? Has the Holy Spirit ever touched your conscience and awakened you to see that you not only do bad things but have wickedness in your very heart? Has the truth of God's Word come to you in a manner that you see the glory of God's Son? Having believed in Jesus Christ alone for salvation, do you know that God is your Father and you are his dear child? These are the works of the Spirit of truth as he testifies through the gospel.

Suggested Song to Sing to the Lord

- "O Spirit of the living God," *THBap*, No. 253

Questions for Meditation or Discussion

1. How was the Holy Spirit involved in the earthly life and ministry of Christ?
2. How did the Holy Spirit give Jesus power to suffer, die, and rise again?
3. What does Christ do through the Spirit today as he reigns at God's right hand?
4. What implications does the Spirit's work in Christ have for the Christian life?
5. What does it mean to be baptized with the Holy Spirit? When did this baptism first take place?
6. According to Pentecostalism, what is the baptism with the Spirit? When may it take place?
7. What arguments are made for Pentecostalism? How can we answer those arguments?
8. When Christ calls the Spirit "another Comforter," what does the word "Comforter" mean?
9. How did the Holy Spirit work as an Advocate on the day of Pentecost?
10. In light of what you learned from this chapter, how should you be praying for the Holy Spirit to work today?

54

The Gifts of the Spirit and Cessationism

Chapter Summary and Key Terms

Christ equips the members of his body to serve by gifts of the Spirit. A *spiritual gift* is a gracious stewardship from God that gives a person power to build up Christ's church by the activity of the Holy Spirit. Each believer has a spiritual gift. He or she should use it to build up the body of Christ in submission to God's Word and the elders of his or her local church. There are gifts for the special revelation of the Word (*apostle* and prophet), gifts for signs and wonders (*miracles*, healing, and speaking in *tongues*), and gifts for ordinary service (teaching, exhorting, leading, helping, giving, and so on). *Continuationism* is the view that the Spirit gives all the gifts today (though some exclude apostles in the sense of Peter and Paul). However, *cessationism* is the more biblical view; it says that the gifts of special revelation and signs and wonders have ceased.

WITH THE OUTPOURING of the Spirit came many spiritual gifts from the ascended Christ (Eph. 4:8). Thus, Paul says that his ministry as an apostle arose from "the gift of the grace of God given unto me by the effectual working of his power" (3:7). He also affirms, "Unto every one of us is given grace according to the measure of the gift of Christ" (4:7).

Those gifts included the grace granted to apostles and prophets (Eph. 4:11) to receive new special revelation from God (3:5). They also included the grace given to the apostles and others to perform works of supernatural power: "Many wonders and signs were done by the apostles" (Acts 2:43). This is why the book of Acts is full of accounts of miracles. There are also gifts for ordinary service, by which believers minister today through word and deed.

In this chapter, we will examine the Bible's teaching on spiritual gifts. We will also argue for the doctrine of *cessationism*, the teaching that God has ceased giving new special revelation and gifts of signs and wonders, though the Spirit still works mightily in the church. The alternative is *continuationism*, the doctrine that God continues to give all or almost all of the spiritual gifts. Examples of continuationism may be found in Pentecostalism (see the last chapter) and the broader charismatic movement.

The Gifts of the Holy Spirit in General

When the New Testament refers to abilities for spiritual service as "gifts," it often uses a word that identifies them as grace freely given by God (1 Cor. 1:7; cf. v. 4). They are also called "spiritual gifts" (12:1; 14:1), literally "spiritual things." That means they are from the Holy Spirit and have to do with Christ's spiritual kingdom. Each gift is "the manifestation of the Spirit" (12:7), a display of his presence and power. All gifts include the power "to profit" other people (v. 7). Therefore, a spiritual gift is a gracious stewardship from God that gives a person power to build up Christ's church by the activity of the Holy Spirit.

The spiritual gifts are both manifestations of common grace and means of saving grace. But they themselves are not saving grace. Spiritual gifts may be exercised by wicked hypocrites, such as Judas (Matt. 10:1–4). Even working miracles will not prevent such people from being condemned on the last day (7:21–23). Saving grace comes from God's election of a person to be his beloved child. Gifts come from God's choice of a person for some work or office.

When God gives a spiritual gift, he imparts ability to an individual so that he or she can exercise a regular ministry by the Spirit's power according to God's will. A gift consists of more than a single action or event. Paul says that people "have," or possess, gifts (1 Cor. 12:30; cf. Rom. 12:6). This implies that a gift is not merely a particular act of God. It is a spiritual stewardship in which the Lord entrusts some of his resources to his servants (1 Pet. 4:10). Different gifts equip different members of Christ's body for different forms of service (Rom. 12:4–6).

Every Christian has a spiritual gift (1 Cor. 12:7; Eph. 4:7; 1 Pet. 4:10). That implies that each person receives at least one gift as soon as he is saved. But God might add gifts or strengthen present gifts in answer to prayer (1 Cor.

14:13; 1 Tim. 4:14). Christians have a responsibility to stir up their gifts (2 Tim. 1:6). The various lists of spiritual gifts in the New Testament show that God gives a diversity of gifts to his church.[1]

The Spiritual Gifts for Extraordinary Ministry of the Word

We may group the spiritual gifts into three main categories. There are gifts for extraordinary ministry of the Word, gifts for signs and wonders, and gifts for ordinary service. We begin with gifts by which the Spirit gave power for the extraordinary ministry of the Word.

Apostleship

The word translated as "apostle" means someone who is sent. Sometimes it has the general sense of "messenger" (2 Cor. 8:23; Phil. 2:25). However, it is most often used in the New Testament for a special group of men directly appointed by Jesus Christ (Luke 6:13). They were eyewitnesses of the risen Lord (Acts 1:22; 1 Cor. 9:1; 15:7–8).

The apostles were extraordinary ministers of the new covenant. God revealed truth directly to them (Gal. 1:1, 11–12). They spoke as God spoke in them (Matt. 10:20; 2 Cor. 13:3), and what they wrote was the word of the Lord (1 Cor. 14:37).

The Lord Jesus appointed apostles to heal, cast out demons, and preach the gospel of the kingdom (Matt. 10:1–8). God confirmed their office with "the signs of an apostle . . . signs, and wonders, and mighty deeds" (2 Cor. 12:12). The apostles also governed the church as its shepherds with the elders (John 21:15–17; Acts 15; 1 Pet. 5:1).

The Cessation of Apostleship

By the beginning of the second century AD, the last of the apostles had died. The New Testament contains no record that they appointed men to succeed them as apostles. Instead, the apostles established a church order consisting of elders and deacons (Phil. 1:1; 1 Tim. 3:1–13).

Therefore, we conclude that the apostles of Christ had a unique ministry in Christian history. There are no apostles today. It is contrary to Scripture

1 For lists of gifts presented in Rom. 12:6–8; 1 Cor. 12:8–10, 28, 29–30; Eph. 4:11; and 1 Pet. 4:10–11, see table 6.1, "Lists of Spiritual Gifts in Original Order," in Beeke and Smalley, *RST*, 3:163.

for Christians to use "apostle" for an office or spiritual gift in the church at the present time. People who call themselves apostles often build personal empires based on their claim to direct revelation and authority from God. These so-called apostles bear little likeness to the apostles of Jesus Christ. They resemble the false apostles against whom Paul warned (2 Cor. 11:13–21). The followers of the true apostles are those who receive the Holy Scriptures as the Word of God.

Prophecy

Prophets received, spoke, and wrote the word of the Lord by the inspiration of the Holy Spirit (see chap. 6). They spoke truth directly "revealed" to them by God (1 Cor. 14:29–31; Eph. 3:5). Old Testament prophets often said, "Thus saith the Lord." A New Testament prophet said, "Thus saith the Holy Ghost" (Acts 21:11).

Paul also lists "discerning of spirits" among the spiritual gifts (1 Cor. 12:10). The word "discerning" means judging between good and bad. The word "spirits" refers to activity connected to prophets (v. 32; cf. 1 John 4:1). There was a need to judge prophecies (1 Cor. 14:29). Therefore, discerning of spirits was the gift of recognizing whether a prophecy was of God.

The Cessation of Prophecy

With the incarnation, humiliation, and exaltation of Jesus Christ, God's final word has come to man. God formerly granted special revelation through mere men. Now he has spoken "by his Son" (Heb. 1:1–2). Christ's coming has started the "last days" (v. 2). The revelation given us through Christ is "the faith which was *once* delivered unto the saints" (Jude 3).

Just as Christ made atonement for sins once for all (Heb. 10:10), so he brought the revelation of God's will for our salvation once for all. The most fundamental reason for cessationism is the sufficiency of Jesus Christ, as revealed in the Word of God (Col. 2:6–10). In Christ "are hid all the treasures of wisdom and knowledge" (v. 3).

The new covenant church is God's new temple, "built upon the foundation of the apostles and prophets, Jesus Christ himself being the chief corner stone" (Eph. 2:20). The context of this verse is the massive advance of God's purpose for the nations through Christ's death (vv. 11–22). Therefore, the "foundation" speaks to the unique place of the apostles and prophets in history. The foundation was laid in their publication of the word of Christ: "The mystery of Christ . . . is now revealed unto his holy apostles and prophets by the Spirit" (3:4–5). Having given the church this foundation of truth, God no longer speaks through prophets today.

True prophets of God were infallible in their prophecies. Moses says, "When a prophet speaketh in the name of the LORD, if the thing follow not, nor come to pass, that is the thing which the LORD hath not spoken, but the prophet hath spoken it presumptuously: thou shalt not be afraid of him" (Deut. 18:22). Those who claim to be prophets today must submit to the Bible's standard of prophecy—that prophecies are inerrant truth.

Someone might object that the New Testament tells us that Christians must "judge" and "prove" the message of prophets (1 Cor. 14:29; 1 Thess. 5:19–21). Therefore, it is said, there was a kind of prophecy that could contain errors, at least after Christ came.

In reply, we argue that Christians were commanded to test and prove prophecies because "many false prophets are gone out into the world" (1 John 4:1). All claims to new revelation had to be tested by prior revelation (Acts 17:11; Gal. 1:8–9). But that does not mean that true prophets of God erred. Rather, false prophets needed to be exposed.

We conclude, therefore, that God no longer gives new special revelation through prophets. He has given us the Holy Scriptures in all their fullness, the "former ways of God's revealing His will unto His people being now ceased," as the Westminster Confession says.[2]

The doctrine of cessationism protects us from spiritual bondage. No church leader has the right to assert the authority of having received direct revelations from God. No believer should pressure another by claiming his advice is a word from the Lord, apart from Scripture.

Christians have the liberty to regard their feelings and inner impressions for what they are—the thoughts of man, not personal directions from the Holy Spirit. The Spirit leads God's children by drawing them along the pathway of love and holiness (Rom. 8:12–17; Gal. 5:19–24). But the Spirit guides us in the right path by the Word. John Calvin said that Christ gives his Spirit not for "the task of inventing new and unheard-of revelations,"

2 The Westminster Confession of Faith (1.1), in *RC*, 4:233–34. Cf. the Second London Baptist Confession (1.1), in *RC*, 4:532.

but of "sealing our minds with that very doctrine which is commended by the gospel."[3]

Gifts for Signs and Wonders

In the New Testament, a miracle is often called a "sign" because it was evidence that a person had been sent by God (Acts 14:3). "Signs" are also called "wonders" because they amazed and awed people (2:43; 5:11–12). They also revealed God's presence (Luke 7:16). Sometimes another word is translated as "miracles," a word literally meaning "powers," because they were mighty acts of God (Acts 2:22). In its full sense in the Bible, a miracle was an extraordinary, observable event caused by God that evoked awe at his presence because it confirmed his word of salvation and judgment.

Gifts of Miracles

In some lists of spiritual gifts, Paul refers to "the working of miracles" and "miracles" (1 Cor. 12:10, 28–29). Almost all the miracles worked through Christ's servants and recorded in the New Testament consisted of healing diseases and disabilities, speaking in tongues, and casting out demons.

Paul also lists "faith" as a spiritual gift (1 Cor. 12:9). Paul does not mean saving faith here. He says, "Though I have all faith, so that I could remove mountains, and have not charity [love], I am nothing" (13:2). So "faith" might mean faith to work miracles. Alternatively, moving a mountain might be a figure of speech for overcoming obstacles to God's kingdom (Zech. 4:6–7). If so, then "faith" might be not a miraculous gift but a gift for ordinary ministry.

Gifts of Healing

Paul writes of "gifts of healing" (1 Cor. 12:9, 28, 30). Healing in the New Testament consisted of the supernatural restoration of the body to health. Christ healed lame legs, blind eyes, deaf ears, leprosy, a withered hand, a serious fever, long-term bleeding, and a severed ear.[4] The apostles healed men who had been lame for years (Acts 3:1–8; 9:32–35; 14:8–10). The effects of such healings were obvious, for they demonstrated the power of the living God.

3 Calvin, *Institutes*, 1.9.1.

4 Matt. 9:27–30; 11:5; 15:30; Mark 3:1–5; Luke 4:38–39; 8:43–44; 22:51.

Speaking in Tongues

Paul speaks of the gift of "kinds of tongues" and those who "speak with tongues" (1 Cor. 12:10, 28, 30). This gift consisted in the supernatural ability to speak a message from God in other languages (Acts 2:11). It was closely related to prophecy (vv. 17–18; 19:6). Speaking in tongues produced words from God that the speaker did not understand and that hearers could not understand unless they spoke the language the speaker was using (1 Cor. 14:2). Tongues was a sign of God's judgment on the nation of Israel for rejecting Christ (Acts 2:33, 36; 1 Cor. 14:21). Yet it was also a sign that God was reversing the judgment at Babel (Gen. 11:7–9) and bringing people from all nations into his covenant (Acts 10:44–47).

God gifted some people to "interpret" words spoken in tongues for the edification of the church (1 Cor. 14:5). To "interpret" means to translate into a language understood by one's hearers or readers (Acts 9:36). The words spoken in tongues were not babble or nonsense but prayers and blessings to God (10:46). They would call forth an "Amen" from other believers if translated into speech they could understand (1 Cor. 14:15–16).

The Cessation of Gifts for Signs and Wonders

Cessationism holds that God has ceased to give gifts for signs and wonders. God decreed that he would administer different seasons of history in different ways. Not every generation saw firsthand his mighty works of redemption or received new special revelation. Some of God's saints have said, "We see not our signs: there is no more any prophet" (Ps. 74:9).

God chose to concentrate his miracles in certain periods of history, especially the days of Moses and Aaron, Elijah and Elisha, and Jesus Christ and his apostles. These miracle workers invoked judgments on nations, divided the sea, obtained miraculous provisions of food, raised the dead, called down fire from heaven, and healed people of major disabilities. These were not common events. Even in the book of Acts, most miracles took place "by the hands of the apostles" (Acts 5:12). People sought the apostles (not just Christians in general) to receive healing (vv. 15–16).

How can we explain these concentrations of miracles? The Bible teaches that signs and wonders served to authenticate the messengers of special revelation (Ex. 4:1–5; 1 Kings 17:24). God was "bearing them witness, both with signs and wonders, and with divers miracles" (Heb. 2:4). These concentrations of miracles also happened at significant moments in history—when the Lord redeemed Israel from its bondage to Egypt and made it his holy nation, when the prophets confronted Israel over its covenant breaking, and when God the Son came in the flesh.

Jonathan Edwards said, "The thing chiefly designed by the extraordinary gifts was to introduce and establish that standing revelation of the mind and will of God by his word, as the grand means of grace and standing rule of faith and practice through all ages." But when that rule of faith was complete, "then those extraordinary influences of the Spirit of God withdrew and vanished away. . . . They are no more to be expected in the Christian church."[5]

What are claimed today to be miraculous gifts are pale shadows of the biblical realities. The messages of so-called prophets prove false. Many sick people have gone to self-proclaimed healers with hearts full of hope but have returned home sadly disappointed. Some promoters of speaking in tongues shamelessly teach congregations to repeat nonsensical syllables, as if babble were a spiritual gift. And where are the dead being raised to life again? As John Chrysostom observed many centuries ago, miraculous gifts have had a "cessation, being such as then used to occur but now no longer take place."[6]

Therefore, we are justified in speaking of a distinct "apostolic age" in which God chose to work a great concentration of miracles. He granted gifts of signs and wonders then because the new covenant was dawning in Christ. God still works powerfully today in answer to prayer, but he no longer gives people gifts or ministries of miracles.

Gifts for Ordinary Service

Even in the apostolic age, not everyone was an apostle, prophet, or miracle worker (1 Cor. 12:29). However, every member of Christ's body has a gift and is needed for the health and growth of the church (v. 21). God the Holy Spirit still works today with great power through the ordinary gifts of his servants.

5 Edwards, "Extraordinary Gifts of the Spirit Are Inferior to Graces of the Spirit," in *WJE*, 25:285, 287. See Owen, *The Duty of Pastors and People Distinguished*, in *WJO*, 13:31–32.

6 Chrysostom, *Homilies on 1 Corinthians*, 29.1, in *NPNF*[1], 12:168.

Gifts for Speaking God's Truth

One precious spiritual gift is teaching the truth of God's Word (Rom. 12:7; 1 Cor. 12:28–29; Eph. 4:11). Another is exhorting—that is, urging people to act on the truth (Titus 2:6, 15). Teaching and exhorting go together (1 Tim. 4:13; 6:2; 2 Tim. 4:2), yet Paul distinguishes between these two gifts (Rom. 12:7–8). This suggests that some people are more gifted in doctrinal instruction and others in practical admonition.

Paul also refers to a "word of wisdom" and a "word of knowledge" (1 Cor. 12:8). These probably refer to gifts used to communicate wisdom and knowledge.

Paul groups "pastors and teachers" together (Eph. 4:11). The word translated as "pastor" means "shepherd," a title describing the work of all elders (Acts 20:28; 1 Pet. 5:2). All pastors and elders must be able to teach (1 Tim. 3:2). But the Scriptures do not say that all teachers must be pastors. There are many ways in which teachers can serve in the church besides being elders or preachers.

Gifts for Practical Service

Paul names the gift of "helps" (1 Cor. 12:28). The Greek word used here means help, assistance, or strength. Thus, "helps" likely refers to spiritual gifts for providing practical assistance and encouragement to the poor, sick, and needy.

The gifts of ministry, giving, and mercy are kinds of help. Paul lists "ministry" as a different gift from teaching (Rom. 12:7), so it refers to the gift of doing good works that meet the physical needs of the church and its members (cf. 1 Pet. 4:11). When Paul speaks of giving (Rom. 12:8), he seems to have in mind a special ability from God's Spirit to give money or material goods for the aid of others. Mercy is the kindness to help others in their weaknesses and sorrows (Matt. 9:27) or to protect them from troubles that threaten to fall on them (Phil. 2:27). The mention of the gift of mercy (Rom. 12:8) implies that the Holy Spirit gives some Christians a much larger capacity to show effective mercy to people in misery.

Gifts for Leadership

Paul says that other gifts that God has set in the church include "governments" (1 Cor. 12:28). This refers to the gift to provide wise direction for a group of Christians serving together. Paul also speaks of a gift of ruling: "he that ruleth, with diligence" (Rom. 12:8). The Greek verb translated as "rule" implies both leadership and care.

It does not appear that government and ruling express two different gifts. They are most likely different descriptions in different passages of Scripture for the same gift. Leadership gifts are important for those who bear office in the church, but they do not require an office in the church to be used. Many forms of service require the ability to organize and give direction.

Practical Applications of Spiritual Gifts

The doctrine of spiritual gifts has significant practical applications for us as we think about our responsibilities as Christians and members of the church.

First, *judge your gifts with humble, sober realism*. Paul says, "For I say, through the grace given unto me, to every man that is among you, not to think of himself more highly than he ought to think; but to think soberly, according as God hath dealt to every man the measure of faith" (Rom. 12:3). Examine yourself and how God has used you in the past. Ask for counsel from wise, godly people who know you. What are your gifts?

Second, *employ your gifts in active church membership*. Christians are members of one another in the body and have different functions (Rom. 12:4–5). They put their gifts into active exercise—not half-heartedly but with "generosity," "zeal," and "cheerfulness" (vv. 6–8 ESV). Be "fervent in spirit; serving the Lord" (v. 11).

Third, *cherish the other gifts and rely on the other members of the body*. Paul teaches, "The eye cannot say unto the hand, I have no need of thee: nor again the head to the feet, I have no need of you" (1 Cor. 12:21). Learn to say to your brothers and sisters, "Please help me. I need you."

Fourth, *treasure and pursue love above any spiritual gift*. If we have the greatest gifts but lack love, we are "nothing" (1 Cor. 13:1–3). So "pursue love" (14:1 ESV).

Fifth, *use your gifts for peace, order, and edification in the church*. Giftedness is no excuse for disrupting the church or disregarding the authority of its officers. Paul says, "Let all things be done unto edifying. . . . For God is not the author of confusion, but of peace, as in all churches of the saints. . . . Let all things be done decently and in order" (1 Cor. 14:26, 33, 40).

Sixth, *submit your gifts to the direction of the Lord Christ through his Word.* Christ gave the ministers of the Word to equip the saints (Eph. 4:10–12). Do not use your gifts as a maverick. Only when church members are listening to the preaching of the Word by Christ's servants are they ready to use their gifts well.

Seventh, *serve as a steward of God's grace for his glory.* Peter says, "As every man hath received the gift, even so minister the same one to another, as good stewards of the manifold grace of God . . . that God in all things may be glorified through Jesus Christ, to whom be praise and dominion for ever and ever" (1 Pet. 4:10–11).

Suggested Song to Sing to the Lord

- Psalm 105, "O praise the Lord, His deeds make known," *Psalter*, No. 289

Questions for Meditation or Discussion

1. What does the New Testament teach us about spiritual gifts in general?
2. What are the three main categories of spiritual gifts?
3. What is an apostle? Are there apostles today? Why or why not?
4. What are the gifts of prophecy and discerning of spirits?
5. How can we argue that God has ceased giving new prophecies or special revelation?
6. Why are miracles called signs, wonders, and powers in the New Testament?
7. What are the gifts of tongues and interpretation?
8. What argument can be made that God has ceased giving gifts for signs and wonders?
9. What are the gifts for ordinary service?
10. What is our duty regarding spiritual gifts? Are you doing your duty? How?

Section 5B

The Spirit and the Application of Salvation

55

Union with Christ and the Order of Salvation

Chapter Summary and Key Terms

Salvation belongs to those who are in Christ. *Union with Christ* is the bond God forms between his Son and his people. God first formed a *federal union* in his eternal decree so that Christ represents the elect in the covenant of grace. By this union, Christ died and rose again for them. Then, in time, God creates *mystical union*. This is not *mysticism* that directly unites God and man so that mere human beings participate in God's uncreated glory (*deification* or *theosis*). Rather, it is union with the incarnate Christ by the work of the Spirit through faith in the Word. The Holy Spirit applies salvation through union with Christ in a series of blessings called the *order of salvation*. This order begins with the general gospel call and often preparation by grace through conviction of sin. It continues with effectual calling and regeneration, faith in Jesus Christ and repentance unto life, justification and adoption, sanctification, perseverance by the grace of preservation, and lastly glorification. By union with Christ, believers enjoy fellowship with God and participation in Christ's sufferings and power.

THE SPIRIT APPLIES SALVATION by bringing people into *union with Christ*.[1] In the mind of the apostle Paul, to be "without Christ" is to have "no hope" and to be "without God in the world" (Eph. 2:12). But "in Christ," we have "all spiritual blessings" (1:3).

1 The Westminster Shorter Catechism (Q. 30); and the Baptist Catechism (Q. 33), in *RC*, 4:357, 577.

John Calvin wrote,

> As long as Christ remains outside of us, and we are separated from him, all that he has suffered and done for the salvation of the human race remains useless and of no value for us. Therefore, to share with us what he has received from the Father, he had to become ours and to dwell within us. . . . The Holy Spirit is the bond by which Christ effectually unites us to himself.[2]

Union with the Last Adam

God gave us a picture of the union between Christ and his people in the oneness of mankind in Adam. Christ stands like Adam as the head of his people. Paul calls Adam "the figure [type] of him that was to come" (Rom. 5:14). Adam's transgression resulted in mankind's condemnation and death. Christ stands as the head of his people so that his righteousness becomes their justification and life (vv. 15–19).

Christ is the covenant officer with whom God's people are one. Adam stood as mankind's representative in God's first covenant (Gen. 2:16–17). Christ represents his people before God. Adam was the first prophet, priest, and king. In a far greater way, Christ is our Prophet, Priest and King (see chap. 45).

Christ is "in" his people, and they are "in" him (John 14:20; 15:4–5). Believers are "in Christ" (1 Cor. 1:2, 30; 2 Cor. 5:17). Paul says, "For since by man came death, by man came also the resurrection of the dead. For as *in Adam* all die, even so *in Christ* shall all be made alive" (1 Cor. 15:21–22). Paul writes of Adam and Christ as the "first man" and "second man" (v. 47). It is as if no one else ever lived. All other human beings are bound up in Adam or in Christ.

Pictures of Union with Christ

God has given us several ways to think about our union with Christ. All of these ways are connected to Adam's experience in the garden of Eden.

First, *believers are God's temple in Christ*. The garden of Eden was the first temple. Adam experienced God's special presence and served the Lord as

2 Calvin, *Institutes*, 3.1.1.

a priest (see chap. 32). After the fall of man, God dwelt with Israel in the tabernacle and temple (Ex. 29:42–46; 1 Kings 8:12–13). In the new covenant, God makes his people into his temple by their union with Christ in the Holy Spirit. Christ is the living temple of God (John 1:14; 2:19–22). Paul wrote to believers in Christ, "Know ye not that ye are the temple of God, and that the Spirit of God dwelleth in you?" (1 Cor. 3:16). How can human beings be God's temple? Believers are joined to the Lord Jesus Christ by the Holy Spirit. The Holy Spirit dwells in their bodies as God's temple for his glory (6:17–20). Believers in union with Christ are the home of God's presence. They behold his glory and worship him.

Second, *believers are God's fruit bearers in Christ*. The garden of Eden was an orchard of many beautiful trees (Gen. 2:9). God delighted in the goodness of these creations (1:12). A fruitful tree became an image of God's righteous people (Pss. 1:3; 52:7; 92:12–15). Israel was to be like a vine that produced fruit pleasing to God (Isa. 5:1–7; 27:2–6). Christ said, "I am the vine, ye are the branches: he that abideth in me, and I in him, the same bringeth forth much fruit: for without me ye can do nothing" (John 15:5). Rowland Stedman said, "If they have strength and ability to work the works of God, it is imparted through him. For they are branches in him, and he is the vine. . . . The whole life that we live, should be by faith on the Son of God."[3]

Third, *believers are God's guests at the feast in Christ*. The garden of Eden was watered by a great river and was lush with good fruit to eat (Gen. 2:9–10). Israel ate manna in the wilderness (Exodus 16), the bread from heaven (Ps. 78:24). Christ alone gives the living water that eternally satisfies (John 4:14), the heavenly streams of the Holy Spirit (7:37–39). Jesus himself is the Bread of Life on whom we feed by faith (6:35). Michael Barrett writes, "We must have a regular, daily diet of eating the Bread of Life and drinking the Living Water if we are going to grow in grace and in the knowledge of God."[4]

Fourth, *believers are dressed in God's clothing in Christ*. Adam and Eve made pitiful attempts to cover their nakedness after the fall (Gen. 3:7). In

3 Rowland Stedman, *The Mystical Union of Believers with Christ* (London: by W. R. for Thomas Parkhurst, 1668), 247.

4 Michael P. V. Barrett, *Complete in Him: A Guide to Understanding and Enjoying the Gospel*, 2nd ed. (Grand Rapids, MI: Reformation Heritage Books, 2017), 103.

his mercy, God clothed them with the skins of animals (v. 21). Clothing became a symbol of salvation itself (Isa. 61:10). Paul says, "Put ye on the Lord Jesus Christ" (Rom. 13:14). He also says, "For as many of you as have been baptized into Christ have put on Christ" (Gal. 3:27). One day, when the trumpet sounds, believers will be clothed with immortality by their union with the risen Lord Jesus (1 Cor. 15:53–54).

Fifth, *believers are Christ's bride*. God made the first woman from Adam's side and presented her to him as his wife (Gen. 2:18–25). The prophets use the image of marriage to describe God's love for Israel (Isa. 54:5; Hos. 2:19–20). Christ calls himself the Bridegroom of his people (Matt. 9:15; 25:6). The union of the church with her heavenly Bridegroom gives her greater honor than that of the angels. John Flavel said, "They are as the barons and nobles in his kingdom, but the saints as the dear spouse and wife of his bosom."[5]

Sixth, *believers are Christ's body*. After recounting how Adam received his wife from God in the garden of Eden, the author of Genesis says, "Therefore shall a man leave his father and his mother, and shall cleave unto his wife: and they shall be one flesh" (Gen. 2:24). Paul applies this statement to Christ and his people:

> For no man ever yet hated his own flesh; but nourisheth and cherisheth it, even as the Lord the church: for we are members of his body, of his flesh, and of his bones. For this cause shall a man leave his father and mother, and shall be joined unto his wife, and they two shall be one flesh. This is a great mystery: but I speak concerning Christ and the church. (Eph. 5:29–32)

Christ is closer to the church than any husband is to his wife because Christ lives in his body by the Holy Spirit.

Union with Christ is the heart of salvation, so we must strive to see if we are truly united to him. Paul writes, "Examine yourselves, whether ye be in the faith; prove your own selves. Know ye not your own selves, how that Jesus Christ is in you, except ye be reprobates?" (2 Cor. 13:5). How are we to examine ourselves? The evidence of union with Christ is fruit. Thomas

5 Flavel, *The Method of Grace*, in *WJF*, 2:42.

Boston said, "They that are barren may be branches of Christ by profession, but not by real implantation. All who are united to Christ bring forth the fruit of gospel-obedience and true holiness."[6]

If we are in union with Christ, we should marvel at God's grace to us. As John Owen said, the Christian should exclaim, "What am I, poor, sinful dust and ashes, one that deserves to be lightly esteemed by the whole creation of God, that I should be thus united unto the Son of God?"[7] C. H. Spurgeon said that the believer has "a living, loving, lasting union" with Christ and owes "everything to that."[8]

Stages of Union with Christ

Many of Paul's "in Christ" statements have to do with a living union between Christ and the church by his Spirit. Thus, Paul says that certain believers "were in Christ before me" (Rom. 16:7). But in other passages, Paul speaks of a person being "in Christ" long before conversion. How are we to understand him?

First, there is *union with Christ in the Father's eternal election.* God has blessed us with every spiritual blessing in Christ "according as he hath chosen us in him before the foundation of the world, that we should be holy and without blame before him in love" (Eph. 1:4). In God's decree, his grace "was given us in Christ Jesus before the world began" (2 Tim. 1:9). The Westminster Larger Catechism says, "The covenant of grace was made with Christ as the second Adam, and in him with all the elect as his seed."[9] This is not a living, justifying, or transforming relationship. It is only a union in God's eternal purpose.

Second, there is *union with Christ in his incarnation.* "For both he that sanctifieth and they who are sanctified are all of one: for which cause he is not ashamed to call them brethren" (Heb. 2:11). Christ's incarnation gave him a common nature with all human beings, but it joins him particularly to the "brethren" whom God gave to him to save. God the Son became "Immanuel" (Isa. 7:14), "God with us" (Matt. 1:23).

6 Thomas Boston, *Human Nature in Its Fourfold State* (Edinburgh: Banner of Truth, 1964), 302.

7 Owen, *WJO-H*, 4:149.

8 C. H. Spurgeon, *The Metropolitan Tabernacle Pulpit*, 57 vols. (Edinburgh: Banner of Truth, 1969), 38:98.

9 The Westminster Larger Catechism (Q. 31), in *RC*, 4:305.

Third, there is *union with Christ in his death, resurrection, and ascension.* Christ died for his people. And they died with him, were buried with him in the tomb, rose with him from the grave, and are seated with him in the heavenly places.[10] This is a matter of historical fact. Paul says, "One has died for all, therefore all have died; and he died for all, that those who live might no longer live for themselves but for him who for their sake died and was raised" (2 Cor. 5:14–15 ESV).

Fourth, there is *union with Christ in the Spirit's works of personal salvation.* "There is therefore now no condemnation to them which are in Christ Jesus," and they have been set free by "the Spirit of life in Christ Jesus" (Rom. 8:1–2). Fallen mankind is in a state of death and hatred against God. The "Spirit of Christ" gives "life and peace" to those who belong to Christ (vv. 6–9). Thus, "if Christ be in you, the body is dead because of sin; but the Spirit is life because of righteousness" (v. 10).

As a result of the Spirit's work to unite us to Christ, what Christ accomplished outside of us is now being applied to us. Paul says, "But of him are ye in Christ Jesus, who of God is made unto us wisdom, and righteousness, and sanctification, and redemption" (1 Cor. 1:30). Richard Sibbes wrote, "Whatsoever Christ hath, or is, or hath done or suffered, it is mine by reason of this union with him by faith, which is the grace of union that knits us to Christ, and the first grace of application."[11]

Therefore, there are two ways that we may speak of being united with Christ. The first is a *federal union.* We are one with him in God's eternal covenant. Federal union joins people to Christ in eternal election, his incarnation, and his death and resurrection. The second is a *mystical union.* We are one with him in the mystery of the Spirit's work. Mystical union is the living, saving relationship that bears fruit in our lives. Federal union is the basis of mystical union. What Christ did *for* us is the basis of what he does *in* us.

Herman Witsius said, "True saving benefits are bestowed on none of the elect, before effectual calling, and actual union to Christ by a lively faith."[12] Owen said that living union with Christ "is the first and principal grace. . . .

10 Rom. 6:1–14; 7:4–6; Gal. 2:19–20; 5:24; 6:14; Eph. 2:4–7; Col. 2:13, 20; 3:1–4; 2 Tim. 2:11; cf. 1 Pet. 2:24.

11 Sibbes, *Spiritual Jubilee*, in *WRS*, 5:242.

12 Herman Witsius, *The Economy of the Covenants between God and Man*, 2 vols. (1822; repr., Grand Rapids, MI: Reformation Heritage Books, 2010), 2.7.8 (1:237).

Hence is our adoption, our justification, our sanctification, our fruitfulness, our perseverance, our resurrection, our glory."[13]

False Views of Union with Christ

Outside of the Trinity, union with Christ is the closest union possible between persons. But there are also important ways in which we are *not* united to the Lord.

Union with Christ does not mean that we are one in essence with him. That is the error of pantheism or panentheism (see chap. 10). A person's human spirit is not God's Spirit. We are not Christ. Nor are all people united to him, for many are "without Christ" (Eph. 2:12).

Union with Christ also does not mean that a believer's personality is absorbed into him. That is the error of *mysticism*. We remain distinct persons from God and know him on a human level. Christ is the Bridegroom. Christians are the bride in relationship with him by the Holy Spirit. Mysticism can also arise from a false view of our union with Christ known as *deification* (or, in Greek, *theosis*). That is the term used in Roman Catholicism and Eastern Orthodoxy to say that Christians share, by grace, in God's glory or uncreated energies.[14] God's people are indeed glorified with the incarnate Christ. But ours is the manifest, created glory of God's living human temple. It is not the eternal, infinite, uncreated glory of the Trinity.

The Order of Salvation by Union with Christ

How does the Spirit apply redemption to individuals through union with Christ? Theologians answer this question by listing a series of acts by which the Spirit applies redemption, collectively called the *order of salvation*. Salvation is like a story that has a beginning, middle, and end. Paul outlines some parts of this order when he says, "Whom he did predestinate, them he also called: and whom he called, them he also justified: and whom he justified, them he also glorified" (Rom. 8:30).

The elect are "called" when they hear the *general gospel call* (2 Thess. 2:14). But Paul means more than this by the word "called." The "called" are those

13 Owen, *WJO-H*, 4:149–50.

14 On the Eastern Orthodox doctrine of uncreated energies, see Gregory Palamas, *The Triads*, ed. John Meyendorff, trans. Nicholas Gendle, The Classics of Western Spirituality (New York: Paulist, 1983), 3.2.5–7 (93–96).

who are not merely informed about but also transformed by God's grace to believe in Christ (1 Cor. 1:22–24). We speak of this as *effectual calling* because God makes it effective in the heart. Through effectual calling, those in federal union with Christ are brought into mystical union with him and begin to receive the saving graces he bought for them.

Paul says that those whom God "called, them he also justified" (Rom. 8:30). *Justification* is by belief in Christ (3:28): "We have believed in Jesus Christ, that we might be justified" (Gal. 2:16). So calling must result in *faith in Jesus Christ*. Next, Paul writes that "whom he justified, them he also glorified" (Rom. 8:30). In the context, *glorification* refers to the gift of perfect happiness that God's children will enjoy when Christ returns (vv. 17–18). In a sense, "glory" has already begun as the Spirit changes believers from the inside out (2 Cor. 3:18). So glorification may include *sanctification*, the process of making believers to be like Christ. Paul has just written of being conformed to Christ's image (Rom. 8:29).

Therefore, a basic order of salvation is the general call of the gospel, effectual calling, faith, justification, sanctification, and glorification.

In other Scripture passages, we see that the gospel call is often accompanied by *preparation by grace through conviction of sin* (John 16:8; Acts 2:37). We also read of *regeneration* (Titus 3:5), the new birth by the Holy Spirit (John 3:1–8). From the new birth springs faith in Christ (1 John 3:9; 5:1). Therefore, regeneration is prior to faith and is closely connected to effectual calling.

With saving faith comes *repentance unto life* (Mark 1:15; Acts 20:21; 26:18). This is turning from sin to God to serve him (Acts 26:20; cf. 1 Thess. 1:9–10).

There is also the grace of *adoption* (Gal. 4:5). This is given to all who have saving faith in Christ (John 1:12; Gal. 3:26).

With sanctification comes *perseverance* through sufferings in hope (Rom. 8:17, 25), while believers are upheld by the grace of *preservation* (vv. 35–39).

Therefore, we can say that the full order of salvation is as follows: first, the general gospel call and often conviction of sin (these are common graces and do not have the power in themselves to save); second, effectual calling and regeneration; third, faith and repentance; fourth, justification and adoption; fifth, sanctification and perseverance by the grace of preservation; and finally, glorification.

The whole order, from effectual calling onward, involves union with Christ. We will discuss these graces in later chapters (glorification will be reserved until our treatment of the doctrine of last things). Here we simply list them and note that the sequence is mostly logical, not necessarily chronological. Some of these things happen at the same time.

Practical Applications of Spiritual Union with Christ

Living, spiritual, mystical union with Christ has important applications for the Christian life.

First, *union with Christ lays the foundation for communion with God.* Jesus says, "He that hath my commandments, and keepeth them, he it is that loveth me: and he that loveth me shall be loved of my Father, and I will love him, and will manifest myself to him" (John 14:21). He also promises, "My Father will love him, and we will come unto him, and make our abode with him" (v. 23). We should desire to fellowship more deeply with our God in Christ.

Second, *union with Christ starts and continues spiritual transformation.* By union with him in his death and resurrection, Christians no longer live for themselves but for the One who died and rose again for them (Rom. 14:7–9; 2 Cor. 5:15). Flavel wrote, "We are married to Christ 'that we should bring forth fruit unto God' (Rom. 7:4)."[15]

Third, *union with Christ brings sharing in Christ's sufferings.* Paul wrote that he aimed to "be found in him [Christ] . . . that I may know him and the power of his resurrection, and the fellowship of his sufferings, being made conformable unto his death" (Phil. 3:9–10). We must suffer with Christ if we desire to be glorified with him (Rom. 8:17).

Fourth, *union with Christ grants a new and noble identity.* Sinclair Ferguson says that union with Christ gives believers great dignity as God's children, confidence in prayer because all in Christ is theirs, and strength in temptation, knowing that as those in Christ they should have nothing to do with sin.[16]

Fifth, *union with Christ connects us to one another as members of one body.* Christians are not isolated individuals. They share one life with other believers. This should move us to depend on one another and value the

15 Flavel, *The Method of Grace*, in *WJF*, 2:41.

16 Sinclair B. Ferguson, *The Christian Life: A Doctrinal Introduction* (Edinburgh: Banner of Truth, 1989), 113.

weakest believers in the church (1 Cor. 12:21–22). Whatever we do for the least of Christ's brothers, we do for Christ (Matt. 25:35–40).

Sixth, *union with Christ empowers pastors with bold faithfulness in ministry*. The apostle Paul says, "For we are not as many, which corrupt the word of God: but as of sincerity, but as of God, in the sight of God speak we *in Christ*" (2 Cor. 2:17). Gospel preachers speak the Word in union with Christ.

Seventh, *union with Christ grants to all Christians hope in trials and temptations*. Flavel said, "Death dissolves the dear union betwixt the husband and wife, friend and friend, yea, betwixt soul and body, but not betwixt Christ and the soul."[17] Therefore, we may say in all our troubles, "Who shall separate us from the love of Christ?" (Rom. 8:35).

Suggested Songs to Sing to the Lord

- Psalm 46, "God is our refuge and our strength," *Psalter*, No. 126; *THBap*, No. 37
- "Amazing grace, how sweet the sound," *THBap*, No. 402

Questions for Meditation or Discussion

1. How is the union between Christ and his people foreshadowed in Adam?
2. How does God's temple reveal union with Christ?
3. What does Christ's parable of the vine (John 15:1–10) teach us about union with Christ?
4. What Scripture passages compare our union with the Lord to wearing clothes and eating food?
5. What does the biblical teaching that the church is the bride and body of Christ imply?
6. In what sense can God's people be said to be "in Christ" from eternity?
7. Where does the Bible teach that Christians died, rose, and ascended with Christ? What do such statements mean? Why is this aspect of union with Christ crucial for our salvation?
8. How does the Holy Spirit make union with Christ into a vital, fruitful relationship?

17 Flavel, *The Method of Grace*, in *WJF*, 2:40.

9. Explain the following terms: (1) federal union and (2) mystical union.
10. What is the full order of salvation?
11. What practical applications does the doctrine of union with Christ have?

56

The General Gospel Call

Chapter Summary and Key Terms

God saves sinners through the gospel. The *general gospel call* consists of the doctrine of the good news about Christ, the command for everyone who hears to respond in repentance and faith, and the promise of salvation to all who do so. God offers his Son to all through the gospel. He sincerely calls them to Christ. Some believe that this offer contradicts God's election, leading them to reject either election (Arminianism) or the gospel offer (*hyper-Calvinism*). But the Word of God teaches both God's sovereignty in saving whom he chooses and the *free offer of the gospel*. The Word gives us many motivations to bring the gospel to all people. These include the sinfulness of all people, the love of God, the office of Christ as the only Mediator, the church's commission from Christ, and the glory of God in saving people through the gospel by his power.

PAUL WROTE TO the converts in Thessalonica, "God hath from the beginning chosen you to salvation through sanctification of the Spirit and belief of the truth: whereunto he called you by our gospel, to the obtaining of the glory of our Lord Jesus Christ" (2 Thess. 2:13–14).

When we speak of the gospel, the word "call" means to summon or invite. God's calling may refer to his effective summons that creates a saved and holy people (Rom. 1:6–7; 8:28, 30; 9:11, 24). This effectual calling is the topic of chapter 58. In this chapter, we will give attention to the *general gospel call* that goes forth through the Word and may or may not result in salvation. Christ said, "I am not come to call the righteous, but sinners to repentance" (Matt. 9:13). This calling is an invitation that can be refused (Luke 14:16–24).

The Characteristics of the Gospel Call

In Christ's parable of the wedding banquet (Matt. 22:1–14), the king has prepared a feast to honor his son at his wedding. He sends out his servants to invite people to the celebration. Those invited reject the invitation and abuse the king's servants. They provoke the king to send his soldiers to destroy them. The king then sends out his servants into the highways to gather all kinds of people into the feast. This parable shows us how God calls sinners through the gospel.

First, *God calls sinners through his word.* The first part of Christ's parable resembles the Lord's sending his prophets to Judah (2 Chron. 36:15–19). It is also like Christ's sending the apostles to Israel. Therefore, the call of God goes out through the Spirit-inspired words of his prophets and apostles, the writers of the Holy Scriptures (2 Pet. 1:20–21; 3:2, 16).

Second, *God calls sinners with authority.* In the parable, the call is brought to people by the servants of a king. Preachers are ambassadors of the King of kings (2 Cor. 5:10, 20).

Third, *God calls sinners to his grace.* In the parable, the servants invite people to a free feast for the wedding of the king's son. Likewise, Christ calls people to unearned riches of grace (Rom. 10:12).

Fourth, *God calls sinners as their Judge.* Christ's parable is about an invitation issued not by a private person but by a king who relates to people as subjects under his justice (Matt. 22:2, 7, 11, 13). The call exposes the rebellion of the king's enemies and brings judgment on them (vv. 5–7). The gospel brings justification to believers but condemnation to unbelievers (John 3:18, 36).

Fifth, *God calls sinners in a general invitation.* The king commands his servants, "Go ye therefore into the highways, and as many as ye shall find, bid [call or invite] to the marriage" (Matt. 22:9). The servants obey and call "all as many as they found" (v. 10). The gospel summons all who hear to come to Christ (11:28).

Sixth, *God calls sinners according to his mercy.* Christ depicts the king in his parable as a man of great patience. When those first invited insult him by refusing to come, the king sends the servants again with sweet words about how good the feast is (Matt. 22:3–4). They prove to be violent traitors. So the king extends the invitation to others, both "bad and good" (v. 10). God calls sinners in his great compassion for them so that they may not perish (Ezek. 33:11).

Seventh, *God calls sinners in a manner that can be resisted.* Though the host of the banquet in the parable is a mighty king, his invited guests not only turn down the invitation but treat his royal hospitality with contempt (Matt. 22:5–6). The Lord's calls are often rejected by sinners who choose not to listen (Isa. 65:2, 12).

Eighth, *God calls sinners through his suffering servants.* The servants of the king give their time, energy, and patience to bring the invitation to people in many places. They suffer contempt, abuse, and death (Matt. 22:5–7). Gospel preachers suffer with and for Christ (2 Cor. 1:3–6; 4:12).

Ninth, *God calls sinners to accomplish his sovereign will.* Christ concludes his parable with the saying "For many are called, but few are chosen" (Matt. 22:14). Many people choose to reject the king's call. But those who respond rightly do so because of God's choice of them. God's word, including his general call, never fails to accomplish his will (Isa. 55:1, 10–11).

The Contents of the Gospel Call

The general call of the gospel contains three essential ingredients: doctrine, command, and promise (Luke 24:48–49; Acts 10:38–43).

First, *the gospel call includes the doctrine of the good news.* Conversion requires submitting to the "doctrine which was delivered [to] you" (Rom. 6:17). The basic doctrine of the gospel can be stated as follows. God has revealed himself to people in "the gospel of God" (1:1). The entire human race has rebelled against our Creator and refuses to glorify him, provoking his wrath (1:18–23). God is still very good to people (2:4), but no one is righteous or seeks him (3:10–12). However, God is working out his plan revealed in Scripture (1:2). He sent his Son, Jesus Christ, to become a man in the line of David, the king of Israel (v. 3). Christ lived a perfectly righteous life of obedience to God's law (5:18–19). He then died on the cross to satisfy God's justice for our sins (3:24–26). After three days, Christ rose from the dead for our salvation (1:4; 4:25; 5:10). He will come again to judge all mankind (2:16). The doctrine of the gospel may be simply summarized in these four words: *God*, *sin*, *Christ*, and *salvation*.

Second, *the gospel call includes the command to repent and believe the gospel.* The call does not merely teach doctrine but urges, exhorts, warns, pleads, and appeals—it demands a right response to that doctrine. Christ commands, "Repent ye, and believe the gospel" (Mark 1:15). God "commandeth all men every where to repent" (Acts 17:30). Paul ministered by "testifying both to the Jews, and also to the Greeks, repentance toward God, and faith toward our Lord Jesus Christ" (20:21). John writes, "This is his commandment, That we should believe on the name of his Son Jesus Christ, and love one another, as he gave us commandment" (1 John 3:23).

Third, *the gospel call includes the promise of salvation.* God uses this promise to encourage people to repent and believe, and to give assurance to those who do. Thus, he says, "whosoever shall call on the name of the Lord shall be saved" (Acts 2:21; cf. Rom. 10:13). Christ promises, "For God so loved the world, that he gave his only begotten Son, that whosoever believeth in him should not perish, but have everlasting life" (John 3:16). The gospel message joins repentance and forgiveness (Luke 24:47), and repentance and life (Acts 11:18).

All who hear the gospel are commanded to repent and trust in Christ immediately, and therefore, they have the right from God to do so. All are promised salvation if they repent and believe. Jesus promises, "All that the Father giveth me shall come to me; and him that cometh to me I will in no wise cast out" (John 6:37)—that is, "I will certainly never cast him out."

The Free Offer of the Gospel

The Bible teaches that God has chosen to save only some sinners—indeed, many sinners, but not all—from the punishment they deserve (see chaps. 22–23). The Bible also teaches that God calls everyone who hears the gospel to repent and believe in Christ alone for salvation, promising salvation to all who do. We should humbly accept both of these truths. We cannot fully understand the infinite God. But some people reject one truth because they cannot understand how it fits with another.

On the one hand, *some people reject God's sovereign grace because they think it contradicts the free offer of the gospel.* They argue that there can be no sincere offer of salvation to everyone unless God chose to save all people and Christ died for all people. This is the teaching of Arminianism (see chaps. 23 and 58).[1]

1 The same argument could be made by people holding to Pelagianism.

In reply, we teach with the Synod of Dort that Christ died for the elect, but his sacrifice was "of infinite worth and value, abundantly sufficient to expiate the sins of the whole world."[2] All who hear the gospel are genuinely called by God, who "seriously promises eternal life and rest to as many as shall come to Him and believe on Him."[3]

Eternal election is God's decision. The gospel call tells us our duty, which is a different matter. God saves sinners through the gospel call. He always keeps his promises to those who repent and believe. Therefore, we must preach the gospel, and we can do so with confidence.

J. I. Packer said,

> The New Testament never calls on any man to repent on the ground that Christ died specifically and particularly for him. The basis on which the New Testament invites sinners to put faith in Christ is simply that they need Him, and He offers Himself to them, and that those who receive Him are promised all the benefits that His death secured for His people.[4]

The confidence that Christ "gave himself for me" belongs to those already in Christ (Gal. 2:20). The confidence that Christ died for them gives believers assurance that nothing can separate them from God's love or stop him from doing them good (Rom. 8:32–35). This assurance does not belong to unbelievers.

On the other hand, *some people reject the free offer of the gospel because they think it contradicts God's election*. They argue that the gospel does not "offer" Christ to anyone but only announces what he has done. This view is sometimes called *hyper-Calvinism*.

In reply, we note that to believe in Christ is to receive him (John 1:11–12; Col. 2:6). Grace is a gift that must be received for salvation (John 1:16; Rom. 5:17). How can anyone receive Christ and salvation if the gospel does not offer Christ and salvation?

John Calvin taught his church, "Just as the merciful Father offers us the Son through the word of the Gospel, so we embrace him through faith

2 The Canons of Dort (Head 2, Art. 3, 8), in *TFU*, 134, 136.

3 The Canons of Dort (Heads 3/4, Art. 8), in *TFU*, 143.

4 J. I. Packer, *Evangelism and the Sovereignty of God* (Downers Grove, IL: InterVarsity Press, 1976), 68.

and acknowledge him as given to us."[5] The Canons of Dort state, "It is not the fault of the gospel, nor of Christ offered therein, nor of God, who calls men by the gospel and confers upon them various gifts, that those who are called by the ministry of the Word refuse to come and be converted."[6] The Westminster Shorter Catechism says that Christ is "freely offered to us in the gospel."[7]

God "is kind to the unthankful and to the evil" because he is "merciful" (Luke 6:35–36). He delights in a right response to his Word (Deut. 5:29). He says, "Have I any pleasure at all that the wicked should die . . . and not that he should return from his ways, and live?" (Ezek. 18:23). Yet he also has righteous pleasure in executing justice (Jer. 9:24).

We should believe in both election and the free offer of the gospel because Christ Jesus taught both. Christ said, "These things I say, that ye might be saved" (John 5:34). But those who heard him were not willing (v. 40). He also said that people will be held responsible for rejecting the gospel (Matt. 11:20–24). He called everyone who was burdened to come to him and find rest (vv. 28–30). But he also rejoiced that God has hidden the truth from some people according to his purpose, and no one can know the Father except those to whom the Son chooses to reveal him (vv. 25–27). The Lord Jesus affirms man's responsibility, God's sovereignty, and the free offer of the gospel.

The Motivations for Missions and Evangelism

Reformed Christianity is a missionary faith because the Bible is a missionary book. The Holy Scriptures give us powerful motivations to engage in the costly work of missions and evangelism.

First, *all people are sinful.* All mankind lies under the dreadful darkness of corruption, sin, alienation from God, and enmity toward him (Rom. 3:10–12; 8:7). Human beings are in a hopeless condition without Jesus Christ, dead in their sins and under God's wrath (Eph. 2:1–3, 12).

Second, *God loves the world.* Even though the world hates God and Christ, God still loved the world so much that he sent his Son to save sinners (John

5 Calvin's Catechism of 1537 (Art. 12), in *RC*, 1:365.

6 The Canons of Dort (Heads 3/4, Art. 9), in *TFU*, 143.

7 The Westminster Shorter Catechism (Q. 31), in *RC*, 4:357. Cf. the Baptist Catechism (Q. 34), in *RC*, 4:577.

3:16–19). Though God's creation reveals his glory, it is only the Word of the Lord that saves souls (Psalm 19; Rom. 1:16, 20).

Third, *Christ is the only Mediator between God and man*. Christ gave himself as a ransom for all (1 Tim. 2:5–6). However, his death does not save people automatically. They must hear of him and call on his name to be saved (Rom. 10:13–15).

Fourth, *the church has a commission from Christ*. He rose with all authority and commissioned the church to make disciples of all nations (Matt. 28:19–20). Sinners must seek the Lord while he may be found (Isa. 55:6). Today is the day of salvation, but that day will come to an end (2 Cor. 6:2).

Fifth, *the salvation of sinners glorifies God*. While we are powerless to change sinners, the Lord can make the dead come to life so that our labors are not in vain (2 Cor. 3:5; Eph. 2:4–5). God will be glorified in the salvation and damnation of men, and his glory should be our highest love and aim (Rom. 9:22–24; 11:36).

Let us therefore give our time, energy, money, skills, children, and very lives to bring the gospel to the world. And let us pray that God will raise up and empower gospel preachers (Matt. 9:38; Eph. 6:19–20) and convert lost sinners (Rom. 10:1).

Suggested Song to Sing to the Lord

- Psalm 96, "O sing a new song to the Lord," *Psalter*, No. 257

Questions for Meditation or Discussion

1. What is the difference between the general gospel call and effectual calling?
2. What are nine things we can learn about the general gospel call from the parable of the wedding banquet?
3. What are the three basic parts of the gospel call?
4. What doctrine is essential to the gospel call?
5. How can we prove that the gospel call includes a command to repent and believe?
6. Why is it important to include the promise of salvation in the gospel call?
7. How can we answer people who say that the free offer of the gospel disproves election?

8. What answer can we give to people who say that election disproves the free offer of the gospel?
9. What motivations does the Bible provide for missions and evangelism?
10. How has reading this chapter motivated you to practice and support evangelism?

57

Preparation by Gracious, Resistible Conviction

Chapter Summary and Key Terms

The doctrine of *preparation by grace* teaches that the Holy Spirit causes people to understand the Word of God and convicts them of sin. This preparation is a form of common grace—it cannot save people, but it awakens them to see their need for salvation. God often works preparation by the preaching of the law. Preparation by grace must be distinguished from *preparationism*. That is the false teaching that God gives saving grace to people if they make good use of the grace he already has given them. In truth, until God gives saving grace, people always resist the Holy Spirit. Hypocrites in the church put the Holy Spirit to the test. Worst of all, some people commit *blasphemy against the Holy Spirit*, the unforgivable sin of permanently hardening their hearts against the gospel and hatefully rejecting Christ and the Spirit as evil despite the Spirit's powerful work to show them Christ and convict them of sin.

THE FREE OFFER OF CHRIST goes out to all who hear the good news of the gospel. Jesus says, "Come unto me, all ye that labour and are heavy laden, and I will give you rest" (Matt. 11:28). But only those who feel the weight of their spiritual burdens seek Christ's rest. Who are they? They are people who, by God's grace, have come to know something of their need for salvation and helplessness to save themselves.

God's *preparation by grace* is a common operation of the Holy Spirit on unbelievers through the Word of God. Through this grace, the Spirit illuminates the mind and convicts the conscience. But this grace does not produce the smallest degree of saving faith or good works pleasing to God. Rather, it simply makes a person more aware of his or her need for salvation. Unless God gives saving grace, the gospel call and the Spirit's conviction will bring no one to Christ.

The Error of Preparationism

A doctrine sometimes confused with preparation by grace is *preparationism*, the idea that people can and must prepare themselves to be fit for salvation. This has been taught by some theologians in both Roman Catholicism and Arminianism. God, they say, will give more grace to people who do what they can with the grace that he has already given everyone.

Reformers such as John Calvin rejected preparationism because people will not take the smallest step toward God until he saves them.[1] The Westminster Confession of Faith denies that man is "able, by his own strength, to convert himself, or to prepare himself thereunto."[2]

In contrast to preparationism, Reformed theology has its doctrine of preparation by common grace. Calvin taught that God "prepareth our hearts to come unto him to receive his doctrine."[3] Herman Bavinck said that "one can speak of 'preparatory grace' in a sound sense."[4]

The Bible's Teachings on Preparation by Grace

According to the Holy Scriptures, some people have been "enlightened" by the Word and the Holy Spirit (Heb. 6:4–5). Yet they are like land that receives the rain but bears only "thorns and briers" and will be burned under God's curse (vv. 7–8). This teaches us that in addition to the saving works of the Spirit, there are "common operations of the Spirit."[5]

God ordinarily convicts sinners of their sin by his law before bringing them to saving faith by his gospel. We see this pattern in Paul's epistle to

1 Calvin, *Institutes*, 2.2.27; 2.3.7.

2 The Westminster Confession of Faith (9.3), in *RC*, 4:246. Cf. the Second London Baptist Confession (9.3), in *RC*, 4:545.

3 John Calvin, *Sermons on Deuteronomy* (1583; facsimile repr., Edinburgh: Banner of Truth, 1987), 423.

4 Bavinck, *RD*, 4:39.

5 The Westminster Confession of Faith (10.4), in *RC*, 4:247. Cf. the Second London Baptist Confession (10.4), in *RC*, 4:546.

the Romans. Before Paul explains the gospel, he proclaims the sinfulness of all people and God's wrath against them (Rom. 1:18–3:20). This is the message of God's law against sinners. Paul writes, "Now we know that what things soever the law saith, it saith to them who are under the law: that every mouth may be stopped, and all the world may become guilty before God. Therefore by the deeds of the law there shall no flesh be justified in his sight: for by the law is the knowledge of sin" (3:19–20).

John Flavel said that Paul was "denying to [the law] a power to justify us," but he was also "ascribing to it a power to convince us, and so prepare us for Christ."[6] The Westminster Larger Catechism says, "The moral law is of use to unregenerate men, to awaken their consciences to flee from the wrath to come, and to drive them to Christ; or . . . to leave them inexcusable, and under the curse."[7]

The Lord Jesus promised his disciples that the Holy Spirit would bear witness to him as they witnessed to him (John 15:26–27). The Spirit would come to convict the world of sin (16:8). When Christ poured out the Spirit at Pentecost, Peter's preaching pierced his hearers to the heart so that they exclaimed, "What shall we do?" (Acts 2:37). He then called them to repentance.

Thus, conviction is not conversion. Sinners may be "cut to the heart" by the preaching of the Word but respond only with hatred (Acts 5:33; 7:54–55). "Felix trembled" when he heard God's Word (24:25–26), but he did not repent and believe.

The Doctrine of Preparation by Grace

Preparation by grace is different from salvation by grace. In preparation, God brings light to people who still love sin: "This is the condemnation, that light is come into the world, and men loved darkness rather than light, because their deeds were evil" (John 3:19). In salvation, God causes his glory to shine in the heart so that people are changed into his image (2 Cor. 3:18; 4:6).

Preparation by grace leaves men in a state of spiritual death. In preparation, God works in people as their Creator and Judge. He created them to

6 Flavel, *The Method of Grace*, in *WJF*, 2:287.

7 The Westminster Larger Catechism (Q. 96), in *RC*, 4:320.

think, so he addresses their minds with the truth. He also created them to make choices, so he gives them reasons why they need Christ. In salvation, God works as the Savior, giving new life.

Preparation is not a requirement that we must fulfill before we come to Christ. Preparation by grace is not legalism. Rather, it is the use of the law to drive sinners to Christ. Therefore, the doctrine of preparation by grace honors Christ.

Practical Applications of the Doctrine of Preparation by Grace

We can identify several practical applications of this doctrine.

First, *pastors must preach the law and the gospel.* The Holy Spirit uses the law to convict sinners of their need for Christ and the gospel to reveal the Savior of sinners. People need to hear both.

Second, *sermons should deal differently with believers and unbelievers.* We should not dangle the children of God over hell. Neither should we speak peace to the unrepentant. Rather, we should search unbelievers' consciences with God's Word to reveal to them their sin and God's wrath.

Third, *sinners must use the means of grace but rest in Christ alone.* Lost sinners should be encouraged to listen to the Word, read the Word, and pray for God's saving grace. These are God's means of conviction and conversion. But sinners must not rest in experiences of conviction. They must rest only in Christ—his death and resurrection for our salvation.

Fourth, *the church must pray for the convicting power of the Holy Spirit.* Flavel observed that without the Spirit's power, God's law preached to unbelievers will "make no more impression than a tennis-ball against a wall of marble," and the gospel will only be a song to lull sinners to sleep.[8] Therefore, let us pray for God to awaken sinners.

Resisting the Holy Spirit

After preaching to a crowd of unbelievers, Stephen said,

> Ye stiffnecked and uncircumcised in heart and ears, ye do always resist the Holy Ghost: as your fathers did, so do ye. Which of the prophets have not your fathers persecuted? And they have slain them which shewed before

8 Flavel, *England's Duty under the Present Gospel-Liberty*, in *WJF*, 4:48.

> of the coming of the Just One; of whom ye have been now the betrayers and murderers: who have received the law by the disposition of angels, and have not kept it. (Acts 7:51–53)

Resisting the Spirit means rejecting the Word inspired by the Spirit and fighting against the Spirit's conviction of sin. It may lead to persecuting Spirit-anointed preachers. Resisting the Spirit comes from being "uncircumcised in heart and ears." People resist the Spirit because they are covenant breakers by nature. They lack God's inner circumcision (Deut. 29:4; 30:6).

Someone might argue that if people can resist the Spirit, salvation ultimately depends on man's will, not God's will. But that assumes God's grace can do nothing more than teach and convict. The root of sinners' resistance is being uncircumcised in heart. Christ gives the circumcision of the heart by the Spirit (Deut. 30:6; Rom. 2:29; Col. 2:11). When God circumcises the heart, he overcomes the sinner's resistance and plants faith and love in his or her heart.

The doctrine of resisting the Spirit warns unbelievers that when they fight against the preachers of God's Word, they are fighting against God. Every time they hear the gospel and walk away unrepentant, they show their hostility to the Lord. Why would anyone resist the Holy Spirit? He is good and kind. He is calling sinners to salvation and eternal happiness.

This doctrine presses believers to ask why they no longer resist the Spirit. It is only because God saved them from their uncircumcised hearts. Therefore, they should praise and thank the Savior forever.

Preachers should soberly consider that sinners will resist the Spirit when the Word is preached. Therefore, preachers must expect rejection and persecution. But sinners are fighting not against them but against God. Therefore, preachers should remain faithful.

Testing the Holy Spirit

In the early history of the church in Jerusalem, some disciples sold houses and lands, and then gave the money to the apostles to help the poor (Acts 4:34–37). Ananias and his wife, Sapphira, likewise sold some property and brought a gift to the apostles. But they secretly kept back part of the money from the sale (5:1–2).

Peter sharply rebuked them. Their sin was not keeping some of the money, for it was theirs (Acts 5:4). Rather, they had pretended to give the whole amount from the sale. Peter said, "Why hath Satan filled thine heart to lie to the Holy Ghost. . . . Thou hast not lied unto men, but unto God. . . . How is it that ye have agreed together to tempt the Spirit of the Lord?" (vv. 3–4, 9). Behind this act of hypocrisy was contempt for the Holy Spirit who dwells in his church. God struck them dead for testing the Holy Spirit. When unrepentant sinners masquerade as godly worshipers, their worship is an abomination to the Lord (Prov. 15:8; 28:9).

The warning against members of the church testing the Spirit should cause them to fear the living God and show him great reverence in the church (Acts 5:11). Unconverted people should beware of professing to be Christians (v. 13). But believers should not hesitate to confess their faith and join the church (v. 14). The Holy Spirit gladly dwells in them (2:38).

Blaspheming the Holy Spirit

Some people so harden their hearts against the gospel that they close the door to salvation. Christ said,

> All manner of sin and blasphemy shall be forgiven unto men: but the blasphemy against the Holy Ghost shall not be forgiven unto men. And whosoever speaketh a word against the Son of man, it shall be forgiven him: but whosoever speaketh against the Holy Ghost, it shall not be forgiven him, neither in this world, neither in the world to come. (Matt. 12:31–32)

Blasphemy against the Holy Spirit is a reaction against the Spirit's powerful work to make known God's grace in Christ. It is committed when an unconverted sinner wholeheartedly condemns Christ and the Spirit as if they were evil. It is an act of settled hatred against God, not just a lapse into unfaithfulness due to outside pressure and persecution.[9]

Herman Bavinck explained, "The blasphemy against the Holy Spirit, therefore, does not simply consist in unbelief, nor in resisting and grieving the Holy Spirit in general." Rather, it is a full and final rejection of the gospel

9 Perkins, *A Golden Chain*, chap. 53, in *WWP*, 6:245.

when it comes with the Spirit's "illumination and conviction" in a manner that is "intense and powerful."[10] Blasphemy against the Spirit is the unpardonable sin because it permanently hardens the heart against the gospel.

It is possible to commit the unpardonable sin today (Heb. 6:4–6; 10:26–27; 1 John 5:16). People who regard Christ as the Savior sometimes wrongly believe they have committed this sin and fear that they may be damned, but by this very fear they show evidence that they have *not* committed it. They should flee to Christ and rest in him. But sinners should be warned that there is a point of no return in rejection of Christ. They should repent and believe now, lest they settle their choice on Satan and receive his fate.

Conclusion

Let us all humble ourselves for our sin. The doctrines of resisting, testing, and blaspheming the Spirit show how corrupt, deceitful, and rebellious the human race is. Man's hatred against God is displayed nowhere more starkly than in our response to his love.

Let us also acknowledge our need for saving grace to change our hearts. The clear light of the truth and the powerful conviction of the Spirit are not sufficient to produce faith and repentance. We need new hearts and new spirits, a new birth by the Holy Spirit.

If God has saved you, you should thank him with a grateful heart. Did God patiently bear with you when you resisted the Holy Spirit? It was sheer mercy, for he could have justly destroyed you instead. Did God restrain you from blindly rushing to damnation by hardening yourself against Christ? It was only his kindness that kept him from giving you over to the darkness you deserved. If the Lord has saved you, you ought to rejoice with trembling at his grace to you, for he saved you despite your resistance and made you willing to be saved in the day of his power (Ps. 110:3). Give him the praise and glory for your salvation and never take it for granted.

Suggested Songs to Sing to the Lord

- Psalm 78, "My people, give ear, attend to my word," *Psalter*, No. 213, stanzas 1, 3, 4, 6; *THBap*, No. 301, stanzas 1, 3, 4, 7
- "Come, ye sinners, poor and wretched," *THBap*, No. 393

10 Bavinck, *RD*, 3:155.

Questions for Meditation or Discussion

1. What is God's work of preparation by grace?
2. What is the error of preparationism?
3. How does the epistle to the Romans show God's ordinary way of preparing sinners for Christ?
4. What can we learn about the Spirit's work from the effect of Peter's preaching at Pentecost?
5. How would you summarize the doctrine of preparation by grace?
6. Of the practical applications of preparation by grace, which is most relevant to you? Why?
7. What does it mean to resist the Holy Spirit?
8. What does it mean to test the Holy Spirit?
9. What does it mean to blaspheme the Holy Spirit?
10. How are these doctrines warnings to unbelievers? Why should they stir believers to grateful love to the Savior?

58

Effectual Calling

Chapter Summary and Key Terms

God's general call goes out to all who hear the preaching of the gospel, but many are not saved. To save sinners, God gives them *effectual calling*, his sovereign summons that unites the elect to Christ by faith and produces the fruit of holiness. Contrary to *Pelagianism*, people do not have the natural ability to choose God. Nor is this calling *prevenient grace* given to all people so that they have the restored ability to choose God and salvation. In the state of sin, people have total inability to turn to God. God alone must turn them (*monergism*). People do not turn until they are turned by God (against *synergism*). Effectual calling is *effectual grace*, with power to effectively save everyone to whom it is given by changing the heart. Effectual grace does not save people against their wills but saves their wills so that they willingly come to Christ.

MANY WHO HEAR the gospel respond with hostility, indifference, or superficial acceptance. But some respond with true faith and repentance. How are we to explain the difference?

Charles Spurgeon said, "How came I to be converted? I prayed, thought I. Then I thought how came I to pray? I was induced to pray by reading the Scriptures. How came I to read the Scriptures? . . . And then, in a moment, I saw that God was at the bottom of all, and that he was the author of faith."[1] God saves sinners by grace alone. He makes unbelievers into believers by

1 C. H. Spurgeon, *The New Park Street Pulpit*, 6 vols. (repr., Pasadena, TX: Pilgrim, 1975), 1:384.

effectual calling. This calling does not bypass the human will but rather transforms the will.

In many passages in the New Testament, to be "called" is to be saved. Paul says, "Whom he did predestinate, them he also called: and whom he called, them he also justified: and whom he justified, them he also glorified" (Rom. 8:30). This calling cannot be the general gospel call, for many who hear the gospel are not justified. Thus, Paul is speaking of a calling that produces faith, for we are justified by faith (3:28). Theologians refer to this calling as *effectual* because it has the power to produce the effect of saving faith in Christ.

The Bible's Doctrine of Effectual Calling

The Holy Scriptures teach many truths about effectual calling.

First, *effectual calling is God's sovereign summons*. God "hath called you out of darkness into his marvellous light," in contrast to those who continue to "stumble at the word, being disobedient" (1 Pet. 2:8–9). Wayne Grudem says, "No powerless, merely human calling is in view," but rather a " 'summons' from the King of the universe . . . [that] has such power that it brings about the response that it asks for in people's hearts."[2]

Second, *effectual calling is executed by the triune God*. The Father, the Son, and the Holy Spirit act together as one God in calling sinners. God the Father is the author who speaks the call (Rom. 1:7; 8:29–30). God the Son is the Father's living Word (John 1:1). The Son's voice raises people from spiritual death (5:25). He calls his sheep, and they follow him (10:3, 16, 27). God the Holy Spirit gives life through the Word (6:63). He makes the gospel powerful to convert the elect (1 Thess. 1:3–5).

Third, *effectual calling is rooted in God's eternal purpose in Christ*. God "hath saved us, and called us with an holy calling, not according to our works, but according to his own purpose and grace, which was given us in Christ Jesus before the world began" (2 Tim. 1:9). God effectually calls the people whom he chose and predestined (Rom. 8:30; 2 Thess. 2:13–14).

Fourth, *effectual calling is particular to elect individuals*. Paul says that he was saved "when it pleased God, who separated me from my mother's

2 Wayne Grudem, *Systematic Theology: An Introduction to Biblical Doctrine*, 2nd ed. (Grand Rapids, MI: Zondervan, 2020), 842–43.

womb, and called me by his grace" (Gal. 1:15). Christ "calleth his own sheep by name" (John 10:3).

Fifth, *effectual calling is gracious and undeserved.* Paul writes, "For ye see your calling, brethren, how that not many wise men after the flesh, not many mighty, not many noble, are called" (1 Cor. 1:26). God calls sinners according to his grace alone, not on the basis of any works that they have done or will do (Rom. 9:11, 16; 2 Tim. 1:9).

Sixth, *effectual calling is fruitful in producing faith and repentance.* Paul says that Jews and Greeks reject the gospel, "but unto them which are called, both Jews and Greeks, Christ [is] the power of God, and the wisdom of God" (1 Cor. 1:24). Faith and repentance are gifts of God. He exalted Christ to his right hand "to give repentance to Israel" (Acts 5:31), and also to the Gentiles God "granted repentance unto life" (11:18). When sinners in Antioch of Pisidia heard the word of the Lord from Paul and Barnabas, "as many as were ordained to eternal life believed" (13:48). This explains why Paul thanked God constantly for the faith and love of the saints (Eph. 1:15–16).

Seventh, *effectual calling is powerful to create a new people.* In the first work of creation, "God said, Let there be light: and there was light" (Gen. 1:3). In his work of new creation, "God, who commanded the light to shine out of darkness, hath shined in our hearts, to give the light of the knowledge of the glory of God in the face of Jesus Christ" (2 Cor. 4:6). God's almighty word creates a divine and supernatural light in the soul. God is creating a new humanity in Christ (5:17). Like Adam but far greater, the Lord Jesus is "the image of God" (4:4). The Spirit joins us to Christ so that we begin to be "changed into the same image" (3:17–18). Believers are "called to be saints" (Rom. 1:7; 1 Cor. 1:2). Thus, by saving grace, God makes us to be "his workmanship, created in Christ Jesus" (Eph. 2:10).

Eighth, *effectual calling is effective to bring people into spiritual union with Christ.* The saints are "called unto the fellowship of his Son Jesus Christ our Lord" (1 Cor. 1:9). The Westminster Shorter Catechism says, "The Spirit applieth to us the redemption purchased by Christ, by working faith in us, and thereby uniting us to Christ in our effectual calling."[3]

3 The Westminster Shorter Catechism (Q. 30), in *RC*, 4:357. Cf. the Baptist Catechism (Q. 33), in *RC*, 4:577.

Ninth, *effectual calling is practical in its implications for holiness.* Though not based on good works, it is a "holy calling" (2 Tim. 1:9). Peter says, "As he which hath called you is holy, so be ye holy" (1 Pet. 1:15). Paul exhorts Christians "that ye would walk worthy of God, who hath called you unto his kingdom and glory" (1 Thess. 2:12).

Tenth, *effectual calling is observable in its effects on heart and conduct.* Peter exhorts believers to increase in faith, virtue, knowledge, self-control, patience, godliness, brotherly love, and Christlike love (2 Pet. 1:5–7). They should do so, he says, to "make [their] calling and election sure" (v. 10). John says, "Hereby we do know that we know him, if we keep his commandments" (1 John 2:3).

Eleventh, *effectual calling is permanent because of God's faithfulness and sovereignty.* God's saving call is based on his eternal purpose (Rom. 8:28–30). Salvation is not based on human will, effort, or works, but only on God's choice and calling (9:11, 16, 18). God will establish the saints until Christ returns, for "God is faithful, by whom ye were called" (1 Cor. 1:8–9).

Twelfth, *effectual calling is heavenly and glorious in its ultimate aim.* God has "called us to glory" (2 Pet. 1:3). He "called you by our gospel, to the obtaining of the glory of our Lord Jesus Christ" (2 Thess. 2:14). Through the gospel, the effectual call summons sinners into the glorious kingdom of God (1 Thess. 2:12). Thomas Watson said, "God calls them to glory, as if a man were called out of a prison to sit upon a throne."[4]

Different Views of God's Grace and the Sinner's Will

Theologians have disagreed sharply over how to teach both salvation by grace and the free choice of man's will. Here we outline the major views on this subject.

First, *Pelagianism teaches the natural ability of mankind to turn to God and trust in Christ.*[5] In fact, according to this view, people have the power to obey God perfectly if they so choose. The Christian church has long considered Pelagianism to be a heresy, but it has reappeared in liberal modernism, which teaches human goodness and progress.

4 Thomas Watson, *A Body of Divinity* (Edinburgh: Banner of Truth, 1965), 222.

5 On Pelagius and his controversy with Augustine, see chap. 34.

Second, *Roman Catholicism and Arminianism teach restored ability by prevenient grace for all.* (The word *prevenient* means "coming before," as in grace that comes before faith.) In this view, original sin destroyed man's ability to seek God and do good. But God gives everyone prevenient grace so that they have the power to either receive or reject salvation. People must cooperate with prevenient grace to be saved.[6]

Third, *Lutheranism teaches restored ability by special grace with the Word.* This is not prevenient grace that goes out to all mankind. Rather, it is grace given to all who hear the gospel of Christ. They can be saved only if they do not resist this grace. But Lutheranism also teaches that sinners are saved by grace alone.[7]

Fourth, *Augustinianism and Reformed theology teach particular and effectual saving grace.* This means that God gives saving grace only to some, and this grace effectively brings those people to faith in Christ.

Augustinian and Reformed theologians teach that God's saving grace overcomes sinful human resistance. Thus, it is sometimes called *irresistible grace*. We should be clear, though, that God never forces a person to believe against his or her will. Augustine said, "Therefore he is drawn in wondrous ways to will, by Him who knows how to work within the very hearts of men. Not that men who are unwilling should believe, which cannot be, but that they should be made willing from being unwilling."[8]

Theologians also use the term *monergism* for the view that God alone works to create saving faith in sinners. Sinners contribute nothing to the first beginning of saving faith in their hearts, for salvation is by grace alone. The term *synergism* refers to the view that sinners must cooperate with God in order to come to faith. Thus, Arminianism is an example of synergism.

Probably the most helpful way to state the Reformed view of salvation is with the term *effectual grace*. God's effectual calling has divine power to effectively produce faith. The Canons of Dort deny "that after God has performed His part, it still remains in the power of man to be regenerated

6 Some Roman Catholic theologians have held to the Augustinian view (see the fourth point). But Augustinianism was dealt a serious blow in the Roman Catholic Church when that church condemned Jansenism.

7 By Lutheranism, we refer to confessional Lutheran orthodoxy holding to the Formula of Concord. We are not commenting on the theology of Martin Luther, who was an Augustinian, or on modern Lutheran theologians.

8 Augustine, *Against Two Letters of the Pelagians*, 1.37.19, in *NPNF*[1], 5:389.

or not." Rather, "all in whose heart God works in this marvelous manner are certainly, infallibly, and effectually regenerated, and do actually believe."[9]

We might imagine asking four professing Christians, representatives of the four positions explained above, "Why are you saved?" All would answer that they are saved because they trust in Christ, who died for their sins and rose again.

We might then ask, "Why did you trust in Christ?" The Pelagian would answer, "I came to Christ by my own free will." The other three would say, "I came to Christ because God's grace drew me."

Finally, we might ask, "Why did you come to Christ when many who hear the gospel do not?" The Roman Catholic or Arminian would say, "I cooperated with the grace that God gives to everyone." The Lutheran would respond, "I did not resist the grace that God gives to all who hear his Word." The Augustinian or Reformed person would answer, "God changed my heart so that I willingly believed in Christ."

The Effectual Power of God's Saving Grace

The doctrine of effectual calling goes hand in hand with the doctrine of total inability (see chap. 35). Adam's disobedience cast all his natural descendants into the state of sin (Rom. 5:12, 19). People in the state of sin hate God and love sin (John 3:19–20; 15:18–25). No one is righteous, seeks God, or does good (Rom. 3:9–12; 5:12). They are dead in sin (Eph. 2:1).

People are so hostile to God that they cannot submit to his law (Rom. 8:5–8). Instead, they are enslaved to sin (John 8:34) and subject to the power of Satan (v. 44; 12:31). They cannot see or enter God's kingdom (3:3, 5). They cannot come to Christ (6:44, 65) or believe in him (12:39). They cannot bear fruit glorifying to God (15:5, 8).

Therefore, to be saved by grace is like being raised from the dead (Eph. 2:1, 5). It is the making of a new creation (v. 10), an act of supernatural power like God's creation of the world (2 Cor. 4:6). As we saw earlier in this chapter, God gives faith and repentance to sinners.

Christ teaches, "No man can come to me, except the Father which hath sent me draw him: and I will raise him up at the last day" (John 6:44). To come to Christ is to trust him with saving faith (v. 35). No one is able to

9 The Canons of Dort (Heads 3/4, Art. 12), in *TFU*, 144–45.

exercise faith in Jesus Christ apart from a powerful work of God. The Greek word translated as "draw" literally means to move by pulling, such as pulling fish in a net (21:11). This drawing is a powerful action that results in spiritual change and eternal salvation.

Christ also says, "*All* that the Father giveth me shall come to me; and him that cometh to me I will *in no wise cast out*" (John 6:37). If saving grace were resistible, we would have to change Christ's words to "*Some people* that the Father giveth me shall come to me; and him that cometh to me I *might later* cast out." But that is not what our Lord said.

Objections to Effectual Calling

People raise several objections to the doctrine of God's effectual calling. Some of these objections have to do with election, and we treated them under that topic (chap. 23). Here we address objections that especially concern effectual calling.

Objection 1: Obligation implies ability. Since people who hear the gospel have the obligation to repent and believe in Christ, they must have the ability to do so.

In reply, we say that we may speak of human ability in terms of a mind to understand and a will to choose—which sinners have. But apart from saving grace, people are dead in sin, ruled by Satan, and "by nature" objects of God's wrath (Eph. 2:1–3). God's Word teaches both human obligation and inability (Rom. 3:12, 19; 8:7–8).

Objection 2: God gives prevenient grace to all people. It is written in John 1:9, "[Christ] was the true Light, which lighteth every man that cometh into the world."

In reply, we deny that this Scripture teaches that a saving light shines in all people. Christ said of the unbeliever, "There is no light in him" (John 11:10). The unsaved are "darkness" (Eph. 5:8). John 1:9 could mean that Christ, as the Creator (v. 3), gives a mind and conscience to every human being. More likely, John 1:9 means that Christ brought truth to this world by his preaching (Matt. 4:12–17). "Every man" need not mean everyone in the world without exception. The words *all* and *every* often refer to many or all kinds of people (John 2:10; 3:26). Paul said that he was "warning every man, and teaching every man" (Col. 1:28), but he did not have a ministry to every human being. The Bible does not teach that God gives prevenient grace to enable all mankind to choose salvation. God does not even give the gospel to everyone.

Objection 3: People can resist God's call in the gospel. Stephen said, "Ye stiffnecked and uncircumcised in heart and ears, ye do always resist the Holy Ghost" (Acts 7:51).

In reply, we agree that people resist the call of the gospel and the conviction of the Holy Spirit (see chap. 57). But the Spirit can do more than convict. He can also give the new birth, which he does to whomever he wills (John 3:8).

Objection 4: Sinners can defeat God's purpose to save them. It is written, "The Pharisees and the lawyers rejected the purpose of God for themselves" (Luke 7:30 ESV).

In reply, we point out that the Greek word translated as "purpose" or "counsel" (KJV) can refer to God's teaching to us about what we should do. The Pharisees rejected the preaching of both John the Baptist and the Lord Jesus Christ (Luke 7:31–34). The Scripture quoted in this objection (v. 30) is not about stopping God's eternal purposes. It is about rejecting the gospel.

Objection 5: People are responsible for their choice to believe or disbelieve. Effectual calling, we are told, treats people as robots without free will.

In reply, we say that the Bible teaches both God's sovereignty and human responsibility. Christ said, "Truly the Son of man goeth, as it was determined: but woe unto that man by whom he is betrayed!" (Luke 22:22). We also note that effectual calling does not force people to do something against their will. God supernaturally creates in the heart a new trust and a new love. When the Father draws a person to Christ, Francis Turretin said, "he is not indeed drawn with a twisted neck, but is conquered by the truth and vanquished by a triumphant delight, than which nothing is sweeter, nothing more efficacious."[10]

Practical Applications of the Doctrine of Effectual Calling

What are some practical applications of this doctrine?

The church must preach the gospel for the salvation of sinners. God's ordinary method of saving sinners does not bypass their minds—he calls

10 Francis Turretin, *Institutes of Elenctic Theology*, trans. George Musgrave Giger, ed. James T. Dennison Jr., 3 vols. (Phillipsburg, NJ: P&R, 1992–1997), 15.6.13 (2:550).

sinners to Christ through the Word. The gospel is "the power of God unto salvation to every one that believeth" (Rom. 1:16). Faith comes "by hearing, and hearing by the word of God" (10:17). J. I. Packer said, "They must be told of Christ before they can trust Him, and they must trust Him before they can be saved by Him. Salvation depends on faith, and faith on knowing the gospel."[11]

The doctrine of effectual calling can give us courage to preach the gospel to the worst sinners. Packer wrote, "The sovereignty of God in grace gives us our only hope of success in evangelism."[12] Paul wrote that though he was in chains for the gospel, "the word of God is not bound. Therefore I endure all things for the elect's sakes, that they may also obtain the salvation which is in Christ Jesus with eternal glory" (2 Tim. 2:9–10).

Yet it is not enough to hear the gospel. A person must be effectually called to be saved—even the children of believers. Archibald Alexander wrote, "The education of children should proceed on the principle that they are in an unregenerate state, until evidences of piety clearly appear."[13] Apart from God's effectual call, no amount of education or moral reformation can save a sinner. Have you been effectually called to Christ? If God has not called you, then call on him to save you before you close this book.

A person's election makes itself known in his effectual calling. The golden chain of salvation shows that God brings salvation to the elect through effectual calling (Rom. 8:30). If you lack assurance, take hold of God's promises by grace and strive by grace to grow in holiness.

Christians should glorify God alone for their conversion. If you are among the called, then give thanks to the Father daily for rescuing you from the power of darkness and transferring you into the kingdom of his beloved Son (Col. 1:12–13).

The called must pursue practical holiness. God's call draws us into the way of holiness. Abraham Booth said, "Happy are you, reader, if you know by experience what it is to be called by grace. If such be your state, it becomes your indispensable duty to walk worthy of your calling, for it is high,

11 J. I. Packer, *Evangelism and the Sovereignty of God* (Downers Grove, IL: InterVarsity Press, 1976), 97.

12 Packer, *Evangelism and the Sovereignty of God*, 106.

13 Archibald Alexander, *Thoughts on Religious Experience* (repr., Edinburgh: Banner of Truth, 1967), 13.

holy, heavenly. Yes, believer, your calling is truly noble."[14] View yourself as part of a caravan of pilgrims summoned by the King to his celestial city and traveling together on the narrow road. Pursue holiness as a faithful member of a local church.

If God has effectually called you to Christ, you can hope in a happy future. Booth said, "What shall I say? You are called from the slavery of sin, to the practice of holiness; into a state of grace here, and to the enjoyment of glory hereafter. . . . It is an unfading inheritance, an eternal kingdom, you are called to enjoy."[15] Rejoice, Christian, for you are called by God!

Suggested Songs to Sing to the Lord

- Psalm 65, "Praise waits for Thee in Zion," *Psalter*, No. 170; *THBap*, No. 306
- "I was a wandering sheep," *THBap*, No. 396

Questions for Meditation or Discussion

1. What do theologians mean by *effectual* calling?
2. How is each person in the Trinity active in effectual calling?
3. How would you prove that God effectually calls his elect to salvation?
4. What Scripture passages show that faith and repentance are gifts of God?
5. What are the practical implications of God's call for the Christian life?
6. What doctrines are taught about God's saving grace and human will by (1) Pelagianism, (2) Roman Catholicism and Arminianism, (3) Lutheranism, and (4) Augustinianism and Reformed theology?
7. How does Christ explain effectual grace in John 6:37, 44?
8. You are explaining effectual calling to someone, and she objects, "That can't be true because people resist the Spirit and frustrate God's purpose to save them." What do you say?
9. What are some practical applications of the doctrine of effectual calling for evangelism and holiness?

14 Abraham Booth, *The Reign of Grace, from Its Rise to Its Consummation*, 1st American ed. (New York: T. Allen, 1793), 92.

15 Booth, *The Reign of Grace*, 93.

59

Regeneration

Chapter Summary and Key Terms

God begins the application of salvation through *regeneration*, the supernatural rebirth into spiritual life. Regeneration is a resurrection from spiritual death that produces a new life of faith, repentance, love, and obedience. It is also a work of new creation and the beginning of the restoration of God's image in his people. Regeneration is a sovereign act of God, not a result of human choice or an effect of baptism. Regeneration and effectual calling seem to be two ways that God's Word describes effectual saving grace. The doctrine of regeneration encourages us to evangelize with confidence and in dependence on the Holy Spirit. It also teaches us to glorify God alone for our salvation and to show the reality of our regeneration by a life of good works.

ONE NIGHT A DEVOUT, strictly law-observant, and highly educated Jewish man came to Jesus and said, "Rabbi, we know that thou art a teacher come from God: for no man can do these miracles that thou doest, except God be with him" (John 3:2). Christ replied, "Except a man be born again, he cannot see the kingdom of God. . . . Ye must be born again" (vv. 3, 7). People cannot be saved by religious devotion and education. They must have a new birth and a new life from God.

The new birth is also called *regeneration*. Sometimes Reformed writers in the sixteenth century used "regeneration" to mean repentance and sanctification.[1] But we use the term in the same way as the Canons of Dort

1 Calvin, *Institutes*, 3.3.9.

and the Westminster Confession of Faith: to mean God's first act to renew a sinner's heart so that he repents of sin and believes the gospel.[2]

The Doctrine of Regeneration

Regeneration is the supernatural rebirth into spiritual life by which God begins salvation in a person. Believers have been "born, not of blood, nor of the will of the flesh, nor of the will of man, but of God" (John 1:13). Therefore, this is not a natural birth or a choice of human will. This birth is an act of God. Without it, Christ says, people "cannot see the kingdom of God" (3:3) and "cannot enter into the kingdom of God" (v. 5). Human nature cannot produce spiritual life. Only the Holy Spirit can give this birth to those dead in sin (v. 6). The Spirit regenerates people with all the freedom of the wind in its blowing (v. 8). We cannot control the new birth.

"Regeneration" (Titus 3:5) is quite literally "genesis again," a new creation. Paul says, "If anyone is in Christ, he is a new creation" (2 Cor. 5:17 ESV). Such people "no longer live for themselves but for him who for their sake died and was raised" (v. 15 ESV). God created the world out of nothing. He then gave it order by his word, making man in his image (Genesis 1). In regeneration, God does not create new parts to human nature, such as a human spirit. But he does create new graces in sinners' hearts, such as hope and love (1 Pet. 1:3, 22–23). God also gives order to their thoughts, affections, and choices by his Word (Eph. 4:20–24). He renews his image in man (Col. 3:10). Regeneration prepares God's people to live in their inheritance in the new heaven and new earth (Titus 3:5–7; 1 Pet. 1:3–4).

When God regenerates someone, he raises him from spiritual death by the resurrection of Christ. Paul says, "But God . . . even when we were dead in sins, hath quickened us [made us alive] together with Christ" (Eph. 2:4–5). "With Christ" means this happens by union with Christ and his resurrection. Regeneration is also an act of God's power to create faith in Christ. The saints believe "according to the working of his mighty power, which he wrought in Christ, when he raised him from the dead" (1:19–20). The life of the risen Lord comes to people through the gospel and gives them eternal spiritual life. Peter says, "Blessed be the God and Father of

2 The Canons of Dort (Heads 3/4, Arts. 11–12, 16), in *TFU*, 144–45, 147; and the Westminster Confession of Faith (13.1), in *RC*, 4:249. Cf. the Second London Baptist Confession (13.1), in *RC*, 4:548.

our Lord Jesus Christ, which according to his abundant mercy hath begotten us again unto a lively hope by the resurrection of Jesus Christ from the dead" (1 Pet. 1:3). As a change from death to life, regeneration is worked by God in an instant.

Regeneration produces conversion in the inner man. The Lord says, "A new heart also will I give you, and a new spirit will I put within you: and I will take away the stony heart out of your flesh, and I will give you an heart of flesh" (Ezek. 36:26). He also says, "I will give them one heart . . . that they may fear me for ever . . . I will put my fear in their hearts" (Jer. 32:39–40). By the new birth, God creates faith in Christ, love, righteousness, and perseverance:

- "Whosoever believeth that Jesus is the Christ is born of God" (1 John 5:1).
- "Every one that loveth is born of God, and knoweth God" (1 John 4:7).
- "Every one that doeth righteousness is born of him" (1 John 2:29).
- "Whatsoever is born of God overcometh the world" (1 John 5:4).

In this way, regeneration restores the image of God in the inner man, for God "is righteous" (1 John 2:29) and "is love" (4:7–8). In regeneration, God renews his spiritual likeness in a person by uniting him to Christ, the Image of God (Rom. 8:29; Col. 1:15).

In regeneration, a person is washed from his sin (Ezek. 36:25–26; Titus 3:5). Paul warns that "the unrighteous shall not inherit the kingdom of God," listing several kinds of sinners, but says, "Such were some of you: but ye are washed" (1 Cor. 6:11). The Lord Jesus Christ told his disciples that they (except Judas) were already "washed" and "clean" (John 13:10–11). Christ warned that anyone whom he does not "wash" has no part with him (v. 8). Peter says that when God saves people, he has "cleansed their hearts by faith" (Acts 15:9 ESV). Regeneration ends a person's continual pattern of rebellion against God's law (1 John 3:4–9).

An internal war begins with the new birth, for Christians still have much remaining sin. Peter tells believers that they have been "born again" (1 Pet. 1:23), but he also warns them to "abstain from fleshly lusts, which war against the soul" (2:11). This inner conflict is not evidence that a person is not born again. Rather, the battle is evidence of regeneration. The Spirit has begun to produce holy desires that are contrary to the desires of sin (Gal. 5:17).

God gives regeneration only because of his mercy and love: "God, who is rich in mercy, for his great love wherewith he loved us, even when we were dead in sins, hath quickened us together with Christ, (by grace ye are saved)" (Eph. 2:4–5). He regenerated us because of his "kindness and love . . . not by works of righteousness which we have done, but according to his mercy" (Titus 3:4–5). The doctrine of regeneration teaches believers to bless God for his great mercy (1 Pet. 1:3). It should amaze us that he gave us life in Christ.

Questions about Regeneration

This doctrine can spark many questions. Here we attempt to answer some of the most common ones.

First, *how is the Trinity involved in regeneration?* Regeneration is one divine act that involves all three persons of the Trinity. God the Father causes the new birth (James 1:17–18; 1 Pet. 1:3). God the Son is the Mediator of the new birth. God has made us alive together with the risen Lord Jesus (Eph. 2:5; Col. 2:13). God the Holy Spirit is sent from the Father through the Son to regenerate sinners (Titus 3:4–6). We are born "of" the Spirit (John 3:5–8).

Second, *how does regeneration relate to God's sovereignty?* We have already argued that God's saving grace is effectual to save all to whom God gives it (chap. 58). So, too, regeneration is a monergistic and effectual act of God. The new birth is produced not by the human will but by God (John 1:13). It is a birth worked by the Holy Spirit (3:3–8). No one causes or controls his own conception and birth. Nor can human nature produce spiritual life (v. 6). The Spirit gives regeneration according to his free and sovereign will (v. 8; James 1:18).

Regeneration is an act of making a new creation (2 Cor. 5:17; Eph. 2:10). Creation is God's work, and he does it alone (Isa. 44:24). The universe did not make itself. In regeneration, God makes the dead come to life in Christ (Eph. 2:5). It is the removal of a stony heart and the gift of a heart of flesh (Ezek. 11:19; 36:26). Thus, it overcomes our resistance and makes us submissive to God. The new birth produces repentance, faith, love, righteous deeds, and victory over the world (1 John 2:29; 3:9; 4:7; 5:1, 4). Therefore, the new birth is the cause of conversion.

John Murray wrote, "Regeneration is the beginning of all saving grace in us, and all saving grace in exercise on our part proceeds from the fountain of regeneration. We are not born again by faith or repentance or conversion; we repent and believe because we have been regenerated."[3]

Third, *does God give regeneration through baptism?* No, baptism is not the means of regeneration. People may be baptized but remain the slaves of sin (Acts 8:13, 20–23). Also, people can be saved and receive the Holy Spirit before baptism simply by hearing the gospel (10:44–48). Paul said, "Christ sent me not to baptize, but to preach the gospel" (1 Cor. 1:17). He would not have said that if baptism were the ordinary means of regeneration.

It is true that Christ taught that we must be "born of water and of the Spirit" in order to enter his kingdom (John 3:5). But it is best to interpret "water" to mean the cleansing of the heart by the Spirit (Ezek. 36:25–27). When Christ went on to say more about regeneration, he spoke only of the Spirit, not of water or of baptism (John 3:6, 8).

If God regenerates people by baptism, the millions of infants taken to the church font have all been born again. But where is the repentance, faith, love, righteousness, and victory over this world that regeneration produces? Thomas Watson said, "It is not baptism [that] makes a Christian; many are no better than baptized heathens."[4]

Fourth, *can God regenerate infants and the mentally handicapped?* Yes, the Holy Scriptures show that God is able to save his elect despite mental disability or even if death takes them away in infancy. John the Baptist was "filled with the Holy Ghost, even from his mother's womb" (Luke 1:15). When Mary, the mother of our Lord, visited Elizabeth when she was pregnant with John, "the babe leaped . . . for joy" (v. 44). Some psalms speak of people trusting God from their earliest days of life, even from the womb (Pss. 22:9–10; 71:5–6). If God is able to regenerate infants, he can also regenerate people with infantile minds—the mentally handicapped.

This doctrine should give great comfort to Christians. But we must be careful not to distort this sweet truth into dangerous error. Believers must not presume that their children are born again. A regenerated child will

3 John Murray, *Redemption Accomplished and Applied* (Grand Rapids, MI: Eerdmans, 1955), 103.

4 Thomas Watson, "Who Are in Christ Are New Creatures," in *A Body of Practical Divinity . . . with a Supplement of Some Sermons* (London: Thomas Parkhurst, 1692), 984 [pagination error beginning at 545].

show his or her salvation by love for God and righteousness. As we noted above, God can save children in infancy, but his ordinary way to save people is through hearing the gospel (Rom. 10:13–17). That means God generally saves people after they have grown up enough to actively disobey him and sin maliciously against one another (Titus 3:3–5).

Fifth, *what is the relationship between regeneration and effectual calling?* We must not separate the two. No one is regenerated at one age and called and converted many years later. Regeneration immediately creates a new life.

It seems best to see regeneration and effectual calling as two ways of describing the same act of God. Herman Bavinck said, "Regeneration . . . is only another name for the call: the efficacious call of God."[5] Both are the effectual act of God's saving grace in Christ to produce faith and love in the heart. But regeneration emphasizes that this act is God's gift of new life applying Christ's resurrection to the spiritually dead. Effectual calling emphasizes that this act is God's summons drawing sinners to come to Christ.

Practical Applications of the Doctrine of Regeneration

The doctrine of regeneration has many practical applications for evangelism and the Christian life.

1. *Applications for evangelism.* We are born again through the word of God, the gospel (James 1:18; 1 Pet. 1:23).[6] Therefore, if we desire for people to be born again, we must labor for them to hear the gospel. We must plant the seeds of truth—though only God can cause those seeds to grow and bear fruit. John Flavel said, "This speaks encouragement to ministers and parents, to wait in hopes of success at last, even upon those that yet give them little hope of conversion at the present."[7] We cannot control the Holy Spirit (John 3:8), but we must pray that he would give life to dead sinners.

In evangelism, the doctrine of the new birth is a powerful weapon to overthrow the self-righteousness and self-sufficiency of sinners. The Lord Jesus says to sinners that, despite all their learning and religion, they "must be born again" (John 3:7). Some proud sinners think that it is easy for them

5 Bavinck, *RD*, 4:77.

6 Regeneration may rightly be said to be mediate (by means) through the word of God as applied to the mind but immediate (without means) as applied to the disposition and choice of the heart. See Beeke and Smalley, *RST*, 3:432–36.

7 Flavel, *The Method of Grace*, in *WJF*, 2:99.

to believe in Christ and be saved. They then manufacture a kind of belief in Jesus that he rejects (2:23–25). They must hear the message of regeneration to challenge their self-confidence and must learn that they cannot be saved by their own willpower, much less their brain power. Stephen Charnock said, "An evangelical head will be but drier fuel for eternal burning, without an evangelical impression upon the heart."[8]

The doctrine of regeneration offers hope for sinners awakened to their deep corruption and stubborn unbelief, for it tells them that God can give them a radical new beginning. Like blind Bartimaeus, they cannot heal themselves of their spiritual darkness, but they can cry, "Son of David, have mercy on me" to the One who is able to save them (Mark 10:47).

2. *Applications for the Christian life.* Those who trust in Christ and repent of their sins find in this doctrine God-glorifying comfort. They ask, "Why am I saved?" The doctrine of regeneration answers, "Not because of anything good in you or done by you, but only because God loved you and made you new by the Holy Spirit" (cf. Titus 3:4–5). And they respond, "Then all glory be to God alone!"

If God has given you this gift of the new birth, then he will give you all good forever. In this world, all the providences of God serve for your good (Rom. 8:28). And if God so loved you when you were dead in your sins, how much more will he show his love to you in the ages to come now that you are alive in Christ (Eph. 2:7)?

Understanding regeneration cultivates dependence on the Spirit. Believers should learn from regeneration that their spiritual life does not come from themselves but from the Lord. Spiritual disciplines and the church's means of grace are just instruments; they have no power to give life or growth. Richard Sibbes said, "Learn this, that you trust not too much to any outward performance or task, to make idols of outward things. . . . All these are things necessary, but they are dead things without the Spirit of Christ. Therefore in the use of all those outward things, whatsoever they be, look up to Christ."[9]

The doctrine of regeneration spurs God's children to do good works. Paul ends his teaching on regeneration by saying, "This is a faithful saying,

8 Charnock, *The Necessity of Regeneration*, in *WSChar*, 3:59.

9 Sibbes, *The Excellency of the Gospel above the Law*, in *WRS*, 4:295.

and these things I will that thou affirm constantly, that they which have believed in God might be careful to maintain good works. These things are good and profitable unto men" (Titus 3:8).

But if God regenerated us apart from "works of righteousness which we have done" (Titus 3:5), why would this doctrine motivate us to do works now? Regeneration displays the remarkable love of God to change his enemies into his friends. If God has so loved us, shall we not love him in return? Regeneration shows that authentic salvation includes not only justification but also transformation. Shall we claim to be justified when our lives are barren of the fruits of regeneration? This doctrine also shows us that the way to glorify the God of regeneration is to "adorn the doctrine of God our Saviour" with an honorable life of doing good (2:10). We must show the world the reality and beauty of the new birth in a life of holy love.

In particular, let us learn to conduct ourselves with patience and gentleness toward the wicked. We were not saved by our religion or righteousness. In fact, we were formerly "foolish, disobedient, deceived, serving divers lusts and pleasures, living in malice and envy, hateful, and hating one another" (Titus 3:3). But God saved us by the washing of regeneration. Therefore, we should strive "to speak evil of no man, to be no brawlers, but gentle, shewing all meekness unto all men" (v. 2). The strongest advocates of the doctrine of sovereign regeneration should be the meekest and most merciful of people.

What God has revealed to us about regeneration shows us his unspeakable glory. Petrus van Mastricht observed that the regeneration of dead sinners requires "infinite power, a superabundant greatness of power, as great, and if possible, even greater, than was exercised in creation, . . . [and] infinite or exhaustless goodness and mercy."[10] Therefore, we should contemplate regeneration with awe and wonder. And we should worship the God of regeneration.

Suggested Songs to Sing to the Lord

- Psalm 87, "Zion, founded on the mountains," *Psalter*, No. 238; *THBap*, No. 369
- "Come, Holy Spirit, come," *THBap*, No. 254

10 Petrus van Mastricht, *A Treatise on Regeneration* (New Haven, CT: Thomas and Samuel Green, 1770), 51.

Questions for Meditation or Discussion

1. What is regeneration?
2. How does the Bible describe regeneration?
3. What does the Bible teach about regeneration as (1) a supernatural rebirth, (2) a new creation, (3) an inward resurrection, (4) the cause of conversion, (5) washing from sin, and (6) the free gift of God's mercy and love?
4. How is regeneration an act of the whole Trinity?
5. What reasons do we have for saying that God is sovereign in regeneration?
6. Why is baptism not the means of regeneration?
7. Can God give regeneration to infants and mentally disabled people? How do we know?
8. What practical applications does the doctrine of regeneration have for evangelism?
9. How can the doctrine of regeneration strengthen the spiritual lives of believers?

60

Conversion: Repentance and Faith

Chapter Summary and Key Terms

The gospel calls sinners to *conversion*, a turning to God with repentance and faith, which are inseparable. *Repentance unto life* is a gift of God's saving grace by which a sinner turns from sin to God. Saving repentance involves the whole person, a turning to God in beliefs, affections, choices, and actions. The exercise of repentance involves looking to God's mercy, confessing one's sins, and grieving over sin because it dishonors and displeases him. *Faith in Jesus Christ* is also a gift of God's saving grace in which a sinner rests on Christ alone for salvation from sin. Saving faith involves knowledge of the gospel, assent to its truth, and trust in Christ. The exercise of faith empties one of self, receives Christ, lives out of his grace, strives against obstacles, and produces good works. Both repentance and faith are necessary for salvation, and believers must continue to exercise repentance and faith in order to grow spiritually.

SALVATION IS BY GRACE ALONE. God's grace produces spiritual life in his people. This life shows itself in their acts of response to God. John Gill said, "Effectual vocation is the call of men out of darkness to light; and conversion answers to that call, and is the actual turning of men from the one to the other."[1] Anthony Hoekema wrote, "Conversion may be defined as the conscious act of a regenerate person in which he or she turns to God in repentance and faith."[2]

1 John Gill, *A Complete Body of Doctrinal and Practical Divinity* (1839; repr. Paris, AR: The Baptist Standard Bearer, 1995), 545.

2 Anthony A. Hoekema, *Saved by Grace* (Grand Rapids, MI: Eerdmans, 1989), 113.

There is variety in people's experiences of conversion. Manasseh turned to the Lord as an adult (2 Chron. 33:11–13). Obadiah feared the Lord from his youth (1 Kings 18:12). Some suffer piercing convictions of sin before coming to faith in Christ (Acts 2:37), while others have their hearts gently opened to him (16:14–15). However, all true conversions have two sides: *repentance unto life* and *faith in Jesus Christ*.

In the Bible, conversion is sometimes described simply as repentance (Matt. 4:17; Acts 2:38) and sometimes simply as faith in Christ (John 1:12; Acts 16:31). In other Scripture passages, faith and repentance appear together (Isa. 30:15; Mark 1:15). Thus, repentance and faith cannot be separated, but they are not identical. Repentance is turning from sin to God. Faith is trusting in Christ as the Mediator of eternal life (Acts 20:21).

Repentance unto Life

Common terms for repentance are the words translated as "turn" and "return" (Deut. 4:30; Matt. 13:15). The Greek words generally translated as "repent" or "repentance" in the New Testament have the meaning of changing one's mind (Matt. 3:2, 8). Repentance involves sorrow for sins, but not all regret for sin is repentance that leads to salvation (2 Cor. 7:9–11).

The Bible speaks of "repentance unto life" (Acts 11:18). The Westminster Shorter Catechism says, "Repentance unto life is a saving grace, whereby a sinner, out of a true sense of his sin, and apprehension of the mercy of God in Christ, doth, with grief and hatred of his sin, turn from it unto God, with full purpose of, and endeavour after, new obedience."[3]

True repentance is a saving grace, given freely by God to sinners through his effectual calling and regeneration (chaps. 58–59). Repentance is turning from sin (1 Kings 8:35; Isa. 59:20) to God (2 Chron. 15:4; 36:13). It is turning "from darkness to light, and from the power of Satan unto God" (Acts 26:18).

Repentance is not merely changing one's beliefs but turning one's whole person from sin to God. The Lord says, "Turn ye even to me with all your heart" (Joel 2:12). Thus, repentance requires the following:

3 The Westminster Shorter Catechism (Q. 87), in *RC*, 4:365. Cf. the Baptist Catechism (Q. 92), in *RC*, 4:585.

- turning the mind from sinful lies to the truth of God (2 Tim. 2:25)
- turning the affections away from sin with grief (2 Cor. 7:10) and shame (Rom. 6:21) to God to rejoice in him (Matt. 13:44; 1 Thess. 1:6, 9)
- turning the will to choose to serve the Lord (Josh. 24:15) and follow Christ (Matt. 16:24)
- turning behavior to stop doing evil and start doing good (Isa. 1:16–17)

That last point is especially important, for repentance must bear fruit in changed behavior or it is not saving repentance at all (Luke 3:8–9; Acts 26:20).

The repenting sinner looks to the just and merciful God. One psalm of repentance begins, "Blessed is he whose transgression is forgiven, whose sin is covered. Blessed is the man unto whom the Lord imputeth not iniquity, and in whose spirit there is no guile" (Ps. 32:1–2). The repenting sinner confesses from the heart his sins against the righteous God. David says, "I will confess my transgressions unto the Lord" (v. 5). In another psalm, he writes with sorrow, "I acknowledge my transgressions: and my sin is ever before me" (51:3). He prays for the cleansing and joy of God's forgiveness (vv. 7–9) and the renewal of his heart (vv. 10–12).

We must discern between true repentance and false repentance. There is such a thing as a false conversion. Sometimes people have a superficial response to God's Word that does not bear fruit (Mark 4:16–19). There is "godly sorrow," literally "sorrow according to God," which "worketh repentance" (2 Cor. 7:10). This sorrow is grief over sin because it dishonors and displeases God. It produces serious and diligent striving against sin, fear of the Lord, and zeal to make things right (v. 11). But there is also "the sorrow of the world" (v. 10). Such sorrow is grief merely over sin's consequences in this world—the loss of human strength, relationships, riches, or honor.

The Need for Repentance

There is no salvation apart from repentance. Peter says, "Repent ye therefore, and be converted, that your sins may be blotted out" (Acts 3:19). The Westminster Confession of Faith says, "Although repentance be not to be rested in, as any satisfaction for sin, or any cause of the pardon thereof, which is the act of God's free grace in Christ; yet is it of such necessity to all sinners, that none may expect pardon without it."[4]

Some theologians say that we need only faith to be saved, not repentance. But John the Baptist warned sinners of "the wrath to come" and exhorted them, "Bring forth therefore fruits meet for repentance" (Matt. 3:7–8). The Lord Jesus warns, "Every tree that bringeth not forth good fruit is hewn down, and cast into the fire" (7:19). He also says, "Except ye repent, ye shall all likewise perish" (Luke 13:3, 5). Paul warns those who do not repent that they are storing up wrath for themselves on judgment day (Rom. 2:4–5). And he writes, "They that are Christ's have crucified the flesh with the affections and lusts" (Gal. 5:24). Only those who repent of their sinful desires truly belong to Christ.

Have your repented of your sins? Let no one deceive you with empty words. Turn from sin before it ruins you forever. Turn to the Lord who gives eternal life through Jesus Christ. Judgment day is coming. Bring forth the fruit of repentance, or you will be found outside of Christ, outside of life, and outside of all hope.

Repentance is also needed for spiritual growth and perseverance. A Christian might need to repent seven times a day (Luke 17:3–4)—or more. Christ speaks some of his most searching calls for repentance to Christian churches (Rev. 2:5, 16; 3:3, 19). The opposite of repentance is hardness of heart. If we allow the deceitfulness of sin to harden our hearts, we will fall away from the faith and prove that we have not been partakers of Christ (Heb. 3:8, 12–14). Martin Luther wrote, "When our Lord and Master Jesus Christ said, 'Repent' (Matt. 4:17), he willed the entire life of believers to be one of repentance."[5]

As Thomas Boston pointed out, God gives us strong reasons to repent.[6] He commands everyone to repent (Acts 17:30). His daily mercies invite us to repent (Rom. 2:4). The restless evil of sin should drive us to repent (Isa. 57:21). The inescapable reality of death urges us to repent (Heb. 9:27). The justice of God's judgment demands that we repent (2 Cor. 5:10–11). The sufferings of Christ for sinners should draw us to repent (Zech. 12:10). The wrong that our sins do against God should move us to repent (Ps.

4 The Westminster Confession of Faith (15.3), in *RC*, 4:251.

5 Luther, *Ninety-Five Theses*, in *LW*, 31:25.

6 Boston, *The Necessity of Repentance*, in *WTB*, 6:431–45.

51:4). The terrors of hell should convince us to repent (Heb. 10:31). And if we repent, we will never perish (Isa. 55:7). Boston said, "There is mercy for thee, if thou wilt repent, and come to Christ. Good news, sinners, if ye repent, all your sins shall be blotted out, ye shall be embraced in the wide and warm arms of mercy."[7]

Faith in Jesus Christ

Faith in Christ is the living heart of a relationship with God. Paul says, "The just shall live by faith" (Rom. 1:17). He adds, "Therefore being justified by faith, we have peace with God through our Lord Jesus Christ" (5:1). J. C. Ryle compared faith to a hand that grasps Christ, an eye that looks to him, a mouth that feeds on him spiritually, and feet that run to him.[8]

Faith is expressed in the Old Testament with words translated as "believe" (to regard as reliable, Gen. 15:6), "lean" (Prov. 3:5), "trust" (Isa. 12:2), and another word for "trust" that means to take refuge (Ruth 2:12). The most common words for faith in the New Testament are used in the sense of relying on the faithfulness of another. Hebrews 11:11 says, "Through faith also Sara herself received strength . . . because she judged him faithful who had promised."

The Bible makes it clear that there are kinds of faith that do not save people:

- Mere mental belief in the truths of God's Word (Acts 26:27). If this were saving faith, people could be saved and remain as wicked as the Devil (James 2:19).
- A short-term emotional commitment. Saving faith is deeply rooted in the heart, for the heart itself has been changed by grace (Luke 8:13, 15).
- Confidence that God will work a miracle. Christ will reject many miracle workers on judgment day, saying, "I never knew you" (Matt. 7:22–23).
- Blind submission to church leaders (Matt. 15:9). Saving faith rests in the gospel revealed by God, not the traditions of men (Gal. 1:11–14).

7 Boston, *The Necessity of Repentance*, in *WTB*, 6:431–45.

8 J. C. Ryle, *Old Paths*, 2nd ed. (London: William Hunt and Co., 1878), 228–29.

- Claiming earthly blessings with confidence. Job lost his health and wealth but said, "Though he slay me, yet will I trust in him" (Job 13:15).
- A physical action such as going to a place or saying a prayer. Paul wrote that "with the heart man believeth unto righteousness" (Rom. 10:10).

Saving faith has as its object what is invisible to us: "Faith is the substance of things hoped for, the evidence of things not seen" (Heb. 11:1). By faith people live "as seeing him who is invisible" (v. 27). Faith gives a present and proven reality in the heart to things we have not seen. Paul says, "We are always confident. . . . For we walk by faith, not by sight" (2 Cor. 5:6–7).

The special object of faith is Jesus Christ and the eternal life he brings (John 3:16). The call of the gospel is, "Believe on the Lord Jesus Christ, and thou shalt be saved" (Acts 16:31). Faith looks to Christ because he is the only Mediator of God and his grace (John 14:6).

In grasping Christ, faith takes hold of God in trust and hope (1 Pet. 1:21). The Lord Jesus said, "He that believeth on me, believeth not on me, but on him that sent me" (John 12:44). Faith rests in God as our supreme good (Ps. 4:5–7). William Ames said, "Faith is the resting of the heart on God. . . . To believe in God, therefore, is to cling to God by believing, to lean on God, to rest in God as our all-sufficient life and salvation."[9]

The Three Parts of Saving Faith

The Bible's teaching enables us to identify three parts of saving faith.

First, *saving faith is the experiential knowledge of God.* Faith must start with the knowledge revealed in God's Word (Rom. 10:14, 17). We cannot base our faith on feelings, for we are saved through "belief of the truth" (2 Thess. 2:13). Christ rebuked people for being "slow of heart to believe all that the prophets have spoken" (Luke 24:25).

The knowledge of God's Word must penetrate the heart. Such knowledge is not merely information but eternal life itself (John 17:3). It is a knowledge

9 William Ames, *The Marrow of Theology*, trans. John D. Eusden (Grand Rapids, MI: Baker, 1968), 1.3.1, 15 (80, 82).

that sets sinners free from their slavery to sin (8:32, 34). Psalm 9:10 says, "They that know thy name will put their trust in thee."

Psalm 34:8 says, "O taste and see that the Lord is good: blessed is the man that trusteth in him." A scientist may know much about the chemistry of food but might never have tasted it. Faith is not just knowing about God but also knowing him with spiritual relish. Saving faith arises when God "hath shined in our hearts, to give the light of the knowledge of the glory of God in the face of Jesus Christ" (2 Cor. 4:6). This divine light, Jonathan Edwards said, gives "a real sense of the excellency of God, and Jesus Christ, and of the work of redemption, and the ways and works of God revealed in the gospel."[10] This is humbling but glorious.

Second, *saving faith is submissive assent to God's Word.* It believes God's ability to do what he promises (Rom. 4:21; Heb. 11:11). Faith assents to the Word because it is God's testimony in Christ, and God is true (John 3:33–34). Paul writes of the "obedience of faith" (Rom. 1:5 ESV; 16:26) and describes this submission to the truth as follows: "Ye have obeyed from the heart that form of doctrine which was delivered you" (6:17). Faith listens to God's Son (Matt. 17:5). Jesus says, "Ye believe not, because ye are not of my sheep. . . . My sheep hear my voice, and I know them, and they follow me" (John 10:26–27).

Through the submission of assent, faith welcomes the Word of God into the heart. True disciples abide in God's Word, and the Word abides in true disciples (John 8:31; 15:7–8). When people receive the Word with a living faith, that Word sanctifies them (17:8, 17). John Calvin said, "For the Word of God is not received by faith if it flits about in the top of the brain, but when it takes root in the depth of the heart."[11]

Third, *saving faith is confident trust in Christ.* The Westminster Shorter Catechism says, "Faith in Jesus Christ is a saving grace, whereby we receive and rest upon him alone for salvation, as he is offered to us in the gospel."[12]

Saving faith in Christ involves receiving him. John writes, "He came unto his own, and his own received him not. But as many as received him, to

10 Edwards, *A Divine and Supernatural Light*, in *WJE*, 17:413. See Edwards, *Religious Affections*, in *WJE*, 2:272.

11 Calvin, *Institutes*, 3.2.36.

12 The Westminster Shorter Catechism (Q. 86), in *RC*, 4:365. Cf. the Baptist Catechism (Q. 91), in *RC*, 4:585.

them gave he power to become the sons of God, even to them that believe on his name" (John 1:11–12). This means accepting Christ not merely as one's friend but as the glorious Lord of grace and truth (v. 14).

Saving faith in Christ may also be described as resting on him. Isaiah 28:16 says, "Therefore thus saith the Lord God, Behold, I lay in Zion for a foundation a stone, a tried stone, a precious corner stone, a sure foundation: he that believeth shall not make haste [or panic]." Christ is the cornerstone of God's temple, and Christians rest on him by faith (1 Pet. 2:6–7).

So faith is receiving and resting on Christ as he is offered to us in the gospel. Christ is the Prophet to teach us the truth (Acts 3:22–23). He is the Priest to give us forgiveness and reconciliation with God by his one sacrifice and perpetual intercession (Heb. 7:25; 10:10). And he is the King to rescue us from sin and rule us by his Spirit through his Word (Psalm 2; Acts 5:31–32). By faith, we receive the whole Christ: Prophet, Priest, and King.[13]

Faith's Experiential Exercise

Martin Luther said, "Faith is not the human notion and dream that some people call faith. . . . Faith, however, is a divine work in us. . . . O it is a living, busy, active, mighty thing, this faith. It is impossible for it not to be doing good works incessantly."[14] Faith is not just *about* Christ, but it unites the soul *to* Jesus Christ in a living union. Here we list some of the exercises of faith, not in a sequence or order in time but as a description of the Christian life from beginning to end.

First, *faith empties us of self.* Faith agrees with Christ that we are not "righteous, but sinners" (Luke 5:32). Faith means the utter despair of everything except Christ to be our righteousness, salvation, and eternal life. Calvin said, "Faith cannot be truly preached, without wholly depriving man of all praise by ascribing all to God's mercy."[15] The language of faith is, "I am not worthy" (Matt. 8:8–10).

Thomas Watson said, "Repentance and faith are both humbling graces; by repentance a man abhors himself; by faith he goes out of himself. . . . [He] sees God's justice pursuing him for sin . . . and . . . he sees nothing in

13 Christ's threefold office as Prophet, Priest, and King is introduced in chap. 45 and studied in chaps. 46–50.

14 Luther, *Preface to Romans*, in *LW*, 35:370.

15 Calvin, *Comm.* on Rom. 3:27.

himself to help, but he must perish unless he can find help in another."[16] Faith renounces self because it embraces Christ.

Second, *faith comes to Christ and receives him.* To come to Christ is to receive him for the satisfaction of our ultimate needs and deepest desires (John 6:35; 7:37). He dwells in the believer's heart by faith (Eph. 3:17). Calvin wrote, "Faith is not a distant view, but a warm embrace of Christ, by which he dwells in us, and we are filled with the divine Spirit."[17]

Faith receives Christ as the One in whom all saving benefits are given (Eph. 1:3; 1 John 5:11–12). John Preston explained, "First remember that you must take Christ himself, and then other things that we have by him."[18] Luther said, "Faith takes hold of Christ and has Him present, enclosing Him as the ring encloses the gem."[19] Faith weds the soul to Christ.

Third, *faith lives out of Christ.* Paul says, "I am crucified with Christ: nevertheless I live; yet not I, but Christ liveth in me: and the life which I now live in the flesh I live by the faith of the Son of God, who loved me, and gave himself for me" (Gal. 2:20).

Faith is obedience to Christ's command "Abide in me" (John 15:4). Faith draws from Christ the life of the soul: "I am the vine, ye are the branches: he that abideth in me, and I in him, the same bringeth forth much fruit: for without me ye can do nothing" (v. 5). Richard Sibbes wrote, "Having the Spirit of Christ, faith fetches all strength from Christ."[20]

Fourth, *faith strives against obstacles.* Saving faith is fighting faith. Paul wrote, "Fight the good fight of faith, lay hold on eternal life, whereunto thou art also called" (1 Tim. 6:12). Faith must overcome the onslaught of unbelieving fear (2 Tim. 1:7; 1 John 4:18). It moves the Christian to cry, "Lord, I believe; help thou mine unbelief" (Mark 9:24).

Faith in Christ must battle against misplaced worldly trust. Some sinners trust in wealth (1 Tim. 6:17). Other sinners have "trusted in themselves that they were righteous" (Luke 18:9). Still other sinners trust in the glory of man (John 5:44). Saving faith wages war against cursed, God-abandoning trust in man so that it may draw living water from the Lord alone (Jer. 17:5–8).

16 Thomas Watson, *A Body of Divinity* (Edinburgh: Banner of Truth, 1965), 216.

17 Calvin, *Comm.* on Eph. 3:17.

18 John Preston, *The Breast-Plate of Faith and Love* (1634; facsimile repr., Edinburgh: Banner of Truth, 1979), 1:45.

19 Luther, *Lectures on Galatians*, on Gal. 2:16, in *LW*, 26:132.

20 Sibbes, *The Life of Faith*, in *WRS*, 5:367.

Faith fights against all sin. John says, "This is the victory that overcometh the world, even our faith" (1 John 5:4). The Belgic Confession notes that "great infirmities" remain in believers, "but they fight against them through the Spirit all the days of their life, continually taking their refuge in the blood, death, passion, and obedience of our Lord Jesus Christ, in whom they have remission of sins through faith in Him."[21]

Fifth, *faith produces good works*. Paul writes of the "work of faith" (1 Thess. 1:3; 2 Thess. 1:11) and "faith which worketh by love" (Gal. 5:6). "Without faith it is impossible to please God" (Heb. 11:6), for by faith, God's people walk in courageous obedience. Abel pleased God in his worship, Abraham obeyed God's calling, Sarah received power to bear a child in her old age, Isaac and Jacob declared the Lord's blessing on their offspring, and Moses chose the reproach of Christ over the riches of Egypt—all by faith (vv. 4–26).

By faith, spiritual warriors can stand against Satan's temptations (Eph. 6:16). By faith, they rejoice in God's promises with hope (Rom. 15:13). By faith, believers draw near to God and enjoy his holy presence mediated through their great High Priest (Heb. 10:19–22). By faith, the prayers of God's children call the power of God down from heaven (James 5:15–16).

Do you have saving faith in Christ? Faith is known in its exercises in the soul and practical results in life. Examine yourself to see if you are in the faith and if faith is in you.

The Need for Faith in Christ

John Flavel wrote, "The soul is the life of the body, faith is the life of the soul, and Christ is the life of faith."[22] Without faith there is only death and damnation (Mark 16:16; 1 John 5:12–13).

To be saved, one must hear the gospel and respond to it with saving faith in Jesus Christ (Rom. 10:13–14). The Westminster Larger Catechism says,

> They who, having never heard the gospel, know not Jesus Christ, and believe not in him, cannot be saved, be they never so diligent to frame their lives according to the light of nature, or the laws of that religion

21 The Belgic Confession (Art. 29), in *TFU*, 49–50.

22 Flavel, *The Method of Grace*, in *WJF*, 2:104.

> which they profess; neither is there salvation in any other, but in Christ alone, who is the Saviour only of his body the church.[23]

As our Lord says, "If ye believe not that I am he, ye shall die in your sins" (John 8:24).

Believers must grow in their faith so that they can grow in every part of their spiritual lives. Christ rebuked his disciples for being people of "little faith." Smallness of faith leads to anxiety about daily needs (Matt. 6:30), terror in crises (8:26), doubts about the power of God (14:31), and weakness in understanding God's Word (16:8). The apostle Paul thanked God for the believers in Thessalonica because their faith "groweth exceedingly" (2 Thess. 1:3).

Therefore, take hold of Christ in the Word. Meditate on him in the Word, and you will feed your soul. Ask God the Father to strengthen you so that Christ dwells in your heart by faith more and more unto the fullness of God (Eph. 3:16–19). Cling to Christ when sorrows come, for suffering is the school of faith (James 1:2–3). Strive to know Christ in "the power of his resurrection, and the fellowship of his sufferings" (Phil. 3:10).

Suggested Songs to Sing to the Lord

- Psalm 51, "God be merciful to me," *Psalter*, No. 140; *THBap*, No. 415
- "Not what my hands have done," *THBap*, No. 403

Questions for Meditation or Discussion

1. What is conversion?
2. What are the two sides of conversion? How would you prove that from Scripture?
3. What is repentance unto life? How is it different from mere regret over sin?
4. Someone says, "Repentance is not needed for salvation. We are saved by grace through faith alone." How do you respond?
5. What are some kinds of faith that do not save?
6. Who is the object of saving faith? Why is that important?
7. What are the three parts of saving faith? What does each part mean?

23 The Westminster Larger Catechism (Q. 60), in *RC*, 4:311.

8. What are the experiential exercises of faith?
9. Do you observe these exercises of faith in your life? Do you have a living faith in Christ?
10. If you are a believer, which of these exercises of faith is an area where you especially need to grow? What steps can you take so that, by God's grace, your faith will grow?

61

Justification

Chapter Summary and Key Terms

When God gives faith to a sinner through effectual calling, he also gives *justification* through faith. Justification is a gift of saving grace in which God counts and declares a believer to be righteous in his sight. The basis of justification is not anything in the believer or done by him, but Christ's active and passive obedience to the law. The execution of justification is not in eternity but only when the elect trust in Christ by God's grace. The means of justification is faith in Jesus Christ. However, faith is not righteousness. Rather, faith receives Christ as one's only righteousness by God's legal reckoning (*imputation*). Believers are justified by faith alone (*sola fide*), but their good works demonstrate that their faith is real and living. Contrary to Roman Catholicism, justification does not include regeneration and is not increased by the merit of good works. Justification by faith brings peace, communion with God, liberty, eternal life, solid ground for assurance, confidence, and hope.

AT THE HEART OF THE GOSPEL is the promise of *justification* by faith alone. Paul says that God is "the justifier of him which believeth in Jesus" (Rom. 3:26). Justification answers the crucial question of salvation: How can a sinful human being be righteous with the just and holy God?

We can understand the need for justification only when we have a clear view of God's justice and mankind's sin. God is not mere love with no concern for justice. The Lord says, "I will not justify the wicked" (Ex. 23:7). He is "a God of law."[1] Mankind is sinful and guilty before God (Rom. 3:9–18), and the law demands punishment for sinners. So the psalmist cries, "If thou, Lord, shouldest mark iniquities, O Lord, who shall stand?" (Ps. 130:3).

The Meaning of Justification

To "justify" is the act of a judge who declares a person to be right in the eyes of the law. We read in the law, "If there be a controversy between men, and they come unto judgment, that the judges may judge them; then they shall justify the righteous, and condemn the wicked" (Deut. 25:1). The Lord judges men, "condemning the wicked . . . justifying the righteous" (1 Kings 8:32). Another meaning of the word *justify* is to publicly demonstrate that someone is righteous (Rom. 3:4). But this term does not mean changing someone into a better person.

As an act of salvation, justification is a gracious, legal declaration by God. Paul speaks much of justification in his letter to the Romans. His concern there is "the righteous judgment of God" (Rom. 2:5). No "guilty" sinner can be "justified" by obeying the law, "for by the law is the knowledge of sin" (3:19–20). In justification, God gives forgiveness of guilt and freedom from condemnation (5:16; 8:1). Notice the opposites: "It is God that justifieth. Who is he that condemneth?" (8:33–34). God also acts as the Judge to count the person as having faithfully obeyed God's law. Thus, "justification" through Christ is the same thing as "by the obedience of one shall many be made righteous" (5:18–19). Justification is a legal counting or reckoning someone to be righteous (4:3–6).

Justification is the amazing reversal of a sinner's legal status before God. It is like taking off filthy clothes that make a person offensive to God and putting on clean clothes that please him (Zech. 3:1–5). God justifies unworthy sinners, not people who think they are righteous (Luke 18:9–14). How can this be?

The Basis of Justification

Paul says that sinners are justified by the righteousness of God. He writes, "For therein [in the gospel] is the righteousness of God revealed from faith

1 Leon Morris, *The Apostolic Preaching of the Cross*, 3rd ed. (Grand Rapids, MI: Eerdmans, 1965), 253.

to faith: as it is written, The just shall live by faith" (Rom. 1:17). Paul adds, "But now the righteousness of God without the law is manifested, being witnessed by the law and the prophets; even the righteousness of God which is by faith of Jesus Christ unto all and upon all them that believe: for there is no difference" (3:21–22). He then explains that sinners can be "justified freely by his grace through the redemption that is in Christ Jesus" (v. 24).

What man's righteousness cannot do, God's righteousness accomplishes. The "righteousness of God" is a shorthand description of how God exercises and glorifies his righteousness in the salvation of sinners. He satisfied the just demands of his law through Christ's righteous life and death for the sins of his people. As a result, God counts them as righteous. Isaiah says, "All we like sheep have gone astray; we have turned every one to his own way; and the Lord hath laid on him the iniquity of us all. . . . By his knowledge shall my righteous servant justify many; for he shall bear their iniquities" (Isa. 53:6, 11).

God credits Christ's passive and active obedience to believers (see chap. 48). Christ suffered the penalty of God's law. By his blood, his people have forgiveness of sins (Eph. 1:7). He perfectly obeyed what God commands in the law. By his obedience, believers are counted worthy of eternal life (Rom. 5:18–19).

Theologians refer to this legal reckoning as *imputation*. In justification, Christ's righteousness is imputed to believing sinners, just as guilt was imputed to him as their surety so that he was punished as their substitute.

Thus, Christ is the righteousness of his people (1 Cor. 1:30). Believers are "justified in Christ" (Gal. 2:17 ESV). Paul says, "For he hath made him to be sin for us, who knew no sin; that we might be made the righteousness of God in him" (2 Cor. 5:21). Wilhelmus à Brakel said, "Believers are thus made righteous in Him, as He has in like manner been made sin for them. Here is a mutual transfer from one to the other."[2]

The Execution of Justification

God planned justification from eternity and has executed his plan over the course of history. God "hath chosen us in him [Christ] before the foundation of the world, that we should be holy and without blame before him in love" (Eph. 1:4). That does not mean that the elect have always been justified.

2 Brakel, *CRS*, 2:352.

No sinner is justified until he or she trusts in Christ (John 3:18). Until God makes the elect alive with Christ, they are "children of wrath, even as others" (Eph. 2:3–5). But God planned their justification, so it cannot fail.

God accomplished justification by Christ's obedience, death, and resurrection. Paul says that Christ "was delivered for our offences, and was raised again for our justification" (Rom. 4:25). He adds, "By the obedience of one shall many be made righteous" (5:19). This work is done. Christ could say in his dying breath, "It is finished" (John 19:30).

God promises justification in the gospel of Christ. The evangelical promise announces "the forgiveness of sins" and that "all that believe are justified" (Acts 13:38–39). God grants actual justification by faith in Christ. Paul says, "We have believed in Jesus Christ, that we might be justified" (Gal. 2:16).

The Westminster Confession of Faith gives a good summary of how God executes justification: "God did, from all eternity, decree to justify all the elect, and Christ did, in the fulness of time, die for their sins, and rise again for their justification: nevertheless, they are not justified, until the Holy Spirit doth, in due time, actually apply Christ unto them."[3]

God can give a felt sense of justification in the conscience of the justified believer. The justifying "blood of Christ," when applied by faith to the heart, can "purge your conscience from dead works to serve the living God" (Heb. 9:14). That is, God gives an inward sense of being clean and acceptable before him so that the believer draws near with "boldness" (10:19, 22).

The Means of Justification

In Genesis 15:6, we read of Abraham, "He believed in the Lord, and he counted it to him for righteousness." Abraham did not merit God's blessing. Paul uses Abraham as an example of how God "justifieth the *ungodly*" (Rom. 4:5). God imputed to Abraham "righteousness without works" (v. 6) before Abraham had even received circumcision (vv. 9–12).

Paul says, "Therefore being justified by faith, we have peace with God through our Lord Jesus Christ" (Rom. 5:1). He adds, "Knowing that a man is not justified by the works of the law, but by the faith of Jesus Christ, even we have believed in Jesus Christ, that we might be justified by the faith of

3 The Westminster Confession of Faith (11.4), in *RC*, 4:248. Cf. the Second London Baptist Confession (11.4), in *RC*, 4:547.

Christ, and not by the works of the law: for by the works of the law shall no flesh be justified" (Gal. 2:16). Where the Bible speaks of the "faith of Christ" (cf. Phil. 3:9), it does not refer to faith exercised *by* Christ but to faith exercised *toward* Christ.

We are justified by faith in Christ. Faith, therefore, is not our righteousness but the means through which we receive the righteousness of God in Christ. Paul never says that God justifies us *because of* faith or *on the basis of* faith. Faith does not fulfill any condition of divine justice to make us acceptable to God. It does not become our merit instead of our good works. On the contrary, faith always looks outside of itself for righteousness in another—namely, Jesus Christ, the Righteous One.

The Heidelberg Catechism says, "Why sayest thou that thou art righteous by faith only? Not that I am acceptable to God, on account of the worthiness of my faith, but because only the satisfaction, righteousness, and holiness of Christ, is my righteousness before God; and that I cannot receive and apply the same to myself any other way than by faith only."[4]

Justification by Faith Alone and the Place of Good Works

The Westminster Confession of Faith says, "Faith, thus receiving and resting on Christ and His righteousness, is the alone instrument of justification: yet it is not alone in the person justified, but is ever accompanied with all other saving graces, and is no dead faith, but worketh by love."[5]

Justification by faith is the opposite of justification by works of obedience to the law. Paul writes, "Therefore by the deeds of the law there shall no flesh be justified in his sight: for by the law is the knowledge of sin" (Rom. 3:20). He adds, "Therefore we conclude that a man is justified by faith without the deeds of the law" (v. 28).

Paul's doctrine of justification by faith alone apart from works seems to contradict James 2:21–24, which says,

> Was not Abraham our father justified by works, when he had offered Isaac his son upon the altar? Seest thou how faith wrought with his works, and by works was faith made perfect? And the scripture was fulfilled which

4 The Heidelberg Catechism (LD 23, Q. 61), in *TFU*, 87.

5 The Westminster Confession of Faith (11.2), in *RC*, 4:248. Cf. the Second London Baptist Confession (11.2), in *RC*, 4:546.

> saith, Abraham believed God, and it was imputed unto him for righteousness: and he was called the Friend of God. Ye see then how that by works a man is justified, and not by faith only.

But James uses "justified" differently from Paul, referring to a public demonstration that someone is righteous. Abraham had a right relationship with God when he trusted in God's promise (Gen. 15:6). Yet Abraham publicly demonstrated that he was in a right relationship with God when he obeyed God's command by a living faith (22:9–12).

Justification by faith can never be separated from the grace of sanctification. Everyone with justifying faith is united to Christ in his death and resurrection. The believer has died to sin and become alive to God. Sin cannot reign over him any longer (Rom. 6:1–14). Christ is not just the believer's righteousness but also his wisdom, sanctification, and redemption (1 Cor. 1:30). John Calvin said that we cannot be justified by faith alone without also living a holy life. These graces are so tied together that to separate them would be to "tear Christ in pieces."[6]

The Reformation Debate on Justification

Medieval Roman Catholicism taught that justification is both forgiveness of sins and an inward change by grace that produces good works to merit more grace. But some medieval theologians also taught sinners to trust in Christ alone for salvation. Bernard of Clairvaux said, "The pitying mercy of the Lord is, then, all my merit. . . . Shall it be my own righteousness that I celebrate? Nay, O Lord; I will make mention of Thy righteousness, even of Thine only (Ps. 71:16). For that is mine also, since Thou Thyself hast become my Righteousness."[7]

In the sixteenth century, the Reformers taught justification by faith alone. Martin Luther said, "We are pronounced righteous solely by faith in Christ, not by the works of the Law or by love."[8] Calvin said, "Our righteousness is not in us but in Christ. . . . The obedience of Christ is reckoned to us

6 Calvin, *Comm.* on 1 Cor. 1:30; cf. *Institutes*, 3.11.6.

7 Bernard of Clairvaux, *Sermons on the Song of Songs*, 61.3, 5, in *The Life and Works of Saint Bernard, Abbot of Clairvaux*, ed. John Mabillon, trans. Samuel J. Eales, 4 vols. (London: John Hodges, 1896), 4:367–68.

8 Luther, *Lectures on Galatians*, on Gal. 2:16, in *LW*, 35:137.

as if it were our own."[9] He also wrote, "Man, accordingly, has no works in which to glory before God; and hence, stripped of all help from works, he is justified by faith alone."[10]

The official Roman Catholic response to the doctrine of justification by faith alone was given at the Council of Trent. The council ruled that justification "is not remission [forgiveness or pardon] of sins merely, but also the sanctification and renewal of the inward man, through the voluntary reception of the grace."[11] Christians "are still further justified" as their personal justice increases in a life of faith and good works.[12] Those persevering in love and use of the sacraments may hope that God may reward "their good works and merits" with eternal life.[13] In affirming the merit of our good works—even good works produced by the power of God's grace—the Roman Catholic Church affirms the very thing that Paul denies: justification by works.

Objections to Justification by Faith Alone

What reasons do people give for rejecting justification by faith alone?

Objection 1: God's word is always effective. If God declares a person righteous, that declaration changes him to be righteous.

In reply, we agree that God's word is always effective to accomplish what he intends (Isa. 55:11). But what God intends by justification is to give a new legal status.

Objection 2: In the Bible, justification includes regeneration. Paul says, "He saved us by the washing of regeneration, and renewing of the Holy Ghost . . . that being justified by his grace, we should be made heirs" (Titus 3:5–7), and, "But ye are washed, but ye are sanctified, but ye are justified in the name of the Lord Jesus, and by the Spirit of our God" (1 Cor. 6:11).

In reply, we note that the Scriptures sometimes list benefits of salvation together without saying they are the same thing (1 Cor. 1:30). Also, Paul

9 Calvin, *Institutes*, 3.11.23.

10 Calvin, *Institutes*, 3.17.8.

11 Council of Trent (Session 6, Decree on Justification, chap. 7), in *The Creeds of Christendom*, ed. Philip Schaff, rev. David S. Schaff, 3 vols. (Grand Rapids, MI: Baker, 1983), 2:94.

12 Council of Trent (Session 6, Decree on Justification, chap. 10), in *The Creeds of Christendom*, ed. Schaff, 2:99.

13 Council of Trent (Session 6, Decree on Justification, chap. 16), in *The Creeds of Christendom*, ed. Schaff, 2:107.

distinguishes between effectual calling and justification (Rom. 8:30). The word *justify* is a term of legal status, not new birth or life.

Objection 3: God speaks no lies. But it would be a lie for God to declare someone righteous with no basis in who the person is or what the person did.

In reply, we insist that God's declaration of sinful believers as righteous is not a lie. Rather, the sinner is righteous because of the legal reality of his union with Christ. The Lord Jesus satisfied God's justice by his obedience and death as the surety of his people (chap. 47).

Objection 4: Only some works are excluded from justification, such as works of the Old Testament law or works before regeneration. But the regenerate are justified by works of love.

In reply, we argue that Paul denies a place to any works in our justification. God saved us "not by works of righteousness which we have done" (Titus 3:5). Paul presents regenerate believers (Abraham and David) as examples of justification "without works" (Rom. 4:1–8).

Objection 5: Faith cannot justify without love. Paul says that "though I have all faith . . . and have not charity [love], I am nothing" (1 Cor. 13:2).

In reply, we note that Paul's statement in 1 Corinthians 13 is not about justification but the importance of love in the Christian life. The faith in view is not saving faith but the faith to work miracles. Paul says, "Though I have all faith, so that I could remove mountains, and have not charity, I am nothing" (1 Cor. 13:2). Justifying faith is always accompanied by love (Gal. 5:6). But that does not prove love is part of justification. Paul nowhere teaches that we are justified by love.

Objection 6: The doctrine of "faith alone" is antinomian. If we are justified merely for believing in Jesus, people may be justified even though they live in unrepentant sin against God.

In reply, we point out that Calvin said, "It is therefore faith alone which justifies, and yet the faith which justifies is not alone."[14] Rather, justifying faith is always accompanied by love. Paul says, "They that are Christ's have crucified the flesh with the affections and lusts. If we live in the Spirit, let us also walk in the Spirit" (Gal. 5:24–25). Those whose lives are characterized

14 John Calvin, *Canons and Decrees of the Council of Trent, with the Antidote*, in *Tracts Relating to the Reformation*, trans. Henry Beveridge, 3 vols. (Edinburgh: Calvin Translation Society, 1844), 3:152.

by the works of the flesh instead of the fruit of the Spirit will not inherit the kingdom of God (vv. 19–23).

Objection 7: Christ's obedience is not our righteousness, for God counts the Christian's faith to be his righteousness. Paul says, "His faith is counted for righteousness" (Rom. 4:5).

In reply, we find a clear statement that Christ's righteousness is counted to believers in Paul's words: "For he hath made him to be sin for us, who knew no sin; that we might be made the righteousness of God in him" (2 Cor. 5:21). When the Bible says that faith is counted as righteousness, it is not because faith is our righteousness. Rather, it is because faith grasps Christ, who is our righteousness.

Justification is not based on anything good in us, including our faith. Our faith would be a very imperfect righteousness. The imputation of righteousness is "of grace" to "the ungodly" (Rom. 4:4–5). John Piper writes, "Paul's conceptual framework is that the thing imputed to us is external to us. . . . Faith receives the gift of righteousness."[15]

Objection 8: Justification is not about our legal standing with God but our acceptance into God's people. This is one teaching of what is called "the New Perspective on Paul."[16]

In reply, we note that we have already shown that the word *justify* has to do with a judge's verdict on one's legal status (Deut. 25:1), and the opposite of justification is condemnation (Rom. 8:33–34). Justification certainly has implications for acceptance in the church (Gal. 2:11–16). But we should not confuse the effect with the cause. Justification is not acceptance in the church but acceptance by God the Judge.

Practical Applications of Justification by Faith Alone

The faith that receives Christ for righteousness grasps hold of many blessings in him.

First, *justification provides peace of conscience.* Paul says, "Therefore being justified by faith, we have peace with God through our Lord Jesus Christ"

15 John Piper, *Counted Righteous in Christ: Should We Abandon the Imputation of Christ's Righteousness?* (Wheaton, IL: Crossway, 2002), 60.

16 On the New Perspective on Paul, a rejection of Reformation theology and reinterpretation of Paul taught by Krister Stendahl, E. P. Sanders, James Dunn, and N. T. Wright, see Beeke and Smalley, *RST*, 3:568–72.

(Rom. 5:1). Objective peace leads to inner peace. As faith increases, so do boldness and confidence in the presence of God (Eph. 3:12).

Second, *justification provides joyful communion with the reconciled God.* Justification opens the door for a sweet relationship with the righteous God. It removes both guilt and wrath so that nothing can separate believers from the love of God in Christ (Rom. 8:33–39). Paul writes that as those "justified by his blood, . . . we also joy in God" (5:9, 11).

Third, *justification provides liberty to confess our sins and seek God's fatherly forgiveness.* The church enjoys the holy fellowship of walking in God's light, for "the blood of Jesus Christ his Son cleanseth us from all sin" (1 John 1:6–7). This involves regular confession, repentance, experience of God's forgiveness through Christ, and renewed resolve to keep God's commandments (1:8–2:3).

Fourth, *justification provides the gift of eternal life and blessing.* Paul writes of the "justification of life," for those who receive "the gift of righteousness shall reign in life" through Jesus Christ (Rom. 5:17–18). God is not against them but for them, and so all things work together for their good (8:28, 31).

Fifth, *justification provides grounds for assurance of salvation.* Since Christians are "justified by faith" and "have peace with God" by the finished work of Christ, they "stand" in the status of divine grace (Rom. 5:1–2). Good works and perseverance are important evidences of salvation (vv. 3–5). But if we attempt to rest on them, we will soon find them to fail us. Justification by an imputed righteousness apart from works is a solid ground for the trembling saint.

Sixth, *justification provides confidence that we are pleasing to God.* Justification by the imputed righteousness of Christ makes believers pleasing to God. He views them in union with Christ and thus clothed with his perfect righteousness (Isa. 61:10; 62:5). By faith they please God (Heb. 11:5–6), as do their good works (13:16).

Seventh, *justification provides the hope of glory.* Paul says that the consequence of "being justified by faith" is that we "rejoice in hope of the glory of God" (Rom. 5:1–2). The anticipation of judgment day no longer should fill believers with dread because they are counted righteous in Christ. While the thought of Christ's judgment should fill his people with holy awe, it is an awe mingled with joy and hope. The Judge has justified them by his blood.

Suggested Song to Sing to the Lord

- "Jesus, thy blood and righteousness," *THBap*, No. 439

Questions for Meditation or Discussion

1. What must we know about God and ourselves to understand our need for justification?
2. What does "justify" mean?
3. What is the basis of justification?
4. How did God make and execute his plan for justification?
5. What is the means of justification?
6. If we are justified by faith alone, what is the place of good works?
7. Someone says that 1 Corinthians 6:11 and Titus 3:5–7 show that justification includes regeneration. How do you respond?
8. How do we know that no works, not even works of love done after regeneration, add anything to our justification?
9. What practical blessings does justification bring?
10. Which of the blessings of justification listed above is most precious to you? Why?

62

Adoption

Chapter Summary and Key Terms

In addition to justification, God gives all believers the saving grace of *adoption*, making them his beloved children with the full rights and inheritance of sons. In the Old Testament, God adopted Israel as his national son. Israelites who feared the Lord were his individual children. He also took the offspring of David to be his royal son. After Christ, the eternal (not adopted) Son of God, came in the flesh, God revealed his fatherly adoption of believers, male and female, as a great benefit of union with Christ. God gives his children the Holy Spirit, who dwells in them as the Spirit of adoption. All of God's acts of salvation, from eternal election through glorification, aim at the adoption of his people. The grace of adoption transforms the believer's relationships with God, himself, the world, and the church.

WHILE JUSTIFICATION BY FAITH lays the foundation for salvation, adoption may be "the apex and epitome of grace," as John Murray said.[1] The apostle John marveled, "Behold, what manner of love the Father hath bestowed upon us, that we should be called the sons of God" (1 John 3:1). In justification, God declares sinners righteous in the court of his legal justice. In adoption, God takes justified believers into his household to be his children.

Adoption is by covenant, not by creation. Liberal modernism claims that God is everyone's Father and that all people are spiritual brothers

1 John Murray, *Collected Writings of John Murray*, 4 vols. (Edinburgh: Banner of Truth, 1982), 2:229.

and sisters. But Christ teaches that there are two kinds of people traveling to either destruction or life (Matt. 7:13–14). Only those saved by grace through faith in Jesus Christ can rightly claim to be God's children (John 1:12; Gal. 3:26).

It is true that God is the Father of all mankind in the sense that he created the human race (Acts 17:28). But the fall broke mankind's relationship with the Creator. Christ warned unbelievers, "If God were your Father, ye would love me: for I proceeded forth and came from God. . . . Ye are of your father the devil, and the lusts of your father ye will do" (John 8:42, 44). Thus, God is no longer the spiritual Father of unbelievers; Satan is (1 John 3:10). God continues to love sinners as his creatures, but they are under his wrath (Rom. 1:18) and counted as his enemies until they are reconciled to him through Christ (5:10).

Adoption is a marvelous grace. William Perkins said that for "such rebels to be made the sons of God—it is a wonderful privilege and prerogative, and no dignity like unto it."[2] Some of the privileges of adoption are explained in the Westminster Confession of Faith:

> All those that are justified, God vouchsafeth [graciously grants], in and for His only Son Jesus Christ, to make partakers of the grace of adoption, by which they are taken into the number, and enjoy the liberties and privileges of the children of God, have His name put upon them, receive the spirit of adoption, have access to the throne of grace with boldness, are enabled to cry, Abba, Father, are pitied, protected, provided for, and chastened by Him as by a Father: yet never cast off, but sealed to the day of redemption; and inherit the promises, as heirs of everlasting salvation.[3]

A Biblical Theology of Adoption

God's Adoption of Sons in the Old Testament

Adoption is rooted in God's creation of man "in our image, after our likeness" (Gen. 1:26). A son is the living image of his father (5:1–3). Adam was made to be a son of God (Luke 3:38). But he disobeyed God and forfeited man's great privilege.

2 Perkins, *An Exposition of the Symbol*, in *WWP*, 5:33.

3 The Westminster Confession of Faith (chap. 12), in *RC*, 4:249. Cf. the Second London Baptist Confession (chap. 12), in *RC*, 4:547–48.

There are hints of adoption in God's covenant with Abraham and his seed (Gen. 17:7–8). God promised that they would "inherit" the land (15:7–8; 28:4), just as a son inherits the property of his father.

When God redeemed Abraham's descendants out of Egypt, the Lord declared, "Israel is my son, even my firstborn" (Ex. 4:22). Israel received the Lord's care (Deut. 1:31), discipline (8:5), and call to holiness (14:1–2) because God had adopted the whole nation as a group to be his "son." Individuals among God's covenant people were not his children if they rejected him and his laws (Deut. 32:5–6 KJV mg., ESV). But people who feared the Lord were under his fatherly compassion (Ps. 103:13) and loving discipline (Prov. 3:11–12).

The Lord especially adopted the offspring of David as his "firstborn, higher than the kings of the earth" (Ps. 89:26–27). This action foreshadowed David's greatest descendant, Jesus of Nazareth (Luke 1:32). But Christ was not adopted by God. He was already God's Son at birth (v. 35). He is the eternal, only begotten Son of the Father (John 3:16; 17:5, 24).

The Hebrew prophets used the doctrine of adoption to rebuke Israel for its failure to honor and obey God (Isa. 1:2; Mal. 1:6). They also clung to God as the faithful Father of his people (Isa. 63:16; 64:8). God promised to restore his sinful and exiled covenant family, the beloved children he had created for his glory (Isa. 43:6–7; Jer. 31:9, 20; Hos. 1:10; Mal. 3:17).

Therefore, in the Old Testament, God revealed his adoptive love for mankind as a whole as those created in his image. After the fall destroyed that relationship, God adopted the covenant seed of Abraham, the nation of Israel. But the focus of adoption in the Old Testament is on the whole covenant people as God's "son" and on the son of David as God's royal "son."

God's Adoption of Sons in the New Testament

With the coming of God the Son incarnate, the Lord revealed his adoption in a far greater way. Christ called God the "Father" of believers dozens of times and taught his disciples to regularly address God as "our Father which art in heaven" (Matt. 6:9). Not all people are God's children, but only those who are peacemakers (5:9), love their enemies (vv. 44–45), and do the will of Christ's Father in heaven (12:50). Jesus revealed God as

- the attentive Father who rewards his children's good works (6:4, 6, 18)
- the caring Father who knows what they need before they ask (v. 8)
- the providing Father who gives them all they need (vv. 25–32)
- the responsive Father who delights to answer his children's prayers (7:9–11).

Christ "came to his own, and his own people did not receive him. But to all who did receive him, who believed in his name, he gave the right to become children of God" (John 1:11–12 ESV). After Christ died for his people's sins and rose from the dead, he said, "I ascend unto my Father, and your Father; and to my God, and your God" (20:17).

Paul often opens his epistles by calling on "God our Father" to bless his people (Rom. 1:7; 1 Cor. 1:3, etc.). He is the only writer to use the Greek word translated as "adoption" in the Scriptures (Rom. 8:15, 23; 9:4; Gal. 4:5; Eph. 1:5). This term means "placement as a son." Paul teaches that not all those descended from Abraham are the children of God, but only those chosen and called by God (Rom. 9:8, 11, 23–26). God adopts those who trust in Christ: "for in Christ Jesus you are all sons of God, through faith" (Gal. 3:26 ESV). Thus, adoption is a benefit of union with Christ ("in Christ"). Gentiles in Christ are grafted into the true Israel and become heirs of God's promises to Abraham (v. 29). Christ redeemed his people so that they would be adopted by God (4:4–5). As a result, God gives them the Spirit of his Son (v. 6). Therefore, the believer in Christ has the status of "a son; and if a son, then an heir of God through Christ" (v. 7). Christians already have the Spirit of adoption (Rom. 8:15), but do not yet enjoy the glory of being "joint-heirs with Christ" (v. 17). The full realization of their adoption awaits their resurrection from the dead (v. 23).

Adoption is not as prominent in the other New Testament writings, but it remains an important theme. For example, we are told that God sent Christ for the purpose of "bringing many sons unto glory" (Heb. 2:10). Peter exhorts God's chosen, redeemed, and born-again people to conduct themselves "as obedient children," for they "call on the Father, who without respect of persons judgeth according to every man's work" (1 Pet. 1:14, 17). As we saw above, John exclaims, "Behold, what manner of love the Father hath bestowed upon us, that we should be called the sons of God. . . . When he shall appear, we shall be like him; for we shall see him as he is" (1 John 3:1–2). John emphasizes that God's adopted children have been born again and thus transformed (v. 9). Consequently, the mark of God's children is their righteousness and love for one another (v. 10). In the last chapters of the Bible, God promises, "He that overcometh shall inherit all things; and I will be his God, and he shall be my son" (Rev. 21:7). Thomas Watson said it well: "Adoption ends in coronation."[4]

Adoption as a Way of Looking at All of Salvation

Stephen Marshall said, "Though sometimes in the Holy Scriptures our sonship is but one of our privileges, yet very frequently in the Scripture all that believers do obtain from Christ . . . is comprehended in this one [privilege], that they are made the children of God."[5] Let us therefore consider how all the aspects of salvation relate to adoption.

Election and predestination are the planning of adoption. In election, God chose whom he would adopt. In predestination, he determined their destiny beforehand to become his sons through Christ's work (Eph. 1:4–5). Adoption reveals the fatherly affection behind election.

Incarnation is Christ's taking on a nature suitable for our adoption. Christ took "flesh and blood" to be like his "brethren" whom he came to save and bring to glory (Heb. 2:10–15). The Son of God became a man so that men might become children of God, as Irenaeus said.[6]

Redemption by Christ's blood is the objective accomplishment of adoption. Christ kept God's law and suffered its penalty to redeem lawbreakers so that they would become God's sons and daughters (Gal. 4:4–5). This reveals the infinite price that God paid to adopt sinners.

Resurrection and ascension are Christ's exaltation as the Mediator of adoption. He ascended to his "God" and "Father" to secure the adoption of his people by their "God" and "Father" (John 20:17). He went "to prepare a place" for them in his "Father's house" (14:2).

4 Thomas Watson, *A Body of Divinity* (Edinburgh: Banner of Truth, 1965), 234.

5 Stephen Marshall, "The High Priviledg [*sic*] of All True Believers to Be the Sons of God," in *The Works of Mr Stephen Marshall . . . The First Part* (London: Peter Cole and Edward Cole, 1661), 37.

6 Irenaeus, *Against Heresies*, 3.19.1, in *ANF*, 1:448.

Calling is the effectual summons to Christ for adoption. God takes those "whom he hath called, not of the Jews only, but also of the Gentiles," and brings them from being "not my people" to be "the children of the living God" (Rom. 9:24–26).

Regeneration is God's giving to sinners a nature suitable to live in the relationships granted by adoption. The new birth implants new life into people so that they trust in Christ and have a disposition to hate sin and love God's children (1 John 3:9–10, 14; 5:1).

Repentance is a sinner's turning to the Father for adoption. Sinners are restored to the Father's household when they come to him in repentance over their sins and discover the greatness of his grace (Luke 15:21–22).

Faith is the human means of receiving adoption. Those who believe in Jesus Christ are granted the right to be counted God's children (John 1:12). People are God's children "by faith" (Gal. 3:26), the same way that they are justified (Rom. 3:30).

Justification is the legal requirement for adoption. Only when people are justified by faith do they have peace with God—a reconciled relationship (Rom. 5:1, 11). Until they are justified, divine justice condemns them to suffer divine wrath. Thus, adoption depends on justification. Sinners must be "justified" to be "made heirs according to the hope of eternal life" (Titus 3:7).

Sanctification is the practical outworking of the relationship of adoption. Since believers in Christ are "the sons of God," they are "led by the Spirit" to live as sons (Rom. 8:14). Having been born again, they begin to learn to live "as obedient children" (1 Pet. 1:3, 14).

Perseverance is the school of adopted children. Through perseverance, God's children mature (Heb. 12:5–6). John Calvin said, "In the very harshness of tribulations we must recognize the kindness and generosity of our Father toward us, since he does not even then cease to promote our salvation."[7]

Glorification is the completion of the aims of adoption. Believers are "heirs of God, and joint-heirs with Christ," and they "suffer with him" so that they will "be also glorified together" with him (Rom. 8:17). Glorification can even be called "adoption" (v. 23).

7 Calvin, *Institutes*, 3.8.6.

Adoption as the Transformation of Relationships

Adoption is thoroughly transformative. It changes a believer's relationships to God, to himself or herself, to the world, and to the church. Let us consider several aspects of each of these transformed relationships.

A Transformed Relationship to the Triune God

First, *God the Father predestined the elect to adoption before time began* (Eph. 1:4–5). He sent his Son to redeem them so that they would receive the adoption of sons (Gal. 4:4–5). He called them to Christ so that adoption would become theirs (Rom. 8:29–30).

By grace, God's adopted children call on him as "Abba, Father" (Rom. 8:15; Gal. 4:6). "Abba" is the Aramaic word that a child used to speak to his father in the home. It was the word Jesus used to pray to the Father in his deepest distress (Mark 14:36). The Son dwells in believers by his Spirit, stirring them to call on his Father as "our Father," as Athanasius said.[8]

God's children should trust their heavenly Father in everything. He knows what they need before they ask (Matt. 6:7, 32). Will not the God who cares for all the birds and flowers in the world take care of his own children (vv. 26–30)? They should revere their Father with childlike fear, reflect his holy character in their lives, and obey his commands (1 Pet. 1:14–17). They should honor him, especially in worship, for he is the great King (Mal. 1:6, 14).

Second, *God the Son accomplished adoption for those in him*. So great is his love for them that "he is not ashamed to call them brethren" (Heb. 2:11). He is "the firstborn among many brethren" (Rom. 8:29). Thomas Houston said, "Christ is the Elder Brother of those that are adopted into God's family. . . . Christ regards His saints with the love of a brother's heart. He takes the tenderest interest in all their concerns, and He never ceases to do them good."[9]

God's children should cooperate with his purpose that they become "conformed to the image of his Son" (Rom. 8:29). They should strive to become like Christ, imitating his obedience to the Father's will. They should seek Christ's honor and good name in all they do (Col. 3:17).

8 Athanasius, *Four Discourses against the Arians*, 4.22, in *NPNF*^{2}, 4:441.

9 Thomas Houston, *The Adoption of Sons, Its Nature, Spirit, Privileges, and Effects: A Practical and Experimental Treatise* (Paisley, Scotland: Alex. Garner et al., 1872), 58.

Third, *God the Holy Spirit applies the blessings of adoption*. He is the Spirit of adoption, who witnesses with believers' spirits that they are the children of God (Rom. 8:15–16). In the Spirit believers have fellowship with one another as the family of God. There is "one Spirit," "one Lord," and "one God and Father of all" (Eph. 4:4–6).

Let the children of God walk carefully to never grieve the Spirit or forfeit any of his comforting, sanctifying, and empowering blessings (Eph. 4:30; 1 Thess. 5:19). They should welcome the work of the Spirit in their lives, for he is "the Spirit of your Father" (Matt. 10:20).

The believer's relationship with the triune God is a treasure of infinite glory and joy. Wilhelmus à Brakel said, "The excellency of the children of God is so great that it exceeds all comprehension," for God "has all glory within Himself . . . and all that He is, He is for His children." Consequently, "a godly beggar is a thousand times more exalted and glorious than the greatest monarch who has ever been in the world."[10]

A Transformed Relationship to Oneself

First, *the believer should view himself or herself as God's son or daughter*. Paul says, "For ye are all the children of God by faith in Christ Jesus" (Gal. 3:26). If it is a great honor to be the son-in-law of a human king (1 Sam. 18:23), it is much more so to be adopted by the King of kings.

Second, *the believer should count himself or herself to be one with the Son of God*. Paul says, "For as many of you as have been baptized into Christ have put on Christ" (Gal. 3:27). The Christian is now bound up in him whom the Father embraces as "the beloved" (Eph. 1:6).

Third, *the believer should understand that he or she has an identity that transcends earthly categories*. Paul says, "There is neither Jew nor Greek, there is neither bond [slave] nor free, there is neither male nor female: for ye are all one in Christ Jesus" (Gal. 3:28). Sinclair Ferguson says, "Our self-image, if it is to be biblical, will begin just here. God is my Father. . . . I am one of his children. . . . His people are my brothers and sisters."[11]

Fourth, *the believer should see himself or herself as an heir of God's promises*. Paul says, "If ye be Christ's, then are ye Abraham's seed, and heirs

10 Brakel, *CRS*, 2:417–18.

11 Sinclair B. Ferguson, *Children of the Living God* (Colorado Springs, CO: NavPress, 1987), 18–19.

according to the promise" (Gal. 3:29). Though perhaps poor now, the child of God is rich in grace (James 2:5; Rev. 2:9).

A Transformed Relationship to the World

First, *adoption sets God's adopted children in opposition to the world.* John says of "the sons of God" that "the world knoweth us not, because it knew him not" (1 John 3:1). "The world" refers to people under the dominion of Satan and sin (v. 8). John concludes, "Marvel not, my brethren, if the world hate you" (v. 13).

Second, *adoption implies a call to live differently from the world.* Believers must be "blameless and innocent, children of God without blemish in the midst of a crooked and twisted generation, among whom you shine as lights in the world" (Phil. 2:15 ESV).

Third, *adoption enables God's children to have a peaceable and kind heart toward enemies in the world.* Christ says, "Blessed are the peacemakers: for they shall be called the children of God" (Matt. 5:9). He adds that people show they are true children of the heavenly Father by their likeness to him in loving their enemies and praying for them (vv. 44–45).

Fourth, *adoption grants God's children participation in the Son's mission to the world.* After Christ said, "I am ascending to my Father and your Father, to my God and your God," he added, "As the Father has sent me, even so I am sending you" (John 20:17, 21 ESV). God's only begotten Son is the great missionary, and God's adopted children share in his mission.

A Transformed Relationship to the Church

First, *God's adopted children must count themselves to have true membership in God's family with their brothers and sisters.* They have one Father (Eph. 4:6), and all who do his will are their brothers and sisters in Christ (Matt. 12:50).

Second, *God's adopted children must recognize their fundamental spiritual equality with their brothers and sisters.* The believer in union with Christ has become united to all people in him, regardless of their ethnicity, social status, or gender (Gal. 3:28; Col. 3:11). Although Christians may have legitimate authority over one another in the family, workplace, church, and state, no Christian is the lord of another, and all Christians are fellow heirs (1 Tim. 6:2; 1 Pet. 3:1, 7).

Third, *God's adopted children must maintain harmonious relationships with their brothers and sisters.* The Lord Jesus rebukes any disciple who is sinfully "angry with his brother" or insults "his brother," and urges him to go quickly to "be reconciled to thy brother" if he realizes that "thy brother hath ought against thee" (Matt. 5:22–24).

Fourth, *God's adopted children must give sacrificial service to their brothers and sisters.* Paul says, "Let us do good unto all men, especially unto them who are of the household of faith" (Gal. 6:10). John urges, "We ought to lay down our lives for the brethren" (1 John 3:16).

Fifth, *God's adopted children must share in giving and receiving exhortation among their brothers and sisters.* Mutual admonition in the family of God is the royal law of love (Lev. 19:17–18) and a great means of preserving believers from falling away (Heb. 3:12–13). The fourth and fifth points imply that every child of God should be an active member of a local church.

Sixth, *God's adopted children must sweeten ministry with affection to their brothers and sisters.* We should cherish partners in ministry as beloved siblings (Eph. 6:21; Phil. 2:25). We should love those to whom we minister as if we were their loving parents (1 Thess. 2:7–12).

Seventh, *God's adopted children should engage in communication with their brothers and sisters.* Much of the New Testament consists of epistles written with warm affection (Rom. 16:14, 23; 1 Cor. 16:20). God's children should communicate with one another through various media—though it is always preferable for them to meet face-to-face (2 John 12).

Although adoption by God is an invisible, heavenly transaction, it transforms every relationship that believers have. Adoption changes everything.[12]

Suggested Song to Sing to the Lord

- "Behold th'amazing gift of love," *THBap*, No. 442

Questions for Meditation or Discussion

1. What is adoption?
2. What did God say about adoption in the Old Testament?
3. How did Jesus Christ reveal God as the Father of his disciples?

12 For a study of Puritan teachings on the benefits and responsibilities of adoption, see Joel R. Beeke, *Heirs with Christ: The Puritans on Adoption* (Grand Rapids, MI: Reformation Heritage Books, 2008).

4. What does Paul teach about adoption by God?
5. Your family attends a funeral where the pastor says, "Everyone is a child of God." What do you say to your family after you return home from the funeral?
6. How do the following aspects of salvation relate to adoption: (1) election, (2) Christ's incarnation, (3) redemption by Christ's blood, (4) Christ's resurrection and ascension, (5) effectual calling, (6) regeneration, (7) repentance, (8) faith, (9) justification, (10) sanctification, (11) perseverance, and (12) glorification?
7. How does adoption transform our relationship with each person in the Trinity?
8. How does adoption transform our relationship with ourselves?
9. How does adoption transform our relationship with the world?
10. How does adoption transform our relationship with the church?

63

Sanctification

Chapter Summary and Key Terms

Sanctification is the saving grace by which God makes his people holy in heart and life. This grace is necessary to enter God's kingdom. The Father chose his people to be holy by union with Christ in the power of the Holy Spirit. By *definitive sanctification*, God has brought all believers into a state of grace. Sin no longer rules over them, for they are *saints* of God. By *progressive sanctification*, God works increasing holiness in believers by their efforts to obey him in *good works*. Errors about sanctification include *sinless perfectionism* (freedom from all sin), *asceticism* (special consecration by poverty, monasticism, celibacy, or severe treatment of the body), *perfectionism* (perfect love for God and people), and *two-level Christianity* (victory over inward conflict by faith). All Christians must strive for greater sanctification by relying on Christ, keeping God's commandments, imitating Christ, and exercising the spiritual disciplines.

HOLINESS IS THE LIFEBLOOD of Christianity. People often mistakenly think of holiness as proud, miserable legalism. But Jonathan Edwards said, "Holiness is a most beautiful, lovely thing. . . . There is nothing in it but what is sweet and ravishingly lovely."[1]

The words translated as "holy," "sanctify," and "consecrate" mean to be or make sacred, set apart for God from what is ordinary and set against

1 Edwards, "The Way of Holiness," in *WJE*, 10:478.

what is unclean (Lev. 10:10; 11:44). Geerhardus Vos said, "Holiness means a relationship with God, a dedication to God." Holiness always "serves for God's glorification."[2]

Sanctification is God's work to make people holy. Justification is a change in legal status before God, but sanctification is a change in heart and life. William Ames said, "Sanctification is the real change in man from the sordidness of sin to the purity of God's image."[3]

The Need for Sanctification

Without holiness, "no man shall see the Lord" (Heb. 12:14). Sanctification is absolutely necessary to behold God's glory in the eternal kingdom (Matt. 5:8). Why is this so?

First, *we must be sanctified because God is holy* (1 Pet. 1:14–16). God's holiness shines forth in his infinite majesty and moral perfection as the supreme King (Ps. 99:1–5). For the Holy One to allow unholy people to dwell with him, he would have to deny his own deity.

Second, *we must be sanctified because we are God's image bearers* (Gen. 1:26–27). At the core of that image is moral likeness to God in knowledge, righteousness, and holiness (Eph. 4:24; Col. 3:10). Holiness is at the heart of God's purpose for mankind.

Third, *we must be sanctified because we are born in the state of sin*. Since the fall, every human being is conceived in sin (Ps. 51:5): "They are all gone aside, they are all together become filthy: there is none that doeth good, no, not one" (14:3).

Fourth, *we must be sanctified because mere outward morality and religion are not holiness*. Despite all the moral and religious works people do, Paul says, "There is none righteous . . . there is none that seeketh after God" (Rom. 3:10–11).

Fifth, *we must be sanctified because regeneration is only the beginning of holiness*. Writing to those who are "born again," Peter says, "See that ye love one another with a pure heart fervently" (1 Pet. 1:22–23). What God planted in regeneration, believers must grow by grace.

2 Geerhardus Vos, *Reformed Dogmatics*, ed. Richard B. Gaffin, trans. Annemie Godbehere et al. (Bellingham, WA: Lexham, 2012–2014), 4:188.

3 William Ames, *The Marrow of Theology*, trans. John D. Eusden (Grand Rapids, MI: Baker, 1968), 1.29.4–5 (168).

Sixth, *we must be sanctified because salvation demands a response of holy love.* Paul says, "I beseech you therefore, brethren, by the mercies of God, that ye present your bodies a living sacrifice, holy, acceptable unto God, which is your reasonable service" (Rom. 12:1).

Seventh, *we must be sanctified because good works demonstrate the reality of salvation by faith.* James says, "Faith, if it hath not works, is dead, being alone," and so, "I will shew thee my faith by my works" (James 2:17–18). Sanctification proves true union with Christ.

The Grace of the Trinity in Sanctification

Election to Holiness by the Father

The deepest root of sanctification reaches back to before time began. Paul says, "[God the Father] hath chosen us in him before the foundation of the world, that we should be holy and without blame before him in love" (Eph. 1:4). God predestined the elect to be "conformed to the image of his Son, that he might be the firstborn among many brethren" (Rom. 8:29).

Therefore, all glory for our holiness must be given to God. All our choices to be holy flow from his eternal choice of us. Man's practical holiness is a response to God's will: "For this is the will of God, even your sanctification, that ye should abstain from fornication: that every one of you should know how to possess his vessel in sanctification and honour. . . . For God hath not called us unto uncleanness, but unto holiness" (1 Thess. 4:3–4, 7).

Union with Christ in His Death and Resurrection

Christ "bare our sins in his own body on the tree, that we, being dead to sins, should live unto righteousness: by whose stripes ye were healed" (1 Pet. 2:24). Herman Bavinck wrote, "By this act, he not only won for them the forgiveness of sins; his self-offering, his death, was also a total consecration to the Father, a perfect act of obedience to his will, a sanctification of himself that by his word they too might be sanctified in the truth (John 17:17, 19)."[4]

Justification by union with Christ does not encourage sin. By that same union with Christ, we died to sin and rose with him to walk in a new life (Rom. 6:1–4). The reigning power of sin has been crucified, and we are

4 Bavinck, *RD*, 4:233.

alive unto God (vv. 5–10). Sin still remains in us, and we must put it to death (8:12–13), but we should not view ourselves as slaves of sin. Paul says, "For sin shall not have dominion over you: for ye are not under the law, but under grace" (6:14).

The Supernatural Power of the Holy Spirit

God applies the accomplishment of Christ's death and resurrection to his elect people by the Holy Spirit. When Christ writes God's law on men's hearts, he does so "not with ink, but with the Spirit of the living God," the Lord and life giver (2 Cor. 3:3, 6). The Spirit of God is "the Spirit of life in Christ Jesus" because he liberates his people from sin and death (Rom. 8:2).

Therefore, to "walk in the Spirit" (Gal. 5:16, 25) is, by the grace of Christ applied by the power of the Spirit, to put to death the wicked works of the flesh and to live in love and self-control—"the fruit of the Spirit" (vv. 19–24). The Christian who is growing in holiness is a "spiritual" person (1 Cor. 2:15; Gal. 6:1), for his whole life is directed by the Holy Spirit.

God's Work of Sanctification

How does God perform his gracious work of sanctification in those whom he is saving?

Holiness begins with *definitive sanctification*. God has brought everyone saved by faith into a state of holiness (Col. 3:12), so that all believers are *saints*. The New Testament often refers to Christians as "saints" or "holy ones." The true members of the church are God's holy temple (1 Cor. 3:17; Eph. 2:21), his "holy priesthood" and "holy nation" (1 Pet. 2:5, 9), and "holy brethren" (1 Thess. 5:27; Heb. 3:1). All true believers are saints, not just an elite group of especially spiritual people in the church.

Although believers are far from perfect, they all have been "sanctified" (Acts 20:32; 26:18; 1 Cor. 1:2; 6:11; Jude 1). This is not just a positional truth about their holy standing before God. Their sanctification has made them obedient to God (1 Pet. 1:2; cf. Rom. 6:17). John Murray wrote that definitive sanctification is "a decisive and definitive breach with the power and service of sin" for those who have "come under the control of . . . grace."[5]

5 John Murray, *Collected Writings of John Murray*, 4 vols. (Edinburgh: Banner of Truth, 1982), 2:280.

Definitive sanctification overlaps with effectual calling (Rom. 1:7; 1 Cor. 1:2; 2 Tim. 1:9) and conversion (Acts 15:9; 26:18; 2 Thess. 2:13–14).

Holiness increases with *progressive sanctification*. Sanctification is both the present state of believers (they have been sanctified in Christ) and their progressive growth (they are being sanctified by Christ). They must exert effort to grow in holiness by faith in God's promises. Paul said, "Having therefore these promises, dearly beloved, let us cleanse ourselves from all filthiness of the flesh and spirit, perfecting holiness in the fear of God" (2 Cor. 7:1).

Progressive sanctification is cooperative, requiring God's grace along with human willing and working. Paul says, "Wherefore, my beloved, as ye have always obeyed, not as in my presence only, but now much more in my absence, work out your own salvation with fear and trembling. For it is God which worketh in you both to will and to do of his good pleasure" (Phil. 2:12–13). On the one hand, Paul commands these children of God to "work"—that is, to do *good works*, which are acts of obedience to God's commandments out of a heart cleansed by faith and motivated by love for the purpose of glorifying God (1 Cor. 7:19; 10:31; Gal. 5:6). On the other hand, Paul assures them that God "worketh" in them. God's work rules over man's work. He causes the believer "both to will and to do," giving both the heart and the hand of obedience. Murray explained, "God's working in us is not suspended because we work, nor our working suspended because God works. . . . The relation is that *because* God works we work."[6]

Common Errors regarding the Doctrine of Sanctification

A common mistake people make is thinking that an elite group of Christians lives on a higher spiritual level than most ordinary believers. This idea takes different forms.

First, *sometimes people go so far as to teach sinless perfectionism*, the claim that it is possible for Christians to be completely righteous and pure of sin in this life. They might quote John's statements, "Whosoever abideth in him sinneth not: whosoever sinneth hath not seen him, neither known him. . . . Whosoever is born of God doth not commit sin; for his seed remaineth in him: and he cannot sin, because he is born of God" (1 John 3:6, 9).

6 John Murray, *Redemption Accomplished and Applied* (Grand Rapids, MI: Eerdmans, 1955), 148–49.

In response, we note that there is no one on earth who does not sin—a truth clearly taught in several passages of Scripture.[7] Among men, Jesus Christ alone has never sinned (Heb. 4:15; 7:26–27; 1 John 3:5). As to 1 John 3:6, 9, John is contrasting the state of everyone who has been born of God to that of people who are still in a state of sin. John uses Greek present tense verbs to state that regeneration breaks the continuous pattern of sin and begins a new pattern of obedience—not perfect obedience but prevailing obedience.

Second, *the Roman Catholic Church teaches the error of asceticism*, the belief that people can follow a path of special consecration to God by taking vows of poverty, obedience to the rules of an order of monks or nuns, and celibacy (abstinence from sexual activity, including in marriage).[8] Asceticism may also involve denying oneself food, sleep, or human companionship for extended periods of time, and striking one's body or otherwise inflicting pain and discomfort on oneself.

In response, we acknowledge that self-denial is essential to Christian discipleship (Luke 9:23). However, this does not justify the mistreatment of the body or mandatory abstinence from the pleasures of God's creation. The Spirit of God warned that false teachers would forbid people to marry and to eat certain foods (1 Tim. 4:1–3). All God's creations are good and can be received in holiness if used with prayer, thanksgiving, and obedience to God's Word (vv. 4–5). Asceticism has no power to overcome inward sin. We conquer sin only by faith in Christ, who died and rose again to save us (Col. 2:18–3:1).

Third, *some Arminian theologians, such as John Wesley, have taught perfectionism*. This is not a claim to absolute sinlessness. Rather, it is a declaration that believers can act with total love so that they do not consciously break any commandment of God.

In response, we find no basis for this doctrine in the Holy Scriptures. When the Bible refers to certain saints on earth as "perfect," it is commending their maturity (Gen. 6:9; Job 1:1). But even these believers sinned (Gen.

7 1 Kings 8:46; Prov. 20:9; Eccles. 7:20; James 3:2; 1 John 1:8, 10.

8 *Catechism of the Catholic Church* (New York: Doubleday, 1994), sec. 915; and Vatican II, *Perfectae Caritatis* (Perfect Love), secs. 1, 5, 12, http://www.vatican.va/archive/hist_councils/ii_vatican_council/documents/vat-ii_decree_19651028_perfectae-caritatis_en.html. Similar teachings are found in the Eastern Orthodox Church.

9:21; Job 40:1–5; 42:6). The most mature Christian must still press on to higher measures of holiness (Phil. 3:12–14).

Fourth, *some evangelical theologians teach the error of two-level Christianity*. They urge Christians to seek what is variously called the second blessing, entire sanctification, the higher Christian life, baptism with the Holy Spirit, or the filling of the Holy Spirit. Of course, some of these expressions are from the Holy Scriptures and can be used in a way that is faithful to sound doctrine. The error lies in the doctrine that there are two levels of Christians. Sanctification, it is said, sometimes begins much later than regeneration and justification. Regenerate and justified believers supposedly can live in a state of defeat under the power of sin (Rom. 7:14–25). But there is said to be a higher level available to Christians through the Holy Spirit (Rom. 8:1–16). Under this view, holiness is attained not by effort and struggle but by surrender and faith. We are told, "Let go, and let God."[9]

In response, we acknowledge that Christians walk in different degrees of sanctification. But there are not two levels of Christians. Romans 7:14–25 describes a believer in Christ who is in the same spiritual state as that described in Romans 8. In Romans 7:14 and following, Paul uses the present tense to describe his experience as a believer in Christ (7:25). He says he loves God's law and serves it willingly (7:16, 19, 22, 25), but he experiences great frustration, an inward conflict that is normal for Christians (Gal. 5:17).

Paul's frustration in Romans 7 does not reflect a total failure to obey. Every Christian is empowered by the Spirit: "For as many as are led by the Spirit of God, they are the sons of God" (8:14). When Paul speaks of "the good I want" (7:19 ESV), he is referring to flawless obedience, which he longs to give to God but is not able. The focus in Romans 7 is on the battle against coveting and evil desire (vv. 7–8), which the believer cannot completely extinguish.

Contrary to a two-level view of Christianity, the new birth produces a new life (1 John 2:29; 3:9; 4:7; 5:4). All in Christ are justified and sanctified (Gal. 2:16–20). No one in Christ is a slave of sin (Rom. 6:14, 17–18). Baptism with the Holy Spirit is already granted to all believers in Christ (1 Cor. 12:13). Sanctification comes by our faith (Heb. 11:6) and by our work (Phil. 2:12). Believers must "be watchful, stand firm in the faith, act like men, be strong"

9 Charles Trumbull, cited in Andrew David Naselli, "Keswick Theology: A Survey and Analysis of the Doctrine of Sanctification in the Early Keswick Movement," *Detroit Baptist Seminary Journal* 13 (2008): 32.

(1 Cor. 16:13 ESV). Christ's obedience to God demanded great struggle, suffering, tears, and cries to God—and Jesus was without sin (Heb. 2:18; 4:15; 5:7–8). Much more, then, is our pathway to holiness full of difficulty and tribulation, and yet also hope (Rom. 5:3–5).

Practical Applications of the Doctrine of Sanctification

Holiness is entirely of grace. But sanctification engages the whole man in strenuous activity. Scripture compares the Christian life to running a race (Heb. 12:1) and fighting in a war (Eph. 6:10–18). Holiness is an absolute imperative for every believer (1 Pet. 1:15–16). God calls Christians to cultivate holiness in all of life. John Calvin said, "The whole life of Christians ought to be a sort of practice of godliness, for we have been called to sanctification."[10]

What are some practical applications of this doctrine?

Sanctification by Faith in Christ

Sanctification is impossible apart from Christ. Jesus says, "I am the vine, ye are the branches: he that abideth in me, and I in him, the same bringeth forth much fruit: for without me ye can do nothing" (John 15:5). Are you in Christ?

If you are in Christ, take to heart Paul's words: "As ye have therefore received Christ Jesus the Lord, so walk ye in him: rooted and built up in him, and stablished in the faith, as ye have been taught, abounding therein with thanksgiving" (Col. 2:6–7). Whatever spiritual needs we may have, we are "complete in him" (v. 10).

We run the race of sanctification "looking unto Jesus" (Heb. 12:2). We look to Christ as our Prophet to make known to us God and his will. We depend on Christ as the Priest who has once for all consecrated his people to God through his blood. We need every day to draw on the power and victory of Christ as the King. On the basis of Christ's death and resurrection, we must count ourselves "to be dead indeed unto sin, but alive unto God" (Rom. 6:11).

The Pattern of Sanctification

The life of holiness is rooted in faith in the promise of the covenant: "I am the Lord that doth sanctify you" (Ex. 31:13). The call of the covenant is to

10 Calvin, *Institutes*, 3.19.2.

separate ourselves from unclean things, for "I am the Lord your God; ye shall therefore sanctify yourselves, and ye shall be holy; for I am holy" (Lev. 11:44; cf. 1 Peter 1:16). The motive of sanctification is the fear of the Lord (Lev. 19:2, 14, 30, 32; 2 Cor. 7:1). The pathway of sanctification is obedience to God's laws (Lev. 20:7–8; 1 Cor. 7:19).

Sanctification requires putting off and putting on (Col. 3:8, 12). As the Heidelberg Catechism reminds us, there is putting sin to death with "a sincere sorrow of heart that we have provoked God by our sins; and more and more to hate and flee from them," and bringing righteousness to life with "a sincere joy of heart in God, through Christ, and with love and delight to live according to the will of God in all good works."[11]

Holiness is found in the imitation of God and Christ (Eph. 5:1–2). Stephen Charnock said, "We do not so glorify God by elevated admirations, or eloquent expressions, or pompous services [magnificent worship] of him, as when we aspire to . . . live *to* him in living *like* him."[12]

The Christian pursuing holiness finds himself in a spiritual war against temptation and sin (Eph. 6:12). If he would win, he must "fight the good fight of faith" (1 Tim. 6:12). John Owen urged, "Make it your daily work; be always at it while you live; cease not a day from this work; be killing sin or it will be killing you."[13]

In sanctification, God writes his law on men's hearts and causes them to obey it by his indwelling Spirit (Jer. 31:33; Ezek. 36:27). Christian holiness is defined by obedience to the moral law of God. The pinnacle of wisdom is "Fear God, and keep his commandments: for this is the whole duty of man" (Eccles. 12:13).

God's adopted sons and daughters must pass through sorrows to come to glory so that they may bear the image of the Son (Rom. 8:17, 28–29). Sanctification requires submission to our Father's will as he sends us through painful training (Heb. 12:5–6).

The heart of holiness is living unto God. Paul says, "Whether therefore ye eat, or drink, or whatsoever ye do, do all to the glory of God" (1 Cor. 10:31). He writes, "For none of us liveth to himself, and no man dieth to himself. For whether we live, we live unto the Lord; and whether we die,

11 The Heidelberg Catechism (LD 33, Q. 88–90), in *TFU*, 99.

12 Charnock, *The Existence and Attributes of God*, in *WSChar*, 2:268.

13 Owen, *The Mortification of Sin in Believers*, in *WJO*, 6:9.

we die unto the Lord: whether we live therefore, or die, we are the Lord's" (Rom. 14:7–8). Calvin said, "We are not our own. . . . We are God's: let all the parts of our life accordingly strive toward him as our only lawful goal."[14]

Obstacles to Holiness

We are often more concerned about sin's consequences for ourselves than its offense to God. Paul says, "Let love be genuine. Abhor what is evil; hold fast to what is good" (Rom. 12:9 ESV). William Plumer wrote, "We never see sin aright until we see it as against God."[15]

We misunderstand living by faith if we take it as an excuse for laziness. J. C. Ryle wrote, "The Scriptures teach us that in following holiness the true Christian needs personal exertion and work as well as faith."[16] Isaiah says, "Cease to do evil; learn to do well" (Isa. 1:16–17).

On the other hand, we fail miserably when we take pride in our strength and holiness. Richard Sibbes said, "There is not the least thought or affection to goodness in us, but it comes from God; we are what we are by his grace."[17] Self-sanctification does not exist.

We are prone to avoid the battle of daily spiritual warfare. But Samuel Rutherford said, "The devil's war is better than the devil's peace."[18] Hence, the wisest course is for us to "submit . . . therefore to God. Resist the devil, and he will flee from you" (James 4:7).

Disciplines to Cultivate Holiness

The Scriptures command the Christian to "exercise thyself . . . unto godliness" (1 Tim. 4:7).[19] How are we to do this?

First, *meditate on God's Word.* Jesus prayed, "Sanctify them through thy truth: thy word is truth" (John 17:17). Peter advises, "As newborn babes, desire the sincere milk of the word, that ye may grow thereby" (1 Pet. 2:2).

14 Calvin, *Institutes*, 3.7.1.

15 William S. Plumer, *Studies in the Book of Psalms* (Philadelphia: J. B. Lippincott and Co., 1867), on Ps. 51:4 (557).

16 J. C. Ryle, *Holiness: Its Nature, Hindrances, Difficulties, and Roots* (Cambridge: James Clarke and Co., 1956), viii.

17 Sibbes, *The Saint's Hiding Place in the Evil Day*, in *WRS*, 1:410.

18 Samuel Rutherford, *The Trial and Triumph of Faith* (Edinburgh: The Assembly's Committee, 1845), 402–3.

19 For a practical guide to the pursuit of holiness, see Joel R. Beeke and Michael P. V. Barrett, *A Radical, Comprehensive Call to Holiness* (Fearn, Ross-shire, Scotland: Christian Focus, 2020).

Second, *pray for more sanctifying grace*. Pray with the psalmists, "Create in me a clean heart, O God" (Ps. 51:10), and, "Incline my heart unto thy testimonies, and not to covetousness. Turn away mine eyes from beholding vanity; and quicken thou me [give me life] in thy way" (119:36–37).

Third, *participate fully in the life of the church*. "He that walketh with wise men shall be wise" (Prov. 13:20). Thomas Watson said, "Association begets assimilation."[20]

Fourth, *flee worldliness as pilgrims on earth*. John warns, "For all that is in the world, the lust of the flesh, and the lust of the eyes, and the pride of life, is not of the Father, but is of the world" (1 John 2:16).

Fifth, *fill your mind with the glory of God*. Man's intelligence, power, and wealth are not worth boasting about, but we should glory in knowing the Lord (Jer. 9:23–24). Such knowledge of God makes us like God in faithful love (Hos. 6:6) and justice (Jer. 22:16).

Sixth, *know your sinful heart*. Keep watch over your heart (Prov. 4:23), for "he that trusteth in his own heart is a fool" (28:26). Welcome admonitions from a loving brother (Ps. 141:5).

Seventh, *look to the blood of Christ*. Owen said, "Set faith at work on Christ for the killing of thy sin. His blood is the great sovereign remedy for sin-sick souls. Live in this, and thou wilt die a conqueror; yea, thou wilt, through the good providence of God, live to see thy lust dead at thy feet."[21] Believe that Christ has the fullness of grace for all your needs (John 1:16).

Pursue holiness because in it you pursue your deepest joy. Christ says, "If ye keep my commandments, ye shall abide in my love; even as I have kept my Father's commandments, and abide in his love. These things have I spoken unto you, that my joy might remain in you, and that your joy might be full" (John 15:10–11).[22]

Suggested Song to Sing to the Lord

- Psalm 119:33–40, "Teach me, O Lord, Thy way of truth," in *Psalter*, No. 325; *THBap*, No. 451

20 Thomas Watson, *A Body of Divinity* (Edinburgh: Banner of Truth, 1965), 249.

21 Owen, *The Mortification of Sin in Believers*, in *WJO*, 6:79.

22 Joel R. Beeke, *Holiness* (Pensacola, FL: Chapel Library, 1999), 8, available at https://www.chapellibrary.org/book/hol2. Also published as a booklet: Joel R. Beeke, *Holiness* (Edinburgh: Banner of Truth, 1994).

Questions for Meditation or Discussion

1. What is sanctification?
2. Why do we need the grace of sanctification?
3. How is each person of the Trinity involved in sanctification?
4. What is the meaning of and basis in the Bible for definitive sanctification and progressive sanctification?
5. What is asceticism? How can we refute its false teachings?
6. What is two-level Christianity? Why is it false?
7. Why must we exercise faith in Christ to grow in holiness?
8. What is the Bible's pattern for sanctification?
9. What are some obstacles to growing in holiness?
10. Of the disciplines to cultivate holiness, which is a strong point for you? Which is a weak point? How can you make your practice of that discipline stronger and more consistent?

64

Preservation and Perseverance

Chapter Summary and Key Terms

The doctrine of the *perseverance of the saints* states that God preserves his elect, redeemed, and called people. Thus, by the grace of *preservation*, they will never fully or finally fall away from him but will persevere in faith and obedience. Christ promises that all who believe in him alone for salvation already have eternal life and will never perish. But believers must persevere to avoid damnation and enter eternal glory. The Bible warns that some people will believe in Christ in a superficial way but later fall away (*apostasy*) because they were never truly united to him. God the Father, the Son, and the Holy Spirit preserve true believers by God's saving grace. God's children may rest in his promise as they run the Christian race, making use of the Word and the church to endure to the end.

IN JOHN BUNYAN'S STORY *The Pilgrim's Progress*, Christian sees a palace of eternal glory. Soldiers stand ready to keep anyone from entering it. A man puts on armor and bravely attacks. He receives many wounds, but he presses forward into the palace, where he is welcomed. Here Bunyan depicts the fierce battle that a Christian must fight to enter Christ's kingdom.

In another place, Christian sees a fire by a wall. A man pours water on the fire, but it does not go out. Hidden on the other side of the wall stands a man who pours oil on the fire. Bunyan thus portrays how the Devil seeks to quench the Christian's faith, hope, and love. But Christ secretly and effectively sustains the souls of his people so that they persevere in the faith.[1]

1 John Bunyan, *The Pilgrim's Progress*, in *The Works of John Bunyan*, ed. George Offor, 3 vols. (1854; repr., Edinburgh: Banner of Truth, 1991), 3:100.

Bunyan's story reflects the two sides of the doctrine that we consider in this chapter: preservation and perseverance. God promises to preserve every true believer in Christ so that he will persevere in repentance and faith until he reaches eternal glory.

The church's understanding of the doctrine of the preservation and perseverance of the saints has developed through history. Augustine said, "The perseverance by which we persevere in Christ even to the end is the gift of God." But he added, "It is uncertain whether any one has received this gift as long as he is still alive."[2] Augustine taught the perseverance of the elect but not the perseverance of all believers. Other theologians have said that perseverance depends both on God and man's free will.

The Roman Catholic Church teaches that perseverance is God's gift. But Roman Catholic doctrine says that apart from direct revelation, no one can know that he or she is one of God's elect or will persevere to the end. Saving grace is lost when a person commits mortal sin, but it can be restored by penance.[3]

Reformed theologians teach the perseverance of all who have saving faith. The Synod of Dort, opposing the Arminians, declared the perseverance of the saints as its fifth head of doctrine.[4] Also, the Westminster Confession of Faith says, "They, whom God hath accepted in His Beloved, effectually called, and sanctified by His Spirit, can neither totally nor finally fall away from the state of grace, but shall certainly persevere therein to the end, and be eternally saved."[5] Believers can partly or temporarily fall away, but their faith does not completely and permanently fail.

Christ's Promises of Eternal Life

Those who trust in Christ with saving faith have already received "eternal life" (John 3:15). Wayne Grudem writes, "Now if this is truly eternal life that believers have, then it is life that lasts forever with God."[6]

2 Augustine, *A Treatise on the Gift of Perseverance*, chap. 1, in *NPNF*[1], 5:526.

3 Council of Trent (Session 6, Decree on Justification, chaps. 13–15, canons 15–17), in *The Creeds of Christendom*, ed. Philip Schaff, rev. David S. Schaff, 3 vols. (Grand Rapids, MI: Baker, 1983), 2:103–6, 113–14.

4 The Canons of Dort (Head 5), in *TFU*, 153–63. On Arminianism, see chaps. 23 and 58.

5 The Westminster Confession of Faith (17.1), in *RC*, 4:253. Cf. the Second London Baptist Confession (17.1), in *RC*, 4:552.

6 Wayne Grudem, *Systematic Theology: An Introduction to Biblical Doctrine*, 2nd ed. (Grand Rapids, MI: Zondervan, 2020), 790.

The Lord Jesus Christ gives his people numerous wonderful promises that nothing will cancel their eternal existence with him:

- "Whosoever drinketh of the water that I shall give him shall never thirst; but the water that I shall give him shall be in him a well of water springing up into everlasting life" (John 4:14). True believers will never be deprived of God's life-giving, heart-satisfying grace.
- "[The believer] hath everlasting life, and shall not come into condemnation; but is passed from death unto life" (John 5:24).
- "All that the Father giveth me shall come to me; and him that cometh to me I will in no wise cast out. . . . This is the Father's will which hath sent me, that of all which he hath given me I should lose nothing, but should raise it up again at the last day" (John 6:37–39).
- "My sheep hear my voice, and I know them, and they follow me: and I give unto them eternal life; and they shall never perish, neither shall any man pluck them out of my hand. My Father, which gave them me, is greater than all; and no man is able to pluck them out of my Father's hand" (John 10:27–29).

Calvin said, "The salvation of all the elect is not less certain than the power of God is invincible."[7]

The Necessity of Perseverance

Although Christ's promises of eternal life are sure for all believers, we abuse them if we promise eternal security to people regardless of whether they continue to follow Christ. The Lord Jesus insists that his disciples must persevere to the end to receive full and final salvation. He says, "The one who endures to the end will be saved" (Matt. 10:22; 24:13 ESV).

Christ calls men to deny themselves, take up their crosses, and follow him, for this is the only way to find life and vindication on judgment day (Luke 9:23–26). Thus, the doctrine of the perseverance of the saints is not a cause of laziness. The Bible demands that converts continue to cling to Christ and endure many tribulations to enter the kingdom (Acts 11:23; 14:22).

7 Calvin, *Comm.* on John 10:28–29.

The epistle to the Hebrews states that we are Christ's house "*if we hold fast* the confidence and the rejoicing of the hope firm unto the end" (Heb. 3:6). Furthermore, "We are made partakers of Christ, *if we hold* the beginning of our confidence stedfast unto the end" (v. 14).

The Warnings against Apostasy

The word *apostasy* refers to falling away from the faith. Jesus gives us vivid pictures of this. He says there are some people, like rocky soil, who, "when they hear, receive the word with joy; and these have no root, which for a while believe, and in time of temptation fall away" (Luke 8:13). He also compares such people to branches and himself to a vine, saying, "If a man abide not in me, he is cast forth as a branch, and is withered; and men gather them, and cast them into the fire, and they are burned" (John 15:6).

It is written in Hebrews 6:4–6,

> It is impossible for those who were once enlightened, and have tasted of the heavenly gift, and were made partakers of the Holy Ghost, and have tasted the good word of God, and the powers of the world to come, if they shall fall away, to renew them again unto repentance; seeing they crucify to themselves the Son of God afresh, and put him to an open shame.

Those who teach that true believers may fall away and be lost forever argue that the spiritual experiences listed here describe true Christians. But the language used in this passage is consistent with the experience of people who come to church but are not truly converted. They are "enlightened" by the knowledge of the truth and have "tasted," or experienced, God's presence with his people. The word translated as "partakers" can simply mean those who accompany someone in an activity (Luke 5:7). The text says nothing about such people being regenerated, brought to faith in Christ, or justified. Rather, they are like the people of Israel in the wilderness (Neh. 9:10–20), who were enlightened by the fiery pillar. They tasted of the heavenly gift of manna. They experienced the presence of the Holy Spirit working through Moses. They tasted God's word and saw his power. But Israel was not a godly nation that fell away from God. It consisted mostly of wicked people who sometimes had a superficial faith but rebelled against the Lord (Numbers 13–14; Psalm 95).

Hebrews 6 refers to people who have received much from God but they do not respond rightly. We read in verses 7–8: "For the earth which drinketh in the rain that cometh oft upon it, and bringeth forth herbs meet for them by whom it is dressed, receiveth blessing from God: but that which beareth thorns and briers is rejected, and is nigh unto cursing; whose end is to be burned." This is not a field that produces good fruit and later becomes overgrown by weeds. Rather, it is a field that responds to the rain of heaven only with the evil effects of Adam's fall: "thorns and briers." As a result, it will fall under the curse and judgment of God.

Therefore, the warning in Hebrews 6 has to do with people who hear the gospel preached with the conviction of the Spirit. They assent to the gospel, temporarily change their behavior, join the church, and even experience the passing joys of temporary faith. But they lack saving grace, and later fall away completely. However, God's true people do not fully and finally fall away from Christ after being united to him for salvation (Heb. 3:6, 14).

The Grace of Preservation

God promised to provide a cure for Israel's apostasy in the "new covenant" (Jer. 31:31–32). He said, "I will put my law in their inward parts, and write it in their hearts" (v. 33). He also said, "I will put my fear in their hearts, that they shall not depart from me" (32:40). The grace promised in the covenant also secures how God relates to his people: "For I will forgive their iniquity, and I will remember their sin no more" (31:34). He said, "I will make an everlasting covenant with them, that I will not turn away from them, to do them good" (32:40).

Believers face many obstacles to their perseverance and final salvation. The Canons of Dort say, "By reason of these remains of indwelling sin, and the temptations of sin and of the world, those who are converted could not persevere in a state of grace if left to their own strength. But God is faithful, who having conferred grace, mercifully confirms and powerfully preserves them therein, even to the end."[8] The Scriptures repeatedly tell us that God preserves his saints because he is faithful (1 Cor. 1:8–9; 1 Thess. 5:23–24; 2 Thess. 3:3).

Paul says that he is "confident of this very thing, that he which hath begun a good work in you will perform it until the day of Jesus Christ" (Phil. 1:6). Peter writes that those whom God has caused to be born again "are kept by

8 The Canons of Dort (Head 5, Art. 3), in *TFU*, 153–54.

the power of God through faith" even as they endure great trials (1 Pet. 1:3, 5). And John says, "Whatsoever is born of God overcometh the world: and this is the victory that overcometh the world, even our faith" (1 John 5:4). Therefore, we can say with Jude, "Now unto him that is able to keep you from falling, and to present you faultless before the presence of his glory with exceeding joy, to the only wise God our Saviour, be glory and majesty, dominion and power, both now and ever. Amen" (Jude 24–25).

Resting in the Triune God, the Preserver of Our Salvation

The Christian's comfort and hope are greatly strengthened by the doctrine of perseverance. But believers do not trust in a doctrine so much as in the triune God who preserves them.

First, *Christians can rest their hope for preservation in God the Father*. He blessed us in Christ, "as he hath chosen us in him before the foundation of the world, that we should be holy and without blame before him in love" (Eph. 1:4). "All things," both good and bad, work to cause God's elect "to be conformed to the image of his Son" (Rom. 8:28–29). The Father supports his chosen children with his mercies and comfort (2 Cor. 1:3–4, 6). They can say, "It is of the LORD's mercies that we are not consumed, because his compassions fail not. They are new every morning: great is thy faithfulness" (Lam. 3:22–23).

Second, *Christians can rest their hope for preservation in God the Son*. Hebrews 10:14 says, "For by one offering he hath perfected for ever them that are sanctified." Christ could say on the cross, "It is finished" (John 19:30). The perfect righteousness of Christ imputed to believers in their justification secures their future with God (Rom. 5:9). His intercession applies his complete redemption, so that "he is able also to save them to the uttermost" (Heb. 7:25). Satan aimed to destroy Peter, but Christ said to Peter, "I have prayed for thee, that thy faith fail not: and when thou art converted [literally turn back], strengthen thy brethren" (Luke 22:31–32). Paul says, "Who is he that condemneth? It is Christ that died, yea rather, that is risen again, who is even at the right hand of God, who also maketh intercession for us" (Rom. 8:34). Therefore, nothing "shall be able to separate us from the love of God" (vv. 35–39).

Third, *Christians can rest their hope for preservation in God the Holy Spirit*. The Lord says, "I will put my spirit within you, and cause you to walk in my statutes, and ye shall keep my judgments, and do them" (Ezek. 36:27). Christ promises that the Holy Spirit will "abide with you for ever" (John 14:16). The Spirit will never leave believers, for God has sealed them with the Spirit until the day of redemption (Eph. 1:13–14). The Holy Spirit is "the Spirit of adoption, whereby we cry, Abba, Father" (Rom. 8:15). By his influence, those in Christ keep panting after the grace of Christ and thus will receive what they need to persevere.

Running with Perseverance for the Heavenly Prize

While the Christian life is certainly one of resting our faith on the Lord, it is a rest that empowers hard work "by faith," as Hebrews 11 tells us. Thomas Watson said, "Christians do not arrive at perseverance when they sit still and do nothing. . . . We arrive at salvation in the use of means; as a man come to the end of a race by running, to a victory by fighting."[9] How are we to do this?

First, *pay careful attention to God's Word.* Hebrews 2:1 warns that we must give "earnest heed to the things which we have heard" so that we do not drift away from the gospel. We must not let ourselves get lazy about reading and listening to the Word. Remember who it is that speaks to us in the Word—the Lord of heaven and earth (12:25).

Second, *establish in your mind the supremacy of Christ.* Hebrews 3:1 says, "Wherefore, holy brethren, partakers of the heavenly calling, consider the Apostle and High Priest of our profession, Christ Jesus." William Gouge said, "If anything in the world is to be seriously considered, surely Christ above all, and that in his excellencies."[10] Think often of Christ.

Third, *lean on Christ's intercession in your own prayers.* Hebrews 2:17–18 says, "Therefore he had to be made like his brothers in every respect, so that he might become a merciful and faithful high priest in the service of God, to make propitiation for the sins of the people. For because he himself has suffered when tempted, he is able to help those who are being tempted" (ESV). Thomas Goodwin wrote, "Christ took to heart all that befell him as deeply as might be."[11] He added, "Your very sins move him to pity more

9 Thomas Watson, *A Body of Divinity* (Edinburgh: Banner of Truth, 1965), 280.

10 William Gouge, *Commentary on Hebrews*, 2 vols. (1866; repr., Birmingham, AL: Solid Ground, 2006), 1:206.

11 Goodwin, *The Heart of Christ in Heaven to Sinners on Earth*, in *WTG*, 4:141.

than to anger." No one hates his own body when it is hurting but is full of compassion for it. We are his body.[12] Therefore, pray to God boldly for the grace you need, knowing that Christ understands your trials and temptations (4:14–16).

Fourth, *stand on the promises of God.* God gave his unbreakable promises to be "an anchor of the soul" so that "we might have a strong consolation, who have fled for refuge to lay hold upon the hope set before us" (Heb. 6:18–19). Here are two precious promises: "The Lord is my light and my salvation; whom shall I fear? The Lord is the strength of my life; of whom shall I be afraid?" (Ps. 27:1) and "No weapon that is formed against thee shall prosper; and every tongue that shall rise against thee in judgment thou shalt condemn" (Isa. 54:17). By believing in such promises, we cling to God's all-sufficiency to give us victory over all evil.

Fifth, *share in the worship, love, and accountability of the church.* Perseverance is not an individual effort but a community project. Hebrews 3:13 says, "Exhort one another daily . . . lest any of you be hardened through the deceitfulness of sin." By meeting regularly with the church, we can provoke one another to perseverance, love, and good works (10:24–25).

Sixth, *run the race with your eyes on Christ the Victor.* Hebrews 12:1–2 says, "Let us run with patience the race that is set before us, looking unto Jesus the author and finisher of our faith; who for the joy that was set before him endured the cross, despising the shame, and is set down at the right hand of the throne of God." All the efforts of a Christian to persevere arise from Christ. We run the race by his grace, and we run the race to meet him in glory. Therefore, let us fill our mind's eye with his glory now. Christ is worth all our efforts.

Suggested Song to Sing to the Lord

- Psalm 17, "Lord, hear the right, regard my cry," *Psalter*, No. 32; cf. *THBap*, No. 735

Questions for Meditation or Discussion

1. Is perseverance in faith and obedience necessary for final salvation? Prove it from the Bible.

12 Goodwin, *The Heart of Christ in Heaven to Sinners on Earth*, in *WTG*, 4:149.

2. What promises of divine preservation do we find in the Gospel of John? What do they mean?
3. Who are the people described in Hebrews 6:4–6 who "fall away"?
4. What does the new covenant promise about preservation (Jer. 31:31–34; 32:39–40)?
5. What promises of preservation are found in the epistles of Paul, Peter, John, and Jude?
6. How can a Christian find hope in God (1) the Father, (2) the Son, and (3) the Holy Spirit?
7. Why is keeping your mind focused on God's Word crucial for perseverance?
8. What special encouragement do believers in Christ have for prayer?
9. Why do we need the church in order to persevere? How can we make use of its help?
10. How would you encourage a believer who fears he may not persevere to the end?

Section 5C

The Spirit and the Experience of Salvation

65

The Indwelling, Leading, and Filling of the Spirit

Chapter Summary and Key Terms

At the heart of Christian experience is the work of the Holy Spirit. The *indwelling of the Holy Spirit* refers to his special presence in every believer in Christ. The indwelling Spirit produces in believers spiritual life in communion with God and obedience to his commandments. The *leading of the Holy Spirit* is his continual work to influence God's children to understand the Holy Scriptures and obey them. The *filling of the Holy Spirit* refers to his special empowerment of believers, whether for godliness, ministry, or fellowship with God. They may experience this filling multiple times and in various degrees. *Revival* is a special season when the Holy Spirit does his usual work in the church through the Word with unusual power for the glory of God. Revival does not consist in signs and wonders but in the Spirit filling the church with abundant grace. This moves believers to repent of sin, trust in Christ, worship in God's presence, and declare the law and gospel with remarkable effects.

THE SPIRIT OF THE LIVING GOD brings God's presence to his people to change them and their relationship to him. The Holy Spirit is central to Christian experience. John Calvin said, "We observe this distinction between the theoretical knowledge derived from the Word of God and what is called the experimental knowledge of his grace." Though God "must first be sought in his Word," he also "shows himself present in operation."[1]

1 Calvin, *Comm.* on Ps. 27:9.

John says, "No man hath seen God at any time. If we love one another, God dwelleth in us, and his love is perfected in us. Hereby know we that we dwell in him, and he in us, because he hath given us of his Spirit" (1 John 4:12–13). Hence, Christian experience flows directly from the work of the Holy Spirit.

The Indwelling of the Holy Spirit

The Belgic Confession says, "The Holy Ghost is our Sanctifier by His dwelling in our hearts."[2] God said, "I will put my Spirit within you, and you shall live" (Ezek. 37:14 ESV). The Lord also promised, "I will put my Spirit within you, and cause you to walk in my statutes and be careful to obey my rules" (36:27 ESV). Thus, the *indwelling of the Holy Spirit* effectively produces life and obedience. By contrast, people "having not the Spirit" will "walk after their own ungodly lusts" (Jude 18–19).

Christ says that the Holy Spirit "dwelleth with you, and shall be in you," and will "abide with you for ever" (John 14:16–17). This is a permanent indwelling. And where the Spirit dwells, there the Father and the Son are also present (v. 23). John writes, "Hereby we know that he abideth in us, by the Spirit which he hath given us" (1 John 3:24).

The Spirit indwells every believer. Paul says, "You, however, are not in the flesh but in the Spirit, if in fact the Spirit of God dwells in you. Anyone who does not have the Spirit of Christ does not belong to him" (Rom. 8:9 ESV). Just as believers are justified by faith (Gal. 3:6), so they have "received . . . the Spirit . . . by the hearing of faith" (v. 2).

The Holy Spirit is infinite and present everywhere (Ps. 139:7). Thus, his indwelling of believers is not about his location but his action. The Spirit makes known God's special presence in his people. He is personally present in believers just as God's glory inhabited the temple in Jerusalem (1 Cor. 3:16; 6:19). Augustine said, "The Holy Spirit is the gift of God, the gift being Himself indeed equal to the Giver."[3] Wilhelmus à Brakel said, "The believer does not merely have the gifts of the Spirit, but he has the Spirit Himself."[4]

The Spirit indwells those in union with Christ: "The Spirit of life in Christ Jesus" has set them free "from the law of sin and death" (Rom. 8:2). As a

2 The Belgic Confession (Art. 9), in *TFU*, 24.

3 Augustine, *The Enchiridion*, chap. 37, in *NPNF*[1], 3:250.

4 Brakel, *CRS*, 1:181.

result, they "walk not after the flesh, but after the Spirit" (v. 4). The fleshly mindset is "enmity against God," rebellion against him and his law (Rom. 8:6–7). The indwelling of the Spirit places believers in a new state. Once they could not please God, but now they obey his laws as Christ dwells in them by the Spirit (vv. 8–10).

Octavius Winslow said, "The work of holiness forms a great and glorious part of His operation as the Indweller of His people. . . . He has come to restore the reign of holiness, to set up the law of God in the soul, to unfold its precepts, and to write them upon the heart."[5]

The Leading of the Holy Spirit

The Spirit of God moves believers in a new spiritual direction by his application of the Word to their hearts. Paul says, "For as many as are led by the Spirit of God, they are the sons of God" (Rom. 8:14). This means that anyone who is not led by the Spirit is not a child of God. The Greek word translated as "led" is the same term used of the Spirit's leading of God's Son in his obedience under temptation (Luke 4:1). Now the same Spirit continually influences believers in the Son (present tense "are led") to live as obedient children of God.

Some Christians say they are being "led by the Spirit" when they feel certain impulses that they think are revealing God's will to them. But there is nothing in Romans 8 about inner promptings from God that guide people to take particular actions. Rather, Paul is writing about obeying God's law and pleasing him (vv. 8–9). He is talking about denying sinful desires and putting sinful deeds to death (vv. 12–13). He is saying we must suffer with Christ in order to be glorified with him (vv. 17–18). Therefore, to be "led by the Spirit" means especially to be influenced by the Spirit so that one aims at obeying God's Word with one's whole life. In other words, to be led by the Spirit is to be "ruled by his Spirit," which, as Calvin said, refers to "sanctification."[6]

The Spirit leads believers by illuminating their minds with God's Word and powerfully motivating their hearts to keep it. Thus, the *leading of the Holy Spirit* is an answer to the psalmist's prayer: "Teach me, O Lord, the way

5 Octavius Winslow, *The Work of the Holy Spirit: An Experimental and Practical View* (Edinburgh: Banner of Truth, 1961), 100.

6 Calvin, *Comm.* on Rom. 8:14.

of thy statutes; and I shall keep it unto the end. Give me understanding, and I shall keep thy law. . . . Make me to go in the path of thy commandments; for therein do I delight. Incline my heart unto thy testimonies, and not to covetousness" (Ps. 119:33–36).

Believers must strive to please the Holy Spirit who works in them. Paul says, "Grieve not the holy Spirit of God, whereby ye are sealed unto the day of redemption" (Eph. 4:30). The Spirit is offended by a refusal to repent of lying, stealing, sinful anger, lack of love, impurity, or other sins (4:25–5:6). John Owen said, "The Holy Ghost, in his infinite love and kindness towards me, hath condescended to be my comforter; he doth it willingly, freely, powerfully. . . . Can I live one day without his consolations? . . . Shall I grieve him by negligence, sin, and folly?"[7]

Paul commands, "Walk in the Spirit, and ye shall not fulfil the lust of the flesh" (Gal. 5:16). Believers must direct their whole conduct according to the rule of God's Word and the holy motions of the indwelling Holy Spirit, who leads them to obey that Word. Walking by the Spirit requires engaging in combat against the lusts and works of the flesh (vv. 17, 19–21). It also requires cultivating and practicing "the fruit of the Spirit . . . love, joy, peace, long-suffering, gentleness, goodness, faith, meekness, temperance" (vv. 22–23).

The Filling of the Holy Spirit

Every Christian has the Holy Spirit and is led by him. But the Spirit works in different degrees in different people, and his work in any one person may vary over time. Sometimes believers experience the *filling of the Holy Spirit.*

In the Old Testament, the Lord "filled" his servants with the wisdom and power to serve him (Ex. 31:3; 35:31; Deut. 34:9; Mic. 3:8). When Christ poured out the Holy Spirit on his disciples at Pentecost, "they were all filled with the Holy Ghost" (Acts 2:4). That filling produces godliness and power for ministry (6:3, 5, 8). Sometimes, God fills people with the Spirit after they have been seeking his grace in prayer (1:14; 2:4; 4:31). Some believers are characteristically filled with the Spirit (6:5; 11:24). In other instances, God fills his servants with the Spirit to meet an immediate need for power without any mention of them seeking it first, as Peter and Paul experienced (4:8; 13:9). Both of those apostles had been filled before (2:4; 9:17).

7 Owen, *Communion with God*, in *WJO*, 2:266.

Paul says, "Be not drunk with wine, wherein is excess; but be filled with the Spirit" (Eph. 5:18). This is a command. All the saints have a constant obligation to receive the influence of the Spirit so that he fills them. Charles Hodge commented, "Men are said to be filled with wine when completely under its influence; so they are said to be filled with the Spirit when he controls all their thoughts, feelings, words, and actions."[8] Drinking too much wine produces a wasteful, self-destructive life. But the power of the Holy Spirit produces a wise, careful, diligent life of doing God's will (vv. 15–18). The Spirit-filled church offers to God Bible-saturated, heart-engaging, Trinity-adoring, and authority-honoring worship (vv. 19–21).

To be filled with the Spirit is not merely to receive power but to be filled with God. We must not pursue the Spirit's filling merely because we find God useful but because he is infinitely glorious (Eph. 3:19–21; 5:18–20). As Augustine said, the triune God is the fountain of love and life, and the Spirit of God calls us "to drink of Himself."[9]

Revival by the Holy Spirit

Revival may be defined as a special season when God the Holy Spirit does his usual works in the church through the Word with unusual power for the glory of God. We cannot plan, cause, trigger, or manipulate revival, but we should ask God to send it. The Spirit of revival is the Spirit of Christ, for the Spirit comes through Christ and works to the glory of Christ (John 14:16–17; 16:14).

Unusual works such as miracles are no proof of revival by the Spirit (2 Thess. 2:9). Rather, as J. I. Packer writes, "Revival is God touching minds and hearts in an arresting, devastating, exalting way. . . . It is God accelerating, intensifying, and extending the work of grace that goes on in every Christian's life. . . . It is the near presence of God giving new power to the gospel of sin and grace."[10]

From the filling of the Spirit at Pentecost (Acts 2), we learn, first, that authentic revival is always a sovereign work of God in Christ through the

8 Charles Hodge, *Ephesians* (1856; repr., Edinburgh: Banner of Truth, 1991), 220.

9 Augustine, *Homilies on the Epistle of John*, 7.6, in *NPNF*[1], 7:503.

10 J. I. Packer, "The Glory of God and the Reviving of Religion: A Study in the Mind of Jonathan Edwards," in *A God-Entranced Vision of All Things: The Legacy of Jonathan Edwards*, ed. John Piper and Justin Taylor (Wheaton, IL: Crossway, 2004), 100.

Holy Spirit (v. 33). Second, authentic revival is usually, though not always, preceded by a remarkable movement of prayer (1:14; 4:31). Third, revival usually begins with those who have already been born again (2:1–4). Fourth, in authentic revival, the Spirit works powerfully through the Word (vv. 14–36). Fifth, during revival, the Holy Spirit searches the heart with the truth to expose sin and incite repentance (vv. 37–38). Sixth, Spirit-worked revival is always accompanied by saving faith in Jesus (v. 21). Seventh, revival moves God's people to worship him with profound reverence (vv. 42–43, 47).

We should desire and seek revival today. When we consider Paul's prayers for the churches, it is difficult to imagine that he is praying for anything less than remarkable revivals of those bodies of believers by God's Spirit (Eph. 1:15–20; 3:14–21; Col. 1:9–12). We see this even in Paul's prayer for a church that he strongly commends (Phil. 1:9–11).

Some generations never see revival. Yet when faithful men and women serve God with perseverance in times of great darkness, they sow the seeds that God causes to grow when he does send revival. And all believers will share in the greatest "revival" of the church: when our Lord returns and raises the dead to enjoy the fullness of life, holiness, and glory in his presence. Therefore, let us pray, "Thy kingdom come" (Matt. 6:10) with an eye on revival but hearts set on Christ's coming in glory.

Suggested Song to Sing to the Lord

- "Come, O come, thou quick'ning Spirit," *THBap*, No. 247

Questions for Meditation or Discussion

1. How do we know that all God's saved people are indwelt by the Holy Spirit?
2. Show from the Scriptures that the indwelling of the Spirit is a sanctifying presence.
3. Whom does the Holy Spirit personally lead today? How does he lead them?
4. What does it mean to grieve the Holy Spirit? How can believers avoid doing that?
5. A friend says, "I know that my pastor is walking in the Spirit because his life is full of miracles." How do you respond? How would you explain what it means to walk in the Spirit?

6. What does the Bible teach about being filled with the Spirit?
7. What is revival? Should we seek revival today? How?
8. Are you indwelt by the Holy Spirit?
9. Are you filled by the Holy Spirit? How do you know?
10. What difference should it make in the lives of Christians to know that the Holy Spirit—not just a power but the divine person—is dwelling in them wherever they go?

66

Assurance of Salvation and the Spirit's Witness

Chapter Summary and Key Terms

Unbelievers may think they are saved. Believers may fear they are not saved. But it is possible for believers to have a true and certain *assurance of salvation*—the confidence that they are saved by grace. The foundations of assurance are God's promises in Christ, the evidence of saving faith, and the testimony of the Holy Spirit. Assurance is possible only by the power of the Spirit. His work to give confident hope to believers is called his *sealing*, *earnest*, *witness*, and *firstfruits*. Believers should cultivate assurance by growing in Christlikeness and examining themselves for the marks of grace. They should wait on the Lord in times of darkness and rest their faith not in their experiences but in the person and work of Jesus Christ.

"ASSURANCE IS THE conscious confidence that we are in a right relationship with God through Christ," writes Sinclair Ferguson.[1] It is described in the Bible as "full assurance of hope" (Heb. 6:11). Having assurance greatly enriches the lives of God's people with peace, hope, and joy. It also stirs up their longing for the world to come.

The doctrine of full assurance has been a point of controversy since the Reformation. The Roman Catholic Church states that "no one can

1 Sinclair B. Ferguson, "The Reformation and Assurance," *The Banner of Truth*, no. 643 (April 2017): 20.

know with a certainty of faith, which cannot be subject to error, that he has obtained the grace of God."[2] But if assurance were unattainable, then Christ could not say, "Rejoice, because your names are written in heaven" (Luke 10:20). The Psalms teach believers to say, "Surely goodness and mercy shall follow me all the days of my life: and I will dwell in the house of the LORD for ever" (Ps. 23:6). And John says, "We do know that we know him," and, "These things have I written unto you that believe on the name of the Son of God; that ye may know that ye have eternal life" (1 John 2:3; 5:13).

There are three possibilities concerning assurance. First, unbelievers can have false assurance (Isa. 48:1–2; Mic. 3:11). Christ says that many will claim to be his followers on judgment day, only to hear him reply, "I never knew you: depart from me, ye that work iniquity" (Matt. 7:22–23). Second, true believers in Christ may enjoy little or no assurance. Peter says, "Give diligence to make your calling and election sure" (2 Pet. 1:10). Third, true believers can have true assurance. The privilege of those who "have peace with God through our Lord Jesus Christ," Paul says, is to "rejoice in hope of the glory of God" (Rom. 5:1–2).

The Foundations of Assurance

The Westminster Confession of Faith says that assurance is "founded upon the divine truth of the promises of salvation, the inward evidence of those graces unto which these promises are made, [and] the testimony of the Spirit of adoption."[3] Let us consider each of these foundations.

First, *God's promises in Christ are the chief ground for a Christian's assurance.* Assurance is the fruit that grows naturally from faith, and "faith cometh by hearing, and hearing by the word of God" (Rom. 10:17). As Thomas Brooks wrote, "The promises are not only the food of faith, but also the very life and soul of faith."[4]

The promises lead us to Christ himself, for all God's promises are yes and amen in Christ (2 Cor. 1:19–20). "Let thy eye and heart, first, most, and last,

2 The Council of Trent (Session 6, Decree on Justification, chap. 9), in *The Creeds of Christendom*, ed. Philip Schaff, rev. David S. Schaff, 3 vols. (Grand Rapids, MI: Baker, 1983), 2:99.

3 The Westminster Confession of Faith (18.2), in *RC*, 4:254. Cf. the Second London Baptist Confession (18.2), in *RC*, 4:553.

4 Thomas Brooks, *A Cabinet of Jewels*, in *The Works of Thomas Brooks*, ed. Alexander Grosart, 6 vols. (1866; repr., Edinburgh: Banner of Truth, 1980), 3:255.

be fixed upon Christ, then will assurance bed and board with thee," said Brooks.[5] Anthony Burgess warned against too much introspection when he wrote, "We should not so gaze upon ourselves to find graces in our hearts that we forget those acts of faith whereby we immediately close with Christ and rely upon Him only for our justification."[6]

Second, *the evidence of saving grace demonstrates that our faith in Christ is genuine*. Jesus Christ says, "Ye shall know them by their fruits" (Matt. 7:16). John Calvin said that since unconverted sinners may have a kind of belief, "believers are taught to examine themselves carefully and humbly, lest the confidence of the flesh creep in and replace assurance of faith."[7] Christ describes the evidence of grace in the Beatitudes (Matt. 5:3–12), as does Paul when he lists the fruit of the Spirit (Gal. 5:22–23). We will study these marks of grace in the next chapter.

The believer uses Spirit-empowered logic to find assurance. John writes, "Hereby we do know that we know him, if we keep his commandments" (1 John 2:3). Thus, by the Spirit's help, a believer can reason as follows: "Those who know God keep his commandments. I keep his commandments. Therefore, I know that I know him." John also says, "We know that we have passed from death unto life, because we love the brethren" (3:14). So the Spirit also enables the believer to reason in this way: "Those who love the brethren have passed from death to life. I cannot deny that I have a love for other Christians that moves me to be with them and serve them. Therefore, I have passed from death to life."

Third, *the testimony of the Holy Spirit brings assurance into the heart so that it is not merely a probable conclusion of the mind but a certainty of faith*. Some Reformed and Puritan theologians have believed that the Spirit simply works through the evidences of grace to establish assurance. Others believe that the Spirit gives a direct testimony to the heart in addition to the evidence of grace. But they agree that the Spirit always works through the Word and never in contradiction to it. To better understand the Spirit's work in assurance, we must consider different ways the New Testament describes it.

5 Brooks, *Heaven on Earth*, in *Works*, 2:524.

6 Anthony Burgess, *Faith Seeking Assurance*, ed. Joel R. Beeke (Grand Rapids, MI: Reformation Heritage Books, 2015), 114.

7 Calvin, *Institutes*, 3.2.11.

Four Pictures of the Spirit's Work in Assurance

We need the power of the Holy Spirit to have assurance. Burgess said that "evangelical confidence" is "wholly supernatural," just as faith in Christ and holiness are supernatural.[8] So our ability to obtain assurance by the Word and evidence of faith comes from the Spirit. Burgess quipped, "There may be pleasant flowers in a garden, yet if we have not light, we cannot see them."[9] The Bible gives us four metaphors (or word pictures) of how the Spirit gives us light for our assurance.

First, *God seals his people with the Holy Spirit.* Paul says, "Now he which stablisheth [confirms] us with you in Christ, and hath anointed us, is God; who hath also sealed us, and given the earnest of the Spirit in our hearts" (2 Cor. 1:20–22). To "seal" is literally to impress an image on clay, wax, or soft metal. A seal serves as a mark of ownership and security. God puts his image on believers to mark them as belonging to him.

Paul says, "In him [Christ] you also, when you heard the word of truth, the gospel of your salvation, and believed in him, were sealed with the promised Holy Spirit" (Eph. 1:13 ESV). Therefore, God seals his people at the time of their conversion, when they first trust in Christ alone for salvation. He marks his elect (v. 4) and redeemed (v. 7) people by giving them his sanctifying and comforting Spirit.

Paul adds, "Grieve not the holy Spirit of God, whereby ye are sealed unto the day of redemption" (Eph. 4:30). On the one hand, God places his seal on every saved person once for all at conversion; that seal can never be broken. On the other hand, a believer can experience the assuring effects of being sealed to a greater or lesser degree. The Holy Spirit is the source of all vital Christian hope (1:17–18; Rom. 15:13). Believers must not grieve the Spirit, or they may temporarily forfeit the hope he supplies.

Second, *God gives his people the earnest of the Holy Spirit.* Paul says that God has "given the earnest of the Spirit in our hearts" (2 Cor. 1:22). God has made us heirs of immortality, for which we "groan," and he "also hath given us the earnest of the Spirit" (5:4–5). The Spirit "is the earnest of our

8 Anthony Burgess, *An Expository Comment, Doctrinal, Controversial, and Practical, upon the Whole First Chapter of the Second Epistle of St Paul to the Corinthians* (London: by A. M. for Abel Roper, 1661), 636.

9 Burgess, *An Expository Comment* [on 2 Corinthians 1], 641.

inheritance until the redemption of the purchased possession, unto the praise of his glory" (Eph. 1:13–14).

The Greek word translated as "earnest" or "guarantee" (ESV) refers to a pledge of future payment. An earnest, then, is a deposit that commits someone to pay the full amount promised. Matthew Henry said, "The earnest is part of payment, and it secures the full sum: so is the gift of the Holy Ghost; all his influences and operations, both as a sanctifier and a comforter, are heaven begun, glory in the seed and bud."[10] John Flavel said that assured believers "enjoy heaven upon earth, a joy beyond all the joys of this world."[11]

Third, *the Spirit testifies to God's people that they are his children*. Paul says, "The Spirit itself beareth witness with our spirit, that we are the children of God" (Rom. 8:16). This witness to our adoption by God is the remedy for spiritual "bondage" that produces "fear" (v. 15). As in a legal courtroom, the Holy Spirit uses God's Word, properly applied, to testify that the believer in Christ is truly loved and adopted by God the Father.

Paul says, "God's love has been poured into our hearts through the Holy Spirit who has been given to us" (Rom. 5:5 ESV). This love is objectively revealed in the gospel of Christ crucified (vv. 6–8), but it is subjectively applied by the Holy Spirit to the heart as we persevere in faith and obedience through many trials (vv. 1–4). Octavius Winslow said, "Your minister, your friend . . . cannot assure your spirit that you are 'born of God.' God the eternal Spirit alone can do this. . . . This alone will do for a dying hour."[12]

Fourth, *believers have the firstfruits of the Spirit*. Paul says that we "which have the firstfruits of the Spirit, even we ourselves groan within ourselves, waiting for the adoption, to wit, the redemption of our body" (Rom. 8:23). The "firstfruits" are the first part of the harvest, which the Lord required Israel to offer to him (Deut. 18:4). Thus, the indwelling of the Spirit is the first taste believers enjoy of the future "glorious liberty of the children of God" (Rom. 8:21).

Christ rose as the "firstfruits" of his people who will rise from the dead at his return (1 Cor. 15:20, 23). He already gives his resurrection life to them

10 Matthew Henry, *Matthew Henry's Commentary on the Whole Bible: Complete and Unabridged in One Volume* (Peabody, MA: Hendrickson, 1994), on Eph. 1:14 (2308).

11 Flavel, *Sacramental Meditations*, in *WJF*, 6:407–8.

12 Octavius Winslow, *The Work of the Holy Spirit: An Experimental and Practical View* (Edinburgh: Banner of Truth, 1961), 173.

by the life-giving Spirit (v. 45). The Lord works through the gospel, "that the offering up of the Gentiles might be acceptable, being sanctified by the Holy Ghost" (Rom. 15:16). When Christ comes again, believers will receive the full harvest of the Spirit. Even their bodies will become "spiritual," completely ruled and filled with eternal life by the Holy Spirit (1 Cor. 15:44).

What an amazing gift of love is the Spirit from the Father in the Son! By God's grace, the believer may enjoy the comfort of confessing that "I with body and soul, both in life and death, am not my own, but belong unto my faithful Savior Jesus Christ," that "without the will of my heavenly Father, not a hair can fall from my head," and that "by His Holy Spirit, He also assures me of eternal life, and makes me sincerely willing and ready, henceforth, to live unto Him."[13]

The Cultivation of Assurance

All saving faith contains the seed of assurance (Heb. 11:1). By faith in Christ, believers have "boldness" to draw near to God (10:19, 22). But there is a difference between faith and assurance. Full assurance grows out of faith as its fruit. It is possible to be justified by a weak faith that lacks full assurance. Therefore, believers must "give diligence" to pursue assurance (2 Pet. 1:10). Confidence in salvation usually increases as believers grow in grace (vv. 5–9).

God has joined assurance to Christlikeness. John says, "Hereby perceive we the love of God, because he laid down his life for us: and we ought to lay down our lives for the brethren. . . . My little children, let us not love in word, neither in tongue; but in deed and in truth. And hereby we know that we are of the truth, and shall assure our hearts before him" (1 John 3:16, 18–19).

Professing Christians should periodically engage in self-examination for the evidence of a living faith in Christ. Paul says, "Examine yourselves, whether ye be in the faith; prove your own selves. Know ye not your own selves, how that Jesus Christ is in you, except ye be reprobates [those who fail the test]?" (2 Cor. 13:5).

Some believe that assurance takes away a Christian's motivation to obey God. But we should not fear assurance but desire it. The Westminster Confession (18.3) stresses that true assurance does not produce loose living but

13 The Heidelberg Catechism (LD 1, Q. 1), in *TFU*, 68.

a close walk with God because the believer's heart is "enlarged in peace and joy in the Holy Ghost, in love and thankfulness to God, and in strength and cheerfulness in the duties of obedience."[14]

Conversely, the Christian cannot enjoy high levels of assurance while he persists in low levels of obedience. The Canons of Dort say that when believers commit great sins, they "interrupt the exercise of faith, very grievously wound their consciences, and sometimes lose the sense of God's favor for a time, until on their returning into the right way of serious repentance, the light of God's fatherly countenance again shines upon them."[15] Through repentance, a believer places himself in a position to receive assurance again from God (Ps. 51:12).

We must also recognize that God, in the mystery of his sovereign will, sometimes withdraws assurance from his child to test him. This may not be a consequence for any sin, but to teach the believer humility before God and dependence on Christ. In such seasons, as William Gurnall wrote, "the Christian must trust in a withdrawing God."[16]

Assurance is sweet and strengthening. However, faith rests not in the experience of assurance but in the person and work of Christ. He is believers' righteousness before God. They must cling to Christ alone as he is offered in the promises of the gospel. Christ is also their hope. When he returns, all the saints will enter an experience of joy and peace of which the highest assurance in this life is but a foretaste.

Suggested Songs to Sing to the Lord

- Psalm 35, "Be Thou my helper in the strife," *Psalter*, No. 92; *THBap*, No. 740
- "Gracious Spirit, Dove Divine," *THBap*, No. 245

Questions for Meditation or Discussion

1. How does God's Word show it is possible for believers to enjoy assurance of their salvation?

14 The Westminster Confession of Faith (18.3), in *RC*, 4:254. Cf. the Second London Baptist Confession (18.3), in *RC*, 4:554.

15 The Canons of Dort (Head 5, Art. 5), in *TFU*, 154.

16 William Gurnall, *The Christian in Complete Armour* (1864; repr., Edinburgh: Banner of Truth, 1964), 2:145.

2. What are three possibilities concerning assurance among professing Christians?
3. How do God's promises provide a foundation for assurance?
4. What are the evidences of grace? What are some Scripture passages that reveal specific evidences?
5. How can believers use the evidences of grace and Spirit-empowered logic to seek assurance?
6. Why do we need the work of the Holy Spirit to enjoy assurance of salvation?
7. What are four pictures of the Spirit's work in assurance? What do they mean?
8. What lessons can we learn about cultivating assurance?
9. How much genuine assurance do you have? What is the basis of that assurance?

67

The Marks of Grace in Christian Character

Chapter Summary and Key Terms

God's saving grace produces Christian character. Christ reveals eight marks of saving grace in the Beatitudes at the beginning of the Sermon on the Mount. The first four of these beatitudes highlight the humble repentance of those to whom the kingdom of God belongs. The last four beatitudes describe how the citizens of the kingdom relate to the world. Paul also records nine marks of grace in Christian character in his list of the fruit of the Spirit. Chief among them is Christian *love*, which can be described as giving oneself to glorify God and to do good to people graciously and righteously with a desire for building friendships. The other fruit of the Spirit—joy, peace, longsuffering (patience), gentleness (kindness), goodness, faith (faithfulness), meekness, and temperance (self-control)—are all aspects of love.

GOD SAVES PEOPLE from many cultures. He works through a remarkable variety of circumstances. But he saves one people by one Christ through one Spirit. This means that there are distinguishing marks of saving grace that every believer has to some extent. They consist of moral character and obedience to God's commandments, all by a living faith in Christ. In this chapter, we will discuss how God's grace manifests itself in Christian character, first by considering Christ's Beatitudes and then Paul's list of the fruit of the Spirit.

The Beatitudes

The Lord Jesus Christ came preaching "the gospel of the kingdom" (Matt. 4:23; 9:35). His Sermon on the Mount focuses on the righteousness required by the kingdom (5:20). The sermon begins with the Beatitudes, eight sayings beginning "Blessed are . . ." (vv. 3–10). These sayings expand on Christ's message: "Repent: for the kingdom of heaven is at hand" (4:17). The first and last take the form "Blessed are . . . for theirs is the kingdom of heaven" (5:3, 10).

Therefore, the Beatitudes describe the marks of people who have the grace of the kingdom now and will inherit its glory in the future. Since they are "blessed," we can conclude that they are justified by faith alone. God can bless only those whom he has delivered from the curse of the law and counted righteous in Christ (Gal. 3:8–14).

In the first four beatitudes, Christ reveals that the way of life is humility, for the kingdom of God is gained through repentance.

First, the Lord Jesus says, "Blessed are the poor in spirit: for theirs is the kingdom of heaven" (Matt. 5:3). The word translated as "poor" has to do with a beggar who depends on charity to survive. The Psalms use the word "poor" for people who trust in God and walk in his ways (Pss. 14:6; 34:6; 37:14). Christ came to bring good news to the "poor" (Isa. 61:1 ESV). This poverty consists of humility before the Holy One, heartbreak over sin, and trembling at his Word (57:15; 66:1–2; cf. Ezra 9:4; 10:3). Jesus blesses the inward poverty of humility.

The "poor in spirit" are those who trust in the Lord for salvation because they have no righteousness of their own. These sinners see themselves as spiritual beggars, unable to live on their own good deeds. Christ gives us an example of such a spiritually poor man in the tax collector who said, "God be merciful to me a sinner" (Luke 18:13). This is the kind of person whom the Lord justifies, not the proud and self-righteous (v. 14).

Second, the Lord Jesus says, "Blessed are they that mourn: for they shall be comforted" (Matt. 5:4). This grieving is over sin, for Christ speaks in the context of his call to repentance and righteousness. It is "godly sorrow" (2 Cor. 7:10–11).

The poor in spirit mourn because their lack of righteousness makes them worthy of the fires of hell (Matt. 5:22, 29–30). They especially mourn over the evil of sin against God, for he is "the great King" (v. 35). His name should be treated as holy and his will should be done (6:9–10; 7:21), but they have violated his holy law (5:17–18). Knowing their sin, they have "a broken and a contrite heart" that moves them to pray, "Against thee, thee only, have I sinned, and done this evil in thy sight" (Ps. 51:4, 17). But Christ promises that "they shall be comforted." Paradoxically, the way to true happiness is to embrace the pain of hating sin—especially one's own sin.

Third, the Lord Jesus says, "Blessed are the meek: for they shall inherit the earth" (Matt. 5:5). Meekness is humility and patience (Eph. 4:2; Col. 3:12; 2 Tim. 2:24–25; James 3:13–17). The words of Christ allude to Psalm 37:9 and 11: "For evildoers shall be cut off: but those that wait upon the Lord, they shall inherit the earth.... The meek shall inherit the earth; and shall delight themselves in the abundance of peace." This psalm calls the godly to refrain from anxiety and anger while trusting in the Lord, for he will punish the wicked and give the godly their inheritance.

Those who are poor in spirit realize they have no right to demand anything, for their sins have made them beggars before God. Those who mourn have had their proud hearts broken over their sins. Thomas Watson said that the "spiritually meek" person "does not quarrel with the instructions of the Word, but with the corruptions of his heart."[1] This disposes such people to bear patiently and gently with others who sin against them. They accept sorrow as their lot in this world but look to the coming kingdom for their full comfort.

Fourth, the Lord Jesus says, "Blessed are they which do hunger and thirst after righteousness: for they shall be filled" (Matt. 5:6). Though the citizens of God's kingdom are meek, they are not apathetic. They hunger for the righteousness that only justification by faith in Christ can supply (Phil. 3:8–9). However, they also hunger for an inner righteousness that goes far deeper than the hypocritical piety of the Pharisees (Matt. 5:20).

Those who hunger for righteousness desire it not only because it brings great benefits. They "see this righteousness [as] lovely and excellent in itself," as Jeremiah Burroughs said.[2] Ultimately, "they shall be filled" (Matt.

1 Thomas Watson, *The Beatitudes: An Exposition of Matthew 5:1–12* (Edinburgh: Banner of Truth, 1971), 106.

2 Jeremiah Burroughs, *The Saints' Happiness, Together with the Several Steps Leading Thereunto: Delivered in Divers Lectures on the Beatitudes* (1867; repr., Ligonier, PA: Soli Deo Gloria, 1992), 109.

5:6)—deeply satisfied—only in a "new heavens and a new earth, wherein dwelleth righteousness" (2 Pet. 3:13).

In the last four beatitudes, Christ shows how the citizens of his kingdom relate to people around them, including a hostile world.

Fifth, the Lord Jesus says, "Blessed are the merciful: for they shall obtain mercy" (Matt. 5:7). To be merciful is to be giving and forgiving to those in need (17:15; 18:33, 35). Mercy flows sweetly from broken hearts when sinners have tasted of God's mercy. In their meekness, they are not preoccupied with their own desires but consider the needs of others. The poor in spirit know that they themselves need mercy from the righteous Judge (James 2:12–13).

When Jesus says that "the merciful . . . shall obtain mercy" (Matt. 5:7), he reminds us that only those marked by mercy to others will be welcomed into his kingdom on judgment day (25:34–40). This does not mean that mercy merits eternal life. Christ says, "They shall obtain mercy," not that they shall get what they deserve. Rather, the play on words between "merciful" and "obtain mercy" suggests that the merciful bear the image of the merciful God. Thus, they show themselves to be God's children (5:9, 44–45), those saved by his grace.

Sixth, the Lord Jesus says, "Blessed are the pure in heart: for they shall see God" (Matt. 5:8). The scribes and Pharisees were very concerned with being outwardly "pure" from the world's contamination (the Greek word can also be translated as "clean"). But Christ criticized them for cleaning the outside but leaving the inside filthy (23:25–26). Poor in spirit and meek, the pure in heart have been cleansed from the inner filth of self-righteousness and pride. Instead, they hunger and thirst for true, God-pleasing righteousness. God has taught them to mourn over sin and repent of it (James 4:8–9). He has made them merciful.

"Pure in heart" could describe moral perfection, but that is impossible in this age (Prov. 20:9). However, it can also mean, as it does in the Beatitudes, having a heart that is washed by God's grace through faith (Acts 15:9; 1 Cor. 6:11) so that it loves God and people (1 Tim. 1:5). As a result, the "pure in heart . . . shall see God" (Matt. 5:8). This is the "one thing" that the godly desire above all else: "to behold the beauty of the LORD" (Ps. 27:4). Augustine said, "To behold God is the end and purpose of all our loving activity."[3]

3 Augustine, Sermon 53.5, cited in *Ancient Christian Commentary on Scripture, New Testament*, ed. Thomas Oden, 12 vols. (Downers Grove, IL: InterVarsity Press, 2005–2006), 1a:86; cf. *NPNF*[1], 6:267.

Seventh, the Lord Jesus says, "Blessed are the peacemakers: for they shall be called the children of God" (Matt. 5:9). Peace refers to harmonious and just relationships with God and one another. Being a peacemaker means working to build a community of peace based on a mutual commitment to love and justice.

James says, "The wisdom that is from above is first pure, then peaceable, gentle, and easy to be intreated, full of mercy and good fruits, without partiality, and without hypocrisy. And the fruit of righteousness is sown in peace of them that make peace" (James 3:17–18). Being peacemakers is a distinguishing mark of "the children of God" (Matt. 5:9). The future "shall be called" points to their future acknowledgment by God on the day of judgment. Their peaceable ways show their likeness to their Father—evidence of his regenerating and adopting grace.

Eighth, the Lord Jesus says, "Blessed are they which are persecuted for righteousness' sake: for theirs is the kingdom of heaven" (Matt. 5:10). Christ adds, "Blessed are ye, when men shall revile you, and persecute you, and shall say all manner of evil against you falsely, for my sake. Rejoice, and be exceeding glad: for great is your reward in heaven: for so persecuted they the prophets which were before you" (vv. 11–12).

Remarkably, the world responds to God's humble, meek, merciful, pure, peaceable children with hatred, insults, and even violence. However, enduring persecution is a mark of grace because it shows that God's people do not belong to this world but to Christ, whom the world hates (John 15:18–20).

In the Beatitudes, we hear the voice of the living Christ addressing us personally. Has God shown you that you are a spiritual beggar, empty of any right to eternal life in yourself? Do you mourn over your sins because sin is hateful to the good and loving God? Has the Lord melted your pride into meekness, at least to some extent? Do you hunger and thirst for the righteousness that only Christ can give you in both justification and sanctification?

How has God's mercy to you moved you to show mercy to others in need? Are you merely concerned with outward forms of religious purity, or has God cleansed your heart with brokenhearted repentance, true faith in Christ, and authentic love? Are you a divisive person who constantly strives with others or does your meek and gentle spirit tend to build relationships of peace? Finally, has God worked in you a practical righteousness that provokes the world's sneers, insults, or worse? It is only to such people that Christ says, "Blessed are you."

The Fruit of the Spirit

Paul lists "the fruit of the Spirit" as "love, joy, peace, longsuffering, gentleness, goodness, faith, meekness, [and] temperance" (Gal. 5:22–23). Believers are engaged in an inward conflict between the Spirit and the flesh (v. 17). There are two ways of life marked by either "the works of the flesh" (vv. 19–21) or "the fruit of the Spirit" (vv. 22–23). Of the works of the flesh, Paul says, "They which do such things shall not inherit the kingdom of God" (v. 21). The phrase "fruit of the Spirit" teaches that these qualities are produced only by the Holy Spirit.

The Central Fruit of the Spirit: Christlike Love

"Love" (*agapē*, Gal. 5:22), sometimes translated as "charity," is the fruit of the Spirit that includes all other fruit. Saving faith "worketh by love" (v. 6). We must "by love serve one another" (v. 13). The duty required by God's law is summed up in the commandment to "love thy neighbor as thyself" (v. 14).

The supreme demonstration of love is the gospel: "For God so loved the world, that he gave his only begotten Son, that whosoever believeth in him should not perish, but have everlasting life" (John 3:16). Christ is our model for imitation in loving one another (Eph. 5:2, 25).

Christlike, Spirit-produced love can be described as giving ourselves to glorify God and do good to people graciously and righteously with a desire for building friendships.

First, *love is giving ourselves to glorify God.* God requires us to love him with all our heart and strength (Deut. 6:5). Paul says, "Whether therefore ye eat, or drink, or whatsoever ye do, do all to the glory of God" (1 Cor. 10:31). Love for God has three major dimensions: (1) seeking the glory of his name, the advance of his kingdom, and the doing of his will (Matt. 6:9–10); (2) adoring and delighting in his beauty (Ps. 27:4); and (3) thanking him for his kindness (116:1, 12).

Second, *love is giving ourselves to do good to people.* Love shows kindness (1 Cor. 13:4). John says, "If anyone has the world's goods and sees his brother in need, yet closes his heart against him, how does God's love abide in him? Little children, let us not love in word or talk but in deed and in truth" (1 John 3:17–18 ESV).

Third, *love is giving ourselves graciously*. Love does not come from any goodness in us but from God. He loves unworthy sinners (Rom. 5:6–8). Christ likewise commands us to love those who hate us (Matt. 5:44–45). Love motivates Christians to do good to others though they anticipate no repayment from them—as a free gift of grace (Luke 6:32–34).

Fourth, *love is giving ourselves righteously*. The same apostle who writes, "God is love," also says, "God is light"—that is, he is truth and righteousness (1 John 1:5; 4:8). Love is not indifferent to evil but hates it (Rom. 12:9). Love "rejoiceth not in iniquity, but rejoiceth in the truth" (1 Cor. 13:6). Jesus Christ says, "He that hath my commandments, and keepeth them, he it is that loveth me" (John 14:21). William Plumer said, "We may know that we love God by our cheerful, earnest obedience to his will."[4]

Fifth, *love is giving ourselves with a desire for building friendships*. Love, if mutual, tends to create relationships of fellowship and partnership. God gave his Son in love to reconcile sinners to himself (Rom. 5:10). Amazingly, the Lord counts his people as his "friends" (John 15:13–15). Christian love leads us to build good relationships with one another in "brotherly love" (Rom. 12:9–16). Friendship involves mutual loyalty, affection, unity, communication, knowledge of one another, joy, and partnership in shared concerns (Phil. 1:3–8, 24–26; 2:19–30).[5]

The Other Fruit of the Spirit: The Beauties of Christlike Love

Paul says, "Love is patient and kind; love does not envy or boast; it is not arrogant or rude. It does not insist on its own way; it is not irritable or resentful; it does not rejoice at wrongdoing, but rejoices with the truth. Love bears all things, believes all things, hopes all things, endures all things" (1 Cor. 13:4–7 ESV). It is evident that the other fruit of the Spirit (patience, kindness, meekness, joy, etc.) are forms and expressions of love.

The next fruit of the Spirit that Paul names after love is *joy*. The Greek word translated as "joy" means happiness or gladness. God's people rejoice

4 William S. Plumer, *Vital Godliness: A Treatise on Experimental and Practical Piety* (1864; repr., Harrisonburg, VA: Sprinkle, 1993), 343.

5 See Joel R. Beeke and Michael A. G. Haykin, *How Should We Cultivate Biblical Friendship?*, Cultivating Biblical Godliness (Grand Rapids, MI: Reformation Heritage Books, 2015).

in the Lord (1 Sam. 2:1; Hab. 3:17–19; Phil. 4:4). The chief distinguishing mark of spiritual joy is that it comes with Christlike love. As Augustine said, joy is having and delighting in what one loves, and the goodness or evil of one's joy depends on what one loves.[6] The Spirit moves people to rejoice because they love God and love their neighbors as themselves. It is the joy of the "cheerful giver" (2 Cor. 9:7).

The fruit of inward *peace* springs from the objective peace believers have with God through Christ (Rom. 5:1; Eph. 2:14–18).[7] Such inward peace gives them quietness and rest as they trust in the Lord (Isa. 26:3; 30:15). To maintain their inner peace, believers must (1) bring all their requests to God with thanksgiving; (2) set their thoughts on his perfections and whatever reflects them; and (3) do what is right (Phil. 4:6–9). The essence of peace is the presence of the reconciled God—"the God of peace shall be with you" (v. 9). Wilhelmus à Brakel said, "Peace consists in fellowship between the believing soul and God, this being characterized by oneness of heart, intimacy, friendliness, and love."[8]

The fruit of *longsuffering* (or *patience*) makes a person slow to anger (Ex. 34:6). Jonathan Edwards said, "A Christian spirit disposes persons meekly to bear ill which is received from others"—that is, to bear such wrongs "without doing anything to revenge them," "with a continuance of love in the heart," "without losing the quietness and repose of our minds," and with a willingness "to suffer considerably in our own interest for the sake of peace."[9] Christlike patience is driven by love, which "endureth all things" (1 Cor. 13:7).

The fruits of *gentleness* (or *kindness*) and *goodness* both consist of a heart to do good to others (Rom. 2:4). Paul says, "As we have therefore opportunity, let us do good unto all men, especially unto them who are of the household of faith" (Gal. 6:10). As we said earlier, the essence of love is the disposition to do good to others. Love "is kind" (1 Cor. 13:4).

The fruit of *faith* does not refer to trust in Christ but to *faithfulness*. Since God is faithful and true, his servants must be faithful (2 Cor. 1:18).

6 Augustine, *The City of God*, 14.7, in *NPNF*[1], 2:267.

7 Here we focus on inward, subjective peace. We have already spoken of the peace believers must cultivate in their relationships in the section on "Blessed are the peacemakers" (Matt. 5:9) above.

8 Brakel, *CRS*, 2:440.

9 Edwards, *Charity and Its Fruits*, in *WJE*, 8:186, 189–92.

A faithful person does not lie (Prov. 14:5). Faithfulness, though, is not mere honesty. Christian faithfulness is Christlike, faithful love. Faithfulness is keeping one's commitments just as God keeps his covenant (Deut. 7:9, 12).

The fruit of *meekness* is the humble self-restraint that makes us deal in *gentleness* with those with whom we might be harsh. We have already discussed meekness in the section on the Beatitudes. Meekness is a form of Christlike love, for meekness makes Christians submissive to God's will and willing to regard the concerns of others as more important than their own.

The last fruit of the Spirit that Paul lists in Galatians 5 is *temperance* (or *self-control*). This is the Spirit-worked power to control oneself to conform to God's will despite desires and circumstances that might lead one to sin. The man who can control himself has greater power than one who conquers a city (Prov. 16:32). But "he that hath no rule over his own spirit is like a city that is broken down, and without walls" (25:28). An area of life needing much self-control is our speech (13:3; 21:23; James 1:26). Christian self-control is motivated by Christlike love. People exercise temperance or self-control based on what they love as their greatest joy. Augustine said, "Temperance is love giving itself entirely to that which is loved."[10]

Practical Conclusion to the Fruit of the Spirit

We should not think that the word "fruit" implies that these qualities arise without effort. Trees invest an enormous amount of energy in the production of fruit. Both before and after listing the fruit of the Spirit, Paul commands believers to "walk in the Spirit" (Gal. 5:16, 25). This requires that they make intentional, disciplined, and prolonged efforts to live according to the Spirit's ways.

Furthermore, we must not be satisfied to bear this fruit in occasional acts and meager degrees. We should pray and labor for a great fullness of ripe, mature fruit in every area of our lives. The fruit of the Spirit is nothing less than the loving character and moral excellence of Jesus Christ. Christians should strive to reach that high and heavenly goal. And they should look forward to heaven, where they will finally attain Christlikeness in perfection.

Cultivate the fruit of the Spirit in the garden of your life, and by God's grace, your life will be increasingly full of the sweet fragrance of Jesus Christ.

10 Augustine, *Of the Morals of the Catholic Church*, 15.25, in *NPNF*[1], 4:48.

You will discover that the Holy Spirit is sculpting and painting the image of Christ in your soul, which is the hope of glory.

Suggested Songs to Sing to the Lord

- Psalm 112, "How blest the man who fears the Lord," *Psalter*, No. 305
- "I've found the pearl of greatest price!," *THBap*, No. 592

Questions for Meditation or Discussion

1. How would you explain the first four of Christ's beatitudes? How does each show that the path to the kingdom is the path of humility and self-denial?
2. How would you explain the last four of Christ's beatitudes? How does each show how a citizen in God's kingdom relates to the world?
3. What description of love do the authors present? How is each part of it based on the Holy Scriptures?
4. How are Spirit-worked joy and peace different from earthly joy and peace?
5. What are longsuffering (or patience) and faith (or faithfulness)? How do we imitate God when we exercise them?
6. What does it mean, practically speaking, to show gentleness (or kindness) and goodness to people?
7. How is meekness an exercise of love?
8. What is the motivation for Christian temperance (or self-control)?
9. Does your life exhibit, to some extent, the qualities described in the Beatitudes and the fruit of the Spirit? If not, how can you obtain them? If so, what is one quality in which you need to grow? What practical steps will you take toward that goal?

68

Introduction to Obedience to God's Law

Chapter Summary and Key Terms

God teaches the promise of salvation in the gospel and our duty to obey him in the law. The *moral law* consists of unchanging commandments of righteousness that apply to all mankind. The *ceremonial law* refers to old covenant forms of external worship that served as types of Christ but no longer bind us. The *judicial law* for civil justice in ancient Israel now offers only general principles of wisdom for righteous conduct. God summarized the moral law in the *Ten Commandments*, also known as the *Decalogue*. These commandments reflect the creation ordinances that God instituted when he made man and the natural law that God embedded in the human conscience. God's law also contains *positive law*, which are commandments by mere authority, not based on divine or human nature. There are *three uses of the moral law*. In its *civil use*, it regulates conduct in families and society. In its *evangelical use*, it convicts the conscience of sin and the need of salvation. In its *didactic use*, it shows believers how to please God after they are saved by grace.

THE EXPERIENCE OF SALVATION transforms the believer's relationship to God's law. The Heidelberg Catechism says that spiritual life in Christ "is a sincere joy of heart in God, through Christ, and with love and delight to live according to the will of God in all good works." And "good works" are "only those which proceed from a true faith, are performed according to the law of God, and to His glory; and not such as are founded on our imaginations or the institutions of men."[1]

1 The Heidelberg Catechism (LD 33, Q. 90–91), in *TFU*, 99–100.

Therefore, we need God's law. In the spiritual darkness of this world, the believer says of God's law, "Thy word is a lamp unto my feet, and a light unto my path" (Ps. 119:105). Paul says, "The law is holy, and the commandment holy, and just, and good" (Rom. 7:12). Christians "delight in the law of God" (v. 22). While the law can neither justify nor sanctify us, we need the revelation of righteousness that God provides in the law.

The Law and the Gospel

It is crucial for us to understand the difference between the law and the gospel. God gave his law to reveal the moral duty of man (Deut. 10:12–13). He gave his gospel to reveal the message of salvation (Rom. 1:16–17). Richard Greenham defined the law as "that part of the Word that commandeth all good, and forbiddeth all evil." The gospel, he said, is "that part of the Word which containeth the free promises of God, made unto us in Jesus Christ, without any respect of our deservings."[2]

The Holy Scriptures contrast law and gospel with respect to our justification. The law demands our works, but the gospel promises life to those with Spirit-granted faith in Christ (Gal. 3:11–12). If sinners seek to be righteous by doing the works of the law, the law curses them (v. 10). By faith in Christ alone, sinners receive salvation from the curse and enjoy the blessing of God (vv. 13–14).

The gospel also reveals the grace of sanctification (2 Thess. 2:14). Those who by grace have come to love God can confess, "His commandments are not grievous" (1 John 5:3). Sadly, "evil is present" in them still to resist God's will, but they "delight in the law of God after the inward man" (Rom. 7:21–22). The godly person loves God's law (Ps. 119:97, 165).

Therefore, the Word of God teaches us the difference between law and gospel. But the Scriptures also teach us that both law and gospel come from God for our good.

The Moral, Ceremonial, and Judicial Law of Moses

The law is as old as human nature (Rom. 2:14–15). Abraham walked with God in obedience to his commandments centuries before Moses was born

2 Richard Greenham, *A Short Forme of Catechising*, in *The Workes of the Reverend and Faithfull Servant of Jesus Christ M. Richard Greenham*, ed. Henry Holland, 5th ed. (London: William Welby, 1612), 72.

(Gen. 17:1; 26:5). But God greatly expanded the revelation of his commandments when he gave the law of Moses.

Christians have long distinguished between *moral*, *ceremonial*, and *judicial* law in the law of Moses. Moral law refers to unchanging principles of righteousness that apply to all mankind. Ceremonial law consists of rules for external worship that foreshadowed Christ. Judicial law has to do with directions for civil justice in ancient Israel's national society.[3]

God summarized the moral law in the *Ten Commandments* (Ex. 20:1–17). These are also called the *Decalogue*, which means "ten words." The commandments are, in brief:

1. Thou shalt have no other gods before me.
2. Thou shalt not make unto thee any graven image.
3. Thou shalt not take the name of the Lord thy God in vain.
4. Remember the Sabbath day, to keep it holy.
5. Honor thy father and thy mother.
6. Thou shalt not kill.
7. Thou shalt not commit adultery.
8. Thou shalt not steal.
9. Thou shalt not bear false witness.
10. Thou shalt not covet.[4]

The Lord set apart the Ten Commandments from the many other rules he gave to Israel (Deut. 4:12–13; 5:22; 9:10; 10:1–4). These ten were the only commandments that God spoke directly to Israel in the majesty of his appearing on Mount Sinai. They were also the only laws God wrote on two tablets of stone, to be kept in the ark of the covenant.

3 Calvin, *Institutes*, 4.20.15; and the Westminster Confession of Faith (19.2–5); and the Second London Baptist Confession (19.2–5), in *RC*, 4:255–56, 554–55.

4 We follow the traditional Reformed numbering of the Ten Commandments. Roman Catholics and Lutherans count the first commandment to be the prohibitions against other gods and idols (vv. 3–6), the ninth to be the prohibition against coveting one's neighbor's house (v. 17), and the tenth as the prohibition against coveting his wife, servants, or possessions (v. 17). However, there is distinction between what we may not worship (false gods, v. 3) and how we may not worship (images, vv. 4–6). Furthermore, Moses's later restatement of the Ten Commandments changes the order in saying we must not covet our neighbor's wife, house, and so on (Deut. 5:21). This makes it impossible to divide "Thou shalt not covet" into two commandments. It is best to treat the prohibition against coveting as one commandment, just as Paul does: "The law had said, Thou shalt not covet" (Rom. 7:7).

Why are the Ten Commandments unique? They express who God is and who we are meant to be as his image bearers. Each commandment reflects the created order revealed in Genesis 1–2:

1. No other gods: God alone is the Creator of all things outside of himself.
2. No idols: The glorious God must not be confused with his visible creation.
3. Reverence: The Creator is powerful and wise, worthy of all honor.
4. Sabbath keeping: God made the world in six days and set apart the seventh as holy.
5. Honoring parents: God is like a father to mankind and instituted the family.
6. No murder: Human life is sacred above that of the animals, for God created man in his image.
7. No adultery: God ordained marriage for one man and one woman to be one flesh.
8. No theft: God gave man authority over the world and thus the right to own property.
9. No perjury: God speaks truth and reality, and man is created to be his image.
10. No coveting: God richly provided for man in the garden; he should be content.

In addition to the Ten Commandments, the Lord gave many statutes and judgments (Deut. 4:13–14). Ceremonies such as the offering of sacrifices were not as important as faithful love (Hos. 6:6), humility and repentance (Ps. 51:17), and obedience to God (1 Sam. 15:22; Ps. 40:6–8; Jer. 7:21–23). Judicial laws, such as those in Exodus 21–22, showed how to make wise applications of general moral principles to specific situations in Israel's ancient society.

Christ taught a distinction between the moral, ceremonial, and judicial law. He said, "Think not that I am come to destroy the law, or the prophets: I am not come to destroy, but to fulfil. For verily I say unto you, Till heaven and earth pass, one jot or one tittle shall in no wise pass from the law, till all be fulfilled" (Matt. 5:17–18). None of the commandments he went on to quote were ceremonial laws, but only moral laws or moral principles drawn from judicial laws.

He also treated the ceremonial law differently from the moral law. He kept the whole law of Moses. But Jesus said that we are not made unclean by what we eat, but only by what comes out of our hearts (Matt. 15:10–20). He "declared all foods clean" (Mark 7:19 ESV).

In addition, Christ taught that the judicial law of Moses contains principles of righteous wisdom. For example, he quoted the Old Testament law that required that judicial verdicts against criminals must rest on testimony from two or three witnesses (Deut. 17:6). However, Christ did not apply this principle to civil law but to church discipline and excommunication (Matt. 18:15–17).

The apostles of Christ followed in their Lord's footsteps regarding the law. Paul quotes one of the Ten Commandments and applies it directly to children in the church: "Honour thy father and mother" (Eph. 6:2). But Paul also warns Christians not to let others judge them according to Old Testament ceremonies, for they are "a shadow" of Christ (Col. 2:16–17). Paul quotes a judicial law requiring the death penalty, "Purge the evil from your midst" (Deut. 17:7 ESV), but he applies it to excommunication from the church, not capital punishment (1 Cor. 5:13).

Three great doctrines of the New Testament support the moral/ceremonial/judicial distinction in the law. First, our great High Priest offered himself as the perfect sacrifice and abolished ceremonial laws about priests and sacrifices (Heb. 7:12, 27). Second, the Son of David was crucified by Israel and enthroned at God's right hand (Acts 2:30–36), ending the theocracy of the nation of Israel and its judicial laws. Third, Christ has ratified the new covenant, in which God promised, "I will put my laws into their mind, and write them in their hearts" (Heb. 8:10). God once wrote the Ten Commandments on tablets of stone. Now he writes them on the heart (2 Cor. 3:3). Christ gives believers the inner motivation to obey the moral law summarized in the Ten Commandments.

Therefore, there are three dimensions to the law of Moses: moral, ceremonial, and judicial. The Ten Commandments are God's summary of the moral law for Israel. We should make good use of Reformed catechisms that explain the Ten Commandments. We also should teach the ceremonial law to point people to Jesus. And we should receive the judicial law, not as legislation for modern nations but as a revelation of principles of wisdom to guide God's people in righteousness.

The Rules of Interpretation for the Ten Commandments

To recognize the Ten Commandments as a summary of the moral law and discern the richness of their instruction, we need to interpret them according to the following rules.[5]

First, *negative prohibitions imply positive duties, and vice versa.* By revealing what he hates and forbids, God also reveals what he loves and requires.

Second, *precepts regarding external acts imply inward attitudes and affections.* The tenth commandment prohibits sinful desires. In the second commandment, the Lord speaks of hating or loving him (Ex. 20:5–6). Therefore, the moral law addresses the heart (Matt. 5:8, 21–22, 27–28).

Third, *the Ten Commandments express God's created order* (Genesis 1). The second and fourth commandments refer to the creation account (Ex. 20:4, 11). As we observed earlier in this chapter, the prohibitions against murder and adultery (vv. 13–14) come from God's creation of man in his image (Gen. 1:26; 9:5–6) and his institution of marriage between one man and one woman (2:18–24). Therefore, the Ten Commandments reveal the ethical implications of God's *creation ordinances*, structures that God built into the life of human beings created in his image (see chap. 28). The Ten Commandments are God's revelation to Israel of the *natural law* embedded in human nature by the Creator (see chap. 4) because of his own divine nature (Rom. 1:32; 2:14–15). Some aspects of God's law are not natural law but *positive law*, requirements added by God's mere authority. For example, the prohibition against eating the fruit of one tree in the garden (chap. 32) was positive law.

Fourth, *specific precepts reveal broadly applicable principles so that we may know what pleases our Creator in all of life.* This follows from the fact, which we already have noted, that the Ten Commandments express God's nature and created order for human attitudes and conduct. For example, the prohibition against bearing "false witness" specifically addresses perjury in judicial cases (Ex. 20:16), but it also reveals God's love for the truth and the value of a good reputation. Thus, it instructs us regarding the evil of gossip,

5 See the Westminster Larger Catechism (Q. 99), in *RC*, 4:320–21.

fraud in business dealings, and so on. Each commandment represents a whole area of righteousness and a whole family of sins.

Fifth, *the Ten Commandments require conduct that helps other people obey the same precepts*. For example, the precept against adultery implies that we should speak or dress in a manner that helps people practice sexual purity (Eph. 5:3–4; 1 Tim. 2:9). The command to honor one's father and mother implies the duty of parents to act in an honorable fashion.

Sixth, *the Ten Commandments are fulfilled in love* (Ex. 20:6; Lev. 19:18; Deut. 6:5). The whole law depends, Christ teaches us, on loving God and loving our neighbors (Matt. 22:37–40).

Seventh, *the Ten Commandments assert the supremacy of God*. God is the Lawgiver (Ex. 20:1). His lordship, covenant, and grace provide the great motivations for obedience (v. 2). The first four commandments all pertain to him (vv. 3–11). These commandments are given three times as much attention as the next six, which pertain to our duties to people. William Ames said that obedience is "towards God, for he is at once its standard, its object, and its end."[6]

The Three Uses of the Moral Law

Just as God's law can be distinguished in its moral, ceremonial, and judicial dimensions, so there are *three uses of the moral law*: the *civil*, *evangelical*, and *didactic* uses.

First, *there is the civil use of the moral law, to restrain sin*. For example, the Ten Commandments prohibit rebellion against proper authority, unjust destruction of human life, adultery, theft, and perjury. The civil government should make and enforce civil laws that reflect these prohibitions. Righteous civil justice restrains evil conduct (Deut. 17:13; Prov. 19:25; 21:11). But only the gospel can change the heart and save the soul.

By what standard should parents direct their children, business owners their employees in their business operations, pastors and elders the members of their churches, and civil leaders the officers and the citizens of their nation? No one can lead well, nor can people flourish, without justice and righteousness (Prov. 8:12–16; 14:34). God alone can provide us

6 William Ames, *The Marrow of Theology*, trans. John D. Eusden (Grand Rapids, MI: Baker, 1968), 2.1.12 (220).

with a standard that will resonate with the consciences of all people. That standard is his moral law.

Second, *there is the evangelical use of the moral law, to convict sinners*. Everything the law says is intended "that every mouth may be stopped, and all the world may become guilty before God. Therefore by the deeds of the law there shall no flesh be justified in his sight: for by the law is the knowledge of sin" (Rom. 3:19–20). The Heidelberg Catechism says, "Whence knowest thou thy misery? Out of the law of God."[7] The law drives sinners to Christ for salvation by showing them their need of him.

The Westminster Larger Catechism says, "The moral law is of use to unregenerate men, to awaken their consciences to flee from the wrath to come, and to drive them to Christ; or, upon their continuance in the estate and way of sin, to leave them inexcusable, and under the curse thereof."[8] Without the evangelical use of the law combined with the call to repentance, the professing church ceases to cherish the gospel. The church then dies from the inside out and becomes puffed up with empty self-righteousness (Rev. 3:1–3, 14–19).

Third, *there is the didactic use of the moral law, to direct saints*. In response to God's amazing grace, believers offer their whole lives to God. They live as those set apart to be holy, seeking to know his good will, and walking in righteousness by the Holy Spirit (Rom. 12:1–2; 14:17). It is God's law that teaches them what is holy, righteous, and good (7:12). The New Testament does not just tell us to love one another; it is full of specific commands. And it quotes the Ten Commandments as binding moral principles for the disciples of Jesus Christ.[9] Christ says, "If ye love me, keep my commandments" (John 14:15). While the old ceremonies do not bind us, "the keeping of the commandments of God" remains crucial to the Christian life (1 Cor. 7:19).

The law puts hands and feet on love, so to speak, so that we can see how Christlike love leads people to act toward their God and their neighbors. It should be our constant conversational partner in life (Deut. 6:6–8) so that we can say, "O how love I thy law! It is my meditation all the day" (Ps. 119:97).

7 The Heidelberg Catechism (LD 2, Q. 3), in *TFU*, 69.

8 The Westminster Larger Catechism (Q. 96), in *RC*, 4:320.

9 Matt. 5:21–22, 27–28; Mark 2:23–3:5; 7:9–10; 10:19; Rom. 7:7; 13:9; Eph. 6:2; James 2:11–12. The New Testament also restates the same principles as the Ten Commandments in other words (as in Eph. 4:25–5:6).

The law does not provide detailed instructions for every situation. However, marinating our minds in its precepts and putting it into practice will cause us by grace to mature in wisdom and discernment (Heb. 5:13–14).

Therefore, study God's law. Meditate on his commandments day and night. Use the law as a mirror to see Christ. Marvel at Christ's perfect obedience to God's law in its every requirement. Glorify God's Son as the perfect law keeper on behalf of his people. Trust him as your only righteousness. And follow him, stumbling at times as you go, down the path of obedience so that your good works may please and glorify God.

Suggested Song to Sing to the Lord

- Psalm 19, "Jehovah's perfect law restores the soul again," *Psalter*, No. 38; *THBap*, No. 448

Questions for Meditation or Discussion

1. What is the difference between the law and the gospel?
2. What is a definition and example of (1) the moral law, (2) the ceremonial law, and (3) the judicial law?
3. How did the Lord especially honor the Ten Commandments?
4. How is each of the Ten Commandments based on Genesis 1–2?
5. What did Jesus say about the moral, ceremonial, and judicial law?
6. What can we learn from Paul about the moral, ceremonial, and judicial law?
7. What rules of interpretation should we use to fully understand the Ten Commandments?
8. What are the three uses of the law? What is an example of each use?
9. What is one way that reading this chapter has helped you to better obey God's law?

69

Obedience to the First Four of the Ten Commandments

Chapter Summary and Key Terms

In the preface to the Ten Commandments, the Lord motivates us to obey his moral law by reminding us of who he is and what he has done to save his people. The first commandment requires us to worship the true God alone. In the second commandment, God regulates how we worship him by his Word. Specifically, he forbids us to make images of him or any god, or to direct our worship to images. The third commandment forbids us to speak of God without due reverence. The fourth commandment requires us to keep the weekly *Sabbath* as a day of rest and worship. Though the Sabbath is a day of rest, God blesses *works of necessity*, *mercy*, and *piety* that are performed on it. Some aspects of the Sabbath are positive law that God specified for a time and that since have changed. With Christ's resurrection, the Sabbath is now the *Lord's Day* on the first day of the week.

THE LORD INTRODUCED the Ten Commandments by saying, "I am the LORD thy God, which have brought thee out of the land of Egypt, out of the house of bondage" (Ex. 20:2). With this preface to the Decalogue, he gave the people of Israel three reasons for obeying his law. First, they must keep his commandments because he was the sovereign and faithful Lord over all his creation. Second, he was "thy God," the One who had given himself in covenant to the seed of Abraham and had taken them to be his people (Gen. 17:7; Ex. 6:7). John Calvin said, "He holds out the promise of grace to draw them by its sweetness to a zeal for holiness."[1] Third, he had saved them from slavery in Egypt, keeping his covenant in a massive display of sovereign grace (Ex. 2:24; 19:4–6).

These grounds, or motives, for obedience, as given to Israel, foreshadowed the great work of salvation for all God's children. Christ gave himself to redeem a people for God and make them zealous to do what pleases him (Titus 2:14; Heb. 13:20–21). Thomas Boston said, "All men are obliged to keep these commandments, for God is Lord of all: but the saints especially; for besides being their Lord, he is their God and Redeemer too."[2]

It is an astounding thing that the holy God says to sinners, "I am the Lord thy God." The Lord's words ground all true obedience to the Ten Commandments on his sovereign grace. Ebenezer Erskine said, "These words, 'I am the Lord thy God,' contain the leading promise of the covenant of grace; and there is more in them than heart can conceive, or tongue express. . . . O what can he give more than himself! And what will he not give when he gives himself!"[3]

Thus, the preface to the Ten Commandments shows that the covenant made at Mount Sinai was not a covenant of works but an administration of the covenant of grace.

Having examined the preface to the Decalogue, we will consider the first four commandments in the remainder of this chapter, then turn to the last six in the next.

The First Commandment: God's Unique Glory

The Lord says, "Thou shalt have no other gods before me" (Ex. 20:3). This commandment forbids the worship of any deity except the God who saved Israel from Egypt (v. 2). While the first four commandments all pertain to worshiping and glorifying God, the first commandment specifies the only God whom we must worship. As Martin Luther said, "We are to fear, love, and trust God above all things."[4]

1 Calvin, *Institutes*, 2.8.13.

2 Boston, *An Illustration of the Doctrines of the Christian Religion*, in *WTB*, 2:90.

3 Ebenezer Erskine, *A Treasure of Gospel Grace Digged out of Mount Sinai*, in *The Whole Works of the Late Rev. Ebenezer Erskine*, 3 vols. (Edinburgh: Ogle & Murray et al., 1871), 2:22.

4 The Small Catechism (1.2), in *The Book of Concord: The Confessions of the Evangelical Lutheran Church*, ed. Robert Kolb and Timothy J. Wengert, trans. Charles Arand et al. (Minneapolis: Fortress, 2000), 351.

This commandment is grounded in God's work of creation: "In the beginning God created the heaven and the earth" (Gen. 1:1) and all that they contain. This shows there is only one true God, and the Holy Scriptures sharply distinguish "the true God" from "the gods that have not made the heavens and the earth" (Jer. 10:10–11). There are, in reality, no other gods. But people manufacture gods out of their imagination by worshiping the creation instead of the Creator.

The prohibition against other gods implies the duty of wholehearted devotion to the Lord: "Hear, O Israel: The Lord our God is one Lord: and thou shalt love the Lord thy God with all thine heart, and with all thy soul, and with all thy might" (Deut. 6:4–5). The repetition of "all" emphasizes that love for the Lord must permeate everything we are and do. Augustine said that God is "the chief end after which we are told to strive with supreme affection."[5]

The first commandment teaches monotheism—that is, belief in the one true God and adoration of him alone. Philosophies and religions contrary to biblical monotheism, such as atheism, polytheism, pantheism, panentheism, and finite theism, offend God and destroy men's souls (chap. 10). We should choose to die rather than to offer worship to a false god (Dan. 3:18, 28) or to forsake praying and giving thanks to the true God (6:1–10). We should not bow down or give worship to saints or angels, put our absolute trust in any mere creature, or seek supernatural power or knowledge from spirits. Rather, we must love God with our whole being and live such lives as give people reason to worship our God (Matt. 5:16).

The Second Commandment: God's Prescribed Worship

The Lord says, "Thou shalt not make unto thee any graven image, or any likeness of any thing that is in heaven above, or that is in the earth beneath, or that is in the water under the earth: thou shalt not bow down thyself to them, nor serve them" (Ex. 20:4–5). He adds this sobering motive: "For I the Lord thy God am a jealous God, visiting the iniquity of the fathers upon the children unto the third and fourth generation of them that hate me; and shewing mercy unto thousands of them that love me, and keep my commandments" (vv. 5–6).

5 Augustine, *Of the Morals of the Catholic Church*, 8.13, in *NPNF*[1], 4:44–45.

This commandment does not forbid all visual art, for God commanded art to be put in the tabernacle (Ex. 25:18; 26:1). Rather, God forbids all visual representation of a divine being or use of images in worship. This includes an image of the true God. Moses says that the Lord appeared on Mount Sinai as fire lest the people make a "graven image" of him (Deut. 4:15–16). But the second commandment presents no obstacle to the use of images of mere human beings or other creatures for the purpose of education or art.

The second commandment pertains to the outward means of worship. The words "thou shalt not make unto thee" teach us that man is prohibited from worshiping God through means that man makes for himself. God chooses to be worshiped by faith and obedience to his Word.

The Creator of heaven and earth cannot be represented in a man-made image (Acts 17:24, 29). An image does not draw people near to God but is "a teacher of lies" (Hab. 2:18). The only image of himself that God has authorized is his living image in righteous human beings, especially his incarnate Son, Jesus Christ (Col. 1:15; 3:10).

Christians in the early church opposed all images of divine beings, including images of Jesus. They did use symbols, such as a fish, a shepherd, grapes, or a dove. However, the use of images in worship crept into the church until the practice became officially blessed in the medieval period. Today, Roman Catholicism uses images of God, Christ, Mary, and the saints in its worship. But early Reformed theologians rejected such images. The Second Helvetic Confession says, "Although Christ took upon Him man's nature, yet He did not, therefore, take it that He might set forth a pattern for carvers and painters. He denied that He came 'to destroy the Law and the prophets' (Matt. 5:17), but images are forbidden in the Law and the prophets."[6]

The Westminster Larger Catechism says that "the sins forbidden in the second commandment" include "the making any representation of God, of all or of any of the three persons, either inwardly in our mind, or outwardly in any kind of image or likeness of any creature whatsoever; all worshipping of it, or God in it or by it; the making of any representation of feigned deities, and all worship of them, or service belonging to them."[7] Even objects

6 The Second Helvetic Confession (chap. 4), in *RC*, 2:815.

7 The Westminster Larger Catechism (Q. 109), in *RC*, 4:324.

not originally designed to be idols should be destroyed if people begin to worship them (Num. 21:8–9; 2 Kings 18:4).

True worship is an act of love for God that aims to please him by following his Word. Moses told the Israelites that when they entered the land of Canaan, they must not ask, "How did these nations serve their gods?" (Deut. 12:30). The rule of worship is "Everything that I command you, you shall be careful to do. You shall not add to it or take from it" (Deut. 12:32 ESV). This rule has come to be known as the regulative principle of worship (see chap. 80).

The prohibition against idols also has surprisingly broad applications, including "covetousness, which is idolatry" (Col. 3:5). Whenever we set our hearts on something visible as the means of obtaining happiness or glory, we make it an idol that directly opposes the love of God (1 John 2:15–17; 5:21).

The Third Commandment: God's Awesome Name

The Lord says, "Thou shalt not take the name of the LORD thy God in vain; for the LORD will not hold him guiltless that taketh his name in vain" (Ex. 20:7). God has revealed himself by various names, including "the LORD," "Most High," "God Almighty," and so on (see chaps. 10 and 15). However, the "name" of the Lord includes every aspect of his revealed glory, such as his attributes of love and justice (33:19; 34:5–7), the majesty shining in his works (9:16; 15:3), and his manifest presence (23:21; Deut. 12:5, 11). To "take the name of the LORD thy God in vain" means to speak about God's names, attributes, works, or presence as if he were nonexistent, distant, powerless, or dead.

God's name is "glorious and fearful" (Deut. 28:58). And so, as the Heidelberg Catechism says, we must "use the holy name of God no otherwise than with fear and reverence."[8] The first commandment specifies the God whom we worship, the second regulates the outward means of worship, and the third mandates reverence for the God whom we worship. The Creator of the universe is awesome and majestic (Amos 4:13; 5:8). Therefore, Christ taught us, the desire of our hearts should be "Hallowed be thy name" (Matt. 6:9).

The most obvious application of the prohibition against taking God's name in vain is to avoid blaspheming or cursing God (Lev. 24:10–16).

8 The Heidelberg Catechism (LD 36, Q. 99), in *TFU*, 103.

Blasphemy is speaking about God in a manner that insults him (Isa. 37:4–6, 23; cf. 36:18–20). The third commandment also forbids speaking of God lightly. Thomas Watson said, "We take God's name in vain . . . when we use God's name in idle discourse. He is not to be spoken of but with a holy awe upon our hearts. To bring his name in at every turn, when we are not thinking of him, to say, 'O God!' or, 'O Christ!' . . . is to take God's name in vain."[9] The positive side of the third commandment is the duty to tell his wonders to our children (Ps. 78:4), praise and thank him among his people (35:18; 111:1), and declare his glory among the nations (96:3).

The Fourth Commandment: God's Holy Day

The Lord says, "Remember the sabbath day, to keep it holy. Six days shalt thou labour, and do all thy work: but the seventh day is the sabbath of the Lord thy God: in it thou shalt not do any work, thou, nor thy son, nor thy daughter, thy manservant, nor thy maidservant, nor thy cattle, nor thy stranger that is within thy gates" (Ex. 20:8–10). He gives this reason: "For in six days the Lord made heaven and earth, the sea, and all that in them is, and rested the seventh day: wherefore the Lord blessed the sabbath day, and hallowed it" (v. 11).

The Hebrew word translated as "sabbath" comes from a verb meaning to "cease" or "rest." The rest that God commanded is cessation not from all activity but only from the ordinary labor of one's daily vocation. One purpose of the *Sabbath* day is that people and their animals may rest and find refreshment (Ex. 23:12; Deut. 5:14). The other purpose of the Sabbath is that a day might be set aside for worship in the assembly of God's people (Lev. 23:3; cf. Psalm 92).

Thus, the first four commandments teach us to worship the holy God by the holy means he ordains with the holy reverence he deserves on the holy day he chooses. Calvin said, "We have one definite day of the week which is to be completely spent in hearing God's word, in prayers and petitions, and in meditating upon his works so that we may rejoice in him."[10]

The Sabbath is not a merely ceremonial law but a creation ordinance (Ex. 20:11). The first creation account concludes, "On the seventh day God ended his work which he had made; and he rested on the seventh day from

9 Thomas Watson, *The Ten Commandments* (Edinburgh: Banner of Truth, 1965), 85.

10 John Calvin, *Sermons on Genesis, Chapters 1–11*, trans. Rob Roy McGregor (Edinburgh: Banner of Truth, 2009), 130.

all his work which he had made. And God blessed the seventh day, and sanctified it: because that in it he had rested from all his work which God created and made" (Gen. 2:2–3). His sanctifying of the day implies man's duty to treat it as holy. God's rest, unnecessary for him, was presented as a model for imitation by his image bearers.

The Lord began calling Israel to practice the Sabbath before making the covenant at Mount Sinai (Ex. 16:22–31). According to the fourth commandment, the obligation to keep the Sabbath was not limited to Israel but included the "stranger that is within thy gates" (20:10)—that is, Gentiles outside the covenant who lived in Israel.

The Pharisees accused Christ and his followers of breaking the Sabbath, especially by his healing of people on that day (Luke 6:7; 14:1–3). Christ did not respond by abolishing the Sabbath. On other occasions, he did abolish the law of clean and unclean things (Mark 7:1–5, 14–23; cf. Luke 11:37–41) and the necessity of worshiping at the old covenant temple (John 4:20–24). But in this case, Christ explained the true keeping of the Sabbath (Mark 2:23–3:6). He said that on the Sabbath God permits us to do *works of necessity* that preserve our lives and health. He also blesses *works of mercy* that prevent or relieve the misery of people and animals. God commands *works of piety* on the Sabbath—the glad labors of worship and gospel ministry. Jesus says, "The sabbath was made for man, and not man for the sabbath" (2:27). Thus, the Sabbath serves to benefit us as human beings; mankind needs this day of rest and sacred worship.

The Lord Jesus says, "The Son of man is Lord also of the sabbath" (Mark 2:28). For Christ to declare himself "Lord" of the Sabbath is to claim to be God. It is also to make himself the focus of the Sabbath celebration. Far from renouncing the Sabbath, Christ's disciples must keep it even more devoutly because of their love and submission to him.

Not every part of the fourth commandment reflects the unchanging moral order of God. Some aspects of the Sabbath are positive law, such as the particular day of the week that is the Sabbath. Under the law of Moses, God also gave additional requirements for the Sabbath (Ex. 35:3), instituted special ceremonial laws concerning it (Lev. 24:8; Num. 28:9–10), added other Sabbath days and even Sabbath years beyond the seventh day (Leviticus 23 and 25), and commanded the death penalty for Sabbath breaking (Ex. 31:14–15; 35:2; Num. 15:30–36).

Several Scripture passages indicate that the Lord moved the Sabbath from the seventh day to the first day of the week. Christ died on the cross as the evening of the Sabbath drew near (Luke 23:54; John 19:31). His great work of accomplishing redemption was "finished" (John 19:30). During the seventh day, his body rested in the grave. Every gospel says that he rose on "the first day of the week," marking that day as particularly important. Christ's resurrection was the dawning of the new creation of life and immortality (2 Tim. 1:10). The risen Christ first appeared to his disciples on "the first day of the week" (John 20:19). He appeared again "after eight days" (v. 26), which in the ancient inclusive method of counting time was again the first day of the week.

Christ poured out the Holy Spirit on the church on the day of Pentecost (Acts 2), which fell on the first day of the week (Lev. 23:16). Luke records that later, "upon the first day of the week, when the disciples came together to break bread, Paul preached unto them" (Acts 20:7). The apostle commanded the churches to take a collection for the poor in Judea on "the first day of every week" (1 Cor. 16:1–2 ESV). John says, "I was in the Spirit on the Lord's day" (Rev. 1:10). The word translated as "Lord's" means that the day is set apart as sacred to the Lord, just as "the Lord's supper" is set apart for him (1 Cor. 11:20).

Therefore, there remains a Christian Sabbath, the *Lord's Day* on the first day of the week. Christians are not under the burden of keeping the many old covenant holy days with their regulations and penalties (Rom. 14:5; Gal. 4:10; Col. 2:16).[11] But the creation ordinance of weekly rest for sacred worship continues and will continue until Christ returns.

The Sabbath is a call to love and joy. God says that if we "call the sabbath a delight . . . then shalt thou delight thyself in the Lord" (Isa. 58:13–14). In the "song for the sabbath day," we are taught to sing, "It is a good thing to give thanks unto the Lord, and to sing praises unto thy name, O Most High," and, "Those that be planted in the house of the Lord shall flourish in the courts of our God" (Ps. 92:1, 13). By union and communion with Christ, believers can already "begin in this life the eternal Sabbath."[12]

Thus, the essence of the Lord's Day is concentrated communion with God. Robert Murray M'Cheyne said, "This is the reason why we love the

11 On these three passages in relation to the Sabbath, see Beeke and Smalley, *RST*, 3:909–11.

12 The Heidelberg Catechism (LD 38, Q. 103), in *TFU*, 105.

Lord's day. This is the reason why we 'call the Sabbath a delight.'" When believers set aside their ordinary work and come to the house of God, it is like the dawn of the resurrection. When they hear the voice of the Shepherd speaking through the Word and feeding their souls, it reminds them of the day when "the Lamb which is in the midst of the throne shall feed them, and shall lead them unto living fountains of waters: and God shall wipe away all tears from their eyes" (Rev. 7:17). When believers join in singing God's praise, it reminds them that one day they will worship God and the Lamb in glory. Thus, M'Cheyne said, "a well-spent Sabbath we feel to be a day of heaven upon earth."[13]

Suggested Songs to Sing to the Lord

- Psalm 92, "How good it is to thank the Lord," *Psalter*, No. 250; *THBap*, No. 535
- Psalm 96, "Sing to the Lord, sing His praise, all ye peoples," *Psalter*, No. 259; *THBap*, No. 65

Questions for Meditation or Discussion

1. What is the preface to the Ten Commandments? What motivations does it give us to obey God's commandments?
2. What does the first commandment say? In your own words, what does it mean?
3. How does the first commandment call us to love God?
4. What does the second commandment say? What does it mean?
5. How did the church's response to the second commandment vary from the early church through the medieval period and in the Reformation?
6. What is the third commandment? What does it mean?
7. What is the fourth commandment? What does it mean?
8. How is the fourth commandment grounded on God's work of creation?
9. When the Pharisees challenged Jesus Christ about the Sabbath, how did he respond? What did he teach about the Sabbath?

13 Robert Murray M'Cheyne, "I Love the Lord's Day," in *Memoirs and Remains of Robert Murray M'Cheyne*, ed. Andrew Bonar (1892; repr., Edinburgh: Banner of Truth, 1995), 596–97.

10. What evidence is there in the New Testament that apostolic Christianity observed the first day of the week as the Lord's Day?
11. What are the most significant ways that you are breaking each of these first four commandments? Make a list, take it to the Lord in confession, and look to Christ for forgiveness by his blood. What are some practical steps you can take, by grace, toward greater obedience?

70

Obedience to the Last Six of the Ten Commandments

Chapter Summary and Key Terms

The last six of the Ten Commandments teach us to love our neighbors as ourselves as an expression of our supreme love for God. The fifth commandment binds us to honor proper human authority, beginning with our parents. The sixth commandment requires us to highly value human life rather than maliciously hating people and seeking to harm them. The seventh commandment requires us to obey God's will that human sexual activity take place only in marriage. In the eighth commandment, we are taught to respect the property of other people. The ninth commandment forbids lying or maliciously harming the reputation of another human being. The tenth commandment prohibits coveting anyone or anything that God has given to one of our neighbors. This final commandment reminds us that God's law directs even our desires.

THE FIRST FOUR COMMANDMENTS direct our love for God. The last six instruct us in how to love our neighbors. These two loves cannot be separated. John says, "If a man say, I love God, and hateth his brother, he is a liar; for . . . he who loveth God [must] love his brother also" (1 John 4:20–21).

The last six commandments are associated with the virtues of civil society, but they are required as acts of obedience to the Lord. John Brown of Haddington noted that civil acts "are religious obedience" when done "from love and regard to God, chiefly for his glory, depending on his promised strength, and hoping for acceptance only through Christ."[1] Sins such as adultery and murder harm people, but they primarily wrong God (Ps. 51:4).

The Fifth Commandment: Proper Human Authority

The Lord says, "Honour thy father and thy mother: that thy days may be long upon the land which the Lord thy God giveth thee" (Ex. 20:12). The fifth commandment requires us to regard our parents as worthy of our respect. Both "father" and "mother" are included (Lev. 19:3). We must honor them because God made them our parents and commands us to honor them.

It is wise to honor one's parents because doing so tends to produce a longer and happier life (Prov. 3:1–2; 4:10). It forms habits of gratitude and submission to authority that foster other virtues and protect against self-destructive vices. Paul tells children to obey their parents "in the Lord" so that it may "be well" with them and they may "live long on the earth" (Eph. 6:1–3). This is another piece of evidence that the Ten Commandments present moral principles for everyone.

The Heidelberg Catechism says that God requires "that I show all honor, love and fidelity, to my father and mother, and all in authority over me, and submit myself to their good instruction and correction, with due obedience; and also patiently bear with their weaknesses and infirmities, since it pleases God to govern us by their hand."[2]

Obedience to the fifth commandment begins with minor children in their parents' households. Paul tells children to "obey your parents" (Eph. 6:1–2; Col. 3:20). The duty of obedience ceases with the onset of adulthood (though an adult child living in his or her parents' home must still observe their household rules.) However, the requirement to honor one's parents is much broader than obedience. The duty of rendering honor continues throughout life.

Sons and daughters should show respect to their parents through their speech, posture, facial expressions, and gestures (Ex. 18:7; 1 Kings 2:19). When their parents speak to them, they should listen with a desire to grow in wisdom (Ex. 18:24; Prov. 1:8). When parents grow old, their children must not despise them (Prov. 23:22). If parents become unable to provide

1 John Brown of Haddington, *Questions and Answers on the Shorter Catechism* (Grand Rapids, MI: Reformation Heritage Books, 2006), 237.

2 The Heidelberg Catechism (LD 39, Q. 104), in *TFU*, 105.

for themselves, their children must care for their needs (Matt. 15:4–6; 1 Tim. 5:4, 8).

The command to honor parents implies that parents should conduct themselves in an honorable fashion. Paul says, "Fathers, provoke not your children to wrath: but bring them up in the nurture and admonition of the Lord" (Eph. 6:4). In another epistle, Paul adds this reason: "lest they be discouraged" (Col. 3:21). Parents should provide what their minor children need to live and flourish. And they must train their children in the ways of God. Parental authority is given by God for the benefit of children, not for their parents' selfish ends (2 Cor. 12:14–15).

We have concentrated on applications to parent-child relationships, for that is the focus of the fifth commandment. But this commandment reveals our duty to respect all human authorities. We live in a world full of relationships structured by authority. Beyond the family, these include the relationships between civil rulers and people (Rom. 13:1), military officers and soldiers (Matt. 8:8–9), business owners and employees (20:1, 15), and elders and church members (Heb. 13:17; 1 Pet. 5:2). All this authority comes from God. It is administrated by Christ the King. And it is rightly exercised by Spirit-empowered obedience to the Word of God. These many kinds of authority remind us, as Jochem Douma says, that human "authority is always limited authority and is bordered by other spheres of authority."[3]

The Sixth Commandment: Sacred Human Life

The Lord says, "Thou shalt not kill" (Ex. 20:13; Deut. 5:17). The word translated as "kill" is never used in the Bible for killing an animal. It refers here to murdering a human being or unlawful manslaughter. Matthew Poole summarized the commandment: "Thou shalt not kill . . . any man or woman, without authority, and without just cause."[4] Human life has special value because God made people in his image (Gen. 1:26–28; 9:6). John Calvin said, "If we do not wish to violate the image of God, we ought to hold our neighbor sacred."[5]

3 J. Douma, *The Ten Commandments: Manual for the Christian Life*, trans. Nelson D. Kloosterman (Phillipsburg, NJ: P&R, 1996), 187.

4 Matthew Poole, *Annotations upon the Holy Bible*, 3 vols. (New York: Robert Carter and Brothers, 1853), on Ex. 20:13 (1:160).

5 Calvin, *Institutes*, 2.8.40.

The sixth commandment exposes the evil of malice against other human beings. Christ teaches that "murders" come "out of the heart" (Matt. 15:19). He also draws out the spirituality of the law, explaining that the commandment "Thou shalt not kill" condemns not just murder but also sinful anger and malicious insults (5:21–22). John says, "Whosoever hateth his brother is a murderer: and ye know that no murderer hath eternal life abiding in him" (1 John 3:15).

Therefore, this commandment prohibits hatred against people because of their ethnicity. John Gill said, "All mankind are our neighbours; they are all the offspring of God, and near akin to one another, being all of one man's blood."[6] God's law says, "The stranger that dwelleth with you shall be unto you as one born among you, and thou shalt love him as thyself" (Lev. 19:34).

It is sin against God to kill an unborn child in the womb (Ex. 21:22–23; Amos 1:13), unless without intervention both the mother and the child would die. Each child is a human person from his or her conception. Job and David each say that in his mother's womb God made "me," a person (Job 10:10–11; Ps. 139:13–16).

The prohibition of murder also condemns suicide, or self-murder.[7] The wrongfulness of killing does not arise from a lack of consent, but from the unjust destruction of a person created in God's image. Francis Turretin explained that suicide is a great sin against God, "who alone is the Lord of life." It is a sin against oneself, against one's nation (by cutting off one of its citizens), against one's family (by plunging loved ones into grief), and, if done by a Christian, against the church (by bringing disgrace on Christianity).[8] When Paul saw his jailer prepare to commit suicide, he shouted, "Do thyself no harm!" (Acts 16:28).

Obedience to the sixth commandment leads us to repent of malicious hatred that delights in the harm of other people: "Let all bitterness, and wrath, and anger, and clamour, and evil speaking, be put away from you, with all malice" (Eph. 4:31). Instead, we must love our neighbors as ourselves

6 John Gill, *A Complete Body of Doctrinal and Practical Divinity* (1839; repr., Paris, AR: The Baptist Standard Bearer, 1995), 770; cf. Acts 17:26, 28.

7 Note the sad cases of wicked Saul (1 Sam. 31:3–4), Ahithophel (2 Sam. 17:23), Zimri (1 Kings 16:18–19), and Judas (Matt. 27:3–5).

8 Francis Turretin, *Institutes of Elenctic Theology*, trans. George Musgrave Giger, ed. James T. Dennison Jr., 3 vols. (Phillipsburg, NJ: P&R, 1992–1997), 11.17.23 (2:116–17).

(Lev. 19:18), even our enemies (Matt. 5:43–45). We should share necessities with those who lack them (Ps. 112:9) and do good to all men (Gal. 6:10).

The Seventh Commandment: Faithful Human Sexuality

The Lord says, "Thou shalt not commit adultery" (Ex. 20:14). Adultery refers to sexual immorality that violates a marriage covenant because at least one of the participants is married to someone else. God ordained marriage as a lifelong covenant between one man and one woman—the only legitimate context for sexual activity (Gen. 1:27–28; 2:18–25). He made the human body good, and the enjoyment of loving sexual activity in marriage is a good gift to "be received with thanksgiving" and "sanctified by the word of God and prayer" (1 Tim. 4:3–5).

The law of God reveals his great displeasure at sexual activity outside of marriage, including fornication (premarital sex), prostitution, adultery, incest, rape, homosexuality, and bestiality.[9]

Sexual purity and faithfulness to one's spouse are crucial aspects of loving one another (Rom. 13:9). The world often confuses sexual lust with love (Prov. 7:18). However, Paul contrasts them by starting his list of "the works of the flesh" with "adultery, fornication, uncleanness, lasciviousness," but then saying that "the fruit of the Spirit is love, joy, peace," and so on (Gal. 5:19, 22).

Sexual purity begins, by grace, in the heart. Our Lord Jesus Christ says, "Whosoever looketh on a woman to lust after her hath committed adultery with her already in his heart" (Matt. 5:28). Samuel Willard said, "We must resist and suppress lascivious thoughts. We ought to withstand them at their first starting, and cast them out as soon as we discover them to have gotten into our minds. . . . If we are consecrated temples to the Spirit of God, we ought to keep the house clean."[10]

Sexual purity in an unclean world requires the diligent use of means. The Westminster Larger Catechism reminds us that "the duties required in the seventh commandment" include "watchfulness over the eyes and all

9 Ex. 22:16–17; Lev. 18:6–23; 19:29; 20:11–12, 14–17; Deut. 22:13–21, 25–27; Rom. 1:24–27; 1 Cor. 5:1; 6:9–10; Heb. 13:4, etc. On human sexuality in general and homosexuality in particular, see chap. 30 of this book.

10 Samuel Willard, *A Compleat Body of Divinity* (1726; facsimile repr., New York: Johnson Reprint, 1969), 671.

the senses; temperance, keeping of chaste company, modesty in apparel; marriage by those that have not the gift of continency, conjugal love, and cohabitation."[11] We must implement this holy resolve: "I will set no wicked thing before mine eyes: I hate the work of them that turn aside; it shall not cleave to me" (Ps. 101:3).

If we are in situations where our sexual desires are frustrated, let us not turn to self-pity or, worse yet, to acts of immorality. Rather, let us devote ourselves to rejoicing in the Lord and serving other people. Whatever our marital status or degree of sexual satisfaction in marriage, we should remember that marriage and sexual activity are temporary gifts from God. His children will advance to greater joys when Christ returns (Luke 20:34–36).

The Eighth Commandment: Rightful Human Property

The Lord says, "Thou shalt not steal" (Ex. 20:15; cf. Deut. 5:19). Stealing is the unlawful taking of another's property. It can be done by fraud and deceit (Lev. 19:11), force (Ex. 22:1; Luke 3:14), or unjust legal and political means (Isa. 1:23). Paul includes "thieves" among those who will not "inherit the kingdom of God" (1 Cor. 6:10).

The prohibition against stealing implies the right to own personal property. This right is grounded on God's creation of man in his image to "have dominion . . . over all the earth" (Gen. 1:26). Man is not the ultimate owner of the other creatures. Rather, he is the Creator's steward, responsible to rule as his representative. As God's servant-kings on earth, human beings have a responsibility to care for the animals and plants.[12] As the Heidelberg Catechism says, the eighth commandment of God forbids, among other things, "all abuse and waste of His gifts."[13]

Love for one's neighbor should engender respect for his rights to own and enjoy his property (1 Tim. 6:17). The law of Moses forbade creditors from walking into a debtor's home to take the collateral for a loan. Creditors had to wait outside while the owner brought it out (Deut. 24:10–11). The law also forbade keeping a poor man's cloak as collateral, lest he be exposed to the cold of the night (Ex. 22:26–27; Deut. 24:12–13). Such laws protect the dignity of all people.

11 The Westminster Larger Catechism (Q. 138), in *RC*, 4:333.

12 Gen. 2:15; Ex. 23:4–5; Lev. 22:28; Deut. 20:19–20; 22:1–4, 6–7; 25:4; Prov. 12:10.

13 The Heidelberg Catechism (LD 42, Q. 110), *TFU*, 108.

The opposite of stealing is not merely avoiding theft but working and giving. Paul says, "Let him that stole steal no more: but rather let him labour, working with his hands the thing which is good, that he may have [something] to give to him that needeth" (Eph. 4:28). Paul exhorts Christians "that with quietness they work, and eat their own bread" (2 Thess. 3:12). However, they must not stop at mere self-love but love their neighbors as themselves. John says, "If anyone has the world's goods and sees his brother in need, yet closes his heart against him, how does God's love abide in him?" (1 John 3:17 ESV). But Paul also says, "If any would not work, neither should he eat" (2 Thess. 3:10).

The Westminster Shorter Catechism summarizes the requirement of the eighth commandment as "the lawful procuring and furthering the wealth and outward estate of ourselves and others."[14] George Swinnock wrote, "In all thy contracts, purchases, and sales, cast an eye upon that golden rule, mentioned by our Saviour."[15] That is, "whatever you wish that others would do to you, do also to them" (Matt. 7:12 ESV).

The Ninth Commandment: True Human Testimony

The Lord says, "Thou shalt not bear false witness against thy neighbour" (Ex. 20:16). This commandment explicitly prohibits giving false testimony in court (perjury). God will most certainly punish the lying witness (Prov. 19:5, 9).

The ninth commandment reveals God's love for the truth. Satan is the original liar (John 8:44). But God cannot lie, as his Word repeatedly tells us.[16] Thus, God's law forbids lying to one another (Lev. 19:11; Eph. 4:24–25). All liars "shall have their part in the lake which burneth with fire and brimstone: which is the second death" (Rev. 21:8).

A lie is an act of verbal communication in which a person intentionally presents something false as if true. However, it is not a lie to hide people in danger of being unjustly killed (1 Kings 18:3–4; 2 Kings 11:1–3) or to disguise oneself to conceal one's identity (1 Kings 20:38, 41). It is also not

14 The Westminster Shorter Catechism (Q. 74), in *RC*, 4:363. Cf. the Baptist Catechism (Q. 79), in *RC*, 4:583.

15 George Swinnock, *The Christian Man's Calling*, in *The Works of George Swinnock*, 5 vols. (1868; repr., Edinburgh: Banner of Truth, 1992), 2:201.

16 Num. 23:19; 1 Sam. 15:29; Titus 1:2; Heb. 6:18.

a lie to speak ambiguously to enemies (2 Kings 6:19) or to tell part of the truth when telling the whole truth would expose people to unjust harm (1 Sam. 16:1–5).

Lying is an act of hatred (Prov. 26:28). One of the most precious gifts we can give to our neighbors is to speak the truth in love (Eph. 4:15). Someone might object that in some cases it is more loving to tell a lie than the truth. But God commands us to speak difficult truths to our brothers and sisters regarding their sins because we love them (Lev. 19:17–18; Prov. 27:5–6). Again, someone might object that sometimes we must tell lies to save people's lives, as the Hebrew midwives and Rahab did (Ex. 1:15–19; Josh. 2:1–7), and were commended by God (Ex. 1:20–21; Heb. 11:31; James 2:25). But they were commended not for lying but for their faith and reverence to God. Augustine said, "It is not the deceit, but their good intention, that is justly praised, and sometimes even rewarded. It is quite enough that the deception should be pardoned."[17] Paul firmly rejects the argument that we should "do evil, that good may come" (Rom. 3:8).

The Westminster Shorter Catechism says, "The ninth commandment requireth the maintaining and promoting of truth between man and man (Zech. 8:16), and of our own and our neighbour's good name (3 John 12), especially in witness-bearing (Prov. 14:5, 25)."[18] To this end, we should avoid gossip and speaking evil of people when it is not necessary.[19] A good reputation has great value, better "than great riches . . . than silver and gold" (Prov. 22:1). Even if we know that someone has sinned, we should desire to deal with his or her sin as privately as possible (Prov. 10:12; 17:9; Matt. 1:19; 18:15). God's prohibition of lying and requirement of speaking the truth should make us slow to speak (James 1:19): "The heart of the righteous studieth to answer: but the mouth of the wicked poureth out evil things" (Prov. 15:28).

The Tenth Commandment: Submissive Human Contentment

The Lord concludes the Ten Commandments by saying, "Thou shalt not covet thy neighbour's house, thou shalt not covet thy neighbour's wife, nor

17 Augustine, *Enchiridion*, chap. 22, in *NPNF*[1], 3:245.

18 The Westminster Shorter Catechism (Q. 77), in *RC*, 4:363. Cf. the Baptist Catechism (Q. 82), in *RC*, 4:584.

19 Lev. 19:16; Ps. 15:2–3; Prov. 11:13; 16:28; 26:20.

his manservant, nor his maidservant, nor his ox, nor his ass, nor any thing that is thy neighbour's" (Ex. 20:17). To "covet" means to desire. What is forbidden here is desiring what rightfully belongs to one's neighbor. The people and objects wrongly desired belong to others. Sinful coveting is rebellion against the God who has forbidden us to have certain relationships or possessions, as when his providence puts them in the rightful possession of others or his law prohibits them to us.

Sexual lust and materialistic greed (prohibited in the seventh and eighth commandments) are sins that involve an intentional *choice* to engage the mind in sinful thoughts (Job 31:24–25; Matt. 5:28). However, the tenth commandment addresses sinful *desires*. These involve the inclination or disposition of the heart but not necessarily a conscious choice. We should distinguish between temptation and sin, but when a person responds to temptation with an inward delight in the idea of sinning, even without the full consent of the will, he has sinned in the heart. He has not loved the Lord his God with all his heart (Deut. 6:5). The "motions of sin"—literally its "passions" or "affections" (plural *pathēma*)—are sin (Rom. 7:5).[20]

The first motion of unbelief in the human heart consisted of coveting: "The woman saw that the tree was good for food, and that it was pleasant to the eyes, and a tree to be desired to make one wise" (Gen. 3:6). God had revealed that the fruit of that tree did not belong to Adam and Eve, but they in effect said, "We need it. We want it. We have a right to it. We will get it." Covetousness is selfishness. Paul warns, "Men shall be lovers of their own selves, covetous" (2 Tim. 3:2). Covetousness takes the greatest love of our hearts and directs it to creatures rather than the Creator (Rom. 1:23, 25).

Repentance from covetousness entails learning "full contentment" with God's will for us:[21] "Let your conversation [manner of life] be without covetousness; and be content with such things as ye have: for he hath said, I will never leave thee, nor forsake thee" (Heb. 13:5). The reason why we need not and must not covet anything belonging to our neighbors is that God says, "I am the Lord thy God. . . . Thou shalt have no other gods before me" (Ex. 20:2–3).

20 The Westminster Confession of Faith (6.5); and the Second London Baptist Confession (6.5), in *RC*, 4:242, 541.

21 The Westminster Shorter Catechism (Q. 80); and the Baptist Catechism (Q. 85), in *RC*, 4:364, 584.

We must look to Christ crucified as the conqueror of all our sin, including its secret lusts (Gal. 5:24). Christ's death is the death of believers to sin (Rom. 6:10–11). John Owen said,

> Consider the sorrows he underwent, the curse he bore, the blood he shed, the cries he put forth, the love that was in all this to your souls, and the mystery of the grace of God therein. Meditate on the vileness, the demerit, and the punishment of sin as represented in the cross, the blood, the death of Christ. Is Christ crucified for sin, and shall not our hearts be crucified with him unto sin? Shall we give entertainment [our warm welcome] unto that, or hearken unto its dalliances [listen to its flirtations], which wounded, which pierced, which slew our dear Lord Jesus? God forbid! Fill your affections with the cross of Christ, that there may be no room for sin.[22]

Suggested Songs to Sing to the Lord

- "Blest be the tie that binds," *THBap*, No. 285
- "Father, I know that all my life is portioned out for me," *THBap*, No. 444

Questions for Meditation or Discussion

1. What does the fifth commandment require of us? What does "honour" mean?
2. What are practical ways that people (children and adults) can show honor to their parents or others in positions above them?
3. Why is it wrong to murder another human being or to desire to do so?
4. What is God's will for the right expression of human sexual activity?
5. How are you guarding yourself against sexual immorality in heart and body? Is there more that you need to do to protect yourself? If so, what?
6. What is stealing? What is the opposite of stealing?
7. What does the ninth commandment require of us in court? In ordinary life?

22 Owen, *The Nature, Power, Deceit, and Prevalency of the Remainders of Indwelling Sin in Believers*, in *WJO*, 6:250–51.

8. What does "covet" mean? What, then, does the tenth commandment prohibit?
9. Someone says, "Coveting cannot be wrong, for it's no sin just to desire something." How do you respond?
10. How can we use the death of Christ to fight against sin? How can you make this practice a regular discipline of your spiritual life?

71

Godly Fear, Prayer, and Hope

Chapter Summary and Key Terms

A crucial part of God's saving grace is the gift of godly fear. The *fear of the Lord* is a childlike awe of him and desire to please him based on love for him and a sanctifying awareness of his holy glory. The fear of God moves believers to practice self-denial to follow Christ. Conscious of his majesty, they exercise sober watchfulness over their lives in expectation of his return. If for a season their faith and obedience decrease and their sins increase (*backsliding*), they must turn back to the Lord to receive his renewing grace. Saving grace also moves believers to pray and to have hope in God. Christian *prayer* is presenting our desires to God through Christ with thanksgiving. Christian *hope* is the believer's expectant desire for God and eternal life with him, exercised through faith in his promises and love that delights in him as one's portion.

IN PREVIOUS CHAPTERS, we have studied several evidences of God's saving grace. In this chapter, we close our discussion of the experience of salvation by highlighting some other evidences. These are the fear of the Lord, self-denial, sober watchfulness, recovery from backsliding, the practice of prayer, and hope. These effects of saving grace both confirm our assurance and call us to grow.

The Fear of the Lord

People today tend to regard the *fear of the Lord* as bad for our emotional health. But God says in his Word that fearing him is necessary to holiness and happiness (Psalm 112). The fear of the Lord springs naturally from faith in his promises and engenders hope in his love (31:19).

Solomon says, "Let us hear the conclusion of the whole matter: Fear God, and keep his commandments: for this is the whole duty of man. For God shall bring every work into judgment, with every secret thing, whether it be good, or whether it be evil" (Eccles. 12:13–14). John Murray said, "The fear of God is the soul of godliness."[1]

The Bible speaks about different ways in which people might fear God. They might fear him with outward acts of worship while their hearts remain far from him (Isa. 29:13). They might be frightened emotionally when they see or hear of God's mighty works (Ex. 15:14–16; Luke 5:26). They might have a conscientious concern to be moral and avoid doing injustice (Gen. 20:11). They might suffer from an accusing conscience and a fearful anticipation of God's wrath (Prov. 28:1; Isa. 33:14). Finally, there is godly, childlike fear of God based on the gospel (Deut. 10:12; Pss. 33:18; 103:10–18). At the heart of this good fear is a desire to please God (2 Cor. 5:9–11). John Brown of Edinburgh said, "It matters little to them that the world frowns on them, if he smiles; and it matters little to them that the world smiles, if he frowns."[2]

Apart from God's saving grace, people do not fear the Lord with faith and love, even if they are afraid of him and his judgment: "There is no fear of God before their eyes" (Rom. 3:18). But the Lord says of his elect, "I will put my fear in their hearts, that they shall not depart from me" (Jer. 32:40). Jesus Christ was anointed by the Spirit "of the fear of the LORD" to pour out that Spirit on his people (Isa. 11:2; 44:3–5; Acts 9:31). Murray said, "The church walks in the fear of the Lord because the Spirit of Christ indwells, fills, directs, and rests upon the church and the Spirit of Christ is the Spirit of the fear of the Lord."[3]

Slave-like fear is a mixture of terror and hatred toward God. It is driven only by self-love. Childlike fear comes with love for God (Deut. 6:1–2, 5). Godly fear arises from knowing the magnificent goodness and merciful

1 John Murray, *Principles of Conduct: Aspects of Biblical Ethics* (Grand Rapids, MI: Eerdmans, 1957), 229.

2 John Brown of Edinburgh, *Expository Discourses on the First Epistle of the Apostle Peter* (New York: Robert Carter and Brothers), 103.

3 Murray, *Principles of Conduct*, 230.

greatness of God. The essence of fearing the Lord is an awareness of his holy glory. Thus, "the fear of the LORD is the beginning of wisdom: and the knowledge of the holy is understanding" (Prov. 9:10). A God-fearing person rejoices in God's majesty (Ps. 2:11). The fear of God is practical "wisdom" that guides a person "to depart from evil" (Job 28:28). Godly fear fills life with boldness and zeal: "In the fear of the LORD is strong confidence. . . . The fear of the LORD is a fountain of life" (Prov. 14:26–27). The fear of God is necessary for the Christian life. Peter commands us, "Fear God" (1 Pet. 2:17). Paul says, "Work out your own salvation with fear and trembling" (Phil. 2:12). He also says, "Let us cleanse ourselves from all filthiness of the flesh and spirit, perfecting holiness in the fear of God" (2 Cor. 7:1).

How can we grow in this precious grace of the fear of God? Let us pray, "Teach me thy way, O LORD; I will walk in thy truth: unite my heart to fear thy name" (Ps. 86:11). Let us think often of the greatness of God and praise him: "There is none like unto thee, O LORD; thou art great, and thy name is great in might. Who would not fear thee, O King of nations?" (Jer. 10:6–7). Murray said that "the controlling sense of the majesty and holiness of God and the profound reverence which" it produces is "the essence of the fear of God."[4] Therefore, we should meditate on God's grace in the gospel: "There is forgiveness with thee, that thou mayest be feared" (Ps. 130:4). John Bunyan said, "There is nothing in heaven or earth that can so *awe* the heart as the grace of God."[5]

Remind yourself that you live each moment before God's eyes (Prov. 15:3). Stay alert to sins that are especially contrary to the fear of God, such as pride (Rom. 11:20). Beware, too, of sinful fears. A legalistic "spirit of bondage" is quite opposite to a childlike reverence toward the Lord (Rom. 8:15). Another sinful fear is the fear of man: "The fear of man bringeth a snare: but whoso putteth his trust in the LORD shall be safe" (Prov. 29:25).

Self-Denial

The fear of the Lord moves us to deny ourselves of anything contrary to God's glory or will. There is no Christianity without self-denial. The Lord Jesus Christ says, "If any man will come after me, let him deny himself,

4 Murray, *Principles of Conduct*, 237.

5 John Bunyan, *The Water of Life*, in *The Works of John Bunyan*, ed. George Offor, 3 vols. (1854; repr., Edinburgh: Banner of Truth, 1991), 3:546, emphasis original.

and take up his cross daily, and follow me" (Luke 9:23). John Calvin said that "the denial of ourselves" is the "first step" of godliness and "the sum of the Christian life."[6] Believers must sacrifice to serve Christ. They must suffer persecution for their confession of him. After all, the cross was an instrument of death (Phil. 2:8). Therefore, we must put away all that is incompatible with Christ's demands on our lives. This includes things that are inherently sinful, but it also includes things good in themselves that must be given up at times to keep Christ's word (Luke 14:25–27).

To take up our crosses also means renouncing our self-righteousness, for only a condemned lawbreaker died on a cross, a sign of God's curse (Deut. 21:22–23). Carrying our crosses means forsaking our pride and lust for honor among men. The cross was an instrument of humiliation and shame (Heb. 12:2) and a display of weakness (2 Cor. 13:4). Thus, the "self" we especially must deny to follow Christ is our self-righteous, self-sufficient pride.

What we gain is worth the pain. After issuing the call to self-denial, Christ says, "For whosoever will save his life shall lose it: but whosoever will lose his life for my sake, the same shall save it. For what is a man advantaged, if he gain the whole world, and lose himself, or be cast away?" (Luke 9:24–25). Christ's disciples renounce themselves and this world to gain eternal life in the age to come (John 12:25). Thus, self-denial is not really self-hatred but self-love. But it is self-love directed by wisdom and love for God.

Paul says that God's grace teaches us that

> denying ungodliness and worldly lusts, we should live soberly, righteously, and godly, in this present world; looking for that blessed hope, and the glorious appearing of the great God and our Saviour Jesus Christ; who gave himself for us, that he might redeem us from all iniquity, and purify unto himself a peculiar people, zealous of good works. (Titus 2:12–14)

By denying ourselves, we gain the eternal enjoyment of God's glory in Christ. And we acknowledge that we were bought at a price (1 Cor. 6:19–20). Calvin said, "We are not our own. . . . We are God's: let us therefore live for him and die for him."[7]

6 Calvin, *Institutes*, 3.7, title and sec. 1.

7 Calvin, *Institutes*, 3.7.1.

Sober Watchfulness

The fear of the Lord is a mindset controlled by the awareness of God. Together with the self-denial of Christian discipleship, this entails spiritual sobriety. The word translated as "soberly" (Titus 2:12) means thinking clearly so as to exercise discretion and self-restraint. True sobriety is a gift of divine grace by the Holy Spirit (2 Tim. 1:7). This spiritual renewal of the mind enables a person to make a realistic assessment of himself and not be puffed up with pride (Rom. 12:2–3).

Spiritual sobriety is closely tied to the virtue of watchfulness. Peter says, "But the end of all things is at hand: be ye therefore sober, and *watch* unto prayer" (1 Pet. 4:7). John Owen defined watchfulness as "a universal carefulness and diligence, exercising itself in and by all ways and means prescribed by God, over our hearts and ways, the baits and methods of Satan, the occasions and advantages of sin in the world, that we be not entangled."[8] Brian Hedges says that spiritual watchfulness has four ingredients: wakefulness (versus spiritual slumber), attentiveness (to Christ, ourselves, and one another), vigilance (against sin and Satan), and expectancy (for the coming of the Lord).[9]

Christians must keep watch against temptation and sin. The Lord Jesus Christ told his disciples, "Watch and pray, that ye enter not into temptation: the spirit indeed is willing, but the flesh is weak" (Matt. 26:41). Watchfulness also keeps us attentive to hearing and keeping God's Word (Prov. 8:34). Believers must also maintain a constant readiness to meet their Lord. Christ says, "Take ye heed, watch and pray: for ye know not when the time is" (Mark 13:33).

Recovery from Backsliding

The Christian life is a race that we run "looking unto Jesus" until by grace we join him in glory (Heb. 12:1–2).[10] However, on the road to heaven, Christians can backslide. *Backsliding* is a season of weakened faith, increasing sin, and decreasing obedience. Wilhelmus à Brakel

8 Owen, *Of Temptation*, in *WJO*, 6:100–101.

9 Brian G. Hedges, *Watchfulness: Recovering a Lost Spiritual Discipline* (Grand Rapids, MI: Reformation Heritage Books, 2018), 18–34.

10 See Joel R. Beeke, *Getting Back in the Race: The Cure for Backsliding* (Adelphi, MD: Cruciform, 2011).

described backsliding as "spiritual winter" in one's life, "the very opposite of growth."[11]

Backsliders must return to the Lord, and returning requires repentance. Hosea 14:1 says, "O Israel, return unto the LORD thy God; for thou hast fallen by thine iniquity." Backsliders must also receive the grace of God. Hosea 14:4 highlights three graces in Christ that are especially precious to those who have wandered from the Lord: the grace of sanctification ("I will heal their backsliding"), the grace of adoption ("I will love them freely"), and the grace of justification ("For mine anger is turned away from him").

By drawing these graces from Christ by faith, backsliders can recover spiritual vitality and fruitfulness. They learn the lesson of Hosea 14:8: "From me is thy fruit found." They have come to experience their constant need for communion with God by union with Christ. The Lord Jesus says, "I am the vine, ye are the branches: He that abideth in me, and I in him, the same bringeth forth much fruit: for without me ye can do nothing" (John 15:5).

Christian Prayer

Nothing is more characteristic of the child of God than that he prays to God (Rom. 8:15; Gal. 4:6). Prayer should be as natural to the regenerate soul as breathing is to a living body. When the Lord told Ananias that Saul of Tarsus had been converted, he said, "Behold, he prayeth" (Acts 9:11). J. C. Ryle said, "A habit of prayer is one of the surest marks of a true Christian."[12]

A Description of Christian Prayer

Prayer is a "necessary" part of the Christian life, as the Heidelberg Catechism reminds us, "because God will give His grace and Holy Spirit to those only, who with sincere desires continually ask them of Him, and are thankful for them."[13]

What is Christian prayer? The Baptist Catechism says, "Prayer is an offering up of our desires to God, by the assistance of the Holy Spirit for things

11 Brakel, *CRS*, 4:159–60.

12 J. C. Ryle, *Home Truths*, 4th ed. (Ipswich, England: William Hunt, 1859), 2:106.

13 The Heidelberg Catechism (LD 45, Q. 116), in *TFU*, 110.

agreeable to His will, in the name of Christ, believing; with confession of our sins and thankful acknowledgment of His mercies."[14] David says, "Trust in him at all times; ye people, pour out your heart before him: God is a refuge for us" (Ps. 62:8). Christian prayer is possible only by the power of the Holy Spirit (Gal. 4:6).

Christ taught his disciples to pray in his name (John 14:13–14; 16:24). That means, as the Westminster Larger Catechism says, "to ask mercy for his sake; not by bare mentioning of his name, but by drawing our encouragement to pray, and our boldness, strength, and hope of acceptance in prayer, from Christ and his mediation."[15]

John says, "This is the confidence that we have in him, that, if we ask any thing according to his will, he heareth us" (1 John 5:14). In the Lord's Prayer, Christ has given us directions for praying according to God's will (Matt. 6:9–13).

Christians are to confess their sins to God, for "if we confess our sins, he is faithful and just to forgive us our sins" (1 John 1:9). And they should thank him for his good gifts. Paul says, "Do not be anxious about anything, but in everything by prayer and supplication with thanksgiving let your requests be made known to God" (Phil. 4:6 ESV).

An Exhortation to Prayerful Praying

Alexander Ross said, "A man may pray with his lips and yet not pray with an intense desire of the soul."[16] We might call this *prayerless praying*. By contrast, James says that Elijah "prayed earnestly" (James 5:17)—literally he "prayed in his prayer" (KJV mg.). This could be called *prayerful praying*.

Is your prayer life a missile that shatters satanic powers or is it like a harmless toy that Satan sleeps beside? We are often more concerned about what our listeners think of our words than the quality of our communication with God. Where is our prayerful passion for the presence of God? We must go beyond complaining about our weak prayers and repent of our coldness. We must confess our prayerless praying to God and plead for the

14 The Baptist Catechism (Q. 105), in *RC*, 4:587. Cf. the Westminster Shorter Catechism (Q. 98) and Larger Catechism (Q. 178), in *RC*, 4:347, 367.

15 The Westminster Larger Catechism (Q. 180), in *RC*, 4:347.

16 Alexander Ross, *The Epistles of James and John*, The New International Commentary on the New Testament (Grand Rapids, MI: Eerdmans, 1954), 102.

renewal of our souls. Prayer is the thermometer of our souls. Let us then take practical steps toward prayerful praying.

Remember the value of prayer. Daniel was ready to die rather than give up prayer (Dan. 6:6–10). Appreciate the value of prayer, even if unanswered, as a means of communing with God. Maintain the priority of prayer. Watch and pray "with all perseverance" (Eph. 6:18).

Keep a blood-washed conscience for boldness in prayer. Go quickly to Jesus Christ as soon as your conscience smites you. Find cleansing, forgiveness, and liberty in his blood to draw near to God (Eph. 3:12; Heb. 9:14; 10:19). Speak with sincerity in prayer. To pray with your mouth what is not truly in your heart is hypocrisy (Isa. 29:13). It would be better to confess the coldness of your heart and cry out for heartwarming grace.

Cultivate a spirit of continual prayer. Paul says, "Pray without ceasing" (1 Thess. 5:17). Keep set times of prayer with others (Acts 3:1) and private devotions (Matt. 6:6). Develop a habit of regularly shooting short prayers up to heaven (Neh. 2:4). Pray for many people and churches, as the apostle Paul calls for "supplication for all saints" (Eph 6:18).

Read the Bible for prayer and pray the Bible to God. Christ says, "If ye abide in me, and my words abide in you, ye shall ask what ye will, and it shall be done unto you" (John 15:7). Use variety in prayer: praise, confession, lamentation, petition, thanks, and intercession for others.

Believe that God answers the prayers of his children. Faith in God is essential to answered prayer (Mark 11:22–24; James 1:5–6). Wrestle with God until he blesses you (Gen. 32:24–30). When you pray, meditate on the gospel of Christ. Paul says, "For through him we both have access by one Spirit unto the Father" (Eph. 2:18). May it not be said of us that "there is none that calleth upon thy name, that stirreth up himself to take hold of thee" (Isa. 64:7).

The Hope of Glorification

The last step in the order of salvation is glorification. We will open up this precious subject later when we study Christ's return, the resurrection of the dead, judgment day, and eternal life with God (chaps. 92, 93, and 95). Here we will end our study of salvation with a meditation on the grace of *hope* and how it shapes the Christian life.

Hope is the expectation of some future good. Christian hope is a saving grace (2 Thess. 2:16). It is produced by the new birth through the power of the risen Christ (1 Pet. 1:3, 21). People outside of God's covenantal promise have "no hope" (Eph. 2:12), but all believers in Christ share "one hope" (4:4). Waiting on the Lord is a defining mark of the people whom God will save and bring to the inheritance (Pss. 25:3, 5, 21; 37:9, 34). Isaac Ambrose said, "If we long for his coming, then will he come to satisfy our longings."[17]

The ultimate object of Christian hope is the living God himself (1 Tim. 4:10; 5:5; 6:17) and eternal life with him (Titus 1:2; 3:7). The "blessed hope" of the church is "the appearing of the glory of our great God and Savior Jesus Christ" (Titus 2:13 ESV). We have such hope when the Lord sanctifies our hearts to desire him supremely (Isa. 26:8): "The LORD is my portion, saith my soul; therefore will I hope in him" (Lam. 3:24).

Hope is closely connected to faith and love (1 Cor. 13:13). By hope, we reach in faith for what we do not yet fully possess (Rom. 8:24–25). However, hope brings into the present an anticipation of the joys promised for the future (12:12; 15:13). It is love that delights in God so much that it waits patiently to obtain his glory. Paul says that love "beareth all things, believeth all things, hopeth all things, endureth all things" (1 Cor. 13:7).

God's means of producing hope is his Word (Rom. 15:4). Hope depends on the confidence that God cannot lie (Titus 1:2; Heb. 6:18). People commonly say "I hope so" as a mere wish. But biblical hope in God is a solid "expectation" with "great certainty" obtained "by faith" in God's true Word, as William Ames said.[18]

Hope has a purifying influence on the whole life: "When he shall appear, we shall be like him; for we shall see him as he is. And every man that hath this hope in him purifieth himself, even as he is pure" (1 John 3:2–3). Brakel said, "The result of hope is holy industry. . . . The end in view causes us to be active and to take the means in hand."[19]

The saints must persevere in hope to the end (Col. 1:22–23; Heb. 3:6; 6:11). Believers wait on the Lord for complete salvation. They also wait on him for present strength to endure to the end (Isa. 40:31): "Wait on the

17 Isaac Ambrose, *Looking unto Jesus: A View of the Everlasting Gospel* (Philadelphia: J. B. Lippincott & Co., 1856), 670–71.

18 William Ames, *The Marrow of Theology*, trans. John D. Eusden (Grand Rapids, MI: Baker, 1968), 2.6.8–9 (247).

19 Brakel, *CRS*, 3:324.

Lord: be of good courage, and he shall strengthen thine heart: wait, I say, on the Lord" (Ps. 27:14).

What amazing blessings come to us through the grace of hope! Owen said, "Hope is a glorious grace.... By it we are purified, sanctified, saved."[20] Therefore, as Paul says, "be ye stedfast, unmoveable, always abounding in the work of the Lord, forasmuch as ye know that your labour is not in vain in the Lord" (1 Cor. 15:58).

Suggested Songs to Sing to the Lord

- Psalm 112, "Praise ye the Lord. The man is blessed," *THBap*, No. 768
- Psalm 130, "From out the depths I cry, O Lord, to Thee," *Psalter*, No. 362; *THBap*, No. 463

Questions for Meditation or Discussion

1. What different kinds of fear toward God do the Holy Scriptures reveal?
2. How should a Christian seek to grow in the fear of God?
3. What did Christ mean when he said, "If any man will come after me, let him deny himself, and take up his cross daily, and follow me" (Luke 9:23)?
4. What does the Bible mean by being "sober"?
5. What is the Christian's duty with respect to being watchful?
6. How does Hosea 14 show us the way that backsliders can be restored?
7. How can we describe Christian prayer?
8. What do the authors mean by "prayerless praying"? What is the antidote to it?
9. What is the grace of hope?
10. How would you describe the influence of hope on your life? What difference would it make if your hope were to increase tenfold? How might you seek to grow in hope?

20 Owen, *Phronēma tou Pneumatos*, in *WJO*, 7:321.

PART 6

THE DOCTRINE OF THE CHURCH

Section 6A

The Church's Identity

72

Introduction to the Doctrine of the Church

Chapter Summary and Key Terms

The doctrine of the church is well worth our study. The true church is God's beloved people, among whom he is present to give spiritual life and growth. By learning what God says about his church, we are equipped to build up the true church for his glory for generations to come. The word translated as *church* means an assembly or congregation. The term is used of God's people under both the Old and New Testaments. The Holy Scriptures reveal that God has had one church throughout history. Yet he has developed it over time to its present form in the new covenant under the ascended Christ and the ministry of the outpoured Holy Spirit.

THE TRUE *CHURCH* is a supernatural work of God. His people are the beginning of the new creation (Isa. 65:17–18; Eph. 2:15–16). The church cannot be explained by merely human factors. God is in her midst (Ps. 46:4–5). And yet, the church is very human due to the many faults and frailties of its members. As Bernard of Clairvaux said, the church is both a "house of clay" and God's "royal palace."[1] In this chapter, we will introduce the doctrine of the church. And by *church*, we do not mean the building where Christians worship, but the true people of God.

1 Bernard of Clairvaux, *St. Bernard's Sermons on the Canticle of Canticles*, 2 vols. (Dublin: Browne and Nolan, 1920), sermon 27 (1:317).

The Importance of the Church

Why is the church worthy of our study? Let's consider some reasons.

First, *the church is God's people, whom he loves.* Just as a husband should have a special love for his wife, Paul says, "Christ also loved the church, and gave himself for it" (Eph. 5:25). If we love God, then we will love what he loves—the church.

Second, *the church is God's plan for his people's spiritual growth.* The Lord Jesus gave ministers of the Word for "the edifying of the body of Christ" (Eph. 4:11–12). Every member of the church must love the others so that the whole church grows (v. 16). The church is "the mother of us all" (Gal. 4:26). John Calvin said that God gathers his children into the church, "that they may be guided by her motherly care until they mature and at last reach the goal of faith."[2]

Third, *the church is God's place, where he is present.* Christ says, "Where two or three are gathered together in my name, there am I in the midst of them" (Matt. 18:20). The Lord Jesus promises that as the church makes disciples of all nations, "Lo, I am with you always, even unto the end of the world" (28:20).

Fourth, *the church is God's purpose for all things.* God created all things for the sake of his Son (Col. 1:16; Heb. 1:2). He sent his Son to redeem his people (Gal. 1:4–5; Titus 2:14). He then exalted Christ to the highest place and "gave him to be the head over all things to the church" (Eph. 1:22). Thus, the church stands at the center of God's purpose for the universe (3:9–11).

The Practical Benefits of the Doctrine of the Church

There are several benefits of studying the doctrine of the church.

First, by learning the doctrine of the church, we are better equipped to *follow God's revelation instead of human ideas.* Paul compared the church to "God's building," and said that to please God on judgment day we must build on the right foundation (Christ) and use the right materials (God's wisdom, 1 Cor. 3:9–13).

Second, by learning the doctrine of the church, we are better equipped to *distinguish true churches from false churches and healthy churches from unhealthy ones.* Christ warns of "false Christs, and false prophets" (Matt. 24:24). Many groups claim to be the true church of God. Churches may have a repu-

2 Calvin, *Institutes*, 4.1.1.

tation for being lively but be quite dead (Rev. 3:1). This doctrine helps us to tell the difference and judge which churches are good for us and our families.

Third, by learning the doctrine of the church, we are better equipped to *benefit from the public means of grace*. It is easy to go through the motions of worship without understanding why we do these things or how to make the best use of them. But the church's ordinances have long been called "the means of grace" because God works through them (John 17:17).

Fourth, by learning the doctrine of the church, we are better equipped to *make visible the invisible realities of our faith*. People cannot see God or our faith in him. But they see the church and how it acts. Christ says, "By this shall all men know that ye are my disciples, if ye have love one to another" (John 13:35).

Fifth, by learning the doctrine of the church, we are better equipped to *pass on a godly heritage to future generations*. The ordinances of the church were designed by God to preserve the memory of great historical events and doctrines. When our children ask, "Why do we do these things?" we tell them about the Lord's great works of salvation (Ex. 12:24–27; 1 Cor. 11:26).

The Meaning of the Term "Church"

The Bible uses many terms for the church. For example, Peter says, "Ye are a chosen generation, a royal priesthood, an holy nation, a peculiar people" (1 Pet. 2:9). These are the same titles given to Old Testament Israel (Ex. 19:5–6; Deut. 7:6).

The Greek word translated as "church" appears in passages of the Septuagint (the Greek translation of the Old Testament) regarding the assembly of Israel. The same phrase translated as "church of God" (1 Tim. 3:5) is used of God's worshipers in Israel (Neh. 13:1).

What does the word translated as "church" mean? The Greek term means an "assembly" or "congregation." The Old Testament often refers to Israel as an "assembly" or "congregation" (Deut. 9:10; 18:16; 23:1–3; etc.). The term especially denotes the assembly of God's people to worship in his special presence. John Murray said, "The assembly is the covenant people of God gathered before him."[3]

In the New Testament, the word *church* often refers to a local church—that is, a particular Christian congregation. Often the singular *church* is

3 John Murray, *Collected Writings of John Murray*, 4 vols. (Edinburgh: Banner of Truth, 1982), 2:321.

identified with a particular city, such as "the church which was at Jerusalem" (Acts 8:1) or "the church that was at Antioch" (13:1)—or a private "house" where it met (Rom. 16:5). Other singular uses of *church* refer to the whole body of people whom Christ is saving (Matt. 16:18; Eph. 5:23–25).

A Biblical Theology of the Church

How did God unfold the doctrine of the church over the course of redemptive history? The Bible shows the church's basic continuity and developing identity from Genesis through the New Testament.

The One Church through History

The New Testament makes it clear that there has been one church or people of God through the ages. The promise of the "seed" that would crush the Serpent's head (Gen. 3:15) is fulfilled in the church. Paul says, "The God of peace shall bruise Satan under your feet shortly" (Rom. 16:20). The physical seed of Abraham, Isaac, and Jacob continues today as the Jewish people. The spiritual seed of Abraham, however, consists of all who belong to Christ, both Jews and Gentiles, and they are the heirs of the promises (Gal. 3:28–29).

When Christ and his apostles spoke of God's people as the "church," they employed a familiar term often applied to Israel's assembly or congregation in the Greek Old Testament (Ezra 2:64; 10:8; Neh. 7:66).

Though the new covenant church is composed of members from many nations and peoples (Rev. 5:9), it is still described as God's "nation" and "people" (Titus 2:14; 1 Pet. 2:9–10), just as Israel was (Ex. 19:5–6; Deut. 7:6). Paul quotes words that the Lord spoke to Israel—"I will walk among you, and will be your God, and ye shall be my people" (Lev. 26:12)—and applies them to the church (2 Cor. 6:16). The title "the people of God" is applied in the same New Testament epistle to both Israel in the days of Moses and believers in Christ today (Heb. 4:9–11; 11:25).

Therefore, we conclude with the Belgic Confession that Christ's "church hath been from the beginning of the world and will continue to the end thereof."[4] In its most essential sense, the church consists of all those for whom Christ died and whom he will present perfect on the last day (Eph. 5:25–27).

4 The Belgic Confession (Art. 27), in *TFU*, 47.

The church did not simply replace Israel. Rather, the New Testament church consists of the remnant of faithful Israel expanded to include the believing Gentiles in Christ as "fellowcitizens" in God's holy nation (Eph. 2:19) and "fellowheirs" of the ancient covenants (3:6). God's church in the Old Testament is not identical in every way to the church in the New Testament (Heb. 12:18–24). But there is one covenant of grace.

The Developing Church through History

In the Holy Scriptures, we find a development in the church as God's eternal covenant of grace was revealed step by step in distinct historical covenants and finally in the new covenant when Christ came (see chaps. 39–41).

The church of God is foreshadowed in the creation of God's image bearers (Gen. 1:27). God created his people as a family, each one bearing his image as sons resemble their father (5:1–3) and multiplying to fill the earth (1:28). But man's breaking of God's covenant showed the need for God to form a church by his saving grace. The Lord revealed his plan to save his church in the promise of the victorious "seed" (Gen. 3:15). The seed of the woman has a twofold meaning, referring to both Christ and the people in union with him.

The Lord gave more definite promises to his church in his covenant with the offspring of Abraham, Isaac, and Jacob (Gen. 12:1–3; 17:1–8). However, not all their physical descendants were part of the blessed seed that God had elected (Rom. 9:6–13). At the heart of God's promise of seed to Abraham were Christ and those in union with him by faith (Gal. 3:16, 26–29).

God grew the seed of Abraham from a family to a people that he then redeemed and called as the national assembly of Israel. At Mount Sinai, the Lord established his direct rule over them through his covenant of law. Geerhardus Vos said, "In essence, the church under the old and new covenant is the same; in form and manifestation there is a difference.... The church under the old dispensation was more than church; it was equally state ... a national church."[5] The Lord also ordered the public worship of his people with many ceremonies that foreshadowed Christ. Through David and his offspring, the Lord established the holy city of Jerusalem as the center of his kingdom and the location of his temple (Ps. 122:1–5; Neh. 11:1).

5 Geerhardus Vos, *Reformed Dogmatics*, ed. Richard B. Gaffin, trans. Annemie Godbehere et al., 5 vols. (Bellingham, WA: Lexham, 2012–2014), 5:7.

After centuries of patience with Israel's disobedience, the Lord judged the covenant seed through the exile, preserved them in it, and brought them back to the land. He also revealed the new covenant promise of a faithful people (Jer. 31:31–34; 32:38–41). God even said, "Many nations shall be joined to the Lord in that day, and shall be my people" (Zech. 2:11).

Christ began to form the new covenant community by calling his disciples. The Lord Jesus preached throughout Israel (Matt. 9:35). Those who rejected him were cut off from the people of God and the messianic kingdom (21:42–43; Rom. 11:20). But his disciples are heirs of the kingdom, the new Israel (Matt. 5:3–12; 19:28).

The new covenant is a testament that went into effect upon the death of the testator (Heb. 9:14–17). Christ gave his life for the church (Eph. 5:25). He offered himself "to make propitiation for the sins of the people" (Heb. 2:17 ESV). Christ's sacrifice abolished the old covenant ceremonies (10:1–6, 18). He then rose from the dead and commissioned the apostolic church for the mission to the nations (Luke 24:44–48; Acts 1:1–8). Thus, the remnant of godly Israel gathered around Christ as his disciples became the core of the international church.

The day of Pentecost inaugurated a new era for the church when Christ, having ascended into heaven, baptized his people with the Holy Spirit (Acts 2). God's people have been regenerated by the Holy Spirit through all ages. However, Pentecost represented a great advance in the Spirit's work to empower every saint to serve God effectively and extend his kingdom throughout the world. Though standing in clear continuity with the godly in ancient Israel, the church in its full New Testament sense is the creation of God the Son incarnate by his Spirit. It is the assembly of God's people in the last days.[6] Its members already gather around the glory of God in Christ. The church on earth now meets as assemblies of exiles and pilgrims in various places among the nations (1 Pet. 1:1; 2:11).

The true identity of the church will one day appear when the returning Lord vindicates and glorifies his saints (Matt. 25:31–34). The ultimate destiny of the church is to dwell with God in the heavenly city and new garden (Revelation 21–22).

6 On the inauguration of the last days with Christ's first coming, see chap. 87.

One practical lesson that we can learn from studying the development of God's people through the ages is the unchanging faithfulness of God. Moses told Israel, "Know therefore that the Lord thy God, he is God, the faithful God" (Deut. 7:9). Solomon said, "There hath not failed one word of all his good promise, which he promised by the hand of Moses his servant" (1 Kings 8:56). Paul says, "God is true.... For all the promises of God in him [Christ] are yea, and in him Amen, unto the glory of God by us" (2 Cor. 1:18–20). If God has been so faithful to his people over the course of thousands of years, then we can trust that he will be faithful to us as well.

Suggested Songs to Sing to the Lord

- "Glorious things of thee are spoken," *THBap*, No. 269
- Psalm 22:23–27, "All ye that fear Jehovah's Name," *Psalter*, No. 48; *THBap*, No. 6

Questions for Meditation or Discussion

1. How would you explain the importance of the church in terms of God's (1) people, (2) plan, (3) place, and (4) purpose?
2. Why is the doctrine of the church important for knowing how to build the church and do evangelism?
3. Of the practical benefits of studying the doctrine of the church, which is most precious to you? Why?
4. What titles are given to the church in 1 Peter 2:9? Where do these titles come from?
5. What does the word translated as "church" mean? How is this word used in the Bible?
6. How do the authors argue that old covenant Israel and the new covenant church are one people?
7. How would you describe the changes in God's people from the garden of Eden through the end of the Old Testament?
8. How did Christ form the new covenant community by his preaching, death, resurrection, ascension, and pouring out of the Holy Spirit?
9. What is one practical lesson that the authors draw out of the development of God's people through the ages? What does that lesson mean to you personally?

73

Describing and Defining the Church

Chapter Summary and Key Terms

The Bible describes the church through various metaphors. The church is the flock of the Good Shepherd. It is the city of God. It is the house of the Lord, where he dwells. It is the *bride* of Christ and the mother of believers. And it is the *body* of Christ. We may define the church as the assembly of God's people in his special presence through his Son by his Spirit. God creates the church by the Father's election, the Son's redemption, and the Spirit's regeneration. We may distinguish between the *church militant* on earth and the *church triumphant* in glory. We may also distinguish between a *particular church* in a specific place and the *universal church* throughout the world. The universal church is both the *invisible church* in its saving grace and the *visible church* in its marks. Not all people who have formal membership in the church are saved, and not all the saved are able to have formal membership in a church.

IF SOMEONE WERE TO ASK, "What is the greatest work that God has ever made?" we would probably point to something grand, such as the galaxies. However, God's most important creation is his people. Francis Turretin said, "The church is the primary work of the holy Trinity."[1] To better understand this glorious work of God, in this chapter we will consider some of the Bible's metaphors for the church and give a definition of the church with some distinctions.

1 Francis Turretin, *Institutes of Elenctic Theology*, trans. George Musgrave Giger, ed. James T. Dennison Jr., 3 vols. (Phillipsburg, NJ: P&R, 1992–1997), 18.1.3 (3:1).

Metaphors for the Church

A metaphor is a word or phrase used to refer to something to which it is similar but not exactly the same. Important metaphors for the church are flock, city, house, bride, mother, and body.

First, one of the oldest metaphors for the church is the *flock* of God (Gen. 49:24). A flock of sheep depends on its shepherd for guidance, provision, and protection. The Lord is the "Shepherd of Israel," who leads his people "like a flock" (Ps. 80:1; cf. 23:1). The hope of Israel is that their Lord and Shepherd will come and lovingly gather his flock (Isa. 40:11). The Son of David is the great human Shepherd of Israel (Jer. 23:1–6; Ezek. 34:1–31).

As the Good Shepherd, Christ laid down his life for the sheep (John 10:11–15). He then took up his life again and calls his sheep together as one flock (vv. 16–18). Those whom the Father has given to him are his sheep, and they listen to him, follow him, and receive eternal life from the Father and the Son, who are one (vv. 26–30). The elders of the church are servants of this great Shepherd who care for his flock (1 Pet. 5:1–4; cf. John 21:15–17).

Second, the church also is called the *city* of God (Ps. 46:4). The city of Jerusalem, built on the hill called Zion, had a central place in God's plan (Ps. 132:13–14). Solomon built God's house there, according to the Lord's covenant with David (2 Sam. 7:4–17). "Jerusalem" and "Zion" can refer to the people of God delivered from all evil and fully blessed (Isa. 35:10; Zeph. 3:14–17). Peter says that God is building his house in Zion by laying believers as living stones on Christ (1 Pet. 2:6; citing Isa. 28:16). Paul writes of the "Jerusalem which is above [and] is free" (Gal. 4:25–26).

Believers look for "a city which hath foundations, whose builder and maker is God," a "heavenly" city (Heb. 11:10, 13, 16). In the new covenant, worshipers already have access to "the city of the living God, the heavenly Jerusalem" (12:22). Those who overcome this world are citizens of "the city of my God, which is new Jerusalem" (Rev. 3:12). Zion is now located at the throne of God, where the assembly of his true Israel worships Christ (14:1–5). Yet "the beloved city" is also on earth, trampled by the nations (11:2; 20:9). In the closing vision of Revelation, "the holy city, new Jerusalem," appears, "coming down from God out of heaven" (21:2).

Third, the New Testament describes the church as the *house* of God. In the Old Testament, God's house was the tabernacle (Ex. 29:42–46; 40:34–38) and later the temple (1 Kings 8:10–13). These were the places where God was with his people in his special presence.

Christ is the living tabernacle, God dwelling with man (John 1:14). Christ abolished the requirement of worship at the temple in Jerusalem (4:19–24) and foretold the temple's destruction (Matt. 24:1–2). When Christ died, God tore the veil of the temple, showing that it was obsolete (27:51). Christ's body is the true and living temple, which sinners destroyed but he raised (John 2:18–22).

By union with Christ through his Spirit, God's people have become the visible home of God's special presence. Paul says to the church, "Ye are the temple of the living God" (2 Cor. 6:16). Believers in Christ "are built upon the foundation of the apostles and prophets, Jesus Christ himself being the chief corner stone; in whom all the building fitly framed together groweth unto an holy temple in the Lord: in whom ye also are builded together for an habitation of God through the Spirit" (Eph. 2:20–22). Paul envisions the church as the heavenly temple where God dwells, extended so that it includes believers still on earth.

The teaching that the church is God's temple by the indwelling Holy Spirit has practical implications. The church's functioning and success depend entirely on the Spirit of God (Zech. 4:6). It must remain separate from and opposed to this wicked world, for "what agreement hath the temple of God with idols?" (2 Cor. 6:16). Church officers and members must obey God's instructions for how "to behave . . . in the house of God, which is the church of the living God" (1 Tim. 3:15). Christians should exult in their great privileges, for they are being "built up [as] a spiritual house, an holy priesthood, to offer up spiritual sacrifices, acceptable to God by Jesus Christ" (1 Pet. 2:5).

Fourth, the church is compared to the *bride* of the Lord and the *mother* of believers. The Old Testament says the Lord is the husband of Israel, his wife (Isa. 54:5; 62:5; Jer. 3:14). Christ calls himself "the bridegroom" of his people (Matt. 9:15; 25:6). This implies that he is the incarnate God of Israel, and the church is his bride. Paul quotes the passage about husband and wife becoming "one flesh" (Gen. 2:24) and applies it to "Christ and the church" (Eph. 5:31–32). Christ is the ideal husband in his sacrificial love for the church (vv. 25–27). The metaphor of the bride woos believers to love Jesus Christ with all their hearts. It also stirs them to hope in Christ's return, which will bring the wedding of Christ and his bride (Rev. 19:7; 21:2, 9; 22:17).

The church is also depicted as our mother (Isa. 50:1; Ezek. 19:2). Though Israel was unfaithful, the Lord promised to receive her again as his spiritual wife so that she would bear many children by his grace (Isa. 54:1–10, 13). Paul quotes that prophecy, adding that the "Jerusalem which is above . . . is the mother of us all" (Gal. 4:26–27). Paul's own ministry was motherly in bringing children to birth and nursing them (v. 19; 1 Thess. 2:7–8). The book of Revelation depicts Israel as a woman whose "seed . . . keep the commandments of God, and have the testimony of Jesus Christ" (Rev. 12:1, 17). She is the church, the people of God, both in her heavenly glory and her endurance of earthly persecution.

Fifth, Paul teaches that the church is the *body* of Christ. Paul says, "As we have many members in one body, and all members have not the same office [function]: so we, being many, are one body in Christ, and every one members one of another" (Rom. 12:4–5). The idea of a "member" here is not membership in an organization but a part of a living body, such as a hand or an eye (cf. Matt. 5:29–30).

Paul emphasizes the unity of the church with the phrase "one body" (Rom. 12:4–5; Eph. 4:4). He explains, "For as the body is one, and hath many members, and all the members of that one body, being many, are one body: so also is Christ. For by one Spirit are we all baptized into one body, whether we be Jews or Gentiles, whether we be bond or free; and have been all made to drink into one Spirit" (1 Cor. 12:12–13).

Christ is "the head of the body, the church" (Col. 1:18). He is "the head over all things" by his exaltation to God's right hand (Eph. 1:20–22; cf. Col. 2:10), but he is specifically the "head" over his "body" in his authority (Eph. 5:23–24), which he uses for its health and growth (4:15–16; Col. 2:19). The union of Christ and his body is a spiritual union. The church is not Christ's continuing incarnation; rather, the church is one with Christ because believers share in the one Spirit of Christ.

William Ames said that we call the church the "body" of Christ to express "the closest union that she has with Christ . . . the dependence that she has from Christ . . . [and] the union and communion that the faithful have among themselves in Christ [by the bonds of] the Spirit, faith, and love."[2]

2 William Ames, *A Sketch of the Christian's Catechism*, trans. Todd M. Rester, Classic Reformed Theology (Grand Rapids, MI: Reformation Heritage Books, 2008), 109.

One practical application of these metaphors for the church is that we should use them in our prayers. For example, we can pray, "Gather thy sheep into one flock and make us one under the leadership of our Good Shepherd. Defend Zion, O Son of David, against her enemies. Fill thy temple with the Holy Spirit. Forget not thy bride, and grant to her a sweet and sanctifying assurance of thy love. Empower each member of thy body to serve effectively, and cause the ministers of the Word to be as nursing mothers caring for thy children."

The Church's Definition and Distinctions

A Basic Definition of the Church

We may define the essence of the church as *the assembly of God's people in his special presence through his Son by his Spirit.* Our definition is trinitarian, relating the church to God the Father, God the Son, and God the Holy Spirit.

As we saw in the previous chapter, the word translated as "church" in the Bible means "assembly." This Greek word was used of any gathering of people (Acts 19:32, 39). However, the church is not just a meeting but the society of people who regularly assemble (14:27; 1 Cor. 14:23). Specifically, the church is the assembly of God's people, "the church of God" consisting of the "saints" (1 Cor. 1:2). The Belgic Confession says of the church, "This holy congregation is an assembly of those who are saved."[3]

The church is the assembly of God's people in his special presence. Under the new covenant, the church of Christ is the living temple in which God dwells (Eph. 2:21–22). God has brought them into his presence through his Son by his Spirit. Paul says, "Through him [Christ] we both [Jews and Gentiles] have access by one Spirit unto the Father" (v. 18).

The Church as the Work of the Trinity

G. H. Kersten said, "The essence of the church is determined by the election of the Father, the purchase of the Son, and the gathering of the Holy Spirit."[4]

First, *the church is God the Father's chosen people.* Election is especially the work of the Father, for he chose whom to adopt into his family (Eph.

3 The Belgic Confession (Art. 28), in *TFU*, 48.

4 G. H. Kersten, *Reformed Dogmatics: A Systematic Treatment of Reformed Doctrine Explained for the Congregations*, trans. Joel R. Beeke and J. C. Westrate, 2 vols. (Grand Rapids, MI: Netherlands Reformed Book and Publishing Committee, 1980), 2:460, punctuation edited.

1:3–5). Paul says, "For whom he did foreknow, he also did predestinate to be conformed to the image of his Son, that he might be the firstborn among many brethren" (Rom. 8:29). Peter says, "Ye are a chosen generation, a royal priesthood, an holy nation, a peculiar people" (1 Pet. 2:9). Augustine wrote of "the bride of Christ . . . in whom is the fixed number of the saints predestined before the foundation of the world."[5]

Second, *the church is God the Son's redeemed people.* Redemption is especially the work of the Son, who is the head of the church and died to save her (Eph. 5:23–25). Paul says that Christ "gave himself for us, that he might redeem us from all iniquity, and purify unto himself a peculiar people, zealous of good works" (Titus 2:14). This is the identity of God's people: they are "the church of God, which he hath purchased with his own blood" (Acts 20:28). Augustine said, "Christ is the head of the Church, which is His body, destined to be with Him in His eternal kingdom and glory."[6]

Third, *the church is God the Spirit's regenerated people.* Regeneration is especially the work of the Holy Spirit (John 3:3–5). The church is the family of God, and each true and living member comes into it through the new birth by the Spirit (John 1:12–13; 1 John 3:9–10).

Therefore, the church is the work of the whole Trinity. John Calvin said, "All those who, by the kindness of God the Father, through the working of the Holy Spirit, have entered into fellowship with Christ, are set apart as God's property and personal possession."[7]

God has elected, redeemed, and regenerated his church for his glory. The Lord says, "This people have I formed for myself; they shall shew forth my praise" (Isa. 43:21). Paul says that God chose his people in Christ "to the praise of the glory of his grace" (Eph. 1:6). Peter writes, "Ye are . . . a peculiar people; that ye should shew forth the praises of him who hath called you out of darkness into his marvellous light" (1 Pet. 2:9). But the church is not merely a means to display God's glory. He designed it to be the people in whom his glory will shine forever (Isa. 60:1–3, 14; Eph. 3:19–21). To study the doctrine of the church is to listen to God's heartbeat, as it were, as it pulses throughout the history of the world.

5 Augustine, *On Baptism, Against the Donatists*, 5.27.38, in *NPNF*[1], 4:477.

6 Augustine, *On Christian Doctrine*, 3.37.55, in *NPNF*[1], 2:573.

7 Calvin, *Institutes*, 4.1.3.

Distinctions regarding the Church

We must make certain distinctions to clarify what we mean by the "church."

First, the church is *militant and triumphant*. The term *militant* refers to the church on earth, which is engaged in continual spiritual warfare against sin (Gal. 5:17; 1 Pet. 2:11), the world (John 15:19; Rev. 17:14), and the Devil (Eph. 6:12). The term *triumphant* refers to the church in glory, which enjoys complete victory and peace in Christ (Rev. 7:15–17; 14:13).

Second, the militant church is *particular and universal*. A particular church is a local congregation. It is an organized expression of the church militant in a certain place, with its own officers, discipline, and meetings for public worship. Most uses of the word translated as "church" in the New Testament refer to particular churches. Paul says, "The churches of Asia salute you. Aquila and Priscilla salute you much in the Lord, with the church that is in their house" (1 Cor. 16:19). The universal church is the church militant throughout the world. Christ says, "I will build my church; and the gates of hell shall not prevail against it" (Matt. 16:18). This promise applies not to particular churches (Rev. 2:5) but to the universal church.

Third, the universal church is *visible and invisible* in different respects. The universal church is visible in the profession of the true gospel, the administration of the true sacraments (baptism and the Lord's Supper) in public worship, and the exercise of true church discipline. We will discuss these marks of the true church in the next chapter. The universal church is invisible in its election, union with Christ, and possession of saving grace in the soul. But though there is one universal church, the visible and the invisible do not always involve the same people. Some members of the church in an external manner are not true and living members of Christ's body (Matt. 7:21–23; Gal. 2:4; 1 John 2:19). However, some members of Christ's body, in union with him, are prevented by God's providence from joining a biblical church (Luke 23:39–43). Some seriously backslidden believers are presently excommunicated from church membership due to persistent, serious sin, but they have not fully or finally fallen away from God's people (1 Cor. 5:2–5).

But we must not think that these are two churches—one visible and the other invisible. Wilhelmus à Brakel said that the church on earth "may be viewed either in her internal, spiritual frame, or in her public gatherings. . . . Thus, in some respects the church is visible, and in some respects invisible. However, one may not divide the church into a visible and invisible church."[8] The invisible church shows itself in visible people and their activities. The visible church reveals the invisible and depends on its reality. The invisible church is to be sought within congregations of the visible church.

Practical Applications of the Church's Definition and Distinctions

What are some practical applications of the doctrine of the church based on this definition and these distinctions?

If the church is the assembly of God's people in his special presence through his Son by his Spirit, then the worship of the church should revolve around communion with the triune God. Our worship should celebrate the grace of the Son, the love of the Father, and the fellowship the Spirit gives us with God and one another (2 Cor. 13:14).

When we are confronted by the church's faults, frailties, and struggles, we must remember that the church on earth is the church militant. Would we be surprised to see wounded soldiers on the front lines of a war? Indeed, would we be astonished to discover that the enemy has agents and saboteurs in the midst of our own forces? Rather than becoming cynical, we should persevere in the battle with great hope. The church militant is on its way to becoming the church triumphant.

Since the church is both particular and universal, our love for the body of Christ should show itself in both ways. We must love the church by committing ourselves to one particular congregation and serving its people loyally. But we must love all of God's people, not merely those of our own congregations, denominations, ethnicities, or nations.

A preacher should never assume all the members of his church are saved, for the visible church is not the same as its invisible, spiritual reality. The preacher should regularly help his listeners to discern their spiritual states by describing the marks of saving grace. But in a biblical and rightly ordered church, the preacher has good warrant to address most of its communicant members as believers and speak freely of the comfort that Christ offers to his people through the gospel.

8 Brakel, *CRS*, 2:5.

Suggested Songs to Sing to the Lord

- Psalm 84, "O Lord of Hosts, how lovely Thy tabernacles are," *Psalter*, No. 227
- "Open now thy gates of beauty," *THBap*, No. 304

Questions for Meditation or Discussion

1. How is the church like the flock of God and the city of God?
2. What do the Scriptures mean when they compare the church to God's house?
3. How is the church the bride of the Lord? How is she the mother of believers?
4. What does Paul mean when he says the church is the body of Christ?
5. How might we use these metaphors for the church in our prayers? Take one metaphor and write a prayer to God for your church based on it. Then pray that prayer for your church.
6. What basic definition do the authors propose for the church? How is the identity of the church rooted in the Trinity?
7. What is the church militant? What is the church triumphant?
8. What is a particular church? What is the universal church?
9. In what sense is the church visible? In what sense is it invisible?
10. What are some applications of the church's definition and distinctions? What practical steps can you take by God's grace to apply these truths to your life?

74

Christ's Church, with Its Attributes and Marks

Chapter Summary and Key Terms

Christ promised to build his church on the doctrine of his person and work. He gave to the church's apostles and elders, as his servants, the *keys of the kingdom*, by which they may welcome people into the church or exclude them from it. These keys are exercised in the preaching of forgiveness of sins and the *discipline of the church*. Christ commissioned the church to make disciples of all nations by going, baptizing, and teaching. The *attributes of the Christian church* are that is it one, *holy*, *catholic* in its worldwide scope, and *apostolic* in its faithfulness to the doctrine and mission of the apostles. The *marks of the true church* are the preaching of the true doctrine of the Holy Scriptures, the administration of the true sacraments, and the exercise of true discipline. These marks all express the church's submission to Christ alone as its head.

ALTHOUGH GOD HAS HAD HIS PEOPLE since the beginning of time, the church received its distinctively Christian form with the coming of Christ. God the Son has come in the flesh, accomplished redemption, and risen from the dead to sit at God's right hand.

What are the properties of the Christian church? In this chapter, we will study Jesus Christ's teachings about his church. We will then examine the attributes of the Christian church and the marks that set the true church apart from false churches.

Christ's Teaching about the Christian Church

The first instances of the word *church* in the New Testament appear on the lips of Christ in Matthew 16 and 18. We must also consider the Great Commission of Matthew 28. These passages give us his manifesto, model, and mission for his church.

Christ's Manifesto for the Church

Jesus said to the apostle Peter, "Thou art Peter, and upon this rock I will build my church; and the gates of hell shall not prevail against it. And I will give unto thee the keys of the kingdom of heaven: and whatsoever thou shalt bind on earth shall be bound in heaven: and whatsoever thou shalt loose on earth shall be loosed in heaven" (Matt. 16:18–19). Let us ask some questions about this passage.

First, what is the "rock" on which Christ builds his church?

Some interpreters say that the rock is Peter. The Greek terms translated as "Peter" (*Petros*) and "rock" (*petra*) are very similar. But the word translated as "Peter" means a piece of stone. The word translated as "rock" means a massive body of stone, such as bedrock under the earth (Matt. 7:24; Luke 6:48). Other interpreters have understood Christ to be referring to himself as the rock on which the church is built. Peter has just said, "Thou art the Christ, the Son of the living God" (Matt. 16:16). Christ is certainly the foundation of the church (1 Cor. 3:11; 1 Pet. 2:4–6). But it would be somewhat confusing if in the same statement Jesus said that he is both the builder and the foundation of the church. This interpretation also does not explain why Jesus connects "Peter" (*Petros*) and "rock" (*petra*) by using such similar words.

Other interpreters, including us, understand "this rock" to refer to Peter's confession about Christ. Peter received this knowledge by divine revelation (Matt. 16:16–17). This interpretation connects Peter with the rock but also distinguishes him from it. Christ's words echo Peter's confession. Peter says, "Thou art the Christ" (v. 16). Jesus says, "Thou art Peter" (v. 18). This is a very old interpretation, taught, for example, by John Chrysostom.[1] The Lord Jesus builds his church on the truth about who he is—the promised Christ, God the Son incarnate.

1 John Chrysostom, *Homilies on Matthew*, 54.3, in *NPNF*[1], 10:333.

Second, what does Christ mean when he says, "I will build my church" (Matt. 16:18)?

Christ alone is the builder of God's house (Heb. 3:1–6). He is "the Son of the living God" (Matt. 16:16). The verb translated as "build" literally means to construct a building, such as the temple (2 Sam. 7:5, 7, 13). The church is nothing less than God's house constructed by his appointed King, the Son of David (Matt. 1:1). It is, Jesus says, "*my* church." The church belongs not to its pastors or people but to Jesus Christ. Old Testament Israel was "the church of the Lord."[2] New Testament Israel is the church of the Lord Jesus. The rule of the church's conduct cannot be our will but must be the Word of its owner, Jesus Christ.

Third, how should we understand Christ's promise to his church that "the gates of hell shall not prevail against it"?

The Greek word translated as "hell" is not the term typically used of everlasting damnation but is instead a term for death (1 Cor. 15:55). The expression "gates of hell" portrays death as a city, like a political or military power. Christ uses this phrase for powers that strive to "prevail" against his church. The church's great enemy is Satan (Matt. 16:21–23). Therefore, Christ promises the church's victory over the forces of Satan that seek to destroy it (Eph. 6:12). By Christ's grace, the church will crush Satan and triumph (Rom. 16:20).

As the Belgic Confession says, "This holy church is preserved or supported by God against the rage of the whole world, even though she sometimes (for a while) appears very small and in the eyes of men, to be reduced to nothing."[3]

Fourth, what does Christ mean by "the keys of the kingdom of heaven" (Matt. 16:19)?

Keys imply authority in Christ's kingdom, authority delegated to the King's steward (Isa. 22:22). Christ gives these *keys of the kingdom* to his servants, the officers of the church who serve as his stewards (1 Cor. 4:1–2; Titus 1:7). Keys lock or unlock the doors of a building. Christ is speaking here of his church like a building. A key can symbolize knowledge or doctrine as a means of entering the kingdom (Luke 11:52; cf. Matt. 23:13). As

2 Deut. 23:2–4, according to the Septuagint (the ancient Greek translation of the Old Testament), which we translate here.

3 The Belgic Confession (Art. 27), in *TFU*, 47.

the Heidelberg Catechism says, the keys of the kingdom are "the preaching of the holy gospel, and Christian discipline, or excommunication out of the Christian church; by these two, the kingdom of heaven is opened to believers and shut against unbelievers."[4]

Christ's Model for the Church

The second reference to the church in the New Testament is found in Matthew 18:15–20. We will return to this passage when treating the subject of church discipline (chap. 85). Here we consider what this Scripture indicates about Christ's purpose for his church.

The church is a gracious family in which there is mutual accountability. Jesus says,

> If thy brother shall trespass against thee, go and tell him his fault between thee and him alone: if he shall hear thee, thou hast gained thy brother. But if he will not hear thee, then take with thee one or two more, that in the mouth of two or three witnesses every word may be established. And if he shall neglect to hear them, tell it unto the church. (Matt. 18:15–17)

Note the repetition of the word "brother." The church consists of brothers and sisters bound together by their obedience to their Father's will (Matt. 12:50). It is a community that seeks out its straying sheep (18:13) and is willing to forgive the repentant (vv. 21–22).

The church is also an organized society with defined membership, standards, and judicial process. Jesus says that if the sinning church brother "refuses to listen even to the church, let him be to you as a Gentile and a tax collector" (Matt. 18:17 ESV). Christ's church has a boundary. He commands his church to exclude those who repeatedly refuse to repent when confronted over serious sins.

As we mentioned above, the church's officers are stewards of God's kingdom. Jesus says, "Whatsoever ye shall bind on earth shall be bound in heaven: and whatsoever ye shall loose on earth shall be loosed in heaven" (Matt. 18:18). Christ already has said this to Peter about the keys of the kingdom (16:19). Now he clearly gives the authority to use these keys to

4 The Heidelberg Catechism (LD 31, Q. 83), in *TFU*, 97.

other officers in the church (plural "ye"), beginning with the apostles and continuing in the elders whom Christ will raise up after them.

The church invokes God's power in Christ's special presence. Jesus says, "If two of you shall agree on earth as touching any thing that they shall ask, it shall be done for them of my Father which is in heaven. For where two or three are gathered together in my name, there am I in the midst of them" (Matt. 18:19–20). In its official meetings, the church shows its nature as the assembly of God's people in his special presence through his Son by his Spirit.

Christ's Mission for the Church

Christ says, "All power is given unto me in heaven and in earth. Go ye therefore, and teach [make disciples of] all nations, baptizing them in the name of the Father, and of the Son, and of the Holy Ghost: teaching them to observe all things whatsoever I have commanded you: and, lo, I am with you always, even unto the end of the world. Amen" (Matt. 28:18–20).

Having accomplished his work of redemption and risen from the dead, Jesus Christ is now invested by God the Father with supreme authority over the entire universe. In light of his supremacy, Christ gives his people a mission to perform. He directly addresses his apostles (Matt. 28:16), but his commission includes the church to the end of the age (v. 20).

The Great Commission centers on one command: "make disciples of all nations" (Matt. 28:19 KJV mg., ESV). Christ's "disciples" give their absolute allegiance to Jesus and follow him as their Master. They conform their beliefs and conduct to his example and teaching (Luke 6:40; 14:25–35). Previously, Christ had directed the apostles to make disciples in Israel alone (Matt. 10:5–6; 15:24). Now the risen Lord launches the mission to "all nations" (cf. Luke 24:47). The reason is that Christ has entered his state of exaltation over all the earth (Ps. 2:2, 6, 8).

This central command to make disciples is modified by three participles (Matt. 28:19–20). "Going" calls for the church to send ministers of the Word to all nations (Mark 16:15; Rom. 10:13–15). "Baptizing" refers to the sign of initiation (Acts 2:38) into the community that worships the triune God: "the name of the Father, and of the Son, and of the Holy Ghost." "Teaching" is further explained as "to observe all things whatsoever I have commanded you." This is instruction for life—not merely doctrine but moral principles and exhortation.

Christ promises to be with his church, even "to the end of the age" (Matt. 28:20 ESV). This implies that Jesus is the omnipresent God. This promise of his presence is the same promise he gave to the gathered church (18:20). Missions must never be separated from the church nor the church from missions.

The Attributes of the Church

The Nicene Creed, in its final form adopted at the Council of Constantinople (AD 381), declares, "I believe one holy catholic and apostolic Church."[5] These are the four attributes of the church.

First, *the church is one*. There is one church because "there is one God, and one mediator between God and men, the man Christ Jesus" (1 Tim. 2:5). The church does not receive its unity by following one man on earth (1 Cor. 1:12–13); its unity comes from the Trinity of God (John 17:21). Paul says, "There is one body, and one Spirit, even as ye are called in one hope of your calling; one Lord, one faith, one baptism, one God and Father of all, who is above all, and through all, and in you all" (Eph. 4:4–6). By its union with Christ, the church is one despite the diversity of its members. Paul writes, "There is neither Jew nor Greek, there is neither bond nor free, there is neither male nor female: for ye are all one in Christ Jesus" (Gal. 3:28).

However, Christian unity is imperfect. The church must continue to grow under the ministry of the Word "till we all come in [attain] the unity of the faith, and of the knowledge of the Son of God, unto a perfect man, unto the measure of the stature of the fulness of Christ" (Eph. 4:13). Every church must work toward the goal that "there be no divisions among you; but that ye be perfectly joined together in the same mind and in the same judgment" (1 Cor. 1:10).

Second, *the church is holy*. Holiness is an absolute necessity for the church, for it is the people of God, and God is holy (Lev. 11:44; 20:26). It is a contradiction to say that the holy God is our God and that we are his people if we are not holy. The body of Christ is set apart as God's "holy temple," where he dwells by the Spirit (Eph. 2:21). Paul says, "The temple of God is holy" (1 Cor. 3:17). Each true and living member of the church is holy: "the church of God . . . sanctified in Christ Jesus, called to be saints, with all that in every place call upon the name of Jesus Christ our Lord" (1:2).

5 The Nicene Creed, in *TFU*, 7.

Therefore, the church has no right to admit into or retain in its membership those known to persist in serious, unrepentant sin despite the admonitions of the brethren (Deut. 13:5; 14:2; 1 Cor. 5:13).

However, the holiness of the church is only beginning and not yet complete. The true citizens of Christ's kingdom "hunger and thirst after righteousness" (Matt. 5:6). The holy Christian church has an obligation to strive together toward "perfecting holiness in the fear of God" (2 Cor. 7:1). Holiness must be cultivated in privacy with God. It must be cherished in the day-to-day relationships of home life. It must be practiced in the pressures of our work. It must be relished in the pleasures of time with friends. It must be evidenced in our interactions with unsaved people. And it must be pursued in public worship on the Lord's Day.

Third, *the church is catholic*. The word *catholic* does not refer to a particular organization, such as the Roman Catholic Church. *Catholic* means "general, universal." The church is called "catholic" in the Nicene Creed because it is not confined to a particular location.[6] Since Christ's ascension into heaven and his pouring out of the Holy Spirit, the church is scattered among the nations, where it makes disciples (Matt. 28:19). Christians are part of an international movement, for the church is the body of believers around the world who share a common evangelical doctrine. The gospel offers salvation to all people, regardless of gender, ethnicity, earthly citizenship, color of skin, culture, or economic status (1 Tim. 2:3–4).

Yet the catholicity of the church is also incomplete. The church has not finished its mission to all nations. There are many peoples not yet present among the worshipers of God. Furthermore, the church fails to express the catholic unity of Christ whenever Christians have prejudice and hatred against one another due to differences in nationality, color, or culture. Therefore, the members of the church must strive to fully embrace one another in humble, brotherly love (Eph. 4:1–3).

Fourth, *the church is apostolic*. Paul says that God's living temple is "built upon the foundation of the apostles and prophets, Jesus Christ himself being the chief corner stone" (Eph. 2:20).

When we say the church is apostolic, we do not mean that it has apostles today (see chap. 54). The apostles served as the church's foundation because

6 See the discussion of the universal church in chap. 73.

they received and proclaimed the revelation of the mystery of Christ concerning his body (Eph. 3:1–6). The church is apostolic because it continues to preach, preserve, and practice "the form of sound words" communicated to it through the apostles (2 Tim. 1:13), "the faith which was once delivered unto the saints" (Jude 3). That is the doctrine found in the Holy Scriptures.

The church is also apostolic because it continues the apostolic mission. The church's teachers must train "faithful men, who shall be able to teach others also" (2 Tim. 2:2). The church must send out preachers of the gospel so that all may hear of Christ (Rom. 10:15).

Some churches claim to be apostolic by *apostolic succession*. This is the claim to an unbroken series of ordinations from Christ's apostles to today. But true apostolic succession consists of faithfulness to the teachings of the Holy Scriptures.

The Marks of the True Church

In the sixteenth century, the Reformers were excommunicated by the pope, who claimed to be the visible head of the true church. The Reformers responded by identifying marks of the true church. The Belgic Confession says,

> The marks by which the true Church is known are these: if the pure doctrine of the gospel is preached therein; if she maintains the pure administration of the sacraments as instituted by Christ; if church discipline is exercised in punishing of sin; in short, if all things are managed according to the pure Word of God, all things contrary thereto rejected, and Jesus Christ acknowledged as the only Head of the Church. Hereby the true Church may certainly be known, from which no man has a right to separate himself.[7]

First, *the true church preaches true doctrine*. Jesus says, "My sheep hear my voice, and I know them, and they follow me" (John 10:27). Those who are of the true flock of Christ follow the voice of its Shepherd, which they hear in the preaching of his gospel (Eph. 2:17). But John warns, "Many false prophets are gone out into the world. . . . They are of the world: therefore

7 The Belgic Confession (Art. 29), in *TFU*, 49.

speak they of the world, and the world heareth them. We are of God: he that knoweth God heareth us; he that is not of God heareth not us" (1 John 4:1, 5–6). How people respond to God's Word shows whether they belong to God (John 8:47).

Second, *the true church administers the true sacraments.* The sacraments are visible ordinances of worship that God instituted to point our faith to Christ and his sacrifice (see chaps. 81–84).[8] When Christ died on the cross, God abolished the obligation to keep the Old Testament ceremonies (Col. 2:14–17). Christ instituted a much simpler pattern of worship with two sacraments, baptism and the Lord's Supper (Matt. 26:26–29; 28:19).

Third, *the true church exercises true discipline.* We have already seen that Christ commanded his church to exercise discipline among its members (Matt. 18:15–20). Church discipline is essential for the health and order of Christ's body (see chap. 85).

True churches have relative purity, not absolute purity in these matters. The Westminster Confession of Faith says, "The purest Churches under heaven are subject both to mixture and error."[9] Therefore, Christians should not leave a church merely because they detect some relatively minor impurity in its doctrine or practice. There are times, though, when Christians must separate from a church due to heresy in doctrine, gross and unrepentant iniquity in practice, or open idolatry in worship.

The marks of the true church show their spiritual reality in Christlike conduct. Wilhelmus Schortinghuis said, "The true church is found where . . . the truth of Jesus is found, confessed, and demonstrated in heart, word, and walk of life (John 10:27; Eph. 4:21–24)."[10]

Though we list three marks of the true church, it has one central quality: the acknowledgment of Christ's sole supremacy over the church so that its doctrine and practice is controlled by the Holy Scriptures. Christ "is the head of the body, the church" (Col. 1:18). Thus, his people are grounded on his Word and must not follow philosophy, tradition, or humanly invented commands or worship, but hold firmly to their Head (2:6–7, 19–23).

8 The Heidelberg Catechism (LD 25, Q. 67), in *TFU*, 89.

9 The Westminster Confession of Faith (25.5), in *RC*, 4:264. Cf. the Second London Baptist Confession (26.3), in *RC*, 4:562.

10 Wilhelmus Schortinghuis, *Essential Truths in the Heart of a Christian*, trans. Harry Boonstra and Gerrit W. Sheeres, ed. James A. De Jong, Classics of Reformed Spirituality (Grand Rapids, MI: Reformation Heritage Books, 2009), 39.10 (126).

Suggested Song to Sing to the Lord

- "Jesus, with thy church abide," *THBap*, No. 278

Questions for Meditation or Discussion

1. What are the three main interpretations of "this rock" in Matthew 16:18? Which is best? Why?
2. What are the implications of Christ's statement "I will build my church; and the gates of hell shall not prevail against it" (Matt. 16:18)?
3. What are the keys of the kingdom?
4. What can we learn from Matthew 18:15–17 about Christ's church?
5. What does Jesus teach us about the church's mission in Matthew 28:18–20?
6. What are the four attributes of the church according to the Nicene Creed? What does each mean, and how is it taught in Scripture?
7. What is often meant by the claim of apostolic succession? What is true apostolic succession?
8. What are three marks of the true church, and what do they mean?
9. Choose one of the attributes or marks of the church. How would you speak devotionally to a group of Christians about what this attribute or mark means for our lives?

75

Membership in the Church

Chapter Summary and Key Terms

A *member of the Christian church* is someone who belongs to God's covenant people. A true and living member is joined to Christ and his church by the Holy Spirit, just as a member is joined to a body and shares its life. Membership is ordinarily lived out in the relationships and ministry of a particular church. The New Testament implies membership by references to those inside and those outside the church, the duty to submit to its officers, and the administration of baptism and the Lord's Supper. Particular churches require a *credible profession of faith* of a *communicant member*—that is, one who may partake of the Lord's Supper. Two hindrances to church membership are false brethren and false churches. Faithful church membership requires participating regularly in public worship, loving and serving one another, giving financial support, submitting to the ministers and elders, and praying with the church.

MEMBERSHIP IN THE CHURCH is essential to the Christian life, unless circumstances make it impossible for a believer to join a faithful church.[1] People will not value or understand church membership if they view the church as a theater in which to see and hear a show, a museum designed to preserve the past, a shopping mall set up to meet their needs, a mission for community service, or a lecture hall in which to hear a talk. The truth is that the church is a body, and true believers are living members joined to it

1 Some believers, though faithful to the Lord, cannot be active members in a biblical church due to location, imprisonment, illness, or other factors outside of their control.

and to one another. In this chapter, we will explain the meaning of church membership and argue for its great importance. Then we will discuss different views as to how membership relates to children. We will consider the requirements for adult communicant membership. Finally, we will explore hindrances to and responsibilities of being a member in the church.

The Meaning and Importance of Church Membership

In the New Testament, the Greek word translated as "member" refers literally to a part of the human body, such as a hand or eye (Matt. 5:29–30). Paul uses the word "members" figuratively when he says, "For as we have many members in one body, and all members have not the same office: so we, being many, are one body in Christ, and every one members one of another" (Rom. 12:4–5). The members share life in "one Spirit" (1 Cor. 12:12–13). They need one another (vv. 17–22). While these principles are true of the whole body of Christ, members live them out practically in particular churches. Paul said to the local church in Corinth, "Ye are the body of Christ" (v. 27).

The church has boundaries between members and nonmembers. Christ instructed his disciples to count someone who persisted in sin despite admonitions as outside the covenant community (Matt. 18:15–17). Paul speaks of people inside and outside of the church (1 Cor. 5:12–13). The addition of people to the church (their joining it) also implies membership (Acts 2:41, 47). Saul sought to "join himself to the disciples" in Jerusalem, but they were not convinced at first "that he was a disciple" (9:26). Barnabas had to verify his conversion (vv. 27–28).

Some duties that the Lord requires of his people imply membership in a local church. Christians must "exhort one another daily" (Heb. 3:13) and "consider one another to provoke unto love and to good works: not forsaking the assembling of ourselves together" (10:24–25). Believers also have a duty to their spiritual leaders: "Obey them that have the rule over you, and submit yourselves: for they watch for your souls" (13:17). Only by having membership in a particular church can a Christian know which elders in all the world are responsible to care for him.

The metaphors for the church imply that it has a membership (chap. 73). The church is Christ's *body*. What kind of body has no members? Christians are living stones in the *house*, or temple, of God. Does a temple consist of stones scattered across the ground or fitted and cemented together as one building?

The sacraments of the church also imply that it has a defined membership. Baptism is the sign of having "put on Christ," by which believers "are all one in Christ Jesus" (Gal. 3:27–28). There is "one body" and "one baptism" (Eph. 4:4–5). In the Lord's Supper, the church shows that it is "one body" by eating "one bread" (1 Cor. 10:17). People without spiritual discernment have no right to participate in the Lord's Supper (11:29).

Therefore, membership in the church is a biblical doctrine, one that is important for the Christian life. Edmund Clowney said, "Those who say that church membership is not necessary, or even that it is unbiblical, fail to grasp what the New Testament teaches about the church and the administration of the sacraments."[2] The Belgic Confession says,

> All men are in duty bound to join and unite themselves with [Christ's congregation], maintaining the unity of the Church; submitting themselves to the doctrine and discipline thereof; bowing their necks under the yoke of Jesus Christ; and as mutual members of the same body, serving to the edification of the brethren, according to the talents God has given them.[3]

Different Views regarding Children and Membership

The Word of God clearly calls children to godliness (Ex. 20:12; Eccles. 12:1; Eph. 6:1–3). But there are widely different approaches to the membership of children in the church.

Churches that teach baptismal regeneration regard the baptism of children as saving them and making them part of the church. Despite their differences, the Roman Catholic Church, Eastern Orthodox churches, and Lutheran churches agree on this point.

Some Baptist churches permit children to join the membership of the church when they reach an age when they can understand God's Word and have received baptism on a profession of faith in Christ. If children are believers in Christ, it is said, we have no right to restrain them from the Lord's Supper and pastoral care (Matt. 19:14).[4]

2 Edmund P. Clowney, *The Church*, Contours of Christian Theology (Downers Grove, IL: InterVarsity Press, 1995), 103–4.

3 The Belgic Confession (Art. 28), in *TFU*, 48.

4 Ted Christman, *Forbid Them Not: Rethinking the Baptism and Church Membership of Children and Young People* (Owensboro, KY: Heritage Baptist Church, 2019), 8–9, 15, 23, 31–32.

Other Baptist churches do not permit children to be baptized or join church membership until they reach a measure of maturity in their middle to upper teen years. These churches argue that young children are immature in their thinking (1 Cor. 13:11). They cannot speak for themselves to make a profession of faith (John 9:20–21) and are easily influenced by others (Eph. 4:13–14).[5]

In the Reformed and Presbyterian tradition, the children of a church member are considered to already possess membership in the church by virtue of the covenant of grace (Gen. 17:7). Baptism begins formal membership and reception into the visible church.[6]

We will discuss this matter in more detail under the topic of baptism (chap. 83).

In the remainder of this chapter, we will focus on adult members who partake of the Lord's Supper (*communicant members*).

The Requirements for Adult Communicant Membership

To become church members who partake of the Lord's Supper, adults must make a *credible profession of faith*. They must also have received Christian baptism. And they must profess their willingness to participate in the work of the church and their submission to the doctrine and discipline of its leaders. Luke says of the church in Jerusalem at Pentecost, "They that gladly received [Peter's] word were baptized: and the same day there were added unto them about three thousand souls. And they continued stedfastly in the apostles' doctrine and fellowship, and in breaking of bread, and in prayers" (Acts 2:41–42).

A credible profession of faith is central to adult communicant church membership. This is recognized in the Lutheran, Reformed and Presbyterian, and Baptist traditions.[7] Saving faith results in a public confession of

5 Greg Nichols, *Lectures in Systematic Theology*, ed. Rob Ventura, 4 vols. to date (Seattle: CreateSpace Independent Publishing Platform, 2023), 4:281–92; and David Merck, "Children and Church Membership" (unpublished paper, rev. ed., 2020, Grace Immanuel Reformed Baptist Church, Grand Rapids, MI), 9–16.

6 The Belgic Confession (Art. 34), in *TFU*, 54.

7 C. F. W. Walther, *American-Lutheran Pastoral Theology*, ed. David W. Loy, trans. Christian C. Tiews, in *Walther's Works* (St. Louis, MO: Concordia, 2017), 303–9 (on confirmation); and the Westminster Confession of Faith (25.2) and the Second London Baptist Confession (26.2), in *RC*, 4:264, 562.

Christ as Lord (Rom. 10:9–10). Such a confession of faith is an important evidence of salvation. Christ warns, "Whosoever therefore shall confess me before men, him will I confess also before my Father which is in heaven. But whosoever shall deny me before men, him will I also deny before my Father which is in heaven" (Matt. 10:32–33).

The word *credible* means that the person's profession is believable. It is informed by true knowledge of the gospel. Furthermore, it is not contradicted by a life of rebellion against God's Word but confirmed by a life marked by obedience to the Lord. Christ's church is his flock (Acts 20:28). He says, "My sheep hear my voice, and I know them, and they follow me" (John 10:27). Many claim to be his disciples, but, Christ says, "ye shall know them by their fruits" (Matt. 7:16, 22).

That is not to say that the church claims to discern conversion in the heart. No mere man can search the heart (1 Kings 8:39; Jer. 17:9–10). Rather, the church's elders must receive a profession of faith consistent with the applicant's life to welcome him into its membership. Without presuming to be judges of regeneration—even the apostles had a "devil" among them and did not know it (John 6:70–71)—elders must exercise discernment in admitting professing Christians into church membership. This is crucial for the life of the church and the glory of God.

Faithful Church Membership

Overcoming Hindrances to Church Membership

One hindrance that discourages people from entering or remaining in church membership is false brethren in the church (Gal. 2:4). Of course, it is possible for all Christians to sin and thus grieve God and his people (Eph. 4:30), but we speak here not of sinning believers but of hypocrites in the visible church. They conceal unrepentant hearts under a show of religion, "having a form of godliness, but denying the power thereof" (2 Tim. 3:5). Their wicked acts or apostasy from the Lord may give people the impression that everyone in the church is a hypocrite or that its elders are grossly unfaithful. When Christians see or hear such things, they should not be shaken but persevere as faithful members of the church of Jesus Christ.

Another major hindrance to church membership is the existence of false churches. Such churches profess to be Christian but do not teach the doctrine taught by Christ and his apostles, do not administer the sacraments ordained by Christ, or do not practice the holy discipline commanded by Christ. A believer may need to travel an hour or more from his or her home to worship according to God's Word. Or if there is no true church available in the area, the believer may—as a last resort—worship privately at home until either the Lord starts a church nearby or the believer is able to move to a place where he or she can worship with a biblical church.

Fulfilling the Responsibilities of Church Membership

As professing Christians, all church members have the duty to live a consistent Christian life in obedience to God's commandments, bearing the fruit of the Spirit. Here we present some major responsibilities of church members with respect to the local church.

First, *feed on the public ministry of the Word.* Peter says, "As newborn babes, desire the sincere milk of the word, that ye may grow thereby" (1 Pet. 2:2). When the worship service begins, "take heed therefore how ye hear" (Luke 8:18). Many hear the Word but bear no fruit from it (vv. 11–15). After the service, meditate on the Word, offer specific prayers, and make specific resolutions.

Second, *nurture saving faith with the Lord's Supper.* Christ commands his disciples, "This do in remembrance of me" (Luke 22:19). Therefore, Christian, participate regularly in the church's celebration of the Lord's Supper. Take the bread and the cup with earnest desire for Christ.

Third, *exercise a growing love for fellow members.* God's reborn children must labor to "love one another with a pure heart fervently" (1 Pet. 1:22–23). Love is one of the great signs to the world that believers are true disciples of Christ (John 13:35).

Fourth, *guard and strengthen the unity of the church.* God has already made the church one in Christ by "the unity of the Spirit in the bond of peace," but it is our duty to make every effort to maintain that unity by "all lowliness and meekness, with longsuffering, forbearing one another in love" (Eph. 4:2–3).

Fifth, *serve in ministry by your spiritual gifts.* Each believer has the responsibility to employ his gifts in service to others by God's grace for God's glory in Christ (1 Pet. 4:10–11).

Sixth, *keep watch over one another in brotherly accountability*. Perseverance is a community project. It requires the regular giving and receiving of exhortation (Heb. 3:12–13). God calls believers to thoughtfully provoke one another to good works of love (10:24–25).

Seventh, *speak the gospel to believers and unbelievers*. While not all Christians are called to be preachers or teachers, all must be "speaking the truth in love" (Eph. 4:15).

Eighth, *support your church with your financial gifts*. Paul says, "The Lord ordained that they which preach the gospel should live of the gospel" (1 Cor. 9:13–14). He adds, "Let the one who is taught the word share all good things with the one who teaches" (Gal. 6:6 ESV).

Ninth, *honor and submit to the ministers and elders of your church*. Paul says, "We beseech you, brethren, to know them which labour among you, and are over you in the Lord, and admonish you; and to esteem them very highly in love for their work's sake" (1 Thess. 5:12–13).

Tenth, *pray for and with your church*. Christ gave a special promise: that he would hear the prayers of his people when they gather as a church (Matt. 18:19–20). Be willing to sacrifice time and convenience to regularly attend the prayer meetings of the church. Whatever limitations you may have, you can still perform the most important ministry—*you can pray*.

Be a faithful member of a faithful church. The demands of church membership are costly. But remember that what you do to the least of Christ's brethren, you do to Christ (Matt. 25:40).

Suggested Song to Sing to the Lord

- Psalm 122, "With joy I heard my friends exclaim," *Psalter*, No. 350

Questions for Meditation or Discussion

1. What does the New Testament mean by a "member" of the church?
2. What do the boundaries and duties of the church teach us about membership?
3. How do the Bible's metaphors for the church imply membership?
4. How do baptism and the Lord's Supper imply membership?
5. How do the following churches view children and membership: (1) Roman Catholic, Eastern Orthodox, and Lutheran, (2) Baptist, (3) Reformed and Presbyterian?

6. Why is a credible profession of faith a requirement for adult communicant membership in a local church?
7. What are two hindrances to church membership? How can we overcome them?
8. What are the responsibilities of adult communicant membership?
9. Which of those responsibilities are you most prone to neglect? Why? What are some steps you can take to become more consistent and faithful in this matter?
10. A friend in your church is considering walking away from the church because another prominent member has fallen into serious unrepentant sin. What do you say to your friend?

Section 6B

The Church's Authority and Work

76

Church Government

Chapter Summary and Key Terms

There are three basic principles of New Testament *polity* (or church government). First, the King of the church is Jesus Christ, the only Mediator. He is the only Head of the church, not the *pope* of Roman Catholicism (the *papacy*). Second, Christ governs the church through *elders*. *Bishops* ("*overseers*") are the same as elders, not leaders who rule over elders in a church or even groups of churches (as in *episcopal polity*). Each church is led by a *plurality of elders*, who serve as its ruling council (the *consistory* or *session*). Third, the members of the church hold one another accountable and elect their officers. In *presbyterianism*, which is the polity of most Reformed churches, particular churches unite in federations overseen by councils of the churches' elders. A regional council is a *classis* or *presbytery*. A broader council is a *synod* or a *general assembly*. In *congregationalism*, no officer or council has authority over more than one particular church, though churches may form associations for fellowship, cooperation, and mutual counsel. The New Testament clearly displays *connectionalism* in networks of relationships among particular churches and their ministers.

TO WHOM SHOULD WE SUBMIT our souls for spiritual guidance? Few questions in life are as important as this one. This is a matter of church government, or *polity*, which has to do with how a church's organization and leadership should be structured.

In this chapter, we will explore basic principles of church government taught in the New Testament. We will discuss denominations or associations of churches in light of the debate between *presbyterianism* and *congregationalism*.[1] We will also examine other forms of church government. Then we will close with some practical applications.

Basic Principles of Church Authority

Authority typically takes the form of *monarchy* (the rule of one over all), *aristocracy* (the rule of those regarded as best able to govern), *democracy* (the rule of the people), or often some combination. In the church, we find all three principles present but transformed by the gospel.

First, *Christ rules his church as its only Mediator-King*. Christ is the "head" of the church, his "body" (Eph. 4:15–16; 5:23). The calling of the church consists of obeying all that the King of the universe has commanded, as he is present with us in his grace (Matt. 28:18–20). Therefore, no mere man is king in Christ's church. The God-man alone is King.

All offices among God's people derive from the office of the Mediator, according to God's covenant of grace (see chap. 45). Any authority or power exercised by church officers comes through Christ (Rom. 15:17–19; 2 Cor. 13:3–4).

Second, *the eldership governs Christ's church as his servant-leaders*. These men act as shepherds who "feed the flock of God" under the supervision of "the chief Shepherd" (1 Pet. 5:2, 4). Paul says to them, "Take heed therefore unto yourselves, and to all the flock, over the which the Holy Ghost hath made you overseers, to feed the church of God, which he hath purchased with his own blood" (Acts 20:28). They are called "them which have the rule over you" (Heb. 13:7, 17, 24), so Christians must "obey" and "submit" to them (v. 17). But they are servants and stewards of the Lord (1 Cor. 4:1–2; Titus 1:7).

The New Testament refers to ruling church leaders primarily with two terms. A "*bishop*" (also translated as "*overseer*") is a man of sound faith and blameless character who teaches and governs the church (1 Tim. 3:1–7; Titus 1:6–9). In the New Testament, a bishop or overseer of the church is the same as an "*elder*." Paul called "the elders of the church" in Ephesus to meet him, and said to them, "The Holy Ghost hath made you overseers"

1 We are not capitalizing terms such as *presbyterianism* and *congregationalism*, for they do not refer in this case to the names of denominations but to doctrines or systems of polity held by denominations that in some cases are called by other names, such as "Reformed" or "Baptist."

(Acts 20:17, 28). Paul instructed Titus to "ordain elders in every city," and then told him the qualifications for a "bishop" or overseer (Titus 1:5, 7). Peter urged "the elders" to be exercising "oversight" over the flock (1 Pet. 5:1–2). The elders include the church's ministers or preachers (1 Tim. 5:17).

The New Testament pattern is a *plurality of elders* serving as a ruling council in each church.[2] The apostles ordained "elders in every church" (Acts 14:23). We constantly read of these elders exercising their ministry as a plurality—"the elders of the church" (James 5:14). There were "overseers" in the church in Ephesus (Acts 20:28) and "bishops" in Philippi (Phil. 1:1). Therefore, the authority of each elder is exercised in partnership with the other elders. This means that each elder is under the authority of the church's eldership as a whole. John Murray said, "Elders are members of the body of Christ and are subject to the very same rule of which they are the administrators."[3]

Third, *all members of Christ's church hold one another accountable as brothers and sisters.* The democratic principle in church government is based on the common profession of faith by church members and the priesthood of all believers (1 Pet. 2:5, 9). All who are in Christ share a basic equality (Gal. 3:28; Col. 3:11). Hence, they share the responsibility to exhort and encourage one another (Matt. 18:15; Rom. 15:14; Heb. 3:13; 10:24–25). The members also have the responsibility to elect the officers of their church.[4] The apostles instructed the Jerusalem church to "pick out from among you seven men of good repute, full of the Spirit and of wisdom, whom we will appoint to this duty" (Acts 6:3 ESV).

Therefore, in Christ's church, we see the principles of monarchy, aristocracy, and democracy all working together. But the way in which these principles come together in the church is unique, given the special character of the kingdom of God. All church authority comes from God through Christ. It is rightly used in obedience to his Word by the power of the Holy Spirit.

2 Note "elders" and "bishops" (or "overseers") in the plural, often with respect to a particular church, in Acts 11:30; 14:23; 15:2, 4, 6, 22, 23; 16:4; 20:17, 28; 21:18; Phil. 1:1; 1 Tim. 5:17; Titus 1:5; James 5:14; 1 Pet. 5:1. The singular form with reference to the church officer is far less common. It is used not of the officer in his active function but in describing his qualifications or in situations when he is accused of misconduct (1 Tim. 3:1–2; 5:19; Titus 1:7).

3 John Murray, *Collected Writings of John Murray*, 4 vols. (Edinburgh: Banner of Truth, 1982), 1:262.

4 Calvin, *Institutes*, 4.3.15; and Polyander, Walaeus, Thysius, and Rivetus, *SPT*, 42.32 (2:637).

Denominations and Associations of Churches

Christ rules his church through the elders. They act as his official stewards among the mutually accountable members of the body. This is the basic pattern for the polity of the local church. But what does this pattern imply about relationships among churches?

Most churches in the Reformed tradition follow a polity known as *presbyterianism*. In this system, local churches join in a federation overseen by assemblies of those churches' elders (including ministers and ruling elders). The *consistory* or *session* is the council of elders overseeing a particular church. An assembly of elders on a regional level is called a *classis* or *presbytery*. On a broader level, it is called a *synod* or *general assembly*. These assemblies function as church courts. They render decisions according to God's Word but ordinarily do not interfere with the proceedings of individual churches. Each local church is directly governed by its own council of elders (its consistory or session).

Some churches in the Reformed tradition, as well as churches outside of that tradition, follow a polity known as *congregationalism*. In this system, each particular church has full authority to govern itself under Christ by his appointed officers. No officer or council, it is said, may exercise authority over more than one local church. But many congregationalist churches form associations with one another for counsel, assistance, agreement in a confession of faith, fellowship, and resolution of matters of doctrine or discipline.

Congregationalist theologians argue that the New Testament teaches the rule of elders over the particular church they serve. A group of elders shepherds each local church (Acts 14:23; 20:17; Phil. 1:1). For example, Peter exhorts elders to shepherd "the flock of God *which is among you*" (1 Pet. 5:2), not people in other places. Congregationalists also argue that the New Testament contains no command for elders to rule over churches other than their own. Nor, they say, do we find in the Bible a system of larger assemblies with authority over local churches.

Presbyterian theologians argue that the council of Jerusalem (Acts 15) is the model of an assembly of representative elders making a decision that bound their churches. In reply, congregationalists argue that the decision was made by the apostles and elders of the church in Jerusalem, not the elders of more than one church (15:2–6, 22–23; 16:4). Congregationalists also argue that the decision was binding on churches that had no representatives at the council (16:1–4). Presbyterians respond that either those churches did have representatives in Jerusalem or they received the council's decision as good advice.

Presbyterians also argue that the broader assemblies can restrain individual ministers or ruling elders from domineering their congregations. It is their conviction that the presbyterian system is the most effective way to control and subdue human nature's depraved tendency to fall into a corrupt use of power that damages the church.

A Case for Strong Connectionalism

The authority of councils that represent federations of churches remains a disputed point between presbyterianism and congregationalism. But both presbyterians and congregationalists may recognize that there is a solid biblical case for *connectionalism* among churches. By connectionalism, we mean the formation of a committed and cooperative network of local churches as an expression of membership in the larger body of Christ.

We see in the New Testament that established churches sent leaders to visit and encourage new churches (Acts 8:14; 11:21–22). Churches shared warm relationships and correspondence (Rom. 16:21–23; 1 Cor. 16:19–20; Col. 4:10–14). Paul shared greetings from a group of "churches," suggesting that he had contact with a gathering of their representatives (Rom. 16:16).

Churches recognized ministers from other churches and welcomed their ministries. We see this in the cases of Barnabas (Acts 11:21–22; 13:1–3; 14:21–23), Philip (6:5; 8:5; 21:8), Timothy (16:1; 17:14–15; 18:5; etc.), and Apollos (18:24–28; 19:1). Churches sent written commendations with traveling ministers and members so that they would be welcomed and assisted by other churches.[5] Such commendations assumed mutual recognition, fellowship, and cooperation among the churches.

We also find in the New Testament that churches collaborated in organized works of benevolence (Acts 11:27–30; Rom. 15:26–27; 1 Cor. 16:1–4). One benevolent collection was administered by Paul, Titus, and "the brother, whose praise is in the gospel throughout all the churches; and not that only, but who was also chosen of the churches to travel with us with this grace" (2 Cor. 8:18–21). They were "the messengers of the churches" (v. 23). This

5 Acts 15:25–27; 18:27; Rom. 16:1–2; 1 Cor. 16:3; Eph. 6:21–22; Col. 4:7–10.

implies that leaders from these churches communicated or assembled to plan cooperative efforts.

There was also unity among the churches with respect to doctrine and missions. Churches and missionaries cooperated in gospel missions while practicing doctrinal discrimination (2 John 7–11; 3 John 5–8). Churches shared apostolic letters and communicated apostolic directives to one another (Col. 4:16). Paul reminded the Corinthian church several times that he instructed all the churches to follow the same doctrines and practices.[6] Whether we take a presbyterian or congregationalist view of the council of Jerusalem, the church in Antioch clearly worked together with the church in Jerusalem to resolve a serious doctrinal dispute (Acts 15:1–6).

We conclude that the New Testament shows a connectionalism consisting of close-knit denominations or associations of churches.

Other Forms of Church Government

Presbyterianism and congregationalism are not the only systems of polity that churches have used. Therefore, in this section, we will consider some other significant forms of church government.

First, *in episcopal polity, a bishop oversees a group of churches in a district called a "diocese."* An archbishop governs a group of bishops and their dioceses. One argument for this polity is based on the singular "angel" in each church that Christ addresses in Revelation 2–3. "Angel" can mean messenger, so this word is taken to mean the bishop of the church. Other arguments for the authority of bishops over elders are drawn from James, the brother of our Lord, who acted as the primary leader of the church in Jerusalem (Acts 12:17; 15:13; 21:18), as did Timothy in Ephesus (1 Tim. 1:3) and Titus in Crete (Titus 1:4–5). It also appears that churches used the episcopal system of polity shortly after the apostles died.

In response, we note that, as we saw earlier in this chapter, "elder" and "bishop" (or "overseer") both refer to the same leaders in the New Testament (Acts 20:17, 28; Titus 1:5, 7). It is not certain whether the seven "angels" in Revelation 2–3 are heavenly messengers (as is commonly the case in Revelation) or human ministers. Even if they are human, it is not clear whether these ministers had greater authority than others or presided as

6 1 Cor. 4:17; 7:17; 11:16; 14:33; 16:1.

first among equals in the eldership. James appears to have been an apostle (1 Cor. 15:7; Gal. 1:19; 2:9). Timothy and Titus were extraordinary officers who assisted the apostles in starting and organizing the New Testament churches and in ordaining bishops (elders) in the church of each city, but they were not themselves called bishops (1 Tim. 3:1–2; Titus 1:7). So there is no biblical basis for episcopal polity. And while it is true that the church elevated bishops to positions of special authority early in its history, it is also true that these bishops often functioned like mediators between God and people. But there is only one Mediator, Jesus Christ (1 Tim. 2:5).

Second, *the polity of civil supremacy makes the king or another civil ruler to be the governing authority over churches and their leaders.* From the fourth century onward, emperors and kings have asserted authority over the bishops and ministers of the church. Sometimes they have appealed to the Scripture passages that teach that civil rulers have authority over Christians (1 Pet. 2:13–14). They also have pointed out that King David and later kings descended from him gave direction to the priests and Levites (1 Chron. 23:1–6; 24:3; 25:1; 2 Chron. 29:1–11).

In response, we acknowledge that God commands everyone to submit to the civil government in civil matters (Rom. 13:1–7). But that does not mean the civil government has authority over the church's worship, organizational principles, ordination of officers, and teaching on doctrine and ethics. God has appointed no king over the church's religious service except the Son of David, Jesus Christ (Matt. 1:1; 16:18). Any king who claims to rule in the church trespasses on Christ's rights as King. Christ gave the keys of the kingdom not to the magistrate but to officers of the church (Matt. 16:19).

Third, *the papacy further develops episcopal polity by concentrating authority in the bishop of Rome.* He is known as the *pope* ("father") or *pontiff* ("high priest"). The pope is also called the *vicar of Christ* because he supposedly sits in Christ's place as the church's supreme teacher, priest, and ruler on earth. The *papacy* asserts supreme authority based on its claim to an unbroken succession of office from the apostle Peter. The pope is supposedly the visible head of the universal church.

In the early centuries of Christian history, the bishop of Rome was greatly respected.[7] But he was not elevated above all other bishops as

7 On the history of the papacy, see Beeke and Smalley, *RST*, 4:243–50, and the sources cited there.

their supreme authority. Over time, the papacy rose in power and influence. The pope gained control not only of other churches but of extensive land in Italy. The medieval papacy claimed to hold supreme power over all churches and all political kingdoms throughout the earth. During the medieval period, many popes lived more like worldly princes than spiritual shepherds serving the church. In the sixteenth century, the Reformation shattered the pope's hold on large sections of Europe. The Roman Catholic reaction resulted in a measure of moral reform but little or no change to the doctrine of papal authority. The First Vatican Council (1868–1870) declared that the pope speaks with infallibility when defining doctrine or morals by his apostolic authority. Today, the Roman Catholic Church teaches, "The Roman Pontiff, by reason of his office as Vicar of Christ, and as pastor of the entire Church has full, supreme, and universal power over the whole Church."[8]

In response, we note that we have already argued that there is no biblical basis to give special authority over multiple churches to a bishop. Furthermore, to proclaim the pope to be the visible head of the church insults its true Head, Jesus Christ. All authority within the church of Christ comes by God's Word. There is no doctrine of the papacy in the Holy Scriptures. Christ's words to Peter about the rock of the church and the keys of the kingdom (Matt. 16:18–19) do not establish a continuing office in the church with the authority of the apostle Peter (see chap. 74). Much less do they establish a supreme vicar of Christ who is head of the church on earth, which Peter never was. Several men who have held the office of pope have proven to be heretical, immoral, or driven by worldly ambition. How can we consider such men to be the vicars of Christ and the successors of the apostles?

Fourth, *theocracy is the direct rule of God through his special presence or leaders to whom he gives supernatural knowledge or power*. Theocracy is not the same as a state-sponsored religion or a government influenced by religious beliefs.

In response, we say that the only true theocracy was Israel under the law of Moses. Theocracy will not come to earth again until Christ returns to make all things new (Rev. 21:1–5).

8 *Catechism of the Catholic Church* (New York: Doubleday, 1994), sec. 882.

Fifth, *anarchy is a lack of organized authority*. In a church with this polity, each Christian acts as an individual independent of all earthly spiritual authority.

In response, we say that the church must have a structured form of leadership. God is the God of order (1 Cor. 14:33, 40). The Holy Spirit provides overseers and teachers to shepherd God's flock (Acts 20:28; 1 Cor. 12:11, 28). God commands his people to submit to their leaders (1 Cor. 16:15–16; Heb. 13:17). Finally, the church needs organization to manage its financial help to the poor and widows (1 Cor. 16:1–4; 1 Tim. 5:9–12).

Sixth, *single-pastor polity is practiced by some congregationalist churches rather than plural-elder polity*. Perhaps this pastor has no fellow elders. Or perhaps he gives direction to one or more assistant or associate pastors under his authority.

In response, we note that the arguments for a single pastor are the same as those for a "bishop" in episcopal polity. There is no basis for this polity in the New Testament. Elders and bishops (overseers) are the same leaders (Titus 1:5, 7). The biblical pattern is for more than one elder in each church (Acts 14:23; Phil. 1:1; James 5:14). Furthermore, single-pastor polity places on the pastor more authority and responsibility than any one man should carry or have to carry.

Seventh, *pure democracy is the polity of some congregationalists who reject both plural-elder and single-pastor polities*. Though the church may have paid staff, most policies are determined by a vote of the members.

In response, we acknowledge that the members have an important function in selecting their leaders (Acts 6:3, 5). But the church is governed not by the will of the people but by the will of Christ (Matt. 28:18–20). Therefore, it must follow the biblical pattern of church government, which we have argued to be the servant-leadership of the council of elders. Attempts to implement pure democracy in the church tend to degenerate into petty dictatorships by members with strong personalities.

Let us never compromise Christ's instructions for the church. Christians can disagree about polity and still have sweet fellowship, assuming that they believe the same gospel of Christ and walk in the Spirit of Christ. But we must also recognize that ordering the church in a manner not commanded by Christ dishonors the King of the church. It also causes the church to drift away from the Word of God, a drift that over the years can lead it to a very dark place.

Practical Applications of Basic Principles of Church Government

Having laid out the basic principles of authority in the church, we close this chapter with some practical applications.

First, *the soul of church government is submission to Christ.* Without a Spirit-worked obedience to the Lord Jesus, there can be no proper exercise of authority in the church or right response to that authority. Therefore, our highest priority in establishing faithful church polity must be to bow before King Jesus. We must present ourselves as his willing servants.

Second, *church authority is given to men so that they might serve, not lord it over others.* Therefore, church officers should meditate often on the unique glory of Christ and learn to love him more. They should labor to care for Christ's bride as servant-leaders so that she may give single-minded devotion to him.

Third, *rejecting the lawful exercise of pastoral authority by the eldership is rebellion against the Lord.* Christ has put overseers into office by the Holy Spirit and has given his servants authority to shepherd the flock of God. Just as we should never treat mere men as if they were gods, so we must not belittle or despise the men whom God puts in authority over us.

Fourth, *the members of Christ's body bear significant responsibility for the church.* If they have the right to choose office bearers and participate in some other major church decisions, then they have the responsibility to do so wisely. Therefore, we must participate in church meetings in a manner that is faithful, informed, prayerful, loving, humble, and God-fearing.

Fifth, *voting is not for personal preference but to do the will of Christ.* Though the Lord has given his servants a voice, it is not for the purpose of advancing their personal agendas or parties in the church. Rather, it is so that his servants, whether in an elders' meeting or a members' meeting, may do the will of Christ for his church. Let us, therefore, conduct ourselves so that, by grace, we will one day hear him say, "Well done, good and faithful servant."

Suggested Song to Sing to the Lord

- "Shout, for the blessed Jesus reigns," *THBap*, No. 298

Questions for Meditation or Discussion

1. What basic principle of church authority has to do with Christ himself?
2. What basic principle of church authority has to do with elders?
3. How would you show from the Bible that "elders" and "bishops" refer to the same people?
4. What is the plurality of elders? How is it seen in the New Testament?
5. What basic principle of church authority has to do with the members of the church?
6. What is presbyterianism (as a form of church polity)? What arguments are presented for it?
7. What is congregationalism (again, as a polity)? What arguments are made for it?
8. What is strong connectionalism? What evidence is there for this in the New Testament?
9. What are the following forms of church government: (1) episcopal polity, (2) civil supremacy, (3) papacy, (4) theocracy, (5) anarchy, (6) single pastor, and (7) pure democracy?
10. What are some practical applications of the principles of church government?

77

Elders and Ministers of the Word

Chapter Summary and Key Terms

Christ rules his church through its ordained officers. Each particular church is governed by a council of spiritual shepherds, some of whom are called to preach (*ministers of the Word* or *teaching elders*) and some of whom do not ordinarily preach (*ruling elders*). All elders, including ministers, must have the qualifications of the ability to teach sound doctrine and blamelessness in moral conduct. God brings men into office by an *internal call to the ministry* (ability and blamelessness) and an *external call to the ministry* (recognition and ordination by the church). *Ordination* is the authorization of a person to serve as an office bearer, often through the laying on of hands. God trains ministers through *theological professors*. Ministers and ruling elders should serve God and his people in love, the Word, prayer, and leadership.

THE ORDAINED OFFICERS of the church are ministers of the Word, elders, and deacons. In *ordination*, the ministers and elders formally recognize a person's calling to bear office in the church and officially authorize him to perform that ministry (Acts 6:3–6; 13:1–3).

The New Testament makes a basic distinction between elders and deacons (Phil. 1:1; 1 Tim. 3:1–13).[1] The word "elders" includes most ministers of the Word, who also serve as shepherds of God's flock (1 Pet. 5:1–2). All elders must be able to teach (Titus 1:9), but only the ministers of the

1 As discussed in the previous chapter (chap. 76), "bishop" and "overseer" are other terms for "elder." See Acts 20:17, 28; Titus 1:5, 7; 1 Pet. 5:1–2.

Word are empowered by the Holy Spirit to preach as Christ's heralds (2 Cor. 3:3–8; 5:18–20).

In this chapter, we will study the elders and ministers of the church. In the next chapter, we will discuss deacons, the question of women in office, and practical applications.

The Elders of the Church

The Responsibilities of Elders

The elders must shepherd God's people (1 Pet. 5:1–2). Paul exhorts elders to "take heed therefore unto yourselves, and to all the flock, over the which the Holy Ghost hath made you overseers, to feed the church of God, which he hath purchased with his own blood" (Acts 20:28). Christ gave to the church "pastors and teachers" (Eph. 4:11), and the Greek word translated as "pastors" literally means "shepherds." Cornelis Van Dam writes, "Since the Lord Jesus is *the* Shepherd of the flock (John 10:11, 14; 1 Pet. 2:25), the elders as servant-shepherds are responsible to him."[2]

The elders shepherd the flock by teaching and ruling it (1 Tim. 3:2, 4–5; Heb. 13:7). An elder must hold firmly to "the faithful word as he hath been taught, that he may be able by sound doctrine both to exhort and to convince the gainsayers" (Titus 1:9). Elders are to "rule" (1 Tim. 5:17), "take care of" (3:5), and exercise "oversight" (1 Pet. 5:2) over the people of God. Elders "watch for your souls" (Heb. 13:17)—that is, they give careful attention to the spiritual condition of individual church members. This responsibility implies giving personal admonition (1 Cor. 16:15–16; 1 Thess. 5:12–13).

The authority of elders is shared in a consistory or council. If possible, every church should be governed by a plurality of elders, following the New Testament pattern (see chap. 76). The Word gives all elders the same titles of authority ("elder" and "overseer"). They share in the ministry of shepherding the church, whether they are *teaching elders* (vocational ministers of the Word) or *ruling elders*. Samuel Miller stressed that every member of the council of elders has an "equal voice" and "equal vote."[3]

2 Cornelis Van Dam, *The Elder: Today's Ministry Rooted in All of Scripture*, Explorations in Biblical Theology (Phillipsburg, NJ: P&R, 2009), 152, emphasis original.

3 Samuel Miller, *An Essay on the Warrant, Nature and Duties of the Office of the Ruling Elder in the Presbyterian Church* (Scarsdale, NY: Westminster Discount Book Service; Dallas, TX: Presbyterian Heritage, 1999), 204, 208. In some church polities, the chairman of the

The Qualifications of Elders

Elders must have certain spiritual qualifications. One major qualification is the ability to teach sound doctrine and refute false doctrine (1 Tim. 3:2; Titus 1:9). Teaching requires understanding Christian truth and an ability to communicate it clearly and compassionately (2 Tim. 2:24–25).

The other major qualification is "blameless" character (1 Tim. 3:2; Titus 1:6–7). This means having moral integrity. Paul lists specific moral qualifications (1 Tim. 3:1–7; Titus 1:5–9).

1. The elder must desire the work of the ministry with sincere love for God and people.
2. He must obey God's will for marriage. He may pursue a sexual or romantic relationship with only one woman—the one he marries.
3. He must lead his household so that his minor children are generally subject to his authority and reliable in their conduct.
4. He must show hospitality by opening his home and sharing his table.
5. He must have a clear and alert mind. He must be respectable and self-controlled.
6. He must be loving, gentle, and patient, not harsh, proud, or violent.
7. He must not get intoxicated with alcohol.
8. He must not grasp greedily after money or wealth.
9. He must love what is good. He must be just, righteous, and devoted to the Lord.
10. He must be mature, seasoned and humbled by the endurance of trials. He must have proven himself in the experience of those who know him—even unbelievers.

There are no perfect Christians. Those who nominate men for office in the church must therefore exercise charity and discernment. These qualifications describe well-rounded maturity in godliness but allow for ways in which a man still needs to grow.

---

consistory or session votes only in cases where there is a tie vote or a paper vote related to action on individuals.

Practical Directions for Elders and Ministers of the Word

We address the following directions to elders and ministers, but we encourage all believers to pray that God would give their leaders the grace to fulfill their responsibilities.

First, *do your ministry as servants of God.* David Dickson said, "We must love the Master, and the work for the Master's sake."[4]

Second, *keep watch over your own souls.* As we noted above, Paul says, "Take heed therefore unto yourselves" (Acts 20:28; cf. 1 Tim. 4:16).

Third, *be lifelong students of sound doctrine.* Read the Bible daily and digest it thoroughly. Study confessions, catechisms, and books of doctrine and systematic theology that are grounded in the Holy Scriptures.

Fourth, *grow as wise and well-informed church leaders.* Become familiar with your church's book of order or constitution. Always be reading, listening, and thinking.

Fifth, *love the church and its members.* Christ loves the church (Eph. 5:25). Should not the servants of Christ do the same? Put to death your impatience, arrogance, and selfishness.

Sixth, *visit, encourage, and admonish church members.* Care for souls (Heb. 13:17). Lovingly inquire into people's faith, obedience, and private devotions, and exhort them in godliness.

Seventh, *pray for the church, interceding for particular people.* Pray daily for the members of the church. Participate in prayer meetings. Pray with people when visiting them.

Eighth, *love your fellow ministers and elders, and hold them accountable.* Though you may have disagreements, stand together as a band of brothers.

The Ministers of the Word

The Doctrine of the Ministers of the Word

God has appointed some, but not all, of the church's elders with a special gift and commission to preach the Word. These men are called *preachers, ministers of the Word*, and *teaching elders.*

The Holy Scriptures speak of *preachers* of the Word. To "preach" means to proclaim, to declare publicly and boldly.[5] It is the word used of the task

4 David Dickson, *The Elder and His Work*, ed. George Kennedy McFarland and Philip Graham Ryken (Phillipsburg, NJ: P&R, 2004), 30.

5 We will discuss preaching in more detail in chap. 81.

of a herald sent by a king. Paul says, "How shall they preach, except they be sent?" (Rom. 10:15). A preacher of the Word, according to Paul, is a "man of God" (2 Tim. 3:17–4:2). The phrase has to do with a man sent by God as his messenger (Deut. 33:1; 1 Sam. 2:27; 1 Kings 12:22; 13:1). Therefore, a preacher is not merely someone who tells others the gospel, but is an official herald or messenger sent by God.

The Bible describes preachers as *ministers* (1 Tim. 4:6). The word translated as "minister" means "servant." Paul writes of the "ministers of the new testament," through whom the Spirit writes the Word on people's hearts (2 Cor. 3:3, 6, 8). Ministers of the Word are covenantal officers through whom the Mediator of the covenant works. A mark of their "ministry" is their plain declaration of "the word of God"; they "preach . . . Christ Jesus the Lord" (4:1–2, 5; cf. 1:19). They have "the ministry of reconciliation" (5:18) and speak as "ambassadors for Christ" (v. 20)—that is, Christ's authorized representatives. The apostles were ministers of the Word (Eph. 3:7–8), as are other preachers (1 Cor. 3:5–6; Col. 1:7).

Most ministers are *elders* in a church,[6] but not all elders are ministers of the Word. Paul makes a distinction within the eldership. He says, "Let the elders that rule well be counted worthy of double honour, especially they who labour in the word and doctrine" (1 Tim. 5:17). Paul here distinguishes the ministers of the Word from the rest of the eldership. John Owen said, "There are two sorts of elders, some that labour in the word and doctrine, and some who do not."[7] The word rendered as "labour" means to "toil, work hard, grow weary at one's task"—an appropriate term for full-time vocational work. This kind of labor in the Word is exactly what Timothy did as a "minister of Jesus Christ" (4:6–16).

After speaking of "double honor," Paul makes it clear that those who labor in the Word should receive financial support—"the laborer deserves his wages" (1 Tim. 5:17–18 ESV). Elsewhere, Paul says, "Let the one who is taught the word share all good things with the one who teaches" (Gal. 6:6 ESV). The phrase "all good things" implies full financial support. Just as the priests lived off the sacrifices at the temple, so also "the Lord ordained that they which preach the gospel should live of the gospel" (1 Cor. 9:13–14). All believers are servants of God, but most labor in other vocations. Only

6 Some ministers may be assigned to church planting, chaplaincies, missions, prisons, or other work.

7 Owen, *The True Nature of a Gospel Church*, in *Works*, 16:116. See Calvin, *Comm.* on 1 Tim. 5:17; and "Form of Ordination of Elders and Deacons," in *Doctrinal Standards, Liturgy, and Church Order*, ed. Joel R. Beeke (Grand Rapids, MI: Reformation Heritage Books, 1999), 145.

certain people are called by God to devote themselves to "the ministry of the word" (Acts 6:4).

God has given ministers of the Word special gifts and responsibilities to labor in the ministry of the Word. However, the church may not treat ministers as if they were mediators or kings. John Murray said, "It cannot be too strongly emphasized that, in respect to ruling, the minister of the Word is on a parity with all the others who are designated elders."[8]

God's Calling of the Ministers of the Word

God places a special calling and commission on those he appoints to the ministry of the Word. The Lord called Christ to be his Servant (Isa. 49:1–6). Christ called his apostles (Matt. 4:21; Mark 1:20). The Holy Spirit called Barnabas and Saul (Acts 13:2). Even today, God sends out ministers (Matt. 9:38), makes men into overseers (Acts 20:28), and gives to the church pastors and teachers (Eph. 4:10–11). God's call is both internal and external.

The *internal call to the ministry* consists of God's gifts of grace to qualify a man for the office. This begins with the holy desire for ministry and the blameless life required of all elders, as we saw earlier in this chapter (1 Tim. 3:1–7; Titus 1:5–8). God stirs within a man a desire so that he serves Christ "willingly" and "of a ready mind," not out of worldly ambitions or pride (1 Pet. 5:1–4). Rather, by God's grace, he has a holy motivation to proclaim the Word for the glory of God's name (3 John 7). Like Christ, his compassionate heart yearns for the salvation of perishing sinners (Matt. 9:36). He is willing to spend and to be spent for the edification of the church (Rom. 1:11; 2 Cor. 12:15). He must be like Ezra, who "set his heart to study the Law of the Lord, and to do it and to teach his statutes and rules in Israel" (Ezra 7:10 ESV). The man of God has an inner sense of obligation to preach the truth of God (Jer. 20:9; Rom. 1:14–15; 1 Cor. 9:16). Yet he may also struggle with his sense of call due to fear or a sense of his own unworthiness (Ex. 4:10–14; Jer. 1:6; 2 Tim. 1:7–8). God also gives him a fitness for the work through the natural gifts of mind to study and of voice to preach, the spiritual gifts of teaching, exhorting, and ruling (Rom. 12:7–8), and a mature grasp of sound doctrine gained by reading and meditating on the Word (1 Tim. 4:6, 13–16).

8 John Murray, *Collected Writings of John Murray*, 4 vols. (Edinburgh: Banner of Truth, 1982), 2:347.

The *external call to the ministry* consists of the demonstration of these gifts by actual ministry in the church and recognition of that giftedness by church officers and members. One reason why Paul chose Timothy to join his ministry team was Timothy's good reputation in the church (Acts 16:2). Paul gave the elders the responsibility to guard the flock against false teachers (20:28–30). This implies that elders supervise the selection of ministers. The external call to the ministry of the Word is sealed by the public act of ordination by the solemn laying of hands on the new preacher (13:3; 1 Tim. 4:14; 5:22). John Calvin said, "It is useful for the dignity of the ministry to be commended to the people by this sort of sign, as also to warn the one ordained that he is no longer a law unto himself, but bound in servitude to God and the church."[9]

God's Training of the Ministers of the Word

Men aspiring to the ministry must have opportunities to develop their gifts through training and mentoring (2 Tim. 1:2; 2:2; 3:10–11). A "good minister" of Christ must be "nourished up in the words of faith and of good doctrine" (1 Tim. 4:6). Teachers must train other teachers if the ministry is to continue and expand. Paul says, "The things that thou hast heard of me among many witnesses, the same commit thou to faithful men, who shall be able to teach others also" (2 Tim. 2:2). Christ's mandate to make disciples of all nations implies that the church must train teachers to the end of the age (Matt. 28:19–20).

Ministers of the Word should seek to encourage and train potential teachers. If qualified to do so, ministers should consider overseeing theological students periodically in pastoral internships. But most of the work of training future ministers falls on *theological professors* at seminaries. Calvin said, "There is a distinct class of teachers, who preside both in the education of pastors and in the instruction of the whole church."[10] Early Dutch Reformed theologians taught that there was a distinct office of "doctor" (or teacher) belonging to professors of theology. We see the power of such a ministry in the life of Laurence Chaderton, who trained generations of English Puritan ministers, including William Perkins, during his career at the University of Cambridge.[11]

9 Calvin, *Institutes*, 4.3.16.

10 Calvin, *Comm.* on Eph. 4:11.

11 See Joel R. Beeke, "Laurence Chaderton: His Life and Ecclesiology," in *Puritan Reformed Theology: Historical, Experiential, and Practical Studies for the Whole of Life* (Grand Rapids, MI: Reformation Heritage Books, 2020), 238–54.

The church needs godly and well-educated professors to train ministers and teachers. Most full-time ministers pastoring congregations do not have the time or the expertise to provide a complete ministerial education. Also, churches suffering severe persecution benefit from ministers trained in seminaries in countries where the church has more liberty. Seminaries must be closely connected to the church, both to hold professors accountable and to train people for practical ministry. Also, seminaries must never become merely academic but must cultivate biblical godliness. A true theologian is a member of Christ's body and a servant in his church.

The Faithfulness of the Ministers of the Word

A minister, by the very definition of the term, is a servant. Paul says, "Let a man so account of us, as of the ministers of Christ, and stewards of the mysteries of God. Moreover it is required in stewards, that a man be found faithful" (1 Cor. 4:1–2). The faithfulness of a minister is crucial for the life of the church. Paul exhorts the minister, "Take heed unto thyself, and unto the doctrine; continue in them: for in doing this thou shalt both save thyself, and them that hear thee" (1 Tim. 4:16). A faithful ministry is one of God's great means to bring his people through all their trials and temptations to receive full and ultimate salvation by grace. What does such a ministry look like?

First, *the minister must be faithful in his love for Christ and people.* Christ demands the heart of his minister. We see this in the question Christ pressed three times on Peter: "Do you love me?" (John 21:15–17 ESV). Love for Christ is the great motivation for ministry. The duty that Christ put on Peter—and which he puts on all the ministers of the Word—is, "Feed my lambs. . . . Tend my sheep. . . . Feed my sheep" (John 21:15–17 ESV). Ministers love Christ by loving his people.

Second, *the minister must be faithful in personal holiness.* The minister of the Word has a duty to set an example for his hearers to imitate, as do all elders (1 Pet. 5:3). Paul says, "Let no one despise you for your youth, but set the believers an example in speech, in conduct, in love, in faith, in purity" (1 Tim. 4:12 ESV). John Boys wrote that preachers should be "walking sermons," quipping, "He doth preach most, that doth live best."[12] Robert

12 John Boys, *An Exposition of the Dominicall Epistles and Gospels Used in Our English Liturgie* (London: by George Miller for William Aspley, 1630), 14.

Murray M'Cheyne said, "It is not great talents God blesses so much as great likeness to Jesus. A holy minister is an awful weapon in the hand of God."[13]

Third, *the minister must be faithful in laboring in the Word and prayer.* The apostolic pattern of ministry is "We will give ourselves continually to prayer, and to the ministry of the word" (Acts 6:4). Every minister should devote large blocks of his time to prayerful intercession, prayerful study of the Word, prayerful preaching of the Word, and prayerful thanksgiving for its Spirit-worked effects. Augustine said of the preacher, "He will succeed more by piety in prayer than by gifts of oratory; and so he ought to pray for himself, and for those he is about to address, before he attempts to speak."[14] To prayer, the minister must add the faithful study and proclamation of the Holy Scriptures. Paul says, "Meditate upon these things; give thyself wholly to them; that thy profiting may appear to all. Take heed unto thyself, and unto the doctrine; continue in them" (1 Tim. 4:15–16). The ministry of the Word also requires God's servants to speak the Word in private settings (Acts 5:42), such as home visitations, personal evangelistic encounters, and pastoral counseling sessions. The minister needs discernment to give each spiritual illness its proper medicine (1 Thess. 5:14).

Fourth, *the minister must be faithful in leadership.* Spiritual leadership is the wise exercise of proper authority to influence people to take united action with biblical intention, motivation, instruction, and association. Ministers and other elders provide leadership by a combination of example, relationship, and communication (1 Thess. 2:9–12). Though he must not try to do everything in the church, the minister must give direction to every area of church life: worship and sacrament, teaching, pastoral care, corrective discipline, pastoral prayer, evangelism and missions, finances and property, leadership development, and leadership health. The minister is Christ's construction worker through whom he builds his church (1 Cor. 3:5, 9–17).

Fifth, *the minister must be faithful in high ideals and imperfect attainment.* The minister must aim high in his pursuit of faithfulness to his Master. Yet the servant of Christ must lean heavily on God's grace. Every minister has shortcomings and weaknesses (2 Cor. 12:9).

13 Robert Murray M'Cheyne, letter to Daniel Edwards of October 2, 1840, in *The Memoir and Remains of Robert Murray M'Cheyne*, ed. Andrew A. Bonar (Edinburgh: Banner of Truth, 1973), 282.

14 Augustine, *On Christian Doctrine*, 15.32, in *NPNF*[1], 2:585.

Sixth, *the minister must be faithful in bearing the cross.* The faithful minister experiences a paradoxical mixture of pain and power. Paul says, "We are afflicted in every way, but not crushed; perplexed, but not driven to despair; persecuted, but not forsaken; struck down, but not destroyed. . . . For we who live are always being given over to death for Jesus' sake, so that the life of Jesus also may be manifested in our mortal flesh" (2 Cor. 4:8–9, 11 ESV).

Sadly, much of the sorrow of the ministry arises from people in the church. The minister must be faithful in responding to criticism with gracious love, humble self-examination, wise discernment, evangelical faith in Christ, and undaunted courage to fulfill his calling.[15] At the end of the day, however, the minister must learn to say with Paul, "It is a very small thing that I should be judged of you . . . but he that judgeth me is the Lord" (1 Cor. 4:3–4). The faithful minister of the Word is a servant of Christ, who will honor his servants with the reward of grace.

Suggested Song to Sing to the Lord

- "Saviour, like a Shepherd lead us," *THBap*, No. 644

Questions for Meditation or Discussion

1. What are the kinds of church officers?
2. What are the responsibilities of elders?
3. What qualifications must a man meet to be an elder?
4. What practical directions do the authors give to elders?
5. How do the Holy Scriptures describe the ministers of the Word?
6. How does God call a man into the ministry of the Word?
7. How does God train men to become ministers of the Word?
8. How must ministers be faithful in (1) love for Christ and people, (2) personal holiness, (3) laboring in the Word and prayer, (4) leadership, (5) high ideals and imperfect attainment, and (6) bearing the cross?
9. Based on what this chapter says about elders and ministers, what reasons do we have to show them love and respect? How can we support them?

15 See Joel R. Beeke and Nick Thompson, *Pastors and Their Critics: A Guide to Coping with Criticism in the Ministry* (Phillipsburg, NJ: P&R, 2020).

78

Deacons, Women in Office, and Duties to Officers

Chapter Summary and Key Terms

Three remaining matters concerning church officers are the office of deacon, the question of whether women should hold office, and the duties of members to officers. A *deacon* is an office bearer who serves Christ by managing the material concerns of the church, especially its ministries of mercy. Like an elder, a deacon must be qualified for office by a morally blameless life. God does not authorize the church to place women in office or allow them to teach the Word to groups of adult men. But God does work through women in many important kinds of ministry, for they are the spiritual equals of men, though different from them. Church members should treat their church's officers with love and respect, submit to their authority, serve under their direction, support their ministries by financial giving, and pray for them.

IN THIS CHAPTER, we conclude our consideration of church officers. We will look first at the biblical teaching on deacons. Then we will take up the controversial subject of whether women may hold office in the church. We will end with applications concerning the duties of church members toward their officers.

Deacons

The Greek word translated as "deacon" means "servant" or "minister." In two passages it is transliterated as "deacon" because it refers to an officer of the church who is distinguished from the "bishop" or "overseer" (Phil. 1:1; 1 Tim. 3:8–13, cf. vv. 1–7).

Unlike elders or overseers (1 Tim. 3:2; 1 Pet. 5:2), deacons do not have an office of teaching or pastoring. Ministers of the gospel and elders address spiritual concerns (true doctrine and righteous conduct). Deacons are ministers of material concerns. We see this division of labor between the apostles and the seven officers that the church in Jerusalem appointed to lead its benevolence ministry to Greek-speaking widows (Acts 6:1–7). Though the word "deacon" does not appear in the passage, these officers may be considered the first deacons.[1]

Therefore, we conclude that deacons are to care for the material concerns of the church, and especially to collect and distribute benevolence toward the poor. "Deacon" literally means "one who serves tables."[2] The office can be summarized in three "tables," so to speak: the table of the poor, the table of the ministers (their financial support), and the table of the Lord (the physical aspects of the Lord's Supper, which implies caring for the facilities and furnishings for public worship).

Deacons are not elders or mere money managers, but ministers of mercy. David Apple says that the deacons' ministry of practical mercy includes their responsibilities to

- "equip and mobilize the saints" to serve those in need,
- "collect the gifts of God's people and distribute them,"
- "come alongside those who are hurting,"
- "prevent poverty within the body,"
- "empower the needy to make good use of all available institutions of mercy," and
- maintain "an inventory of gifts and talents" in the congregation to help people.[3]

When administering relief to the afflicted, deacons should speak "comfortable words from Scripture."[4] They should especially remind the suffering of God's promises to his children of present provision and future fullness of joy.

1 Calvin, *Comm.* on Acts 6:1.

2 *TDNT*, 2:82–84, 87, 91.

3 David S. Apple, *Not Just a Soup Kitchen: How Mercy Ministry in the Local Church Transforms Us All* (Fort Washington, PA: CLC Communications, 2014), 140–51.

4 "Form of Ordination of Elders and Deacons," in *Doctrinal Standards, Liturgy, and Church Order*, ed. Joel R. Beeke (Grand Rapids, MI: Reformation Heritage Books, 1999), 146.

Both elders and deacons are servants of Christ who bear distinct but complementary offices from him as King of the church. However, deacons serve under the authority of the elders, who have oversight over the whole church (Acts 20:28; 1 Pet. 5:2).[5]

Deacons must have a good reputation and be full of the Holy Spirit and wisdom (Acts 6:3). Like elders, they must meet the moral qualifications set down in Scripture (1 Tim. 3:8–12). They must be blameless, worthy of respect, not drunkards or greedy men, honest in speech, and adherents of sound doctrine. They must be faithful to their wives ("husbands of one wife") and good managers of their households. Deacons must be tested before entering office.

Deacons who serve well obtain "a good degree, and great boldness in the faith which is in Christ Jesus" (1 Tim. 3:13). The first refers to public honor in the church. The second has to do with the confidence and liberty of an increased assurance of salvation. Great are the blessings of Christ on his faithful deacons!

Women in Office

Some of the most admirable figures in the Bible are women. But God has prohibited the church from placing women in positions of office or permitting them to teach the Word to groups of adult men.

God created male and female human beings in his image (Gen. 1:27). Therefore, men and women are equal in value and dignity. However, men and women are not identical but are two distinct genders. God created the man first, then the woman (2:7, 22), which Paul explains to mean that man has a leadership function (1 Tim. 2:12–13). God gave his commandment to the man before making the woman (Gen. 2:15–17), implying that the man had the duty to teach the woman. The Lord made the woman to be a "help meet" for the man (v. 18), or "a helper fit for him" (ESV). This means she is a powerful partner who complements him with her equal dignity as a human being and distinct strengths as a woman. The man gave the woman her name (2:23), another sign of his relative authority (1:5, 8, 10). Though the Serpent tempted the woman directly and she sinned first, the Lord called the man first to account (3:9).

5 In some Reformed churches that have only a few elders, deacons participate in most or even all consistory decisions.

Wives are called to submit to their husbands as their heads, and husbands to love their wives as their own bodies (Eph. 5:22–25; Col. 3:18–19). Ordinarily, wives serve as mothers and homemakers (1 Tim. 5:14; Titus 2:4–5). The influence of mothers on future generations of the church is incalculable (Prov. 1:8; 4:3; 2 Tim. 1:5).

Women are certainly not spiritually inferior to men. Paul says, "There is neither Jew nor Greek, there is neither bond nor free, there is neither male nor female: for ye are all one in Christ Jesus" (Gal. 3:28). Men and women share the same union with Christ, sealed by baptism (v. 27); the same adoption by God through faith in Christ (v. 26); and the same rights as heirs of God's covenant promises (v. 29). But spiritual equality does not erase all distinctions between them.

God chose men to be the primary teachers and rulers of Israel. All of the priests were men; there were no priestesses in Israel. All rightful monarchs in Israel were men. It is true that God gifted women to serve as prophets (Ex. 15:20; Judg. 4:4; 2 Kings 22:14), but the Scriptures give no indication that the prophetesses were involved in public preaching or teaching. Deborah also served as a judge (Judg. 4:4–5, 10), but she was the only female judge—hardly a pattern in Scripture.

Christ had many female disciples, but he selected only men to serve as his apostles (Matt. 10:1–4). When others were added to the apostolic office, such as Matthias, James, and Paul, they too were all men (Acts 1:26; Rom. 1:1; Gal. 1:19). Paul's statement that "Junia" was "of note among the apostles" (Rom. 16:7) is unclear. Was this person a woman or a man ("Junias")? Does Paul mean this person was one of the apostles or simply known to the apostles? Were these apostles like Peter and Paul or merely "messengers" or "missionaries," which are other meanings of the Greek term (cf. Phil. 2:25)? We have no clear evidence that there were any female apostles of Christ.

Paul's instructions about the qualifications of elders and deacons assume that they are men (1 Tim. 3:1–13). He uses masculine terms and says the office bearer must be the "husband" of one wife (vv. 2, 12). The officer must rule his household well (vv. 4, 12). The apostles instructed the church in Jerusalem to appoint men to minister to widows, and only men were selected (Acts 6:3, 5). Thus, these offices should be filled by men.

Some theologians allow for female deacons. In the qualifications for deacons, Paul also gives qualifications for women (1 Tim. 3:11). But these women are not called deacons (or deaconesses) there. It is more likely that Paul refers to deacons' wives or women who assist the deacons. Paul calls Phoebe "a servant of the church," using the same word translated as "deacon" or "minister" (Rom. 16:1). But this verse need not refer to an office in the church. Rather, Paul may be saying that Phoebe used her wealth and social position to help people and strengthen the ministries of the church (v. 2).

Paul says, "Let a woman learn quietly with all submissiveness. I do not permit a woman to teach or to exercise authority over a man; rather, she is to remain quiet" (1 Tim. 2:11–12 ESV). Thus, Paul forbids any ministry in the church of public teaching or spiritual authority by women over adult men. This prohibition appears just before Paul gives the qualifications of elders, who must be able to teach (3:2). Only men are to be elders or ministers of the Word.

Women can serve in many forms of ministry, though. They can labor to spread the knowledge of the gospel (John 4:28–30, 40–42; Phil. 4:2–3). They can do many good works for the poor (Prov. 31:20; Acts 9:36, 39). Women often are at the forefront of teaching biblical truth to children, beginning with their own (Prov. 6:20). Older women can train younger women in sound thinking and good works (Titus 2:3–4). On occasion, a woman may privately instruct a man (Prov. 31:1–9; Acts 18:26). Women can financially support the ministry (Luke 8:1–3). There are many ways that women can and do engage in ministry for the glory of God and the good of the church.

The Duties of Church Members to Officers

As we close our treatment of church government, we present applications for church members regarding their duties to officers.

First, *give officers your esteem, love, and honor*. Paul says, "We beseech you, brethren, to know them which labour among you, and are over you in the Lord, and admonish you; and to esteem them very highly in love for their work's sake" (1 Thess. 5:12–13). To "know" them probably means to give them attention and affection. Faithful ministers and elders who labor and suffer for the church should be received with joy, valued highly, and given double honor (Phil. 2:29; 1 Tim. 5:17). Robert Murray M'Cheyne said, "Love your pastor. . . . You little know the anxieties, temptations, pains and wrestlings, he will be called to bear for you."[6]

6 Robert Murray M'Cheyne, *Memoir and Remains of Robert Murray M'Cheyne*, ed. Andrew Bonar (1892; Edinburgh: Banner of Truth, 1966), 407.

Second, *recompense well the minister of the Word.* Paul writes that nature itself teaches this (1 Cor. 9:7), for what soldier serves at his own expense, or what farmer does not enjoy the fruit of his fields and flocks? Shall the minister share with you precious and eternal spiritual goods, and you not share with him material goods (v. 11)? Our goal should be to give "double honour" to those who rule well and labor in the Word (1 Tim. 5:17–18).

Third, *be slow to accuse officers, but support the removal of wicked leaders.* Paul says to Timothy, "Against an elder receive not an accusation, but before two or three witnesses. Them that sin rebuke before all, that others also may fear" (1 Tim. 5:19–20). Do not repeat gossip about officers or be quick to criticize them of wrongdoing. Do not expect a mere servant of Christ to be Christ. But support the removal of leaders who have proven to be disqualified by evil conduct.

Fourth, *consider your officers' example and imitate their faithfulness.* Follow them as they follow Christ (1 Cor. 4:16; 11:1; Heb. 13:7). Paul says, "Brothers, join in imitating me, and keep your eyes on those who walk according to the example you have in us" (Phil. 3:17 ESV).

Fifth, *submit to each officer's authority according to his office.* The author of Hebrews says, "Obey them that have the rule over you, and submit yourselves: for they watch for your souls, as they that must give account, that they may do it with joy, and not with grief: for that is unprofitable for you" (Heb. 13:17). Sheep who rebel against their God-given shepherds endanger themselves.

Sixth, *do not expect your officers to do everything.* The church is the body of Christ, in which every member has a spiritual gift that he or she must use for the edification of all (Rom. 12:4–8). Paul says, "The eye cannot say unto the hand, I have no need of thee" (1 Cor. 12:21). Consider how God has gifted you in talents and resources, make yourself available to the officers to serve as they think best, and take up every lawful opportunity to do good.

Seventh, *pray for your officers and their ministries.* Pray for ministers, that they would preach the Word faithfully, boldly, and with powerful effect. Pray for elders, that they would have holy motivation and skill to shepherd the flock of God among them and guard it against false teachers. Pray for deacons, that they would be filled with the Holy Spirit and wisdom for practical ministry, so that God would be glorified through works of mercy. Pray for all officers, that God would give them holiness and comfort. Ask

God to be their strength and peace, a fountain of living water that constantly irrigates their souls.

Suggested Song to Sing to the Lord

- Psalm 46, "God is our refuge and our strength," *Psalter*, No. 126; *THBap*, No. 37

Questions for Meditation or Discussion

1. What is the office of deacon? How can we deduce it from the Holy Scriptures?
2. What are the three "tables" that deacons serve?
3. What qualifications must a man fulfill to be considered for the office of a deacon?
4. What arguments support the teaching that women may not hold office in the church?
5. Someone says, "I know that Paul said he does not permit a woman to teach or exercise authority over a man (1 Tim. 2:12), but I don't think that one obscure verse, written by a man influenced by his sexist culture, should control what we think today. After all, the Bible says many positive things about women serving God." How do you respond?
6. What are some examples of ministry that women may perform in the church?
7. How should we think and feel about our church officers?
8. Why should churches pay their ministers of the Word full salaries if at all possible?
9. What does it mean to submit to the authority of (1) the deacons of your church, (2) the elders, and (3) the minister(s) of the Word? Be practical and specific in your answers.
10. Make a list of the officers in your church and specific ways you can pray for them. Keep the list in your Bible or devotional book and use it to make regular intercession for them.

79

Churches in Relation to Families and Civil Government

Chapter Summary and Key Terms

God instituted the family, the church, and the civil government—each with a distinct sphere of authority. The family arose first, when God created man. Fathers and mothers have the authority and responsibility to raise their children. God later made civil government to use coercive power to punish those who do evil and to praise those who do good. Civil standards and rights should come from God's moral law. According to *theonomy*, all nations must also follow the judicial law of Moses. But the judicial law no longer binds us to specific statutes; rather, it guides us in principles of moral and judicial wisdom. We should honor our civil rulers, pay them taxes, urge them to do justice, and pray for them. Civil rulers should acknowledge the Lord and follow his Word regarding civil justice. But contrary to the *establishment principle*, they should not punish false worship and open heresy or set up a national church and require people to worship in it.

THE POET JOHN DONNE once observed, "No man is an island."[1] We might also say, "No church is an island." Each church participates in a network of connections with individuals and groups. Among these groups, two of the most important are the family and the civil government. How does the church relate to these institutions? This is the question that this chapter will address.

1 John Donne, *Devotions upon Emergent Occasions*, ed. John Sparrow (Cambridge: Cambridge University Press, 1923), 98.

Churches and Families

God designed both the church and the family for our good. These institutions have different spheres of authority under him. Neither is under the other or independent of it. Rather, the church and the family support and complete each other.

The family is based on God's work of creation (Gen. 1:26–28; 2:18–25). The church is based on God's work of redemption in Christ. The nature and particular duties of the church are known only through the special revelation of God's Word.

God made the family before the church. Thus, the family is the original unit of society. This means it does not depend on the church for its legitimacy and authority. In its ministry to children, the church assists the heads of households, who have the responsibility to bring up sons and daughters "in the nurture and admonition of the Lord" (Eph. 6:4).

Our first circle of responsibility is our family, from birth (Ex. 20:12) through adulthood (Eph. 6:4; 1 Tim. 5:4, 8). However, the family is not our highest allegiance. Rather, we must love the Lord our God with all our hearts (Deut. 6:5; Matt. 10:37).

The church's shepherds have the authority to teach husbands, wives, parents, and children concerning their duties to one another (Col. 3:18–21). Ministers and elders may not exercise parental discipline on children. But they may exercise church discipline on members who persist in sin, including members who disobey God's commands about the family.

The gospel of Christ often divides families (Matt. 10:34–36). However, the gospel also creates a new family united by obedience to the Father (12:46–50) by the Spirit of Christ (Rom. 8:9, 14–15). The church is a spiritual family by the grace of adoption in Christ (Gal. 4:4–6). Christ's church is the only family that will last forever.

The Church and the Civil Government

God instituted the ministry of the church in the religious sphere of life and the civil government in the political sphere of life to maintain a just and well-ordered society. Paul and Peter both give extended instruction concerning civil magistrates (Rom. 13:1–7; 1 Pet. 2:13–17). In this section, we will outline biblical principles about the civil government and how the church should relate to it.

The Doctrine of Creation and Civil Government

God alone is the Creator, Lord, and Savior (Gen. 1:1; Deut. 4:35, 39). We should not look to any civil ruler to save us, for only God can do so (Isa. 45:21–22). No form of government can conquer the evils of human life, for they spring from the corruption of the heart.

God created man in his image to rule as his servants (Gen. 1:26–28). This means human authority is limited, not absolute. It is essentially good in proper relationships, and every human ruler is accountable to God for its right exercise.

All God's image bearers are essentially equal. Rulers and the ruled are under God, who made them both (Job 31:13–15; 34:19; Prov. 22:2). Peter says, "Honour all men. Love the brotherhood. Fear God. Honour the king" (1 Pet. 2:17). Therefore, we owe our civil rulers relative subjection fitting for one image bearer to show to others.

God created the family before civil government (Gen. 1:28; 2:18–25). Therefore, the civil government has no authority to change the God-given definition of marriage. Heads of households derive their authority not from civil government but from God.

God also authorized cultural dominion before civil government (Gen. 1:28–29). The rights of people to own and enjoy private property, engage in personal vocations, develop private businesses, and study and practice the arts and sciences depend not on civil government but on the Creator. Civil authority coexists with individual equality, family authority, and voluntary associations as a distinct and equally important sphere of human life.

The Moral Foundations for Civil Government

God instituted civil government. After mankind's fall into sin, the Lord instituted a new order with Noah: "Whoso sheddeth man's blood, by man shall his blood be shed: for in the image of God made he man" (Gen. 9:6). Obeying this command required judgment and execution by recognized authority. Thus, civil government originated from God, not as a social contract among men. It is a gift of God's goodness and wisdom to prevent anarchy. It is not inherently evil or demonic, but is a common grace of "our gracious God."[2]

God's moral law defines standards for civil justice. His law is "holy, and just, and good" (Rom. 7:12). The moral law is essential for civil government, for the ruler's authority is founded on justice and righteousness (Prov. 16:12; 25:4–5). Only when civil law is based on moral law can it appeal to the sense of right and wrong in the conscience (Rom. 1:32; 2:14–16). The rule of law over all citizens, including civil rulers, restrains corruption and tyranny.

According to *theonomy* (or Christian reconstruction), modern societies should be conformed to the Old Testament judicial law. But the Son of David does not rule an earthly nation. He sits at God's right hand in heaven, and his church has been multiplied into many churches among the nations. Yet even though the judicial law of Moses does not give us universal civil standards, we still can learn wisdom for civil justice from it. For example, it teaches restitution for stolen or damaged property (Ex. 22:1, 4–15). It distinguishes intentional murder and manslaughter (Num. 35:15–23). And it warns against convicting someone of a crime on the testimony of only one witness (Deut. 19:15).

God's moral law implies fundamental human rights. The first four of the Ten Commandments imply the human right to worship the true God as he appoints in his Word. The fifth commandment implies the right to exercise authority over one's children. The sixth implies the right to the preservation of one's life from unjust harm. The seventh implies the right to the faithfulness of one's spouse. The eighth and tenth imply the right to the possession and enjoyment of one's property. The ninth implies the right to speak the truth in public discourse and the preservation of one's good name from unjust slander.

Civil society is upheld by truthfulness and faithfulness. Societies composed of treacherous people are neither safe nor just (Jer. 9:2–5; Mic. 7:1–6). Trust is the very fabric of human society. Lies destroy the just administration of civil rulers (Prov. 17:7; 29:12). "Steadfast love and faithfulness preserve the king, and by steadfast love his throne is upheld" (20:28 ESV).

2 The Belgic Confession (Art. 36), in *TFU*, 60.

The Authority of Civil Rulers under God

The authority of every civil ruler comes from God. Christ told Pontius Pilate that he would have no civil authority "except it were given [him] from above" (John 19:11). Paul says, "There is no power but of God: the powers that be are ordained of God" (Rom. 13:1).

Paul commands everyone to "be subject" to civil rulers (Rom. 13:1; cf. 1 Pet. 2:13). The Greek verb translated as "be subject" means to honor someone's superior authority and voluntarily act as his subordinate. But no one should be counted a rebel for refusing to obey when it would mean sinning. Submission is due to rulers as obedience to God.

People have a true obligation to civil rulers but a total obligation to God. The Pharisees and Herodians asked, "Is it lawful to give tribute to Caesar, or not?" (Mark 12:14). Christ took a Roman coin and asked, "Whose is this image and superscription?" When they answered "Caesar's," Jesus said, "Render to Caesar the things that are Caesar's, and to God the things that are God's" (vv. 16–17). We bear God's image. Thus, we pay taxes to the government (Rom. 13:7), but we must give ourselves to God.

The civil ruler is God's servant. Paul says the civil official is God's "minister," literally his "servant" (Rom. 13:4, 6). This applies even to wicked kings—the Lord spoke of "Nebuchadnezzar the king of Babylon, my servant" (Jer. 27:5–6).

The Responsibility of Civil Rulers to God

God appoints the civil ruler for the public good. Paul says, "He is the minister of God to thee for good" (Rom. 13:4). John Calvin said, "They are not to rule for their own interest, but for the public good; nor are they endued with unbridled power, but what is restricted to the wellbeing of their subjects."[3] Augustine said, "Even those who rule serve those whom they seem to command."[4]

God gives authority to civil rulers "for the punishment of evildoers, and for the praise of them that do well" (1 Pet. 2:14). Paul says much the same: "Rulers are not a terror to good works, but to the evil. . . . Do that which is good, and thou shalt have praise of the same" (Rom. 13:3). Civil justice

3 Calvin, *Comm.* on Rom. 13:4.

4 Augustine, *The City of God*, 19.14, in *NPNF*[1], 2:411.

pertains to "works," visible and bodily actions that people "do" (v. 4). Since the magistrate is God's servant, the standard for good and evil is God's moral law.

Civil rulers may use force against evildoers. Paul says that the ruler is "a terror . . . to the evil. . . . For he beareth not the sword in vain" (Rom. 13:3–4). The "sword" represents deadly force (cf. Gen. 9:6). The Old Testament also authorized nonlethal corporal punishment consistent with human dignity (Deut. 25:1–3; Prov. 10:13; 19:29) and financial penalties (Ex. 21:18–19; 26–27). A ruler may also lead his people to engage in just war when it is necessary (Deut. 20:1–20).

Civil rulers often do evil. This is evident in the Pharaoh of the exodus (Ex. 1:15–22; 5:1–2), Jezebel (1 Kings 21:1–16), Manasseh (2 Kings 21:16), the king of Assyria (Isa. 36:18–20), and Herod the Great (Matt. 2:16). Civil government can degenerate into an evil persecuting power intoxicated with the blood of the saints (Rev. 17:6).

Those who hold civil office should share power and restrain one another. Since all men are sinful (Rom. 3:23), no one should be given absolute power. Kings tend to take more and more from their subjects until the people cry out for relief (1 Sam. 8:11–18). Thus, it is safest for a group of civil rulers to help, counsel, and rein in one another. Israel's government combined monarchy, aristocracy, and democracy (1 Sam. 11:15; 2 Sam. 5:3; Ezra 10:14)—a combination long recognized for its stability and wisdom.[5]

Civil rulers are subject to the law. Nothing in Romans 13 exempts the civil ruler from the same accountability due to others who do evil. Rather, Paul's reference to "every soul" (v. 1) includes the magistrate, who also must be subject to civil authority. God's law warns judges against favoritism toward the great and powerful (Lev. 19:15; Deut. 1:17). Civil rulers, too, may be condemned and punished by lawful authority (Judg. 3:8–30; 2 Kings 9).

The Lordship of Jesus Christ and Civil Government

Christ is Lord of all and should be acknowledged by all (Eph. 1:21). He is "the ruler of kings on earth" (Rev. 1:5 ESV), the "King of kings" (17:14; 19:16). The gospel call goes out to civil authorities: "Be wise now therefore,

5 On elements of monarchy, aristocracy, and democracy in church government, see chap. 76.

O ye kings: be instructed, ye judges of the earth. Serve the Lord with fear, and rejoice with trembling. Kiss the Son, lest he be angry, and ye perish from the way, when his wrath is kindled but a little. Blessed are all they that put their trust in him" (Ps. 2:10–12). A kiss here expresses honor (1 Sam. 10:1) and worship (1 Kings 19:18). Therefore, civil rulers should publicly honor Jesus Christ as God's Son and the supreme King (Ps. 2:6–7).

The *establishment principle* asserts that civil rulers in each country should set up a national church in sound doctrine and discipline. This principle would require rulers to punish idolaters and heretics, and to require all members of society to attend public worship in the national church. Supporters of this principle point to the sacred society of ancient Israel.

But the establishment principle contradicts the New Testament administration of God's church. Christ's kingdom advances by biblical teaching, not civil force. Christ told Pilate,

> My kingdom is not of this world: if my kingdom were of this world, then would my servants fight, that I should not be delivered to the Jews: but now is my kingdom not from hence.... Thou sayest that I am a king. To this end was I born, and for this cause came I into the world, that I should bear witness unto the truth. Every one that is of the truth heareth my voice. (John 18:36–37)

Likewise, Paul says, "Faith cometh by hearing, and hearing by the word of God" (Rom. 10:17). Therefore, the civil government should never seek to compel faith or attendance in worship.

Christ's correction of false worship and doctrine is not by civil power. As we noted above, the authority of civil rulers pertains to works and public justice, not beliefs, affections, and worship (Rom. 13:3–4). Disciplining people for false doctrine or worship belongs to the authority of the church, to which Christ gave the keys of the kingdom (Matt. 16:19; 18:15–17).

Christ's people should be protected by civil government against persecution. Civil rulers should not be persecutors but protectors of public justice, liberty, and peace so that churches can serve God freely without suffering unjust violence (Isa. 49:23; 60:16; Acts 25:11).

These truths illustrate the fact that Christ's church is a sphere of authority distinct from that of civil government. The Lord constituted the church and the state as different organizations with different officers. No civil ruler should intrude into the reign of Christ over his church. Nor do officers of the church have authority to rule over the civil government.

The Special Duties of Christians to Civil Government

Civil government must exercise its authority by God's wisdom (Prov. 8:15–16). Therefore, Christians should speak God's Word to civil rulers. When God provides opportunity, Christians working in the civil government ought to graciously remind their superiors of God's sovereignty and urge them to repent of their sins and practice righteousness and mercy to the poor (Dan. 4:17, 19, 27). Though ministers of the Word possess no ruling authority in civil government, they have the responsibility to teach God's Word to all people, including civil rulers.

Christian submission to civil authority supports the church's witness. By submitting to proper governmental authority, believers take away any basis for unbelievers to accuse them of being rebels or criminals (1 Pet. 2:13–16). God instructs his people to respect the ruler's power to take life, seek to live at peace with him, and avoid rebellious people (Prov. 16:14–15; 24:21–22; Eccles. 10:20).

Christians may work in civil or military service under wicked rulers. We have righteous examples to follow in the conduct of Daniel (Dan. 1:8–16; 2:17–18), Joseph (Genesis 41, 48), Obadiah (1 Kings 18:3–16), and Esther and Mordecai (Esther 7–9). God's prophets did not require soldiers to resign from military service when they turned to the Lord (2 Kings 5:1, 15–19; Luke 3:7–14). Instead, soldiers must honor and obey God in their military service.

However, Christians must disobey and resist sinful civil decrees (Acts 4:19; 5:29). Believers must worship God alone, even at the cost of their lives (Dan. 3:18, 28). They must persevere in their duties toward God, such as daily prayer, even if such activities become illegal (6:10–13). The godly have rightly disobeyed wicked orders from kings (Ex. 1:17, 20; 2 Kings 1:11–12), resisted unjust and unholy actions by rulers (1 Sam. 14:44–45; 2 Kings 6:32; 2 Chron. 26:16–20), and rebuked them for unwise courses of action (2 Sam. 20:18–20). They have hidden believers from persecuting rulers (1 Kings 18:3–4) and engaged in secret resistance against a wicked usurper until a rightful ruler could be established (2 Kings 11:1–16).

Christians should love and pray for civil rulers. Paul tells Timothy to see that in the church "supplications, prayers, intercessions, and giving of thanks, be made for all men; for kings, and for all that are in authority" (1 Tim. 2:1–2). In all our interactions with the civil government, we must remember that we are dealing with real people created in God's image.

Though Christians are citizens of their earthly homelands, they must remember that only Christ's kingdom lasts forever (Isa. 9:6–7). Believers are "strangers and pilgrims on the earth" (Heb. 11:13–16). Augustine said, "As far as this life of mortals is concerned, which is spent and ended in a few days, what does it matter under whose government a dying man lives, if they who govern do not force him to impiety and iniquity?"[6] God will bring both "small and great" to judgment (Rev. 20:12). All will answer to him who shows no partiality (Eph. 6:9; Col. 3:25).

Suggested Songs to Sing to the Lord

- Psalm 82, "Where'er His creatures gather the unseen God is near," *Psalter*, No. 223
- Psalm 133, "How pleasant and how good it is," *Psalter*, No. 369

Questions for Meditation or Discussion

1. What does it mean that the church and the family are different spheres of authority under God?
2. How should pastors assist parents and hold them accountable while respecting their authority in the home?
3. What are the implications of the doctrine of creation (Genesis 1) for civil government?
4. What are the moral foundations for civil government?
5. What obligations do people have toward their civil rulers? Why?
6. What is the responsibility of civil rulers to God? What is their God-given task?
7. How can civil rulers best honor Christ's lordship and kingdom?
8. Why is it wrong for the civil government to use its coercive force to convert people to true religion and punish those who teach heresy or practice false worship?

6 Augustine, *The City of God*, 5.17, in *NPNF*[1], 2:98.

9. What special responsibilities do Christians have toward civil rulers?
10. Under what circumstances is it right to disobey or resist an order from a civil ruler? What is the difference between principled Christian resistance and sinful rebellion?

80

The Work of the Church

Chapter Summary and Key Terms

Christ has commissioned the church to perform three works: public worship, edification, and evangelism. *Public worship* is the exercise of love for God through outward expressions of his honor and worthiness in the assembly of his people in his special presence. God's people must offer him only the *elements of public worship* that he commands in the Bible (the *regulative principle of worship*). *Edification of the church* is the building up of God's people in love to full maturity in Christ. God edifies the church through the public means of grace, the private means of grace, and works of benevolence to the saints. *Evangelism* is communicating the gospel to unbelievers in love to call them to salvation through repentance and faith in Christ. God works through evangelism by means of the Word and prayer. God also uses believers' works of love and their holy and submissive conduct despite unjust suffering as evidence of the truth of the gospel.

THE GREAT COMMISSION summarizes the work that Christ has called the church to do in dependence on his lordship while it waits for his return. This work has three aspects. First, the command to "go therefore and make disciples of all nations" requires the work of *evangelism*. Second, "baptizing them in the name of the Father and of the Son and of the Holy Spirit" requires the work of *public worship*. And third, "teaching them to observe all that I have commanded you" requires the work of *edification of the church* (Matt. 28:19–20 ESV). In this chapter, we will examine the threefold work of the church.

The Public Worship of God

Worship revolves around God from beginning to end. It is the act of his creatures to celebrate his unique glory according to his will. Worship belongs to God alone.

The Meaning of Public Worship

We may distinguish between three senses of the term *worship*, like three concentric circles. In its broadest sense, worship is offering all of one's life to God to do his will in response to his mercies (Rom. 1:9; 12:1–2). In a more focused sense, worship refers to loving God from the heart by outward expressions of his worthiness, such as singing his praises (Rev. 5:9). In its narrowest sense, worship is the exercise of love for God through outward expressions of his honor in the assembly of God's people. That is public worship.

Public worship is superior to private worship. Christ promises his special presence to the gathered church (Matt. 18:20). God is glorified by more people in a more open manner in public worship (Pss. 22:22–25; 96:1–3). Also, Christ works more powerfully in public worship, as the ministry of the Word builds up the church and every member builds up one another (Eph. 4:10–16).

Public worship is an open and affectionate work of honoring God, offered as a believing and obedient response to his Word by the assembled church because of his mercies in Christ. We can see each of these aspects of worship in Psalm 100:

- *an open and affectionate work of honoring God.* "Make a joyful noise unto the Lord, all ye lands. Serve the Lord with gladness: come before his presence with singing" (vv. 1–2).
- *offered to God as a believing and obedient response to his Word.* "Know ye that the Lord he is God: it is he that hath made us, and not we ourselves" (v. 3). Worship is obedience: note the commands to "make," "serve," "come," and "know" (vv. 1–3).
- *by the assembled church.* "We are his people, and the sheep of his pasture" (v. 3). It is the work of the church gathered in his holy presence: "Enter into his gates with thanksgiving, and into his courts with praise: be thankful unto him, and bless his name" (v. 4).

- *because of his mercies in Christ*. "For the LORD is good; his mercy is everlasting; and his truth endureth to all generations (v. 5).

God has designated one day in seven as the day of worship—the holy Sabbath (see chap. 69 on the fourth commandment). The Sabbath is the day of assembly for sacred worship (Lev. 23:3; Psalm 92). Therefore, God warns against "forsaking the assembling of ourselves together, as the manner of some is" (Heb. 10:25). Reformed churches have traditionally held worship services in the morning and the evening (or sometimes in the afternoon) of the Lord's Day. The second service, while not commanded in Scripture, is a great help for taking full advantage of the means of grace and sanctifying the whole day. A vibrant love for God moves believers to ask not how much time they *must* spend in public worship but how much they *can* spend there.

The Rule of Public Worship

In most areas, God allows us to order our lives as we choose, as long as we keep his law in love. However, in public worship, we enter the house of God to engage in holy, priestly work in his special presence. Therefore, we are not at liberty to worship as we please. We must offer to God only the worship that he has commanded. This rule of Reformed worship is known as the *regulative principle of worship*. The Heidelberg Catechism says God requires that we not "worship Him in any other way than He has appointed in His Word."[1]

God instituted Israel's first ordinance of worship, the Passover, with detailed instructions (Ex. 12:1–18). Israel followed them "as the LORD commanded" (v. 50). In the first four of the Ten Commandments, the Lord asserted his authority to regulate the object, means, attitude, and time of his people's worship by his Word (Ex. 20:3–11). In Exodus 39–40, we read fifteen times that the tabernacle was constructed "as the LORD commanded." Later, Moses warned Israel that it must not copy the worship of the nations and said, "Everything that I command you, you shall be careful to do. You shall not add to it or take from it" (Deut. 12:30–32 ESV).

When two priests offered incense to the Lord that he did not command, God took their lives and insisted that he must be honored as holy by his

1 The Heidelberg Catechism (LD 35, Q. 96), in *TFU*, 102.

worshipers (Lev. 10:1–3). Centuries later, God struck down a man who transported the holy ark of the covenant in a manner that he had not commanded and even dared to touch it (1 Chron. 13:6–10; 15:2). Afterward, David commented, "The LORD our God broke out against us, because we did not seek him according to the rule" (vv. 12–15 ESV). Among the sins of Jeroboam and Ahaz was their institution of forms of worship that they invented or copied from other nations (1 Kings 12:31–33; 2 Kings 16:10–16).

Christ quotes Isaiah, saying, "In vain do they worship me, teaching for doctrines the commandments of men" (Matt. 15:5–9; cf. Isa. 29:13). Worship based on human inventions is worthless. Paul admonishes believers not to submit to religious ordinances "after the commandments and doctrines of men," condemning "will worship" (Col. 2:20–23)—that is, "self-chosen worship."

New covenant worship is much simpler than old covenant worship, but we must still "serve God acceptably with reverence and godly fear: for our God is a consuming fire" (Heb. 12:28–29). Furthermore, we have not yet arrived in the new Jerusalem, the "holy city" where all things are holy (Rev. 21:2; cf. Zech. 14:20). There remains a distinction between daily devotions and the public worship of the assembled church. For example, when God's people celebrate the Lord's Supper, it is a holy activity. Thus, when some people in Corinth profaned the Supper, God struck many with illness and some with death (1 Cor. 11:20–22, 30–31).

The regulative principle of worship does not hinder "thanksgivings upon special occasions," as the Westminster Confession of Faith says.[2] For example, the Scriptures also approve of the Feast of Purim, which was instituted by Esther and Mordecai without a specific command from God (Est. 9:20–32).

The Westminster Confession of Faith says, "The acceptable way of worshipping the true God is instituted by Himself, and so limited by His own revealed will, that He may not be worshipped according to the imaginations and devices of men, or the suggestions of Satan, under any visible representation, or any other way not prescribed in the holy Scripture."[3]

2 The Westminster Confession of Faith (21.5), in *RC*, 4:259. Cf. the Second London Baptist Confession (22.5), in *RC*, 4:558.

3 The Westminster Confession of Faith (21.1), in *RC*, 4:258. Cf. the Second London Baptist Confession (22.1), in *RC*, 4:559.

To clarify the application of the regulative principle, Reformed theologians distinguish between an element of worship, its form, and its circumstances.

An *element of public worship* is something that God sets apart as holy and blesses as a means of grace. It is a way to commune with God by faith in Christ. For example, God dwells in the praises of his people (Ps. 22:3). The elements of public worship under the new covenant include the following:

- reading the Holy Scriptures (Col. 4:16; 1 Thess. 5:27; 1 Tim. 4:13; Rev. 1:3)
- praying together to God (Isa. 56:7; Acts 2:42; 4:23–31; 1 Tim. 2:1–4, 8)
- preaching and teaching the Word (1 Tim. 4:11; 2 Tim. 4:2)
- singing God's praise (Eph. 5:19; Col. 3:16)
- offering financial gifts (1 Cor. 16:1–2; Phil. 4:18; Heb. 13:16)
- administering baptism (Matt. 28:19; Acts 2:41; Eph. 4:5)
- celebrating the Lord's Supper (1 Cor. 10:16–17; 11:17–34)

The *form of public worship* is the content of an element. For example, the words used in prayer are its form. The form or content of Christian worship should be richly biblical. As Terry Johnson says, we are to "read the Bible, preach the Bible, sing the Bible, pray the Bible, and see the Bible" (in baptism and the Lord's Supper).[4]

A *circumstance of public worship* is an ordinary thing that assists God's people in worshiping him in an organized way without distractions. It is not something regarded as sacred or spiritually powerful. Circumstances include such things as a building, seating, lighting, service times, audio amplification, audio and video recording, and so on. The Westminster Confession of Faith says that "there are some circumstances concerning the worship of God . . . common to human actions and societies, which are to be ordered by the light of nature, and Christian prudence, according to the general rules of the Word, which are always to be observed."[5] Matters

4 Terry L. Johnson, "The Regulative Principle," in Terry L. Johnson et al., *The Worship of God: Reformed Concepts of Biblical Worship* (Fearn, Ross-shire, Scotland: Christian Focus, 2005), 24–26.

5 The Westminster Confession of Faith (1.6), in *RC*, 4:235. Cf. the Second London Baptist Confession (1.6), in *RC*, 4:533.

of circumstance are not limited by the regulative principle. They vary from church to church.

In the new covenant, the regulative principle directs the church to worship God in a spiritual and simple manner. Christ says that people no longer need a sacred place or holy temple for worship, for "God is a Spirit: and they that worship him must worship him in spirit and in truth" (John 4:24). Old covenant worship had many outward ceremonies that were types of Christ. In the new covenant, worship has few ceremonies. It focuses on receiving and rejoicing in the knowledge of Christ applied to our hearts by the Holy Spirit. Spiritual and simple worship is a joy to those who have received "the spiritual renovation of the affections that gives [us] delight in God through Christ," as John Owen said.[6]

God the Son incarnate is the great High Priest of the church and its supreme worship leader (Heb. 2:12; 13:15). Christ directs public worship through the people whom he appoints to shepherd the church (1 Pet. 5:2). Therefore, ministers and elders have the authority and responsibility to lead the worship services of the church. That is not to say that they must do everything. But Christ will call them to account for how the congregations under their care worshiped God (Heb. 13:15–17).

The Heavenly Glory of Public Worship

Though remaining on earth, the church militant draws near to God's "throne of grace" through Jesus Christ (Heb. 4:15–16). By faith in Christ, believers have "boldness to enter into the holiest" and to "draw near" to God (10:19, 22). When they do so, they "come unto mount Sion, and unto the city of the living God, the heavenly Jerusalem . . . and to Jesus the mediator of the new covenant" (12:22–24). Amazingly, the church on earth worships with the church in heaven before the face of God, so public worship is a foretaste of heaven on earth. William Perkins said, "The church of God upon earth is as it were the suburbs of the city of God, and the gate of heaven."[7] Therefore, public worship is a sacred activity of the church. It must be conducted with joy in God, fear toward him, and gratitude for the great privilege of drawing near to his throne.

6 Owen, *The Grace and Duty of Being Spiritually Minded*, in *WJO*, 7:423–30.

7 Perkins, *Divine Worship*, in *Works*, 7:496; cf. Gen. 28:17.

The Edification of True Believers

Edification corresponds to God's work of sanctifying his people by grace. Since we have already addressed that topic (chap. 63), our treatment of edification will be briefer and will focus on the ministry of the church. Paul says in his instructions for the church, "Let all things be done unto edifying" (1 Cor. 14:26). The words translated as "edify" (1 Thess. 5:11) and "edification" (Rom. 15:2) literally refer to "building," as in a physical house or its construction. Used metaphorically for people, "edify" means to strengthen or cause to grow to maturity (Eph. 4:12–13, 16). Edification never ceases until Christ is finished building his church (Matt. 16:18).

God motivates the members of his church to engage in the work of edification by placing in their hearts a Christlike love for one another. Christ works in his body "unto the edifying of itself in love" (Eph. 4:16). Believers' efforts to edify one another ultimately aim at glorifying God (Rom. 15:2, 5–6).

The aim of the church's work of edification is nothing less than our bearing Christ's perfect image and becoming full of his glory (Rom. 8:17, 29). Therefore, the goal of edification is full maturity in Christ (Col. 1:28), an ideal that the church will pursue until Christ returns. Edification aims to develop Christlike doctrinal beliefs, moral character, and communion with God (Eph. 4:13). It also seeks after unity, stability, and ministry in Christ (vv. 13–16).

The primary instruments that Christ employs to edify his church are his appointed ministers and shepherds. Paul says, "He gave some . . . pastors and teachers; for the perfecting of the saints, for the work of the ministry, for the edifying of the body of Christ" (Eph. 4:11–12). The Lord uses pastoral ministry to apply his Word to the church through the public means of grace (see the following chapters), private means of grace (reading, meditation, prayer, etc.), and works of benevolence to the saints.

God gives effective power to the church's work of edification. Paul writes of his ministry to "present every man perfect in Christ Jesus," then adds, "I also labour, striving according to his working, which worketh in me mightily" (Col. 1:28–29). Therefore, the church should do the work of edification with dependence, prayer, faithfulness, perseverance, joy, and thanksgiving. All growth is from God (1 Cor. 3:7), so all glory for edification must go to him.

The Evangelism of the Unsaved

The word *evangelize* comes from a Greek term that means "to announce good news"—that is, to tell people the gospel. J. I. Packer defined evangelism as "going out in love, as Christ's agent in the world, to teach sinners the truth of the gospel with a view to converting and saving them." He added, "If, therefore, we are engaging in this activity, in this spirit, and with this aim, we are evangelizing, irrespective of the particular means by which we are doing it."[8] If we would do evangelism, we must keep the focus on telling people about Jesus Christ, his saving work, and the command to respond to him in faith and repentance (see chap. 56).

Two great motivations spur on Christians to evangelize the unsaved. First, we should evangelize out of love for the Lord in his glory (Ps. 96:3–4). Second, we should communicate the gospel in love for the lost in their desperate need (Matt. 9:36).

Satan labors to distort the church's evangelism in various ways. Preachers may tell people that they are saved simply because they prayed a prayer to ask Jesus into their hearts—though they may lack saving faith and repentance (chap. 60). Preachers may add to the gospel the false promise that faith in Christ will bring them health and wealth in this world (chap. 88). Or preachers may fail to preach the whole Christ: they may offer the Priest to forgive sins but neglect the Prophet to teach us and the King to rule us and make us holy (chap. 45).

God has provided two great means of evangelism, which go hand in hand. One is the knowledge of the Holy Scriptures. We must use the Bible in evangelism, reading it to unbelievers, quoting its very words, and explaining its meaning (Acts 8:27–35; 2 Tim. 3:15). The other means of evangelism is prayer. We should regularly pray for the salvation of lost and perishing sinners (Rom. 10:1). We should also pray regularly that we and other Christians would do evangelism and that it would be effective (Col. 4:3–4; 2 Thess. 3:1).

God also uses two forms of evidence to draw attention to his gospel and grace. One is the practice of Christian love to other people (John 13:34–35). Jesus says, "Let your light so shine before men, that they may see your good

8 J. I. Packer, *Evangelism and the Sovereignty of God* (Downers Grove, IL: InterVarsity Press, 1961), 53.

works, and glorify your Father which is in heaven" (Matt. 5:16). Another evidence is holy and submissive conduct despite suffering (1 Pet. 2:12, 15; 3:1–4, 15–16). It has been rightly said, "Evangelism is pre-eminently dependent upon the quality of the Christian life which is known and enjoyed in the church."[9]

We should sow the gospel as broadly as we can. Methods of evangelism include the following:

- preaching in public worship
- preaching outside the church
- raising our children in the knowledge of God's law and gospel
- witnessing personally to non-Christians
- teaching the Bible and a catechism
- starting church programs of gospel outreach
- forming parachurch organizations
- engaging in polemics against false teaching and apologetics to defend Christianity
- running ministries of mercy that include communicating the gospel
- publishing gospel truth in print and electronic form
- sending preachers to unreached communities
- planting new churches
- training new preachers and teachers

Christ says, "This gospel of the kingdom shall be preached in all the world for a witness unto all nations; and then shall the end come" (Matt. 24:14). Therefore, all those who love Christ and long for his coming must do what they can to spread the gospel throughout the world. It is indeed a daunting task. But Christ promises, "All power is given unto me in heaven and in earth. . . . And, lo, I am with you always, even unto the end of the world" (Matt. 28:18, 20). Therefore, God's servants must do evangelism by faith in Christ. Let us be faithful to preach his Word (not our own ideas) and to walk in obedience to his commandments. And let us devote ourselves to prayer that "thy kingdom come" (Matt. 6:10), so that "Satan's kingdom may

9 Iain H. Murray, *David Martyn Lloyd-Jones: The First Forty Years, 1899–1939* (Edinburgh: Banner of Truth, 1982), 246.

be destroyed; and that the kingdom of grace may be advanced, ourselves and others brought into it, and kept in it; and that the kingdom of glory may be hastened."[10]

Suggested Songs to Sing to the Lord

- Psalm 67, "O God, to us show mercy," *Psalter*, No. 176; *THBap*, No. 385
- Psalm 100, "All people that on earth do dwell," *Psalter*, No. 268; *THBap*, No. 1

Questions for Meditation or Discussion

1. How do the authors explain the meaning of public worship?
2. What is the regulative principle of worship? What are some key biblical texts that support it?
3. Explain the distinction between the elements, form, and circumstances of public worship. What are examples of each?
4. In what sense is the public worship of the church "heavenly"?
5. What do the words "edify" and "edification" mean? What is the goal of edification?
6. What good motives drive both edification and evangelism?
7. What are the practical implications of the fact that God alone has the power of edification?
8. What is evangelism? How might Satan distort the church's evangelism?
9. What are the means of evangelism? What are the confirming evidences of the gospel?
10. Which methods of evangelism do you use? How else could you do evangelism?

10 The Westminster Shorter Catechism (Q. 102), in *RC*, 4:367. Cf. the Baptist Catechism (Q. 109), in *RC*, 4:588.

Section 6C

The Church's Means of Grace

81

The Means of Grace and the Ministry of the Word

Chapter Summary and Key Terms

The *means of grace* are the sacred activities that God appointed as his instruments to give saving grace to people by the work of the Holy Spirit. Some means of grace are *sacraments*, covenantal signs and seals of the grace of Christ. According to the *sacramental system* of Roman Catholicism and *Eastern Orthodoxy*, there are seven sacraments by which the church mediates the grace of Christ. But the Bible speaks of only two signs of grace in the new covenant: baptism and the Lord's Supper. The primary means of grace is God's Word. Christ, the only Mediator, gives grace by the Spirit working through faith by means of the Word. The other means of grace are ways of applying the Word through faith. The public means are the preaching and teaching of the Word, prayer, praise, fellowship, church discipline, and the sacraments of baptism and the Lord's Supper. Foremost among them is preaching, which should be biblical, doctrinal, experiential, and practical. To profit from the preaching of God's Word, we should prepare ourselves with prayer, receive the Word with humility, and practice the Word with obedience.

GOD DOES NOT NEED any instruments to accomplish his will. But he generally works through means. Thus, he directs us to seek his blessing by a diligent use of means. The means of grace, Charles Hodge explains, are those sacred activities that "God has ordained to be the ordinary channels of grace, i.e., of the supernatural influences of the Holy Spirit, to the souls of men."[1] Some means of grace are called "sacraments," which are sacred acts of public worship that God appointed as covenantal signs and seals of the grace of Christ.

A balanced approach to the means of grace is necessary for healthy Christianity. If we separate God's grace from the means, we fall into mysticism. We may then seek direct experiences of God's indwelling presence or inner light. But if we bind grace to the rites of the church, we will think that all saving grace comes "through the sacraments" and "increases through them or, when lost, is regained through them," as Roman Catholicism teaches.[2]

The Sacramental System

In the medieval period, the church developed a system of seven sacraments that, according to Roman Catholicism and Eastern Orthodoxy, administer God's grace. This list of sacraments first appeared in the writings of Peter Lombard in the twelfth century. The seven sacraments of this system are as follows:

- *baptism* in water for forgiveness of sins and regeneration by the Holy Spirit
- *confirmation* (or chrismation) with holy oil for strengthening by the Holy Spirit[3]
- *the Eucharist* (or Mass) to increase grace by receiving the Lord's body and blood
- *penance* for sin by contrition, confession, and satisfaction for temporal punishment[4]
- *extreme unction* with holy oil to increase grace in preparation for death
- *holy orders* to set men apart to be clergy (bishops, priests, and deacons)

1 Charles Hodge, *Systematic Theology*, 3 vols. (1871–1873; repr., Peabody, MA: Hendrickson, 1999), 3:466.

2 Council of Trent (Session 7, Decree on the Sacraments, foreword), in *Denzinger*, sec. 1600 (388).

3 In Eastern Orthodoxy, chrismation is performed immediately upon baptism, not later as confirmation.

4 Eternal punishment for sin is said to be taken away by Christ's blood, but temporal punishment must be taken away by making satisfaction through works of penance or by suffering in purgatory (chap. 89).

- *marriage* to sanctify sexual union and the procreation and education of children

According to Roman Catholicism, the elements of the Eucharist are transformed by the miracle of transubstantiation into the body and blood of Christ (see chap. 84). It is said that the Lord instituted the Eucharist to "perpetuate" his sacrifice and make it "present" on earth as priests offer it to God for the forgiveness of sins.[5] Thus, the sacrifice of the Eucharist is "truly propitiatory" and provides "satisfaction" for the sins of the living and the dead.[6]

In this system, the sacraments "contain the grace they signify" and "confer that grace on those who do not place an obstacle in the way," and such grace is given "by the performance of the rite itself" (*ex opere operato*).[7]

The Reformation Criticism of the Sacramental System

The Reformers argued that the only sacraments revealed in the Holy Scriptures are baptism and the Lord's Supper. As to the Supper, transubstantiation has no basis in the Bible. The claim that the Mass makes satisfaction to God for sins by offering up Christ denies his finished work on the cross (Heb. 9:26; 10:10). Thus, the Lord's Supper is no sacrifice for sins, but a sacrifice of praise (13:15). In the Supper, God's people exercise faith in Christ's finished work and offer themselves as living sacrifices in response to his mercies in Christ (Rom. 12:1).

The Reformers also rejected the doctrine that the sacraments confer grace by the performance of the ceremony itself (*ex opere operato*). Instead, they said that the sacraments present Christ for the strengthening of faith by the power of the Holy Spirit through the gospel. The Belgic Confession says:

> [God] ordained the sacraments for us . . . to nourish and strengthen our faith, which He hath joined to the Word of the gospel. . . . For they are

5 *Catechism of the Catholic Church* (New York: Doubleday, 1994), secs. 611, 1323, 1362–1366; cf. Council of Trent (Session 22, Doctrine and Canons on the Sacrifice of the Mass), in *Denzinger*, sec. 1740 (417).

6 Council of Trent (Session 22, Doctrine and Canons on the Sacrifice of the Mass), in *Denzinger*, sec. 1743 (418).

7 Council of Trent (Session 7, Canons on the Sacraments in General), in *Denzinger*, secs. 1606, 1608 (389).

> visible signs and seals of an inward and invisible thing, by means whereof God worketh in us by the power of the Holy Ghost. . . . For Jesus Christ is the true object presented by them.[8]

A Biblical, Reformed Perspective on the Means of Grace

Let us consider now what the Bible teaches about the means of grace. We begin with the truth that Christ alone is the Mediator of God's saving grace (1 Tim. 2:5; Heb. 8:6). In the sacramental system, the officers of the church function as mediators between the Mediator and the people. The pope, bishops, and priests claim to be the sacrament behind the sacraments.[9] In reality, the officers of the church are merely ministers (servants) of the new covenant, not its mediators (2 Cor. 3:6). They have no sufficiency of themselves (v. 5).

God saves through internal and external means. The internal means is faith in Jesus Christ (John 1:12–13; Eph. 2:8). The primary external means by which God creates and nurtures faith is his Word. Paul says, "Faith cometh by hearing, and hearing by the word of God" (Rom. 10:17). The Word of God is his power to save (1:16) and to sanctify (John 17:17).

Though the great means of grace is the Word, God has ordained other external means to bring the Word into people's lives through faith. The most prominent public means are the *preaching* and *teaching* of the Word (1 Thess. 2:13). True *prayer* is a believing response to God's Word (Matt. 21:22; John 15:7). In prayer, we lift holy desires to God in requests that reflect his will revealed in the Word (1 John 5:14). A particular form of prayer is the public *praise* of God. By praising God, Christians edify themselves and one another (Pss. 34:2; 92:1; Col. 3:16). Christ works through all the members of the church as they are "speaking the truth in love" to one another in *fellowship* (Eph. 4:15). Church *discipline* has the gracious purpose that, as God wills, the disciplined party may repent and "may be saved in the day of the Lord Jesus" (1 Cor. 5:5).

Christ also ordained two visible signs of the gospel for the church to use until he returns. The first is *baptism* (Matt. 28:18–20). This is a sign of union with Christ in his death and resurrection (Rom. 6:3–4). The

8 The Belgic Confession (Art. 33), in *TFU*, 53–54.

9 *Catechism of the Catholic Church*, secs. 1118, 1120.

second is the *Lord's Supper*. Paul says, "As often as you eat this bread and drink the cup, you proclaim the Lord's death until he comes" (1 Cor. 11:26 ESV).

Baptism is a means of grace. That is not to say that baptism is necessary for salvation or is the way God gives regeneration.[10] But Paul says that remembering one's baptism helps a believer to know that he has died to sin and risen with Christ to a new life (Rom. 6:1–11). Baptism is a sign that believers are God's adopted children by union with Christ (Gal. 3:26–27). Thus, it is a means of increasing faith and assurance.

The Lord's Supper is also a means of grace. Paul says, "The cup of blessing which we bless, is it not the communion of the blood of Christ? The bread which we break, is it not the communion of the body of Christ?" (1 Cor. 10:16). As we will argue later in this book (chap. 84), communicants do not receive Christ's physical body or blood. But they can fellowship with Christ spiritually in the Supper (cf. v. 20). Such fellowship is by faith, when, in obedience to Christ's command, we celebrate the Supper "in remembrance of me" (11:25). Here again, we must understand that the sacraments serve as means of grace only through faith in the Word.

Some Baptists and other evangelicals prefer not to use the term *sacrament* because it is associated with Roman Catholicism. They may prefer another term, such as *ordinance*.[11] We do not want to quarrel about words. What is important is that we make clear what we mean by the terms that we use for baptism and the Lord's Supper.

The Westminster Larger Catechism summarizes:

> A sacrament is an holy ordinance instituted by Christ in his church, to signify, seal, and exhibit unto those that are within the covenant of grace, the benefits of his mediation; to strengthen and increase their faith, and all other graces; to oblige them to obedience; to testify and cherish their love and communion one with another; and to distinguish them from those that are without.[12]

10 See our discussion of regeneration and baptism in chaps. 59 and 82.

11 Compare "sacrament" in the Westminster Confession of Faith (27.1) to "ordinance" in the Second London Baptist Confession (28.1), in *RC*, 4:265, 566. However, some Baptists have spoken of "sacraments."

12 The Westminster Larger Catechism (Q. 162), in *RC*, 4:342.

The Preaching of God's Word

Let us now consider specific means of grace, beginning with preaching. Richard Sibbes said, "Preaching is the chariot that carries Christ up and down the world."[13] To preach is to publicly proclaim the King's message as his herald. It involves both teaching the truth of God's Word and exhorting one's hearers to believe and obey it (2 Tim. 4:2).

Preaching as God's Primary Means of Grace

The New Testament indicates that preaching is the main vehicle by which God sends forth his Word to save lost sinners. Christ teaches that preaching is central to the church's mission: "This gospel of the kingdom shall be preached in all the world for a witness unto all nations; and then shall the end come" (Matt. 24:14). Similarly, Paul says, "How then shall they call on him in whom they have not believed? And how shall they believe in him of whom they have not heard? And how shall they hear without a preacher?" (Rom. 10:14).

Through the efforts of ministers to "preach . . . Christ," God causes "the light of the knowledge of the glory of God" to dawn in the darkness of the human heart (2 Cor. 4:5–6). The Holy Spirit then works to change God's people "into the same image from glory to glory" (3:18). God speaks through his preachers, for as Paul says, "we are ambassadors for Christ, as though God did beseech you by us" (5:20). Augustine said, "Let us therefore hear the gospel, just as if we were listening to the Lord himself present."[14]

Essential Qualities in Faithful Preaching

In order to be faithful to his calling from God, a minister must strive after the following qualities in his preaching.

First, *preaching must be biblical.* The apostolic injunction is to "preach the word" (2 Tim. 4:2). Since "all Scripture is breathed out by God" (3:16 ESV), it is his Word, given by God to fully equip "the man of God" (v. 17). Thus, preachers must study the Bible with meditation and prayer (1 Tim. 4:15; 2 Tim. 2:7). Edward Dering said, "The faithful minister, like unto Christ, [is] one that preacheth nothing but the word of God, not for any cause, but

13 Sibbes, *The Fountain Opened*, in *WRS*, 5:508.

14 Augustine, *Tractates on the Gospel of John*, 30.1, *NPNF*[1], 7:186.

God's glory."[15] Christ must be the great theme of preaching (1 Cor. 2:2), even as the preacher addresses the many topics taught in the Holy Scriptures.

Second, *preaching must be doctrinal.* Ministers must "preach the word" with "doctrine" (2 Tim. 4:2). "All Scripture is . . . profitable for doctrine" (3:16). A doctrine, or teaching, is a clear explanation of a particular truth in the Bible. The apostles gave to the church "the form of sound words" that we must "hold fast" today (1:13). The preaching of doctrine should be plain and understandable, an open "manifestation of the truth" (2 Cor. 4:2).

Third, *preaching must be experiential.* It must not only speak to the head but also affect the heart with a sense of God's glory. Paul says to the preacher, "I charge thee therefore before God, and the Lord Jesus Christ, who shall judge the quick and the dead at his appearing and his kingdom" (2 Tim. 4:1). He directs the minister to preach as one seeing an invisible majesty. Martyn Lloyd-Jones said, "What is preaching? . . . It is theology on fire. . . . What is the chief end of preaching? . . . It is to give men and women a sense of God and His presence."[16] Experiential preaching searches the soul, "for the word of God is quick [living], and powerful, and sharper than any twoedged sword" (Heb. 4:12). Over the course of a ministry, preaching should address conviction of sin, conversion by the Spirit's regenerating power, the inner conflict of faith, the comfort of Christian joy and peace, the deceitfulness of sin, and Satan's crafty temptations. Experiential preaching conveys idealism, realism, and optimism.[17]

Fourth, *preaching must be practical.* Preaching requires the preacher to "reprove, rebuke, [and] exhort with all longsuffering" (2 Tim. 4:2). The Holy Scriptures are "profitable" not only for doctrine but "for reproof, for correction, [and] for instruction in righteousness" (3:16). Thomas Brooks said, "Doctrine is but the drawing of the bow; application is the hitting of the mark."[18] Hence, the Westminster divines said that the preacher "is not

15 Edward Dering, *XXVII Lectures, or Readings, upon Part of the Epistle to the Hebrues*, in *M. Derings Workes* (Amsterdam: Theatrum Orbis Terrarum; New York: Da Capo, 1972), no pagination [M6v].

16 D. Martyn Lloyd-Jones, *Preaching and Preachers* (Grand Rapids, MI: Zondervan, 1971), 97.

17 For more on Reformed experiential preaching, see Joel R. Beeke, *Reformed Preaching: Proclaiming God's Word from the Heart of the Preacher to the Heart of His People* (Wheaton, IL: Crossway, 2018).

18 Thomas Brooks, *The Crown and Glory of Christianity: or Holiness, the Only Way to Happiness*, in *The Complete Works of Thomas Brooks*, ed. Alexander Grosart, 6 vols. (Edinburgh: James Nichol, 1867), 4:23.

to rest in general doctrine . . . but to bring it home to special use, by application to his hearers."[19] The goal of preaching is "love that issues from a pure heart and a good conscience and a sincere faith" (1 Tim. 1:5 ESV).

Additional Ways of Using God's Word as a Means of Grace

God has provided a variety of ways by which he brings the truths of the Holy Scriptures into our lives.

First, *God works through the public reading of his Word.* The public reading of the Holy Scriptures was an established practice of the church in the old covenant (Ex. 24:7; Deut. 31:10–13; Josh. 8:30–35). Christ read the Scriptures in the synagogue during his preaching ministry (Luke 4:16–19). Paul commands the minister of the Word to continually and attentively apply himself to "reading" (1 Tim. 4:13). In the context of "exhortation" and "doctrine," this refers to the public reading of the Word in the worship of the church. In short, the reading of the Scriptures to the congregation is a means of grace. Christ says, "Blessed is he that readeth, and they that hear the words of this prophecy, and keep those things which are written therein" (Rev. 1:3).

Second, *God works through the private reading of his Word.* The Lord's favor rests on the man who, turning away from the sins of this world, meditates daily on God's Word (Ps. 1:1–2). All those who love God study his ways and words to obtain a deeper understanding of them and a more obedient walk with the Lord (111:2; 119:45, 94, 155). Since "all scripture . . . is profitable" (2 Tim. 3:16), it is wise to regularly read through the whole Bible.

Third, *God works through parental instruction and family worship.* Christian fathers must "bring [their children] up in the nurture and admonition of the Lord" (Eph. 6:4). Moses says, "These words, which I command thee this day, shall be in thine heart: and thou shalt teach them diligently unto thy children" (Deut. 6:6–7). An important tool in cultivating family godliness is the regular practice of family worship. This requires the head of the household to gather the family for a brief time daily to read the Word, discuss it in an age-appropriate manner, pray, and sing God's praises.[20]

19 The Westminster Directory for the Publick Worship of God, in *Westminster Confession of Faith* (Glasgow, Scotland: Free Presbyterian Publications, 1994), 380.

20 See Joel R. Beeke, *Family Worship*, Family Guidance Series (Grand Rapids, MI: Reformation Heritage Books, 2021). For a helpful resource, see the *Family Worship Bible Guide*, ed. Joel R.

Fourth, *God works through small group Bible studies*. Christ taught small groups of disciples in private homes (Mark 7:17–18; Luke 10:38–39). The apostles imitated him in their ministry of the Word "every day, in the temple and from house to house" (Acts 5:42 ESV). Small group Bible studies can enhance the fellowship shared by believers in the Word. Small groups also serve as platforms to evangelize lost people. And small groups help to preserve the church during intense persecution when larger assemblies are very dangerous. It is important, though, not to make a small group a substitute for a church, elevate its teacher to undue authority, abuse it as a forum to criticize the minister, or allow it to become an elitist faction within a church.

Fifth, *God works through Bible and doctrine classes for children or adults*. Ministers and elders bear the primary responsibility for teaching the Word (1 Tim. 3:2; Titus 1:9). But God also gives the gift of teaching to various members of the body (1 Cor. 12:27–28). Christian churches have a long history of holding classes to teach children and adults. For centuries, catechism classes have instilled in people a basic understanding of Christian doctrine and ethics. God calls churches to be "warning everyone and teaching everyone with all wisdom, that we may present everyone mature in Christ" (Col. 1:28 ESV).

Sixth, *God works through letters, articles, and books*. Much of the New Testament consists of epistles (letters). God's people can enlighten and refresh one another by writing notes and letters. Believers who have the gift of teaching and skill in writing can write articles for publication online or in print media. They can also write books of sound doctrine, spiritual biographies, accounts of church history, and works of fiction illustrating moral and evangelical truths. Articles and books can go to places where their authors never visit and continue to teach long after their authors die.

Seventh, *God works through advanced theology classes*. Paul wrote his epistles to the Romans and the Ephesians—which are full of profound theology—to all saints, not just theological students (Rom. 1:7; Eph. 1:1). The church must also train new teachers in theology. Paul says, "The things that thou hast heard of me among many witnesses, the same commit thou to faithful men, who shall be able to teach others also" (2 Tim. 2:2). Churches must have some means to train prospective elders to be "holding fast the

---

Beeke, Michael P. V. Barrett, Gerald M. Bilkes, and Paul M. Smalley (Grand Rapids, MI: Reformation Heritage Books, 2016).

faithful word as [they] hath been taught, that [they] may be able by sound doctrine both to exhort and to convince the gainsayers" (Titus 1:9). Therefore, churches might collaborate to form schools of theology, in which godly and gifted seminary professors train ministers of the Word.

Practical Directions for Profitable Listening to Preaching and Teaching

Christ says, "Take heed therefore how ye hear" (Luke 8:18). We offer the following advice for profitable hearing of the Word.[21]

First, *prepare for the Word.* The evening before the Lord's Day, avoid filling your mind with media that would distract you from the Word. Try to get a good night's sleep. Before coming to church, pray for the minister. And prepare your heart, praying, "Speak, Lord; for thy servant heareth" (1 Sam. 3:9).

Second, *receive the Word.* Depending on God's help (Acts 16:14), listen attentively to the Word (Isa. 55:3). James says, "Receive with meekness the engrafted word, which is able to save your souls" (James 1:21). The Lord promises, "To this man will I look, even to him that is poor and of a contrite spirit, and trembleth at my word" (Isa. 66:2). Remember that ministers are God's ambassadors, and Christ himself speaks to you through them (2 Cor. 5:20). Inasmuch as the preacher is faithful to God's Word, let us soak up the message like sponges.

Third, *practice the Word.* James says, "Be ye doers of the word, and not hearers only, deceiving your own selves" (James 1:22). Talk with other people about the Word and encourage one another to put it into practice (Mal. 3:16; Heb. 10:25). Set a good example as a Christian who walks in the blessed way of diligent obedience to the Word (Ps. 119:1–3).

Suggested Song to Sing to the Lord

- "The Spirit breathes upon the Word," *THBap*, No. 258

Questions for Meditation or Discussion

1. What are the seven sacraments of the sacramental system?
2. What does the phrase *ex opere operato* teach about the sacraments?

21 For more detail, see Joel R. Beeke, *The Family at Church: Listening to Sermons and Attending Prayer Meetings*, Family Guidance Series (Grand Rapids, MI: Reformation Heritage Books, 2008), 9–35.

3. How did the Reformers criticize the sacramental system?
4. Who is the only Mediator of grace? What is the internal means of grace?
5. What is the primary external means of grace? What are other external means of grace?
6. How does the Westminster Larger Catechism define a "sacrament"?
7. How does the Bible show us that preaching is a means of grace?
8. What are the four essential qualities of faithful preaching?
9. What are other ways of using God's Word as a means of grace?
10. Based on the practical directions for profitable listening, what are some specific resolutions you can make to become a better listener to preaching and teaching?

82

Baptism, Part 1: Why and What

Chapter Summary and Key Terms

The sacrament of *baptism* with water is the sign and seal of initiation into Christ and his church. Baptism is not necessary for salvation, which is by grace alone through faith in Christ alone. But baptism is a duty that must be exercised for full obedience to Christ. It is a sign to the baptized person of union with Christ in his death and resurrection, salvation and spiritual cleansing in him, union with other members of his church, and participation in the new covenant. Christians should practically apply their baptism by humbling themselves over their sins, seeking greater assurance of salvation, and drawing power from Christ by faith to walk in obedience and love.

BAPTISM IS THE SACRAMENT or ordinance of initiation into Christianity by the outward sign of washing of the body with water (Acts 8:36, 38; 10:47). Baptism stands at the heart of the Great Commission (Matt. 28:18–20).

In this chapter, we will discuss the necessity and meaning of baptism and present some practical applications of the doctrine. In the next chapter (chap. 83), we will discuss who should be baptized and how it should be done.

The Necessity of Baptism

Baptism is not necessary or effectual for salvation. After all, the ordinance did not even exist in the Old Testament. And Christ promised the unbaptized but repentant thief dying on the cross next to him, "Today shalt thou be with me in paradise" (Luke 23:43).

Some theologians, especially those in Roman Catholicism and Lutheranism, have taught that baptism is necessary for salvation under ordinary circumstances. They quote Scripture passages such as these: "Except a man be born of water and of the Spirit, he cannot enter into the kingdom of God" (John 3:5); "Repent, and be baptized every one of you in the name of Jesus Christ for the remission of sins, and ye shall receive the gift of the Holy Ghost" (Acts 2:38); and, "Baptism doth also now save us" (1 Pet. 3:21).

However, there are several reasons to reject the teaching that baptism is ordinarily necessary for salvation.

First, *baptism is not the means of regeneration*. We discussed this matter and the meaning of John 3:5 in our study of regeneration (chap. 59).

Second, *God saves sinners through repentance and faith*. When the Holy Scriptures associate baptism with salvation (Acts 2:38; 1 Pet. 3:21), in the context they also speak of repentance or faith. Many passages speak of salvation through repentance or faith while making no mention of baptism at all. But baptism is not presented as a means of salvation apart from repentance or faith.

Third, *baptizing is not as important as evangelizing*. Paul says, "Christ sent me not to baptize, but to preach the gospel" (1 Cor. 1:17).

Fourth, *many receive baptism and yet perish*. The people of Israel received many outward signs of God's mercy, but many of them fell under God's wrath (1 Cor. 10:1–11). In the same way, people can participate in baptism but remain unconverted enemies of God.

Fifth, *salvation is by grace apart from works* (Eph. 2:8–9; 2 Tim. 1:9). Baptism is a work of obedience to God's command, but such works do not save. Paul denies that God regenerates us on account of "works of righteousness which we have done" (Titus 3:5).

Sixth, *regeneration produces faith, which adult candidates for baptism must already have* (John 1:12–13; 1 John 5:1). Baptism cannot regenerate those who are already regenerated.

Seventh, *regeneration brings a new creation, which many baptized in infancy never exhibit*. Regeneration produces faith, repentance, obedience, love, and power to overcome the world (1 John 2:29; 3:9; 4:7; 5:1, 4). This evidence is sadly lacking among many baptized people.

Eighth, *God's ordinary means of regeneration is the gospel, which infants cannot understand* (1 Pet. 1:23–24; James 1:18). If God ordinarily regenerates infants at their baptism, then it would not be true that most Christians have been born again through hearing the Word.

Therefore, we conclude that baptism is not necessary for salvation, for it is not God's appointed means for regeneration.

But baptism is necessary for obedience to Christ. He commanded the church to be "baptizing" in its mission that continues "to the end of the age" (Matt. 28:19–20 ESV). Peter commanded the Jews at Pentecost to "be baptized" (Acts 2:38), and Ananias commanded Saul of Tarsus to "be baptized" (22:16).

Disobedience to Christ is a serious matter. Refusing to repent of sin provokes the Father's discipline (Heb. 12:5) and the Son's rebuke (Rev. 3:19), and it grieves the Spirit (Eph. 4:30). Persistent disobedience to the requirement of baptism raises the question of whether a person is saved. Saving faith expresses itself by confessing Christ (Matt. 10:32–33; Rom. 10:9–10).

The Meaning of Baptism

Though it may have some precedents in Jewish ritual washings and John's baptism, Christian baptism has its own special meaning.

First, Christian baptism is *a sign of union with Christ crucified and risen.* Paul says, "For as many of you as have been baptized into Christ have put on Christ" (Gal. 3:27). Baptism itself cannot cause this union, for Paul has just said, "Ye are all the children of God by faith in Christ Jesus" (v. 26). Thus, baptism is a sign to "the party baptized" of "his ingrafting into Christ."[1]

Baptism has great practical significance for the Christian's sanctification. Paul anticipates that someone will say, "Shall we continue in sin, that grace may abound?" Paul answers, "God forbid. How shall we, that are dead to sin, live any longer therein?" Then, he appeals to baptism: "Know ye not, that so many of us as were baptized into Jesus Christ were baptized into his death? Therefore we are buried with him by baptism into death: that like as Christ was raised up from the dead by the glory of the Father, even so we also should walk in newness of life" (Rom. 6:1–4). By union with Christ, the believer has died to the reigning power of sin and begun to live

1 The Westminster Confession of Faith (28.1), in *RC*, 4:266. Cf. the Second London Baptist Confession (29.1), in *RC*, 4:566.

to God. Through baptism, God reinforces in his children the awareness that they share in Christ's victory over sin and that his power is presently at work in them.

Since baptism is a sign of dying and rising with Christ in his once-for-all work, it should not be repeated like the Lord's Supper. Baptism is an ordinance to be received once.

Second, Christian baptism is *a sign of salvation and spiritual cleansing.* After saying that in Noah's ark "eight persons, were brought safely through water," Peter adds, "Baptism, which corresponds to this, now saves you, not as a removal of dirt from the body but as an appeal to God for a good conscience, through the resurrection of Jesus Christ" (1 Pet. 3:20–21 ESV). The water of baptism symbolizes death by divine judgment. Baptism thus symbolizes salvation—passing through death with Christ and rising with him. What saves a person is not the outward ceremony with water but calling on the Lord to grant a clean conscience.

Baptism with water naturally lends itself to the idea of washing away sin's defilement. Ananias said to Saul of Tarsus, "Arise, and be baptized, and wash away thy sins, calling on the name of the Lord" (Acts 22:16). Such washing is granted by calling on Christ with faith. As the Belgic Confession reminds us, this cleansing is not "effected by the external water, but by the sprinkling of the precious blood of the Son of God."[2]

Third, Christian baptism is *a sign of union with one another as the church of Christ*. Paul says, "There is one body, and one Spirit, even as ye are called in one hope of your calling; one Lord, one faith, one baptism, one God and Father of all" (Eph. 4:4–6).

Baptism functions as a distinguishing mark of the community of disciples under the triune God, where Christ is honored as Lord, his Word is taught as the rule of life, and his presence is powerfully manifest (Matt. 28:18–20). At Pentecost, "they that gladly received his word were baptized: and the same day there were added unto them about three thousand souls" (Acts 2:41). John Calvin said, "Baptism serves as our confession before men. Indeed, it is the mark by which we publicly profess that we wish to be reckoned God's people."[3]

2 The Belgic Confession (Art. 34), in *TFU*, 54–55.

3 Calvin, *Institutes*, 4.15.13.

Fourth, Christian baptism is *a sign of participation in the new covenant.* The New Testament never explicitly connects Christian baptism to God's covenant. But both baptism and the covenant of grace center on Christ and union with him. Baptism is the sign that those who are "Christ's" are "Abraham's seed, and heirs according to the promise" of the eternal covenant of grace, brought to fruition in the new covenant (Gal. 3:27–29).

In summary, the Westminster Confession of Faith says,

> Baptism is a sacrament of the new testament, ordained by Jesus Christ, not only for the solemn admission of the party baptized into the visible Church; but also, to be unto him a sign and seal of the covenant of grace, of his ingrafting into Christ, of regeneration, of remission of sins, and of his giving up unto God, through Jesus Christ, to walk in newness of life.[4]

Practical Applications of Baptism

The Westminster Larger Catechism offers the following ways by which Christians should make use of their baptism "all our life long, especially in time of temptation, and when we are present at the administration of it to others":

- "by being humbled for our sinful defilement, our falling short of, and walking contrary to, the grace of baptism, and our engagements." It is humbling to consider the cross of Christ. Baptism reminds us that salvation comes through judgment.
- "by growing up to assurance of pardon of sin, and of all other blessings sealed to us in that sacrament." Reflecting on our baptism should motivate us to seek and cherish a strong assurance of salvation. This requires the exercise of faith and obedience.
- "by drawing strength from the death and resurrection of Christ, into whom we are baptized, for the mortifying of sin, and quickening of grace." We should apply our baptism by resting on Jesus for liberty from sin's enslavement and daily victory.

4 The Westminster Confession of Faith (28.1), in *RC*, 4:266. Cf. the Second London Baptist Confession (29.1), which says, "Baptism is an ordinance of the New Testament, ordained by Jesus Christ, to be unto the party baptized, a sign of his fellowship with Him, in His death and resurrection; of his being engrafted into Him; of remission of sins; and of his giving up unto God, through Jesus Christ, to live and walk in newness of life" (*RC*, 4:566).

- "by endeavouring to live by faith, to have our conversation [conduct] in holiness and righteousness, as those that have therein given up their names to Christ and to walk in brotherly love, as being baptized by the same Spirit into one body."[5] Shall we receive the mark of Christ and not strive to live in imitation of him? Whenever we think of baptism, we should renew our commitment to love and serve the church of Christ.

How blessed is baptism! Delight in Christ's ordinance. John Bunyan said, "Do you think that love-letters are not desired between lovers? Why these, God's ordinances, they are his love-letters, and his love-tokens too. No marvel then if the righteous do so desire them."[6]

Suggested Song to Sing to the Lord

- "Come, ye who bow to sov'reign grace," *THBap*, No. 353

Questions for Meditation or Discussion

1. How do we know that baptism is not necessary for salvation?
2. In what sense is baptism necessary? How seriously should we take the obligation to be baptized? Why?
3. What can we learn about the meaning of baptism from Galatians 3:27 and Romans 6:1–4?
4. Show from the Holy Scriptures that baptism is a sign of spiritual washing from sin.
5. How does baptism function as a sign of the church's unity?
6. How is baptism a sign of God's covenant?
7. How would you summarize the meaning of Christian baptism in a short paragraph?
8. What are the practical applications of the necessity and meaning of baptism?
9. How can you make use of baptism to strengthen your own spiritual life at this time?

5 The Westminster Larger Catechism (Q. 167), in *RC*, 4:343, division into bullet points added.

6 John Bunyan, *The Desire of the Righteous Granted*, in *The Works of John Bunyan*, ed. George Offor, 3 vols. (1854; repr., Edinburgh: Banner of Truth, 1991), 1:757.

83

Baptism, Part 2: Who and How

Chapter Summary and Key Terms

The subjects and mode of baptism are disputed among Christians. The doctrine of *paedobaptism* teaches that the church should baptize the young children of believers. (Paedobaptists also teach that adults giving a credible profession of faith should be baptized if they were not previously baptized as the children of believers.) Why should infants be baptized? According to Reformed paedobaptism, the children of believers are included within God's covenant people. This is in keeping with God's revelation to Abraham, with whom he made an everlasting covenant (and provided the sign of circumcision). The New Testament is said to confirm this principle. Most paedobaptists teach that baptism may be done by immersion, pouring, or sprinkling with water. The doctrine of *credobaptism*, on the other hand, teaches that the church should baptize only people who make a credible profession of faith. According to credobaptism, the New Testament does not permit the baptism of infants because baptism is the sign of union with Christ and his body, the church, through saving faith. Circumcision, it is said, was a temporary arrangement with Abraham. Most credobaptists teach that baptism may be done only by immersion.

BAPTISM, the sign of union with Christ, has been the occasion of sad disunity in the body of Christ. Two questions stand at the heart of this disagreement: Who should the church baptize? and How should the church baptize them? There are two main positions on these matters.[1]

1 The argument for paedobaptism in this chapter expresses the views of Joel R. Beeke and Jonathon D. Beeke, PhD, the academic dean at Puritan Reformed Theological Seminary. The

The majority position within Reformed Christianity is *paedobaptism*, the belief that the church should baptize the infant children of believers. This position further holds that unbaptized adults desiring to join the church (the covenant community) should be baptized only after they make a credible profession of faith. Paedobaptists generally teach that baptism may be done in a variety of ways: dipping (*immersion*), pouring (*affusion*), or most commonly, sprinkling (*aspersion*).[2]

Baptists, on the other hand, hold to *credobaptism*, the belief that the church should baptize only those people who make a credible profession of faith. Credobaptists generally teach that baptism may be done only by immersion in water.[3]

In this chapter, we will present the arguments for each position. It is our aim to conduct this discussion in a spirit of humility and brotherly love.

The Case for Reformed Covenantal Infant Baptism

Should children born or adopted into a household of faith receive baptism as a sign and seal of God's covenant of grace? Reformed paedobaptist theology teaches that such children should receive baptism because they are part of the covenant community ("covenant children").

Answers to Objections to Paedobaptism

What follows are five common objections to covenantal infant baptism, with brief responses to each.

First, *it is argued that there is no explicit command or example in the New Testament of an infant child being baptized*. Therefore, some argue, infant baptism has no biblical basis and contradicts the regulative principle of worship (chap. 80).

In response, we note that there is equally no express command or example of baptism for an adult who is already part of a household of faith. Furthermore, there is no explicit command or example of a woman taking part in the Lord's Supper. Paedobaptism, as well as women taking part in the Lord's Supper, can be established by way of good and necessary inference.[4]

---

argument for credobaptism by immersion expresses the view of Paul M. Smalley. All other parts of this chapter are cowritten by Joel R. Beeke and Paul M. Smalley.

2 An exception is Eastern Orthodoxy, which baptizes infants by immersion, unless medically prohibitive.

3 An exception would be those Anabaptists who baptize believers by pouring.

4 On the idea of "good and necessary consequence," see the Westminster Confession of Faith (1.6), in *RC*, 4:235.

Second, *it is asserted that the pattern of New Testament baptism is for a person to repent and then be baptized.* Baptism, it is said, is for disciples of Jesus Christ.

In response, we affirm that "Repent, and be baptized" (Acts 2:38) is the necessary order for all those who are not in covenant relation with God, but then, in later years of life, are called by God into covenantal fellowship with him. But this order does not apply to infants who are already in covenant relation with God. Furthermore, not every example of baptism recorded in the New Testament is necessarily a pattern for all to imitate. Christ's own baptism is a case in point.

Third, *it is argued that paedobaptists do not apply the same logic to both New Testament sacraments.* In the Old Testament, male children were both circumcised and invited to participate in the Passover. Why, then, it is asked, do paedobaptists bar children from the Lord's Supper?

In response, we say that it must be recognized that baptism and the Lord's Supper signify and seal distinct things. Baptism, administered once, focuses on the initiatory act of union with Christ. The Lord's Supper, repeated often, focuses on the continuing benefits of this union. The Scriptures outline certain requirements of a worthy recipient of the Lord's Supper: he or she must remember Christ's sacrifice, discern his body, and exercise self-examination (1 Cor. 11:23–29). Furthermore, as both the typological and national elements of the old covenant sacraments do not continue into the new covenant, baptism and the Lord's Supper are not *exact* replacements of circumcision and the Passover. (If it were an exact replacement, for example, we would need to restrict baptism to males only.)

Fourth, *it is objected that infant baptism is founded on a view of the covenants that overemphasizes continuity between the two testaments.* The covenant with Abraham, it is said, cannot be equated to the covenant of grace, for the Abrahamic covenant has national and physical elements that are types of spiritual realities. Circumcision is not simply replaced by baptism.

In response, as already noted, we agree that it is imprecise to use the term *replacement* when comparing the church with Israel or baptism with circumcision. But it is also too simplistic to say that the old covenant was only about physical and national matters, and the new covenant about spiritual and church matters. While certain elements of circumcision certainly pointed forward to Christ's redeeming work, circumcision was not itself a type of a *future* circumcision of the heart. Thus, the continuity between the two sacraments is striking: circumcision of the old covenant and baptism of the new covenant are symbols that point to the spiritual circumcision of the heart experienced by Old Testament and New Testament believers alike.

Fifth, *some Baptists argue that the old covenant was not a covenant of grace*. Rather, as Jeffrey Johnson asserts, "It was a conditional covenant based upon works—that eventually led to the condemnation of its participants."[5] Thus, circumcision, and the principle of including children in the covenant, is said to not be part of the covenant of grace or the new covenant.

In response, we note that this book has already argued for the essential unity of God's covenant of grace while acknowledging diversity in each covenantal administration and context (chaps. 38–41). Furthermore, the covenant of works was definitively broken by Adam (chaps. 32–33). To say that later covenant arrangements revert once again to a covenant-of-works order denies this fact. In addition, the conditions that God attached to his covenants with Abraham, Moses, and even the new covenant do not prove that these covenant administrations belong to the covenant of works.

Major Arguments for Paedobaptism

Covenant children should receive the New Testament sacrament of baptism as a sign and seal of God's covenant of grace. Covenantal infant baptism can best be defended as the scriptural position by presenting multiple arguments that involve careful consideration of all the evidence that needs to be taken together.

First, *young children under the authority of a believing parent are members of God's covenant people*. It is an indisputable fact that young children occupied a significant place in the covenantal community of the Old Testament. As a sign of their inclusion, eight-day-old male children received the covenantal sign of circumcision (Gen. 17:11–12). As Genesis 17 indicates, circumcision did not begin the covenantal relationship, but it

5 Jeffrey D. Johnson, *The Fatal Flaw of the Theology behind Infant Baptism* (Conway, AR: Free Grace Press, 2010), 70.

was given as confirmation of an already established covenant between God and Abraham and his seed.

Second, *in both the Old and New Testaments, membership among God's covenant people depends on God's will, not necessarily a profession of faith.* Covenant membership in the Old Testament was not founded on the professed faith of the individual, but on the sovereign and gracious choice of God (Deut. 7:6–7). But there are some covenant members—who for a time are called "holy" and "special" to God—who in time reject and hate God, and thus finally and ultimately encounter his wrath (vv. 10–11).

The same pattern of mixed covenant membership appears in the New Testament. To someone who counts "the blood of the covenant, wherewith he was sanctified, an unholy thing," this warning is given: "It is a fearful thing to fall into the hands of the living God" (Heb. 10:31). A mixed covenant community is possible also in a new covenant context. Some who have been sanctified (or set apart) by the blood of the new covenant—that is, counted as covenant members—are unbelievers who ultimately will reject the covenant blessings and thus will surely experience the vengeance of God. God's free and gracious choice is the cause of their membership in the new covenant (Hebrews 8–10), and their inclusion in that covenant demands a response of faith (10:19–25).

Third, *circumcision and baptism are signs and seals not just of blessing but of curse as well.* Circumcision did not initiate a covenantal relationship with God, and neither does baptism. Rather, God gave both as pledges or tokens of an already-established relationship (Gen. 17:11–14). Nor was circumcision a sign of Abraham's faith, but instead a sign of the promise of righteousness (Rom. 4:11). Mark Ross elaborates, "Circumcision is the authenticating mark that certifies the truth of God's promise, that he will give righteousness to the one who has faith. What is certified is not so much a truth about Abraham, or any other circumcised person, but a truth about God."[6] As the circumcision knife drew blood, it promised either life or death—life through Christ's ultimate circumcision on the cross, but death if this gospel was rejected.

6 Mark E. Ross, "Baptism and Circumcision as Signs and Seals," in *The Case for Covenantal Infant Baptism*, ed. Gregg Strawbridge (Phillipsburg, NJ: P&R, 2003), 94.

Baptism signifies and seals the same essential covenant promises given to Abraham—promises that offer life through another but threaten death upon unbelief. Colossians 2:11–12 establishes the link between circumcision and baptism. Both point to the spiritual reality of someone dead in sin who is made alive when he or she is united to Christ, who died on account of sin but victoriously rose again. Thus, both sacraments culminate not in the subjective experience of the individual but in the objective finished work of Jesus Christ. It is also evident that New Testament baptism follows the blessing/cursing formula that also was true of circumcision. The only two New Testament references to Old Testament baptisms have to do with the flood and the crossing of the Red Sea (1 Pet. 3:20–21; 1 Cor. 10:1–2). The waters of these two great baptismal events signified a dual purpose: judgment for all those in opposition to God, but extraordinary and gracious deliverance for all those who trusted in him. Thus, the spiritual significance of circumcision and baptism are the same. If united in Christ through his death and resurrection, you are an heir of the gospel promise given to Abraham (Gal. 3:29). If you are not, however, circumcision and baptism threaten the very same judgment that fell on Jesus Christ.

Additional Arguments for Paedobaptism

In addition to the three arguments above, we would add seven other brief arguments.

First, *the new covenant is more expansive, not more restrictive, than the old covenant.* The new covenant now encompasses all nationalities (Gal. 3:28). If the covenant sign was more restrictive, this would certainly need to be explained. Imagine that a Jewish father heard that his children were no longer covenant members under the new covenant. Would he not ask, "How is this a *better* covenant?" John Murray said, "If infants are excluded now, it cannot be too strongly emphasised that this change implies a complete reversal of the earlier divinely instituted practice. So we must ask: do we find any hint or intimation of such reversal in either the Old or the New Testament?"[7] The exclusion of children from the New Testament church's covenant (and the covenantal sign of inclusion—that is, baptism) would seem to argue that children of professing believers no longer have a place

7 John Murray, *Christian Baptism* (Phillipsburg, NJ: P&R, 1980), 49.

sacramentally in the covenant community. In other words, nothing distinguishes them from the heathen children of the world. If the new covenant is indeed more expansive and wider than the old covenant, as the Scriptures teach, how strange it would be if children of believers in the New Testament had no place within the covenant community when Old Testament children, who were under a more restrictive covenantal context, were included.

Second, *Peter confirms in Acts 2 that children are included in the covenant.* He says, "For the promise is unto you, and to your children, and to all that are afar off, even as many as the Lord our God shall call" (v. 39). Echoing the covenant formula—"between me and thee and thy seed after thee" (Gen. 17:7)—Peter underscores the "identity of the covenant of grace under all dispensations and continuity of the covenant pattern in which promises made to believers are extended to their children."[8] Adding that the promise is also "to all that are afar off," Peter says the pattern will be repeated from nation to nation. Adults will confess Christ and be baptized, and their children will then be baptized as well.

Third, *Christ welcomed children.* He prayed for them and placed his hands on them—sure indications of covenant blessing and inclusion—and declared, "Suffer [permit] little children, and forbid them not, to come unto me: for of such is the kingdom of heaven" (Matt. 19:13–14; cf. Mark 10:13–14; Luke 18:15–16).

Fourth, *the New Testament records four household baptisms* (Acts 16:15, 31–33; 18:8; 1 Cor. 1:16). There were, no doubt, many others. It is highly unlikely that not one of these households had within it an infant or young child. We must remember that a household in New Testament times included not just the nuclear family we are familiar with but also a significant number of family members and relatives (equivalent to our concept of an extended family.)

Fifth, *Paul confirms that children of a believing parent are holy* (1 Cor. 7:14). Paul is not teaching here about their eternal state. Rather, he is affirming that children of at least one believing parent are set apart as covenant members.

Sixth, *Paul includes children within his instructions to the church*, an entire group that he refers to collectively as "saints" (Eph. 1:1; 6:1; Col. 1:2; 3:20).

8 Joel R. Beeke and Ray B. Lanning, "Unto You and Your Children," in *The Case for Covenantal Infant Baptism*, ed. Strawbridge, 55–56.

Seventh, *an overwhelming majority of Reformed theologians have argued for infant baptism*. This argument is, of course, of less weight than the authority of Scripture. But it should at least give us pause that most theologians since the Reformation (and countless before that) held to a paedobaptist position.

Baptism by a Variety of Legitimate Modes

Most of this section has concerned the question of who is to receive baptism. Another disputed question is, *What is the proper mode of baptism?* It is evident that the Greek word *baptizō* denotes submerging or immersion under water. But it is also apparent that *baptizō* has a range of meanings. Jesus, it is said, baptizes with the Holy Spirit and fire (Matt. 3:11). He also speaks of his death on the cross as "the baptism that I am baptized with" (20:22). When Scripture refers to the Jewish custom of washing hands before eating, it twice uses the word *baptizō* or a derivative of it (Mark 7:4; Luke 11:38). The author of Hebrews refers to a variety of Old Testament "washings" (*baptismois*; Heb. 9:10), which included sprinkling unclean people, ordinary vessels, and even the covenant document "the book" with blood and water (vv. 13, 19, 21). It is clear from its uses in Scripture that the word has a fairly wide range of meanings, including immersion, washing a part of the body, and sprinkling.

When we consider the instances of New Testament baptisms, it is striking that the mode of baptism is never mentioned. The concern of Scripture is that water is used, but never *how much* water. Furthermore, there is no *express* command or example of a New Testament baptism by immersion. It would seem, based on the range of meaning of *baptizō* as well as Scripture's silence as to the exact mode, that immersion, pouring, and sprinkling are all appropriate methods of baptism. This is evident for the following reasons.

First, immersion is an appropriate mode of baptism because it symbolizes the believer's identification with the death, burial, and resurrection of Jesus Christ (Rom. 6:3–4). But Paul's point here is not to argue for one mode of baptism to the exclusion of any other.

Second, pouring is an appropriate mode of baptism because it pictures the Holy Spirit's work in effecting spiritual union with Christ. Peter quotes from Joel 2:28, where God promised to "pour out [his] Spirit upon all flesh" (Acts 2:16–17). At that time, many called on the Lord to be saved and were baptized (vv. 21, 37, 41).

Third, sprinkling is an appropriate mode of baptism because it represents purification from sin. Ezekiel 36:25 records the promise of God to "sprinkle clean water upon you" with this desired effect: "Ye shall be clean." Hebrews 12:24 and 1 Peter 1:2 both refer to Christ's blood as the "blood of sprinkling."

Since Scripture does not command one mode to the exclusion of others—nor does it give a clear example of any one mode—and due to the biblical symbolism found in all three, the exact mode of baptism is left as a matter of Christian freedom. We must be careful not to bind the conscience beyond what the Scriptures require.

The Reformed Baptist Case for Believers' Baptism Alone

This section presents an argument for the doctrine of baptizing only professing believers, and that by immersion. It is written from a Reformed Baptist perspective that affirms the unity of the covenant of grace but also affirms a Baptist view of the New Testament church.

The Silence of the Holy Scriptures on Infant Baptism

God's Word has much to say about baptism. If we look up all the occurrences of "baptize" and "baptism" in the Bible, we see that believers should be baptized as a sign of their union with Christ and his people. But there is no explicit command, teaching, or example in the entire Bible about baptizing infants. Paedobaptists admit this. Louis Berkhof said, "There is no explicit command in the Bible to baptize children, and . . . there is not a single instance in which we are plainly told that children were baptized."[9]

The silence of the Bible is weighty evidence against infant baptism. God gave us his Word to teach us all we need to know to worship him rightly. We have no authority to worship God in a way he has not commanded. To do so is to violate the regulative principle of worship (chap. 80).

Paedobaptists object that there is also no explicit command or example of women taking the Lord's Supper. That is true. But it is clear in Scripture that the Lord's Supper is for Christ's "one body" (1 Cor. 10:17), "the church of God" for whom he died and with whom God made the new covenant (11:20–25). Female believers are included with male church members in

9 Louis Berkhof, *Systematic Theology* (Edinburgh: Banner of Truth, 1958), 632.

that group. Logically, their participation is implied. But when the New Testament says that baptism is for professing believers in Christ, the children of believers are not included in that category. They are in another category of people who have no warrant from God's Word to receive baptism.

Paedobaptists answer that infant baptism, though not explicitly taught in the Bible, is rightly deduced by logical implication from the Bible. John Murray said, "The evidence for infant baptism falls into the category of good and necessary inference."[10]

In response, I will argue that infant baptism is not logically implied by the Scriptures. In other words, the paedobaptist argument by good and necessary consequence is not convincing. Furthermore, paedobaptism contradicts the New Testament doctrine of baptism.

An Examination of the Reformed Paedobaptist Argument

Reformed paedobaptists make the following argument. God made a covenant with Abraham and his offspring. The Lord commanded that the infant children of believers be given circumcision, the sign of the covenant (Gen. 17:1–14). The covenant with Abraham is the eternal covenant of grace in Christ (Gal. 3:16, 29). Therefore, the infant children of believers are part of the church and have a right to its sign.

The problem with this argument is that the baptism of the infant children of believers does not fit with what God said to Abraham. The covenant with Abraham did not require the circumcision of *all* the children of *each believer*. Rather, it required the circumcision of all *males* in *Abraham's* household, including his servants (Gen. 17:12–13). A boy's parents did not need to be believers for him to be circumcised. The ceremony was later applied to the whole nation of Israel (Josh. 5:2–8). If we were to apply the covenant of circumcision to baptism today, we would baptize entire nations if they were descended from a believing ancestor.

Also, it is true that there is one covenant of grace (chap. 41). But the covenant of grace has had different administrations through history. The Bible speaks of specific historical "covenants" (Rom. 9:4; Eph. 2:12). These historical covenants are one in essence. They present the same saving gospel of Christ and the same moral law of God, but they have different forms of

10 Murray, *Christian Baptism*, 69.

administration. We cannot assume that God always requires a sign of the covenant to be placed on our children. There was no such requirement in the thousands of years before Abraham.

Therefore, paedobaptism does not follow by good and necessary consequence from the circumcision of male children under the covenant with Abraham. Neither Genesis 17 nor the doctrine of the covenant of grace requires it.

Paedobaptists try to strengthen their argument with the following observations. First, God promises to bless the offspring of believers (Deut. 7:9; Ps. 112:2). Second, the New Testament includes children in the covenant people of God (Luke 18:15–16; 1 Cor. 7:14).

Baptists can joyfully agree that God blesses the children of believers. But this blessing might not include salvation or church membership. God saves whom he chooses, sometimes dividing families (Rom. 9:6–13).

When Christ says of "infants" that "of such is the kingdom of God" (Luke 18:15–16), he is not saying that all children of believers are in God's kingdom. All children naturally descended from Adam begin life in the state of sin (Pss. 51:5; 58:3).

It is true that Paul says the children of a believer are "holy," but he says the same thing about the unsaved spouse of a believer (1 Cor. 7:14). This holiness gives neither the child nor the unconverted spouse a place in God's covenant or Christ's church. The passage may mean that the whole family is influenced by the Holy Spirit who dwells in the believer (6:19). In any case, Paul says nothing in this context about baptism or church membership.

Paedobaptists also argue that in the New Testament, baptism corresponds to circumcision (Col. 2:11–12). They claim that the New Testament strongly implies the baptism of the infant children of believers. Peter says that God's promise is "unto you, and to your children" (Acts 2:39). There are examples of whole households being baptized (Acts 16:15, 31–34, and so on). Therefore, it is said, God commands that the infant children of believers should be baptized.

On the contrary, Paul says that baptism is the sign of *spiritual circumcision*: "the circumcision made without hands, in putting off the body of the sins of the flesh by the circumcision of Christ" (Col. 2:11). Unlike physical circumcision, baptism is for people who have received spiritual rebirth, not just natural birth in a Christian family.

Peter says, "Repent, and be baptized every one of you in the name of Jesus Christ for the remission of sins, and ye shall receive the gift of the Holy Ghost. For the promise is unto you, and to your children, and to all that are afar off, even as many as the Lord our God shall call" (Acts 2:38–39). Peter offers this promise not only to the Jews and their children but also to those "afar off," the Gentiles. The promise is not that these people are in the covenant or have a right to baptism, but that forgiveness and the gift of the Holy Spirit will be given to those who repent.

The baptism of households in the New Testament also does not prove infant baptism. These Scripture passages do not tell us that infants were in those households or that infants were baptized. It is better to take the household baptisms as referring to people who believed the gospel. Luke writes, "Crispus, the chief ruler of the synagogue, *believed on the Lord with all his house*; and many of the Corinthians hearing believed, and were baptized" (Acts 18:8).

Therefore, the arguments offered to prove paedobaptism fall short of the "good and necessary consequence" required to prove that God requires infant baptism. Without such solid proof, Christians have no warrant from Christ to practice infant baptism as an ordinance of his church, much less to require it of others.

The New Testament Doctrine of Baptism

So far, I have argued that there is no basis for infant baptism in the Holy Scriptures. I add another line of argument: paedobaptism contradicts what the Bible does teach about baptism.

First, *the New Testament teaches that baptism is for Christ's disciples.* "Jesus was making and baptizing more disciples than John (although Jesus himself did not baptize, but only his disciples)" (John 4:1–2 ESV). Christ says, "Go therefore and make disciples of all nations, baptizing them" (Matt. 28:19 ESV).

Second, *the New Testament teaches that baptism is for those who repent of sin and believe in Christ.* We often find this in the book of Acts: "Repent, and be baptized" (Acts 2:38); "they that gladly received his word were baptized" (v. 41); and "When they believed . . . they were baptized" (8:12; see also vv. 36–38; 10:44–48; 16:14–15, 31, 33; 18:8; 22:16). Those who are "baptized" are the same people who are "the children of God by faith in Christ Jesus" (Gal. 3:26–27).

Third, *the New Testament teaches that baptism marks people in union with Christ.* Paul says, "So many of us as were baptized into Jesus Christ were baptized into his death" (Rom. 6:3). He adds, "For as many of you as have been baptized into Christ have put on Christ" (Gal. 3:27). He says that those "buried with him in baptism" have also "risen with him through the faith of the operation of God, who hath raised him from the dead" (Col. 2:11–12).

Fourth, *the New Testament teaches that the baptized church is Christ's body.* The church is united in "one body, and one Spirit . . . [and] one baptism" (Eph. 4:4–5). Its members are "baptized into Jesus Christ" (Rom. 6:3) and, though "many, are one body in Christ" (12:5). Therefore, the church should baptize only those united by the Spirit to Christ and his other living members.

Fifth, *the New Testament teaches that the baptized church is God's new covenant people.* God promised that in the new covenant his people would no longer be covenant breakers, as many were under the old covenant (Jer. 31:31–32). Saving grace would be given to all the new covenant people (v. 33), and "they shall *all* know me, from the least of them unto the greatest of them" (v. 34). This new covenant is in force today (2 Cor. 3:3, 6).

The baptism of infants contradicts these principles. Infants cannot express a commitment to follow Christ as his disciples, understand gospel preaching, or make a credible profession of faith. We have no biblical basis to presume that all infant children of believers are in union with Christ, are members of his body by the Spirit, or know the Lord under the new covenant.

Therefore, the Holy Scriptures do not permit us to baptize infant children. Christ commands us to baptize only people who have a credible profession of faith.

Baptism Only by Immersion

Why do Baptists believe that baptism must be done by immersing the whole body in water, and not by pouring or sprinkling water on the head?

The most basic reason is that the verb translated as "baptize" has the literal meaning of "immerse" by dipping, sinking, plunging, or flooding.[11] In the

11 *LSJ*, 305; *TDNT*, 1:530; and *BDAG*, 164

Greek translation of the Old Testament, it is used for "taking a ritual bath for cleansing."[12] First-century Jewish writings use the word for pushing an inflated skin under water, drowning someone in a sea or pool, and sinking a ship into the sea.[13] Therefore, to "baptize" literally means to "immerse."

Someone might object that the word translated as "baptize" simply means to "wash" (Mark 7:4). We read in that passage that the Pharisees "wash" (literally baptize themselves) before eating. They also practiced the "washing" (literally baptism) of objects, even "tables" or "beds" (KJV mg.).

In reply, I note that ancient Jewish homes often had cleansing pools where people and objects could be immersed for ritual cleansing (cf. Lev. 11:32).[14] The word translated as "tables" or "beds" refers to furniture for reclining that a man could easily pick up and carry (Matt. 9:6). It is quite reasonable to understand Mark 7:4 to refer to the immersion of people and objects in water.

That "baptize" means "immerse" is confirmed by the way that the New Testament describes baptism. People were "baptized" by John "in the river of Jordan" (Mark 1:5). In another place, we read, "John also was baptizing in Aenon near to Salim, because there was *much water* there" (John 3:23). When Philip evangelized the Ethiopian eunuch as he traveled home in his chariot, Luke records, "They came unto a certain water: and the eunuch said, See, here is water; what doth hinder me to be baptized? . . . And they went down both into the water, both Philip and the eunuch; and he baptized him" (Acts 8:36, 38). It is difficult to make sense of these passages if baptism required only a little water for sprinkling. Furthermore, baptism by immersion is a picture of dying and rising with Christ, of which baptism is a sign (Rom. 6:3–4; Col. 2:12).

The interpretation of "baptize" to mean "immerse" was not invented by Baptists. Immersion was the normal mode of baptism in the church for many centuries. It is still practiced by the Eastern Orthodox Church today,

12 *NIDNTTE*, 1:460. Thus, 4 Kingdoms (2 Kings) 5:14; Judith 12:7; Sirach 34:25 LXX.

13 Philo of Alexandria, *Every Good Man Is Free*, 97, in *The Works of Philo*, trans. C. D. Yonge, new ed. (Peabody, MA: Hendrickson, 1995), 691; and Josephus, *Life of Flavius Josephus*, 15; *Antiquities of the Jews*, 4.81; 9.212; 15.55; and *Wars of the Jews*, 1.437; 2.475, 556; 3.368, 423, 525, 527, in *The Works of Josephus*, trans. William Whiston (Peabody, MA: Hendrickson, 1987), 2, 107, 259, 401, 578, 628, 633, 656, 658, 663 (twice).

14 James R. Edwards, *The Gospel according to Mark*, The Pillar New Testament Commentary (Grand Rapids, MI: Eerdmans; Leicester, England: Apollos, 2002), 208.

even for infants. Both Martin Luther and John Calvin said that the Greek word translated as "baptize" means "immerse."[15]

Therefore, the only proper subjects for baptism are people who make a credible profession of faith in Christ, and the only proper way to baptize is by immersion.

Conclusion

In this chapter, we have presented the cases for paedobaptism and credobaptism by immersion. Each side has made its arguments based on the Holy Scriptures and theological reasoning. It is important to weigh these arguments and come to a solid conclusion. Our doctrine of baptism has significant implications for our view of the covenants and our practice of church life.

But we also recognize that both paedobaptist believers and credobaptist believers embrace the Holy Scriptures as God's Word and love the glory of the sovereign Savior. We should appreciate and respect one another despite our differences. It should humble us that godly Christians sincerely disagree on such an important matter. We all should walk humbly, speak meekly, and pray often, "Open thou mine eyes, that I may behold wondrous things out of thy law" (Ps. 119:18), and, "Who can understand his errors? Cleanse thou me from secret faults" (19:12).

Though the doctrine of baptism still divides believers, baptism points to the union with Christ that makes them one with each other. Let us not rest in our baptism, whether it was received as infants or as professing believers. Rather, let us rest and rejoice in Christ alone.

Suggested Song to Sing to the Lord

- Psalm 105, "Unto the Lord lift thankful voices," *Psalter*, No. 425; *THBap*, No. 763

Questions for Meditation or Discussion

1. What are paedobaptism and credobaptism? What do people who hold to these positions generally teach about how baptism may be done?

15 Luther, *The Babylonian Captivity of the Church*, in *LW*, 36:64, 67–68; and Calvin, *Institutes*, 4.15.19.

2. How do Reformed paedobaptists argue for infant baptism based on Genesis 17 and God's covenant of grace? How do credobaptists respond?
3. How do credobaptists argue from the Bible's lack of explicit references to infant baptism? How do paedobaptists respond?
4. How do paedobaptists argue for infant baptism based on (1) Matthew 19:13–14, (2) Acts 2:39, (3) Acts 16:15, (4) 1 Corinthians 7:14, and (5) Colossians 2:11–12? How do credobaptists respond?
5. How do credobaptists argue that only believers should be baptized based on (1) Matthew 28:19, (2) Acts 2:38, 41, (3) Romans 6:3, (4) Ephesians 4:4–5, and (5) Jeremiah 31:31–34? How do paedobaptists respond?
6. How do paedobaptists argue that baptism may be done by sprinkling, pouring, or immersion?
7. How do credobaptists argue that baptism must be done by immersion?
8. How have you benefited from reading this chapter?

84

The Lord's Supper

Chapter Summary and Key Terms

Christ instituted the *Lord's Supper* by setting apart bread and a cup of the fruit of the vine as signs of his body and blood. Roman Catholicism teaches the *real physical presence* of Christ in the Supper, claiming that the elements become Christ's body and blood in substance without changing in outward form (*transubstantiation*). Lutheranism denies transubstantiation but teaches the real physical presence of Christ's body and blood under, with, and in the bread and wine. According to *memorialism*, the Supper serves merely as a ceremony of remembrance, with no promise of Christ's real presence. Reformed theology denies Christ's real physical presence in the Supper but teaches his *real spiritual presence* with believers by the Holy Spirit. The benefit of the Lord's Supper is communion with Christ as both God and man in his saving grace by faith. Believers should prepare for the Supper with self-examination, partake with faith in Christ, and respond with reflection and thanksgiving.

THE SECOND SACRAMENT of the church's worship is the Lord's Supper (1 Cor. 11:20), also known as the Lord's Table (10:21), Holy Communion (v. 16), the Eucharist,[1] or breaking bread (11:23–24). The Supper is a sign and seal of feeding on Christ by faith in his Word.

In this chapter, we will study Christ's institution of the Supper, the nature of his presence in it, the spiritual benefits of the Supper, and some practical directions for partaking of it.

1 "Eucharist" comes from the Greek word meaning to "give thanks" (1 Cor. 11:23–24).

Christ's Institution of the Lord's Supper

In 1 Corinthians 11:23–25, Paul says,

> The Lord Jesus the same night in which he was betrayed took bread: and when he had given thanks, he brake it, and said, Take, eat: this is my body, which is broken for you: this do in remembrance of me. After the same manner also he took the cup, when he had supped, saying, This cup is the new testament in my blood: this do ye, as oft as ye drink it, in remembrance of me.[2]

At the time, Jesus was eating the Passover meal with his twelve apostles (Matt. 26:17–20). The Lord designed the Passover to be a "memorial" of his redemption of Israel from bondage in Egypt (Ex. 12:14). By saying "this do . . . in remembrance of me" and speaking of the new covenant, Christ created a new ordinance that centers on him as Lord and Redeemer.

Christ took bread, blessed it with a prayer of thanksgiving, broke it into pieces, and gave it to his disciples to eat, saying, "This is my body" (1 Cor. 11:24). According to Luke's account, Christ's body was "given for you" (Luke 22:19), implying his voluntary surrender to death (Mark 10:45). In Paul's account, his body was "broken for you" (1 Cor. 11:24). The breaking of bread was the way a host began a meal (Matt. 14:19). In using this language, Christ alluded to both the Passover lamb and the manna. The Passover lamb was a sacrifice that turned away God's judgment (Ex. 12:12–13, 27). Manna was the heavenly "bread" by which God fed his people in the wilderness after the exodus (16:4, 15; Ps. 78:24–25).

After distributing the bread, Christ took a cup, identified it with the new covenant and his blood, and gave it to his disciples to drink (Luke 22:20; 1 Cor. 11:25). The blood of the Passover lamb shielded the households of Israel from God's wrath (Ex. 12:7, 13). The sacrificial blood sprinkled on Israel in the ratification of the Mosaic covenant was called the "blood of the covenant" (24:8). Christ inaugurated the new covenant by his death; he said his blood would be "shed for many for the remission of sins" (Matt. 26:28), which was sacrificial language (Leviticus 4). But Christ did not offer

2 See also Matt. 26:26–29; Mark 14:22–25; Luke 22:19–20.

up a sacrifice during the Supper. Rather, he pointed to the sacrifice of his once-for-all death.

Christ said he would not drink again of the fruit of the vine "until that day that I drink it new with you in my Father's kingdom" (Matt. 26:29). His words forecast a time of separation followed by the coming of his kingdom. Paul says, "For as often as you eat this bread and drink the cup, you proclaim the Lord's death until he comes" (1 Cor. 11:26 ESV).

Various Views of Christ's Presence in the Lord's Supper

Roman Catholicism and Lutheranism teach the *real physical presence* of Christ's body and blood in the Supper, though in different ways. Reformed theology denies his physical presence but affirms his *real spiritual presence.* Other Christians deny his real presence, physically or spiritually, and teach that the Supper is a mere memorial of Christ's death.

Roman Catholicism teaches the doctrine of *transubstantiation*, which holds that the substance of the elements is supernaturally changed into Christ's body and blood while retaining the outward appearances of bread and wine. The Fourth Lateran Council (1215) made transubstantiation the official doctrine of the Roman Catholic Church,[3] and this doctrine is still taught today.[4] Christ's physical body is said to not be limited by distance and location in its sacramental presence. At least some theologians in Eastern Orthodoxy also teach this doctrine.

Lutheranism rejects transubstantiation but still teaches that "in the Holy Supper the body and blood of Christ are truly and essentially present."[5] Christ's body is said to be present "under the bread," "with the bread," and "in the bread" by "the sacramental union of the unchanged essence of the bread and the body of Christ."[6]

Reformed theologians deny that Christ is present in a bodily or corporal manner but affirm that he is present by the Spirit uniting believers to the ascended Christ through faith. The Westminster Confession of Faith says,

3 The Fourth Lateran Council (chap. 1), in *Denzinger*, sec. 802 (267).

4 *Catechism of the Catholic Church* (New York: Doubleday, 1994), sec. 1376.

5 The Formula of Concord (Epitome, 7.6), in *The Book of Concord*, 505.

6 The Formula of Concord (Solid Declaration, 7.35), in *The Book of Concord*, 599. Sometimes the term *consubstantiation* is used of the Lutheran view, but Lutheran theologians generally avoid that word.

> Worthy receivers, outwardly partaking of the visible elements, in this sacrament, do then also, inwardly by faith, really and indeed, yet not carnally and corporally but spiritually, receive, and feed upon, Christ crucified, and all benefits of His death: the body and blood of Christ being then, not corporally or carnally, in, with, or under the bread and wine; yet, as really, but spiritually, present to the faith of believers in that ordinance, as the elements themselves are to their outward senses.[7]

Reformed Baptists believe the same.[8]

A fourth approach, called *memorialism*, denies that there is a special presence of Christ in the Lord's Supper. The Supper, it is said, is simply a ceremony done "in remembrance" of Christ (Luke 22:19). This view prevails in many Baptist and Pentecostal churches today.

Arguments against Christ's Real Bodily Presence in the Supper

We should not interpret Christ's words in the Supper to mean that his body and blood are physically present in the bread and cup. His words allow for a nonliteral meaning. Christ said, "This is my body," but the words "this is" can be used of symbolism (Matt. 13:19; Ezek. 5:1–5). When Jesus said these words, he was standing in his physical body before his disciples. They knew the bread was not his body. Also, Christ often spoke in figures of speech. Indeed, a literal interpretation of "blood" would make Christ a transgressor of the law of Moses, which forbade eating blood (Lev. 17:10).

Christ said, "This cup is the new testament" (Luke 22:20; 1 Cor. 11:25). But a physical cup could not literally be the covenant. And Christ spoke of the contents of the cup as real wine ("this fruit of the vine," Matt. 26:28–29; Mark 14:25). Similarly, Paul says, "We are all partakers of that one bread" (1 Cor. 10:17) and "as often as ye eat this bread" (11:26). The elements are still bread and wine.

Christ's body ascended to heaven and is not here (Acts 1:9–11). He said, "I go to prepare a place for you.... I go away.... I depart.... I go to my Father" (John 14:2; 16:7, 10). If Christ's body is present in millions of locations at once, it no longer is a human body but a kind of spirit with properties that even the angels do not possess.

7 The Westminster Confession of Faith (29.7), in *RC*, 4:269.

8 The Second London Baptist Confession (30.7), in *RC*, 4:568.

Arguments for Christ's Real Spiritual Presence in the Supper

Though Christ is not bodily present in the Lord's Supper, the sacrament is not merely a memorial but a means of communion with Christ, who is really present in a spiritual sense.

First, *Christ invites his disciples to receive him.* Jesus commands, "Take, eat; this is my body. . . . Drink ye all of it; for this is my blood" (Matt. 26:26–28). His words resemble other invitations to eat and drink that refer to receiving spiritual blessings (Isa. 55:1). Therefore, Christ's command in the Supper is not merely for believers to receive food with the mouth but to receive him with the heart by faith.

Second, *Paul says the Supper is communion with Christ.* The apostle writes, "The cup of blessing which we bless, is it not the communion of the blood of Christ? The bread which we break, is it not the communion of the body of Christ?" (1 Cor. 10:16). The word translated as "communion" means fellowship, sharing, or participation. Compare this with the warning that follows: "The things which the Gentiles sacrifice, they sacrifice to devils, and not to God: and I would not that ye should have fellowship [the same word translated as "communion"] with devils" (v. 20). Idolaters fellowship with demons, but Christians fellowship with the Lord in his Supper. Such communion is possible because the Holy Spirit joins Christ to his people (1 Cor. 6:17, 19).

Third, *the Supper is a visible word preaching the gospel.* Paul says that in the Supper, "you proclaim the Lord's death until he comes" (1 Cor. 11:26 ESV). The Supper is the gospel made visible. Christ dwells in the heart by faith in the gospel (Eph. 3:17). Thus, the Supper offers believers communion with God through Christ by a Spirit-worked faith in the gospel. Benjamin Keach said, "The sacrament is a feast for our souls . . . a soul-reviving cordial."[9]

The Administration of the Lord's Supper

Like baptism with water, the Lord's Supper is a simple ordinance, requiring no other physical elements than "bread" and a cup containing the "fruit of the vine" (Matt. 26:26, 29). We should avoid adding rituals not instituted

9 Benjamin Keach, *Preaching from the Types and Metaphors of the Bible* (1855; repr., Grand Rapids, MI: Kregel, 1972), 632, 637. A "cordial" was a drink given to stimulate, cheer, or invigorate.

by Christ. In the Bible, "bread" may be made of wheat (Ex. 29:2) or of other grains, such as barley (Judg. 7:13) and millet (Ezek. 4:9). The "fruit of the vine" is an apt expression for wine made of grapes.[10] But wine was often mixed with water, greatly diluting its alcoholic content. Paul includes drinking wine among morally indifferent matters (Rom. 14:21). Therefore, churches have liberty to use wine or grape juice.

The Lord's Supper is not for everyone, but only for believers seeking Christ's grace as members of his church in the fear of God. Christ gave the Supper to "the disciples" (Matt. 26:26). Sharing in "one bread" is a sign of being "one body" in Christ (1 Cor. 10:17). A communicant must "examine himself, and so let him eat of that bread, and drink of that cup" (11:28). Therefore, the church's officers should "fence" the table by prohibiting the very young, ignorant, unconverted, uncommitted, wicked, unbelieving, or irreverent from participating.

The Lord's Supper is to be celebrated by the gathered church under the direction of its elders. Christ instituted the Supper when his disciples were together, not when he was with each one of them individually. Christ commanded "all" of them to drink of the cup, for his blood was "shed for many" (Matt. 26:27–28). Paul writes of the Supper taking place "when ye come together in the church . . . when ye come together therefore into one place" (1 Cor. 11:18, 20). To profane the Supper as if it were a common meal is to despise "the church of God" (v. 22).

Personal Benefits of the Lord's Supper

The Supper centers around union and communion with Christ. All its benefits are contained as a vast spiritual treasure hidden in his person as the incarnate Son of God (John 1:16; Eph. 1:3; Col. 2:3). In the Supper, we do not feast on one benefit or another, but on Christ himself. Edward Reynolds wrote, "The main end of the Sacrament . . . is to unite the faithful unto Christ."[11] The precise nature of how this works is a mystery too grand for our feeble minds to comprehend.

10 In the Jewish Mishnah (circa AD 200), the prescribed blessing over the "wine" gives thanks to the God who "creates fruit of the vine." Mishnah Berakhot 6:1; Mishnah Pesachim 10:2, both available at Sefaria, https://www.sefaria.org/texts/Mishnah. See *TDNT*, 3:733.

11 Edward Reynolds, *Meditations on the Holy Sacrament*, in *The Whole Works of the Right Rev. Edward Reynolds*, 6 vols. (1826; repr., Morgan, PA: Soli Deo Gloria, 1999), 3:73.

The following list presents several particular benefits of the Lord's Supper.[12]

1. *Focus on the gospel of Christ crucified.* The Lord's Supper places the fact of Christ's death for sinners before the eyes of all in a tangible way (1 Cor. 11:24–26).
2. *Divine pledge and confirmation of grace.* The Supper is a sign and seal that we have free and full forgiveness by the blood of the new covenant (Matt. 26:28).
3. *Covenant renewal.* The Supper reaffirms the benefits of God's covenant to us, and we respond by reaffirming our part in the covenant—our grateful response to his grace.
4. *Intimate communion with Christ.* In the Supper, Christ's bride proclaims, "Let him kiss me with the kisses of his mouth: for thy love is better than wine" (Song 1:2).
5. *Thanksgiving and praise.* When Christ took the bread at the Last Supper, he "gave thanks" (Matt. 26:27). How much more should we!
6. *Unity in Christ's body.* Paul said to the church at Corinth, "For we being many are one bread, and one body: for we are all partakers of that one bread" (1 Cor. 10:17).
7. *Growth in particular virtues.* The Supper spurs us to repentance of our sins, faith and love toward Christ, joy in God's presence, zeal to serve him, and hope in his return.

Directions for Partaking of the Lord's Supper

The benefits of the Supper do not come automatically, as if a bare ceremony or ritual could confer the grace of God. We must partake with a right heart in a right manner. Drawing near to God's special presence calls for sanctifying the name of God with reverence (Lev. 10:3).

The Danger of Partaking Unworthily

What did Paul mean when he cautioned the Corinthians about partaking "unworthily" (1 Cor. 11:27, 29)? Paul is not speaking of worthiness in an

12 See Joel R. Beeke and Ray B. Lanning, *How Can I Benefit from the Lord's Supper?*, Cultivating Biblical Godliness (Grand Rapids, MI: Reformation Heritage Books, 2019); and Joel R. Beeke and Paul M. Smalley, eds., *Feasting with Christ: Meditations on the Lord's Supper* (Darlington, England: Evangelical Press, 2012).

absolute sense (merit based on law). The Christian's works are worthy in the sense that the Father accepts for Christ's sake our imperfect yet sincere obedience arising from the gracious influences of the Spirit. Our access to the table, like our salvation, is by grace alone (Eph. 2:8–9). Furthermore, "unworthily" is an adverb describing our manner of partaking, not an adjective describing our persons. It implies taking the Supper in a manner inappropriate to its meaning as a sign of Christ's death for our sins (1 Cor. 11:27), the unity of the church (10:17), and communion with our Lord (v. 16). Hence, partaking unworthily involves eating and drinking without exercising faith in Christ alone; while living in conscious refusal to repent of sin; when acting in a way that divides Christ's church; or with irreverent disregard for his holy presence. But if we come humbly, conscious of our faults and weaknesses, looking to Christ, we have every reason to partake of the Supper.

Preparing for the Lord's Supper

In the time leading up to the Supper, make use of your devotions to prepare to partake. Wilhelmus à Brakel said that preparation requires practicing three matters.

First, there should be a "stimulating of desire."[13] Like David, we should stir up strong desire to be in God's presence with his people (Pss. 27:4; 42:2, 4; 122:1–2).

The second aspect of preparation is self-examination, which Paul explicitly commands (1 Cor. 11:28–29). Jonathan Edwards taught that self-examination before the Lord's Supper should include asking ourselves the following questions: (1) Am I living in willful rebellion against the will of God in any known commandment? (2) Do I have a "serious resolution to avoid all sin and live in obedience to all known commands" as long as I live? (3) Do I "entertain a spirit of hatred or envy or revenge" toward my neighbor? (4) Is my motive in coming to grow in holiness?[14]

Brakel called the third aspect of preparation "spiritual adornment," writing, "A bride will adorn herself in a most excellent manner so that she may be desirable to her husband and honor him. Much more must a believer do this in order that the King may delight in his beauty."[15] This "adornment"

13 Brakel, *CRS*, 2:572.

14 Edwards, "Self-Examination and the Lord's Supper," in *WJE*, 17:267–69.

15 Brakel, *CRS*, 2:582.

consists in reflection on redemption, meditation on our unworthiness of God's love, evangelical shame over our sin, confession of sins, prayer for forgiveness and peace of conscience, renewal of our covenantal commitment to our God, resolution to grow in holiness, love for Christ's church, and prayer for the Spirit to fill the church.[16]

Partaking of the Lord's Supper

The spiritual exercises that begin in preparation should intensify as we partake of the Supper. When the church's worship transitions to the observance of the Supper, we should pray for God to grant his people a deeper experiential knowledge of his grace in Christ. When the Supper is administered, the time has come to meditate more intensely on the Lord Jesus Christ, especially his sufferings and death. "This do in remembrance of me," our Lord said (1 Cor. 11:24).

Brakel gave this counsel:

> Do not focus on the external signs only, for you know that they cannot feed your soul. . . . Behold in them the breaking of the body of Christ and the shedding of His blood, and with that, His love and the efficacy of His suffering unto the forgiveness of your sins. . . . While eating and drinking, apply Christ to yourself . . . saying, "My beloved is mine, and I am His" (Song of Sol. 2:16).[17]

Responding after the Lord's Supper

Further reflection, thanksgiving, praise, self-examination, meditation, prayer, and watchfulness should follow our participation in the Supper. We should continue to make holy resolutions to walk with God and follow Christ fully, renouncing the world and its pleasures.

Brakel said that we should continue to meditate on the core truths of the Supper as we reflect on our experience in partaking of it. This includes reflecting further on our condition during preparation and participation. Did we prepare adequately or haphazardly? When we partook, were we presumptuous or penitent, insensitive or tenderhearted?[18]

16 Brakel, *CRS*, 2:582–89.

17 Brakel, *CRS*, 2:591–92.

18 Brakel, *CRS*, 2:593–94.

Furthermore, did we receive some conscious benefit from the Supper? If we can answer yes to this question, we should give thanks to God, celebrating the work that God has done in our souls. Behold his glory, be transformed by his likeness, be enamored with gratitude for his salvation, and be content with his providence.[19] If we come away from the Supper with little conscious sense of blessing, we must fall back on the objective promises of the covenant of grace, signed and sealed to us in the Supper.[20]

Conclusion: Purposes of the Feast

May God grant us to taste and see that he is good and gracious in his holy Supper. May he allow us to experience it as a genuine feast for us. It is a *commemorative* feast to remember his Son and a *strengthening* feast to nurture our faith. It is a *covenanting* feast to covenant ourselves back to him who covenants himself to us and a *witnessing* feast to declare our need of him. And it is a *love* feast through which to be loved by him and to love him from whom all blessings flow.

Suggested Songs to Sing to the Lord

- Psalm 116, "I love the Lord, the fount of life and grace," *Psalter*, No. 426
- "'Twas on that night when doomed to know," *THBap*, No. 359

Questions for Meditation or Discussion

1. What is the meaning of Christ's words of institution regarding his body and blood?
2. What are the major approaches to Christ's presence in the Lord's Supper?
3. What arguments can be made against the doctrine of Christ's real bodily presence?
4. What arguments can be made in favor of Christ's real spiritual presence in the Supper?
5. What is the proper way to administer the Supper?
6. How does rightly partaking of the Supper benefit the believer?

19 Brakel, *CRS*, 2:593–600.

20 Brakel, *CRS*, 2:596.

7. What does it mean to partake unworthily?
8. How should a believer (1) prepare for the Supper, (2) partake of the Supper, and (3) respond after the Supper?
9. How has reading this chapter changed the way that you view the Lord's Supper? What will you do differently in the future in regard to the Supper?

85

Prayer, Praise, Fellowship, and Discipline

Chapter Summary and Key Terms

Christ works through other public means of grace besides the ministry of the Word and the sacraments. When God's people gather for *corporate prayer*, they commune with him and obtain blessings in answer to their requests. The church glorifies God through *songs of praise*. According to the principle of *exclusive psalmody*, the church should sing only psalms in public worship. In Christian *fellowship*, believers strengthen one another through friendships, mutual service, and partnership in the gospel. *Formative church discipline* matures the body of Christ by the Word. There are four levels of *corrective church discipline*: (1) personal reproof; (2) private meeting with witnesses; (3) church *censure*, an official rebuke, often with the temporary *suspension* of privileges such as taking the Lord's Supper; and (4) *excommunication*, the removal of a person from church membership due to prolonged refusal to repent of heinous sin despite repeated appeals from the church. The aims of corrective discipline are the repentance and spiritual restoration of the offender, the holiness of the visible church, and the glory of God.

AS GOD'S WORD goes out to his people, it generates a holy echo as their prayers and praises return to him. It also generates a community of fellowship and discipline. Corporate prayer, songs of praise, fellowship, and discipline, if rightly done, are full of God's Word. Therefore, they are means of grace by which the Lord strengthens the faith and obedience of his church. In this chapter, we will examine these four public means of grace.

Corporate Prayer in the Bible

By *corporate prayer* we mean prayer done together with other believers, especially in a meeting of the church. The Lord requires that "supplications, prayers, intercessions, and giving of thanks, be made" (1 Tim. 2:1) in "the church of the living God" (3:15). Christ came to make God's people into a "house of prayer" (Isa. 56:7; Matt. 21:13).

After Pentecost, the members of the church "continued stedfastly . . . in prayers" (Acts 2:42). Under the threat of persecution, the members of the church "lifted up their voice to God with one accord" (4:24). When Peter was imprisoned, "prayer was made without ceasing of the church unto God for him" (12:5). This involved a meeting in a private home, "where many were gathered together praying" (v. 12). As Paul journeyed toward possible martyrdom, he met with the elders of Ephesus, "kneeled down, and prayed with them all" (20:36).

As Paul teaches (Eph. 2:18), corporate prayer requires us to exercise the following:

- faith in Christ, who reconciles us to God and to one another by his blood
- faith in the Father, who sent Christ and welcomes all who come in Christ
- faith in the Spirit as the living bond of union that joins us to God and one another

We should pray to please the Father (Matt. 6:5–6) and to edify those with us (John 11:42; 17:13). It is best to pray with minds full of the Bible (15:7) and hearts in awe of God (Acts 4:24–28). We should pray for ministers of the gospel and their preaching (Eph. 6:19–20). We should intercede for all kinds of people, including rulers in civil government (1 Tim. 2:1–2). We should especially ask God to cause the gospel to advance in the salvation of sinners (vv. 4–7). We should petition the Lord for awakening and revival in our souls, our families, our churches, our nations, and the world. As we come together for prayer, let us make sure that we are walking in holiness and are at peace with one another (v. 8). We should also pray for the sanctifying work of the Holy Spirit in God's children (Luke 11:13).

We may join together in corporate prayer with great expectation. Christ says, "If two of you shall agree on earth as touching any thing that they shall ask, it shall be done for them of my Father which is in heaven" (Matt. 18:19). God has graciously confirmed this promise many times in church history. He has granted remarkable seasons of revival in response to the cries of his needy people.

Let us, therefore, go eagerly to prayer meetings.[1] Charles Spurgeon said, "Brethren, we shall never see much change for the better in our churches in general till the prayer meeting occupies a higher place in the esteem of Christians."[2]

Corporate Singing of Praises

The Singing of Praise

God made singing central to the worship of his people when he raised up David, "the sweet psalmist of Israel" (2 Sam. 23:1). David organized the Levites to minister at the temple in song and music (1 Chron. 15:16–24; 16:41–42). One way that God manifested his special presence at the temple was through the praises of his people. David says, "Thou art holy, O thou that inhabitest the praises of Israel" (Ps. 22:3). The verb translated as "inhabitest" is used in the book of Psalms of the Lord's sitting as a king on his throne (47:8; 99:1).

In the new covenant, believers in Christ act as a "holy priesthood" to offer God spiritual sacrifices (1 Pet. 2:5). They offer "the sacrifice of praise to God . . . the fruit of our lips giving thanks to his name" (Heb. 13:15). God the Son incarnate now leads his people in singing (2:12). God the Holy Spirit fills God's church as believers are singing praises and giving thanks to God the Father in the name of Jesus Christ (Eph. 5:18–20; Col. 3:16).

The Songs of Praise

True worship is a response to God's truth (John 4:24). Songs of worship, therefore, should be full of doctrinal truth. Good songs of worship celebrate God's glory in his attributes and works (Ps. 95:1–6).

Today, there are four main approaches to choosing songs for public worship:

1 For a more detailed treatment of corporate prayer, see Joel R. Beeke, *The Family at Church: Listening to Sermons and Attending Prayer Meetings*, Family Guidance Series (Grand Rapids, MI: Reformation Heritage Books, 2008), 39–77.

2 C. H. Spurgeon, *Only a Prayer Meeting* (Fearn, Ross-shire, Scotland: Christian Focus, 2000), 9.

1. Some churches sing only the Psalms (exclusive psalmody). This is the approach taken by several Presbyterian churches, especially those originating in Scotland.
2. Some churches sing the Psalms and, on occasion, a few other parts of the Bible. This is the approach taken by the Dutch Reformed Church based on the Synod of Dort.
3. Some churches sing songs of the Bible (including the Psalms) and doctrinally rich hymns written by men and women over the centuries. This approach has been taken by many Lutheran, Baptist, and other evangelical churches.
4. Some churches sing few if any of the Psalms or older hymns, but mostly sing songs composed in the last few decades.

God's Word clearly requires that the church sing the Psalms. This was the practice of God's people under the old covenant (2 Chron. 29:30). More than one-third of the psalms bear titles referring to music (e.g., Pss. 4:1; 5:1; 6:1). Some psalms directly command us to sing (95:2; 105:2). Indeed, they call all the earth to sing to the Lord (96:1; 100:1; 117:1). In the new covenant, Paul says, "Be filled with the Spirit, addressing one another in psalms and hymns and spiritual songs, singing and making melody to the Lord with your heart" (Eph. 5:18–19 ESV; cf. Col. 3:16). The word transliterated as "psalms" refers to the book of Psalms.[3] The words translated as "hymns" and "songs" are often, though not always, used of the Psalms. Therefore, by "psalms, hymns, and spiritual songs," Paul teaches that it is God's will for the church to sing the Psalms.

Should the church sing only the Psalms in public worship? Those who oppose exclusive psalmody argue that the Scriptures contain other songs of praise besides the Psalms. The standard for songs of worship, they say, should be the same as that for sermons and prayers—namely, that they express biblical truth. They also say that the church needs songs that can express the much clearer revelation of the Trinity and salvation found in the New Testament.

Theologians in favor of exclusive psalmody argue that the book of Psalms is the inspired songbook of the Holy Scriptures. It is the only hymnal, so to speak, that God has authorized. Singing the Psalms, it is argued, allows the

3 Luke 20:42; 24:44; Acts 1:20; 13:33; and seventy-two instances in titles in the Psalms.

whole church to sing with a good conscience. Christians may disagree about the theology of other songs, but the Psalms are God's Word. The Psalms also teach the person and work of Christ and the Holy Spirit, and stress salvation by grace.

Even if we cannot agree on whether the church should sing *only* the Psalms, Paul's words to the Ephesians and the Colossians show that singing the Psalms is God's revealed will for the church. Benjamin Keach, a Baptist theologian who defended singing hymns, said, "The Holy Ghost hath enjoined the singing of psalms particularly."[4]

Practical Directions for Singing to God's Glory and Man's Edification

We offer these guidelines for singing that helps God's people to lift their hearts to the Lord:

1. Sing as a response to God's grace in the gospel (Eph. 1:3, 6).
2. Sing privately at home to train your heart and voice (James 5:13).
3. Sing with understanding of what you are singing (1 Cor. 14:15).
4. Sing with integrity, not as a hypocrite living in sin (Prov. 15:8).
5. Sing as an act of obedience, even if your emotions are not yet engaged (Eph. 5:19).
6. Sing with affection and energy insofar as you can (Ps. 100:1–2).
7. Sing in unity with the whole congregation in pitch, meter, and volume as best you can (Rom. 15:6).
8. Sing with your heart set on Christ and his kingdom (Col. 3:1–4).

Fellowship with the Saints

After Pentecost, the church "continued stedfastly in the apostles' doctrine and *fellowship*, and in breaking of bread, and in prayers" (Acts 2:42). Fellowship has three main dimensions.

First, *the church has fellowship in spiritual friendships*. Christians are holy companions to one another. The believers in the early church "were of one heart and of one soul" (Acts 4:32). This unity is a supernatural gift from God to his covenant people (Jer. 32:39). The Holy Spirit draws them together in humility and Christlike love (Phil. 2:1–5). To develop and preserve these

4 Benjamin Keach, *The Breach Repaired in God's Worship: Or, Singing of Psalms, Hymns, and Spiritual Songs, Proved to Be an Holy Ordinance of Jesus Christ* (London: for the author, 1691), 96.

friendships, believers must forgive and patiently bear with one another (Eph. 4:2; Col. 3:13). An excellent means to cultivate godly friendship is meeting in small groups for intimate fellowship, edifying discussion, and corporate prayer.

The Lord gives a remarkable promise to people who gather for Christian fellowship:

> Then they that feared the LORD spake often one to another: and the LORD hearkened, and heard it, and a book of remembrance was written before him for them that feared the LORD, and that thought upon his name. And they shall be mine, saith the LORD of hosts, in that day when I make up my jewels; and I will spare them, as a man spareth his own son that serveth him. (Mal. 3:16–17)

The holy companionship of Christian fellowship marks people for God's blessing.

Second, *the church has fellowship in mutual service*. Paul counts "helps" to be one of the gifts by which the Holy Spirit builds the church (1 Cor. 12:28). God gives people the ability to repair a car, cook a meal, clean a house, listen with compassion to a hurting person, give a ride in a vehicle, and help someone properly fill out forms. These Christians, too, can use their gifts "as good stewards of the manifold grace of God . . . that God in all things may be glorified through Jesus Christ" (1 Pet. 4:10–11).

Third, *the church has fellowship in missions and evangelism*. Christians become partners with one another in the gospel (Phil. 1:5, 7). They can support missions by their financial gifts (4:15). They can also stand together as a church "in one spirit, with one mind striving together for the faith of the gospel" (1:27). Fellowship in missions requires doctrinal discernment—Christians must take care not to partner with people who do not hold to sound doctrine (2 John 9–11). However, Christians should support those who "have gone out for the sake of the name [of the Lord] . . . that we may be fellow workers for the truth" (3 John 6–8 ESV).

The Discipline of the Church

Discipline refers not just to punishment but more broadly to the training of people. The discipline of the church is done by the triune God: the Father (Heb. 12:5–11), the Son (Rev. 3:19), and the Holy Spirit (Acts 5:3–5, 11).

Ministers and elders are God's servants to perform this discipline. Christ entrusted to the church's shepherds "the keys of the kingdom of heaven" (Matt. 16:19; see chap. 74). In addition, all members of the church exercise mutual discipline toward one another (Rom. 15:14; Gal. 6:1). Church discipline has two sides: formative and corrective.

Formative Discipline

Through formative discipline, God strengthens and matures the body into the image of Christ (Eph. 4:13). The power for formative discipline comes from the grace of God (Titus 2:11–12). Its primary means is the ministry of the Word (Eph. 4:10–12; 1 Thess. 2:11). Another important means of formative discipline is mutual exhortation and encouragement. It is written, "Exhort one another daily, while it is called To day; lest any of you be hardened through the deceitfulness of sin" (Heb. 3:13). And again, "Let us consider one another to provoke unto love and to good works: not forsaking the assembling of ourselves together, as the manner of some is; but exhorting one another: and so much the more, as ye see the day approaching" (10:24–25).

Corrective Discipline

By corrective discipline, God cures spiritual diseases that attack Christ's body. Christ reveals four levels of corrective discipline.

First, *personal reproof.* Christ says, "If thy brother shall trespass against thee, go and tell him his fault between thee and him alone: if he shall hear thee, thou hast gained thy brother" (Matt. 18:15). A private sinful offense should be resolved privately if possible.

Second, *private meeting with witnesses*. Christ says, "If he will not hear thee, then take with thee one or two more, that in the mouth of two or three witnesses every word may be established" (Matt. 18:16). Additional people are introduced to motivate the person who committed the sinful offense to listen. If that fails, they serve as "witnesses" concerning his impenitence.

Third, *church censure* (official rebuke). If admonition from two or three brethren fails to win over the sinning offender, Christ says, "Tell it unto the church" (Matt. 18:17).[5] If the church judges this matter to be of sufficient

5 Congregationalists interpret "church" in Matt. 18:17 to refer to the membership of a particular church. Presbyterians interpret "church" to refer to the assembly of the elders. On this matter

clarity and weight, it will also admonish the offender who has refused to repent. This is implied by the phrase "if he refuses to listen even to the church" (v. 17 ESV).

When the offense is a public, plain, and heinous sin, the earlier steps of meeting privately may be waived. The church may proceed directly to public censure (Gal. 2:11–16).

With censure comes suspension, the loss of some privileges of membership. This may involve suspension from taking the Lord's Supper or participating in ministry functions. The propriety of suspension is implied by Paul's severe rebuke to the Corinthians for their misconduct at the Supper, call to self-examination, and warning to the one who ate and drank "unworthily" (1 Cor. 11:20–22, 27–29). The suspension of someone still regarded as a brother should be only a short-term measure leading to either restoration or excommunication.

Church censure may also require removing people from church office if they no longer have the moral qualifications for that office (1 Tim. 3:1–13; 5:19–21), even if their offenses do not require excommunication. Churches should not be too quick to restore former officers after repentance (5:22). It takes time to demonstrate proven character and rebuild a good reputation.

Fourth, *excommunication*. Christ says that if the offender refuses to hear the church and to repent, "Let him be to you as a Gentile and a tax collector" (Matt. 18:17 ESV). Gentiles and tax collectors were considered outsiders to God's covenant people (cf. 5:46–47; 6:7, 32). Christ solemnly says, "Verily I say unto you, Whatsoever ye shall bind on earth shall be bound in heaven: and whatsoever ye shall loose on earth shall be loosed in heaven" (18:18). Insofar as the church's judgment reflects God's Word and the true circumstances of the case, it expresses the judgment of God himself. Christ's words "Let him be unto thee as an heathen man" (18:17) imply social avoidance.[6] But church discipline does not dissolve the bond of marriage or require the shunning of family members. Under ordinary circumstances, excommunication also does not prohibit someone from

as well as the particular procedure of discipline according to the Synod of Dort, see Beeke and Smalley, *RST*, 4:657–60.

6 Law-observant Jews did not associate or eat with Gentiles (Acts 10:28; 11:3). On social avoidance, see also Rom. 16:17–18; 1 Cor. 5:9–13; Titus 3:10; 2 John 10.

attending public worship. The church should reserve excommunication for heinous sins (1 Cor. 5:1–2, 11; cf. 6:9–10).

The aim of church discipline is the restoration of the offender. Christ's comparison of excommunicated members to Gentiles and tax collectors (Matt. 18:17) reminds us of his mercy to those very people if they repented and believed in him (8:5–13; 9:9–13). Paul says that the aim of excommunication is "to deliver such an one unto Satan for the destruction of the flesh, that the spirit may be saved in the day of the Lord Jesus" (1 Cor. 5:5). If the offender repents and manifests the fruit of "godly sorrow" (2 Cor. 7:10–11), the church should forgive him and welcome him warmly back into membership (2:7). Restoration may require ongoing mentoring and encouragement. After Paul tells the "spiritual" to "restore" someone who has fallen into sin, he adds, "Bear ye one another's burdens" (Gal. 6:1–2).

Whether or not the sinning offender repents, church discipline preserves the purity of the church. If a church will not purify itself by disciplining its members, the Lord Jesus may purify it by disciplining the church (Rev. 2:14–16, 20–23). Faithfulness in discipline shows a church's love for "the name of our Lord Jesus Christ" (1 Cor. 5:4), which would be dishonored by tolerating serious sin. Excommunicating unrepentant sinners is an important way that believers "keep the feast" in sincere holiness (v. 8)—that is, live for the glory of God.

John Calvin summarized the purposes of excommunication as follows: (1) "that they who lead a filthy and infamous life may not be called Christians, to the dishonor of God, as if his holy church were a conspiracy of wicked and abandoned men"; (2) "that the good be not corrupted by the constant company of the wicked"; and (3) "that those overcome by shame for their baseness begin to repent."[7] This strong medicine aims to preserve the purity of churches and to heal souls.

Conclusion on Fellowship and Discipline

We end our study of fellowship and discipline with a few practical reflections from the book of Proverbs. Christians should learn to be true friends (Prov. 17:17). Finding good friends takes discernment (13:20). Let us be careful in what we say to one another, for words are powerful (18:21; 21:23). It is wise

7 Calvin, *Institutes*, 4.12.5.

to avoid unnecessary conflict (17:14; 18:19; 19:11), but true friendship can endure hard conversations (27:5–6, 17). If we are going to correct a friend, we must be willing to listen to him or her and hear both sides of the story (18:13, 17). And when we are corrected, let us remember that confession of sin and repentance are far sweeter than hiding sin (28:13–14).

Suggested Song to Sing to the Lord

- Psalm 146, "Hallelujah, praise Jehovah," *Psalter*, No. 400; *THBap*, No. 53

Questions for Meditation or Discussion

1. How does the Bible encourage us to join with other believers in corporate prayer?
2. What biblical principles should guide our prayer meetings?
3. How do the Holy Scriptures show us that the church should sing God's praises?
4. What are four approaches that churches today use to choose songs?
5. Someone says, "I don't see why our church needs to sing the Psalms." How do you respond?
6. How are you nurturing godly friendships with other believers?
7. How are you using your abilities and resources to serve other Christians and support missions?
8. What is formative discipline? What does the Bible teach us about it?
9. What is corrective discipline? What are its four levels?
10. Someone says, "Excommunication is so unloving!" How do you respond?

86

The Reformation of the Church

Chapter Summary and Key Terms

The *reformation of the church* is not about innovation but the restoration of the church to the standards revealed by Christ in his Word. In the sixteenth century, God brought about the Protestant Reformation through preachers such as Martin Luther, Ulrich Zwingli, and John Calvin. Even when churches are already Reformed in doctrine, they should seek greater conformity to God's Word in Christian experience and practice. The church needs reformation because it is the temple of God, the bride of Christ, and God's army in conflict with the Devil. Key areas for reformation today include the prayer meeting, church discipline, pastoral care by the elders, women's ministry, godliness in the heart, doctrines and moral precepts especially under attack today (such as the sufficiency of the Scriptures, the doctrine of creation, and the second, fourth, seventh, and tenth commandments), and the five *sola* doctrines that were central to the Protestant Reformation. The great means of reformation is the Word of God.

WHEN WE SPEAK OF the *reformation of the church*, we mean its restoration to conformity to the standard of God's Word. The Protestant Reformation took place in the sixteenth century as ministers such as Martin Luther and Ulrich Zwingli preached the Bible and protested against serious corruptions and errors in Roman Catholicism. John Calvin, a second-generation Reformer, later said that the Reformation arose because the church had become seriously ill in matters central to true

Christianity. The church, he said, was sick in its "soul," the doctrines of right worship and salvation, as well as in its "body," the sacraments and the form of church government.[1]

The aim of reformation is not constant innovation. That often leads to error and worldliness. The goal is that the Bible's teachings would be restored to the church by its reformation. Even when a church's official teachings are already Reformed, it should strive to make its experiential and practical life more consistent with sound doctrine.

The Warrant for Reformation from the Nature of the Church

If the church were a social club or a voluntary organization for charitable purposes, it would not need reformation as long as its members were satisfied. But the church is God's holy temple (1 Cor. 3:16). Sometimes the visible church of God becomes like the temple as King Hezekiah found it—filled with unclean things and idols (2 Kings 18:1–4; 2 Chron. 29:1–19). Reformation means cleansing God's temple and restoring it to holiness to honor the Lord who dwells in it.

The church needs reformation because it is Christ's. He says, "I will build my church" (Matt. 16:18). Therefore, it is Christ's possession (Titus 2:14). He is with his servants as they teach the church "to observe all things whatsoever I have commanded you" (Matt. 28:20). The church's task will not be done until all its members are conformed to Christ's will.

We also see the importance of reformation in the church's glorious calling to be Christ's bride. She is to keep herself purely and entirely his as she waits for his return, but she is constantly endangered and sometimes deceived by false teachers (2 Cor. 11:2–4).

Finally, the Scriptures provide warrant for reformation when they tell us that the body of Christ is God's army at war with the Devil. The book of Revelation reminds us that the Lamb slain for our sins now leads the church in a spiritual war against Satan (Rev. 17:14). The Lord Jesus corrected churches for lacking love (2:4), tolerating false teaching (vv. 14–15), failing to discipline a false prophetess (v. 20), being dead though appearing to be alive (3:1), and proudly trusting in themselves (v. 17).

1 John Calvin, *The Necessity of Reforming the Church*, trans. Casey Carmichael (Orlando, FL: Ligonier Ministries, 2020), 5–6.

Therefore, the Bible gives us warrant for the work of reformation. Likewise, the very nature of the church in its present state shows us the need for reformation. Gospel ministers can lead reformation with confidence, for God is with his people.

The Church's Need for Reformation Today

In every age or season, there are areas in the life of the church that especially require reformation. In this section, we present some admonitions to Christians to pursue reformation in the church in areas of particularly urgent need at this present time.

First, *renew the church's prayer meeting.* In too many cases, the prayer meeting has declined into a few old people praying for a few sick people. Every member who is able should regularly attend the church's stated prayer meeting. Parents should also strive to bring their children to prayer meetings. Prayers may certainly be lifted for medical and financial needs, but the priority of the prayer meeting should be that people would honor God's holy name, receive the power of his kingdom, and become doers of his will "in earth, as it is in heaven" (Matt. 6:9–13).

Second, *practice church discipline with both righteousness and mercy.* Some churches need reform because they neglect church discipline. Their elders allow serious sin to continue and spread in Christ's church without calling members to repent. Other churches need reform because they implement discipline in a ruthless manner. Churches must practice discipline with a combination of biblical love, meekness, compassion, and the fear of the Lord (Gal. 6:1; Jude 22–23).

Third, *restore the ministers and elders to their ministry of home visitation and pastoral care.* Far too often, churches view their spiritual leaders as a board of directors. Church members need to be taught to view their ministers and elders as shepherds who care for their souls (Heb. 13:17). They should welcome visits in their homes and receive counsel as coming from brothers who seek their eternal good.

Fourth, *obey God's instructions for women's ministry in the church.* In some churches, biblical reformation will require removing women from church office and beginning to obey the biblical prohibition against women teaching or exercising authority over men (1 Tim. 2:12). In other churches, reformation may require the members to recall that female believers have spiritual gifts and should exercise them.

Fifth, *cultivate heart religion and a close walk with God in the church.* An external form of religion can replace the power of a living faith (2 Tim. 3:5). Reformation results in congregations that live as aliens and pilgrims headed for glory (Heb. 11:13). Also, reformation nurtures the authentic experience of misery over our sins, confidence and joy in our deliverance in Christ, and gratitude that responds to God's love with obedience to his commandments.

Sixth, *hold fast to the Bible in those doctrines and commandments where the world attacks it.* In every season, there are certain battlefronts where Satan most fiercely assaults the church. In the twentieth century, it was the inerrancy of the Bible. Today the battle focuses more on the sufficiency of the Bible.

Another area where the Christian faith is under attack is the doctrine of God's creation of the universe in six days and his special creation of the first man from the dust of the earth (Genesis 1–2).

We must also uphold the moral law summarized in the Ten Commandments, especially in those areas where the law is most under attack.

Regarding the second commandment (Ex. 20:4–6), it has become common for evangelical Christians to break it by using manmade images of God the Son incarnate and even to display these pictures in places of prayer and worship.

In the fourth commandment, we learn our duty to keep the Sabbath holy (Ex. 20:8–11). Many evangelical churches today profane the Sabbath by treating it like any other day, except for an hour or two of worship in the morning.

With respect to the seventh commandment (Ex. 20:14), the church faces tremendous pressure to accept all forms of sexual expression among consenting people, including fornication, pornography, adultery, homosexuality, and transgenderism.

With regard to the tenth commandment (Ex. 20:17), the church must warn its members of the deadly sin of "covetousness, which is idolatry" (Col. 3:5). The age of consumerism is upon us, and we are surrounded by enticements to discontent and a longing for new things.

Seventh, *preach the five* solas *of the sixteenth-century Reformation. Sola scriptura* means that "Scripture alone" is God's rule to direct our faith, obedience, and worship. This includes following the regulative principle of worship and filling our praises with God's own Word (chap. 85). *Sola gratia* means that we are saved, made holy, and brought to glory by God's "grace alone." *Solus Christus* teaches us that all our salvation comes to us through "Christ alone." *Sola fide* accompanies *solus Christus* with the truth that we are justified before God "by faith alone" in Jesus Christ, apart from our own goodness, merit, or works. *Soli Deo gloria* ends the five *solas* with doxology: "to God alone be the glory." The emphasis in this phrase falls on the word *alone*. There is no place in the church of Christ for worshiping saints or praying to them, or for lifting up a living leader as if he were the church's Lord.

The Means of Reformation in the Church

Whatever specific aspects of church life need reform, the means of reformation is the great and essential means of grace: the Word of God (chap. 81). Jean-Henri Merle d'Aubigné said,

> The only true Reformation is that which emanates from the word of God. The Holy Scriptures, by bearing witness to the incarnation, death, and resurrection of the Son of God, create in man by the Holy Ghost a faith which justifies him. That faith, which produces in him a new life, unites him to Christ. . . . This Reformation by the word restores that spiritual Christianity which the outward and hierarchical religion had destroyed; and from the regeneration of individuals naturally results the regeneration of the church.[2]

We conclude with practical advice on how to use the Word to reform the church:

- Know, sing, and memorize the Word of God. Begin reformation with yourself.
- Model the Word as a living example of love. Practice what you preach.
- Pray God's promises to the church. Lift up God's commands to the church as requests with the confidence that it is God's will for the church to obey them.

2 J. H. Merle d'Aubigné, *History of the Reformation of the Sixteenth Century*, trans. H. White, 5 vols. (New York: Robert Carter & Brothers, 1853), 5:149.

- If you are a minister, preach the Word faithfully. Preach Christ.
- If you are an elder or teacher, teach the sound doctrines of the Word.
- Catechize children and adults in the basic teachings of the Word.
- Build friendships with believers who love the Word.
- Train elders and other teachers to serve the church by the Word.
- Write articles that explain and defend the doctrines of the Word.
- Implement changes to further conform the church to the Word. Reformation requires changes in the practice and worship of the church.
- Suffer willingly for the sake of the Word. Just as the Word is always opposed, so reformation according to the Word will be opposed.
- Wait prayerfully and patiently for the Holy Spirit to work through the Word. You cannot cause reformation or control its pace or extent.
- Finally, give the triune God all the praise for the reforming effects of the Word. You are but a servant, an instrument in the hands of the Master.

Reformation is not just a restoration of the doctrines of grace alone for the glory of God alone. It is a powerful illustration of grace alone for the glory of God alone. Luther said, "I simply taught, preached, and wrote God's Word. . . . I did nothing; the Word did everything."[3]

Suggested Song to Sing to the Lord

- "A mighty Fortress is our God," *THBap*, No. 81

Questions for Meditation or Discussion

1. What does *reformation* mean with respect to the church?
2. What warrant does the Bible give us to reform the church based on its very nature?
3. What needs are there for reformation in many churches' prayer meetings, discipline, and women's ministries?
4. Why is the cultivation of heart religion critical to reformation?
5. What doctrinal and ethical matters in the church today call for reformation?

3 Luther, "Eight Sermons at Wittenberg," 1522, the Second Sermon, March 10, in *LW*, 51:77.

6. What are the five *solas*? How is each *sola* affirmed or denied by your church?
7. What are some ways that we should begin reformation with ourselves?
8. Why is it shortsighted to attempt reformation without catechizing children, building friendships, and training elders?
9. Why is it crucial for reformation that we suffer willingly, wait patiently, and glorify God sincerely?
10. Given your gifts and circumstances, what is your duty to seek reformation in the church? What are a few practical steps you can take to begin now?

PART 7

THE DOCTRINE OF THE LAST THINGS

Section 7A

Introduction and Special Issues in the Last Things

87

Introduction to the Doctrine of the Last Things

Chapter Summary and Key Terms

The doctrine of the last things is the message of Christian hope. All people have some expectation for the future. It may be about maintaining order and prosperity in this life, a cycle of death and rebirth (*reincarnation*), the progress of evolution, or the intervention of God. The center of the Christian hope is Christ. He came once to redeem his people from sin, and he will come again. In Christ, God will fulfill the purpose for which he created man. Christ has already begun his kingdom and the *last days*, but his kingdom has not yet arrived in glory (*inaugurated eschatology*). We should rest in Christ's work of redemption and look forward to the age to come with hope and the pursuit of holiness.

CHRISTIAN HOPE gives believers power to become holy (1 John 3:3). Hope comforts the soul with joy and peace (Rom. 15:13). The hope of the godly especially looks to a future age of glory (8:17–18), for "hope that is seen is not hope" (v. 24). The truths that the Bible teaches about our future hope come under the doctrine of the last things—the final part of systematic theology.

In this chapter, we will introduce the doctrine of the last things by considering the hopes of this world, the center of Christian hope, the dangers and benefits of studying the doctrine of the last things, the connection of this doctrine to creation and Christ, and this doctrine's complexity. We will close with some practical applications.

The Hopes of the World

All human beings have hope in something, even if those hopes are as flimsy as "a spider's web" (Job 8:13–14). We can identify four basic kinds of worldly hope.[1]

First, there is *hope in the maintenance of order*. In religions honoring two or more gods or powers in the world (polytheism), the main concern may be to preserve balance, peace, and prosperity. We can see this in African traditional religions and popular Western culture, with their many gods—both secular and spiritual.

Second, there is *hope in the cycle of existence*. Religions teaching that all things are one (pantheism) or that all things share one spirit (panentheism) often say that history consists of a series of cycles. For example, there is the cycle of *reincarnation*, in which people die and are reborn as other people or other living things. The whole universe may go through cycles of creation and destruction. We find such views in Hinduism, Buddhism, Daoism, and European paganism (both ancient and modern).

Third, there is *hope in the progress of evolution*. Atheism might lead to a philosophy of despair—all things are ultimately meaningless. But people might find hope in the theory of biological evolution, concluding that life will develop into higher forms. Others may look to political evolution, as in Marxism. This is the hope that a revolution will overthrow the powers of oppression, leading to a society of equality and social justice. Evolution and Marxism need not be atheistic but may trust in the spirit of all life (panentheism) that prompts people to work for social progress.[2] Other people hope in technological evolution. They believe that advances in machines, information systems, and medicine will overcome mankind's problems. They may even hope that technology will set us free from the limitations of our bodies to enter a new kind of existence (transhumanism).

Fourth, there is *hope in the intervention of God*. Religions that believe that there is one God, the Creator of the universe (monotheism), may teach that God will judge people by their works. God will then bring about a new,

1 On polytheism, pantheism, panentheism, and other views of God, see the discussion of false gods in chap. 10.

2 Jürgen Moltmann, *Theology of Hope: On the Ground and the Implications of a Christian Eschatology*, trans. James W. Leitch (New York: Harper & Row, 1967); and *God in Creation: A New Theology of Creation and the Spirit of God*, trans. Margaret Kohl (Minneapolis: Fortress, 1993).

perfect world for those who deserve it. We see this in traditional Judaism and in Islam.

In contrast to the hopes of this world, Christianity teaches that our hope is in Christ alone. Sorrow and death come from sin (Rom. 6:23) that corrupts our very hearts (Gen. 6:5) and minds (Rom. 8:7–8). Neither order in society nor political revolution can solve our greatest problems. We are not evolving toward a higher form of life; indeed, we have fallen from our created innocence. Our lives are not endless cycles, and we will not be reincarnated. On the contrary, "it is appointed for man to die once, and after that comes judgment" (Heb. 9:27 ESV). And no one will be justified before God by good works of obedience (Gal. 2:16). Christ is all our salvation.

The Center of Christian Hope

Paul expresses the heart of the doctrine of last things when he says,

> For the grace of God that bringeth salvation hath appeared to all men, teaching us that, denying ungodliness and worldly lusts, we should live soberly, righteously, and godly, in this present world; looking for that blessed hope, and the glorious appearing of the great God and our Saviour Jesus Christ; who gave himself for us, that he might redeem us from all iniquity, and purify unto himself a peculiar people, zealous of good works. (Titus 2:11–14)

From this passage, we learn that Jesus Christ, God in the flesh, is the center of our hope. There is a double appearing of Christ in this world. He has already come once to redeem his people. Hope rests on salvation by grace alone in Christ alone. But he also will come again. His second coming will bring a visible display of God's glory. This good news of hope trains believers to live in holiness.

Christ's first coming inaugurated (or officially began) his reign as the exalted Mediator (chap. 50). His kingdom of grace is *already* expanding into the world to make people holy. But his glory is *not yet* openly revealed. That will take place at his second coming.[3]

3 Theologians refer to this teaching of "already" and "not yet" as "inaugurated eschatology." See Anthony A. Hoekema, *The Bible and the Future* (Grand Rapids, MI: Eerdmans, 1979), 18.

The Dangers and Benefits of the Doctrine of the Last Things

The biblical hope is a beautiful and sanctifying topic to study. But the doctrine of the last things can be harmful if it is misused. We should build doctrine not on speculation but only on what God says in the Bible. Also, we must not try to set a date for Christ's return but cultivate a hope that is always watchful. And we should not be divisive toward other Christians who disagree with us about specifics of Christ's return; rather, we should be humble and meek. Finally, we must never rest in theoretical ideas but apply the doctrine of the last things to practical life.

There are many good reasons to study the doctrine of the last things:

1. To understand the Creator's purpose (Eph. 3:9, 11)
2. To see more of Christ's glory by faith (Col. 3:3–4)
3. To know history's direction (Rom. 8:28–30)
4. To avoid being shaken by false doctrine (2 Thess. 2:2)
5. To grow in the joy and peace of hope (Rom. 15:13)
6. To nurture holiness (1 John 3:2–3)
7. To be able to comfort one another (1 Thess. 4:16–18)
8. To stop loving this world (Matt. 6:19–20)
9. To find motivation to pray more for Christ's return (Rev. 22:20–21)
10. To labor in ministry with anticipation (1 Cor. 15:58)
11. To desire to devote oneself to worship (Phil. 2:11)
12. To exult in the expectation of God's glory (Rom. 5:2)

Given these reasons to study the doctrine of the last things, we encourage you to pause your reading now and pray for God to fulfill these good purposes in your life.

Creation, Christ, and the Doctrine of the Last Things

To understand the last things, we must begin with the first things. A right perspective on the second coming of Christ recognizes that God will fulfill the purposes for which he created the world.

God made human beings to bear his image as his children, rule as his servant-kings over a "very good" world, and multiply into families (Gen. 1:26–28, 31; 5:1–3). Adam, the first man, received God's commandment but became a transgressor who brought death into the world (Gen. 2:17; Rom. 5:12). All of Adam's descendants by natural generation followed in his footsteps as sinners (Rom. 3:10). The human race is subject to spiritual death (Rom. 8:5–8), physical death (5:14), and eternal death in hell (Rev. 21:8). The doctrine of the last things answers the question, How will God fully and ultimately deliver his people from the ruin into which Adam plunged his descendants?

The answer to that question is "Thanks be to God, which giveth us the victory through our Lord Jesus Christ" (1 Cor. 15:57). Christ is "the last Adam" (v. 45). The new beginning for humanity arrived in him. Irenaeus said that Christ crushed the power of "him who had at the beginning led us away captives in Adam, and trampled upon his head . . . in order that, as our species went down to death through a vanquished man, so we may ascend to life again through a victorious one."[4] Thus, "we see Jesus . . . crowned with glory and honour" (Heb. 2:9). God's purpose for Adam is restored in Jesus Christ, to whom God subjected "the world to come" (v. 5).

When God the Son became a man, it was the high point of history. Paul says, "When the fulness of the time was come, God sent forth his Son, made of a woman, made under the law, to redeem them that were under the law, that we might receive the adoption of sons" (Gal. 4:4–5). Adam, "the son of God" (Luke 3:38), was conquered by Satan. Christ came as the last Adam and overcame the temptations of Satan (4:1–13). Later, Christ came to a garden and submitted himself to suffer the wrath of God that was coming because of the disobedience of the man in the first garden (Mark 14:36; John 18:1).

In his passion and death, Christ both suffered the ultimate tribulation and won the final victory. While he hung on the cross, darkness came over the land, the earth shook, and some people rose from the dead (Matt. 27:45, 50–53). These were all signs of the end of the age (24:29; Luke 21:11; John 5:28–29). Christ's death on the cross accomplished total victory over the powers of evil (John 12:31; Col. 2:14–15; Heb. 2:14).

The resurrection of Christ was his triumph over every power (Matt. 28:18). Christ ascended into heaven and sat down at God's right hand in

4 Irenaeus, *Against Heresies*, 5.21.1, in *ANF*, 1:548.

absolute supremacy (Ps. 110:1; Eph. 1:20–22). In Christ's ascension, his people were seated with him in heavenly places (Eph. 2:6). John Calvin commented, "He is the 'firstborn from the dead' [Col. 1:18]; for in the resurrection there is a restoration of all things, and in this manner the commencement of the second and new creation, for the former had fallen to pieces in the ruin of the first man."[5]

Christ's first public act as the Lord seated at the Father's right hand was to pour out the Holy Spirit on his people (Acts 2:33–36). This was a *last days* event foretold by the prophets (vv. 16–21, citing Joel 2:28–32). God had promised to send the Holy Spirit to establish Christ's kingdom of peace (Isa. 11:1–9) and restore all things in righteousness (32:15–17). The gift of the Spirit was at the heart of God's blessing promised in the covenant with Abraham (Gal. 3:14). As we discussed earlier (chap. 65), the Holy Spirit is the "earnest" (or down payment) of the inheritance (2 Cor. 1:22; 5:5; Eph. 1:14). He is the "firstfruits" of the age to come (Rom. 8:23).

With the gift of the Spirit, Christ also launched his mission to all nations (Acts 1:8). This mission is one of the great themes of the Old Testament (Luke 24:47). It fulfills God's promise to Abraham: "In thee shall all families of the earth be blessed" (Gen. 12:3). The commission that Christ gave his church to make disciples of all nations is both part of the last days and a work that must be fulfilled before the end of the age (Matt. 24:14; 28:18–20).

Finally, Christ's second coming is the center of Christian hope. His sitting at God's right hand is a position of complete victory, but it is also a posture of waiting until God utterly subjugates his enemies (Ps. 110:1). That conquest will be finalized in the day of judgment (vv. 5–6). Jesus Christ says, "The Son of man shall come in the glory of his Father with his angels; and then he shall reward every man according to his works" (Matt. 16:27).

In summary, Christ is our hope. His work bridges the gap between the first creation and the new creation. He is the head over God's world, fulfilling God's purposes for it. Thus, the doctrine of the last things tells us the history of Jesus Christ, past and future. This means that our study of this doctrine should encourage us to trust, love, obey, and hope in Christ.

5 Calvin, *Comm.* on Col. 1:18.

The Complexity of the Doctrine of the Last Things

The kingdom of God has already come but has not yet fully arrived. During his earthly ministry, Jesus Christ said, "Repent: for the kingdom of heaven is at hand" (Matt. 4:17). Christ also says, "If I cast out devils by the Spirit of God, then the kingdom of God is come unto you" (12:28). In his parables, Jesus reveals that the kingdom has come. The kingdom is like a seed that bears fruit only in some hearers (Matt. 13:19–23). But at the end of the age, the wicked will be cast into fire and the righteous will shine "as the sun in the kingdom of their Father" (vv. 39–43).

Geerhardus Vos explained that in the present, the kingdom comes gradually, works in the internal and invisible life of people, and is subject to imperfections. But at the end, the kingdom will come suddenly and perfectly in an outward, visible display of glory.[6] As the Heidelberg Catechism explains, the prayer "Thy kingdom come" means, "Rule us so by Thy Word and Spirit, that we may submit ourselves more and more to Thee; preserve and increase Thy church; destroy the works of the devil . . . till the full perfection of Thy kingdom take place, wherein Thou shalt be all in all."[7]

The New Testament presents history as a sequence of two ages: this age and the age to come (Matt. 12:32; Mark 10:30; Eph. 1:21). This present age is the time of ordinary human relations, such as marriage. The age to come is the era of resurrection life without marriage or death (Luke 20:34–35). Jesus calls the transition between the two ages "the end of the age," when he will come (Matt. 13:39–41, 49; 24:3; 28:20 ESV).

The first coming of Christ and the outpouring of the Spirit mean that the two ages presently overlap. Paul says that the Old Testament was "written for our admonition, upon whom the ends of the world [age] are come" (1 Cor. 10:11). The times of the end are upon us because Christ accomplished redemption: "Now once in the end of the world [age] hath he appeared to put away sin by the sacrifice of himself," though he will "appear the second time" (Heb. 9:26, 28).

Therefore, since Christ's incarnation, death, and resurrection, we have been living in the last days (James 5:3, 8–9; 1 Pet. 1:20; 1 John 2:18). The

6 Geerhardus Vos, *Biblical Theology* (1948; repr., Edinburgh: Banner of Truth, 1975), 384, 386.

7 The Heidelberg Catechism (LD 48, Q. 123), in *TFU*, 112–13.

epistle to the Hebrews opens, "God . . . hath in these last days spoken unto us by his Son" (Heb. 1:1–2). Peter says that Joel's prophecy was fulfilled at Pentecost because it was "the last days" (Acts 2:17).

Practical Applications of the Introduction to the Doctrine of the Last Things

We conclude this chapter with a few practical applications.

First, *rest on the finished work of Christ in accomplishing redemption.* Christ's work is so complete that he inaugurated the age to come. By the Spirit's grace, place your full trust in him.

Second, *relish the presence of the Spirit as a foretaste of eternal glory.* The Heidelberg Catechism says, "Since I now feel in my heart the beginning of eternal joy, after this life, I shall inherit perfect salvation."[8]

Third, *endure the pain of this present age.* "For our light affliction, which is but for a moment, worketh for us a far more exceeding and eternal weight of glory" (2 Cor. 4:17).

Fourth, *evangelize because today is the day of salvation.* We live in the unique era when God is gathering his elect from all nations. Therefore, let us make use of every opportunity to tell others the gospel.

Fifth, *rejoice in the wonder of the age to come.* Oh, to be with the One who died for us and to see his glory! Nurture this hope in your heart, and it will give you strength to persevere.

Suggested Songs to Sing to the Lord

- Psalm 98, "Sing a new song to Jehovah," *Psalter*, No. 261
- "Rejoice, the Lord is King," *THBap*, No. 226

Questions for Meditation or Discussion

1. What are four ways that the world seeks to find hope?
2. What is the center of Christian hope? What can we learn from Titus 2:11–14?
3. What are some dangers in studying the doctrine of the last things?
4. What are some reasons why we should study the doctrine of the last things?

8 The Heidelberg Catechism (LD 22, Q. 58), in *TFU*, 86.

5. What can we learn from the doctrine of creation about the doctrine of the last things?
6. How does the fall of Adam raise the question that the doctrine of the last things answers?
7. How are these events part of the doctrine of the last things: (1) Christ's incarnation, (2) his sufferings and death, (3) his resurrection and ascension, and (4) his pouring out of the Holy Spirit?
8. How do we see the complexity of the New Testament doctrine of the last things with respect to God's kingdom and the two ages?
9. Which of the practical applications at the end of this chapter is most helpful to you? Why?

88

The Error of Prosperity Theology

Chapter Summary and Key Terms

The main teaching of *prosperity theology* is that Christ purchased for believers the right to enjoy health and wealth by speaking words of positive confession and giving tithes and offerings. Prosperity theology is an error about the doctrine of the last things. It claims that believers can now gain the glory that belongs to the age to come. Prosperity theology also makes mere men into gods who control reality by their words of faith. By these teachings, prosperity preachers exploit people for financial gain and harm them spiritually through false assurance, false guilt, doubts about God, greed, and neglect of the glory of Christ, the believer's true treasure.

A VERY POPULAR FORM of Pentecostal theology is *prosperity theology*, also known as the health-and-wealth gospel or the Word of Faith movement. Prosperity theology may be defined as "the teaching that believers have a right to the blessings of health and wealth and that they can obtain these blessings through positive confessions of faith and the 'sowing of seeds' through the faithful payments of tithes and offerings."[1] Prosperity preachers claim that the outward benefits of Christ's kingdom have already come for those who have faith. Therefore, at its heart, prosperity theology is an error about the doctrine of the last things.

1 The Africa Chapter of the Lausanne Theology Working Group, "A Statement on the Prosperity Gospel," January 16, 2010, Lausanne Movement, https://lausanne.org/content/a-statement-on-the-prosperity-gospel.

On this doctrine, various teachers have built personal spiritual empires, beginning with Kenneth Hagin and expanding to include others such as David Yonggi Cho, Kenneth and Gloria Copeland, Creflo Dollar, "Benny" Hinn, Benson Idahosa, Joyce Meyer, and Joel and Victoria Osteen. Made rich by the donations of their followers, such teachers have become icons of their message of prosperity. Their wealth gives a false appearance of reality to their message.

In this chapter, we will examine some major doctrinal problems with prosperity theology, as well as the practical problems it causes in the Christian life.

Doctrinal Problems of Prosperity Theology

We have already argued, against Pentecostalism, that God no longer gives spiritual gifts of prophecy or miracles (chap. 54). Here we present false teachings in the prosperity doctrine.

First, *prosperity theology claims glory before Christ returns*. Hagin said that believers are to "reign as kings" over "circumstances, disease, sickness, sin, hatred," and so on. "Those things will not dominate us. We will dominate them."[2] We reign, he said, by "the confession of our rights and privileges in Christ Jesus." Therefore, confessing healing actualizes healing; confessing illness nullifies healing. Hagin said, "Your confession must absolutely agree with the Word. . . . Do not destroy the effects of your own prayer by a negative confession."[3] He also claimed that God said to him, "Whatever you need, claim it in Jesus' Name. And then you say, 'Satan, take your hands off my money.' And then say, 'Go, ministering spirits, and cause the money to come.' "[4]

In response, we say that Christians do not yet exercise earthly dominion. Paul says sarcastically, "Now ye are full, now ye are rich, ye have reigned as kings without us: and I would to God ye did reign, that we also might reign with you" (1 Cor. 4:8). The example of the apostles shows that suffering is still our lot: "Even unto this present hour we both hunger, and thirst, and are naked, and are buffeted, and have no certain dwellingplace; and labour, working with our own hands: being reviled, we bless; being persecuted,

2 Kenneth E. Hagin, *The Name of Jesus* (Tulsa, OK: Faith Library, 1979), 119.

3 Hagin, *The Name of Jesus*, 136–39, 144.

4 Kenneth E. Hagin, *Biblical Keys to Financial Prosperity* (Tulsa, OK: Faith Library, 1995), 58.

we suffer it" (vv. 11–12). Our bodies are not yet filled with immortality, glory, and power, but are dying, dishonored, and weak (15:42–44). Christ's glorification of our bodies awaits his return (Phil. 3:20–21). It is then that we will experience the full effects of the promise "with his stripes we are healed" (Isa. 53:5).

Second, *prosperity theology wrongly interprets God's promises.* Its teachers say that to be "snared with the words of thy mouth" (Prov. 6:2) means that negative speech will bring a bad future. But that verse is warning about the danger of becoming a "surety" for someone so that you are financially liable for his debts and obligations, somewhat like cosigning a loan (vv. 1–5).

Prosperity preachers say that a little faith can move a mountain (Mark 11:23). But Christ's promise here is not literal. No miracle worker in the Bible cast mountains into the sea. The symbolism means that by faith, God's kingdom will advance despite opposition. But neither Christ nor his disciples conquered by physical victory; rather, they overcame by enduring hardship by faith.

Prosperity preachers also say that praying in faith will obtain for us whatever we ask. Christ says, "What things soever ye desire, when ye pray, believe that ye receive them, and ye shall have them" (Mark 11:24). But faith must rest in the promises of God, which focus on our eternal good for his glory, not our glory in this world.

Paul's teaching that the person who "believeth" in Christ with saving faith also will "confess" the Lord Jesus with his mouth (Rom. 10:8–10) has nothing to do with the doctrine of positive confession. The passage is about salvation from sin, not earthly success.

John writes, "Beloved, I wish above all things that thou mayest prosper and be in health, even as thy soul prospereth" (3 John 2). But this is not a promise; it is a wish, a loving desire that believers have for one another.

Therefore, none of these Scripture passages teach prosperity theology. The doctrine of the Word of Faith is not grounded on God's Word. It is a human philosophy imposed on the Bible.

Third, *prosperity theology says that Christ suffered damnation in hell and was reborn.* Hagin said that Christ's "spirit, His inner man, went to hell in our place." He wrote, "Jesus is the first person ever to be born again," for he experienced "spiritual death," which "means separation from God" and "also means having Satan's nature." He also said, "Jesus became sin. His spirit was separated from God. And He went down into hell in our place."[5]

It is sheer mythology to say that the soul of Jesus was tormented in hell after his death. Christ's suffering and death on the cross were fully sufficient for the forgiveness of sins (John 19:30; Eph. 1:7). Furthermore, it is blasphemy to say that Christ died spiritually and needed to be born again. Spiritual death is "enmity against God" (Rom. 8:6–7) and subjection to the corrupting power of sin and Satan (Eph. 2:1–3). Christ's identity and nature did not change on the cross. He is ever "the Holy One," "the Just," and "the Prince of life" (Acts 3:14–15).

These errors show the extremes to which teachers can go when they regard their own thoughts as direct revelations from God.

Fourth, *prosperity theology makes human beings into gods.* Hagin said, "This everlasting, eternal life Jesus came to give us is the nature of God. . . . It is God imparting his very nature, substance, and being to our human spirits. . . . Man is a spirit. We know he is in the same class as God, because God is a Spirit."[6] This is not monotheism but panentheism (see chap. 10). Hagin added, "The believer is just as much an incarnation as Jesus was." Copeland says, "You don't have a God living in you; you are one!"[7]

Copeland also says of Genesis 1,

> Every time God spoke, He released His faith—the creative power to bring His words to pass. . . . Man was created from the faith-filled words of God—words of power, dominion, and life. Those words came from the very insides of God where the dominion and authority lies; so that all of the power that it took to have dominion over the earth was a part of man from the very beginning. . . . Man had total authority to rule as a god over every living creature on earth, and he was to rule by speaking words.[8]

5 Hagin, *The Name of Jesus*, 29–33.

6 Kenneth E. Hagin, "The Zoe Life of God," *Word of Faith* (December 2016), Kenneth Hagin Ministries, https://www.rhema.org/index.php?option=com_content&view=article&id=2603:the-zoe-life-of-god&catid=261&Itemid=862.

7 Cited in Michael J. McClymond, "Prosperity Already and Not Yet: An Eschatological Interpretation of the Health and Wealth Emphasis in the North American Pentecostal-Charismatic Movement," in *Perspectives in Pentecostal Eschatologies: World without End*, ed. Peter Althouse and Robby Waddell (Cambridge: James Clarke & Co., 2012), 303–5.

8 Kenneth Copeland, *The Power of the Tongue* (Fort Worth, TX: Kenneth Copeland Publications, 1980), 4–6.

On the contrary, God—not man's boasting words—controls the future. James says, "Come now, you who say, 'Today or tomorrow we will go into such and such a town and spend a year there and trade and make a profit.' . . . Instead you ought to say, 'If the Lord wills, we will live and do this or that'" (James 4:13, 15 ESV).

To assert that we are gods or to put mere men on the same level as God the Son incarnate is a gross violation of the first commandment, "Thou shalt have no other gods before me" (Ex. 20:3). It is also to rob ourselves of our only hope, that "there is one God, and one mediator between God and men, the man Christ Jesus; who gave himself a ransom for all" (1 Tim. 2:5–6). Though prosperity theology uses Christian language, no religious system that turns mere men into gods is true Christianity.

Practical Problems with Prosperity Theology

The serious problems with the health-and-wealth teaching are not limited to the realm of theology but extend to the practical Christian life.

First, *prosperity theology encourages false assurance*. It is possible that a listener to prosperity preaching might trust in Christ alone for salvation and eternal life. But it is likely that many listeners depend on Christ for earthly success and think of themselves as being saved by their own words and financial gifts. It is a grave concern that prosperity theology may have communicated a false assurance to millions of people who are not saved by grace.

Second, *prosperity theology builds spiritual empires for false teachers*. The prosperity movement is well designed to lift its so-called prophets onto pyramids of enormous wealth and power. Paul says that the church must oppose those who teach false doctrine "for shameful gain" (Titus 1:11 ESV). Peter warns of wildly popular "false teachers" who "through covetousness" will "make merchandise of you" (2 Pet. 2:1–3)—that is, exploit people for their own financial profit. Sadly, some prominent preachers in this movement have proven to have "eyes full of adultery" and "hearts trained in greed" (v. 14 ESV).

Third, *prosperity theology sells God's blessings for money*. In the Holy Scriptures, no prophet or apostle ever required anyone to give a financial gift to receive God's blessing. Peter severely rebuked Simon Magus for offering to pay money for the power to confer the Holy Spirit (Acts 8:18–23). When

Gehazi, the servant of the prophet Elisha, secretly convinced a man to give him wealth because the prophet had healed him, Elisha cursed Gehazi with leprosy (2 Kings 5:15–27). Gehazi's fate should haunt prosperity preachers.

Fourth, *prosperity theology breeds false guilt and doubt about God.* Cho said that it was Job's fault that his children died and he lost his wealth. Job received "severe punishment" for his lapse of faith, but when he confessed his faith again, he was restored to wealth.[9] The bitter fruit of this false teaching is that it places heavy burdens of false guilt on suffering believers. It may lead people to doubt God's goodness when he does not do what they think he has promised. The truth about Job is that the Lord said he was an upright and God-fearing man before and after his children died (Job 1:1, 8; 2:3). Like Job, believers must patiently endure trials in this age (James 5:11). Rather than accuse believers of a lack of faith, let us come alongside them in their sorrows, weep with them, pray for God's mercy to relieve their suffering, and wait for Christ to wipe every tear from our eyes when he returns.

Fifth, *prosperity theology cultivates greed instead of rejoicing in Christ.* Paul says,

> Godliness with contentment is great gain, for we brought nothing into the world, and we cannot take anything out of the world. But if we have food and clothing, with these we will be content. But those who desire to be rich fall into temptation, into a snare, into many senseless and harmful desires that plunge people into ruin and destruction. (1 Tim. 6:6–9 ESV)

Likewise, Christ warns, "Lay not up for yourselves treasures upon earth. . . . No man can serve two masters. . . . Ye cannot serve God and mammon [wealth]" (Matt. 6:19, 24).

Prosperity theology makes much of the name of Jesus, but it dishonors him in many ways. Perhaps its greatest insult to Christ is neglecting him as the believer's great treasure. Paul counted everything as worthless compared to "the excellency of the knowledge of Christ Jesus my Lord" (Phil. 3:8). Thus, he says, "To live is Christ, and to die is gain" (1:21). In prosperity theology, the name of Jesus is the key to unlock earthly riches and glory

9 Paul (David) Yonggi Cho, *Salvation, Health & Prosperity: Our Threefold Blessings in Christ* (Altamonte Springs, FL: Creation House, 1987), 14–15.

for us. In the Bible, Christ *is* God's riches and glory for us (Eph. 3:16–17; Col. 1:27).

Suggested Song to Sing to the Lord

- Psalm 73, "In sweet communion, Lord, with Thee," *Psalter*, No. 203; *THBap*, No. 557
- "Sometimes a light surprises the Christian while he sings," *THBap*, No. 520

Questions for Meditation or Discussion

1. What is prosperity theology?
2. How does prosperity theology claim glory before its proper time?
3. What promises do prosperity preachers often claim? How do they wrongly interpret them?
4. What does prosperity theology teach about Christ's saving work? Why is that blasphemy?
5. How does prosperity theology confuse human beings with God?
6. Why does prosperity theology encourage false assurance of salvation?
7. How does prosperity theology build spiritual empires for its teachers?
8. Why should the story of Gehazi frighten prosperity preachers?
9. How can prosperity theology cause false guilt or doubts about God?
10. How does prosperity theology turn people away from Christ to indulge greed?

89

Death and the Afterlife

Chapter Summary and Key Terms

Death entered the world because of Adam's sin. Physical death separates the human body from the soul until the resurrection. The soul does not lose conscious existence, remain on earth as a ghost, or become an angel, but continues in the *intermediate state*. It is also false to say, with Roman Catholicism, that the souls of believers who die imperfectly purified by penance must suffer in a state of *purgatory* until they are ready to enter heaven. At death, the souls of believers are made perfect in righteousness and rest in the presence of God and Christ in heaven. The souls of the wicked suffer the wrath of God. We must prepare for death by trusting Christ alone for salvation and living in faithfulness to keep a good conscience. When death draws near, let us endure whatever trials may come. Let us look to Christ and imitate him in death as in life.

DEATH PERPLEXES MANKIND. It ends earthly dreams and ambitions. It breaks contact with loved ones. The Bible calls it "the king of terrors" (Job 18:14). And it is unavoidable: "What man can live and never see death?" (Ps. 89:48 ESV).

There is much that we do not understand about death and the state of those who are now dead. But God has revealed enough about death that, in Christ, we may face it with courage, peace, and even triumphant victory.

In this chapter, we will explore what the Bible teaches about the physical death of the body and the resulting state of the soul after death. We will also examine errors about the afterlife and offer guidance for facing death.

The Death of the Body

God imposed death as the just punishment for sin (Rom. 6:23). The deaths of animals and human beings were not part of God's original creation (Gen. 1:29–31). Death came because of Adam's transgression of God's law in the covenant of works (2:17; Rom. 5:12; 1 Cor. 15:22). Death sweeps away each generation of mankind after its brief span of life on this earth (Ps. 90:5–6).

However, the death of the body is not the end of the human person. Death is the ruin of the body (Gen. 3:19) and the separation of the body from the spirit or soul (Eccles. 12:7; James 2:26). The soul continues after death, for men "kill the body, but are not able to kill the soul" (Matt. 10:28). The condition of a soul after death is called the *intermediate state* because it takes place between a person's earthly life and the resurrection of the dead at Christ's return. The dead body remains a part of the deceased person and will be reunited with his or her soul at the resurrection, so it should be treated with respect.

The Souls of Believers after Death

What is the state of believers after their death? God's Word reveals enough about the intermediate state for his people to trust him, though it does not answer all our questions.

The Old Testament Scriptures offer hope of a life with God that continues beyond death. The Lord took Enoch and Elijah from earth to heaven without death (Gen. 5:24; 2 Kings 2:11). Though these were exceptional cases, they show the reality of life in heaven.

Abraham died without having received the promised inheritance (Heb. 11:13). Centuries afterward, the Lord still said, "I am . . . the God of Abraham, the God of Isaac, and the God of Jacob" (Ex. 3:6). Jesus comments, "God is not the God of the dead, but of the living" (Matt. 22:32). Thus, the fathers "all live unto him" (Luke 20:38).

David says his enemies are "men of the world, which have their portion in this life," but "as for me, I will behold thy face in righteousness: I shall be satisfied, when I awake, with thy likeness" (Ps. 17:14–15). He also prays, "Yea, though I walk through the valley of the shadow of death, I will fear no evil: for thou art with me. . . . And I will dwell in the house of the Lord for ever" (23:4, 6). When a righteous man dies, "he enters into peace" (Isa. 57:2 ESV).

The hope of the Old Testament shines even brighter in the New with the coming of Christ. Jesus says, "I am the resurrection and the life. Whoever believes in me, though he die, yet shall he live, and everyone who lives and believes in me shall never die" (John 11:25–26 ESV). Those who trust in Christ already possess eternal life (6:47). This life consists of knowing God (17:3), and being eternal, it cannot be extinguished.

When Christ was transfigured in glory, Moses and Elijah appeared with him, talking about his approaching death (Luke 9:30–31). Moses had died more than a thousand years previously. Elijah had been taken directly to heaven. Yet here were both men, alive, conscious, and informed of the progress of God's plan in Christ.

Jesus spoke of a poor man named "Lazarus," who "died, and was carried by the angels into Abraham's bosom," where he was "comforted" (Luke 16:22, 25–28).

While hanging on the cross, Jesus said to the repentant thief dying beside him, "Today shalt thou be with me in paradise" (Luke 23:43). The word translated as "paradise" means a garden and refers to heaven (2 Cor. 12:2–4; Rev. 2:7). Just before Jesus died, he prayed, "Father, into thy hands I commend my spirit" (Luke 23:46). Similarly, while Stephen was being killed by an angry mob, he prayed, "Lord Jesus, receive my spirit" (Acts 7:59).

Paul says that "we walk by faith, not by sight," but affirms, "we are confident, I say, and willing rather to be absent from the body, and to be present with the Lord" (2 Cor. 5:7–8). He adds, "For to me to live is Christ, and to die is gain" (Phil. 1:21). Though remaining "in the flesh" would allow for more ministry to people, Paul also desired "to depart, and to be with Christ; which is far better" (vv. 22–23).

The epistle to the Hebrews tells us that the "spirits" of believers join with a vast group of "angels" in the presence of God and Christ (Heb. 12:22–24). These spirits of "just" or "righteous" people have been "made perfect" (v. 23). They have attained pure "holiness, without which no man shall see the Lord" (v. 14).

Therefore, "Blessed are the dead which die in the Lord from henceforth: yea, saith the Spirit, that they may rest from their labours; and their works do follow them" (Rev. 14:13).

The Westminster Shorter Catechism summarizes, "The souls of believers are at their death made perfect in holiness, and do immediately pass into glory; and their bodies, being still united to Christ, do rest in their graves till the resurrection."[1] The Westminster Larger Catechism adds that when believers die, their souls are "received into the highest heavens, where they behold the face of God in light and glory, waiting for the full redemption of their bodies."[2]

The Souls of the Wicked after Death

All that we have said so far about the state of the soul after death pertains to those who are in Christ. But what about the unbeliever and the wicked person? After death, their spirits go to hell, where they suffer for their sins as they wait for the resurrection and judgment day.

In the Old Testament, the word translated as "hell" (KJV) or "Sheol" (ESV) can mean death and the grave, but it can also refer to the state of the wicked after death (Pss. 9:17; 49:14–15). Even death will not give them a hiding place, for God's wrath will reach them in the realm of the dead. The Lord says, "For a fire is kindled in mine anger, and shall burn unto the lowest hell" (Deut. 32:22).

In the New Testament, "hell" sometimes translates a term that refers to the final punishment of the wicked after judgment day (chap. 94). Another word translated as "hell" (literally *hades*) can mean death or the grave, but it can also mean the realm of the deceased spirits of the wicked. After speaking of the death of the poor man Lazarus, Christ says, "The rich man also died, and was buried; and in hell he lift up his eyes, being in torments, and seeth Abraham afar off, and Lazarus in his bosom. And he cried and said, Father Abraham, have mercy on me . . . for I am tormented in this flame" (Luke 16:22–24). The rich man's request for help was denied (vv. 25–26). After death, the wicked experience intense conscious suffering without relief.

Peter writes of the people who ignored Noah's preaching before the flood as now being "spirits in prison" (1 Pet. 3:19). He adds that the Lord "knows how to . . . keep the unrighteous under punishment until the day of judgment" (2 Pet. 2:9 ESV). The police arrest a crime suspect and hold him in jail until he can be tried in court. In a far more frightening way, the Lord

1 The Westminster Shorter Catechism (Q. 37), in *RC*, 4:358. Cf. the Baptist Catechism (Q. 40), in *RC*, 4:578.

2 The Westminster Larger Catechism (Q. 86), in *RC*, 4:317.

and Judge of all seizes the wicked by what Isaac Ambrose called "death's arrest" and holds them in hell until he issues the sentence of everlasting punishment against them.[3]

The Baptist Catechism summarizes the state of unconverted sinners after their decease: "The souls of the wicked shall at their death be cast into the torments of hell, and their bodies lie in their graves till the resurrection and judgment of the great day."[4]

Errors concerning the State of Souls after Death

There are a number of false beliefs about human life after death.

First, *some people teach the end of conscious existence at death.* They may say that the soul sleeps until Christ returns. Others say that the human mind or spirit ceases to exist when the body dies. That might mean the end of the person, as in atheism. Or they may believe that God will resurrect the soul with the body on the last day, as the Jehovah's Witnesses teach.[5]

In response, we note that the human soul is a distinct substance that survives the death of the body (Matt. 10:28). As we saw, Christ promised the penitent thief immediate entrance into paradise to be with him after death (Luke 23:43). If death were soul sleep, then Paul would not have considered death to be "gain," nor would he have desired "to depart, and to be with Christ; which is far better" (Phil. 1:21–23). The Bible uses sleep as a way of speaking about death (1 Thess. 4:13–15), but this is not because the soul becomes unconscious; rather, it is because the body becomes inactive, as in sleep. When the Scriptures describe death as the end of thought and work (Eccles. 9:5–10), they refer to the end of our interactions with this world "under the sun" (vv. 6, 9).

Second, *some people teach that the spirits of the dead become ghosts on earth.* This is a popular and ancient belief.

In response, we say that ghost stories are often connected with a belief in many spirits or gods (polytheism). However, the Bible does not teach

3 Isaac Ambrose, *Prima, Media, and Ultima: The First, Middle, and Last Things* (London: by T. R. and E. M. for Nathan. Webb and Will. Grantham, 1654), 3:44.

4 The Baptist Catechism (Q. 42), in *RC*, 4:578. Cf. the Westminster Larger Catechism (Q. 86), in *RC*, 4:317.

5 Watch Tower Bible and Tract Society, *What Does the Bible Really Teach?* (Wallkill, NY: Watch Tower Bible and Tract Society of New York, 2014), 6.5; 7.13 (58, 71), Jehovah's Witnesses, https://www.jw.org/en/library/books/bible-teach/.

us to expect to find the spirits of the dead on earth. Someone might point to the account of the medium of Endor as proof that ghosts visit the earth (1 Sam. 28:7–19). But this was an extremely rare event in the Holy Scriptures, and it is debated whether the speaker was Samuel or a demon. The Lord says that those who seek the dead should instead seek God's truth in his Word (Isa. 8:19–20).

Third, *another popular idea is that the righteous become angels in heaven*, sometimes sent to earth to help people here.

In response, we assert that the Bible does not portray angels as men lifted up to heaven. Angels are a different kind of being created by God as invisible spirits (Col. 1:16; Heb. 1:7, 14).

Fourth, *Roman Catholicism teaches that many believers must experience purgatory before entering heaven. Purgatory* is supposedly the cleansing fire that purges the sin of "all who die in God's grace . . . but [are] still imperfectly purified."[6] According to Roman Catholic doctrine, believers must endure in purgatory the temporal punishment for sins for which they did not make satisfaction in this life by penance. The doctrine of purgatory is said to be based on the Holy Scriptures and ancient church tradition.

In response, we declare that there is no basis for purgatory in the Holy Scriptures. The passages cited by Roman Catholic theologians as proof either are in the Apocrypha instead of the Bible (2 Macc. 12:39–45) or have to do with making peace with people (Matt. 5:25–26), the unforgiveable sin (12:31–32), judgment day (1 Cor. 3:11–15), or trials in this life (1 Pet. 1:7). Purgatory contradicts God's promises that believers enter Christ's presence upon death (Luke 23:43; 2 Cor. 5:6–8; Phil. 1:21–23). As for church tradition, the doctrine of purgatory seems to have emerged in the fifth and sixth centuries—long after the apostles died.[7]

Christ has redeemed his people from God's wrath by offering himself once for all as the perfect sacrifice (Col. 2:13–14; Heb. 10:10–12). As a result, there are two possible outcomes when a person dies. If the person is not in Christ by saving faith, his or her spirit will go to hell to suffer until

6 *Catechism of the Catholic Church* (New York: Doubleday, 1994), secs. 1030–31. See the Council of Trent (Session 25, Decree on Purgatory), in *Denzinger*, sec. 1820 (428–29).

7 On the historical development of the doctrine of purgatory, see Beeke and Smalley, *RST*, 4:808–9.

judgment day. If he or she is in Christ, the person's spirit will join the angels and spirits of other saints in heaven to rejoice until even greater joy dawns at the resurrection of the dead.

The Experience of Death

In this section, we will offer some practical encouragements for those who walk through the valley of the shadow of death and for the pastors who care for them.

Preparing for Death

We must prepare for death while we yet live. There will be no preparing after we die, for death seals each person's destiny. William Perkins said, "As death leaves a man, so shall the last judgment find him, and so shall he abide eternally."[8]

The greatest obstacle to facing death with peace is the guilt of our sins. We know that death is God's penalty for sin (Rom. 1:32). Consequently, humanity is "subject" to the "fear of death" (Heb. 2:15), for "it is appointed unto men once to die, but after this the judgment" (9:27).

Only Christ can cleanse the conscience. He offered himself as a sacrifice for our sins to give us the liberty to draw near to God (Heb. 9:14; 10:19). This means we must prepare for death by trusting in Christ alone to save us from our sins. It is the Christian's great comfort to say, "I with body and soul, *both in life and death*, am not my own, but belong unto my faithful Savior Jesus Christ; who, with His precious blood, hath fully satisfied for all my sins."[9] Death is indeed "the last enemy," but Christ's resurrection conquered death for all in him (1 Cor. 15:26, 54–57).

Therefore, live by faith in Christ. Invest your life well, knowing that it is temporary. Allow the reality of death to drive you to be "exceedingly diligent in duty," "exceedingly active in duty," and "exceedingly mortified to the things of a present world," as Andrew Gray said.[10]

8 Perkins, *A Salve for a Sick Man, or a Treatise Containing the Nature, Differences, and Kinds of Death, as also the Right Manner of Dying Well*, in *WWP*, 10:418–19.

9 The Heidelberg Catechism (LD 1, Q. 1), in *TFU*, 68, emphasis added.

10 Andrew Gray, "A Sermon concerning Death," in *The Works of the Reverend and Pious Andrew Gray* (Aberdeen: George King and Robert King, 1839), 104–5. Gray died at twenty-two years of age.

Aim to live so that when you die you can say with Paul, "I have fought a good fight, I have finished my course, I have kept the faith: henceforth there is laid up for me a crown of righteousness, which the Lord, the righteous judge, shall give me at that day: and not to me only, but unto all them also that love his appearing" (2 Tim. 4:7–8).

Passing through Death

Death is not easy, but it is possible, by God's grace, to die as "more than conquerors" (Rom. 8:35–37). When death threatened Paul, he said, "I know that this shall turn to my salvation through your prayer, and the supply of the Spirit of Jesus Christ, according to my earnest expectation and my hope, that in nothing I shall be ashamed, but that with all boldness, as always, so now also Christ shall be magnified in my body, whether it be by life, or by death" (Phil. 1:19–20).

When the news of imminent death arrives, we need not pretend to be stronger than we are. We may weep. But by God's grace, we can also confess, "My flesh and my heart faileth: but God is the strength of my heart, and my portion for ever" (Ps. 73:26).

Though death is the gateway to glory for believers, it may be a hard trial to endure. Yet the Lord knows how to use trials to refine our faith (James 1:2–4). By his grace, "though our outward man perish, yet the inward man is renewed day by day" (2 Cor. 4:16).

Let us look to Christ as our example in how to die. Imitate his submission to the Father's will (Mark 14:36). Also, let us learn to think of others rather than becoming self-absorbed in our suffering (John 19:26–27). Though the pains of death seize us, let us pray for the salvation of sinners, including those who have wronged us (Luke 23:34). Let us commit our souls to the care of our eternal Father (v. 46).

Above all, let us look to Jesus as the pioneer of our faith, who willingly embraced death by crucifixion for the joy set before him (Heb. 12:2). Christ himself is the joy set before us as we persevere through death by faith in him (vv. 22–24).

Suggested Songs to Sing to the Lord

- Psalm 89, "Remember, Lord, how frail I am, how few my years," *Psalter*, No. 422, stanzas 5, 6, 8

- "Abide with me: fast falls the eventide," *THBap*, No. 335

Questions for Meditation or Discussion

1. What does the Bible teach about the death of the body?
2. What are some Old Testament passages that show us the state of the souls of believers after death?
3. According to the New Testament, what is the state of the souls of believers after death?
4. How does the Old Testament depict the state of the souls of the wicked after death?
5. What does the New Testament teach us about the state of the souls of the wicked after death?
6. What are four errors concerning the state of souls after death?
7. What arguments does Roman Catholicism present for purgatory? How can we answer them?
8. Of the directions the authors give about preparing for death, what is one that is particularly helpful to you now? What practical steps can you take to put it into practice?
9. What directions do the authors give about passing through death?
10. How has reading this chapter affected your thoughts and feelings about death?

90

Signs, the Man of Sin, and the Book of Revelation

Chapter Summary and Key Terms

In Matthew 24, the Lord Jesus said that between his first and second comings there would be wars and disasters, the destruction of Jerusalem, persecution, and false prophets and false Christs. Paul teaches in 2 Thessalonians 2 that the *man of sin* (the *antichrist*) will come and seek to take the place of God in the visible church until Christ comes and destroys him. The book of Revelation has been interpreted as ancient history (*preterism*), church history (*historicism*), spiritual principles (*idealism*), or a prophecy of future tribulation (*futurism*). It is best to take an *eclectic approach* that combines insights from all four of these views. Revelation is a book of symbols that are best understood by comparison with other passages of the Scriptures. The book has seven parts that repeatedly bring the reader to Christ's second coming and the end of the age. Revelation teaches us about God's sovereignty, Christ as the Lamb of God, the church's witness, and victory by perseverance.

AT THE CENTER OF the Christian hope are the great truths of Christ's coming, the resurrection of the dead, judgment day, eternal damnation, and the glory of God's kingdom. However, there are also certain issues in the doctrine of the last things that often prove controversial. Sincere and godly Christians may disagree about such matters but should still treat one another with love and respect.

In this chapter and the next, we will present our understanding of what God's Word teaches about these issues. We begin in this chapter by considering Christ's teaching about the signs of his coming (Matthew 24), Paul's teaching about the man of sin (2 Thessalonians 2), and principles for interpreting the book of Revelation.

The Signs of Christ's Kingdom

When Christ predicted that the temple in Jerusalem would be destroyed, his disciples asked, "Tell us, when shall these things be? And what shall be the sign of thy coming, and of the end of the world?" (Matt. 24:3). In what he said in the rest of that chapter, Jesus predicted the future of his people in these last days with an eye on both the destruction of Jerusalem in AD 70 and his second coming.[1]

In this passage, Christ called his disciples to prepare their hearts so that they would not be shaken by deception or tribulation (Matt. 24:4–14). Many false teachers would come and deceive many (vv. 5, 11). These things began in the days of the apostles (7:15; 1 John 2:18). But Christ also said believers must not be troubled when they heard of wars and disasters, for "the end is not yet" (Matt. 24:6–7). These troubles would be just "the beginning of the birth pains" (v. 8 ESV).

Christ said that his disciples must prepare themselves to endure (Matt. 24:13). Persecution would come on the apostles and the church (v. 9), many professing Christians would fall away (v. 10), and people would become corrupt and cold (v. 12), but the church would press on to complete its mission. Christ said, "This gospel of the kingdom shall be preached in all the world for a witness unto all nations; and then shall the end come" (v. 14).

The Lord Jesus next spoke of the destruction of Jerusalem (Matt. 24:15–21). He foretold the desecration of the temple (v. 15). This was the "abomination of desolation" prophesied by Daniel (Dan. 8:13; 9:27; 11:31; 12:11). When Christ's disciples in Judea saw that this would soon happen, they were to "flee into the mountains" (Matt. 24:16). Jesus said, "When ye shall see Jerusalem compassed with armies, then know that the desolation thereof is nigh" (Luke 21:20).

Christ added that this would be a time of "great tribulation, such as was not since the beginning of the world to this time, no, nor ever shall be"

1 On the interpretation of Matthew 24, see D. A. Carson, "Matthew," in *The Expositor's Bible Commentary*, ed. Frank E. Gaebelein, 12 vols. (Grand Rapids, MI: Zondervan, 1984), 8:488–511 (see vol. 9 of the 2010 revised edition); and Jonathan Menn, *Biblical Eschatology*, 2nd ed. (Eugene, OR: Wipf and Stock, 2018), 107–48.

(Matt. 24:21). The phrase "great tribulation" means "a great distress." Saying that it would be worse than anything before or after is the language of divine judgment used of the plagues on Egypt (Ex. 9:18, 24; 10:6, 14; 11:6) and the destruction of Jerusalem by Babylon in 586 BC (Ezek. 5:9; Dan. 9:12). It was a fitting description of the horrible massacre that took place when the Romans destroyed Jerusalem in AD 70.

Christ then returned to his warning against those who would pretend to be Christs and prophets (Matt. 24:23–28). One such false messiah was Simon bar Kokhba (d. 135), who led a Jewish revolt against Rome. The Lord Jesus taught us not to believe future claims that the Messiah had come. The "coming of the Son of man" will not be a hidden event but a public appearance as plain to see as a flash of "lightning" (v. 27).

The tribulation of God's people will end when Christ comes. Jesus foretold that darkness and disruption will come on the sun, moon, and stars (Matt. 24:29). These signs cannot have been symbols of Jerusalem's destruction because they will be accompanied by the "distress of nations" (Luke 21:25). Christ added, "They shall see the Son of man coming in the clouds of heaven with power and great glory. And he shall send his angels with a great sound of a trumpet, and they shall gather together his elect from the four winds, from one end of heaven to the other" (Matt. 24:30–31). Christ will send out his angels at the end of the age when he punishes the wicked and rewards the righteous in the kingdom (13:40–43, 49–50; 25:31).

Jesus said, "When ye shall see all these things, know that it is near, even at the doors. Verily I say unto you, This generation shall not pass, till all these things be fulfilled" (Matt. 24:33–34). "This generation" referred to people alive in Israel at the time when Jesus said this (11:16; 12:41–42; 23:36). Christ was saying that when his disciples saw the rise of false prophets and the destruction of Jerusalem in their lifetimes, they should recognize that these were signs that Christ had begun his kingdom. In a parallel passage, Christ said, "When ye see these things come to pass, know ye that the kingdom of God is nigh [near] at hand" (Luke 21:31).

Christ said, "Of that day and hour knoweth no man, no, not the angels of heaven, but my Father only" (Matt. 24:36). The end of the age will surprise people as they go about their ordinary business, just as the flood of Noah caught men unprepared (vv. 37–41). But Jesus called us to "watch" so that his return does not surprise us like a thief in the night (vv. 42–43):

"Therefore be ye also ready: for in such an hour as ye think not the Son of man cometh" (v. 44).

The Man of Sin, or the Antichrist

Paul writes about the coming of the "man of sin" (2 Thess. 2:3),[2] also called "the lawless one" (v. 8 ESV) or "that Wicked" (KJV). These titles mean that he will be the greatest sinner in human history. Just as Christ will be revealed at his second coming, so this man of sin will be "revealed" at his own "coming" (vv. 3, 6, 8–9). Thus, the man of sin is the *antichrist*, a figure like Christ in some ways but his adversary.

The church in Thessalonica had been alarmed that perhaps "the coming of our Lord Jesus Christ and our being gathered together with him" had already taken place (2 Thess. 2:1–2 ESV), most likely as an invisible spiritual event (cf. 1 Cor. 15:12; 2 Tim 2:18). Paul reminded them that the man of sin and great apostasy must come before Christ returns (2 Thess. 2:3). There will be "a falling away," a breaking of former allegiances and rebellion, especially by those who are outwardly part of God's people but forsake him. This cannot refer to the unbelieving Jews, for they had already rejected Christ (1 Thess. 2:14–16). Paul predicted a rebellion against God that will begin in the professing Christian church (1 Tim. 4:1–3; 2 Tim. 3:1–9). Christians should be vigilant, for the greatest enemies of the church arise from within.

The man of sin will seek to take God's place (2 Thess. 2:4), just as Daniel said a king would "exalt himself, and magnify himself above every god" (Dan. 11:36). He will also be a false leader of God's people. Paul says, "He as God sitteth in the temple of God, shewing [displaying] himself that he is God" (2 Thess. 2:4). Paul consistently uses "temple" for the people of the church (1 Cor. 3:16–17; 6:19; 2 Cor. 6:16; Eph. 2:21). The man of sin will take a position of divine honor and authority in the professing church. But Christ will destroy him "with the spirit of his mouth, and . . . the brightness of his coming" (2 Thess. 2:8; cf. Isa. 11:4).

Before Christ's "coming," the antichrist will first have his own "coming" according to "the working of Satan with all power and signs and lying wonders" (2 Thess. 2:8–9). The man of sin will be the supreme example of the false

2 The translation "the man of lawlessness" (ESV) reflects a difference among the ancient Greek manuscripts.

christs that Christ warns us about (Matt. 24:24). Just as the man of sin will be a self-anointed king and an idolatrous priest, so he will also be a false prophet. He will deceive the wicked so that they will perish forever (2 Thess. 2:10).

Be warned, unbelievers. Those who reject the gospel of Jesus Christ are wide open to the influence of the antichrist (2 Thess. 2:10–12). Will you follow the man of sin straight into hell? O sinner, trust in the Lord Jesus Christ as Savior before he comes to be your Judge.

Who will the antichrist be? He will be a leader of the professing church of Christ, "the temple of God" (2 Thess. 2:4). From the Reformation onward, many have believed that the "man of sin" refers to the office of the pope in Roman Catholicism. The papacy usurps the offices of Christ as Prophet, Priest, and King. But Paul speaks of a particular individual, "the man of sin" and "the son of perdition" (v. 3), whom Christ will destroy at "his coming" (v. 8 ESV). Therefore, it seems best to understand the man of sin to be a future leader who will arise in a professing Christian church, possibly in Roman Catholicism, shortly before Christ returns.

The proper response to the doctrine of the man of sin is not to speculate endlessly about who he will be and when he will arise. Rather, Christians must stand courageously against every antichrist who draws people away from the true gospel and the true church. Those who are being sanctified by the Spirit and who believe in the truth of the gospel have been chosen by God for salvation and eternal glory in Christ (2 Thess. 2:13–14). They can and must stand fast in the truths of God's Word and cling to the hope of Christ's coming. The man of sin may be Satan's greatest attack on the truth, but he also will be the Devil's last desperate gasp before Christ returns.

The Interpretation of the Book of Revelation

If any book of the Bible is especially associated with the doctrine of the last things, certainly it is the book of Revelation. But this book has received a wide variety of interpretations.

General Approaches to the Interpretation of Revelation

There are several approaches to interpreting the book of Revelation.

First, *preterism views Revelation as fulfilled in the ancient world.* It may be entirely fulfilled (*full preterism*) or mostly fulfilled (*partial preterism*). A strength of preterism is that it makes the symbols of Revelation understandable and relevant to the people to whom John originally wrote. It also takes seriously the statement that this book concerns "things which must shortly come to pass" (Rev. 1:1). A major problem with preterism is that it does not recognize prophecies of Christ's future return (chaps. 19–22).

Second, *historicism views Revelation as presenting a sequence of events in church history*. Historicism helps us to recognize fulfillments of Revelation in current events. But it is often arbitrary in interpreting the book's symbols. One historicist says that the "locusts" brought by the fifth trumpet (Rev. 9:1–11) represent the invasion of Christian lands by Muslims. Another says they represent the increasing error and idolatry of the church. Neither interpretation is grounded in the wider context of the Scriptures.

Third, *idealism views most of Revelation as teaching general spiritual principles*. Idealism makes this ancient book relevant to Christians of all times. But it tends to overlook the historical context of Revelation. It also may not lead to an appreciation for Revelation's emphasis on the future coming of Christ in glory.

Fourth, *futurism views Revelation as a message about a future time of tribulation just before Christ's return*.[3] Many futurists interpret the book as literally as possible. The strength of futurism lies in its recognition that Revelation looks ahead to Christ's return. Futurism faces the difficulty that under its interpretation, most of Revelation would have no direct relevance to people until the final generation.

Lastly, *an eclectic approach combines elements of these four views*.[4] John wrote Revelation to first-century churches under the Roman Empire. The book teaches principles that are true of the church through the ages. Revelation invites us to see God's plan already being executed in our world through multiple fulfillments. Yet it predicts a great conflict between God's servants and the forces of evil just before Christ's return. For these reasons, an eclectic approach is the best option for interpreting Revelation.

The Symbolism of Revelation's Visions

The key to interpreting Revelation is understanding its word pictures as symbols. They are like the dreams and visions of Joseph and Daniel. The

3 See the discussion of dispensationalism in chap. 91.

4 A helpful commentary that takes this approach is G. K. Beale with David H. Campbell, *Revelation: A Shorter Commentary* (Grand Rapids, MI: Eerdmans, 2015).

Lord Jesus does not have a literal sword sticking out of his face (Rev. 1:16), but his Word is powerful like a sword (Isa. 49:2; Heb. 4:12). Numbers are also symbolic in Revelation: seven is the number of perfection (Gen. 2:1–3), ten of fullness (Job 19:3; Eccles. 7:19), and twelve of God's people (Gen. 49:28; Matt. 10:2). Understanding Revelation as a book of symbols is not to question its truthfulness or reliability as part of God's written Word. Rather, it is to recognize that Revelation was not written as a historical account, but as a form of literature that uses graphic symbols to communicate truth.

Apocalyptic symbols are best interpreted by comparison to similar figures of speech elsewhere in the Bible. Consider the "two witnesses," of whom it is said that "fire proceedeth out of their mouth, and devoureth their enemies" (Rev. 11:3–5). Are they human flamethrowers? No. The Lord says of Jeremiah's ministry, "I will make my words in thy mouth fire, and this people wood, and it shall devour them" (Jer. 5:14). The two witnesses symbolize the preaching of God's Word, which brings his judgment on those who reject it.

Images of supernatural events in Revelation may indicate natural events during the period between Christ's comings. For example, we do not need to take the effect of the second trumpet literally as a meteor strike that turns a third of the sea into blood (Rev. 8:8). Blowing a trumpet and casting a burning mountain into a sea are symbols of God causing nations to suffer defeat by their enemies (Jer. 51:25–29, 63–64).[5]

The Structure of Revelation

Futurists often view Revelation as a chronological sequence of events. But the birth of Christ appears halfway through the book (Rev. 12:5). Revelation consists of seven parts, with each part after the first bringing the reader to the end of the age, like a series of cycles.[6]

1. *The seven churches* (Revelation 1–3). These were real churches in Asia Minor.
2. *The seven seals* (Rev. 4:1–8:1). This cycle begins with the Lamb slaughtered at Christ's first coming. The opening of the first seals

5 For notes on how the symbols of Revelation draw from Old Testament images, see *The Reformation Heritage KJV Study Bible*, ed. Joel R. Beeke, Michael P. V. Barrett, Gerald M. Bilkes, and Paul M. Smalley (Grand Rapids, MI: Reformation Heritage Books, 2014), notes on Revelation (1867–99).

6 See Anthony A. Hoekema, *The Bible and the Future* (Grand Rapids, MI: Eerdmans, 1979), 223–26.

unleashes events that Christ calls the beginning of the birth pangs (6:1–11; cf. Matt. 24:6–14). The sixth seal brings the disruptions of heaven and earth just before his second coming (Rev. 6:12–14). The seventh seal brings silence, a symbol of awe at the day of the Lord (8:1; Zeph. 1:7).

3. *The seven trumpets* (Rev. 8:2–11:19). Blowing a trumpet sounds an alarm and calls people to action (Jer. 4:5–9, 19, 21). The trumpets in Revelation symbolize physical and spiritual judgments that warn of the coming final judgment and call sinners to repentance. The seventh trumpet again brings the reader to the end of the age, when God's kingdom and judgment day arrive (Rev. 11:15–19).
4. *The great conflict* (Revelation 12–14). This cycle begins with the birth and ascension of Christ (12:5), which starts the last days. Satan attacks the church through the "beast" from the sea and the "beast" from the earth (12:17–13:18). These creatures symbolize civil and religious persecution. This cycle ends with the coming of "the Son of man" on a "cloud" at the end of the age (14:14–20; cf. Matt. 13:39–41).
5. *The seven vials or bowls of wrath* (Revelation 15–16). These severe judgments are like the plagues on Egypt. They appear quickly, one after another, which suggests the sudden destruction of the wicked when Christ returns. The seventh vial again brings the reader to the end of the age, when even the mountains are overthrown (16:17–21). The seventh vial also points to God's final judgment against Gog, the enemy of God's people (Ezek. 38:2, 18–22).
6. *The destruction of Babylon* (Revelation 17–19). The wicked world that persecutes God's people is portrayed as a seducing prostitute and a rich city. There are partial fulfillments of this vision in the fall of Jerusalem (11:7–8) and later the fall of Rome (17:9–10). But God's judgment will ultimately come on Babylon by the return of the King, symbolized as a warrior leading an army on white horses (19:1–16). The end of this cycle (vv. 17–21) again points to the final battle against Gog (Ezek. 39:17–20).
7. *The glorification of Jerusalem* (Revelation 20–22). This cycle begins by returning to the defeat of Satan at Christ's first coming (20:2–3), depicted earlier in the great conflict (12:9). At the close of this age, Satan is permitted for "a little season" (20:3) to lead the whole world

> to attack the church (v. 9). The forces of "Gog" (v. 8) appear again, showing that the same final conflict at the end of the age is in view (16:14). As before, we see the disruption of creation (20:10). Then comes judgment day (vv. 11–15) and the new Jerusalem in the new heaven and new earth (21:1–22:5).

Practical Applications of the Book of Revelation

The book of Revelation says much concerning Christ's coming, judgment day, and the glories to follow. These teachings will occupy our attention in the last section of this book. Here we look at five lessons that show how Revelation centers on God's glory and aims at godliness.

First, *Revelation teaches us about God's sovereignty.* The Greek word translated as "throne" or "seat" appears forty-six times in Revelation. Evil powers sit on thrones as they claim sovereignty and use their strength to increase sin. But the throne that dominates Revelation is the throne of God. Therefore, do not allow the "thrones" of this world to distract you from the One who alone is worthy of your worship. Revelation summons you to join with the saints and angels to sing to him who sits on the throne, "Thou art worthy" (Rev. 4:11; 5:9).

Second, *Revelation teaches us about Christ, the Lamb of God.* In Revelation, Christ has many titles, but he is especially called the "Lamb" (twenty-eight times). This is a picture of his priestly self-sacrifice (Rev. 5:6), when he died to redeem his people from their sins ("blood," 1:5; 5:9; 7:14; 12:11). The title Lamb is associated not just with Christ's death but also with his victory, power, and eternal glory. Therefore, put your trust in Christ alone for salvation and eternal life. Marvel at his love, that he would die for sinners and gladly take them to himself as his spiritual bride forever. Meditate often on the glory of the Lamb.

Third, *Revelation teaches us about spiritual warfare.* Terms translated as "war," "battle," and "fight" appear fifteen times in the book. The satanic "beast" seems to be an invincible warrior (Rev. 13:4). Its persecution of the saints is nothing less than total war (11:7; 13:7). But Christ, too, is a warrior (19:11). His saints conquer "by the blood of the Lamb, and by the word of their testimony; and they loved not their lives unto the death" (12:11). Therefore, fight the most important battle—to believe, speak, and live the truth of Christ.

Fourth, *Revelation teaches us about evangelistic witness.* God calls the church to serve and suffer as witnesses to Christ in the world. Greek words translated as "testify," "testimony," "witness," and "martyr" appear seventeen times in Revelation. Christ is the great "faithful witness" (Rev. 1:5; 3:14). The gospel will gather "a great multitude, which no man could number, of all nations" into salvation (7:9) and make them worshipers of God (15:4). Therefore, do your part in Christ's church to proclaim the gospel. The church is never more faithful to the doctrine of the last things than when it labors to make disciples of all nations.

Fifth, *Revelation teaches us about victory by perseverance in Christ.* The Greek word translated as "overcome," "conquer," "prevail," or "gotten the victory" appears seventeen times. Christ has overcome, so he is worthy to bring salvation, the kingdom, and judgment (Rev. 5:5). By union with Christ, God's elect, called, and faithful people share in Christ's victory (17:14). The church can persevere in joyful hope, for those who overcome the world will also share in the new creation (21:7). Therefore, Christian, do not allow Satan and his persecutors and tempters to draw you away from following Christ. Do not love your life as much as you love Jesus and his kingdom. Cling to the finished work of the cross and do not compromise your testimony to Christ. Press on, dear believer. To persevere in Christ is to escape hell and enter eternal joy.

Suggested Songs to Sing to the Lord

- Psalm 119:19–23, "Thy servant, blest by Thee, shall live," *Psalter*, No. 323; *THBap*, No. 260
- "Blessing and honor and glory and power," *THBap*, No. 219

Questions for Meditation or Discussion

1. What should we learn from Jesus's statement that wars and earthquakes are "the beginning" of the birth pangs?
2. How does Christ describe the coming of the Son of Man (Matt. 24:29–31)?
3. How does Matthew 24 prepare Christ's people to wait for him to return in glory?
4. What does Paul mean when he refers to a person as the "man of sin" and the "lawless one"?

5. How is the man of sin the "antichrist"—that is, a counterfeit messiah?
6. Why did the Reformers identify the man of sin with the papacy?
7. How is Revelation interpreted according to (1) preterism, (2) historicism, (3) idealism, (4) futurism, and (5) the eclectic approach?
8. What evidence is there that Revelation consists of cycles that repeatedly bring the reader to the second coming of Christ?
9. What five practical lessons does Revelation teach us? Which is more important to your life right now? Why?

91

The Future of Israel and the Millennium

Chapter Summary and Key Terms

There are three views of the *millennium* (the "thousand years" in Revelation 20). First, according to *premillennialism*, Christ will return to reign on earth before the final judgment. One form of this view, *dispensationalism*, teaches the *rapture* of the church, the *tribulation*, Christ's second coming, the resurrection of Old Testament and tribulation saints, Israel's exaltation during the millennium, a final revolt by Satan, and the resurrection and judgment of unbelievers. But this system is not taught in the Bible. The New Testament says that the fulfillment of all God's promises and the resurrection and judgment of all people will take place at Christ's second coming. Second, according to *postmillennialism*, Christ will return after a time of righteousness and peace on earth. People of any view of the millennium may hold to the doctrine of the *preeminence of the church*, the belief that God will give his church supreme spiritual influence before the second coming. But the church will suffer persecution, not enjoy preeminence, in this evil world. Third, according to *inaugurated millennialism* (or *amillennialism*), the millennium is happening now, for Christ has already bound Satan and begun his kingdom. Therefore, the church should bring the gospel to all nations with confidence and endurance, hoping also in God's promise that one day all Israel will be saved.

WITH THE COMING OF JESUS CHRIST, the great "son of Abraham" (Matt. 1:1), what place do the physical descendants of Abraham, Isaac, and Jacob have in God's plans? Furthermore, does the Bible teach us to expect an age of righteousness and peace on earth before the final judgment? Such an age is called the *millennium* ("a thousand years," cf. Rev. 20:1–10). In this chapter, we consider the future of ethnic Israel and the doctrine of the millennium. These, too, are controversial issues in the doctrine of the last things, matters about which godly Christians disagree.

Dispensationalism and the Future of Israel

In considering Israel's future, we must also consider the dispensationalist doctrine of the last things. *Dispensationalism* is an evangelical system of doctrine that teaches that Israel and the Christian church are two distinct people for whom God has two different plans (chap. 38).[1]

A Summary of the Dispensationalist Doctrine of the Last Things

Dispensationalist theologians teach the following about God's plan for this age and the next. The Lord promised Israel an earthly kingdom of political power and wealth in the land of Canaan for the blessing of all nations. This kingdom would come through Christ, the Son of David. But when Israel rejected Christ, it fell under God's judgment and the kingdom was delayed. Instead, Christ began the church and its mission to the Gentiles, which were not explicitly foretold in the Old Testament.

To fulfill God's purpose for Israel, according to dispensationalism, Christ will come to "*rapture*" the church from the earth (and also raise up dead Christians) so that believers may escape God's wrath and join Christ in heaven. Then will come the "*tribulation*," seven years when the antichrist will reign and God will send supernatural judgments on the earth, according to a very literal reading of Revelation.

Christ, according to dispensationalism, will return to judge Israel and the Gentile nations. He will raise the Old Testament saints and believers who died during the tribulation and begin the millennium of earthly prosperity,

1 For a presentation of the dispensationalist doctrine of the last things, see J. Dwight Pentecost, *Things to Come: A Study in Biblical Eschatology* (Grand Rapids, MI: Zondervan, 1958). For a briefer treatment, see John MacArthur, ed., *Essential Christian Doctrine: A Handbook on Biblical Truth* (Wheaton, IL: Crossway, 2021), 431–72.

righteousness, and peace. The nation of Israel, with Jerusalem as its capital city, will lead the nations while a restored priesthood ministers in a rebuilt temple. The millennium will conclude with a revolt led by Satan, but God will crush the rebellion and raise unbelievers from the dead to judge and damn them to hell. Believers will then enter the state of eternal glory.

Objections to Dispensationalism from the New Testament

Dispensationalists view the Bible as the inerrant Word of God, inspired by the God who knows the future. But their doctrine of the last things is subject to serious objections.

First, *dispensationalism teaches doctrine that is not taught plainly anywhere in the New Testament.* The Holy Scriptures never say that Christ will return twice, once to rapture the church and seven years later to judge the world. The system classifies passages in the Bible as belonging to the rapture, the tribulation, or the second coming, but those passages do not teach the system itself.

Second, *dispensationalism complicates the simple New Testament hope in Christ's second coming.* Christ says he will come in glory to judge the world, welcome his people into eternal life, and send the wicked to everlasting fire (Matt. 25:31–46). He promises to raise the righteous and the wicked from the dead when he judges the world (John 5:27–29). Paul teaches that Christ will be revealed from heaven to punish the wicked with flaming fire and give relief and glory to his persecuted church (2 Thess. 1:5–10). But dispensationalism proposes two comings of Christ and several resurrections of the dead and judgment days.

Third, *dispensationalism misunderstands Revelation's symbolism.* The book of Revelation consists of symbolic visions. These visions must be interpreted according to the use of metaphorical images in the Old Testament, especially the dreams and visions of Daniel. Dispensationalism fails to do this.

Fourth, *dispensationalism wrongly divides Israel and the church.* The Christian church is the new covenant Israel. Peter applies to the church the very titles of Israel: "Ye are a chosen generation, a royal priesthood, an holy nation, a peculiar people" (1 Pet. 2:9; cf. Ex. 19:5–6). The living members of the church are the heirs of God's promises to Abraham and Israel (Gal. 3:29; Heb. 8:8–12). This is because of the church's union with Jesus Christ. He destroyed the division between Jews and Gentiles who believe in him

(Gal. 3:28; Eph. 2:11–15). But dispensationalism divides Jewish and Gentile believers again during the millennium.

Therefore, we conclude, the dispensationalist doctrine of the last things is not supported by the New Testament.

The Old Testament Promises to Israel

Dispensationalists may object that their system stands on the Old Testament promises to Israel of a golden age of prosperity. For example, the Lord promised to bring Israel and Judah back to the land after the exile, bless them with abundant crops and livestock, make a new covenant with them in saving grace, and restore the city of God forever (Jer. 31:5–17, 31–34, 38–40).

In response, we argue that God has been fulfilling this prophecy step by step from the end of the exile, and he will continue to do so until Christ's second coming. The Lord restored Israel to the Promised Land in the sixth century BC by the decree of the Persian emperor (Ezra 1:1). When Christ came, he began the new covenant by offering up his sacrificial blood to atone for sin (Luke 22:20). Great prosperity and joy await his redeemed in the new heaven and new earth (Isa. 65:13–19; Rev. 22:1–5). Only then will they "not sorrow any more at all" (Jer. 31:12; cf. Isa. 35:10).

Dispensationalists may also object that Isaiah 60 foretells the victory and exaltation of Israel over the Gentiles. Therefore, it is said, national Israel must be restored and honored in a future millennial kingdom. But a comparison of Isaiah 60 with Revelation 21 shows that those very promises are fulfilled in the church—"the bride, the Lamb's wife" (v. 9). Even the promise that the wicked Gentiles who have afflicted godly Israelites will bow down before them and call them God's beloved people (Isa. 60:14) will be fulfilled in the church (Rev. 3:9).

The New Testament Promise of Israel's Salvation

The coming of Christ and his sending out of the apostles launched an evangelistic mission to ethnic Israel (Matt. 10:5–6). But it is not to build a nation separate from the church. Rather, it is a mission of salvation. Though relatively few of the Jewish people have responded to the gospel with faith, the New Testament offers a remarkable promise of Israel's future salvation. Paul says, "Blindness in part is happened to Israel, until the fulness of the Gentiles be come in. And so all Israel shall be saved" (Rom. 11:25–26).

What does Paul mean when he says, "All Israel shall be saved"? It cannot mean that every Jewish person who has ever lived will be saved. Christ said that it would have been better for Judas if he had never been born (Mark 14:21). All people must be saved by faith in Jesus Christ (John 14:6; Acts 4:12; Rom. 10:13–15).

Some theologians have interpreted "Israel" to mean God's people regardless of ethnicity. But Paul clearly has ethnic Israel in view. He is discussing the unbelief of many Israelites toward Christ (Rom. 9:1–3; 10:1–3). In Romans 11, he contrasts "Israel" and the "Gentiles" as distinct groups.

Some interpreters have taken "all Israel" to refer to all the elect in ethnic Israel. This is a possible interpretation, for Paul writes of the elect Israelites as the true Israel: "They are not all Israel, which are of Israel" (Rom. 9:6). But as we said above, "Israel" in Romans 11 refers to ethnic Israel as distinct from the Gentiles. And it seems too obvious to say that all the elect will be saved.

Therefore, we agree with those interpreters who understand "all Israel shall be saved" (Rom. 11:26) to refer to a future spiritual awakening in ethnic Israel. God will save a large number of the Jewish people alive at the time. One day, instead of a "fall," there will be a "fulness" for Israel (v. 12), and instead of a "casting away," there will be a "receiving" (v. 15). The phrase "all Israel" appears dozens of times in the Old Testament for Israel as a corporate people, though not necessarily every individual (Josh. 10:29–38; 2 Sam. 16:22; 1 Chron. 11:1). Thus, Paul seems to be promising that one day the Jews will turn to Christ in large numbers.

But Paul describes the salvation of Jews not as the restoration of a Jewish state distinct from the Gentile nations. Rather, he says this will be the grafting of branches back into the same tree into which the wild branches of Gentile believers were grafted (Rom. 11:23–24). In other words, the salvation of "all Israel" will bring ethnic Israel into the church of Christ.

Implications for Christians' Attitude and Actions toward the Jews

What are some implications of the doctrine that we have observed concerning the future of Israel?

First, *Christians should love the Jewish people and reject anti-Semitism.* Paul says, "As touching the election, they are beloved for the fathers' sakes" (Rom. 11:28). We should be examples before the Jews of love, righteousness, and pure worship of the true God.

Second, *Christians should believe that Jews will be saved only by faith in Christ.* Paul says, "There is no difference between the Jew and the Greek: for the same Lord over all is rich unto all that call upon him. For whosoever shall call upon the name of the Lord shall be saved" (Rom. 10:12–13).

Third, *Christians should earnestly pray for the salvation of the Jewish people.* Paul says, "My heart's desire and prayer to God for Israel is, that they might be saved" (Rom. 10:1).

Fourth, *Gentile Christians and Jewish Christians should welcome one another as brethren in one church.* We should not intentionally have Gentile churches and Jewish churches. Paul says, "Receive ye one another, as Christ also received us to the glory of God" (Rom. 15:7).

Fifth, *Christians should joyfully expect that one day all Israel will be saved.* Let us begin to praise God in anticipation that "all Israel" (Rom. 11:26)—not necessarily all Jewish people, but a great number of them—will be saved through faith in Christ. The salvation of Israel will glorify God, who sent Christ "a servant to the circumcised to show God's truthfulness, in order to confirm the promises given to the patriarchs" (15:8 ESV).

The Millennium and Expectations for the Church

Only one passage in the Bible explicitly speaks of the millennium, or "thousand years" (Rev. 20:1–10). People who hold to orthodox, biblical Christianity have held to a wide variety of beliefs about this subject.[2]

Different Views of the Millennium

To understand what a person believes about the millennium and the future influence of the church, we need to ask two, or possibly three, questions.

First, when is the "thousand years" of Revelation 20? There are three main views:

- *Premillennialism.* The millennium will be a future era after Christ returns to reign with the saints in righteousness and peace before the final judgment and eternal state. Dispensationalists are premillennialists, but not all premillennialists are dispensationalists.

2 For a survey of millennial views through the history of the church, see Beeke and Smalley, *RST*, 4:924–33.

- *Amillennialism.* The millennium is the present era in which Christ has begun his kingdom before he returns to resurrect and judge mankind. This view might better be called *inaugurated millennialism.*
- *Postmillennialism.* The millennium will be a future era of righteousness and peace brought about by God's grace before Christ returns to raise the dead and judge mankind.

Second, will Christ give his church supreme spiritual influence in the world before his second coming? We might call this the doctrine of *the preeminence of the church.* This is the view of postmillennialism, but it is also compatible with the other interpretations of Revelation 20, whether premillennialism or inaugurated millennialism.

Third, if one believes the doctrine of preeminence, what kind of results does one expect from this influence? Possibilities include the following:

- *cultural transformation*—righteousness in society, education, and the arts
- *economic and scientific advance*—a golden age of prosperity and health
- *political dominion*—the reign of the saints over the nations of the world

There are many possible combinations of these views. All of them could be consistent with evangelical Christianity.

However, we believe that the Holy Scriptures do not teach premillennialism, postmillennialism, or the doctrine of preeminence. Rather, we find in the Scriptures the doctrine of inaugurated millennialism.

Evidence against Premillennialism

We have already argued that Old Testament promises, such as those in Isaiah 60 and Jeremiah 31, do not require a golden age for Israel but are fulfilled in the church, and ultimately in the new heaven and new earth. As to the New Testament, the Gospels and Epistles do not teach a period of a thousand years between Christ's return and the day of judgment, different judgment days for believers and unbelievers, or an initial day of judgment that does not send people to eternal damnation or eternal life. Rather, the New Testament teaches a single day of resurrection and judgment (Matt. 12:41; 2 Tim. 4:1), "the last day" (John 6:39–40; 12:48). This is the day of Christ's coming (Matt. 16:27; 2 Thess. 1:6–7; James 5:8–9).

When Christ returns, all people will be raised from the dead and judged (Dan. 12:2; John 5:28–29; Acts 24:15; Rev. 20:11–15). Both believers and unbelievers will be recompensed at the day of judgment (Rom. 2:5–10; 14:10–12). The judgment will lead directly to either eternal punishment or eternal life with Christ (Matt. 25:31, 34, 41, 46).

This is strong evidence against premillennialism.

Evidence against Postmillennialism and the Doctrine of Preeminence

The New Testament provides a view of the church's mission that is both optimistic and realistic. Jesus says, "This gospel of the kingdom shall be preached in all the world for a witness unto all nations" (Matt. 24:14). He adds that God's kingdom will grow from a little "seed" into a mighty influence in the world (13:31–33). He promises that evil will not prevail against his church (16:18). As a result, God will save "a great multitude, which no man could number, of all nations" (Rev. 7:9).

But there will also be persecution, apostasy, deception, the increase of sin, and the weakening of love (Matt. 24:9–12, 24). These troubles will continue to the end, for Christ will come "immediately after the tribulation of those days" (vv. 29–30). Most people will be dwelling in carnal security when Christ appears (vv. 37–39). Paul warns, "In the last days perilous times shall come. For men shall be lovers of their own selves, covetous, boasters, proud, blasphemers, disobedient to parents," and so on (2 Tim. 3:1–2).

This is strong evidence against postmillennialism and the doctrine of preeminence.

The Millennium in Revelation 20:1–10

As we noted above, there is only one passage in the Bible that speaks of the "thousand years." It is found in Revelation, a book of symbols (Rev. 20:1–10). The number one thousand (10 × 10 × 10) is a symbol of fullness (Deut. 7:9; Ps. 105:8). This millennium is best understood as the kingdom that Christ began with his finished work of redemption. Thus, this view may be called inaugurated millennialism.

As we argued in the previous chapter, Revelation is a symbolic vision in seven parts that repeatedly take the reader to the end of this age. The sixth part ends with Christ's appearing as the warrior on a white horse in Revelation 19. This symbol is not about Christ's ascension or the mission of the church. Rather, it is Christ's second coming to destroy the wicked with the "wrath of Almighty God" (v. 15). The vision depicts the slaughter of the nations, "*all* men . . . both small and great" (vv. 18, 21).

It is clear that Revelation 20 does not follow chapter 19 in time because the nations are not yet slaughtered but very much alive (Rev. 20:3). Instead, chapter 20 starts a new cycle of visions, the seventh and final part of Revelation.

An angel uses a "key" and a "chain" to bind "the dragon" in "the bottomless pit" (Rev. 20:1–3). These symbols represent Christ using his victory over evil (1:18) to restrain Satan's attacks against the church and to give her success (3:7–9). The phrase "the dragon, that old serpent, which is the Devil, and Satan" quotes an early vision of Christ's first coming and ascension (12:5–6, 9). At that time, Satan was "cast out" and Christ began to reign (vv. 9–10). Revelation 20 returns to this theme of Satan's defeat at Christ's first coming.

Someone might object that it is not possible that Satan is bound from deceiving the nations, for he is very active in the world. But the symbolic binding of the dragon fits well with the language used elsewhere for Christ's work at his first coming. Christ "first binds the strong man" so that Satan's captives are set free (Matt. 12:29 ESV). The "prince of this world" is judged and "cast out" (John 12:31). Christ died to "destroy" the Devil (Heb. 2:14). None of these statements mean that Satan was annihilated or made powerless. Rather, they announce Christ's victory. Christ is now sending the gospel to save his elect in all nations, and Satan cannot stop him.

Christ's kingdom has already begun. In heaven, the "souls" of the martyrs reign with Christ, symbolized by their sitting on "thrones" (Rev. 20:4). They have already experienced the "first resurrection" (v. 5). That might refer to the spiritual resurrection of salvation (Eph. 2:5–6) before the physical resurrection of the dead (John 5:25–29). Or it might mean the beginning of heavenly life for the souls of believers. But Scripture never speaks of two physical resurrections.

After the "thousand years," Satan will be released "to deceive the nations" and "to gather them together to battle" (Rev. 20:8). This is the language used in earlier passages of Revelation for the mobilization of the forces of evil before

Christ's second coming (16:13–14; 19:19).[3] Satan draws the whole world into persecuting God's people. God will stop this persecution with "fire" (Rev. 20:9). This is the second coming. Next is judgment day (vv. 11–15).

Therefore, the millennium in Revelation 20 is best understood not as a future era but as the present age, when the church experiences the victory of the inaugurated kingdom in Christ and waits for his second coming. Inaugurated millennialism presents a simple doctrine of the last things based on clear New Testament teachings that Christ will return to raise the dead, judge mankind, and begin the eternal state.

By contrast, premillennialism claims that the glorious Christ and resurrected saints will live side by side with mortal, flesh-and-blood people during the millennium. It also says Christ will rule a political kingdom on earth—even though he says, "My kingdom is not of this world: if my kingdom were of this world, then would my servants fight" (John 18:36). Finally, premillennialism places the complete fulfillment of God's promises a thousand years after Christ's return. But the New Testament teaches that Christ's coming is our blessed hope (Titus 2:13). When Christ comes, he will give us all that we have been waiting for.

Practical Applications of Biblical Millennialism and Expectations

Although the question of the millennium is controversial, the doctrine of inaugurated millennialism offers very practical hopes for Christians.

First, *trust in Christ's complete conquest of Satan as the basis of missions.* Christ has bound the strong man! Before we are ready to "make disciples of all nations" for Christ, we must believe that "all authority in heaven and on earth has been given to" him (Matt. 28:18–19 ESV). John Calvin said, "Our doctrine must tower unvanquished above all the glory and above all the might of the world, for it is not of us, but of the living God and his Christ whom the Father has appointed King to 'rule from sea to sea, and from the rivers even to the ends of the earth.' "[4] John Owen said, "Though our persons fall, our cause shall be as truly, certainly, and infallibly victorious, as that Christ sits at the right hand of God."[5]

3 On "Gog and Magog" (Rev. 20:8), see the great battle of Ezekiel 38–39. This same event also is alluded to earlier in Rev. 16:17–21 (cf. Ezek. 38:18–22) and Rev. 19:17–18 (cf. Ezek. 39:17–20).

4 Calvin, *Institutes*, Prefatory Address to King Francis, sec. 2. He quotes Ps. 72:8.

5 Owen, "The Use of Faith, If Popery Should Return upon Us," in *WJO*, 9:507.

Second, *rejoice that the faithful dead live and reign with Christ in heaven.* For believers, death is not the end of existence but the beginning of a new and better existence in which they live and reign with Christ (Rev. 20:4). They enter the new Jerusalem to join the angels and spirits of righteous men made perfect around the throne of Christ (Heb. 12:22–24).

Third, *expect great things for the church and prepare for persecution.* The New Testament simultaneously inculcates a belief that sinners will grow worse as the last days progress and that the church will advance under Christ's blessing. Therefore, do not think the church will set up a lasting Christian society and culture. Rather, prepare to face satanic opposition and persecution, for these characterize the heirs of God's kingdom in this age (Matt. 5:10–12). Be optimistic about Christ's kingdom and realistic about Satan's resistance against it to the end.

Fourth, *wait eagerly for Christ's return as the answer to all your desires.* It is God's way to make Christ everything to the believer. Therefore, focus your hope on the coming of Jesus Christ. Beware of letting millennial doctrines distract you from Jesus, the Bridegroom of the church. Believe with all your heart that when Jesus returns, you will have everything you could possibly desire. This will motivate you to live wholly and solely for him.

Suggested Songs to Sing to the Lord

- Psalm 68, "Blest be the Lord! For us He cares," *Psalter*, No. 181
- Psalm 98, "Come, let us sing unto the Lord," *THBap*, No. 15

Questions for Meditation or Discussion

1. What is the doctrine of the last things taught in dispensationalist theology?
2. What objections can be raised against dispensationalism from the New Testament teaching about the last things?
3. How will God keep his Old Testament promises to Israel, such as those in Isaiah 60 and Jeremiah 31?
4. What does Romans 11:25–26 teach us about the future of Israel?
5. What kind of attitude should we have toward the Jewish people? Why?
6. How would you define the following terms? (1) premillennialism; (2) inaugurated millennialism (amillennialism); and (3) postmillennialism.

7. What is the doctrine of the preeminence of the church? What three expectations might be connected to it?
8. What evidence do we find in the Bible against (1) premillennialism and (2) postmillennialism and the doctrine of preeminence?
9. What is the best interpretation of Revelation 20:1–10?
10. What are one or two practical applications of biblical millennialism that are especially relevant to your life right now? What steps can you take to put them into practice?

Section 7B

The Glorious Hope of Christ

92

The Coming of Christ in Glory

Chapter Summary and Key Terms

The *second coming* of Jesus Christ is denied by scoffers and false teachers (as in *full preterism*), but it is an essential doctrine of true Christianity. The New Testament often speaks of the visible and public coming of the Son of Man with clouds, angels, fire, and glory. He will come to display God's glory, destroy his enemies, raise the dead, judge the world, renew the creation, fulfill God's promises, and dwell with his beloved people. All angels and human beings will be subjected to him, to the terror of the wicked and the joy of the righteous. The *imminency* of Christ's return means the events preceding his second coming could begin suddenly and he could appear very soon. Therefore, we should exercise trust in the promises of our King and Judge, faithful obedience to him, and a watchful, expectant longing for him like that of a bride longing for her bridegroom.

THE HEARTS OF GOD'S PEOPLE long for the return of their Lord. By his grace, his second coming is their great hope. Christ taught that he is the "bridegroom" of his people (Matt. 9:15). His presence is their joy, just as his absence is a cause for their mourning and fasting (v. 15). Waiting for Christ's second coming is like waiting for a bridegroom and a wedding feast (25:1–13; cf. Rev. 19:7–9).

God's Son came once to begin his kingdom. He will come again to complete it: "Christ was once offered to bear the sins of many; and unto them that look for him shall he appear the second time without sin unto salvation"—that is, not to bear sin but to fully save his redeemed (Heb. 9:28). Christ's first coming accomplished redemption by his sacrifice (vv. 15, 26). His second coming will finish the application of redemption and start the new age of glory.

Denials of the Doctrine of Christ's Second Coming

Peter warns, "There shall come in the last days scoffers, walking after their own lusts, and saying, Where is the promise of his coming?" (2 Pet. 3:3–4). Scoffers assume that we cannot expect major changes in the world because "all things continue as they were from the beginning" (v. 4). But they ignore the great changes that God has already worked. God created the world and later destroyed it by the flood (vv. 5–7). The delay of Christ's return must be viewed according to God's eternity. To him, "a thousand years [are] as one day" (v. 8). We must also remember the patience of God—he is giving people time for repentance (v. 9).

Opposition to the doctrine of Christ's coming can also be more subtle, as in spiritualizing the promises. Jesus's apostles had to combat a tendency in their own time to deny the physical reality of Christ's presence and work. Some false teachers denied that he had come "in the flesh" (1 John 4:3; 2 John 7)—that is, in a real, physical human body. Others asserted that "the resurrection has already happened" (2 Tim. 2:18 ESV; cf. 1 Cor. 15:12). They probably thought of a spiritual resurrection instead of the physical resurrection of the dead.

According to the error of *full preterism*, all the promises of the Bible were fulfilled in the first century. Supposedly the scriptural passages predicting Christ's return are symbolic of the desolation of ancient Jerusalem; descriptions of invisible spiritual events; or predictions of an actual coming of Christ to rapture away his people prior to AD 70. Full preterism robs God's people of their hope, for it denies that Christ will return to raise the dead, judge mankind, inflict just punishment on the wicked, and bring all his people into everlasting bliss.

The second coming of Christ lies at the heart of the Christian faith. John Murray said, "An adjustment of the gospel that discards this tenet of faith and hope is an abandonment of Christianity . . . not a version of the Christian faith but its contradiction."[1]

1 John Murray, *Collected Writings of John Murray*, 4 vols. (Edinburgh: Banner of Truth, 1982), 1:90.

The Bible's Terms for Christ's Second Coming

There are several terms in the New Testament that appear repeatedly in passages about Christ's return. Many of these terms are rooted in Christ's references to a prophecy of Daniel, who had a vision of the "Ancient of days" enthroned in "fire" (Dan. 7:9–10). One "like the Son of man came with the clouds of heaven" to the Ancient of days and received "glory" and everlasting dominion (vv. 13–14).

Christ quotes Daniel's vision when he says that the nations will see "the Son of man coming in the clouds of heaven with power and great glory" (Matt. 24:30). He adds that the Son of Man "shall send his angels with a great sound of a trumpet" to "gather" his elect (v. 31). Later Jesus says, "When the Son of man shall come in his glory, and all the holy angels with him, then shall he sit upon the throne of his glory," and all nations will be "gathered" to either enter the eternal kingdom or go away into "everlasting fire" (25:31–32, 34, 41).

Paul uses similar language when he says,

> The Lord himself shall descend from heaven with a shout, with the voice of the archangel, and with the trump of God: and the dead in Christ shall rise first: then we which are alive and remain shall be caught up together with them in the clouds, to meet the Lord in the air: and so shall we ever be with the Lord. (1 Thess. 4:15–17)

Clouds point to God's glorious presence (Ex. 40:34–38). Christ is often said to come with power and fire (2 Thess. 1:7–8), and with angels (Luke 9:26).

Several Scripture passages say that Christ will "come," a word commonly used for moving from one place to another (Matt. 25:19; John 14:2–3). Three terms especially refer to Christ's second coming. The Greek noun translated as "coming" (*parousia*) is used many times for Christ's return.[2] The word suggests that his return will be like the official visit of a king in grand splendor. Christ will "appear" (Col. 3:4), and his coming is called his "appearing" (2 Tim. 4:1). He will be "revealed" (Luke 17:30), and his return will be his "revelation" (1 Pet. 1:13).

2 Matt. 24:3, 27, 37, 39; 1 Cor. 15:23; 1 Thess. 2:19; 3:13; 4:15; 5:23; 2 Thess. 2:1, 8; James 5:7–8; 2 Pet. 1:16; 3:4, 12; 1 John 2:28.

Terms such as these are used in many places in the New Testament.[3] The passages in which they appear teach us that Christ will come from heaven with public glory—his official arrival as the Lord of all. He will be accompanied by his heavenly servants, the angels, in the clouds. On that day, he will be revealed for who he truly is. He will take the kingdom granted him by his Father, rule with power, and judge with eternal fire.

Christ's Visible, Public Coming

Jesus teaches that his disciples must ignore all claims that he will come secretly. He says, "For as the lightning cometh out of the east, and shineth even unto the west; so shall also the coming of the Son of man be" (Matt. 24:23, 26–27). Currently, the church has "not seen him," but that will change at "the revelation of Jesus Christ" (1 Pet. 1:7–8 ESV).

Cornelis Venema says, "The return of Christ will be an event, at the close of the present age, in which the present splendour, honour and authority that belong to the risen and ascended Lord will be visibly, personally and publicly displayed in his being revealed from heaven."[4]

The Holy Scriptures emphasize that Christ's return will be public by repeating the theme of the blowing of a trumpet. We are told that Christ will "send his angels with a great sound of a trumpet" (Matt. 24:31). Believers alive at that moment "shall all be changed, in a moment, in the twinkling of an eye, at the last trump: for the trumpet shall sound, and the dead shall be raised incorruptible" (1 Cor. 15:51–52). Also, "the Lord himself shall descend from heaven with a shout, with the voice of the archangel, and with the trump of God: and the dead in Christ shall rise first" (1 Thess. 4:16).

People will see Christ personally returning. Jesus says, "Then shall all the tribes of the earth mourn, and they shall see the Son of man coming in the clouds of heaven" (Matt. 24:30). John says, "We know that, when he shall appear, we shall be like him; for we shall see him as he is" (1 John 3:2). He adds, "Behold, he cometh with clouds; and every eye shall see him" (Rev. 1:7).

Christ ascended into heaven as a man, and he will descend to earth one day still as a man. Luke records,

3 See Table 34.1, "Common Terms in Some New Testament Passages on Christ's Return," in Beeke and Smalley, *RST*, 4:946.

4 Cornelis P. Venema, *The Promise of the Future* (Edinburgh: Banner of Truth, 2000), 83.

> While they beheld, he [Jesus] was taken up; and a cloud received him out of their sight. And while they looked stedfastly toward heaven as he went up, behold, two men stood by them in white apparel; which also said, Ye men of Galilee, why stand ye gazing up into heaven? This same Jesus, which is taken up from you into heaven, *shall so come in like manner* as ye have seen him go into heaven. (Acts 1:9–11)

The Purposes of Christ's Second Coming

We will expand on the purposes of Christ's return in later chapters. Here we list them briefly.

First, *Christ will come to display God's glory.* Jesus says, "The Son of man shall come in the glory of his Father" (Matt. 16:27). Paul writes, "Our blessed hope [is] the appearing of the glory of our great God and Savior Jesus Christ" (Titus 2:13 ESV). William Ames said, "The glory of Christ at that time will be incomparable."[5]

Second, *Christ will come to destroy the wicked and the persecutors of his church.* God will punish persecutors and give relief to his suffering church "when the Lord Jesus shall be revealed from heaven with his mighty angels, in flaming fire taking vengeance on them that know not God, and that obey not the gospel of our Lord Jesus Christ" (2 Thess. 1:6–8).

Third, *Christ will come to raise mankind from the dead.* Jesus says, "The hour is coming, in the which all that are in the graves shall hear his voice, and shall come forth" (John 5:28–29).

Fourth, *Christ will come to judge everyone.* Jesus says, "When the Son of man shall come in his glory . . . before him shall be gathered all nations. . . . [And the wicked] shall go away into everlasting punishment: but the righteous into life eternal" (Matt. 25:31–32, 46).

Fifth, *Christ will come to renew and reign over God's creation.* Believers are "heirs of God and fellow heirs with Christ, provided we suffer with him in order that we may also be glorified with him . . . [when] the creation itself will be set free from its bondage to corruption and obtain the freedom of the glory of the children of God" (Rom. 8:17, 21 ESV).

Sixth, *Christ will come to fulfill all God's promises.* God "shall send Jesus Christ . . . whom the heaven must receive until the times of restitution of

5 William Ames, *A Sketch of the Christian's Catechism*, trans. Todd M. Rester, Classic Reformed Theology (Grand Rapids, MI: Reformation Heritage Books, 2008), 99.

all things, which God hath spoken by the mouth of all his holy prophets since the world began" (Acts 3:20–21).

Seventh, *Christ will come to live with his people.* Jesus promises, "I will come again, and receive you unto myself; that where I am, there ye may be also" (John 14:2–3). Toward that end, he prayed, "Father, I will that they also, whom thou hast given me, be with me where I am; that they may behold my glory" (17:24).

Christians should not dread the second coming. John Bunyan said, "A Saviour he was at his first coming, and a Saviour he will be at his second coming. At his first coming, he bought and paid for us; at his second coming, he will fetch us to himself."[6]

Responses of Men and Angels to Christ's Second Coming

The appearing of Jesus Christ in divine glory will have an awesome effect on everyone. God will make his Son to be central to and supreme over the whole universe (Col. 1:16, 18).

God will bring about the subjection of all to Christ the Lord. Since the Son became a man and obeyed his Father even unto death on the cross, "God also hath highly exalted him, and given him a name which is above every name: that at the name of Jesus every knee should bow, of things in heaven, and things in earth, and things under the earth; and that every tongue should confess that Jesus Christ is Lord, to the glory of God the Father" (Phil. 2:9–11).

Christ's coming will be the terror and grief of the wicked. When Christ appears in glory, "all tribes of the earth will wail on account of him" (Rev. 1:7 ESV). From the greatest to the least, the wicked will prefer to be crushed by the mountains than to face "the wrath of the Lamb: for the great day of his wrath is come; and who shall be able to stand?" (6:16–17). What will you do if he comes and you are not yet saved—still an enemy of God? Repent of your sin and turn to Christ today to save you.

Christ will appear to the wonder and joy of the righteous. Paul says, "He shall come to be glorified in his saints, and to be admired in all them that believe" (2 Thess. 1:10). The people born of God to share in his righteous image will not need to be ashamed when Christ returns. They will welcome him with confidence (1 John 2:28–29).

6 John Bunyan, *Light for Them That Sit in Darkness*, in *The Works of John Bunyan*, ed. George Offor, 3 vols. (Glasgow: Blackie and Son, 1855), 1:428.

The Imminency of Christ's Second Coming

Christ made it clear that no one will be able to predict when he will come again (Matt. 24:36, 42, 44; cf. Acts 1:7). The world will be continuing in its ordinary course of life when suddenly the end will come. Christ's return will be unexpected like Noah's flood (Luke 17:26–27), the destruction of Sodom (vv. 28–30), or a thief breaking into a house at night (Matt. 24:43).

Christ's coming is near. Paul says, "The Lord is at hand" (Phil. 4:5). He also writes, "The night is far spent, the day is at hand" (Rom. 13:12). James says, "The coming of the Lord draweth nigh," and presents the vivid image of the Judge standing at the door, out of sight but positioned to enter without warning (James 5:8–9).

This is called the doctrine of the *imminency of Christ's return*. The word *imminent* means impending—it could happen soon, though not necessarily at this very moment. Christ says three times at the end of the Bible, "I come quickly" (Rev. 22:7, 12, 20). "Quickly" probably means that he will arrive suddenly and at a time one cannot anticipate.

Someone might object that certain signs must take place before Christ comes in glory. But the desolation of Jerusalem occurred in AD 70 (Luke 21:20). We cannot know exactly when the gospel will reach "all the world" (Matt. 24:14). It may not be possible to identify the final antichrist until the end is almost upon us, for many antichrists have come (1 John 2:18). The conversion of ethnic Israel might begin quietly and happen quickly. And it seems the prophesied cosmic disturbances may take place just before the Lord returns (Matt. 24:29–31; Rev. 6:12–17).

Thus, we can say that the events that will happen immediately before Christ's coming could begin or escalate at any time, and Christ could appear very soon.

Therefore, we should live in a state of expectancy, anticipation, and readiness for Christ to come in his glory. We must beware lest our hearts become overwhelmed with the concerns of this life and our sense of eternal realities grows dim (Luke 21:34).

Practical Applications of the Second Coming

In the New Testament, Christ's second coming has many practical applications. We list some of them here.

First, *receive this doctrine with faith.* Thomas Manton said, "Would Jesus Christ assure us of that which shall never be?" Rest your mind in what God has revealed about the future: "God's word is sufficient. Faith is built on God's testimony, and nothing else."[7]

Second, *allow the anticipation of Christ's return to instill in you a holy fear.* Herman Witsius said that this doctrine "is useful to awaken men from their security, and to generate in their minds a salutary dread [healthy fear]; that, trembling at the thought of so splendid and awful a day, they may turn with the whole heart unto God."[8]

Third, *make Christ's coming your fascination.* Let it be a holy obsession that colors all your thinking (Col. 3:1–4). Be one of those "who are eagerly waiting for him" to "appear a second time" (Heb. 9:28 ESV). Thomas Vincent said, "Consider that Christ will appear; meditate on this thing, let it dwell on your thoughts, let it lie down with you at night, and rise with you in the morning."[9] He added, "Believers look for the appearance of Christ with an eye of love and desire, they love and long for his appearance."[10]

Fourth, *seriously labor to produce the fruit of good works in response to this truth* (Titus 2:13–14). Vincent said, "If thou art careful to please the Lord . . . and are afraid of sin, because it is grievous to him; and are diligent in the use of means to fit and prepare yourselves, and make all things ready for the receiving of him, it is a sign you do both look for his coming, and do desire it."[11]

Fifth, *find motivation to live in faithfulness by hope in his coming.* Richard Sibbes said, "If we desire the second coming of Christ, we will prepare for it . . . as the bride for the coming of the bridegroom."[12] Manton said, "There is no such powerful help to the mortification of your lusts as to consider the day of judgment, [and] no such special encouragement in your difficulties as the comfort, glory, and sweetness of it."[13]

7 Thomas Manton, *Several Sermons upon Matthew 25*, in *The Complete Works of Thomas Manton*, 22 vols. (London: James Nisbet & Co., 1873), 10:30–31.

8 Herman Witsius, *Sacred Dissertations on the Apostles' Creed*, trans. Donald Fraser (1823; repr., Grand Rapids, MI: Reformation Heritage Books, 2010), 22.43 (2:299).

9 Thomas Vincent, *Christ's Certain and Sudden Appearance to Judgment* (Greenfield, MA: by Ansel Phelps for Timothy Frary, 1816), 344.

10 Vincent, *Christ's Certain and Sudden Appearance to Judgment*, 324.

11 Vincent, *Christ's Certain and Sudden Appearance to Judgment*, 327.

12 Sibbes, *The Bride's Longing for Her Bridegroom's Second Coming*, in *WRS*, 6:550–51.

13 Manton, *Several Sermons upon Matthew 25*, in *Works*, 10:31.

Sixth, *draw fortitude from this hope to deny yourself and patiently endure dishonor and disappointment in this world.* Manton said, "Have no cause to think shame of Christ's service, though you suffer disgrace for it; he will appear worthy of all the respect you show to his person and ways. . . . The judgment of the blind world is not to be regarded."[14]

Seventh, *meditate on Christ's coming to inflame your fervor toward him.* Stir up your heart to answer the promises of his Word with your longing and prayer: "He which testifieth these things saith, Surely I come quickly. Amen. Even so, come, Lord Jesus" (Rev. 22:20). Sibbes said, "These desires are the breathings and motions of the Spirit in the soul, tending to further union."[15] Jesus says, "For where your treasure is, there will your heart be also" (Matt. 6:21). Sibbes added, "Now where is the church's treasure but in Christ?"[16]

Suggested Song to Sing to the Lord

- Psalm 97, "Jehovah reigns; let earth be glad," *Psalter*, No. 260; *THBap*, No. 59

Questions for Meditation or Discussion

1. What are some ways that people have denied the doctrine of Christ's second coming?
2. What passages of the New Testament include key terms used for Christ's second coming?
3. What are three special terms or word groups used for Christ's return? What does each mean?
4. Someone says, "I believe that Christ has come—in our hearts." How do you respond?
5. For what purposes will Christ come again?
6. How will Christ's appearing affect everyone? The wicked? The righteous?
7. What does the doctrine of imminency mean?
8. Of the seven applications at the end of this chapter, select one as especially important for your spiritual growth at this time. Write a personal prayer asking God to work this in your soul.

14 Manton, *Several Sermons upon Matthew 25*, in *Works*, 10:32–33.

15 Sibbes, *The Bride's Longing for Her Bridegroom's Second Coming*, in *WRS*, 6:543.

16 Sibbes, *The Bride's Longing for Her Bridegroom's Second Coming*, in *WRS*, 6:547.

9. If the second coming of Christ were not taught in the Bible, what difference would it make to the Christian faith and life? What difference would it make to you?

93

The Resurrection of the Dead and the Day of Judgment

Chapter Summary and Key Terms

At his second coming, Christ will restore all mankind, both the wicked and the righteous, to physical life by the *resurrection of the dead*. People in union with Christ will rise to share in his glory in the immortal life given by the Spirit (*glorification*). Believers yet alive when Christ returns will be changed into the same immortality and caught up with the resurrected saints to meet him in the air (the rapture). After the resurrection will come the *day of judgment*, when God will glorify his authority and justice through Christ. He will judge each person by his works and motives according to the standards of general revelation and, insofar as the person knows it, God's Word. Christ will vindicate the righteous and welcome them into their eternal inheritance by grace. He will condemn the wicked and banish them to eternal punishment. Therefore, let us obtain confidence for judgment day by trusting in Christ alone for salvation and doing good works by the Spirit.

CHRISTIANITY IS A SUPERNATURAL FAITH. Our faith in the supernatural power of God is plainly seen in the doctrines of the resurrection of the dead and of judgment day. Christians for centuries have confessed that Christ "shall come again, with glory, to judge the quick [living] and the dead" and their belief in "the resurrection of the body."[1]

1 The Nicene Creed, in *TFU*, 7.

The resurrection was part of the ancient hope of God's people (Job 19:25–27; Isa. 25:8; 26:19). It is a foundation of the Christian faith (Heb. 6:1–2). If there is no resurrection, our faith is worthless (1 Cor. 15:12–19). The Christian life is motivated in part by the expectation of judgment and reward. Paul says, "We shall all stand before the judgment seat of Christ. . . . Every one of us shall give account of himself to God" (Rom. 14:10, 12).

The General Resurrection of the Dead

The resurrection of the dead will take place at the end of the age, when Christ will return to judge the world. The dead will "rise up in the judgment" (Matt. 12:42). We live in "this age," but at "the resurrection from the dead," "that age" will have begun (Luke 20:34–35 ESV). Christ promises that those who extend hospitality to the poor "shalt be recompensed at the resurrection of the just" (Luke 14:14). He also says that he will raise up his people "at the last day" (John 6:39–40, 44, 54), which also will be the time of judgment (12:48).

Paul teaches that Christ's people will be raised "at his coming" (1 Cor. 15:23). Death, "the last enemy," will be destroyed (v. 26) and "all things shall be subdued unto him" (v. 28). This will happen "at the last trump: for the trumpet shall sound, and the dead shall be raised" (v. 52). Then "the Lord himself shall descend from heaven . . . and the dead in Christ shall rise" (1 Thess. 4:16).

There will be a resurrection "both of the just and unjust" (Acts 24:15). Daniel prophesies, "Many of them that sleep in the dust of the earth shall awake, some to everlasting life, and some to shame and everlasting contempt. And they that be wise shall shine as the brightness of the firmament; and they that turn many to righteousness as the stars for ever and ever" (Dan. 12:2–3). Christ teaches that both the repentant and the unrepentant will rise together on judgment day (Matt. 12:41–42). He adds, "The hour is coming, in the which all that are in the graves shall hear his voice, and shall come forth; they that have done good, unto the resurrection of life; and they that have done evil, unto the resurrection of damnation" (John 5:28–29).

Objections to the Resurrection of the Dead

The doctrine of the physical resurrection is a central feature of biblical religion. But it is alien to most other religions and philosophies. Skeptics have raised various objections, such as these:

First, *the resurrection is unnecessary.* We can believe instead simply that the human soul or mind lives forever after the body dies.

In reply, we note that God made man to exist as a unified body and spirit. Our complete salvation requires "the redemption of our body" (Rom. 8:23).

Second, *the resurrection is impossible.* The bodies of some people have been burned to ashes, vaporized, or eaten by animals.

In reply, we answer that the resurrection will be accomplished by God, who "is able to do exceeding abundantly above all that we ask or think" (Eph. 3:20). Not an atom of the universe escapes his attention or sovereign control. Furthermore, it is not necessary that every particle of the original body be remade into the resurrection body, just a part.

Third, *the resurrection is unbiblical.* Job says, "Man lieth down, and riseth not: till the heavens be no more, they shall not awake, nor be raised out of their sleep" (Job 14:12). Paul writes, "Flesh and blood cannot inherit the kingdom of God; neither doth corruption inherit incorruption" (1 Cor. 15:50).

In reply, we observe that Job says that death is final "till the heavens be no more." Thus, death is ordinarily a permanent state in this age, but that does not rule out the resurrection at the beginning of the age to come. "Flesh and blood" in Paul's statement do not refer to the body itself but to its present state of "corruption" under the power of death. Christ's "flesh" was raised in his resurrection (Luke 24:39).

Fourth, *the resurrection is unnatural.* It is said to be contrary to biological science. Resurrection is the stuff of mythology or science fiction.

In reply, we note that the resurrection of the dead is not a natural resuscitation but a supernatural intervention of God. The general resurrection comes with the arrival of the new age of glory, when the natural course of this age will cease (Luke 20:34–36).

The Resurrection of Those in Union with Christ

Christ will raise all the dead by his power (John 5:28). But only "they that are Christ's" will rise "in Christ," in union with him and his resurrection (1 Cor. 15:21–23). John Calvin said, "Having obtained immortality, he [Christ] is the pledge of our coming resurrection. . . . There was begun in the Head what must be completed in all the members. . . . He was raised by the power of the Holy Spirit, who in us has the common office of giving life."[2]

If Christ will raise dead believers at his coming, what will happen to believers who are alive? Paul says, "We shall not all sleep, but we shall all be changed, in a moment, in the twinkling of an eye, at the last trump: for the trumpet shall sound, and the dead shall be raised incorruptible, and we shall be changed" (1 Cor. 15:51–52). Not all Christians will experience "sleep," a figure of speech for death; those alive at Christ's coming will be changed to share in resurrection life. Paul explains that when the Lord returns, "the dead in Christ shall rise first: then we which are alive and remain shall be caught up together with them in the clouds, to meet the Lord in the air" (1 Thess. 4:16–17). This will not be a secret rapture, but one done with "a shout, with the voice of the archangel, and with the trump of God" (v. 16).

What will the resurrected body of a believer be like? Paul says, "It is sown in corruption; it is raised in incorruption: it is sown in dishonour; it is raised in glory: it is sown in weakness; it is raised in power: it is sown a natural body; it is raised a spiritual body" (1 Cor. 15:42–44). The word "spiritual" means influenced by the Holy Spirit (2:13–15; 12:1–3). So "spiritual" bodies are not spirits like ghosts, but material bodies made alive and sanctified by God's Spirit. When Christ comes, he will "change our vile body, that it may be fashioned like unto his glorious body" (Phil. 3:21). Christ's resurrection body is still a human body, with hands, feet, flesh, and bones (Luke 24:36–43). But he is glorious, and so will be his people. Thus, the resurrection and rapture of the saints will complete their salvation by the grace of *glorification*, so that they will share in the glory of the risen Lord Jesus (Rom. 8:17, 29–30; Col. 3:4).

Practical Applications of the Resurrection

The doctrine of the resurrection has powerful practical applications for believers.

First, *it affords a high view of God.* Andreas Rivetus said, "The primary and ultimate goal of the resurrection is the glory of God."[3] The doctrine of the resurrection shows us God's infinite power to do his will, his immutable

2 Calvin, *Institutes*, 3.25.3, translation altered in the last phrase.

3 Polyander, Walaeus, Thysius, and Rivetus, *SPT*, 51.41 (3:561).

faithfulness to keep his promises, and his immortal life, by which he will bless his people with eternal life in union with Christ.

Second, *it shows us the value of the human body*. Our bodies are a permanent part of who we are. We learn from the resurrection not to see ourselves as mere spirits who live in bodies, but as whole human beings with bodies and souls. Therefore, what we do with our bodies is of great importance. Indeed, what each person has "done in his body" will have eternal consequences (2 Cor. 5:10). But the resurrection also gives us boldness to sacrifice our bodies for the cause of Christ (4:14). And when death comes, the hope of the resurrection enables us to entrust our bodies to God.

The Day of Judgment

Judgment day is a "revelation of the righteous judgment of God" (Rom. 2:5). God must judge because he is God—perfect in moral excellence and supreme in authority. Abraham asks, "Shall not the Judge of all the earth do right?" (Gen. 18:25). He is "God, the Judge of all" (Heb. 12:23).

God will show his glory on the "day of the LORD" (Isa. 2:11–12; Zech. 14:1, 9). He will disrupt and dissolve this present creation.[4] The day of the Lord also will be the time of his righteous anger against all who have not honored his supremacy.[5]

The "day of the Lord" is "the day of judgment" (2 Pet. 3:7, 10). On that day, the King will come and summon all to his court. Human courts are formal assemblies. So, too, the final judgment will be the greatest and most solemn assembly ever to take place in history.

The Lord God, supreme in authority, infinite in power, and perfect in justice, will be the Judge of all (Pss. 50:6; 75:7). In the Trinity, it is particularly God the Son who will judge the world (John 5:22, 30). Christ will judge as the glorious "Son of man" (Matt. 16:27; John 5:27). The fact that he will be the Judge should greatly comfort believers. Calvin said, "We shall be brought before no other judgment seat than that of our Redeemer."[6]

The assistants of the Judge will be his holy angels (Mark 8:38). Jesus says, "When the Son of man shall come in his glory, and all the holy angels with him, then shall he sit upon the throne of his glory" (Matt. 25:31). The

4 Ps. 97:5–6; Nah. 1:5; Matt. 24:29–30; 2 Pet. 3:10, 12; Rev. 6:12–14; 20:11–12.

5 Isa. 13:6, 9, 13; Zeph. 1:14–16, 18; 2:2.

6 Calvin, *Institutes*, 2.16.18.

angels will be witnesses of Christ's legal verdicts (Luke 12:8–9). They will also act somewhat as law-enforcement officers do in human courts (Matt. 13:41–42; 24:31).

Christ's holy people will also participate in the judgment (Dan. 7:22; Matt. 19:28). Paul says, "Do ye not know that the saints shall judge the world?" (1 Cor. 6:2). Christ will act as supreme Judge, declaring God's verdict and sentence for each person, for he alone is the mediatorial King (Matt. 25:34, 41). Christ's people will speak their approval to his condemnation of unrepentant sinners, at least in cases especially relevant to them (12:41–42).

On judgment day, Christ will judge angelic spirits and all human beings. The fires of hell are prepared not just for sinful men but for "the devil and his angels" (Matt. 25:41). Paul says, "Know ye not that we shall judge angels?" (1 Cor. 6:3). This may refer only to evil spirits or to all angels—it is difficult to be sure. Christ will also judge "every man" (Matt. 16:27; Rom. 2:5–6). Paul says, "We shall all stand before the judgment seat of Christ . . . [and] every one of us shall give account of himself to God" (Rom. 14:10, 12).

The expectation of judgment day should direct all our earthly activities, even when we are young and healthy. It is written, "Rejoice, O young man, in thy youth; and let thy heart cheer thee in the days of thy youth, and walk in the ways of thine heart, and in the sight of thine eyes: but know thou, that for all these things God will bring thee into judgment" (Eccles. 11:9).

The Proceedings of the Final Judgment

The day of judgment is the day of Christ's coming (James 5:8–9). The Lord Jesus says, "When the Son of man shall come in his glory, and all the holy angels with him, then shall he sit upon the throne of his glory" and judge mankind (Matt. 25:31). Christ will summon all human beings to stand before his judgment seat. He will resurrect the dead so that they, too, may appear for the judgment to receive either "life" or "damnation" (John 5:28–29).

The Lord will separate the righteous from the wicked (Matt. 25:32–33). Christ says, "The Son of man . . . shall send his angels . . . and they shall gather together his elect" (24:30–31). This corresponds to the resurrection and rapture of the church to meet the Lord in the air (1 Thess. 4:15–17).

God will publicly display his perfect righteousness in executing justice (Ps. 50:6; Rev. 19:2, 11). He will judge with unanswerable truth concerning the facts of each case (Heb. 4:13). Thomas Boston said, "This trial will be righteous and impartial, accurate and searching, clear and evident. The Judge is the righteous Judge, and He will do right to every one."[7]

Christ will judge each person according to his works (Ps. 62:12; Prov. 24:12; Matt. 16:27). He describes the judgment according to works in the parable of a man who calls his servants to account for their stewardship. To one, he says, "Well done, thou good and faithful servant: thou hast been faithful over a few things, I will make thee ruler over many things: enter thou into the joy of thy lord" (Matt. 25:21, 23). But another is rebuked as a "wicked and slothful servant," and punished (vv. 24–30). God's wrath will come on unbelievers because of their acts of disobedience, not merely because of their unbelief (Eph. 5:6; Col. 3:6).

The Lord will also judge according to each man's motives (Jer. 17:9–10). Christ says, "I am he which searcheth the reins and hearts: and I will give unto every one of you according to your works" (Rev. 2:23). Paul says, "Therefore judge nothing before the time, until the Lord come, who both will bring to light the hidden things of darkness, and will make manifest the counsels of the hearts" (1 Cor. 4:5).

God's judgment will be according to his righteous standards. He will judge men by the standard of general revelation (see chap. 4). General revelation testifies to us outwardly in the visible creation (Rom. 1:18–21) and inwardly in the conscience (2:14–15). As a result, "as many as have sinned without law shall also perish without law" (v. 12). Those ignorant of God's Word will still be condemned for sinning against God when they violated their consciences.

The Lord will also judge people according to the standard of special revelation (see chap. 5), insofar as they had access to the Word of God (Rom. 2:12; James 2:12). Christ says, "He that rejecteth me, and receiveth not my words, hath one that judgeth him: the word that I have spoken, the same shall judge him in the last day" (John 12:48). William Bates said, "When the Lawgiver himself shall expound the law in its full extent and perfection, with respect to the duties it commands, and sins it forbids, how guilty will men appear?"[8]

7 Thomas Boston, *Human Nature in Its Fourfold State* (Edinburgh: Banner of Truth, 1964), 412.

8 William Bates, *The Four Last Things*, in *The Whole Works of the Rev. W. Bates*, ed. W. Farmer, 4 vols. (repr., Harrisonburg, VA: Sprinkle, 1990), 3:329.

The Vindication of the Righteous

Christ will judge the righteous for their vindication and the wicked for their condemnation on judgment day. However, the judgment of the righteous will not proceed on exactly the same principles as that of the wicked. Both the righteousness and the reward of believers are by grace.

The evidence for vindication will be the good works of the righteous. The Lord will "render to every man according to his deeds: to them who by patient continuance in well doing seek for glory and honour and immortality, eternal life . . . glory, honour, and peace, to every man that worketh good" (Rom. 2:6–7, 10). Only "they that have done good" will be raised from the dead "unto the resurrection of life" (John 5:29). Their fruitfulness in producing good works will prove that they abide in vital union with Christ (15:4–5; cf. Phil. 1:11).

The divine cause of vindication will be God's grace and justice. His people are saved by grace from first to last. The works by which they will be vindicated on the last day are also of grace. God elected them to holiness (Eph. 1:4). He redeemed them for holiness by Christ's death (5:25–27). And he made them alive with Christ (2:1–5) so that they are "his workmanship" (v. 10). God will magnify his justice when he welcomes the redeemed into his kingdom on the basis of Christ's satisfaction of the law's demands (Rom. 3:25–26; 5:8, 19). His reward of their obedience will glorify him as the holy Father of his children (1 Pet. 1:16–17).

Contrary to Roman Catholicism, the righteous will not have "truly merited eternal life," not even by God's grace working in them.[9] God's servants can never merit God's reward, for they owe him every good work they do (Luke 17:10). Furthermore, they are imperfect in all their service (Phil. 3:12). Their works are gifts of God's grace (2 Cor. 8:1). These works are done by people worthy of damnation (Ps. 143:2) but redeemed at infinite cost by Christ's blood (1 Pet. 1:18–19). He alone saves believers from the coming wrath of God (Rom. 5:9; 1 Thess. 1:10; 5:9). It is on account of Christ's redeeming death that believers will receive the eternal inheritance (Heb. 9:15).

The verdict of vindication will be God's blessing on his people. The King will tenderly say, "Come, ye blessed of my Father" (Matt. 25:34).

9 The Council of Trent (Session 6, Decree on Justification, chap. 16), in *Denzinger*, secs. 1545–46 (383).

William Perkins said, "Though Christ now sit in glory and majesty in judgment, yet He ceases not to show His tender affection of love unto His chosen."[10] His almighty voice will seal on their consciences their everlasting blessedness. Christ depicts this joyful moment in the parable of the talents when the master says, "Well done, thou good and faithful servant" (Matt. 25:21).

The joyful consequence of vindication will be the believers' reception of the inheritance and reward of God (Col. 3:24). His adopted children are "heirs of God, and joint-heirs with Christ" (Rom. 8:17).

There will be degrees of reward (Luke 19:17, 19; 1 Cor. 3:8). Christians who by grace become most like Christ in serving others will be exalted to higher honor than others (Mark 9:34–35; 10:40–45). Paul says, "He which soweth sparingly shall reap also sparingly; and he which soweth bountifully shall reap also bountifully" (2 Cor. 9:6).

The promise of the saints' vindication gives them hope that sanctifies them. Believers ought to take the doctrine of judgment day to heart and think often of the day of the Lord. George Swinnock said, "Could the Christian but . . . hear the sound of the last trumpet in his ears at all times, it would encourage him in his spiritual warfare, and enable him to fight manfully, and to cause the enemies of his salvation to flee before him."[11]

The Condemnation of the Wicked

The Lord Jesus will call the ungodly before his judgment seat to condemn them as guilty and to sentence them to eternal punishment.

The evidence for condemnation will be their lives of evil deeds. Paul says that the day of judgment will be "unto them that are contentious, and do not obey the truth, but obey unrighteousness, indignation and wrath, tribulation and anguish, upon every soul of man that doeth evil, of the Jew first, and also of the Gentile" (Rom. 2:8–9). God will demonstrate the absolute justice of their condemnation and silence all their excuses and arguments (3:19).

The divine cause of condemnation will be God's wrath arising from his impartial justice (Rom. 2:5). God does not show partiality to the rich or

10 Perkins, *An Exposition of the Symbol*, in *WWP*, 5:298.

11 George Swinnock, *The Christian Man's Calling*, in *The Works of George Swinnock*, 5 vols. (1868; repr., Edinburgh: Banner of Truth, 1992), 3:132.

the poor, to one ethnic group or gender above another, when he renders judgment (v. 11). The Judge will be praised for his righteousness in giving sinners what they deserve (Rev. 15:3–4; 16:5–7; 19:2).

The verdict of condemnation will be God's curse on guilty lawbreakers. The sentence of condemnation will be banishment and punishment forever. Christ will say, "Depart from me, ye cursed, into everlasting fire, prepared for the devil and his angels" (Matt. 25:41). Thomas Manton said, "When they came to attack Christ, as soon as he had told them, 'I am he,' they went backward and fell to the ground (John 18:6). . . . If the Lamb's voice be so terrible, how dreadful will he be when he roareth as a lion!"[12]

There will be degrees of punishment inflicted in condemnation (Luke 10:12, 14; 12:47–48). Various sins have different degrees of heinousness (see chap. 36). Each sin will receive its due recompense.

Therefore, "flee from the wrath to come" (Luke 3:7). Wilhelmus à Brakel said, "It is amazing that people who are so desirous to know future things and so careful to make provision for their own old age as well as for their children and grandchildren—and if possible gather treasures—are nevertheless so careless about this great and terrible day."[13]

Consider the horrifying doom to fall on the wicked: "Who among us can dwell with the consuming fire? Who among us can dwell with everlasting burnings?" (Isa. 33:14 ESV). The only way of escape is Jesus Christ. Have you received him and rested your faith in him alone for salvation? Are you walking in repentance?

Beware, impenitent sinner! No matter what you may say with your mouth, if your life does not show the fruit of true repentance and a living faith, judgment day will expose you as an enemy of God. Then there will be nothing for you "but a fearful expectation of judgment, and a fury of fire that will consume the adversaries" (Heb. 10:27 ESV).

Suggested Songs to Sing to the Lord

- Psalm 50, "The mighty God, the Lord," *Psalter*, No. 139; compare *THBap*, No. 239
- "Lo! he comes, with clouds descending," *THBap*, No. 237

12 Thomas Manton, *Several Sermons upon Matthew 25*, in *The Complete Works of Thomas Manton*, 22 vols. (London: James Nisbet & Co., 1873), 10:24.

13 Brakel, *CRS*, 4:349.

Questions for Meditation or Discussion

1. How does the Bible show that the Old Testament saints hoped in the resurrection of the dead?
2. When will the resurrection take place? Prove it from Scripture.
3. How does the Bible show that there will be a general resurrection of the just and unjust?
4. How can we answer objections that the resurrection is (1) unnecessary, (2) impossible, (3) unbiblical, and (4) unnatural?
5. What does God promise believers about their future sharing in his Son's resurrection?
6. Who will be present on the day of judgment? What will they do there?
7. What evidence will be used in the final judgment?
8. How are both God's grace and justice glorified in the vindication of his people?
9. What will happen on judgment day to all who do not repent of sin and trust in Christ?
10. Are you sure that you will escape the condemnation coming on the wicked? Why?

94

Eternal Punishment in Hell

Chapter Summary and Key Terms

At the end of the age, Christ will cast wicked angels and human beings into *hell* for the *eternal punishment* of their sins. They will lose all good and suffer greatly forever. Eternal punishment is perfect justice for the unspeakable evil of sin against the loving and holy God. Christ will not save everyone (*universal salvation*). Once he condemns sinners to hell, there will be no hope for them. God will not end the conscious life of the wicked after a time (*annihilationism*), and those without eternal life will not cease to exist (*conditional immortality*). Rather, the wicked will suffer eternal conscious punishment. We should respond to the doctrine of eternal punishment by trusting in Christ alone for salvation, not fretting over temporal wealth and health, and fearing God rather than man. In the light of this doctrine, we also should hate sin and repent of it, urge sinners to be saved by faith and repentance, thank God for Christ with profound gratitude, and humbly worship the God of glorious justice.

BEFORE POLYCARP was burned to death as a Christian martyr, he said to his persecutors, "You threaten me with fire which burns for an hour, and after a little while is extinguished, but you are ignorant of the fire of the coming judgment and of eternal punishment, reserved for the ungodly."[1] In this chapter, we consider what the Bible says about the *eternal punishment* of the wicked that will commence after the resurrection of the dead and judgment day.

1 *The Martyrdom of Polycarp*, chap. 11, in *ANF*, 1:41.

Someone might ask how the doctrine of *hell* can be part of our glorious hope in Christ. We do not hope in human suffering in itself. But we do hope in God's justice and merciful salvation of his people from the influence of the wicked. Though thoughts of hell make us tremble, we must be faithful to what God says in his Word.

Eternal Punishment in the Holy Scriptures

God's wrath is against sinners. Isaiah speaks of the coming of "the name of the LORD," his revealed glory, "burning with his anger . . . as a devouring fire" (Isa. 30:27). The prophet exclaims, "Who among us shall dwell with the devouring fire? Who among us shall dwell with everlasting burnings?" (33:14).

Isaiah also speaks of judgment as deprivation: God's presence is light (Isa. 2:5; 9:2; 60:1), but the wicked will suffer "trouble and darkness" (8:22). Furthermore, the wicked will lose all joy, for the Lord says, "Ye shall be hungry . . . thirsty . . . ashamed . . . ye shall cry for sorrow of heart, and shall howl for vexation of spirit" (65:13–14). Edward Donnelly said, "Hell is a place of absolute poverty," for God will remove all the good things he has given people to enjoy in this world.[2]

At the close of Isaiah's prophecy, after mentioning the new heaven and new earth, God says, "They shall go forth, and look upon the carcases of the men that have transgressed against me: for their worm shall not die, neither shall their fire be quenched; and they shall be an abhorring unto all flesh" (Isa. 66:22, 24). Daniel similarly says that some people will rise from the dead "to shame and everlasting contempt" (Dan. 12:2).

The Lord Jesus Christ speaks more often about eternal punishment than anyone else in the Bible. Christ warns that sins as seemingly minor as angry thoughts and words make a person liable to "hell fire" (Matt. 5:22). He here uses the term *gehenna* ("hell") for the place of final punishment, as distinct from the state of dead spirits now (*hades*, see chap. 89). To be sentenced to hell is "damnation" or judicial condemnation (23:14–15, 33). Evildoers will rise to "the resurrection of damnation" (John 5:29). Christ calls people to radical repentance, for hell is so horrible that it would be

2 Edward Donnelly, *Biblical Teaching on the Doctrines of Heaven and Hell* (Edinburgh: Banner of Truth, 2001), 35–36.

better to have one's body maimed than to go there (Matt. 5:29–30; 18:8–9; Mark 9:43–47).

Christ says that "wide is the gate, and broad is the way, that leadeth to destruction," and "many" enter it (Matt. 7:13). He adds, "Fear not them which kill the body, but are not able to kill the soul: but rather fear him which is able to destroy both soul and body in hell" (10:28). The word translated as "destruction" does not mean annihilation but ruin (the same word is translated as "waste" in 26:8).

Just as weeds are gathered at harvest time and "burned in the fire," even so, at the end of the age, "the Son of man shall send forth his angels" to seize the wicked and "cast them into a furnace of fire" (Matt. 13:40–42; cf. vv. 47–50). "Hell fire" is "everlasting fire" (18:8–9; 25:41), the infliction of "everlasting punishment" (25:46). "Hell" is "the fire that never shall be quenched" (Mark 9:43, 45). Jesus adds that "their worm dieth not, and the fire is not quenched" (v. 48, a quotation of Isa. 66:24).

Like Isaiah, as we saw above, Christ also teaches that the wicked will be deprived of all good things that they desire. They "shall be cast . . . into outer darkness" (Matt. 8:12; 22:13; 25:30). Jesus says, "Woe unto you that are full! For ye shall hunger. Woe unto you that laugh now! For ye shall mourn and weep" (Luke 6:25). The Lord will reject them, saying, "Depart from me" (Matt. 7:23; 25:41).

Eternal punishment, according to our Lord Jesus, causes great pain and sorrow. He says, "There shall be weeping and gnashing of teeth."[3] Weeping means strong crying, such as at a death or disaster. Gnashing of teeth expresses hatred or self-destructive anger (Ps. 112:10; Mark 9:18–22). Matthew Henry said, "Comfortless sorrow, and an incurable indignation at God, themselves, and one another, will be the endless torture of damned souls."[4]

J. C. Ryle said,

> We need to be reminded, that there is a hell as well as a heaven, and an everlasting punishment for the wicked, as well as everlasting life for the godly. We are fearfully apt to forget this. We talk of the love and mercy of God, and we do not remember sufficiently His justness and holiness.

3 Matt. 8:12; 13:42, 50; 22:13; 24:51; 25:30; Luke 13:28.

4 Matthew Henry, *Commentary on the Whole Bible: Complete and Unabridged in One Volume* (Peabody, MA: Hendrickson, 1994), on Matt. 12:24–43 (1681).

> . . . It is good for us all to be taught that it is possible to be lost for ever, and that all unconverted people are hanging over the brink of the pit.[5]

The same doctrine of final punishment taught by Christ appears also in the New Testament Epistles. Paul says that on judgment day, God will express his "indignation and wrath" toward the wicked, inflicting "tribulation and anguish" on them (Rom. 2:8–9). He will display his "wrath" and "power" in the "destruction" of sinners (9:22). Paul writes, "The Lord Jesus shall be revealed from heaven with his mighty angels, in flaming fire taking vengeance on them that know not God, and that obey not the gospel of our Lord Jesus Christ: who shall be punished with everlasting destruction" (2 Thess. 1:7–9).

The last book of the Bible warns that the damned sinner "shall drink of the wine of the wrath of God, which is poured out without mixture into the cup of his indignation; and he shall be tormented with fire and brimstone in the presence of the holy angels, and in the presence of the Lamb: and the smoke of their torment ascendeth up for ever and ever: and they have no rest day nor night" (Rev. 14:10–11). To "drink" God's wrath depicts receiving punishment in one's innermost experience. Drinking this cup "without mixture" implies that God's wrath will come in its full intensity without mercy. There is no common grace in hell. The last statements, "and the smoke of their torment ascendeth up for ever and ever: and they have no rest day nor night," emphasize the perpetual nature of this punishment. William Perkins said, "They are wholly in body and soul tormented with an incredible horror and exceeding great anguish through the sense and feeling of God's wrath poured out upon them forever."[6]

The eternal wrath of God is depicted as the "lake of fire" (Rev. 19:20). To be immersed in liquid fire would mean suffering severe pain throughout one's whole being. "Fire" represents being "tormented day and night for ever and ever" (20:10). The lake of fire is the "second death," and all who are "not found written in the book of life" will be cast into it (vv. 14–15). And again, John writes, "The fearful, and unbelieving, and the abominable, and murderers, and whoremongers, and sorcerers, and idolaters, and all liars,

5 J. C. Ryle, *Expository Thoughts on the Gospels: St. Matthew* (New York: Robert Carter & Brothers, 1860), 20.

6 Perkins, *A Golden Chain*, chap. 57, in *WWP*, 6:260.

shall have their part in the lake which burneth with fire and brimstone: which is the second death" (21:8).

Hell is the logical and just consequence of all sin. The essence of sin is hatred toward God and his will (Rom. 8:7). Having rejected God, the source of all good, sinners should not be surprised to be rejected by God and excluded from all good. Anselm of Canterbury said, "To reject the supreme good is to rush headlong into eternal unhappiness."[7]

Christ alone delivers people from God's wrath (Rom. 5:9; 1 Thess. 1:10; 5:9). He is the propitiation for sin (1 John 2:2; 4:10), the sacrifice that satisfies God's justice and turns away his wrath. Consequently, those who trust in Christ alone for salvation are justified and have peace with God (Rom. 5:1). However, it is also true that Christ inflicts God's wrath on the wicked (Rev. 6:16; 14:10), for he is the righteous Judge (Acts 17:31; 2 Tim. 4:1, 8).

The "everlasting fire" (Matt. 25:41) of hell cannot be understood to refer to literal combustion, which consumes its fuel after a time and is done. The fire of hell assaults both body and soul (10:28). It also burns the Devil and his demons (25:41; Rev. 20:10), though they are spirits and have no bodies. Therefore, "fire" should be interpreted as an image of God's supernatural and powerful punishment of his enemies. It is the punishment of the age to come, and so, like the glory of God's children, it transcends our full comprehension.

The punishment of God's wrath will last forever (Rev. 14:10–11). The fire is "unquenchable" (Matt. 3:12; Luke 3:17) and "everlasting" (Matt. 18:8–9; 25:41). Damnation brings "everlasting contempt" (Dan. 12:2), "everlasting punishment" (Matt. 25:46), "eternal damnation" (Mark 3:29), "everlasting destruction" (2 Thess. 1:9), "eternal judgment" (Heb. 6:2), and "darkness for ever" (Jude 13).

The horrors of hell reveal the evil of sin. There is no evil in God; he is all love and light (1 John 1:5; 4:8). He does not afflict men out of any malice in his holy heart (Lam. 3:33). Rather, sin demands hell. Jeremiah Burroughs said, "There is more evil in the least sin, than there is in the greatest affliction," for "sin is most opposite unto God himself, the chiefest good."[8]

7 Anselm of Canterbury, *Monologion*, chap. 71, in *The Major Works*, ed. Brian Davies and G. R. Evans, Oxford World Classics (Oxford: Oxford University Press, 1998), 76.

8 Jeremiah Burroughs, *The Evil of Evils, or the Exceeding Sinfulness of Sin* (London: Peter Cole, 1654), 31.

Objections to the Doctrine of Eternal Punishment

Many people who doubt or reject the doctrine of eternal punishment do so because it seems to contradict what they believe about God's justice and love.

First, *some people object that God would be unjust to send people to hell.* No sin committed over a limited time on earth, they say, deserves everlasting torment.

In reply, we would point out that the question is not how long the sin took to commit—someone can commit murder in less than a minute—but the seriousness of the wrong done.[9] How do we know what sin justly deserves? Shall lawbreakers who despise God be the judges? The proper response to the severity of eternal judgment is not to question God's justice but to marvel at the unspeakable evil of sin. Sin deserves hell because it is hatred and treason against the Most High.

Donnelly said, "The ultimate proof of the seriousness of sin and the justice of everlasting punishment is provided by the cross of Christ."[10] If justice does not demand that sin be punished severely, why did God send his Son to suffer horribly in body and soul under the curse of his law (Gal. 3:13)? Donnelly added, "If we lose hell, we will eventually lose the cross, for if there is no hell, there is no real point in the cross."[11]

Second, *some people object that God would be unloving to send people to hell.* They argue that the doctrine of eternal torment in hell depicts God as cruel. But "God is love" (1 John 4:8).

In reply, we rejoice that God is love. He has showered his kindness on all humanity, including the wicked (Matt. 5:44–45). God delights in their repentance, not their death (Ezek. 18:23). But he loves righteousness and justice (Ps. 33:5). Furthermore, true love is always accompanied by hatred and revulsion toward moral evil (Rom. 12:9; 1 Cor. 13:6). Yes, God is love, but it is equally true that "God is light" (1 John 1:5)—absolute righteousness and truth.

In the end, we put to rest our doubts about how God's love fits with the reality of hell by trusting Jesus Christ. Herman Bavinck said, "No one in Scripture speaks of it [eternal punishment] more often and at greater

9 Augustine, *The City of God*, 21.11.1, in *NPNF*[1], 2:462–63.

10 Donnelly, *Biblical Teaching on the Doctrines of Heaven and Hell*, 27.

11 Donnelly, *Biblical Teaching on the Doctrines of Heaven and Hell*, 27.

length than our Lord Jesus Christ, whose depth of human feeling and compassion no one can deny and who was the meekest and most humble of human beings. It is the greatest love that threatens the most severe punishments."[12]

The greatest obstacle to believing the doctrine of hell, however, is not our belief in God's love but our belief in our own greatness joined with our boundless self-love. Donnelly said,

> Man-centredness is at the root of objections to hell. . . . The highest imaginable value in our society is human well-being. . . . Hell smashes this façade to pieces. Hell tells us that there is an awesome, holy God in whose eyes we are dreadfully guilty. . . . This is why it is so vital that we think about hell. It brings us face to face with the living God. Here is a litmus test for our souls. Are you God-centered? Hell will test you.[13]

False Alternatives to the Doctrine of Eternal Punishment

The rejection of the doctrine of hell has led people to embrace alternative views of the ultimate future of the wicked.

First, *some people say that hell is merely the absence of God*. They say that the Bible's descriptions of hell are metaphors. Hell, we are told, is just losing God, the source of all joy.

In reply, we acknowledge that the Lord uses metaphors for hell. Literal fire cannot burn spirits such as Satan or burn people forever. Fire is a symbol of a reality beyond our full understanding. But the meaning of the symbol is clear—God's enemies will be "tormented" (Rev. 14:10–11; 20:10). "There shall be wailing and gnashing of teeth" (Matt. 13:42). This is more than the mere absence of God; it is the infliction of his wrath on the wicked.

Second, *some people say that hell will be empty because God will save everyone*. They hope that God will either save all in this life or that he will bring sinners to repentance in the life to come. Such people argue that we should believe in *universal salvation* because Paul says in various passages that God will save "all" (Rom. 5:18; 11:32; 1 Cor. 15:22, 28; Col. 1:20).

12 Bavinck, *RD*, 4:709.

13 Donnelly, *Biblical Teaching on the Doctrines of Heaven and Hell*, 9–14.

In reply, we point to the clear statements in the Bible that hell lasts forever, such as Revelation 14:11: "The smoke of their torment ascendeth up for ever and ever: and they have no rest day nor night." Sinners do not repent even under horrible afflictions (9:20–21; 16:9), for repentance unto life is the gift of God's grace (Acts 11:18; 2 Tim. 2:25). Once the Lord Jesus rejects the wicked, pronounces a curse on them, and sends them into everlasting fire, there is no hope that he will grant them grace (Matt. 25:41). Hell is no purgatory. If Christ believes that all men will join him in heaven, why does he say, "You will die in your sin. Where I am going, you cannot come" (John 8:21 ESV)?

As to Paul's statements, sometimes he uses "all" to refer to all "in Christ" (Rom. 5:18; 1 Cor. 15:22, 28) and sometimes to people of all nations (Rom. 11:32). God's reconciling "all things" in earth and heaven (Col. 1:20) probably refers to the restoration of peace, which includes the defeat of evil powers (2:15). In other passages, Paul teaches the everlasting destruction of unbelievers (2 Thess. 1:8–9) and the crushing of Satan under the feet of believers (Rom. 16:20). In short, the Scriptures do not teach universal salvation. Rather, those who teach universal salvation imitate the Tempter, who taught our first father and mother to doubt what God said about judgment, saying instead, "Ye shall not surely die" (Gen. 3:4).

Third, *some people say that hell is merely the end of existence, not eternal torment.* They claim that God will extinguish the life of the wicked. *Annihilationism* is the belief that God will end their conscious life. A slightly different view, *conditional immortality*, holds that people continue to exist only if God grants them eternal life. According to people who hold such views, the pictures of "everlasting" and "eternal" hellfire communicate that the wicked are burned up and cease to exist. Eternal judgment is eternal destruction, which, we are told, means that the damned will disappear.

In reply, we say that "everlasting" damnation indicates that it has no end, for the same word is used in the same passages for the eternal life of the blessed. Daniel says, "Many of those who sleep in the dust of the earth shall awake, some to everlasting life, and some to shame and everlasting contempt" (Dan. 12:2 ESV). Christ says, "These will go away into eternal punishment: but the righteous into eternal life" (Matt. 25:46 ESV). The fire of hell is not like earthly fire, which burns up its fuel and goes out, but rather it is "everlasting" (v. 41) and "unquenchable" (Luke 3:17). The words translated as "destroy" and "destruction" do not mean annihilation but ruin and wreck, like something broken (Mark 2:22).

At the end of the day, all these arguments are attempts to evade the plain meaning of the Holy Scriptures. The doctrine of the eternal conscious punishment of the wicked is sobering and humbling. But it is the clear teaching of Christ, as well as his prophets and apostles.

Practical Applications of the Doctrine of Hell

The most pressing practical application of the doctrine of hell is to flee the wrath to come by trusting in Christ alone for salvation. Do not be offended by the God who speaks of eternal fire. Instead, take his warning to heart. George Whitefield said, "If the bare mentioning [of] the torments of the damned is so shocking, how terrible must the enduring of them be!"[14] Thomas Brooks said, "Oh, but this word *eternity, eternity, eternity*; this word *everlasting, everlasting, everlasting* . . . will even break the hearts of the damned in ten thousand pieces!"[15]

Furthermore, once you have come to Christ, allow the doctrine of hell to continue to shape your life. This doctrine has many other practical applications for believers.

First, *fear God, not people*. Our Lord Jesus says, "Fear not them which kill the body, but are not able to kill the soul: but rather fear him which is able to destroy both soul and body in hell" (Matt. 10:28). The fear of God can make us fearless before men.

Second, *do not envy the rich and healthy or dread poverty or illness*. What do such temporary things matter compared to an eternity of hell or happiness? Donnelly said, "The doctrine of hell should make believers supremely contented, grateful to God in every circumstance of life."[16]

Third, *cast off sin at all costs*. Christ says, "If thine eye offend thee, pluck it out, and cast it from thee: it is better for thee to enter into life with one

14 George Whitefield, *The Sermons of George Whitefield*, ed. Lee Gatiss, 2 vols. (Wheaton, IL: Crossway, 2012), 1:451.

15 Thomas Brooks, *The Golden Key to Open Hidden Treasures*, in *The Works of Thomas Brooks*, ed. Alexander Grosart, 6 vols. (1866; repr., Edinburgh: Banner of Truth, 1980), 5:130, italics original.

16 Donnelly, *Biblical Teaching on the Doctrines of Heaven and Hell*, 53.

eye, rather than having two eyes to be cast into hell fire" (Matt. 18:9). While destroying a bodily organ will not put off sin (the language is figurative), we must deny ourselves to escape eternal punishment.

Fourth, *warn sinners of hell with tender urgency.* Robert Peterson says, "Jesus speaks frequently about hell because he is the Savior of the world. He warns of unspeakable torment in order to move his hearers to flee from the wrath to come."[17]

Fifth, *thank God for salvation in his Son.* Augustine said, "When reprobate angels and men are left to endure everlasting punishment, the saints shall know more fully the benefits they have received by grace. . . . For it is only of unmerited mercy that any is redeemed."[18]

Sixth, *worship the God of justice.* Sin and its destructive consequences should grieve us and draw forth our compassion for the perishing. But God's retribution against sinners is not evil. It is good, beautiful, and magnificent. Let us therefore glorify him for his just judgment on sinners and do so with hearts that rejoice in him as the righteous Judge.

Suggested Songs to Sing to the Lord

- Psalm 11, "In God will I trust," *Psalter*, No. 20
- "When this passing world is done," *THBap*, No. 600

Questions for Meditation or Discussion

1. What indications of the fires of hell do we find in the prophecy of Isaiah?
2. What did Christ teach about eternal punishment?
3. What do we learn about eternal punishment in Paul's epistles and in Revelation?
4. What do the authors mean when they say, "Hell is the logical and just consequence of all sin"?
5. How can we respond to the objections that God would be unjust and unloving to send people to hell?
6. How does the doctrine of hell test whether we are man-centered or God-centered?

17 Robert A. Peterson, *Hell on Trial: The Case for Eternal Punishment* (Phillipsburg, NJ: P&R, 1995), 55.

18 Augustine, *Enchiridion*, chap. 94, in *NPNF*[1], 3:267.

7. Why is it inadequate to say that sinners in hell suffer merely because they lose God?
8. How can we prove from the Holy Scriptures that the doctrine of universal salvation is false?
9. Someone says, “The wicked will be destroyed and exist no more.” How do you respond?
10. How has reading this chapter affected your attitude toward sin? Toward Christ?

95

Eternal Life with God

Chapter Summary and Key Terms

The great hope of believers is Christ's second coming to bring them into the enjoyment of *eternal life with God.* After the resurrection of the dead and the day of judgment, believers in Christ will enter their eternal inheritance in the new heaven and the new earth. By his Spirit, God will renew creation into a righteous paradise with Christ as the last Adam. In the world to come, believers will know and show forth the riches of God's infinite love and glory in Christ. They will enjoy friendships with the saints and angels, and everlasting rest from hardship and oppression. Believers will serve God forever as revealing prophets, worshiping priests, and reigning kings. Therefore, let us set our minds on things above, where Christ reigns, and on the hope of his coming. Let us also love one another with patience and endurance, believing that the saints will be one family forever.

JUDGMENT DAY WILL LAUNCH each person into one of two destinies: eternal punishment or eternal life (Matt. 25:46). Eternal life is far more than unending existence. It is the state of blessedness in God's kingdom (v. 34). God gives the beginning of eternal life to believers in Christ now (John 3:16; 5:24), but the fullness of that life awaits the age to come (Col. 3:3–4).

The teaching concerning eternal life is also called the doctrine of *heaven*. But the word *heaven* is also used of the place where the spirits of deceased believers presently live with Christ (see chap. 89). Here we focus on the state of resurrected believers in the new heaven and new earth after Christ returns.

The World to Come

God promises his people that their present state in this world will not continue forever. They will enter eternal happiness in his presence when Christ returns. This is their hope.

God has begun the new creation in Christ and those in union with him (2 Cor. 5:17; Eph. 2:10). But the scope of the new creation will ultimately extend to the new heaven and the new earth (Isa. 65:17; 66:22). There God will fulfill the promises of the kingdom that his people will inherit (9:6–7; Dan. 2:34–35, 44; 7:14, 27; Rev. 11:15–18).

The new creation will be the old creation made new. There are several reasons to believe this. First, the dead will not receive entirely new bodies. Rather, their old bodies will be raised from the dead to new life (1 Cor. 15:42–44). Second, God says that he will "make all things new," which is different from destroying this creation and making another one (Rev. 21:5). Third, creation will be set free to share in the glory of God's children (Rom. 8:21). Fourth, the burning of heaven and earth will be like the refining of metals by fire to purify them, not to annihilate them (2 Pet. 3:5–13).[1]

The Holy Spirit will renew creation. The Spirit of God brought order and blessing to the first creation (Gen. 1:2). In the future, he will restore peace to God's world so that none of God's creatures will harm another (Isa. 11:1–9). The earth that was made into a wilderness by God's curse on our sin will be transformed by the Holy Spirit into a beautiful and fruitful place (32:15–17; cf. Isaiah 35). The "desert" will become "like Eden . . . like the garden of the Lord" (51:3; cf. Ezek. 36:28–30, 35). John Calvin said, "There will be a blessed restoration of the world."[2]

Jesus Christ will be the center of the world to come. He is "the last Adam" (1 Cor. 15:45). In him, God will achieve his purpose for humanity to have dominion over the earth (Heb. 2:6–10). The Son is the heir of all things (1:2). All things were made through him and for him (Col. 1:15–17). John writes, "The Father loveth the Son, and hath given all things into his hand" (John 3:35). Thomas Boston said, "As we derive our grace from the Lamb, so we shall derive our glory from Him too." He added that Christ may be

1 Francis Turretin, *Institutes of Elenctic Theology*, trans. George Musgrave Giger, ed. James T. Dennison Jr., 3 vols. (Phillipsburg, NJ: P&R, 1992–1997), 20.5 (3:590–96); and Cornelis P. Venema, *The Promise of the Future* (Edinburgh: Banner of Truth, 2000), 460–69.

2 Calvin, *Comm.* on Isa. 11:6.

called "the centre of the divine glory in heaven, from whence it is diffused unto all the saints."[3]

The centrality of Jesus will not diminish the supremacy of God. Christ is the Mediator of the triune God. It is the God of glory, God the Father, the Son, and the Holy Spirit, who will give himself to us in Christ. Then God will be "all in all" (1 Cor. 15:28). Thus, the new world will resound with Paul's heartfelt praise: "Thanks be to God, which giveth us the victory through our Lord Jesus Christ!" (v. 57).

The new world will be the place of perfect righteousness. Peter says, "We, according to his promise, look for new heavens and a new earth, wherein dwelleth righteousness" (2 Pet. 3:13). There will be no sin and no sinners in the eternal city of God (Isa. 52:1; Rev. 21:27). It will truly be "the holy city" (Rev. 21:2), "the city of righteousness, the faithful city" (Isa. 1:26), for the Lord will dwell there (Zech. 8:3). God will completely conform each one of his people to his image (Rom. 8:29; 1 John 3:2).

God wants his saints to set their thoughts and affections on the world to come. Peter says, "Therefore, preparing your minds for action, and being sober-minded, set your hope fully on the grace that will be brought to you at the revelation of Jesus Christ" (1 Pet. 1:13 ESV). Paul likewise commands believers to focus their minds on Christ and to pursue his glory (Col. 3:1–2, 4). Richard Baxter said, "A heavenly mind is a joyful mind," and "a heart in heaven will be a most excellent preservative against temptations." He added, "The frequent, believing views of glory are also the most precious refreshment in all afflictions."[4]

The World of Love

We now turn to specific themes about the world to come. The first is God's love toward his people. Jonathan Edwards said, "Heaven is a world of love."[5]

God's love will heal and comfort his people. Their healing springs from God's Son dying as the substitute under the penalty for their sins (Isa. 53:5), but the complete healing of believers awaits the perfect consolation of the age to come. At the resurrection of the dead and the beginning of

3 Thomas Boston, *Human Nature in Its Fourfold State* (Edinburgh: Banner of Truth, 1964), 449.

4 Richard Baxter, *The Saints' Everlasting Rest*, ed. Tim Cooper (Wheaton, IL: Crossway, 2022), 96–99.

5 Edwards, *Charity and Its Fruits*, in *WJE*, 8:368.

"a new heaven and a new earth, . . . God shall wipe away all tears from their eyes; and there shall be no more death, neither sorrow, nor crying, neither shall there be any more pain: for the former things are passed away" (Rev. 21:1, 4).

Christ will become our holy companion. The Lord Jesus promises, "In my Father's house are many mansions: if it were not so, I would have told you. I go to prepare a place for you. And if I go and prepare a place for you, I will come again, and receive you unto myself; that where I am, there ye may be also" (John 14:2–3). He prays, "Father, I will that they also, whom thou hast given me, be with me where I am" (17:24). Paul concludes his teaching on the resurrection and rapture of the church by saying, "So shall we ever be with the Lord" (1 Thess. 4:17).

In Christ, we will have God. Augustine said,

> God Himself, who is the Author of virtue, shall there be its reward; for, as there is nothing greater or better, He has promised Himself. What else was meant by His word through the prophet, "I will be your God, and ye shall be my people," than, I shall be their satisfaction, I shall be all that men honorably desire—life, and health, and nourishment, and plenty, and glory, and honor, and peace, and all good things?[6]

The day of Christ's return will be his wedding day to his people (Rev. 19:7–8; 21:2, 9). The prophet Isaiah declares, "As the bridegroom rejoiceth over the bride, so shall thy God rejoice over thee" (Isa. 62:5). And Zephaniah says, "The LORD thy God in the midst of thee is mighty; he will save, he will rejoice over thee with joy; he will rest in his love, he will joy over thee with singing" (Zeph. 3:17). Bernard of Clairvaux said,

> [God will] intoxicate his dearest ones with the torrent of his delight. . . . Here is fullness without disgust, insatiable curiosity which is not restless, an eternal and endless desire which knows no lack, and lastly, that sober intoxication which does not come from drinking too much, which is no reeking of wine, but a burning for God.[7]

6 Augustine, *The City of God*, 22.30, in *NPNF*[1], 2:510.

7 Bernard of Clairvaux, *On Loving God*, 11.33, in *Selected Works*, trans. G. R. Evans (New York: Paulist Press, 1987), 199.

Are you preparing for the marriage of the Lamb? Make sure that you are betrothed to Christ. Do you trust him alone for salvation from sin (Matt. 1:21)? By grace, do you love Christ more than this world and your life in it (Matt. 10:37–39; 13:44)? If so, then meditate often on God's eternal love for you. And respond to God's love with many works of love. Prepare for the great wedding day by living wholeheartedly in devotion to him. Fill your time, by his grace, with good works that you will be privileged to present to him on that day for his pleasure. As you wait for his return, let your love for God overflow in daily praise (Ps. 136:1). This will be your preparation for the eternal worship in the new heaven and the new earth.

The World of Glory

Another theme of eternal life is the glory of God. Saved by grace, believers exult "in hope of the glory of God" (Rom. 5:2). God's glory is his majestic presence displayed to his creatures. Edward Donnelly said, "Heaven does not exist primarily for our sake. . . . Heaven exists for God's own glory."[8]

Though the revelation of God's glory in the world to come is a profound mystery, the Holy Scriptures reveal certain truths about it to stir our hope.

First, *believers will see God's glory in a far greater way than they do now.* Presently, they see his glory dimly, as in a reflection, but in that day they will see him "face to face" (1 Cor. 13:12). In the Bible, God's "face" refers to a powerful display of his presence, whether in mercy (Ps. 67:1) or in wrath (Rev. 6:16). In our mortal state, no one can see the majesty of God's face and live (Ex. 33:20), but in the new creation, his saints "shall see his face" (Rev. 22:4).

Second, *believers will see God's glory in his incarnate Son.* Christ says, "Father, I will that they also, whom thou hast given me, be with me where I am; that they may behold my glory, which thou hast given me: for thou lovedst me before the foundation of the world" (John 17:24). The "blessed hope" of the saints is "the appearing of the glory of our great God and Savior Jesus Christ" (Titus 2:13 ESV). The Son of God is "the brightness of his glory, and the express image of his person" (Heb. 1:3). Christ will be the central, supreme, and pervasive display of God's glory in the new heaven and the new earth (Rev. 21:23).

8 Edward Donnelly, *Biblical Teaching on the Doctrines of Heaven and Hell* (Edinburgh: Banner of Truth, 2001), 77.

Third, *believers will see God's glory with an inward, experiential knowledge.* Christ will be physically visible to the eyes of everyone when he returns. But God will also grant his people a special spiritual vision of his glory, called the *beatific vision of God*. John says, "Beloved, now are we the sons of God, and it doth not yet appear what we shall be: but we know that, when he shall appear, we shall be like him; for we shall see him as he is" (1 John 3:2). This seeing of God must be more than a physical sight because it will transform us. God reserves this vision for those he purifies by grace to commune with him. Christ says, "Blessed are the pure in heart: for they shall see God" (Matt. 5:8).

Fourth, *believers will see God's glory in every part of the new creation.* Under Christ's influence, the entire new creation will radiate God's glory. This is symbolized in John's vision of a city of gems and transparent gold (Rev. 21:11, 18, 21). The angels will be there (v. 12), and they are means by which God's glory shines (Luke 2:9; 9:26). The saints will be the flawless visible images of God (Rom. 8:29). Each believer will be a marvelous display of God's glory to one another (Matt. 13:43). Even their bodies will be glorified in resurrection life (1 Cor. 15:43; Phil. 3:21). Thus, the whole redeemed creation will be fine-tuned for the worship of the God of glory.

Since the world to come is the world of glory, learn that God's glory is the purpose of your existence. In all that you do, you should strive to glorify God (1 Cor. 10:31) and to delight in his glory as he shows it in your life (Ps. 37:4). You will never be satisfied apart from God's glory. Augustine said, "Thou hast formed us for Thyself, and our hearts are restless till they find rest in Thee."[9] Live especially for Christ. In the new world, everything you see and everyone you meet will remind you of Christ and help you know him better. But this joy will belong only to those who have been sanctified. Therefore, the proper preparation for eternal glory is holiness. Exercise yourself in godliness to train yourself for eternity (1 Tim. 4:7–8).

The World of Friendship

Another reason why heaven is a world of love is because of the friendships that we will share with other believers. The redeemed will be "a great multitude, which no man could number, of all nations, and kindreds, and

9 Augustine, *Confessions*, 1.1.1, in *NPNF*[1], 1:45.

people, and tongues" (Rev. 7:9). Donnelly said, "Throughout eternity we will have the joy of meeting millions of brothers and sisters of whose existence we had previously been unaware. . . . We will encounter Christians from every century, nationality and culture."[10] We will be rich in relationships.

All believers will live together in perfect love and harmony. William Bates said, "Love is the beauty and strength of societies, the pleasure of life. How excellent is the joy of the blessed, when the prayer of Christ shall be accomplished, that they all may be one; 'as thou, Father, art in me, and I in thee, that they also may be one in us' [John 17:21]."[11]

The saints will still have their personal identities (Matt. 17:3; Luke 13:28). The friendships they share with one another now will last forever (Philem. 15–16). Marriage ends with death and will not continue after the resurrection (Luke 20:35), but the love and friendship between godly spouses in this life will be better than ever. When believers meet one another in the new world, what joy, gratitude, and love they will share! Paul says, "For what is our hope, or joy, or crown of rejoicing? Are not even ye in the presence of our Lord Jesus Christ at his coming? For ye are our glory and joy" (1 Thess. 2:19–20).

Every person in heaven will be like a gem through which God's glory will sparkle and like a channel through which his love will flow. All our kindness and delight in one another will serve to express and intensify our love for God and knowledge of his love for us. As we mentioned earlier, angels also will be citizens of the new Jerusalem and worshipers in God's presence (Heb. 12:22; Rev. 21:12), and it will be part of the blessedness of the saints to know them and enjoy fellowship with them. Living in the company of so many blessed and glorious friends will multiply the eternal happiness of God's saints. And all this happiness will be from God, in him, and for his glory.

Therefore, believers, regard your spiritual family—the worldwide people of God—as part of your reward in Christ. Invest in Christian friendships, knowing that you will be friends forever. Perhaps you are suffering from loneliness. If so, rejoice that by faith in Christ you are part of a great family whom you will enjoy forever. Thus, seek unity among the children of God.

10 Donnelly, *Biblical Teaching on the Doctrines of Heaven and Hell*, 118.

11 William Bates, *The Four Last Things*, in *The Whole Works of the Rev. W. Bates*, ed. W. Farmer, 4 vols. (repr., Harrisonburg, VA: Sprinkle, 1990), 3:397.

Christopher Love said, "This is a great blemish to this estate, that believers, that shall partake of the same glory, and have fellowship in the same happiness, yet while they live a life in this world, cannot live in love, that there should be jars [quarrels] and contentions among us."[12]

The World of Rest

The kingdom of God will be a place of rest from our hard labor and spiritual warfare against the world, the flesh, and the Devil. The church will experience the fulfillment of Christ's invitation: "Come unto me, all ye that labour and are heavy laden, and I will give you rest" (Matt. 11:28).

God revealed the saints' everlasting rest in two ancient types: the Sabbath day and the promise of rest in the land of Canaan (Heb. 3:7–4:11). The Sabbath is a creation ordinance of weekly rest from ordinary work (Gen. 2:1–3).[13] One day, the saints' hard labor will be done because "there shall be no more curse" (Rev. 22:3). As a result, as Boston said, "their work is their rest, and continual recreation, and toil and weariness have no place there."[14]

God promised rest to Israel in the land of Canaan (Ex. 33:14; Deut. 3:20). He especially gave his people rest when they enjoyed their inheritance without being attacked or oppressed by their enemies (Deut. 12:9–10; Josh. 21:44). Israel's rest in the land foreshadowed the rest that believers will enter when they will "inherit the kingdom" (Matt. 25:34). Christ the King will reign over his kingdom of peace forever (Isa. 9:6–7). The saints will then enjoy absolute safety from evil (Rev. 21:12) and stability in an unshakeable kingdom (Heb. 12:26–28). There will be no more unjust oppression. The wicked will be in hell. God's people will be like the resurrected Christ, free forever from all temptation, sorrow, and sin (Rom. 8:29; 1 Cor. 15:45–49).

Since believers hope in the everlasting rest of God, we should labor hard for the Lord in this life. We should also keep the weekly Sabbath for refreshment of body and soul, and in anticipation of the everlasting Sabbath. Believers can endure injustice with patience and hope, knowing that Christ will liberate us from all oppression. When fear and anxiety disturb us, we can find our stability in the Lord and his eternal kingdom.

12 Christopher Love, *Heavens Glory, Hells Terror* (London: John Rothwell, 1653), 1:24.

13 On the Sabbath, see our discussion of the fourth commandment in chap. 69.

14 Boston, *Human Nature in Its Fourfold State*, 441.

The World of Service

God made human beings in his image for activity and service (Gen. 1:26–28; 2:15). Restored to paradise, redeemed men and women will serve the Lord forever (Rev. 22:1–3).[15]

First, *the saints will serve God as revealing prophets*. God will constantly reveal himself through his people because they will be perfectly conformed to the image of Christ (Rom. 8:29). John says, "His name shall be in their foreheads" (Rev. 22:4). This is a symbol for reflecting God's character.[16] Christ says, "The righteous [will] shine forth as the sun in the kingdom of their Father" (Matt. 13:43). Thus, they will be like the prophet Moses (Ex. 34:29–35) and Jesus Christ, the Son of God and the great Prophet (Matt. 17:1–5). God's people will see him "face to face" and "know even as also [they are] known" (1 Cor. 13:8–12). God has called the church to "proclaim the excellencies of him who called you out of darkness into his marvelous light" (1 Pet. 2:9 ESV). Thus, all human activities in the new creation will show the greatness and goodness of God. John Piper says, "As each of us sees Christ and delights in Christ with the delight of the Father, mediated by the Spirit, we will overflow with visible actions of love and creativity on the new earth. In this way we will see the revelation of God's glory in each other's lives in ever new ways."[17]

Second, *the saints will serve God as worshiping priests* (Rev. 1:6; 5:10; 20:6). They will eternally offer sacred worship in God's presence for his pleasure and blessing. God makes them a "holy priesthood, to offer up spiritual sacrifices, acceptable to God by Jesus Christ" (1 Pet. 2:5). In the eternal city of God, there will be no temple because his glorious presence will fill all things (Rev. 21:3, 23). Augustine said, "There shall we rest and gaze, gaze and love, love and praise."[18] God's glory will shine in the saints'

15 The idea of serving God in the eternal kingdom may not make sense if people think that the saints will exist in a state of timeless eternity. But glorification does not make human beings into God. Believers will continue to experience time in some sense even in the new heaven and the new earth.

16 G. K. Beale with David H. Campbell, *Revelation: A Shorter Commentary* (Grand Rapids, MI: Eerdmans, 2015), 68–70, 503.

17 John Piper, *God Is the Gospel: Meditations on God's Love as the Gift of Himself* (Wheaton, IL: Crossway, 2005), 162.

18 Augustine, *The City of God*, 22.30, cited in K. E. Kirk, *The Vision of God: The Christian Doctrine of the Summum Bonum*, 2nd ed. (1932; repr., New York: Harper & Row, 1966), 330; cf. *NPNF*[1], 2:511.

expressions of adoration to God and his expressions of sovereign pleasure toward them. They will draw ever closer to him in the infinite depths of his goodness and love. God has saved us "so that in the coming ages he might show the immeasurable riches of his grace in kindness toward us in Christ Jesus" (Eph. 2:7 ESV). This will move us into ever increasing heights of "the praise of the glory of his grace" (1:6).

Third, *the saints will serve God as reigning kings* (Rev. 1:6; 5:9–10). They will reign with Christ (2 Tim. 2:12; Rev. 3:21; 22:5). Boston said, "All Christ's subjects will be kings . . . not that the great King shall divest Himself of His royalty, but He will make all His children partakers of His kingdom."[19] They will "inherit the earth" (Matt. 5:5). They will eat and drink with Christ in the kingdom (Luke 22:16, 18, 30). They will rule over whatever living creatures God may be pleased to put in the new world (Ps. 8:4–8; Heb. 2:5–10). Some believers may exercise higher authority than others in kingdom society (Luke 13:30; 19:17, 19).

The glory to come is beyond comparison to the sufferings of this life (Rom. 8:18; 2 Cor. 4:17). Heavenly treasures are far more valuable than earthly treasures (Matt. 6:19–20; 13:44–46). Therefore, we may conclude that the honor, majesty, riches, and authority to be granted to the least of the saints will make the greatest king on earth look like a beggar.

Given that Christians can look forward to serving the Lord forever as his prophets, priests, and kings, how should we live now? Let us begin by regarding service and work as blessings, not curses. Be faithful today in hope of greater service in eternity. Christ will say to his faithful servant, "Thou hast been faithful over a few things, I will make thee ruler over many things: enter thou into the joy of thy lord" (Matt. 25:21). Invest thought and effort in the service of worship, for it is the business of heaven.

Child of God, believe that you are in training to reign with Christ. Great kings may put their children through rigorous training to prepare them to rule. Never be ashamed of Christianity, for though its way passes through the valley of humiliation, it leads to glory. Calvin said, "The Lord will receive his faithful people into the peace of his Kingdom, will wipe away every tear from their eyes, will clothe them with a robe of glory and rejoicing, will feed them with the unspeakable sweetness of his delights, will elevate them

19 Boston, *Human Nature in Its Fourfold State*, 434.

to his sublime fellowship—in fine, will deign to make them sharers in his happiness."[20] Hallelujah! *Soli Deo gloria!*

Suggested Song to Sing to the Lord

- "The sands of time are sinking," *THBap*, No. 599

Questions for Meditation or Discussion

1. Why should we think that the new creation will be the old creation made new?
2. Why is it important for Christians to meditate on the world to come?
3. How will the world to come be a world of love?
4. How should we prepare for the marriage of the Lamb?
5. What is the beatific vision?
6. What can we learn from the hope that the new world will be full of God's glory?
7. How will our friendship with other believers enrich our joy in the kingdom?
8. What can we learn about the saints' everlasting rest from the Sabbath and Israel's rest in the land of Canaan?
9. How will God's people serve in the world to come as (1) prophets, (2) priests, and (3) kings?
10. How has reading this chapter affected your view of heaven? How has it increased your hope?

20 Calvin, *Institutes*, 3.9.6.

Glossary of Theological Terms

This glossary lists the key terms highlighted in the chapter summaries, along with other words important in theological discussions. Most terms are followed by a brief definition, a sentence or two explaining the doctrine, and a reference to the main chapter(s) in which they are discussed. Where a definition or explanation uses another term that is included in the glossary, that term is placed in *italics*, except for commonly used words such as *Christ* and *sin*.

For Greek and Latin terms, we recommend consulting Richard A. Muller, *Dictionary of Greek and Latin Theological Terms*, 2nd ed. (Grand Rapids, MI: Baker Academic, 2017).

active obedience: the perfect keeping of all God's commandments. Christ's active obedience as the *surety* of the *covenant of grace* was necessary to make *satisfaction* to the law's demand for full compliance to God's *preceptive will* so that believers would be forgiven of sin by Christ's *passive obedience* and counted righteous for his sake (chap. 48).

actual sins: thoughts, words, or deeds that are sin against God or people. Actual sins, the evil fruit produced by *original sin*, include *sins of omission* and *sins of commission* (chap. 36).

***actus purus*:** Latin for "pure act." God, in his *spirituality*, *simplicity* and *aseity*, is his own infinite life, having no unrealized potential but instead being the fullness of actualized perfection. Thus, God is pure act because God is love.

***ad extra*:** Latin for "to the outside," referring to God's acts of *creation* and *providence*.

***ad intra*:** Latin for "to the inside," referring to God's acts within himself. God's *decree* is *ad intra* in his will and knowledge, but *ad extra* in its orientation to the world.

adoption: the *saving grace* by which God takes sinners to be his beloved children. Adoption gives all believers the full rights and inheritance of the sons of God by their *union with Christ*, the eternal and only begotten (not adopted) Son of God (chap. 62).

adoptionism: the *heresy* that Jesus is a mere man whom God adopted as his Son at his baptism and glorified as Lord at his resurrection (chap. 44).

advocate: a person appointed to speak in court on behalf of another. The term is a common translation of the Greek word *paraklētos*, used as a title for Christ and the Holy Spirit (chaps. 49, 53).

aesthetics: the philosophical study of the nature of beauty, whether in nature or art.

affections of God: the attitudes and actions of God expressing his *attributes* in a way analogous to human emotions. These are God's affections with respect to his relationships to the created world, which include his *compassion*, *wrath*, *jealousy*, and delight, all exercised according to his *impassibility* and *beatitude* (chap. 18).

affusion: pouring. Affusion with water, especially on the head, is seen as a valid mode of *baptism* in *Anabaptism* and as one mode among others by many people holding to *paedobaptism* (chap. 83).

agnosticism: with regard to theology, the belief that we have no certain knowledge of God or his will. Agnosticism may be doubtful but open to the possibility of such knowledge, or it may assert the impossibility of knowing God and deny the doctrine of divine *revelation*.

amillennialism: another term for *inaugurated millennialism*, the doctrine that there will be no future *millennium* on earth because the millennium consists of Christ's present reign between his first and *second coming* (chap. 91).

Amyraldianism: the doctrine taught by Moïse Amyraut that God made a conditional *decree* to save all people if they have *faith in Jesus Christ* and, with his *foreknowledge* that no one would believe apart from *regeneration*, also decreed the *election* of some people to regeneration—placing tension in God's decree between his will to save all and his will to elect some.

Anabaptism: various Christian religious movements, such as the Amish and the Mennonites, that began in Europe during the *Protestant Reformation* of the sixteenth century. Anabaptism is characterized by *credobaptism*, seeking to follow Christ's ethical teachings, and separation from the world (including civil government and the military). Anabaptism should not be confused with *Baptist theology*.

analogical language: the use of words to describe God in a manner similar to human beings (not *equivocal language*) but not identical (*univocal language*). For example, God's "love" is like human love but only as is fitting for his *infinity*, *eternity*, *immutability*, and *incomprehensibility*. All true human language about God is analogical (chap. 9).

analogy of faith: the principle of interpreting Scripture according to an established *rule of faith*, such as the *Apostles' Creed* or the *Nicene Creed*.

analogy of Scripture: comparing one Scripture passage with another. This is the principle of interpretation, assuming *plenary, verbal inspiration*, that a passage of the Bible can be better understood by considering other passages that speak to the same topic (chap. 6).

anarchy: the lack of any recognized authority in a group of people, such as a church without *officers* or constitution (chap. 76).

angels: created, intelligent, heavenly spirits. Angels are not the spirits of human beings but a distinct order of beings who serve as God's worshipers, messengers, and warriors (chap. 27).

anhypostatic: term used to indicate that the human nature of Christ never existed as a *person* distinct from the Son but from its beginning was assumed by the person of the Son (*enhypostatic*). The word "anhypostatic" does not mean "impersonal."

animism: the belief that the world is full of spirits that must be appeased or manipulated to avoid suffering and gain knowledge and power. Animism is a form of *polytheism*, often leads to sorcery and spiritism, and may involve on a deeper level a philosophy of *pantheism* or *panentheism* (chap. 10).

annihilationism: the doctrine that God will destroy the conscious existence of the wicked in *hell*. Annihilationism is contrary to the Bible's teaching of *eternal punishment* (chap. 94).

anthropology: the doctrine of man or human nature (part 3).

anthropomorphism: metaphorical language describing God as if he were human, and especially as if he had a human body, such as biblical references to his "hand" despite his *infinity* and *spirituality* (chaps. 9, 11).

anthropopathism: metaphorical language describing God as if he had human emotions and *passions*, such as biblical references to God grieving despite his *beatitude* and *impassibility* (chaps. 9, 18).

antichrist: false teacher in professing Christianity. In the last days between Christ's *incarnation* and *second coming*, many antichrists have arisen, but it appears that one final antichrist will arise at the end of the age, the *man of sin* (chap. 90).

Apocrypha: several ancient books, written by Jews or Christians, not included in the Old Testament or New Testament of the *Holy Scriptures*. Such books were not produced by *inspiration* and thus lack the *authority* and *inerrancy* of the *Word of God* (chap. 6).

***apokatastasis*:** another term for *universal salvation*.

Apollinarianism: the *heresy* that Christ has no human soul. Apollinarius taught that Christ's incarnation consists of the union of the *Word* to a human body, with the Word functioning as Jesus's mind (chap. 44).

apologetics: the study of how to defend Christian doctrine or *ethics* against attacks from other religions and philosophies. Apologetics cannot produce *conversion*, but it can be a means of overcoming the objections of the unconverted and reassuring the saved.

apostasy: fully falling away from faith in Christ. Some people in the *visible church* will fall away from Christ, but God keeps everyone whom he has saved by *effectual calling*, resulting in the *perseverance of the saints* by God's *preservation* (chap. 64).

apostle: authorized messenger. In the New Testament, the word *apostles* especially refers to a group of men selected by Christ to be eyewitnesses of his resurrection, receive and speak new *special revelation*, write the *Word of God*, work *miracles*, and govern the church as its shepherds with its *elders*. Christ no longer gives apostles to the church (chap. 54).

Apostles' Creed: an ancient confession of Christian *dogma*. The creed, though often divided into twelve articles, was not written by the *apostles*, but does summarize *catholic* Christian beliefs (chap. 2).

apostolic: an *attribute of the Christian church*, that it is faithful to the doctrine and mission of the *apostles* of Jesus Christ (chap. 74).

apostolic succession: the doctrine that the true church is *apostolic* because of its historical connection with the apostles. Some churches claim apostolic succession by a supposedly unbroken series of ordinations from Christ's apostles to the bishops of today, but true apostolic succession consists of following the apostles' teaching in the *Holy Scriptures*.

applied revelation: God's work through *special revelation* to apply revealed truth for the renewal of the heart. Applied revelation does not add new content to special revelation, but opens the heart to receive the truth by the *illumination* of the Holy Spirit (chaps. 3, 8).

appropriations: in the doctrine of the *Trinity*, the teaching that though all the acts of God outside himself involve all three *persons* of the Trinity (*inseparable operations*), certain acts are especially appropriated to a particular *person*, such as the *indwelling of the Holy Spirit*.

arguments for God's existence: see *cosmological arguments*, *five ways of Thomism*, *ontological argument*, and *teleological argument*.

Arianism: the *heresy* that God the Father created the Son. Arius asserted that there was a time when the Son was not, contradicting the Bible's witness that Christ is God and so falling under the condemnation of the Council of Nicaea in AD 325 (chaps. 19, 44).

aristocracy: rule by gifted leaders. Christ has authorized the council of the *elders* to rule the church, but only as servants under his Word for the good of the people.

Arminianism: a view of salvation, named after Jacob Arminius, that seeks in *synergism* a middle road between *Pelagianism* and *Reformed theology*. Arminianism teaches *conditional* or *corporate election*, *unlimited atonement*, *prevenient grace*, and the possibility of the saved falling away to suffer *eternal punishment* (chaps. 23, 56–58, 64).

ascension of Christ: his physical, bodily going up to *heaven* forty days after his *resurrection*. Christ's ascension is an important step in his *exaltation*, for he sat down at God's right hand (*session*) to make *intercession* for his people and reign as *King* (chap. 45).

asceticism: severe treatment of the body for *sanctification*, especially in a life of poverty, submission to a religious order (as a monk or nun), and celibacy. Asceticism distorts Christ's call for self-denial into a supposedly higher form of holiness (chap. 63).

aseity of God: the *attribute of God* that he is independent from all other things. The aseity of God means that he exists, lives, and acts from himself as the "I AM" (Ex. 3:14), without being caused or receiving any good from any being outside of himself (chap. 12).

aspersion: sprinkling. Aspersion with water, especially on the head, is considered to be one valid mode of *baptism* by most theologians holding to *paedobaptism* (chap. 83).

assurance of salvation: a true and certain confidence that one is saved by grace. Unbelievers can have false assurance. Believers may lack assurance. True assurance stands primarily on God's promises in Christ. Assurance stands secondarily on the evidence of *saving faith* (the *mystical* and *practical syllogisms*), and the *witness of the Holy Spirit* (chap. 66).

Athanasian Creed: a confession of Christian *dogma*, especially faith in the *Trinity* and the *incarnation* of Christ. Despite its name, this *creed* was not written by Athanasius, but rather it reflects the theology of Augustine and is widely used in Western Christianity.

atheism: the belief that there is no God or divine being. Atheists still give worship to something, such as man (as in *secular humanism*) or government (as in *Marxism*) (chap. 10).

atonement: Christ's work to accomplish *reconciliation* for sinners. In the Bible, the word "atonement" (KJV) often translates Hebrew terms for *propitiation* (chap. 47).

attributes of God: the characteristics, virtues, and perfections that belong to God by his *divine nature*. God's attributes are inseparable from him as God. We may take any attribute and say, "By nature, God is . . . ," such as, "By nature, God is love" (chap. 9).

attributes of the Christian church: the characteristics of the church by God's grace. The Nicene Creed confesses one *holy*, *catholic*, and *apostolic* church (chap. 74).

authority of God: the *attribute of God* that he has the right to do and command what he pleases with his creatures. An aspect of his *sovereignty*, God's absolute authority arises from his nature as the only God and his relationship to the world as its Creator (chap. 15).

authority of the Holy Scriptures: the moral power of the *Word of God* to obligate people to believe all that it teaches and obey all that it commands them (chap. 6).

backsliding: a season in a believer's life when *faith in Jesus Christ* and obedience to him decrease and sin increases. Restoration from backsliding requires a believer to turn back to the Lord in *repentance* and to seek fresh supplies of *saving grace* through Christ (chap. 71).

baptism: the *sacrament* or *ordinance* of initiation into Christ and his church. Baptism with water does not save but is a sign to the person baptized of *union with Christ* in his death and resurrection for salvation and of union with the church under the *new covenant*. There are different views of the subjects of baptism: *paedobaptism* and *credobaptism*. Churches also baptize in different modes: *immersion*, *affusion*, and *aspersion* (chaps. 82–83).

baptism with the Holy Spirit: the pouring out of the Holy Spirit and *spiritual gifts* from the ascended Christ. Contrary to *Pentecostalism* and some other forms of *two-level Christianity*, baptism with the Spirit is granted to all *new covenant* believers upon conversion and unites them as the one *body of Christ* (chap. 53).

Baptist theology: *theology* holding to *credobaptism* by *immersion* and *congregationalism*. Baptist theology began with seventeenth-century English theologians who held views of God and salvation ranging from *Reformed theology* to *Arminianism*.

beatific vision of God: the intuitive knowledge of God granted to the *souls* of believers when they enter heavenly glory. The beatific vision makes the soul perfectly holy and happy (chap. 95).

beatitude of God: the *attribute of God* that he has infinite and perfect joy. Divine joy, one of the *affections of God*, is his limitless happiness arising from the fullness of his own perfection and his *sovereignty* over the world to manifest his *glory* in it (chap. 18).

biblical theology: the study of how a doctrine or theme of the Bible appears in a particular book or author of the Holy Scriptures and how it develops over the history of God's *special revelation*.

bishop: overseer. In *episcopal polity*, "bishop" is the title of an *office* over multiple elders and churches, but in the New Testament it refers to the same office as *elder* (chaps. 76–77).

blasphemy against the Holy Spirit: the unforgiveable sin of permanently hardening one's heart against the gospel and hatefully rejecting Christ and the Holy Spirit. This blasphemy is not merely speaking against the Spirit or resisting him but a settled disposition of rejecting him as evil despite his powerful work to convict a person (chap. 57).

body of Christ: a metaphor for the church, comparing its *union with Christ* to that of a body and its head (chap. 73).

born again: another term for *regeneration*.

bride of Christ: a metaphor for the church, comparing its *covenant* and relationship to the Lord to those of a wife to her husband (chap. 73).

Buddhism: religion of *panentheism* or a nonreligious philosophy originating in Asia from the teachings of Siddhartha Gautama. Buddhism seeks escape from craving and *reincarnation* by attaining *nirvana*. Some kinds of Buddhism are *Mahayana*, *Theravada*, and *Vajrayana* (chap. 10).

caesaropapism: another term for *civil supremacy*, literally meaning "the emperor is pope."

calendar day view: the interpretation of Genesis 1 as teaching the *creation* of all things in six literal days at the beginning of the history of the universe (chap. 24).

calling: God's summons. Calling may be to salvation (either the *general gospel call* or *effectual calling*), to *office* in the church (the *internal call* and the *external call to the ministry*), or to some other labor.

Calvinism: another term for *Reformed theology*, due to the influence of John Calvin on the movement, though he was not its first teacher. Sometimes, the term *Calvinism* is used to refer specifically to the *five points of Calvinism*.

canon: a rule or standard. The canon of the *Holy Scriptures* is the list of books belonging to the Bible because they are the *Word of God*. The canon consists of thirty-nine Old Testament books and twenty-seven New Testament books (chap. 6).

catastrophism: in geology, the belief that many major geological structures were formed by rapidly unfolding events. Biblical catastrophism includes the events of the *creation* week and the worldwide flood. Catastrophism contrasts with geological *uniformitarianism*.

catholic: universal, not limited to one place or people. *Catholic* does not refer to *Roman Catholicism* but to the *universal church* throughout the world, as recognized by the *marks of the true church*. *Catholic* is one of the *attributes of the Christian church*. The term is also used of fundamental doctrine that unites Christians, such as the *Nicene Creed* (chaps. 2, 74).

censure: an official rebuke of a church *member* as an act of *corrective church discipline* for *actual sin* that is either publicly known or has not been repented of after repeated appeals for *repentance*. Censure is often accompanied by *suspension* (chap. 85).

ceremonial law: *old covenant* forms of worship. The ceremonial law provides *types* of Christ and his work but no longer binds us to obedience now that Christ has come (chap. 68).

cessationism: the view that extraordinary *spiritual gifts* for *special revelation* (apostleship and prophecy) and signs and wonders (*miracles*, healing, and speaking in *tongues*) have ceased. Cessationism recognizes that the Spirit still gives power to speak and to serve through other gifts (chap. 54).

Chalcedon, Council of: a gathering of church leaders in AD 451 that explained Christ's *incarnation* as the joining of two natures in Christ without changing his *divine nature* or his human nature but uniting them indivisibly and forever in one *person* (chap. 44).

charismatic movement: forms of *continuationism* that spread in denominations that were not part of *Pentecostalism*. Charismatic theologians may or may not affirm the doctrine of *subsequence*, which says that believers must receive a distinct *baptism with the Holy Spirit* (chap. 54).

chrismation: anointing. According to the *sacramental system* of *Eastern Orthodoxy*, the *sacrament* of chrismation with holy oil is done with *baptism* to confer the gift and *sealing of the Holy Spirit*, somewhat like *confirmation* in *Roman Catholicism* (chap. 81).

Christ: a title of *office* for the Son of God. "Christ" is not Jesus's last name but a title meaning "anointed," for he is anointed by the Holy Spirit to serve as the *Prophet*, *Priest*, and *King* of the people given him by the Father in eternal *election* (chap. 42).

Christian: an adjective meaning related to the disciples of Christ. Christian theology is an act of discipleship done in submission to Christ by listening to his words (the *Holy Scriptures*) and imitating his example. Thus, it is an exercise of faith in Jesus Christ as the Son of God (chap. 2).

Christology: the doctrine of Christ (part 4, especially section 4B).

***Christus Victor*:** Latin for "Christ the Conqueror." See the *victory view of the atonement*.

church: the assembly of God's people in his *special presence* through the Son in the Holy Spirit. We distinguish between the *church militant* and the *church triumphant*, a *particular church* and the *universal church*, and the *visible church* and *invisible church* (chap. 73).

church militant: the church of Christ on earth before his second coming. The term *militant* means that the church on earth is constantly striving spiritually against the world, the flesh, and the Devil. The church militant is *particular* or *universal* (chap. 73).

church triumphant: the church of Christ in glory. The saints in *heaven* already experience the complete victory of Christ in their *souls*. At the *resurrection of the dead* at Christ's *second coming*, the whole church will enter glory with both soul and body (chap. 73).

***circumincessio*:** the Latin term for *perichoresis*.

circumstance of public worship: an ordinary thing used to assist *public worship* but not regarded as a holy act or *means of grace*. It need not be commanded in Scripture (*regulative principle of worship*). Examples include a building, seating, lighting, and amplification (chap. 80).

civil supremacy: a form of church government in which a ruler in the civil government has authority over the church's doctrine, officers, worship, ministry, and discipline. Civil supremacy is sometimes called *Erastianism* or *caesaropapism* (chap. 76).

civil use of the moral law: the application of the *moral law* to regulate conduct in society. One of the *three uses of the moral law*, the civil use is especially helpful to civil government in restraining sin, an aspect of *common grace* (chap. 68).

classis: according to the *polity* of *presbyterianism*, another term for a *presbytery* or a council of *elders* (including both *ruling elders* and *ministers of the Word* or *teaching elders*) governing a regional federation of *particular churches* (chap. 76).

Comforter: a translation of the Greek word *paraklētos*, used as a title for the Holy Spirit (chap. 53).

common grace: God's undeserved gifts to people in general, including life, knowledge, skill, conscience, and externally good behavior. Common grace, though a work of the Holy Spirit, is different from *saving grace*, which alone can bring salvation and eternal glory (chap. 52).

communicable attributes: the *attributes* of God classified by some theologians as being most like the *image of God* in man. Examples of attributes often considered to be communicable are the moral excellencies of goodness, love, truth, and righteousness.

communicant member: a church *member* who partakes of the *Lord's Supper* (chap. 73).

***communicatio idiomatum*:** Latin term for the *communication of properties* in the *incarnation*.

communication of properties: the sharing in the one *person* of Christ of all the *attributes of God* and all the properties of his human nature because of the *hypostatic union* of the *incarnation*. Thus, we can say, "God became man," and, "They crucified the Lord of glory," but not, "The divine nature became human nature," or "Man became God." *Lutheran theology* adds that Christ's human nature, without becoming God, partakes of the infinite divine majesty (*genus majestaticum*).

compassion of God: the affection of God's mercy to the suffering. God's compassion is often expressed in physical terms in the Bible to communicate his delight in showing kindness to those in misery, but it does not imply physical feelings or suffering in God (chap. 18).

compatibilism: the belief that *determinism* is consistent with the *free choice of the will.*

complementarianism: a modern statement of the classic doctrine that God created the two human *genders* to function in distinct but complementary ways in church and *marriage*. Thus, men and women are equally valuable but designed to be different.

concupiscence: sinful desire, either desire for sin or inordinate desire for a created good.

concurrence: God's working in and through his creatures by their natural properties. In the concurrence of his *providence*, God gives his creatures their power and directs them to fulfill his purposes, whether they act necessarily, freely, or contingently (chap. 26).

conditional election: the doctrine often taught in *Arminianism* that in *election* to salvation God chose individuals because he knew that they would believe in Christ and follow him to the end. *Reformed theology* asserts that God's eternal election is unconditional, being based on his will and grace alone (chap. 23).

conditional immortality: the doctrine that only those persons given *eternal life with God* continue in conscious existence forever, and the rest cease to exist. Conditional immortality is contrary to the Bible's teaching of *eternal punishment* in *hell* (chap. 94).

confirmation: a religious rite of initiation subsequent to *baptism*. According to the *sacramental system* of *Roman Catholicism*, in the *sacrament* of confirmation a *bishop* anoints a baptized person with holy oil to seal and strengthen him by the Holy Spirit (chap. 81).

congregationalism: a church *polity* in which each *particular church* has full authority to govern itself according to God's Word without being subject to any officer or council outside of itself. Congregationalist churches may still form associations with one another for fellowship, cooperation, and mutual counsel. The term *congregationalism* does not indicate whether a church is governed by a single pastor, elders, or democracy (chap. 76).

connectionalism: networks of committed and cooperative relationships among *particular churches* and their *ministers*, whether according to *presbyterianism* or *congregationalism* (chap. 76).

conscience: the inner sense of having pleased or displeased God, the righteous Judge. God created the conscience in human nature to act as a witness of *general revelation* against sin and for righteousness, and it continues to do so today, albeit imperfectly (chap. 4).

consistory: according to the *polity* of *presbyterianism*, another term for a *session* or a council of *elders* (including both *ruling elders* and *ministers* or *teaching elders*) governing a *particular church. Consistory*, like *classis* and *synod*, is a term used in Reformed churches originating from continental Europe. In some Reformed churches (especially smaller ones), *deacons* also serve in the consistory (chap. 76).

consubstantiation: another term for the *Lutheran view of the Lord's Supper*. Lutheran theologians have generally rejected this term as an inaccurate summary of their view (chap. 84).

contingency: something not taking place by *necessity* but rather in a manner not predictable based on factors preceding it in the created order. On the level of *secondary causes*, some things are contingent and appear random or accidental, though planned in God's *decree* (chaps. 21, 26).

continuationism: the view that all *spiritual gifts* named in the New Testament continue today, including *miracles*, healing, speaking in *tongues*, and the gifts of being a *prophet* and perhaps even an *apostle*. The alternative to continuationism is *cessationism* (chap. 54).

conversion: turning to God with *repentance unto life* and *faith in Jesus Christ*. Conversion is both the response demanded by the *gospel* and the first fruit of *regeneration* (chap. 60).

corporate election: the doctrine of some forms of *Arminianism* that God chose to save believers as a category or group. Corporate election denies that God chose individuals, saying instead that he chose to save believers, whoever they might be (chap. 23).

corporate prayer: a *public means of grace* in which believers engage in *prayer* together, especially in a meeting of the church (chap. 85).

corrective church discipline: a *public means of grace* for the cleansing of sin in the church. Corrective discipline has four levels: personal reproof, private meeting with witnesses, *censure* (which some Reformed churches do in multiple steps), and *excommunication*. Its purposes are to manifest the *glory of God*, to keep the *visible church* pure and *holy*, and to seek the *repentance* and spiritual restoration of the offender (chap. 85).

cosmological arguments: arguments for God's existence as the only rational explanation for the motions, causation, and contingent existence of the observable universe. See the first three of the *five ways of Thomism*.

counsel of peace: the eternal plan of salvation in Christ made among the *persons* of the *Trinity*, also called the *covenant of redemption*. Some Reformed theologians regard it to be the *covenant of grace* from eternity, others a separate covenant (chap. 39).

covenant: a solemn promise that legally defines a relationship of loyalty. God's covenants define a Lord-servant relationship and often include laws to obey, a grant of authority to perform an *office*, representation of a group by an individual, and visible signs (chap. 32).

covenant of grace: according to *covenant theology*, God's solemn promises concerning Christ and salvation that bind together God and his saved people in all ages. God made various redemptive *historical covenants* with his people, each of which is considered an administration of the one covenant of grace (chap. 38).

covenant of redemption: another term for the *counsel of peace*. In this covenant, the Father promised to the Son an *elect* people and a *kingdom*, the Son promised the Father he would perform the work of *redemption*, and the Holy Spirit promised his effectual working of salvation in all the elect (chap. 39).

covenant of works: the covenant that God made with Adam as his official servant. God promised life or death to Adam and his offspring depending on whether he honored God as Lord by obeying his law regarding the covenant sign of the tree of the knowledge of good and evil (chap. 32).

covenant theology: the teachings of *Reformed theology* about the *covenant of grace*. Covenant theology says that God has revealed one *moral law*, one *gospel*, and one covenant of grace for the salvation of one people (the church) throughout history (chap. 38).

creation: God's act to make the universe and all that is in it, all very good. God's act of creation was the first step in executing his *decree* for his *glory*, began time and history, and demonstrates that God, the Creator, is infinitely greater than his creatures (chap. 24).

creation *ex nihilo*: God's making of the universe "out of nothing." God did not form the world out of matter that already existed but created its very substance (chap. 24).

creationist view of the soul: the belief that God creates a new *soul* out of nothing at the beginning of each human life. The origin of each soul is a mystery not revealed to us. (This term has nothing to do with one's view of the *creation* of the universe.)

creation ordinances: the ordered structures of human life ordained by the Creator. The first two chapters of Genesis reveal that at *creation* God established human work to subdue the earth, *Sabbath* rest, and *marriage* and procreation (chaps. 28, 68).

credible profession of faith: a testimony of one's *repentance unto life* and *faith in Jesus Christ*, confirmed by a life of obedience to God's law. Most churches require a credible profession of faith to receive someone as a *communicant member* (chap. 75).

credobaptism: the doctrine that *baptism* should be administered only to those who give a *credible profession of faith*. Credobaptists argue that baptism is the sign of *union with Christ* and his *body*, and that the Bible gives no command or example of the baptism of infants (*paedobaptism*) (chap. 83).

creed: a statement of Christian *dogma*. Ancient creeds that have long defined Christian *orthodoxy* include the *Apostles' Creed*, the *Nicene Creed*, the Definition of the *Council of Chalcedon*, and the *Athanasian Creed*.

Daoism: a religion of *pantheism* originating in China. Daoism teaches the oneness of all things, expressed in *dualism*, for life energy consists of the opposites of dark/passive and light/active, in which all gods and other beings participate and seek to maintain balance (chap. 10).

day-age view: the interpretation of Genesis 1 that explains each "day" as a long age, so that the six days represent a sequence of eons and eras. This would allow for the time necessary for the development of geological formations according to *uniformitarianism*. It also fits with either the *evolution* of biological life or *progressive creationism* (chap. 24).

day of judgment: the time when the Lord will glorify his *justice* by judging everyone according to his or her works. Christ will bless his *elect* with *eternal life* by his *saving grace*. He will condemn *Satan*, the *demons*, and unrepentant sinners to *eternal punishment* for their sins (chap. 93).

day of the Lord: another term for the *day of judgment*, emphasizing that God will openly display and exalt his *glory* on that day (chap. 93).

deacon: a person bearing *office* in the church to manage its material concerns, especially its ministries of mercy. Deacons have an office distinct from *elders* and *ministers of the Word,* and serve under their pastoral authority (chap. 78).

death: the punishment deserved by sin. Spiritual death separates the *soul* from God to be ruled by sin. Physical death separates the body from the soul to be ruled by decay. Eternal death separates the resurrected body and soul from all happiness to be ruled by God's *wrath* (chap. 33).

Decalogue: another term for the *Ten Commandments. Decalogue* means "ten words," which is a literal translation for the Hebrew phrase rendered "ten commandments" in the Bible (chap. 68).

decree of God: God's sovereign plan of all that will come to pass. God's decree is his eternal and sovereign will, according to his *wisdom* and *goodness,* in which he has decided everything that will take place outside of himself for his *glory* (chap. 21).

decretive will: God's *decree* of all that will take place. As distinct from his *preceptive will,* God's decretive will pertains to his power, not our responsibility (chap. 15).

definitive sanctification: God's *saving grace* by which he makes sinners into *saints* at the time of their *effectual calling* and *conversion.* In definitive sanctification, people die with Christ to sin and rise with him to a new life in the *state of grace* (chap. 63).

deification: the doctrine that believers can attain such union with God through Christ as to participate in his *uncreated energies* or *glory* while remaining human. *Reformed theology* speaks instead of *adoption* and *glorification* through *union with Christ* (chap. 55).

deism: in common usage, the belief in God as the Creator but not the God of *providence.* In more precise historical usage, deism is the belief in a God of nature and moral virtue, known by human reason, with the rejection of *special revelation* and *miracles.*

democracy: rule by the people. Christ has given the members of the church some authority, such as in voting for *officers,* but members are to use their authority not to do their own will but to follow the will of Christ revealed in the *Word of God* and to act in submission to the *elders* (chap. 76).

demons: *angels* that rebelled against God and now rule over this sinful world. The leader of the demons is known as *Satan* or the *Devil,* who works largely through deception (chap. 27).

descent into hell: the teaching of the *Apostles' Creed* that Christ "descended into hell." *Reformed theology* interprets this clause to mean not that Christ went to hell literally but that he experienced the essence of hell spiritually when he bore the full penalty of sin in his *state of humiliation*, culminating in his death and burial.

determinism: the belief that all events, including human choices, are fully determined by prior causes. Some people say that the doctrine of God's *sovereignty* implies determinism, but others do not because classic *Reformed theology* affirms *secondary causes* in the created order, with their *contingency* and liberty (*free choice of the will*), whereas God acts as the primary cause over that order.

Devil: the chief of the *demons*. The Greek word translated as "devil" means "accuser." This fallen *angel*, also known as *Satan*, rules over fallen mankind and opposes the church *militant* (chap. 27).

dialectical theology: another term for *neoorthodoxy*. The word *dialectical* refers to the relationship between opposites, such as the finite and the infinite, because neoorthodoxy emphasizes the infinite qualitative difference between man and God (chap. 5).

didactic use of the moral law: the application of the *moral law* to show believers how to please God after being saved by grace. One of the *three uses of the moral law*, the didactic use shows that the law continues to speak to believers as a rule to direct their lives (chap. 68).

diocese: the territory where a *bishop* has jurisdiction, according to *episcopal polity* (chap. 76).

discipline of the church: a *public means of grace* involving both *formative church discipline* and *corrective church discipline* (chaps. 74, 85).

dispensationalism: an *evangelical* theological system that teaches an absolute distinction between Israel and the New Testament church. It denies the one *covenant of grace* and teaches that God has two plans for his two peoples. Its doctrine of the last things teaches the *rapture* of the church (with the *resurrection* of Christians), the *tribulation*, Christ's *second coming*, the *resurrection* of Old Testament and tribulation saints, Israel's exaltation during the *millennium* (a form of *premillennialism*), a final revolt led by Satan, the *resurrection* and judgment of unbelievers, and then the eternal state (chaps. 38, 91).

divine nature: God's being or essence. The divine nature, which distinguishes God from all other beings, is known by the *attributes of God* (chap. 9).

docetism: the *heresy* that Christ only appeared human. Marcion taught that Christ did not have a body and did not experience suffering, for he was a spirit (chap. 44).

doctor: in its old sense, a teacher. The term *doctor* is sometimes used for a *theological professor* (chap. 77).

doctrine: teaching. Christian doctrine is the church's teaching based on the Bible, and a particular doctrine is teaching on a specific topic (chap. 1).

doctrines of grace: another term for the *five points of Calvinism*.

dogma: official doctrine established in a church's confessional statements.

dogmatics: another term for *systematic theology*, often used by Dutch Reformed theologians.

double predestination: a view of *predestination* that affirms both *election* and *reprobation*.

dualism: the belief that there are two eternal principles in the universe, such as God and the world, or spirit and matter. Dualism may express an underlying philosophy of *pantheism* (as in *Daoism*) or *panentheism* (as in *process theology*).

***dulia*:** in *Roman Catholicism*, the veneration appropriate to give to a created person, such as a saint in *heaven*, as opposed to the *latria* given to God alone.

dynamic monarchianism: another term for *adoptionism*.

earnest of the Holy Spirit: the work of the Spirit to produce *assurance of salvation*, in which his *indwelling* is compared to the down payment on a future inheritance (chap. 66).

Eastern Orthodoxy: a religious system originating in Eastern, Greek Christianity. Eastern Orthodoxy is characterized by belief in the *Nicene Creed* (without the *filioque*), the doctrine of the *Council of Chalcedon*, *mysticism* (participating in God's *uncreated energies* by *theosis*), *episcopal polity*, the use of *icons*, and a *sacramental system*. Against *Roman Catholicism*, it rejects the supreme authority of the *papacy* (chaps. 55, 81).

ecclesiology: the doctrine of the church (part 6).

eclectic approach to Revelation: an interpretation of the book of Revelation that combines insights from *preterism* (ancient context), *historicism* (partial fulfillments), *idealism* (spiritual principles), and *futurism* (events around the *second coming*) (chap. 90).

economic Trinity: the *Trinity* as revealed in God's actions toward the created world. The economic Trinity is not identical to the *immanent* or *ontological*

Trinity because of the *incarnation* of the Son and the accommodation of *special revelation* to human limits in *analogical language*, but God's acts still reveal much about who he is in himself.

edification of the church: the church's work to build up true believers into full maturity in Christ in doctrine, moral character, communion with God, unity, stability, and ministry. The whole work of the church is *public worship*, edification, and *evangelism* (chap. 80).

effectual calling: God's sovereign and effective summons of elect sinners to Christ. Effectual calling is *effectual grace* and not resistible *prevenient grace*, and so it has God's power to create *faith in Jesus Christ* and *repentance unto life* in all to whom it is given (chap. 58).

effectual grace: God's *saving grace* that not only offers salvation, as in the *general gospel call*, but effectively saves the sinner by changing the heart. Effectual grace is given only to God's *elect* in the execution of his *decree* of *election* through Christ (chap. 58).

efficacy of Christ's sacrifice: Christ's effective accomplishment of the salvation of all for whom he died. Christ did not merely make salvation possible but actually redeemed the *elect* so that they will be saved by *faith in Jesus Christ* and glorified (chap. 48).

efficient cause: an agent or power that produces an effect, such as the carpenter who makes a chair.

egalitarianism: a view of human *gender* that men and women should exercise the same authority and functions in the church (especially regarding holding *office*) and in the family (insofar as biology permits).

elder: a person bearing the *office* to shepherd a church as a member of its governing council. Elders may be distinguished as either *ministers of the Word* (*teaching elders*) or *ruling elders*. Another term for elder is *bishop* (chaps. 76–77).

elect: the people chosen by God in eternal *election*.

election: God's selection of those whom he will save by grace in Christ. Election is part of the *decree of God*, being an eternal act of love by the Trinity to choose certain individuals freely and unconditionally, not because of any *merit* or *faith in Jesus Christ* seen in them by God's *foreknowledge*, for salvation by his appointed means to the praise of his grace (chap. 22).

element of public worship: an act that God has set apart as holy in his Word and blesses as a *means of grace* in *public worship*. The elements of *new covenant* worship include Scripture reading, prayer, *preaching* and teaching the Word, singing God's praise, offering gifts, administering *baptism*, and celebrating the *Lord's Supper* (chap. 80).

emotions of God: another term sometimes used for the *affections of God*, but *emotion* may wrongly connote changes in God caused by the created world, *passions*, or physical sensations (contrary to God's *aseity*, *eternity*, *immutability*, *impassibility*, and *spirituality*) (chap. 18).

empiricism: the belief that observation by the senses is the sole (or at least the primary) source and final judge of knowledge. While empirical observation is very important to physical science, empiricism as a philosophy for all knowledge leads to *atheism* and *materialism*.

energies of God: the acts of his *divine nature*. See also *uncreated energies of God*.

enhypostatic: a term used to indicate that the human nature of Christ from its beginning was assumed by the *person* of the Son and never had an independent existence as a person distinct from him (*anhypostatic*).

episcopal polity: a form of church government in which a *bishop* has authority over a group of churches and their elders in a territory called a *diocese*. Multiple dioceses and their bishops are overseen by an archbishop or metropolitan (chap. 76).

epistemology: the philosophical study of the nature of knowledge.

equivocal language: the use of the same words but with different meanings, such as "I love fried potatoes" and "I love my wife." If our language about God were equivocal instead of *analogical*, we would have no certain knowledge of him (chap. 9).

Erastianism: another term for *civil supremacy* over the church, named after Thomas Erastus, though he only taught that the church should leave the discipline of sin to the state.

eschatology: the doctrine of the last things, especially Christ's *second coming* (part 7).

essential presence: the presence of God's being, which is not confined to his *special presence* where he manifestly reveals his glory but is unlimited by space (*immensity*) and is present in every location (*omnipresence*) (chap. 12).

establishment principle: the doctrine that civil government should punish false worship and open *heresy*, set up a national church in sound doctrine and discipline, and require all members of society to attend it (chap. 79).

eternal generation: the Father's act to "beget" the Son in the *divine nature* without a beginning in time. The only begotten Son is thus not created by

God but is God himself, sharing the same essence (*homoousion*) and yet distinct from the Father in the *Trinity* (chap. 19).

eternal life with God: the everlasting enjoyment of God's *glory* in Christ in the new creation. Though God gives eternal life immediately with *saving grace*, believers wait with *hope* for their deliverance from all evil and entrance into their eternal inheritance (chap. 95).

eternal procession: the Spirit's always being "breathed" from the Father and the Son. The Holy Spirit is not a creature or God's energy but a distinct *person* in the *Trinity*, sharing the same divine life and essence as the Father and the Son (chap. 19).

eternal punishment: the execution of God's *justice* against *Satan*, *demons*, and sinful human beings in *hell* (*gehenna*) forever. Eternal punishment consists in the loss of all good and the infliction of great suffering in body and *soul* according to one's sins (chap. 94).

eternal security: the doctrine that no one who receives *saving grace* can lose that salvation. Eternal security can refer to the *perseverance of the saints*, but it may wrongly suggest that people cannot go to *hell* if they pray for salvation or make a profession of faith.

eternity of God: the *attribute of God* that he cannot be limited in any way by time. God possesses the fullness of his infinite life as one complete whole and has no beginning, no end, and no succession of moments, but is fully present at all times (chap. 12).

ethics: the systematic study of human moral obligations to God and one another. Biblical ethics is closely related to the *moral law* of God, especially in its *didactic use*.

Eucharist: another term for the *Lord's Supper*, derived from the Greek term for "thanksgiving" (chap. 84).

Eutychianism: the *heresy* that Christ is one *person* with one divine-human nature (*monophysitism*). Eutyches overreacted to the error of *Nestorianism* and taught that Christ's human nature became divine by union with his *divine nature* (chap. 44).

evangelical: characterized by the *gospel*. *Evangelical theology* centers on the proclamation of the *gospel* according to the *Reformation* teachings of *sola Scriptura*, *sola gratia*, *solus Christus*, *sola fide*, and *soli Deo gloria* (chap. 2).

evangelicalism: various movements in the modern Western world that affirm the *Trinity*, the *inspiration* of the Bible, salvation through Christ's death, and the need for *evangelism* and *conversion* for salvation.

evangelical use of the moral law: the use of the *moral law* to convict the *conscience* of sin and the need for salvation. One of the *three uses of the moral law*, this is helpful in *preaching* the *gospel* to unbelievers and keeping believers dependent on Christ (chap. 68).

evangelism: communicating the *gospel* to unbelievers with the loving desire for their conversion. Christ commissioned his church to do the work of evangelism, together with the works of *edification of the church* and *public worship* (chap. 80).

evolution: the biological theory that all life on earth developed from common ancestors by a natural process over billions of years. Evolution contradicts the doctrine of *creation* that God supernaturally created each kind of plant and animal, and lastly made man of the earth. Biological evolution has spawned similar ideas concerning political evolution (such as *Marxism*) and technological evolution (such as *transhumanism*) (chaps. 25, 87).

exaltation of Christ: see *state of exaltation.*

exclusive psalmody: the principle that the only *songs of praise* permitted in *public worship* are songs taken from the book of Psalms. Early *Reformed theology* taught the practice of either exclusive psalmody or the singing of the Psalms and a few other songs (chap. 85).

excommunication: the removal of a person from being a *member of the Christian church* as an act of *corrective church discipline*. Excommunication is done after several unsuccessful appeals and steps of discipline seeking the person's repentance from *heinous sin* (chap. 85).

exegesis: the study of the meaning of a written text, especially the *Holy Scriptures.*

***ex nihilo*:** Latin phrase meaning "out of nothing"; see *creation ex nihilo.*

***ex opere operato*:** Latin phrase meaning "by the performance of the work." This phrase is used in *Roman Catholicism* to teach that the *sacramental system* imparts grace effectively by the ceremonies themselves, unless the recipient places an obstacle in the way (chap. 81).

experiential knowledge: the knowledge of the triune God and his saving truth revealed in the *Holy Scriptures* and applied by the Holy Spirit to the *sanctification* of the believer's mind, will, and affections. God works through the *means of grace* (both *public* and *private*) to produce an experiential knowledge of misery in sin, deliverance in Christ, and grateful love to God so that the believer yearns to live fully for the *glory of God.*

experimental knowledge: another term for *experiential knowledge*. The word *experimental* draws attention to the need to test spiritual experience by the *Holy Scriptures*.

expiation: the removal of legal guilt and liability to punishment. Christ accomplished the expiation of his people's sins by making *satisfaction* to the *justice* of God (chap. 47).

external calling: another term for the *general gospel call*.

external call to the ministry: God's confirmation through the church of a man's calling to bear *office* in the church. The external call, which is made official by *ordination*, validates the *internal call to the ministry* but is no substitute for it (chap. 77).

***extra Calvinisticum*:** doctrine in the early church and *Reformed theology* that Christ's *divine nature* continued to exist and operate beyond the limits of his human nature after the *incarnation*, in contradiction to the doctrine of the *genus majestaticum* in *Lutheran theology*.

extreme unction: the *sacrament* of healing the sick or preparation for death in the *sacramental system* of *Roman Catholicism* and *Eastern Orthodoxy*. Extreme unction involves anointing with holy oil and is said to provide forgiveness of sins and increase of grace (chap. 81).

faithfulness of God: see *truth of God*.

faith in Jesus Christ: a *saving grace* in which a sinner receives Christ and rests on him alone for salvation from sin. Saving faith involves knowledge of the *gospel*, assent to its truth, and trust in Christ. Faith comes with *repentance unto life* and produces *good works* (chap. 60).

fall of man: the human race's loss of the *state of innocence* and being imprisoned in the *state of sin* as the result of Adam's breaking the *covenant of works*, in which he stood as the covenant representative of mankind (chap. 33).

fatalism: the belief that everything moves toward predetermined results, regardless of what we choose or do. Fatalism destroys human responsibility, but the doctrine of God's *decree* establishes responsibility, for God decrees causes and effects, means and ends (chap. 21).

Father: the first *person* of the *Trinity*. He is "first" not in time or in greatness but in personal relations in the Trinity because he begets the Son (*eternal generation*) and with the Son breathes forth the Holy Spirit (*eternal procession*) in the *divine nature* (chaps. 19–20).

fear of the Lord: a childlike awe of God and desire to please him. Unlike other kinds of fear toward God, which unbelievers may have, the godly fear of the Lord is a *saving grace* based on *love* for him and a sanctifying awareness of his holy *glory* (chap. 71).

federal union: the bond between Christ and his *elect* in the *covenant of grace*. Federal union establishes Christ as their representative before God so that he died for their sins and rose for their *justification*, but it does not give life (as does *mystical union*) (chap. 55).

fellowship, Christian: a *means of grace* in which believers share life together for mutual *edification* and service. Christian fellowship involves friendships with spiritual conversations, mutual service for practical help, and partnership in *evangelism* (chap. 85).

***filioque*:** Latin phrase meaning "and from the Son." Western theologians added this phrase to the *Nicene Creed* to express the Holy Spirit's *eternal procession* not only from the Father but also from the Son, which offended *Eastern Orthodoxy* (chap. 19).

filling of the Holy Spirit: a large degree of the Spirit's empowerment of God's people. This filling may be experienced multiple times and in various measures. It may result in increased godliness, wisdom, effective ministry, and communion with God (chap. 65).

final cause: the purpose or end of an effect, such as making a chair to provide a place for someone to sit.

finality of Christ's sacrifice: the completion of the accomplishment of *redemption* with Christ's death. This finality means that no other sacrifice for sins needs to be added (chap. 48).

final judgment: another term for the *day of judgment*.

finite theism: the belief in a limited God who is distinct from the world. Finite theists might believe that God is limited in power and knowledge (*open theism*) or that God's power consists entirely in the ability to offer emotional support and spiritual guidance (*moralistic therapeutic deism*) (chap. 10).

firstfruits of the Holy Spirit: the work of the Spirit to produce *assurance of salvation*, compared to the first part of a harvest. The *indwelling of the Holy Spirit* is the first taste that believers enjoy of the coming glory that will be theirs in Christ (chap. 66).

five points of Calvinism: a popular summary of the doctrine of salvation in *Reformed theology* as set forth in the Canons of Dort against *Arminianism*.

In recent times, the five points have been stated with the acronym TULIP: *total depravity*, *unconditional election*, *limited atonement*, *irresistible grace*, and the *perseverance of the saints*.

five ways of Thomism: arguments made by Thomas Aquinas for the existence of God from the observable world: (1) all motion must come from a mover, so there must be a first unmoved mover; (2) everything must have a cause, so there must be a first cause; (3) things in the world do not necessarily exist, so their existence must come from something that does necessarily exist; (4) every good comes from something better, so there must be something perfect behind all good; and (5) things show a wise design, so there must be a wise designer.

folk religion: another term for *animism*.

foreknowledge of God: the *attribute of God* that he has complete knowledge of all future events. The foreknowledge of God is well established by many predictive prophecies in Scripture but is contradicted by *process theology* and *open theism* (chap. 14).

formal cause: the design or essential idea of an effect, such as the drawings for a chair made by a carpenter or the idea he has in his mind of what the chair will be.

formative church discipline: the use of the ministry of the Word and mutual exhortation among members for the purpose of *edification* in the church (chap. 85).

form of public worship: the content of the *elements of public worship*. For example, the form of prayer consists of the words and tone used. The form must be biblical but need not be specifically commanded in the *Holy Scriptures* (*regulative principle of worship*) (chap. 80).

fourfold state of man: the different spiritual conditions of human beings in relation to God. The four states are the *state of innocence*, the *state of sin*, the *state of grace*, and the *state of glory* (chaps. 28, 35).

framework view: the interpretation of Genesis 1 as if it were a parable or poem, so that the passage teaches that God formed and filled the world but says nothing about how long it took or in what order God made things (chap. 24).

free choice of the will: the liberty of human beings to choose what they believe is good without being compelled by outside forces or acting like machines. How people use this liberty depends on their spiritual condition according to the *fourfold state of man* (chap. 35).

free offer of the gospel: God's offer of his Son to all who hear the *general gospel call*. Though rejected by *hyper-Calvinism* and misused by *Arminianism* to reject sovereign *election*, the free offer is taught by Scripture alongside God's *sovereignty* in salvation (chap. 56).

full preterism: the *heresy* that all the teachings of the *Holy Scriptures* regarding the last things were fulfilled in ancient times. Some forms of *preterism* still affirm Christ's future *second coming* to raise the dead and judge the world (*partial preterism*), but full preterism does not (chap. 92).

futurism: the interpretation of the book of Revelation as an account of a future *tribulation* period immediately before Christ's *second coming*. Futurism is often associated with *dispensationalism* and a very literal interpretation of Revelation (chap. 90).

gap theory: the teaching that long ages passed between *creation* in Genesis 1:1 and all things becoming "without form, and void" in verse 2. During this "gap" time, it is supposed that the earth's geological structures and many fossils formed (chap. 24).

***gehenna*:** a Greek term (adapted from Hebrew), translated as "hell," referring to the place of *eternal punishment* in fire after Christ's *second coming* (chap. 94).

gender: the aspect of God's creation order of being male or female. There are only two genders among human beings, corresponding to their biological sex at conception (chap. 30).

general assembly: a gathering of representatives. In *presbyterianism*, it is a council of *elders* (including *ruling elders* and *ministers of the Word* or *teaching elders*) governing a broad (often national) federation of *particular churches* (chap. 76).

general gospel call: God's message of salvation in his Word. The *gospel* call consists of the doctrine of the good news about Christ, the command for everyone who hears to respond in *repentance unto life* and *faith in Jesus Christ*, and the promise of salvation to all who do so by God's *effectual grace* (chap. 56).

general revelation: divine *revelation* given naturally through the created world. God shows something of his *divine nature* and will to all people through the works he made, but this *revelation* does not make known the *gospel* by which we must be saved (chaps. 3, 4).

***genus majestaticum*:** according to *Lutheran theology*, the category (Latin *genus*) of the *communication of properties* that involves the gift of infinite divine majesty to Christ's human nature. Christ's *divine nature* is said to enable his humanity to function with *omniscience*, *omnipotence*, and *omnipresence*, though his humanity remains in itself a finite, created essence.

gifts of the Holy Spirit: see *spiritual gift*.

glorification: the grace of God to bring his *elect* to share, body and soul, in the glory of Christ forever. Glorification is the final blessing in the *order of salvation* and completes God's application of salvation through Christ by the Spirit (chaps. 55, 93).

glory of God: God's infinite greatness in himself, or the *revelation* of God's *attributes* to others. When we glorify God, we do not add to his greatness but serve as instruments by which he makes himself known.

Gnosticism: a modern term for a variety of ancient Greek religious movements that taught such things as the emanation of all things from a supreme and unknowable deity, the creation of the physical world by a lesser god, the descent of the Christ-Spirit (another lesser god) on the righteous man Jesus, and salvation by obtaining secret knowledge.

goodness of God: the *attribute of God* that he is morally excellent and beautiful in all he is and in all his ways to his creatures. The goodness of God includes his *mercy*, *grace*, *patience*, *love*, *truth*, and *righteousness* (chap. 16).

good works: acts done in obedience to the right standard, from a right character, and for the right purpose. People in the *state of sin* cannot do good in God's sight, though they might bring temporal benefits to society. People in the *state of grace* do good works when they obey God's law from a heart purified by *faith in Jesus Christ* and directed by *love*, for the *glory of God*. *Justification* is by faith alone (*sola fide*) apart from our works, but *sanctification* produces good works in the lives of all who are saved by grace alone (*sola gratia*) (chap. 63).

gospel: good news. The gospel proclaimed throughout the *Holy Scriptures* is the good news that God sent his Son, Jesus Christ, to die for the sins of his people and to rise from the dead (chap. 2).

governmental view of the atonement: the teaching that Christ died to publicly honor God's moral government over mankind, which was dishonored by sin. This view is incomplete unless one also affirms Christ's *satisfaction* to God's *justice* by *penal substitution*.

grace of God: the *attribute of God* that he gives favor and help to those who do not deserve it. Grace may also refer to the action of God in giving unmerited favor and help. God's grace includes both his *common grace* and his *saving grace* (chap. 16).

guardian angel: an *angel* supposedly assigned to guard and guide a specific human being. The doctrine of guardian angels has no clear biblical support (chap. 27).

***hades*:** Greek term (often translated as "*hell*") for death, the grave, or the realm of the *souls* of the wicked dead, where they suffer for their sins and wait for the *resurrection of the dead* and the *day of judgment* (chap. 89).

hamartiology: the doctrine of sin (section 3B).

heaven: can refer to the skies visible from the earth, the place where the *angels* and *souls* of the dead *saints* dwell in God's *special presence*, or the final state of *eternal life with God* (chaps. 89, 95).

heinous sin: an *actual sin* of especially great evil and offensiveness to God. All sin is *mortal* in the sense of deserving *death*, but there are degrees to the wickedness of sin (chap. 36).

hell: in the Bible, a translation of the terms *sheol*, *hades*, and *gehenna*. The last term refers to the place of *eternal punishment* after the *second coming* (chap. 94).

helper: another translation of the Greek word *paraklētos*, also rendered *advocate* and *comforter*.

heresy: serious departure from Christian *orthodoxy* while still professing to be Christian. Not all error is heresy, but only that which denies the Christian faith in its fundamentals.

hermeneutics: the study of how to interpret the *Holy Scriptures*.

higher criticism: the study of the Bible's sources, historical contexts, and literary forms on the assumption that the *Holy Scriptures* are not the *Word of God* given by God's *inspiration* but are subject to human error. Higher criticism, as distinct from *lower criticism* or *textual criticism*, characterizes the scholarship of *theological liberalism* (chap. 5).

Hinduism: the major religion of India. Hinduism teaches the existence of many gods (practical *polytheism*), *reincarnation* according to a law of *merit* (karma), the unity of all things as expressions of the one impersonal divine being (*pantheism*), and salvation through escape from "self" (*moksha*) by *good works*, meditation, or religious devotion (chap. 10).

historical covenants: specific *covenants* God made at points in history, such as the covenants with Noah, Abraham, Israel, David, and the *new covenant* in Christ. The redemptive covenants of promise with Abraham, Israel, and David were *old covenant* forms of the *covenant of grace* in *temporary administrations* and *types* (chap. 40).

historical theology: the study of the doctrines taught and theological methods used by professing Christians, churches, and other groups in the past.

historicism: the interpretation of the book of Revelation as a symbolic account that traces the events of church history in chronological order from Christ's first coming to his *second coming*. Historicism was most popular in the sixteenth and seventeenth centuries (chap. 90).

historic premillennialism: *premillennialism* that is not *dispensationalism*, though there is such variety in premillennial views that it may not be best to label one of them as "historic."

holiness of God: the incomparable glory of the *divine nature*. God's holiness sets him above all else in his majesty, sets him apart for his own honor in his moral excellence, sets him against all that dishonors him, and sets him with the humble to lift them up (chap. 10).

holy (the church): one of the *attributes of the Christian church*, which defines it as God's temple by the *indwelling of the Holy Spirit*, who works the *sanctification* of believers (chap. 74).

holy orders: see *orders, holy*.

Holy Scriptures: the sacred writings of the *Word of God*, the Bible given by divine *inspiration*. The Holy Scriptures consist of the thirty-nine books of the Old Testament and the twenty-seven books of the New Testament (*canon*).

Holy Spirit: the Spirit of God, who by *eternal procession* from the Father and the Son is a distinct *person* in the *Trinity*. He is called "holy" because he is fully God, he is distinct from evil spirits (*demons*), and he makes God's people holy (*sanctification*) (chap. 19).

***homoousion*:** Greek term meaning "same in essence." This term was used by the Council of Nicaea to declare that the Son has the same *divine nature* as the Father and thus is eternally and fully God, though a distinct *person* in the *Trinity* (chap. 19).

hope, Christian: a *saving grace* consisting of expectant desire for God and *eternal life* with him. Christian hope is not a mere wish that what one "hopes" will happen but confident and sanctifying *faith in Jesus Christ* and *love* for God's *glory* (chap. 71).

humiliation of Christ: see *state of humiliation*.

hyper-Calvinism: a rejection of the doctrine of the *free offer of the gospel.* Hyper-Calvinism reasons from *election* and *particular redemption* that God does not offer Christ to all who hear the *gospel.* With this view is sometimes associated the denial of *common grace* and the affirmation of the eternal *justification* of the *elect* before *conversion* (chap. 56).

hyperdulia: in *Roman Catholicism*, the supreme veneration (*dulia*) given to the virgin Mary, as opposed to the *latria* given to God alone.

hypostasis: Greek term meaning "a specific instance of something," used in the doctrine of the *Trinity* for a *person* or *subsistence.*

hypostatic union: the joining of the *divine nature* and a human nature in one *person* (Greek *hypostasis*) in the *incarnation.* The two natures are united in such a way as preserves their distinct attributes, so that Christ is fully God and truly man, not a hybrid (chap. 43).

icon: an image of Christ or a saint used in religious devotion and *public worship.* The term *icon* is especially prominent in *Eastern Orthodoxy.*

idealism: in the doctrine of the last things (*eschatology*), an interpretation of Revelation as a symbolic depiction of general spiritual principles relevant throughout the time between Christ's first coming and his *second coming* (chap. 90).

illumination: the grace of spiritual light in the soul given through Christ by the Spirit. Illumination can be either a *common grace* that grants an understanding of the Bible and some passing affections or, more commonly, a *saving grace* that gives *faith in Jesus Christ* and *love* in the heart (chap. 46).

image of God: the likeness of God in man. God's image makes human beings unique among the creatures as visible expressions of God's *attributes*, relationships, and activities, especially in man's knowledge, righteousness, and holiness (chap. 29).

immanence of God: the nearness of God to every part of his created world (*omnipresence*).

immanent Trinity: another term for the *ontological Trinity.*

immensity of God: the *attribute of God* that he cannot be limited by location or distance. God's *infinity* with respect to space means that he has a fullness of being that *heaven* and earth cannot contain but that coexists with and sustains every place (*omnipresence*) (chap. 12).

immersion: dipping something entirely in a fluid. People holding to *paedobaptism* often see immersion of the body in water as one valid mode of *baptism* (*Eastern Orthodoxy* uses immersion except when it raises health concerns), but those who hold to *Baptist theology* believe that baptism is properly done only by immersion (chap. 83).

imminency: the doctrine that Christ's *second coming* could take place very soon, and the events preceding it, such as disturbances in the heavens, could begin suddenly. The doctrine of imminency encourages believers to watch for their Lord (chap. 92).

immutability of God: the *attribute of God* that he does not change. God's immutability means that he is unchangeable in his *attributes*, life, *will*, and *decree*, though God's relationships and actions toward his creatures change, such as when they repent of sin (chap. 13).

impassibility of God: the *immutability of God* with respect to his *affections*. God shows distinct affections (delight, *wrath*, *compassion*, etc.) to different people at different points in their lives, but he has no *passions* and does not pass through changing emotional states (chap. 18).

impeccability: inability to sin. Though human nature short of *glorification* is capable of sin, Christ has impeccability due to his being a *person* with a *divine nature*.

impulsive cause: the motivation of someone that causes an effect, such as the generosity of a carpenter that motivates him to make a chair for his mother.

imputation: the legal reckoning of sin or righteousness to a person. Adam's sin of breaking the *covenant of works* was imputed to all his natural offspring for their condemnation. The sins of God's *elect* were imputed to Christ, their *surety*, by *penal substitution*, and Christ's *active obedience* and *passive obedience* are imputed to believers in their *justification* (chaps. 34, 48, 61).

inaugurated eschatology: the doctrine that Christ's kingdom began with his first coming but has not yet come in glory. Thus, we presently live in the *last days*, during the overlap of this present age and the age to come (chap. 87).

inaugurated millennialism: the interpretation of the *millennium* ("thousand years") in Revelation 20 as a symbol of Christ's present *kingdom* after his victory over *Satan* by his death and *resurrection* and before his *second coming* (chap. 91).

incarnation: the Son of God's taking a human nature, body and *soul*, to himself. The incarnation of God the Son resulted in one *person* with two natures, the *divine nature* with all the *attributes of God* and a human nature with human qualities and limitations (chap. 43).

incommunicable attributes: those *attributes* of God classified by some theologians as being least like the *image of God* in man. Examples of attributes considered incommunicable are God's *aseity*, *eternity*, *omnipresence*, and *immutability*.

incomprehensibility of God: the *attribute of God* that he is far beyond the full understanding of any of his creatures, though they can know him truly. The incomprehensibility of God teaches us to humble ourselves before him rather than judging him (chap. 12).

independence of God: another term for God's *aseity*.

indwelling of the Holy Spirit: the *special presence* of the Holy Spirit in every believer in Christ. The Father sends the Spirit through Christ to dwell in his people to produce spiritual life in communion with him and obedience to his commandments (chap. 65).

inerrancy of the Bible: the Bible's complete truthfulness without error. We should hold as truth all that the Bible affirms. The Bible's inerrancy includes the truthfulness of not only the *gospel* but all its teachings, including morality and *ethics*, history, and the *creation* of the world (chap. 7).

infant baptism: see *paedobaptism*.

infinity of God: the *attribute of God* that he is matchlessly perfect in every way without any limitation. Each of God's other attributes is infinite; he is infinite with respect to knowledge (*omniscience*), time (*eternity*), space (*immensity*), and so on (chap. 12).

infralapsarianism: the doctrine that predestination follows the fall in the logical order of God's eternal *decree*, though not in the order of time. Infralapsarianism is a distinct view from *supralapsarianism* and emphasizes that *election* and *reprobation* treat men as sinners.

inherited corruption: another term for the aspect of *original sin* pertaining to sinful pollution of human nature due to the *fall of man*.

inseparable operations: the principle that the three *persons* of the *Trinity* act with one *will* and power, and so all God's acts toward the world (*ad extra*) involve all three *persons*—the Father, the Son, and the Holy Spirit—though each acts in a distinct manner.

inspiration: the work of God through people to produce the human words that are the *Word of God*. By inspiration, the *prophets* and *apostles* wrote the Scriptures so that they have the properties of *self-authentication*, *inerrancy*, *perspicuity*, and *sufficiency* (chap. 6).

instrumental cause: the means used to produce an effect, such as a tool that a carpenter employs to make a chair.

intercession of Christ: Christ's work as *Priest* to appear before God and obtain all *saving grace* as the representative of his people in the *covenant of grace*. In his *state of exaltation*, Christ prays for the application of his sacrifice in its full *efficacy* (chap. 49).

intermediate state: the conscious state of the human *soul* between physical *death* and the *resurrection*. The souls of believers are made perfect in righteousness and rest in God's presence, but the wicked suffer the wrath of God. There is no *purgatory* (chap. 89).

internal calling: another term for *effectual calling*, though some theologians would consider *preparation by grace* through conviction of sin to be part of internal calling.

internal call to the ministry: God's graces that qualify and motivate a man to bear *office* in the church. The internal call consists of godly character, desire, and fitting *spiritual gifts*. The internal call must be confirmed by an *external call* from the church (chap. 77).

invisible church: the *universal church* considered according to its *election*, *union with Christ*, and possession of *saving grace*—none of which people on earth can directly observe. Some members of the invisible church are prevented by circumstances from having formal membership in the *visible church* (chap. 73).

irresistible grace: another term for *effectual calling*. Until God saves by *effectual grace*, sinners resist God and his Word, and God does not save them against the *free choice of the will* but by changing their wills in *regeneration* so that they come to Christ willingly (chap. 58).

Islam: a religion of *monotheism* based on the Arabic Qur'an and traditions about Muhammad. Islam confesses one God (Allah), denies the *Trinity*, teaches that Jesus is a *prophet* but not the Son of God, and commands regular prayer, charity to the poor, fasting in the month of Ramadan, and pilgrimage to Mecca (if possible). Islam promises a paradise of pleasures to those whose good deeds are found weighty on *the day of judgment*.

Jansenism: a theological and devotional movement named after Cornelius Jansen in seventeenth- and eighteenth-century *Roman Catholicism*. Jansenism taught *effectual grace* according to the doctrine of Augustine of Hippo and called for earnest devotion and piety. It was condemned by the *pope* of Rome in 1653 and again in 1713.

jealousy of God: the intensity of the *affections of God*. God's jealousy expresses the ardent zeal of his *love* for his *glory* and his people, but it does not imply the evil and destructive kind of *passions* often seen in sinful human beings (chap. 18).

Jesus: the human name of the Son of God since his *incarnation*. The name Jesus is a form of Joshua and means "the Lord is salvation." Christ was given this name by God because he will save his people from their sins (chap. 42).

Judaism: a religion of *monotheism* based on Jewish traditions and the law of Moses, as interpreted by Jewish rabbis. There is a wide range of views within modern Judaism, including Orthodox Judaism, Conservative Judaism, and Reform Judaism. But all forms of Judaism deny the *Trinity* and that Jesus is the Son of God.

judgment day: see *day of judgment*.

judicial law: God's statutes of civil justice for *old covenant* Israel. The judicial or civil law of Israel was a righteous expression of God's will for the ancient *theocracy* of Israel, but now provides only general principles of wisdom for a just and righteous life (chap. 68).

justice of God: another term for the *righteousness of God*, with emphasis on his authority and acts as the Judge of all (chap. 17).

justification: a gift of *saving grace* in which God counts and declares a believer to be righteous in his sight. Justification is based on Christ's *active* and *passive obedience* to the law and is applied through *faith* alone (*sola fide*) in Christ alone (*solus Christus*) (chap. 61).

kenosis theory: the error that Christ emptied himself of the *attributes of God* when he became a man. A kenotic view of the *incarnation* teaches that the Son of God temporarily set aside some or all divine attributes during his *state of humiliation* (chap. 44).

keys of the kingdom: authority entrusted to the church's *apostles* and *elders* as Christ's servants to welcome people into God's church or exclude them from it. The keys are exercised by the *preaching* of forgiveness of sins and the exercise of *discipline* (chap. 74).

king: in God's *covenants*, the *office* of ruling and defending God's people by his power. The *old covenant* kings were *types* of Christ the King, who conquered sin and death and reigns by the Holy Spirit in his *state of exaltation*. Believers are a kingly people in Christ, overcoming the world and anticipating their reign with Christ in glory (chaps. 45, 50, 51).

kingdom of God: the reign of God, ordinarily not his *sovereignty* over all things as God (*providence*) but his reign through human servants directed by the Spirit through his Word. Christ's coming as the *King* has already brought the promised kingdom of God, but it will not arrive in open glory until his *second coming* (chap. 50).

last days: the time between Christ's first coming and *second coming*. According to *inaugurated eschatology*, the last days are the season of the outpouring of the Holy Spirit, the mission of the church to all nations, and the *tribulation* of the church (chap. 87).

***latria*:** in *Roman Catholicism*, the adoration given to God alone. The distinction between giving *latria* to God and *dulia* to created persons is used to justify offering prayer and praise to the virgin Mary and other *saints* in *heaven*.

leading of the Holy Spirit: the Spirit's continual work to influence God's children. This leading does not consist of inward impulses directing people to specific actions. Instead, it is the influence of the Spirit to cause believers to understand and obey God's Word (chap. 65).

liberalism: see *theological liberalism* and *modernism*.

libertarian free will: the view of the human will that its choices are free and morally accountable only if they are not subject to God's *sovereignty* and *providence*, in contrast to the *free choice of the will* affirmed by *Reformed theology*.

***limbus infantium*:** the place where the *souls* of infants go after death if they are not baptized because they were not cleansed of *original sin* and cannot receive the *beatific vision*, according to many teachers of *Roman Catholicism*, though not its official *dogma*.

***limbus patrum*:** the place where the *souls* of Old Testament saints remained after death until Christ descended into hell and brought them to *heaven*, according to *Roman Catholicism*. *Eastern Orthodoxy* teaches a similar doctrine.

limited atonement: another term for *particular redemption*, the doctrine that Christ died for the *redemption* of God's *elect*.

loci: the major categories of doctrine studied in *systematic theology*. The word *locus* literally means "place," as in location.

logic: the philosophical study of the correct principles of reasoning.

***Logos*:** Greek for "word" or "speech," used especially for Christ as the *Word*.

Lord's Day: the first day of the week, the day set apart as sacred to the Lord. *Reformed theology* teaches that the Lord's Day is the Christian *Sabbath* (chap. 69).

Lord's Supper: the *sacrament* of communion with Christ in the *new covenant*, using bread and a cup as signs of Christ's body and blood given for his people. People differ as to whether the Supper contains Christ's *real physical presence* or his *real spiritual presence*, or is a mere remembrance of his death (*memorialism*) (chap. 84).

love, Christian: giving oneself to glorify God and to do good to people, graciously and righteously, with a desire for building friendships. Love is the central duty of the Christian life and the chief mark of *saving grace* in Christian character (chap. 67).

love of benevolence: the *love of God* exercised in kindness to his creatures out of the abundance of his goodness. The benevolence of God includes his *grace* and *mercy*, and its highest display is in the gift of his Son to save sinners (chap. 16).

love of complacency: the *love of God* exercised in delighting in those whom he loves and has brought into saving *union with Christ*. God's delight expresses his *holiness*: he delights in that which displays his majesty and moral excellence (chap. 16).

love of God: the *attribute of God* that he gives of himself to others. The three *persons* of the *Trinity* love one another infinitely and have a general love for all mankind and a special love for God's people, shown in the *love of benevolence* and the *love of complacency* (chap. 16).

lower criticism: another term for *textual criticism*, in contrast to *higher criticism*.

Lutheran theology: the *evangelical* theology of the Lutheran churches, which emerged from the *Reformation* in Germany. Classic Lutheran theology is defined by the documents of the Book of Concord, such as the Augsburg Confession, the catechisms of Martin Luther, and the Formula of Concord. It emphasizes *sola Scriptura*, *sola fide*, and *sola gratia*.

Lutheran view of the Lord's Supper: a view of the Supper that denies *transubstantiation* but still asserts the *real physical presence* of Christ. The Lord's body and blood are said to be present in, with, and under the elements of the Supper. This requires that his human body be supernaturally present in many places at once (*ubiquity*) (chap. 84).

Mahayana: a form of *Buddhism*, popular in China, Japan, and Korea, that emphasizes religious devotion and dependence on gods, buddhas, and enlightened ones (practical *polytheism*) as the way to attain *nirvana*.

man of lawlessness: the reading in some English versions of 2 Thessalonians 2:3 for the *man of sin*. The different translation arises from variant readings in the Greek manuscripts.

man of sin: the great sinner who, by *Satan's* power, will seek to take God's place during the time before Christ's *second coming*. The man of sin is also known as the *antichrist* (chap. 90).

Marcionism: the *heresy* that the Old Testament and New Testament present two Gods. The God of the Old Testament was said to be the evil maker of the physical world, and the God of the New Testament is the good Father of Christ (chap. 38).

marks of the true church: the external signs of the *visible church* of Christ. The marks are the *preaching* of the true doctrine of the *Holy Scriptures*, the administration of biblical *sacraments* of the *new covenant*, and the exercise of biblical church *discipline* (chap. 74).

marriage: the union of one man (male human being) and one woman (female human being) in an exclusive, lifelong covenant. The purposes of marriage include mutual help, intimate companionship, and procreation (bearing and raising children). Marriage is regarded as a *sacrament* in *Roman Catholicism* and *Eastern Orthodoxy* (chaps. 30, 81).

Marxism: an ideology of hope that political revolution will bring a society of equality and justice. More than a political theory, Marxism is a philosophy of life based on *atheism*, *pantheism*, or *panentheism*. It teaches that material economic forces drive human life, evil results from one class oppressing another, and revolution will establish a government that controls property, education, and production to bring an ideal society (chaps. 10, 87).

material cause: the material acted upon to produce an effect, such as the wood cut and shaped by a carpenter to make a chair.

materialism: the belief that physical matter and energy are all that exist. Materialism is a form of *atheism* and destroys the objective basis for *ethics*.

means of grace: God's external instruments to give *saving grace*. The *Word of God* is the primary external means and is effective only by the work of the Holy Spirit. Specifically, *means of grace* refers to the *public* and *private means* of applying the Word: *preaching*, *prayer*, the *sacraments*, etc. (chap. 81).

mediator: a person assigned the *office* to establish a good relationship between two parties. Christ, by his *incarnation* being both God and man, is the only Mediator between God and man, for God gives the *saving grace* promised in the *covenant of grace* through Christ alone (*solus Christus*) (chap. 45).

member of the Christian church: someone who belongs to God's *covenant* people. A true and living member is joined to Christ and his church by the Holy Spirit, just as a member is joined to a body and shares its life. Membership in the *universal church* is ordinarily lived out in relationships in a *particular church* under its *officers* (chap. 75).

memorialism: a view of the Lord's Supper that denies Christ's *real physical presence* and his *real spiritual presence* but asserts that the Supper is merely a remembrance of his death. This view is commonly held among Pentecostals and many Baptists today.

mercy of God: the *attribute of God* that he has *compassion* and acts in kindness to prevent or deliver from suffering. God's mercy to his people is like the love of a father and a mother to their dear children (chap. 16).

merit: worthiness to receive deserved blessing because of obedience to God's law. No merely human acts have merit before God, but Christ alone merits *eternal life with God* for his people by his *active* and *passive obedience.*

metaphysics: the philosophical study of the nature of reality, including being (*ontology*), causation and change, mind and matter, time and space, and necessity and possibility.

miaphysitism: the doctrine that Christ has only one nature, in which his deity and humanity remain distinct, like a *soul* and a body in one human being—unlike *monophysitism*. This is *Oriental Orthodoxy's* alternative doctrine to that of *Chalcedon*.

middle knowledge: the doctrine that God eternally knows what any possible person would do in any possible situation. According to some teachers in *Roman Catholicism* and *Arminianism*, middle knowledge is the basis of God's *conditional election*.

midtribulational rapture: the belief that Christ will catch up the church (and raise dead Christians) and take it to *heaven* partway through a final *tribulation* preceding his *second coming*. This is a minority view in *dispensationalism*.

millennium: the "thousand years" of Revelation 20. There are three main interpretations of the millennium: *premillennialism* (including *dispensationalism*), *inaugurated millennialism* (also called *amillennialism*), and *postmillennialism* (chap. 91).

minister of the Word: a person bearing *office* in the church to be a *preacher* of God's Word as his vocation. Most ministers of the Word are also *elders* of *particular churches*, though some may be assigned to a mission, church plant, chaplaincy, or school (chap. 77).

miracle: an extraordinary, observable event caused by God that evokes awe at his presence because it confirms his word of salvation and judgment. In the Scriptures, miracles are often called "signs," "wonders," and (in Greek) "powers" (chap. 54).

modalism: the *heresy* that the Father, the Son, and the Holy Spirit are one *person*. The one God is said to appear under three different names, as opposed to the doctrine of the *Trinity*, which says the one God is three distinct *persons* in relation to one another (chap. 20).

modalistic monarchianism: another term for *modalism* in the doctrine of God.

modernism: another term for *theological liberalism*, emphasizing its attempt to make Christian beliefs fit modern *rationalism*.

Molinism: another term for *middle knowledge*, named after Luis de Molina.

monarchy: rule by a single supreme leader, such as a king. Christ is the only *King* of the church, which is subject to his Word, but he reigns for the good of his *body* and works through the leading authority of the *officers* and the consenting authority of the *members* (chap. 76).

monergism: the work of God alone. The doctrine of monergism is that the first act of turning a sinner back to God is by God's grace alone (*sola gratia*) without any contribution from man, who is in a condition of *total inability*, as opposed to *synergism* (chap. 58).

monism: the belief that all is one. See *pantheism* and *panentheism*.

monophysitism: the doctrine of "only one nature" in Christ, another term for *Eutychianism*.

monotheism: the belief that there is only one true God. Biblical monotheism distinguishes between the Lord as the one true God and all other false gods, while asserting that the one God exists in three *persons* as the *Trinity* (chaps. 10, 19–20).

monothelitism: the *heresy* that Christ has no human will but only a divine will. Monothelitism is a partial compromise with *Eutychianism* or *monophysitism*, the idea that Christ's humanity was made divine by the *incarnation* so that he has only one nature (chap. 44).

moral influence view of the atonement: an interpretation of Christ's suffering and death as his work as *Prophet* to reveal God to promote godliness. The moral influence view is true but incomplete without also acknowledging Christ's work as *Priest* to accomplish *penal substitution* (chaps. 46, 47).

moral law: God's unchanging *preceptive will* for humanity that expresses his *righteousness* and *creation* of man in his *image*. The moral law is impressed on the human *conscience* in *natural law*, summarized in the *Ten Commandments*, and fully revealed in the *Holy Scriptures*, which have complete *sufficiency* for our moral guidance (chap. 68).

moralistic therapeutic deism: a form of *finite theism* in which God helps people to be kind and feel good about themselves but exercises no *sovereignty* or *providence*, only offering empathy for the suffering and encouraging people to be empathetic (chap. 10).

mortal sin: sin that, according to *Roman Catholicism*, puts a person out of God's *saving grace*. Mortal sin after *baptism* must supposedly be cleansed by *penance* in this life, or a person will suffer *eternal punishment* in hell (chap. 36).

mother of God: see *theotokos*.

mystical syllogism: a means of *assurance of salvation* by the application of God's Word through the Spirit's *illumination* to recognize the inward evidence of *regeneration*. One might reason, "According to the *Holy Scriptures*, only those with *faith in Jesus Christ* receive the *witness of the Holy Spirit* that they have inward godliness. I know by the Spirit's witness that I have a measure of inward godliness. Therefore, I have *faith in Christ*."

mystical union: the bond of life in which the Holy Spirit joins people to Christ through *faith*. Mystical union with Christ is the means through which God applies all blessings of salvation. It is grounded in the *federal union* between Christ and the *elect* (chap. 55).

mysticism: an unhealthy emphasis on directly experiencing God that tends toward *pantheism* or *panentheism*. Mysticism might involve an unbiblical view of union between the *soul* and God's essence or *uncreated energies*, and a seeking after visions (chap. 55).

natural law: moral principles that the Creator embedded in human nature. Natural law is part of God's *general revelation* of himself and his will through the *conscience* (chaps. 4, 68).

natural revelation: another term for *general revelation.*

necessity: something that must be. There are different kinds of necessity: absolute necessity (God's existence and *attributes*), consequent necessity (Christ's death, given God's *decree* to save sinners), natural necessity (the laws of nature), and the necessity of coaction or compulsion (forcing someone against his will). Thus, God's *providence* carries out his *decree* with necessity, but not in such a way that forces people to act against their wills.

neoorthodoxy: a theological movement (also known as *dialectical theology*), begun in the early twentieth century, that reacted against *theological liberalism* but did not return to true *Reformed theology*. According to *neoorthodoxy*, God revealed himself through Jesus Christ, but God's *revelation* is not words in a book but an encounter with God (chap. 5).

Neoplatonism: a Greek philosophy of *panentheism* and *mysticism* that arose in the third century AD, asserting that the various spiritual entities that animate the world emanated from the one ultimate reality.

Nestorianism: the *heresy* that Christ is two *persons*, one God and the other a man. Scholars debate whether Nestorius taught this view (chap. 44).

New Age movement: an eclectic form of *pantheism* popular in Western nations. New Age teaching combines elements of *Hinduism*, *Daoism*, and Native American spirituality with Western individualism, emphasizing the assertion that "you are god" (chap. 10).

new covenant: the last of the *historical covenants*, promised by the prophets and instituted when Christ accomplished *redemption*. The *saving grace* of the new covenant was given through the *covenant of grace* in all ages, but now comes with greater glory (chap. 40).

new covenant theology: a view of the *covenants*, according to a form of *Baptist theology*, that affirms the fulfillment of God's promises to Israel in the church (against *dispensationalism*) but denies the one *covenant of grace* and the obligation to keep the *moral law* of the Old Testament unless it is repeated in the New Testament (against *covenant theology*).

Nicene Creed: an ancient confession of faith defining *catholic* Christian belief in the *incarnation*, the *Trinity*, and other central doctrines. This creed was composed at the Council of Nicaea (325), expanded at the Council of Constantinople (381), and (for Western churches) further clarified at the Council of Toledo (589) (chaps. 2, 19, 44).

nirvana: a Sanskrit term literally meaning "blown out" like an extinguished flame. Nirvana is the goal of *Hinduism* and *Buddhism* to extinguish the illusion of the individual self, attain enlightenment that all things are one (*pantheism* or *panentheism*), escape the cycle of *reincarnation* in its various degrees of misery and craving, and thus attain happiness.

normative principle of worship: the doctrine that the church may offer to God whatever *elements of public worship* it believes to be helpful, as long as the church does not do anything prohibited in the *Holy Scriptures* or invent *sacraments* not instituted by Christ in the Scriptures. The normative principle is the historic position of the Lutheran churches and the Church of England, and contradicts the *regulative principle of worship*.

office: a special trust or commission to exercise authority on behalf of another person or group. Christ alone bears the office of the *Mediator* of *saving grace* as *Prophet*, *Priest*, and *King*. Christ also appoints men to be *officers of the church* (chaps. 45, 76).

officers of the church: Christ's servants bearing *office* in the church. Since the end of the apostolic age and the end of extraordinary gifts (*cessationism*), the officers of the church have been the *ministers of the Word* (*teaching elders*), the other (*ruling*) *elders*, and the *deacons* (chaps. 77–78).

old covenant: the covenants of promise prior to the *new covenant*: the *historical covenants* with Abraham, Israel, and David. The term especially emphasizes the *temporary administration* and *types* (*ceremonial law*) given to Israel through Moses (chap. 40).

omnipotence of God: the *attribute of God* that he is infinite in power to do all his *decretive will*. The omnipotent God is able to do anything consistent with his *holiness*, gives to creatures any power they have, and exercises *sovereignty* over all things (chap. 15).

omnipresence of God: the *attribute of God* that he is fully present in every location. God's omnipresence means that he is always with us in all his *attributes*, even when we do not sense his presence (chap. 12).

omniscience of God: the *attribute of God* that he knows all things—past, present, and future. In God's *infinity*, he has perfect knowledge of himself, of all possible things and events, and of all actual things and events, including his *foreknowledge* of the future (chap. 14).

ontological argument: a philosophical argument made by Anselm of Canterbury for God's existence. God is, by definition, the supreme being, so that no one greater can be conceived in the mind. A being that exists by absolute *necessity* is greater than one that might not exist. Therefore, it is argued, God exists by absolute *necessity*.

ontological Trinity: the *Trinity* as God is in himself, the *immanent Trinity* as distinct from the *economic Trinity*.

ontology: the philosophical study of the nature of being or reality.

open theism: a form of *finite theism* developed in the late twentieth century. Open theists teach that God's power and *foreknowledge* are severely limited by our choices, and so he changes his plans as he lives in relationships with people (chaps. 10, 13–14).

order of salvation: the series of blessings by which the Holy Spirit applies salvation through *union with Christ*. The order of salvation includes the *gospel* call and conviction of sin, *effectual calling* and *regeneration*, *faith in Jesus Christ* and *repentance unto life*, *justification* and *adoption*, *sanctification* and *perseverance*, and *glorification* (chap. 55).

orders, holy: a *sacrament* in the *sacramental system* of *Roman Catholicism* and *Eastern Orthodoxy* that is said to convey the grace to be a *bishop*, a *priest*, or a *deacon* (chap. 81).

ordinance: something decreed by authority. In Christian usage, *ordinance* often serves as another term for an *element of public worship* or more specifically for a *sacrament*.

ordination: official and public authorization of a person to bear *office* in the church, often done by *officers* laying hands on the person with *prayer* (chap. 77).

***ordo salutis*:** Latin phrase for "order of salvation."

Oriental Orthodoxy: the religious system of the Coptic Orthodox Church in Egypt and several other Eastern churches that rejected the doctrine of *Chalcedon* and instead embraced *miaphysitism*. Oriental Orthodoxy is not to be confused with *Eastern Orthodoxy*.

original sin: not man's first sin, but the guilt and corruption resulting from the *fall of man*. It is the guilt from Adam's breaking the *covenant of works* and the corruption consisting of the lack of original righteousness and the *total depravity* of man's nature, from which come all *actual sins* (chap. 34).

orthodoxy: adherence to the doctrines of the true Christian faith, especially as defined by creeds, confessions, and catechisms. *Orthodoxy* as a general term is not to be confused with *Eastern Orthodoxy* (chap. 2).

overseer: a term for a church *officer*, also translated as "*bishop*," the equivalent of *elder* (chaps. 76, 77).

paedobaptism: the *baptism* of young children. Reformed paedobaptism teaches that the young children of believers are part of the *covenant of grace* and should receive its sign, as revealed to Abraham in the covenant sign of circumcision, with baptism in the *new covenant* understood as corresponding to circumcision in the *old* (chap. 83).

panentheism: the belief that God is the life and spirit of all things, like a *soul* and body. Panentheists may view many beings as gods (*polytheism*), as in some kinds of *Buddhism*, but combine this with the belief that they all share one divine spirit (chap. 10).

pantheism: the belief that everything is God, and so all is one, even good and evil. Pantheists may honor many gods (*polytheism*) but believe all are manifestations of one divine being, as in *Hinduism*, leading to the worship of people, animals, and objects (chap. 10).

papacy: the *office* of the *pope*, or the system of doctrine affirming that office in *Roman Catholicism*. The papacy is a further unbiblical development of *episcopal polity* that concentrates all church power in one man (chap. 76).

Paraclete: an Anglicized form of the Greek word *paraklētos* (see below), used as a title for the Holy Spirit.

paradox: something that seems a contradiction, causing inner tension. Christians experience the paradoxes of loving righteousness while grieving over remaining sin, and of knowing they are God's beloved children while enduring great suffering (chap. 37).

paraklētos: Greek term translated as "*Advocate*," "*Comforter*," or "*Helper*." The word appears to mean a person appointed to speak in court on behalf of another. Used of Christ, it refers to his office as the *Priest* for *intercession* (chap. 49). It also refers to the Spirit of truth sent by the Father and the Son to bear witness of Christ for the conviction of unbelievers and the comfort of believers (chap. 53).

partial preterism: the interpretation of the book of Revelation and other passages as symbolic accounts of events that mostly took place in the first century. In contrast to *full preterism*, partial preterism understands the Scriptures to foretell a future *resurrection of the dead* at the *second coming of Christ*.

Particular Baptist covenant theology: a view of the covenants held by most, if not all, original subscribers to the Second London Baptist Confession, though not explicitly taught in the confession itself or by all *Reformed Baptist* churches holding that confession today. This view affirms the *covenant of works* and the *covenant of grace* revealed in all ages through the *gospel*, but states that the *old covenant* was only a shadow and promise of the *covenant of grace*, which was fulfilled in the *new covenant*. Also called "1689 federalism."

Particular Baptist theology: seventeenth-century *Baptist theology* that was largely in agreement with *paedobaptist Reformed theology*. Particular Baptists expressed their beliefs in the First London Baptist Confession and the Second London Baptist Confession.

particular church: a local congregation of God's people. A particular church, as distinct from the *universal church*, is an organized expression of the *church militant*, ordinarily with its own *officers*, *discipline*, and meetings for *public worship* (chap. 73).

particular redemption: Christ's payment of the ransom price for the *elect* alone. Christ's *redemption* is both particular and universal because he redeemed God's chosen ones from all kinds of people in all nations (chap. 48).

passions: strong emotions or, in the classic meaning of the term, emotions not regulated by wisdom, righteousness, and peace. In this classic sense, passions involve foolishness, sin, and suffering, and thus are inconsistent with God's *attributes* and the *immutability* of his *affections* (*impassibility*) or with the state of the saints after *glorification* (chap. 18).

passive obedience: willing endurance of the law's penalty against sin to do God's will. Christ's passive obedience as the *surety* in the *covenant of grace* was necessary for the *satisfaction* of the law's demand that sin be punished with the *wrath of God*, so that believers are forgiven of sin and counted righteous by the *imputation* of Christ's *active obedience* (chap. 48).

pastor: shepherd. Though *ministers of the Word* are often called pastors, in the New Testament the term often includes all the *elders* of the church (both *ministers* and *ruling elders*) in their work of teaching, admonishing, leading, and disciplining its *members* (chap. 77).

patience of God: the *attribute of God* that he is slow to anger (or "longsuffering"). God is not driven by *passions*, but waits to punish sinners, delights in forgiving those who repent, and chooses to execute his *wrath* according to his *wisdom* (chap. 16).

patripassianism: the *heresy* that the Father suffered and died on the cross. See *modalism* and *Sabellianism*.

Pelagianism: the doctrine that the *fall of man* did not bring mankind into a *state of sin*, but human beings by nature always have the power to choose to be good. Pelagius opposed Augustine's teaching of salvation by *effectual grace* according to *election* (chaps. 23, 34).

penal substitution: a *view of the atonement*, according to which Christ's sacrifice as a *Priest* involves his taking the place of sinners to suffer the penalty their sins deserve. Christ also suffered and died as a *Prophet* (*moral influence view*) and a *King* (*victory view*) (chap. 47).

penalty of loss: the just punishment of sin consisting in the loss of God's good gifts. The greatest loss that unsaved sinners will experience is God himself, for they were created to fellowship with him but will be separated from him forever (chap. 36).

penalty of sense: the just punishment of sin consisting in the infliction of God's *wrath*. Unsaved sinners may suffer various afflictions under God's judgment in this life, but their ultimate judgment will be to suffer forever under the righteous anger of God (chap. 36).

penance: the *sacrament* of reconciliation for sin after *baptism* according to the *sacramental system* of *Roman Catholicism* and *Eastern Orthodoxy*. Penance is said to be the only remedy for *mortal sin* and requires contrition, confession, and making *satisfaction* in order to receive absolution or forgiveness (chap. 81).

Pentecostalism: a combination of *continuationism* and *two-level Christianity* teaching the *baptism with the Holy Spirit* according to the doctrine of *subsequence*. This baptism is said to be distinct and separable from salvation and to manifest itself at first by speaking in *tongues* and then in a fullness of power for holiness and ministry (chap. 53).

perfectionism: the doctrine that believers can attain perfect love for God and people. Some branches of *Arminianism*, while not asserting *sinless perfectionism*, claim it is possible to live in perfect love without any conscious violations of God's commandments (chap. 63).

***perichoresis*:** Greek term for the mutual indwelling of each *person* in the *Trinity* in the other *persons*, sharing one *divine nature*, life, and activity. In the classic doctrine of the *Trinity*, perichoresis is grounded in the Son's *eternal generation* and the Spirit's *eternal procession*. In *social Trinitarianism*, perichoresis is merely perfect empathy.

perseverance of the saints: God's *saving grace* to keep believers in the *state of grace*. Everyone saved by God's *election*, *redemption*, and *effectual calling* will never fully or finally fall away from him but will persevere in faith and obedience to the end through his or her diligent use of the *means of grace* (chap. 64).

person: someone unique, rational (thinking), and volitional (choosing) by nature and in relationships with other persons. This definition of a person is important both for the doctrine of the *Trinity* and for our understanding of human nature (chap. 20).

perspicuity of the Bible: the clarity of the *Holy Scriptures*. Though some parts of the Bible are hard to understand, everything needed for salvation by *faith in Jesus Christ* and pleasing God by obedience is clearly revealed in the Scriptures and can be understood by the ordinary use of means (chap. 6).

piety: godliness and the use of the *means of grace* to pursue it. The heart of Christian piety is living unto God by his grace according to his will, as revealed in the *Holy Scriptures*.

plenary, verbal inspiration: the *inspiration* of the whole Bible, so that every word of the original manuscripts is the *Word of God*. Plenary, verbal inspiration is an important doctrine because some teachers say that only parts of the Bible are inspired (chap. 6).

plurality of elders: the New Testament pattern of multiple church *elders* serving together as a governing council. Plurality of elders is contrary to *single pastor polity*, in which one leader has supreme spiritual authority in each *particular church* (chap. 76).

pneumatology: the doctrine of the Holy Spirit (part 5, especially section 5A).

polemics: the study of how to demonstrate the error of false doctrines or *ethics*. Like *apologetics*, polemics cannot produce *conversion*, but it can be a means of turning people away from false religious and philosophical systems so that they can consider the truth.

polity: a form of government. Various church polities include *presbyterianism*, *congregationalism*, *episcopalian polity*, *civil supremacy*, the *papacy*, *theocracy*, *anarchy*, *single pastor polity*, and pure *democracy* (chap. 76).

polytheism: the belief in many gods. Polytheists may fear or worship many spirits associated with animals and objects (*animism*), practice sorcery, and believe that all things are ultimately one (*pantheism*) or that one spirit fills all things (*panentheism*) (chap. 10).

pontiff: another title of the *pope*, meaning "high priest" (chap. 76).

pope: the *bishop* of Rome in the *episcopal polity* of the Roman Catholic Church. According to *Roman Catholicism*, the pope is the visible head of the *church* *militant* throughout the world, the *vicar of Christ* who has apostolic authority and the ability to speak infallibly when defining doctrine and *ethics* (chap. 76).

positive law: commandments by mere authority, not *natural law*. Positive law does not arise necessarily from the *divine nature* or from our human nature. An example of God's positive law is the particular day of the week designated as the *Sabbath* (chaps. 68, 69).

postmillennialism: the interpretation of the *millennium* ("thousand years") in Revelation 20 as a future period of righteousness and peace on earth before Christ's *second coming*. Postmillennialism is one example of the doctrine of the *preeminence of the church* (chap. 91).

post-tribulational rapture: the belief that Christ will *rapture* the church (and raise dead Christians) at the end of the *tribulation* period preceding his *second coming*. This is a common belief in *premillennialism* outside of *dispensationalism*.

practical syllogism: a means of *assurance of salvation* by the application of God's Word through the Spirit's *illumination* to recognize the outward fruit of *regeneration*. One might reason, "According to the *Holy Scriptures*, only those with *faith in Jesus Christ* receive the *witness of the Holy Spirit* that they bear fruit in *good works*. I know by the Spirit's witness that I bear fruit in *good works*. Therefore, I have faith in Christ."

prayer, Christian: presenting one's desires to God through *faith in Jesus Christ* with thanksgiving. Christian prayer is evidence of *saving grace*, only possible by the Holy Spirit. It is also a *means of grace*, for in prayer God's children draw near to their Father (chaps. 71, 85).

preacher: a herald of Christ with *spiritual gifts* of teaching and exhortation who boldly and publicly proclaims the *Word of God*. A preacher serves as Christ's ambassador and a *minister* of the *new covenant* by the power of the Spirit (chap. 77).

preaching: the work of a *preacher* to explain and apply God's Word as an act of bold, official, and public proclamation (chap. 81).

preceptive will: God's choice of what his rational creatures, including both men and *angels*, should do as their duty to him. God's preceptive will is distinguished from his *decretive will*, for his precepts or laws define our responsibility (chap. 15).

predestination: God's *decree* of *election* of some people to *eternal life with God* and *reprobation* of others to *eternal punishment*, executed by God's *sovereignty* in his work of *providence*, all to the manifestation of his *glory* in *grace* and *justice* (chaps. 22–23).

preeminence of the church: the doctrine that before Christ's *second coming*, God will give the church supreme spiritual influence over the world, whether with cultural transformation, economic and scientific advance, or political dominion. This doctrine is part of *postmillennialism* but is also consistent with some kinds of *premillennialism* and *inaugurated millennialism* (chap. 91).

preexistence of Christ: the life and activity of the Son of God before his *incarnation* (chap. 19).

preexistence of the soul: the belief that the human *soul* existed in a spiritual state before entering this world by conception in its mother's womb. This view has no biblical basis.

premillennialism: the interpretation of the *millennium* ("thousand years") in Revelation 20 as a time of Christ's reign on earth after his *second coming* and before the *day of judgment*. *Dispensationalism* is a form of premillennialism that focuses on Israel (chap. 91).

preparation by grace: the work of the Spirit to awaken sinners to their need of Christ. Preparation by grace is a *common grace* granting *illumination* of the mind to understand God's Word and conviction of the *conscience* to sense one's sins (chap. 57).

preparationism: the false teaching that sinners can prepare themselves for *conversion*. *Preparation by grace* is consistent with *total inability*, but preparationism asserts that God gives *saving grace* to those who make good use of *prevenient grace* (chap. 57).

presbyterianism: a system of *polity* in which churches are governed by councils of *elders* on the levels of the *particular church* (a *consistory* or *session*), a regional federation (a *classis* or *presbytery*), and a broader federation (a *synod* or *general assembly*) (chap. 76).

Presbyterian theology: for the whole system of *theology*, see *Reformed theology*; for the view of church *polity*, see *presbyterianism*.

presbytery: according to the *polity* of *presbyterianism*, another term for a *classis* or a council of *elders* (including both *ruling elders* and *ministers of the Word* or *teaching elders*) governing a regional federation of *particular churches* (chap. 76).

preservation of the saints: another term for the *perseverance of the saints*, emphasizing God's gracious work to cause the *saints* to willingly persevere in faith and obedience (chap. 64).

preterism: interpretation of the book of Revelation and other passages as symbolic accounts of events that took place in the first century. *Full preterism* sees all these events foretold in Scripture as fulfilled, but *partial preterism* only most events (chap. 90).

pretribulational rapture: the belief that Christ will catch up the church (when he also raises dead Christians) and take them all to *heaven* before the beginning of a final *tribulation* preceding his *second coming*. This is the majority view of *dispensationalism*.

prevenient grace: the doctrine of *Roman Catholicism* and *Arminianism* that God gives sufficient *grace* to all humanity that, despite the *fall of man* into the *state of sin*, all people have a restored ability to cooperate with God and be saved if they choose (chap. 58).

priest: in God's *covenants*, the *office* of offering a *sacrifice* to God for sin and interceding for sinners. The *old covenant* priests were *types* of Christ the High Priest, who gave himself as a sacrifice for sin once for all and makes *intercession* at God's right hand. Believers are a priestly people in Christ, given access to God in *worship* and *prayer* (chaps. 45, 47–49, 51).

private means of grace: *means of grace* used outside of *public worship*, whether alone, in family worship, or with friends. The private means of grace include reading, meditation on the Word, *prayer*, fasting, godly conversation, and singing psalms and hymns.

problem of evil: the argument that an all-good and all-powerful God would not permit evil to exist; but evil exists, and therefore, there must not be such a God. Logically, the problem of evil is not compelling because God can have good reasons to permit evil (chap. 26).

process theology: a modern philosophy of *panentheism* that teaches a God of *love* who exists in two poles: the universal, absolute spirit of love and the particular love in each individual person or thing. This deity has *compassion* but no *sovereignty* or *foreknowledge*.

progressive covenantalism: a middle way between *dispensationalism* and *covenant theology* held by some teachers of *Baptist theology*. This view teaches a *covenant* with Adam and a fulfillment of God's promises to Israel in the church but denies that there is one *covenant of grace* or that we must keep the *Sabbath* (chap. 38).

progressive creationism: the teaching that God created different kinds of biological life at different points in history over billions of years rather than in six days. This belief is consistent with the *day-age view* of Genesis 1 and contradicts the *calendar day view*.

progressive dispensationalism: a modification of *dispensationalism* that allows for the fulfillment of some Old Testament promises to Israel in the *new covenant* church while asserting that Christ's reign over Israel will begin at the *millennium* (see *premillennialism*).

progressive sanctification: the *saving grace* by which God causes believers in Christ to grow in holiness. In progressive sanctification, the work of God produces and cooperates with the work of believers—unlike *regeneration*, which is entirely *monergistic* (chap. 63).

prolegomena: the doctrine of our knowledge of God, including questions about the nature and method of *theology* and the doctrine about *revelation* and the *Word of God* (part 1).

prophet: in God's *covenants*, the *office* of receiving the word of God by *special revelation* and communicating it without error. The *old covenant* prophets were *types* of Christ as the supreme Prophet, who is the living *Word* of God and the light of the world to illuminate the mind. Believers are all prophetic people in Christ, anointed to know God's truth and speak it to others, though not by new *special revelation* (chaps. 45, 46, 51, 54).

propitiation: the appeasing of anger by a gift to the offended party. Christ accomplished propitiation as the *Priest* of his people, turning away the *wrath of God* by offering his *active* and *passive obedience* to the law as *satisfaction* to God's *justice* (chap. 47).

prosperity theology: the error that believers in Christ can obtain health and wealth by speaking words of positive confession and paying tithes and offerings. Prosperity theology is at root *panentheism*, the belief that men can share in the *divine nature* (chap. 88).

providence: God's work of executing his *decree* in history by his *preservation* and control of his creatures and *concurrence* with their actions. In providence, God exercises his *omnipotence* according to his *wisdom* and *goodness* to work all things for his *glory* in the good of his people (chap. 26).

public means of grace: the *means of grace* used in *public worship*. The public means of grace are the *preaching* and teaching of God's Word, *prayer*, praise, fellowship, *discipline of the church*, and the *sacraments* of *baptism* and the *Lord's Supper* (chap. 81).

public worship: *worship* as the gathered church. Public worship is the exercise of love for God through outward expressions of his worthiness according to his will in the assembly of his people in his *special presence*. It is directed by the *regulative principle* (chap. 80).

pure act: see *actus purus*.

purgatory: according to *Roman Catholicism*, the state of the faithful dead who have not yet been fully purified of *venial sin* by *penance*. The faithful are said to suffer in purgatory the temporal punishment of sin until prepared to enter *heaven*. This doctrine is not taught in the *Holy Scriptures* (chap. 89).

ransom to the Devil: view of some early church theologians that in Christ's death he paid the price of *redemption* to *Satan* to release sinners. On the contrary, Christ offered his *sacrifice* to God as a *satisfaction* of God's *justice* by *penal substitution* (chap. 47).

rapture: Christ's catching up the church (living and dead) to meet him in the clouds. There are various views of the timing of the rapture: *pretribulational* (majority *dispensationalism*), *midtribulational* (minority *dispensationalism*), *post-tribulational* (non-dispensational *premillennialism*), or at the general *resurrection of the dead* at the *second coming* (*amillennialism/inaugurated millennialism, postmillennialism*) (chaps. 91, 93).

rationalism: the belief that human reason is the primary source and final judge of knowledge. Rationalism opposes doctrines such as the *Trinity*, which is not a logical contradiction but transcends reason because of the *incomprehensibility* of God.

real physical presence: the view of the *Lord's Supper* that Christ's body and blood are physically present with all who partake. Two views of how this takes place are *transubstantiation* and the *Lutheran view of the Lord's Supper* (chap. 84).

real spiritual presence: the view of the *Lord's Supper* that Christ is spiritually present with believers by the Holy Spirit so that they commune with him as both God and man. This is the view of *Reformed theology* (chap. 84).

reconciliation: the work of changing a relationship of hostility to a relationship of peace. Christ, the *Priest* of his estranged people, made reconciliation for them by his death so that they are no longer counted as God's enemies but as his beloved friends (chap. 47).

redemption: releasing prisoners by the payment of a price. Christ, the *Priest* of his guilty people, accomplished redemption by laying down his life as the ransom to God, bearing the curse of God's law against lawbreakers so that they receive his blessing (chap. 47).

reformation of the church: the restoration of the church to the doctrinal and practical standards of God's Word. Reformation is not innovation but a return to the old ways (chap. 86).

Reformation, Protestant: the renewal of biblical doctrine and life in the sixteenth-century church. The Reformers left *Roman Catholicism*, often being excommunicated by the *pope*, and formed the Lutheran churches, the Reformed churches, and the Anabaptist churches.

Reformed Baptist theology: an adaptation of *Reformed theology* according to belief in *credobaptism* and *congregationalism*. Reformed Baptist theology (formerly known as *Particular Baptist theology*) follows the Second London Baptist Confession.

Reformed theology: the *theology* of the Reformed churches that arose from the *Reformation* in Switzerland and soon became an international movement. Like *Lutheran theology*, Reformed theology embraces the *catholic orthodoxy* of the ancient creeds and the *evangelical* doctrines of *sola Scriptura*, *sola gratia*, *solus Christus*, *sola fide*, and *soli Deo gloria*. Reformed theology centers on God's *sovereignty* as he works all things for his *glory*. Reformed *hermeneutics* interprets the Bible according to its great theme of God's *covenant* with his people through Christ (*covenant theology*). The Reformed doctrine of *saving grace* emphasizes that salvation is of the Lord alone by his *unconditional election*, *particular redemption* in Christ, *effectual calling* of sinners perishing in their *total depravity* and *total inability*, and *preservation* of his children resulting in the *perseverance of the saints* (the *five points of Calvinism*). Reformed *worship* is directed by the *Holy Scriptures*, not human ideas, according to the *regulative principle of worship*. Reformed *piety* springs from the *experiential knowledge* of God as the Holy Spirit produces in the soul a sense of misery in sin, deliverance in Christ, and grateful love to God. Reformed theology presents a comprehensive view of the Christian life expressed in the Reformed confessions, such as the Belgic Confession, Heidelberg Catechism, Second Helvetic Confession, Canons of Dort, Westminster Confession of Faith, Westminster Shorter Catechism, and Westminster Larger Catechism (chap. 2).

regeneration: supernatural rebirth into spiritual life. Regeneration is like a *resurrection of the dead* and a new creation, and so it is a work of *monergism* and *effectual grace* that produces a new life of *faith in Jesus Christ*, *repentance unto life*, *love*, and obedience to God's law (chap. 59).

regulative principle of worship: the doctrine that the church must offer to God only those *elements of public worship* that he commands in the *Holy Scriptures*. The principle distinguishes between elements, the *form of public worship*, and the *circumstances of public worship*. The regulative principle is the historic position of Reformed churches (chap. 80).

reincarnation: the teaching that the *soul* of a living being is reborn after death in a new existence according to its *merit* or demerit. Reincarnation is part of the cycle of existence taught in many religions of *pantheism* and *panentheism* (chap. 87).

religious pluralism: the belief that God draws people to himself through many religions, not just one. Since religions contradict one another, religious pluralism claims that no religion has truth directly from God but that all religions represent humanity's groping after God (chap. 5).

repentance unto life: a *saving grace*, by which a sinner turns from sin to God. Saving repentance involves a change in beliefs, affections, choices, and actions, comes with *faith* in God's mercy in Christ, and is necessary for salvation (chap. 60).

reprobation: God's selection in his *decree* of those who will suffer *eternal punishment* for their sins. In reprobation, God eternally chose to abandon certain individuals to hardness of heart by not giving them *saving grace*, so that they would receive the punishment their sins deserve, to the praise of his *justice* (chap. 22).

resurrection of Christ: the raising of Jesus from physical *death* with a living human body and *soul*. Christ's resurrection was the beginning of his *state of exaltation* and is the cause of the *regeneration* of sinners and the future *resurrection of the dead* (chap. 45).

resurrection of the dead: the restoration of mankind to physical life, reuniting body and *soul* forever. Christ will raise the wicked dead and the righteous dead and will change the righteous who yet live so that all his *elect* share in his *glory* by the Holy Spirit (chap. 93).

revealed will of God: another term for his *preceptive will*, emphasizing that God has made known our duty to believe and do certain things.

revelation: God's communication of truths that people would not know or at least not know with certainty, whether through *general revelation* or *special revelation*. God reveals himself and his will on a level that human beings can understand and communicate to one another so that they may know his *glory* (chap. 3).

revival: a special season when the Holy Spirit does his usual works of *regeneration* and *sanctification* through the Word with unusual power in the church, often producing effects in the larger community, all for the *glory of God*. Revival does not consist in *miracles* but in more abundant *saving grace* (chap. 65).

righteousness of God: the *attribute of God* that he is the standard of moral perfection. God commands righteousness in his laws, rules in righteousness, punishes acts contrary to righteousness, honors righteousness in salvation, and rewards righteousness (chap. 17).

Roman Catholicism: a religious system characterized by belief in the *Apostles' Creed* and the *Nicene Creed*, the *papacy*, the *sacramental system*, and the reception of official church tradition as God's *special revelation*. Roman Catholicism developed in the medieval period from the churches of Western, Latin-speaking Europe (chap. 76).

rule of faith: a short summary of Christian *orthodoxy*, such as the *Apostles' Creed*, often used as a guide for interpreting the Bible correctly (*analogy of faith*) and maintaining *orthodoxy*.

ruling elder: an *elder* who is ordinarily not called to preach. Though not *ministers of the Word* (*teaching elders*), ruling elders have equal authority in the church's ruling council (*consistory* or *session*) and share to some extent in the ministers' task of pastoring the flock (chap. 77).

Sabbath: the weekly day on which God requires rest and *public worship* but permits *works of necessity*, *mercy*, and *piety*. The Sabbath is a *creation ordinance* and *moral law*, though which day it must be observed is *positive law*—it was formerly the seventh day of the week, but now is the first day (the *Lord's Day*) because the *resurrection of Christ* happened on that day (chap. 69).

Sabellianism: the *heresy* that Christ is the same *person* as the Father. Sabellius taught a form of *modalism* in which the Father came to earth and died on the cross (*patripassianism*). A similar error is taught today by oneness *Pentecostalism* (chap. 44).

sacrament: a ceremony instituted by Christ in the church as a covenantal sign and seal of *saving grace*. The sacraments serve as *public means of grace* through faith in the *gospel*. The sacraments of the *new covenant* are *baptism* and the *Lord's Supper* (chap. 81)

sacramental system: the efficacious administration of God's *grace* by the church through the seven *sacraments*, according to *Roman Catholicism* and *Eastern Orthodoxy*. In this system, the seven sacraments are *baptism*, *confirmation* (or *chrismation*), the *Eucharist* (the *Lord's Supper*), *penance*, *extreme unction*, *holy orders*, and *marriage* (chap. 81).

sacrifice: something offered to God at one's own expense as an act of obedient *worship*. Animal sacrifices, as under the *old covenant*, were *types* of Christ. Jesus Christ's sacrifice was his work as *Priest* to offer his *active* and *passive obedience* to God, culminating in his death and burial, for *redemption*, *reconciliation*, and *propitiation* by *penal substitution* for the *satisfaction* of God's justice against sinners. Christ's people offer *spiritual sacrifices*, not for sins but to express thanksgiving and praise (chaps. 47–48, 51).

saints: God's holy ones. In *Roman Catholicism* and *Eastern Orthodoxy*, *saint* especially refers to a person who attained unusual holiness on earth and continues to have spiritual influence and to work *miracles* as an intercessor in *heaven*, recognized by the church by official canonization. In the Bible, true saints are not an elite group in the church but all those given *saving grace*, including the grace of *sanctification* (chap. 63).

sanctification: the *saving grace* of God by which he makes his people holy in heart and life. Sanctification takes place first in *definitive sanctification* at *conversion* and then in *progressive sanctification* throughout life, both by *union with Christ* (chap. 63).

Satan: another name for the *Devil*. Satan means "adversary" (chap. 27).

satisfaction: the payment of someone's debt to God's *justice*, often by a priestly *sacrifice*. According to *Reformed theology*, Christ made satisfaction by *penal substitution* as the *surety* for his people by his *active* and *passive obedience* to the law. According to the *sacramental system* of *Roman Catholicism*, the *Eucharist* is a *sacrifice* that makes satisfaction for the sins of the living and the dead, and *penance* makes satisfaction for the temporal punishment of sin (chaps. 47, 81).

saving faith: see *faith in Jesus Christ*.

saving grace: the work of God's undeserved kindness to sinners to save them from sin and bring them to himself. *Common grace* is given to all people in various ways, but saving grace is granted only to God's *elect* and is received only through *union with Christ* (chap. 52).

Scripture: see *Holy Scriptures.*

sealing of the Holy Spirit: the Spirit's work of objectively marking believers as belonging to God forever, performed in their *regeneration* to bear the renewed *image of God*, on which basis the Spirit subjectively produces *assurance of salvation* through his inner *witness* to their transformation (chap. 66).

secondary causes: factors and agents in God's created world that act as true causes of events, though under God's *providence* as the primary cause (*concurrence*). *Reformed theology* teaches that secondary causes can act by *necessity*, *contingency*, or *free choice of the will* under God's *sovereignty.*

second coming of Christ: the return of the Lord Jesus as a visible man in his majesty as the Son of God. Christ will come again with his *angels* to reveal the *glory of God* and bring about the end of the age with the *resurrection of the dead* and the *day of judgment* (chap. 92).

secret will of God: another term for his *decretive will*, emphasizing that we know relatively little about God's *decree*, compared to the full *revelation* of his *preceptive will.*

secular humanism: a modern form of *atheism* that makes humanity into its own deity and object of *worship*. Secular humanism should be distinguished from "humanism," an academic movement beginning in the Renaissance to return to classical literary sources (chap. 10).

self-authentication of the Bible: the Bible's authority to demonstrate itself to be the *Word of God*. We do not depend on the church or human reasoning to know that the Scriptures are God's Word but need only the *illumination* of the Holy Spirit to open our eyes (chap. 6).

self-existence of God: another term for the *aseity of God.*

Septuagint: a translation of the Old Testament into Greek in the second or third century BC, often abbreviated as LXX (the Roman numeral for seventy).

session: according to the *polity* of *presbyterianism*, another term for a *consistory* or a council of *elders* (including both *ruling elders* and *ministers of the Word* or *teaching elders*) governing a *particular church*. *Session*, like *presbytery* and *general assembly*, is a term used by Reformed churches originating from Great Britain (chap. 76).

session of Christ: the sitting of Christ at God's right hand after his *resurrection* and *ascension* into *heaven*. From this position in his *state of exaltation*, Christ acts as the glorified *Prophet*, *Priest*, and *King*—the *Mediator* of *saving grace* to his people (chap. 45).

***sheol*:** Hebrew term (often translated as "hell") for death, the grave, or the realm of the wicked dead, where they suffer for their sins and wait for the *resurrection of the dead* and the *day of judgment* (chap. 89).

simplicity of God: the *attribute of God* that he is not composed of parts but is one in the *divine nature*. God's simplicity means that his *attributes* are his very essence—he is *love*, *righteousness*, *wisdom*, power, life, and so on (chap. 11).

sin: hatred against God, whether in disposition, thought, or action. All sin involves rebellion against God's law, unbelief toward his word, and the *worship* of his creatures, especially ourselves, instead of him, the Creator (chap. 33).

single pastor polity: a form of church government in which authority over a *particular church* is concentrated in one *minister of the Word* who has no equals (no *plurality*) (chap. 76).

sinless perfectionism: the teaching that a believer can be free of all sin. Even after *regeneration* and deliverance from the *state of sin*, believers still have the remaining corruption of *original sin* that results in them doing *actual sins* until *death* and *glorification* (chap. 63).

sins of commission: *actual sins* consisting of doing what God forbids (chap. 36).

sins of omission: *actual sins* consisting of not doing what God commands (chap. 36).

skepticism: another term for *agnosticism*.

social Trinitarianism: the doctrine that defines the oneness of the Trinity in terms of a community of *persons* sharing perfect mutual love and empathy rather than in terms of sharing one substance (*homoousion*) by *eternal generation* and *eternal procession*.

Socinianism: a form of *theological liberalism* that arose in the sixteenth century from the teachings of Lelio Sozini and Fausto Sozzini. Socinianism denied the *Trinity*; God's *infinity*, *spirituality*, *omnipresence*, and *foreknowledge*; *original sin*; and *penal substitution* while teaching that Christ is merely a glorified man (*adoptionism*).

***sola fide*:** Latin for "by faith alone." Only *faith in Jesus Christ*, not works, is the instrument by which God forgives a sinner and counts him as righteous in *justification* (chaps. 2, 61).

sola gratia**:** Latin for "grace alone." Only God's *saving grace*, not human goodness or effort, saves sinners, for people are corrupted by sin and cannot save themselves (chaps. 2, 58).

sola Scriptura**:** Latin for "Scripture alone." Only the *Holy Scriptures* are the supreme and divine rule of faith and life, and thus have *sufficiency* to instruct us in saving faith and spiritual life, for the Bible is the *Word of God* (chaps. 2, 7).

soli Deo gloria**:** Latin for "glory to God alone." All praise for any good in believers must be given to God alone through Jesus Christ, for it is all the gift of God's *grace* (chap. 2).

solus Christus**:** Latin for "Christ alone." Only the Lord Jesus Christ is the *Mediator* of *saving grace* to sinners, not the *saints*, the *angels*, or the *ministers* of the church (chaps. 2, 39).

songs of praise: a *public* and *private means of grace* in which believers sing of the *attributes* and acts of God. The Lord reveals his *special presence* in his people's praises (chap. 85).

Son of God: the only begotten Son of the Father. Christ is not a son created or adopted at a point in time but God's natural Son by *eternal generation* so as to share in the fullness of the one *divine nature* as the second *person* in the *Trinity* (chaps. 19, 42).

soteriology: the doctrine of salvation (part 5, especially sections 5B and 5C).

soul: an invisible, intelligent, immortal human spirit. A whole human person consists of a body and a soul, but the soul is a distinct substance from the body and continues in conscious existence after the body dies (chap. 31).

soul sleep: the doctrine that after death the human *soul* is unconscious until the *resurrection of the dead*. This is contradicted by the Bible's doctrine of life after death (chap. 89).

sovereignty of God: his effectual rule as supreme Lord over all things. God's sovereignty includes his *preceptive will*, *decretive will*, *authority*, and *omnipotence* (chap. 15), and is exercised in his *decree* and works of *creation* and *providence* (chaps. 21–26).

special presence of God: the dwelling of God with people by making known his *glory*. God's special presence in *heaven* and his earthly temple does not confine him to those places, as is clear from his *attributes* of *immensity* and *omnipresence* (chap. 12).

special revelation: divine *revelation* given supernaturally to select people. God has made known himself, his works, his law, and his *gospel* to his *prophets* and *apostles*, who wrote the *Holy Scriptures* so that the church could bring their message to the world (chaps. 3, 5).

spirit, human: see *soul.*

spiritual gift: a gracious stewardship from God that gives a person power to build up Christ's church by the activity of the Holy Spirit. Gifts of new *special revelation* and working *miracles* have ceased (*cessationism*), but other gifts continue (chap. 54).

spirituality of God: the *attribute of God* that he is spirit, analogous to *angels* and *human spirits.* The spirituality of God implies that he has no body and is an invisible, living, intelligent, personal being (chap. 11).

spiritual presence: regarding the *Lord's Supper*, see *real spiritual presence.* See also *special presence of God.*

spiritual sacrifices: offerings to God through Christ in the Holy Spirit by his priestly people. Spiritual *sacrifices* include offering to God oneself as a living sacrifice, one's repentance, praise, care for others, financial gifts, missions, and martyrdom (chap. 51).

state of exaltation: the second of Christ's *two states*, in which his divine glory is being revealed through the glorification of his human nature as the reward of his *satisfaction* of the demands and penalties of the law. The state of exaltation includes Christ's *resurrection* from the dead, *ascension*, *session* at God's right hand, and *second coming* (chap. 45).

state of glory: man's spiritual condition after the *state of grace*, having been delivered from remaining sin by death or Christ's return. This final stage of man's *fourfold state* consists of the glorious liberty that always freely chooses God and cannot sin (chap. 35).

state of grace: man's spiritual condition after being delivered from the *state of sin* by *saving grace.* In this third stage of man's *fourfold state*, human nature is renewed in its ability to freely choose God and his will but does so imperfectly due to remaining sin (chap. 35).

state of humiliation: the first of Christ's *two states*, in which his divine glory was hidden by the suffering and death of his human nature as the consequence of his subjection to the demands and penalties of the law. The state of humiliation began with Christ's *incarnation* and included his sufferings, crucifixion, death, and burial (chap. 45).

state of innocence: man's spiritual condition as created by God in righteousness. In this first stage of the *fourfold state of man*, human nature was very good and had the ability to freely choose God and his will but also could change by choosing sin (chap. 35).

state of sin: man's spiritual condition due to *original sin* after the *fall of man*. In this second stage of the *fourfold state of man*, human nature is corrupt, having *total inability* to choose God and his will, so that it always freely chooses to do *actual sins* (chap. 35).

states of Christ: see *two states of Christ*, *state of humiliation*, and *state of exaltation*.

Stoicism: an ancient Greek philosophy of *pantheism*, which asserted that the physical universe and its rational order are all that exist and that man should cultivate virtue to attain happiness.

subordinationism: the teaching that Christ is in some sense divine but is less than God the Father, not sharing the full *divine nature* in all its *attributes*.

subsequence: the doctrine taught in *Pentecostalism* that the *baptism with the Holy Spirit* is distinct from the initial graces that come with salvation and may be received later, after *conversion* (chap. 53).

subsistence: in the doctrine of the *Trinity*, an individual instance of the *divine nature*—another term for the *person* of the Father, the Son, or the Holy Spirit.

substitutionary atonement: the doctrine that Christ died in the place of sinners. More specifically, he died as the *penal substitution* for the *elect* (*particular redemption*).

sufficiency of Christ's sacrifice: the infinite worth of Christ's offering of himself for sin. This sufficiency, based on the *hypostatic union* of God and man in the *incarnation*, means that Christ's suffering and death have unlimited *merit* to save all who trust in him (chap. 48).

sufficiency of God: the *attribute of God* that he is the infinite fullness of *goodness* and *glory*. Closely related to God's *aseity*, his sufficiency means that he is the overflowing fountain of all good to his creation, but he himself needs nothing (chap. 12).

sufficiency of Scripture: the completeness of the *Holy Scriptures* for instruction in faith and obedience toward God. Though we still need teachers to help us to study the Bible, the Bible contains all the truths we need to know about how to be saved and please God (chap. 7).

supralapsarianism: the doctrine that *predestination* precedes the *fall* in the logical (not temporal) order of God's eternal *decree*, as distinct from *infralapsarianism*. Supralapsarianism emphasizes God's aim to glorify himself in *election* and *reprobation*.

surety: someone who binds himself to fulfill a legal obligation belonging to another. In the *covenant of grace*, Christ is the surety of God's people, having been appointed in the *counsel of peace* to save them by *penal substitution* (chap. 47).

suspension: the temporary loss of the privileges of church *membership*, especially the *Lord's Supper*, as an act of *corrective church discipline*. Suspension often accompanies *censure* after repeated refusals to listen to calls to *repentance* of serious sin (chap. 85).

syllogism: a form of logical proof through reasoning based on certain premises. A categorical syllogism consists of a major premise, a minor premise, and a conclusion. For example: "All men are mortal. John is a man. Therefore, John is mortal."

synergism: the cooperation of God's *saving grace* and man's *free choice of the will*. There is no synergism in *election* or *regeneration*, which are only God's work (*monergism*). In *progressive sanctification*, believers must will and work by the *grace of God* to grow more holy (chaps. 23, 58, 63).

synod: a council of leaders from multiple churches. In the *polity* of *presbyterianism*, a synod is a council of *elders* (including both *ruling elders* and *ministers of the Word* or *teaching elders*) governing a federation of *particular churches*, sometimes a federation broader than a *classis* or *presbytery* (chap. 76).

systematic theology: a presentation of all the doctrines of Christianity organized by topic. Systematic theology answers the question What does the whole Bible teach about each of its major topics and its relation to other topics? The many topics of systematic theology are organized under eight *loci*: *prolegomena*, *theology proper*, *anthropology*, *Christology*, *pneumatology*, *soteriology*, *ecclesiology*, and *eschatology* (chap. 1).

Taoism: another spelling of *Daoism*.

teaching elder: another term for a *minister of the Word* (chap. 77).

teleological argument: an argument for God's existence stating that the wise design of the observable universe and the biological life in it demonstrates the existence of a wise designer, the Creator. See the last of the *five ways of Thomism*.

teleology: the study of the purpose, aim, or end of something (*final cause*).

temporary administrations: the outward elements of the *old covenant*. By these elements, God administered the grace of the *covenant of grace* to his people under *historical covenants* before Christ came and established the *new covenant* in place of the *old* (chap. 40).

Ten Commandments: the summary of the *moral law*, which God spoke to Israel (Ex. 20:1–17). They are, in brief: (1) You shall have no other gods before me. (2) You shall not make any graven image. (3) You shall not take the name of the Lord in vain. (4) Remember the *Sabbath* day, to keep it holy. (5) Honor your father and mother. (6) You shall not murder. (7) You shall not commit adultery. (8) You shall not steal. (9) You shall not bear false witness. (10) You shall not covet (chaps. 68–70).

textual criticism: the study of a literary work seeking to establish its original text. The textual criticism of the *Holy Scriptures* examines differences among ancient manuscripts and quotations of Scripture in ancient writings to determine the original text of the Bible since the original manuscripts are no longer available.

theistic evolution: the belief that God, in his *providence*, used *evolution* to make all forms of biological life on earth over billions of years. This view is inconsistent with a *calendar day view* of Genesis 1 and a literal reading of Genesis 2 (chap. 25).

theocracy: the direct rule of God over a community through a supernaturally empowered leader. True theocracy has been found on earth only in *old covenant* Israel, but it will return in the kingdom of Christ after he returns (chap. 76).

theological liberalism: an alternative belief system to Christianity that denies the *inerrancy* of the Bible and bases religion on human reasoning and felt experience. Developed in the nineteenth century, theological liberalism claims to accommodate Christianity to modern beliefs (and so is called *modernism*) but denies central doctrines of Christianity (chap. 5).

theological professor: a teacher set apart to train future *preachers*, *pastors*, and other teachers. The theological professor may be considered either as a kind of *minister of the Word* or as a distinct *office* in the church (chap. 77).

theology: the study of God and the doctrines he gave by *revelation*. Christian theology is the church's description of the authoritative knowledge and wisdom revealed in the *Word of God* so that we may know him and live unto him through Jesus Christ (chap. 1).

theology proper: the doctrine of God (part 2).

theonomy: the doctrine that the *judicial law* of Moses continues to bind all nations to follow its statutes in civil government. On the contrary, the *judicial law* pertained directly to God's ancient *theocracy* over Israel and today only gives principles of moral and judicial wisdom (chap. 79).

theophany: an appearance of God to people. God is an invisible spirit (*spirituality*), but he is able to manifest his *glory* and *special presence* in a manner visible to the human eye or as a vision or dream in the mind of a *prophet* or seer (chap. 5).

***theosis*:** the Greek equivalent of *deification*.

***theotokos*:** a Greek term meaning "one who gave birth to God." This title is given to Mary to identify Jesus as God the Son incarnate. It is best to clarify that Mary is the mother of our Lord according to his human nature, lest someone think that Mary is part of the *Trinity*.

Theravada: a kind of *Buddhism*, popular in Sri Lanka, Myanmar, Thailand, Laos, and Cambodia, that emphasizes self-denial and meditation rather than dependence on the gods as the way to attain *nirvana*.

Thomism: the system of philosophy and *theology* developed by Thomas Aquinas, an influential medieval theologian of *Roman Catholicism*. On Thomas's arguments for God's existence, see the *five ways of Thomism*.

threefold kingdom of Christ: the reign of the *Mediator* with universal power, spiritual *grace*, and heavenly *glory* to fulfill his office as *King* (chap. 50).

threefold office of Christ: the *office* given to Christ as the *Mediator* of the *covenant of grace* to serve as the *Prophet*, *Priest*, and *King* of his people (chap. 45).

three uses of the moral law: the applications of the *moral law* in its *civil use*, *evangelical use*, and *didactic use* (chap. 68).

tongues: languages. The *spiritual gift* of speaking in tongues enables a person to declare God's excellencies in languages that his or her mind does not understand even as he or she speaks (chap. 54).

total depravity: the corruption of man's whole nature by sin. Total depravity does not mean that everyone is as bad as he can be; rather, it means that every part of who we are is stained by sin and unacceptable to God apart from the *saving grace* of Christ (chap. 34).

total inability: the complete lack of inclination and power to please God. Being dead in sin, people in the *state of sin* cannot submit to God's law in its spiritual demands, cannot come to Christ in *saving faith*, cannot receive the Holy Spirit, and cannot bear fruit in *good works* acceptable to God (chap. 35).

traducian view of the soul: the belief that the *soul* of a child comes from its parents when they generate its physical body by sexual reproduction. The origin of each soul is a mystery not revealed in the *Holy Scriptures*.

transcendence: the quality of being far above or beyond (the opposite of *immanence*). Transcendence is often used for God's *infinity* or *holiness*, by which he is immeasurably greater than the world he created.

transhumanism: the hope that technology will allow human minds to escape the limitations of human bodies. Transhumanism says that using machines and information technology to enhance or replace the human body is the next step of *evolution* (chap. 87).

transubstantiation: the doctrine that in the *Lord's Supper* the bread and wine are transformed in substance into Christ's physical body and blood while retaining their outward forms. This is the teaching of *Roman Catholicism* and at least some in *Eastern Orthodoxy* (chap. 84).

tribulation: trouble or distress. *Dispensationalism* teaches a worldwide tribulation lasting seven years between the *rapture* of the church and the *second coming*, featuring catastrophic supernatural judgments (according to a very literal, futurist reading of Revelation). *Reformed theology* says that the church always faces tribulation and will do so until Christ's return, though there may be intensified persecution at the end (chap. 91).

trichotomy: the teaching that human beings consist of three parts: body, *soul*, and spirit. Contrary to trichotomy, the Scriptures often use *soul* and spirit for the same thing, indicating that human beings have two parts, not three (chap. 31).

Trinity, doctrine of the: the biblical teaching that the one true God eternally exists as three *persons*. The Father, the Son, and the Holy Spirit are distinct *persons* who share one *divine nature* so that each is fully God in all the *attributes of God* (chaps. 19–20).

tritheism: the belief in three gods, a *heresy* contrary to the *Trinity* (chaps. 20, 44).

triune: adjective describing God as the *Trinity*. *Triune* comes from Latin roots that literally mean "three-one," for God is three *persons* but one in the *divine nature*.

truth of God: the *attribute of God* that he is real and reliable. The truth of God means that he is the true God, not a fiction; he is true to reality in all that he thinks and says, without error or falsehood; and he is faithful to act consistently with what he says (chap. 17).

two-level Christianity: a view of *sanctification* that Christians, by faith and surrender to God, can leave behind struggle and defeat (Romans 7) and walk in victory and power (Romans 8). This is also called the second blessing, entire sanctification, the higher Christian life, *baptism with the Holy Spirit*, or the *filling of the Holy Spirit* (chap. 63).

two states of Christ: the two conditions of Christ's incarnate life defined with respect to fulfilling God's law and revealing his divine *glory*. Christ's two states consist of his *state of humiliation* and *state of exaltation* (chap. 45).

types: people, events, institutions, and religious rites designed by God to foreshadow Christ, his work, and his kingdom. A type is an imperfect but instructive picture of Christ and his *saving grace* as promised in the *covenant of grace* (chap. 40).

ubiquity: presence everywhere or in many places at the same time. The ubiquity of Christ's body is said to be a result of the *communication of properties* between his *divine nature* and humanity, according to the *Lutheran view of the Lord's Supper.*

unchangeableness: another term for the *immutability of God.*

unconditional election: the doctrine of *election* according to *Reformed theology*, which holds that God chose whom he would save in Christ apart from his *foreknowledge* of their future actions. However, *unconditional* does not mean that God saves them apart from *faith in Jesus Christ.*

uncreated energies of God: the eternal light of God's *glory*, as distinguished from his essence. Participation in God's uncreated energies is an important feature of *mysticism* in *Eastern Orthodoxy*, but this doctrine contradicts the *simplicity of God*, who is light (chap. 55).

uniformitarianism: in geology, the belief that most major geological structures formed gradually over millions or billions of years by the same slow processes presently observable in the earth. Uniformitarianism is contrasted with geological *catastrophism.*

union with Christ: the bond God forms between his Son and his people for their salvation and his *glory*. Union with Christ has two dimensions: *federal union* in the eternal *decree* and the *covenant of grace*, and *mystical union* in the life-giving work of the Spirit (chap. 55).

universal church: the *church militant* throughout the world, as distinct from *particular churches* or local congregations. The universal church is considered from two perspectives: either the *visible church* or the *invisible church* (chap. 73).

universal redemption: the teaching that Christ died for the salvation of every human being who has ever lived, a doctrine of *Arminianism* and other theological systems in contradiction to *particular redemption.* Universal redemption is sometimes held with *substitutionary atonement* but is more consistent with other *views of the atonement* (chap. 48).

universal salvation: the doctrine that God will save all people whom he created. Universal salvation contradicts *election*, *particular redemption*, the necessity of *saving grace* and *faith in Jesus Christ* in this life, and *eternal punishment* in *hell* (chaps. 48, 60, 94).

univocal language: the consistent use of a word with the same meaning, such as "I love my aunt" and "I love my uncle." If human language about God were univocal instead of *analogical*, he would be a creature on our level and not the infinite Creator (chap. 9).

unlimited atonement: another term for *universal redemption.*

unpardonable sin: another term for *blasphemy against the Holy Spirit.*

uses of the law: see *three uses of the moral law.*

Vajrayana: a kind of *Buddhism*, popular in parts of Asia, that emphasizes the use of tantric rituals and mantras as the way to attain *nirvana.*

venial sin: sin that, according to *Roman Catholicism*, does not destroy *saving grace* as *mortal sin* does. Venial sin must supposedly still be cleansed by the *sacramental system* in this life or *purgatory* in the next before a believer can enter *heaven* (chap. 36).

vicarious atonement: another term for *substitutionary atonement.*

vicar of Christ: another title of the *pope*, meaning the representative or substitute of Christ in the *church militant.* The pope claims without biblical basis to sit in Christ's place as the supreme teacher, *priest*, and ruler of the church on earth (chap. 76).

victory view of the atonement: an interpretation of Christ's sufferings and death as his kingly conquest of the powers of evil. This view, also called the *Christus Victor* view, is true but incomplete unless one also affirms the doctrine of *penal substitution* (chaps. 47, 50).

view of the atonement: an explanation for how Christ's death saves sinners, such as the *governmental*, *moral influence*, *ransom to the Devil*, *substitutionary atonement* (or more specifically, *penal substitution*), and *victory* views.

virgin birth: the birth of Christ after his miraculous conception in the womb of the virgin Mary. Jesus has no physical human father, but his human nature was formed from Mary's body without sexual intercourse by the power of the Holy Spirit (chap. 43).

visible church: the *universal church* as considered according to the *marks of the true church* that people on earth can observe. Not all people who are formal *members* in the visible church are partakers of the *saving grace* of Christ (the *invisible church*) (chap. 73).

will of God: God's holy pleasure, choices, and purposes as a personal being. God's will toward the created world is always characterized by his *sovereignty*, and it can be distinguished into his *decretive will* and *preceptive will* (chap. 15).

wisdom of God: the *attribute of God* that he has infinite skill to create the world and rule it well. The wisdom of God is his ability in his *decree* to choose excellent goals and excellent means to accomplish them, sometimes in mysterious and surprising ways (chap. 14).

witness of the Holy Spirit: the Spirit's work to produce *assurance of salvation*, comparable to testimony in a courtroom. The Spirit testifies by applying the promises of the *Word of God* to the *soul* to show a person that he or she is God's beloved child, evidenced by the fruits of *regeneration* in inward godliness (the *mystical syllogism*) and *good works* (the *practical syllogism*). Some Reformed theologians teach that the Spirit may also add his direct testimony to a *soul* by speaking through the *Word of God* apart from evidence (chap. 66).

Word: a title of the Son of God, drawing attention to his distinct *person* as the self-expression of the Father (*eternal generation*), in whom he acts in *creation*, *providence*, and *revelation*.

Word of God: God's speech or message. When the Bible speaks of the message of the *prophets* and *apostles* as the Word of God, it does not mean that it is man's word about God but God's Word to man (*inspiration*), coming with the *truth* and *authority* of God (chap. 6).

works of mercy: activity approved by God on the *Sabbath* because it is done to prevent or relieve the misery of human beings or animals (chap. 69).

works of necessity: activity approved by God on the *Sabbath* because it is done to preserve human health and life (chap. 69).

works of piety: activity approved by God on the *Sabbath* because it is done to worship God and communicate his *Word* to people (chap. 69).

worship: offering of one's self, service, and resources to God according to his will because of his worthiness and in gratitude for his kindness. We distinguish between worship in all of life, worship through outward expressions of praise, and *public worship* (chap. 80).

wrath of God: the affection of God's righteous hatred of sin and will to punish sinners. God's wrath is the attitude and action against sin that his *attribute* of *righteousness* demands, consistent with his *wisdom*, *goodness*, and *beatitude*, unlike human *passions* (chap. 18).

Select List of Theologians

In this book, we often quote or mention theologians who lived in past times but continue to have influence today. We provide here a list of their names, birth and death dates (if known), and brief biographical statements about them.[1] Some theologians of the ancient and medieval periods are listed under their first names, for their second "names" identify the places where they originated (such as Peter Lombard and Thomas Aquinas).

Though our list spans church history, it is certainly not exhaustive, and it especially focuses on Reformed and Puritan theologians. For short biographies of English Puritan divines, together with some Scottish and Dutch writers of a similar mindset, see Joel R. Beeke, Fraser Jones, and Randall J. Pederson, *Meet the Puritans: With a Guide to Reprints*, 2nd ed. (Grand Rapids, MI: Reformation Heritage Books, forthcoming).

Archibald Alexander (1772–1851) was a Presbyterian theologian from Virginia who served as the first professor of Princeton Theological Seminary.

Ambrose of Milan (c. 339–397) was a theologian, defender of Nicene orthodoxy, hymn writer, and bishop who was instrumental in the conversion of Augustine of Hippo.

Isaac Ambrose (1604–1664) was an English Puritan Presbyterian minister and theologian who was the author of *Looking unto Jesus* and other treatises on the spiritual life.

William Ames (1576–1633) was an English Puritan Congregationalist theologian who taught theology at the University of Franeker in the Netherlands.

1 We are indebted to Fraser Jones, research assistant to Joel Beeke, for compiling this information. The abbreviation "fl.," for *floruit* ("flourished"), refers to the approximate time when a person was active. The abbreviation "c.," for *circa* ("about"), indicates that the exact date is not known.

Moïse Amyraut (1596–1664) was a French Reformed theologian and professor at the University of Saumur who modified Reformed theology to teach a decree of hypothetical universal salvation for all who might believe, a system known as Amyraldianism.

Anselm of Canterbury (c. 1033–1109) was an Italian monk, philosopher, and theologian who served as a teacher in France and later as the archbishop of Canterbury, England.

Apollinarius of Laodicea (fl. 360) was the bishop of Laodicea who taught that Christ had no human soul but that his incarnation consisted in the union of the rational Word (*Logos*) with a human body.

Arius (d. 336) was a priest who taught that God the Father created the Son as his first work, a heresy condemned by the Council of Nicaea (325).

Jacob Arminius (1560–1609) was a Dutch theologian in the Reformed church and professor at the University of Leiden who taught a form of synergism known as Arminianism.

Athanasius of Alexandria (293–373) was a theologian and the bishop of Alexandria who suffered exile because of his adamant opposition to the heresy of Arianism.

Augustine of Hippo (354–430) was a theologian and bishop from North Africa whose writings greatly influenced medieval theologians and the Reformers with his emphasis on God's Trinity, beauty, and sovereignty in salvation.

Karl Barth (1886–1968) was a neoorthodox Swiss theologian who taught systematic theology at the University of Basel and was the author of *Church Dogmatics*.

Basil the Great (c. 329–379), brother of Gregory of Nyssa and author of the treatise *On the Holy Spirit*, was one of the Cappadocian fathers, theologians from what is modern-day Turkey who defended Trinitarian orthodoxy against Arianism.

William Bates (1625–1699) was an English Puritan minister known for his excellent preaching and theological writing.

Herman Bavinck (1854–1921) was a Dutch Reformed minister and theologian who taught systematic theology at the Free University of Amsterdam.

Richard Baxter (1615–1691) was an English Puritan Presbyterian minister who served in Kidderminster and published many valuable practical writings, though his doctrinal writings on redemption and justification departed from Reformed orthodoxy.

Louis Berkhof (1873–1957) was a Dutch American theologian who taught systematic theology at Calvin Theological Seminary in Grand Rapids, Michigan.

Bernard of Clairvaux (1090–1153) was a theologian, mystic, monk, and the founding abbot of the Cistercian monastic community of Clairvaux, France.

Gabriel Biel (c. 1420–1495) was a German philosopher and theologian who helped to found the University of Tübingen.

Abraham Booth (1734–1806) was an English Particular Baptist minister and theologian known for his works in favor of the doctrine of sovereign grace and the abolition of slavery.

Thomas Boston (1676–1732) was a Scottish Presbyterian minister and theologian who defended the free offer of the gospel in the "Marrow Controversy" in the Church of Scotland.

John Boys (1571–1625) was a minister and theologian in the Church of England whose writings display the evangelical, Reformed, and experiential emphasis of Puritan piety.

Thomas Bradwardine (c. 1300–1349) was a philosopher and theologian who served briefly as the archbishop of Canterbury and is known chiefly for his opposition to medieval Pelagianism.

Wilhelmus à Brakel (1635–1711) was a Reformed pastor who was part of the Dutch Further Reformation movement and was the author of *The Christian's Reasonable Service.*

William Bridge (c. 1600–1671) was an English Puritan minister who served in England and then was exiled to Rotterdam, where he ministered in a Congregationalist church until he returned to England and served as a member of the Westminster Assembly.

Thomas Brooks (1608–1680) was an English Congregationalist Puritan who ministered in London and whose writings, such as *Precious Remedies against Satan's Devices*, are treasures of practical divinity.

John Brown of Edinburgh (1784–1858), a grandson of John Brown of Haddington, was a Scottish Presbyterian minister and Bible commentator.

John Brown of Haddington (1722–1787) was a Scottish Presbyterian minister and theologian who served in the Secession Church (Associate Burgher Synod).

F. F. (Frederick Fyvie) Bruce (1910–1990) was a Scottish scholar of biblical studies who taught at the University of Sheffield and the University of Manchester.

Emil Brunner (1889–1966) was a neoorthodox Swiss theologian who taught at the University of Zurich.

Martin Bucer (1491–1551) was a Reformed theologian, Bible commentator, and Reformer who served in Strasbourg and later in Cambridge, England.

Heinrich Bullinger (1504–1575) was a Swiss minister and theologian who succeeded Ulrich Zwingli and widely influenced the Reformation by his letters and published sermons.

John Bunyan (1628–1688) was an English Baptist tinker, preacher, and writer of many books who is best known for his allegories *The Pilgrim's Progress* and *The Holy War*.

Anthony Burgess (d. 1664) was an English Puritan minister, theologian, and member of the Westminster Assembly.

Jeremiah Burroughs (1599–1646) was an English Puritan theologian and member of the Westminster Assembly who served as a Congregationalist minister in London and Rotterdam.

John Calvin (1509–1564) was a French minister, scholar, and second-generation Reformer who served in Geneva and became one of the most influential theologians in the development of the Reformed branch of the Protestant Reformation.

John Cassian (c. 360–c. 433) was a monk and theologian who served in southern Gaul (France) and whose writings asserted salvation by grace plus human cooperation.

Laurence Chaderton (c. 1536–1640) was an English Reformed theologian whose preaching, teaching, and leadership at the University of Cambridge directly influenced generations of ministers (such as William Perkins) and leaders in English law and politics.

Stephen Charnock (1628–1680) was a Puritan pastor who ministered in London and is best known as the author of *The Existence and Attributes of God*.

John Chrysostom (c. 344–407), whose name means "golden-mouthed," was an archbishop of Constantinople who championed expositional preaching.

David Clarkson (1622–1686) was an English Puritan minister who served as copastor with John Owen in London.

Edmund Clowney (1917–2005) was an American Presbyterian pastor and theologian who served as the first president of Westminster Theological Seminary in Philadelphia.

John Cotton (1585–1652) was a Puritan Congregationalist preacher and author who ministered in both England and New England.

Nehemiah Coxe (d. 1689) was a Particular Baptist minister and theologian who pastored a church in London and was an original editor of the Second London Baptist Confession.

Jean-Henri Merle d'Aubigné (1794–1872) was a French Reformed minister and historian of the Reformation who served in Geneva.

Edward Dering (c. 1540–1576) was a Puritan-minded minister in the Church of England who strongly advocated for a godly and biblically learned ministry.

David Dickson (1583–1663) was a minister in the Church of Scotland, a Bible commentator, and a professor at the University of Glasgow and the University of Edinburgh.

John Donne (1572–1631) was an English poet and minister in the Church of England.

Edward Donnelly (1943–2023) was a Presbyterian minister and principal of Reformed Theological College in Belfast, Northern Ireland.

Jochem Douma (1931–2020) was a Reformed theologian and ethicist from the Netherlands who taught at the Theological University of the Reformed Churches in Kampen.

John Duncan (1796–1870) was a Scottish Presbyterian minister, Hebrew scholar, and missionary to the Jewish people.

John Eadie (1810–1876) was a Scottish minister in the United Presbyterian Church and a professor of biblical studies.

Jonathan Edwards (1703–1758) was a Congregationalist minister and Puritan-minded theologian from New England who lived and preached during the First Great Awakening.

Thomas Erastus (1524–1583) was a Swiss professor of medicine best known for arguing that the civil government has authority over all punishment of sin, thus removing from the church its authority to excommunicate unrepentant sinners.

Ebenezer Erskine (1680–1754) was a Scottish Presbyterian minister who left the Church of Scotland and helped to found the Secession Church after the "Marrow Controversy."

Eutyches of Constantinople (c. 378–454) was a leader of a monastery in Constantinople who, in reaction against Nestorianism, taught that Christ has only one divine-human nature.

Dudley Fenner (c. 1558–1587) was an early English Puritan who was forced to spend part of his life ministering on the European continent due to persecution in England.

Charles Grandison Finney (1792–1875) was an American Presbyterian pastor who rejected much of Reformed theology and promoted a Pelagian form of revivalism.

John Flavel (1628–1691) was an English Puritan minister and theologian whose writings exhibit remarkable doctrinal clarity and spiritual warmth.

John Gill (1697–1771) was an English Particular Baptist minister, systematic theologian, and author of a commentary on the entire Bible.

Thomas Goodwin (1600–1680) was an English Puritan minister; theologian; member of the Westminster Assembly; advocate of congregationalist polity; president of Magdalen College, Oxford University; and major contributor to the Savoy Declaration.

Gottschalk of Orbais (c. 804–c. 869) was a Saxon monk and preacher who suffered persecution from church authorities for teaching election and reprobation.

William Gouge (1575–1653) was an English Puritan minister, theologian, Bible commentator, and member of the Westminster Assembly.

Andrew Gray (1633–1656) was a Scottish minister who died after two years of service but whose preaching and printed sermons were treasured as both insightful and powerful.

Richard Greenham (c. 1542–1594) was a Reformed minister in England and a pioneer in Puritan practical divinity, applying Reformed doctrine to the pastoral care of souls.

William Greenhill (1598–1671) was an English Puritan preacher who served with Jeremiah Burroughs in churches in England and the Netherlands and was a member of the Westminster Assembly.

Gregory of Nazianzus (329–389), author of *Five Theological Orations*, was one of the Cappadocian fathers, theologians from what is modern-day Turkey who defended Trinitarian orthodoxy against Arianism.

Gregory of Nyssa (c. 330–c. 395), brother of Basil the Great, was one of the Cappadocian fathers, theologians from what is modern-day Turkey who defended Trinitarian orthodoxy against Arianism.

William Gurnall (1616–1679) was an English Puritan minister who wrote *The Christian in Complete Armour*.

Carl F. H. Henry (1913–2003) was a Baptist theologian who had a major influence in launching the modern evangelical movement in the United States.

Matthew Henry (1662–1714) was a Welsh-born Puritan known for his doctrinal and practical Bible commentary.

Charles Hodge (1797–1878) was an American Presbyterian theologian and Bible commentator who served as the principal of Princeton Theological Seminary.

Anthony Hoekema (1913–1988) was a Dutch American Reformed theologian who taught systematic theology at Calvin Theological Seminary in Grand Rapids, Michigan.

Ezekiel Hopkins (1634–1690) was an English Puritan minister and theologian who served in England and Ireland.

Thomas Houston (1803–1882) was a Reformed Presbyterian minister from Ireland.

John Howe (1630–1705) was an English Puritan who ministered in England, Ireland, and the Netherlands.

Jan Hus, or John Huss (c. 1372–1415) was a Czech (Bohemian) preacher, reformer, and martyr influenced by the writings of John Wycliffe.

Irenaeus of Lyon (c. 140–c. 200) was a Greek-born bishop who ministered in Gaul (modern-day France) and refuted Gnostic heresies in the early church.

Cornelius Jansen (1585–1638) was a Dutch Roman Catholic theologian who revived interest in the teachings of Augustine of Hippo on saving grace.

John of Damascus (c. 675–c. 749) was a Greek theologian, priest, and apologist best known for defending the use of religious icons and writing *On the Orthodox Faith*.

Franciscus Junius (1545–1602) was a French minister who lived during the Protestant Reformation and became a leading figure in the development of Reformed orthodoxy.

Justin Martyr (c. 100–c. 165) was a philosopher and apologist for the Christian faith, so named because he died as a martyr during a time of religious persecution in the Roman Empire.

Benjamin Keach (1640–1704) was a Particular Baptist minister and theologian who suffered persecution for his Baptist beliefs, pastored a church in London, advocated singing psalms and hymns in church, and was a signatory to the Second London Baptist Confession.

Gerrit Hendrik Kersten (1882–1948) was a Reformed minister, theologian, and politician in the Netherlands, best known for his *Reformed Dogmatics*.

Abraham Kuyper (1837–1920) was a Dutch journalist, politician, and Reformed theologian best known for his extensive studies on the doctrine of common grace.

Edward Leigh (1602–1671) was an English Reformed theologian and a member of the English Parliament.

Martyn Lloyd-Jones (1899–1981) was a Welsh medical doctor who became a well-known Reformed preacher, ministered in London, and widely promoted the study of Puritan theology and piety.

Christopher Love (1618–1651) was a Welsh Presbyterian minister who was executed for conspiring against the English Commonwealth to restore the monarchy.

Martin Luther (1483–1546) was a German theologian, Bible translator and commentator, and Reformer residing at Wittenberg who, after his excommunication by the Roman Catholic Church, was the primary founder of Protestantism in general and the Lutheran evangelical movement in particular.

J. Gresham Machen (1881–1937) was an American Presbyterian scholar who taught at Princeton Theological Seminary and helped found Westminster Theological Seminary in Philadelphia and the Orthodox Presbyterian Church.

Thomas Manton (1620–1677) was an English Puritan Presbyterian minister whose preaching resulted in the publication of extended commentaries on portions of Scripture.

Marcion of Pontus (fl. 145) was a theologian in Rome who taught the heresy that the Old Testament Creator was not the same deity as the loving Father of Jesus Christ.

Stephen Marshall (c. 1594–1655) was an English Presbyterian Puritan minister and a member of the Westminster Assembly.

Hugh Martin (1822–1885) was a Scottish mathematician, minister, and theologian who served in the Free Church of Scotland.

Petrus van Mastricht (1630–1706) was a Dutch Reformed orthodox theologian renowned for his *Theoretical-Practical Theology*.

Robert Murray M'Cheyne (1813–1843) was a minister in the Church of Scotland who is remembered for his Christ-centered, experiential letters and mission to the Jews.

Samuel Miller (1769–1850) was an American Presbyterian minister and theologian who taught church history and church government at Princeton Theological Seminary.

Luis de Molina (1535–1600) was a Spanish Jesuit theologian and professor at Coimbra, Evora, and Madrid who argued that God predestined people based on his middle knowledge of what they would do in any hypothetical situation.

Leon Morris (1914–2006) was an Anglican New Testament scholar and Bible commentator from Australia.

John Murray (1898–1975) was a Scottish-born Presbyterian theologian and Bible commentator who taught at Princeton Theological Seminary and Westminster Theological Seminary in Philadelphia.

Nestorius (fl. 428) was a monk, theologian, and patriarch of Constantinople who objected to calling Mary the "mother of God" (*theotokos*) and was accused of teaching that Christ was two persons, one God and the other a man.

Caspar Olevianus (1536–1587) was a German Reformed theologian who coauthored the Heidelberg Catechism with Zacharias Ursinus.

John Owen (1616–1683) was an English Puritan theologian who served as a Congregationalist minister, a chaplain to Oliver Cromwell, and the vice-chancellor of the University of Oxford.

J. I. (James Innell) Packer (1926–2020) was a British-Canadian theologian who ministered in the low-church Anglican tradition, helped revive interest in Puritanism in the twentieth century, and taught at Regent College in Vancouver, British Columbia.

Pelagius (fl. 380) was a British monk active in Rome and Palestine who taught that Adam's sin did not deprive mankind of the ability to freely choose good, in opposition to the teaching of Augustine.

William Perkins (1558–1602) was an English Reformed theologian whose preaching influenced many students at Cambridge and who is now regarded as a father of Puritanism, especially in its wedding of Reformed orthodox theology with practical piety.

Peter Lombard (c. 1096–1160) was an Italian theologian who taught in Paris and whose book *The Sentences* became the central text of theological study for centuries in the West.

William Plumer (1802–1880) was an American Presbyterian minister who taught theology at Pittsburgh Theological Seminary and Columbia Theological Seminary.

Polycarp of Smyrna (d. c. 160) was the bishop of Smyrna, a disciple of the apostle John, and a martyr who died for the Christian faith.

Matthew Poole (1624–1679) was an English Puritan minister who wrote a commentary on the entire Bible.

John Preston (1587–1628) was an English Puritan who was active in politics and served as master of Emmanuel College, Cambridge.

Edward Reynolds (1599–1676) was an English Puritan who served as a member of the Westminster Assembly, vice-chancellor of the University of Oxford, and the bishop of Norwich (although he was a Presbyterian).

Richard of St. Victor (d. 1173) was a Scottish theologian who lived, taught, and wrote at the Abbey of St. Victor in Paris.

Andreas Rivetus (1572–1651) was a French Reformed theologian who taught Old Testament exegesis at the University of Leiden and contributed to the *Synopsis of a Purer Theology*.

Ralph Robinson (1614–1655) was an English Puritan Presbyterian minister.

Robert Rollock (c. 1555–1599) was a Scottish Presbyterian minister, Bible commentator, covenant theologian, and the first regent and principal of the University of Edinburgh.

Alexander Ross (1888–1958) was a Scottish Presbyterian minister in the Free Church of Scotland and a professor at Free Church College, Edinburgh.

Samuel Rutherford (1600–1661) was a Scottish Presbyterian minister who served as a commissioner at the Westminster Assembly and is remembered for his Christ-centered, experiential letters.

J. C. (John Charles) Ryle (1816–1900) was a Reformed minister in the Church of England who served as the bishop of Liverpool and wrote the book *Holiness* and expositions of the four Gospels.

Charles Ryrie (1925–2016) was an American dispensationalist Baptist theologian who taught at Dallas Theological Seminary.

Friedrich Schleiermacher (1768–1834) was a German theologian and one of the founders of modern theological liberalism.

Wilhelmus Schortinghuis (1700–1750) was a Dutch Reformed minister and theologian who ministered during the latter part of the Dutch Further Reformation movement.

Richard Sibbes (c. 1577–1635) was an English Puritan preacher and master of St Catherine's College, Cambridge, whom many nicknamed "the heavenly doctor."

Fausto Socinus (Sozzini) (1539–1604), nephew of Lelio Socinus (Sozini), was an Italian theologian active especially in Transylvania and Poland to promote the anti-Trinitarian views of his uncle, now known as Socinianism.

Lelio Socinus (Sozini) (1525–1562) was an Italian theologian who denied the Trinity, the deity of Christ, and other fundamental doctrines of the Christian faith.

R. C. Sproul (1939–2017) was an American Presbyterian theologian, a prolific author of works on Reformed theology, and the founder of Ligonier Ministries.

C. H. (Charles Haddon) Spurgeon (1834–1892) was an English Reformed Baptist pastor regarded as one of the greatest preachers of all time.

Rowland Stedman (c. 1630–1673) was an English Puritan minister who wrote *The Mystical Union of Believers with Christ.*

William Strong (d. 1654) was an English Puritan Congregationalist minister and member of the Westminster Assembly who was frequently called on to preach before the English Parliament.

George Swinnock (1627–1673) was an English Puritan minister whose preaching explored the practice of Christianity in every aspect of daily life.

Tertullian (fl. 200) was a North African lawyer, theologian, and apologist for the Christian faith.

Thomas Aquinas (1225–1274) was an Italian Dominican theologian, Bible commentator, and philosopher who taught in Paris and Rome, and whose writings profoundly shaped the teachings of the Roman Catholic Church.

Antonius Thysius (1565–1640) was a Dutch Reformed theologian, delegate to the Synod of Dort, Old Testament Bible translator, professor at Leiden University, and contributor to the *Synopsis of a Purer Theology.*

Robert Traill (1642–1716) was a Scottish Presbyterian minister who suffered religious persecution from the civil government and also served in the Netherlands and among English Puritans in London.

Francis Turretin (1623–1687) was a Reformed orthodox theologian who taught in Geneva and wrote the *Institutes of Elenctic Theology.*

William Tyndale (c. 1494–1536) was an English scholar, theologian, and martyr. He provided the first English translation of the Bible from the original Hebrew and Greek text instead of the Latin Vulgate.

Zacharias Ursinus (1534–1583) was a German Reformed theologian who coauthored the Heidelberg Catechism with Caspar Olevianus.

James Ussher (1581–1656) was an Irish bishop, historian, and Reformed theologian.

Johannes VanderKemp (1664–1718) was a Dutch Reformed minister whose exposition of the Heidelberg Catechism became a classic work of Reformed experiential theology.

J. Van Genderen (1923–2004) was a Dutch Reformed theologian who taught dogmatics at the Theological University of the Christian Reformed Churches in Apeldoorn, the Netherlands.

W. H. Velema (1929–2019) was a Dutch Reformed theologian who taught apologetics and ethics at the Theological University of the Christian Reformed Churches in Apeldoorn, the Netherlands.

Peter Martyr Vermigli (1499–1562) was an Italian Reformed theologian who taught in Oxford, Strasbourg, and Zurich.

Thomas Vincent (1634–1678) was an English Puritan minister and theologian who showed great courage and compassion in visiting the ill when the plague came to London.

Geerhardus Vos (1862–1949) was a Dutch American Reformed theologian who taught dogmatics (systematic theology) at Calvin Theological Seminary and biblical theology at Princeton Theological Seminary.

Benjamin B. Warfield (1851–1921) was an American Presbyterian theologian who taught at Princeton Theological Seminary and promoted conservative, Reformed orthodoxy.

Thomas Watson (c. 1620–1686) was an English Puritan minister whose writings are treasured for their simple, clear, and heartfelt expressions of sound doctrine.

John Wesley (1703–1791) was a minister in the Church of England, an itinerant preacher, and the primary organizer of the Arminian Methodist movement.

George Whitefield (1714–1770) was a minister in the Church of England who embraced Reformed doctrine and labored as an itinerant preacher in England, Scotland, and the American colonies.

Samuel Willard (1640–1707) was a New England Puritan whose sermons on the Westminster Shorter Catechism were published as *A Compleat Body of Divinity*.

William of Ockham (c. 1285–1347) was an English Franciscan philosopher and theologian who taught at Oxford University.

Octavius Winslow (1808–1878) was an English Baptist (later Anglican) pastor renowned for his Christ-exalting, experiential writings.

Gerard Wisse (1873–1957) was a Dutch Reformed pastor who ministered in the Netherlands and served as a professor at the Theological University of Apeldoorn.

Herman Witsius (1636–1708) was a Dutch Reformed theologian who taught at the University of Franeker, the University of Utrecht, and the University of Leiden and was the author of numerous theological treatises, such as *The Economy of the Covenants*.

Johannes Wollebius (1589–1629) was a Swiss preacher and theologian whose *Compendium* of Reformed orthodox theology was widely influential.

John Wycliffe, or Wyclif (c. 1324–1384), was an English theologian and reformer who oversaw the translation of the Latin Bible into English.

Edward Young (1907–1968) was an Old Testament scholar and Reformed theologian who taught at Westminster Theological Seminary.

Ulrich Zwingli (1484–1531) was a Reformed preacher and Reformer of the church, as well as the original founder of the Reformed movement in Switzerland.

Guide to Further Reading in *Reformed Systematic Theology*

PERHAPS AFTER READING a chapter in this book, you would like to read a fuller treatment of the same topic. The following list shows where to find the same topics addressed in our four-volume *Reformed Systematic Theology* (*RST*). There you will find a much more robust biblical and theological discussion. Furthermore, there we quote and cite many other sources, especially books in the classical, Reformed, and Puritan traditions. By consulting the footnotes in the relevant chapters of *RST*, you will find a wealth of resources for further study.

Chapters and Topics in This Book	Location in *Reformed Systematic Theology*
PART 1: THE DOCTRINE OF THE KNOWLEDGE OF GOD	
1–2: Questions about Theology	Vol. 1, chaps. 1–9
3: Introduction to God's Revelation	Vol. 1, chap. 10
4: General Revelation	Vol. 1, chaps. 11–13
5: Special Revelation	Vol. 1, chaps. 14–16
6–7: The Inspiration and Properties of the Bible	Vol. 1, chaps. 17–22
8: Applied Revelation for Practical Fruit	Vol. 1, chap. 25
PART 2: THE DOCTRINE OF GOD	
9: Introduction to the Doctrine of God	Vol. 1, chaps. 26–28

Chapters and Topics in This Book	Location in *Reformed Systematic Theology*
10: The Holy "I Am," the Only God	Vol. 1, chaps. 29–31
11–18: God's Attributes and Affections	Vol. 1, chaps. 32–44
19–20: The Trinity	Vol. 1, chaps. 45–47; Vol. 2, chap. 38; Vol. 3, chap. 1
21–23: God's Decree and Predestination to Salvation	Vol. 1, chaps. 48–51
24–25: God's Work of Creation	Vol. 2, chaps. 2–5
26: God's Work of Providence	Vol. 1, chaps. 52–53
27: Angels and Demons	Vol. 1, chaps. 54–55
PART 3: THE DOCTRINE OF MAN	
28: God's Creation of Man	Vol. 2, chaps. 1, 6–7
29: The Image of God	Vol. 2, chaps. 8–10
30: Human Gender and Sexuality	Vol. 2, chap. 11
31: The Human Body and Soul	Vol. 2, chaps. 12–13
32: God's Covenant with Adam	Vol. 2, chaps. 14–16
33: Sin and the Fall of Man	Vol. 2, chaps. 17–18
34–35: Original Sin, Total Depravity, and Free Choice	Vol. 2, chaps. 19–22
36: Actual Sins and God's Punishment of Sin	Vol. 2, chaps. 23–24
37: Sin, Suffering, and the Believer	Vol. 2, chaps. 25–26
PART 4: THE DOCTRINE OF CHRIST	
38–41: Covenant Theology and the Covenant of Grace	Vol. 2, chaps. 27–33, 35
42: Introduction to the Person and Work of Christ	Vol. 2, chaps. 36–37
43–44: Christ's Incarnation	Vol. 2, chaps. 39–42
45: Christ's Two States and Introduction to His Threefold Office	Vol. 2, chaps. 43–44

Chapters and Topics in This Book	Location in *Reformed Systematic Theology*
46: Christ's Work as Prophet	Vol. 2, chaps. 45–47
47–49: Christ's Work as Priest	Vol. 2, chaps. 48–52
50: Christ's Work as King	Vol. 2, chaps. 53–54
51: Christ's Prophetic, Priestly, and Kingly People	Vol. 2, chaps. 47, 52, 55–56
PART 5: THE DOCTRINES OF THE HOLY SPIRIT AND SALVATION	
52: The Spirit in Creation, Common Grace, and Israel	Vol. 3, chaps. 1–3
53: The Spirit of Christ and of Pentecost	Vol. 3, chaps. 4–5
54: The Gifts of the Spirit and Cessationism	Vol. 1, chaps. 23–24; Vol. 3, chaps. 6–7
55: Union with Christ and the Order of Salvation	Vol. 3, chaps. 9–11
56: The General Gospel Call	Vol. 3, chap. 12
57: Preparation by Conviction	Vol. 3, chaps. 13–14
58: Effectual Calling	Vol. 3, chaps. 15–16
59: Regeneration	Vol. 3, chaps. 17–18
60: Conversion: Repentance and Faith	Vol. 3, chaps. 19–21
61: Justification	Vol. 3, chaps. 22–24
62: Adoption	Vol. 3, chaps. 25–26
63: Sanctification	Vol. 3, chaps. 27–29
64: Preservation and Perseverance	Vol. 3, chaps. 30–31
65: The Indwelling, Leading, and Filling of the Spirit	Vol. 3, chap. 32
66: Assurance of Salvation and the Spirit's Witness	Vol. 3, chaps. 33–34
67: The Marks of Grace: The Beatitudes and the Fruit of the Spirit	Vol. 3, chaps. 35–36
68–70: Obedience to the Ten Commandments	Vol. 2, chap. 34; Vol. 3, chaps. 37–40

Chapters and Topics in This Book	Location in *Reformed Systematic Theology*
71: Godly Fear, Prayer, and Hope	Vol. 3, chaps. 41–42
PART 6: THE DOCTRINE OF THE CHURCH	
72: Introduction to the Doctrine of the Church	Vol. 4, chaps. 1–2
73–74: The Church's Description, Attributes, and Marks	Vol. 4, chaps. 3–6
75: Membership in the Church	Vol. 4, chap. 7
76–78: Church Government and Officers	Vol. 4, chaps. 8–12
79: Churches in Relation to Families and Civil Government	Vol. 4, chaps. 13–14
80: The Work of the Church	Vol. 4, chaps. 15–16
81: The Means of Grace and the Ministry of the Word	Vol. 4, chaps. 17–18
82–83: Baptism	Vol. 4, chaps. 19–20, appendix
84: The Lord's Supper	Vol. 4, chaps. 21–22
85: Prayer, Praise, Fellowship, and Discipline	Vol. 4, chaps. 23–24
86: The Reformation of the Church	Vol. 4, chap. 25
PART 7: THE DOCTRINE OF THE LAST THINGS	
87: Introduction to the Doctrine of the Last Things	Vol. 4, chaps. 26–27
88: The Error of Prosperity Theology	Vol. 4, excursus after chap. 27
89: Death and the Afterlife	Vol. 4, chaps. 28–29
90: Signs, the Man of Sin, and the Book of Revelation	Vol. 4, chaps. 30–31
91: The Future of Israel and the Millennium	Vol. 4, chaps. 32–33, excursus after chap. 33
92: The Coming of Christ in Glory	Vol. 4, chap. 34
93: The Resurrection of the Dead and the Day of Judgment	Vol. 4, chaps. 35–37

Chapters and Topics in This Book	Location in *Reformed Systematic Theology*
94: Eternal Punishment in Hell	Vol. 4, chaps. 38–39
95: Eternal Life with God	Vol. 4, chaps. 40–41

General Index

Scripture Index